Hugh Johnson's
Wine
Companion

MITCHELL BEAZLEY

Hugh Johnson's
Wine
Companion

The Encyclopedia of Wines, Vineyards, & Winemakers

Fully revised and updated by Stephen Brook

Hugh Johnson's Wine Companion
Fully revised and updated by Stephen Brook

First published in Great Britain in 1983 by Mitchell Beazley, an
imprint of Octopus Publishing Group Limited, 2–4 Heron Quays,
London E14 4JP.

Revised editions 1987, 1991, 1997, 2003

Reprinted 1998, 2002
Copyright © Octopus Publishing Group Ltd 1987, 1991,
1997, 2003
Text copyright © Hugh Johnson 1987, 1991, 1997, 2003

A CIP catalogue record for this book is available from the
British Library.

ISBN: 1 84000 704 4

The author and publishers will be grateful for any information
which will assist them in keeping future editions up-to-date.
Although all reasonable care has been taken in the preparation
of this book, neither the publishers nor the author can accept
any liability for any consequences arising from the use thereof,
or the information contained therein.

Commissioning Editor   Hilary Lumsden
Executive Art Editor   Yasia Williams
Managing Editor   Emma Rice
Design   Peter Gerrish
Editor   Rebecca Hull
Production   Alexis Coogan
Index   Nigel D'Auvergne

Typeset in Trade Gothic and Garamond

Printed and bound by Toppan Printing Company in China

Contents

Introduction

1

Introduction

It has been twenty years since the first publication of this book: beyond argument, the twenty most eventful years in the history of wine. Four previous editions have done their best to keep up with ever-accelerating change. For this fifth edition I have recruited one of the best-informed and most polished minds in the world of wine: Stephen Brook, himself the author of five books on the subject, to scan all my accumulated work and correct and update it for the twenty-first century with all the resources at the publisher's disposal. I have been involved all the way through, making corrections of my own, but the task of describing – even sketching – the modern wine world, its methods, and its personnel is now too much for one person.

For all its air of seamless and senior tradition, its classifications and regulations, nothing ever stands still in the world of wine. It is a constant fascination that every vintage is different, and then keeps changing in barrel or bottle with every year of maturity – and not, by any means, at a predictable pace. It has all the excitement of a moving target.

But much more is on the move than just vintage quality and maturity. The ownership of vineyards and wineries, laws and regulations, winemakers and their techniques and philosophies are all in constant flux, and with them the quality of what they produce.

There is one constant in all this: – the terroir; the soil – but more than that; the whole natural environment in which the vines grow and the wine is made and cellared. Terroir is the ultimate factor in deciding both character and quality. Not at all constant, however, is the market. Today, wine-drinkers – their tastes, perceptions, and demands – have a major role in the ever-changing scene that must be added to all the other factors.

All these are potent reasons why a *Wine Companion* published in 2003 is a changed animal from its 1997 edition – let alone its first one in 1983. Then, I compared recent changes with those that led the nineteenth century writer Cyrus Redding to coin the term "modern wine". To Redding, the word "modern" distinguished the wines of his time from those of the Ancients. His "modern" methods are now old-fashioned. They created most of the wines now referred to as "classics", but history has moved on again. Modern wine to us is the creation of the technology evolving in the last years of the twentieth century and the first of the twenty-first (though perhaps the word technology is too brutal). The way the great winemakers proceed today could be described as scientific philosophy.

This modern world began with such radical discoveries as the effects of different temperatures on fermentation. (We should remember that the nature of fermentation itself was discovered by Pasteur only in the 1860s.) The ability to slow down fermentation by refrigeration was the first great breakthrough. Without it, the New World of wine, essentially those regions whose Mediterranean climates had limited their potential in the past, would never have challenged the Old.

Their challenge, though, from the mid-1960s on, has made the Old World look again at its entrenched ideas, has made it modify, adapt, and discard old dogma to the point where the simple concept of Old World and New has only a geographical meaning. Old World and New, in fact, have met in what is becoming the global wine village.

Such neighbourliness carries its dangers. The first is the inclination to make the same sort of wine as everyone else: the principal trend of the 1980s, still a danger, but happily less inexorable than it was. Its most obvious manifestation was the near-universal planting of Cabernet Sauvignon and Chardonnay. A more insidious one was the fashion of using oak, not as it was originally intended – for conditioning the wine ready for bottling – but actually to flavour it like a dash of ketchup by adding oak chips or even essence. A generation grew up under the delusion that Chardonnay actually tastes of oak – while in reality if it does, it is either badly made or not ready to drink.

At the end of the twentieth century, it appears, too, that a fundamental difference in taste threatens to divide consumers on the two sides of the Atlantic. To simplify, influential American critics are judging wines more for the impact they make than for those traits that make them good companions: the power to tempt and beguile, to accompany food, and quench thirst. Europe so far is unmoved, but it is a question to follow with interest.

This book is a portrait of this world of modern wine: its methods, its planting of vineyards and cellars, and above all, its practitioners. It is designed to be a practical companion in choices that become more varied and challenging all the time. Like any portrait, it tries to capture the reality of a single moment. The moment is past as soon as the shutter has clicked. The closer the focus and the greater the detail the more there is to change and grow out of date. This edition has been revised and updated to reflect the reality of 2003.

To make it a practical companion I try to give the essential information about each wine country and wine region you are likely to encounter or which is worth making an effort to know. I have shunned a catalogue of the legislation that surrounds the wine business increasingly each year. It casts little light and does nothing to add to the pleasure of our subject – which is, after all, either a pleasure or a failure.

The essentials, it seems to me, are the names and, as far as possible (which is not very far), descriptions of the world's worthwhile wines: who makes them, how much there is of them, how well they keep, and where they fit into our lives – which are too short, alas, to do justice to anything like all of them. You will also find answers to the recurring questions about grape varieties, production methods, and the ways of the wine trade. You will not find a historical survey or a technical treatise, but just enough information, I hope, to indicate essential differences and the trends of change in winemaking today.

The heart of the book is arranged by countries on the same system as my annual *Pocket Wine Book*, with the Index as the alphabetical alternative to find a name you cannot immediately place in a national or regional context. The *Wine Companion* is updated far less frequently than its annual pocket-sized stablemate, leaving to its more ephemeral editions the questions of current vintages, their quality, and maturity. Both will be much clearer if you possess the current (fifth) edition of *The World Atlas of Wine*, in which the regions are geographically displayed.

Each section provides the essential background information about the wines in question, then lists the principal producers with succinct details. In a few well-trodden areas the lists make themselves. In most others, a complete catalogue would be as unhelpful as it would be unmanageable. My (now "our") method, then, is to consult first our own experience, then the advice of friends, local brokers, and officials whom we have reason to respect. We have corresponded with as many producers as possible, asking them specific questions about their properties or firms, their methods, products, and philosophies. Often, unfortunately, the exigencies of space have forced us to leave out good producers we would have liked to include. In a few countries, we have also employed intermediaries to research, interview, and pass us their findings. We have tasted as many of the wines described as we could (which is why some specific tasting notes go back ten years or more).

The enjoyment of wine is a very personal thing. Yet if you love it, and spend your life among wine-lovers, you will find a remarkable consensus about which wines have the power to really thrill and satisfy us. Prejudice and narrow-mindedness have no place; preferences are what it is all about. We have not tried to hide ours among the fabulous variety described in this book.

How to Follow the Star-Rating System

The *Wine Companion* has introduced a new star-rating system for each producer listed.

☆☆☆☆	Exceptionally fine or great quality, consistent over many vintages
☆☆☆	Consistently high quality
☆☆	At least good quality
☆	Sound and steady wines

Any rating given in orange denotes particular good value. No rating is given to new producers whose wines are too new or too few to allow assessment; or to wineries that have recently changed hands.

Modern Wine

At its simplest, wine is made by crushing grapes and allowing the yeast naturally present on the skins to convert the sugar in their juice to alcohol. This is the process of fermentation. No more human intervention is needed than to separate the juice from the skins by pressing. Crushed and fermented like this, white grapes make white wine, and red grapes red.

The art of the winemaker can be equally simply expressed. It is to choose good grapes, to carry out the crushing, fermenting, and pressing with scrupulous care and hygiene, and to prepare the wine for drinking by cleaning it of yeasts and all foreign bodies. For some sorts of wine this entails ageing it as well; for others, the quicker it gets to market the better.

These are the eternal verities of wine and winemaking, well-understood for hundreds of years. They can be carried to perfection with no modern scientific knowledge or equipment whatever – with luck. Great wines came to be made in the places where nature, on balance, was kindest. Given a ripe crop of grapes in a healthy state, the element that determined success more than any other was the temperature of the cellar during and after the fermentation. France (but not the south), Germany, the Alps, and Hungary had these conditions. The Mediterranean and places with a similar climate did not.

If there is one innovation that has made the most difference between old and modern winemaking, it is refrigeration. Refrigeration and air-conditioning have added the whole zone of Mediterranean climate to the world of potentially fine wine.

Yet technology has advanced on a broad front. Every aspect of grape-growing and winemaking is now under a degree of control undreamed of before. These controls are now common practice in almost all the bigger and newer wineries where wine is made. Its scientific basis is widely understood even in traditional areas and among small properties.

One California professor confesses that winemakers now have more possible controls than they know how to use. In leading-edge California, white winemaking is so clinically perfected that one of the main problems is deciding what sort of wine you want to make.

On the other hand, as Professor Emile Peynaud of Bordeaux University has said, "The ultimate goal of modern oenology is to avoid having to treat the wine at all."

The following pages summarize some of the more important modern techniques and currently held views on the many factors that affect the qualities of wine. They follow the processes of grape-growing and winemaking more or less sequentially, so that they can be read as an account or referred to as a glossary. Some processes apply to white wine only, some to red, some to both. The stages of making wine are shown diagrammatically on pages 30–31.

The Vine

A wine-grower in the Clos de Vougeot has no choice about what grapes to plant. It has been a sea of Pinot Noir for centuries. Nothing else is permitted. A wine-grower in the Médoc has an important choice to make: half a dozen varieties within the family of the Cabernets are allowed. The emphasis he places on the harsher or the smoother varieties is the basis of his house style.

A wine-grower in the New World is as free as the air. His own taste and his view of the market are his only guide. This choice, together with the debates it has started, has made all wine-lovers far more grape-conscious than ever before. Not only are more wines named by their grape varieties, but this very fact has made the clear ascendancy of some varieties over others public knowledge.

What is a grape variety? It is a selection from among the infinity of forms a plant takes by natural mutation. In the basic economy of viticulture, a wine-grower looks first for fruitfulness, hardiness, and resistance to disease in his plants. Then he looks for the ability to ripen its fruit before the end of the warm autumn weather. Lastly, he looks for flavour and character.

There has been plenty of time since the discovery of wine to try out and develop different varieties. In the botanical genus *Vitis*, the vine, there are more than twenty species. The wine vine is only one: a wild woodland plant of Europe and

eastern Asia, *Vitis vinifera*. It was scrambling through the treetops of France long before the idea of crushing and fermenting its grapes was imported, via Greece, from the near East.

Nobody knows the precise origins of any of the varieties of vine that were developed locally in France, Italy, Spain, along the Danube, and in the rest of wine-growing Europe. But the assumption is that they started as selections by trial from local vine varieties, possibly interbreeding with imported ones of special quality. In Germany, for instance, the Romans made the brilliant discovery of a grape variety with habits perfectly adapted to the cool northern climate: the Riesling, or its ancestor. Selections, adaptations or descendants from it have become all the other grapes in the German style.

There are now 4,000 or more named varieties of wine grape on earth. Perhaps 100 have really recognizable flavour and character. Of these, a bare dozen have moved into international circulation, and the dozen can be narrowed again to those that have personalities so definite (and so good) that they form the basis of a whole international category of wine. They are the principal red and white grapes of Bordeaux, the same of Burgundy, the Riesling of Germany, the Gewurztraminer of Alsace, the Syrah of the Rhône, and the grandfather of them all: the Muscat.

Today, there is an increasing temptation to plant the champion grapes everywhere. It is a difficult argument between quality and that most precious attribute of wine – variety.

Classic Grapes

Riesling

Johannisberg Riesling, Rhine Riesling, White Riesling

The classic grape of Germany competes with Chardonnay for the title of the world's best white grape. The Riesling produces wines of crisp fruity acidity and transparent clarity of flavour. Even the aromas it gives off are refreshing. In Germany, it ranges from pale green, fragile, and sharp on the Mosel to golden, exotically luscious wines, especially in the Rheinpfalz. It is remarkably versatile in warmer climates, perhaps at its most typical in Alsace and Austria, becoming more buxom when grown in California and Australia, where it ages more rapidly to its unique mature bouquet of lemons and petrol.

Chardonnay

The white burgundy grape makes fatter, more winey, and potent-feeling wine than Riesling, less aromatic when young, maturing to a rich and broad, sometimes buttery, sometimes smoky or musky smell or flavour. The finesse of blanc de blancs Champagne, the mineral smell of Chablis, the nuttiness of Meursault, the ripe-fruit smells of Sonoma Valley wines show its unique versatility. It is a grape that is adapting superbly to Australia, Oregon, New Zealand, and northern Italy.

Cabernet Sauvignon

The Médoc grape. Most recognizable and most versatile of red grapes, apparently able to make first-class wine in any warm soil, in just about any winegrowing region of the world. Small, dark, rather late-ripening berries yield an intense colour, a strong blackcurrant and sometimes herbal aroma, and much tannin, which makes it the slowest wine to mature. It needs age in oak and bottle, and is best of all blended with Merlot, etc., as in Bordeaux. Outside Bordeaux, it is still common to find examples of pure varietal Cabernet, but increasingly, winemakers in areas as diverse as California, South Africa, and Italy, are opting for more subtle claret-style blends.

Pinot Noir

This is the red burgundy and Champagne grape. So far, it is apparently less adaptable to foreign vineyards, where the fine Burgundian balance is very hard to achieve. Sweeter, less tannic, and richer-textured than Cabernet, and therefore enjoyable at a far younger age. It is rarely blended, except in Champagne. It has proved especially successful in Oregon, California, and New Zealand, less so in Mediterranean countries.

Syrah or Shiraz

Widespread, and the great grape of the Rhône Valley. Makes tannic, peppery, dark wine, which can mature superbly. It is very important as Shiraz in Australia. Grown increasingly in the Midi, both for AC wines and *vins de pays* and in South Africa and California.

Gewu(ü)rztraminer

The beginner's grape due to its forthright spicy smell and flavour. Once almost unique to Alsace (without the umlaut), but now also encountered in Italy, Austria, Germany, New Zealand, and North America.

Sauvignon Blanc

The name derives from *sauvage*, – wild – which could well describe its grassy or gooseberry flavour. It it widespread in Bordeaux, where it is blended with Sémillon for both sweet and dry wines, but is most characteristic in Sancerre. A successful transplant to the New World, New Zealand, and South Africa in particular: it can be light and aromatic, or with fuller winey like Chardonnay.

Muscat

Muscat Blanc à Petits Grains, Moscato Canelli

The finest of the ancient tribe of Muscats is the "small white" used for sweet *vins doux naturels* from the south of France and for Asti Spumante. Most of the dry Muscats of Alsace come from a more regular-yielding variety, Muscat d'Ottonel.

Europe's Principal Grapes

France

All eight classic grapes are grown to perfection in France. The Muscat, Riesling, and Gewurztraminer are long-established imports, but the remaining five, the reds and whites of Burgundy, the Rhône, and Bordeaux, appear to be natives of France, representing an eastern and a western tradition: that of the Alps and that of the Atlantic. (They meet on the Loire.)

Nobody can say with any confidence how many other grapes make up this great tradition. A single variety may have four or five different names in different areas quite close together – or indeed, the grape may be a local strain and not quite the same variety. These local characters range from such common plants as the red Carignan of the Midi to the delicate white Viognier, once restricted to the Rhône, but now being more widely used for *vins de pays*; and such rare ones as the white Tresallier (limited to one tiny zone in the upper reaches of the Loire).

Red Grape Varieties

Abouriou grown in the Côtes du Marmandais in South West France.

Aleatico red Muscat variety of Corsica. Makes a wine of the same name.

Alicante-Bouschet prolific variety of southern table wine vineyards.

Aramon high-yielding southern table-wine variety, now in decline.

Aspiran an old variety of the Languedoc.

Auxerrois synonym of Malbec in Cahors.

Bouchet synonym of Cabernet Franc in St-Emilion.

Braquet main variety of Bellet, near Nice.

Brocol synonym of Valdiguié in Gaillac.

Cabernet Franc high-quality cousin of Cabernet Sauvignon used in Bordeaux (especially St-Emilion) and in the Loire.

Cabernet Sauvignon *see* page 11.

Carignan leading bulk-wine producer of the Midi; dull except from very old vines. Greatly improved by carbonic maceration.

Carmenère old Bordeaux variety, now rare.

César tannic traditional variety of Irancy (Yonne).

Cinsaut (or **Cinsault**) prominent southern Rhône variety, that is used in Châteauneuf-du-Pape, etc, and the Midi.

Cot synonym of Malbec in the Loire.

Duras local Gaillac variety.

Fer (or **Fer Servadou**) used in several wines of the South West, notably Marcillac.

Fuelle Noir (or **Folle Noire**) Bellet variety.

Gamay Beaujolais grape: juicy, light, and fragrant. Also grown in the Loire esp. Touraine, and in central France.

Grenache powerful red used in Châteauneuf-du-Pape and Côtes du Rhône, and for rosés (*e.g.* Tavel) and dessert wines in Roussillon.

Grolleau (or Groslot) common Loire red used in, for example, Anjou Rosé.

Jurançon Noir Gaillac (Tarn) grape – not used in Jurançon.

Malbec important variety now fading from the best Bordeaux, but central to Cahors.

Mataro synonym of Mourvèdre.

Merlot essential element in fine Bordeaux; the dominant grape of Pomerol.

Meunier (or **Pinot Meunier**) inferior "dusty-leaved" version of Pinot Noir "tolerated" in Champagne.

Mondeuse chief red of Savoie.

Mourvèdre key variety of Bandol in Provence – one of the improving *cépages améliorateurs* of the Midi.

Négrette variety peculiar to Frontonnais and Gaillac.

Nielluccio Corsican variety, possibly related to Sangiovese.

Petit Verdot high-quality subsidiary grape of Bordeaux.

Pineau d'Aunis local to the Loire Valley, especially Anjou and Touraine.

Pinot Noir *see* page 11.

Portugais Bleu once widespread in Gaillac, now declining in importance.

Poulsard pale-red Jura variety.

Pressac St-Emilion synonym for Malbec.

Sciacarello Corsican variety.

Syrah *see* page 11.

Tannat tannic variety of the South West, especially Madiran.

Tempranillo Spanish (Rioja) variety grown in the Midi.

Trousseau majority grape in Jura reds, but inferior to Poulsard.

White Grape Varieties

Aligoté secondary Burgundy grape of high acidity. Wines for drinking young.

Altesse Savoie variety. Wines are often sold as "Roussette".

Arrufiac Béarnais variety (Pacherenc du Vic-Bilh).

Auvergnat (or **Auvernat**) Loire term for the Pinot family.

Baroque used in Béarn to make Tursan.

Beaunois synonym of Chardonnay at Chablis.

Beurot synonym in Burgundy of Pinot Gris.

Blanc Fumé synonym of Sauvignon Blanc at Pouilly-sur-Loire.

Blanquette synonym of Mauzac Blanc and Clairette Blanc.

Bourboulenc Midi (Minervois, La Clape) variety, also goes into (red and white) Châteauneuf-du-Pape.

Camaralet rare Jurançon variety.

Chardonnay *see* page 11.

Chasselas neutral variety used in Savoie, Pouilly-sur-Loire, and Alsace.

Clairette common neutral-flavoured Midi grape, also makes sparkling Rhône Clairette de Die.

Colombard minor Bordelais grape most common in the Côtes de Gascogne. Also distilled for cognac and armagnac.

Courbu Jurançon variety (alias Sarreat).

Folle Blanche formerly the chief Cognac grape, also grown in Bordeaux and Brittany.

Gamay Blanc synonym of Chardonnay in the Jura.

Gewürztraminer *see* page 11.

Gros Manseng one of the main grapes of Jurançon.

Gros Plant synonym of Folle Blanche in the western Loire.

Jacquère the grape of Apremont and Chignin in Savoie.

Jurançon Blanc minor armagnac variety (not in Jurançon).

Klevner name used for Pinot Blanc in Alsace.

Len-de-l'El (or **Loin de l'Oeil**) variety used in Gaillac.

Maccabeu (or **Maccabéo**) Catalan variety used in Roussillon for dessert *vins doux naturel.*

Malvoisie synonym of Bourboulenc in the Languedoc, of Torbato in Roussillon, and Vermentino in Corsica.

Marsanne with Roussanne, the white grape of Hermitage and the Northern Rhône.

Mauzac used in Blanquette de Limoux and Gaillac.

Morillon synonym of Chardonnay.

Muscadelle minor, slightly Muscat-flavoured variety used in Sauternes and some dry white Bordeaux.

Muscadet gives its name to the wine of the western Loire. Also called Melon de Bourgogne.

Muscat *see* page 11.

Ondenc Gaillac variety.

Petit Manseng excellent South West variety used in the wines of Jurançon, etc.

Petite Sainte-Marie synonym of Chardonnay in Savoie.

Picpoul synonym of Folle Blanche in Armagnac; in the Southern Rhône and the Midi (Picpoul de Pinet) it is a different variety: Picpoul Blanc.

Pineau de la Loire synonym in the Loire of Chenin Blanc (not a Pinot).

Pinot Blanc closely related to Pinot Noir, grown in Burgundy, Champagne, and Alsace.

Pinot Gris (Tokay d'Alsace) a mutation of the Pinot Noir, widespread in Alsace.

Piquepoul *see* Picpoul.

Riesling *see* page 11.

Rolle Italian Vermentino in Provence.

Romorantin grown only at Cheverny; dry, often sharp wine.

Roussanne (with Marsanne) makes white Hermitage.

Roussette synonym of Altesse in Savoie.

Sacy minor variety of the Yonne.

St-Emilion synonym of Ugni Blanc in cognac.

Sauvignon Blanc *see* page 11.

Savagnin the "yellow wine" grape of Château-Chalon (Jura).

Sylvaner the workhorse light-wine grape of Alsace.

Traminer *see* Gewürztraminer.

Tresallier variety of the extreme upper Loire (St-Pourçain-sur-Sioule) now fading.

Ugni Blanc common Midi grape; Italy's Trebbiano; "St-Emilion" in cognac.
Vermentino Italian grape, known in Provence as Rolle; possibly the Malvoisie of Corsica.
Viognier aromatic grape of Condrieu in the Northern Rhône. Increasingly common in the Midi, especially as a varietal *vin de pays*.

Italy

Italy's grape catalogue is probably one of the longest of all. With wine-growing so universal a factor of Italian life, uninterrupted for millennia before phylloxera, local selection has completely blurred the origins and relationships of many varieties beyond recall. Similarly, is the fish caught off Tunisia and called by an Arab name the same as a similar one caught in the Adriatic and called by a name peculiar to the Romagna? In truth, Italian grapes are scarcely less slippery a subject.

In general, their selection has been on the grounds of productivity and good health, along with adaptability to the soil and reliable ripening, rather than great qualities of flavour or ability to age. The mass of Italian grapes are, therefore, sound rather than inspiring, their flavours muted or neutral. The only international classic to (maybe) come from Italy is the (Gewürz) Traminer, from the South Tyrol.

But once you start to list the exceptions, the Italian grapes with personality and potentially excellent quality, it does seem strange that more of them have not yet made a real name for themselves in the world. Nebbiolo, Barbera, Teroldego, Sangiovese, Montepulciano, and Aglianico are reds with much to offer. There are fewer first-class whites, but Ribolla, Cortese, Greco, Tocai, Verdicchio, and Vermentino all make original contributions, and the Moscato of Piedmont, while not exclusively Italian, is a very Italian interpretation of the most ancient of grapes.

At the same time, more and more is being heard of Cabernet, Merlot, Pinot Bianco, and even Chardonnay and Riesling, while Pinot Grigio has become wildly popular in Germany and North America. The northeast is now almost as international in its ampelography as any of the wine areas of the New World. The appearance of Cabernet Sauvignon, Syrah, and Chardonnay in Tuscany in recent years is an important sign of changes in the wind.

The central question over the future of Italian wine is how far she will defend her traditions (which is the purpose of the DOC legislation) in sticking to her indigenous grapes, and how far she will bow to the international trend – as she is tending to do in winemaking techniques.

The world has begun to appreciate just what variety Italy has to offer. She will do well to develop her native flavours to the full. They include as wide a range as the wines of any country – France included.

There is no general rule on the mention of grape varieties on labels; local custom dictates whether the wine is labelled by place, grape, or a name entirely unrelated to either. With the current increase in variety consciousness, however, it does seem likely that producers will start to make more of the grape varieties in future – at least on wines destined for export.

Red Grape Varieties

Aglianico source of full-bodied Taurasi in Campania, and Aglianico del Vulture in Basilicata.
Aleatico Muscat-flavoured grape used for dark dessert wines in Elba, Latium, Apulia, and elsewhere.
Barbera dark, acidic Piedmont variety widely grown in the northwest.
Bombino Nero used in Apulia's Castel del Monte *rosato*.
Bonarda minor variety widespread in Lombardy and Piedmont.
Brachetto makes fizzy, perfumed Piedmont wines.
Brunello di Montalcino a noble strain of Tuscany's Sangiovese.
Cabernet (especially Franc) widespread in the northeast; increasing elsewhere.
Calabrese synonym of Sicilian Nero d'Avola.
Cannonau leading dark variety of Sardinia for DOC wines, the Grenache of France.
Carignano (French Carignan), prominent in Sardinia.
Cesanese good Latium red.
Chiavennasca Nebbiolo in Valtellina, Lombardy.
Corvina Veronese main grape of Valpolicella.
Croatina much used in Lombardy's Oltrepò Pavese and in Emilia-Romagna.
Dolcetto low-acid Piedmont variety, source of several DOCs.
Freisa Piedmont variety, makes sweet, often fizzy wines, and occasional dry ones.
Gaglioppo source of most Calabrian reds, including Cirò.
Grignolino makes light, pleasant wines around Asti in Piedmont.
Guarnaccia red variety of Campania, especially Ischia.
Lagrein grown in Alto Adige: faintly bitter reds and dark rosés.
Lambrusco prolific source of Emilia's effervescent wines.
Malbec seen occasionally in Apulia and Venezia.
Malvasia Nera makes sweet, fragrant, sometimes sparkling reds in Piedmont; also a fine dessert wine in Apulia.
Marzemino dark grape grown in Trentino and Lombardy.
Merlot Bordeaux native widely grown in Italy, especially in the northeast.
Monica makes Sardinian reds, dry and sweet.
Montepulciano dark variety of central Italy, widely planted.
Nebbiolo the great grape of Piedmont, the base of Barolo, Barbaresco, Gattinara, etc. Its wine varies from smoothly fruity to biting black, ageing superbly.
Negroamaro potent Apulian variety of the Salento peninsula.
Nerello Mascalese Sicilian grape, for Etna reds and rosés.
Petit Rouge used in some Valle d'Aosta reds.
Piedirosso (or **Per'e Palummo**) features in Campania reds.
Pinot Nero Burgundy's Pinot Noir (*see* page 11), grown in much of northeast Italy.
Primitivo Apulian grape, the same as Zinfandel.
Raboso worthy, if tannic, Veneto native.
Refosco source of dry, full-bodied Friuli reds. Known as Mondeuse in France.
Rossese fine Ligurian variety, makes DOC at Dolceacqua.
Sangiovese mainstay of Chianti and one of Italy's most widely planted vines, with many clones and *noms de verre*. At best magnificent, astringent but full-bodied, ageing many years.
Schiava widespread in Alto Adige.
Spanna synonym for Nebbiolo.
Teroldego unique to Trentino, makes Teroldego Rotaliano.
Tocai Rosso (or **Tocai Nero**) makes DOC red in Veneto's Colli Berici.
Uva di Troia main grape of several DOC wines in north Apulia.
Vespolina often blended with Nebbiolo in east Piedmont.

White Grape Varieties

Albana Romagna makes dry and semi-sweet wines.

Arneis Piedmont variety that is enjoying a revival.

Biancolella native of Ischia.

Blanc de Valdigne source in Valle d'Aosta of Blanc de Morgex, Blanc de la Salle.

Bombino Bianco main grape of Apulia and Abruzzi, where it is known as Trebbiano d'Abruzzo.

Bosco in Liguria, the main ingredient of Cinqueterre.

Catarratto widely grown in west Sicily, often used in Marsala.

Chardonnay grown in Trentino-Alto Adige, Veneto, and Friuli and now used for IGT (*indicazione geografica tipica*) in Tuscany, Umbria, Piedmont, and elsewhere.

Cortese used in south Piedmont's finest whites: found also in Lombardy's Oltrepò Pavese.

Fiano in Campania makes Fiano di Avellino.

Forestera partners Biancolella in Ischia bianco.

Garganega main grape of Soave.

Grechetto variety of Umbria, important in Orvieto.

Greco Campania's best white.

Grillo figures, usually with Catarratto, in Marsala.

Inzolia used in Sicilian whites, as well as Marsala.

Malvasia common for both dry and sweet wines, especially in Latium (for Frascati etc.).

Moscato (Muscat, *see* page 11) widespread in sparkling wines (*e.g.* Asti Spumante) and dessert wines (*e.g.* Moscatos of Sicily).

Müller-Thurgau encountered in Friuli, Trentino-Alto Adige.

Nuragus ancient Sardinian grape.

Picolit source of Italy's most expensive dessert wines from Friuli.

Pigato grown only in southwest Liguria; good table wine.

Pinot Bianco Burgundy's Pinot Blanc, grown all over north Italy. Weisser Burgunder in Alto Adige.

Prosecco prominent in Veneto, mainly for sparkling wines.

Rheinriesling *see* Riesling Renano.

Riesling Italico not a true Riesling, probably native to the northeast.

Riesling Renano Rhine Riesling, and thus authentic.

Sauvignon Blanc grown in parts of the northeast, and exceptional in Friuli.

Tocai Friulano used for DOC whites in Lombardy and Veneto, as well as in its native Friuli.

Traminer native of Alto Adige.

Trebbiano d'Abruzzo *see* Bombino Bianco.

Verdeca Apulian grape used in southern whites.

Verdicchio main grape of the Marches.

Verduzzo Friulian variety used also in the Veneto for both dry and dessert wines.

Vermentino source of DOC white in Sardinia, and good table wines in Liguria.

Vernaccia di Oristano in Sardinia, makes sherry-like dessert wine.

Vernaccia di San Gimignano ancient Tuscan variety, wine of the same name.

Germany

The international reputation of German wine for a unique effect of flowery elegance is based on one grape alone: Riesling. But the widespread use of Riesling as we know it, is probably no more than 200 or 300 years old. Germany has several old varieties of local importance, which continue to hold their own. More significantly, her vine-breeders have been struggling for a century to produce new vines that offer Riesling quality without its inherent disadvantage: ripening so late in the autumn that every vintage is a cliffhanger. The centenary of the first important Riesling cross (with Silvaner) was celebrated in 1982. The past 100 years have seen its fruit, the Müller-Thurgau, become so prolific that, for a time, it surpassed Riesling as Germany's most popular grape.

Yet none of the new varieties, not even Müller-Thurgau, has supplanted Riesling in the best and warmest vineyards. None has achieved more than either a sketch or a caricature of its brilliant balance and finesse. Nor have any survived such ultimate tests of hardiness as January 1979, when the temperature dropped by forty degrees to -20°F (-29°C) in twenty-four hours. Thousands of vines were killed. Riesling survived.

Seventy-six per cent of the German vineyard is white. Of the twenty-four per cent that is red, Spätburgunder (Pinot Noir) long ago overtook the inferior Portugieser.

Red & White Grape Varieties

Albalonga Rieslaner x Silvaner. Needs to be ultra-ripe. Now in decline.

Bacchus an early ripening cross of (Silvaner x Riesling) x Müller-Thurgau. Spicy but rather soft wines, best as Auslesen, frequently used as *süssreserve*.

Cabernet Cubin One of a number of Cabernet crosses developed in the 1990s in Franken, with the intention of creating dark-red wines with high ripeness levels. Being adopted with caution.

Domina Pinot Noir x Portugieser. A deep-coloured cross, gradually being planted in the Ahr and southern Germany.

Dornfelder A complex cross, developed in the 1950s, but only widely planted in the 1990s, especially in the Pfalz. Gives dark, quaffable red wines even from high yields.

Ehrenfelser Riesling x Silvaner. A good cross, between Müller-Thurgau and Riesling in quality.

Elbling once the chief grape of the Mosel, now only grown high upriver. Neutral and acidic, but clean and good in sparkling wine.

Faber Weissburgunder x Müller-Thurgau, with a certain following in Rheinhessen and the Nahe.

Frühburgunder A small-berried mutation of Pinot Noir, its advantage being that it ripens earlier and has lower acidity. Good quality.

Gewürztraminer *see* page 11.

Gutedel south Baden name for the Chasselas, or Swiss Fendant. Light, refreshing, but short-lived wine.

Huxelrebe Gutedel x Courtiller Musqué. A prolific variety, very aromatic, with good sugar and acidity. Popular in Rheinhessen, but in gradual decline.

Kerner Trollinger x Riesling. One of the better new varieties, widely planted. When not over-cropped, it tastes like a blend of Silvaner and Riesling.

Lemberger Synonym for Austrian Blaufränkisch. Gives complex wine with good acidity in Württemberg.

Morio-Muskat It is hard to believe that this early ripening cross of Silvaner and Weisser Burgunder has no Muscat blood. The wine it makes in Rheinpfalz and Rheinhessen is often too blatant and blowsy.

Müller-Thurgau Riesling x Sylvaner. Created in 1882, but only widely planted after 1930. Immensely popular, despite suffering chronic insipidity, unless yields are heavily reduced. Also known as Rivaner.

Optima Silvaner x Riesling x Müller-Thurgau. This is an improvement on Bacchus, particularly in the Rheinpfalz. Delicately spicy.

Ortega Müller-Thurgau x Siegerrebe. Very early ripening, aromatic, and spicy with superb balance. Planted in the Mosel and in Franken. Gives rather cloying, sweet wines, however.

Perle Gewürztraminer x Müller-Thurgau. An extremely aromatic new cross, planted in Rheinhessen and Franken. In decline.

Portugieser Very popular, high-yielding red grape, but essentially insipid.

Regent One of the better new red varieties, becoming popular in the Pfalz and Rheinhessen.

Reichensteiner Müller-Thurgau x (Madeleine Angevine x Calabreser Fröhlich). A Euro-cross, slightly better for both sugar and acid than Müller-Thurgau.

Rieslaner Silvaner x Riesling. A brilliant variety, created in 1921, but hard to grow. Gives superb sweet wines with higher acidity even than Riesling.

Riesling *see* page 11.

Samtrot A mutation of Pinot Meunier found in Württemberg. Soft, but elegant wines.

Scheurebe the second cross Silvaner x Riesling to become celebrated, now well-established (Rheinhessen, Rheinpfalz) for highly aromatic, often unsubtle wine. At its best when made sweet.

Schwarzriesling German synonym for Pinot Meunier. Found in Baden and Württemberg.

Silvaner a late-ripener like the Riesling, also badly affected by drought in light or thin soils, steadily giving ground to Müller-Thurgau and others. Scarcely noble, but at its best (in Franken and Rheinhessen) the true yeoman: blunt, trustworthy, with unsuspected depths.

Trollinger The favourite grape of Württemberg, giving light red wine consumed in industrial quantities within the region, and regarded with bafflement outside it.

Weisser Burgunder (Pinot Blanc) makes good fresh full-bodied wine in Baden.

Spain & Portugal

Spain and Portugal have been net exporters, rather than importers, of grape varieties. A few of the international varieties have been planted, but they have certainly not yet taken hold in a way that radically alters the wine, whereas their grapes exported to the world include the Palomino (to California, South Africa, and Australia), the Verdelho (to Australia) and, probably, the Carignan, much the most widespread red grape of the South of France.

Traditionally, there are few "varietals" in Spain and Portugal, although, as with elsewhere, this is starting to change. Most wines contain proportions of at least three grapes, balanced for their qualities. The most notable exceptions are the four varietals of Madeira: Sercial, Verdelho, Bual, and Malmsey.

Red Grape Varieties

Agua Santa early ripening red of Bairrada, giving stronger wine than the Baga.

Alfrocheiro Preto prized red variety in Dão and Alentejo.

Alvarelhão Dão variety, and grown for port. Also found in Galicia.

Aragonez variant of Tempranillo, popular in Alentejo.

Azal Tinto red grape with high tartaric acid, used for *vinho verde*.

Baga dark, tannic, potentially noble grape of Bairrada. Gives berry-fruit flavours.

Bastardo a rather pale and low-acid, but aromatic and well-balanced, grape, used for port and in Dão.

Borraçal red Vinho Verde grape providing high malic acidity.

Cabernet Sauvignon (*see* page 11) increasingly being planted in Spain, *e.g.* in Penedès for Torres's "Mas a Plana", in Navarra by Sarría, at Vega Sicilia in Ribera del Duero, and by Riscal in Rioja, along with many others.

Cariñena Carignan in France, originated in Cariñena (Aragón) but now more grown in Catalonia.

Castelão a minor Bairrada red, soft and neutral.

Castelão Frances preferred synonym of Periquita since 2002; widely planted grape of southern Portugal.

Cencibel synonym in La Mancha and Valdepeñas for Tempranillo.

Garnacha Tinta used in Rioja Baja for powerful, if pale Riojas, also Penedès, and Navarra, where it dominates. French synonym is Grenache Noir.

Graciano the most elegant and aromatic of Rioja grapes; gives quick-maturing wine.

Jaen a constituent of red Dão.

Mazuelo a Riojan red grape, possibly a synonym for Cariñena.

Mencía used in Léon and Galicia for light reds.

Monastrell a widely grown red of good colour and texture, especially in Penedès, the Levante, and Valdepeñas.

Periquita *see* Castelão Frances.

Pinot Noir (*see* page 11) Torres grows Pinot for his red "Santa Digna". Also found in Navarra.

Ramisco the tannic, blue-black secret of Colares. Needs very long ageing.

Samsó Penedès variety.

Souzão deeply coloured and excellent port grape.

Tempranillo fine, aromatic, early ripening, and basis for Rioja. Grown throughout Spain under a variety of synonyms.

Tinta Barroca high-yielding but robust port grape.

Tinto Cão low-yielding red variety used for port and Dão.

Tinta Pinheira minor Bairrada variety; pale, low acid, but alcoholic.

Tintorera one of the Valdepeñas grapes.

Touriga Franca perfumed red used for port; previously called Touriga Francesa.

Touriga Nacional deep-coloured, big-yielding port variety, also used in Dão.

Trincadeira gives rich reds in Alentejo; known in the Douro as Tinta Amarela.

Ull de Llebre Penedès synonym for Tempranillo.

Vinhão Vinho verde red grown for its relatively high alcohol.

White Grape Varieties

Airén the main white grape of Valdepeñas and La Mancha.

Albariño the best Galician variety for clean, dry, fragrant and often *pétillant* whites; also grown in Portugal (Alvarinho) for Vinho Verde.

Albillo used, with red grapes, in "Vega Sicilia".

Arinto used for lemony white Dão and Bairrada and to make the rare, dry Bucelas and sweet Carcavelos.

Barcelos recommended white Dão variety.

Bical fragrant and fine Bairrada white, complementary to the sharper Arinto.

Bual sweet Madeira grape, with luscious flavours, also used in Carcavelos and Alentejo.

Chardonnay (*see* page 10) becoming more established in Spain with wines from Penedès, Somontano, and elsewhere. Also the occasional Portuguese example.

Fernão Pires widely planted aromatic Portuguese white.

Gouveio minor white port variety, thought to be Verdelho.

Lairén *see* Airén.

Listan synonym of Palomino.

Loureiro high-yielding grape for Vinho Verde.

Macabeo synonym in Catalonia of Viura. For sparkling wines.

Malvasia important white grape in port, Rioja, Navarra, Catalonia, and the Canary Islands.

Maria Gomes the principal white grape of Bairrada.

Moscatel widespread sweet wine grape.

Pansa grown in Alella. Synonym of Xarel-lo of Penedès.

Parellada used in Penedès for delicately fruity whites and sparklers.

Pedro Ximénez grown for blending in Jerez, Málaga, and the principal grape in Montilla: dried, it adds intense sweetness and colour.

Traminer used (with Moscatel) by Torres for "Viña Esmeralda".

Verdelho white Dão variety, better known in Madeira.

Viura the principal grape of white Rioja, also Navarra. Alias Macabeo.

Xarel-lo Catalan grape, important in Penedès.

Zalema main variety in *vino generoso* of Huelva, being replaced by Palomino.

Southeast & Central Europe

The grape varieties of southeast Europe and the countries fringing the Black Sea are as old as those of the west. The Romans colonized the Danube at the same time as the Rhine. Under the Austro-Hungarian Empire, the only wines to reach international fame were those of Hungary, led by Tokaji. The local grapes, therefore, evolved slowly on their own course, making spicy, often sweetish whites and dry tannic reds. The eastern fringes of the Alps in Slovenia, Austria, and north into Bohemia (Czech Republic) are essentially white wine country, dominated by their low-key namesake, the Riesling (variously known as Italian, Welsch, Olasz or Laski), and Austria by its sappy, vigorous Grüner Veltliner. Hungary is most prolific in native white grapes of strength and style, led by the Furmint of Tokaji. Its red, the Kadarka, is widespread in the Balkans, more recently joined by the Pinot Noir and Gamay. Warmer climates near the Adriatic and Black Seas have reds and sweet whites. The last two decades or so have seen an invasion of classics from the west.

Red & White Grape Varieties

Ezerjó a white variety making fine wine at Mór, in Hungary. Also a bulk producer from the Serbian border region with Hungary and Romania. One of the best Hungarian dry whites.

Furmint classic white grape of Tokaji. (Sipon in Slovenia.)

Hárslevelü second main variety for making Tokaji. Full and aromatic.

Kadarka the common red grape of Hungary, but it is widespread throughout the region, producing a stiff, spicy red that is built especially for ageing. Known as Gamza in Bulgaria.

Kékfrankos (Austrian Blaufränkisch) more reliable than Kadarka and hence being planted as a substitute, especially in Hungary.

Kéknyelü white low-yielding variety of Hungary's vineyards north of Lake Balaton, making concentrated golden-green wines.

Kraski Teran the Refosco of Italy, makes crisp, tangy red in Slovenia.

Leányka delicate, dry white esp. from Eger in the north of Hungary.

Lunel (or **Yellow**) **Muscat** Sargamuskotály in Hungarian. One of the four grape varieties permitted for use in Tokaji.

Mavrud makes Bulgaria's best red, dark and plummy, can last twenty years.

Mezesfehér Hungarian white grape ("little honey") but less grown now.

Misket indigenous to Bulgaria, both red and white often used to make a fatter blend.

Muscat Ottonel the East European Muscat, a specialty of Romania.

Olaszrizling Hungarian name for Riesling Italico. Widely planted. Grasevina in Slovenia and Croatia.

Oremus Furmint x Bouvier, authorized for use in Tokaji since 1994.

Plovdina dark-skinned red grape, native to Macedonia.

Prokupac red grape of Serbia and Macedonia, blended to make Zupsko Crno, and much used to make rosé.

Rebula (or **Ribolla**) an Italian export which makes slightly creamy yellow wine in Slovenia.

Rkatsiteli Russian variety that is good for for strong white wines, preferred sweet by local market. Also used in notheast Bulgaria.

St Laurent deep-coloured variety, of Alsatian origin, but now found only in Austria and Germany.

Saperavi variety indigenous to Georgia, giving intense, peppery wines akin to Syrah.

Smederevka chief white of Serbia and Kosovo for fresh dry whites.

Szürkebarát a form of Pinot Gris grown in the Badacsonyi region of Hungary for rich, not necessarily sweet, wine.

Vranac makes vigorous reds in Montenegro.

Zilavka white variety with faint apricot flavour, grown in southern Serbia.

Zweigelt red grape making deep-coloured, pleasantly scented, spicy wine, especially in Austria.

In the Vineyard

Grape Varieties

The choice of grape varieties is the most fundamental decision of all. *See* pages 11–16.

Source of Grapes

For a winemaker there are arguments both for and against growing your own grapes. Those in favour are that you have total control over the management of the vineyard, and thus decide the quality of the grapes. The argument against is that an independent winemaker can pick and choose among the best grapes of specialist growers in different areas.

In France, and throughout most of Europe, almost all quality wine (except for most champagne) is "home-grown". In California and Australia, the debate is more open. Winemakers who buy their grapes (almost always from the same suppliers) include some of the very best. It is becoming more common for wineries to work on a contract basis with suppliers, dictating crucial factors such as yields and picking dates – and guaranteeing a higher price.

Virus-free Vines

Certain authorities (notably at the University of California at Davis) are convinced that the only way to achieve a healthy vineyard is to "clean" the vine stocks in it of all virus infections. Until recently, the beautiful red colour of vine leaves in autumn was not known to be a symptom of a virus-infected plant.

Plants can now be propagated free of virus infection by growing them very fast in a hot greenhouse, then using the growing tips as mini-cuttings (or micro-cuttings, growing minute pieces of the plant tissue in a nutrient jelly). The virus is always one pace behind the new growth, which is thus "clean" and will have all its natural vigour.

Virus elimination is no substitute for selection of the best vines. The *Office International du Vin* declared in 1980 that "It is a fantasy to try to establish a vineyard free of all virus diseases", and recommended its members to "select clones resistant to dangerous virus diseases and which will still be capable, after infection, of producing a satisfactory crop both as to quality and quantity" (*see* Cloning, below).

Cloning

Close observation of a vine will show that some branches are inherently more vigorous, bear more fruit, ripen earlier, or have other desirable characteristics. These branches (and their buds) are "mutations": genetically slightly different from the parent plant. The longer a variety has been in cultivation the more "degenerate" and thus genetically unstable it will be, and the more mutations it will have. The Pinot family is extremely ancient and notoriously mutable.

A recent technique is to select such a branch and propagate exclusively from its cuttings. A whole vineyard can then be planted with what is, in effect, one identical individual plant, known as a clone. There is thus not one single Pinot Noir variety in Burgundy, but scores of clones selected for different attributes. Growers who plant highly productive clones will never achieve the best-quality wine.

Those who choose a shy-bearing, small-berried clone for colour and flavour must reckon on smaller crops.

One advantage of a single-clone vineyard is that all its grapes will ripen together. A disadvantage is that one problem, pest, or disease will affect them all equally. Common sense seems to indicate that the traditional method of selecting cuttings from as many different healthy vines as possible (known as "massal selection") rather than one individual, carries a better chance of long-term success.

The Choice of Rootstocks

The majority of modern vineyards are of a selected variety of European vine, grafted onto a selected American rootstock, which has inbuilt resistance to phylloxera. Compatible rootstocks have been chosen and/or bred and virus-freed to be ideal for specific types of soil. Some are recommended for acid-to-neutral soils (such as most in California), while others flourish on the limey or alkaline soils common to most of Europe's best vineyards. Some parts of the world, notably South America, are free of phylloxera, so it is a common (but declining) practice to plant vines on their own roots.

Grafting

The grafting of a "scion" of the chosen vine variety onto an appropriate rootstock is either done at the nursery before planting ("bench grafting") or onto an already-planted rootstock in the vineyard ("field grafting"). Recently, in California, it has become common practice for growers to change their minds after a vine has been in production for several years, deciding that they want (say) less Zinfandel and more Chardonnay. In this case they simply saw off the Zinfandel vine at rootstock level, just above the ground, and "T-bud" graft a Chardonnay scion in its place. Within two years they will have white wine instead of red. Not only do growers lose less production, but they also take advantage of the well-established root system of the mature vines.

Hybrid Vines

After the phylloxera epidemic in Europe a century ago, some French biologists started breeding hybrid vines by marrying the European classics to phylloxera-resistant American species. Once the technique of grafting the French originals onto American roots was well-established, the French establishment rejected these *producteurs directes*, or "PDs" (so-called because they produced "directly" via their own roots). Good, hardy, and productive as many of them are, they are banned from all French appellation areas for fear of altering their precious identity. Their American parenthood, however, has made them highly suitable for use in the eastern United States, where hardiness is a perpetual problem (*see* pages 469–71). These hybrid vines were also once popular in New Zealand, and some of the better ones are quite extensively planted in England.

New Crossings of European Vines

Germany is the centre of a breeding programme which is quite distinct from "hybrid" vines. It aims to find, within the genetic pool of varieties of *Vitis vinifera*, a combination of desirable qualities which could supplant, in particular, the

Riesling. It is Germany's finest vine, but Riesling ripens relatively late, thus carrying a high risk element at vintage time. So far, no cross has even remotely challenged Riesling for flavour or hardiness – though many have for productivity, strongly aromatic juice, and early ripening. Müller-Thurgau was the first, and is still, the best-known example.

The University of California also has a *vinifera* breeding programme which has produced some useful additions, particularly in the form of high-yielding grapes for hot areas, capable of retaining good aromas and acidity. The best-known examples resulting from this programme include Ruby Cabernet (Cabernet Sauvignon/Carignan); Carnelian and Centurion (Cabernet Sauvignon/Grenache); Carmine (Cabernet Sauvignon/Merlot); Emerald Riesling (Riesling/Muscadelle); and Flora (Gewürztraminer/Sémillon), all produced by Dr. Harold Olmo at Davis.

South Africa has produced the Pinotage, said to be a cross between Pinot Noir and Cinsaut (though, unfortunately, with few of the qualities of the former). With over 3,000 named varieties already in circulation to choose from, there seems to be a limited point in breeding for the sake of breeding.

Soil

Soil is always given pride of place in French discussions of wine quality. It is considered from two aspects: its chemical and its physical properties. Current thinking is that the latter is much the more important. Most soils contain all the chemical elements the vine needs.

The physical factors that affect quality are texture, porosity, drainage, depth, and even colour. In cool climates, anything that tends to make the soil warm (*i.e.* absorb and store heat from the sun) is good. Stones on the surface store heat and radiate it at night. Darker soil absorbs more radiation. In Germany, vine rows are oriented to expose the soil to maximum sunlight. Dry soil warms up faster. Another important advantage of good deep drainage (*e.g.* on Médoc gravel) is that it makes the vine root dig deep to find moisture. Deep roots are in a stable environment: a sudden downpour just before harvest will not instantly inflate the grapes with water. On the other hand, recent experiments at Davis, California, have shown that where the soil is cooler than the above-ground parts of the vine, the effect can be good for the grape pigments and give deep-coloured red wine. (Château Pétrus on the iron-rich clay of Pomerol would seem to bear this out. St-Estèphe also has more clay, and its wines often more colour, than the rest of the Médoc.)

In California, clay also seems to produce stable white wines that resist oxidation and therefore have a greater ability to mature. But here also, over-rapid ripening often leads to wines that are low in acidity and easily oxidized. The cool of clay may simply be slowing the ripening process: the very opposite of the effect required in, say, Germany.

A reasonable conclusion would be that the best soil is the soil that results in the grapes coming steadily to maturity: warm in cool areas, reasonably cool in hot areas. It should be deep enough for the roots to have constant access to moisture, since a vine under acute stress of drought closes the pores of its leaves. Photosynthesis stops, and the grapes cannot develop or ripen fully. Expert opinion seems to be that if the soils of the great vineyards (*e.g.* Bordeaux First Growths) have more available nutrients and minerals (especially potassium), it is because over the years their owners have invested more in them. Scrutiny of the Côte d'Or has not revealed any chemical differences between the soils of the different *crus* which would account for their acknowledged differences of flavour.

Sites, Slopes, & Microclimates

It is conventional wisdom that wine from slopes is better. The words *côtes* and *coteaux* – meaning slopes – constantly recur in France. The obvious reasons are the increased solar radiation on a surface tipped toward the sun (meaning warmer soil), and the improved cold-air drainage, reducing the risk of frost. A south-facing slope (in the northern hemisphere) is almost always the ideal, but local conditions can modify this. In areas with autumn morning fog, a westerly slope is preferable, since the sun does not normally burn through the fog until the afternoon. The best slopes of the Rheingau are good examples. But, in Burgundy and Alsace, easterly slopes have the advantage of sun all morning to warm the ground, which stores the heat while the angle of the sun decreases during the afternoon. Alsace also benefits from a particularly sunny local climate caused by the "rain shadow" of the Vosges mountains to its west.

Many of the best Old World vineyards (*e.g.* in Germany, the Rhône Valley, the Douro Valley) were terraced on steep slopes to combine the advantages of slope with some depth of soil. Being inaccessible to machinery, terraces are largely being abolished. In Germany, huge earth-moving projects have rebuilt whole hills to allow tractors to operate. The Douro Valley is being remodelled with wide, sloping terraces instead of the old, narrow, flat ones. Experiments with "vertical" planting on the steep Douro slopes – doing away with terraces altogether – have been inconclusive. Heavy rains can wash soil nutrients to the bottom of the slope. A flat valley floor (as in the Napa Valley) is the most risky place to plant vines, because cold air drains into it on spring nights, at a time when the vines have tender shoots (see Frost Protection, right).

It is noteworthy that, in Burgundy, the *grands crus* vineyards have a lower incidence of frost damage than the *premiers crus* – presumably because growers have observed the cold spots and lavished their attentions on the safer ones. The same distinction is even true of the incidence of hail. The term microclimate refers to the immediate surroundings of the vine. The slightest difference can become important in the long period between bud-break and harvest. In the Rheingau, wind is considered a principal enemy, since it can blow out accumulated warmth from the rows – which are therefore planted across the prevailing summer southwesterly wind.

Another microclimatic factor is the shade and possible build-up of humidity under a dense canopy of leaves (*see* Training & Trellising, right). Yet another is the greater incidence of frost over soil covered with herbage than over bare earth, which makes it worth cultivating the vine rows in spring. Microclimatic factors are difficult to pin down with exactitude, but there is no doubt that exposure to sun and wind, elevation and luminosity, susceptibility to frost or erosion, are all vital factors in defining not only the quality, but also the flavour of the wines that will eventually result.

Frost Protection

A dormant *vinifera* vine in winter can survive temperatures down to -28°C (-18°F). In regions where lower temperatures regularly occur, it is common practice to bury the lower half of the vines by "earthing-up" in late autumn. A vine is most vulnerable to frost in spring, when its new growth is green and sappy. The only old means of protection (still widely practised) was to light stoves (or "smudge pots") in the vineyards on clear spring nights. It was often a forlorn hope. An improvement introduced in the frost-prone areas of California, for example, was a giant fan to keep the air in the vineyard moving and prevent cold air accumulating, but it has proved ineffectual without heaters. Helicopters are also an efficient, if expensive, way of circulating freezing air to prevent frost damage. Then there is the sprinkler, which simply rains heavily on the almost-freezing vine. The water freezes on contact with the young shoots and forms a protective layer of ice, which acts as insulation against frosts. Such sprinklers can be an excellent investment, doubling as a (somewhat crude) method of irrigation during dry, hot summers.

Training & Trellising

Most vineyards used to consist of innumerable individual bushes, "head"- or "gobelet"-pruned to a few buds from the short trunk after each harvest. With a few famous exceptions (among them the Mosel, parts of the Rhône, and Beaujolais) most modern vineyards are "cordoned" – that is, with the vines trained onto one or more wires parallel to the ground, supported at intervals by stakes. The wish to use mechanical harvesters has encouraged the use of higher trellising systems, often designed to spread the foliage at the top by means of a crossbar supporting two parallel wires four feet apart. The first such trellis was developed in Austria in the 1930s by Lenz Moser. High trellises are not suitable for cool areas such as Germany, where heat radiation from the ground is essential for ripening. On the other hand, they have been used immemorially in northern Portugal to produce deliberately acidic wine. Widespread "curtains" of foliage, or "double curtains" where the vine is made to branch onto two high supporting wires, have several advantages in warm areas. They expose a larger leaf surface for photosynthesis, at the same time as shading bunches of grapes from direct sunlight. In fertile soils which can support vigorous growth, the so-called "lyre" system, spreading the vine top into two mounds of foliage, is very successful – if not for top-quality wine, at least for good quantities of ripe grapes.

Canopy Management

Viticulturists, especially in newer wine regions, have become much more aware of the concept of canopy management. They appreciate how it is possible to manipulate the vine, to give the grapes more or less direct exposure to sunlight, and control the amount of vegetation, so that humidity within the canopy does not cause disease. Any number of ingenious trellising methods are being developed (especially by the Australian guru of the canopy, Dr. Richard Smart), not only the "double curtain" and "lyre" system, but also Scott Henry and Sylvoz, all with the same intent of obtaining the best fruit without curtailing yields to uneconomic levels.

Pruning Methods

Pruning methods have been adapted to new methods of vine training. The most significant new development is mechanical pruning, which dispenses with the skilled but laborious hand-work in the depths of winter, by treating the vine row as a hedge. Aesthetically appalling, results (initially in Australia) show that a system of small circular saws straddling the vine and cutting all wood extending beyond a certain narrow compass can be as satisfactory as the practised eye and hand. Although some hand pruning may be necessary it is certain to become more common in vineyards. Experience in California, for example, has shown that mechanical pruning costs as little as fifteen per cent of the cost of hand pruning.

Growth Regulators

For many years it has been customary to trim excessively long, leafy shoots from the tops and sides of vines in summer. The growth-regulating spray, a chemical which slowly releases ethylene gas, inhibits further leaf growth, prevents the canopy from becoming too dense, and encourages the plant to make its carbohydrate reserves available to the fruit, instead of allowing it to waste them on useless long shoots. It apparently also encourages ripening, and makes it easier for a mechanical harvester to detach the grapes from their stems.

Excessive vigour is a problem and can be combated with various trellising and pruning methods. Good vineyard management also helps: for example, planting crops such as chicory, which has a deep tap root that takes up excess water and competes against the vines, reducing their vigour.

Systemic Sprays

The traditional protection against fungal diseases such as mildew in the vineyard is "Bordeaux mixture", a bright-blue copper-sulphate solution, sprayed from a long-legged tractor (but washed off again by the next rain). New "systemic" sprays are absorbed into the sap-stream of the plants and destroy their fungal (or insect) victim from inside the leaf or grape. Unfortunately, fungal diseases, and such pests as red-spider mites, can rapidly develop resistance, making it necessary for manufacturers to vary the formula (at great expense). The best-known systemic fungicide, benomyl, is now of limited use for this reason.

Organic Cultivation

Wine can be grown by organic methods, just as any other crop. This cuts out artificial fertilizers, insecticides, and other sprays. Three years must pass since the vineyard was last artificially fertilized before the wine can be called "organic". Some sprays can be used – old-fashioned copper-sulphate is one. The organic logic must also be followed through into the winery. More exacting than organic is biodynamic viticulture, which follows principles laid down by a guru of the 1930s, Rudolph Steiner. There is a complete viticultural calendar, which advises on the most appropriate time to treat the vines, based on the phases of the moon, among other criteria. Some see bio-dynamism as a return to nature, others as almost a witchcraft, but such excellent wines are made this way (which is extremely demanding on the grower) that none can ignore it. Organic and biodynamic cultivation are on the increase as growers respond to public concerns about the use of toxic materials in the vineyard. "Pest management" schemes seek to combat insect damage by introducing other natural predators – in Western Australia for instance, guinea fowl gobble up destructive mites.

Making Wine

Controlling Yield

Higher quantity means lower quality. Acceptance of this golden rule is built into the appellation regulations of France, Italy, and most European wine-producing nations. In France, some areas limit the yield to thirty-five hectolitres per hectare (about two tons per acre) or even less, although Bordeaux is cropped at a more generous fifty to sixty hectolitres per hectare. *Vins de pays* are allowed to produce up to eighty hl or even more. In Italy, the limits are expressed in a similar way as so many quintals (100kg) of grapes per hectare, with a limit on the amount of juice that may be extracted from each quintal. It is widely accepted that in parts of Germany and Italy, officially sanctioned yields are too high for the production of good-quality wine, and the best growers' associations, such as Germany's VDP, insist on far lower yields for their members.

The New World, as yet, has no regulations in this regard – which, in view of its *laissez-faire* philosophy, is not surprising. However, conscientious growers are keenly aware of the detrimental effect of too high a yield, and many, if their crop looks like being excessive, will carry out a green harvest come mid-summer. This entails the removal of part of the potential crop so that the vine concentrates its energy on ripening what is left. Others may suggest that this upsets the natural balance of the vine, and ideally the crop should be regulated by intelligent pruning. Nonetheless, "global warming" and the planting of productive rootstocks and clones often oblige even the most conscientious growers to green-harvest. The practice has additional advantages: the remaining bunches will ripen earlier (useful in northerly climates where rain or hail can occur during harvest) and the better-spaced grapes will be less susceptible to rot in wet weather.

Irrigation

Irrigation used to be considered utterly incompatible with quality wine. But such important regions as Argentina, Chile, Washington State, and large parts of Australia could not grow grapes at all without it. No one can deny the quality of their best wines. Once again, it is a question of understanding the metabolism of the vine and using intelligence and moderation. Modern viticulturists can use techniques such as neutron probes and "pressure bombs" to ensure the vines receive the right amount of water at the right time. Sensible irrigation can give better results than the natural but random downpours of rain that are the sole recourse in regions where the practice is forbidden.

Mechanical Harvesting

A machine for picking grapes, saving the stiff backs (and high wages) of the tens of thousands who turn out to the harvest each year, only became a reality in the 1960s (in New York State, picking Concord grapes). By the 1980s, machines harvested a third of all America's wine grapes, and the percentage is now higher still. The mechanical harvester is an inevitable advance. In France, it has gained wide acceptance in big vineyards, though some quality areas still resist, especially where steep terrain makes the use of a machine impractical. Similarly, many sites in Germany, Portugal, and northeast Italy are too steep to permit any alternative to manual harvesting.

The machine works by straddling the vine row and violently shaking the trunks, while slapping at the extremities of the vine with flexible paddles or striker bars. The grapes fall onto a conveyor belt, which carries them from near ground level to a chute above the vine tops. Here they pass in front of a fan, which blows away any loose leaves, and the grapes are then shot into a hopper towed by a tractor in the next alley between the vines. In many cases, the hopper leads straight to a crusher, and the crusher to a closed tank, so that the grapes leave the vineyard already crushed, sheltered from sunlight and insects, and dosed with sulphur dioxide (SO_2) to prevent oxidation.

The harvester has many advantages. Firstly, it can operate at night, when the grapes are cool, and secondly, it needs only two operators. Whereas a traditional team may have to start while some grapes are still unripe, and finish when some are overripe, the machine works fast enough to pick a whole vineyard at ideal maturity. The harvesting rate in California is up to 150 tons (or up to about sixteen hectares) a day. The disadvantages of the harvester include the need for especially robust trellising, the loss of perhaps ten per cent of the crop, and the slight risk of including leaves, insects, and other unwanted matter in the crush. In addition, skin contact is inevitable, and for this reason machines are not permitted in Champagne, or in Beaujolais, where whole bunches are essential to the vinification process. Although mechanical harvesters are becoming more refined, their use remains controversial, especially in regions with a reputation for very high quality.

Botrytis Infection

The benevolent aspect of the fungus mould *Botrytis cinerea*, as the "noble rot" which produces great sweet wines, receives so much publicity that its malevolent appearance in the vineyard at the wrong time can be forgotten. In some regions (particularly in Germany), its prevalence has made it the most serious and widespread disease the grower has to confront. The more fertile the vineyard and luxuriant the vine, the more likely it is to strike at the unripe or (most vulnerable) semi-ripe grapes and rot the bunch. It starts by attacking grapes punctured by insects or "grape worm"; controlling the bugs is therefore the most effective protection. Only when the sugar content in the grapes has reached about 70° Oechsle or 17° Brix (enough to make wine of about nine per cent natural alcohol) does evil rot become noble rot. For a description of noble rot see page 66 (Château d'Yquem). Some New World regions have experimented with inducing botrytis infection artificially by spraying spores onto the vineyards. Results are inconclusive, though some good sweet wines have been produced by this method.

Sugar & Acid Levels

The crucial decision of when to pick the grapes depends on the measurement of their sugar and acid contents. As they ripen, sugar increases and acid decreases. For each type of wine there is an ideal moment when the ratio is just right.

Ripening starts at the moment called *véraison*, when the grape, which has been growing slowly by cell division, still hard and bright green, grows rapidly by the enlargement of each cell. This is when red grapes begin to change colour.

Sugar content is usually measured with a handheld "refractometer". A drop of juice is held between two prisms. Light passing through it bends at a different angle according to its sugar content; the angle is read off on a scale calibrated as degrees Brix, Oechsle, or Baumé, the American, German, and French systems, respectively, for measuring ripeness.

In warm weather, sugar content may increase by up to 0.4° Brix a day, while there may be a significant drop in acidity. "Ripe" grapes vary between about eighteen and twenty-sic degrees Brix (*i.e.* with a potential alcohol level of 9.3 to fourteen per cent by volume). Different levels of acidity are considered ideal for different styles of wine. In Germany, acid levels as high as 0.9 per cent would be commendable for a wine of 11.3 per cent potential alcohol (ninety degrees Oechsle). In France or California, the recommended acidity level for grapes with the same sugar content would be approximately 0.7 per cent for white wine and slightly lower for red. One risk in hotter regions is rapidly rising sugar levels, which induce growers to pick before the whole grape is fully mature, resulting in harsh, "green", tannic flavours. The trick is to achieve "phenolic" ripeness (*i.e.* ripe seeds and tannins) before sugar levels become so high that "hot", over-alcoholic wines result.

The third variable taken into account is the pH of the juice. This is a measure of the strength, rather than volume, of its acidity. The lower the figure, the sharper the juice. Normal pH in wine is in the range 2.8–3.8. Low pH readings are desirable for stability and (in red wines) good colour.

Although scientific measurements can be invaluable aids in deciding when to pick, many growers cling to the time-honoured method of sampling the grapes throughout the vineyard, relying on taste above all.

Handling the Fruit

A good winemaker will not accept grapes that have been badly damaged on the way from the vineyard, or with a high proportion of mouldy bunches, or what the Californians call MOG (matter other than grapes, *e.g.* leaves, stones, and soil). For winemaking at the highest standard the bunches are picked over by hand – *triage* – and rotten grapes thrown out. Some producers do this in the vineyard, but most have conveyor belts at the winery, where a team of sharp-eyed workers can spot and remove unworthy fruit. With large quantities, a degree of imperfection must be accepted.

Several regions of Europe specify the size and design of container that must be used for bringing in the grapes. The object here is to prevent the weight of large quantities from crushing the grapes at the bottom. The huge "gondolas" often used for transporting grapes in California, frequently under a hot sun, have the distinct drawback in that many of the grapes at the bottom will be broken and macerating in juice long before they even reach the carefully controlled hygienic conditions of the winery.

SO$_2$

The first step in winemaking procedures is usually the addition of a small dose of sulphur dioxide (SO$_2$) to the crushed grapes, or must. Nothing has supplanted this universal and age-old antiseptic of the winemaker in protecting the must from premature or wild fermentation, and both must and wine from oxidation, though some advanced winemakers use very little and strive to use none – putting instead physical barriers (*e.g.* inert gases) between the juice or wine and the oxygen in the atmosphere.

The amount of SO$_2$ allowed is regulated by law. Wine with too much has a sharp, brimstone smell and leaves a burning feeling in the throat – a common occurrence in the past, particularly in semi-sweet wines where the sulphur was used to prevent refermentation in the bottle. Sterile filters have now eliminated the need for this, and the consumer should be unaware that wine's old preservative is used at all. Some people may suffer ill-effects from SO$_2$: hence the USA regulation that labels state "contains sulfites".

White Wine – "Skin-Contact" or Not

Light, fresh, and fruity white wines are made by pressing the grapes as soon as possible after picking. The aim is to prevent the juice from picking up any flavours ("extract") from the skin. The grapes are gently crushed, just hard enough to break their skins. This pomace is then loaded directly into the press. In wineries looking for maximum freshness, the juice or even the grapes may be chilled.

Many bigger wineries now use a "de-juicer" between the crusher and the press. This may consist of a mesh screen, sometimes in the form of a conveyor belt, through which the "free" juice falls. A de-juicer reduces the number of times the press has to be laboriously filled and emptied, but it increases the chance of oxidation of the juice. One de-juicer that avoids oxidation is a stainless-steel tank with a central cylinder formed of a mesh screen. The crushed pomace is loaded into the space around this cylinder and carbon dioxide (CO$_2$) is pumped under pressure into the headspace. The free juice is gently forced to drain out via the central cylinder, leaving relatively little pomace to be pressed. Up to seventy per cent can be free-run juice, leaving only thirty per cent to be extracted by pressing.

Fuller, more robust wines with more flavour and tannins to preserve them while they age, are made by holding the skins in contact with the juice in a tank for up to twenty-four hours after crushing. This maceration (at low temperature, before fermentation starts) extracts some of the elements that are present in the skins but not the juice. The pomace is then de-juiced and pressed as usual. Few winemakers go further and ferment white wines with their skins, like red wines; the resulting wine would be too heavy for today's taste. Skin contact has fallen from fashion, since it is only beneficial when the grapes are in perfect health. Modern winemakers worry that skin contact can impart a phenolic or tannic flavour and texture to a wine, diminishing its freshness.

White Wine – Stems or No Stems

White grapes are usually pressed with their stems, unless they are machine-harvested. The reason is that unfermented grape flesh and juice are full of pectins and sugar, making them slippery and sticky. The stems make the operation of the press easier, particularly when it comes to breaking up the "cake" to press a second time. The press should not be used at a high enough pressure to squeeze any bitter juice out of stems or pips. Many top-quality wines are now being made by whole-bunch pressing, with no crushing or destemming. The technique helps to retain aroma and maintain a low pH.

Types of Press

There is a wide choice of types of press, ranging from the old-fashioned vertical (or hydraulic or basket) model, in which a plate is forced down onto the pomace contained in a cylindrical cage of vertical slots to the mass-production continuous press. The first is the most labour-intensive, but still produces the clearest juice; the second is very cheap and easy to run, but cannot make better than medium-grade wine. Until recently, many wineries chose a horizontal press, which works on a principle similar to the old vertical press, squeezing the pomace by means of plates which are brought together by a central screw.

This has been superceded technically by a "bladder" or "membrane" press. This contains a long rubber balloon which, when inflated, squeezes the pomace against the surrounding fine grille. Both are "batch" presses, meaning that they have to be filled and emptied anew for each batch of pomace, whereas the continuous press spews forth an unending stream of juice below and "cake" at the end.

White Wine – Cold Fermentation

The most revolutionary invention in modern winemaking is controlled-temperature fermentation, particularly for white wines, which used to be flat and low in acid, in warm climates. What was done naturally by using small barrels in the cold cellars of Europe is now practised industrially in California, Australia, and elsewhere by chilling the contents of often huge, stainless-steel vats. Most vats are double-skinned or "jacketed" with a layer of glycol or ammonia as a cooling agent between the skins. Another technique is to dribble cold water down the outside surface. A second-best method is to circulate the wine through a heat exchanger (or a coil submerged in cold water) outside the vat.

Each winemaker has his own idea about the ideal temperature for fermentation. Long, cool fermentation is reputedly good for fruity flavours, though when practised to extremes on certain grapes – particularly non-aromatic sorts – it seems to leave its mark on the wine as a "pear-drop" smell. A number of modern Italian white wines, and even occasionally red ones, are spoilt by over-enthusiastic refrigeration. In Germany, to the contrary, very cold fermentation has gone out of fashion. The normal temperatures for white wine fermentation in California are between 8° and 15°C (46°–59°F). In France, 18°C (64°F) is considered cold. If the temperature is forced down too far, the fermentation will "stick" and the yeasts cease to function. It can be difficult to start again, and the wine will almost certainly suffer in the process.

A completely different approach is used to make "big", richer, smoother, and more heavy-bodied wines from Chardonnay and sometimes Sauvignon Blanc. They are fermented at between 15° and 20°C (59°–68°F), or in barrels even as high as 25°C (77°F). However, the small volumes in a wooden barrel mean that temperatures will never rise to excessive levels.

White Wine – Clarifying the Juice

Modern presses are more efficient than old models but often produce juice with a higher proportion of suspended solids (pieces of grape skins, flesh, pips or dirt). Fermentation of white wine with these solids tends to produce bitterness, so the juice must be cleaned first. This can be done by holding it for a day or more in a "settling" tank, at a cool temperature, allowing particles to sink to the bottom; by filtering through a powerful "vacuum" filter; or (fastest) by use of a centrifuge pump, which uses centrifugal force to throw out all foreign bodies. Over-centrifuged wine can be stripped of desirable as well as undesirable constituents; great care is needed, and many wineries once equipped with the technology have abandoned it.

White Wine – Adjusting Acidity

Either de- or re-acidification of white-wine must may be necessary, depending on the ripeness of the crop. Overacid juice is de-acidified by adding calcium carbonate (chalk) to remove tartaric acid, or a substance called Acidex, which removes malic acid as well by "double-salt precipitation". In Germany, the addition of sugar and (up to fifteen per cent) water to wines of QbA level (*see* page 237) and below naturally lowers the proportion of acidity. In France, chaptalization with dry sugar (permitted in the centre and north) has the same effect to a lesser degree. In the south of France, however, only concentrated must, not sugar, is allowed for raising the alcoholic degree; it naturally raises the acid level at the same time.

In Australia and other warm countries where the usual problem is too little acid, it is permitted to add one of the acids that naturally occur in grapes: malic, citric, and tartaric. Tartaric is preferred, since it has no detectable flavour and also helps towards tartrate stability (*see* Cold Stabilization, right). But it is more expensive.

Tanks & Vats

The unquestioned grandeur and nobility of traditional fermenting vats of oak (or sometimes chestnut, acacia or redwood) is accompanied by many disadvantages. Most important are the problems of disinfecting them and keeping them watertight between vintages.

Early in the twentieth century, concrete began to replace them in newer and bigger wineries. It is strong, permanent, and easy to clean. Moreover, it can be made in any shape to fit odd corners and save space. Although considered obsolete after the installation of stainless-steel vats in recent decades, winemakers are coming to respect the advantages of concrete, in which the wine is never subjected to extremes of temperature. In 2003, a new winery, kitted out with new concrete tanks, opened in Argentina.

Nonetheless, in almost all modern wineries, stainless steel is the king. It is strong, inert, simple to clean and to cool. Moreover, it is also extremely versatile; the same tank can be used for fermentation and, later in the year, for storage, ageing, or blending. Its high initial cost is thus quite quickly recouped.

To make good wine, a winery must have ample capacity. It often happens that in an abundant vintage there is a shortage of space. Grapes cannot be stored, so the only answer is to cut short the fermenting time of the early batches. With red wines this will mean shorter maceration on the skins and thus lighter wine. Well-designed modern wineries not only have plenty of tank space, they have tanks in a variety of sizes to avoid leaving small lots of wine in half-full containers or being obliged to mix them.

Wooden fermenters are also making a comeback, not only in Bordeaux, but in the New World, where Mondavi has installed them, at great expense, in its new winery. They are expensive to maintain, but purists insist they are still the ideal medium for prolonged, even fermentation.

Yeasts

There are yeasts naturally present in every vineyard and winery, which will cause fermentation if they are allowed to. Some consider them part of the stamp, or personality, of their locality, and believe they help to give their wine its individuality. Indeed, an experiment in swapping the yeasts of different Bordeaux château showed how distinct each strain was: Graves could be made to resemble Pauillac. Many modern wineries, wanting to keep total control, take care to remove the natural yeast (by filtering or centrifuging), or at least to render it helpless with a strong dose of SO_2. Some even flash-pasteurize the juice by heating it to 55°C (131°F) to kill off bacteria and inhibit the wild yeasts. They then proceed to inoculate the must with a cultured yeast of their choice, which is known to multiply actively at the temperature they choose for fermentation. Some of the most popular yeasts in California go by the promising names of "Montrachet", "Champagne", and "Steinberg". The secret is to start the fermentation with a generous amount of active yeast; once the whole vat is fermenting, such problems as oxidation can temporarily be forgotten. The activity of yeast increases rapidly with rising temperature. For each additional degree Celsius, yeast transforms ten per cent more sugar into alcohol in a given time. The ceiling to this frantic activity occurs at about 30°C–35°C (86°F–95°F) when the yeasts are overcome by heat. A "run-away" fermentation can "stick" at this temperature, just as most yeasts will not function below about 10°C (50°F). There is no doubt that using cultivated yeasts is less risky than relying on natural yeasts. But there are drawbacks. The use of the same yeast for every wine can impart a uniform flavour to those wines. Moreover, some cultivated yeasts are so effective that their "conversion rate" of sugar into alcohol can be very high, resulting in wines with worryingly high alcohol levels: a frequent problem with wines from Australia and California.

Specialized use of *flor* yeast for producing sherry is now greatly advanced. New ways have been found to produce the sherry effect much faster and with more certainty than the traditional way of leaving the naturally occurring layer of *flor* floating on the wine.

White Wines – Malolactic Fermentation

Secondary or malolactic fermentation (*see* Red Wine – Malolactic Fermentation) is less common with white wine than with red. It is sometimes encouraged, to reduce excess acidity in wines from cool climates (*e.g.* Chablis and other parts of Burgundy, Loire, Switzerland, but less commonly in Germany). Its complex biological nature may help to add complexity to flavours. In warmer regions where acidity tends to be low, such as California and Australia, malolactic fermentation in white wines is often avoided.

White Wines – Residual Sugar

A completed natural fermentation makes a totally dry wine, all its sugar converted to alcohol. The only exceptions are wines made of grapes so sweet that either the alcohol level or the sugar, or both, prevents the yeasts from functioning. To make light, sweet wines, either the fermentation has to be artificially interrupted or sweet juice has to be blended with dry wine. The former was the old way. It needed a strong dose of SO_2 to stop the fermentation, and more in the bottle to prevent it starting again. The invention of filters fine enough to remove all yeasts, and means of bottling in conditions of complete sterility, now solve the sulphur problem.

Some winemakers in Germany used to prefer a different method: blending with "sweet reserve". This became the standard procedure for producing the sweet and semi-sweet wines of Germany up to Auslese level. The method used is to sterilize a portion of the juice instead of fermenting it. The majority of the wine is made in the normal way, fermented until no sugar is left. The "sweet reserve" (in German *süssreserve*) is then added to taste, and the blend bottled under sterile conditions. The addition of unfermented juice naturally lowers the alcohol content of the wine. At top estates in Germany, *süssreserve* is no longer used. Instead, wines are allowed to cease fermentation naturally, with varying degrees of residual sugar, and different lots are then blended to produce the best-balanced wine.

Although it is fashionable to prefer dry wines to sweet, many consumers would be surprised to know that many so-called dry wines, such as a large number of New World Chardonnays, contain a small amount of residual sugar. The sweetness may not be discernible, but adds roundness and texture to the wine.

White Wine – After Fermentation

After white wine has fermented, it must be clarified. The traditional method was to allow it to settle and then rack it off its lees (composed largely of dead yeast cells). When Muscadet is bottled *sur lie* this is exactly what is happening. Modern wineries, however, tend to use a filter for this clarification, if necessary with the additional precaution of fining with a powdery clay from Wyoming called bentonite, which removes excess proteins: potential causes of later trouble in the form of cloudy wine. Bentonite fining is also sometimes used on the must before fermentation.

White wines not intended for ageing (*i.e.* most light commercial wines) then need only to be stabilized and filtered before they can be bottled and distributed. Those intended for ageing are usually transferred into barrel for clarification, so that they enjoy the same benefits of barrel-ageing as red wines. They may be left for several months on the fine lees, which may be regularly stirred up, in a process called *bâtonnage*, so that the wine benefits from the effects of yeast autolysis, whereby the lees, including dead yeast, impart extra complexity to the flavour of the wine.

White Wine – Cold Stabilization

The tartaric acid, which is a vital ingredient in the balance and flavour of all wines, has an unfortunate habit of forming crystals in combination with either potassium (quite big sugary grains) or calcium (finer and whiter, powdery crystals). In former times, wine was kept for several years in cool cellars, and these crystals formed a hard deposit on the walls of their casks, known in Germany as *weinstein* – "wine stone". With faster modern methods, most large wineries consider it essential to prevent the crystals forming after the wine is bottled. Although the crystals have no flavour at all, and are totally natural and harmless, there are ignorant and querulous customers who will send back a bottle with any sign of deposit.

Unfortunately, it is a costly business to remove the risk of tartrate crystals. The simplest way is to chill the wine to just above freezing point in a tank for several days. The process is accelerated by "seeding" with added tartrate crystals to act as nuclei for more crystals to form. More efficient ways of achieving this strictly unnecessary object will keep research chemists busy for years to come.

Red Wine – Stems or No Stems

Each red winemaker has his own view about whether the grape stems should be included, wholly or in part – and it changes with the vintage. In the Rhône, the stems are sometimes included; in Burgundy only rarely; in Bordeaux few or none; in Chinon on the Loire, the stems are left on the vine. Outside Europe, stems are usually excluded.

The argument for destemming is that stalks add astringency, lower the alcohol content, reduce the colour, and take up valuable space in vat. The argument for keeping some of them in is that they help the process of fermentation by aerating the mass, they lower the acidity, and they make pressing easier. In any case, the stems must be thoroughly ripe, or they will add "green" flavours to the wine.

Must Concentration

In the late 1980s, French oenologists developed systems for removing water from grapes harvested in wet conditions. The most popular technology was reverse osmosis. Its careful use could eliminate the dilution that water, on or beneath the skins, could cause. It could also increase the potential alcohol of the concentrated must, so European authorities would not allow concentrated must to be chaptalized. The technique has been legal in France for some years, and was permitted in Germany from 2002 onwards. Must concentrators are now clearly part of the standard equipment at many wineries.

The technique remains controversial, as it is open to abuse. It can encourage lazy growers to pick too early or during wet spells, on the grounds that they can then correct any deficiencies by concentration. This reasoning is flawed, since the technology concentrates all components in the wine, and any unripe flavours would only be augmented. But used with care and discretion, must concentration can be a positive development in improving overall wine quality in difficult vintages.

Red Wine – Pumping Over

When a vat of red wine ferments, the grape skins float to the surface, buoyed up by bubbles of CO_2 which attach themselves to solid matter. The "cap" (French, *chapeau*, Spanish *sombrero*) that they form contains all the essential colouring matter – and is prone to overheating and being attacked by bacteria. It is therefore essential to keep mixing the cap back into the liquid below. There are several methods.

In Bordeaux, the cap is often pushed under by men with long poles. In Burgundy, with smaller vats, it is trodden under (*pigeage*) by men, formerly naked, who jump into the vat. Another widespread method is to fit a grille below the filling level, which holds the cap immersed (*chapeau immergé*). Mechanical "plungers" are also used. But the most widespread method now used is "pumping over": taking wine by a hose from the bottom of the vat and spraying it over the cap, usually several times a day.

Several ingenious alternatives have been invented. The "Rototank" is a closed horizontal cylinder which slowly rotates, continually mixing the liquids and solids inside. Its advantage is speed of extraction, but most quality-conscious winemakers prefer a slower fermentation with frequent pumping over.

An automatic system developed in Portugal, where the traditional way of extracting the colour was night-long stomping by all the village lads to the sound of accordions, involves an ingenious gusher device activated by the build-up of CO_2 pressure in a sealed tank.

Micro-oxygenation

This controversial technique was developed in Madiran in the late 1980s by wine producer Patrick Ducournau. Madiran wine is produced from the notoriously tannic Tannat grape, and the technique was aimed at softening those tannins by introducing a controlled dose of oxygen during fermentation and/or during the ageing process in barrels. There seems no doubt that the technique works, and that its use can greatly subdue harsh tannins and unripe flavours. Micro-oxygenation has become a useful weapon in the armoury of industrial winemakers.

However, it is also widely used at some of the top properties in Bordeaux and elsewhere. The idea of "dosing" the wine during barrel maturation is to lessen the need for racking, which, the proponents of micro-oxygenation argue, is a more brutal and less controllable method of introducing oxygen into the wine. This may be so, but what is still unknown is the overall effect of the technique on the ageing potential of wines that are intended to be kept for years or decades before being drunk.

Red Wine – Pressing

By the time fermentation is finished, or nearly finished and merely simmering slightly, most (up to eighty-five per cent) of the red wine is separated from the solid matter and will run freely from the vat. This free run or *vin de goutte* is siphoned out of the vat into either barrels or another tank. The remaining *marc* is pressed. Red wine is pressed in the same types of presses as white, but after fermentation the pulp and skins have partly disintegrated and offer less resistance.

Relatively gentle pressure will release very good quality vin de presse, which is richer in desirable extracts and flavours than the *vin de goutte*. It may need such treatment as fining, to reduce astringency and remove solids, but in most cases it will be a positive addition and make better wine for longer keeping. Wine from a second, more vigorous, pressing will almost always be too astringent, and will be sold separately, or used in a cheap blend. The amount of press wine blended into the free-run will vary from vintage to vintage, and be affected by the stylistic preference of the winemaker.

The Value of Barrels

The development of winemaking in the New World, with its more questioning approach, has drawn attention to what has long been known, but taken for granted, in France and elsewhere: that new barrels have a profound effect on the flavour of wine stored in them – and even more on wine fermented in them. California Chardonnays, fermented in the same French oak as white burgundy, can have an uncanny resemblance to its flavour.

Barrels were invented (probably by the Gauls) of necessity as the most durable and transportable of containers, supplanting the amphora and the goatskin in regions that could afford them. They have developed to their standard sizes and shapes over centuries of experience. The 200-odd-litre barrels of Bordeaux, Burgundy, and Rioja are the largest that one man can easily roll or two men carry – but they also happen to present the greatest surface area of wood to wine of any practicable size.

The advantages of this contact lie partly in the very slow transfer of oxygen through the planks of the barrel, and partly through the tannin and other substances that the wine dissolves from the wood itself. The most easily identified (by taste or smell) of these is vanillin, which has the flavour of vanilla. Oak tannin is useful in augmenting and slightly varying the tannins naturally present in wine as preservatives. Other scents and flavours are harder to define, but can be well-enough expressed as the "smell of a carpenter's shop".

Which wines benefit from this addition of extraneous flavours? Only those with strong characters and constitutions of their own. It would be disastrous to a fragile Mosel or a Beaujolais Nouveau. The "bigger" the wine and the longer it is to be matured, the more oak it can take.

New barrels are extremely expensive. A typical 2002 price is 510 euros. The full impact of their oak flavour diminishes rapidly after the first two or three years' use, but there is a lively trade in secondhand barrels, particularly those that have contained great wines. Barrels can also be renewed to full pungency by shaving the wine-leached interior down to fresh wood. A cheap but effective way of adding oak flavour to wine is to use oak chips. These are still strictly forbidden in France – and indeed, considered shocking – but chips are widely accepted in the New World for cheaper wines. They vary in size from sawdust granules to matchsticks, and must be properly seasoned to avoid any harsh flavours. Winemakers must calculate how much they need, according to the volume of the wine and the desired degree of oakiness, and the chips are added to the wine in a muslin bag. Properly used, they are very effective in flavouring both Chardonnay and red wine for those who like the extraneous flavour of oak (I don't). A better but still questionable method is to introduce toasted wooden staves into the tank.

A quite different role is played by the huge permanent oak barrels, (*foudres*, or *demi-muids* in French, *fuders* or *stücks* in German), which are common in southern France, Germany, Italy, Spain, and eastern Europe. Their oak flavour has been minimized or neutralized by constant impregnation with wine, and often by a thick layer of tartrate crystals. Their value seems to lie in offering an ideal environment, with very gradual oxidation, for the maturing and slow stabilizing of wine. Before the advent of sterile bottling, an oak vat was simply the safest place for a grower to store wine, sometimes for years, topped up with fresh wine as necessary.

Cooperage has become something of a fetish. Winemakers frequently compare the same wine aged in oak from different French forests, even from the same forest but different barrel makers. The names of Demptos and Nadalié of Bordeaux, of Taransaud and Séguin-Moreau of cognac, and François Frères and the Tonnelleries de Bourgogne of Burgundy are just as familiar in the Napa Valley as in France. (Seventy per cent of all French barrels are exported.) Current opinion seems to be that Limousin oak, which is faster growing with wider rings, imparts coarser flavours to wine, whereas the much tighter-grained oaks of the forests of the Massif Central, Tronçais, Allier, and Nevers, and from the Vosges, provide much more refined flavours for both red and white wines. American white-oak, uncharred, Bourbon barrels are also used. They offer less flavour and tannin but a higher tannin/flavour ratio – good for Cabernet and Zinfandel, less so for white wines. American oak is significantly cheaper than French oak, which has encouraged some French coopers, such as Demptos and Séguin-Moreau to establish cooperages in California, where they use French methods to treat American oak, with some success.

Baltic, Balkan, and other oaks are also used, and much has been written about their relative merits. Since there is no visual difference, and a cooper's shop contains oak from many sources, one may well be sceptical about such fine distinctions in any case. Other factors, such as the thickness of the staves, whether they have been split or sawn, air-dried or kiln-dried, steamed or "toasted" with varying degrees of toasting, even whether the barrel is washed in hot water or cold, can all start arguments among the initiated. Consequently, some people place more emphasis on the type of oak, while others attach more importance to the individual cooper.

Red Wine – Carbonic Maceration

The technique of fermenting uncrushed grapes, known as *macération carbonique*, has been developed in France since 1935 by Professor Michel Flanzy and others. The method is described on page 128. It began to make a real impact in the early 1970s in dramatically improving the quality of the better Midi wines, especially from intrinsically tough grape varieties such as Carignan. It is now well-established in France as the best way to produce fruity, supple, richly coloured reds for drinking young, but its acceptance has been surprisingly slow in other countries. Low acidity tends to make such wines short-lived, which is inappropriate for the finest growths. But a proportion can be a valuable element in a blend with a particularly tannic and/or acidic red component.

Racking

Once the lees, or sediment, in a barrel or vat have sunk to the bottom, the wine is "racked" off them simply by pouring the clear liquid from a tap above the level of the solids. In wines that are kept over a length of time in barrels, racking is repeated every few months, as more solids are precipitated.

If the wine is judged to need more oxygen, racking is done via an open basin; if not, it is done by a hose linking one barrel directly to another.

Red Wine – Malolactic Fermentation

Growers have always been aware of a fresh activity in their barrels of new wine in the spring following the vintage. Folklore put it down to a "natural sympathy" between the wine and the rising sap in the vineyards. It seemed to be a further fermentation, but it happened in wine that had no sugar left to ferment.

The science of microbiology has found the answer. It is a form of fermentation carried on by bacteria, not yeasts, which are feeding on malic ("apple") acid in the wine and converting it to lactic ("milk") acid, giving off CO_2 bubbles in the process. It has several results: a lowering of the quantity of acidity and of its sharpness (lactic acid is milder to taste than malic); and increase of stability, and a less quantifiable smoothing and complicating of the wine's flavour. For almost all red wines, therefore, it is highly desirable, and winemakers take steps to make sure that it takes place.

In most cases, a gentle raising of the temperature in the cellar to about 20°C (68°F) is sufficient. Sometimes it is necessary to import the right bacteria, and it is now possible to seed the malolactic fermentation artificially. Sometimes, the malolactic fermentation can be encouraged to happen concurrently with the first (alcoholic) fermentation.

Blending for Complexity

Champagne, red and white Bordeaux, Southern Rhône reds, Chianti, Rioja, and port, are all examples of wines made of a mixture of grapes. Burgundy, Barolo, sherry, German and Alsace wines are examples of one-grape wines. American varietal-consciousness has tended to put a premium on the simplistic idea that "100 per cent is best". But recent research has shown that, even among wines of humble quality, a mixture of two is often better than the lesser of the two, and generally better than either. This is taken to prove that complexity is in itself a desirable quality in wine; that one variety can "season" another, as butter and salt do eggs.

There is a general trend in Bordeaux-admiring regions, such as California and Tuscany, towards claret-style blending of Merlot with Cabernet. On the other hand, no other grape has been shown to improve Pinot Noir, Chardonnay, or Riesling. Added complexity in their already delicious flavours either comes with the help of barrel-ageing, in Riesling with "noble-rot", or simply with years in bottle.

Fining

The ancient technique of pouring whipped egg-whites, gelatin, isinglass (fish gelatin), blood, or other coagulants into wine is still widely used both on must and finished wine, despite modern filtration systems. Its object is to clean the liquid of the finest suspended solids (which are too light to sink) and to reduce excessively high tannins. The "fining", poured onto the surface, slowly sinks like a superfine screen, carrying any solids to the bottom. Certain finings such as bentonite (see White Wine – After Fermentation, page 23) are specific to certain undesirable constituents. "Blue" fining (potassium ferrocyanide) removes excess iron from the wine.

Filtration

The Seitz Company of Bad Kreuznach, Germany, has been the pioneer in developing ever finer and finer filters capable of removing almost everything, even the flavour, from wine if they are not used with discretion. Most filters consist of a series of "pads" alternating with plates, through which the wine is forced under pressure. The degree of filtration depends on the pore size of the pads. At 0.65 microns they remove yeast, at 0.45 bacteria as well. To avoid having to change them frequently, wine is nearly always clarified by such other means as fining, before filtration.

Pasteurization

Louis Pasteur, the great French chemist of the late nineteenth century who discovered the relationship of oxygen to wine, and hence the cause of vinegar, gave his name to the process of sterilization by heating to kill off harmful organisms. In wine, this means any yeast and bacteria that might start it re-fermenting.

A temperature of 60°C (140°F) for about thirty minutes is needed – although an alternative preferred today (for bulk wine only) is "flash" pasteurization at a much higher temperature – 85°C (185°F) – for up to one minute. Normally, pasteurization is used only on cheap wines not intended to mature further, although there is evidence that it does not permanently inhibit further development. Modern sterile handling and filtration is steadily phasing out pasteurization from modern wineries.

Ageing

There are two separate and distinct ways in which wine can age: "oxidative" ageing in contact with oxygen, and "reductive" ageing, when the oxygen supply is cut off. Barrel-ageing is oxidative; it encourages numerous complex reactions between the acids, sugars, tannins, pigments, and multifarious polysyllabic constituents of wine.

Bottle-ageing is reductive. Once the wine is bottled, the only oxygen available is the limited amount dissolved in the liquid and trapped between the liquid and the cork. (No oxygen enters through a cork.) In wines with a high CO_2 content (e.g. Champagne) there is not even this much oxygen. Life-forms depending on oxygen are therefore very limited in their scope for activity. "Reductive" means that the oxygen is reduced – eventually to zero. In these conditions different complex reactions between the same constituents occur at a much slower rate. The ultimate quality and complexity in most wines is arrived at only by a combination of these two forms of ageing, though the proportions of each can vary widely. Many white wines are bottled very young, but improve enormously in bottle. Champagne and vintage port are matured almost entirely in bottle. Fine red wines may spend up to three years in barrel, and then perhaps two or three times as long in bottle. Tawny port and sherry are matured entirely in barrel, and are not normally intended for any further bottle-age.

Closures

The traditional way of sealing a bottle has always been with a cork. The closure it achieves is just about perfect, permitting age-worthy wines to mature in bottle over years or even decades. Unfortunately, many corks do come impregnated with a taint known as TCA (trichloroanisole), which can either render the wine entirely undrinkable or, at best, mute its aromas and flavours. Whether TCA is the consequence of chance or negligence is hotly debated, and cannot be resolved here.

However, the high incidence of TCA has led to experimentation with alternative closures such as crown caps, plastic "corks", and screwcaps. The latter have been adopted with enthusiasm by, for example, Australian Riesling producers and Sauvignon Blanc producers in New Zealand. Comparative tastings of the same wine bottled with various closures seem to confirm that screwcaps (also known as Stelvin closures) work best. The move towards screwcap closures for wines destined for immediate consumption is surely to be welcomed. What is less certain is how such closures will affect the development of great red wines, such as Burgundy and Bordeaux.

Bottling

The question of where, and by whom, wine should be bottled has always been much debated, but since the introduction in France of the mobile bottling unit in the 1960s, it has become the rule, rather than the exception, for producers even on a small scale to bottle their own wine. The bottling unit is simply a lorry equipped as a modern semi-automatic bottling plant. Its arrival meant that the evocative words *mis en bouteille au château* or *au domaine*, widely supposed (especially in America) to be a guarantee of authenticity and even quality, could be used by all the little properties that used to rely on merchants to bottle for them. The change rubbed both ways: some merchants' names were a guarantee of well-chosen, well-handled wine; others were not.

Modern automatic bottling lines can be like a cross between an operating theatre and a space shuttle, with airlock doors for total antiseptic sterility. The wine is often "sparged", or flushed out with CO_2 or an inert gas such as nitrogen, to remove any oxygen. The bottle is first filled with nitrogen, and the wine filled into it through a long nozzle (a "Mosel cock") to the bottom, pushing out the gas as the level rises. A once popular device with commercial wines is "hot-bottling": heating the wine to about 54°C (130°F) at the point of filling the bottle. All this is to avoid any chance of refermentation. For naturally stabilized wines that have spent a long time in barrel, such precautions should not be needed.

CO_2 for "Spritz"

Many light white, rosé, and occasionally red wines benefit greatly from being bottled with a small degree of CO_2 dissolved in them – just enough for a few faint bubbles to appear at the brim or the bottom of the glass. In many wines, this is a natural occurrence. In others, it is an easy and effective way of giving a slight prickle of refreshing sharpness to wines that would otherwise be dull, soft, and/or neutral.

Cooperatives

Arguably the most important development for the majority of winemakers in Europe has been the rise of the cooperative movement. By pooling resources and qualifying for generous government grants and loans, the peasant wine-farmers of the past are now nearly all grape-growers who deliver their whole harvest to a well-equipped central winery. Most are now extremely up-to-date, with vats, presses, and bottling lines far better than the district would otherwise have, and a qualified oenologist to make the wine.

A few are outright leaders in their regions; nobody else can afford such heavy investment in modern plant. Nearly all use premiums to encourage farmers to produce riper, healthier, cleaner grapes and charge fines for rot, leaves, and soil in the crop.

However, cooperatives are run for, and sometimes by, their members, who can be stubbornly conservative in their refusal to adapt their vineyards to the requirements of the market. In the absence of firm management, some cooperatives, especially in regions such as the Languedoc, still allow their members to produce vast quantities of overcropped and unsaleable wine.

Flying Winemakers

The trend for what are now called "flying winemakers" first began among the co-ops of southern France and Italy, which have greatly benefited from an input of New World technology and know-how, particularly concerning hygiene and temperature control. The concept (and the term) were invented by the pioneering English wine merchant, Tony Laithwaite.

Many of the young graduates of the Roseworthy College in Australia begin their winemaking experience by clocking up as many vintages as possible on both sides of the world. Central and Eastern Europe, in particular, have benefited from their input.

Often the graduates are employed by established flying winemakers (among them Kym Milne and Jacques Lurton) to produce a specific wine for a specific customer, more often than not for a British supermarket. There is disquiet that some flying winemakers will simply impose a formula on all the wineries for which they work, thus standardizing the wines, but this risk has been overstated. The wines will reflect the quality and character of the grapes from which they are made – however perfect the technology.

Chemical Analysis

Whoever coined the phrase "a chemical symphony" described wine perfectly. (There are, of course, string quartets, too.) Good wine gets its infinitely intriguing flavour from the interweaving of innumerable organic and inorganic substances, in amounts so small that they have hitherto been untraceable.

But this is no longer the case. A gas chromatograph is an instrument capable of identifying and measuring up to 250 different substances in wine so far.

It (and similar instruments) can produce a graphic chemical profile. University of California researchers are playing the fascinating computer game of trying to match the sensory (*e.g.* smell and taste) perception of teams of tasters with the drawings of the chromatograph to discover which substance is responsible for which taste – the idea presumably being that once we know, vineyards and grapes will become obsolete. At a more humdrum level, it is normal to do simple laboratory checks on about twenty constituents, from alcohol and acidity to sugar and sulphur, before giving any wine a clean bill of health.

The Critical Audience

A catalogue of the influences and advances in modern wine would be one-sided without a mention of the consumer. At least as striking as the technological changes of the past twenty-five years has been the snowballing interest in wine as a topic, as well as a drink.

This snowballing began in Britain, spread rapidly to America, Holland, Germany, Scandinavia, and in the past few years has even stirred the great bastions of conservatism and complacency: France, Italy, and Spain, the major wine-producing nations.

Books and articles about wine, comparative tastings, newsletters, and reviews have turned the spotlight on the individual winemaker. The motivation is there not just to sell, but also to excel. The spirit of rivalry and the friendly confrontation between producer and consumer may be the most important driving force of all. We are all the beneficiaries.

Wine Styles

Wine is simply fermented grape juice. The basic stages in making white and red wines are shown on pages 20–28; variations on the main theme are explained here.

Dry White Wines

Plain dry wine of no special character, fully fermented, not intended to be aged. Usually made with non-aromatic grapes, especially in Italy, southern France, Spain, and California. Outstanding examples are Muscadet and Soave. Winemaking is standard, with increasing emphasis on freshness by excluding oxygen and fermenting cool.

Fresh, fruity, dry to semi-sweet wines for drinking young are made from aromatic grape varieties: Riesling, Sauvignon Blanc, Gewürztraminer, Muscat Blanc, for example. Extreme emphasis on picking at the right moment, clean juice, cool fermentation, and early bottling.

Dry but full-bodied and smooth whites are usually made with a degree of skin contact, fermented at higher temperatures, sometimes in barrels. Bottled after a minimum of nine months and intended for further ageing. Chardonnay from Burgundy is the classic example, which the New World aspires to emulate. Sauvignon Blanc is occasionally treated in this way.

Sweet White Wines

Fresh, fruity, light in alcohol, semi-sweet to sweet in the German style. Sometimes made by fermenting to dryness and "back-blending" with unfermented juice.

The same style, but made by stopping fermentation while some sugar remains, usually has higher alcohol and a more winey, less obviously grapey flavour. Most French, Spanish, Italian, and many New World medium-sweet wines are found in this category.

Botrytis (noble rot) wines have a balance of either low alcohol with very high sugar (German style), or very high alcohol and fairly high sugar (Sauternes style). Hungary's Tokaji Aszú lies in the middle, balancing high sugar and moderate alcohol with high acidity.

Very sweet wines are made from extremely ripe or partially raisined grapes, where the sugars are concentrated. Italian *vin santo* is the classic example.

Rosé Wines

Pale rosé is made from red grapes pressed immediately to extract juice with very little colour, sometimes called *vin gris* (literally "grey wine") or blanc de noirs in the case of sparkling wines.

Rosé with more colour is made from red grapes crushed and *saigné* (or bled), so that the juice is run off the skins after a short red-wine-type maceration or vatting, then pressed and fermented like white wine. This is the more common method used for Tavel rosé, Anjou rosé, Italian Chiaretto, and *vin d'une nuit*.

Champagne rosé is made in two ways: the "maceration process" is when skins of black grapes are left in contact with the juice during the initial fermentation, producing a delicate, pale-pink wine. The wine then undergoes a second fermentation in the bottle to produce the sparkle. The second method is to blend still red and still white wines together after the initial fermentation. The second fermentation follows once the wine has been bottled.

Red Wines

Light, fruity wines made with minimum tannin by a short maceration period. Should be drunk early, as the extract, pigments, and tannin necessary for maturation are absent. Can be made with aromatic grapes, but are more commonly made of simple, fruity or neutral grapes.

Softer, richer, more savoury and deep-coloured wines (but still low in tannin) are made by carbonic maceration or interior fermentation of the grapes before pressing. Heating the must is another method of producing colour and smoothness. Full-blooded reds for maturing (known as *vins de garde*) made by long contact of the skins with the juice to extract pigments, tannins, phenols, etc. All great red wines are made this way.

Fortified Wines

Vin doux naturel is naturally very sweet wine, its fermentation stopped (*muté*) by adding spirits, leaving residual sugar and high alcohol (fifteen to sixteen per cent). Port follows the vin doux naturel procedure, but fermentation is stopped earlier, at four to six per cent, by a larger dose of spirits: a quarter of the volume. Sherry is naturally strong white wine fully fermented to dryness. Then a small quantity of spirits is added to stabilize it while it matures in contact with air. Madeira is white wine with naturally high acidity. Sweeter styles have their fermentation arrested with the addition of alcohol, before it stops of its own accord. Then it is heated before being aged in barrels or big glass jars.

Sparkling Wines

White (or sometimes red) wines made to ferment a second time by the addition of yeast and sugar. The gas from the second fermentation dissolves in the wine. In the classic Champagne method the second fermentation takes place in the bottle in which the wine is sold, involving complicated and laborious processing, which inevitably makes it expensive. The *méthode champenoise* (or classic method as we must now call it, since the Champenois have properly claimed the term as belonging to their region) is not susceptible to many short cuts or labour-saving devices, although machines have been devised for most of the laborious hand work involved. The latest and most notable is an automatic "riddling rack" to replace the unremitting chore of shaking and turning each bottle regularly. The massive framework, which vibrates and tips automatically at intervals, is known in France as a *gyropalette*, in the USA simply as a "VLM" – Very Large Machine. Wines from elsewhere, however good, can only be described as being made by the "classic method" or, in French, *méthode traditionnelle*. Cheaper methods, none of which achieves the same degree of dissolved gas as the classic method, include:

The transfer process. wine is transferred, via a filter, under pressure to another bottle.

Cuve close or Charmant. the second fermentation takes place in a tank; the wine is then filtered under pressure and bottled.

Carbonization. CO_2 is pumped into still wine (although the bubbles are scarcely long-lived).

White Wine

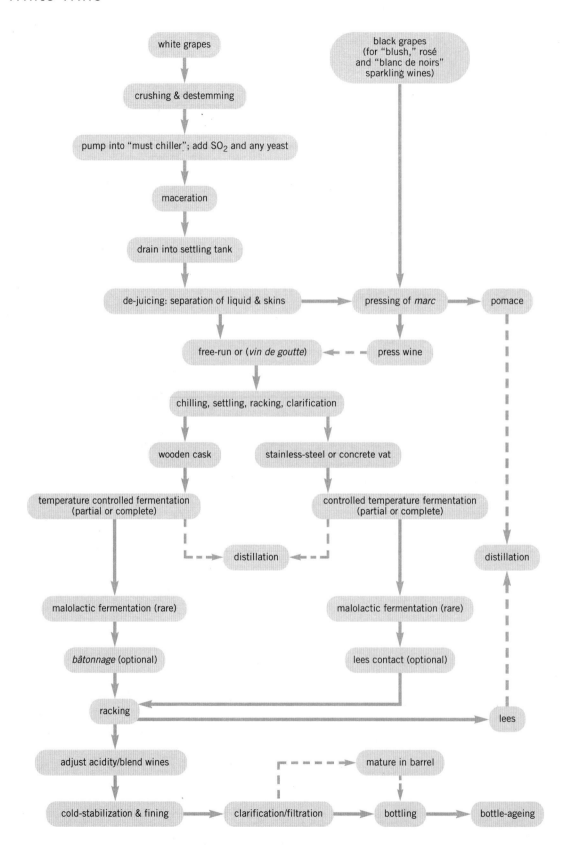

Red Wine

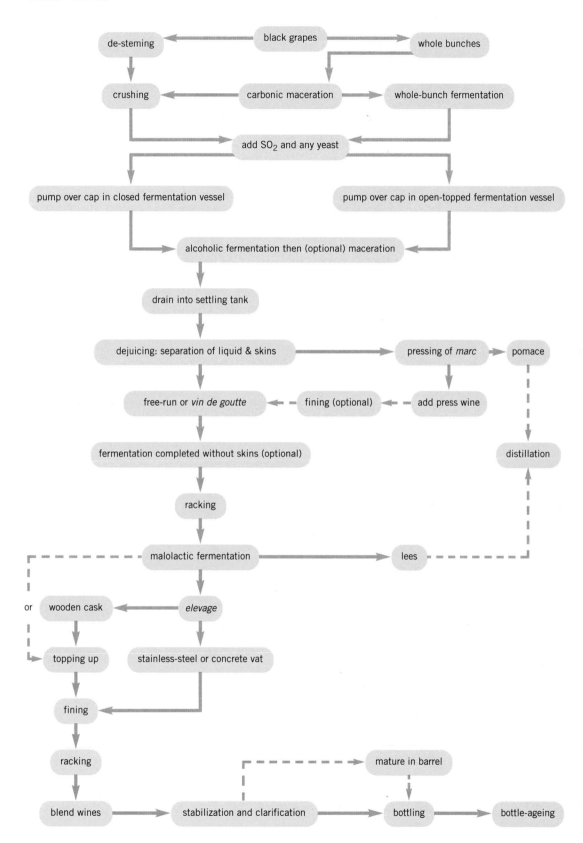

Wines, Vineyards, & Winemakers of the World

2

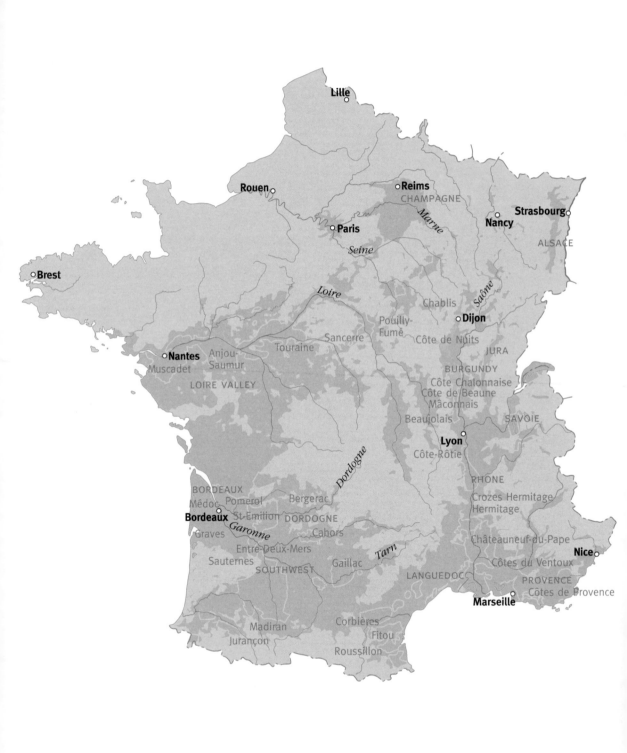

Lille

Rouen

Reims

CHAMPAGNE

Marne

Strasbourg

Nancy

Paris

ALSACE

Seine

Brest

Loire

Chablis

Saône

Pouilly-
Fumé

Dijon

Sancerre

Côte de Nuits

JURA

Touraine

BURGUNDY

Nantes

Anjou-
Saumur

Côte Chalonnaise
Côte de Beaune
Mâconnais

Muscadet

LOIRE VALLEY

Beaujolais

SAVOIE

Lyon

Côte-Rôtie

Dordogne

RHONE

BORDEAUX

Crozes Hermitage
Hermitage

Médoc

Pomerol

Bergerac

Bordeaux

St-Emilion

DORDOGNE

Châteauneuf-du-Pape

Garonne

Cahors

Nice

Graves

Côtes du Ventoux

Entre-Deux-Mers

Tarn

Sauternes

Gaillac

PROVENCE

Côtes de Provence

SOUTHWEST

LANGUEDOC

Marseille

Madiran

Corbières

Jurançon

Fitou

Roussillon

France

Nobody argues with the primacy of France as the country that set the international standards by which wine is judged. Germany's Rieslings, Spain's sherry, and Portugal's port are the only non-French wines accepted as universal models. This is not to invalidate Chianti or Barolo or Rioja; but they remained vernacular styles long after Bordeaux, Burgundy, Champagne, and certain Loire, Rhône, and Alsace wines were targets that winemakers everywhere aimed at – in the first instance by planting their grape varieties.

A form of natural selection gave France these ideas of what wine can be. Her first vineyards were planted in the Midi in the sixth or seventh centuries BC. The Romans established what are now the highest-quality areas – Burgundy, Bordeaux, Champagne, the Rhône and Loire valleys, and Alsace. They chose them for their promising-looking slopes near centres of population with reasonable transport facilities; ideally water but failing that by main trade routes. They planted them, after trying Italian vines, with woodland vines, native to Gaul, Spain, the Rhineland, and the Alps. It is fairly certain today's vines are their descendants.

The soils, climate, and conditions of cellarage are the same so, with allowances for different techniques and tastes, we can speculate that French wines have honed their identities over almost 2,000 years. Identity and fame once established, there is the inevitable problem of maintaining standards, not to mention preventing fraud. For every person who knows what a given wine ought to taste like, there are a hundred who are ready to pay for something they will be unable to identify.

The problem is age-old. Many laws have been passed (and taxes raised) to regulate wine – how much, when, where, by whom, of what grapes, under what name, and at what price it can be sold. At the start of the twentieth century the problem was acute, since phylloxera had left Europe with a serious shortage. The need for a national system of control was clear and in 1932 the *Institut National des Appellations d'Origine* (INAO) was founded to regulate the entire quality wine industry. The first ACs were created in 1936 and the *Office National Interprofessionnel des Vins de Table* was founded to keep order.

These distinctions are now central to the whole wine system in Europe. In EU terms every wine is either a *Vin de Qualité Produit dans Une Région Determinée* (VQPRD) or a *vin de table* – an absurd choice of category, incidentally: almost all wines are made to be drunk at table, and it is perfectly fair to say that Château Lafite is a table wine. The French system itself has become more elaborate. Apart from *vin de consommation courante*, where the price depends solely on the alcoholic degree, there are three classification categories for all the wines of France:

Appellation (d'Origine) Contrôlée (AC or AOC)

A more or less strict control of origin, grape varieties and methods used, alcoholic strength, and quantity produced. Most AC wines are limited to a basic production in the region that ranges approximately from twenty-five to fifty hectolitres per hectare but a complicated system of annual reassessment usually allows more, sometimes considerably more.

The nature of appellation control varies. In Bordeaux, the most specific and restricted appellation is a whole village, within which individual properties ("châteaux") are given liberties to plant where, and what (within the regional tradition) they like. In the best sites of Burgundy each field has its own appellation. The appellation Champagne covers a whole region and its method of working. Each region is particular with its own logic. The number of ACs is constantly expanding as regions sub-divide and local growers petition the INAQ for their own AC, sometimes successfully.

The ceiling on production, or *Plafond Limite de Classement* (PLC), is always lower for *grands crus* (in regions that have them) than for humbler appellations. The differences used to provide manouvering space for notorious fiddles but stricter controls now try to ensure that each appellation is treated entirely separately in the grower's and merchant's cellar.

The AC system was not instituted originally to provide quality control, only guarantees of origin and authenticity. Quality control by compulsory tasting has now been introduced, at least in theory. In practice, as much as ninety-seven per cent of wines submitted for tasting are nodded through: relations between growers and inspectors are far too close for the good of the system. This is a problem the INAO has undertaken to solve. It is not hurrying. The result? An AC is a sure indicator of origin, but it is only the producer's name that even indicates, let alone guarantees, quality.

Vins Délimités de Qualité Supérieure (VDQS)

The second rank of appellations was instituted in 1945 for regions with worthwhile identities and traditions producing "minor" wines. It has similar systems of control, and in practice became a sort of training ground for true ACs. Without further recruits it will gradually disappear as VDQS producers petition for, and obtain, promotion to full AC status.

Vins de Pays

Vins de pays are now in reality the dynamic second tier after AC. The notion of "country wines" was crystallized in the 1970s, organized like ACs on several levels of precision; the regional being the broadest, Vins de Pays de Zone the most precise, usually with the highest standards.

There are four regional *vins de pays*: Jardin de la France for the Loire Valley; Comté Tolosan for the South West; Comtés Rhodaniens for the Rhône region; and d'Oc for the whole of the Midi. Thirty-nine *départements* give their names to *vins de pays* grown within their borders and (up to a point) their viticultural traditions. As many as 100 defined districts, with a great concentration in the Midi, produce Vins de Pays de Zone. This is the logical breeding ground for new ideas, whether based on grape variety or distinctive terroir.

Those that succeed in producing attractive quality and consistent identity, and perhaps eventually go on to matriculate as ACs, will inevitably combine both grape variety (or varieties) and terroir in their definition. In the end, there is no other way to define and delimit what is distinctive about any wine.

Bordeaux

Four factors make Bordeaux the most important vineyard region of all: its quality, size, variety, and unity. The last two are not contradictory but complementary. They are the reason we keep coming back for more. The range of styles and types of Bordeaux is sufficiently wide for everybody; no two are ever identical, and yet there is an unmistakable identity among all of them, a clean-cut, appetizing, easily digestible, and stimulating quality that only Bordeaux offers.

The Bordeaux character comes as much from grapes and climate as from the soil (which varies from gravel to limestone to clay). And, of course, it comes from traditions of making, handling, and enjoying wine in a certain way, an amalgam of the tastes of the French and their northern neighbours, the British, Belgians, Dutch, Germans, and Scandinavians, who have paid the piper since the Middle Ages.

In 2001, thirty-six per cent of Bordeaux production was exported. But the proportion among the best growths (Pauillac, Graves, and Margaux, for example) is considerably higher. Over seven times as much red wine is made as white, and red is worth five times as much as white on the export market.

Bordeaux supplies four basic styles of wine: light, everyday red; fine red; dry white; and sweet, "liquorous" white. There is not a great deal to be said about the first, except that there is a vast supply: up to 2,500,000 hectolitres (330 million bottles) a year, varying from the excitingly tasty to the merely

passable or occasionally poor and watery. It may be offered under a brand name or as the production of a *petit château*.

There is a degree of overlap between this everyday red and "fine" red, where the former excels itself or the latter lets the side down, but the fine red is really a distinct product, a more concentrated wine made for keeping and matured in oak. This is where the distinctions between different soils and situations produce remarkable differences of flavour and keeping qualities, more or less accurately reflected in the system of appellations and of classifications within the appellations. The total quantity available in this category is even more impressive for this class of wine: approaching one bottle for every two of the everyday red.

The dry whites belong, in the main, alongside the light reds. A very few rise to the level of fine white burgundy, but this is an area where Bordeaux has recently made exciting progress. Modern techniques are finding great character in Bordeaux's traditional white grapes, and fermenting in oak is adding to their stature. There is less than half as much made as there is of comparable red. The sweet whites are a drop in the ocean, only about one bottle in forty, but a precious specialty capable of superlative quality, and much appreciated in Bordeaux even at a humble level as an aperitif.

Every Bordeaux vintage is subject to the most fickle of climates. Overriding all other considerations is the unpredictable seaside weather. A great vintage will give even the commonest wines an uncommon vitality, but conversely, the category of fine wines can be sadly depleted by a really bad one, and the sweet whites can be eliminated altogether. This shifting pattern of vintages against the already

complex background of appellations and properties, and the long lifespan of the good wines, make the appreciation of Bordeaux a mesmerically fascinating pursuit.

Bordeaux in Round Figures

Over the thirty years from 1963 to 1993, the total area of *appellation contrôlée* vineyards in Bordeaux dwindled for a while, then recently began to increase. In 2001, it reached 119,669 hectares, producing 6.56 million hectolitres. A mere one per cent of the entire Gironde vineyard is now non-appellation. Red wine currently accounts for eighty-eight per cent of Bordeaux's production, while white wine has dropped dramatically as a proportion of this total – from sixty per cent in the 1950s to twelve per cent by 2001. About twenty-four per cent of all wine production was undertaken by cooperatives.

Meanwhile, the number of individual properties continues steadily to decrease. In 1950 the total was 60,327 and in 1994, it was just 13,957: a drop of seventy-seven per cent. By 2001, it was down again, to 11,385. The average size of holding, though, is edging up: from 1.3 ha in 1950 to 13.5 in 2000.

With this concentration of ownership, efficiency has improved. Vintages of the 1950s (admittedly including a disastrous frost in 1956) produced an average crop of thirty hectolitres per hectare; the decade 1985 to 1994, an average of fifty-two. But disastrous years can still occur, as in 1991, when spring frosts eliminated around two-thirds of the crop.

Classifications

The appellations of Bordeaux are themselves a sort of preliminary classification of its wines by quality, on the basis that the more narrowly they are defined, the higher the general level of the district. This is as far as overall grading has ever (officially) gone. More precise classifications are all local to one area, without cross-referencing.

The most effective way of comparing the standing of châteaux within different areas is by price – the method used for the first and most famous of all classifications, that done for the Médoc for the Paris Exhibition of 1855.

In 1855, the criterion was the price each wine fetched, averaged over a long period, up to 100 years, but taking into account its recent standing, and the current condition of the property. The list is still so widely used that it is essential for reference almost 150 years later.

A few châteaux have fallen by the wayside; the majority have profited by their notoriety to expand their vineyards, swallowing lesser neighbours. It is certain that the original classification located most of the best land in the Médoc and gave credit to the proprietors who had planted it.

What they subsequently did with it has proved to be less important than the innate superiority of the gravel banks they chose to plant.

The Concept of a Château

The unit of classification in Bordeaux is not the land (as in Burgundy) but the property on the land, the estate or château. It is the château that is either a First or a Fourth Growth or a *cru bourgeois*. A proprietor can buy land from a neighbour of greater or lesser standing, add it to his own and, given that it is suitable, it will take his rank. Vineyards can go up or down the scale according to who owns them.

An example. Château Gloria is an estate of high quality in St-Julien, formed since World War II by buying parcels of land from neighbouring *crus classés*. When the land changed hands it was "classed", but because the buyer had no classed château, the vines were demoted to *cru bourgeois*.

Conversely, many classed growths have added to their holdings by buying neighbouring *cru bourgeois* vines. When the Rothschilds of Château Lafite bought the adjacent Château Duhart-Milon, they could theoretically have made all its wine as Lafite.

The justification for this apparent injustice is that a château is considered more as a *marque* than a plot of ground. Its identity and continuity depend so much on the repeated choices the owner has to make, of precisely when and how to perform every operation from planting to bottling, that he has to be trusted with the final decision of what the château wine consists of. A recent sign of how seriously owners take this is the proliferation of "second labels" for batches of wine that fail to meet self-imposed standards. There is also a large handful of classed-growth proprietors who, out of idleness or ignorance, churn out indifferent wine. Neighbours say, only half-jokingly, that their problem is an allergy to paying taxes.

This is the Médoc method. St-Emilion is different. Some of its châteaux, the *premiers grands crus*, have a semi-permanent classification renewable (in theory) after ten years – and last reviewed in 1996. Others, the *grand crus*, have to submit each vintage for tasting.

Only the Médoc and the single Château Haut-Brion in Graves were classified in 1855. The list divides them into five classes, but stresses that the order within each class is not to be considered significant. Only one official change has been made since: the promotion in 1973 of Château Mouton-Rothschild from Second to First Growth.

Crus Bourgeois and Petits Châteaux

Whether an unclassed château has any official rank or not is not simple, either. It depends partly on whether the owner is a loner or a joiner, since membership of the *Syndicat de Crus Bourgeois*, the next ranking authority, is purely voluntary. The list of members of the *Syndicate of Crus Bourgeois* of the Médoc, revised in September 1996, includes 321 properties, of which 108 are Médoc AC, 109 Haut-Médoc (twenty-four from St-Seurin de Cadourne), sixteen Moulis AC, twenty-four Listrac AC, thirty-four St-Estèphe AC, ten Pauillac AC, six St-Julien AC and fourteen Margaux AC. The confusing concepts of *cru grand bourgeois* and *cru grand bourgeois exceptionnel* no longer exist – perhaps one of the better minor rulings of the EU – although these terms are still seen on labels.

The terms *cru artisan* and *cru paysan* are sometimes used for properties below *cru bourgeois* in size and/or quality. In 1989, the *Syndicat des Crus Artisans* was formed for properties of less than seven hectares. It has 236 members. The wine trade tends to lump them all together as *petits châteaux* – a relative term, since no doubt Rothschilds consider *crus bourgeois* in these terms.

In the early 2000s, the entire concept of the *cru bourgeois* was being re-examined, and an independent panel will determine which candidates for this status are worthy of it. In 2001, the ministry of agriculture decreed that there should be three categories: *crus bourgeois*, *crus bourgeois supérieurs*, and *crus bourgeois exceptionnels*, membership of each being subject to revision every ten years. However, many of the

The Unique Bordeaux Wine Market

With few exceptions, you cannot buy a bottle of wine from a top Bordeaux estate. There are none of the tasting rooms and picnic tables so common in the Californian and Australian wine regions. This is because, for over two centuries, Bordeaux proprietors did not wish to be involved with such tawdry matters as commerce. They preferred to entrust the selling of their wine to specialist merchants (négociants) based in the city of Bordeaux itself.

The system has been maintained, more or less intact, to this day. Proprietors were often politicians or bankers or noblemen who lacked or scorned the commercial contacts that would facilitate the selling of large quantities of wine. Merchant houses, often founded by the English or Irish, the Dutch or Germans, had access to distribution networks throughout Europe and were prepared to undertake the job on behalf of the château owners. They would also nurture the young wine in barrel in their own warehouses, and then bottle it.

Today, as centuries ago, the owner will suggest an opening price for his or her new vintage. A broker, known in France as a *courtier*, would, for a modest fee, act as a go-between for the owners and the merchants. The merchant would buy part, or even the entirety, of the new crop, and then sell it, if possible at a good profit, to a whole network of importers, retailers, restaurateurs, and so forth.

Most of the time, everyone was happy. The proprietors gained a good deal of cash fast, and could be reasonably sure that their wine was widely distributed; moreover, they did not need to bother with a sales force and the irksome overheads that entailed. The *courtier* pocketed his two-per-cent commission for doing – well, not very much. And the merchants made as much money as they thought they could get away with.

The balance of power shifted from time to time; sometimes the merchants had the whip hand, sometimes the proprietors. The strength of the system is that the merchants would usually undertake to buy wine from all vintages, good or bad. Failure to do so could be punished by the proprietor, who could deny the merchant access to the next really good vintage.

The system still flourishes, with slight modifications. Most châteaux now bottle their own wines, and there has been a growth in direct sales to consumers, especially in less prestigious regions such as Côtes de Bourg and the St-Emilion satellite districts. Nonetheless, the descendants of those ancient families – the Lawtons and Schylers and many others – are still deeply involved in the Bordeaux wine trade. In good times, everyone profits – and the consumer, at the end of the line, pays.

very best *crus bourgeois* do not like these terms (they prefer, with some justification, to think of themselves as near-miss *crus classés*) and do not wish to be associated with it, and have no wish to join a *Syndicat* or to use these terms on their label. So the situation remains in a state of flux.

To add to the confusion, a number of estates in the Côtes de Bourg and Côtes de Blaye also used the term *cru bourgeois*, which the Médocains had always assumed was their exclusivity. They took the matter to court, and lost.

A great number of the thousands of lesser châteaux that used to exist are now allied to the *caves coopératives*, but more and more are sought out by wine merchants and given

the dignity of their own labels. Many, indeed, lose their identity in the anonymity of the cooperative and then miraculously find it again later. There is no object in listing their endless names, however evocative, but to the claret-lover with an open mind they are always worth exploring, offering some of the best bargains in France. In good vintages, drunk at no more than three or four years old, they can be both delicious and reasonable in price.

The Bordeaux Classification of 1855

First Growths (premiers crus)
Château Lafite-Rothschild, Pauillac
Château Latour, Pauillac
Château Margaux, Margaux
Château Haut-Brion, Graves
Château Mouton-Rothschild, Pauillac
(elevated to First Growth in 1973)

Second Growths (deuxièmes crus)
Château Rauzan-Ségla, Margaux
Château Rauzan-Gassies, Margaux
Château Léoville-Las-Cases, St-Julien
Château Léoville-Poyferré, St-Julien
Château Léoville-Barton, St-Julien
Château Durfort-Vivens, Margaux
Château Lascombes, Margaux
Château Gruaud-Larose, St-Julien
Château Brane-Cantenac, Cantenac-Margaux
Château Pichon-Longueville, Pauillac
Château Pichon-Lalande, Pauillac
Château Ducru-Beaucaillou, St-Julien
Château Cos d'Estournel, St-Estèphe
Château Montrose, St-Estèphe

Third Growths (troisièmes crus)
Château Giscours, Labarde-Margaux
Château Kirwan, Cantenac-Margaux
Château d'Issan, Cantenac-Margaux
Château Lagrange, St-Julien
Château Langoa-Barton, St-Julien
Château Malescot-St-Exupéry, Margaux
Château Cantenac-Brown, Cantenac-Margaux
Château Palmer, Cantenac-Margaux
Château la Lagune, Ludon
Château Desmirail, Margaux
Château Calon-Ségur, St-Estèphe
Château Ferrière, Margaux
Château d'Alesme, Margaux
Château Boyd-Cantenac, Cantenac-Margaux

Fourth Growths (quatrièmes crus)
Château St-Pierre, St-Julien
Château Branaire, St-Julien
Château Talbot, St-Julien
Château Duhart-Milon-Rothschild, Pauillac
Château Pouget, Cantenac-Margaux
Château la Tour-Carnet, St-Laurent
Château Lafon-Rochet, St-Estèphe
Château Beychevelle, St-Julien
Château Prieuré-Lichine, Cantenac-Margaux
Château Marquis-de-Terme, Margaux

Fifth Growths (cinquièmes crus)
Château Pontet-Canet, Pauillac
Château Batailley, Pauillac
Château Grand-Puy-Lacoste, Pauillac
Château Grand-Puy-Ducasse, Pauillac
Château Haut-Batailley, Pauillac
Château Lynch-Bages, Pauillac
Château Lynch-Moussas, Pauillac
Château Dauzac, Labarde-Margaux
Château d'Armailhac, Pauillac (formerly known as Mouton
 d'Armailhacq and Mouton Baronne-Philippe)
Château du Tertre, Arsac-Margaux
Château Haut-Bages-Libéral, Pauillac
Château Pedesclaux, Pauillac
Château Belgrave, St-Laurent
Château de Camensac, St-Laurent
Château Cos-Labory, St-Estèphe
Château Clerc-Milon-Rothschild, Pauillac
Château Croizet-Bages, Pauillac
Château Cantemerle, Macau

The Red Grapes of Bordeaux

The particulars given in the following pages of each of the principal Bordeaux châteaux include the proportions of the different grape varieties in their vineyards, as far as they are known.

The classic Bordeaux red-wine varieties are all related, probably descended from the ancient *biturica*, whose name is still preserved as Vidure (a synonym for Cabernet Sauvignon in the Graves). Over the centuries, four principal varieties have been selected for a combination of fertility, disease resistance, flavour, and adaptability to the Bordeaux soils.

Cabernet Sauvignon is dominant in the Médoc. It is the most highly flavoured, with small berries making dark, tannic wine that demands ageing, but then has both depth and "cut" of flavour. It flowers well and evenly, and ripens a modest crop relatively late, resisting rot better than softer and thinner-skinned varieties. Being a late ripener it needs warm soil. Gravel suits it well, but the colder clay of Pomerol is unsatisfactory.

Its close cousin, the Cabernet Franc, is a bigger, juicier grape. Before the introduction of Cabernet Sauvignon in the eighteenth century, it was the mainstay of Bordeaux, and is still widely planted, particularly in Pomerol and St-Emilion, where it is known as the Bouchet. Cabernet Franc wines have delicious, soft-fruit flavours (which are also vividly seen in Chinon and Bourgueil, wines made from this grape on the Loire) but less tannin and depth. Less regular flowering and a thinner skin are also drawbacks, at least in the Médoc.

More important today is the Merlot, a precocious grape that buds, flowers, and ripens early, making it more vulnerable in spring but ready to pick sooner, with an extra degree of alcohol in its higher sugar. Unfortunately, at harvest, its tight bunches need only a little rain to start them rotting.

Merlot wine has good colour and an equally spicy but softer flavour than Cabernet Sauvignon, making wine that matures sooner. In the Médoc, a judicious proportion – rarely above forty per cent – is used; rather more in the Graves; more again in St-Emilion, and in Pomerol up to ninety-five per cent. This is the grape that gives Château Pétrus its opulent texture and flavour.

A fourth red grape that is still used in small amounts in the Médoc is the Petit Verdot, another Cabernet cousin that ripens late with good flavour and ageing qualities, but flowers irregularly and has other quirks. A little in the vineyard is nonetheless a source of added complexity and "backbone" in the wine.

A fifth variety, once important but now found more in St-Emilion and largely in the minor areas, is the Malbec (alias Pressac), a big, juicy, early ripening grape, which has serious flowering problems (*coulure*). It is grown in the Gironde more for quantity than quality. Paradoxically, under its synonym Auxerrois (or Cot), it is the grape of the historically famous "black wines" of Cahors. The arid climate of the Andes suits it better than either.

In the long run, a château proprietor designs his wine by the choice and proportions of varieties he plants.

The White Grapes of Bordeaux

The classic white wine vineyard in Bordeaux is a mixture of two principal varieties, and one or two subsidiary ones as variable in proportions as the red.

Sauvignon Blanc and Sémillon make up at least ninety per cent of the best vineyards, Sauvignon for its distinct flavour and good acidity, Sémillon for its susceptibility to noble rot. Thus the sweet wine vineyards of Sauternes tend to have more Sémillon, and often a small plot of the more highly flavoured Muscadelle.

Unfortunately, Sauvignon Blanc has flowering problems in Bordeaux, which makes it an irregular producer; to keep a constant proportion of its grapes means having a disproportionate number of vines. A variant known as Sauvignon Gris is also interesting, and has been planted at some top estates in the Graves. Recently, some excellent fresh, dry white has been made entirely of Sémillon. Other white grapes include Ugni Blanc, Folle Blanche, Colombard, and Riesling.

The Wine Trade in Bordeaux

Since Roman times, when a *negotiator britannicus* was reported buying wine in Burdigala, Bordeaux's overseas trade has been one of the mainstays of the life of the city. In the Middle Ages, the chief customer was England. From the seventeenth century, it became the Dutch, and later the Germans, then the English again, and latterly the Americans. In the 1980s, the Japanese joined in. The north of France, and above all Belgium, now absorb the biggest share, much of it by direct sales.

For two centuries up to the 1960s, the trade was largely in the hands of a group of négociants, nearly all of foreign origin, with their offices and cellars on the Quai des Chartrons, on the river just north of the centre of the city. The oldest firm still in business is the Dutch Beyermann, founded in 1620. The "Chartronnais" families, including Cruse, Calvet, Barton & Guestier, Johnston, and Eschenauer, were household names, and their power was considerable.

Most of these firms have been taken over or their names absorbed, their importance diminished with the growth of direct sales from the châteaux, of bottling at the châteaux, and above all, with the sheer cost of holding stock. New ways of selling new kinds of brand name wines to fewer but more powerful retailers have created a new class of trade. Most of them have also moved out of Bordeaux to more accessible warehouses. The following are among the most influential.

Alias

Bordeaux. Principal: Pierre Lawton. www.aliasbordeaux.com
Dynamic company founded in 1992, and specializing in *crus classés*, especially for the Far East market.

Barton et Guestier

Blanquefort. Principal: Etienne Brault.
www.barton-guestier.com
Owned by Diageo. Only a third of the business is now Bordeaux and the connection with the original firm, founded in 1725 by an Irishman whose descendants still own Château Langoa-Barton, is only in the name. The firm exports two million cases of wine per annum.

Bordeaux Millésimes

Bordeaux. Principal: Dominique Renard
A specialist in *crus classés*, and a major stockholder of current and older vintages.

Borie-Manoux

Bordeaux. Principal: Philippe Castéja
Major supplier of Bordeaux to hotels, restaurants, and specialist retailers on the home market. Owner of "Beau Rivage'", the second-largest Bordeaux brand; controls over 240 hectares of vines in the major appellations: Châteaux Batailley, Haut-Bages-Monpelou, Beau-Site, Trottevieille, Bergat, Domaine de l'Eglise.

Calvet SA

Bordeaux. Principal/owner: Jacques Drounau. www.calvet.com
Founded in 1870, but originally from the Rhône and still with connections there and in Burgundy. The range has been revitalized by a team of young winemakers.

Castel Frères

Offices in Blanquefort. Principal: Pierre Castel.
www.castel-freres.com
A shipper with enormous turnover, but wine sales are overshadowed by those of beer and water. Castel owns or manages 600 hectares of vineyards in Bordeaux and owns, among other properties, the Château d'Arcins in the Haut-Médoc and Domaines Virginie in the Languedoc.

Cheval Quancard

Lagrave d'Ambares. www.cheval-quancard.com
Family firm that owns Château Terrefort Quancard (among others) and brand "Le Chai des Bordes". The firm owns 200 hectares of vineyards in Bordeaux.

Cordier

Blanquefort. www.cordier-wines.com
In 1984, the Cordier family sold to a big financial group, Suez Lyonnaise des Eaux. Now a subsidiary of the Val d'Orbieu group. The firm owns Châteaux Lafaurie-Peyraguey, Meyney, Clos des Jacobins, etc. and, in all, controls 450 hectares of Bordeaux vineyards.

C.V.B.G. (Consortium Vinicole de Bordeaux et de Gironde)

Parempuyre. Principal: Jean-Marie Chadronnier. www.cvbg.com
Including Dourthe and Kressmann, this major player on the Bordeaux scene has its offices and cellars at Parempuyre in the Médoc. CVBG owns Château Belgrave and Château la Garde, and has developed successful brands such as "Dourthe No 1" and "Essence".

Madame Jean Descaves

Bordeaux
During her lifetime, Mme. Descaves owned the biggest stock of rare, old, top wine, which she proceeded to sell at ever-increasing prices. After her death in 1999 at the ripe old age of ninety-seven, the business was acquired by Duclot (*q.v.*).

Duclot

Bordeaux. Principal: Jean-François Moueix. www.duclot.fr
Jean-François Moueix, the brother of Christian Moueix and part of the powerful family firm in Libourne, owns a group of companies specializing in top-quality Bordeaux. These are sold largely to private customers. The smart Bordeaux wine shops, Badie and L'Intendant, are also in the same ownership.

Dulong Frères & Fils

Floirac. Principal: Eric Dulong. www.dulong.com
A family company exporting an increasing quantity of table wine as well as AC Bordeaux in bottle and bulk.

Robert Giraud

St André de Cubzac. Principal: Philippe Giraud.
www.robertgiraud.com
A major player on the French market with its "Blason Timberlay" brand.

Grands Vins de Gironde

St Loubes. Principal: Pierre-Michel Alsac. www.gvg.fr
A group formed by Rémy Cointreau in 1991 from de Luze, de Rivoyre, Diprovin, and Chantecaille and bits of the defunct S.D.V.F., with a fine-wine arm, la Grande Cave.

Joanne

Fargues St Hilaire
The three Castéja brothers, Pierre-Antoine, Olivier, and Eric, successfully specialize in *crus classés* and château-bottled wines.

Nathaniel Johnston & Fils

Bordeaux. www.nath-johnston.com
Family firm, founded 1734. Denis and Archibald Johnston are the ninth generation. Sixty per cent export, mostly fine wines.

Mähler-Besse

Bordeaux. Principal: Franck Mähler-Besse.
www.mahler-besse.com
A family firm in Bordeaux, Holland, Belgium, Spain, and Portugal with the majority holding in Château Palmer, and a formidable stock of old vintages.

Yvon Mau

Gironde sur Dropt. Principal: Jean-Francois Mau.
www.yvonmau.fr
Dynamic producer, acquired by Spanish drinks giant Freixenet in 2001. Commercially astute policy of brands and châteaux exclusivities has brought success with major

retailers. "Yvescourt" is France's best-selling rosé. Owner of Château Preuillac.

Mestrezat
Bordeaux. Principal: Alain Duhau

Merchants dealing primarily in bottled Bordeaux wine from *petits châteaux* to First Growths. This is part of the Paribas group that owns properties that include Châteaux Grand-Puy-Ducasse, Rayne Vigneau, Lamothe Bergeron, etc. Now part of the Val d'Orbieu group, as is Cordier (*q.v.*).

Millésima
Bordeaux. Principal: Patrick Bernard. www.millesima.com

An atypical merchant, specializing in direct mail-order sales to the public of *crus classés*.

J.-P. Moueix
Libourne. Principal: Christian Moueix

A leading Right Bank merchant house, but better known as the owner of Château Pétrus and numerous other top estates in Pomerol and St-Emilion. In 2000, Moueix sold all the properties he owned in Fronsac.

Baron Philippe de Rothschild SA
Pauillac. www.bpdr.com

Managed for Philippine de Rothschild by Xavier de Eizaguirre, who in 1996 succeeded Philippe Cottin, one of the wisest heads in the whole of Bordeaux. The company, based in the Médoc, commercializes Bordeaux's best-known brand "Mouton Cadet" and the "Baron Philippe" range, and has recently acquired estates in the Languedoc. It is co-owner of the Napa wine, "Opus One", and the Chilean "Almaviva".

William Pitters
Lormont. Principal: Bernard Magrez. www.williampitters.com

An enterprising merchandizing house: its "Malesan" is the most important Bordeaux brand within France. Also owns the Algerian brand, "Sidi Brahmin", and vineyards in Morocco, China, and South America. Bernard Magrez has also acquired numerous Bordeaux estates, notably Château Pape-Clément.

André Quancard
St André de Cubzac. Principal: Joel Quancard. www.andrequancard.com

A house with a good reputation, especially for *bourgeois* growths and *petits châteaux*.

Sichel
Bordeaux. Principal: Allan Sichel. www.sichel.fr

Part owner of Château Palmer, and sole owner of Château d'Angludet. Its pioneering Cave Bel Air winery in the Premières Côtes makes fruity modern claret and "Sirius", a brand of excellent, barrel-fermented white and oak-aged red Bordeaux.

Taillan
Bordeaux. Principal: Merlaut

Founded by Jacques Merlaut, this respected firm also owns Ginestet, and Châteaux Gruaud-Larose, Chasse-Spleen, and Haut-Bages-Libéral.

Médoc

The Médoc is the whole of the wedge of land north of Bordeaux between the Atlantic and the wide estuary of the Gironde, the united rivers Garonne and Dordogne. Its vineyards all lie within a mile or two of its eastern estuarine shore, on a series of low hills, or rather plateaux, of more or less stony soil separated by creeks, their bottom land filled with alluvial silt.

Dutch engineers in the seventeenth century cut these *jalles* to drain the new vineyards. Their role is vital in keeping the water table down inland, which, despite its gravel content, can be very heavy clay six to nine feet (1.8–2.7 metres) down where the vine roots go.

The proportion of *graves* (big gravel or small shingle) in the soil is highest in the Graves region, upstream of Bordeaux, and gradually declines as you go downstream along the Médoc. But such deposits are always uneven, and the soil and subsoil both have varying proportions of sand, gravel, and clay. The downstream limit of the Haut-Médoc is where the clay content really begins to dominate the gravel, north of St-Estèphe.

The planting of the *croupes*, the gravel plateaux, took place in a century of great prosperity for Bordeaux under its *parlement*, whose noble members' names are remembered in many of the estates they planted between 1650 and 1750. The Médoc was the Napa Valley of the time, and the Pichons, Rauzans, Ségurs, and Léovilles were the periwigged Krugs, Martinis, de la Tours, and Beringers.

The style and weight of wine these grandees developed have no precise parallel anywhere else. In some marvellous way, the leanness of the soil, the vigour of the vines, the softness of the air, and even the pearly seaside light seem to be implicated. Of course, it is a coincidence (besides being a terrible pun) that "clarity" is so close to "claret" – but it does sound right for the colour, smell, texture, weight, and savour of the Médoc.

The centuries have only confirmed what the original investors apparently instinctively knew: that the riverside gravel banks produce the finest wine. The names that started first have always stayed ahead. The notion of "First Growths" is as old as the estates themselves.

Today, the Médoc is divided into eight appellations: five of them limited to one commune (St-Estèphe, Pauillac, Moulis, Listrac, and St-Julien), one (Margaux) to a group of five small communes, one (Haut-Médoc) a portmanteau for parts of equal merit outside the first six, and the last, Médoc, for the northern tip of the promontory.

Margaux

The Margaux appellation covers a much wider area than the village: vineyards in the Margaux commune, plus neighbouring communes Cantenac, Labarde, Arsac and Soussans – a total of 1,408 hectares, rather more than Pauillac or St-Estèphe, with more *crus classés* than any other, and far more high-ranking ones.

Margaux is a big, sleepy village, with a little *maison du vin* to direct tourists. Wine from Margaux itself comes from the lightest, most gravelly land in the Médoc, and is considered potentially the finest, most fragrant of all. That of Cantenac, in theory, has slightly more body, and that of Soussans, on marginally heavier, lower-lying land going north, less class. The châteaux of Margaux tend to huddle together in the village, with their land much divided into parcels scattered around the parish.

Margaux Premier Cru

Château Margaux ☆☆☆☆
Owner: SCA Château Margaux. 78 hectares – red, 12 hectares – white. Grapes red: Cab.Sauv. 75%, Merlot 20%, Petit Verdot and Cab.Fr. 5%. White: Sauv.Bl. 100%.
www.chateau-margaux.com
With Château Lafite, the most stylish and obviously aristocratic of the First Growths, both in its wine and its lordly premises. The wine is never blunt or beefy, even in great years; at its best, it is as fluidly muscular as a racehorse and as sweetly perfumed as any claret – the very taste and smell of elegance.

Like Lafite, Margaux emerged in the late 1970s from fifteen-odd years of unworthy vintages. The late André Mentzelopoulos, whose daughter Corinne directs the estate today, bought the property (for sixty million francs) in 1977, and invested huge sums in a total overhaul of château, vineyards, and winemaking facilities. His ambition for perfection showed immediately with the excellent 1978. Professor Peynaud advised the sweeping changes that put Château Margaux back at the very top. In 1983, the young Paul Pontallier became general manager of the estate, an inspired appointment that has ensured that Margaux is always one of the top wines of any vintage.

The château is a porticoed mansion of the first empire, unique in the Médoc; the *chais* and cellars, pillared and lofty, are in keeping. Magnificent avenues of plane trees lead through the estate. Some of the lowest riverside land is planted with white (Sauvignon) grapes to make a light, fittingly polished dry wine, "Pavillon Blanc". The second label for red is "Pavillon Rouge".

Margaux Crus Classés

Châteaux Boyd-Cantenac ☆
3ème Cru Classé. Owner: Pierre Guillemet. 18 hectares. Grapes: Cab.Sauv. 67%, Cab.Fr. 7%, Merlot 20%, Petit Verdot 6%. www.boyd-cantenac.fr
The strange name, like that of Cantenac-Brown, came from a nineteenth century English owner. A small property not widely seen, nor much acclaimed, can be long-lasting and highly flavoured in such top years as 1970, '82, '86, '89, and '90.

Château Brane-Cantenac ☆☆–☆☆☆
2ème Cru Classé. Owner: Henri Lurton. 85 hectares. Grapes: Cab.Sauv. 70%, Cab.Fr. 10%, Merlot 20%.
www.lucienlurton.com
One of the most respected names of the Margaux Second Growths; a very big and well-run property on a distinct, pale gravel plateau. The wine is generally enjoyable and supple at a fairly early stage, but lasts well. Good vintages of the '80s

hold their own among the good Second Growths. After Lucien Lurton turned over the estate to his son Henri, the latter returned to manual harvesting and improved the *cuverie*. Quality has improved markedly since 1998. The second labels are "Château Notton" and "Baron de Brane".

Château Cantenac-Brown ☆☆–☆☆☆
3ème Cru Classé. Owner: AXA Millésimes. 52 hectares. Grapes: Cab.Sauv. 65%, Cab.Fr. 10%, Merlot 25%.
www.cantenacbrown.com
A great, prim pile of a building, like an English public school, on the road south from Margaux. Conservative wines capable of terrific flavour. It went through a bad patch, until a change of owner (1987) invested heavily in both vineyards and cellar. Still a way to go, and most Cantenac is a coarser and more rudely tannic wine on the finish than classic Margaux. The second label is "Canuet".

Château Dauzac ☆☆–☆☆☆
5ème Cru Classé. Owner: MAIF insurance group. 40 hectares. Grapes: Cab.Sauv. 58%, Cab.Fr. 5%, Merlot 37%.
In 1992, MAIF brought in André Lurton of la Louvière to advise, and a new cellar was built in 1994. Has been reliably smooth if uninspiring, but 1998 and 1999 vintages show signs of improvement. Second wine is "La Bastide Dauzac".

Château Desmirail ☆☆
3ème Cru Classé. Owner: Denis Lurton. 30 hectares. Grapes: Cab.Sauv. 80%, Cab.Fr. 5%, Merlot 15%
A Third Growth that disappeared for many years into the vineyards and vats of Châteaux Palmer and Brane-Cantenac. Now established in its own right. So far, delicate, fragrant wines to drink young. Second label: Château de Fontarney.

Château Durfort-Vivens ☆☆–☆☆☆
2ème Cru Classé. Owner: Gonzague Lurton. 30 hectares. Grapes: Cab.Sauv. 65%, Cab.Fr. 15%, Merlot 20%
The name of Durfort, suggesting hardness and strength, used to sum up the character of this almost all-Cabernet wine – which seemed to want keeping for ever. A Second Growth in name only. The new generation took over in 1992 and increased the proportion of Merlot. The wine usually has more structure than Brane-Cantenac, but has been gaining in refinement since 1998.

Château Ferrière ☆☆–☆☆☆
3ème Cru Classé. Owner: Claire Villars/Merlaut family. 8 hectares. Grapes: Cab.Sauv. 80%, Merlot 15%, Petit Verdot 5%. www.ferriere.com
Until 1992, this was part of Lascombes. Now it is in the same capable hands as Haut-Bages-Libéral. Exciting quality from old vines since 1995.

Château Giscours ☆☆–☆☆☆
3ème Cru Classé. Owner: Eric Albada Jelgersma. 80 hectares. Grapes: Cab.Sauv. 60%, Cab.Fr. 5%, Merlot 35%.
www.chateau-giscours.fr
A success story of the 1970s when it made an outstanding '70 and much better '75 than most. The '80s were decidedly shaky. The vast Victorian property was virtually remade since the 1950s by the Tari family, including making a large lake to alter the microclimate. By creating turbulence between the vines and the neighbouring woodland, it helps to ward off

spring frosts. The wines are tannic, robustly fruity, often dry, but at best full of the pent-up energy that marks first-class claret – not the suavely delicate style of Margaux. Since 1995, under new Dutch owners, wine has become more consistent.

Château d'Issan ☆☆☆
3ème Cru Classé. Owners: Emmanuel Cruse. 30 hectares. Grapes: Cab.Sauv. 70%, Merlot 30%. www.chateau-issan.com

One of the (few) magic spots of the Médoc: a moated seventeenth-century mansion down among the poplars, where the slope of the vineyard meets the riverside meadows. Issan is never a big wine, but old vintages have been wonderfully, smoothly persistent. Some recent ones appear rather too light to last as well, though '82, '83, '85, '88, '89, '90, '95, and 2000 are excellent.

Château Kirwan ☆☆☆
3ème Cru Classé. Owners: the Schyler family and partners. 35 hectares. Grapes: Cab.Sauv. 40%, Cab.Fr. 20%, Merlot 30%, Petit Verdot 10%. www.chateau-kirwan.com

The Third Growth neighbour to Brane-Cantenac. Until recently, Kirwan had few friends among the critics, although it is carefully run and at its best ('61, '70, '75, '79) is as long-lived and classic as any of the Margaux Second Growths, making elegant, feminine claret. Michel Rolland has consulted here since 1992, and its wine has gained fruit, weight, and oak. '98, '99, and 2000 were first-rate.

Château Lascombes ☆☆
2ème Cru Classé. Owner: Colony Capital. 83 hectares. Grapes: Cab.Sauv. 60%, Cab.Fr. 4%, Merlot 35%, Petit Verdot 1%. www.chateau-lascombes.com

A potentially superb, great property (one of the biggest in the Médoc) restored by the energy of Alexis Lichine in the 1950s to making delectable, smooth, and flavoury claret. Some of the vineyards Lichine assembled were far from Second Growth standard. New owners installed Dr. Alain Raynaud as general manager in 2001, with controversial results. Judgment on the success of his approach (huge extraction, more new oak) will have to wait. The second label is "Château Ségonnes".

Château Malescot-St-Exupéry ☆☆–☆☆☆
3ème Cru Classé. Owner: Jean-Luc Zuger. 31 hectares. Grapes: Cab.Sauv. 50%, Cab.Fr. 10%, Merlot 35%, Petit Verdot 5%. www.chateau-malescot.com

A handsome house in the main street of Margaux, with vineyards scattered north of the town. For many years it was run in tandem with Marquis d'Alesme-Becker, but since 1979 has taken flight on its own, showing signs of becoming even finer – with fruity flavour hidden by the tannic hardness of youth. Excellent results in '96 and 2000.

Château Marquis d'Alesme Becker ☆☆
3ème Cru Classé. Owner: Jean-Claude Zuger. 18 hectares. Grapes: Cab.Sauv. 30% and Cab.Fr. 30%, Merlot 30%, Petit Verdot 10%

A small vineyard in Soussans, owned by the same family as Château Malescot (*q.v.*). The wines are known for their old-fashioned toughness; the flavour of the heavier soil of Soussans giving them long life. The winemaking is modern, but Margaux should have more charm than this.

Château Marquis de Terme ☆☆
4ème Cru Classé. Owner: Philippe Sénéclauze. 38 hectares. Grapes: Cab.Sauv. 55%, Cab.Fr. 3%, Merlot 35%, Petit Verdot 7%. www.chateau-marquis-de-terme.com

A respected old name, not seen often enough in commerce; the greater part is sold direct to French consumers. It is made notably tannic for very long life, although since 1985 a more delicate touch has given it more charm.

Château Palmer ☆☆☆–☆☆☆☆
3ème Cru Classé. Owner: Société Civile du Château Palmer. 51 hectares. Grapes: Cab.Sauv. 47%, Merlot 47%, Petit Verdot 6%. www.chateau-palmer.com

A possible candidate for promotion to First Growth, whose best vintages ('61, '66, '70, '78, '83, '86, '88, '90, '96, 2000) set the running for the whole Médoc. They combine finesse with most voluptuous ripeness, the result of a superb situation on the gravel rise just above Château Margaux, and old-fashioned long fermentation with not too many new barrels, but, probably most of all, the very skilful selection by the owners, French, Dutch, and English, whose flags fly along the romantic roof-line of the château.

Château Pouget ☆
4ème Cru Classé. Owner: Pierre Guillemet. 10 hectares. Grapes: Cab.Sauv. 66%, Merlot 30%, Cab.Fr. 4%

Under the same ownership, and with the same lacklustre results, as Boyd-Cantenac.

Château Prieuré-Lichine ☆☆–☆☆☆
4ème Cru Classé. Owner: Ballande group. 70 hectares. Grapes: Cab.Sauv. 52%, Cab.Fr. 4%, Merlot 40%, Petit Verdot 4%

The personal achievement of the late Alexis Lichine, who assembled a wide scattering of little plots around Margaux in the 1950s and created a reliable and satisfying modern Margaux, harmonious and even rich at times. Then things slid.

Sacha Lichine sold in 1999, now Libourne oenologist Michel Rolland advises here, and St-Emilion winemaker, Stéphane Derenoncourt, makes the wine. A well-defined new style has yet to emerge. The second label is "Château de Clairefont".

Château Rauzan-Gassies ☆–☆☆

2eme Cru Classé. Owner: Jean-Michel Quié. 30 hectares.
Grapes: Cab.Sauv. 65%, Cab.Fr. 10%, Merlot 25%

Disappointing over the last two decades, but signs of improvement since 1996. The owners seem to like it as it is.

Château Rauzan-Ségla ☆☆☆–☆☆☆☆

2ème Cru Classé. Owners: the Wertheimer family (Chanel).
51 hectares. Grapes: Cab.Sauv. 54%, Merlot 41%, Cab.Fr.
1%, Petit Verdot 4%

The larger of the two parts of the estate that used to be second only to Château Margaux, but lagged behind from the '50s to the '90s. At its best ('61, '75, '83, '86, '90) exceedingly fragrant in the Margaux manner. New owners (since 1994) have rebuilt and restored the property to second-growth quality in all respects. The second label is "Ségla".

Château du Tertre ☆☆–☆☆☆

5ème Cru Classé. Owner: Eric Albada Jelgersma. 50 hectares.
Grapes: Cab.Sauv. 85%, Cab.Fr. 5%, Merlot 10%

This backwoods vineyard at Arsac has performed spottily, but new owners since 1997 have invested heavily, with very promising results. The percentage of Cabernet is high.

Other Margaux Châteaux

Château d'Angludet ☆☆

Cantenac. Owner: Benjamin Sichel. 32 hectares.
www.chateau-angludet.fr

Home of the English partner of Château Palmer and, like it, badly undervalued in the official classification. Firm wines, that take time to show their unquestionable class and elegance.

Château Bel-Air-Marquis d'Aligre ☆☆

Margaux. Owner: Pierre Boyer. 17 hectares

Despite its grand name, one of the more basic and backward Margaux, but much improved since the mid-1990s. It usually rewards patience.

Château Deyrem-Valentin ☆☆

Soussans. Owner: Jean Sorge. 12 hectares

Elegant, mid-weight Margaux, sometimes rather stretched.

Château la Gurgue ☆☆

Margaux. Owner: Claire Villars/Merlaut family. 10 hectares.
www.lagurgue.com

A formerly run-down château in the centre of Margaux. Since

1978 under the same ownership as Château Chasse-Spleen. Modern and approachable in a full, fruity style.

Château Haut-Breton-Larigaudière ☆–☆☆

Soussans. Owner: Jacques de Schepper. 13 hectares

A tiny property, better known as one of the few good restaurants in the Médoc.

Château Labégorce ☆☆

Margaux. Owners: Hubert and Joel Perrodo. 41 hectares.
www.chateau-labegorce.com

Potential frontrunner, grand mansion and all. At present, wines have less than real Margaux elegance, but the excellent 2000 may mark the beginning of its renaissance.

Château Labégorce-Zédé ☆☆

Soussans. Owner: Luc Thienpont. 28 hectares.
www.labegorce-zede.com

Among the best unclassified Margaux. The same Flemish family as Vieux-Château-Certan. The 1978 was still fine in 1999.

Château Marojallia

Arsac. Owner: Philippe Porcheron. 2.5 hectares

Margaux's first *vin de garage*. The brainchild of Jean-Luc Thunevin, with advice from Michel Rolland.

Château Marsac-Séguineau ☆–☆☆

Soussans. Owner: Société Civile du Château/Mestrezat.
10 hectares

Part of the same group as Château Grand-Puy-Ducasse (Pauillac). Forward wines.

Château Martinens ☆–☆☆

Cantenac-Margaux. Jean-Pierre Seynat-Dulos. 31 hectares

A good property, which is getting better, re-equipped in 1989. The eighteenth-century château was built, I am told, by three English sisters, the Whites (of Limerick fame).

Château Monbrison ☆☆–☆☆☆☆

Arsac. Owner: Laurent Vonderheyden. 21 hectares

Jan Luc Vonderheyden, who died too young, made a reputation for this property in the '80s with wines of density and finesse. His brother maintains this tradition.

Château Paveil de Luze ☆–☆☆

Soussans. Owner: Baron Geoffrey de Luze. 27 hectares

A gentlemanly estate with smooth, well-mannered wine to match. For drinking relatively young.

Château Siran ☆☆–☆☆☆

Labarde. Owner: William Alain Miaulhe. 24 hectares.
www.chateausiran.com

Fine estate, making most attractive and consistent wine and obsessed with winning classed-growth status (which 40% of this vineyard had before changes in ownership). M. Miailhe has commissioned an historical map to prove that many classed growths have less of 1855 land than Siran. Heliport and antinuclear cellar seem to point to a man who means business. So does the wine.

Château la Tour de Mons ☆☆
Soussans. Owner: Bertrand Clauzel. 35 hectares
Romantic, old-fashioned property long owned by the family who sold Château Cantemerle in 1981. Rounded, well-structured wines (45% Merlot).

Moulis & Listrac

Moulis and Listrac are two communes of the central Haut-Médoc whose appellations (each commune has its own individual one) are more stalwart than glamorous. Between Margaux and St-Julien, the main gravel banks lie farther back from the river with heavier soil. No château here was classified in 1855, but a dozen *crus bourgeois* make admirable wine of the more austere kind. The best soil is on a great dune of gravel stretching from Grand Poujeaux in Moulis (where Châteaux Chasse-Spleen and Maucaillou are both among the best value in the Haut-Médoc) inland through Listrac.

The total area of vines is 608 hectares in Moulis, 694 in Listrac. Both saw rapid expansion in the heady atmosphere of the 1980s. The leaner years of the early '90s were a tough testing ground for these inland Médoc châteaux, where Cabernet ripens later than in vineyards closer to the Gironde. Closer to the river, the villages of Arcins, Lamarque, and Cussac have only the appellation Haut-Médoc (*q.v.*).

Leading Moulis & Listrac Châteaux

Château Baudan ☆☆
Listrac. Owner: Alain Blasquez. 4.5 hectares
Small property that sells concentrated wine directly to restaurants and retailers.

Château Biston-Brillette ☆☆–☆☆☆
Moulis. Owner: Michel Barbarin. 22 hectares
Elegant, medium-bodied wine of high and consistent quality.

Château Brillette ☆☆
Moulis. Owner: Jean-Louis Flageul. 36 hectares
Located on the next plateau to the various Poujeaux, Brillette's wine is supple and gently oaky.

Château Cap Léon Veyrin ☆–☆☆
Listrac. Owner: Alain Meyre. 17 hectares
An improving property, boasting vineyards with an average age of twenty-five years.

Château Chasse-Spleen ☆☆–☆☆☆
Moulis. Owners: the Merlaut family. 83 hectares.
www.chasse-spleen.com
A big property, regularly compared with *crus classés* for style and durability. Expertly made and highly consistent wines for a ten-year haul.

Château Clarke ☆☆
Listrac. Owner: Baron Benjamin de Rothschild. 55 hectares
Completely replanted in the late 1970s, Clarke, despite the investment, has had difficulty producing consistent wines. In some vintages they are delicious: in others, tough and tannic.

Château la Closerie du Grand-Poujeaux ☆
Moulis. Owner: Jean-Paul Bacquey. 7 hectares
Small property, delivering long-lived wines.

Château Ducluzeau ☆☆
Listrac. Owners: the Borie family. 4.5 hectares
Tiny production, but admirable, 90%-Merlot wine, made by the owner of Ducru-Beaucaillou.

Château Duplessis-Fabre ☆
Moulis. Owner: Philippe Dourthe. 17 hectares
Same ownership as Château Maucaillou.

Château Duplessis-Hauchecorne ☆
Moulis. Owner: Marie-Laure Lurton-Roux. 18 hectares
Lighter, more easygoing wine than most here.

Château Dutruch Grand Poujeaux ☆☆–☆☆☆
Moulis. Owner: François Cordonnier. 25 hectares
Old family property, delivering well-structured wine typical of Moulis, for long maturing.

Château Fonréaud ☆
Listrac. Owner: Jean Chanfreau. 30 hectares.
www.chateau-fonreaud.com
Well-known property, but the wines are often astringent and charmless.

Château Fourcas ☆☆–☆☆☆
Loubaney. Owner: Altus Finance. 46 hectares
Classy wine. A substantial estate producing substantial wines with class and discreet oakiness.

Château Fourcas-Dupré ☆☆
Listrac (Part of the vineyard is in Moulis.). Owner: Patrice Pagès. 44 hectares. www.chateaufourcasdupre.com
Sound wine, often with succulent fruit, but sometimes afflicted with hard tannins.

Château Fourcas-Hosten ☆☆–☆☆☆
Listrac. Owners: Bertrand de Rivoyre and Patrice Pagès. 43 hectares
Marked by cassis and oak, but tends towards austerity. Needs bottle-age for its tannins to become more supple.

Château Gressier Grand-Poujeaux ☆☆–☆☆☆
Moulis. Owner: Bertrand de Marcellus. 22 hectares
A rich weighty wine from a neighbour of Château Chasse-Spleen; it repays cellaring.

Château Lafon ☆
Listrac. Owner: J.-P. Théron. 13 hectares
Sound, rather rustic wine.

Château Lestage ☆
Listrac. Owners: the Chanfreau family. 44 hectares
Same owners as Château Fonréaud. Well-known; unremarkable.

Château Malmaison ☆–☆☆
Moulis. Owner: Baronne Nadine de Rothschild. 24 hectares
Borders Château Clarke. Sound, supple wine.

Château Maucaillou ☆☆–☆☆☆
Moulis. Owner: Philippe Dourthe. 68 hectares.
www.chateau-maucaillou.com
Important property with a winemaking museum. Good, deep wine: velvety, chewy, and essentially fruity.

Château Mauvesin ☆
Moulis. Owner: Société Viticole de France. 60 hectares
A big estate, but the wine generally lacks excitement.

Château Mayne-Lalande ☆☆
Listrac. Owner: Bernard Lartigue. 16 hectares
Full-bodied wine and a sometimes exceptional "Grande Réserve", given longer barrel-ageing.

Château Moulin à Vent ☆☆
Moulis. Owner: Dominique Hessel. 25 hectares.
www.moulin-a-vent.com
Sound, fruity wine, steadily improving.

Château Peyre-Lebade ☆–☆☆
Listrac. Owner: Baron Benjamin de Rothschild. 56 hectares
Once home of the painter Odilon Redon, replanted in 1989. Neighbour to Château Clarke.

Château Poujeaux ☆☆☆
Moulis. Owners: the Theil family. 52 hectares.
www.chateaupoujeaux.com
Principal property of the Poujeaux plateau. Vies with Chasse-Spleen as the leading wine of its commune. Recent vintages increasingly fine. The excellent 1988 was at its peak in 2002.

Château Ruat-Petit-Poujeaux ☆
Moulis. Owner: Pierre Goffre-Viaud. 16 hectares
Rather rustic wines.

Château Sansarot-Dupré ☆–☆☆
Listrac. Owner: Yves Raymond. 14 hectares
A full-bodied, Merlot-based wine. Also two hectares of Bordeaux Blanc.

Château Sémeillan Mazeau ☆☆
Listrac. Owners: the Mazeau family. 15 hectares.
www.vignobles-jander.com
Rich, burly wine that needs a few years to become accessible.

Cave Coopérative de Listrac ☆–☆☆
Listrac. 160 hectares
One of the biggest Médoc co-ops. Good reputation.

St-Julien

St-Julien, with a high proportion of *crus classés*, is the smallest of the top-level Médoc appellations. It has only 880 hectares, but eighty per cent of this is classed Second, Third, or Fourth Growth (no First and no Fifth, and very little *cru bourgeois*). Its prominent gravel plateau by the river announces itself as one of the prime sites of Bordeaux.

St-Julien harmonizes force and fragrance with singular suavity to make the benchmark for all red Bordeaux, if not the pinnacle. Farther inland, towards the next village, St-Laurent, the wine is less finely tuned.

The two villages of St-Julien and Beychevelle are scarcely big enough to make you slow your car.

St-Julien Crus Classés

Château Beychevelle ☆☆☆
4ème Cru Classé. Owners: Grands Millésimes de France and Suntory. 90 hectares. Grapes: Cab.Sauv. 60%, Merlot 28%, Cab.Fr. 8%, Petit Verdot 4%. www.beychevelle.com
A regal château built in the seventeenth century, with riverside vineyards on the hill running up to St-Julien from the south. Its silky, supple wine is the one I most associate with the better class of English country house; Blandings must have bulged with it. Famous vintages of the '50s and '60s were touchstones of the sort today's corporate ownership does not match. The curious boat on the label commemorates its admiral founder, to whose rank passing boats on the Gironde used to *baisse les voiles* – hence, they say, the name. The second label is "Amiral de Beychevelle".

Château Branaire ☆☆☆
4ème Cru Class. Owner: Patrick Maroteau. 50 hectares.
Grapes: Cab.Sauv. 70%, Cab.Fr. 5%, Merlot 22%, Petit Verdot 3%. www.branaire.com
Vineyards in several parts of the commune; the château opposite Beychevelle. Model St-Julien, relying more on flavour than force; notably fragrant and attractive wine with a track-record of reliability. Manager Philippe Dhalluin quietly sustains the quality of this exceptionally pure, dignified wine. The second label is "Château Duluc".

Château Ducru-Beaucaillou ☆☆☆–☆☆☆☆
2ème Cru Classé. Owner: Francois-Xavier Borie. 49 hectares.
Grapes: Cab.Sauv. 65%, Cab.Fr. 5%, Merlot 25%, Petit Verdot 5%
Riverside neighbour of Château Beychevelle, with a château almost rivalling it in grandeur, if not in beauty, built over its barrel cellars. The Borie family also owns Ch'x Grand-Puy-Lacoste and Haut-Batailley in Pauillac. After a bad patch around 1990, the estate has been back on top form since '95, with the firm but seductive flavour of the best St-Juliens.

Château Gruaud-Larose ☆☆☆–☆☆☆☆
2ème Cru Classé. Owner: Jean Merlaut. 82 hectares. Grapes: Cab.Sauv. 57%, Cab.Fr. 7%, Merlot 32%, Petit Verdot 4%.
www.chateau-gruaud-larose.fr
This magnificent vineyard on the south slope of St-Julien was long the pride of the merchant house Cordier, until its sale in 1997. Manager Georges Pauli remains in charge. Consistently one of the fruitiest, smoothest, easiest to enjoy of the great Bordeaux, although as long-lived as most, and better value than almost any. Superlative quality since 1995. Second wine: "Sarget de Gruaud-Larose".

Château Lagrange ☆☆–☆☆☆
3ème Cru Classé. Owner: Suntory. 113 hectares.
Grapes: Cab.Sauv. 67%, Merlot 26%, Petit Verdot 7%.
www.chateau-lagrange.com
A magnificent wooded estate inland from St-Julien. The Japanese owners took over in 1983, and started to expand and re-equip. Now the largest St-Julien producer. Discreet, supple wines, always enjoyable, rarely thrilling. The second label is "Les Fiefs-de-Lagrange".

Château Langoa-Barton ☆☆–☆☆☆
3ème Cru Classé. Owners: the Barton family. 15 hectares.
Grapes: Cab.Sauv. 72%, Cab.Fr. 8%, Merlot 20%
The noble sister château of Léoville-Barton and home of the Bartons. Similar excellent wine, although by repute always a short head behind the Léoville.

Château Léoville-Barton ☆☆☆–☆☆☆☆
2ème Cru Classé. Owners: the Barton family. 45 hectares.
Grapes: Cab.Sauv. 72%, Cab.Fr. 8%, Merlot 20%
This third of the original Léoville estate has been owned by the Irish Barton family since 1821. One of the finest and most typical St-Juliens, often richer than Léoville-Las-Cases, made by a conservative philosopher in old-oak vats at the splendid eighteenth-century Château Langoa, built over its barrel cellars. Major investments recently are raising standards even higher – while prices have remained commendably steady. A cornerstone of the Anglo-Saxon cellar.

Château Léoville-Las-Cases ☆☆☆☆
2ème Cru Classé. Owner: Jean-Hubert Delon. 97 hectares.
Grapes: Cab.Sauv. 65%, Cab.Fr. 12%, Merlot 20%,
Petit Verdot 3%
The largest third of the ancient Léoville estate on the boundary of Pauillac, adjacent to Château Latour. A top-flight Second Growth and a favourite of the critics, consistently producing connoisseur's claret, extremely high-flavoured and dry for a St-Julien, needing long maturing and leaning towards austerity. The vineyard's stone gateway is a landmark, but the *chais* are in the centre of St-Julien beside the château, which belongs to Léoville-Poyferré. Severe selection means that the *grand vin* often represents less than half the total. The second wine is "Clos du Marquis". *See also* Château Potensac (Médoc).

Château Léoville-Poyferré ☆☆☆
2ème Cru Classé. Owners: the Cuvelier family. 80 hectares.
Grapes: Cab.Sauv. 60%, Merlot 30%, Petit Verdot 8%,
Cab.Fr. 2%. www.leoville-poyferre.fr

The central portion of the Léoville estate, including the château. Potentially as great a wine as Léoville-Las-Cases, and Didier Cuvelier is set on rivalling his neighbour with oenologist Michel Rolland's help. The second wine takes the name of a *cru bourgeois*, "Château Moulin-Riche".

Château St-Pierre (-Sevaistre) ☆☆☆
4ème Cru Classé. Owner: Domaines Martin. 17 hectares.
Grapes: Cab.Sauv. 70%, Cab.Fr. 10%, Merlot 20%
The smallest and least-known St-Julien classed growth, but superbly situated. The property was bought in 1982 by Henri Martin of Château Gloria (*q.v.*), who raised it to new heights, and is now run by his son-in-law, Jean-Louis Triaud. No glamour, but fruity, deep-coloured wine from old vines.

Château Talbot ☆☆☆
4ème Cru Classé. Owners: the Cordier family. 102 hectares.
Grapes: Cab.Sauv. 66%, Cab.Fr. 3%, Merlot 24%,
Petit Verdot 5%, Malbec 2%. www.chateau-talbot.com
One of the biggest and most productive Bordeaux vineyards, just inland from the Léovilles. Marshal Talbot was the last English commander of Aquitaine. Like Gruaud-Larose, a rich, fruity, smooth wine, but without the same plumpness or structure. Small quantity of dry white "Caillou Blanc" is produced on five hectares and challenges the notion that the Médoc can't do white. Second label is "Connétable Talbot".

Other St-Julien Châteaux

Château la Bridane ☆☆
Owner: Pierre Saintout. 15 hectares
Solid wine, with blackcurrant fruit. Very attractive wine for medium-term drinking.

Château du Glana ☆☆
Owner: Vignobles Meffre. 42 hectares
Oddly unrenowned as one of St-Julien's only two big unclassed growths. The owner is a wine merchant with several properties, who has built a giant *chai* more like a warehouse just north of St-Julien. His splendidly sited vineyards produce respectable wine from grapes picked mostly by machine.

Château Gloria ☆☆–☆☆☆☆
Owner: Francoise Triaud. 48 hectares
The classic example of the unranked château of exceptional

Commanderie du Bontemps de Médoc et des Graves

The Médoc unites with the Graves in its ceremonial and promotional body, the *Commanderie du Bontemps de Médoc et des Graves*. In its modern manifestation it dates from 1950, when a group of energetic château proprietors, on the initiative of the regional deputy, Emile Liquard, donned splendid red velvet robes and started to "enthronize" dignitaries and celebrities, wine merchants, and journalists at a series of protracted and very jolly banquets held in the *chais* of the bigger château estates.

The Commanderie claims descent from an organization of the Knights-Templar of the Order of Malta at St-Laurent in the Médoc

in 1154 – a somewhat tenuous link. Its three annual banquets are the festivals of St Vincent (the patron saint of wine) in January, the *Fête de la Fleur* (when the vines flower) in June, and the *Ban des Vendanges*, the official proclamation of the opening of the vintage, in September. Male recruits to the Commanderie are usually entitled *Commandeur d'Honneur*, and female, *Gourmettes* – a pun meaning both a woman gourmet and the little silver chain used for hanging a cork around the neck of a decanter.

The Commanderie cleverly blends a knack for wine promotion with a refusal to take itself or its members too seriously.

quality, the creation of the illustrious mayor of St-Julien. The late Henri Martin assembled the vineyard in the 1940s with parcels of land from neighbouring *crus classés*, particularly Château St-Pierre. The wine is rich and long-lasting; being partly aged in large casks, it is not overtly oaky. Quality has made another leap forward since the mid-'90s. "Château Haut-Beychevelle-Gloria" and "Château Peymartin" are names for selections made for certain markets.

Château Lalande Borie ☆☆
Owners: the Borie family. 18 hectares
A vineyard created from part of the old Lagrange in 1970 by the owner of Château Ducru-Beaucaillou, where the wine is made. In effect, a baby brother of Ducru.

Château Moulin de la Rose ☆☆
Owner: Guy Delon. 4.5 hectares
A little-known property surrounded by *crus classé* vineyards. Well-made wines.

Château Terrey-Gros-Caillou & Château Hortevie ☆☆
Owner: Henri Pradère. 15 hectares
A union of two small properties, producing very creditable St-Julien.

Pauillac

Pauillac is the only town in the vineyard area of the Médoc, and a pretty quiet one at that. Its riverside site was marred by a huge Shell Oil refinery subsequently closed and partially dismantled. The town's few hotels face the estuary across a tree-lined quay. Only the *maison du vin* (worth a visit) on the quay gives a hint of this town's world renown. That, and the famous names on signs everywhere you look in the open steppe of the vineyards.

The wine of Pauillac epitomizes the qualities of all red Bordeaux. It is the virile aesthete; a hypnotizing concurrence of force and finesse. It can lean to an extreme either way (Latour and Lafite representing the poles) but at its best, strikes such a perfect balance that no evening is long enough to do it justice. There are 1,200 hectares of vineyards with more *crus classé* than any other commune except Margaux, surprisingly weighted towards Fifth Growths – some of which are worth much better than that.

Pauillac Premiers Crus

Château Lafite-Rothschild ☆☆☆☆
Owner: Domaines Baron de Rothschild. 100 hectares.
Grapes: Cab.Sauv. 70%, Cab.Fr. 3%, Merlot 25%, Petit Verdot 2%. www.lafite.com
See **The Making of a Great Claret, page 50**

Château Latour ☆☆☆☆
Owner: Pinault-Printemps group. 65 hectares. Grapes: Cab.Sauv. 78%, Cab.Fr. 4%, Merlot 16%, Petit Verdot 2%. www.chateau-latour.fr
Château Latour is in every way complementary to Château Lafite. They make their wines on different soils in different ways; the quality of each is set in relief by the very different qualities of the other. Lafite is a tenor; Latour a bass. Lafite is a lyric; Latour an epic. Lafite is a dance; Latour a parade. Lafite lies on Pauillac's northern boundary with St-Estèphe, Latour on the southern, St-Julien limit of the commune 6.5 kilometres (four miles) away on the last low hill of river-deposited gravel, before the flood plain and the stream that divides the two parishes. The ancient vineyard, taking its name from a riverside fortress of the Middle Ages, surrounds the modest mansion, its famous domed stone tower and the big, square, stable-like block of its *chais*. Two other small patches of vineyard lie half a mile inland near Château Batailley.

For nearly three centuries the estate was in the same family (and up to 1760, connected with Lafite). Its modern history began in 1963, when the de Beaumonts sold the majority share to an English group headed by the banker Lord Cowdray, and including the wine merchant Harveys of Bristol. They set in hand a total modernization, starting with temperature-controlled, stainless-steel fermenting vats in place of the ancient oak. Combined English and French talent has since rationalized and perfected every inch of the property, setting such standards that Latour has, rather unfairly, become almost more famous for the quality of its lesser vintages than for the splendour of such years as 1961, '66, '70, '78, '82, '86, '88, '89, '90, '95, '96, and 2000. Its consistency and deep, resonant style extends into its second label, "Les Forts de Latour", which fetches a price comparable to a Second Growth château. "Les Forts" comes partly from vats of less than the *grand vin* standard, but mainly from two small vineyards (eighteen hectares) farther inland towards Batailley. These were replanted in 1966, and their wine first used in the blend in the early 1970s. In the '90s there was also a third wine, modestly labelled "Pauillac", which by no means disgraced its big brothers.

In 1989, Allied-Lyons Ltd (owners of Harveys) bought the Cowdray-Pearson share, valuing the property at around US\$100 million and making it the world's most expensive vineyard. The thirty-year English occupation ended when Allied-Lyons sold Latour in 1994 to the French entrepreneur François Pinault, for 680 million *francs*, ten times the price Mentzelopoulos had paid for Margaux in 1977. Pinault's lieutenant, Frédéric Engerer, has supervised another complete modernization of the winemaking facilities, completed in 2002. There is no sign of compromise.

Château Mouton-Rothschild ☆☆☆☆
Owner: Baronne Philippine de Rothschild. 80 hectares (including 4 of white grapes). Grapes: Cab.Sauv. 80%, Cab.Fr. 10%, Merlot 8%, Petit Verdot 2%. www.bpdr.com
Mouton-Rothschild is geographically neighbour to Lafite, but gastronomically closer to Latour. Its hallmark is a deep concentration of the flavour of Cabernet Sauvignon, often described as resembling blackcurrants, held as though between the poles of a magnet in the tension of its tannin – a balancing act that can go on for decades, increasing in fascination and grace all the time. In 1976, I noted of the 1949 Mouton: "Deep, unfaded red; huge, almost California-style nose; resin and spice; still taut with tannin, but overwhelming in its succulence and sweetness. In every way magnificent."

More than any other château, Mouton-Rothschild is identified with one man, the late Baron Philippe de Rothschild, who came to take it over as a neglected property of his (the English) branch of the Rothschild family in 1922, and died in 1989. This remarkable man of many talents (poet, dramatist, racing-driver among them) determined to raise Mouton from being first in the 1855 list of Second Growths to parity with Lafite. It took him fifty-one years of effort, argument, publicity, and above all, perfectionist winemaking. He gained official promotion in 1973, the only change ever made to the 1855 classification.

Baron Philippe and his American wife, Pauline, created a completely new house in the stone stable block and collected in the same building a great museum of works of art relating to wine, displayed with unique flair (and open to the public by appointment). He was succeeded in 1989 by his daughter Philippine, who has inherited her father's unquenchable zest for life, and has brilliantly nurtured the New World empire he inaugurated with Robert Mondavi in the 1980s.

The baron's love of the arts (and knack for publicity) led him to commission a different famous artist to design the top panel of the Mouton label every year from 1945 on. Of these vintages, the most famous are the 1949 (the owner's favourite), '53, '59, '61, '66, '70, '75, '82, '85, '86, '88, '89, '90, '95, '98, and 2000.

The baron's Bordeaux domaine expanded over the years to include Châteaux d'Armailhac and Clerc-Milon, and la Baronnie, his company that produces and markets "Mouton-Cadet", the best-selling branded Bordeaux. Mouton itself had no second label until the launch in 1994 of "Le Petit Mouton". Since 1991, a small quantity of intense, dry white, "Aile d'Argent", has been made. It has yet to prove itself.

Pauillac Crus Classés

Château d'Armailhac ☆☆☆
5ème Cru Classé. Owner: Baronne Philippine de Rothschild. 52 hectares. Grapes: Cab.Sauv. 55%, Cab.Fr. 25%, Merlot 20%
Originally Mouton-d'Armailhacq, bought in 1933 by Baron Philippe de Rothschild and twice renamed. The vineyard is south of Mouton, next to Pontet-Canet, on lighter, even sandy soil, which, with a higher proportion of both Cabernet Franc and Merlot, gives a rather lighter, quicker-maturing wine, but a star nonetheless, made to the customary Mouton standards.

Château Batailley ☆☆–☆☆☆
5ème Cru Classé. Owner: Emile Castéja. 52 hectares. Grapes: Cab.Sauv. 70%, Cab.Fr. 5%, Merlot 25%
The name of the estate, another of those divided into easily confusable parts, comes from an Anglo-French disagreement in the fifteenth century. Charles II's favourite wine merchant was called Joseph Batailhé – I like to think he was a son of this soil, the wooded inland part of Pauillac. Batailley is the larger property and retains the lovely little mid-nineteenth-century château in its "English" park. Its wine is tannic, never exactly graceful, but eventually balancing its austerity with sweetness; old (twenty-year) bottles keep great nerve and vigour. These are the Pauillacs that approach St-Estèphe in style. The wine is usually excellent value.

Château Clerc-Milon ☆☆☆
5ème Cru Classé. Owner: Baronne Philippine de Rothschild S.A.. 30 hectares. Grapes: Cab.Sauv. 70%, Cab.Fr. 10%, Merlot 20%
An obscure little estate known as Clerc-Milon-Mondon until 1970, when it was bought by Baronne Philippine de

Rothschild. The vineyard (there is no château) is promisingly positioned close to Château Lafite and Château Mouton-Rothschild. Typical Rothschild perfectionism, energy, and money have made a series of good vintages, starting with a remarkably fine 1970. After an uneven patch, Clerc-Milon is once again classic and consistent; the 2000 is a model wine.

Château Croizet-Bages ☆–☆☆
5ème Cru Classé. Owner: Jean-Michel Quié. 30 hectares. Grapes: Cab.Sauv. 50%, Cab.Fr. 10%, Merlot 40%
A property belonging to the owners of Château Rauzan-Gassies, Margaux (q.v.). No château, but vineyards on the Bages plateau between Lynch-Bages and Grand-Puy-Lacoste. Compared with the firmness and vigour of the Lynch-Bages of the same year, the 1961 at twenty years old was rather old-ladyish, sweet but fragile. Recent vintages have been distinctly light, even in top years.

Château Duhart-Milon-Rothschild ☆☆☆
4ème Cru Classé. Owners: Domaines Baron de Rothschild. 50 hectares. Grapes: Cab.Sauv. 65%, Cab.Fr. 5%, Merlot 30%. www.lafite.com
The little sister of Château Lafite, on the next hillock inland, known as Carruades, bought by the Rothschilds in 1964 and since then completely replanted and enlarged. Its track record was for hard wine of no great subtlety, but as the young vines age, this is becoming a great château again, making long-living claret. The second label is "Moulin de Duhart".

Château Grand-Puy-Ducasse ☆☆
5ème Cru Classé. Owner: Mestrezat. 37 hectares. Grapes: Cab.Sauv. 62%, Merlot 38%
Three widely separated plots of vineyard, one next to Grand-Puy-Lacoste, one by Pontet-Canet, the third nearer Batailley, and *chais* and château on the Pauillac waterfront. Much replanted and renovated, but already known for big, well-built, and long-lived wine (*e.g.* '61, '64, '66, '67, '70). The 1986 and 1989 vintages were stars of the '80s, but the wines have often lacked flair. The 1996 is a welcome exception. "Artigues-Arnaud" is a second label.

Château Grand-Puy-Lacoste ☆☆☆–☆☆☆☆
5ème Cru Classé. Owners: the Borie family. 50 hectares. Grapes: Cab.Sauv. 70%, Cab.Fr. 5%, Merlot 25%
Sold in 1978 by the Médoc's greatest gastronome, Raymond Dupin, to one of its most dedicated proprietors, Jean-Eugène Borie (of Ducru-Beaucaillou, Haut-Batailley, etc.), whose son, François-Xavier, lives at the château and runs it. Rather remote but attractive property with an extraordinary romantic garden, a thousand miles from the Médoc in spirit, on the next "hill" inland from the Bages plateau. The wine has tremendous attack, colour, structure, and class. The second label is "Lacoste-Borie".

Château Haut-Bages-Libéral ☆☆–☆☆☆
5ème Cru Classé. Owner: Claire Villars. 28 hectares. Grapes: Cab.Sauv. 75%, Merlot 22%, Petit Verdot 3%. www.hautbagesliberal.com
A vineyard bordering Château Latour to the north. The Merlaut family has invested heavily here, and this property is making much better wine than its rather limited reputation suggests. It is a true Pauillac: forthright, tannic, and long-lived. The second label is "Chapelle de Bages".

Château Lafite-Rothschild – The Making of a Great Claret

This is the place to study the author's control of his superlatives. Wine for intelligent millionaires has been made by this estate for well over 200 years, and when a random selection of thirty-six vintages, going back to 1799, was drunk and compared in recent times, the company was awed by the consistency of the performance. Underlying the differences in quality, style, and maturity of the vintages, there was an uncanny resemblance between wines made even a century and a half apart.

It is easy to doubt, because it is difficult to understand the concept of a Bordeaux *cru*. As an amalgam of soil and situation with tradition and professionalism, its stability depends heavily on the human factor. Sometimes even Homer nods. Lafite had its bad patch in the 1960s and early 1970s. Since 1976, it has once again epitomized the traditional Bordeaux château at its best.

As a mansion, Lafite is impeccably chic rather than grand; a substantial but unclassical eighteenth-century villa, on a terrace above the most businesslike and best vegetable garden in the Médoc. There are no great rooms; the red drawing room, the pale-blue dining room, and the dark-green library are comfortably cluttered and personal. The Rothschild family of the Paris bank bought the estate in 1868. It has been the apple of their corporate eye ever since. In 1974, the thirty-four-year-old Baron Eric de Rothschild took over responsibility for the estate.

Grandeur starts in the *cuvier*, the vat house, and low barns of the *chais*, where the barrels make marvellous perspectives of dwindling hoops seemingly for ever. In 1989, a unique and spectacular new circular *chai*, dug out of the vineyards and supported by columns to test Samson, was inaugurated. History is most evident in the shadowy, moss-encrusted bottle cellars, where the collection stretches back to 1797 – probably the first Bordeaux ever to be château-bottled, still in its original bin.

Quality starts with the soil: deep, gravel dunes over limestone. It depends on the age of the vines: at Lafite an average of forty years. It depends even more on restricting their production: the figure of forty to forty-five hectolitres is achieved by stern pruning.

Vintage in the Médoc starts at any time between early September and late October. In a big vineyard (Lafite has 100 hectares), it is impossible to pick every grape at precisely the ideal moment. Picking teams, some 250 strong, begin with the Merlot, which ripens first, and move as quickly as they can.

The vital work of selection starts in the vineyard, discarding bunches that are unevenly ripe or infected with rot. It continues at the *cuvier*, where they are inspected before being tipped in the *égrappoir-fouloir*, a simple mill that first strips the grapes off the stalks, then half-crushes them (most estates use a *fouloir-égrappoir* that crushes and de-stems at the same time: perfectionists remove stalks first). By controlling the speed of the rollers it is possible to prevent green grapes being crushed at all.

The crushed grapes, each variety separately, are pumped into upright oak vats, each holding between 15,750 and 20,250 litres. If the grapes lack sufficient natural sugar, the must will be chaptalized. In mild weather, the juice and pulp start to ferment within a day. In cold weather, the whole *cuvier* is heated.

The temperature of fermentation is controlled to rise no higher than 30°C (85°F) – enough to extract the maximum colour from the skins; not enough to inhibit the yeasts and stop a steady fermentation. If it threatens to go higher, the must wine is pumped from the bottom of the vat to the top through a cooling system and over the floating "cap" of skins which also helps extract colour.

Fermentation can take from one to three weeks, depending on the yeasts, the ripeness of the grapes, and the weather. The wine may be left on the skins for up to twenty-one days, if necessary, to leach the maximum colour and flavour. By this time, the malolactic fermentation may be underway or even finished. The juice is run off into new 225-litre barriques made at the château of oak from the forest of Tronçais in the Allier in central France. The remaining *marc* of skins and pips is pressed in a hydraulic press. Some of this, exaggeratedly tannic, can be blended if necessary, usually between ten per cent and none at all.

The barriques, up to 1,100 of them in a plentiful year, stand in rows in the *chai*, loosely bunged at the top, while the malolactic fermentation finishes. Early in the new year, the proprietor, his manager, the *maître de chai*, and consultant oenologist (Professor Boissenot) taste the inky, biting new wine to make the essential selection: which barrels are good enough for the château's *grand vin*, which are fit for the second wine, "Carruades de Lafite", and which will be bottled as mere "Pauillac". This is the moment for the *assemblage* of the wines of the four different varieties, up to now still separate. Once assembled, the wines are put back into clean barrels.

For a further year they stand with loose bungs, being topped up weekly to make good any "ullage", or loss by evaporation. During this year they will be racked into clean casks two or three times and fined with beaten egg whites. The white froth poured onto the top coagulates and sinks, taking any floating particles with it to the bottom. When the year is up, the bungs are tapped tight and the casks turned *bondes de côte* – with their bungs to the side. From now on the only way to sample them is through a tiny spiggot hole plugged with wood at the end of the cask.

At Lafite, the wine is kept in cask for a further nine to twelve months, until the second summer or autumn after the vintage, then racked into a vat, which feeds the bottling machine. If it were bottled from individual casks there would be too much variation.

Complicated as it is to relate, there is no simpler or more natural way of making wine. The factors that distinguish First Growth winemaking from more modest enterprises are the time it takes, the number of manoeuvres, and the rigorous selection.

In recent years, Rothschild enterprise has been at work to use the technical (as well as financial) strength of Lafite in new fields both near and far. The neighbouring Château Duhart-Milon has been bought and renovated; Château Rieussec in Sauternes and leading Pomerol Château L'Evangile acquired; and joint ventures started in Chile (1988), California (1989), and Portugal (1992).

Château Haut-Batailley ☆☆–☆☆☆
5ème Cru Classé. Owners: the Borie family. 22 hectares.
Grapes: Cab.Sauv. 65%, Cab.Fr. 10%, Merlot 25%
A wine of charm rather than weight, as much St-Julien in style as Pauillac. For sheer tastiness there are few wines you can choose with more confidence. The second label of Haut-Batailley is "La Tour l'Aspic".

Château Lynch-Bages ☆☆☆–☆☆☆☆
5ème Cru Classé. Owners: the Cazes family. 90 hectares.
Grapes: Cab.Sauv. 75%, Cab.Fr. 10%, Merlot 15%.
www.lynchbages.com
An important estate, fondly known to its many English friends as "lunch-bags"; a perennial favourite for sweet and meaty, strongly Cabernet-flavoured wine, epitomizing Pauillac at its most hearty. The Bages plateau, south of the town, has relatively strong soil over clay subsoil. The best vintages ('82, '85, '86, '88, '89, '90, and all vintages from '95 onwards) are very long-lived; the '61 is perhaps now at its peak.
Jean-Michel Cazes, who doubles as Pauillac's leading insurance broker, rebuilt the crumbling château and the former cavernous, gloomy *chais* in the '80s and raised the name of his property to new heights. He was also the founding director of the AXA wine estates, until he retired from that position in 2001. His other property is Les Ormes-de-Pez in St-Estèphe. The second label is "Haut-Bages-Averous".

Château Lynch-Moussas ☆–☆☆
5ème Cru Classé. Owner: Emile Castéja. 50 hectares.
Grapes: Cab.Sauv. 60%, Merlot 40%
Stablemate since 1969 of its neighbour Château Batailley. M. Castéja has replanted and totally renovated the château and *chais*. As the young vines age, vintages of the '90s show more depth of flavour, but this is essentially a lightweight.

Château Pedesclaux ☆
5ème Cru Classé. Owner: Bernard Jugla. 20 hectares. Grapes: Cab.Sauv. 65%, Cab.Fr. 7%, Merlot 25%, Petit Verdot 3%
The least renowned classed growth of Pauillac, scattered around the commune like Grand-Puy-Ducasse, and making suave wines that lack stuffing but are much to the taste of its principal customers, the Belgians. M. Jugla (*see* Château Colombier-Monpelou) uses the names of two of his *crus bourgeois*, "Grand Duroc Milon" and "Belle Rose", as second labels.

Château Pichon-Longueville ☆☆☆–☆☆☆☆
2ème Cru Classé. Owner: AXA Millésimes. 68 hectares.
Grapes: Cab.Sauv. 70%, Cab.Fr. 5%, Merlot 25%.
www.pichonlongueville.com
The following entry gives the background to the unwieldy name. New owner (the insurance company AXA) since 1987 set lustily about competing with the Comtesse across the road, which for years had made much better wine. With Jean-Michel Cazes (*see* Château Lynch-Bages) as director, and a seemingly bottomless purse, an aggressive building programme has transformed the place. The wine is now an earnest contender with its neighbour, and more full-bloodedly Pauillac in style, with its preponderance of Cabernet. Brilliant quality since the magnificent '90. Second wine is "Les Tourelles de Longueville".

Château Pichon-Longueville, Comtesse de Lalande ☆☆☆–☆☆☆☆
2ème Cru Classé. Owner: Mme. May-Eliane de Lencquesaing. 75 hectares. Grapes: Cab.Sauv. 45%, Cab.Fr. 12%, Merlot 35%, Petit Verdot 8%. www.pichon-lalande.com
Two châteaux share the splendid estate that was planted in the seventeenth century by the same pioneer who planted the Rauzan estate in Margaux. The châteaux were long owned by his descendants, the various sons and daughters of the Barons de Pichon-Longueville. Two-thirds of the estate eventually fell to a daughter who was Comtesse de Lalande – hence the lengthy name, which is often shortened to Pichon-Lalande. The family of the present owner bought it in 1925.
The mansion lies in the vineyards of Château Latour, but most of its vineyard is across the road, on gravelly soil with clay below, surrounded by the vines of the other Pichon château and parts of the vineyards of Châteaux Latour, Ducru-Beaucaillou, and Léoville-Las-Cases. The southern portion of the vineyard is actually in St-Julien. With its relatively generous proportion of Merlot, the wine lacks the concentrated vigour of Château Latour, but adds a persuasive perfumed smoothness that makes it one of the most fashionable Second Growths.
The Pichon-Lalande team is now making fabulously good wine of the kind everyone wants: stylish Pauillac of the St-Julien persuasion, not so rigid with tannin and extract that it takes decades to mature. Each vintage since 1975 is among the best of its year, with spectacular successes in '81, '82, '83, '84, '85, '86, '89, and almost all vintages since '95. The second label is "Réserve de la Comtesse".

Château Pontet-Canet ☆☆☆
5ème Cru Classé. Owner: Alfred Tesseron. 79 hectares.
Grapes: Cab.Sauv. 62%, Cab.Fr. 6%, Merlot 32%.
www.pontet-canet.com
Sheer size has helped Pontet-Canet to become one of Bordeaux's most familiar names. That, and over a century of ownership by the shippers Cruse & Fils Frères. Its situation near Mouton promises top quality; the 1929 was considered better than the Mouton of that great year. But 1961 was the last great vintage Pontet-Canet has made, and that, like all its wines of that epoch, varied considerably from bottle to bottle. The Cruse family did not believe in château bottling. In 1975, the estate was sold to Guy Tesseron of cognac, son-in-law of Emmanuel Cruse. The 1980s saw steady improvement, and fanatical selection has brought the wines to an impressive new level in the late 1990s. They have swagger, power, and concentration. The double-decker *cuvier*, *chais*, and bottle cellars are on an enormous scale, even by Médoc standards. The second label, "Les Hauts de Pontet", was introduced in 1982.

Other Pauillac Châteaux

Château la Bécasse ☆–☆☆
Owner: Roland Fonteneau. 4.2 hectares
Tiny but admirable estate making deep-flavoured Pauillac in good years.

Château Colombier Monpelou ☆
Owner: Bernard Jugla. 17 hectares
Usually attractive, if lightweight, stablemate of the *cru classé* Château Pedesclaux (*q.v.*).

Château Cordeillan Bages ☆☆–☆☆☆
Owner: J.M. Cazes. 2 hectares
A mere 1,000 cases from the château hotel vineyard.

Château la Fleur Milon ☆☆
Owners: the Mirande family. 13 hectares.
www.lafleurmilon.com
Robust, long-lived wine with rustic overtones but also with Pauillac typicité.

Château Fonbadet ☆☆–☆☆☆
Owner: Pierre Peyronie. 20 hectares.
www.chateaufonbadet.com
A good growth, producing rich, dense, traditional wines from very old vines. Can be outstanding in top years.

Les Forts de Latour ☆☆☆
See Château Latour
The first of the "second" wines of the Médoc, and still the best.

Château Gaudin ☆
Owner: Mme. Capdevielle. 10 hectares
Fruity wines that lack complexity.

Château Haut-Bages Monpelou ☆–☆☆
Owner: Emile Castéja. 15 hectares
Until 1948, part of Château Duhart-Milon, now in the same hands as Château Batailley and effectively its second wine.

Château Pibran ☆☆–☆☆☆
Owner: AXA Millésimes. 19 hectares
Fleshy, robust, at times opulent wine. In 2001, neighbour Château Tour Pibran was purchased and incorporated.

Château Plantey ☆
Owner: Claude Meffre. 26 hectares
Formerly part of Château Fonbadet. The Meffre family also owns Château du Glana (St-Julien *q.v.*). A commercial wine, that lacks elegance.

La Tour l'Aspic ☆
Owners: the Borie family
Second label of Château Haut-Batailley.

Cave Coopérative la Rose Pauillac ☆–☆☆
Growers' cooperative drawing on seventy-eight hectares. Well-made, if rustic, Pauillac.

St-Estèphe

St-Estèphe is more pleasantly rural than Pauillac; a scattering of six hamlets with some steepish slopes and (at Marbuzet) wooded parks. It has 1,378 hectares of vineyards, mainly *crus bourgeois*, on heavier soil planted with, as a rule, a higher proportion of Merlot to Cabernet than the communes to the south. Typical St-Estèphe keeps a strong colour for a long time, is slow to show its virtues, has less perfume and a coarser, more hearty flavour than Pauillac, with less of the tingling vitality that marks the very best Médocs. With a few brilliant exceptions, the St-Estèphes are the foot soldiers of this aristocratic army.

St-Estèphe Crus Classés

Château Calon-Ségur ☆☆☆
3ème Cru Classé. Owner: Philippe Capbern-Gasqueton. 74 hectares. Grapes: Cab.Sauv. 65%, Cab.Fr. 15%, Merlot 20%. www.calon-segur.com
The northernmost classed growth of the Médoc, named after the eighteenth-century Comte de Ségur, who also owned Lafite and Latour, but whose "heart was at Calon" – and is remembered by a red one on the label. After years when the wine was somewhat dour and tannic, quality leapt ahead in the mid-1990s, and Calon-Ségur is now indisputably one of the top wines of the region. The walled vineyard surrounds the fine château.

Château Cos d'Estournel ☆☆☆–☆☆☆☆
2ème Cru Classé. Owner: Taillan group and investors. 64 hectares. Grapes: Cab.Sauv. 58%, Cab.Fr. 2%, Merlot 40%. www.cosdestournel.com
Superbly sited vineyard sloping south towards Château Lafite. No house, but a bizarre chinoiserie *chai*. The most (perhaps the only) glamorous St-Estèphe, one of the top Second Growths with both the flesh and the bone of great claret and a fine record for consistency. Despite a change of ownership in 1998, Jean-Guillaume Prats, the son of the previous owner, remains at the helm.

This is one of the finest modern-style clarets, with the estate using all the technology at its disposal to focus on quality. It remains a powerful, long-lived wine with an abundance of fruit and oak. Fifteen to twenty years is a good age to drink it. The second label is "Les Pagodes de Cos". The "s" of Cos is sounded, like most final consonants in southwest France.

Château Cos-Labory ☆☆–☆☆☆
5ème Cru Classé. Owner: Bernard Audoy. 18 hectares. Grapes: Cab.Sauv. 55%, Cab.Fr. 10%, Merlot 35%
A businesslike little classed growth next door to Cos d'Estournel, but only geographically. The rather scattered vineyards with a high proportion of Merlot vines make a blunt, honest St-Estèphe, relatively soft and fruity for drinking in four or five years. What the wines lack is finesse.

Château Lafon-Rochet ☆☆☆
4ème Cru Classé. Owner: Michel Tesseron. 40 hectares. Grapes: Cab.Sauv. 55%, Merlot 41%, Cab.Fr. 4%.
www.lafon-rochet.com
A single block of vineyard sloping south towards the back of Château Lafite on the south bank of St-Estèphe. The château was rebuilt in the 1960s by the cognac merchant, Guy Tesseron, whose son Michel (brother of Alfred Tesseron of Château Pontet-Canet), spares no expense to make good wine, and has steadily improved the property. He makes full-bodied, lush, powerful wine, which is worth keeping for smoothness, but does not seem to find great finesse. Superb quality in '98 and 2000.

Château Montrose ☆☆☆–☆☆☆☆
2ème Cru Classé. Owner: Jean-Louis Charmolüe. 68 hectares. Grapes: Cab.Sauv. 65%, Cab.Fr. 10%, Merlot 25%
Isolated, seemingly remote property overlooking the Gironde north of St-Estèphe with a style of its own; traditionally one of the firmest of all Bordeaux, hard and forbidding for a long time, notably powerful in flavour even

when mature. The deep colour and flavour of the wine probably come from the clay subsoil under reddish, iron-rich gravel. Being right on the river also helps the grapes to early ripeness. Wines of the period 1978–85 let the standard drop, being much softer and easier, but in the early '90s the tone has again been sterner, tempting some to call Montrose the "Latour of St-Estèphe". Superb in '90, '95, '96, and 2000. The second label is "La Dame de Montrose".

Other St-Estèphe Chateaux

Château Andron-Blanquet ☆
Owner: Bernard Audoy. 16 hectares
Made at Cos-Labory (*q.v.*). Inexpensive but lacklustre.

Château Beau-Site ☆☆
Owners: Borie-Manoux. 35 hectares
A fine situation in the hamlet of St-Corbin. Good, sturdy wines, but most enjoyable fairly young.

Château le Boscq ☆☆
Owner: CVBG. 16 hectares
Very good, supple wines for medium-term drinking.

Château Capbern-Gasqueton ☆–☆☆
Owners: Philippe Capbern-Gasqueton. 20 hectares
Rich, burly wine from same stable as Château Calon-Ségur.

Château Chambert-Marbuzet ☆–☆☆
See **Château Haut-Marbuzet**

Château Coutelin-Merville ☆–☆☆
Owner: Bernard Estager. 20 hectares
Light wine, not for long keeping.

Château le Crock ☆☆
Owners: the Cuvelier family. 33 hectares.
www.cuvelier-bordeaux.com
Classical mansion; same ownership as Château Léoville-Poyferré (*crus classé*, St-Julien). Consistent and well-made, with ample density and fruit. Can be enjoyed fairly young.

Château Haut-Beauséjour ☆☆
Owner: Roederer. 18 hectares
A property re-created in 1992 by Jean-Claude Rouzaud, who also owns Château de Pez (*q.v.*).

Château Haut-Marbuzet ☆☆☆
Owner: Henri Duboscq. 58 hectares
Today the outstanding *cru bourgeois* of St-Estèphe: oaky, fleshy, luxurious, and instantly appealing. Château Chambert-Marbuzet and Château MacCarthy are *cru bourgeois* with the same owners. Second label: "Château Tour de Marbuzet".

Château Houissant ☆
Owner: Jean Ardouin. 28 hectares
Fruity, Merlot-dominated wine.

Château Laffitte-Carcasset ☆–☆☆
Owner: Vicomte de Padirac. 42 hectares
Well-made wine with a fairly high proportion of new oak.

Château Lilian Ladouys ☆☆
Owners: institutional investors. 40 hectares.
www.chateau-lilian-ladouys.com
New owners in 1989 made substantial investments, and initial vintages were splendid, if very oaky. The property went bankrupt in the late 1990s, and wine is sound if less flamboyant than before.

Château MacCarthy ☆–☆☆
See **Haut-Marbuzet**

Château (de) Marbuzet ☆☆
Owner: Taillan group and investors
No longer the second label of Cos d'Estournel (*q.v.*), though under the same ownership.

Château Meyney ☆☆
Owner: Cordier. 50 hectares
One of the best-sited and most long-lived of the many reliable *cru bourgeois* in St-Estèphe. Firm, dark wine, sometimes a bit tough. Second label: "Prieur de Meyney".

Château Morin ☆
Owners: the Sidaine family. 10 hectares
An ancient property, but the wine can be rustic.

Château Les Ormes-de-Pez ☆☆–☆☆☆
Owner: Jean-Michel Cazes. 33 hectares. www.ormesdepez.com
Extremely popular and highly regarded property. Deservedly so, as the wine is rich, fleshy, elegant, and beautifully balanced.

Château de Pez ☆☆
Owner: Louis Roederer. 24 hectares
Noble, very long-lived wine, sometimes of classed growth standard. At twenty years, the 1970 was magnificent. Since Champagne Roederer bought the property in 1995, the wine has become softer and more elegant.

Château Phélan-Ségur ☆☆–☆☆☆
Owner: Xavier Gardinier. 70 hectares
Important property, totally rebuilt, and full of ambition since the Gardiniers (former owners of Pommery) bought it in 1985. Sometimes underrated, as the wine is elegant rather than powerful or dramatic. Best enjoyed within ten years.

Château Pomys ☆☆
Owner: François Arnaud. 10 hectares
A well-known property (and hotel) producing classic, well-structured St-Estèphe.

Château Ségur de Cabanac ☆☆
Owner: Guy Delon. 6 hectares
Only 3,000 cases of excellent quality.

Château Tour de Pez ☆☆
Owner: the Bouchara family. 23 hectares
Improving property, producing wine with ample fruit and reasonable intensity.

Château Tronquoy-Lalande ☆☆
Owner: Mme. Arlette Castéja. 17 hectares
Once dark and tannic, the wine has become more supple in the 1990s – a change in style rather than quality.

Haut-Médoc

Haut-Médoc is the catch-all appellation for the fringes of the area that includes the most famous communes. It varies in quality from equal to some of the best in the very south, where Château la Lagune in Ludon and Château Cantemerle are out on a limb, to a level only notionally higher than the best of the lower, northerly end of the Médoc. Some of this land lies along the river in the middle of the appellation, in the low-lying communes of Arcins, Lamarque, and Cussac – which also, it must be said, have some very good gravel. Some lies back inland along the edge of the pine forest.

With a total of 4,380 hectares, the Haut-Médoc appellation is only an indication of high quality – not a guarantee .

Haut-Médoc Crus Classés

Château Belgrave ☆☆–☆☆☆
5ème Cru Classé. Owner: CVBG. 55 hectares. Grapes: Cab.Sauv. 55%, Cab.Fr. 12%, Merlot 32%, Petit Verdot 1%
A lost property until 1980, and since then it has produced consistently attractive wine. In the late 1990s, quality improved further, and the wine has much more intensity and class.

Château de Camensac ☆–☆☆
5ème Cru Classé. Owners: the Forner family. 75 hectares. Grapes: Cab.Sauv. 60%, Merlot 40%
Neighbour of Châteaux Belgrave, la Tour-Carnet, and Lagrange (qq.v.) in the St-Laurent group, inland from St-Julien. Largely replanted since 1965 by M. Forner, former owner of the neighbouring Château Larose-Trintaudon. The result is good, full-bodied, forthright wine with plenty of vigour.

Château Cantemerle ☆☆–☆☆☆
5ème Cru Classé. Owner: SMABTP group. 87 hectares. Grapes: Cab.Sauv. 45%, Cab.Fr. 10%, Merlot 40%, Petit Verdot 5%. www.chateau-cantemerle.com
The next château north from la Lagune, within a wooded park of mysterious beauty. The tree beside the house on the pretty engraved label is a plane that now dominates the house completely – a monster.

The vineyards, with light soil and a good deal of Merlot, yield wine of incredible charm yet formidable stability. Vintages of the '50s and '60s were marvellous; those of the '70s not quite so good, but quality was regained with '82 and '83 and now stands high. The 2000 is especially fine, but is the charm still there? Second wine: "Les Allées de Cantemerle".

Château la Lagune ☆☆–☆☆☆
3ème Cru Classé. Owners: the Ducellier family. 70 hectares. Grapes: Cab.Sauv. 55%, Cab.Fr. 15%, Merlot 20%, Petit Verdot 10%
The nearest important Médoc château to Bordeaux, and a charming eighteenth-century villa. The vineyard had almost disappeared in the 1950s, when it was totally replanted and equipped with the latest steel vats and pipes. In 1961, the owners of Ayala Champagne bought it and have been making better and better wine as the vines have rooted deeper in the light, sandy gravel. Sweetness, spiciness, and fleshiness are all qualities found in it by critics. In poor vintages it can almost caricature itself with a rather jammy effect; in great ones it can rival many more prestigious growths. La Lagune uses new barrels for all the wine every year, so the wines can be excessively oaky.

Château la Tour-Carnet ☆–☆☆☆
4ème Cru Classé. Owner: Bernard Magrez. 48 hectares. Grapes: Cab.Sauv. 47%, Cab.Fr. 10%, Merlot 39%, Petit Verdot 4%. www.latour-carnet.com
A moated medieval castle in the relatively rolling, wooded back country of St-Laurent, restored in the 1960s. The wine used to be light in colour and pretty in style, but négociant Bernard Magrez acquired the estate in 1997 and moved swiftly to improve quality in the vineyard and winery. Excellent quality since 1998.

Other Haut-Médoc Châteaux

Château d'Agassac ☆☆
Ludon. Owner: Groupama. 38 hectares
The Médoc's most romantic château, medieval, moated, and deep in the woods. The new owner, an insurance company, bought Agassac in 1996 and invested substantially. The wines are fleshy, but still lack some concentration.

Château d'Arche ☆–☆☆
Ludon. Owner: Mähler-Besse. 8 hectares
A good wine with pure fruit and sweet oak.

Château d'Arcins ☆–☆☆
Arcins. Owner: Castel Frères. 97 hectares
The important wine-merchant family of Castel has restored the property and built a stone-clad warehouse that seems to dominate the village. A lean, vigorous wine with a touch of oak.

Château d'Arnauld ☆☆
Arcins. Owners: the Theil family. 35 hectares (See Château Poujeaux, Moulis)
A very good wine (50% Merlot).

Château Barreyres ☆
Arcins. Owner: Castel Frères. 109 hectares
An imposing property near the river, now linked with Château d'Arcins (q.v.).

Château Beaumont ☆–☆☆
Cussac. Owner: GMF. 105 hectares. www.chateau-beaumont.com
Grand château in the woods north of Poujeaux, in the same hands as Beychevelle (q.v.), making stylish, good-value claret for early drinking.

Château Bel-Orme-Tronquoy-de-Lalande ☆
St-Seurin. Owner: Jean-Michel Quié. 26 hectares
Well-sited property of the family that owns Châteaux Rauzan-Gassies and Croizet-Bages (qq.v.). A tough, tannic wine in the '70s and '80s; more supple since mid-'90s. Easily confused with Château Tronquoy-Lalande, St-Estèphe.

Château Bernardotte ☆☆
Owner: Château Pichon-Lalande. 30 hectares
Property on the fringes of Pauillac, acquired by Château Pichon-Lalande in '97, since when quality, already sound, has improved further. Second wine: "Château Fournas-Bernardotte".

Château le Bourdieu ☆
Vertheuil. Owner: Guy Bailly. 55 hectares
Lies just inland from St-Estèphe on similar clayey gravel. A big property, including the château with the promising name Victoria, can make good, St-Estèphe-style wine.

Château du Breuil ☆–☆☆
Cissac. Owner: Danielle Vialard. 25 hectares
On the edge of the parish just behind the Carruades plateau of Pauillac. Stylish wines.

Château Cambon-la-Pelouse ☆☆
Macau. Owner: Jean-Pierre Marie. 60 hectares.
www.cambon-la-pelouse.com
Large estate between Cantemerle and Giscours (*q.v.*), with 50% of the vineyard planted with Merlot. Increasingly substantial wines.

Château Caronne-Ste-Gemme ☆–☆☆
St-Laurent. Owners: Jean and François Nony. 45 hectares
A substantial property delivering well-made, somewhat lean wine, capable of charm with time. Rounder since 1995.

Château Charmail ☆☆
St-Seurin. Owner: Olivier Sèze. 22 hectares
Full, fruity claret with a silky texture.

Château Cissac ☆☆
Cissac. Owner: Louis Vialard. 50 hectares.
www.chateau-cissac.com
A pillar of the bourgeoisie. Reliable, robust, mainstream Médoc at its best after ten years or so (it used to take twenty), thanks to the preponderance of Cabernet Sauvignon in the wine.

Château Citran ☆☆
Avensan. Owner: Antoine Merlaut. 90 hectares. www.citran.com
Pace-setting *cru exceptionnel*. Wide following and long record of good vintages. Round, full wine (42% Merlot) with ageing potential, benefited from Japanese investment from 1987 until bought by Merlaut (of the Taillan group) in 1996.

Château Clément Pichon ☆–☆☆
Parempuyre. Owner: Clément Fayat. 25 hectares
Formerly exhibited a bland, upfront style, but since mid-'90s has gained in weight and complexity.

Château Coufran ☆☆
St-Seurin. Owners: the Miailhe family. 75 hectares
The northernmost estate of the Haut-Médoc, it is unusual in being 85% Merlot to make softer, more "fleshy" wine than its neighbouring sister – Château Verdignan (*q.v.*).

Château Dillon ☆
Blanquefort. Owner: Ecole d'Agriculture. 35 hectares.
www.chateau-dillon.com
The local agricultural college. Some good wines, including dry white Château Linas.

Château Fontesteau ☆☆–☆
St-Sauveur. Owners: the Fouin and Renaud families.
22 hectares
A good, conservative wine in the classic Médoc style, for long keeping.

Château de Gironville ☆
Macau. Owners: the Fouin and Raoult families. 9 hectares
Uprooted in 1929, and not replanted until '87.

Château Grandis ☆
St-Seurin-de-Cadourne. Owner: François-Joseph Vergez.
9 hectares
Simple and sometimes rather dry wines from very old vines.

Château Grand Moulin ☆
St-Seurin. Owner: Robert Gonzalvez. 18 hectares
Also appears under the name Château la Mothe. Rounded wine with little complexity.

Château Hanteillan ☆–☆☆
Cissac. Owner: Catherine Blasco. 55 hectares.
www.chateau-hanteillan.com
Old property, lavishly restored and replanted since 1973. Easygoing, well-balanced wine for early drinking.

Château Hourtin-Ducasse ☆
St-Sauveur. Owner: Maurice Marengo. 25 hectares
An elegant wine.

Château Lamarque ☆☆
Lamarque. Owner: Pierre-Gilles Gromand. 50 hectares
The finest remaining medieval fortress in the Médoc, in the village where the ferry leaves for Blaye. The wine is supple and spicy, with a flavour of blackberries; it establishes the potential of the central Médoc. "Cap de Haut" is the second label.

Château Lamothe-Bergeron ☆–☆☆
Cussac. Owner: Mestrezat. 66 hectares
The same owners as Château Grand-Puy-Ducasse produce a sturdy, well-balanced wine.

Château Lamothe-Cissac ☆
Cissac. Owners: the Fabre family. 33 hectares
A fairly austere wine, lacking finesse.

Château Lanessan ☆☆–☆☆☆
Cussac. Owners: the Bouteiller family. 40 hectares
An extravagant Victorian mansion and park with a popular carriage museum. The best-known estate in Cussac, which occasionally reaches *cru classé* quality. Polished rather than exciting wine. Ages well.

Château Larose-Trintaudon ☆
St-Laurent. Owner: Assurances Générales de France.
172 hectares. www.chateau-larose-trintaudon.fr
The biggest estate in the Médoc, planted since 1965, built up by the Forner family (who still owns Château de Camensac *q.v.*) until its sale in '86. Modern methods include mechanical harvesting. Quantity does not seem to impede steady, enjoyable quality, even if the wine is essentially bland.

Château Larrivaux ☆

Cissac. Owners: the Carlsberg family. 24 hectares

Light and rather nondescript wine.

Château Lestage Simon ☆☆

St-Seurin. Owners: the Simon family. 40 hectares

Concentrated, fruity, and reliable.

Château Lieujean ☆

St-Sauveur. Owners: the Lieujean and Penot families. 66 hectares

Tannic wine; also appears as the Château Haut-Laborde label.

Château Liversan ☆–☆☆

St-Sauveur. Owner: Prince Guy de Polignac. 40 hectares

Charming property including Château Fonpiqueyre. Conscientious winemaking backed by new investment.

Château Magnol ☆

Blanquefort. Owner: Barton et Guestier. 17 hectares

Half Cabernet, half Merlot; supple and medium-bodied.

Château Malescasse ☆☆

Lamarque. Owner: Alcatel Alsthom. 37 hectares.

www.chateau-malescasse.com

Replanted in the 1970s by the Tesseron family, who sold the property in '92. Very good in '82, '85, '86, and investments by the new owners have led to a more intense and sophisticated wine, now well-distributed and popular.

Château de Malleret ☆–☆☆

Le Pian. Owner: Comte Bertrand du Vivier. 31 hectares

Well-balanced wine, full of fruit and charm.

Château Maucamps ☆–☆☆

Macau. Owner: Alain Tessandier. 18 hectares

A gentle wine of some finesse for medium-term drinking.

Château le Meynieu ☆

Vertheuil. Owner: Jacques Pédro. 16 hectares

A burly wine, with ample tannin and oak, if little elegance.

Château du Moulin Rouge ☆

Cussac. Owner: Guy Pelon. 16 hectares

A hefty, well-structured wine.

Château Peyrabon ☆–☆☆

St-Sauveur. Owner: Patrick Bernard. 41 hectares

Bought in 1998 by Patrick Bernard of Millésima, the wine has yet to shed a distinct gawkiness.

Château Pontoise-Cabarrus ☆–☆☆

St-Seurin. Owner: François Tereygeol. 30 hectares

A serious, well-run property.

Château Puy-Castéra ☆

Cissac. Owners: the Marès family. 25 hectares

After complete renovation in '73, the property has steadily produced sound but simple wine.

Château Ramage la Batisse ☆

St-Sauveur. Owner: MACIF. 56 hectares

A vineyard since 1961. The estate employs modern methods to make a traditional yet rapidly maturing style of wine.

Château Reysson ☆

Vertheuil. Owner: Mercian Corporation. 67 hectares

Japanese owners since 1987 favour an easygoing style for early drinking.

Château Saint-Ahon ☆

Blanquefort. Owner: Comte Bernard de Colbert. 31 hectares. www.saintahon.com

Sleek, enjoyable wine; not too extracted.

Château de St-Paul ☆–☆☆

St-Seurin. Owner: M. Boucher. 20 hectares

An old-fashioned style requiring considerable bottle-age.

Château Ségur ☆

Parempuyre. Owner: Jean-Pierre Grazioli. 38 hectares

Early maturing claret from vines on good, deep gravel in the extreme south of the Médoc. Popular in Holland.

Château Sénéjac ☆☆

Le Pian. Owner: Thierry Rustmann. 28 hectares

Seriously good in '89 and '90, but shakier since. Bought in 1999 by one of the owners of Château Talbot. Sénéjac had a good reputation for its white wine, but these vines were grubbed up by the new owner. However, from '99 there is a *prestige cuvée* called "Karolus".

Château Senilhac ☆

St-Seurin. Owner: M. Grassin. 20 hectares

Straightforward claret for early consumption.

Château Sociando-Mallet ☆☆☆

St-Seurin. Owner: Jean Gautreau. 58 hectares

Bought by Jean Gautreau in '69, and by the early '80s a major success, thanks to excellent location of the vineyards and exacting winemaking. Recent vintages, needing long maturation, have outshone many *crus classés*. Second wine: "Demoiselle de Sociando-Mallet".

Château Soudars ☆–☆☆

St-Seurin. Owner: Eric Miailhe. 26 hectares

Essentially a new estate, created by Jean Miailhe's son since '73. Well-made, supple wine, with an abundance of ripe fruit.

Château du Taillan ☆

Le Taillan. Owner: Mme. Henri-François Cruse. 30 hectares

Pleasant red, 40% Merlot, from a charming estate north of Bordeaux. "La Dame Blanche" is the estate's white wine.

Château Tour du Haut Moulin ☆–☆☆

Cussac. Owner: Laurent Poitou. 30 hectares

Full-flavoured wine (50% Merlot) from an estate near Beaumont; enjoys a wide following.

Château la Tour du Mirail ☆

Cissac. Owners: Hélène and Danielle Vialard (*see* Château Cissac). 18 hectares

Undemanding wine with some charm.

Château Tour du Roc ☆

Arcins. Owner: Philippe Robert. 12 hectares

A slightly rustic wine for drinking young.

Château la Tour St-Joseph ☆
Cissac. Owners: the Quancard family. 10 hectares
Sturdy wine, with a fair amount of oak.

Château Verdignan ☆–☆☆
St-Seurin. Owner: Jean Miailhe. 60 hectares
In contrast to its sister-château Coufran (*q.v.*), Verdignan has the classic Médoc proportion of Cabernet, and needs keeping two or three years longer.

Château Villegeorge ☆☆
Avensan. Owner: Marie-Laure Lurton-Roux. 15 hectares
Another Lurton property. Deep, rich-flavoured wine from a 60% Merlot vineyard. Fine '90.

Caves Coopérative Fort Médoc ☆
Cussac. 60 hectares
Sound cooperative cellar at the impressive riverside fort built by Vauban to command the Gironde.

Appellation Médoc

The lower Médoc (being farther down the Gironde) was formerly called Bas-Médoc, which made it clear that it was this area and not the whole peninsula under discussion. The soil, and therefore the wines, are considered inferior here. The last of the big-calibre gravel has been deposited by glaciers higher up between Graves and St-Estèphe.

Although the ground continues to heave gently, the humps become more scattered and their soil much heavier, with a high proportion of pale, cold clay, suited to Merlot rather than Cabernet (although patches of sandier soil persist).

The wine has distinctly less finesse and perfume, but good body and structure with some of the tannic "cut" that makes all Médocs such good wines at table. Good vintages last well in bottle, without developing the sweet complexities of the Haut-Médoc at its best.

The last decade has seen a great revival of interest in this productive area. Half a dozen big properties have already made the running and now offer a good deal, if not an absolute bargain. In 1972, there were 1,836 hectares in production in the appellation Médoc. By 2000, this figure had risen to 5,040 hectares.

Much the most important commune is Bégadan, with several of the most prominent estates and a very big growers' cooperative. Nearly a third of the whole appellation comes from the one parish. Next, in order of production, come St-Yzans, Prignac, Ordonnac, Blaignan, St-Christoly, and St-Germain.

The principal producers are given here in alphabetical order, followed by the names of their communes. The central town for the whole area is Lesparre.

Leading Lower Médoc Châteaux

Château Bellevue ☆
Valeyrac. Owner: Yves Lassalle. 23 hectares
Black fruits and spice mark this Merlot-dominated wine.

Château Blaignan ☆
Blaignan. Owner: Mestrezat. 75 hectares
Blaignan's largest vineyard, yielding easygoing wines for early drinking.

Château le Boscq ☆
St-Christoly. Owner: Jean-Michel Lapalu (*see also* Château Patache d'Aux)
The basic wine lacks interest, but the "Cuvée Vieilles Vignes" has more complexity and structure.

Château Bournac ☆
Civrac. Owner: Bruno Secret. 13 hectares
Solid, even rustic wines.

Château la Cardonne ☆☆
Blaignan. Owner: Guy Charloux. 86 hectares
This estate was restructured in the early 1970s by the Rothschilds. This provided a great boost to the lower Médoc with its prestige and predictably well-made wine. However, the property has changed hands repeatedly and is now grouped with Châteaux Ramafort and Grivière (*qq.v.*). Frankly commercial: machine-picked and never sold *en primeur*. Nonetheless, it does produce well-focused wines, impeccably made.

Château Castéra ☆
St-Germain. Owner: Deugro. 63 hectares
A lovely old place with a real drawbridge – a relic of more exciting times when it was besieged by the English during the fourteenth century. German owners, producing flavoury wines.

Château la Clare ☆
Bégadan. Owner: Paul de Rozières. 27 hectares
Chewy wine, Cabernet-dominated.

Château d'Escurac ☆☆
Civrac. Owner: Jean-Marc Landureau. 10 hectares
Has only bottled its wines since '90. Brilliant wine in '96.

Château les Grands Chênes ☆☆–☆☆☆
St. Christoly. Owner: Bernard Magrez. 7 hectares
Since 1998, Magrez and his team have lavished their resources and skill on this already elegant wine. The "Cuvée Prestige" is splendid if heavily oaked.

Château Greysac ☆☆
Bégadan. Owner: Domaine Codem. 60 hectares
Big, efficient property making sound wine, well-known in the USA. Greysac is approachable young but capable of ageing.

Château Grivière ☆–☆☆
Prignac. Owner: Guy Charloux. 22 hectares
(*See* Château la Cardonne)
A rounded wine, with almost 60% Merlot.

Château Haut-Condissas ☆☆–☆☆☆
Bégadan. Owner: Jean Guyon (owner of Château Rollan de By).
5 hectares. www.rollandeby.com
A parcel within Rollan de By, given luxury treatment, and a very high price.

Château Laujac ☆
Bégadan. Owners: the Cruse family. 27 hectares.
www.laujac.com
A home of the famous family of shippers, hence well-known abroad long before most of the other châteaux in the district. The wine is straightforward but stylish.

Château Livran ☆
St-Germain. Owners: the Godfrin family. 52 hectares
A lovely old country house with old vines (55% planted with Merlot). Large quantities of usually undistinguished wine.

Château Loudenne ☆–☆☆
St-Yzans. Owner: Jean-Paul Lafragette. 65 hectares
A low, pale pink château on a hill of gravelly clay overlooking the river. Loudenne was in English hands (it was Gilbey's French HQ) for over a century, an informal clubhouse for visiting merchants and journalists. The estate produced well-balanced and long-lived red, and one of Bordeaux's best dry whites, until it changed hands in 1999.

Château Monthil ☆
Bégadan. Owner: Domaine Codem. 20 hectares
A fresh, medium-bodied wine.

Château les-Ormes-Sorbet ☆☆
Couquêques. Owner: Jean Boivert. 21 hectares
Rich, highly oaked wines with fine depth of fruit.

Château de Panigon ☆
Civrac. Owners: the Leveilley family. 50 hectares
Lean, sometimes green, wines.

Château Patache d'Aux ☆☆
Bégadan. Owner: Claude Lapalu. 43 hectares
Popular, full-flavoured Médoc with 70% Cabernet Sauvignon, now linked with the aristocratic Château Liversan (*q.v.*).

Château Potensac ☆☆☆
Ordonnac. Owner: Jean-Hubert Delon. 53 hectares
A very successful enterprise of the owners of Château Léoville-Las-Cases. Well-made, fruity, structured claret with a stylish flavour of oak and surprising longevity, if no real finesse.

Château Preuillac ☆–☆☆
Lesparre. Owner: Yvon Mau. 30 hectares
Acquired by the Mau négociant company in 1998. The terroir is not exceptional, but scrupulous work in vineyard and winery is delivering good results.

Château Ramafort ☆☆
Blaignan. Owner: Guy Charloux. 24 hectares
Another property in the group based at la Cardonne (*q.v.*). Stylish wines with some complexity.

Château Rolland de By ☆☆–☆☆☆
Bégadan. Owner: Jean Guyon. 37 hectares.
www.rollandeby.com
Guyon's determination to produce something exceptional in the Médoc shows through in this tightly structured, oaky wine. *See also* Château Haut-Condissas.

Visiting Châteaux

Visitors to the Médoc will have no difficulty in finding châteaux willing to show them how they make their wine, and to let them taste it from the barrel. One simple way of arranging a château visit is to call at one of the little offices called *maison du vin*. The principal one is in the heart of Bordeaux near the Grand Théâtre. Margaux, Pauillac, St-Estèphe, and several other villages have local ones. They will suggest an itinerary and, if necessary, make contacts. This is the best method of arranging a visit, as you can be sure of a proper welcome when you arrive.

An even simpler method, but only really practicable for those who speak some French, is to stop at any of the many châteaux that advertise *dégustation* (tasting) and *vente directe* – direct sales – on roadside signs. They include some important châteaux as well as many modest ones. At any reasonable time (*i.e.* not during the harvest or any period of frantic activity, and not at lunch-time: from noon to two o'clock) you can expect a more or less friendly welcome.

At some properties you may be received by the *maître de chai*, the cellar master. In big châteaux he is a man of considerable dignity and responsibility. He has seen many visitors pass and will make up his own mind, rightly or wrongly, about how much to show you. He will expect moderate praise for the chilly, tannic, and (to the non-expert) almost untastable sample he draws from the barrel and hands you in a glass. Unless an obvious receptacle (often a tub of sawdust) is provided you may – indeed, must – spit it out on the floor. I tend to wander off ruminating to the doorway and spit into the outside world. It gives me a chance to compose my thoughts – and recover from my grimace.

At some larger properties, you may be invited to participate in a tour, either with a public relations official or as part of a group. This can be an effective if slightly impersonal way to learn a great deal in a painless and often interesting fashion. Clearly the idea of *vente directe* is that you should buy a bottle or two, but you need not feel obliged. Many châteaux do not sell their wine to the public, and those that do often charge more for a bottle than any retailer. So do not get carried away with your purchases.

Do not expect a lavish tasting. The Bordelais may offer you a barrel sample or a taste of the current vintage. You are unlikely to be offered anything more.

Château St-Bonnet ☆
St-Christoly. Owner: Gérard Soliverès. 52 hectares
Reliable and medium-bodied.

Château Sestignan ☆
Jau-Dignac-et-Loirac. Owner: Bertrand de Rozières.
20 hectares
A medium-bodied wine with some finesse.

Château Sigognac ☆
Yzans. Owner: Mme. Colette Bonny. 47 hectares
A good if light wine.

Château la Tour-Blanche ☆
St-Christoly. Owner: Dominique Hessel (*see also* Château
Moulin à Vent, Moulis). 36 hectares
Pleasant but scarcely distinguished wine.

Château la Tour-de-By ☆☆
Bégadan. Owner: Marc Pagés. 55 hectares
Extremely successful estate with a high reputation for enjoyable and durable, if not literally fine, wine.

Château la Tour-Haut-Caussan ☆☆–☆☆☆
Blaignan. Owner: Philippe Courrian. 17 hectares
Fine off-vintages give this property one of the best records in the Médoc. Utterly traditional winemaking, with consistently satisfying results.

Château la Tour-Prignac ☆
Prignac. Owner: Philippe Castel Frères. 140 hectares
Vast new enterprise of the Castelvin family, whose Haut Médoc headquarters is at Arcins (*see* Château d'Arcins).

Château la Tour St-Bonnet ☆
St-Christoly. Owner: Jacques Merlet. 40 hectares
One of the pioneers of the lower Médoc renaissance. Good-value, traditional Médoc, tannic when young.

Vieux-Château Landon ☆–☆☆
Bégadan. Owner: Philippe Gillet. 36 hectares
An energetic proprietor with ambitions. Sound, lively wine.

Château Vieux-Robin ☆☆
Bégadan. Owner: Maryse Roba. 18 hectares.
www.chateauvieuxrobin.com
"Cuvée Bois de Lunier", aged in new oak, is better than the regular wine. Conscientious winemaking, often impressive results.

Médoc Caves Coopératives

Bégadan
The largest cooperative in the area, sourcing grapes from about 500 hectares. Labels include "Château Bégadanais".

Prignac
About 300 hectares.

St-Yzans
About 200 hectares. As an example of the quality of its production, the 1970 was excellent at twelve years old.

Graves

Wine was first made at Bordeaux in what is now the city and the suburbs, immediately across the river and to the south. Graves was the name given to the whole of the left (city) bank of the Garonne for as far as sixty-five kilometres (forty miles) upstream, beyond the little town of Langon, and back away from the river into the pine forests of the Landes – an area not much different in size from the wine-growing Médoc, but more cut up with woodland and farms and containing few extensive vineyards or big châteaux.

Graves' distinguishing feature (hence its name) is its open, gravelly soil, the relic of Pyrenean glaciers in the ice ages. In fact, the soil varies within the region just as much as that of the Médoc. Sand is common. Pale clay and red clay are both present. But, as in the Médoc, it is pretty certain that by now most of the potentially good vineyard land is being put to good use. In all, there are some 5,040 hectares of vineyards. In 1983, it was 1,494.

But Graves is too diffuse to grasp easily. It would be helpful (and accurate) if the authorities established an appellation "Haut-Graves" to distinguish the few communes of the northern section where all the *crus classés* are situated. Instead, they established the AC Pessac-Léognan for a rather wider area. An enclave in the south of the region has quite different styles – of landscape, ownership, and wine. This is Sauternes.

Although Graves is divided between two-thirds red wine and one-third white, most of the top-quality wine is red. The words commonly used to explain how red Graves differs from Médoc make it sound less fine; "earthy", "soft", "maturing sooner" all sound more homely than inspiring. The late Maurice Healey got it in one when he said that Médoc and Graves were like glossy and matt prints of the same photograph. The matt picture can be equally beautiful, but less crisp and sharp-edged, with less glittering colours.

White Graves, at its best, is a rare experience – and an expensive one. Very few estates even aim for the unique combination of fullness and drive that comes to white Graves with time. The best is equal in quality to the great white burgundies. Opinion is divided even on the grapes to make it with. Some favour all Sémillon, some all Sauvignon Blanc, and some a mixture, in various proportions. Some make it in stainless steel and bottle it in the early spring. Others (including the best) make it and mature it, at least briefly, in new-oak barrels. The tendency among the lesser growths making dry wine has been to pick too early to obtain full ripeness. Sauvignon Blanc in any case tends to ripen unevenly here. The best makers now concentrate on getting full ripeness and a complete fermentation to give clean, dry wine with plenty of flavour.

The communes of what might be called "Haut-Graves" are as follows, starting in the north on the doorstep of Bordeaux: Pessac and Talence (in the suburbs); Gradignan and Villenave-d'Ornon (with very little wine today); Léognan, the most extensive, with six classed growths; Cadaujac and Martillac. Up to 1987, all shared the single appellation Graves. In that year, the new AC Pessac-Léognan was created, to include fifty-five châteaux and domaines in ten communes; a total of 1,150 hectares of red vines, 250 of white. South of this district, but increasingly important for similar wine, is Portets. Cérons, on the threshold of Barsac and Sauternes, makes both sweet and dry white wine, the dry now gaining in quality and popularity. Red has been steadily increasing at the expense of white, whether dry or sweet.

The châteaux of Graves were first classified in 1953 and 1959 in a blunt yes-or-no fashion, which gives little guidance. Château Haut-Brion having been included in the Médoc classification 100 years earlier (in 1855), twelve other châteaux were designated *crus classés* for their red wine, in alphabetical order.

In 1959, six of them and two additional châteaux were designated *crus classés* for white wine. There is no other official ranking in Graves, so all the rest can call themselves *crus bourgeois*.

Graves Premier Cru

Château Haut-Brion ☆☆☆☆
Pessac. Owner: Domaine Clarence Dillon. AC: Pessac-Léognan. 46 hectares. Grapes: Cab.Sauv. 45%, Cab.Fr. 18%, Merlot 37%. www.haut-brion.com

The first wine château to be known by name, late in the seventeenth century, and although now surrounded by the suburbs of Bordeaux, still one of the best, regularly earning its official place beside the four First Growths of the Médoc.

The situation of the sixteenth-century manor house of the Pontacs is no longer particularly impressive, but its nine-metre- (thirty-foot-) deep gravel soil gives deep-flavoured wine that holds a remarkable balance of fruity and earthy flavours for decades. Mouton has resonance, Margaux has coloratura; Haut-Brion just has harmony – between strength and finesse, firmness and sweetness. I shall never forget the taste of an Impériale of the 1899 – the most spellbinding claret I have ever drunk.

The present owners, the family of American banker Clarence Dillon, bought the estate in a near-derelict condition in 1935. In 1983, they added the next-door Château la Mission-Haut-Brion (*q.v.*). The current president is Dillon's granddaughter, the Duchesse de Mouchy. Haut-Brion was the first of the First Growths to install stainless-steel vats for the quite quick and relatively warm fermentation, which is its policy. Rather than select the "best" strain of each vine, M. Delmas, the administrator, believes in diversity. He therefore reckons to have nearly 400 different clones in the vineyard. This, and the fairly high proportion of Cabernet Franc, contribute complexity and harmony to the wine. As for age, Haut-Brion demands it. The good vintages of the 1970s – '71, '75, '78, '79 – only recently reached their peak; the apogee of the 1980s is still some time away. The '89 Haut-Brion is already a legend. A tiny quantity of very good white Graves (37:63 Sauvignon/Sémillon; from three hectares) is also made and sold at an extravagant price. The second wine of Haut-Brion, "Bahans-Haut-Brion", was unusual in being a non-vintage blend until 1983.

Graves Crus Classés

Château Bouscaut ☆☆
Cadaujac. Owner: Sophie Lurton. AC: Pessac-Léognan. 47 hectares, of which 7 white. Grapes red: Merlot 50%, Cab.Sauv. 35%, Cab.Fr. and Malbec 15%. white: Sém. 70%, Sauv. 30%

A handsome eighteenth-century house with rather low-lying vineyards, which was bought from its American owners in 1979 by Lucien of the ubiquitous Lurton family. The style is rather understated and there may be a tendency to overproduce, but the '90 is delicious, and more recent vintages made by the new generation look good, if lean in structure.

Château Carbonnieux ☆☆–☆☆☆
Léognan. Owner: Antony Perrin. AC: Pessac-Léognan. 90 hectares, of which 45 red. Grapes red: Cab.Sauv. 60%, Merlot 30%, Cab.Fr. 7%, Malbec 2%, Petit Verdot 1%. white: Sauv. 60%, Sém. 39%, Musc. 2%. www.carbonnieux.com

An old embattled monastery built around a courtyard, restored and run by a family who left Algeria in the 1950s. Bigger, and hence better known, than most Graves properties, particularly for its white wine, one of the flag-carriers for white Graves. The white is aged briefly in new oak barriques, then bottled young, thus keeping freshness while getting some of the proper oak flavour. Quality took a marked step forward during the late '80s. Three or four years in bottle are needed to perfect it. The red faces more competition, but is well-made typical Graves, dry and persistent.

Château le Sartre (*q.v.*) is also in the family. "La Tour Léognan" is the second wine.

Domaine de Chevalier ☆☆☆–☆☆☆☆
Léognan. Owner: Olivier Bernard. AC: Pessac-Léognan. 38 hectares, of which 5 white. Grapes: Cab.Sauv. 65%, Cab.Fr. 5%, Merlot 30%, white: Sauv. 70%, Sém. 30%

This is rather a strange place to find a vineyard, in the middle of a frost-prone wood. Total rebuilding, however, revolutionized a sombre old place in the 1980s. The soil and the style of the red wine are similar to the nearby Haut-Bailly (*q.v.*); starting stern, maturing dense and savoury. The 1961, '64, and '66 were all magnificent, and the 1980s have been very fine. The château often succeeds when others fail, for example in '84 and '91. The red epitomizes finesse, not fat, and often fares poorly in blind tastings. But it's hard to think of a wine that gives more pleasure at the dinner table.

The white wine is second only to Laville-Haut-Brion in quality and is designed for an astonishingly long life. It is made with the care of a great Sauternes, fermented and matured in barrels. To drink it before five years is a waste, and the flavours of a fifteen-year-old bottle can be breathtaking.

Château Couhins
Villenave-d'Ornon. Owner: Institut National de la Recherche Agronomique (INRA). 13.5 hectares, of which 6 white. Grapes: Sauv. 80%, Sém. 20%

The *Institut National de la Recherche Agronomique* bought the land in 1968 for viticultural research.

Château Couhins-Lurton ☆☆–☆☆☆
Léognan. Owner: André Lurton. AC: Pessac-Léognan. 6 hectares. Grapes: 100% Sauvignon Blanc

In 1970, André Lurton bought six hectares of this classed growth which he had farmed since 1967. The wine, unusually, is pure Sauvignon, fermented and aged in oak. It rewards keeping five to ten years. The Lurtons also bought the château and original cellar in 1992.

Château de Fieuzal ☆☆☆
Léognan. Owner: Lochlainn Quinn. AC: Pessac-Léognan. 48 hectares, of which 8 white. Grapes red: Cab.Sauv. 60%, Merlot 33%, Petit Verdot and Cab.Fr. 7%. white: Sauv. 50%, Sém. 50%

Until its sale in 2001, Fieuzal had been nurtured by Gérard Gribelin to tune the masculine, tannic, earthy style of the region to fine harmony; since the mid-1980s a regular top performer.

The production of white is not technically "*classé*" although it is better than some that are.

Château Haut-Bailly ☆☆☆
Léognan. Owner: Robert Wilmers. AC: Pessac-Léognan. 28 hectares. Grapes: Cab.Sauv. 65%, Cab.Fr. 10%, Merlot 25%. www.chateau-haut-bailly.com

A modest-looking place with a farmyard air, until 1998 the property of the Belgian Sanders family, generally considered one of the top five châteaux of (red) Graves. It makes no white wine. One-quarter of the vineyard is a mixed plantation of very old vines. Relatively shallow, stony soil over hard clay is an unusual site for a great vineyard, and the result can be problems during drought.

The great years ('66, '70, '78, '79, '86, '88, '89, '96, 2000) I can best describe as nourishing, like long-simmered stock; deep, earthy, and round. I love them. Second label: "La Parde de Haut Bailly". Despite the change of ownership, the Sanders family, who have cared for this property so deeply, stay on to run the estate.

Bordeaux Glossary

Barrique the standard Bordeaux barrel for ageing, and sometimes shipping the wine; holds 225 litres.

Cépage; encépagement grape variety; choice of grape varieties in a vineyard.

Chai; maître de chai the storage place for wine in barrels, in the Médoc usually a barn above ground or slightly sunk in the earth for coolness; in St-Emilion frequently a cellar. The cellar master in charge of all winemaking operations.

Chef de culture in larger properties, the outdoor equivalent of the *maître de chai*; the foreman of the vineyard.

Collage fining; clarification of the wine, usually with beaten egg white.

Cru "growth" – any winemaking property, as in *cru classé*, *cru bourgeois*, etc.

Cuve, cuvier, cuvaison vat, vat-house, vatting (*i.e.* time the wine spends fermenting in the vat).

Engrais (*chimique, biologique*) fertilizer (chemical, organic).

Fouloir-égrappoir (*foulage, éraflage*) rotary machine for tearing the grapes off their stalks and crushing them. *Foulage* is crushing, *éraflage* removing the stalks.

Gérant general manager of a property, the man in charge.

Grand vin not a recognized or regulated term, but generally used to mean the first or selected wines of a property, in contrast to the second or other wines.

Millésime the vintage year (*e.g.* 1990).

Monopole a contract between a grower and shipper for the monopoly in handling his wine.

Négociant a merchant or "shipper".

Oenologue oenologist or technical winemaking consultant.

Porte-greffe root-stock of phylloxera-resistant vine onto which the desired variety is grafted.

Propriétaire owner.

Récolte harvest.

Régisseur manager or bailiff of an estate.

Rendement (*à l'hectare*) crop (measured in hectolitres per hectare).

Taille pruning.

Tonneau the measure in which Bordeaux is still bought and sold from the château (900 litres, or four barriques, or 100 dozen bottles) although such big barrels are no longer in use.

Viticulteur a wine-grower.

Château Laville-Haut-Brion ☆☆☆☆
Talence. Owner: Domaine Clarence Dillon. AC: Pessac-Léognan. 3.5 hectares. Grapes: Sém. 70%, Sauv. 27%, Muscadelle 3%. www.haut-brion.com

The white wine of la Mission-Haut-Brion (*q.v.*), first made in 1928 on a patch where former owner M. Woltner decided the soil was too heavy for red. Bordeaux's best dry white wine. Drunk young, its quality may go unnoticed – and its price will certainly seem excessive. The wine is fermented in new oak barriques, and bottled from them the following spring. Its qualities – apart from an increasingly haunting flavour as the years go by – are concentration and the same sort of rich-yet-dry character as "Ygrec", the dry wine of Château d'Yquem, but with more grace. '88, '89, '94, '96, and '98 stand out.

Château Malartic-Lagravière ☆☆☆
Léognan. Owner: Alfred-Alexandre Bonnie. 44 hectares, of which 7 white. Grapes: red: Cab.Sauv. 40%, Cab.Fr. 10%, Merlot 50%, white: Sauv. 85%, Sém.15%. www.malartic-lagraviere.com

Underrated château of notable quality for both red and white wine. A square stone house in a typical Graves landscape, patched with woods and gently tilted vineyards. The red is a firm, austere, dark-coloured *vin de garde*, finishing fine rather than fleshy, though since 1994 the style appears rounder.

The white (unusual in being mostly Sauvignon) is dazzling when young, but becomes even better – and more typical of Graves – with five or ten years in bottle. Enormous investments since 1998 by the new owner, M. Bonnie, are already paying off in terms of even higher quality and finesse.

Château la Mission-Haut-Brion ☆☆☆–☆☆☆☆
Talence. Owner: Domaine Clarence Dillon. AC: Pessac-Léognan. 21 hectares. Grapes: Cab.Sauv. 48%, Cab.Fr. 7%, Merlot 45%. www.haut-brion.com

The immediate neighbour and former rival to Haut-Brion, equally in the Bordeaux suburbs of Pessac and Talence with the Paris-Madrid railway running in a cutting (good for the drainage) through the vineyard. Owned since 1983 by the proprietors of Haut-Brion. The claim is that the urban surroundings give the advantage of 1°C (1.8°F) higher temperature than the open country, and also a large harvesting force at short notice.

The wines show the effect of warm and dry conditions: concentration and force. Beside Haut-Brion, which is no weakling, they can appear almost butch. Michael Broadbent makes use of the words "iron", "earth", "beef", and "pepper" in his notes on various vintages. After due time (often twenty years or more), they combine warmth with sweetness in organ-like tones that make it a "super second" in quality. The white wine, "Laville-Haut-Brion", is discussed separately.

Château Olivier ☆☆
Léognan. Owner: Jean-Jacques de Bethmann. AC: Pessac-Léognan. 48 hectares, of which 12 white. Grapes red: Cab.Sauv. 51%, Cab. Fr. 8%, Merlot 41%, white: Sém. 48%, Sauv. 44%, Musc. 8%. www.chateau-olivier.com

A moated fortress with vineyards, operated for the owner

until 1981 by the shipper Eschenauer & Co, but now under the control of the family again. Its lean red wine has never enjoyed the fame of its white, which is of the modern school of easy-come, easy-go Graves; a good, light meal-opener. Quality has improved in the 1990s, but to a lesser extent than many of Olivier's neighbours.

Château Pape-Clément ☆☆☆

Pessac. Owner: Bernard Magrez. AC: Pessac-Léognan. 33 hectares, of which 3 white. Grapes red: Cab.Sauv. 60%, Merlot 40%. white: Sém. 45%, Sauv. 45%, Musc. 10%. www.pape-clement.com

One-time property of Bertrand de Goth, the fourteenth-century Bishop of Bordeaux who, as Clement V, brought the papacy to Avignon. The vineyard is in scattered plots and one large block at the extreme edge of Pessac, where it is quasi-rural and the gravel soil finer, but no less deep. No Cabernet Franc in the vineyard, but a high proportion of Merlot.

New barrels are used for 70–95% of the crop, depending on the vintage. Wines used to be lacklustre, but in the 1990s quality improved beyond recognition, and the 2000 is magnificent. The property also makes a tiny quantity of spicy, oaky white.

Château Smith-Haut-Lafitte ☆☆☆

Martillac. Owner: Florence and Daniel Cathiard. AC: Pessac-Léognan. 56 hectares, of which 11 white. Grapes red: Cab.Sauv. 45%, Cab.Fr. 20%, Merlot 35%. white: Sauv.Bl. 95%, Sauv.Gris 5%. www.smith-haut-lafitte.com

With cash from their sportswear business and considerable flair and enthusiasm, the Cathiards have, since 1990, transformed the reputation of their famous old estate with modernization of vineyard, cellar, château, and wine. The white (not a classed growth) is one of the best (and most frankly oaky) of the region, and the red improves steadily. The second wine is the good-value "Les Hauts de Smith". The property includes a hotel, restaurant, and luxury spa.

Château la Tour-Haut-Brion ☆☆–☆☆☆

Talence. Owner: Domaine Clarence Dillon. AC: Pessac-Léognan. 5 hectares. Grapes: Cab.Sauv. 42%, Cab.Fr. 35%, Merlot 23%. www.haut-brion.com

Formerly the second label of Chateau la Mission-Haut-Brion (*q.v.*), but now run as a separate vineyard. Up to '93, it used to be powerful and tannic, but recent vintages have been more elegant, with the proportion of Cabernet Franc increased.

Château la Tour-Martillac ☆☆–☆☆☆

Martillac. Owner: Domaines Kressmann. AC: Pessac-Léognan. 40 hectares, of which 10 white. Grapes red: Cab.Sauv. 60%, Merlot 35%, Malbec 1%, and Cab.Fr. 4%. white: Sém. 55%, Sauv. 40%, Muscadelle 5%. www.latour-martillac.com

A property once in the Montesquieu family (who owned the magnificent moated la Brède nearby). The Kressmanns, a Bordeaux négociant family, patiently cultivate old vines for quality. The white wine is classic Graves, vigorous and toasty and best with bottle-age; the red is a good example of the robust, savoury style of the region.

Other Graves Châteaux

Château d'Archambeau ☆☆

Illats. Owners: the Dubourdieu family. 10 hectares

Good, fruity dry white, and fragrant, barrel-aged reds.

Château d'Arricaud ☆–☆☆

Landiras. Owner: Albert Bouyx. 23 hectares

Property overlooking the Garonne Valley from the south of Barsac. The *cuvées prestige* red and white are oakier and more concentrated than the regular bottlings.

Château Baret ☆☆

Villenave-d'Ornon. Owners: the Ballande family. AC: Pessac-Léognan. 20 hectares

Property in the heart of "Haut-Graves", formerly high among Graves' Second Growths, producing earthy reds and oaky whites. An exclusivity of Borie-Manoux.

Château Brown ☆☆

Léognan. Owner: Bernard Barthe. AC: Pessac-Léognan. 27 hectares. www.chateau-brown.com

Revived by new owners, who have invested heavily since 1994. Elegant and well-balanced whites and reds.

Château Cantelys ☆☆

Martillac. Owners: Florence and Daniel Cathiard. AC: Pessac-Léognan. 31 hectares. www.smith-haut-lafitte.com

Leased by the Cathiards, who make the wine at Château Smith-Haut-Lafitte (*q.v.*). Less complex wines than the classed growth, but well-made and good for medium-term drinking.

Château les Carmes Haut-Brion ☆☆

Pessac. Owner: Didier Furt. AC: Pessac-Léognan. 4 hectares. www.les-carmes-haut-brion.com

A miniature neighbour of Haut-Brion with a new lease of life since Furt took over in 1986. Good, savoury wine that has yet to attain complexity.

Château Cazebonne ☆☆

St-Pierre-de-Mons. Owner: Jean-Marc Bridet. 13 hectares

Rich, oaky reds, and a perfumed white.

Château de Chantegrive ☆☆–☆☆☆

Podensac. Owners: Henri and Françoise Lévêque. 90 hectares. www.chantegrive.com

A substantial property, using modern methods. The family farms several other properties, including Château Moulin de Marc and Domaine du Bourdieu. Reliable wines, especially the opulently oaky white "Cuvée Caroline".

Château Cheret-Pitres ☆–☆☆

Portets. Owner: Pascal Dulugat. 14 hectares

Firm, earthy red wines.

Château Chicane ☆

Toulenne. Owner: François Gauthier. 6 hectares

Although the red is Cabernet-dominated, the wine is delicate and best enjoyed young.

Château de Cruzeau ☆☆

St-Médard-d'Eyrans. Owner: André Lurton. AC: Pessac-Léognan. 60 hectares

A Lurton property bought and replanted in 1973. St-Médard has deep, pebbly soil, which should mean good wine. The red is a touch austere but the white plump and spicy.

Château Ferrande ☆–☆☆
Castres. Owner: Castel Frères. 43 hectares
The principal property of Castres, just north of Portets. Red and white wines for drinking young.

Clos Floridène ☆☆–☆☆☆
Bequey. Owners: Denis and Florence Dubourdieu. 16 hectares
Original, full, and richly characterful white made by Denis Dubourdieu, who has done for Bordeaux whites what Emile Peynaud did for reds. Keeps for five years. Attractive red, too.

Château de France ☆☆
Léognan. Owner: Bernard Thomassin. AC: Pessac-Léognan. 32 hectares. www.chateau-de-france.com
A large property among some of the best of the district, modernized and enlarged since 1971. Investments paid off in the late 1990s, when the wines, both red and white, gained in flesh and complexity.

Domaine de Gaillat ☆–☆☆
Langon. Owners: the Coste family. 11 hectares
A plump, savoury red for early drinking.

Château la Garde ☆☆
Martillac. Owner: Domaines Kressmann. AC: Pessac-Léognan. 55 hectares
The red, in good vintages, is robust and flavoury. The white is grapey and oaky. Quality, however, has much improved since mid-1990s.

Château du Grand Abord ☆–☆☆
Portets. Owner: Marc Dugoua. 20 hectares
Succulent red wine, almost pure Merlot, and a fragrant, lemony white.

Château Haut-Bergey ☆☆
Léognan. Owner: Sylviane Garcin-Cathiard. AC: Pessac-Léognan. 26 hectares. www.chateau-haut-bergey.com
The sister of Daniel Cathiard of Château Smith-Haut-Lafitte (*q.v.*) bought this property in 1991. Steadily improving smoky reds, and grapefruity whites.

Château Haut-Gardère ☆☆
Léognan. Owners: Banque Populaire. AC: Pessac-Léognan. 25 hectares
Reborn in 1979, this property near Fieuzal produces sound, oaky reds and toasty whites.

Château Haut-Lagrange ☆☆
Léognan. Owner: Francis Boutemy. AC: Pessac-Léognan. 17 hectares
Completely replanted in the early 1990s, so full potential has yet to be realized. Boutemy defies modern trends by ageing in tank. The reds are supple, the whites markedly citric.

Château Haut-Nouchet ☆–☆☆
Martillac. Owner: Louis Lurton. AC: Pessac-Léognan. 38 hectares. www.louis-lurton.fr
Pleasant, inexpensive wines from rather young vines. Organic.

Château Haut-Selve ☆–☆☆
Cadillac-en-Fronsadais. Owner: Jean-Jacques Lesgourgues. 68 hectares
A large property, making medium-bodied wines; the white is fresher and more lively than the hard-edged red.

Château Jean Gervais ☆
Portets. Owners: the Counilh family. 54 hectares
Restrained wines with little complexity.

Château Larrivet-Haut-Brion ☆☆
Léognan. Owner: Philippe Gervoson. AC: Pessac-Léognan. 50 hectares
One of the better second-rank Graves, although a long way from Haut-Brion in every sense. New owners have expanded the vineyards and hired Michel Rolland as a consultant. Lean, racy whites and fairly tannic, chocolatey reds.

Château la Louvière ☆☆–☆☆☆
Léognan. Owner: André Lurton. AC: Pessac-Léognan. 48 hectares
The show place of M. Lurton's considerable estates, a noble eighteenth century mansion where he makes avant-garde dry white, Sauvignon-dominated, of Loire-like freshness; and typically masculine, earthy red of *cru classé* standard.

Château Millet ☆
Portets. Owners: Henri and Thierry de la Mette. 78 hectares
The most imposing château in Portets. Modest wines: a smooth, supple red and balanced white.

Château Montalivet ☆☆
Pujols-sur-Ciron. Owners: Pierre Coste and Pierre Dubourdieu. 14 hectares
Fresh, well-made wines.

Château Pique-Caillou ☆☆
Mérignac. Owner: Calvet Paulin. AC: Pessac-Léognan. 20 hectares
The only *cru* in Mérignac, near the airport. Fairly tannic wines with black-cherry flavours.

Château Piron ☆☆
St-Morillon. Owner: Paul Boyreau. 20 hectares
An old family property in the hinterland of Graves, on gravel slopes with a chalk content that favours white wine, but the red wine is savoury and complex, too.

Château de Portets ☆☆
Portets. Owner: Jean-Pierre Théron. 38 hectares
Reputation of Portets is growing, particularly for the red, a spicy blend of Cabernet and Merlot in equal proportions.

Château Rahoul ☆☆
Portets. Owner: Alain Thienot. 20 hectares
Estate with a deserved reputation for stylish, wood-aged reds and crisp whites.

Château Respide ☆☆
Langon. Owner: Franck Bonnet. 35 hectares
Long-established vineyards on the sandy soil of Langon, producing wines of some complexity, especially the barrique-aged "Cuvée Callipyge".

Château Respide-Médeville ☆☆–☆☆☆

Toulenne. Owner: Christian Médeville. 12 hectares
A small property that has, for many years, been producing
red wines with depth and concentration, and whites with a
pronounced citric character.

Château de Rochemorin ☆☆

**Martillac. Owner: André Lurton. AC: Pessac-Léognan.
90 hectares**
A major old estate abandoned in the 1930s, replanted since 1973
by M. Lurton. Modern, fruity reds and dry, aromatic whites.

Château Roquetaillade la Grange ☆☆

Mazères. Owners: the Guignard family. 45 hectares
A very reliable property, established for many years.

Château St-Robert ☆☆–☆☆☆

Pujols. Owner: Crédit Foncier de France. 34 hectares
Same ownership as Chateaux Bastor-Lamontagne in nearby
Sauternes, this is a very reliable property, and the top *cuvée*,
"Poncet Deville", both red and white, is confidently oaky.

Château le Sartre ☆☆

**Léognan. Owner: Antony Perrin. AC: Pessac-Léognan.
25 hectares. www.chateau-le-sartre.com**
Identical vinification to Perrin's other wine, Château
Carbonnieux, but in a lighter style.

Château Tourteau-Chollet ☆

Arbannats. Owner: Mestrezat. 67 hectares
Large property, producing pleasant, commercial red and
white wines.

Château le Tuquet ☆☆

Beautiran. Owner: Paul Ragon. 52 hectares
This is Beautiran's principal property on the main Bordeaux
to Langon road. In ripe years, the red is supple and charming.

Château la Vieille France ☆–☆☆

**Portets. Owner: Michel Dugoua. 24 hectares.
www.chateau-la-vieille-france.com**
A sound and enterprising property, with the best wines being
oak-aged and released as "Cuvée Marie".

Vieux-Château Gaubert ☆☆–☆☆☆

Portets. Owner: Dominique Haverlan. 16 hectares
Ever since Haverlan bought this property in 1988, he has
made excellent wines, both white and red, and both
unusually intense and complex.

Villa Bel Air ☆☆

**St-Morillon. Owner: Jean-Michel Cazes. 46 hectares.
www.villabelair.com**
These are wines designed for immediate pleasure: medium-
bodied red, and ripe, barrique-fermented whites.

Sauternes

Towards the south of the Bordeaux region, red winemaking
dwindles to insignificance compared with white. A slightly
warmer and drier climate, and very limey soil, are ideal for
white grapes; the wine naturally has what the French call
great *sève* – sap – a combination of body and vitality.

The best of the region is the relatively hilly enclave of
Sauternes, an appellation that applies to five villages just
south of a little stream called the Ciron. On the other side of
the Ciron, on flatter land, lies Barsac, which also has the right
to the Sauternes appellation. As the cold waters of the Ciron
meet the warmer flow of the Garonne, autumnal mists
develop, conditions that give rise to the famous noble rot,
and the possibility of *vin liquoreux*. For the last 250 years,
Sauternes has specialized in this extraordinarily concentrated,
golden dessert wine. Between 1982 and 1990, the tide of
fortune turned strongly in its favour with a string of excellent
years, but this was cruelly balanced by a number of bad years
in the early 1990s.

Unlike most of the Graves region, Sauternes has big estates
in the manner of the Médoc. Historically, its position on the
inland route up the Garonne gave it military importance.
Later, its fine climate and its good wine made it a desirable
spot to replace castles with mansions. A score of these were
already famous for their "sappy" white wine when the 1855
classification was made for the Paris Exhibition. They were
classified in three ranks, with Château d'Yquem alone in the
first, nine classed as *premiers crus*, and another nine as
deuxièmes crus – which is, broadly speaking, still a fair
classification, except that divisions of property have
increased the *premiers crus* to eleven and the *deuxièmes* to
fourteen. They are surrounded by a host of unofficial *crus
bourgeois*, some of a comparable quality. The combined
vineyard area of the six communes is 2,240 hectares. There
is no *cave coopérative*.

The laborious procedure for making great Sauternes is
described on the opposite page. With sweet wines out of
fashion in the '60s and '70s, it became unrealistic for most
proprietors, who could not afford the labour needed to pick
single grapes at a time, or the new barrels, or the years of
waiting. But fashion, and apparently climate, have both
changed so radically recently that Sauternes is entering a new
golden age.

The ultimate short cut, used by many of the humbler
growers, is simply to wait for fully ripe grapes (hoping that
at least a few are "nobly rotten"), pick them all together, add
sugar to bring the potential alcohol up to about eighteen
per cent, then stop the fermentation with SO_2 when the
fermentation has produced thirteen or fourteen actual
degrees, leaving the wine sweet. It is a bastard approach to
winemaking, with predictably mediocre results. The wine has
none of the classic Sauternes flavour and should, in fairness,
be called something else.

What is the classic flavour? It depends on the vintage.
In some it is forceful, hot, and treacly. In others, it is rich
and stiff with flavour, but almost literally sappy and not
sweet. In the best, with all the grapes "nobly rotten", it is
thick with sugar yet gentle, creamy, nutty, honeyed. Barsacs
tend to be a little less rich than Sauternes, but can produce
their own spellbinding equilibrium of the rich and the
brisk. Bottles can be better than ever after as much as forty
or fifty years.

Yields of Sauternes vary worryingly according to the
weather. Some years hardly any sweet wine is made, or a whole
crop is declassified to another label. An average harvest, even
in a good year, might give thirty dozen bottles per hectare,

whereas a St-Julien classed growth for example, will make about ninety-five dozen per hectare with much less trouble.

Sauternes Premier Cru Supérieur

Château d'Yquem ☆☆☆☆
Owner: LVMH. AC: Sauternes. 103 hectares. Grapes: Sém. 80%, Sauv. 20%. www.chateau-yquem.com

Indisputably the greatest sweet wine of France, but also recognized as the best white wine of Bordeaux long before the fashion for sweet wine was initiated in the nineteenth century. The extreme pains that go into its making are described in detail on the previous page.

In certain vintages, Château d'Yquem also makes "Y" (which is pronounced "Ygrec"), its rare dry wine, made from 50% Sauvignon, 50% Sémillon. It has some of the concentration of Yquem, and the same alcohol content, but only a trace of sweetness for balance. After centuries of ownership by the Lur-Saluces family, the property was sold to luxury-goods group LVMH in 1999. The struggle for control was a bitter one, but resolved amicably, with Comte Alexandre de Lur-Saluces remaining as manager of the estate he has so admirably run for decades. *See also* page 66.

Sauternes Premiers Crus

Château Climens ☆☆☆☆
Owner: Bérénice Lurton. AC: Barsac. 29 hectares. Grapes: Sém. 100%

Barsac's sweetest and richest wine, made by the old methods with a crop nearly as derisory as that at Yquem, giving it almost caramel concentration as it ages, yet with a touch of elegance typical of Barsac. The property changed hands in 1971 (a superb vintage). Since then it has only enhanced its reputation, with such wines as the '83, '86, '88, '89, '90, '97, and 2001. The locals pronounce the final "ns" emphatically, with a sort of honking effect. The second label is "Les Cyprès de Climens".

Château Coutet ☆☆☆–☆☆☆☆
Owners: the Baly family. AC: Barsac. 39 hectares. Grapes: Sém. 75%, Sauv. 23%, Muscadelle 2%. www.chateau-coutet.com

With Château Climens, the leading growth of Barsac, using traditional barrel fermentation to make exceptionally fine and stylish wine. The old manor house dates back to the English rule of Aquitaine. In the best years ('71,'75, '83, '86, '88, '89, '90), a selection of the richest wine is labelled "Cuvée Madame". "Chartreuse de Coutet" is the second wine.

Château Guiraud ☆☆☆
Owners: the Narby family. AC: Sauternes. 100 hectares. Grapes: Sém. 70%, Sauv. 30%. www.chateau-guiraud.fr

The southern neighbour of Yquem, but distinctive in having a fairly high proportion of Sauvignon in the vineyard. Vintages of the 1980s had mixed success: power sometimes outweighed finesse. Guiraud is now hitting its stride under long-term winemaker Xavier Planty; '90 and '99 are superb.

Château Clos Haut-Peyraguey ☆☆☆
Bommes. Owner: Jacques Pauly. AC: Sauternes. 12 hectares. Grapes: Sém. 90%, Sauv. 10%

Formerly the upper part of the same estate as Château Laufaurie-Peyraguey, separated in 1879 and in the Pauly family since 1914. A modest estate, making relatively light but extremely elegant wine. Château Haut-Bommes has the same owner and has effectively become the second wine.

Château Lafaurie-Peyraguey ☆☆☆–☆☆☆☆
Bommes. Owners: the Cordier family. AC: Sauternes. 40 hectares. Grapes: Sém. 90%, Sauv. 5%, Muscadelle, 5%. www.cordier-wines.com

A fortress to challenge Yquem – militarily, that is – with a fine reputation for beautifully structured, long-lived Sauternes, particularly since 1979. The 1983 was the first of a run of great wines.

Château Rabaud-Promis ☆☆–☆☆☆
Bommes. Owner: Philippe Dejean. AC: Sauternes. 30 hectares. Grapes: Sém. 80%, Sauv. 20%

The larger part of the formerly important Rabaud estate, making rich wine, fat without being heavy. Since 1986, a reliably good property to follow, but rarely exceptional.

Château Rayne-Vigneau ☆☆–☆☆☆
Bommes. Owner: Mestrezat. AC: Sauternes. 80 hectares. Grapes: Sém. 74%, Sauv. 24%, Muscadelle, 2%

A big estate, now detached from its château but celebrated in history for its soil being – literally – full of precious stones. The fortunate Vicomte de Roton (a Pontac, whose descendants still have the château) found himself picking up sapphires, topaz, amethysts, and opals by the thousand. (The rest of the soil is gravel.) Modern methods produce rich and good, but not the most ambitious, Sauternes, and a little "Rayne-Vigneau Sec". The second label is "Clos L'Abeille".

Château Rieussec ☆☆☆–☆☆☆☆
Fargues. Owner: Domaines Barons de Rothschild. AC: Sauternes. 75 hectares. Grapes: Sém. 90%, Sauv. 8%, Muscadelle, 2%. www.lafite.com

Yquem's eastern neighbour, perched even higher on the same line of hills. Rieussec, traditionally aromatic, elegant yet powerful, changed significantly in the '70s under its previous owner, when it became darker and richer with a honeyed, botrytis character. The '62 has been a favourite of mine for years. the '71, '75, '79, '88, and '89 are all first-class. A dry white, inspired by Yquem's "Y", is called "R". The Lafite-Rothschilds bought the property in 1985, and the style became more classic and less tarry. Vintages of the late 1990s have been outstanding. The second wine is "Clos Labère".

Château Sigalas Rabaud ☆☆☆
Bommes. Owner: Marquis de Lambert des Granges. AC: Sauternes. 14 hectares. Grapes: Sém. 85%, Sauv. 15%. www.cordier-wines.com

One-third of the former Rabaud estate, descended for over a century in the Sigalas family. The wine was mainly made and aged in tanks until 1988 to avoid oaky flavours; thereafter more oak was used, but the emphasis was always on retaining the wine's freshness and fruit. In 1994, the Cordier team leased the property and the wine has gained in complexity without losing its distinctive character. The

Château d'Yquem – The Making of a Great Sauternes

Wine has few legends more imposing than the hilltop fortress of Yquem and its golden nectar. Only France could produce such a monument to aristocratic craftsmanship.

In 1785, Josephine Sauvage d'Yquem, whose family would retain the estate for over 200 years, married the Comte de Lur Saluces. Two years later Thomas Jefferson paid a famous visit to the château and rated the wines so highly that he ordered a consignment for America. Whether the wine he so admired was as exactly liquorous, intensely sweet as Yquem is today remains a mystery. It was certainly as sweet as possible. The question is when it became worth using the pains and patience that now make the wine so extraordinary. Today, the painstaking care at Yquem is difficult to exaggerate. A description of its methods is a description of the ideal – which other châteaux only approximate to a greater or lesser degree.

The principle must first be understood. Under certain autumnal conditions of misty mornings and sunny afternoons, one of the forms of mould common in vineyards reverses its role; instead of ruining the grapes, it is entirely beneficial. Given a healthy, ripe, and undamaged crop without other fungus infections, it begins to feed on the sugar and the tartaric acid in each grape, probing with roots so fine that they penetrate the microscopic pores of the grapeskin. The grapes rapidly shrivel, turning first grey with fungus spores, then warm, violet-brown, their skins mere pulp. By this time they have lost more than half their weight, but less than

half their sugar. Their juice is concentrated, extremely sweet, and rich in glycerine. If conditions are perfect (as they were in 1967, 1989, and 2001) the process is sudden and complete; not a grape in the bunch is recognizable. They are a repulsive sight.

Unfortunately, in most years the process is gradual; the berries rot patchily – even one by one. At Yquem, the pickers, in four gangs forty-strong, move through the vines at a snail's pace gathering the grapes, if necessary, one at a time, then going back over the same vines again and again, up to ten (once up to eleven) times. The final crop amounts to about one glass of wine per vine.

In the *cuvier* the grapes are slightly sulphured, put through a gentle wooden *fouloir* (crusher), then immediately pressed in old-fashioned vertical presses three times, the "cake" being cut up with shovels and thrown into a mill to remove the stalks between pressings. The whole day's picking – up to forty barrels – is assembled together in one vat, then poured straight into new-oak barriques, filling them three quarters full, to ferment. The day's crop, the *journée*, is the critical unit to be tasted again and again to see whether it has the qualities of the *grand vin*. If it does not have those qualities, it will be sold to the trade as anonymous Sauternes. There is no court of appeal, no second wine, at Yquem.

The *chai* is heated to 20°C (68°F) to encourage a steady fermentation which lasts between two and six weeks. When it reaches around fourteen degrees of alcohol, the yeasts gradually stop working, leaving up to 120 grammes of sugar to a litre. The sums are critical here. Twenty-per-cent total sugar ("potential alcohol") in the juice is ideal. With twenty-five per cent, the fermentation might stop at nine to ten degrees – as in Trockenbeerenauslese. (The extreme example is Tokaji Essencia, with so much sugar that the potential alcohol content is thirty-five degrees but fermentation barely starts at all.)

Château d'Yquem is kept for no fewer than 3.5 years in cask, racked every three months, and never bunged tight – which means twice-weekly topping up over the whole period, and a loss by evaporation of twenty per cent. The wine is so thick that it never "falls bright", or clears itself fully by gravity. The sediment, at the same density as the liquid, remains in suspension, so it must be "fined" – but never with egg whites, says Alexandre de Lur Saluces; one of the eggs might be bad.

This stupendous property is no longer owned by the Lur Saluces family, but Alexandre de Lur Saluces remains as general manager, maintaining the perfectionist standards at this national treasure.

---

winemaking is identical to that used at the other Cordier property of Château Lafaurie-Peyraguey (*q.v.*).

Château Suduiraut ✩✩✩–✩✩✩✩
Preignac. Owner: AXA Millésimes. AC: Sauternes. 90 hectares. Grapes: Sém. 90%, Sauv. 10%. www.suduiraut.com
A château of great splendour within equally splendid parkland and the next vineyard to Yquem, going north. One of the most respected names, despite a period of relative neglect in the early 1970s.

Manager Alain Pascaud succeeded his father Pierre at the helm here, and has quietly imposed a consistently high standard on the winemaking. Suduiraut at its best ('67, '76,

'82, '88, '90, '97, and '99) is plump and unctuous, truly *liquoreux*; the poor man's Yquem. Second wine since '93: "Castelnau de Suduiraut".

Château la Tour Blanche ✩✩✩
Bommes. Owner: Ministère de l'Agriculture. AC: Sauternes. 37 hectares. Grapes: Sém. 77%, Sauv. 20%, Muscadelle, 3%. www.tourblanche.com
Probably the first estate on which sweet Sauternes was made, and placed first after Yquem in the 1855 classification. Bequeathed to the French state in 1912 by M. Osiris (an umbrella tycoon), whose name still appears on the label. The vineyard slopes steeply westwards towards the River

Ciron. Winemaking was, from 1983, run dynamically and to the great benefit of quality by Jean-Pierre Jausserand, until he retired in 2001.

Since 1989, the entire crop has been fermented in new oak – before 1983 it was all in steel tank. There is a college of viticulture here, but clearly separated from the wine estate.

Sauternes Deuxièmes Crus

Château d'Arche ☆☆–☆☆☆
Owners: consortium of investors. AC: Sauternes. 29 hectares. Grapes: Sém. 90%, Sauv. 10%
Exceedingly luscious, sometimes heavy Sauternes at its best ('83 and '90). Jean Perromat has directed since 1980.

Château Broustet ☆☆–☆☆☆
Owner: Didier Laulan. AC: Barsac. 15 hectares. Grapes: Sém. 63%, Sauv. 25%, Muscadelle 12%
Remembered as the property of the cooper who standardized the now-universal Bordeaux barrique. His descendants (who also ran the great Château Canon, St-Emilion) made an adequate but scarcely distinguished wine. Didier Laulan has profited from the string of good vintages since 1996 to improve quality considerably.

Château Caillou ☆–☆☆☆
Owner: Marie-Josée Pierre. AC: Barsac. 16 hectares. Grapes: Sém. 90%, Sauv. 10%. www.chateaucaillou.fr
A very businesslike property on the higher ground of "Haut" Barsac, near Château Climens. A small amount of superior "Private Cuvée" is produced in top years. Humdrum quality in the 1980s and unfortunate family rows meant that this estate was seriously underperforming for many years, but since the mid-1990s there has been a welcome improvement.

Château Doisy-Daëne ☆☆☆
Owner: Pierre Dubourdieu. AC: Barsac. 15 hectares. Grapes: Sém. 80%, Sauv. 20%
Doisy-Daëne is in the forefront of modern winemaking with sophisticated use of steel and new oak to make fresh, lively sweet wines of real class. Pierre Dubourdieu, now assisted by his celebrated oenologist son Denis, affects to dislike sweet wines, but nonetheless produces supremely elegant examples. In top vintages, tiny quantities of truly extreme wine, rightly called "L'Extravagant" and priced accordingly, are produced. The estate also produces excellent dry Graves.

Château Doisy-Dubroca ☆☆–☆☆☆
Owner: Louis Lurton. AC: Barsac. 4 hectares. Grapes: Sém. 100%. www.louis-lurton.fr
A small property linked for a century to the neighbouring Château Climens and now made with the same traditional techniques of intense care.

Château Doisy-Védrines ☆☆☆
Owner: Pierre Castéja. AC: Barsac. 27 hectares. Grapes: Sém. 80%, Sauv. 15%, Muscadelle 5%
I always assumed from its quality that this was a First rather than a Second Growth. It is one of the rich Barsacs that is fermented in barrels and built for a good long life.

Château Filhot ☆☆
Owner: Comte Henri de Vaucelles. AC: Sauternes. 60 hectares. Grapes: Sém. 60%, Sauv. 35%, Muscadelle 5%. www.filhot.com
A palace, or nearly, built by the Lur Saluces family in the early nineteenth century on the edge of the woods south of Sauternes. The big vineyard on sandy soil produces wines that are distinctively light by classical Sauternes standards. They are all the more appetizing and savoury for it. A reluctance to age the wines in wood diminished their complexity, but in the mid-1990s this began to change, a process that is continued by Comte Henri's son, Gabriel, who took over managment of the property in 2002.

Château Lamothe-Despujols ☆
Owner: Guy Despujols. AC: Sauternes. 7.5 hectares. Grapes: Sém. 85%, Sauv. 10%, Muscadelle 5%. www.guy-despujols.free.fr
Minor Sauternes, bottled within a year for early drinking.

Château Lamothe Guignard ☆
Owners: the Guignard family. AC Sauternes. 18 hectares. Grapes: Sém. 90%, Sauv. 5%, Muscadelle 5%
The Guignards, a winemaking family from the Graves, bought this part of the vineyard from the proprietor of Château d'Arche (*q.v.*) in 1981. They were soon producing excellent, spicily fruity, luscious Sauternes at a fair price, but for some reason quality has unfortunately slipped throughout the 1990s.

Château de Malle ☆☆☆
Preignac. Owner: Comtesse Nancy de Bournazel. AC: Sauternes (plus Graves). 29 hectares. Grapes white: Sém. 75%, Sauv. 25%. www.chateau-de-malle.fr
The most beautiful house and garden in Sauternes – possibly in Bordeaux – and much appreciated by tourists. Built for the owner's family (related to the Lur Saluces) about 1600. Italian gardens were added 100 years later. The vineyard, on light sandy soil, is in Sauternes and Graves, and produces roughly equal quantities of sweet white and red.

Until the late 1980s, quality was sound rather than distinguished, but the wine has gained in richness and complexity throughout the 1990s. The second wine is "Château de Sainte-Hélène", and the excellent white Graves is "M de Malle".

Château de Myrat ☆–☆☆
Barsac. Owners: the de Pontac family. AC Barsac. 22 hectares. Grapes: Sém. 85%, Sauv. 10%, Muscadelle 5%
The father of the present owners uprooted all the vines in 1976. The vineyard was replanted in 1988, but the first vintages were the disastrous years of the early '90s. The better vintages of the late '90s produced good but inconsistent wines.

Château Nairac ☆☆☆
Barsac. Owner: Mme. Nicole Tari-Heeter. AC: Sauternes. 17 hectares. Grapes: Sém. 90%, Sauv. 6%, Muscadelle 4%
A young American, Tom Heeter, made this formerly run-down estate one of the leaders of the district, with wines of the racy, less sticky Barsac style that bear keeping ten years or more.

The wine is now made by his son, Nicolas Tari-Heeter, who is a perfectionist – harvesting only truly botrytized grapes and ruthlessly selling off barrels that don't please him. The resulting wine is highly concentrated and of imposing quality.

Château Romer-du-Hayot ☆–☆☆
Owner: André du Hayot. AC: Sauternes. 16 hectares.
Grapes: Sém. 70%, Sauv. 25%, Muscadelle 5%
The château was demolished for the new *autoroute*, and the wine is made at the owner's Château Guiteronde in Barsac. For many years the wine has been simple, having been aged only in tanks, but now a year of barrique-ageing has given them more complexity.

Château Suau ☆
Owner: Roger Biarnès. AC: Barsac. 8 hectares.
Grapes: Sém. 80%, Sauv. 10%, Muscadelle 10%
The relic of a more important property, near the Garonne sited on heavier soil than the best growths. The wine is aged in a mixture of wood and tanks, and, regrettably, is rather coarse.

Other Sauternes Producers

Château d'Armajan des Ormes ☆–☆☆
Preignac. Owners: the Perromat family. 19 hectares
Good, apricotty wine, and a "Crème de Tête" bottling in top years.

Château Bastor-Lamontagne ☆☆
Preignac. Owner: Crédit Foncier de France. 58 hectares.
www.bastor-lamontagne.com
A substantial and well-kept property with a history of good vintages to substantiate its claim to be "as good as a Second Growth".

Château Cantegril ☆–☆☆
Barsac. Owners: Messieurs Dubourdieu and Masencal.
20 hectares
Part of the former Château de Myrat (*q.v.*) vineyard, beautifully kept but rather unambitious until 1988. The '90 is fabulous. Made by Pierre Dubourdieu.

Cru Barréjats ☆☆☆
Barsac. Owner: Dr. Mireille Daret. 5 hectares
Tiny, high-quality estate between Climens and Caillou, which went live in 1990.

Château de Fargues ☆☆☆
Fargues. Owner: Comte Alexandre de Lur Saluces. 15 hectares.
Grapes: Sém. 80%, Sauv. 20%. www.chateau-de-fargues.com
A proud castle in ruins, with a diminutive vineyard, but the perfectionist standards of Yquem. Lighter wine, but impeccable and sometimes brilliant (*e.g.* '67, '75, '80, '86, '90, '95).

Château Gilette ☆–☆☆☆
Owner: Christian Médeville. 5 hectares
A unique producer of long-aged Sauternes of great splendour: *e.g.* '49, '55, '59, '61, '62, '67, aged in large tanks and not bottled until its idealistic owner considers it ready to drink – at twenty-five years or so. Monsieur Médeville also produces the far more conventional "Château les Justices".

Château Haut-Bergeron ☆☆–☆☆☆
Preignac. Owners: the Lamothe family. 29 hectares
Sumptuous peachy wines of classed growth quality.

Château Liot ☆
Barsac. Owner: J. David. 20 hectares
Large property on the best slopes in Barsac. The general level is "good commercial", sometimes over-sulphured.

Château du Mayne ☆–☆☆
Barsac. Owner: Jean Sanders. 8 hectares
Ancient vines (many eighty years old) cultivated for small amounts of very good wine.

Château Piada ☆☆
Barsac. Owner: Jean Lalande. 10 hectares
One of the better-known lesser Barsacs, and a wine of great finesse. "Clos du Roy" is a second label.

Château Raymond-Lafon ☆☆☆
Sauternes. Owners: the Meslier family. 16 hectares.
www.chateau-raymond-lafon.fr
Owned by the ex-manager of Château d'Yquem, neighbour to the great château, made with similar care and aged three years in oak. Regularly first-class (*e.g.* '75, '78, '88, '89, '90, '97).

Château de Rolland ☆–☆☆
Barsac. Owners: Jean and Pierre Guignard. 17 hectares.
www.chateauderolland.com
Attractive wines, honeyed but somehow lacking in elegance and complexity.

Château Roumieu ☆
Barsac. Owner: Olivier Bernadet. 19 hectares
Although the vineyard neighbours Château Climens, the wines have been respectable rather than exciting.

Château Roumieu-Lacoste ☆☆
Barsac. Owner: Hervé Dubourdieu. 12 hectares
The nephew of the owner of the excellent Doisy-Daëne makes good, rich wine here.

Château St-Amand ☆–☆☆
Preignac. Owners: the Ricard family. 20 hectares
Admirable quality in the style of Barsac, with the emphasis on fruit rather than oak or complexity. Sold by Sichel as "La Chartreuse".

Château Simon ☆–☆☆
Barsac. Owners: the Dufour family. 17 hectares
A well-run property, producing dry Graves as well as sweet wine from an additional twenty-three hectares.

St-Emilion

As a town, every wine-lover's idea of heaven; as an appellation, much the biggest for high-quality wine in France, producing not much less than the whole of the Côte d'Or of Burgundy. Nowhere is the civic and even the spiritual life of a little city so deeply imbued with the passion for making good wine.

St-Emilion, curled into its sheltered corner of the hill, cannot expand. Where other such towns have spread their nondescript streets over the countryside, around St-Emilion there are priceless vineyards, most of its very best, lapping up to its walls, which prevent any sprawl. It burrows into its yielding limestone to find building blocks and store its wine – even to solemnize its rites. Its old church is a vast-vaulted cave, now used for the meeting of the Jurade, St-Emilion's ceremonial organization (*see* below).

The vineyards envelop several distinct soils and aspects, while maintaining a certain common character. St-Emilion wines are a degree stronger than Médocs, with less tannin. Accessible, solid tastiness is their stamp, maturing to warm, gratifying sweetness. They are less of a puzzle than Médocs when young and mature faster, but are no less capable of asking unsolvable questions as they age.

The best St-Emilions come from the relatively steep *côtes*, the hillside vineyards and the cap of the escarpment around the town, and from an isolated patch of gravel soil on the plateau two miles northwest, almost in Pomerol. The *côtes* wines are the more smiling, in degrees from enigmatic to beaming; the wines of the graves more earnest and searching. Michael Broadbent defines the difference as "open" (*côtes*) and "firm" (*graves*). But they can easily be confused with one another, with Médocs, with Graves, and even with burgundy. And some of the same qualities are found in vineyards on substantially different soils, both down in the sandy (*sables*) region in the Dordogne Valley below St-Emilion town itself, and in the five "satellite" villages to the north and east.

The classification of St-Emilion follows a pattern of its own. It was settled in 1954 and is the only one planned to be regularly revised – the third category is to be revised every year.

There are now, since the 1985 vintage, two appellations, simple AC St-Emilion and AC St-Emilion Grand Cru. The *crus classés* come in two classes: *premier grand cru classé* and *grand cru classé*. The top class is divided into two: "A" and "B". The current classification names two châteaux (Cheval Blanc and Ausone) as *premiers grands crus classés* "A", and eleven as "B". Bs are the approximate equivalent in value to Médoc Second and Third Growths. Then come fifty-five *grands crus classés*, elected for (about) ten years. They were revised in 1969, in 1986, and again in 1996.

The St-Emilion Grand Cru, for which proprietors have to re-apply every year by submitting their wines for tasting belongs to the AC.

Obviously, St-Emilion is not an area of big estates. The average size of holding is about eight hectares, the biggest not much more than forty, and many as small as two or three, making a mere few hundred cases. In fact "*grand cru*" in St-Emilion, unqualified, is the same broad category as *crus bourgeois* in the Médoc.

Since the early 1990s, there has been an unsubtle transformation in the style of many St-Emilion wines.

Nowhere else in Bordeaux have techniques such as must concentration and micro-oxygenation been adopted with such enthusiasm. Applied to wine cropped at very low yields, the result is opaque colour, immense concentration and power, high alcohol, and jammy flavours. There is no doubt that there is a wide following for such wines, especially among American wine critics, but others might argue that St-Emilion is in danger of losing not just its elegance, but also its *typicité*.

St-Emilion Premiers Grands Crus

Château Ausone ☆☆☆☆
Owner: Alain Vauthier. 7 hectares. Grapes: Merlot 50%, Cab.Fr. 50%. www.chateau-ausone.com
If you were looking for the most obviously promising vineyard site in the whole Bordeaux area, this would be first choice. No wonder its name is associated with the Roman poet Ausonius (also connoisseur of the Moselle). It slopes south and east from the rim of the St-Emilion escarpment, whose limestone cap has been quarried for building and provides perfect cool, commodious cellars. The soil is pale alkaline clay, in a shallow layer over permeable limestone (which vine roots love). The château is a dainty building perched above and among the vines, where an old white mare shambles around doing the cultivating, hull-down in the green leaves.

Ausone went through a long eclipse when its wine was good, but not good enough. Its neighbours seemed to dim their lamps at the same time. Matters were put right from 1975 by a new manager, Pascal Delbeck, and each good vintage now takes its proper place among the First Growths. '76, '78 and '79 were all confirmed excellent, and '82, '83, '89, and '90 continue the high standards. 1995, the first vintage made by Alain Vauthier with Michel Rolland's advice, shows a new rich, seductive Ausone, with a revelatory density and complexity repeated in every subsequent vintage, culminating in the superb 2000.

Winemaking here is exactly the same in principle as in the Médoc. New barrels are used for the whole, pathetically small crop. (I was present by chance at a cellar tasting of Ausone from barrels washed before filling with steam, hot water, and cold water. The differences were astonishing. Hot water won.) The wine is bottled slightly sooner than Médoc First Growths and its whole evolution to drinkability is slightly quicker, yet its potential lifespan, judging by very rare old bottles, is no shorter. The final result is the pure magic of claret: sweet, lively harmony with unfathomable depths.

Château Cheval Blanc ☆☆☆☆
Owners: Bernard Arnault and Albert Frère. Administrator: Pierre Lurton. 37 hectares. Grapes: Cab.Fr. 58%, Merlot 41%, Cab. Sauv. 1%. www.chateau-cheval-blanc.com
Although it shares the first place in St-Emilion with Ausone, the soil and situation (and tradition) of Cheval Blanc are totally different. It lies back on the plateau near the boundary of Pomerol on much deeper soil, an irregular mixture of gravel, sand, and clay with clay subsoil. The main grape is Cabernet Franc (known in these parts as Bouchet).

There is no white horse here, and the château is an unfanciful, cream-painted residence that for some reason always reminds me of Virginia. The new *chais* make a more imposing building. The same family had owned the property since its nineteenth-century beginning, but in 1998, a private partnership of two very rich businessmen altered all that.

Cheval Blanc is the Mouton of St-Emilion: the blockbuster. The 1947 is a legend, a wine of heroic style and proportions, with the combined qualities of claret, port, sculpture, and Hermès or Gucci – or is this *lèse-majesté*? The '61 is only just ready; a tough piece of beef that needed to marinate for years. Not all vintages are so awe-inspiring: but '75, '82, '83, '89, '90, '95, and '98 are in the grandest tradition. Pierre Lurton has been running the property since 1991 and has not put a foot wrong. The second wine is "Le Petit Cheval" (which was the only wine released in frost-struck '91).

Château l'Angélus ☆☆☆☆
Owners: the Boüard de Laforest family. 23 hectares. Grapes: Merlot 50%, Cab.Fr. 47%, Cab.Sauv. 3%. www.angelus.com
On the slope below Château Beauséjour where the soil is heavy. The owners' passionate pursuit of excellence caused Angélus's promotion in 1996 after a series of high-grade vintages in the second half of the '80s and the more difficult early '90s. The wine is as opulent and explosive as any in Bordeaux.

Château Beau-Séjour-Bécot ☆☆☆
Owners: Gérard and Dominique Bécot. 17 hectares. Grape var: Merlot 70%, Cab.Fr. 24%, Cab.Sauv. 6%. www.beausejour-becot.com
Two-thirds of an estate that was divided in 1869 (the smaller part got the house). The vineyard slopes west from the crest behind Château Ausone. Since 1969, the property has been modernized, with a complete new *cuvier*, and its dimmed reputation restored to that of a leader in the tight circle of the St-Emilion *côtes*, making the sort of rich wine for the medium term (say, ten years) that makes St-Emilion so popular. Demoted in the 1985 classification because M. Bécot had extended the property by buying two other vineyards,

but now rightly reinstated in 1996. The flavours are lush, almost plummy, and all recent vintages have been excellent, other than '99.

Château Beauséjour (Duffau-Lagarrosse) ☆☆–☆☆☆
Owners: Duffau-Lagarrosse heirs. 7 hectares. Grapes: Merlot 65%, Cab.Fr. 25%, Cab.Sauv. 10%
The smaller part of Beauséjour, but with the charming house and garden. Run in the traditional, small, family château style; full-bodied, well-extracted, but tending to be short of finesse, though the '90 has a sensational reputation.

Château Belair ☆☆–☆☆☆
Owner: Mme. J. Dubois-Challon. 12.5 hectares. Grapes: Merlot 80%, Cab.Fr. 20%
Until 1995, the bigger but junior brother of Château Ausone with the same owner. Part of the same sloping vineyard, plus a patch on the flat top of the hill behind. It has its own quarry caves, which once caused a serious landslip of the vines, and, like many St-Emilion châteaux, its own chapel (full of lumber). The wine is now excellent (*e.g.* the '89, '95, and '98), close to Ausone but perhaps, to split hairs, a shade less deft. Ten years is a good age for it.

Château Canon ☆☆–☆☆☆
Owners: the Wertheimer family (Chanel). 22 hectares. Grapes: Merlot 65%, Cab.Fr. 35%
My instinct is to spell the name with two "n"s: a great bronze gun-barrel (rather than a genteel cleric) expresses the style of Canon nicely. If production were only bigger this would be one of the most famous Bordeaux; generous, masculine, not too aggressive young, but magnificent with twenty years in bottle.

The Fournier family sold to the Wertheimers of Chanel, also owners of Château Rauzan-Ségla (*q.v.*), in 1997. Much of the vineyard needed to be replanted, and, rather to the surprise of some in St-Emilion, the INAO permitted the vineyards of Château Curé-Bon, another property purchased by the Wertheimers, to be promoted in status and incorporated into those of Canon.

Emile Peynaud and His Successors

No single man had such a direct influence over the style and standards of winemaking in Bordeaux over forty years up to 1990 as Emile Peynaud. A former director of the *Station Oenologique* of the University of Bordeaux, he became France's most celebrated consultant oenologist, with an astonishing list of clients among the châteaux of Bordeaux.

He encouraged his clients to be selective in harvesting, reserving only the best grapes for the *grand vin*. He also encouraged harvesting the grapes as ripe as possible, then adding to the "free-run" wine at least some of the more tannic, pressed wine to give a firm, tannic structure. He was also the first oenologist to understand the complexities of malolactic fermentation.

His advice was based on solid research undertaken at the university. Others have followed in his footsteps, such as Pascal Ribéreau-Gayon and Denis Dubourdieu. Dubourdieu is the master of white-wine fermentation, having conducted research projects into skin contact and lees-stirring.

Bordeaux as a whole – and indeed the wider world of wine – has benefited immeasurably from the contributions of its academic oenologists, some of whom have developed techniques, such as must concentration, that have kept Bordeaux at the forefront of oenological innovation. Bordeaux proprietors like to affect a certain disdain for "technological" wines (shorthand for Australian), but no region is more adept at technology than Bordeaux itself.

Other consultant oenologists are almost as influential, although they do not hold academic appointments. Michel Rolland is known throughout the world, and regularly advises estates in Argentina, California, and South Africa, as well as Bordeaux. Others, such as Jacques Boissenot and Gilles Pauquet, stay closer to home.

Nor are these top oenologists airy theoreticians. Rolland has his own property in Pomerol, and Dubourdieu has two estates in the Graves. Their understanding of winemaking is rooted in the *terroir* of Bordeaux, and refined in the laboratory.

Château Figeac ☆☆☆

Owner: Thierry Manoncourt. 40 hectares. Grapes: Cab.Sauv. 35%, Cab.Fr. 35%, Merlot 30%. www.chateau-figeac.com

Château Figeac has the aristocratic air of a Médoc Cru Classé and once had an estate on the grand Médoc scale, including what is now Château Cheval Blanc, and two others which still bear the name of Figeac. The house could be called a mansion and the park has a seigneurial feeling absent in most of the Libournais. The owner even has the features of an old-school aristocrat. The present vineyard, still among the biggest in St-Emilion, has stonier ground and a higher proportion of Cabernet Sauvignon than the others – which may account for its different style from Cheval Blanc. Figeac is more welcoming, less dense and compact; closer to a Médoc (again) in its structure of sweet flesh around a firm spine. It is big but not strapping, maturing relatively early and beautifully sweet in maturity – always individual. The 1970 was deceptively easy-drinking even at five years old. The '82, '85, '86, '89, '90, and '98 have been notably successful.

The second wine, "La Grange Neuve de Figeac", was launched in 1983. It was formerly a wine drunk only by the de Manoncourt family, production having started in 1954.

Clos Fourtet ☆☆–☆☆☆

Owner: Philippe Cuvelier. 20 hectares. Grapes: Merlot 80%, Cab.Fr. 8%, Cab.Sauv. 12%

The first *crus classé* that visitors stumble on as they walk out of the lovely old walled town into the vineyards. A modest-looking place, but with a warren of limestone cellars. (The old quarry-cellars are said to run for miles, one château's cellars connecting with another. Paradise for an oenospeleologist-burglar.) Old vintages of Clos Fourtet were tough going for many years. The 1966 was still immature in 1982. More recently, the wine has been made a bit kindlier, but without reaching the peaks of quality or price. The year in which the property was sold by the Lurton family to a genial businessman, Philippe Cuvelier – 2000 – turned out to be a magnificent vintage here.

Château la Gaffelière ☆☆☆

Owner: Comte Léo de Malet-Roquefort. 22 hectares. Grapes: Merlot 65%, Cab.Fr. 30%, Cab.Sauv. 5%. www.chateau-la-gaffeliere.com

The tall Gothic building at the foot of the hill up to St-Emilion, with vineyards at the foot of Ausone and Pavie. Three centuries have passed in the de Malet-Roquefort family, a history of noble vintages which aged well and gracefully ('55 was a favourite). Recent experience has been less consistent, but both '82 and '83 are fine wines. From 1995, when Michel Rolland was hired as a consultant, the wine showed more overt cassis and blackberry fruit, but by 2000, Rolland was no longer involved, and it remains to be seen whether the high standard he set will be maintained.

Château Magdelaine ☆☆☆

Owner: Etablissements Jean-Pierre Moueix. 10 hectares. Grapes: Merlot 85%, Cab.Fr. 15%

An impeccably conducted little property situated next to Château Belair, with a vineyard on the plateau and another on the south slope. The wine is made by Christian Moueix and Jean-Claude Berrouet, the brilliant resident oenologist of the house of J.P. Moueix. Its high proportion of Merlot makes it almost a Pomerol, but less plummy,

with the "meat" of St-Emilion and great finesse. There can scarcely be a more reliable or fascinating St-Emilion to watch vintage by vintage.

Château Pavie ☆☆☆

Owner: Gérard Perse. 37 hectares. Grapes: Merlot 80%, Cab.Fr. 15%, Cab.Sauv. 5%. www.chateaupavie.com

A priceless site, the whole south-by-west slope of the central St-Emilion *côtes*; the biggest vineyard on the hill, with the advantage of both top and bottom as well. The spacious cellars are dug under the top part of the vineyard, whose vine roots can be seen rejoicing in their fragrant humidity. Pavie was formerly known for warm, round claret of medium weight, more delicious than deeply serious: "supple" is the technical term. Since supermarket tycoon Gérard Perse bought the property (and its neighbour Château Pavie-Decesse), the changes have been radical. A splendid new *chai* was built, but more importantly, Perse opted for low yields, and maximum ripeness and concentration. In the course of a few vintages, the price trebled. The wine world is now divided in its opinion. Generally speaking, the Americans adore it, the Brits deplore its atypical fat.

Château Trottevieille ☆☆

Owners: the Castéja family. 10 hectares. Grapes: Merlot 50%, Cab.Fr. 45%, Cab.Sauv. 5%

Detached from the solid block of *crus classés* along the *côtes*, on the plateau east of the town, on richer-looking but still shallow clay with pebbles over limestone. Full-flavoured wine with plenty of character, and better since '85 as a result of stricter selection in vineyard and cellar. Yet Trottevieille never seems to be as good as it ought. It simply lacks flair.

St-Emilion Grands Crus Classés

Château L'Arrosée ☆☆

Owner: François Rodhain. 10 hectares. Grapes: Merlot 55%, Cab.Sauv. 30%, Cab.Fr. 15%

At the bottom of the *côtes* near the town. The name 'l'Arrosée' means "watered" (by springs). The wine itself, on the contrary, is medium-bodied but concentrated and serious, if not entirely consistent.

Château Balestard la Tonnelle ☆☆

Owners: the Capdemourlin family. 11 hectares. Grapes: Merlot 70%, Cab.Fr. 25%, Cab.Sauv. 5%

The Capdemourlin family has owned this property since the fifteenth century, when the poet Villon described its wine as *le divin nectar*. I have been more prosaically satisfied with this full-bodied, meaty wine. A new cellar was built in 1995.

Château Bellevue

Owners: daughters of Louis Horeau. 6 hectares. Grapes: Merlot 80%, Cab.Fr. 20%

Well named for its situation high on the west slope of the côtes. In 2000, Stéphane Derenoncourt (*see* Château Canon-La-Gaffaliere) became consultant winemaker. There was a dramatic change, for the better, from the light, fruity '99s to the dark, dense exotic 2000. A property to watch.

Château Bergat ☆–☆☆
Owners: the Castéja and Preben-Hansen families. 4 hectares. Grapes: Merlot 55%, Cab.Fr. 35%, Cab.Sauv. 10%
Tiny vineyard in the sheltered gully east of the town, linked by ownership with Château Trottevieille (*q.v.*).

Château Berliquet ☆☆–☆☆☆
Owner: Vicomte Patrick de Lesquen. 9 hectares. Grapes: Merlot 67%, Cab.Fr. 25%, Cab.Sauv. 8%
Old estate modernized in the 1970s, promoted in 1985, and made and marketed by the St-Emilion cooperative until the early 1990s. Since 1997, consultant winemaker Patrick Valette has given the wine more oak and concentration.

Château Cadet-Bon ☆☆
Owner: Bernard Gans. 5 hectares. Grapes: Merlot 80%, Cab.Fr. 20%
The terroir here doesn't permit enormous richness, but recent vintages have shown good fruit and ample finesse.

Château Cadet-Piola ☆–☆☆
Owners: the Jabiol family. 7 hectares. Grapes: Merlot 51%, Cab.Sauv. 28%, Cab.Fr. 18%, Malbec 3%
Memorable as the only Bordeaux label to portray (prettily) the female bosom. But a sturdy, even masculine, wine.

Château Canon-La-Gaffelière ☆☆☆
Owner: Graf zu Neipperg. 19 hectares. Grapes: Merlot 55%, Cab.Fr. 40%, Cab.Sauv. 5%. www.neipperg.com
German-owned property on sandy soil by the railway under the *côtes*. Total renovation in 1985 brought some startlingly good wines. Manager Stephan von Neipperg and his winemaker, Stéphane Derenoncourt, are in the forefront of modern winemaking in St-Emilion, favouring very low yields and harvests at optimal ripeness; also ardent believers in the virtues of micro-oxygenation. Wines are rich, plump, and velvety, sumptuous but possibly a tad too voluptuous to give pleasure to the last drop. *See also* La Mondotte.

Château Cap-de-Mourlin ☆☆–☆☆☆
Owners: the Capdemourlin family (*see* Château Balestard). 14 hectares. Grapes: Merlot 65%, Cab.Fr. 25%, Cab.Sauv. 10%
Situated one mile north of town on clay soil. For several years until 1982 this estate was divided, but is now one again, and is making strikingly high-flavoured wine.

Château Chauvin ☆☆–☆☆☆
Owners: Marie-France Février and Béatrice Ondet. 15 hectares. Grapes: Merlot 80%, Cab.Fr. 15%, Cab.Sauv. 5%. www.chateauchauvin.com
Inconsistent property being given a face-lift with Michel Rolland's help. Much improved since 1995.

Château Clos des Jacobins
Owner: Gérard Frydman. 7.5 hectares. Grapes: Merlot 70%, Cab.Fr. 30%
Located in the centre of the commune where *côtes* begins to shade into *graves*. After years of ownership by the house of Cordier, the Clos was sold in 2001. Perfumier Frydman brought in Hubert de Bouard of Château l'Angélus to supervise the winemaking, and the style is, therefore, likely to change.

Clos St Martin ☆☆–☆☆☆
Owners: the Reiffers family. 1.3 hectares. Grapes: Merlot 65%, Cab.Fr. 20%, Cab.Sauv. 15%
The smallest of the *grands crus classés*. Minute production: essentially a *garage* wine, made by Sophie Fourcade.

Château la Clotte ☆–☆☆
Owners: Héritiers Chailleau. 4 hectares. Grapes: Merlot 70%, Cab.Fr. 30%
Beautifully situated in the fold of the hill east of the town.

Château la Clusière ☆☆
Owner: Gérard Perse. 2.5 hectares. Grapes: Merlot 100%
Part of the vineyard of Château Pavie (*q.v.*), not quite up to *premier grand cu* standard. Same style as Pavie since 1998.

Château Corbin ☆☆
Owner: Domaines Giraud. 13 hectares. Grapes: Merlot 80%, Cab.Fr. 17%, Malbec 3%
Corbin is the northern hamlet of graves St-Emilion, near the Pomerol boundary and sloping gently northeast. Some flesh, some tannin, but, on balance, not very distinctive wine.

Château Corbin-Michotte ☆☆
Owner: Jean Noël Boidron. 7 hectares. Grapes: Merlot 65%, Cab.Fr. 30%, Cab.Sauv. 5%
See previous entry; but this seems to me more delicate and supple. For drinking fairly young.

Château la Couspaude ☆☆–☆☆☆
Owner: Vignobles Aubert. 7 hectares. Grapes: Merlot 70%, Cab.Fr. 15%, Cab.Sauv. 15%. www.la-couspaude.com
Re-established in the classification in 1996. Now that the wine is château-bottled, this well-placed property is taking a new lease of life under Michel Rolland's direction. Very concentrated and oaky (and expensive) 1998.

Château Couvent-des-Jacobins ☆☆–☆☆☆
Owners: the Joinaud-Borde family. 10 hectares. Grapes: Merlot 65%, Cab.Fr. 25%, Cab.Sauv. 10%
Excellent *côtes* vineyard right under the town walls to the east, with venerable cellars in the town centre. The wine is well-structured, ripe, and juicy.

Château Dassault ☆☆–☆☆☆
Owner: SARL Château Dassault. 24 hectares. Grapes: Merlot 65%, Cab.Fr. 30%, Cab.Sauv. 5%
One of the biggest *graves* vineyards, northeast of the town. Steady rather than distinguished, although since 1995 the wines show more concentration and elegance.

Château la Dominique ☆☆☆
Owner: Clément Fayat. 22 hectares. Grapes: Merlot 80%, Cab.Fr. 15%, Cab.Sauv 5%
this is the neighbour of Château Cheval Blanc (*q.v.*) reflecting its privileged position in an almost unbroken sequence of concentrated, fleshy, wines, with the Michel Rolland touch.

Château Faurie-de-Souchard ☆☆
Owners: the Jabiol family. 11 hectares. Grapes: Merlot 65%, Cab.Fr. 26%, Cab.Sauv. 9%
Confusingly, the neighbour of Petit-Faurie-de-Soutard (*q.v.*).

Same owners as of Château Cadet-Piola and Château Cadet-Peychez; now tightening its grip on quality.

Château Fonplégade ☆☆

Owner: Armand Moueix family. 18 hectares. Grapes: Merlot 60%, Cab.Fr. 35%, Cab.Sauv. 5%

One of the grander châteaux, on the *côtes* among the very best, yet never one of the great names. Delicious, meaty wine that seems persistently underrated. Excellent in 2000.

Château Fonroque ☆☆

Owners: Ets. J.-P. Moueix. 18 hectares. Grapes: Merlot 85%, Cab.Fr. 15%. www.chateaufonroque.com

A relatively modest member of the impeccable Moueix stable. Fonroque is dark, firm wine of definite character that ages well.

Château Franc-Mayne ☆☆

Owner: Georgy Fourcroy. 7 hectares. Grapes: Merlot 90%, Cab.Sauv. 10%. www.chateau-francmayne.com

A serious little property on the western *côtes*, sold to Belgian wine merchant Fourcroy in 1996. He lowered yields and opted for ageing in all new oak, which tends to overwhelm the fruit.

Château Grand Mayne ☆☆☆

Owner: Jean-Pierre Nony. 19 hectares. Grapes: Merlot 76%, Cab.Fr. 13%, Cab.Sauv. 11%. www.chateau-grand-mayne.com

A well-placed property realizing its considerable potential for rich-tasting, serious claret. Michel Rolland is the consultant oenologist.

Château Grandes Murailles ☆☆

Owners: the Reiffers family. 2 hectares. Grapes: Merlot 70%, Cab. Fr. 30%

Wines from a tiny plot below the ruined wall of the thirteenth-century Dominican church, a well-known local landmark outside the town.

Château Grand-Pontet ☆☆

Owners: the Bécot and Pourquet families. 14 hectares. Grapes: Merlot 75%, Cab.Fr. 15%, Cab.Sauv. 10%

Next to Beau-Séjour Becot and, like it, revitalized since 1985. Showy wine.

Château Guadet-St-Julien ☆☆

Owner: Robert Lignac. 6 hectares. Grapes: Merlot 75%, Cab.Fr. 25%

Vineyard out of town to the north. Delicate wines with finesse.

Château Haut-Corbin ☆☆

Owner: Soc Haut-Corbin. 7 hectares. Grapes: Merlot 70%, Cab.Sauv. 20%, Cab.Fr. 10%

The least of the Corbins up near the Pomerol border, but improving in the late '90s.

Château Haut-Sarpe ☆☆

Owners: the Janoueix family. 12 hectares. Grapes: Merlot 70%, Cab.Fr. 30%. www.j-janoueix-bordeaux.com

The Janoueix family are merchants in Libourne with six small properties in Pomerol. Haut-Sarpe lies east of St-Emilion, and is one of several good properties making firm, earthy wine.

Château Laniote ☆

Owners: the de la Filolie family. 5 hectares. Grapes: Merlot 70%, Cab.Sauv. 20%, Cab.Fr. 10%

One of the many little properties so appreciated in Belgium that they are unknown elsewhere. Rather rustic wine. The estate includes the grotto where the monk St Emilion lived in the eighth century.

Château Larcis-Ducasse ☆☆–☆☆☆

Owner: Mme. H. Gratiot-Alphandery. 11 hectares. Grapes: Merlot 65%, Cab.Fr. 25%, Cab.Sauv. 10%

The best vineyard of St-Laurent-des-Combes, splendidly sited on the *côtes* just east of Château Pavie (*q.v.*). Elegant wine that needs patience before it shows its complexity. Exceptional in 2000. Changes in personnel in 2002 may signal a more fruit-driven wine in future.

Château Larmande ☆☆

Owner: Groupe d'Assurance la Mondiale. 25 hectares. Grapes: Merlot 65%, Cab.Fr. 30%, Cab.Sauv. 5%. www.chateau-larmande.com

Lovely wines in the 1980s ('83, '85, '86, and '88) made its reputation, which was then enhanced by new ownership in 1991. In the late 1990s, the wines seemed very tannic and extracted, but they may well become harmonious with time.

Château Laroque ☆☆

Owners: the Beaumartin family. 27 hectares. Grapes: Merlot 87%, Cab.Fr. 11%, Cab.Sauv. 2%. www.chateau-laroque.com

A substantial property on the St-Emilion *côtes* in St-Christophe. A reliable, medium-bodied wine.

Château Laroze ☆☆

Owner: Guy Meslin. 27 hectares. Grapes: Merlot 59%, Cab.Fr. 38%, Cab.Sauv. 3%

Lying low on the western *côtes* on sandy soil. Not one of the outstanding vineyards, but modern and well-managed, and capable of very good wine for four to five years' maturing.

Château Matras ☆–☆☆

Owner: Véronique Gaboriaud. 8 hectares. Grapes: Cab.Fr. 50%, Merlot 50%

Beautifully sited château at the foot of the western *côtes* next to Château l'Angélus (*q.v.*). Modest quality; drink young.

Château Moulin du Cadet ☆☆

Owner: Ets J.-P. Moueix. 5 hectares. Grapes: Merlot 90%, Cab.Fr. 10%

Impeccably made wine typical of the Moueix establishment. A combination of clay soil and a *côtes* situation gives solidity and sweetness.

Château Pavie-Decesse ☆☆☆

Owners: Gérard Perse. 9 hectares. Grapes: Merlot 90%, Cab.Fr. 10%

The junior partner of Château Pavie, from the flatter land at the top of the *côtes*. The estate was bought by Perse in 1997, and is now made in the same way as Pavie, with the same controversial results.

Château Pavie-Macquin ☆☆☆

Owners: the Corre-Macquin family. 15 hectares. Grapes: Merlot 70%, Cab.Fr. 30%

Organically farmed vineyard and fine winemaking by Nicolas Thienpont and Stéphane Derenoncourt. A sumptuous and highly concentrated wine, built for long ageing.

Château Petit-Faurie-de-Soutard ☆–☆☆

Owner: Mme. Françoise Capdemourlin. 8 hectares. Grapes: Merlot 60%, Cab.Fr. 30%, Cab.Sauv. 10%

Neighbour of the Cap-de-Mourlin. Readily confused with next-door Faurie-de-Souchard. Technically *côtes* wines, but like Château Soutard (of which it was once a part) harder to penetrate.

Château le Prieuré ☆

Owner: SCE Baronne Guichard. 5.5 hectares. Grapes: Merlot 60%, Cab.Fr. 30%, Cab.Sauv. 10%

On the eastern *côtes* in an ideal situation, but apparently ticking over at present.

Château Ripeau ☆☆

Owner: Mme. Françoise de Wilde. 15 hectares. Grapes: Merlot 60%, Cab.Fr. 30%, Cab.Sauv. 10%

A well-known *graves* château in the past, considered on a par with Château la Dominique (*q.v.*). Less prominent recently, but heading for a revival, with severely reduced yields in 2000.

Château St-Georges (Côte-Pavie) ☆–☆☆

Owner: Jacques Masson. 5.5 hectares. Grapes: Merlot 75%, Cab. Fr. 25%

An enviable spot between Châteaux Pavie and la Gaffelière. Fresh, medium-bodied wines that are worth seeking out.

Château la Serre ☆–☆☆

Owner: Luc d'Arfeuille. 7 hectares. Grapes: Merlot 80%, Cab.Fr. 20%

Just outside the town on the *côtes* to the east. Despite its surprisingly high proportion of Merlot, this lacked charm in the 1980s, but things seem to be looking up.

Château Soutard ☆☆–☆☆☆

Owners: the des Ligneris family. 27 hectares. Grapes: Merlot 65%, Cab.Fr. 35%

An important property on a rocky outcrop northeast of the town. Can be well-made, warm, and powerful wine. The great vintages are long-keeping classics. A problem with TCA caused by woodwork treatments in the cellar has been solved.

Château Tertre-Daugay ☆☆

Owner: Comte Léo de Malet-Roquefort. 18 hectares. Grapes: Merlot 60%, Cab.Fr. 40%. www.chateau-tertre-daugay.com

Spectacularly well-sited on the final promontory of the *côtes* west of Château Ausone, in disarray for some years, but since 1978 in the same hands as Château la Gaffelière and replanted. Some recent vintages have shown the true class of the property.

Château la Tour Figeac ☆☆–☆☆☆

Owner: Otto Rettenmaier. 15 hectares. Grapes: Merlot 60%, Cab.Fr. 40%

Formerly part of Château Figeac, now owned and run on biodynamic principles by a German, with the help of Stéphane Derenoncourt. This is a worthy wine, sleek and concentrated.

Château la Tour-du-Pin-Figeac ☆☆–☆☆☆

Owner: Jean-Michel Moueix. 9 hectares. Grapes: Merlot 70%, Cab.Fr. 30%

Powerful, pungent wines from a privileged situation among the great plateau vineyards.

Château la Tour-du-Pin-Figeac (Giraud-Bélivier) ☆–☆☆

Owner: GFA Giraud-Bélivier. 11 hectares. Grapes: Merlot 70%, Cab.Fr. 30%

A vineyard north of Figeac, beside Cheval Blanc, but not above average in quality.

Château Troplong-Mondot ☆☆☆

Owner: Christine Valette. 30 hectares. Grapes: Merlot 80%, Cab.Sauv. 10%, Cab.Fr. 10%

A famous vineyard on the crest of the *côtes* east of the town, above Château Pavie. Reliably good in the '80s and, since '88, powerfully concentrated, oaky wines. Enthusiastic following.

Château Villemaurine ☆☆

Owner: Robert Giraud. 76 hectares. Grapes: Merlot 70%. Cab.Sauv. 30%. www.robertgiraud.com

At the gates of the town, a côtes vineyard with more Cabernet Sauvignon than most; consequently less easy wine but worth waiting for. There are splendid cellars.

Château Yon-Figeac ☆☆

Owner: Bernard Germain. 25 hectares. Grapes: Merlot 80%, Cab.Fr. 20%. www.ygas.com

A former part of the Figeac domaine in the Graves. Not especially concentrated but enjoyable in the medium term. Aged in new 400-litre barrels.

St-Emilion Grands Crus & Other Château

The quality of such a number of châteaux obviously varies very widely. Only those with particularly high and consistent standards are listed, together with some of the *vins de garage* that became fashionable in the mid-1990s.

Château L'Archange ☆☆–☆☆☆

Owner: Pascal Chatonnet

A property revived by Chatonnet and, since 2000, producing acclaimed wine.

Château Barde-Haute ☆☆

Owner: Sylviane Garcin-Cathiard. 17 hectares

Property next to Château Troplong-Mondot. Acquired in 2000 by the owner of Château Haut-Bergey in the Graves. Sweet oak and spice in 2000.

Château Bellefont-Belcier ☆☆–☆☆☆

Owner: Jean Labusquière. 13 hectares

Medium-bodied wine with a good dose of oak, made by Louis Mitjavile.

Château Cardinal Villemaurine ☆–☆☆

Owner: Jean-Francois Carrille. 7 hectares

Toasty wine for medium-term drinking.

Château Carteau-Côtes-Daugay ☆☆
Owner: Jacques Bertrand. 16 hectares
A traditional wine, solid and benefiting from bottle-age.

Clos de l'Oratoire ☆☆–☆☆☆
Owner: Stephan von Neipperg. 10 hectares. www.neipperg.com
Acquired by the owner of Château Canon-La-Gaffelière in 1991, and now making dark, dense, chocolatey wines. A *côtes* property that has grown in size recently, it is now making solid, unassuming wines in mainstream St-Emilion style.

Château Cormeil-Figeac ☆–☆☆
Owners: the Moreaud family. 10 hectares
Vineyard on sandy soil west of the town. Quite rustic wine.

Château Faugères ☆☆
Owner: Corinne Guisez. 55 hectares.
www.chateau-faugeres.com
A complex property, energetically run by Mme. Guisez, since about half of it lies within the Côte de Castillon. A small sector of the St-Emilion vineyard is used to make the ultra-concentrated "Péby-Faugères". The regular St-Emilion is very good value.

Château de Ferrand ☆–☆☆
Owners: the Bich family. 28 hectares
A fine property – the wine is more modest, though well made.

Château Fombrauge ☆☆–☆☆☆
Owner: Bernard Magrez. 52 hectares. www.fombrauge.com
Fombrauge is a large property that changed hands in 1999. Quality was previously humdrum, but Magrez and Michel Rolland have invested heavily, with some very impressive results. A tiny amount of *garage* wine, "Magrez-Fombrauge", is now produced, although at a very high price.

La Gomerie ☆☆–☆☆☆
Owner: Gérard and Dominique Bécot. 2.5 hectares
A no-holds-barred *garage* wine produced since '95 by the owners of Château Beau-Séjour-Bécot. Voluptuous, but low in acidity.

Château Grand-Corbin-Despagne ☆☆
Owner: Francois Despagne. 26 hectares.
www.grand-corbin-despagne.com
Conscientious property aiming for reinstatement as *cru classé*.

Château Haut Brisson ☆☆
9 hectares
Under new ownership; the wine is becoming more fleshy and concentrated.

Château Monbousquet ☆☆–☆☆☆
Owner: Gérard Perse. 31 hectares
Everyone acknowledges that most of the vineyard is on mediocre land near the river, but after Gérard Perse bought the property in '93, quality soared, thanks in large part to advice from Michel Rolland and very low yields.

La Mondotte ☆☆☆
Owner: Stephan von Neipperg. 4.5 hectares.
www.neipperg.com
Neipperg was refused permission by INAO to incorporate these few hectares of well-located vines into Château Canon la Gaffelière, so in '96 he created a kind of *garage* wine from its production. Inky, voluptuous wines, perhaps exaggerated, but fetching very high prices.

Château Moulin St-Georges ☆☆–☆☆☆
Owner: Alain Vauthier. 8 hectares
Excellent new-oaked wines from a small property under the same ownership as Château Ausone (*q.v.*).

Château Quinault ☆☆
Owner: Dr. Alain Raynaud. 15 hectares.
www.chateau-quinault.com
Fifty-year-old vines on unremarkable alluvial soil. Made in the same way as a *garage* wine for maximum concentration.

Château Rochebelle ☆☆–☆☆☆
Owner: Philippe Faniest. 3 hectares
A rising star since the superb '98.

Château Rol Valentin ☆☆–☆☆☆
Owner: Eric Prissette. 4 hectares
Small property near Cheval Blanc, vinified by Stéphane Derenoncourt with intense attention to detail. Owes its notoriety both to its owner (a famous footballer) and to its undoubted quality.

Château Sansonnet ☆☆
Owner: François d'Aulan. 7.5 hectares
An estate near Château Trottevieille (*q.v.*), bought by industrialist D'Aulan in '99.

Château Tertre-Rôteboeuf ☆☆☆
Owner: François Mitjaville. 5 hectares
As a pioneer of very late harvesting, Mitjaville was, arguably, the first *garagiste*.

Château Teyssier ☆–☆☆☆
Owner: Jonathan Maltus. 17 hectares. www.teyssier.fr

The Jurade de St-Emilion

The ceremonial and promotional organization of St-Emilion is probably the oldest in France. The Jurade de St-Emilion was formally instituted by King John of England and France in 1199, as the body of elders to govern the little city and its district – a dignity granted to few regions at the time. Nobody seriously pretends that the modern institution is a linear descendant, but its impressive processions to Mass in the great parish church and to its own candle-lit solemnities in the cloisters cut out of the solid limestone in the centre of the town, are full of dignity as well as good humour.

The Jurade also played an important role in the control of quality and administration of the various categories of châteaux. Its annual tastings give a boost to St-Emilion quality in a similar way to the *tastevinage* undertaken by the Chevaliers de Tastevin in Burgundy. On a memorable autumn weekend in 1981, the Jurade visited the great medieval city of York, arriving by river in a state barge, to process to the Minster for a service conducted by the archbishop, and to dine in the splendour of Castle Howard. They do these things with style.

On the plain near Vignonet, Teyssier makes an easy-drinking wine of no pretensions. Maltus has parcels elsewhere in St-Emilion, from which he produces two very expensive and admired wines: the 90% Merlot "La Forge" and the 75% Cabernet Franc "Le Dôme".

Château Valandraud ☆☆☆
Owner: Jean-Luc Thunevin. 8 hectares. www.thunevin.com
The archetypal *garage* wine: some undistinguished parcels (and some on much better soil) cropped very low and vinified for maximum sumptuousness. But overpriced.

Château Vieux-Sarpe ☆☆
Owners: the Janoueix family. 7 hectares.
www.j-janoueix-bordeaux.com
Wines with charm rather than weight.

The St-Emilion Satellites
Apart from the five saintly villages (St-Emilion, St-Laurent, St-Christophe, St-Etienne, and St-Hippolyte) that are considered part of the appellation St-Emilion, four more to the north and east are granted the privilege of adding St-Emilion to their names. They are known as the satellites.

They lie just north of the little River Barbanne, which forms the northern boundary of glory and renown. Their citizens argue that the formation of the valley gives two of them, St-Georges (183 hectares) and Montagne (1,430 hectares), a better situation than some of St-Emilion.

Be that as it may, those two, plus Puisseguin (740 hectares) and Lussac (1,440 hectares), are honoured. Proprietors in St-Georges may call their wines Montagne St-Emilion if they wish. St-Georges has a splendid château that gives it pride in its own name. Its wine is indeed like St-Emilion and can be made almost equally meaty and long-lived.

More growers, however, prefer using a good deal of Merlot and making softer (still strong) wine that can be delicious in two or three years. Unfortunately, many properties are still producing decidedly rustic wines.

Leading Puisseguin-St-Emilion Châteaux

Château Bel-Air ☆–☆☆
Owners: Adoue Frères. 42 hectares
A large property, with a special "Cuvée de Bacchus" with more richness and power.

Château Branda ☆☆–☆☆☆
Owners: Arnaud Delaire and Yves Blanc. 6 hectares
Oaky and ultra-concentrated.

Château Durand-Laplagne ☆–☆☆
Owner: J. Bessou. 14 hectares
The best wine here is the "Cuvée Sélection".

Château Guibeau la Fourvieille ☆–☆☆
Owner: Henri Bourlon. 10 hectares
Almost pure Merlot, with soft tannins.

Château des Laurets ☆☆
Owner: SA Château des Laurets. 70 hectares
Rich yet surprisingly elegant wines.

Château la Mauriane ☆☆
Owner: Josette Taix. 3.5 hectares
Vin de garage. Careful selection has brought the wine to a high standard: supple and generous.

Château Soleil ☆
Owner: Jean Soleil. 20 hectares
Rounded, ripe wines with a touch of oak.

Leading Lussac-St-Emilion Châteaux

Château de Barbe Blanche ☆–☆☆
Owner: André Lurton. 28 hectares
The regular bottling is fresh and elegant, the "Cuvée Henri IV" (renamed "Réserve" from 2000) shows the influence of new oak.

Bel-Air ☆☆
Owner. Jean-Noel Roi. 21 hectares
Half the wine is aged in oak, but in 1998 Roi launched his "Cuvée Jean-Gabriel", aged solely in new barriques.

Château du Courlat ☆☆
Owner: Pierre Bourotte. 17 hectares
A well structured wine that can be drunk young or aged five years. "Cuvée Jean-Baptiste" is from older vines and is more dense.

Château Lyonnat ☆
Owners: the Milhade family. 45 hectares
Large property, of which 80% is planted with Merlot.

Château Mayne-Blanc ☆–☆☆
Owner: Jean Boncheau. 23 hectares
"Cuvée Tradition" is aged in used barrels, "Cuvée St Vincent" (from old vines) in mostly new barriques.

Château du Moulin Noir ☆
Owners: the Tessandier family. 15 hectares
A well-equipped property making good, lightly oaked wines.

Château Tour de Grenet ☆
Owners: the Brunot family. 33 hectares
Light, charming wine.

Leading Montagne-St-Emilion Châteaux

Château Beauséjour ☆☆
Owner: Bernard Germain. 14 hectares
The "Clos de l'Eglise" is a modern-style, Merlot-dominated wine from old vines.

Château Faizeau ☆☆
Owner: Chantal Lebreton. 10 hectares
Aged in 50% new oak, this is a ripe, plummy wine. An abundance of old Merlot vines and the counsel of Michel Rolland keep quality high.

Maison Blanche ☆–☆☆
Owner: Nicolas Despagne. 32 hectares
Most of the wine is aged in older barrels, but "Cuvée Louis Rapin" is aged in new oak.

Château Montaiguillon ☆–☆☆
Owner: Roger Amart. 28 hectares
A well-known property making good, spicy wines for medium-term drinking.

Château Roudier ☆
Owner: Jacques Capdemourlin. 30 hectares
Reliable wine from the owner of two leading properties.

Château Teyssier ☆
Owners: the Durand Teyssier family. 8 hectares
Managed by the négociant CVBG. Plenty of new oak is used here, but the wine remains essentially rustic.

Vieux-Château St-André ☆☆
Owner: Jean-Claude Berrouet. 10 hectares
The personal property of the winemaker at Pétrus. Fruity, well-balanced wines.

Leading St-Georges-St-Emilion Châteaux

Château Belair ☆☆
Owner: Nadine Pocci-le Menn. 4 hectares
Small but highly regarded, mostly planted with Merlot.

Château Griffe de Cap d'Or
A Belgian-owned property, run by Jean-Luc Thunevin, who produces a dense *vin de garage* here.

Château St Georges ☆☆–☆☆☆
Owners: the Desbois family. 45 hectares.
www.chateau-saint-georges.com
The eighteenth century mansion here is one of the show places of the region. The estate produces wine to match: elegant and imposing.

Pomerol

If there are doubters (and there are) about the differences that different soils make to wine, they should study Pomerol. In this little area, flanked by the huge spread of St-Emilion like a market-garden to Libourne on the north bank of the Dordogne, there are wines as potent and majestic as any in France, cheek by jowl with wines of wispy, fleeting fruitiness and charm – and dull ones, too.

The soil grades from shingly sand around the town of Libourne through increasingly heavy stages to a climactic plateau, where the clay subsoil is very near the surface. A yard down, the clay is near-solid and packed with nuggets of iron. This, at the giddy height of fifteen metres (fifty feet) above its surroundings, is in every sense the summit of Pomerol.

Despite its (recent) international reknown, Pomerol will always be an abstruse, *recherché* corner of the wine world. Its whole vineyard area is no larger than St-Julien, the smallest of the great communes of the Médoc. Perhaps half of this (as against two-thirds of St-Julien) is of truly distinctive, classed-growth standard.

The size of the properties is correspondingly small. There are 126 members of the growers' syndicate, sharing 800 hectares: six hectares each on average. The biggest estate is fifty hectares. The total annual production is about 358,000 cases entitled to the appellation. There is no cooperative; small growers tend to make their wine and sell it directly to consumers all over France, and particularly to Belgium.

It is only 100 years since the name of Pomerol was first heard outside its immediate area, yet tradition has already provided it with a clear identity. Its best soil is clay; therefore cold. The early ripening Merlot does better than the later Cabernet, and of the Cabernets, the Franc (alias Bouchet) rather than the Sauvignon. The mellow, brambly Merlot and the lively, raspberryish Bouchet pick up the iron from the clay, are matured in fragrant oak – and *voilà*, you have a greatly over-simplified recipe for Pomerol. Where does it get its singular texture of velvet, its chewy flesh, its smell of ripe plums and even cream, and even honey? Wherever, it was more than an edict from the bureaucracy that fixes appellations.

Authorities put Pomerol between St-Emilion and the Médoc in style. To me, it is closer to St-Emilion: broader, more savoury, and with less "nerve" than Médocs of similar value, maturing in five years as much as Médocs do in ten – hence tending to overlay them at tastings, as California wines do French. Great Pomerols, however, show no sign of being short-lived.

No official classification of Pomerol has ever been made. Professor Roger published a personal one in 1960, in *The Wines of Bordeaux*, dividing sixty-three châteaux into four ranks, with Château Pétrus on its own, Yquem-like, at the head.

Pomerol First Growth

Château Pétrus ☆☆☆☆
Owner: Ets J.-P.Moueix. 11 hectares. Grapes: Merlot 95%, Cab.Fr. 5%
See Pétrus, Pomerol's First Growth, page 79.

Leading Pomerol Châteaux

Château Beauregard ☆☆☆
Owner: Credit Foncier de France. 17 hectares. Grapes: Merlot 65%, Cab.Fr. 35%. www.chateau-beauregard.com
In contrast to most of the modest châteaux of Pomerol, the seventeenth-century Château Beauregard is so desirable that

Mrs Daniel Guggenheim had it copied stone for stone on Long Island. Richer and fruitier than before, under new ownership since 1991. Opulent and boldly flavoured in 2000.

Château Bonalgue ☆☆–☆☆☆
Owner: Pierre Bourotte. 6.5 hectares. Grapes: Merlot 80%, Cab.Fr. 20%

Full-bodied wines of good consistency, if not among the most elegant of Pomerol.

Château le Bon-Pasteur ☆☆☆
Owner: Michel Rolland. 7 hectares. Grapes: Merlot 90%, Cab.Fr. 10%

Michel Rolland not only makes his own richly sensuous Pomerol, but is also a valuable consultant partly responsible for a new era of more luscious Pomerols and, more recently, Médocs, too.

Château Bourgneuf-Vayron ☆☆–☆☆☆
Owners: the Vayron family. 9 hectares. Grapes: Merlot 90%, Cab.Fr. 10%

Within the heart of Pomerol, lying between Trotanoy and Latour. Potent, plummy wine; not the most stylish, although there are signs of more finesse and harmony in the later 1990s.

Château la Cabanne ☆☆
Owner: Jean-Pierre Estager. 10 hectares. Grapes: Merlot 92%, Cab.Fr. 8%

The name means "the hut" or the "shanty", which seems excessively modest for an estate situated in the heart of Pomerol with Trotanoy as a neighbour. The soil gravel and clay; the wine is not remarkable. Recently modernized.

Château le Caillou ☆–☆☆
Owner: André Giraud. 7 hectares

Grown on iron-impregnated soils of gravel and sand, this is a tannic wine with grip rather than charm.

Château Cantelauze ☆☆–☆☆☆
Owner: Jean-Noel Boidron. 1 hectare. Grapes: Merlot 90%, Cab.Fr. 10%

Tiny vineyard, tiny production, but what there is of Cantelauze is elegant and balanced.

Château Certan de May ☆☆
Owner: Mme. Barreau-Bader. 5 hectares. Grapes: Merlot 70%, Cab.Fr. 25%, Cab.Sauv. 5%

Formerly called Château Certan. Perfectly sited next to Vieux-Château-Certan and Pétrus (*qq.v.*); but verging more towards Pétrus in richness and concentration. Recent vintages have been inconsistent and lacking in fruit.

Château Certan-Giraud
See Hosanna.

Château Clinet ☆☆☆
Owner: Jean-Marie Laborde. 9 hectares. Grapes: Merlot 80%, Cab.Sauv. 10%, Cab.Franc 10%

Close to Pétrus and Lafleur. Formerly a lean, almost Médoc-style wine, but recently much fatter. Late harvesting gives the wines their richness and power, perhaps at the expense of some finesse.

Bordeaux Trade Measures

For official and statistical purposes, all French wine production is measured in hectolitres, but each region has its traditional measures for maturing and selling its wine. In Bordeaux, the measure is the *tonneau*, a notional container since such big barrels are no longer made.

A tonneau consists of four barriques – the barrels used at the châteaux, and still sometimes for shipping. A barrique *bordelaise* must by law contain 225 litres, which makes twenty-five cases of a dozen 75 cl. bottles each. The *tonneau* is therefore a simple and memorable measure: 100 cases of wine.

Château la Conseillante ☆☆☆
Owner: Héritiers Louis Nicolas. 12 hectares. Grapes: Merlot 80%, Cab.Fr. 20%

The splendid silver-on-white label is designed around an "N" for the family that has owned the château for more than a century. Coincidentally, London's Café Royal has the same motif for the same reason. La Conseillante lies between Pétrus and Cheval Blanc, but makes a more delicate, high-pitched wine – sometimes as fine and fragrant as any Pomerol, but less plummy and fat. Recent vintages are first-class.

Château la Croix ☆–☆☆
Owner: J. Janoueix. 10 hectares. Grapes: Merlot 60%, Cab.Sauv. 20%, Cab.Fr. 20%. www.j-janoueix.bordeaux.com

Another 2.5 hectares is la Croix-Toulifaut. These crosses are in the south of the commune on relatively light soil with a high iron content, not to be confused with la Croix-de-Gay on the northern edge. Sturdy, generous wine not noted for great finesse but repaying bottle age. The same firm owns the 3.5-hectare Château la Croix-St-Georges.

Château la Croix-du-Casse ☆☆
Owners: the Audy family. 9 hectares. Grapes: Merlot 70%, Cab.Fr. 30%. www.chateau-lacroixducasse.com

Grown on light soils, this is a ripe fleshy wine, made until his death in 2001 by Jean-Michel Arcaute of Château Clinet.

Château la Croix-de-Gay ☆☆–☆☆☆
Owners: the Raynaud family. 10 hectares. Grapes: Merlot 90%, Cab.Sauv. 5%, Cab.Fr. 5%

A well-run vineyard on the gravelly clay sloping north down to the River Barbanne. As in so many Pomerol properties, its wines are being made with more care for a more demanding market. There is (since 1982) a costly 100% Merlot *cuvée prestige* "Fleur du Gay", that is the best part (about 1,200 cases) of the crop. The regular wine suffers, it seems, as a consequence.

Château du Domaine de l'Eglise ☆–☆☆
Owners: the Castéja and Preben-Hansen families. 7 hectares. Grapes: Merlot 90%, Cab.Fr. 10%

Medium-bodied wine with a marked flavour of oak.

Château L'Eglise-Clinet ☆☆☆–☆☆☆☆
Owner: Denis Durantou. 5.5 hectares. Grapes: Merlot 80%, Cab.Fr. 20%. www.eglise-clinet.com

Generally rated above Clinet; a stouter production with tannin, even brawn. Recently reaching higher: luscious deep wines of top class. Second label "La Petite Eglise" is from young vines, some from other properties.

Château l'Enclos ☆☆–☆☆☆
Owner: Société Civile du Château L'Enclos. 10 hectares. Grapes: Merlot 82%, Cab.Fr. 17%, Malbec 1%
With Clos René, one of the most respected châteaux of the western half of Pomerol, with the sort of deeply fruity and rewarding wine that impresses you while young, but needs at least seven or eight years in bottle to do it justice.

Château l'Evangile ☆☆☆
Owners: Dom. Baron de Rothschild. 14 hectares. Grapes: Merlot 78%, Cab.Fr. 22%. www.lafite.com
In the top ten of Pomerol for quality and size. At its best (*e.g.* '90, '95, '98) a voluptuous, concentrated wine for a long life. The (Lafite) Rothschilds bought a majority share in 1990. Its situation between Pétrus and Cheval Blanc is propitious.

Château Feytit-Clinet ☆☆
Owners: the Domergue family. 7 hectares. Grapes: Merlot 85%, Cab.Fr. 15%
I have had some wonderful old wines from this little château,

across the road from the illustrious Château Latour à Pomerol (*q.v.*). Under Moueix management since '66.

Château la Fleur-Gazin ☆☆
Owner: Mme. Delfour Borderie. 9 hectares. Grapes: Merlot 80%, Cab.Fr. 20%
Northern neighbour of Château Gazin, making elegant, smooth, well-bred wine. The property is managed and the wine vinified by J.-P. Moueix.

Château la Fleur-Pétrus ☆☆☆
Owner: Ets J.-P. Moueix. 7 hectares. Grapes: Merlot 85%, Cab.Fr. 15%
The third-best Moueix Pomerol – which is high praise indeed. The vineyard is more gravelly than Pétrus and Trotanoy, the wine less fat and fleshy with more obvious tannin at first, poised, taut, asking to be aged. Enlarged in 1985 to take in part of its neighbour, le Gay, planted with very old vines.

Château Franc-Maillet ☆☆
Owner: G. Arpin. 5 hectares. Grapes: Merlot 80%, Cab.Fr. 20%
Owned by the Arpin family since 1919, this is a solid, tannic wine. The "Cuvée Jean-Baptiste" receives more oak-ageing.

Château Pétrus – Pomerol's First Growth

As Château Yquem is to Sauternes, so Château Pétrus is to Pomerol; the perfect model of the region and its aspirations. Like its region, Pétrus is a miniature; there are 4,000 cases in a good year, and often less. Among First Growths it is unique in that it has never been officially classified, and that its emergence as a wine worth as much or more than any other red Bordeaux only started in 1945. The Loubat family were the promoters of its quality and status. Since 1961 it was owned jointly by Madame Loubat's niece, Madame Lacoste, and Jean-Pierre Moueix, until the house of Moueix became the majority owner. Moueix died in 2003; his son Christian now holds centre stage. The modest

Moueix offices and vast *chais* on the Libourne waterfront have a position of prestige without an exact equivalent anywhere in France. The resident oenologist, Jean-Claude Berrouet, has technical control of a score of the best properties both in St-Emilion and Pomerol.

Pétrus is the flagship. Outwardly it is a modest little place. The *cuvier* is a cramped space between batteries of narrow concrete vats. The *chais*, recently rebuilt, are more spacious, but by no means grand.

The magic lies in the soil. No golf course or wicket is more meticulously tended. When one section of ancient vines (the average age is forty years) was being replaced I was astonished to see the shallow topsoil bulldozed aside from the whole patch and the subsoil being carefully graded to an almost imperceptible slope to give a shade more drainage. It was a remarkable opportunity to see how uninviting this famous clay is.

The principle of winemaking at Pétrus is perfect ripeness, then ruthless selection. If the October sun is kind, the Merlot is left to cook in it. It is never picked before lunch, to avoid diluting the juice with dew. The crop is small, the new wine so dark and concentrated that fresh-sawn oak, for all its powerful smell, seems to make no impression on it. At a year old the wine smells of blackcurrant. At two, a note of tobacco edges in. But any such exact reference is a misleading simplification. Why Pétrus (or any great wine) commands attention is by its almost architectural sense of structure; of counterpoised weights and matched stresses. How can there be such tannin and yet such tenderness?

Because Pétrus is fat, fleshy, not rigorous and penetrating like a Médoc but dense in texture like a Napa Cabernet, it appears to be "ready" in ten years or less. Cigar smokers probably should (and anyway do) drink it while it is in full vigour. To my mind it takes longer to become claret. In a sense the great vintages never do.

Château le Gay ☆☆–☆☆☆
Owners: Jacques and Sylvie Guinadeau. 9 hectares. Grapes: Merlot 80%, Cab.Fr. 20%
See Château Lafleur

Château Gazin ☆☆☆
Owner: Nicolas de Bailliencourt. 24 hectares. Grapes: Merlot 90%, Cab.Fr. 3%, Cab.Sauv. 7%. www.chateau-gazin.com
One of the biggest Pomerol properties, despite selling a section to its neighbour, Château Pétrus, in 1970. The quality record was uneven; at best a fittingly fruity, concentrated wine, but usually a shade full. Then, in 1987, machine-harvesting was abandoned and the grapes began to be picked at higher ripeness levels. The '89 seemed to mark a turning point toward an excellent long-term wine, and the nineties have been excitingly good. Second label is "Château l'Hospitalet".

Château Gombaude-Guillot ☆☆
Owners: the Laval family. 7 hectares. Grapes: Merlot 68%, Cab.Fr. 30%, Malbec 2%
An organically cultivated property (listed by Prof. Roger as a First Growth) right in the centre near the church. A leaner style than most, but the wine is harmonious and ages well.

Château la Grave (Trigant de Boisset) ☆☆–☆☆☆
Owner: Ets J.-P. Moueix. 9 hectares. Grapes: Merlot 89%, Cab.Fr. 11%
A fabulous wine in the 1920s, but the Moueix family acquired some of the best parcels for la Fleur Pétrus and other properties. Today, not the most full-bodied Pomerol, but particularly well balanced and stylish with tannin to encourage long development. The soil here is graves, not clay – hence finesse rather than flesh.

Château Guillot ☆☆–☆☆☆
Owner: GFA Luquot Frères. 4.7 hectares. Grapes: Merlot 70%, Cab.Fr. 30%
Usually less marked by new oak than neighbours such as Clinet, but richly fruity in years like '85, '89, and '90. After an erratic patch, quality has been excellent in the late 1990s.

Hosanna ☆☆☆
Owner: Ets J.-P. Moueix. Grapes: Merlot 80%, Cab.Fr. 20%
This is part of the former Château Certan-Giraud, which Moueix bought in 1999, restructured, and renamed. Silky wine that gains intensity from the old Cabernet Franc vines.

Château Lafleur ☆☆☆–☆☆☆☆
Owners: Jacques and Sylvie Guinadeau. 4.5 hectares. Grapes: Merlot 50%, Cab.Fr. 50%
The two adjacent properties are united in the statistics, but distinct in quality. Lafleur (next to la Fleur-Pétrus *q.v.*) is a model of balance, body with finesse, and considerable style. One the most massive wines of Pomerol, it ages superbly. Le Gay (seven hectares, across the road) is a shade plainer and less potent, needing a good eight years' ageing. Both are carefully nurtured by their owner, and are among the most consistently good Pomerols. Second wine is "Les Pensées de Lafleur".

Château Lafleur du Roy ☆–☆☆
Owner: Yvon Dubost. 4 hectares. Grapes: Merlot 80%, Cab.Fr. 10%, Cab.Sauv. 10%
Little property on the outskirts of Libourne, near Château Plince. A minor wine with a good name.

Château Lagrange ☆☆
Owner: Ets J.-P. Moueix. 8 hectares. Grapes: Merlot 95%, Cab.Fr. 5%
Another Moueix property in the Pétrus group on the plateau. Less spectacularly flavoursome than some of its neighbours, but has been good recently.

Château Latour à Pomerol ☆☆☆
Owner: Mme. Lacoste-Loubat. 8 hectares. Grapes: Merlot 90%, Cab.Fr. 10%
The property is run by the house of Moueix for one of the family who once owned a share of Pétrus. It shows a fuller, fruitier style than la Fleur-Pétrus: more fat, less sinew – words can be very misleading. Paradoxically, it is a *graves* wine, from westwards of the fat band of clay. Very long-lived.

Château Mazeyres ☆☆
Owner: Société Générale. 20 hectares. Grapes: Merlot 80%, Cab.Fr. 20%. www.mazeyres.com
Located close to Libourne, this large property is managed by Alain Moueix. The sandy, gravelly soils give wines of elegance rather than power.

Château Montviel ☆☆
Owner: Catherine Peré-Vergé. 5 hectares. Grapes: Merlot 80%, Cab.Fr. 20%
A modest wine, but well-made and consistently pleasurable. For medium-term drinking.

Château Moulinet ☆–☆☆
Owner: Nathalie and Marie-José Moueix. 18 hectares. Grapes: Merlot 60%, Cab. Sauv 30%, Cab.Fr. 10%
An isolated estate on the northern edge of Pomerol where both the soil and the wine are lighter; the wine is stylish notwithstanding.

Château Nenin ☆–☆☆☆
Owner: Jean-Hubert Delon. 34 hectares. Grapes: Merlot 70%, Cab.Fr. 30%
One of the biggest properties, lying between the great Châteaux Trotanoy and la Pointe (*qq.v.*), but lacklustre for many years. The Delons of Château Léoville-Las-Cases bought Château Nenin in 1997 and restored the neglected vineyards. Quality will surely rise, but patience is required.

Château Petit-Village ☆☆☆
Owner: AXA Millésimes. 11 hectares. Grapes: Merlot 80%, Cab.Sauv. 10%, Cab.Fr. 10%. www.petit-village.com
Uppermost Pomerol from the Cheval-Blanc zone. In 2002, AXA Millésimes agreed to sell the property to Gérard Perse of Château Pavie, but the deal fell through. Nonetheless, changes in ownership could be imminent. Fine, powerful wine in 1998 and 2000, but the style may change should the estate be sold.

Château le Pin ☆☆☆
Owners: the Thienpont family. 2.3 hectares. Grapes: Merlot 100%

The Thienponts bought this tiny property on top of the Pomerol plateau next to Certan de May in 1979. Their aim was to make a wine to rival Pétrus. They have achieved superb results, with the '82 being perhaps the top wine of the vintage and recent vintages selling (mainly in Asia) for prices to make you blanch. Sumptuous, mocha-tinged wine, but its capacity to age has been called into question.

Château Plince ☆☆
Owners: the Moreau family. 10 hectares. Grapes: Merlot 75%, Cab.Fr. 20%, Cab.Sauv. 5%
The same owner as at Clos L'Eglise, producing a more supple, fruity wine on sandier soil.

Château la Pointe ☆☆–☆☆☆
Owner: Bernard d'Arfeuille. 25 hectares. Grapes: Merlot 80%, Cab.Fr. 20%
Sister château of la Serre in St-Emilion, and big enough to be widely known. The vineyard is on the doorstep of Libourne, in gravel and sand over the famous iron-bearing clay. Much improved throughout the 1990s.

Château Rouget ☆☆–☆☆☆
Owners: Jean-Pierre Labruyère. 17.5 hectares. Grapes: Merlot 85%, Cab.Fr. 15%
I cast envious eyes on Château Rouget each time I pass; it has the prettiest situation in Pomerol in a grove of trees leading down to the River Barbanne. Ideas here are conservative; the wine was tough by modern standards, but has gained in richness and texture in the later 1990s.

Château de Sales ☆–☆☆
Owner: Bruno de Lambert. 48 hectares. Grapes: Merlot 70%, Cab.Fr. 15%, Cab.Sauv. 15%
The only noble château of Pomerol, remote down long avenues to the northwest, then rather disconcertingly having the railway line running right through the garden. The big vineyard is beautifully run and the wine increasingly well-made, yet without the concentration and sheer personality of the great Pomerols.

Château du Tailhas ☆☆
Owners: Nebout & Fils. 11 hectares. Grapes: Merlot 80%, Cab.Fr. 10%, Cab.Sauv. 10%
This is the southernmost Pomerol vineyard, a stone's throw from the edge of the sandy riverside area of St-Emilion. It still has Pomerol's iron-rich clay subsoil, and consequently has a dense, if somewhat rustic, character – which is very popular in Belgium.

Château Taillefer ☆☆–☆☆☆
Owner: Bernard Moueix. 10 hectares. Grapes: Merlot 80%, Cab.Fr. 20%
Owned by the Moueix family since 1923. Unremarkable for many years, Taillefer is, since the later 1990s, showing much more finesse.

Château Trotanoy ☆☆☆–☆☆☆☆
Owner: Ets J.-P. Moueix. 7.5 hectares. Grapes: Merlot 90%, Cab.Fr. 10%
Generally allowed to be the runner-up to Château Pétrus, made by the same hands to the same Rolls-Royce standards. The little vineyard is on the western slope (such as it is) of the central plateau. The vines are old, the yield low, the darkly concentrated wine matured in new barriques (which lend it a near-Médoc smell in youth). For ten years or more the best vintages have a thick, almost California-Cabernet texture in your mouth. Tannin and iron show through the velvet glove. The '71, '79, '76 '82, '89, '90, '95, and '98 are among the best recent vintages.

Vieux-Château-Certan ☆☆☆–☆☆☆☆
Owners: the Thienpont family. 13.5 hectares. Grapes: Merlot 60%, Cab.Fr. 30%, Cab.Sauv.10%. www.vieux-chateau-certan.com
The first great name of Pomerol, though overtaken at a canter by Pétrus in the last thirty or forty years. The style is quite different: drier and less fleshy but balanced in a Médoc or Graves manner. At early tastings, substance can seem to be lacking, to emerge triumphantly later. The '45 was unforgettable in 1980. The handsome old château lies halfway between Pétrus and Cheval Blanc. Its Belgian owners take intense pride in its unique personality. '85, '89, '90, '98, and 2000 are recent triumphs.

Château Vray-Croix-de-Gay ☆–☆☆
Owner: SCE Baronne Guichard. 3.6 hectares. Grapes: Merlot 90%, Cab.Fr. 10%
The name means "the real Croix-de-Gay", implying that the neighbours pinched the name. Jockeying for position seems appropriate here on the northern rim of the precious plateau. Good easygoing Pomerol, but I have no record of very notable bottles.

Clos du Clocher ☆☆
Owners: the Audy family. 4 hectares. Grapes: Merlot 80%, Cab.Fr. 20%
Central vineyard next to the Certans, making well-balanced, middle-weight wine with plenty of flavour.

Clos L'Eglise ☆☆☆
Owner: Sylviane Garcin-Cathiard. 6 hectares. Grapes: Merlot 60%, Cab.Fr. 40%
A superb little vineyard located on the north rim of the plateau, bought in 1997 as part of a shopping spree that took in estates in the Graves and St-Emilion. Old Clos l'Eglise vintages were backward, long-lived wines. The new style is very concentrated, lush, and oaky.

Clos René ☆☆–☆☆☆
Owners: Garde and Lasserre families. 12 hectares. Grapes: Merlot 70%, Cab.Fr. 20%, Malbec 10%
Unpretentious and on the unfashionable (western) side of the commune, yet unmistakably serious Pomerol. The style of wine became lusher in the '80s.

Lalande-de-Pomerol
On the northern boundary of Pomerol is the little river of Barbanne. The two communes on its other bank, Lalande and Néac, share the right to the name Lalande-de-Pomerol for red wine which, at its best, is certainly of junior Pomerol class. Traditionally, they have grown more of the Malbec (or Pressac), a difficult grape, which is now going out of fashion. But the gravel-over-clay in parts is good, and some

châteaux have high reputations. Altogether there are 1,120 hectares of vines; 840 more than Pomerol. Some 195 growers (without a cooperative) make an average total of 600,000 cases.

Leading Lalande-de-Pomerol Châteaux

Château des Annereaux ☆☆
Lalande-de-Pomerol. Owners: the Milhade family. 20 hectares
Firm wines with black-fruits overtones.

Château de Bel-Air ☆–☆☆
Lalande-de-Pomerol. Owner: Jean-Pierre Musset. 16 hectares
This is fairly tannic wine that requires a few years ageing to become harmonious.

Château Belles-Graves ☆–☆☆
Néac. Owners: the Theallet family. 16 hectares.
www.belles-graves.com
Plump, oaky wine that gives immediate pleasure.

Château Bertineau St-Vincent ☆☆
Néac. Owner: M. Rolland. 6 hectares
Elegant wines that are vinified at Michel Rolland's main property at Château le Bon-Pasteur in Pomerol (*q.v.*).

Château la Croix-St-André ☆☆
Néac. Owners: the Carayon family. 17 hectares
Full-bodied wine from a popular property.

Château la Fleur de Boüard ☆☆–☆☆☆
Néac. Owner: Hubert de Boüard de Laforest. 17 hectares.
www.lafleurdebouard.com
De Boüard, of Château L'Angélus, bought this property in 1998 and gave it its present name. Rich, dark wine that sets new standards for the appellation.

Château Garraud ☆☆
Néac. Owner: Jean-Marc Nony. 37 hectares
Low yields and serious winemaking have ensured a high standard here for some years.

Château Grand Ormeau ☆☆–☆☆☆
Lalande-de-Pomerol. Owner: Jean-Claude Beton. 12 hectares
Since the 1980s, this estate has produced rich, well-structured wines, especially the old-vine "Cuvée Madeleine".

Château Haut-Chaigneau ☆☆
Lalande-de-Pomerol. Owner: André Chatonnet. 21 hectares
Chatonnet is a skilled winemaker, and it shows in this supple wine packed with fruit.

Château les Hauts-Conseillants ☆–☆☆
Lalande-de-Pomerol. Owner: Pierre Bourotte. 10 hectares
Oaky wine from Château Bonalgue owner in Pomerol (*q.v.*).

Château Moncets ☆–☆☆
Néac. Owners: the de Jerphanion family. 24 hectares.
www.moncets.com
Rich, velvety wines for medium-term drinking.

Château la Sergue ☆☆
Néac. Owner: André Chatonnet. 5 hectares
Made mostly from Merlot, and vinified in wooden vats. Intense wine.

Château les Templiers ☆
Néac. Owner: Jean Servant. 7 hectares
Solid, spicy wine.

Bordeaux's Minor Regions

The vast extent of the Gironde vineyards begins to sink in when you look at the number and size of growers' cooperative cellars dotted over the *département*. Most communes have one or two well-established châteaux: old manor houses whose wine has long been made in the manner of a not-very-ambitious family business.

In many cases, the small grower has sold his vineyard to the bigger grower as an alternative to joining the co-op. A number of well-run larger châteaux are thereby adding to their hectarage, revising their methods, and starting to specialize in either red or white instead of dabbling in both. Several now offer a proportion of their best vats as a top *cuvée* – aged in oak and at a higher price than their basic wine. In some cases, they have switched from third-rate

Garage Wines

In the early 1990s a new phenomenon occurred: the *vin de garage*. As the name implied, these were wines made in an artisanal fashion in tiny quantities. The scale of the operation allowed for a fanatical attention to detail – very low yields, exhaustive selection, destemming by hand, and so forth – which supposedly resulted in wines of exceptional quality.

Le Pin in Pomerol has often been described as Bordeaux's first *garage* wine. Although a small property with a rudimentary winery, Le Pin is a proper, reasonably homogeneous estate. The prototype for a *garage* wine is surely Valandraud (*q.v.*) in St-Emilion, which was, as its creator happily confesses, made from vines planted on mediocre terroir. A mixture of extreme concentration and lashings of new oak helped the wine to gain recognition and, like Le Pin, it sold for very high prices.

This set a trend. More and more growers would separate a small section of their vineyard, or purchase a small undistinguished parcel, and crop and vinify in the garagiste manner. Small quantities were used to justify a very high price. By 2000, however, there were at least sixty *vins de garage* and the novelty was wearing off. It also contradicted the very foundation of Bordeaux: the notion that exceptional terroir produces exceptional wine.

Vins de garage are a specialty of the Right Bank. The proprietors of the much larger estates of the Médoc and Graves are utterly opposed to the whole idea. In the end, the consumer will decide whether the wines are worth the prices being demanded for them.

sweet wines to second-rate (occasionally even first-rate) dry ones. Unquestionably, a new understanding of winemaking techniques, coupled with a far more demanding generation of wine-buyers and -drinkers, is transforming these outlying regions. Wine-loving investors have found affordable properties here, and many small estates that used to sell fruit to the cooperatives are now producing wine of improving quality under their own label.

Fronsac & Canon-Fronsac

The town of Libourne lies on the Dordogne at the mouth of its little northern tributary, the Isle. It has Pomerol as its back garden, St-Emilion as its eastern neighbour, and only a mile to the west another, surprisingly different, little wine area.

Fronsac is a village on the Dordogne, at the foot of a jumble of steep bumps and hollows, and a miniature range of hills up to ninety metres (292 feet). Several of the châteaux were obviously built as country villas rather than as plain farms. Under it all there is limestone. The vines are nearly all red, the usual Bordeaux varieties, traditionally with more stress on the soft and juicy Malbec than elsewhere. Having plenty of colour and alcohol, Fronsac wine has been much used in the past as *vin médecin* for weaklings from more famous places.

Historically, Fronsac took precedence over Pomerol. During the eighteenth century, its wines were even drunk at court. Circumstances gave Pomerol the advantage it has exploited well, and it is only over the past twenty years that Fronsac has begun to climb back – and only in the past ten years that real investment has been able to change its image.

There are 1,350 hectares of vineyards. Over two-thirds of the hills (the lower parts) are AC Fronsac; the rest, where the soil is thinner with more lime, is AC Canon-Fronsac. Its wines can be delectable, full of vigour and spice, hard enough to resemble Graves or St-Emilion more than Pomerol, and worth a good five years' ageing. The style has been changing, bringing these wines into line with the prevailing trend on the Right Bank towards fatter, plumper, oakier wines – sometimes at the expense of acidity and finesse.

Leading Fronsac & Canon-Fronsac Chateaux

Château Barrabaque ☆–☆☆
Fronsac. Owners: the Nöel family. 9 hectares
Pleasant, rounded wines, and an oakier *cuvée prestige*.

Château Canon ☆☆
Canon-Fronsac. Owner: Jean Halley. 1.3 hectares
Deep-coloured wine that ages well.

Château Canon-de-Brem ☆–☆☆
Canon-Fronsac. Owner: Jean Halley. 4.5 hectares
A high proportion of Cabernet Franc gives the wine its unusual fragrance.

Château de Carles ☆☆
Saillans. Owner: Antoine Chastenet de Castaing. 8 hectares

Supple enjoyable wines, although the best fruit goes into "Château Haut Carles".

Château Cassagne-Haut-Canon ☆–☆☆
St-Michel de Fronsac. Owner: Jean-Jacques Dubois.
13 hectares
Soft oaky wines, ripe, but lacking in vigour.

Château Coustolle ☆–☆☆
Fronsac. Owner: Alain Roux. 20 hectares
Large property; produces wines with some tannic grip.

Château Dalem ☆☆
Saillans. Owner: Michel Rullier. 13 hectares
With advice from Michel Rolland, this estate is producing soft, juicy, velvety wines, mostly Merlot.

Château de la Dauphine ☆–☆☆
Fronsac. Owner: Jean Halley. 33 hectares
Formerly owned by Moueix, but sold in 2000. Medium-bodied wines.

Château Fontenil ☆–☆☆
Saillans. Owner: Michel Rolland. 9 hectares
Rather jammy wines, aged in 50% new oak.

Château du Gaby ☆☆
Fronsac. Owner: Antoine Khayat. 9.5 hectares
A new owner making fine wine in a prime site.

Château Grand Renouil ☆☆–☆☆☆
Fronsac. Owner: Michel Ponty. 11 hectares
Full-bodied wines of considerable complexity.

Château Mazeris ☆–☆☆
St-Michel-de-Fronsac. Owners: the de Cournuaud family.
14 hectares
Top wine here is "La Part des Anges", from old Merlot vines.

Château Mazeris-Bellevue ☆
St-Michel-de-Fronsac. Owner: Jacques Bussier.
11 hectares
Rather light wines, with supple, raspberry fruit.

Château Moulin ☆–☆☆
Haut-Laroque. Owner: Jean-Noël Hervé. 15 hectares.
www.moulinhautlaroque.fr
A ripe style, but with weight and structure.

Château Moulin Pey-Labrie ☆☆
Fronsac. Owner: Gregoire Hubau. 6.5 hectares
Michel Rolland advises here; distinctly oaky wines.

Château de la Rivière ☆☆–☆☆☆
La Rivière, Fronsac. Owner: Jean Leprince. 59 hectares.
www.chateau-de-la-riviere.com
The region's most important estate, with an opera-set château producing very well-balanced wines that age well. Since 2000, an opulent all-Merlot *cuvée*, "Aria", has been released.

Château la Rousselle ☆
Fronsac. Owner: Jacques Davau. 4.5 hectares
Oaky wines for drinking fairly young.

Château les Trois Croix ☆☆–☆☆☆
Canon-Fronsac. Owners: Patrick Léon. 14 hectares
The personal property of the winemaker of Château Mouton-Rothschild. Rich, well-structured wines.

Château la Vieille Cure ☆–☆☆
Saillans. Owner: Colin Ferenbach. 18 hectares
This estate is american-owned. Producing very ripe wines with good concentration.

Château Villars ☆☆–☆☆☆
Saillans. Owner: Jean-Claude Gaudrie. 20 hectares
Some impressive wines with ripe toastiness being balanced by fine tannins.

Côtes de Castillon & Côtes de Francs

Two areas adjoining the St-Emilion satellites to the east, still within the general appellation area of Bordeaux, were granted their own independent *appellations d'origine contrôlée* in 1989. The larger is the Côtes de Castillon in the hills to the north of the Dordogne valley overlooking Castillon-la-Bataille, where the French defeated the English forces in 1452 and ended English rule in Aquitaine. Ten communes are affected, with a total of some 3,019 hectares of vines. To its north, the Côtes de Francs is much smaller, with 512 hectares under vine. The appellation takes in parts of the communes of Francs, Les Salles, St-Cibard, and Tayac; tranquil and remote country long known as a good producer of Bordeaux Supérieur, but only now recognized on its distinctive merits.

Côtes de Castillon and Côtes de Francs wines in general are like lightweight St-Emilions. Many wines have only remained rustic because the property owners could not afford necessary investments. But these regions should not be dismissed out of hand. Several châteaux are beginning to show real ambition and are making wine to mature five years or more.

Leading Côtes de Castillon Châteaux

Château d'Aiguilhe ☆☆
St-Philippe-d'Aiguilhe. Owner: Stephan von Neipperg. 37 hectares
Under the same ownership as Château Canon-La-Gaffelière (*q.v.*). Very oaky wines.

Château Ampélia
St-Philippe d'Aiguille. Owner: François Despagne. 4 hectares
First vintage was 2000.

Château Beauséjour ☆☆
St-Magne-de-Castillon. Owners: the Verger family. 20 hectares
Biodynamic estate. Supple wines.

Château Cap de Faugères ☆☆
Ste-Colombe. Owner: Corinne Guisez. 27 hectares
The extension of Château Faugères in St-Emilion (*q.v.*). Attractive wines for medium-term consumption.

Château la Clarière-Laithwaite ☆☆–☆☆☆
Ste-Colombe. Owner: Tony Laithwaite. 5 hectares
Like several of these properties, occupies splendid quarry-like cellars. Perfectionist wines since 1998, sold mostly through Laithwaite's Direct Wines company in Britain. "Le Presbytère" is a splendid old-vines *cuvée*.

Château Côte Montpezat ☆
Belvès-de-Castillon. Owner: D. Bessineau. 30 hectares.
www.cote-montpezat.com
Charming, easy-drinking wines.

Château Lapeyronie ☆–☆☆
Ste-Colombe. Owner: Jean-Frédéric Lapeyronie. 8 hectares
Rich, supple wines of consistent quality.

Château Pervenche Puy Arnaud ☆
Belvès-de-Castillon. Owner: Thierry Valette. 8 hectares
Organic property, with Stéphane Derenoncourt as consultant.

Château de Pitray ☆☆
Gardegan. Owner: Comtesse de Boigne. 36 hectares.
www.pitray.com
Powerful, cherry-scented wines.

Château Robin ☆
Belvès-de-Castillon. Owner: Sté Lurckroft. 12 hectares
Well-balanced wines, with some use of new oak.

Clos de l'Eglise ☆☆
Owners: Gérard Perse and Alain Raynaud. 17 hectares
The owners of Pavie and Quinault (*qq.v.*) vinify the wines as though they were top St-Emilion. Rather too extracted.

Domaine de l'A ☆☆
Ste-Colombe. Owner: Stéphane Derenoncourt. 4 hectares
The personal property of one of St-Emilion's top winemakers. Cultivated biodynamically. In effect, a private, experimental station for Derenoncourt to try out his ideas.

Vieux-Château-Champs de Mars ☆–☆☆
St-Philippe-d'Aiguilhe. Owner: Regis Moro. 17 hectares
Nothing rustic about these perfumed wines. Good value except for costly "Cuvée Johanna". Also makes Côtes de Francs.

Leading Côtes de Francs Châteaux

Château les Charmes-Godard ☆–☆☆
St-Cibard. Owners: Nicolas Thienpont. 4 hectares
Small property, producing good white as well as rich red.

Château de Francs ☆☆
Francs. Owners: the Hébrard and de Boüard families.
29 hectares
Sumptuous wines for medium-term drinking. The top wine is "Les Cerisiers".

Château Laclaverie ☆–☆☆
St-Cibard. Owner: Nicolas Thienpont. 10 hectares
Forward, oaky wines.

Château Marsau ☆–☆☆
Owner: Jean-Marie Chadronnier. 10 hectares
All-Merlot property belonging to the boss of CVBG.

Château Puyguéraud ☆☆
St-Cibard. Owners: the Thienpont family. 30 hectares
Solid, but not inelegant wines, they are among the best of
the region.

Côtes de Bourg

The right bank of the Gironde was a thriving vineyard long
before the Médoc across the water was planted. Bourg, lying
to the north of the Dordogne where it joins the Garonne
(the two form the Gironde), is like another and bigger
Fronsac: hills rising steeply from the water to sixty metres
(180 feet) or more, but unlike the hills of Fronsac, almost
solidly vine covered.

The Côtes de Bourg (3,876 hectares) makes as much wine
as the lower Médoc – and so does its immediate neighbour to
the north, the Côtes de Blaye (5,800 hectares). Bourg
specializes in red wine of a very respectable standard, made
largely of Merlot and Cabernet Franc, round and full-bodied
and ready to drink at four or five years – but certainly not in
a hurry. The châteaux that line the riverbank have, to all
appearances, a perfect situation. Farther back from the water
is largely cooperative country, with an increasing proportion
of white wine of no special note.

Leading Côtes de Bourg Châteaux

Château de Barbe ☆
Villeneuve. Owner: Sovivi. 64 hectares
Large property, sound wines.

Château du Bousquet ☆
Bourg. Owner: Castel Frères. 62 hectares
Light wines.

Château Brûlesécaille ☆☆
Tauriac. Owners: the Rodet family. 27 hectares
The 55% of Merlot in this wine contributes suppleness
and harmony to an otherwise traditional wine of the region.

Château Falfas ☆☆
Bayon. Owner: John Cochrane. 22 hectares
Biodynamic estate, producing quite tannic wines. The top
wine, "Cuvée Chevalier", is made from seventy-year vines
and aged in new oak.

Château Grand-Jour ☆
**Prignac-et-Marcamps. Owner: Vignobles Rocher-Cap.
98 hectares**
Large producer of rather soft, Merlot-dominated wines.

Buying Wines "En Primeur"

In the 1980s a new way of buying wine became fashionable.
Instead of buying wines once they were in bottle, it was possible
to buy the wine about six months after the vintage, and many
more months before it was bottled. The advantage to the
consumer was, supposedly, an opportunity to buy the wine at a
cheaper price, and, of equal importance, to secure a case or
two of rare wine (*e.g.* Pomerol) that might be harder or
impossible to find after its release. For the château proprietor
and négociant, the advantage was cash flow: instead of waiting
two or three years for their money, they could bank cheques
after six months.

In some vintages the system worked well. Anyone who bought
the 1995 vintage *en primeur* (or, in American parlance, as
futures) would have secured some bargains. In other years,
such as 1997, when quality was modest but prices very high,
the consumer would have lost out.

Bordeaux loves the *en primeur* system. It creates a buzz
of excitement around almost every new vintage. However, all
judgments, whether by the trade or the press, on the new wines
must inevitably be based on cask samples, which are drawn
from barrel without any monitoring or control. Most proprietors
are honest, but the temptation to show the best or richest
barrel is surely high. Buying *en primeur* is always risky, if only
because the wine is still in an unfinished state when assessed
and purchased.

Château de la Grave ☆–☆☆
Bourg. Owner: Philippe Bassereau. 40 hectares
This estate makes quite stylish wines and a special *cuvée*
ambitiously named "Nectar".

Château Guerry ☆☆
Tauriac. Owner: Bernard de Rivoyre. 22 hectares
Robust, flavoury wine of consistent quality with a fair
proportion of Malbec.

Château Guionne ☆
Lansac. Owner: Alain Fabre. 23 hectares
Two bottlings: one unwooded, the other oaked. A new
owner in 2000 may bring changes.

Château Haut-Macô ☆☆
**Tauriac. Owners: Bernard and Jean Mallet.
50 hectares**
The "Cuvée Jean-Bernard" is aged in new oak.

Château Labadie ☆
Mombrier. Owner: Joel Dupuy. 45 hectares
Large commercial property, mechanically harvested. Various
cuvées, all of sound quality.

Château Macay ☆
Samonac. Owner: Eric Latouche. 30 hectares
Old vines and fairly low yields deliver good wines.

Château de Mendoce ☆
**Villeneuve. Owner: Philippe Darricarrère.
15 hectares**
Rather light, easy-drinking wines.

Château Mercier ☆–☆☆
St-Trojan. Owner: Christophe Chéty. 23 hectares
The *cuvée prestige* here is noteworthy.

Château Peychaud ☆☆
Berson. Owner: Bernard Germain. 29 hectares. www.vgas.com
The "Cuvée Maisonneuve" is fleshy and oaky.

Château le Roc des Cambes ☆☆–☆☆☆
Bourg. Owner: Francois Mitjaville. 10 hectares
Among the best and most expensive wines of the region, from the same stable as Château Tertre-Rôteboeuf (*q.v.*). Very dense and concentrated.

Château Tayac ☆☆☆
Bourg. Owner: Pierre Saturny. 30 hectares
Forceful, tannic wines that benefit from five years' cellaring.

Premières Côtes de Blaye

Two miles of water, the widening Gironde, separates Blaye from the heart of the Médoc. Blaye is the northernmost vineyard of the "right bank"; the last place, going up this coast, where good red wine is made. North of this is white-wine country; the fringes of cognac. Blaye already makes about one third white wine.

Premières Côtes de Blaye is the appellation reserved for the better vineyards, nearly all red, whose wine is to all intents like that of Bourg – although generally considered not quite as good or full-bodied. A new AC Blaye was created in 2000, requiring slightly higher minimal ripeness. There are five cooperatives, the following châteaux are worth noting.

Leading Premières Côtes de Blaye Châteaux

Châteaux Bertinerie and Haut-Bertinerie ☆☆
Cavignac. Owner: Daniel Bantegnies. 60 hectares
Very well-run property with immediately appealing wines, white and red. The "Haut-Bertinerie" label is used for the best wines, and priced accordingly.

Château les Bertrands ☆
Reignac. Owner: Laurent Dubois. 80 hectares
Large commercial property, all machine-harvested. Cleanly made if frequently dilute wines, with the exception of the *prestige cuvée* "Nectar".

Château Chante Alouette ☆
Plassac. Owner: Georges Lorteaud. 25 hectares
Robust wine, aged in a good deal of new oak.

Château Charron ☆☆
St-Martin-Lacaussade. Owner: Bernard Germain. 26 hectares
Many old vines on the property give wines, white as well as red, of considerable weight and richness. Their "Cuvée Acacia" is the best white, and "Les Gruppes" their most impressive red.

Château du Grand Barrail ☆–☆☆
Cars. Owner: Denis Lafon. 33 hectares
Since 1998, Lafon has produced "Cuvée Révélation", from the oldest vines and aged, perhaps excessively, in new oak.

Château Haut-Sociondo ☆
Cars. Owners: the Martinaud family. 16 hectares
Accessible wines for drinking young.

Château les Jonqueyres ☆☆–☆☆☆
St-Paul. Owner: Pascal Montaut. 15 hectares
One of the top properties, the wines are much in demand.

Château le Menaudat ☆
St-Androny. Owner: Mme. Edouard Cruse. 15 hectares
Gentle wine, best enjoyed young.

Château Mondésir-Gazin ☆☆
Plassac. Owner: Marc Pasquet. 14 hectares
This is a serious property run by an equally serious man. Concentrated wines are produced, and a good Côtes de Bourg, too.

Château Prieuré Malesan ☆
St-Genès. Owner: William Pitters International. 53 hectares
Supple, fruity wines.

Château la Rivalerie ☆
St-Paul-de-Blaye. Owner: Georges Gillibert. 35 hectares
An abandoned property revived in 1972. Fairly light wines, white and red.

Château Roland la Garde ☆☆
St-Seurin. Owner: Bruno Martin. 28 hectares
Martin only bottles the best wines from his estate, and gives them luxury treatment in new oak.

Château Segonzac ☆–☆☆
St-Genès. Owner: Jacques Marmet. 30 hectares.
www.chateau-segonzac.com
The top wine is the *cuvée prestige*, aged in new barriques.

Château des Tourtes ☆–☆☆
St-Caprais. Owners: the Raguenot family. 47 hectares
The *cuvée prestige* whites and reds are rich, supple wines for short-term drinking.

Premières Côtes de Bordeaux

A long, narrow strip of the east bank of the Garonne facing Graves enjoys the doubtful prestige of this appellation. Its hinterland is Entre-Deux-Mers. At their northern end they were some of Bordeaux's Roman and medieval vineyards – now buried under houses. At their southern end, at Cadillac and into Ste-Croix-du-Mont, they are known for sweet wines, at their best up to Sauternes standards. Along the way the mix is about eighty per cent red and twenty per cent white, the white recently made much drier and fresher than formerly. (Château Reynon is perhaps the best example.) Red Premières Côtes is potentially much better than plain Bordeaux Supérieur from less well-placed vineyards, and this is beginning to be recognized. Lack of incentive is a real problem. Nonetheless, there are ambitious owners, and some very grand and prosperous names appear among the owners who are improving this area. A notable pioneer in the region is the négociant Sichel, which has a New World-style winery at Verdelais where it vinifies the grapes it buys in the district to make very fruity and attractive Cave Bel Air claret for drinking young. Oddly, the practice of buying grapes is almost unknown in Bordeaux except in the cooperative, profit-sharing system.

Leading Châteaux of the Premières Côtes & Cadillac

Château de Birot ☆☆
Béguey. Owners: the Fournier and Castéja families. 17 hectares
Serious wines from vineyards overlooking the Garonne.

Château Brethous ☆☆
Camblanes. Owners: the Verdier family. 13 hectares
Well-balanced wines, especially the *cuvée prestige*.

Château Carsin ☆☆
Rions. Owner: Juha Berglund. 55 hectares. www.carsin.com
Very good, modern-style wines from a Finnish-owned estate.

Château Cayla ☆☆–☆☆☆
Rions. Owner: Patrick Doche. 30 hectares
Excellent Cadillac, aged in new oak.

Château de Chelivette ☆–☆☆
Ste-Eulalie. Owner: Jean-Louis Boulière. 10 hectares
Red wines only: elegant and medium-bodied.

Château Fayau ☆–☆☆
Cadillac. Owner: Jean Médeville. 140 hectares
Perhaps the outstanding property of the region, offering a wide range of wines, including a long-lived Cadillac.

Château Grand Moueys ☆
Capian. Owners: the Bömers family. 80 hectares
A wide range of wines, mostly for drinking young.

Château Haut-Rian ☆
Rions. Owner: Michel Dietrich. 76 hectares
Crisp modern wines; Cadillac, too.

Château de Haux ☆☆
Haux. Owners: the Jorgensen family. 28 hectares
Very good red wine; firm and balanced.

Château du Juge ☆–☆☆
Cadillac. Owner: Chantal Dupleich. 30 hectares. www.chateau-du-juge.com
Red fruits characterize the red wine from this property.

Château Lagarosse ☆
Tabanac. Owner: Gérard Laurencin. 32 hectares
Gently oaked red wines.

Château Lamothe de Haux ☆–☆☆
Haux. Owner: Fabrice Néel. 71 hectares www.chateau-lamothe.com
"Première Cuvée" is the best wine at this well-run property.

Château Laroche ☆–☆☆
Baurech. Owner: Julien Palau. 25 hectares. www.chateaularoche.com
Firm wines, worth brief cellaring.

Château Lezongars ☆
Villenave de Rions. Owner: SC Château Lezongars. 10 hectares. www.chateau-lezongars.com
Good red wine, though sometimes hard.

Château de Marsan ☆
Lestiac sur Garonne. Owner: Paul Gonfrier. 30 hectares
A rather mild red wine and a charming *clairet*.

Château du Peyrat ☆
Capian. Owners: the Lambert family. 100 hectares
A huge estate offering a wide range of wines.

Château Plaisance ☆–☆☆
Capian. Owner: Patrick Bayle. 25 hectares
Serious wines, red and white, some showing plenty of oak.

Château Puy Bardens ☆–☆☆
Cambes. Owner: Yves Lamiable. 17 hectares
Red fruits and oak characterize these appealing wines.

Château Reynon ☆☆
Béguey. Owners: Denis and Florence Dubourdieu. 35 hectares
Sound light reds, and very good whites, especially the "Cuvée Vieilles Vignes" and the Cadillac.

Château Suau ☆☆
Capian. Owner: Monique Bonnet. 60 hectares
Fresh red wines but the *cuvée prestige* has more weight.

Château Tanesse ☆
Langoiran. Owner: Domaines Cordier. 40 hectares
Light red wines for early drinking.

Entre-Deux-Mers

The two "seas" in question are the rivers Dordogne and Garonne, whose converging courses more or less define the limits of this big, wedge-shaped region; the most diffuse and, territorially, the most important in Bordeaux, with some 23,000 hectares under vine. The appellation Entre-Deux-Mers is now reserved for dry white wine only. Growers tend to declare their best white wines as Entre-Deux-Mers, while other wines they produce are given the Bordeaux or Bordeaux Supérieur appellation, which are, of course, shared with the whole Bordeaux region. Three-quarters of production is red, also sold as Bordeaux or Bordeaux Supérieur.

The south of the region is relaxed patchwork countryside with as much woodland and pasture as vineyard. The north is almost a monoculture of the vine. Its biggest cooperative, at Rauzan, makes 1.4 million cases a year. The cooperatives make a third of the production of Bordeaux dry white.

Entre-Deux-Mers is the one wine Bordeaux has succeeded in redesigning in modern marketing terms. The region was bogged down with cheap, sweet wine nobody wanted any more. Some bright spark thought of the catchphrase *"Entre deux huitres, Entre-Deux-Mers"* ("Between two oysters," etc…) and a rosy future opened up for dry white: the Muscadet of the southwest.

I have yet to taste an Entre-Deux-Mers of the sort of quality that would win medals in California – but the world needs its staples, too. It varies from the briskly appetizing to the thoroughly boring, but in ways that are hard to predict. A good cooperative is just as likely to produce a clean and bracing example as a property with a long name. A handful of private growers, like Francis Courselle of Thieuley, and Jean-Louis Despagne of Tour de Mirambeau (*qq.v.*) set a standard that others emulate. "La Gamage" has been a consistently good cooperative wine, as have merchant brands like "Dourthe No 1".

No sooner had the growers adroitly replanted their vineyards with white varieties than the "French paradox" was propounded, and demand switched from white to red wines worldwide. This has led to the bizarre situation whereby Bordeaux produces some of the world's most expensive red wine, and some of the cheapest white.

Within the appellation, an area limited to the southern communes with theoretically superior wine, producers can use the appellation "Haut-Benauge" in addition to "Entre-Deux-Mers" or "Bordeaux". However, it is very rarely encountered on a label.

Leading Entre-Deux-Mers Châteaux

(and some properties using the Bordeaux appellation)

Château Bauduc ☆–☆☆
Créon. Owner: Gavin Quinney. 30 hectares. www.bauduc.com
Charming, floral white wines.

Château Bel-Air Perponcher ☆☆
Naujan et Postiac. Owner: J.-L. Despagne. 30 hectares. www.vignobles-despagne.com
Excellent white wines, with unusual complexity for the region. The red "Grande Cuvée" is intensely fragrant.

Château Bonnet ☆☆
Grézillac. Owner: André Lurton. 225 hectares
André Lurton has demonstrated for many years that it is possible to make simple but delicious wines, white and red, from Entre-Deux-Mers vineyards. In 2000, he launched a special *cuvée* called "Divinus".

Château de Camarsac ☆–☆☆
Camarsac. Owner: Bérénice Lurton. 50 hectares
Delicate wines from the vineyards of this medieval fortress.

Clos Chaumont ☆☆–☆☆☆
Haux. Owner: Pieter Verbeek
A small property, bought and replanted by a Dutch merchant. Ambitious wines, both whites and reds being aged in a high proportion of new oak.

Château Ducla ☆–☆☆
Gironde-sur-Dropt. Owner: Yvon Mau. www.chateau-ducla.com
Sound if rather unexciting wines from a conscientious négociant house.

Château Fonchereau ☆
Montussan. Owner: Mme. Georges Vinot-Postry. 25 hectares. www.fonchereau.com
Good red wine, Merlot-dominated.

Château Grand Monteil ☆
Salleboeuf. Owner: Jean Téchenet. 130 hectares
A large property that was once owned by Gustave Eiffel. Attractive red wines.

Château Guibon ☆
Daignac. Owner: André Lurton. 30 hectares
Another of the Lurton properties, which produces red and white wines.

Château Launay ☆–☆☆
Soussac. Owner: François Greffier. 61 hectares
Mostly white wines, fresh and well-made.

Château Marjosse ☆
Tizac de Curton. Owner: Pierre Lurton. 6 hectares
When not making fabulous wine at Château Cheval Blanc (*q.v.*), Lurton relaxes by producing fresh white wine from his personal property.

Château Queyret-Pouillac ☆
Ste-Antoine de Queyret. Owner: M. Charland. 65 hectares. www.queyret-pouillac
Founded in 1783, producing white, red, and *clairet*.

Château Rauzan-Despagne ☆☆–☆☆☆
Naujan-et-Postiac. Owner: J.-L. Despagne. 64 hectares. www.vignobles-despagne.com
Some remarkable red wines are made here, notably the "Cuvée Passion", which is built to last. And a delightful Sauvignon Blanc.

Château Sainte-Marie ☆☆
Targon. Owner: Gilles Dupuch. 40 hectares
Two fine white wines: one oaked, the other not. There is also a supple, red Bordeaux.

Château Thieuley ☆☆–☆☆☆
La Sauve. Owner: Francis Courselle. 80 hectares
The outstanding producer of the region. The top wine is the "Cuvée Francis Courselle", fermented and aged in new barriques.

Château Tour de Mirambeau ☆☆
Naujan-et-Postiac. Owner: J.-L. Despagne. 109 hectares. www.vignobles-despagne.com
A huge supply of very consistent wines, red and white.

Domaine de Courteillac ☆☆
Ruch. Owner: Dominique Méneret. 27 hectares
A new owner took over this property in 1998. It is best-known for supple red wines and the oaky white named "Cuvée Antholien".

Vignobles Ducourt ☆–☆☆
Ladaux. Owners: the Ducourt family. 250 hectares
An important merchant house, producing about two million bottles. They use the labels of various properties, including Château de Beauregard.

Ste-Croix-du-Mont & Loupiac

The southern end of the Premières Côtes de Bordeaux faces Barsac and Sauternes across the Garonne. From Cadillac southwards the specialty is sweet white wine, growing more "liquorous" the nearer it gets to Sauternes.

Ste-Croix-du-Mont gazes across at the hills of Sauternes from its higher riverbank and often shares the same autumnal conditions that lead to noble rot and sticky wines. Without quite the same perfection of soil, or pride of tradition, it cannot afford the enormous investment in labour needed to make the greatest wines, but it succeeds remarkably often in producing wine at least as good as run-of-the-mill Sauternes, and often better. And they are a good deal less expensive than Sauternes.

To my surprise, I have been given Ste-Croix-du-Mont in the German Palatinate by a grower famous for his Beerenauslesen, who told me he thought it compared well with his wines. (I must admit the Riesling said more to me.)

The only difference in the regulations between Sauternes and these right-bank wines is the quantity allowed. The same grapes and alcohol content are required, but the grower is allowed forty hectolitres per hectare as against only twenty-five for Sauternes. This is not to say that perfectionist growers make their full quota. They also make dry wines of potentially fine quality, and a little light red sold as Bordeaux. There are 429 hectares of vines with about 100 estates.

Loupiac is not quite so well-placed, and makes slightly less liquorous wines on 400 hectares. About seventy properties make Loupiac, though only fifty bottle their own production. Growers make dry white and red, too.

Leading Ste-Croix-du-Mont Châteaux

Château Crabitan-Bellevue ☆☆
Owner: Bernard Solane. 22 hectares
Lush, orangey wines, and in top vintages an excellent barrique-aged "Cuvée Spéciale".

Château la Grave ☆☆
Owner: Jean-Marie Tinon. 15 hectares
Oaked and unoaked styles here, and Château Grand Peyrot from a different soil.

Château Loubens ☆☆–☆☆☆
Owner: Arnaud de Sèze. 21 hectares
Exceedingly rich, sometimes rather alcoholic wines, that see no oak.

Château Lousteau-Vieil ☆
Owners: the Sessacq family. 17 hectares
A long-established estate. Wines lack real concentration.

Château des Mailles ☆–☆☆
Owner: Daniel Larrieu. 14 hectares
Many old vines contribute to this lush wine. In top vintages an oaked *cuvée* is produced.

Château du Pavillon ☆☆
Owner: Alain Fertal. 4 hectares
An ambitious estate, aiming for fully botrytized wines whenever possible.

Château la Rame ☆☆–☆☆☆
Owner: Yves Armand. 40 hectares (20 in Ste-Croix)
The top producer here. The honey-scented, oaked "Réserve" could easily be mistaken for a fine Barsac.

Leading Loupiac Châteaux

Clos Jean ☆
Owner. Lionel Bord 17 hectares
Well-known property that produces commercial wines with little noble-rot character.

Château du Cros ☆☆
Owner: Michel Boyer. 43 hectares. www.chateauducros.com
An enthusiastic producer of good-quality Loupiac, partially barrel-aged.

Château Grand Peyruchet ☆–☆☆
Owner: Bernard Queyrens. 8 hectares
Half the wine is aged in barriques. It has a fresh apricot character.

Château Loupiac-Gaudet ☆☆
Owner: Marc Ducau. 26 hectares
Good, straightforward wine, now set to become more complex since barrel-ageing was adopted in 1998.

Domaine de Noble ☆☆–☆☆☆
Owner: Patrick Dejean. 15 hectares.
The leading producer in this area, producing both oaked and unoaked wines with good concentration and a zesty acidity.

Château de Ricaud ☆
Owner: Alain Thienot. 70 hectares (14 in Loupiac)
Medium-bodied wines, from a property owned by a leading Champagne producer.

Château les Roques ☆☆
Owner: Alain Fertal. 3.5 hectares
Same ownership as Château du Pavillon in Ste-Croix (*q.v.*).

Graves de Vayres & Ste-Foy-Bordeaux

Within the same block of vineyard, two smaller zones have separate appellations defined with Gallic precision: one on the basis of its soil and potential for something out of the rut, the other, I suspect, for political reasons.

Graves de Vayres (360 hectares), across the river from Libourne, has more gravel than its surroundings. Unfortunately, its name invites comparison with Graves, which it cannot sustain. Whites are sometimes made sweeter than Entre-Deux-Mers. The quickly maturing reds have been compared in a charitable moment to minor Pomerols.

The other appellation, Ste-Foy-Bordeaux (358 hectares), looks like a natural part of the Bergerac region cobbled on to Bordeaux. Its wines are not notably different from the wines of Bergerac, and its history is identical. For centuries, the Dutch came for the two commodities most in demand: sweet wine and wine for distilling.

Côtes de Bordeaux St-Macaire

Ten villages beyond Ste-Croix-du-Mont rejoice in this appellation for semi-sweet wine, a trickle of which finds its way to Belgium. Red sold as Bordeaux or Bordeaux Supérieur is much more important.

Cérons

Cérons applies to the three Graves villages (Podensac and Illats are the other two) that abut Barsac on the north and have a natural tendency to make sweet wines.

Their wines are classified according to their natural degree of alcohol as either Graves or Graves Supérieures (at eleven to twelve degrees and naturally dry), or at half a degree more as Cérons, which inclines to be *moelleux*, the grey area which is sweet but not *liquoreux*. Occasionally it attains *liquoreux* stickiness. All depends on the autumn and the vinification, which previously used sulphur as its crutch and left much to be desired. Modern methods can mean much cleaner and better wine, as the growing reputations of some of the properties indicate.

Production of Cérons has been in decline, as growers have the option to produce dry white wine (Graves) from the same vineyards, without all of the risks attendant upon sweet wine production and at higher yields. Only twenty producers bottle Cérons; even good examples fetch only a moderate price. France consumes nearly all of it.

Leading Cérons Châteaux

Château de Cérons ☆☆–☆☆☆
Cérons. Owner: Jean Perromat. 10 hectares
Jean Perromat is a passionate defender of the appellation and produces one of its best wines, with a pronounced apricot or citric character. Age becomes it as well as it does good Sauternes.

Château de Chantegrive ☆☆
Podensac (*see* Graves)
Not made every year. Wines of finesse and concentration.

Château Huradin ☆–☆☆
Cérons. Owner: Daniel Lafosse
Spicy, lively wines, sometimes with botrytis character.

Clos Bourgelat ☆
Cérons. Owner: Dominique Lafosse
Simple, fresh, lively wines.

Grand Enclos du Château de Cérons ☆☆–☆☆☆
Cérons. Owner: Olivier Lataste
Fine quality, but not produced every year.

Bordeaux & Bordeaux Supérieur

The basic appellations underlying all the more specific and grander names of Bordeaux are available to anyone using the approved grapes, achieving a certain degree of alcohol, and limiting the harvest to a statutory maximum (which varies from year to year). The standing definitions for red wines are as follows. Bordeaux must have a minimum ten degrees alcohol after fermentation at a maximum of fifty-five hectolitres per hectare. Bordeaux Supérieur: 10.5 degrees at a maximum of forty hectolitres per hectare – hence more concentration and flavour. For white wines: Bordeaux must have 10.5 degrees at sixty-five hectolitres per hectare. Bordeaux Supérieur needs 11.5 degrees at forty hectolitres per hectare. In practice, the PLC raises these crop levels significantly.

Cubzac

The districts that regularly carry the simple appellation, having no other, include St-André-de-Cubzac and the nearby Cubzac-Les-Ponts, and Guitres and Coutras. Cubzac is where the great iron bridge built by Eiffel (of the tower) crosses the Dordogne on the way from Bordeaux to Paris. It lies between the hills of Fronsac and those of Bourg, on flat land which can nonetheless make respectable wine.

Guitres & Coutras

Guitres and Coutras are very much on the fringe, to the north of Cubzac where wine-growing used to be directed towards cognac. One property in the area uses a typically Pomerol mix, with seventy-five per cent Merlot on clay soil with encouraging results.

Burgundy

Burgundy has the best-situated shop window in France, if not in Europe. The powerful, the influential, the enterprising, and the curious have been filing by for two millennia along the central highway of France, from Paris to Lyon and the south, from the Rhine and the Low Countries to Italy. Every prince, merchant, soldier, or scholar has seen the Côte d'Or, rested at Beaune or Dijon, tasted, and been told tall tales about the fabulous wine of this narrow, scrubby hillside.

Whether any other hillside could do what the Côte d'Or can is a fascinating speculation – without an answer. What it does is to provide scraps of land and scattered episodes of weather that bring two grape varieties to a perfection not found anywhere else. In certain sites and in certain years only, the Pinot Noir and Chardonnay achieve flavours valued as highly as any flavour on earth.

So specific are the sites and the conditions needed that the odds are stacked quite strongly against them. It is an uncertain way to make a living. So Burgundy has organized itself into a system that makes allowances – for crop failures, for human errors, for frailties of all kinds. Its legislation is a delicate structure that tries to keep the Burgundian one jump ahead of his clients without them tumbling to the fact.

The Burgundy of wine falls into five distinct parts. What is true of the Côte d'Or is equally true of Chablis, its northern outpost, but much less so of the Côte Chalonnaise and the regions of Mâcon and Beaujolais to the south. The chapters on these areas summarize the local issues and conditions.

There is no simple or straight answer to the conundrum of Burgundy. The essential information is presented here in the form of geographical lists of the vineyards, their appellations, and official ranking, and alphabetical lists of selected growers and merchants.

The Classification of Burgundy

Bordeaux has a random series of local classifications of quality. Burgundy has a central system by which every vineyard in the Côte d'Or and Chablis (although not in Beaujolais and the Mâconnais) is precisely ranked by its appellation. Starting at the top, there are over forty *grands crus* which have their own individual appellations. They

do not (except in Chablis) use the names of their communes. They are simply and grandly Le Corton, Le Musigny, Le Montrachet. In the nineteenth century, the villages that were the proud possessors of this land added the *grand cru* name to their own, so that Aloxe became Aloxe-Corton; Chambolle, Chambolle-Musigny; Puligny and Chassagne both added Montrachet to their names. Hence the apparent anomaly that the shorter name in general means the better wine.

In parentheses it must be said that the decisions about which sites are *grands crus* are old and, in a few cases, unfair. They were taken on observations of performance over many years. Their soil is ideal. They are generally the places that suffer least from spring frost, summer hail, and autumn rot. But they can be well or badly farmed. There are certainly some of the next rank, *premier cru*, which reach or exceed the level of several *grands crus*. The rank of *premier cru* is given with much deliberation over detail to 562 plots of land in the best non-*grand cru* vineyards of all the best communes. For several years a review was in progress that entailed nit-picking over minute parcels of vines. It was only finally completed in 1984. The upshot is, for example, that in the Pommard vineyard (or *climat*) of Les Petits Epenots plots two to eight and thirteen to twenty-nine are classed as *premier cru*, while plots nine to twelve are not. I give this instance not to confuse the issue, but to show how extremely seriously the authorities take the matter.

The biggest and best *premiers crus* have reputations of their own, particularly in the Côte de Beaune (where Le Corton is the only red *grand cru*). Such vineyards as Volnay Caillerets and Pommard Rugiens can be expected to produce fabulously good wine under good conditions. In such cases the producer proudly uses the name of the vineyard. The law allows the vineyard name to be printed on the label in characters the same size as the commune name. There are smaller *premiers crus*, however, without the means to acquire a great reputation, whose wine is sometimes just sold as, for example, Volnay Premier Cru. Often a grower's holdings in some vineyards are so small that he is obliged to mix the grapes of several holdings in order to have a vatful to ferment. This wine will have to settle for an unspecific name.

The *grands crus* and *premiers crus* form an almost unbroken band of vineyards occupying most of the east-facing Côte d'Or slope, perfectly exposed to the morning sun. The villages with their evocative names – Gevrey-Chambertin, Aloxe-Corton, Pommard – generally sit at the foot of the slope, encompassing in their parish boundaries both the best (upper) land and some less good (or even distinctly inferior) either on the flat at the bottom or in angles of the hills that face the "wrong" way. This also is classed. The best of it, but not up to *premier cru* standard, is entitled to use the name of the village and the vineyard. In practice not many vineyards below *premier cru* rank are cited on labels. The law in this case demands that a vineyard name be printed in characters only half the size of the commune name. This allows a distinction on the labels of, say, Denis Mortet between his Gevrey-Chambertin Champeaux (a *premier cru*) and Gevrey-Chambertin "Matrot" (a village vineyard or *lieu-dit*). The *appellation contrôlée* here applies to the village name, not the vineyard. In the descriptions of properties that follow, I refer to these as "village" wines.

Inferior land within a village is not even allowed the village name. It falls under the rubric of *appellations régionales*: the most specific name it can have is Bourgogne (when it is made from the classic grapes, red and white, of the region), Bourgogne Passe-tout-grain, Bourgogne Aligoté, or Bourgogne Grand Ordinaire. These terms are explained on page 94.

Grapes & Wine

Burgundy is easier wine to taste than Bordeaux, but harder to judge and understand. The Pinot Noir, which gives all the good reds of the Côte d'Or, has a singular and memorable smell and taste, sometimes described as "pepperminty", sometimes as showing aromas of raspberries or violets, yet also rooty, as in beetroot, and warm as in alcohol, but in any case beyond the reach of my vocabulary.

Singular as it is, it varies in "pitch" more than most grapes from one site to another and one vintage to another. In unripe years it smells mean, pinched, and watery (German red wines give a good idea of the effect). At the other extreme it roasts to a raisiny character (many California Pinot Noirs are out of key in this way).

The ideal young red burgundy has the ripe-grape smell with neither of these defects, recognizably but lightly overlain with the smell of oak. And it tastes very much as it smells: a little too astringent for total pleasure but with none of the impenetrable tannin of a great young Bordeaux. Good burgundy tastes good from birth.

The object of keeping it in barrels is not simply to add a flavour of oak, but to bolster the tannins, to encourage a gentle oxidation, and to allow the wine to stabilize naturally. The object of maturing it in bottle is to achieve softness of texture and a complex alliance of flavours that arise from the grape, yet seem to have little to do with it. Fine old red burgundy arrives at an intense, regal red with a note of orange (the decorator's "burgundy" is that of young wine). It caresses the mouth with a velvet touch that loses nothing of vigour by being soft. And it smells and tastes of a moment of spring or autumn just beyond the grasp of your memory.

Strange to say, white burgundy can have a distinct resemblance to red – not exactly in smell or taste, but in its texture and weight, and the way that it evolves.

Chardonnay wine is not markedly perfumed when it is new: just brisk and, if anything, appley. The traditional burgundian method of fermenting it in small barrels adds the smell of oak immediately, but a skilled winemaker will ensure that the oak influence is integrated and harmonious, not overwhelming. Thereafter, the way the wine develops in barrel and bottle depends very much on which district it comes from, and on the acid/alcohol ratio of the particular vintage.

An ideally balanced vintage such as '90, '95, or '99 keeps a tension between the increasingly rich flavours of maturity and a central steeliness, year after year. A sharp, barely ripe vintage such as '87 leans too far towards the steel – and not very springy steel at that. A very ripe vintage such as '76 and '92 produced many wines that were too fat and lacked "cut". All in all, however, the success rate of white burgundy vintages is very much higher than that of red.

How Burgundy is Made

Red burgundy is normally made in an open-topped cylindrical wooden vat filled to about two-thirds of its capacity with grapes crushed in a mill (*fouloir/égrappoir*) which removes some or all of the stalks. Every grower has his own theory of how much or little of the stems should be included, depending on the ripeness of the grapes (and of their stalks), the colour and concentration of the vintage, and whether he wants to make a tannic *vin de garde* or a softer wine to mature more quickly. Ultra-conservative growers still tend to include all the stalks.

Among the arguments in favour are that it makes the pressing easier – to the contrary that it robs the wine of colour and can add bitter tannin. Many growers today often use "cold maceration" – keeping the skins in the juice at a low temperature that prevents fermentation for a few days but extracts fruity flavours and colour.

To start the pulpy mass fermenting, it is sometimes necessary to add a measure of actively fermenting wine from another vat, with a teeming yeast population – known as a *pied de cuve*. In cold weather it may also be necessary to break up the cap and redistribute it evenly across the vat. The ancient way to get things moving was for all (male) hands to strip naked and jump in, lending their body heat to encourage the yeast. In an account of the Côte d'Or in 1862 by Agoston Haraszthy, reporting to the government of California, "Five days is generally sufficient for the fermenting of wine in this part, unless it is cold weather, when the overseer sends his men in a couple of times more in their *costume à l'Adam* to create the necessary warmth." He adds that "This, in my eyes, rather dirty procedure could be avoided by throwing in heated stones or using pipes filled with steam or hot water." And indeed it is. Pinot Noir needs a warm fermentation to extract all the colour and flavour from the skins.

The operation of *pigeage*, or mixing the floating cap of skins with the fermenting juice, is still sometimes performed in small cellars by the *vigneron* or his sons, scrupulously hosed down, in bathing shorts, but more up-to-date establishments use a mechanical plunger to perform the operation. In addition, or as an alternative, some producers will either pump the juice from the bottom of the vat over the *chapeau* (*remontage*) or use a grille which prevents the cap from floating to the top (*chapeau immergé*). I am told by practitioners that it is the positively physical rubbing of the *marc* by *pigeage* that is important. It liberates elements that *remontage* or *chapeau immergé* cannot possibly obtain.

Individual ideas on the right duration of this maceration of the skins in the *cuve* vary from a very few days to up to almost three weeks, depending to a large extent on the degree and kind of extraction sought by the winemaker. The free-run wine is then drawn off and the *marc* pressed. The wine of the first pressing is usually added to the free-run juice and the ensemble filled into barrels, old or new according to the means and motives of the proprietor, to settle down and undergo its quiet secondary – malolactic – fermentation. The malolactic fermentation is often encouraged by raising the cellar temperature, but many growers are in no rush, and it's not unusual to hear the wine perking away well into the spring following the vintage. Once they have finished this infantile fretting they are racked into clean barrels.

Fine red burgundies are usually kept in barrel for between twelve and eighteen months. Unlike Bordeaux, they are racked as little as possible to avoid contact with the air. Two months before bottling they may need to be fined to remove the very faintest haze. Some cellars use filters to clarify the wine, but other producers avoid this.

Making White Burgundy

The procedure for making all dry white wines, white burgundy included, is virtually standardized today (*see* page 30). The object is maximum freshness, achieved by minimum contact with the air. Careful, clean, and cool handling of the grapes is followed by a quick pressing and slow, cool fermentation.

In big, modern plants in Chablis, and the best of the big cooperative cellars of the Mâconnais, this clinical procedure is carried out and the flavours of the resulting wines owe everything to grape and soil. Chablis, having more acidity and a more distinctive flavour, can benefit from maturing in a steel or concrete vat and then in bottle for a considerable time. The simpler, rounder taste of Mâcon wines has little to gain by keeping.

But the classic white burgundies of the Côte d'Or are another matter. They are fermented in small oak barrels. A *grand cru* or top *premier cru* will often be aged in a high proportion of new oak, but there are no firm rules. The pungent smell of new oak is part of the personality of the wine from the start, but should moderate with age.

The majority of growers, those with good but not the finest land, settle for older barrels, perhaps replacing a few each year. In this case, the oak has less of the obvious carpenter's-shop effect on the wine; the barrel is simply the ideal size and shape of container for maintaining fermentation at an even, low temperature, cooled by the humid ambience of the cellar. A greater volume of wine would generate too much heat as fermentation progresses.

Fermentation over, the wine stays in the barrel, on its yeasty sediment, or lees. The tradition in Burgundy is to stir those lees regularly so that the wine can "feed" off the nutrients they contain and gain in body and richness. According to the winemaker's judgment, it is then racked off the lees into clean barrels and kept until the maker deems it ready for bottling. What he is doing is allowing a gentle and controlled oxidation of the wine to introduce nuances and breadth of flavour that would otherwise not develop. It is then ready for drinking – unless the buyer wants to continue the ageing process in the bottle. To me, the possibility of this reductive ageing is the whole point of buying the great white burgundies. No other white wines (with the exception of Riesling) reward patience so well.

Adding Sugar

It is regular practice in Burgundy, as in most of France, to add sugar to the unfermented grape juice. The long experience of growers has shown that slightly more than the natural degree of sugar can produce a better fermentation and a more satisfactory final wine. It is not purely the extra one to two degrees of alcohol but the evolution and final balance of the wine that is affected (they say). Climatic changes in the 1990s have reduced the need for routine chaptalization, but the number of producers who eschew it altogether is tiny.

All chaptalization is strictly controlled by law. Nobody in any appellation may add more than two degrees alcohol to any wine by adding sugar. (There is a temptation to add the maximum; sugar makes the wine easier to sell. The extra alcohol makes it taste more impressive and flattering in its youth when buyers come to the cellar to taste.)

In 1987, the regulations stipulated that to use the humblest appellation for red wine, Bourgogne, the wine must have a natural alcoholic degree of ten. The maximum degree allowable, after chaptalization, was thirteen degrees. So a ten-degree wine was permitted to be raised to twelve degrees, 10.5 to 12.5, and eleven and upwards to thirteen. The equivalent figures for white wine are always 0.5 degrees higher: *e.g.* Bourgogne Blanc must be naturally 10.5 degrees and may be pushed up to 13.5 degrees.

It has always been illegal to add acidity to a chaptalized wine. You can follow either procedure but not both. However, it has been an open secret that most Burgundian winemakers frequently perform both, not to cut corners but to produce a better-balanced wine. When one of Burgundy's most celebrated winemakers admitted to the practice in the late 1990s, all hell broke loose, but he won the moral argument simply by admitting to a procedure widely practiced. (Winemakers could legally chaptalize one vat, and add acidity to another, and then blend the two – thus demonstrating that the law is an ass.)

The Burgundy Revolution

This fine-tuning during vinification and ageing pales in comparison with the major changes in viticulture over the past decade or so. There has been a widespread recognition that, during the 1960s and 1970s, serious errors were made: too much fertilizer was used, and clones adapted for productivity rather than quality were planted. Today there are few quality-oriented growers who do not accept that the choice of plant material – whether massal or clonal selection – is of crucial importance. The routine use of herbicides has also declined, severe pruning or green harvesting (or both) are employed to keep yields low, and some top estates have

Biodynamism

It was the Loire producer Nicolas Joly who first became convinced that the ideas of educationalist and theorist Rudolf Steiner were applicable to grape farming. Biodynamics is hard to explain because of its mystical elements. It counsels an approach to viticulture than is essentially organic, but with some added ingredients. Biodynamism argues that cosmic forces such as lunar positions have a direct influence on natural growing seasons here on earth. This is hardly a cranky idea, since such processes as racking and bottling were traditionally performed according to the position of the moon, which growers knew could affect the turbidity of the wine.

Biodynamism also recommends – indeed insists upon – a return to ploughing the soil, the use of precisely composed compost, and the addition of homeopathic doses of minerals or materials such as manure buried within a cow's horn for a specified time. Treatments are dissolved in a solution and ritually stirred (or "dynamized") before being applied at precisely prescribed times of the day (or night) and month. This is the mumbo-jumbo aspect (in outlying farms even witchcraft is mentioned) of biodynamism that many conscientious growers find hard to swallow. Yet some of the most prestigious (and hard-headed) of Burgundy's growers – including Leflaive, Leroy, and Lafon – have fervently adopted the system. Some of them admit they don't really understand how it functions, yet they find that their vineyards are healthier. Micro-organisms and nutrient elements in the soil begin to multiply, and because the soil is enjoying optimal health, so the proponents of biodynamism argue, the fruit, too, will be healthier and more intense in flavour. In some vintages biodynamic vineyards can be more susceptible to diseases such as mildew; in other years they seem to resist disease better than vines that are conventionally farmed. The jury is still out, but biodynamism is fast winning converts, not just in Burgundy but throughout France.

adopted biodynamism (*see* box below). The consequence of all these developments is that the overall quality of Burgundy's wines has risen sharply in recent years, and is no longer confined to a handful of top estates.

General Appellations

There are four appellations that are available to growers in the whole of Burgundy with certain provisos:

Bourgogne

Red, white, or rosé wines. The whites must be Chardonnay, or Pinot Beurot. The reds must be Pinot Noir or Pinot Liébault, except in the Yonne, where the César and the Tressot are traditional and are admitted, and the *crus* of Beaujolais, whose Gamay may be sold as Bourgogne. A few villages, such as Epineuil and Chitry have the right to add their name to Bourgogne on the label. There are also separate appellations for Bourgogne Côte Chalonnaise and Bourgogne Côte du Couchois.

The maximum crop is fifty-five hectolitres per hectare for red and rosé, sixty for white. Minimum natural strength: ten degrees for red and rosé, 10.5 degrees for white. It is worth ageing Bourgogne Rouge at least two years. Bourgogne AC made by top growers in the major villages from vines grown just outside the village boundaries represent the best-value wine. In Burgundy, the name of the producer is everything.

Bourgogne Passe-tout-grains

Red or rosé wines from any area made of up to two-thirds Gamay and at least one-third Pinot Noir fermented together. Maximum crop: fifty-five hectolitres per hectare. Minimum natural strength: 9.5 degrees. Bourgogne Passe-tout-grains can be delicious after at least one-year's ageing, and is not as heady as Beaujolais.

Bourgogne Aligoté

White wine of Aligoté grapes, with up to fifteen per cent Chardonnay, from anywhere in Burgundy. Maximum crop sixty hectolitres per hectare. Minimum natural strength 9.5 degrees. One commune, Bouzeron in the Côte Chalonnaise, has gained its own appellation for Aligoté; the permitted maximum crop is forty-five hectolitres per hectare. Aligoté often makes a sharp wine with considerable local character when young – the classic base for a *vin blanc* cassis, or Kir.

Bourgogne Grand Ordinaire (or Bourgogne Ordinaire)

Red, white, or rosé from any of the permitted Burgundy grape varieties. Maximum crop is fifty-five hectolitres per hectare for red and rosé, sixty for white. Minimum natural strength nine degrees for red and rosé, 9.5 degrees for white. This appellation is now not often used.

A new AC was approved in 2002 – St-Bris. This is an oddity among Burgundian appellations, since its 895 hectares are dedicated to Sauvignon Blanc and not to Chardonnay. Its vineyards and producers are located in five villages of the Yonne: St-Bris, Chitry, Irancy, Quenne, and Vincelottes.

Burgundy in round figures

"Greater Burgundy", the region including not only the Côte d'Or but Beaujolais, the Mâconnais, Mercurey, and the Yonne (Chablis), now produces fifteen per cent of all *appellation contrôlée* wines. In Burgundy (excluding Beaujolais), there are some 25,000 hectares of AC vineyards under vine, and a further 22,500 in Beaujolais. While red wine production has remained fairly stable, white wine production has expanded, especially in Chablis and the Mâconnais. Vineyards producing the non-appellation *vins de consommation courante* have decreased sharply.

The trend in Burgundy, as in Bordeaux and elsewhere in France, has been towards more specialization and fewer but bigger holdings of vines. For example, in the Côte d'Or in 1955, 16,500 farmers had vineyards amounting to less than one hectare. The figure today is less than 2,000. In contrast, the number of *exploitations* of between five and ten hectares has more than doubled, of those between ten and twenty almost trebled, and of those of twenty hectares and upwards quadrupled. Similar trends – if anything, more marked – apply to the other areas of Burgundy. Today the total production in the region, including Beaujolais, is 2.9 million hectolitres (the equivalent of almost thirty million cases).

The average annual production for the five years 1995–9 is summarized below for the principal brackets of Burgundy appellations.

WHITE WINES	Hectolitres	Cases
Côte d'Or Grands Crus	3,800	42,180
Côted d'Or Premiers Crus	22,230	246,750
Côte d'Or other (village) wines	55,500	616,000
Chablis	248,000	2,752,000
Côte Chalonnaise	33,270	370,000
Mâcon Crus (*e.g.* Pouilly-Fuissé)	92,800	1,030,000
Mâcon Blanc (other)	209,300	2,323,000
Beaujolais	13,000	144,000
Regional appellations (simple Bourgogne, etc.)	225,000	2,497,500
Total production of white wines	**902,900**	**10,021,430**

RED WINES	Hectolitres	Cases
Côte d'Or Grands Crus	13,000	144,400
Côte d'Or Premiers Crus	65,641	728,615
Côte d'Or other (village) wines	189,000	2,097,900
Côte Chalonnaise	40,310	447,400
Mâcon	47,625	528,600
Beaujolais and Beaujolais-Villages	980,000	10,878,000
Beaujolais Crus (*e.g.* Fleurie)	360,000	3,996,100
Regional appellations (simple Bourgogne, etc.)	286,640	3,181,700
Total production of red wines	**1,982,216**	**22,002,715**
Total production, red & white	**2,885,116**	**32,024,145**

Chablis

Chablis and the few other scattered vineyards of the Yonne *département* are a tiny remnant of what was once the biggest vineyard area in France. It was the 40,000 hectares of the Yonne, centred around the city of Auxerre, that supplied the population of Paris with its daily wine before the building of the railways brought them unbeatable competition from the Midi. Whether one is to draw any conclusion from the fact that its best vineyard was called La Migraine is hard to say.

Any vineyard so far north is a high-risk enterprise. When falling sales were followed by the phylloxera disaster, Auxerre turned to other forms of agriculture. Chablis dwindled yet held on. When it was first delineated as an appellation in the 1930s, there was not much more than 400 hectares, but they included the hillside of the seven *grands crus*. Nobody could ignore the quality of their wine. I remember a forty-five-year-old half-bottle of Les Clos 1923 as being one of the best white wines I ever drank.

It was the merchants of Beaune who made Chablis famous. In the simple old days when Beaune, being a nice, easy name to remember, meant red burgundy, Chablis meant white. The name was picked up and echoed around the wine-growing world as a synonym for dry white wine.

But the real thing remained a rarity. Year after year, spring frosts devastated the Chablis vineyards and discouraged replanting. Only in the 1960s did new methods of frost control turn the scales. The introduction of sprinkler systems to replace stoves among the vines on cold spring nights finally made Chablis profitable. Advances in weed and rot control made it very attractive to invest in a name that was already world-famous. Within a decade, the planted area doubled, with each hectare yielding far more wine more reliably than ever before. It continues to grow. Today there are over 4,000 hectares, and an average crop is around a quarter to one-third of all white burgundy.

Inevitably, the old guard strongly resists the granting of the appellation to so much new land. However, as in the rest of Burgundy, the *grands* and *premiers crus* are more or less sacrosanct; it is in Chablis simple or village, with no vineyard name, that there is room for more expansion.

Unqualified village Chablis, as it is generally made today, competes in the marketplace with Mâcon-Villages. In style it is lighter, sharper, drier, and cleaner. A good example is distinctly fruity with a quality that only Chardonnay gives. A poor one is simply neutral and more or less sharp. A small amount of wine from inferior plots is only allowed the appellation Petit Chablis. A good Petit Chablis has the regional style, can even be gentle and juicy; but you must find a first-class maker. Many say it should not be called Chablis at all.

Premier cru and *grand cru* Chablis are different wines; there are distinct steps upward in body, flavour, and individuality. Some people find the best *premiers crus* the most satisfyingly typical, with plenty of flavour and a distinctive "cut" of acidity. The *grands crus* add a richness and strength which round them out; occasionally too much so. To be seen at their best, the *grands crus* need at least four and sometimes up to ten years ageing in bottle.

In the 1980s, the fashion for ageing in new oak came to Chablis. Opinions were sharply divided, as much among producers as among their customers. Fortunately, the trend is in retreat, and estates that once aged their *grands crus* in 100 per cent new oak are now more judicious. Certainly a skilful use of barriques, including a proportion of new barrels, can add complexity and structure to the wine. The trick is not to end up with a wine that, however splendid and attention-grabbing, has lost its Chablisienne *typicité*. Many growers ignored the trend altogether and still vinify and age the wine entirely in steel tanks, with no evident loss in quality.

The scent and flavour that develop are the quintessence of an elusive character you can miss if you only ever drink Chablis young. I can only define it as combining the fragrances of apples and hay with a taste of boiled sweets and an underlying mineral note that seems to have been mined from the bowels of the earth. A good vintage in due course gains a golden richness that reminds me of Sauternes.

The price of Chablis has not kept pace with its value. *grand cru* Chablis is happily in much better supply than Bâtard-Montrachet, otherwise, it could well fetch as high a price. *Premier cru* Chablis from a good grower is the best value in white burgundy.

In 2001, eighteen top growers formed an association called the *Union des Grands Crus*. The idea was to impose stricter controls than the AC rules require, and thus enhance the image and quality (and no doubt price) of *grand cru* Chablis. After much debate, the Union members agreed to outlaw machine-picking on *grand cru* sites, the main surprise being that it was ever permitted in the first place.

Leading Chablis Producers

Billaud-Simon ☆☆☆
Chablis

Most of the estate's twenty hectares are *premiers* or *grands crus*, the latter including 1.7 hectares in Les Clos, Les Preuses, and Vaudésir. Almost all the wines are unoaked, spend a long time in vat or barrel before being bottled, and have a steely brilliance.

Jean-Marc Brocard ☆☆–☆☆☆
Préhy. www.brocard.fr

Brocard is a self-made man who has built up a large domaine of eighty hectares. He is also a négociant, buying in about two-thirds of his requirements. The range of wines is very extensive and, in addition to Chablis, he produces some fascinating Bourgogne Blancs, each from a different soil type and labelled accordingly. The Chablis wines are unoaked, but the top wines can age very well, although they are styled to be enjoyable young.

Cave Coopérative la Chablisienne ☆☆–☆☆☆
Chablis. www.chablisienne.com

A quarter of all Chablis comes from this cooperative, founded in 1923. No fewer than 278 members provide grapes from 1,130 hectares (not only in Chablis), of which thirteen are *grands crus*. Of the *grands crus* vineyards, the most significant are 3.3 hectares of Les Preuses, and the 7.2-hectare monopoly known as Château Grenouille, owned by the cooperative since 2000. Fourchaume is much their most important *premier cru*. Their methods are modern and their wine well-made, clean, and surprisingly sophisticated. Vinification and ageing are adapted to the *crus* and fruit quality, with no firm rules about barrique-ageing. Oak fans should look out for the "Grande Cuvée", a *premier cru* blend that is barrel-fermented. So is the Château Grenouille.

René & Vincent Dauvissat ☆☆☆☆
Chablis

Vincent Dauvissat's great-great-grandfather was a cooper, so it is no surprise that his cellars, unlike many in Chablis today, are still full of barrels, including the traditional *feuillettes*, which are smaller than regular Burgundian barrels. Dauvissat ages the wine from his eleven hectares for about eight months in mostly older wood in the old style. His best wines are the *grands crus* Les Clos and Les Preuses. His remaining vineyards are mostly *premier cru*. This is an utterly reliable source of exceptional Chablis.

Etienne Defaix ☆☆–☆☆☆
Château de Milly

About half this estate, twenty-five hectares, is in *premier cru* sites, with many parcels of old vines. The *premiers crus*, unusually, are aged in tanks for up to three years, with lees-stirring to enrich the wine. The Defaix family insists that this is a traditional method. Interestingly, it gives the wine a character akin to oakiness.

Jean-Paul Droin ☆☆–☆☆☆☆
Chablis. www.jeanpaul-droin.fr

Droin's great-grandfather presented his wines to Napoléon III when he visited Auxerre in 1866. His cellars have not changed overmuch. Droin is fortunate enough to own seven hectares of *premiers crus* (mainly Vaillons), as well as parcels in four *grands crus*. Once a champion of new-oak fermentation and ageing, he has moderated his views, and the wines since the mid-1990s are much better balanced. They are some of the finest Chablis made today.

Joseph Drouhin ☆☆☆
Beaune

The famous Beaune négociant has, since 1979, added thirty-six hectares of Chablis to his domaine and makes immaculate, beautifully tender, and aristocratic wine from the *grands crus* Vaudésir, Les Clos, Les Preuses, and vividly typical *premier cru* from a number of sites.

Jean Durup ☆☆–☆☆☆
Maligny

The huge estate of Jean Durup, president of the lobby that favours expanding the appellation Chablis. He has 170 hectares, of which thirty-five are in *premiers crus* (principally Fourchaume and Vau de Vey). All the wines are unoaked. An impeccable modern winery whose wines appear under the names "Domaine de l'Eglantière" and "Château de Maligny".

William Fèvre ☆☆☆–☆☆☆☆☆
Chablis

Fèvre was the largest owner of *grands crus* and a fervent advocate of new-oak fermentation. The estate's sixteen hectares of *grands crus* include four of Les Clos, six of Bougros, and three of Les Preuses, with smaller but significant parcels in Valmur, Vaudésir, and Grenouilles. There is a similar amount of *premiers crus*, split among seven vineyards, and twenty hectares of Chablis "simple". In 1998, the property was purchased by Bouchard Père et Fils of

The Vineyards of Chablis

Chablis comes in four tiers: Chablis AC (also known as village), Petit Chablis (1,550 hectares in 2001), *premier cru* (750), and *grand cru* (102). *Premier cru* vineyard names (listed here) are sometimes used in conjunction with *premier cru* names. In the 1990s, new vines were planted at such a rate that by 2000 the area exceeded 4,000 hectares (there were only 2,280 as recently as 1988).

Premiers Crus

Premier cru Chablis may be sold either with the names of individual vineyards or those of certain vineyards grouped together. The latter is generally the case, so in practice there are only a small number of names. In alphabetical order, together with the names of the vineyards that have the right to use the name in question (since 1986): Les Beauregards (Côte de Cuissy); Beauroy (Troesmes, Côte de Savant); Berdiot; Chaume de Talvat; Fourchaume (Vaupulent, Côte de Fontenay, l'Homme Mort, Vaulorent); Les Fourneaux (Morein, Côte des Prés-Girots); Côte de Jouan; Les Landes et Verjuts; Côte de Léchet; Mont de Milieu; Montée de Tonnerre (Chapelot, Pied d'Aloup, Côte de Bréchain); Montmains (Forêts, Butteaux); Vaillons (Châtains, Séchet, Beugnons, Les Lys, Mélinots, Roncières, les Epinottes); Côtes de Vaubarousse; Vaucoupin; Vau de Vey (Vaux Ragons); Vau Ligneau; and Vosgros (Vaugiraut).

Grands Crus

Blanchot (12 hectares); Bougros (13); Les Clos (25); Grenouilles (10); Preuses (11.5); Valmur (13); and Vaudésir (15 hectares). La Moutonne is a vineyard of 2.5 hectares within Vaudésir and Les Preuses. Learning the differences between them is one of life's sustaining pleasures.

Beaune (*q.v.*). From 1999, yields were diminished, hand-picking was made *de rigueur*, and the amount of new oak was severely reduced. The wines are now among the very finest of the region.

Alain Geoffroy ☆☆
Beines. www.chablis-geoffroy.com

A third of the forty-hectare domaine is *premier cru*, mainly Beauroy (seven hectares), as well vines in *grands crus* Les Clos and Vaudésir. Geoffroy is no fan of wood, and likes to bottle young to preserve the wines' freshness and *typicité*.

Jean-Pierre & Corinne Grossot ☆☆–☆☆☆
Fleys

Enthusiastic growers with eighteen hectares, including holdings in *premiers crus* Fourchaume, Vaucoupin, Mont de Milieu, and the rarely encountered Côte de Troemes. Vinification is mostly in stainless steel, although some oak is used for the better wines.

Domaine Laroche ☆☆–☆☆☆☆
Chablis. www.michellaroche.com

Michel Laroche is the fifth-generation owner of an estate of ninety-nine hectares. There are six hectares of Chablis Grand Cru, notably Les Blanchots, and twenty-eight of *premier cru*. Modern equipment makes Chablis in an austere, vigorous style, though some new oak is used for the *grands* and *premiers crus*. The *grands crus* should be kept for between three and eight years. The top wine is a selection from old Blanchot vines labelled "Réserve de l'Obédiencerie". The name "Laroche" also appears on a wide range of non-domaine wines, including a good brand of simple Chablis, "St Martin". They also blend good, non-regional Chardonnay and have now embarked on a range of wines from the Languedoc. Laroche remains a keen defender of the appellation and was the driving force behind the new *Union des Grands Crus*.

Long-Depaquit ☆☆☆
Chablis

This family estate was bought in 1967 by the négociant Bichot (*q.v.*) of Beaune but is still run autonomously. Of their sixty-two hectares, fifteen are *premiers crus* and nine *grands crus*, including over two of Vaudésir. The most famous property is the two-hectare Moutonne vineyard, a part of the *grands crus* Vaudésir and Les Preuses, whose history goes back to the Abbey of Pontigny and its monks, who apparently skipped like young sheep under its inspiration. Long-Depaquit wines are very thoughtfully and professionally made with modern methods, but not for instant drinking. Since 1993, there has been a very cautious use of oak-ageing for the *grands crus*.

Domaine des Malandes ☆☆☆
Chablis

A twenty-three-hectare domaine with 0.9 hectares in *grand cru* Vaudésir, and seven hectares of *premiers crus* including Fourchaume and Montmains. Modern-style Chablis: bright, fresh, and untouched by oak.

Louis Michel & Fils ☆☆–☆☆☆☆
Chablis

Louis and son Jean-Loup have built up a sizeable estate from small beginnings. They now have twenty hectares, thirteen in *premiers crus* (some in Montmains and Montée de Tonnerre) and two in *grands crus* (Vaudésir, Grenouilles, and Les Clos). Michel believes in letting the wine make itself as far as possible. He uses no barrels, but by modest yields and careful handling makes concentrated wines that repay years of bottle-age.

Jean-Marie Raveneau ☆☆☆☆
Chablis

A 7.5-hectare domaine entirely composed of *grands crus* (Blanchots, Valmur, Les Clos) and *premiers crus*, considered by some to be the best in Chablis. The wines are fermented in tanks, but aged in barrels of various sizes and ages for at least one year. They can be austere and minerally when young but age superbly.

A. Regnard & Fils ☆
Chablis

A family firm of négociants, founded in 1860 and now partly owned by Loire wine magnate Patrick de Ladoucette. The best wines are often the *grands crus* Vaudésir and Valmur. As well as Chablis they sell Aligoté and Sauvignon de St-Bris. Other labels used are "Michel Rémon" and "Albert Pic".

Simonnet-Febvre & Fils ☆☆
Chablis

This small domaine of four hectares is better known as a négociant going back five generations. The company makes wine from bought-in juice as well as its own sites in *grand cru* Preuses and a range of *premiers crus*.

Robert Vocoret ☆☆
Chablis

A century-old family domaine of forty-five hectares, four in *grands crus* (Les Clos, Valmur, Blanchots) and fifteen in *premiers crus*. Some of the better wines are aged in large casks but bottled fairly young. The result is wine with less of the immediately appealing fruit but a firm grip that rewards keeping.

Other Chablis Producers

Other leading Chablis producers include: Barat, Jean-Claude Bessin, Pascal Bouchard, Jean Collet, Daniel Dampt, Gérard Duplessis, Bernard Legland, Gilbert Picq, Louis Pinson, Denis Race, Olivier Savary, Servin, Gérard Tremblay, Tribut-Dauvissat, and Domaine de Vauroux.

The Côte d'Or – Côte de Nuits

The heart of Burgundy is the forty-eight kilometre (thirty-mile) line of hills running south from Marsannay on the southern outskirts of Dijon, inclining westwards as it goes and presenting a broadening band of southeast-facing slopes until it stops at Santenay. The eight villages of the northern sector, ending at Prémeaux, are the Côte de Nuits. The twenty villages running south from Aloxe-Corton are the Côte de Beaune. The Côte de Nuits is almost exclusively devoted to red wine – almost all Pinot Noir. On these steep slopes, but particularly their middle curves, the most potently flavoured, concentrated, eventually smooth and perfumed wines are made.

The villages are listed here from north to south. Each is briefly described with an appreciation of its wine and a list of its *grands crus* (if any) and *premiers crus*. The hectarage figures given are those arrived at in 1984 after a long process of official deliberation. Growers are no longer listed under each village entry, as they have become too numerous, but there is an expanded section listing the major Côte d'Or growers, beginning on page 108. It is by no means an exhaustive list. The details of growers' holdings give a vivid picture of the infinitely complex structure of the world's most highly prized vineyards.

(NB: all *grands/premiers crus* entries include hectare figures in brackets.)

Marsannay-la-Côte

Formerly known only for its excellent Rosé de Marsannay, this village now has, uniquely in Burgundy, an appellation for all three colours. The whites mostly lack interest, the rosés are deliciously perfumed and elegant, the reds on the light side but extremely pretty. A few more serious reds are now being produced, too. Marsannay also covers the few remaining vineyards (*e.g.* Clos du Roy) of Chenove, which is now a light industrial suburb of Dijon. Marsannay covers 188 hectares but has no designated *premier cru* vineyards.

Fixin

The *premiers crus* are splendidly situated and capable of wines as good as those of Gevrey-Chambertin. Even the village wines are stout-hearted and long-lived. The commune has ninety-seven hectares under vine. Between Fixin and Gevrey-Chambertin, the village of Brochon has no appellation of its own. Its better vineyards are included in Gevrey-Chambertin. The lesser ones are plain Côte de Nuits-Villages.

PREMIERS CRUS

Arvelets (3.4)
Clos du Chapitre (4.8)
Clos Napoléon (1.8)
Clos de la Perrière (6.8)
Hervelets (4.3)

Gevrey-Chambertin

There is a very wide range of quality in the production of Gevrey – the biggest of any of the townships of the Côte d'Or. Some of its flat vineyards beyond the valley road are of middling quality only. But there is no questioning the potential of its constellation of *grands crus*. Chambertin and the Clos de Bèze are acknowledged to lead them; an extra charge of fiery concentration gives them the edge. The seven others must always keep the Chambertin after their names; Clos de Bèze may put it before, or indeed simply label itself Chambertin. They are all stern, essentially male (since everything in France has a gender) wines that I cannot imagine even Astérix himself tossing back in bumpers (Obélix, perhaps). French critics claim for Chambertin the delicacy of Musigny allied to the strength of a Corton, the velvet of a Romanée and the perfume of the Clos Vougeot. I have certainly tasted fabulous complexity, but delicacy is not the word I would choose. Great age is probably the key. Among the *premiers crus* on the hill behind the village, Clos St-Jacques is widely thought to be on the same level of quality as the bevy of hyphenated Chambertins.

GRANDS CRUS

Chambertin (12.6)
Chambertin Clos de Bèze (15.4)
Chapelle-Chambertin (5.4)
Charmes- (and/or Mazoyères-) Chambertin (30.4)
Griotte-Chambertin (2.4)
Latricières-Chambertin (7.4)
Mazis-Chambertin (9)
Ruchottes-Chambertin (3.1)

PREMIERS CRUS

Bel Air (2.6)
La Boissière*
Cazetiers (9)
Champeaux (6.7)
Champitonnois (also called Petite Chapelle) (4)

Champonnets (3.2)
Cherbaudes (2)
Clos du Chapitre (1)
Clos Prieur (part) (2)
Clos St-Jacques (6.7)
Clos des Varoilles (6)
Closeau (0.5)
Combe-aux-Moines (4.7)
Combottes (4.5)
Corbeaux (3)
Craipillot (2.7)
Ergot (1.2)
Estournelles (2)
Fonteny (3.6)
Gémeaux*
Goulots (1.8)
Issarts (0.6)
Lavaux St Jacques (10)
Perrière (2.4)
Petits Cazetiers (0.45)
Poissenot (2.2)
Clos Prieur-Haut (2)
La Romanée (1)
*No hectarage specified in the latest official documents.
Appellation communale: 330 hectares.

Morey-St-Denis

The least-known of the Côte de Nuits villages, despite having four *grands crus* to its name and part of a fifth. Clos de la Roche is capable of making wine with the martial tread of a Chambertin; Clos St-Denis marginally less so; Clos des Lambrays is unusually opulent; Clos de Tart was much lighter, but has taken on weight in recent vintages. All the wines are worth a study, for authenticity and the chance of a bargain.

GRANDS CRUS
Bonnes Mares (a small part) (1.5)
Clos des Lambrays (8.6)
Clos de la Roche (16)
Clos St-Denis (6.6)
Clos de Tart (7.5)

PREMIERS CRUS
Blanchards (2)
Bouchots
Maison Brûlée (1)
Calouères
Chabiots
Chaffots (2.6)
Charmes (1.2)
Charrières (2.3)
Chénevery (3)
Chéseaux (1.5)
Clos Baulet (0.9)
Clos de la Bussière (2.6)
Clos des Ormes (3.2)
Clos Sorbé (3.5)
Côte Rôtie (1.2)
Façonnières (1.7)
Fremières
Froichots

Genavrières (1.2)
Gruenchers (0.5)
Meix-Rentiers
Les Millandes (4.2)
Monts-Luisants (5.4)
Riotte (2.5)
Ruchots (2.6)
Les Sorbés (2.6)
Le Village (0.9)
Appellation communale: 64 hectares.

Chambolle-Musigny

The lilt of the name is perfectly appropriate for the wines of this parish – as is the apparent evocation of the muse. It is hard to restrain oneself from competing in similes with the much-quoted sages of Burgundy, but Gaston Roupnel seems to have it precisely right. Musigny, he says, "has the scent of a dewy garden… of the rose and the violet at dawn." Le Musigny is my favourite red burgundy, closely followed by *premiers crus* Les Amoureuses and Les Charmes, and the other *grand cru*, Bonnes Mares. A contributory reason is that some particularly good winemakers own this land.

GRANDS CRUS
Bonnes Mares (13)
(*see also* Morey-St-Denis)
Musigny (9.3)

PREMIERS CRUS
Amoureuses (5.4)
Les Baudes (3.4)
Aux Beaux Bruns (1.5)
Borniques (1.4)
Carrières
Chabiots (1.5)
Charmes (9.5)
Châtelots (3)
Combe d'Orveau (2.4)
Combottes (1.6)
Aux Combottes (2)
Cras (3.4)
Derrière la Grange (0.4)
Echanges
Feusselottes (4.5)
Fuées (4.4)
Grands Murs
Groseilles (1.3)
Gruenchers (2.8)
Hauts Doix
Lavrottes (0.9)
Noirots (2.8)
Plantes (2.6)
Sentiers (4.9)
Veroilles (0.37)
Appellation communale: 99 hectares.

Vougeot

The great vineyard of the Clos (de) Vougeot has the most resounding reputation in Burgundy. Fifty hectares within a single wall built by the fourteenth century monks of Cîteaux add a certain presence. The land at the top of the slope, next to Musigny and Grands-Echézeaux, is equal to the best in Burgundy, but with its present fragmented ownership among eighty growers it is not easy to meet a bottle that answers this description. Classical references always stress its perfume. My impression is of a more meaty, extremely satisfying but less exotic wine than those of its great neighbours.

GRAND CRU
Clos de Vougeot (50)

PREMIERS CRUS RED
Clos de la Perrière (2.2)
Cras (3)
Petits Vougeots (3.5)

PREMIER CRU WHITE
Clos Blanc (3)
Appellation communale: 5 hectares.

Flagey-Echézeaux

Exists as a village but not as an appellation, despite the fact that it has two *grands crus* in the parish. They are effectively treated as being in Vosne-Romanée, having the right to declassify their wine under the Vosne name. In reality, Grands-Echézeaux is at *grand cru* level – an ideal site adjacent to the best part of the Clos Vougeot. Its wines can have all the flair and the persuasive depths of the greatest burgundy. But the huge thirty-four-hectare Les Echézeaux would be more realistically classified as one or several *premiers crus*. Its lack of any readily spotted identity joined with its apparently unmanageable name means that it sells for a reasonable price. There is a lightness of touch, a gentle sweetness, and airy fragrance about a good Echézeaux which make it less of a challenge than the biggest burgundies.

Vosne-Romanée

If Chambertin has the dignity, the name of Romanée has the glamour. Only the very rich and their guests have ever even tasted La Romanée-Conti. The Domaine de la Romanée-Conti, sole owner of that vineyard and the next greatest, La Tâche, casts its exotic aura equally over Richebourg, Romanée-St-Vivant, and Grands-Echézeaux, where it also owns or manages property. The domaine's wines are marked with a character that seems to be their own, rather than that of Vosne-Romanée as a whole. Out of the torrent of words that has poured around Vosne and its sacred ground over the centuries I would pick three: "fire", "velvet", and "balance". In the excitement of the *grands crus*, the *premiers crus* of Vosne-Romanée can be unwisely overlooked.

GRANDS CRUS
Echézeaux (34)
Grande Rue (1.6)
Grands-Echézeaux (8.6)
Richebourg (7)
La Romanée (0.8)
Romanée-Conti (1.8)

Romanée-St-Vivant (9.3)
La Tâche (6)

PREMIERS CRUS
Beaux Monts (11.4)
Aux Brûlées (4.5)
Chaumes (6.5)
Clos de Réas (2.1)
Croix Rameau (0.6)
Cros Parantoux (1)
Gaudichots (1)
Malconsorts (7)
En Orveaux (1.8)
Petits Monts (3.7)
Reignots (1.6)
Rouges du Dessus (2.6)
Suchots (13)
Appellation communale: 97 hectares, of which 13.3 are in Flagey-Echézeaux.

Nuits-St-Georges

As a town, Nuits-St-Georges does not bear comparison with the alluring city of Beaune; its walls have long gone and it has no great public monuments. But it is the trading centre of the Côte de Nuits, the seat of a dozen négociants, its endless silent cellars maturing countless big-bellied *pièces*. In another way, too, it echoes Beaune; its long hill of vines produces highly prized and famous wine without a single peak. If Nuits had a *grand cru*, it would be Les St-Georges, and possibly Les Vaucrains, Les Cailles, and Les Porrets on the slope above and beside it. But none of these vineyards has convinced the world that its wine alone rises consistently above the *premier cru* level.

Compared with the wines of Beaune, which they sometimes are, those of Nuits-St-Georges are tougher and less fruity and giving in their youth – often for many years. It is hard to understand why they should be so popular in Anglo-Saxon countries, since ten years is often needed to turn toughness to warmth of flavour. The best Nuits has marvellous reserves of elusive character that demand leisurely investigation.

Prémeaux, the village to the south, is part of the appellation Nuits-St-Georges and itself has a run of *premiers crus* of equal merit, squeezed on to a steep and narrow slope between the road and the woods.

PREMIERS CRUS
Aux Argillas (1.8)
Les Argillières, Prémeaux (0.2)
Boudots (6.2)
Bousselots (4.2)
Cailles (7)
Chaboeufs (3)
Chaignots (5.8)
Chaines-Carteaux (3)
Champs Perdrix (0.7)
Château Gris (*monopole* within Les Crofts) (2.8)
Clos de l'Arlot, Prémeaux (4)
Clos des Argillières, Prémeaux (4.2)
Clos des Corvées, Prémeaux (5)
Clos des Corvées Pagets, Prémeaux (1.5)

Clos des Forêts St-Georges, Prémeaux (7)
Clos des Grandes Vignes (2.1)
Clos de la Maréchale, Prémeaux (9.5)
Clos des Porrets St-Georges (3.5)
Clos de Thorey (4.1)
Corvées, Prémeaux (7.7)
Cras (3)
Crots (1.2)
Damodes (8.5)
Didiers, Prémeaux (2.5)
Haut-Pruliers (0.4)

Murgers (5)
Aux Perdrix, Prémeaux (3.5)
Perrières (3)
Perrière-Noblot (0.3)
Porrets (4)
Poulettes (2)
Procès (1.4)
Pruliers (7)
Richemone (2)
Roncières (1)
Rue de Chaux (2)

Romanee-Conti – A Great Burgundy Estate

All the conundrums of wine come to a head at this extraordinary property. It has been accepted for at least three centuries that wine of inimitable style and fascination comes from one small patch of hill, and different wine, marginally but consistently less fascinating, from the sites around it. Romanée-Conti sounds like a super-successful public relations exercise. In some ways it is even organized as one. But there is no trick. On such a small scale, and with millionaires eager for every drop, it is possible to practise total perfectionism. Without the soil and the site, the opportunity would not be there; without the laborious pursuit of perfection, it would be lost. A great vineyard like this is largely man-made, the practice in the days of the eighteenth century. Prince de Conti, who gave it his name, brought fresh loam up from the pastures of the Saône Valley in wagonloads to give new life to the soil.

Ironically, today the authorities would forbid so much as a bucketful from outside the appellation. Does this condemn the great vineyard to a gradual decline?

The co-proprietors of the domaine today are the Leroy and de Villaine families. Aubert de Villaine manages the estate; his home is at Bouzeron, near Chagny, where he makes particularly good Aligoté. After a spectacular in-house row and court case in 1992, Mme. Bize-Leroy was removed from her role within the company and replaced by her nephew Henry-Frédéric Roch.

The vineyards are cultivated organically, with new plant material carefully selected from existing vines. The domaine's policy is to delay picking until the grapes are consummately ripe, running the gauntlet of the autumn storms and the risk of rot, simply rejecting all the grapes that have succumbed. The proportion of stems put in the vat depends on the season. Fermentation is exceptionally long: from three weeks to even a full month. All the wine is matured in new barrels every year. There is a minimum of racking and filtration. It is indeed the grapes that do it.

As the prices of the domaine's wines are so spectacularly high, one expects to find them not only exceptional in character but in perfect condition. They are essentially wines for very long bottle-ageing. It is almost the hallmark of "D.R.C." wines that they are instantly recognizable by their exotic opulence. It used to be the case that bottles were filled directly from each barrel, which led to inconsistencies and some frankly poor bottles. These errors have been corrected, and since 1993 the domaine has hardly put a foot wrong.

Of a bottle of La Tâche 1962, which has been one of the very best burgundies for many years (at least in my view), I noted in 1982: "Overwhelming high-toned smell of violets to start with, changing within twenty minutes to a more deep and fruity bouquet which seemed at first like oranges, then more like blackcurrants. The flavour was best about half an hour after opening – exotically rich and warm – then seemed to become a bit too alcoholic and lose some of its softness. Very exciting wine – not least for the speed and range of its metamorphoses."

The holdings, and average production figures, of the domaine are as follows:

La Romanée-Conti: 1.8 hectares, 6,000 bottles.
La Tâche: 6 hectares, 17,000 bottles.
Richebourg: 3.5 hectares, 13,000 bottles.
Grands-Echézeaux: 3.5 hectares, 13,000 bottles.
Echézeaux: 4.67 hectares, 19,000 bottles.
Romanée-St-Vivant: 5.28 hectares, 21,000 bottles.
Le Montrachet: 0.67 hectares, 3,500 bottles.

Les St-Georges (7.5)
Terres Blanches, Prémeaux (0.9)
Vallerots (0.8)
Vaucrains (6)
Vignes Rondes (3.8)
Appellation communale: 161 hectares.

Côte de Nuits-Villages

This appellation is a consolation prize for the parishes at either end of the main *côtes*: Prissey, Comblanchien, and Corgoloin next to Prémeaux on the road south, and Fixin, Brochon, and Marsannay on the Dijon road beyond Gevrey-Chambertin. Fixin and Marsannay have appellations of their own.

For the others this is the highest aspiration. Stone quarries are more in evidence than vineyards on the road to Beaune. The marble from the hill here is some of France's best. Only one important vineyard stands out as a *premier cru manqué*: the Clos des Langres, property of la Reine Pédauque, at the extreme southern tip of the Côte de Nuits.

Côte d'Or – Côte de Beaune

The heartland of great white Burgundy, home to the fabulous vineyards of Corton-Charlemagne, Meursault, and Montrachet. But its red wines are distinguished too, from the powerful wines of Pommard, the refined Volnays, and the consistently underrated vineyards around Beaune itself. It is also a good region for bargain-hunters to explore, with increasingly elegant and substantial wines from lesser-known villages such as Savigny, Monthelie, and St Aubin.

Nonetheless its most treasured wines are likely to remain its rich, buttery Meursaults, the racy wines of Puligny and Chassagne, the high-powered minerally whites of Corton, and the mighty *grands crus* of Batard-Montrachet and Montrachet itself.

Ladoix-Serrigny

The Côte de Beaune starts with its most famous landmark, the oval dome (if you can have such a thing) of the hill of Corton. The dome wears a beret of woods but its south, east, and west flanks are all vines, forming parts of three different parishes: (in order from the north) Ladoix-Serrigny, Aloxe-Corton, and – tucked round the corner out of sight – Pernand-Vergelesses. The best vineyards of all three are those on the mid- and upper slopes of the hill, which share the appellation Corton Grand Cru (the only red *grand cru* of the Côte de Beaune) and in parts, for white wine, Corton-Charlemagne.

Ladoix-Serrigny has the smallest part of "Corton", and not the best, in its vineyards of Rognet-Corton and Les Vergennes, names which are rarely encountered but often subsumed in the general title of Corton, as all the *grand cru* territory can be. Similarly the village wines of Ladoix, which few people have ever heard of, often take advantage of the appellation Côte de Beaune-Villages.

GRANDS CRUS
Corton-Charlemagne white wines only:
Basses Mourottes (1)
Hautes-Mourottes (1.8)
Le Rognet-et-Corton (3.2)

Corton red and white:
Les Carrières (0.4)
Les Grandes Lolières (3)
Les Moutottes (0.8)
Le Rognet et Corton (8.4)
La Toppe au Vert (0.1)
Les Vergennes (3.4)
Parts of Ladoix-Serrigny may be sold under the appellation Aloxe-Corton, the rest may be sold as Côte de Beaune-Villages.

PREMIERS CRUS
Total area 24 hectares:
Basses Mourottes (0.9)
Bois Roussot (1.8)
Les Buis
Le Clou d'Orge (1.6)
La Corvée (7)
Les Grenchons et Foutrières
Hautes-Mourottes (0.6)
Les Joyeuses (0.8)
Les Lolières
La Micaude (1.6)
En Naget
Le Rognet
Appellation communale: 118 hectares.

Aloxe-Corton

The major part of the *grands crus* Corton and Corton-Charlemagne dominates this parish, but still leaves a substantial amount of lower land with the appellation Aloxe-Corton, both *premier cru* and village. It is important to remember that Corton *tout-court* is always a superior appellation to Aloxe-Corton.

It is almost impossible (and, in any case, not really essential) to grasp the legalities of the *grands crus* here. "Corton" embraces a dozen different adjacent vineyards, the top of which is actually called Le Corton. The others may be labelled either Corton, or, for example, Corton-Clos du Roi, Corton-Bressandes. On such a big hillside there is inevitably a wide range of style and quality. Bressandes, lowest of the *grands crus*, is considered to produce richer wine (from richer soil) than Clos du Roi above it… and so on.

There are 120 hectares of *grand cru* in Aloxe-Corton, of which forty-nine are entitled to produce Corton-Charlemagne. But growers have the right to plant red grapes within Corton-Charlemagne if they wish, though few do so. This makes it impossible to give precise figures for areas planted, as we have done for other communes. But it may be useful to know that about two-thirds of *grand cru* vineyards are released as red Corton (including its sub-vineyards such as Les Bressandes), about one-third as Corton-Charlemagne, and just over one per cent as white Corton.

Corton-Charlemagne is a white *grand cru* from some of the same vineyards as red Corton: those on the south slope and the top ones where the soil is paler and more impregnated with lime. Perversely enough, there is also an appellation for white *grand cru* Corton, although this is rarely seen.

True to their national inclinations, the French rate (red) Corton the best wine of the hill, comparing it for sheer force of personality with Chambertin, whereas the British speak of Corton-Charlemagne in the same breath as Le Montrachet. I have certainly been surprised to see French authors mildly liken it to Meursault. It expresses great driving vigour of a kind closer to a *grand cru* Chablis made in oak, though with more spice, even earth, and correspondingly less of the simple magic of ripe fruit. It is in the nature of Corton-Charlemagne to hide its qualities and show only its power, as red wines do, for as many as seven or eight years. Red Corton needs keeping as long as the *grands crus* of the Côte de Nuits.

The dominant name among Corton growers, both red and white, is that of Louis Latour, whose press house and cellars are cut into the foot of the hill itself and who gives the name of his château, Grancey, to a selection of Corton of even greater than usual power.

GRANDS CRUS
Lieu-dits for red Corton:
Bressandes (17.4)
Maréchaudes (4.2)
Perrières (10)
Renardes (11.3)
Clos du Roi (10.7)
Parts (smaller than 4 hectares) of Chaumes and Voirosses, Combes, Fiètres, Grèves, Meix, Meix Lallemand, Pauland, Le Village, and La Vigne au Saint in Aloxe-Corton.

PREMIERS CRUS
Chaillots (4.6)
Clos des Maréchaudes (1.4)
Coutière (2.5)
Les Fournières (5.5)
Les Guérets (2.5)
Les Maréchaudes (2.3)
Les Meix (2)
Moutottes (0.9)
Paulands (1.6)
Petits Lolières (1.6)
Yoppe au Vert (1.7)
Les Valozières (6.6)
Les Vercots (4.2)
Appellation communale: 89 hectares.

Pernand-Vergelesses

The *grand cru* of Pernand-Vergelesses is Corton-Charlemagne; there is no red Corton on the western slope of the hill (the only western slope in the whole of the Côte d'Or). But its *premiers crus* are in a completely different situation, directly facing Corton-Charlemagne across the narrow valley that leads up to this hidden village. The *premiers crus* are red; they continue the best vineyards of neighbouring Savigny, and in a sense those of Beaune.

GRAND CRU
Charlemagne (white only) and Corton (red only) are both in the same parcel.

PREMIERS CRUS
Basses Vergelesses (also known as Les Vergelesses) (18)
Caradeux (12)
Clos Berthet
Clos Le Village
Creux de la Net (3.4)
Croix de Pierre (2.8)
Fichots (11)
Ile des Vergelesses (9)
Sous Frétille
Appellation communale: 137 hectares.

Savigny-lès-Beaune

Savigny, like Pernand-Vergelesses, stops the head of a little valley cut back into the *côte* and grows vines on both sides of it. On the Pernand side they face south, on the Beaune side northeast. The best are at the extremities of the parish, where both incline most to the east: respectively, Les Vergelesses and Lavières, and La Dominode and Marconnets. The valley is drained by the little River Rhoin.

Savigny has a substantial château, a great number of good growers, and best of all a tendency to more moderate prices than its neighbours. Its wines could be called light classics, apt to age, yet never ultra-chic. They need a good vintage to bring them up to their full strength – but whose do not?

PREMIERS CRUS
Bas Marconnets (3)
Basses Vergelesses (1.7)
Bataillere (1.8)
Champ-Chevrey (1.5)
Charnières (2)
Clous (10)
Dominode (8)
Fourneaux (6.4)
Gravains (6)
Guettes (14)
Hauts-Jarrons (4.5)
Hauts-Marconnets (5.4)
Jarrons (1.4)
Lavières (17)
Narbantons (9.5)
Petits Godeaux (0.7)
Peuillets (16)
Redrescut (0.5)
Rouvrettes (2.8)
Serpentières (12)
Talmettes (3)
Aux Vergelesses (15)
Appellations communales: 212 hectares.

Beaune

Beaune offers more temptation than any town to turn a wine encyclopedia into a guide book. It begs to be visited. Walking its wobbly streets between its soothing cellars is one of the great joys. The oldest, biggest, grandest, and most of the best négociants have their warrens here. They also own the greater part of its wide spread of vineyards. Do not look to Beaune for the most stately or the most flighty wines. "*Franc de gout*" is the classic description, which is almost impossible to translate. *Franc* signifies straight, candid, open, real, downright, forthright, and upright. Not dull, though. Young Beaune is already good to drink; as it ages, it softens and broadens its bouquet.

If there is a pecking order among the *premiers crus*, the following are near the top of it: Les Grèves, Fèves, Cras, Teurons, Marconnets, and Clos des Mouches (which also produces an excellent white wine). But nobody would claim to be able to distinguish them all, and more depends on the maker than the site. For this reason, the various *monopoles* of the négociant*s* are usually worth their premium. Their names are usually prefixed with the word *clos*. The three biggest landowners are Bouchard Père & Fils, Chanson, and the Hospices de Beaune.

PREMIERS CRUS

Aigrots (18)
Avaux (11.5)
Bas Teurons (6.3)
Beaux Fougets (0.3)
Bélissand (5)
Blanche Fleur (0.4)
Boucherottes (8.5)
Bressandes (17)
Cent Vignes (24)
Champs Pimont (16)
Chouacheux (5)
Clos des Avaux (3.7)
Clos de l'Ecu (2.4)
Clos de la Féguine (1.9)
Clos Landry (2)
Clos des Mouches (25)
Clos de la Mousse (3.4)
Clos du Roi (8.4)
Clos Ste Anne (0.7)
Coucherias (7.7)
Cras (5)
A l'Ecu (2.6)
Epenottes (8)
Fèves (4.5)
En Genèt (4.5)
Grèves (32)
Marconnets (9.5)
Mignotte (2.4)
Montées Rouges (3.7)
Montrevenots (8)
En l'Orme (2)
Perrières (3.2)
Pertuisots (5.2)
Reversées (4.8)
Seurey (1.2)
Sizies (8.6)
Sur les Grèves (3)
Teurons (21)

Toussaints (6.5)
Tuvilains (9)
Vignes Franches (10)
Appellation communale: 128 hectares.

Chorey-lès-Beaune

The little appellation of Chorey-lès-Beaune slips off the map down into the plain. Its wine is often commercialized as Côte de Beaune-Villages. The wines can be delicious but should be drunk young.

Côte de Beaune

This appellation was instituted, as it seems, to discover who was dozing during the complexities of Côte de Beaune-Villages (*see* page 108). It applies only to wine from Beaune (which has no reason to use it) or from another nine hectares adjoining, which appear to be just as deserving. La Grande Châtelaine, the Clos de Topes, and Clos de Monsnières are the only vineyards I know that use it, for an admirable white as well as red. There's only thirty hectares in production, so it's not often seen.

Pommard

In the war of words that continually tries to distinguish one village from another, the wines of Pommard seem to have been labelled "*loyaux et marchands*", which translates as "loyal and commercial". The suggestion is not of poetic flights. Pommard makes solid, close-grained wines of strong colour, aggressive at first, bending little even with age. Les Rugiens, with its iron-red soil, is the vineyard with most of these qualities, considered the best of the village. Les Epenots, on the edge of Beaune, gives rather easier wine. There are some proud and decidedly loyal growers in the parish, but few of them have mastered the art of taming the Pommard tannins.

PREMIERS CRUS

Argillières (4)
Arvelets (8.5)
Bertins (3.5)
Boucherottes (1.5)
Chanière (2.8)
Chanlins Bas (4.4)
Chaponnières (2.8)
Charmots (9.7)
Clos Blanc (4.2)
Clos de la Commaraine (3.8)
Clos des Epeneaux (5.2)
Clos Micot (2.8)
Clos de Verger (2)
Combes-Dessus (2.7)
Croix Noires (1.3)
Fremiers (5)
Grands-Epenots (10)
Les Jarollières (3.2)
Petits Epenots (15)
Pézerolles (6)
Platière (2.5)

Poutures (4.1)
Refène (2.3)
Rugiens-Bas (5.8)
Rugiens-Hauts (6.8)
Saussilles (3.9)
Appellation communale: 210 hectares.

Volnay

Corton and Volnay are the extremes of style of the Côte de Beaune: the first regal, robust, deep-coloured, and destined to dominate; the second ideally tender, "lacy", a lighter red with a soft-fruit scent, all harmony and delight. The dictum goes that Volnay is the Chambolle-Musigny of the Côte de Beaune. Personally, I find it exact: each is my favourite from its area. To shift the ground a little, Château Latour answers to Corton; Lafite lovers will want Volnay – though some Volnay growers are carried away with the search for power and extract these days. A pity. Indeed, a crying shame.

The lovely little village hangs higher in the hills than its neighbours, its 136 hectares of *premiers crus* on the mid-slopes below. The long ramp of vines that leads down to Meursault contains Les Caillerets, probably the closest any Volnay Premier Cru gets to *grand cru* quality. Champans, beside it under the village, reaches the same class, as does Clos des Chênes. There is no clear division between Volnay and its southern neighbours, Meursault in the valley and Monthélie on the hill. The same style of wine, even the same vineyard names continue. Meursault is allowed to use the name of Volnay for red wine grown in its part of Caillerets, Santenots, Pitures, and Cras (as long as it uses Pinot Noir). To taste them beside the white *premiers crus* of Meursault is to discover that red and white wine are by no means chalk and cheese.

PREMIERS CRUS
Angles (3.4)
Aussy (1.7)
Brouillards (5.6)
Caillerets (14.4)
Carelle Sous la Chapelle (3.7)
Carelles Dessous (1.5)
Champans (11)
Chanlins (2.9)
Chevret (6.4)
Clos de l'Audignac (1.1)
Clos de la Barre (1.3)
Clos de la Bousse d'Or (2.2)
Clos du Château des Ducs (0.6)
Clos des Chênes (15)
Clos de la Cave des Ducs (0.6)
Clos des Ducs (2.4)
En l'Ormeau (4.3)
Frémiets (7.4)
Gigotte (0.5)
Grand-Champs (0.2)
Lurets (2)
Mitans (4)
Pitures Dessus (4)
Pointes d'Angles (1.2)
Robardele (3)
Ronceret (1.9)
Santenots (22)

Taille Pieds (7)
Clos du Verseuil (0.7)
Appellation communale: 100 hectares.

Monthélie

Just as Corton-Charlemagne goes on round the corner into Pernand-Vergelesses, so the best Volnay vineyard flows into the lesser-known Monthélie. It changes its name to Les Champs-Fulliot. The centre of interest in the village of Monthélie is its château, the property of one of its most distinguished growers: Robert de Suremain.

PREMIERS CRUS
Cas Rougeot (0.6)
Champs Fulliot (8)
Château Gaillard (0.5)
Clos Gauthey (1.8)
Duresses (6.7)
Meix-Bataille (2.3)
Riottes (0.7)
Sur la Velle (6)
Taupine (1.5)
Vignes Rondes (2.7)
Appellation communale: 110 hectares.

Meursault

If Meursault has convinced itself that it is a town, it fails to convince visitors looking for amenities – still less action. Its streets are a bewildering forest of hoardings to cajole the tourist into the cellars that are its whole *raison d'être*. Levels of commercialism vary. In one property half-hidden with invitations to enter I was told, curtly, that I could not taste unless I was going to buy. There was no answer to my mild protest that I could not tell if I was going to buy until I had tasted.

There is a mass of Meursault, and it is mixed. Its model is a drink that makes me thirsty even to think of it: a meeting of softness and succulence with thirst-quenching clarity and "cut". A village Meursault will be mild; the higher up the ladder you go the more authority and "cut" the wine will have. I am thinking of a 1978 *premier cru* Charmes from Joseph Matrot, which, at three years old (I can still remember it), was almost painful to hold in your mouth. This is the authority and concentration of a first-class wine of a great vintage. With age comes rounding out, the onset of flavours people have described with words like "oatmeal" and "hazelnuts", and "butter"; things that are rich but bland.

The white wine vineyards of Meursault are those that continue unbroken into Puligny-Montrachet to the south, and the best are those that are nearest to the parish line: Les Perrières, Les Charmes, Les Genevrières. The hamlet of Blagny, higher on the same hill, also contains Meursault Premiers Crus of the top quality: Sous le Dos d'Ane and La Pièce Sous le Bois – names that seem to express a rustic crudity, which is far from being the case.

Village wines from high on the hill (Les Tillets, Les Narvaux) are excellent, with sharper acidity. Like Blagny, they are slow to develop. The best red wines of Meursault sell as Volnay-Santenots.

PREMIERS CRUS

Bouchères (4.4)
Charmes (31)
Clos des Perrières (1)
Cras (3.5)
Genevrières (16.5)
Gouttes d'Or (5.4)
Jeunelotte (5)
Perrières (Dessous and Dessus) (13.7)
La Pièce Sous le Bois (11)
Poruzots (11.4)
Santenots (22)
Sous Blagny (2.2)
Sous le Dos d'Ane (5)
Appellation communale: 305 hectares.

Blagny

Blagny has no appellation of its own, but possesses excellent vineyards in both Meursault and Puligny-Montrachet.

PULIGNY-MONTRACHET PREMIERS CRUS

La Garenne (10)
Hameau de Blagny (4.2)
Sous le Puits (6.8)
Appellation communale: 8 hectares.

MEURSAULT PREMIERS CRUS

La Jeunelotte (5)
La Pièce Sous le Bois (11)
Sous Blagny (2.2)
Sous le Dos d'Ane (5)
Appellation communale: 2 hectares.

Auxey-Duresses

This is the village above and behind Meursault where a valley at right angles to the *côte* provides a south slope at the correct mid-point of the hill for a limited patch of *premier cru* vineyard, mostly planted with Pinot Noir. Among other growers, the Duc de Magenta produces white like very crisp Meursault, which I find more exciting than Auxey red. Much of the red, I gather, is sold as Côte de Beaune-Villages. The village also shelters the fabulous stocks of Mme. Bize-Leroy, the "Gardienne des Grands Millésimes" (*see* Maison Leroy).

PREMIERS CRUS

Bas des Duresses (2.4)
Bréterins (1.7)
Chapelle (1.3)
Climat du Val (8.4)
Clos du Val (1)
Duresses (8)
Ecusseaux (3.1)
Grands Champs (4)
Reugne (2)
Appellation communale: 138 hectares.

St-Romain

A pretty little village lurking in the second wave of hills, behind Auxey-Duresses, and only promoted to Côte de Beaune-Villages status in 1967. It has no *premier cru* land, being too high on the hills, and makes more and better white wine than red. In cool years the wines can be too sharp for comfort.

Puligny-Montrachet

Puligny and Chassagne appear at first sight like Siamese twins linked by their shared *grand cru*, Le Montrachet. But the impression is a false one. Puligny is a dedicated white-wine parish. Chassagne, despite the Montrachet of its name, used to earn most of its living from red, and about forty per cent of the vineyards are still planted with Pinot Noir.

There is no magic by which white wine from Meursault Charmes must taste different from the Puligny Les Combettes, which meets it at the boundary. Yet I would expect the Puligny-Montrachet to have a slightly more lively taste of fruit, a bit more bite, and perhaps a floweriness which is not a Meursault characteristic. Sheaves of old tasting notes tend to contradict each other, so my description is pure impressionism – all that airy metaphor in dabs of paint representing orchards does seem to have something to do with the taste I cannot describe.

What is more tangible is the superiority of the *premiers crus*. Those of Combettes and Champs Canet at the Meursault end of Puligny, and the part of Blagny that lies in this parish with the appellation Blagny Premier Cru, can be expected to be closer to Meursault in style. A slightly higher premium is normally put on the ones that border the *grands crus*: Cailleret and Pucelles.

Two of the *grands crus* that are the white-wine climax of Burgundy lie entirely within Puligny-Montrachet: Chevalier-Montrachet (the strip of hill above Montrachet), and Bienvenues-Bâtard-Montrachet: half the shallower slope below. The accepted appreciation of Chevalier is that it has the fine flavour of Montrachet but in less-concentrated form (concentration being the hallmark of this grandest of all white wines). The critics do not normally distinguish between Bienvenues and Bâtard (to shorten their unwieldy names). Any such generalization is inevitably overturned by the next tasting of a different vintage or a different grower's wine.

As for Puligny-Montrachet village without frills – it is still expensive. Is it worth more than Meursault? Probably not, as there is more excitement to be had from the better village wines of Meursault. The Puligny-Montrachet is likely to be slightly the more expensive of the two.

GRANDS CRUS

Bâtard-Montrachet (6)
Bienvenues-Bâtard-Montrachet (3.6)
Chevalier-Montrachet (7.25)
Montrachet (4)

PREMIERS CRUS

Caillerets (3.4)
Chalumeaux (5.8)
Champs Canet (4)
Champ Gain (10.7)
Clavoillon (5.6)
Clos de la Garenne (1.5)
Clos des Meix (1.6)
Combettes (6.8)
Demoiselles (0.6)
Folatières (17.7)
Garenne (10)
Hameau de Blagny (4.3)
Perrières (8.4)
Pucelles (5.1)
Referts (5.5)
Sous le Puits (6.8)
Truffière (2.5)
Appellation communale: 114 hectares.

also known as Chassagne, produces white only:
Abbaye de Morgeot (8.5)
Baudines (3.6)
Blanchot Dessus (1.3)
Bois de Chassagne (4.4)
Bondues (1.7)
Boudriotte (part of Morgeots)
Brussonnes (part of Morgeots)
Caillerets (20)
Champs Gain (4.6)
Chaumées (7.5)
Chenevottes (9.3)
Clos St Jean (14.2)
Dents de Chien (0.65)
Embrazées (5.2)
En Remilly (1.6)
Grande Montagne (2.8)
Grandes Ruchottes (2.1)
Macherelles (5)
Maltroie (11.6)
Morgeot (54)
Romanée (3.4)
Vergers (9.4)
Vide-Bourse (1.2)
Appellation communale: 180 hectares.

Chassagne-Montrachet

Almost half of the *grands crus* Le Montrachet and Bâtard-Montrachet and the whole of Criots-Bâtard-Montrachet occupy the hill corner that ends the parish to the north. Unfortunately, the steep south-facing slope that runs at right angles to them, along the road to St-Aubin in the hills, has not enough soil for vines. If this were the Douro, there would be terraces. Between here and the village there is some *premier cru* land, but the famous wines begin again where the *côte* picks up its momentum and its tilt in the Clos St-Jean above the little township. Caillerets, Ruchottes, and Morgeot are names seen on expensive and memorable white bottles. Clos St-Jean, La Boudriotte… in fact, all the rest stress red.

Any association of ideas that suggests that red Chassagne should be a light wine is quite wrong. Far from being a gentle fade-out from Volnay, Chassagne returns to the meat and muscle of Corton or the Côte de Nuits. The best example I know of the brilliant duality of this land is the Duc de Magenta's Clos de la Chapelle, part of the *premier cru* Abbaye de Morgeot, which is half red and half white, and (at least in the early 1970s) was brilliant on both counts. Red Chassagne, moreover, sells at the price of the lesser-known villages – much cheaper than the grand names of the Côte de Nuits and every bit as satisfying.

Many of the *premiers crus* can be bottled under the names of better-known Premiers, which is why some of the names are rarely, or never, glimpsed on labels.

GRANDS CRUS

Bâtard-Montrachet (6)
Criots-Bâtard-Montrachet (1.6)
Montrachet (4)

PREMIERS CRUS

Red and white, but En Cailleret produces red only; Cailleret,

St-Aubin

St-Aubin is a twin to St-Romain, a village tucked into the first valley behind the Côte but with a slight advantage of situation that gives it some *premiers crus*. The village of Gamay (the presumed source of the grape that makes Beaujolais, which is a taint to the Côte d'Or) contributes about half the land in this appellation. There are some good whites in a sub-Puligny (or is it sub-Meursault?) style, and most of the best sites (En Remilly, Murgers des Dents de Chien, Chatenière, and Charmots) border those of Puligny and Chassagne. The wines have improved greatly in recent years and can be excellent value. The area under vine is 142 hectares.

Santenay

It is a conceit, I know, but I have always found the names of the villages of Burgundy to be a useful clue to the nature of their wines. Chambertin has a drum-roll sound, Chambolle-Musigny a lyrical note; Pommard sounds precisely right for its tough, red wine, and so does Volnay for its more silky produce. Santenay sounds like good health. (Funnily enough, it has a far-from-fashionable spa for the treatment of rheumatism and gout.)

Healthiness seems just the right sort of image to attach to the wines of Santenay. They are rather plain, even-flavoured, with no great perfume or thrills but good, solid drinking. At their best, in Les Gravières, La Comme, and Le Clos de Tavannes, they are in the same class as Chassagne-Montrachet: weighty and long-lived. Other parts of the parish with stonier, more limey soil have paler reds and a little white wine.

PREMIERS CRUS

Beauregard (18)

Beaurepaire (15.5)
Clos Faubard (5.2)
Clos des Mouches (1.5)
Clos Rousseau (10)
Clos de Tavannes (5.3)
Comme (22)
Fourneaux (6)
Grand Clos Rousseau (7.7)
Gravières (24)
Maladière (13.5)
Passe Temps (11.5)
Appellation communale: 254 hectares.

Maranges

This new (1989) appellation covers the three rather forlorn little villages which share the vineyard Les Maranges, along the hill just west of Santenay and to their regret, just over the *département* line of the Côte d'Or, in the outer darkness of Saône-et-Loire. Their names are Sampigny, Dézize, and Cheilly – but Côte de Beaune-Villages is more likely to appear on their labels. The wines are well-structured with deep colour, and are generally quite tannic. They age well and make splendid drinking when eight years old, as the local clientele buying direct has proved time and again.

CHEILLY-LES-MARANGES PREMIERS CRUS

Boutières, Maranges, and Plantes de Maranges (together 42 hectares)

DEZIZE-LES-MARANGES PREMIER CRU

Maranges (60 hectares)

SAMPIGNY-LES-MARANGES PREMIERS CRUS

Clos des Rois, Maranges (together 28 hectares)

Le Montrachet

All critics agree that the best Montrachet is the best white burgundy. In it, all the properties that make the mouth water in memory and anticipation are brought to a resounding climax. The first quality that proclaims it at a tasting with its neighbours is a concentration of flavour. I have wondered how much this is due to its singular site and its soil and how much to the regulations (and common sense) that keep its crop to a minimum. There is little doubt that other good vineyards could pack more punch if their keepers kept them more meanly pruned and fertilized, picked late, and used only the best bunches. Such economics only work for a vineyard whose wine is as good as sold before it is made, at almost any price. The principal owners of Le Montrachet are the Marquis de Laguiche (whose wine is handled by Drouhin of Beaune), Baron Thénard, Bouchard Père & Fils, Jacques Prieur, and the Domaine de la Romanée-Conti.

Côte de Beaune-Villages

All the villages of the Côte de Beaune, with the exception of Beaune, Pommard, Volnay, and Aloxe-Corton, have this as a fall-back appellation in red wine (only).

Leading Côte d'Or Producers

The almost literally priceless land of the Côte d'Or is broken up into innumerable small units of ownership, variously expressed as *ares* (a hundredth of a hectare) or as *ouvrées* (an old measure which is one twenty-fourth of a hectare, or about a tenth of an acre). These little plots have come about by the French system of inheritance, by the amount of capital needed to buy more, and by the dread of local disasters, which make it inadvisable to put all your eggs in one basket. They mean that a grower who has, say, ten hectares may well have them in thirty different places – often just a few rows of vines separated from his others in the same vineyard.

The precious land is also divided by ancient custom into a jigsaw of *climats*, or fields, sometimes with natural and obvious boundaries, sometimes apparently at random. Each *climat* is a known local character with a meaning and value to the farmers that is hard for an outsider to grasp.

Overlay the one pattern on the other and you have the fragmentation of ownership that bedevils buyers of burgundy. Whereas in Bordeaux a château is a consistent unit doing one or, at most, two things on a reasonably large scale, a Burgundy domaine is often a man and his family coping with a dozen or more different wines with different needs and problems. If he is a good husbandman of vines, his talent does not necessarily extend to the craftsmanship of the cellar – or vice versa. For any number of reasons, inconsistency is almost inevitable.

There are major exceptions in the form of bigger vineyards with richer owners. But the concept of the little man trying to do everything is fundamental. It explains the importance of the négociants or shippers, whose traditional role is to buy the grower's grapes or newly made wine, mature it, and blend it with others of the same vineyard or village or district to make marketable quantities of something consistent.

It takes little imagination to see that an unscrupulous merchant could get away with almost anything under these conditions. Consumers have probably always, since Roman times, had grounds for complaint. The old and profitable game of stretching the limited supplies with imports from the south is now made very much harder by the application of the strict appellation laws. But there is still plenty of room for manoeuvre in the area of quality. There are inspections but nobody pretends they are comprehensive or effective.

When most consumers hear that merchants are venal, their reaction is to look directly for authenticity from the growers. Bottling at the domaine has been presented as the answer. It brings us back, though, to the basic question: who is more competent and more conscientious? Ownership of a corner of a fine and famous field does not carry with it a technical degree in winemaking or *élevage* – the bringing up of wine in the cellar – or bottling.

It can be a depressing experience to taste a set of broker's samples submitted to a négociant from good vineyards, even after a good vintage. A considerable proportion of the wines are likely to be either over-sugared or in poor condition, or both.

The greatest change of the past fifteen years in Burgundy, though, has been the growing competence of a younger generation of growers, well-schooled and innovative, who are often making far better wine than Burgundy has probably ever seen. They are more conscious than many of their fathers of the need to return to a balanced viticulture, free from a dependency on fertilizers, productive clones, and yields pushed to the maximum.

Ambroise ☆☆–☆☆☆
Nuits-St-Georges. www.ambroise.com
The exuberant Bertrand Ambroise approaches winemaking with gusto. Half the seventeen hectares he works is leased, and he also buys in grapes. There are dense, cherryish wines from Nuits (especially the splendid *vieilles vignes*), as well as *grands crus*, white and red, from Corton. Ambroise ages almost all his wines in new oak – which can be too much of a good thing.

Guy Amiot ☆☆
Chassagne-Montrachet
This little-known estate owns twelve hectares in numerous *premiers crus* of Chassagne, with most vines older than thirty years. The style is solid, oaky, powerful, and minerally, with Baudines and Caillerets often among the best *crus*.

Pierre Amiot ☆☆
Morey-St-Denis
A traditionalist grower with small plots totalling 8.5 hectares in *grands crus* Clos de la Roche and Clos St-Denis as well as Gevrey-Chambertin Les Combottes and Chambolle-Musigny. Pierre's two sons now run the estate, and quality has improved since the late 1990s.

Robert Ampeau ☆☆–☆☆☆
Meursault
Outstanding ten-hectare domaine respected particularly for its white wines. The best known are from Meursault Perrières, Charmes, and La Pièce Sous le Bois (partly in Blagny), and a parcel in Puligny Combettes. Unusually, Ampeau only sells wines well-bottle-aged in his own cellars. Reds include Beaune Clos du Roi, Savigny Premier Cru (Lavières and Fourneaux), Pommard, and Volnay Santenots. The reds are less consistent, and, like the whites, are sold when M. Ampeau thinks them ready to drink.

Pierre André ☆–☆☆☆
Château de Corton-André, Aloxe-Corton
Négociant and grower on the largest scale. Pierre André founded La Reine Pédauque. His château at Corton is the centre for the estate, which consists of fifty-six hectares on the Côte d'Or and more vineyards in other regions. The *grand cru* sites include six hectares of Corton. These Cortons are easily the best wines.

Marquis d'Angerville ☆☆☆
Volnay. www.angerville.com
The impeccable domaine of a totally dedicated nobleman: fifteen hectares mostly in Volnay. The present marquis's father was a pioneer of domaine-bottling as a way of countering fraudulent practice by négociants abusing the good name of Volnay.

The *monopole* Clos des Ducs is an unusual, steep, and chalky 2.4-hectare vineyard whose wine tends to miss the velvet of the best Volnay, but can age magnificently. I prefer the more sumptuous Champans (produced from four hectares) and Caillerets. All its wines are beautifully made,

yet recent vintages have been a touch disappointing: elegant but light.

Hervé Arlaud ☆☆☆
Morey-St-Denis
This estate was founded in 1949 and has expanded to twelve hectares. Since 1998, Cyprien Arlaud has been making the wines, aiming for a fruity, supple style without too much extraction. Arlaud's first vintages got the balance right: voluptuous fruit and ripe tannins.

Domaine de l'Arlot ☆☆
Nuits-St-Georges
The insurance company AXA owns this Prémeaux estate, but it has been run (and co-owned) for over fifteen years by Jean-Pierre de Smet. The Clos de l'Arlot is a *monopole* site (four hectares), as is the seven-hectare Clos des Forêts St-Georges. The wines are elegant but a touch light.

Comte Armand ☆☆☆–☆☆☆☆
Pommard. www.domaine-d-epeneaux.com
New life was breathed into this domaine, which owns the excellent monopoly vineyard, Clos des Epeneaux, when the young Québecois Pascal Marchand was put in charge in 1985. These are deeply coloured, intense wines, which require significant ageing.

Since 1995 the domaine has added vineyards in Auxey-Duresses (red and white), Volnay, and Meursault through share-cropping agreements. Since 1999, Marchand has been winemaker at Domaine de la Vougeraie (*q.v.*), his place here taken by young Benjamin Leroux, who seems equally competent. Since 2002, the estate has been cultivated biodynamically.

Robert Arnoux ☆☆☆
Vosne-Romanée
Arnoux died in 1995, but his son-in-law, Pascal Lachaux, runs this thirteen-hectare estate, which is endowed with *grands crus* Echézeaux, Romanée-St-Vivant, and Clos de Vougeot, as well as a parade of *premiers crus* in Nuits and Vosne. The best wines are often the Vosne Suchots and the Romanée-St-Vivant. The style is elegant and oaky, and although the wines are extremely expensive, they are certainly among the best in the village.

Marc de Bourgogne & Cassis

The pulpy residue of skins, pips, and stalks left in the press after the juice has been run off is often distilled to produce a spirit known as *marc*. The clear spirit is matured in oak to give it colour and, with luck, a little finesse. Most *marc* is made by growers for private consumption. Some of the larger houses, such as Bouchard Père & Fils and Louis Latour, make carefully aged commercial versions. There are also some high-priced versions aged for many years in new oak, from prestigious domaines such as de Vogüé.

Cassis is an alcoholic blackcurrant liqueur that soften the sharpness of white wine – in Burgundy, usually Aligoté – in a proportion of one of cassis to three or four of wine. The resulting drink is often called Kir after a brand of cassis developed by Canon Félix Kir, one-time mayor of Dijon.

Domaine d'Auvenay ☆☆☆☆
Meursault

This small, four-hectare domaine is the personal property of the Leroy family, and is separate from the more recent Domaine Leroy (*q.v.*). But the wines are made in the same way, with tiny yields, especially from the *grands crus* such as Chevalier-Montrachet. The wines are superb, all but unobtainable, and very expensive.

Denis Bachelet ☆☆☆
Gevrey-Chambertin

One man's tiny enterprise in Gevrey-Chambertin, *premier cru* Les Corbeaux, and Charmes-Chambertin. But brilliantly stylish wines.

Bart ☆
Marsannay

This family-run domaine has twenty hectares, mostly at Marsannay, but also in Fixin, and with some sizeable parcels in *grands crus* Bonnes Mares and Clos de Bèze. The wines have become more concentrated and less rustic than in the past.

Ghislaine Barthod ☆☆☆
Chambolle-Musigny

From six hectares of mostly *premiers crus*, Mme. Barthod makes a fine range of wines that achieve the right balance between structure and seductiveness. The new oak is held in check, rarely exceeding 30%. Les Cras is often the best of the *crus*.

Domaine de Beaumont ☆☆
Morey-St-Denis

A rarity in Burgundy, a new estate, with its first vintage in 1999 from five hectares of mostly *premiers crus*. It's too early to make a definitive judgment, but the first releases were ripe, oaky, and svelte.

Roger Belland ☆
Santenay

One of a number of Belland estates in the village, this is widely regarded as the best, offering a wide range of wines from all over the Côte de Beaune. It is best to focus on the wines of Santenay and Maranges, which are rich but never rustic.

Domaine Bertagna ☆☆☆
Vougeot

Owners of some Vougeot Premier Cru (white as well as red), including the *monopole* Clos de la Perrière (two hectares), the hill just below Le Musigny. Bertagna has a total of sixteen hectares, with a fair selection of *grands crus* such as Chambertin, Clos St-Denis, Corton, and Corton-Charlemagne. A new winemaker, Claire Forestier, arrived here in 1999, and quality, already good, has taken a firm step upwards. The Bertagna style revels in new oak.

Besancenot ☆
Beaune

A ten-hectare domaine created by a Beaune citizen of great repute and scholarship, M. Besancenot, who died, alas, in 1981. Most of the vineyards are in Beaune Premiers Crus (Bressandes, Clos du Roi, Toussaints, etc.), of which half is a parcel of Cent-Vignes with fifty-year-old vines. The wines can lack flair.

Albert Bichot ☆–☆☆
Beaune

The firm was founded in Beaune in 1831 and grew to become one of the biggest exporters of burgundy in 1927. Bichot also trades under the names of several of the companies it has taken over: Paul Bouchard, Charles Drapier, Rémy Gauthier, etc. As a grower, Bichot owns two domaines: Clos Frantin in Vosne, and Long-Depaquit (*q.v.*) in Chablis. At the top levels, and especially from their own domaines, quality can be high.

Simon Bize ☆☆
Savigny

A domaine of twenty-two hectares almost entirely in Savigny (there's a parcel of Corton-Charlemagne too), with holdings in the *premiers crus* Vergelesses, Guettes, and Marconnets. Patrick Bize ages the wine in 30% new oak. Quality can be variable, but the Vergelesses is usually reliable and there are some good white wines, too.

Blain-Gagnard ☆☆☆
Chassagne-Montrachet.

Jean-Marc Blain is an utterly reliable grower, and all his Chassagne Premiers Crus are aged in about 30% new oak. Boudriottes and Cailleret can be exceptional. Blain also has small parcels of Bâtard-Montrachet, Criots, and, since 2000, Montrachet itself.

Jean Boillot ☆☆–☆☆☆
Volnay

Henri Boillot presides over a major domaine with holdings not only in Volnay, but also in Puligny-Montrachet (four hectares, including the *monopole* Clos de la Mouchère), Beaune Premiers Crus, and Pommard. The Volnays are unusually rich.

Jean-Marc Boillot ☆☆–☆☆☆
Pommard

Jean-Marc came into his inheritance in 1988, acquired partly through his paternal grandfather, Henri, and partly from his maternal grandfather, the late Etienne Sauzet (*q.v.*). He is equally at home making richly oaked white wines from various vineyards mostly in Puligny-Montrachet, or clearly defined reds from Volnay and Pommard. He also runs a négociant business; the labels for these wines omit the word *propriétaire*.

Lucien Boillot ☆☆☆
Gevrey-Chambertin

Two grandchildren of Henri Boillot, Louis and Pierre, run this flourishing fourteen-hectare domaine in Gevrey, Nuits, Pommard, Volnay, and Fixin. Excellent quality.

Pierre Boillot
Meursault

The respected veteran Pierre Boillot is gradually transferring his domaine to his nephew Francois Mikulski.

Jean-Claude Boisset ☆
Nuits-St-Georges. www.boisset.com

A recent (in Burgundian terms – 1961) foundation which has since swallowed up many long-established names, including Charles Viénot, Bouchard Aîné, Pierre Ponnelle,

Jaffelin, Ropiteau, Moreaux in Chablis, and the Cellier des Samsons in Beaujolais. In general, Boisset has been more praised for commercial skills and marketing acumen than for attaining peaks of quality with its wines. Their best-known brand is "Charles de France", a white burgundy sourced from outside the Côte d'Or, but vinified as though it were Meursault. In 1999 the various holdings of the company were assembled under the name of Domaine de la Vougeraie (*q.v.*).

Bonneau du Martray ✫✫✫✫
Pernand-Vergelesses
The largest producer of the inimitable Corton-Charlemagne, with a solid block of 9.5 hectares of old vines, and an adjacent 1.5 in Corton (red). The famous "Cuvée François de Salins", the costliest wine of the Hospices de Beaune, comes from the same prime hill corner site. This is the only estate in Burgundy, other than Domaine de la Romanée-Conti, to own nothing but *grand cru* vineyards.

Quality has always been fine, but a new generation in charge – Jean-Charles Le Bault de la Morinière having succeeded his father – has raised standards even higher. He introduced lees-stirring and expanded the cellars, and avoids filtration whenever feasible. The Corton-Charlemagne behaves more like a red, ageing majestically. It reaches its sublime peak at ten years and can be kept longer.

Bouchard Père & Fils ✫✫–✫✫✫✫
Beaune
The biggest domaine in Burgundy, with 130 hectares in the Côte d'Or alone, and one of the best négociants, run by Bouchards from father to son since 1731, until the company was sold to Henriot (of Champagne fame) in 1995. Joseph Henriot immediately set in train a series of measures to raise the standing of the wines, including the declassification of some *grand cru* stocks such as Le Montrachet, which he thought not up to scratch – a move typical of the complex character of a man who is at once an agile businessman and a passionate guardian of quality.

Bouchard's biggest holdings are in Beaune, where their *premiers crus* include the *monopoles* of the famous 4-hectare Grèves Vigne de l'Enfant Jésus, the 3.5-hectare Clos de la Mousse, and the 2-hectare Clos Landry. They are also the largest proprietor of vineyards in Meursault. Inevitably, they have some impressive *grands crus* in their portfolio: Montrachet, of course, but also two hectares of Chevalier-Montrachet, and substantial parcels in Corton. Other notable wines are Volnay Caillerets labelled as Ancienne Cuvée Carnot, atypically foursquare and long-lived Volnay from very old vines.

In the early 1990s, the firm was going through a very bad patch, beset by scandal and a dwindling reputation. In just a few years Henriot has restored this great name, and the prestigious wines are once again all that they should be.

Pierre Bourée & Fils ✫
Gevrey-Chambertin
Pierre Bourée is a négociant-grower. Most of the 4-hectare domaine is in the *monopole* Clos de la Justice. The wines are made in a decidedly rustic way, with no de-stemming, and ageing in old barrels. Also known as Vallet Frères.

Michel Bouzereau ✫✫✫
Meursault
Michel and his son, Jean-Baptiste, produce rich, spicy *premiers crus* from Genevrières and Charmes, but the village wines from Teurons and Limozins can be very fine, too, with a discreet oaky fragrance. Even his Aligoté is notable.

Alain Burguet ✫✫–✫✫✫
Gevrey-Chambertin
A small domaine of mostly village vines, made remarkable by the fact that the average age of these vines is fifty years. The Cuvée Vieilles Vignes is as good as some *premiers crus* in the village. Burguet's only *premier cru* is Champeaux.

Louis Carillon ✫✫–✫✫✫
Puligny-Montrachet
A proud family domaine of twelve hectares, going back 350 years, now run by Louis with his two sons. The vineyards include a little patch of Bienvenues-Bâtard-Montrachet, three hectares of Puligny Premier Cru, and five of Puligny village, with smaller parcels of Chassagne and Mercurey. The Pulignys have an attractive citric quality and plenty of zest. Only 20% new oak is used, so the fruit comes shining through.

Carré-Courbin ✫✫
Beaune
A small 4.5-hectare estate, but with fine vineyards in Volnay and Pommard Premiers Crus. The wines are gently oaky and well-balanced, and succulent.

Château de Chambolle-Musigny ✫✫✫
Chambolle-Musigny
Four hectares in some of the village's best sites deliver first-class delicate Chambolle-Musigny. The domaine includes half a hectare of *premier cru* Amoureuses as well as 1.1 hectares of Musigny and a parcel of Bonnes-Mares. The diffident Frédéric Mugnier has been running the property since 1984.

Although he himself rarely seems content with his own wines, everyone else who tastes them tends to be more than satisfied. In 2002, the large Nuits-St-George *monopole* of Clos de la Maréchale, leased to Faiveley for many years, returned into Mugnier's hands.

Champy ✫✫–✫✫✫
Beaune
Probably Beaune's oldest négociant house, founded in 1720, Champy was sold in 1990 to respected wine broker Henri Meurgey and his son, Pierre. They only own ten hectares, so they buy in most of their requirements and offer some sixty different wines. Quality is high, on the same level as many fine domaines.

Domaine Chandon de Briailles ✫✫✫
Savigny-lès-Beaune
An important thirteen-hectare property, largely in the best red wine vineyards of Savigny (Les Lavières) and the neighbouring Ile des Vergelesses in Pernand, now run by mother and daughter to a very high standard. Also considerable owners in Corton, with 1.7 hectares in Bressandes, plus Clos du Roi and a little Corton Blanc. These are discreet, ultra-refined wines, poised and elegant.

Chanson Père & Fils ☆–☆☆☆
Beaune

Négociants and growers (founded 1750) with a fine domaine of thirty-eight hectares, many of them in Beaune Premiers Crus, and substantial holdings in Savigny and Pernand-Vergelesses. Their best wines are perhaps their Beaune Clos des Fèves (3.8 hectares) and Clos des Mouches. Wines tasted in 2002 from the early decades of the twentieth century showed how marvellously the supposedly lightweight wines of Beaune could age. However, towards the end of the century quality had slipped, and in 1999 the company was bought by Bollinger. The new team moved rapidly to lower yields and to eliminate practices such as machine-harvesting. The wines showed an immediate improvement.

Philippe Charlopin ☆☆–☆☆☆☆
Gevrey-Chambertin

A new star in the Côte de Nuits, whose success with wines from Gevrey and Marsannay has allowed him to expand his fourteen-hectare domaine, already endowed with Clos St-Denis and Chambertin, with small parcels in Echézeaux, Clos Vougeot. Charlopin picks as late as possible, and produces rich, fleshy, even voluptuous, wines.

Chartron & Trebuchet ☆
Puligny-Montrachet. www.chartron-trebuchet.com

The marriage of the Chartron domaine and the négociant Trebuchet resulted in much talked about oaky wines. Quality was sound but rarely inspired, despite impressive holdings, especially in Puligny-Montrachet. But a new generation, Jean-Michel Chartron, seems to be leading to better quality.

Robert Chevillon ☆☆☆
Nuits-St-Georges

A typical, family run thirteen-hectare estate, part owned and part rented. Very old vines and outstanding winemaking produce splendid *premier cru* Nuits-St-Georges from (especially) Les Cailles, Les St-Georges, Les Vaucrains, etc. Plus a little white Nuits.

Bruno Clair ☆☆–☆☆☆☆
Marsannay

When Domaine Clair Daü was divided in 1985, Bruno Clair received twenty-one hectares dispersed over 230 appellations, and now sells very good wines under his own name. He has just under one hectare of Chambertin Clos de Bèze with some ninety-year-old vines, and 3.5 hectares of *premiers crus* in Gevrey-Chambertin and Savigny-lès-Beaune (the excellent Les Dominodes). There are also 5.5 hectares of red Marsannay, from which he makes three single-vineyard wines that are among the finest of the village. Since 1993, Clair has leased some vines in Corton-Charlemagne. A very reliable source across the range.

Denis Clair ☆☆
Santenay

Although based in Santenay, most of Clair's eleven hectares of vineyards are located in good sites in St-Aubin. These are excellent wines, with the rich minerality of good white burgundy, and they are attractively priced.

Bruno Clavelier ☆☆
Vosne-Romanée

A rising star in the Côte de Nuits, with six hectares of organic vineyards in Vosne, Chambolle, Gevrey-Chambertin, and Corton. These are full-bodied, well-structured wines, sometimes ungainly, but rich and full of fruit.

Christian Clerget ☆☆–☆☆☆
Vougeot

A small six-hectare domaine with some very old vines in Chambolle and Echézeaux as well as Vougeot. The ripeness and tannin can wage war when the wines are young, but this is red Burgundy with considerable density and stuffing.

Yves Clerget ☆☆☆
Volnay

A domaine of six hectares with an incredibly long history: the Clergets apparently were making wine in Volnay in 1268. The pride of the house is their resounding Pommard Rugiens. The Volnay parcels are in the *premiers crus* Carelle Sous la Chapelle, the *monopole* Clos du Verseuil, and Caillerets. For some reason this is a seriously underestimated estate.

Clos de Tart ☆☆☆☆
Morey-St-Denis

This famous 7.5-hectare *monopole grand cru* has been owned since 1932 by the Beaujolais growers Mommessin. Quality was disappointing until Sylvain Pitiot was appointed as director in 1995. The vines are organically cultivated and yields are kept low; the wine is aged at least eighteen months in new oak. Pitiot's methods have paid off, and the wine is sumptuous and concentrated, if very oaky in its youth.

Jean-François Coche-Dury ☆☆☆
Meursault

Jean-François is the third generation to own this eleven-hectare domaine that has both vineyards in Meursault and in Corton-Charlemagne. He has an almost fanatical following for his powerful and oaky white wines – even his Bourgogne Blanc. The Corton-Charlemagnes fetch extravagant prices at auction, but the wines don't quite live up to their exalted reputation.

Marc Colin ☆☆–☆☆☆
St-Aubin

Half Colin's twenty hectares of vineyards are in St-Aubin, where he makes firm, well-structured, but nonetheless fruity white wines. There are also vines in *premiers crus* in Chassagne- and Puligny-Montrachet, and a little Montrachet as the icing on the cake.

Colin-Deléger ☆☆
Chassagne-Montrachet

As well as six *premiers crus* in Chassagne, Michel Colin has vines in Puligny and Santenay. The style of the white wines is consistently fruity, with exotic tones of mango and banana in ripe years. He is also a négociant, buying in mostly red grapes to supplement his production.

Jean-Jacques Confuron ☆☆–☆☆☆
Nuits-St-Georges

A Confuron daughter married Alain Meunier, who now runs this estate, as well as a small négociant business called Féry-Meunier. The wines are expressive and very well-made. The domaine owns two *grand cru* sites: Romanée-St-Vivant and Clos de Vougeot.

Confuron-Coteditot ☆☆–☆☆☆
Vosne-Romanée

This eleven-hectare domaine embraces a wide range of appellations, from Chambolle to Charmes-Chambertin. Jean-Pierre Confuron practised some controversial vinification techniques in the early 1990s, which gave dark, extracted wines that lacked some *typicité*. But the 1999 vintage marked a return to a more classic style.

Coste-Caumartin ☆–☆☆
Pommard

A good source of full-bodied yet not over-tannic Pommard, especially from the monopoly *premier cru*, Les Boucherottes.

Domaine de Courcel ☆☆☆
Pommard

The Courcels have made Pommard here for 400 years. Their eight-hectare domaine includes the five-hectare "Grand Clos des Epenots" within the *premier cru* Epenots, and one hectare of Rugiens. I opened a sixteen-year-old bottle of 1966 Rugiens to find out where I should be pitching my enthusiasm; Pommard is not normally my favourite burgundy. This wine was astonishingly dark; the smell and taste were stubborn and inaccessible on first opening. After two hours in a decanter it began to give off a seductive, creamy smell of nuts and damsons, which developed into what Michael Broadbent describes as fish glue – in any case, the smell of very fine old burgundy. Yet curiously, the flavour remained austere and straight-backed. Good but not great. Recent vintages such as 1999 remain hefty and tannic, certainly imposing but perhaps too extracted for their – and our – good.

Pierre Damoy ☆☆☆
Gevrey-Chambertin

The biggest single share of Chambertin and Clos de Bèze (six hectares) belongs to the Damoy family. Yet the wines were indifferent until Pierre Damoy took over in 1992 and ended the domaine's Rip van Winkel phase. He ruthlessly cut yields and moved towards biodynamism. The result was dense tannic wines that were impressive but severe. Over the years the style has moderated and has more vigour. As well as a host of *grands crus*, Damoy makes excellent village wine from his *monopole* Clos du Tamisot.

Darnat ☆☆
Meursault

Henri Darnat is the owner of the tiny "Clos Richemont", and a small parcel of the *premier cru* Goutte d'Or.

Doudet-Naudin ☆
Savigny

A house associated with old-fashioned, very dark-coloured, concentrated, almost jammy wines which have had a great following in Britain in the past. They last, and twenty-year-old bottles can be richly velvety and full of character. Lately the style has been more in tune with today's taste for greater freshness. Their six-hectare domaine includes *premiers crus* in Savigny and Beaune Clos du Roi, and *grands crus* in Corton-Charlemagne and Corton-Maréchaudes.

Joseph Drouhin ☆☆–☆☆☆☆
Beaune

A leading négociant (founded in 1880) with one of the biggest domaines in Burgundy, with twenty-five hectares of *grands* and *premiers crus* in the Côte d'Or and a further forty in Chablis. Cultivation has been organic since 1988. The head of the house is Robert Drouhin, now ably assisted by his three children, though the majority shareholder has been Japanese since 1994.

The whole gamut of Drouhin wines is made very conscientiously, rising to the appropriate peaks and never falling below fine quality in the *grands crus*. The specialty of the house is the excellent Beaune Clos des Mouches: long-lived, full-bodied wine, red and white. Drouhin also has sole rights on the superb Montrachet of the Marquis de Laguiche.

The Drouhins are wary about excessive new oak, and take the *élevage* very seriously, air-drying their own wood before cooperage. The house style gives preference to finesse, so those more used to rich, extracted red burgundies are sometimes disappointed by the Drouhin wines. But they age very well and gain in complexity, as anyone who has tasted a mature Griotte-Chambertin or Musigny can confirm. Drouhin was the first Burgundian to plant Pinot Noir in the USA – in Oregon's Willamette Valley (*q.v.*).

Robert Dubois ☆☆
Nuits-St-Georges

A family estate with twenty-two hectares, including one in the *premiers crus* Les Porêts and Clos des Argillières. The wines can be rather chunky and tough.

Dubreuil-Fontaine ☆
Pernand-Vergelesses

Bernard Dubreuil, the present manager, is the grandson of the founder of this twenty-hectare domaine, with 3.5 hectares of *grand cru* Corton (principally Bressandes) and Corton-Charlemagne, as well as Savigny-Vergelesses Premier Cru and the one-hectare Clos Berthet in the village of Pernand. Many of the vines are young, having been recently replanted, so it may be a few years before this domaine is running at full steam again.

Claude Dugat ☆☆☆
Gevrey-Chambertin

Claude Dugat has a 3.5-hectare domaine making wines of the highest class. Premiers and *grands crus* (Griottes-Chambertin, Charmes-Chambertin) are aged entirely in new oak.

Dugat-Py ☆☆☆☆
Gevrey-Chambertin

Bernard Dugat makes very good wine from seven hectares of vines from Vosne-Romanée to Gevrey, where he has *grands crus* in Mazis and Charmes-Chambertin. Like his cousin Claude (*q.v.*), he ages his top wines entirely in new oak. An impressive range.

Dujac ☆☆☆–☆☆☆☆
Morey-St-Denis. www.dujac.com

Jacques Seysses is the "Jac" of the name. Rather to his surprise, since he is an ex-banker turned winemaker in 1969, he is widely regarded as a mentor by dozens of Burgundy's best winemakers. He has always experimented tirelessly, in the vineyard as well as the winery, and has few preconceived ideas. His methods are essentially noninterventionist: fermenting stems and all for as long as possible, using new barrels, never filtering. The result is elegance with depth, as red burgundy should be. Clos de la Roche, where he has two hectares, is usually the best wine, but Bonnes Mares is becoming better with every year, as the vines age.

There are also *premiers crus* from Chambolle and Gevrey-Chambertin, plus *grands crus* Charmes-Chambertin and Echézeaux. Dujac wines are never overtly tannic or dark, as Seysses favours finesse over extraction. The wines seem too exquisite to age well, but thirty-year-old bottles have remained fresh and delightful.

René Engel ☆☆☆
Vosne-Romanée

Philippe Engel runs this highly regarded estate, which was founded in 1901. The domaine of seven hectares includes 1.5 on the upper slope of the Clos Vougeot and plots in Grands-Echézeaux, Echézeaux, and Vosne-Romanée (both *premier cru* and village). The wines are fine, masculine, and powerful.

Michel & Sylvie Esmonin ☆☆–☆☆☆
Gevrey-Chambertin

This estate only began bottling in 1989, after Sylvie completed her studies and returned to the family domaine. The top wine is Clos St Jacques, where the Esmonins own 1.6 hectares.

Faiveley ☆☆–☆☆☆☆
Nuits-St-Georges

The Faiveleys, an unbroken family succession since 1825, own one of the biggest domaines in Burgundy: 122 hectares divided among 35 appellations in the Côte d'Or alone. Seventy-five hectares are in Rully and Mercurey, where their 6.3 hectare *monopole* Clos des Myglands is their best-known wine, and Clos du Roi usually their best wine. As for *grands crus*, Faiveley can boast of substantial holdings in Mazis, Latricières, and Clos de Bèze, well as Clos Vougeot, Corton-Charlemagne, and Corton. Faiveley has become well known for its 9.5-hectare Nuits-St-Georges *monopole* Clos de la Maréchale, but this property was only leased, and in 2002 was returned to its owner, the Château de Chambolle-Musigny (*q.v.*). In those communes where they own no vines, they buy in grapes and make the wine themselves at Nuits-St-Georges.

François Faiveley, who is also at the helm of his family's large industrial business, is very serious about his wines, and prepared to take pains, even to the extent of bottling his top wines directly from the barrel by gravity. Indeed, during the early 1990s the wines seemed almost too dense and solidly structured, but today the balance is much finer. These are wines built to last, and they do.

Fougeray de Beauclair ☆
Marsannay

Although based far to the north, this estate owns 1.5 hectares of Bonnes Mares, from which it produces a good but usually not outstanding wine, imbued with new oak.

Jean-Marie Fourrier ☆
Gevrey-Chambertin

A change of generations in 1997 has led to a marked improvement at this nine-hectare domaine. The one *grand cru* (Griottes-Chambertin, with ninety-year-old vines) is often rivalled by the svelte and concentrated Clos St Jacques.

Vieilles Vignes

Although this term, meaning old vines, is quite often seen on labels, there is no legal definition. It would be assumed that vines need to be at least thirty years old before they can be considered *vieilles vignes*, but it is entirely up to the producer to provide his own definition. It is worth bearing in mind that in Chablis, where there has been much vineyard expansion, seventy-two per cent of vines are under twenty years of age. In the Côte d'Or about sixty per cent of the vines are over thirty years old, with red vines attaining greater age than white.

Jean-Noel Gagnard ☆☆☆–☆☆☆☆
Chassagne-Montrachet

Gagnard's daughter Caroline Lestimé makes the wines here, from 7.5 hectares of splendid Chassagne vineyards, including a fine parcel of Bâtard. They are utterly consistent, with a vigorous, limey character that is appealing young, yet the wines age very well. An excellent source.

Jean-Michel Gaunoux ☆☆
Meursault

François Gaunoux has handed over running the domaine to his son, Jean-Michel. His six-hectare domaine includes *premiers crus* Perrières and Goutte d'Or, as well as Volnay Clos des Chênes and Corton-Renardes. The Meursaults are pure and not too oaky.

Michel Gaunoux ☆☆
Pommard

Half of Gaunoux's ten hectares are in Pommard Premier Cru with the biggest part in Epenots and the best in Rugiens. There are also 1.2 hectares of Corton-Renardes and vineyards in Beaune include *premier cru* Boucherottes. The wine is firm, robust, and long-lived.

Géantet-Pansiot ☆☆☆
Gevrey-Chambertin

Vincent Géantet presides over a thirteen-hectare domaine endowed with many very old vines. The wines are ripe and fleshy, with the one *grand cru*, Charmes-Chambertin, showing additional layers of elegance and length of flavour.

Pierre Gelin ☆☆
Fixin

Fixin's leading domaine was run until 1995 by Stéphane Gelin (son of Pierre) and André Molin. After André retired, the domaine was split between the two families. Gelin has ownership of parcels in Clos de Bèze and Mazis-Chambertin.

Germain Père et Fils ☆☆☆
Château de Chorey-lès-Beaune

François Germain's turreted medieval château, just north of Beaune, has five hectares in Chorey and seven in Beaune Premier Cru, where some parcels date from 1948. His Beaune includes Teurons, Cent Vignes, Vignes Franches, Cras, and Boucherottes. Today the estate is run by Benoît Germain, who makes surprisingly serious wines from these often overlooked sites. The proportion of new oak is high, even for the Chorey. The best wine is usually Les Cras, followed by Teurons. They are concentrated wines that need age, yet show real finesse.

Vincent Girardin ☆☆–☆☆☆
Santenay

Girardin owns fourteen hectares in appellations as varied as Rully, Echézeaux, and Corton-Charlemagne, as well as Santenay itself. In addition he buys in grapes for his négociant business. These are modern-style burgundies, with a large dose of new oak, even for simpler wines such as Bourgogne Blanc. But Girardin is a skilled winemaker, and these offer great satisfaction.

Camille Giroud ☆
Beaune

An extraordinary house founded in Beaune in 1865 and specializing in wines intended for very long ageing. The wines, mostly from the Côte de Beaune, are sturdy and frequently impressive. Much of the stock is only released when the wine is ready to drink – hence a 1979 Pouilly-Fuissé on offer in 1996. In 2002, the company was bought by a group of American investors, so its future is uncertain.

Henri Gouges ☆☆☆☆
Nuits-St-Georges. www.gouges.com

In many minds and for many years the top grower of Nuits, with almost all his fifteen hectares in the *premiers crus*, including the whole of the Clos des Porrets. During the 1980s, the property went through a bad patch, but has fully recovered, often producing wines close to *grand cru* quality: powerful, slow to develop, and long in the finish. There is also a rare white Pinot Noir from vines that have mutated in the vineyard.

Alain Gras ☆
St-Romain

From his twelve-hectare domaine, Alain Gras produces some of the best wines – red and white – from this often forgotten village.

Albert Grivault ☆☆☆
Meursault

A small five-hectare domaine focused around the *monopole* Clos des Perrières, which gives rich but racy wines with a strong personality.

Jean Grivot ☆☆☆–☆☆☆☆
Vosne-Romanée

Etienne Grivot (son of Jean) is a deeply dedicated grower with a number of small parcels of exceptionally good land – fifteen hectares in twenty-one appellations. The holdings include 1.9 hectares in Clos Vougeot and four in Vosne-Romanée, notably the excellent *premier cru* Beaumonts and bits of Suchots and Brûlées, which are sandwiched between the *grands crus* Richebourg and Echézeaux.

In the late 1980s, the wines were too dense and extracted and even lacked *typicité*, but Etienne Grivot has corrected this, and they are now superb: very concentrated, yet not too heavy or dense. The fruit quality is vivid without flashiness, and these are clearly wines that will age very well.

Robert Groffier ☆☆☆
Morey-St-Denis

An excellent eight-hectare domaine in the best sites of Bonnes Mares, Clos de Bèze, and above all the owner's favourite: Chambolle-Musignys, Les Amoureuses, and Les Sentiers. Delicious wines but very expensive.

Anne Gros ☆☆☆–☆☆☆☆☆
Vosne-Romanée

A small domaine of only five hectares, but the vineyards are fabulous: 0.6 hectares of Richebourg, 0.9 of Clos Vougeot, and a little Echézeaux and Chambolle-Musigny. So are the wines, which are unctuous and toasty yet with underlying finesse.

Jean Gros ☆☆☆
Vosne-Romanée

After Jean Gros retired in 1995, his son Michel took over running this domaine. At the same time another son, Bernard, became responsible for Domaine Gros Frère et Soeur, while daughter Anne-Françoise (at Domaine A.-F. Gros) and niece Anne (*q.v.*) began to make excellent wines at their share of the domaine. Here the best-known wine is the *monopole* Clos des Réas, a walled vineyard of over two hectares. These are wines of ripeness and charm rather than power.

Antonin Guyon ☆☆
Savigny-lès-Beaune

A very substantial domaine of fifty hectares, including three of Corton Grand Cru, 2.5 in Pernand-Vergelesses Premier Cru, and 3.5 in Chambolle-Musigny; and a tiny parcel of Charmes-Chambertin. Altogether a remarkable spread of good sites, so it is strange that the name is not better known. Their Cortons are their particular pride. The wines can be hard-edged when young, but age well.

Hudelot-Noëllat ☆☆–☆☆☆
Vougeot

Well-reputed ten-hectare estate, endowed with parcels in Clos Vougeot, Richebourg, and Romanée-St-Vivant, and *premiers crus* in Chambolle-Musigny and Nuits. The owner is Alain Hudelot, who produces concentrated, oaky wines, especially from the *grands crus*.

Louis Jadot ☆☆–☆☆☆☆
Beaune. www.louisjadot.com

The American concern Kobrand now owns this firm based in the medieval Couvent des Jacobins, but the previous owners, the Gagey family, continue to run the property. The domaine of Louis Jadot now covers almost sixty hectares, including the original holding, the 2.7 hectare Clos des Ursules in Les Vignes Franches. In Beaune, it also has substantial holdings in various other *premiers crus*. In Aloxe-Corton it has vineyards in Corton Pougets (*grand cru*) and Corton-Charlemagne; in Puligny-Montrachet parcels of Les Folatières and Chevalier-Montrachet (a plot called Les Demoiselles, after the spinster sisters Adèle and Julie Voillot, who sold it in 1846).

Since 1985, the company has purchased the Chassagne grapes of Domaine du Duc de Magenta (*q.v.*), although the wine is sold under that label. The brilliant white wines are probably the greatest pride: especially the Corton-Charlemagne or Chevalier-Montrachet. But Jadot reds are equally reliable.

A Jadot Musigny 1972 was perfection in 2002; the domaine wines lead a first-class list of classic burgundies, united for over thirty years by the passionate care of winemaker Jacques Lardière. This is a shining example of a grower-cum-négociant.

Jaffelin
Beaune

An old company of négociants, occupying the magnificent thirteenth century cellar of the canons of Notre Dame in Beaune. The company was bought by Joseph Drouhin (*q.v.*) in 1969 and subsequently sold to Jean-Claude Boisset (*q.v.*). Its strength used to lie in village wines such as Monthélie and Rully, but recent vintages have been unimpressive.

François Jobard ☆☆☆
Meursault

Everybody in Meursault has great respect for the quiet, lean, wiry François Jobard, than whom no grower is more meticulous. Superb Meursault from such vineyards as Poruzots, Charmes, and Genevrières. The wines are naturally high in acidity, and the cellars are exceptionally cool, which means that these bottles are slow to evolve, and definitely repay keeping.

Rémi Jobard ☆☆☆
Meursault

Since François's nephew, Rémi, took over in 1997, quality has soared, with brilliant Meursault Premiers Crus from Genevrières and Charmes. Rapidly becoming as reliable a source for long-lived wines as François Jobard (*q.v.*).

Labouré-Roi ☆☆
Nuits-St-Georges

A négociant emerging as one of the most consistent and reliable at quite modest prices. But the wines do not dazzle.

Michel Lafarge ☆☆☆☆
Volnay

An old family estate which survived the doldrums of Burgundy in the mid-1930s by the initiative of Michel Lafarge's grandfather, who bottled his wine and attacked the Paris market with it in person. Of the ten hectares, most are in Volnay, but there are also some in Meursault and Beaune Grèves. The *premiers crus* include Clos des Chênes (always outstanding here) and the *monopole* site Clos du Château des Ducs. Painstaking viticulture and vinification, and a judicious use of one-third new barrels produce elegant and long-lived wines, surely the best in Volnay. Since 2000, the estate has been biodynamic and is now run by Michel's son, Frédéric.

Comtes Lafon ☆☆☆☆
Meursault

One of the rare producers to excel with both red and white wines. Dominique Lafon took over as full-time winemaker here in 1984, producing sublime Meursault from the *premier cru* Charmes, Genevrières, and Perrières vineyards plus their own "back garden", Clos de la Barre, and a tiny amount of *grand cru* Montrachet.

Since 1999 the vineyards have all been biodyamically cultivated. His reds were all from Volnay: Champans, Clos des Chênes, and especially a large holding of Santenots-du-Milieu, to which some Monthélie has been added. Other red burgundies can match, even surpass, Lafon's, excellent though they are, but when it comes to white burgundy there is surely no one to match Dominique Lafon.

Laleure Piot ☆
Pernand-Vergelesses

This is a ten-hectare domaine producing reputable but unremarkable Pernand-Vergelesses and *premier cru* Vergelesses from Savigny.

Lamarche ☆☆–☆☆☆☆
Vosne-Romanée

A fourth-generation family domaine with the good fortune to own the *monopole* of La Grande Rue, a narrow strip of 1.6 hectares running up the hill between Romanée-Conti and La Tâche. A bottle of the 1961 at twenty-one years old was a miracle of subtle sensuality: understated beside La Tâche, but in its quieter way among the great bottles of my experience.

The rest of the nine-hectare property includes one of Clos de Vougeot, and parcels of Grands-Echézeaux and the Vosne-Romanée Premiers Crus Malconsorts and Suchots. Lamarche produced dull wines until the mid-1990s, when, perhaps stimulated by the promotion of La Grande Rue to *grand cru* status in 1990, quality improved dramatically.

Domaine des Lambrays ☆☆☆☆
Morey-St-Denis

The domaine owns almost the entire *grand cru* Clos des Lambrays. Thierry Brouin makes the wine, with the encouragement of German tycoon Gunter Freund, who bought the property in 1996.

Since 1996, quality has been stellar. The domaine also produces small quantities of Puligny Folatières and Cailleret, superb but expensive.

Hubert and Olivier Lamy ☆☆☆
St-Aubin

Ever since Olivier Lamy took over the family domaine in 1995, quality has soared. Even the red wines from St-Aubin, rarely exceptional, are very good here, though not quite at the level of the delicious white *premiers crus*. About 30% new oak is employed.

Louis Latour ☆–☆☆☆
Beaune. www.louislatour.com

One of Burgundy's names to conjure with, founded in 1797 and since 1867 owned and directed, father-to-son, by Latours called Louis. The centre of their domaine is the Château de Grancey at Aloxe-Corton, one of the first large-scale, purpose-built wineries in France. The domaine totals fifty hectares, of which thirty-five are in Corton and Aloxe-Corton, including ten of Corton-Charlemagne and a two-hectare *monopole* of *grand cru* Clos de la Vigne au Saint. Other *grands crus* include Romanée-St-Vivant and 0.5 hectares of Chevalier-Montrachet Les Demoiselles.

Latour is most celebrated for his white wines, above all Corton-Charlemagne, which he almost literally put on the map at the end of the nineteenth century. They are powerful and must be kept. Latour stubbornly continue to employ an unusual method of vinification for the reds, subjecting the must briefly to a form of flash pasteurization. This may account for the fact that the red wines are considerably lighter and less complex than the splendid whites.

Domaine wines account for one-tenth of their production. Latour's selections of other wines, particularly whites, are reliable. Montagny is a specialty to look out for, and the Chardonnay Vin de Pays de l'Ardèche is remarkable in character and volume.

Dominique Laurent ☆☆☆
Nuits-St-Georges

This former *pâtissier* is passionate about what he considers authentic burgundy: wines made from old and unproductive vines. To this end, this unusual négociant works very closely with proprietors who own exceptional parcels of vines, and pays top prices. Although Laurent has started to participate in the winemaking at some estates, his real gift is as an *éleveur*. He has his own cooperage, and his wines spend at least eighteen months on the fine lees in barrels, with a high percentage of new oak. Bottling is done directly from barrel.

This is old-fashioned winemaking at its best, and the results are impressive: concentrated, rich, and dense, with numerous *cuvées* that demonstrate the sheer variety to be found in a single commune such as Nuits-St-Georges.

Production of each wine tends to be tiny. Laurent has developed a cult following, and although some doubt has been cast about the ageing potential of some of the wines, they are nonetheless bold and personal expressions of burgundy.

Philippe Leclerc ☆☆
Gevrey-Chambertin

Dynamic wines are made *chez* Philippe Leclerc. But you need to like a significant amount of new wood, garish labels, and a brash, in-your-face style.

Domaine Leflaive ☆☆☆☆
Puligny-Montrachet

The grand old man of Puligny-Montrachet, Vincent Leflaive, established a fabulous reputation for his Puligny-Montrachet from such vineyards as Clavoillons, Combettes, and Pucelles plus *grands crus* Bâtard-, Bienvenue-Bâtard-, and Chevalier-Montrachet. The jewel in the crown, Le Montrachet, has now been added. In Vincent's later days quality slipped, but his daughter, Anne-Claude, assisted by a revitalized team and a firm belief in biodynamic methods, has rapidly restored the image of this great domaine.

Olivier Leflaive ☆☆
Puligny-Montrachet

Nephew of Vincent Leflaive, Olivier is now the most highly-regarded négociant in the area, thanks to winemaker Franck Grux, with brilliant Pulignys and excellent St-Romain, St-Aubin, Auxey-Duresses, etc. – model wines from the Côte de Beaune. Leflaive is best known for his stylish white wines, and deservedly so, but the red wines, mostly found on the domestic market, can be good, too.

Lejeune ☆
Pommard

A renowned name in Pommard, yet even after ten years or more in bottle, these wines can remain tough and austere. Not for the pleasure-seeking.

Domaine Leroy ☆☆☆☆
Vosne-Romanée

Mme. Lalou Bize-Leroy, a restless and ambitious woman of extraordinary energy, was already co-directing the Domaine de la Romanée-Conti (D.R.C.), as well as running her family's négociant business Maison Leroy (*q.v.*), when she began to acquire excellent vineyards by buying up moribund domaines such as Charles Noëllat. The expansion of her domaine (it now encompasses 22.5 hectares) was a contributory factor to her bust-up with and eventual dismissal from the D.R.C. in 1992. Undaunted, Mme. Bize-Leroy continued in her purpose of establishing a truly great domaine. She now has a range of *grands crus* scarcely matched by any other property in Burgundy, and a quiverfull of excellent *premiers crus*. Since the early 1990s, she has adopted biodynamism with a passion, and insists on yields so low that they can scarcely be economical. Most of the wines are aged for eighteen months in new oak, yet such is their concentration that oakiness is not an obvious characteristic of the wines. A few hours tasting the entire range in her cellars, a privilege granted to few, is a dazzling and humbling experience, as one perfect wine succeeds another. If Domaine Leroy is now among the very top domaines of France, you can be sure that the prices reflect this.

Maison Leroy ☆☆☆
Auxey-Duresses

Mme. Lalou Bize-Leroy inherited this family négociant business in 1955, and specialized in releasing wines only when fully mature. They need patience, and they cost a fortune. The self-styled "Gardienne des Grands Millésimes" is believed to have a stock of 2.5 million bottles.

Chantal Lescure ☆☆–☆☆☆
Nuits-St-Georges. www.domaine-lescure.com

This estate was founded in 1975 and has eighteen hectares of vineyards from Chambolle to Volnay. It used to be allied to the négociant house Labouré-Roi, but that arrangement ceased in 1996, when a new team took over. In 1999, a new winery was built. The investments have paid off and the wines are now very impressive, the Vosne Suchots often outshining the Clos Vougeot.

Vicomte Ligier Belair ☆☆
Vosne-Romanée

Until 2000, the wines of this estate were marketed by Bouchard Père & Fils (*q.v.*), but now the domaine is making and distributing its wines itself. The vineyards are all in Vosne, and include a *monopole* site, the "Clos du Château". The 2000s show promise, especially the Vosne Chaumes, but these are early days.

Hubert Lignier ☆☆–☆☆☆
Morey-St-Denis

Once Domaine Georges Lignier was highly reputed in Morey, but quality slipped badly in the 1990s, while the Hubert Lignier estate has improved dramatically. There are now eight hectares, one in Clos de la Roche, and small holdings in Chambolle-Musigny and Gevrey-Chambertin Premiers Crus. Under Romain Lignier, the style has become rich and concentrated, underpinned by a fair amount of new oak.

Bertrand Machard de Gramont ☆☆
Nuits-St-Georges

The Machard de Gramont vineyards have, over the years, been divided among various family members. This five-hectare remnant produces rich, robust wines from top sites in Nuits-St-Georges.

Duc de Magenta ☆☆☆
Meursault

The descendant of the French victor of the battle of Magenta (1859, with Piedmont against the Austrians) owns the Clos de la Chapelle, as well as the *premier cru* Clos de la Garenne in Puligny, along with other vineyards in Auxey-Duresses and Meursault. Since 1985, all the Domaine's wines have been made by Maison Louis Jadot (*q.v.*).

Château de la Maltroye ☆☆☆
Chassagne-Montrachet

The source of some outstanding white Chassagne under the *monopole* label of the château. In addition, the fifteen-hectare estate has a small piece of Bâtard-Montrachet as well as red wine vineyards in Chassagne Clos St-Jean.

Matrot ☆☆–☆☆☆
Meursault

An eighteen-hectare domaine now run by Thierry Matrot. It is best-known for its whites from the Meursault section of Blagny, and for Meursault Premiers Crus Charmes and Perrières, and Puligny Premiers Crus Combettes and Chalumeaux. There are also 1.5 hectares of red Volnay-Santenots and an unusual red Blagny from La Pièce Sous le Bois, which makes a vivid, somewhat harsh wine, as a change from the gentler Volnay.

The whites can be austere in their youth, but with age they become harmonious and complex.

Prosper Maufoux ☆☆–☆☆☆
Santenay

A respected family négociant, the company was sold in 1994 to its American importer, Robert Fairchild. Maufoux red wines are designed to age, but their performance of late has been patchy. Marcel Amance is another trade name.

Maume ☆☆☆
Gevrey-Chambertin. www.domaine-maume.com

Bernard Maume is a professor of biochemistry at Dijon University as well as being proprietor of this four-hectare domaine. He is assisted by his son, Bertrand. The largest and best parcel is of Mazis-Chambertin Grand Cru. There is also a small site of Charmes-Chambertin Grand Cru and three *premiers crus*.

Louis Max ☆–☆☆☆
Nuits-St-Georges

A négociant house founded in 1859 by Russian immigrant Louis Max, and now run by his descendant Laurent Max. In the 1990s, the company improved its performance and packaging and began building up a portfolio of its own vineyards.

Méo-Camuzet ☆☆☆–☆☆☆☆
Vosne-Romanée

For many years, Jean Méo leased out his vineyards, but since 1983 they have been back in family hands, and his son, Jean-Nicolas, with much advice from legendary winemaker Henri Jayer, has been turning out majestic and very rich wines from some outstanding vineyards.

The *grands crus* here are Richebourg, Echézeaux, Clos Vougeot, and Corton. There are two *premiers crus* in Nuits, and three in Vosne, including the rare and wondrous Cros Parantoux. A splendid tasting in 2001 showed how well these wines can age, and how complex they become.

Prince Florent de Mérode ☆
Ladoix-Serrigny

Although based in Serrigny, most of this domaine's holdings are in Corton, with nearly four hectares of *grands crus*. After many years of mediocrity, these wines are now made in a rich, full-bodied style.

Mestre Père & Fils ☆
Santenay

One of Santenay's bigger domaines (twenty hectares), in the fifth generation, with *premiers crus* in all the best vineyards, and smaller holdings in Aloxe-Corton, Chassagne-Montrachet, and Ladoix (appellation Côte de Beaune). A well-established source of medium-bodied wines.

Château de Meursault ☆☆
Meursault

A sixty-hectare domaine bought in 1973 by the négociant Patriarche of Beaune and turned into a showplace for visitors. The Meursault Premiers Crus are blended and sold as Château de Meursault. There are also red wines from *premiers crus* in Pommard, Savigny, and Beaune. Prices are high.

Moillard ☆–☆☆
Nuits-St-Georges

A family firm in the fifth generation (the name is now Thomas) with a forty-hectare domaine, Domaine Charles Thomas (*q.v.*). Also making wine from purchased grapes from a much larger area (including Beaujolais and the Rhône) and playing the traditional role of négociant with stocks of no fewer than eight million bottles – certainly the biggest in Nuits.

Mongeard-Mugneret ☆☆–☆☆☆
Vosne-Romanée

A 25-hectare estate making sound and long-lived Vosne Suchots, Echézeaux, Grands-Echézeaux, Vougeot, and Richebourg, as well as a slate of *premiers crus* from Vosne, Nuits, Vougeot, and Savigny.

René Monnier ☆☆
Meursault

The Monnier family has built up a large private domaine in the Côte de Beaune – seventeen hectares – over 150 years. The biggest plots are in Meursault Chevalières and the *premier cru* Charmes, Beaune Cent Vignes, and Toussaints and Puligny Folatières. Other plots are in Pommard, Volnay, and Santenay. The reds are fermented for as long as possible and aged in 30% new oak.

Domaine Monthélie-Douhairet-Porcheret ☆☆
Monthélie

Nonagenarian Mlle. Armande Douhairet, the domaine's current proprietor, is a figure of living history in Burgundy. The estate of six hectares includes some *premiers crus* in Pommard, Volnay, and Meursault.

Hubert de Montille ☆☆☆
Volnay

This seven-hectare property owned by a Dijon lawyer is now run by his son, Etienne. The vineyards are scattered among the *premiers crus* of Volnay (Champans, Taille-Pieds,

Crémant

Three high-quality French white-wine regions successfully established a new appellation for their best-quality sparkling wine. The term *crémant*, originally used in Champagne for wines produced at about half the full sparkling-wine pressure, thus gently fizzing instead of frothing in the glass, has been borrowed (with the consent of Champagne) as a controlled term for these full-sparklers of high quality. A new term was needed because the old one, *mousseux*, had acquired a pejorative ring; any old fizz made by industrial methods could (and can) use it. Burgundy and the Loire in 1975, and Alsace in 1976, joined in agreeing that *crémant* had to be made with Champagne-type controls. Specifically, they concern the grape varieties used, the size of the crop, the way it is delivered to the press-house with the bunches undamaged, and the pressure that should be applied (with a limit of two-thirds of the weight of the grapes being extracted as juice). Thereafter, the Champagne-method rules apply, with the minimum time in bottle with the yeast being specified as nine months in Burgundy and Alsace and twelve in the Loire. (An influential lobby wants to increase the nine months to twelve, but so far its efforts have been resisted.)

The result of these controls is a category of sparkling wine of good if rarely exceptional quality. Heavy initial investment has deterred some cellars from upgrading from *mousseux* to *crémant*. The wines tend to be made from grapes of insufficient quality to fetch a decent price for still wines such as Bourgogne Blanc. *Crémant* from southern Burgundy tends to be fuller and richer than examples from northern areas such as the Yonne, just as Montagny is broader than Chablis. In 2001, total *crémant* production was over eight million bottles: confirmation that the term *crémant*, in its new meaning, is well understood.

Among the hundred or so concerns producing Crémant de Bourgogne are:

Ambroise, Nuits-St-Georges
André Bonhomme, Mâcon
Louis Bouillot, Nuits-St-Georges
Cave d'Azé, Azé
Caves de Bailly, St-Bris-le-Vineux
Cave des Grands Crus Blancs, Vinzelles
Cave de Lugny, Lugny
Cave de Viré, Viré
Bernard Cros, Cercot
Deliance
André Delorme, Rully
Roger Luquet, Fuissé
Domaine des Moirots, Bissey-sous-Cruchard
Picamelot, Rully
Simonnet-Febvre, Chablis
Lucien Thomas, Prissé
Verret, St Bris-le-Vineux
Vitteaut-Alberti, Rully

Mitans) and Pommard (Epenots, Rugiens, Pézerolles). Both the Pommard and Volnay are richly coloured, flavoursome, wines that age well. De Montille opposes chaptalization, so the character of the wines can be lean and rather tough in their youth.

More than any other Volnays, they need ten years in bottle to develop their remarkable complexity – a useful lesson. Strength does not equal longevity.

Bernard Morey ☆☆–☆☆☆
Chassagne-Montrachet

An old family domaine of fourteen hectares, largely in Chassagne and almost equally divided between white and red wines. The best-known white wine is *premier cru* Les Embrasées, though the Caillerets and Morgeot are excellent, too. The wines are fruity and powerful, but not the most elegant from Chassagne.

Marc Morey ☆☆–☆☆☆
Chassagne-Montrachet

Morey's son-in-law, Bernard Mollard, has been making the wines here for fifteen years. There are a number of *premiers crus*, and small parcels in Bâtard-Montrachet and Chevalier-Montrachet. In general, the style of the wines is fruity, balanced, and accessible, so they can be enjoyed young, though they will age.

Pierre Morey ☆☆☆
Meursault

Morey has been the winemaker for Domaine Leflaive (*q.v.*) since 1989, and produces fine Meursault and Bâtard-Montrachet from his own eight hectares. He also buys in grapes for his négociant label, Morey Blanc.

Albert Morot ☆☆–☆☆☆
Beaune

Seven hectares of Beaune Premiers Crus in Teurons, Grèves, Cent Vignes, Toussaints, Bressandes, and Marconnets and two at Savigny-Vergelesses Clos la Bataillère. In 2000, Mlle. Françoise-Guigone Choppin handed responsibility for making the wines to her nephew, Geoffroy de Janvry. He has introduced greater selection at harvest and up to 50% new oak, and eliminated fining and filtration. A fine property through which to discover the characters of top-level Beaune.

Denis Mortet ☆☆☆☆
Gevrey-Chambertin

Denis Mortet is probably the best of the modernist winemakers of the village, practising essentially organic viticulture, harvesting only very ripe grapes, and using a great deal of new oak. But the wines, even from village sites such as Motrot and En Champs are rich, dark, concentrated, and finely balanced. But they all benefit from cellaring. Strong international demand has inevitably led to high prices.

Thierry Mortet ☆☆
Gevrey-Chambertin

Thierry has been somewhat overshadowed by the success of his older brother, Denis, (the family domaine was divided in 1992). The wines are good, with sweet fruit and spiciness.

Mugneret-Gibourg ☆☆☆
Vosne-Romanée

Of the seven Mugneret estates in Vosne, this is probably the finest. After the death of Georges Mugneret (some wines still appear under his label), the property has been managed by his widow Jacqueline and her two daughters. Yields are low at this nine-hectare domaine, and the proportion of new oak barrels varies, but never exceeds 80%. These are succulent wines: firm Vosne, delicious Feussellottes with all the charm of Chambolle, exotic Echézeaux, more tannic Clos Vougeot, and some rich Ruchottes-Chambertin. An impeccable source.

Jacques-Frédéric Mugnier
See Château de Chambolle-Musigny.

André Mussy ☆
Pommard

Very much a family business, this six-hectare domaine includes Pommard Epenots Grand Cru, and Beaune Epenottes Premier Cru. But the wines are on the rustic side.

Lucien Muzard ☆
Santenay

This family estate of twenty-two hectares produces splendid, gently oaky wines at a fair price.

Michel Niellon ☆☆–☆☆☆
Chassagne-Montrachet

A small but highly regarded estate, much in demand in the United States. The style is ripe and rounded, but, other than the *grands crus*, these are rarely wines for long cellaring.

Hospices de Nuits-St-Georges ☆☆
Nuits-St-Georges

The lesser-known and smaller Nuits counterpart of the great Hospices de Beaune, founded in 1634 and now endowed with eight hectares, mostly Nuits Premier Cru. The best *cuvées* are sold by auction in March. As with the Hospices de Beaune, the final quality of the wine is largely dependent on which domaine is the *éleveur*.

Domaine Parent ☆☆
Pommard. www.domaine-parent.com

A fifteen-hectare domaine founded in 1750, and best-known for its firm Pommards and medium-bodied wines from Volnay and Beaune. In 1999, the domaine was split, with Francois Parent vinifying his one-third share separately.

Patriarche ☆–☆☆
Beaune

Possibly the biggest firm in Burgundy (it claims to have the biggest cellars) with a history going back to 1780 and an annual production of twenty million bottles. Patriarche, which is still family owned, has a paradoxical image: on one hand, proprietor of the excellent Château de Meursault (*q.v.*) and the Château de Marsannay, domaines that amount to 110 hectares, and regularly a major buyer at the Hospices de Beaune auctions; and on the other a brand which the snob in me would describe as definitely downmarket. Its greatest success must be "Kriter Brut de Brut", created in the early 1960s as a high-quality, non-appellation sparkling wine. In 2000, it launched a new range of regional wines as "Terroirs et Secrets de Bourgogne". Brand names include "Père Patriarche", "Cuvée Jean Baptiste", "Noémie Vernaux".

Pavelot ☆☆
Savigny

The Pavelots have been growers in Savigny since the eighteenth century. Their domaine comprises twelve hectares, a little under half of it in the *premier cru* vineyards of the slopes, with very old vines in Dominode. The wines are soundly made and consistent, but lack some excitement.

Domaine des Perdrix ☆☆–☆☆☆
Nuits-St-Georges

Acquired by Maison Rodet (*q.v.*) in 1996, this twelve-hectare domaine includes the *monopole* site "Aux Perdrix". The wines are rich, dense, and extracted.

Domaine de la Perrière ☆
Fixin

An unusually simple property making only one wine: the famous Fixin Clos de la Perrière, established by the Cistercian monks of Citeaux in the twelfth century. The original manor, its cellars, and the great press, 700 years old, are still here. The seven hectares produce bold, uncompromising wine, made by long fermentation and long barrel-ageing. The wine has been compared with Chambertin for power, if not for finesse.

Perrot-Minot ☆☆–☆☆☆
Morey-St-Denis. www.perrot-minot.com

The finest site of this ten-hectare domaine is the 1.5-hectare parcel in Charmes-Chambertin, and there are two *premiers crus* in Chambolle-Musigny: Fuées and Combe d'Orveau. Christophe Perrot-Minot is a modernist, and his wines are fleshy and bold – perhaps not very subtle, but undoubtedly concentrated.

Château de Pommard ☆☆–☆☆☆
Pommard

The château is very much in evidence from the main road, with a label and a sales approach that might lead one to think it is strictly for tourists. In fact, it is extremely serious. The wine comes from the largest *clos* in Burgundy: a walled vineyard of twenty-five hectares. The owner, Jean-Louis Laplanche, an expert on Freud, uses new barrels every year, keeps the wine two years in wood, and does not filter. In 2002, Laplanche, who has no heirs, granted management of the property to Daniel Cathard of Château Smith Haut-Lafitte (*q.v.*) in Bordeaux.

Jean-Marie Ponsot ☆☆–☆☆☆
Morey-St-Denis

A nine-hectare domaine over a century old, all in Morey-St-Denis except for a small parcel of Latricières-Chambertin and Le Chambertin. Almost half of the total is in the splendid Clos de la Roche, making concentrated, long-lived wine without recourse to new oak. White *premier cru* Morey Monts-Luisants is Ponsot's other specialty, made mostly from venerable Aligoté vines. Its high acidity demands bottle-age. At their best, Ponsot's wines are remarkable, but they can be dismayingly inconsistent.

Nicolas Potel ☆☆–☆☆☆
Nuits-St-Georges

Nicolas Potel grew up in Volnay as the heir-apparent of the Domaine Pousse d'Or (*q.v.*). But the premature death of his father and the sale of the estate in 1997 led to his departure. With a reservoir of good will among the growers of Burgundy, and their confidence in his rare skills as a winemaker with international experience, Potel set himself up as a négociant.

The winemaking is non-interventionist, and he seeks out parcels of old vines whenever possible, paying good prices. In 2000, instead of expanding in response to the enthusiastic reception of his first vintages, he cut back production to improve quality even further.

Domaine de la Pousse d'Or ☆☆
Volnay. www.la-pousse-d-or.fr

A twelve-hectare domaine entirely in the *premiers crus* of Volnay, Pommard, and Santenay; recently supplemented with red *grands crus* in Corton. Its reputation, as high as any in the Côte de Beaune, was made by Gérard Potel. In 1997, Potel died unexpectedly and the domaine was sold. It has three *monopoles* in Volnay: Clos de la Bousse [sic] d'Or, Clos des 60 Ouvrées, and Clos d'Audignac. The first and last are typically gentle, sociable Volnays, delicacy and elegance that reaches its peak in the "Bousse d'Or"; the "60 Ouvrées", however, is a prime piece of Caillerets, more forceful wine demanding maturity. Another parcel of Caillerets of the same size produces lighter wines. Two similar plots in Santenay's best *premiers crus* (Tavannes and Gravières) and one hectare of Pommard Jarollières complete the domaine. The new owner, Patrick Landanger, knew from the outset that Potel would be a hard act to follow, and his first vintages were disappointing. But quality is now improving, if not yet at the supremely elegant level established by Potel.

Jacques Prieur ☆☆☆
Meursault

One of Burgundy's most remarkable properties, including parts of both Chambertin and Montrachet, with all its fifteen hectares in great vineyards. Its architect was Jacques Prieur, whose grandson Martin now runs it together with Bertrand Devillard, the director of Antonin Rodet (*q.v.*), which bought half the estate in 1988. The vines include 1.1 hectares in Chambertin and Clos de Bèze, 0.75 in Musigny, 1.25 in Clos Vougeot, 0.75 in Corton-Bressandes, two in Beaune (Clos de la Féguine), as well as extensive holdings in Volnay Premiers Crus (notably Clos des Santenots) and in Meursault Clos de Mazeray, Puligny Les Combettes, and Chevalier-Montrachet. Not to mention 0.6 hectares of Le Montrachet. The domaine had a fading reputation for both red and white wines which Antonin Rodet has restored with determination. Until recently, the style of the red wines was powerful and extracted, but the latest vintages have been better-balanced.

Ramonet ☆☆☆
Chassagne-Montrachet

A distinguished old name in Chassagne. Half of the fourteen-hectare domaine is white, including Bâtard-, Bienvenues-Bâtard-Montrachet, and Le Montrachet, racy Chassagne Premier Cru from Les Ruchottes and other sites, and Chassagne village. The red wines are less famous but remarkably fine; Clos de la Boudriotte, Clos St-Jean, and red Chassagne village are as good as any red wines of the southern Côte de Beaune. The grand old man, Pierre Ramonet, died in 1995 and his grandsons, Noël and Jean-Claude, now make the wine.

Rapet ☆
Pernand-Vergelesses

A highly reputed twelve-hectare domaine including parcels of Corton-Charlemagne and (red) Corton Grand Cru, and Pernand-Vergelesses Premier Cru. Not five-star quality, but good value. Now run by Vincent Rapet.

La Reine Pédauque ☆
Beaune

A well-known commercial house owned by Pierre André. It owns fifty hectares, including the four-hectare Clos des Langres, and parcels in Corton-Renardes and Corton-Charlemagne. In the late 1990s, it opened a new winery in Savigny. Quality has never been remarkable, but there are some efforts to improve. However, the nature of the market, overwhelmingly domestic, is looking for consistency rather than excellence.

Remoissenet ☆
Beaune

A small domaine of 2.5 hectares in Beaune Premier Cru (the best being Grèves and Toussaints) but an important broker and négociant who supplies burgundies to the French firm of Nicolas and the Bristol one of Avery's. Through the latter I have had many good bottles, particularly of white wines.

Remoriquet ☆
Nuits-St-Georges

The Remoriquets are an established family of growers (now headed by Gilles Remoriquet) in Nuits with *premiers crus* Les St-Georges, Rue de Chaux, Les Bousselots, and Les Damodes. This is a conservative domaine, using little new oak; but the wines are robust and age well.

Daniel Rion ☆☆
Nuits-St-Georges

An eighteen-hectare domaine with a solid reputation, with vineyards in Vosne-Romanée, Chambolle-Musigny, and Clos Vougeot, as well as Nuits. In 2001, Patrice Rion sold his share of the property to his brothers, and developed his own property (and négociant business) under the name Michèle and Patrice Rion.

Domaine de la Romanée-Conti ☆☆☆☆
Vosne-Romanée

See Romanée-Conti – A Great Burgundy Estate, page 101.

Ropiteau Frères ☆
Meursault

This once-distinguished firm, specializing in white wines from Meursault and Puligny, was bought by Boisset (*q.v.*) in 1994 and the range was severely pared down. Since the early 2000s the range has once again been expanded.

Philippe Rossignol ☆☆
Gevrey-Chambertin

Six hectares of mostly village vines do not give Rossignol great scope, but he makes the most of what he has, and quality is high.

Joseph Roty ☆☆☆
Gevrey-Chambertin

The impassioned Roty makes lush, full-bodied wines from his eight hectares, almost all in Gevrey. His *grands crus* are all aged in new oak.

Emmanuel Rouget ☆☆☆
Flagey-Echézeaux

The nephew and inheritor of Henri Jayer's legendary estate, including *grand cru* Echézeaux, Vosne-Romanée Premiers Crus Beaumonts and Cros Parantoux, and Nuits-St-Georges. These are splendid wines (especially the Cros Parantoux), but very expensive.

Guy Roulot ☆☆
Meursault. www.domaineroulot.com

This is a family domaine that owns eleven hectares, mostly in Meursault, including *premiers crus* Charmes and Perrières, but also village wines from excellent sites such as Tessons, Luchets, and Les Meix Chavaux.

There are also vineyards in Auxey-Duresses and Monthélie. These are serious, well-judged wines, made since 1989 by Jean-Marc Roulot.

Domaine G. Roumier ☆☆☆–☆☆☆☆
Chambolle-Musigny

Christophe Roumier took over the family property in 1982, and has raised it to the highest level. There are twelve hectares, mostly in Chambolle, but there is also a *monopole premier cru* in Morey-St-Denis (Clos de la Bussière), and some small parcels in Ruchottes- and Charmes-Chambertin. Roumier is unhappy with the quality of his Clos Vougeot vines and no longer produces this wine. Although all his wines are classics of depth and harmony, his finest effort is invariably the Bonnes Mares, where he owns various parcels that amount to 1.45 hectares.

Since 1999, the estate has been organic, though Roumier doesn't publicize this fact. Most of his efforts are directed at the vineyards, as the winemaking is uncontroversial and not reliant on large amounts of new oak. Roumier's thoughtful, modest, pragmatic approach has brought the estate to the top rank.

Armand Rousseau ☆☆☆☆
Gevrey-Chambertin

Charles Rousseau is unquestionably the most respected grower of Chambertin. The fourteen-hectare property includes 2.2 hectares in Chambertin, 1.5 in Clos de Bèze, as well as parcels in Mazis and Charmes-Chambertin and in the Clos de la Roche in Morey, and (his particular pride) 2.2 hectares of Gevrey Clos St-Jacques.

The wines might not be the most powerful of Burgundy's, but their perfume and finesse are incomparable.

Etienne Sauzet ☆☆–☆☆☆☆
Puligny-Montrachet

Etienne Sauzet (who died in 1975) was the third of the five generations to have built up a reputation for richly flavoured white burgundy wines.

For almost thirty years the domaine has been run by his son-in-law, Gérard Boudot. Family feuding among Sauzet's grandchildren led to the original domaine being divided, so Boudot has had to buy in grapes to make up for the loss of some vineyards.

The house style is to keep the wines on their lees for a year to develop flavour and fat. The main holding is in Puligny Premiers Crus, with about 1.5 hectares each of Combettes (the best-known wine) and Champ-Canet; and a small parcel of Bâtard-Montrachet. Although enjoyable young, the Sauzet Pulignys are even better at five or more years of age.

The Hospices de Beaune

vineyards and much more farmland. The wine from its scattered vineyard plots is made in *cuvées,* not necessarily consisting of the wine of a single *climat* but designed to be practicable to make and agreeable to drink. Each *cuvée* is named after an important benefactor of the Hospices. There are thirty-eight *cuvées,* all but one in the Côte de Beaune.

The wine is sold, *cuvée* by *cuvée* and cask by cask, at a public auction on the third Sunday of November in the market hall opposite the Hospices. The profits are spent on running the hospital, which now has every sort of modern equipment. Its original wards, chapel, and works of art are open to the public.

Buyers include merchants, restaurants, individuals, and syndicates from all over the world, who are attracted by the idea of supporting this ancient charity, and the publicity that accompanies it. The winemaking of the Hospices was much criticized in the early 1990s but is now back on course. However, it is exceedingly difficult to judge the wines so soon after the harvest, when buyers have to make their choice. After the sale the wine passes into the hands of local merchants, who are responsible for its *élevage.* Not surprisingly, the upbringing of the wine is a major factor in its eventual quality.

The third weekend in November is the most important date in the Burgundy calendar, known as Les Trois Glorieuses from the three feasts which make it a stiff endurance test. On Saturday the "Chevaliers de Tastevin" hold a gala dinner at the Clos de Vougeot. On Sunday after the auction the dinner is at the Hospices, and Monday lunch is a wine-growers' feast known as the Paulée at Meursault: this last a gigantic bottle party, at which even the guests are expected to bring something interesting for all their neighbours to share.

The Hospices de Beaune has a unique role as a symbol of the continuity, the wealth, and the general benevolence of Burgundy. It was founded as a hospital for the sick, poor, and aged of Beaune in 1443 by the Chancellor to the Duke of Burgundy, Nicolas Rolin, and his wife Guigone de Salins. They endowed it with land in the Côte de Beaune for its income; a practice that has been followed ever since by rich growers, merchants, and other citizens. The Hospices now owns sixty-two hectares of

Comte Senard ☆☆
Beaune. www.domainessenard.com

Philippe Senard's nine-hectare domaine includes substantial holdings in Corton's *grands crus* of Corton, Clos du Roi, and Bressandes, and the entire two-hectare "Clos Meix". After a bad patch in the early 1990s, the wines are now fresh and vigorous, benefitting from a new modern winery.

Domaine de Suremain ☆
Château de Monthélie

A small, old-fashioned but famous estate whose eleven hectares of old vines in Monthélie produce a red wine comparable with good Volnays. Since 1995, the estate has been biodynamic. In other respects its winemaking is conservative, with no more than 20% new oak. At their best, they are perfumed and elegant.

Domaine Thénard
See **Domaine Thénard, Côte Chalonnaise**

Charles Thomas ☆☆
Nuits-St-Georges

The forty-hectare domaine belongs to the Thomas family of Maison Moillard (*q.v.*), and has also been confusingly bottled under other names. It owns vines in eight different Nuits Premiers Crus (Clos de Thorey and Clos des Grandes Vignes are *monopoles*), Chambertin and Clos de Bèze, Bonnes Mares, Clos Vougeot, Romanée St-Vivant and Vosne-Romanée Beaux Monts and Malconsorts, Corton Clos du Roi and Corton-Charlemagne.

Tollot-Beaut ☆☆
Chorey-lès-Beaune

A family property since 1880 with impeccable standards. Of a total of twenty-two hectares, one-third at Chorey and the remainder divided among various *premiers crus* of Beaune, Savigny, and Aloxe-Corton, with *grands crus* from Corton-Bressandes, Le Corton, and Corton-Charlemagne.

No secrets here, but careful, traditional winemaking. The special pride of the house is in the Corton-Bressandes and Beaune Clos du Roi. The wines can seem light initially but they age well.

Trapet ☆☆–☆☆☆
Gevrey-Chambertin. www.domaine-trapet.com

Jean Trapet and his son, Jean-Louis, now own half of the original Louis Trapet domaine which was divided in 1990. The viticulture has been biodynamic since 1997. The pride of the house is still its Chambertin, made in the traditional way, and showing great delicacy and finesse.

Domaine des Varoilles ☆☆
Gevrey-Chambertin

A fourteen-hectare domaine once known for serious *vins de garde* that really must be matured. It takes its name from its *premier cru* Clos des Varoilles, planted by monks on the south-facing hill above Gevrey.

The Clos du Couvent, Clos du Meix des Ouches, and La Romanée are other *monopoles* in Gevrey, besides parcels of Charmes- and Mazoyères-Chambertin, Bonnes Mares, and Clos de Vougeot. The property is now owned by a Swiss company, and the wines have acquired more flesh to balance the always firm tannins.

Henri de Villamont ☆
Savigny

Négociant and grower founded by the huge Swiss firm of Schenk in 1964, when it bought domaines at Savigny and Chambolle-Musigny, and Grands-Echézeaux. In 1969, it purchased the business of Arthur Barolet in Beaune. The name "Barolet" figures largely in company's annals since they found and marketed the extraordinary hoard of fine old burgundies of the late Dr. Barolet in 1968.

Michel Voarick ☆
Aloxe-Corton

A nine-hectare family domaine which includes farming the famous Corton "Cuvée Dr. Peste" for the Hospices de Beaune. Voarick owns 2.5 hectares of Corton Grand Cru (Clos du Roi, Bressandes, Languettes, Renardes) and one of Corton-Charlemagne, besides vineyards in Pernand-Vergelesses and Aloxe-Corton.

Old-fashioned methods include fermenting stalks-and-all in oak *cuves* to make *vins de garde* that have body but not much finesse.

Domaine Comte Georges de Vogüé ☆☆☆☆
Chambolle-Musigny

Considered by some to be the finest domaine in Burgundy, descended by inheritance since 1450. The name "de Vogüé" appears in 1766.

Splendid vaulted cellars under the fifteenth century house hold the production of twelve hectares, of which 7.2 are in Musigny, 2.7 in Bonnes Mares, 0.6 in the *premier cru* Les Amoureuses, and two in the appellation Chambolle-Musigny. Some 3,000 Chardonnay vines in Musigny produce a minute quantity of a unique Musigny Blanc.

The estate replanted these vines in 1994, and is selling the wine as a costly Bourgogne Blanc until the vines are old enough to merit the *grand cru* appellation. After a flat patch in the 1970s and '80s, the wines are once again superlative.

The "Amoureuses" is the most seductive wine, but the greatest is the sublime "Musigny Vieilles Vignes". It's indicative of the exacting standards of this estate that Musigny vines under twenty years of age are bottled as Chambolle Premier Cru. Since 1990, the domaine is back on form as one of France's greatest estates.

Domaine de la Vougeraie ☆☆–☆☆☆
Nuits-St-Georges. www.domainedelavougeraie.com

This new domaine was established by the négociant house Boisset (*q.v.*) as a way of unifying the substantial thirty-seven hectares of vineyards it had collected over the years. Pascal Marchand was recruited as winemaker, and organic viticulture was introduced.

Marchand admits he is lucky to be working with a splendid range of vineyards, from old vines in village appellations to the noblest of *grands crus* such as Corton-Charlemagne and Musigny. Initial releases were dark and rich, but certainly reflected their vineyard origins.

Côte Chalonnaise

Santenay brings the Côte d'Or to a close at its southern end. There is scarcely time for lunch at the luxurious Lameloise at Chagny before the wine scout has to be alert again for the five villages that make up the Côte Chalonnaise. Chalon-sur-Saône has little to do with the district today, but in antiquity it was one of the great wine ports of the empire. It was the point where wine coming or going north to or from Paris or the Moselle had to be trans-shipped from river to road – 25,000 amphoras were found in one dredging operation in the Saône at Chalon.

A new appellation, Bourgogne Côte Chalonnaise, was introduced in 1990, which distinguishes the wines of the Côte Chalonnaise from the rather large and undefined appellation of Bourgogne itself. The Côte from Chagny southwards is less distinct and consistent than from Santenay northwards. So is its wine. Rising demand and prices have only recently made winegrowing profitable rather than marginal, and encouraged replanting of land abandoned after phylloxera. About 1,500 hectares are planted, although the appellation authorizes the planting of considerably more. Pinot Noir dominates, but there are villages such as Montagny or Bouzeron where white grapes are more important. Although its best wines are up to minor Côte de Beaune standards, it is difficult to pin them down with a regional character. They vary remarkably from village to village.

Mercurey and Givry are dedicated ninety per cent to red wine, which should be firm and tasty Pinot Noir at least on a level with, say, a good Côte de Beaune-Villages; if anything harder and leaner, with Givry, traditionally the bigger, demanding longer keeping. The tannins, especially in Mercurey, can have an earthy edge to them, but more modern winemaking techniques are now producing wines that are considerably less rustic than in the past.

Two-thirds of Rully's vineyards now produce white wine, which, at its best, is marvellously brisk, with a touch of real class. The red, at least as most growers make it today, can be rather thin compared with Mercurey. High acidity in Rully whites makes them ideal for sparkling wines.

Montagny is entirely a white wine appellation, with the peculiarity that almost all its wines of 11.5 degrees alcohol or more are entitled to be labelled *premier cru* – which seems scarcely fair to the carefully limited *premiers crus* of the other villages. Montagny whites tend to have a little more body and less finesse than those of Rully. They are certainly more in fashion.

The fifth appellation of the Côte Chalonnaise is the only specific one of the Aligoté grape in Burgundy. The village of Bouzeron, between Rully and Chagny, has made a specialty of what is elsewhere a plain, sharp café wine. In 1979, it was granted the appellation Bourgogne Aligoté de Bouzeron.

Besides these specific appellations, the Région de Mercurey makes a considerable quantity of honourable Bourgogne Rouge, most of which is sold in bulk.

The other regional specialty is Crémant de Bourgogne, sparkling wine whose quality will amaze those who think that Champagne is first and the rest nowhere. (*See* box on page 119.) Three sizeable producers account for most of the *crémant* production. They are Delorme at Rully, R. Chevillard at La Rochepot on the road to Paris, and Parigot-Richard at Savigny-lès-Beaune.

THE REGION IN ROUND FIGURES

Appellation	Average Annual Production		
Bouzeron	3,603 hl	40,000 cases	(white)
Rully	11,000 hl	122,00 cases	(white)
	6,000 hl	66,600 cases	(red)
Mercurey	29,230 hl	325,000 cases	(mainly red)
Givry	11,700 hl	130,000 cases	(mainly red)
Montagny	15,500 hl	172,000 cases	(white)

Leading Côte Chalonnaise Producers

Brintet ☆
Mercurey
This estate produces good, solid reds from a wide range of vineyards, including *monopole premier cru* La Levrière.

Chateau de Chamirey ☆☆
See **Antonin Rodet**

Daniel Chanzy ☆
Bouzeron
This is a particularly considerable domaine of thirty-six hectares, based in Bouzeron, but with vineyards in Rully and Mercurey, too. Chanzy's Bourgogne (*i.e.* Pinot Noir and Chardonnay) vineyards in Bouzeron are called Clos de la Fortune, and he also produces good Aligoté. The quality of the wines is average.

Clos Salomon ☆☆
Givry
This is one of the most historic and best-known vineyards of Givry, and its renown has been restored in the course of the 1990s.

Domaine de la Renarde (Jean-François Delorme) ☆–☆☆
Rully
The most remarkable enterprise in the region; a sixty-nine hectare estate built from scratch over recent decades, largely by reclaiming vineyards abandoned long ago and turned to scrub.

Delorme is equally well-known as one of Burgundy's best sparkling wine specialists. The Rully *monopole* Varot is the seventeen-hectare vineyard that gives his best white, notable for freshness and finesse.

Michel Derain ☆
St-Désert
This small-scale producer makes serious Bourgogne Rouge and Givry Blanc from six hectares.

Dureuil-Janthial ☆
Rully
This is a six-hectare domaine and it produces both white and red wines in more or less equal quantities. The quality of the wines is sound.

Domaine de la Folie ☆
Rully

A substantial property with 1,000 years of history, in the parish of Chagny but in the appellation of Rully. The eighteen hectares are in one block around the house, with Chardonnay in a majority, producing Rully Blanc Clos St-Jacques, plus Rully Rouge Clos de Bellecroix, and a smaller patch of Aligoté. The wines, especially the whites, have a good reputation.

Michel Goubard ☆
St-Désert

An example of how good Bourgogne Côte Chalonnaise without a specific appellation can be in this part of the *côtes*.

Paul & Henri Jacquesson ☆☆–☆☆☆
Rully

Father and son together take great pride in this small domaine of seven hectares, making wine in the old way. The best wines are the *premiers crus*, notably Les Pucelles (white) and Les Clous (red). No corners are cut here: for instance, oak staves for their barrels are dried at the winery to ensure optimal quality. Excellent value.

Joblot ☆☆
Givry

There is strong demand for the wines from Jean-Marc Joblot, and for good reason. His thirteen hectares, with nine of *premiers crus*, produce some of the best wines of the Côte Chalonnaise.

Michel Juillot ☆☆
Mercurey. www.domaine-michel-juillot.fr

For many years Juillot has been one of Mercurey's best winemakers, winning acclaim for his red Clos des Barraults and Champs Martin from his thirty hectares. He also produces Corton Perrières and Corton-Charlemagne. Nowadays Michel's son Laurent is increasingly in charge.

Lorenzon ☆
Mercurey

Splendid if somewhat oaky wines from Champs Martin, the top *cuvées* from this five-hectare domaine.

Jean Maréchal ☆
Mercurey

Maréchals have made Mercurey for 300 years. Most of their ten hectares are *premiers crus*, almost all red. These are long-lived wines.

Maurice Protheau & Fils
Mercurey

A major domaine of sixty hectares in Mercurey and Rully, but in 2002 it went bankrupt and its assets were acquired by a company called Béjot in Meursault.

Ragot ☆☆
Givry

An eight-hectare domaine in its fourth generation with a dignified château. The proportion of white is unusually high for Givry, and the keeping qualities of the wine are remarkable – particularly in years of high acidity.

J. & F. Raquillet ☆☆–☆☆☆
Mercurey

Robust wines from various *crus*. Clos l'Eveque is often the best of them.

Antonin Rodet ☆☆–☆☆☆
Mercurey

An important négociant as well as proprietor in Mercurey. The fourth generation of the Rodet family is represented by the Marquis de Jouennes d'Herville, whose daughter is married to the company's respected director, Bertrand Devillard. Rodet has distributed the excellent wine from Château de Chamirey in Mercurey since 1934, and leases the imposing Château de Rully.

In 1988, Rodet bought a half-share in Domaine Jacques Prieur (*q.v.*), and in 2000 acquired a leading property in Limoux. As a négociant house, Rodet deals in wines from all parts of Burgundy, taking special pride in its Bourgogne Rodet, Mercurey, Meursault, and Gevrey-Chambertin. The very best wines from any appellation are labelled "Cave Privé".

Château de la Saule ☆
Montagny

An eleven-hectare property almost entirely devoted to fresh, vigorous, Montagny. Freshness is the aim, but big vintages have been known to improve for eight-ten years. Some of the wines are bottled under the name of the owner Alain Roy.

Hugues de Suremain ☆☆
Mercurey

A leading proprietor whose twenty-five hectares, all in Mercurey, are known for concentrated and age-worthy wines.

Domaine Thénard ☆☆–☆☆☆
Givry

Much the grandest estate of Givry, with twenty hectares in the village (almost all red *premiers crus*), but better known to the world as the owner of the second-biggest single plot, 1.8 hectares, of Le Montrachet as well as substantial plots in Corton Clos du Roi, Iles des Vergelesses, and Grands-Echézeaux. The property has been in the family for almost 250 years. All the wine is made in the atmospheric, oak-beamed *cuverie* and cellars at Givry.

Caves des Vignerons de Buxy ☆–☆☆
Buxy

Important and very modern growers' co-op for Buxy and Montagny, founded in 1931. Its members own 750 hectares of vines, less than half with generic appellations (Bourgogne Rouge, Passe-tout-grains, and Aligoté are its main productions.) The remainder include white Montagny, Rully, red Côte Chalonnaise, and Crémant de Bourgogne.

A. & P. de Villaine ☆☆☆
Bouzeron

Aubert de Villaine, better known as co-proprietor of the Domaine de la Romanée-Conti, but equally proud to have helped win the formerly obscure Bouzeron its own appellation for Aligoté in 1979.

This forthright wine remains the flagship of the property, but there is also good Bourgogne Côte Chalonnaise called "La Digoine". Since 1994, white Rully and red Mercurey have been added to the list.

Mâconnais

Say Mâconnais to most wine-drinkers today and their knee-jerk response will be *blanc*. The region is riding high on the reliability and uncomplicated pleasantness of its Chardonnay whites. They have the advantage of being recognizably white burgundy but far cheaper than Côte d'Or wines, and marvellously easy to choose – since most of them are made by skilful cooperatives which welcome visitors.

The Mâconnais is a widespread and disjointed region, taking its name from the important commercial city on the Saône just outside its limits to the east. It has little of the monoculture of Beaujolais; its mixed farming land is more attractive, and in places geologically spectacular. Pouilly-Fuissé is its only appellation with *grand vin* aspirations.

Most Mâcon wine used to be red, made of Gamay, but grown on heavy chalky soil which prevented it from ripening to Beaujolais softness and vitality. Mâcon Rouge was indeed merely *vin ordinaire* with an appellation until Beaujolais methods of fermentation were introduced. Recently, there have been some much better wines up to Beaujolais-Villages standards.

Pinot Noir from the Mâconnais can aspire no higher than the appellation Bourgogne Rouge or (mixed with Gamay) Passe-tout-grains. High yields are common, and much of the wine is thin and boring. With minimum must weights set at a derisory nine to ten degrees, the temptation for all but the most conscientious growers is to pick at minimum ripeness levels and chaptalize to the maximum – not a formula for good winemaking.

Chardonnay now occupies two-thirds of the vineyards, including (in the more northerly communes in particular) a strain of Chardonnay known as the "Musqué" for its decidedly richer, melony-musky flavour. Used to excess it can produce a blowzy, unsubtle wine. In due proportion it adds a hint of richness to otherwise rather straight, dry white: undoubtedly an element in the popularity of Mâcon-Villages or with the name of a particular village.

Pouilly-Fuissé rises higher in the quality league for local reasons of soil and situation – but not as high as its price infers. The four villages in the appellation area have been prominent over the centuries, partly for their proximity to Mâcon, partly as a tourist attraction for the mighty limestone bluffs that dominate them and the prehistoric traces that litter the district, partly for the chalky clay and sunny slopes that make their wine at least as good as any south Burgundy white.

Generalizations about Pouilly-Fuissé are risky, as the wine varies greatly according to the precise location of the vineyard in a country that is all bumps and dips. Such variations are not easy to follow where there are very few domaines of more than a few hectares. The growers' cooperative of Chaintré is much the biggest source of Pouilly-Fuissé.

The fact that wines of more or less equal value are produced in the surrounding area has given rise to two other appellations. The smaller Pouilly-Vinzelles (which includes Pouilly-Loché) has somehow failed to catch the public's eye. The much larger St-Véran, which scoops in six communes, including the northern fringe of the Beaujolais country, was added in 1971 and now offers extremely good value.

Throughout the 1990s there has been a discernible change in style. Whereas most Mâcon was fresh and unpretentious, some growers in the more prestigious appellations, are harvesting as late as possible to obtain high potential alcohol levels, and ageing the wine in new-oak barrels with *bâtonnage*. The result is a fat, opulent wine, certainly rich but sometimes vulgar and blowzy. Such wines can be excellent, but often lack the sustaining acidity that underpins the richness of a top Côte de Beaune white.

The Appellations of Mâconnais

The Mâconnais has seven appellations of its own and shares the right to five more with the rest of Burgundy. Its own appellations are:

FOR WHITE WINES

Mâcon Blanc. Chardonnay wine from delimited areas with a minimum ten degrees of natural alcohol.

Mâcon Supérieur. The same with one more degree of alcohol.

Mâcon-Villages (or Mâcon- followed by the name of one of forty-three villages in the eastern half of the region). The best known of these – Clessé and Viré – were awarded their own AC in 1999: Viré-Clessé, with 196 hectares in production. The minimum degree is 11, as for Mâcon Supérieur. All the Mâcon appellations together amount to 3,100 hectares.

St-Véran. 560 hectares. The same as for Mâcon-Villages but from six of the southernmost communes, overlapping into Beaujolais at St-Amour. The six are Chânes, Chasselas, Davayé, Leynes, Prissé, and St-Vérand [sic]. Davayé and Prissé lie to the north and are based on classic Burgundian limestone, which gives the wines weight and concentration, the rest are to the south of Pouilly-Fuissé on the granitic sand of the Beaujolais, which is much less suited to white wine production.

They offer lighter, thinner wines, which can also be sold as Beaujolais Blanc, Mâcon-Villages, or Bourgogne Blanc if the customer prefers one of these names. If a particular vineyard is named on the label, the minimum degree is twelve, with the implication that the wine is better and more concentrated.

Pouilly-Fuissé. 767 hectares. Chardonnay wine of eleven degrees from specified parts of the villages of Pouilly, Fuissé, Solutré, Vergisson, and Chaintré. If a vineyard name is used, it must have twelve degrees.

Pouilly-Loché. Twenty-eight hectares. May be sold as itself or labelled as...

Pouilly-Vinzelles. Fifty-four hectares. The same rules as for Pouilly-Fuissé, but for wine from the two villages of Vinzelles and Loché to the east – marginally less good but more than marginally cheaper.

FOR RED WINES

Mâcon Rouge. Gamay red wine of at least nine degrees. It can also be made pink and offered as Mâcon Rosé.

Mâcon Supérieur. The same as previous entry with an extra degree of alcohol and from certain specified zones. It can also be labelled as...

Mâcon- (followed by a village name), but not Mâcon-Villages, and must have at least eleven degrees. The two appellations together account for 750 hectares.

GENERAL APPELLATIONS
Aligoté. As in the rest of Burgundy.

Bourgogne. For Chardonnay whites and Pinot Noir reds.

Crémant de Bourgogne. As in the rest of Burgundy.

Passe-tout-grains. For Gamay and Pinot Noir (2:1) reds.

Leading Mâconnais Producers

The great bulk of Mâcon, both white and red, is produced by the eighteen growers' cooperatives of the area. The best known are those of Chaintré (for Pouilly-Fuissé), Lugny (for Mâcon-Lugny and Mâcon Rouge Supérieur), Mancey (red and white Mâcon), Prissé (Mâcon-Prissé and St-Véran), and Viré (Viré-Clessé).

The following are the few individual producers with more than a local reputation.

Pouilly-Fuissé

Auvigue
Charnay
Numerous bottlings from this five-hectare domaine.

Daniel Barraud
Vergisson
Numerous *cuvées*, some barrique-fermented.

Christophe Cordier
Fuissé
Various *cuvées* of Pouilly-Fuissé and Pouilly-Loché.

Domaine Corsin
Davayé

Ferret
Fuissé
Fifteen hectares of mostly old vines permit the Ferrets to produce numerous *cuvées* of Pouilly-Fuissé with varying degrees of new-oak ageing.

Château de Fuissé
Fuissé
Jean-Jacques Vincent is the outstanding grower of the area. However he is facing ever stronger competition from his neighbours.

Lassarat
Vergisson
Lavish, oaky wines.

Manciat-Poncet
Levigny
High-lying vineyards – excellent wines, some are oaked.

Saumaize-Michelin
Vergisson
Good St-Véran, too.

Domaine de la Soufrandise
Fuissé

Gérard Valette
Chaintré
Splendid range of wines from some of the appellation's best sites.

Pouilly-Loché

Alain Delaye
Loché

Pouilly-Vinzelles

Domaine de la Soufrandière
Davayé
Rich ripe wines.

St-Véran

Domaine de la Croix Senaillet
Davayé
Produces good unoaked.

Mâcon-Davayé
St-Véran & Pouilly-Fuissé

Lycée Agricole Davayé
Pouilly-Vinzelles

Domaine des Deux Roches
Davayé

Viré-Clessé

André Bonhomme
Viré
A dependable source.

Laurent Huet
Clessé

René Michel
Clessé

Domaine Rijckaert
Leynes

Jean Thévenet
Quintaine-Clessé

Also produces remarkable sweet wines from botrytized Chardonnay. Labels include "Domaine Emilian Gillet" and "Domaine de la Bongran".

Mâcon

Guffens-Heynen
Vergisson

Domaine des Heritiers des Comtes Lafon
Milly-Lamartine
Dominique Lafon has acquired a domaine here from which he produces three *cuvées*. 2001 was the first vintage. Quality is high, but prices are reasonable.

Olivier Merlin
La Roche Vineuse
Seven hectares, scrupulously tended and vinified.

Alain Normand
La Roche Vineuse
An ambitious young grower.

Domaine de Roally
Viré

Domaine de la Sarrazinière
Bussières

Verget
Sologny
Founded by Belgian broker Jean-Marie Guffens in 1991 as a high-quality négociant house.

In addition, very good wines are offered by several of the négociants well-known for their Beaujolais, notably Georges Duboeuf, Thorin, and Piat, and by Louis Latour, Robert Drouhin, and Louis Jadot of Beaune.

Caves Coopératives

Azé
Lugny

Chaintré
Chaintré
Produces a huge range of appellations, Beaujolais and St-Véran included. But best-known for Pouilly-Fuissé.

Cave des Grands Crus Blancs
Pouilly-Vinzelles

Igé
Pierreclos

Lugny
Lugny
The largest producer of all.

Mancey Sennecey-Le-Grand
Sennecey-le-Grand

Prissé
Pierreclos

Viré
Viré

Beaujolais

The Beaujolais region is no more complex than its light-hearted wine. Thirteen appellations take care of the whole 22,500 hectares. They could really be reduced to half a dozen without greatly grieving anyone but the gastronomes of Lyon. What is needed is a grasp of the essential grades of quality and a good address list – which need not be long.

The great majority of Beaujolais is made either by a growers' cooperative or by tiny properties. There are over 3,600 estates, with average holdings varying from seven to ten hectares. Inevitably, few of those properties can bottle and market their wines, so they earn their living by selling grapes or wines to the many large merchant houses within the region. Only seventeen per cent of the crop is domaine-bottled; the rest is bottled and marketed by merchants and nineteen cooperatives.

The world's perception of Beaujolais today is very different from what it was twenty or so years ago. Beyond its own region and Paris, where it was the café wine, Beaujolais used to be traded as a cut-price burgundy, imitating the weight of the Pinot Noirs of the Côte d'Or, by dint of picking as ripe as possible and adding plenty of sugar, achieving strength without grace. I have always been mystified by mid-nineteenth century figures showing Beaujolais *crus* with fifteen degrees of alcohol (while Médocs had nine or ten degrees). Very few red wines need anything like that strength, and least of all Gamay, which lacks the flavour to countenance it. The Gamay of Beaujolais has no great fruity flavour; well-made and in the modern manner, it lures you in with its sappy smell and a combination of soft juiciness and a slight nip – the perfect recipe for quenching thirst.

Beaujolais, or its image, has lost some of its lustre in recent years, and the market for *nouveau* styles has greatly diminished, which may be no bad thing. There is now a glut of production, and some major changes in the structure of the region's vineyards may be imminent. In 2002, over 100,000 hectolitres were ordered to be sent for distillation in order to stabilize prices, since so much wine from the two previous vintages remained unsold. Growers had routinely produced the maximum yields at the expense of vinosity and quality, and many of them had remained complacently unaware that the market for dilute and rapidly ageing red Beaujolais was shrinking. There is certainly a decline in the amount of wine being made by carbonic maceration (*see* below) as the leading growers do their best to show that, on these slopes, Gamay is capable of producing serious red wine.

How Beaujolais is Made

The secret of the fresh, grapey fruitiness of Beaujolais lies in the way the Gamay grape – a variety of modest pretensions to quality – is handled and fermented. Winemaking in the Beaujolais combines the classic method of making burgundy with *macération carbonique*: the activity of enzymes inside an uncrushed grape, which, provided it is surrounded by CO_2, causes an internal fermentation and the extraction of colour and flavour from the inner skin.

The trick is to fill the fermentation vat with whole bunches, stalks and all, with as few grapes crushed and damaged as possible. The weight of the upper grapes crushes the lower ones, which start a normal fermentation with their natural yeasts. The CO_2 given off by this process (helped along with gas from a bottle, if necessary) blankets off the air from the uncrushed upper layers. Here the grapes quietly feed on themselves, many of them splitting in the process.

After six or seven days of spontaneous fermentation, the vat is about one-third full of juice, known as "free-run". This is run off, and the solid matter pressed to extract the remaining juice. The two products are blended together, and fermentation continues to completion. In normal red-winemaking, the *vin de presse* is in a minority (and may not be used at all). In the Beaujolais method it accounts for between two-thirds and three-quarters of the total, and the resulting wines tend to be softer and less astringent than those fermented traditionally.

At this stage, the juice still has unfermented sugar in it. Fermentation has to finish before the juice is stable enough to be called wine. The law regulating Beaujolais Nouveau says that this will happen by the third Thursday in November, although in years with a late harvest, some brutal methods of stabilization are needed to "finish" the wine in time.

A few growers still produce the wine by old-fashioned methods, scarcely distinguishable from those further north in the Côte d'Or. The resulting wines have more structure and complexity, especially if barrique-aged, but lack the exuberant *typicité* of a fresh, youthful Beaujolais-Villages.

The Appellations of Beaujolais

The most basic Beaujolais is from the southern half of the region, south of Villefranche, where the Gamay is encouraged to produce large quantities on heavy soil (although there is nothing to stop growers anywhere in Beaujolais using the appellation). This is a now-or-never wine, originally destined to be sold on draught in local cafés and by the carafe in restaurants. It is best drunk as young as possible. The term *nouveau* really only means the wine of the last-harvest, until the next. The minimum alcoholic degree is nine, but this is regularly exceeded, either naturally or by chaptalizing.

For this reason, the appellation Beaujolais Supérieur, only different in that it requires ten degrees, is little used. "Beaujolais" applies to red, white, or rosé, but only one per cent is white. Total area is 10,480 hectares.

Beaujolais-Villages

Beaujolais-Villages AC has a total of 6,020 hectares. The northern half of the region, or Haut-Beaujolais, has steeper hills, warmer soil (because it is lighter and more sandy), and makes better wine. Beaujolais-Villages is the appellation that covers the whole of this area, thirty-eight villages in all, but ten small zones in the north, identified by combinations of slopes and soils that are peculiar to themselves, are singled out as the Beaujolais *crus* – the aristocrats.

Beaujolais-Villages makes a better *vin de primeur* than plain Beaujolais, except in atypically hot vintages. It has a minimum of ten degrees alcohol and more backing of fruit and body – more flavour, in fact – to complement the rasp of new fruit juice. It is almost always worth its fairly modest premium both *en primeur* and even more when it has been, or will be, kept. Good Beaujolais-Villages is at its best in the summer after the vintage, and can hold for another year. Besides the *crus*, the region as a whole has some producers whose wines are regularly up to *cru* standards.

The Beaujolais Crus

Between the railway along the Saône Valley and the 450-metre (1,463-foot) contour line in the Beaujolais mountains to the west, from just south of Belleville to the boundary with the Mâconnais, the vine has the landscape to itself. Sandy, stony, or schistose granite-based soils without lime give the Gamay a roundness and depth of flavour it lacks elsewhere. Here it is pruned hard, and the plants are trimmed individually. Minimum natural strength of the wine is ten degrees, but when it is sold with a vineyard name the required minimum is a degree higher. It will almost always be chaptalized up to thirteen degrees or more.

Cru Beaujolais can be offered *en primeur*, but not until a month after Beaujolais and Beaujolais-Villages, from the fifteenth of December. It would be a pity to prevent it being poured for Christmas. The best *crus* are never treated in this way; they are kept in barrel or vat until at least the March after the vintage. Their full individuality and sweet, juicy smoothness take anything from six months to six years in bottle to develop. Three of the *crus* – Morgon, Chénas, and above all Moulin-à-Vent – are looked on as *vins de garde*, at least by Beaujolais standards.

Brouilly 1,315 hectares. The southernmost and the largest of the *crus*, enveloping areas in six villages (Odenas, St-Lager, Cercié, Charentay, St-Etienne-la-Varenne, and Quincié) grouped around the isolated Mont de Brouilly (*see* Côtes de Brouilly). The word "typical" is most often used for Brouilly – not surprising for the biggest-producing *cru* lying in the very heart of the region. This means the wine is full of grapey flavour and vigour, but is not aggressive in its first year.

Chénas 285 hectares. The smallest *cru*, sheltered from the west by a wooded hill (Chénas is derived from *chêne*, meaning oak) and including part of the commune of La Chapelle-de-Guinchay. Certain Chénas wines achieve formidable strengths, but its vineyard sites are too varied for the appellation to be readily identifiable, or its style reliable.

Chiroubles 374 hectares. All the vineyards are southeast-facing on the higher slopes, making some of the best-balanced and most prized Beaujolais, in limited quantities. In some years, the elevation can mean that the vines struggle to ripen fully. This is the first *cru* to be "supple and tender" for the eager restaurateurs of Paris.

Côte de Brouilly 325 hectares. The slopes of the Mont de Brouilly give a stronger, more concentrated wine than the surrounding appellation Brouilly, but in smaller quantities. The minimum degree here is 10.5 – the highest in Beaujolais. The wines are said to develop the high-toned scent of violets after two to three years in bottle. After warm vintages, they benefit from keeping that long.

Fleurie 875 hectares. The pretty name, a substantial supply, and a singular freshness of flavour all contribute to making this the most memorable and popular Beaujolais *cru* emanating from red, granitic, sandstone soils. Fleurie is often irresistible in its first year, with the result that the full, sweet silkiness of its maturity at three or four years is little-known.

Juliénas 600 hectares. With St-Amour, the northernmost *cru* (the *département* boundary of Rhône and Saône-et-Loire runs between them). Substance, strong colour, and vigour, even tannin, mean that Juliénas needs two years or more to age. It is generally considered to be a mealtime Beaujolais rather than a thirst quencher.

Morgon 1,115 hectares. The spread of vineyards around Villié-Morgon, between the *crus* Brouilly and Fleurie, are credited with a character so peculiar that *morgonner* has become a verb for a way that other wines sometimes (when they are lucky) behave. The soil is schistose, and the peculiarity is described as a flavour of wild cherries. I have not found them so identifiable, but they are among the bigger and longest-lasting wines of Beaujolais.

Moulin-à-Vent 676 hectares. There is no village of Moulin-à-Vent, but a sail-less windmill among the hamlets between Romanèche-Thorins and Chénas gives its name to the most "serious" and expensive Beaujolais appellation. Moulin-à-Vent *en primeur* is almost a contradiction in terms. It should be a firm, meaty, and savoury wine that has less of the surging scent of Beaujolais in its first year, but builds up a bouquet resembling burgundy in bottle. Some authorities attribute its power to the presence of manganese in the soil. Some growers age it briefly in small oak barrels to add to its structure and longevity. Moulin-à-Vent is always served last in a Beaujolais meal, often with the cheeses, which will dominate the lighter wines.

Régnié 746 hectares. The newest Beaujolais *cru*, to the west of Brouilly and Morgon from the commune of Régnié-Durette. While it shows a particular resemblance to Brouilly, it nonetheless has a personality of its own, with its well-defined aroma of red fruits. The soils of Régnié are sandier than the other *crus*. The *cru* has had difficulty establishing a reputation for itself, and bulk prices have sometimes dipped below those for Beaujolais-Villages.

St-Amour 317 hectares. The one Beaujolais appellation in the Mâconnais – its white wine is entitled to the appellation St-Véran. The power of suggestion is strong, so its name may have some bearing on my predilection for this wine. I find it next to Fleurie and Chiroubles in delicacy and sweetness – pleading to be drunk young, yet tasting even better after two or three years in bottle. As one of the smaller areas it is not often seen.

Enjoying Beaujolais

Beaujolais Nouveau is often served alone, slightly chilled, as a party wine, but it can be very fatiguing and thirst-making – especially when its alcoholic degree is particularly high. Its cheerful properties are better appreciated with terrines or cheeses, picnic or buffet food. Beaujolais *crus* of good vintages, aged three or four years in bottle, often begin to resemble fine Rhône wines or, more rarely, Côte d'Or wines. They are best served at the same temperature as red Burgundy and with similar food. An increasing number of these wines are being aged in barriques. They can be highly rated by wine critics and are capable of fetching high prices, but whether you enjoy the combination of Gamay fruitiness and new oak barrels is very much a matter of personal taste.

Leading Beaujolais Producers

Jean-Marc Burgaud ☆☆
Villié-Morgon. 12.5 hectares
Burgaud is based in Morgon, where he makes powerful wines from the Côtes du Puy. But he has more to offer: a rounder Morgon Charmes, a fruity Beaujolais-Villages, and a rare example of a striking wine of complexity from Régnié.

F. & J. Calot ☆☆–☆☆☆
Villié-Morgon. 10 hectares
Jean Calot has little time for carbonic maceration, declaring that his aim is to make structured wines. He is aided by the ownership of some very old vines, and his "Cuvée Vieilles Vignes" is made from vines at least seventy years old. It's a spicy, concentrated wine with aromas of blackberries. Also memorable is the plummy "Cuvée Jeanne", picked slightly overripe and given a short but very warm *cuvaison*.

Domaine Emile Cheysson ☆☆
Chiroubles. 26 hectares
Extensive vineyards allow Jean-Pierre Large to compose his Chiroubles blends with care. The basic wine shows to the full the charm of which Chiroubles is capable, while the oak-aged "Prestige" has greater weight and complexity, but perhaps at the expense of *typicité*.

Michel Chignard ☆☆
Fleurie. 8 hectares
Rich, seductive wines, among the finest from this popular *cru*. The "Cuvée Spéciale" will be too oaky for many Beaujolais enthusiasts. Prices are relatively high.

Domaine Desperrier ☆☆–☆☆☆
Romanèche-Thorins. 10 hectares
Copybook Moulin-à-Vent, bold in flavour and rich in tannin. The top *cuvée*, "Clos de la Pierre", benefits from bottle-ageing.

Louis-Claude Desvignes ☆☆
Villié-Morgon. 13 hectares
A respected producer of Morgon, making wines with fruit and depth, especially the Côtes du Puy.

Jean Foillard ☆☆
Villié-Morgon. 8 hectares
A small domaine, but Foillard is fortunate to have vines in the Côte du Puy, one of the best vineyards in the region. This is a wine made at optimal ripeness levels, and it repays ageing.

Château des Jacques ☆☆☆
Romanèche-Thorins. 36 hectares
The Burgundy négociant, Jadot, bought this large Moulin-à-Vent estate in 1996. It is divided into five separate sites (plus vineyards in Mâcon-Villages and Beaujolais-Villages) that are vinified and sometimes marketed separately. The vinification is essentially Burgundian, and the grapes are de-stemmed. These are dense, complex wines, with little initial primary fruit, so they need time to age.

Paul Janin ☆☆–☆☆☆
Romanèche-Thorins. 12 hectares
One-third of this estate is in Beaujolais-Villages, the rest in Moulin-à-Vent. Part of the property is farmed biodynamically.

Janin ferments his wines at a high temperature and ages them either in tanks or large casks. The result is dense wines with varying aromas of cherries and liquorice, and the best of them is usually the "Clos du Tremblay". The Beaujolais-Villages vines lie just across the border from the *cru*, and they give wines of surprising guts and structure.

Hubert Lapierre ☆☆
La Chapelle-de-Guinchay. 7.5 hectares.
www.domaine-lapierre.com
Lapierre's estate is divided almost equally between Chénas and Moulin-à-Vent. The wines are given a fairly long fermentation, and aged in tanks, with the exception of one *cuvée* of Chénas, which is aged in oak for ten months. It is arguable whether it is actually superior to the unoaked wines. The wines all age well.

Domaine des Marrans ☆☆
Fleurie. 10 hectares
The Mélinand family have vines with an average age of forty years. They also produce a Juliénas, and both their wines have rich, dense, black-fruits flavours.

Domaine Gilbert Picolet ☆☆
Moulin-à-Vent
Much of Picolet's wine is sold to négociants, leaving only the best to be bottled. He has some extremely old vines, from which he makes "Vieilles Vignes" bottlings, both in Moulin-à-Vent and Chénas.

Jean-Charles Pivot ☆☆
Quincié. 13 hectares
A good grower in the Côte de Brouilly, who is also well-known for his Beaujolais-Villages.

Domaine des Terres Dorées ☆☆☆
Crière. 17 hectares
Jean-Paul Brun is certainly the most original and creative winemaker of the region, though some may dismiss him as a mere eccentric. It was he who led what has now become a fashion: to return to traditional methods of vinification far removed from the carbonic maceration and flashy fruitiness of most Beaujolais production. So much of Brun's wine is denied the AC, which does not seem to bother him greatly. He also produces weighty white wine from Chardonnay, and a Pinot Noir sold under the pitifully minor AC of Bourgogne Grand Ordinaire. And yet the wines have remarkable concentration and finesse that mark them out as among the most interesting and characterful of all the wines of Beaujolais.

Michel Tête ☆☆–☆☆☆
Juliénas. 13 hectares
Half the estate lies within Juliénas, the rest in St-Amour and Beaujolais-Villages. The latter is planted on granitic soils, so it is a wine with some stuffing. In 1990, he introduced a Juliénas "Cuvée Prestige", half of which is oak-aged. The crisp, cherryish St-Amour is consistently good.

Château Thivin ☆☆–☆☆☆
Odenas. 26 hectares. www.chateau-thivin.com
The Beaujolais-Villages is the bargain here, but the best wines are certainly the impressive *cuvées* from the Côte de Brouilly,

which have depth of flavour without excessive extraction. "Cuvée Zacharie" is aged in barriques.

Domaine du Vissoux ☆☆
Fleurie. 20 hectares

Pierre-Marie Chermette vinifies his wines with minimum manipulation, avoiding chaptalization and the addition of cultivated yeasts whenever possible. He produces two bottlings of Fleurie, and a good Moulin-à-Vent. The various *cuvées* of simple Beaujolais are bargains, for drinking young.

Leading Beaujolais Merchants

Georges Duboeuf ☆–☆☆☆
Romanèche-Thorin. www.duboeuf.com

Duboeuf's family has been embedded in the region for four centuries. Beaujolais is in his blood. In the early 1950s, he made wine from his brother's vineyards and sold it to local restaurants. The great chef, Georges Blanc, bought the wine with enthusiasm, and young Georges Duboeuf never looked back. Over the decades, his small winery has expanded into an extremely slick and successful company, buying in wines from 400 growers and fifteen cooperatives, mostly in the Beaujolais and Mâconnais, but also from the Rhône. Even in his seventies, Georges, now aided by his son Franck, tastes for over two hours a day in order to compose their blends. He also designs his own labels, including the famous flower labels that adorn many of his best wines. Duboeuf effortlessly combines excellent winemaking and blending with first-rate marketing, and his "Hameau du Vin" in Romanèche-Thorin is one of France's most delightful wine museums.

Eventail de Vignerons Producteurs
Corcelles

A marketing group, working with the production of a large number of mostly good-quality independent estates. Not rated as a group of producers.

Henry Fessy ☆–☆☆
St-Jean-d'Ardières. 11 hectares. www.vins-henry-fessy.com

Fessy produces a very wide range of wines from all over Beaujolais, and at all quality levels. The basic Beaujolais bottlings have drive and excellent fruit, the *crus* are inevitably more varied in quality and subtle in expression. All wines are vinified by the Fessy team, and total production is around two million bottles.

Loron & Fils ☆–☆☆
Fleurie. www.loron-et-fils.com

A large, high-quality family business, formerly mainly dealing in bulk but now selling more and more in bottle, under several brand names. Offers some good domaine wines and good-value, non-appellation *vins de marque*.

Mommessin ☆–☆☆
Charnay-lès-Mâcon

Until recently this was a very traditional family business. Now it is diversifying into *vins de marque* as well as Beaujolais, where it has exclusive arrangements with several good domaines.

Potel-Aviron ☆☆

An unusual joint venture between Burgundy négociant Nicolas Potel and Stéphane Aviron, from a Beaujolais wine-broking family. Their aim is to produce wines made in the true Burgundian fashion. First releases from the 2000 vintage displayed considerable oakiness these were less noticeable in 2001.

Louis Tête ☆☆
St-Didier sur Beaujeu. www.tete-beaujolais.com

A specialist in the high-class restaurant trade, particularly well-known in Britain and Switzerland. The properties it markets include Château des Alouettes in Beaujolais-Villages and Domaine de la Chapelle in Brouilly-Villages.

Other Beaujolais Producers

Domaine Noël Aucoeur ☆–☆☆
Villié-Morgon

A good property in Morgon, with a good Beaujolais-Villages and an oaked "Cuvée Jean-Claude Aucoeur" from Morgon.

Paul Beaudet ☆–☆☆
La Chapelle-de-Guinchay. www.paulbeaudet.com

Négociant firm, well-known in top restaurants and in the USA for about ten *cru* bottlings as well as other good wines.

Christian Bernard ☆–☆☆
Fleurie

Lush, highly approachable wines from Moulin-à-Vent and Fleurie.

Clos de la Roilette ☆☆–☆☆☆
Fleurie

The Coudert family makes lush Fleurie from very old vines.

Bernard Diochon ☆☆
Romanèche-Thorins

A small property focused on very old vines in Moulin-à-Vent.

Domaine du Granit ☆–☆☆
Chénas

A small estate based in Chénas but producing robust Moulin-à-Vent.

Marcel Lapierre ☆☆
La Chapelle-de-Guinchay. www.marcel-lapierre.com

Intense yet fruit-packed wines from his vineyards in Morgon.

Domaine de la Madone ☆–☆☆
Fleurie

Jean-Marc Desprès from de la Madone produces both a regular Fleurie and a "Cuvée Vieilles Vignes", which has considerably more concentration.

Dominique Piron ☆
Villié-Morgon

In addition to his own vineyards, Dominique Piron farms smallholdings that belong to owners with other careers, and then he purchases their grapes, giving him access to around fifty hectares.

Jura

Connoisseurs of the French countryside each have their favourite corner. I hope never to be forced to make a final choice, but I have a shortlist ready, and the Jura is on it. These limestone mountains (they give their name to a whole epoch of geology, the Jurassic) roll up towards Switzerland from the plain of the Saône in Burgundy. Halfway in a straight line from Beaune to Geneva you come to the delicious timbered and tiled little town of Arbois (where Pasteur lived), then Poligny, then Château-Chalon, the heart of a completely original wine country. The Jura vineyards are small (much smaller than they once were; currently 1,828 hectares). But their origins are as old as Burgundy's, their climate and soil singular, and their grapes their own.

Jura producers are fond of making a wide range of wines, from *méthode traditionnelle* sparkling to *vin jaune*. The overall appellation is Côtes du Jura. This appellation covers a long strip of country from north of Arbois to south of Cousance. Arbois is another general AC with higher alcohol stipulated. L'Etoile covers whites and *vins de paille* from the valley around the village of L'Etoile to the south. As an AC, the forty-five hectare Château-Chalon is for *vin jaune* exclusively.

The vineyard sits on a band of heavy clay, rich in lime, exposed along the mountain slopes between 275 and 410 metres (885 and 1,165 feet) high. Woods, bovine pastures, and limestone cliffs constantly interrupt the continuity of the vines. Unlike Alsace to the north, which lies in the rain shadow of the Vosges, the west-facing Jura is often deluged by summer rain. Hail is a frequent problem here, but September and October are usually sunny. Jura grapes have been selected because they thrive in deep, damp soil, given a good, sun-warmed slope. The most widespread is the Poulsard (confusingly referred to as Plousard in the Pupillin region): a pale red, which is the nearest thing to a rosé grape. Another obscure red, the tannic Trousseau, is grown with it to stiffen its too "supple" wine. Pinot Noir is increasingly added to give more colour and backbone to red wine – but red is in a minority here; most of the wine is rosé, fermented on its pale skins as though intended to be red.

Nowadays, the Chardonnay is the standard grape for light white wines; it performs well (under the alias of Melon d'Arbois or Gamay Blanc) but certainly not spectacularly. Much of it is made into sparkling wine. But the real specialty is Savagnin or Naturé. It is said to be related to the Alsatian Traminer, but doesn't taste much like it. Savagnin is a late ripener and a small cropper, but its wine is powerful in alcohol and flavour. Used merely for topping up barrels of Chardonnay it gives them, as they age, a marvellously rustic style, sometimes described as *vin typé*.

Used alone, it behaves in a most peculiar way that makes it comparable with *fino* sherry. The end result is the oxidative *vin jaune*, and can only be made from vines cropped at no more than twenty hectolitres per hectare. The young wine is left in old barrels with a history of making *vin jaune*, not filled to the top but in the normally perilous state of "ullage". A *flor* yeast, presumably residing in the barrel wood, rapidly grows as a film on the surface of the wine, excluding direct contact with oxygen. The wine is left thus for a statutory minimum of six years and three months, without being topped up. At the end of this ageing period, it has lost thirty

per cent of its volume, but a miraculous stability has (or should have) come over it. A finished *vin jaune* is an impressive apéritif, intense in flavour, obviously slightly oxidized, but long and fine and altogether worthwhile. The village (not château) of Château-Chalon and a few adjacent communes are famous for the best, although good *vins jaunes* are made all over the area.

Wine produced in such restricted quantities (and by no means every year) and by such drawn-out methods is inevitably expensive. Like Tokaji, *vin jaune* comes in smaller-than-standard bottles that help to disguise the price. (The *clavelin* of the Jura, long-necked and hunch-shouldered, holds sixty-two centilitres.) I cannot pretend it is anything like as good value, as reliable, or even as delicious, as a first-class *fino* sherry. But it exists – and as wine-lovers, we should be grateful for variety and support it, especially in such time-honoured forms as this.

Another time-honoured regional specialty, *vin de paille*, was under threat of extinction but has been revived. It is made by hanging bunches of grapes in the rafters (or laying them on straw – *paille* – mats) to dry and concentrate their sweetness in the manner of Italian *vin santo*. The drying requires at least two months, and then the wine must be barrel-aged for at least three years; the tradition was ten. The result is a wine with 15.5 to sixteen degrees of alcohol and around 100 grams of residual sugar.

The Jura vineyard was decimated by phylloxera and took many years to recover. Today it thrives – largely on the tourist trade and faithful private customers in France. There are 250 growers, and only about twenty with more than thirteen hectares. One of the biggest is merchant-grower Henri Maire, who has been a significant force in achieving recognition for the region and its wines.

A local specialty is MacVin, which is not an offshoot of a well-known fast-food chain, but a blend of two-thirds grape juice with one-third *marc*, aged up to thirty months in casks. Since 1991, this product has had its own AC.

Leading Jura Producers

Château d'Arlay ☆–☆☆
Arlay. 25 hectares. www.arlay.com
The Jura's one lordly estate, descended in the same family since the twelfth century, when it was a Hapsburg stronghold. The present owner, Comte Alain de Laguiche, has family ties with the Marquis de Laguiche of Montrachet, the de Vogüés of Champagne and Chambolle-Musigny, and the Ladoucettes of Pouilly-Fumé. Château d'Arlay uses traditional Jura varieties to produce an excellent range of wines, including an unusual, dark-coloured red blend of Poulsard, Trousseau, and Pinot Noir, and an excellent nut- and spice-filled *vin jaune*, as well as *vin de paille*.

Berthet-Bondet ☆☆–☆☆☆
Château-Chalon. 9 hectares
This domaine was only created in 1985. It makes earthy Chardonnay and rather austere Savagnin, and an unusually elegant *vin jaune*.

Jean Bourdy ☆☆–☆☆☆
Arlay. 7 hectares

A cornerstone of the Jura wine industry, dating back to the sixteenth century, with bottles of such famous vintages as 1865 still offered for sale. Jean Bourdy retired in 1979 after fifty-two years to be succeeded by his son, Christian. Their model Jura wines come from Savagnin grown in Château-Chalon and Arlay, where they make red, rosé, and Chardonnay white as well as superlative *vin jaune*.

Caveau des Jacobins ☆–☆☆
Poligny. 35 hectares
Small cooperative producing a range of Côtes du Jura wines and good *crémant*. Its traditional Poulsard has a good following. Also good Chardonnay aged in barriques.

Pascal Clairet ☆☆
Arbois. 6 hectares
Clairet worked for years as the oenologist of the chamber of commerce and, in 1991, founded his own property. Wines include very powerful Savagnin, and pretty, strawberry-scented Poulsard.

Château de l'Etoile ☆–☆☆☆
L'Etoile. 25 hectares
The Château de l'Etoile exists no more, but the name has been used by the Vendelle family since 1883. Famous for its traditional-method sparkling wines, *vin jaune* with tremendous attack, and Côtes du Jura white. A small amount of red is also produced. The best wines are probably the white blends, which are vibrant, nutty, and have great depth.

Fruitière Vinicole d'Arbois ☆–☆☆☆
Arbois. 200 hectares
Founded in 1906, it has 140 members, making it the oldest and biggest of the Jura co-ops, producing red, white, and *jaune* wines, all AC, both *tranquilles* and *mousseux*. Good Savagnin and Chardonnay, and a "Cuvée Bethanie" that blends the two. The largest producer of *vin jaune*, the cooperative also began making *vin de paille* in 1989.

Fruitière Vinicole de Pupillin ☆☆
Pupillin. 50 hectares
A small co-op with thirty-five members producing especially interesting whites; also known for special barrels of spicy *vin jaune*. Pupillin is a perfect example of a Jura country village, with some 200 inhabitants, all living by and for the vine.

Michel Geneletti ☆–☆☆
L'Etoile. 11 hectares
Mostly Chardonnay produced here, toasty and spicy. But the Savagnin and *vin jaune* are also fine.

Château Gréa ☆☆
Rotalier. 6 hectares
The pride of the Gréa family for nearly 300 years and a leading property in the southern Côtes du Jura.
   Their specialties are a *méthode traditionnelle brut*; "Le Chanet", a blend of Chardonnay with Savagnin; and a *vin jaune* of pure Savagnin.

Labet ☆☆–☆☆☆
Rotalier. 9 hectares
Alain Labet specializes in very rich Côtes du Jura whites from single vineyards.

Jean Macle ☆☆–☆☆☆
Château-Chalon. 12 hectares
A major producer of Château-Chalon of exceptional quality, and a fine Côtes du Jura white.

Henri Maire ☆–☆☆
Château-Montfort, Arbois. 300 hectares. www.henri-maire.com
Very much the biggest producer of Jura wines, marketing half the region's production. Maire's imaginative and aggressive sales strategy has made Maire a household name. His modern domaines produce a vast range of wines under all the Jura appellations, plus many other wines. Sparkling "Vin Fou" is perhaps the best-known; its name is on street corners all over France. One of my favourites is the pale, dry rosé, or *vin gris*, called "Cendré de Novembre". Some of the reds are distinctly sweet – not to my taste.

François Mossu ☆☆–☆☆☆
Voiteur, Château-Chalon. 4 hectares
Passionately committed producer, with a finely balanced *vin jaune*, with a distinctive seawater tang, and rather alcoholic *vin de paille*, tinged with iodine, barley sugar, and caramelized orange.

Pierre Overnoy ☆☆
Pupillin. 2 hectares
Organic estate, producing fine Chardonnay and aromatic Savagnin. But the reds, made without SO_2, can be weird.

Désiré Petit ☆☆
Pupillin, Arbois. 12 hectares
An old family property scattered within the sheltered coomb of Pupillin, and neighbouring Arbois and Grozon. Stainless-steel and old casks stand side by side. The investment in modern equipment means that the wines – red, white, and rosé – can now be drunk young. The firm, minerally Chardonnay can be aged.

Pignier ☆–☆☆
Montaigu. 15 hectares
Exquisitely cellared in a former Carthusian monastery. Most of their wines are varietal, and the whites can be rather heavy and oily. Very citric *vin jaune*.

Domaine de la Pinte ☆–☆☆☆
Arbois. 30 hectares. www.domainedelapinte.com
A large, modern estate created by Roger Martin in 1955 on abandoned vineyard land of the chalky clay loved by the Savagnin, which occupies almost half the vineyards. The domaine occupies some of the best terroir in Arbois. The estate produces a complete range of Arbois wines, and both the *vin jaune* and *vin de paille* are exceptional.

Jacques Puffeney ☆–☆☆☆
Montigny-lès-Arsures. 7.5 hectares
Exceptional nutty white Arbois, much preferable to the reds, and very intense *vin jaune*.

Xavier Reverchon ☆–☆☆☆
Poligny. 6 hectares
Xavier Reverchon produces a typically wide range of hand-made wines in small quantities – including intense *vins jaunes*, *méthode traditionnelle*, and MacVin (red and white),

as well as many small lots of red, white, and rosé. Rather woody Chardonnay, but deliciously pure Savagnin, traditionally made and aged without topping up. Prize-winning *vins jaunes* that need to be cellared to calm their assertive acidity.

Domaine Rolet ☆☆–☆☆☆
Arbois. 65 hectares. www.rolet-arbois.com
One of the most important producers in the Jura after Henri Maire (*q.v.*), making wines in all the major appellations. Concentrates on single-grape-variety wines including Chardonnay, Poulsard, and a Trousseau built to last. Experiments with a shorter vinification period for the Poulsard have produced a fresh, fruity rosé, something of a departure from the traditional Jura style. The "Tradition" whites blend Savagnin and Chardonnay and are aged up to thirty-six months in barrel; the result is tangy and minerally. Powerful *vin jaune*, too.

André & Mireille Tissot ☆☆–☆☆☆
Montigny-lès-Arsures. 29 hectares
Organic family domaine making good Arbois and *côtes* wines of all colours including nutty *vin jaune*, and a sumptuous, honeyed *vin de paille* from all four traditional varieties. The whites, especially the Arbois Chardonnay, are exemplary.

Jacques Tissot ☆–☆☆
Arbois. 30 hectares. www.domaine-jacques-tissot.fr
Louis Pasteur made some of his fermentation experiments in this *chai* in the centre of Arbois. All Jacques Tissot's wines are well-made, but his red-berry-scented Trousseau is especially good. Rich, full *vin jaune*, with an alluring aroma of mango.

Savoie

The wine country of Savoie follows the River Rhône south from the Lake of Geneva, then lines the Lac du Bourget (the biggest lake in France) around Aix-les-Bains, then hugs the sides of the valley south of Chambéry and turns the corner eastwards into the Val d'Isère. The whole wine zone is affected by the proximity of the Alps. It exists more as opportunistic outbreaks occurring in four *départements* than as a cohesive vineyard. Its appellations, encompassing 1,800 hectares of vineyards, are consequently complicated: more so than its simple, fresh, and invigorating wine.

Three-quarters of Savoie wine is white, based on half a dozen different grapes. Along the south shore of Lake Geneva (Haute-Savoie) it is the Chasselas, the grape the Swiss know as Fendant. Crépy is the best-known *cru*, with Marignan, Ripaille, and Marin, all light and often sharp wines. Crépy is an all-white appellation that might have disappeared but for the efforts of Léon Mercier and his son Louis. The better wines are bottled *sur lie*, giving them a slight spritz. Ayze, too, has a name for its sharpish *pétillant*.

Seyssel is your chance to win a bet. Few people realize or remember that it is France's northernmost Rhône wine. The grapes here are Roussette (alias Altesse) for still wines and Molette for fizz. Roussette, the aristocrat, reaches a relatively high degree of sugar, body, and flavour; Molette is a mild little thing. Seyssel has built an international reputation by developing its naturally fizzy tendency into fully fledged, classic-method sparkling. The specialist is Varichon & Clerc.

Still or *pétillant*, dry or sometimes slightly sweet, Roussette wines with local reputations are made along the Rhône Valley and Lac du Bourget at Frangy, Marestel, Monterminod, and Monthoux. Occasional super-vintages put them on a level with Vouvray.

The third principal white grape, and the commonest of the region, is the Jacquère. South of Seyssel, still on the Rhône, the district of Chautagne, centred on its cooperative at Ruffieux, makes Jacquère white, and the grape dominates the vineyards south of Chambéry: Chignin, Apremont, Abymes, and Montmélian. Chignin has the best southern hillside exposure. Its Jacquère fetches a franc (remember them?) or two more a bottle than its neighbours, Apremont and Les Abymes. Red Gamay, Pinot Noir, and Mondeuse are also important.

Suburbia is invading these lovely vineyards fast. Montmélian, a little Alpine village a few years ago, is now hideous with housing estates. So far the red-wine vineyards on the slopes of the Val d'Isère are almost intact, but for how long? Their centre is the *cave coopérative* at Cruet, serving Cruet, Arbin, Montmélian, and St-Jean de la Porte. Much its best wine, to my mind, is its Mondeuse (especially that of Arbin). Gamay costs a little more, and Pinot Noir more again, but Mondeuse is the character: a dark, slightly tannic, smooth, but intensely lively wine that reminds me a little of Chinon, the "raspberry" red of the Loire.

There are other local specialties too: Roussette is the highest priced white of the Cruet cooperative; a yellow, full-bodied, slightly bitter wine you might take for an Italian. And Chignin grows the Bergeron, either a rare local grape or (say some) the Roussanne of the (lower) Rhône. This is the only Savoyard white wine that ages with distinction.

Savoie's ACs are shadowed by the VDQS Bugey to the west on the way to Lyon, a mere 240 hectares with an even more complex set of names, which is hard to justify in reality. The white VDQS is Roussette de Bugey, although the regulations only demand Roussette grapes if a village name is used (the *crus* are Anglefort, Arbignieu, Chanay, Langieu, Montagnieu, and Virieu-Le-Grand). Plain Roussette de Bugey can contain Chardonnay, as can Roussette du Savoie. Jacquère, Aligoté, and Chardonnay are allowed in Vin de Bugey Blanc. VDQS Vin de Bugey is red, rosé, or white and also has its *crus*: Virieu-Le-Grand, Montagnieu, Manicle, Machuraz, and Cerdon. Cerdon, in turn, is also an individual VDQS for *mousseux*, including a rosé, and merely fizzy *pétillant*.

Leading Savoie Producers

Abymes

Cave Coopérative "le Vigneron Savoyard" ☆
Apremont
(Also for Apremont, Gamay, Mondeuse, Vin de Pays de Grésivaudan.)

Claude Tardy ☆
Chapareillan. 3 hectares
These wines come from high vineyards in the Isère.

Apremont

Pierre Boniface ☆☆
Les Marches. 7 hectares
Good reputation for his Jacquère.

Michel Magne ☆☆
Chapareillan
Lush Apremont "Tête de Cuvée".

Jean Perrier ☆–☆☆
Apremont. 21 hectares. www.vins-perrier.com
Good-value wines from Apremont.

Gilbert Tardy ☆–☆☆
Apremont
Flowery wines.

Ayze

Domaine Belluard ☆–☆☆
Ayze
Specializes in *méthode traditionnelle* and a rare white from the Gringet grape.

Marcel Fert ☆
Marignier

Chautagne

Cave Coopérative de Chautagne ☆
Ruffieux
A cooperative that unites 180 growers.

Chignin and Chignin-Bergeron

The Quénard Family ☆☆
Chignin. (Five separate branches: André and son Michel, Claude, Jean-Pierre, Raymond and son Pascal, René.)
Raymond, with ten hectares, is widely acknowledged as the best, with André and Michel (twenty hectares) hot on his heels. However, all the branches maintain high standards.

Crépy

L. Mercier & Fils ☆
Douvaine

Cruet

Cave des Vins Fins ☆
Cruet. www.cavedecruet.com
Makes a range of reds such as Roussette de Savoie, Gamay, Mondeuse, and Pinot; also Jacquère, *mousseux*, and *pétillant*.

Domaine de l'Idylle ☆–☆☆
Cruet. 8 hectares
Good Jacquère from the Tiollier brothers.

Frangy

Domaine Dupasquier ☆☆–☆☆☆
Aimavigne, Jongieux. 12 hectares
Excellent Roussette.

Marestel

Henri Jeandet ☆
Jongieux

Monterminod

Château de Monterminod ☆
Challes-les-Eaux

Monthoux

Michel Million Rousseau ☆☆
St-Jean-de-Chevelu
Fine whites wines, especially Jacquère, on the Coteau de Monthoux.

Montmelian

Cave Coopérative de Vente des Vins Fins ☆
Montmélian
The co-op also produces a wide range of wines from other districts.

Louis Magnin ☆☆–☆☆☆
Arbin. 6 hectares
Good Roussette and Mondeuse, the latter capable of ageing.

J. Perrier & Fils ☆–☆☆
Montmélian

Ripaille

Château de Ripaille ☆–☆☆
Thonon-les-Bains
Good Chasselas.

Seyssel

Maison Mollex ☆☆
Corbonod. 25 hectares
This estate is a major producer in the appellation, producing fine *méthode traditionnelle* wines as well as a toasty wine called Altesse.

Varichon & Clerc ☆–☆☆
Seyssel. www.boisset.com
Owned by Burgundian négociant Boisset, this is a general négociant for sparkling Savoie wines. In 1999, it launched a prestige wine called "Brut des Cimes" from Molette and Altesse.

The Loire Valley

It is marvellous with what felicity, what gastronomic *savoir-vivre*, the rivers Rhône and Loire counter-balance one another on their passage through France. For 160 kilometres (100 miles) or so they even run parallel, flowing in opposite directions forty-eight kilometres (thirty miles) apart.

They decline the notion of rivalry: in every way they are complementary. The Rhône gives France its soothing, warming, satisfying, winter-weight wines. The Loire provides the summer drinking.

The Loire rises within 160 kilometres (99 miles) of the Mediterranean. Wine is made in earnest along some 400 kilometres (248 miles) of its course and on the banks of its lower tributaries. It is a big stretch of country, and one might expect a wide variety of wines. The long list of the appellations encourages the idea, but it is not difficult to simplify into half-a-dozen dominant styles based on the grape varieties.

The Loire has three principal white and two red grapes (but only one that gives fine wine). Among the whites, the centre stage is held by the Chenin Blanc (alias Pineau de la Loire). It dominates in Touraine and even more so in Anjou, its produce ranging from neutral/acidic base material for sparkling Saumur to toffee-rich, apparently immortal, dessert wines. It is so versatile because it has such subtle flavours (quince, citrus fruits, green apples); its qualities lie more in balance and vitality. It keeps a high acid content even when it ripens (which it can do) to extremely high levels of sugar. Aromatically it is noncommittal – until it matures. Even then, it has fruit salad and *crème brûlée* both within its repertoire.

Downstream from Anjou the dominant white grape is the Muscadet – again a low-profile variety. Early ripening and (in contrast) low acidity, rather than any great aroma, make it ideal for instant drinking with *fruits de mer*.

Upstream in Touraine, east of Vouvray-Montlouis and beyond to Pouilly and Sancerre, is the country of the Sauvignon Blanc, in this climate one of the most intensely aromatic grapes in France.

The Cabernet Franc is the quality red grape of the Loire, at its very best at Chinon in Touraine and almost equally successful in parts of Anjou. It is shadowed everywhere by the Gamay, which is made into juicy, fresh, light-to-medium-bodied reds which can be delicious. Both, along with Grolleau, are responsible for large quantities of more or less amiable rosé, one of the region's great money-spinners.

A number of grapes are named on Loire labels: the white Gros Plant of the Muscadet region (a sharp grape which might be described as its Aligoté); the Pinot Noir, grown to make red wine in Sancerre; Chardonnay in Haut-Poitou. A couple are traditional and accepted; a white variety called Romorantin gives the thin wine of Cheverny. A great number of ignoble plants used to be grown, but in the last thirty-odd years they have been slowly ousted from the vineyards in favour of the principal types and an understudy cast of Cabernet Sauvignon, Malbec (here called Cot), Pinot Meunier, and such local characters as Arbois and Pineau d'Aunis, and even Furmint from Hungary and Verdelho from Madeira.

As with its grapes, so with its regions, the Loire is simply divisible into its upper waters, above Orléans, which – together with their hinterland near Bourges – are best-known for producing whites from Sauvignon Blanc; its famous slow-moving centre, where it passes in infinite procession among the many châteaux of Touraine and Anjou; and its broad maritime reaches, where the wind carries the hint of shrimps far inland.

Wine Areas of the Loire Valley

All Loire AC and VDQS wines are listed below. There is a total vineyard area of 73,000 hectares, cultivated by 13,000 growers. The production figures given refer to the 2000 vintage.

Coteaux d'Ancenis (red, white, and rosé) VDQS. Lower Loire. 254 ha. 16,500 hl. Light Gamay, occasionally Cabernet, reds and rosés from the north bank opposite Muscadet. The white is marginal, and is produced from Chenin Blanc and a miniscule quantity of Malvoisie (Pinot Gris).

Anjou (red and white) AC. West-Central. 164,500 hl. Light, mainly Cabernet Franc, reds from a wide area (an alternative to Saumur). Slightly less white is produced: mainly Chenin Blanc and often slightly sweet. There is no special quality.

Anjou-Coteaux de la Loire (white) AC. West-Central. 600 hl. A limited area along both banks of the river west of Angers. Chenin Blanc of variable quality, but often quite delicious off-dry or sweet wines. Only a handful of producers.

Anjou Gamay (red) AC. West-Central. 16,640 hl. Light yet tasty reds for first-year drinking, which can often have more character than many a Beaujolais.

Anjou Mousseux (white and rosé) AC. West-Central. 3,400 hl. Made throughout the entire Anjou zone. Chenin Blanc is the base of the whites though Cabernet, Cot, Gamay, Grolleau, and Pineau d'Aunis are permitted (to a maximum of 60%). A small quantity of rosé is made from Cabernet, Cot, Gamay, Grolleau, and Pineau d'Aunis.

Anjou-Villages (red) AC. West-Central. 17,350 hl. There are forty-eight communes entitled to this appellation for the production of Cabernet Franc and Cabernet Sauvignon. The wines cannot be sold before the September after the harvest. Since 1998, about a dozen producers can use the appellation Anjou-Villages Brissac, named after one of the best-known villages.

Cabernet d'Anjou (rosé) AC. West-Central. 167,300 hl. The best-quality rosé, normally rather sweet; at its best from Martigné-Briand, Tigné, and La Fosse-Tigné in the Coteaux du Layon.

Rosé d'Anjou (rosé) AC. West-Central. 190,000 hl. Pale, sweet rosé mainly from Grolleau.

Coteaux de l'Aubance (white) AC. West-Central. 4,710 hl. Chenin Blanc, in a range of styles from off-dry to *doux*, from the south bank opposite Angers, north of the (not automatically superior) Coteaux du Layon. Quality is increasing steadily.

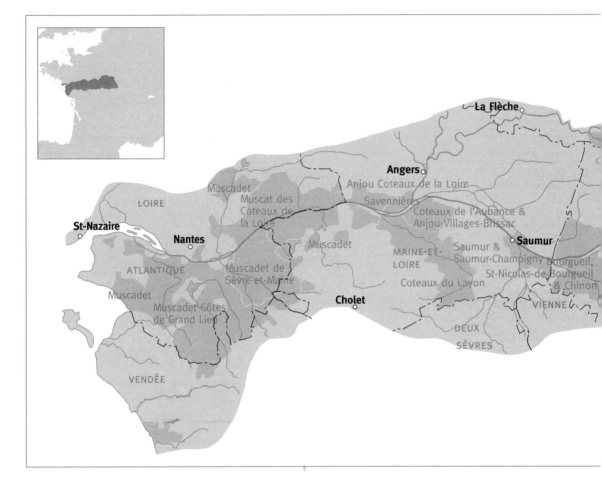

Côtes d'Auvergne (red, white, and rosé) VDQS. Extreme upper Loire. 374 ha. 17,360 hl. Near Clermont-Ferrand. Chanturgues, Châteaugay, Corent, and Madargues are considered *crus* and their names are used on the labels. Easy-drinking wines made principally from Gamay and Pinot Noir. The white is relatively unimportant: a very light Chardonnay.

Bonnezeaux (white) AC. West-Central. 130 ha. 1,965 hl. *Grand cru* of Chenin Blanc in the Coteaux du Layon, Anjou. In fine years, with noble rot or super-ripe grapes, a great sweet wine; otherwise "nervy" and fine.

Bourgueil (red and rosé) AC. Central. 1,250 ha. 77,860 hl. Excellent red of Cabernet Franc from the north bank facing Chinon, Touraine. For drinking young and cool or maturing like Bordeaux.

Châteaumeillant (red and rosé) VDQS. Upper Loire. 84 ha. 4,770 hl. Minor area of Gamay and Pinot Noir south of Bourges. Light reds or very pale *gris rosés*.

Cheverny (red, white, and rosé) AC. East-Central. 400 ha. 22,370 hl. Small but growing supply of light Gamay and Pinot Noir blends with up to 15% Cabernet or Cot for the red, and pure or blended Gamay for the rosé. The white is mainly rather sharp Sauvignon with a dash of Chardonnay from south of Blois.

Chinon (red, white, and rosé) AC. Central. 2,000 ha. 118,880 hl. Fine Cabernet Franc red, sometimes superb and capable of ageing many years, but generally drunk young and cool. The most important Loire red. A small quantity of white is produced from Chenin Blanc.

Cour-Cheverny (white) AC. 2,320 hl. A pungently vinous wine made from the local Romorantin grape in the heart of the Cheverny zone.

Fiefs Vendéens (red, white, and rosé) VDQS. West. 450 ha. 26,000 hl. Light reds and rosés made principally from Gamay, Pinot Noir, and Cabernet. About one-quarter of production is white, mostly quaffable Chenin Blanc.

Côtes du Forez (red and rosé) AC. Extreme Upper Loire. 181 ha. 6,860 hl. The southernmost Loire vineyards, south of Lyon: Gamay, Beaujolais-style.

Coteaux du Giennois (red, white, and rosé) AC. Upper Loire. 148 ha. 7,000 hl. Light- to medium-bodied reds from just downstream of Pouilly/Sancerre towards Gien. Well-made, they can be delicious. A recent ruling states they must be a Pinot Noir and Gamay blend. About one-third of production is white, solely from Sauvignon.

Haut-Poitou (Vin du) (red, white, and rosé) VDQS. South-Central. 28,325 hl. Flourishing vineyard south of Anjou, mainly Gamay and Cabernet Sauvignon, with some Merlot, Pinot Noir, Cot, and Grolleau. There is an expanding production of Sauvignon Blanc, Chardonnay, Chenin Blanc, and Pinot Blanc.

Jasnières (white) AC. North-Central. 2,630 hl. A *cru* within Coteaux du Loir. Small Chenin Blanc area north of Tours. Wine like Vouvray, if less rich. Ages very well.

Coteaux du Layon (white) AC. West-Central. 50,250 hl. The biggest area of quality Chenin Blanc, south of Angers, generally fully sweet, *moelleux* or *liquoreux*; it includes the Grands Crus Quarts de Chaume and Bonnezeaux.

Coteaux du Layon-Villages must have an extra degree of ripeness and come from one of six communes: Beaulieu-sur-Layon, Faye-d'Anjou, Rochefort-sur-Loire, Rablay-sur-Layon, St-Aubin-de-Luigné, and St-Lambert-du-Lattay.

Coteaux du Layon-Chaume (white) AC. West-Central. 78 ha. 1,270 hl. A superior appellation for Coteaux du Layon with an extra degree of ripeness, comparable to a villages AC in the Rhône.

Coteaux du Loire (red, white, and rosé) AC. North-Central. 3,270 ha. Small area of Pineau d'Aunis and Gamay with some Cot and Cabernet north of Tours on the Loir, a tributary of the Loire. About one-third is white from Chenin Blanc.

Crémant de Loire (white and rosé) AC. Anjou-Saumur-Touraine. 38,000 hl. Appellation for high-quality sparkling wine, which must be aged at least twelve months on the yeasts.

Rosé de Loire (rosé) AC. Anjou-Saumur-Touraine. 65,000 hl. An appellation for dry rosés with thirty per cent Cabernet – not widely used, but can be good. About twenty producers.

Menetou-Salon (red, white, and rosé) AC. Upper Loire. 374 ha. 24,500 hl. Red and rosé rival to Sancerre, with similar light Pinot Noir. The more important white production is Sauvignon, like Sancerre.

Montlouis (white) AC. East-Central. 1,000 ha. 16,900 hl. The reflected image of Vouvray across the Loire: dry, semi-sweet, and occasionally sweet wines. Also made as *pétillant* and *mousseux* sparkling wines.

Muscadet (white) AC. Lower Loire. 3,077 ha. 200,500 hl. A large area but a small part of Muscadet production (*see* Muscadet de Sèvre-et-Maine).

Muscadet Coteaux de la Loire (white) AC. Lower Loire. 284 ha. 15,000 hl. The smallest section of Muscadet, upstream of Muscadet de Sèvre-et-Maine.

Muscadet Côtes de Grand Lieu (white) AC. Lower Loire.

320 ha. 18,400 hl. The newest Muscadet sub-region stretches west of Nantes airport.

Muscadet de Sèvre-et-Maine (white) AC. Lower Loire. 9,360 ha. 528,300 hl. Much the biggest Loire AC: the best part of Muscadet, east and south of Nantes.

Gros Plant du Pays Nantais (white) VDQS. Lower Loire. 2,213 ha. 162,870 hl. Sharp white of Gros Plant (or Folle Blanche) from the Muscadet area.

Orléanais (Vin de l') (red, white, and rosé) VDQS. Upper Loire. 107 ha. 5,700 hl. Very light reds of Pinot Meunier, Cabernet Franc, and Pinot Noir. The white wine is a light-style Chardonnay.

Pouilly-Fumé (white) AC. Upper Loire. 1,078 ha. 72,000 hl. Powerful, aromatic Sauvignon Blanc from opposite Sancerre.

Pouilly-sur-Loire (white) AC. Upper Loire. 38 ha. 2,400 hl. Neutral white of Chasselas from the same vineyards as Pouilly-Fumé – must be drunk young.

Quarts de Chaume (white) AC. West-Central. 40 ha. 575 hl. *Grand cru* of the Coteaux du Layon, with maximum yields set at 20 hl/ha. In certain years, glorious rich wines of Chenin Blanc.

Quincy (white) AC. Upper Loire. 171 ha. 10,300 hl. Small source of attractive Sauvignon Blanc west of Bourges.

Reuilly (red, white, and rosé) AC. Upper Loire. 138 ha. 8,700 hl. White from Sauvignon Blanc, and Pinot Noir and Pinot Gris reds and rosés.

Côte Roannaises (red and rosé) AC. Extreme upper Loire. 183 ha. 11,350 hl. Gradually expanding Gamay region not far from Beaujolais, in distance or style.

St-Nicolas-de-Bourgueil (red and rosé) AC. Central. 790 ha. 58,460 hl. Neighbour to Bourgueil with similar excellent Cabernet Franc.

St-Pourçain-sur-Sioule (red, white, and rosé) VDQS. Extreme upper Loire. 512 ha. 32,680 hl. The well-known local wine of Vichy: Gamay and Pinot Noir from chalk soil – good café wine.

A great deal is very pale rosé. The white, which can be better, is made from Tresallier, Chardonnay, and Sauvignon. Commendable country wines.

Sancerre (red, white, and rosé) AC. Upper Loire. 2,540 ha. 162,630 hl. Light Pinot Noir red and rosé from chalky soil. Known for white. Making real progress: the best wines are richer and longer-lived. About five times as much white is produced: fresh, eminently fruity and aromatic Sauvignon Blanc.

Saumur (red and white) AC. West-Central. 91,440 hl. Light Cabernet reds from south of Saumur – can also be sold as Anjou. The white is crisp Chenin Blanc with up to twenty per cent Chardonnay and/or Sauvignon. About one third of the grapes are made into sparkling wine.

Cabernet de Saumur (rosé) AC. West-Central. 3,174 hl. The upstream, slightly drier, equivalent of Cabernet d'Anjou. Wines must be vinified by a method that direct presses for early consumption.

Saumur-Champigny (red) AC. West-Central. 1,300 ha. 85,820 hl. Possibly the best Cabernet reds of Anjou, from the northern part of the Saumur area just east of the city.

Coteaux de Saumur (white) AC. West-Central. 110 hl. Rare Chenin Blanc, often off-dry, sometimes *moelleux*, from a similar but slightly more widespread area than Saumur-Champigny.

Saumur Mousseux (rosé) AC. West-Central. 88,140 hl. *Méthode traditionnelle* rosé of Cabernet, Gamay, Grolleau, Pinots Noir, and d'Aunis. The white is mostly Chenin Blanc (though up to sixty per cent can be Grolleau, Pinots Noir, and d'Aunis). Increasingly popular and sometimes excellent.

Savennières (white) AC. West-Central. 4,770 hl. Sometimes splendid, powerful, long-lived, dry Chenin Blanc from west of Angers. It includes the Grands Crus Roche aux Moines (19 ha) and Coulée de Serrant (6.8 ha).

Vins de Thouarsais (red, white, and rosé) VDQS. West-Central. 24 ha. 1,000 hl. Vineyards in the Thouet Valley south of Saumur produce red and rosé from Gamay, and white from Chenin Blanc.

Touraine (red, white, and rosé) AC. East-Central. 5,250 ha. 343,800 hl. Principal grapes for red and rosé are Gamay, Cabernet, and Cot (the label will name the grape). Gamays can outshine many a Beaujolais – at least in warm years. In west Touraine, pure Cabernet is generally bottled; in the east, the authorities are encouraging blends.

For rosés, Pineau d'Aunis and Grolleau may also be used. The white is usually Sauvignon Blanc, in a tolerable imitation of Sancerre. Chenin Blanc, Menu Pineau (alias Arbois), and Chardonnay now play a supporting role. Semi- and full-sparkling versions are of some importance.

Whites are based on Chenin Blanc with up to thirty per cent black grapes, including Cabernet, Pinot Noir, Pinot Gris, Pinot Meunier, Pineau d'Aunis, Cot, and Grolleau. Reds are made from Cabernet Franc; rosés from Cabernet Franc, Cot, Gamay, and Grolleau.

Touraine-Amboise (red, white, and rosé) AC. East-Central. 208 ha. 12,600 hl. Light reds made from Gamay, Cabernet, and Cot from just east of Vouvray. The white is Chenin Blanc, sometimes capable of Vouvray-like quality.

Touraine-Azay-Le-Rideau (white and rosé) AC. East-Central. 150 ha. 2,660 hl. Tiny Chenin Blanc vineyard, occasionally as rich as Vouvray. The rosé is a minor outpost of Grolleau with some Gamay, Cot, or Cabernet, made between Tours and Chinon.

Touraine-Mesland (red, white, and rosé) AC. East-Central. 200 ha. 6,200 hl. Rather good blends of Gamay, Cabernet Franc, and Cot for the red, and eighty per cent Gamay for the rosé, from the north bank of the Loire opposite Chaumont. Less important is the dry white chiefly of Chenin Blanc, sometimes blended with Chardonnay and Sauvignon.

Touraine Noble Joué (rosé) AC. East-Central. 25 ha. 1,030 hl. An almost extinct historic appellation that has been recently revived. Small production of rosé from Pinot Meunier, Pinot Noir, and/or Pinot Gris.

Valençay (red, white, and rosé) VDQS. Upper Loire. 300 ha. 4,700 hl. Dry white of Chenin Blanc, Sauvignon, and others. The reds and rosés are an outpost of Gamay on the eastern border of Touraine.

Coteaux du Vendômois (red, white, and rosé) AC. North-Central. 8,750 hl. The wines, particularly the rosés, are made chiefly from Pineau d'Aunis supported by Gamay, Cabernet, and Pinot Noir. The white is Chenin Blanc, pure or blended with Chardonnay.

Vouvray (white) AC. East-Central. 2,000 ha. 116,400 hl. Dry, semi-sweet, or sweet Chenin Blanc of potentially superb quality, according to the vintage. There are also sparkling versions.

Muscadet

It is hard to resist the notion of Muscadet as Neptune's own vineyard, nowhere is the gastronomic equation quite so simple and clear-cut – or appetizing. Britanny provides the fruits de mer; the vineyards clustering south and east of Nantes provide oceans of the ideal white wine.

Muscadet is both the grape and the wine – as well as the zone. The grape came from Burgundy (where it is still sometimes found as the Melon de Bourgogne) as an early ripener that was satisfied with thin, stony soil. Early ripening (about 15 September) gets it in before the autumn rain in this often cloudy and windswept vineyard. The Muscadet (or Melon) has low natural acidity that makes it particularly vulnerable in contact with air. To avoid oxidation and to bottle the wine as fresh and tasty as possible, the local tradition is to leave the new wine in its tank or barrel at the end of fermentation, lying on its own yeasty sediment (*sur lie*) and to bottle it in March or April from the barrel – racking it, as it were, straight into bottles without fining or filtering. A certain amount of CO_2 is still dissolved in the wine and helps to make it fresh and sometimes faintly prickly to the tongue.

With modern quantities and economics, such careful bottling barrel by barrel is becoming rare, but the aim is still the same – except among certain growers who look for a more fully developed wine for further ageing. Regulation changes have effectively made bottling *sur lie* an appellation in itself: now there are generic Muscadets and generic Muscadets *sur lie*, Muscadets de Sèvre-et-Maine and Muscadets de Sèvre-et-Maine Sur Lie, etc. A specially moulded bottle is now used to denote *sur lie* wines. The key differences are in the yield and in the timing of bottling following the harvest. Yields for *sur lie* wines, for example, cannot exceed fifty-five hectolitres per hectare (for generic Muscadets the yield can be up to sixty-five hectolitres per hectare). As from 1997, *sur lie* wine must be bottled off its lees in the cellar in which it was vinified.

Thus there are different styles of Muscadet, but it is hard to pin them down except by tasting each producer's wares. The extremes are a light, fruity but essentially rather mild wine or, by contrast, one with a pungently vegetable and somehow "wild" flavour, that can be very exciting with oysters or clams. The latter style can mature surprisingly well: I have had a five-year-old bottle that had achieved a sort of quintessential soft dryness I found delectable with turbot. Wines that have been bottle-aged can be marketed by their producers with the words Muscadet Haute Expression on the label.

Much the greatest concentration of Muscadet vineyards is just east of Nantes and south of the Loire, in the area named for the rivers Sèvre and Maine. About seventy-five per cent of the 13,041 hectares of vineyards are Sèvre-et-Maine; the rest is divided among the Coteaux de la Loire with 284 hectares scattered eastwards towards Anjou, Côtes de Grand Lieu with 320, and plain Muscadet with 3,077 dotted over a wide area south of Nantes.

All four appellations are interspersed with plantations (2,213 hectares in all) of the secondary white grape of the area, the Gros Plant or Folle Blanche, which stands in relation to Muscadet as Aligoté does to Chardonnay: an acknowledged poor relation, but with a faithful following of its own. Gros Plant du Pays Nantais is a VDQS, not an appellation wine like Aligoté. It is always sharp, often "green", sometimes coarse, but can be made by a sensitive hand into a very fresh if fragile wine. It would be a natural Breton progression to drink a bottle of Gros Plant with oysters, then Muscadet with a sole. Gros Plant has a maximum alcoholic degree of 11; Muscadet a maximum of 12. Controlling the maximum degree is unusual, but particularly necessary in a region where chaptalization is normal and natural acidity low. Over-sugared Muscadet would be a graceless brute.

So, some would argue, is Muscadet aged in new oak. This fad gained some ground in the late 1990s, but has not really caught on. It should not be dismissed out of hand as an abberation, but it does seem an unnecessary embellishment of a wine that has won friends with its uncomplicated charm. A more subtle tendency among some producers is deliberately to bottle the wine with some residual sugar.

For red wine, the region has little to offer: about 250 hectares among the Muscadet vineyards of the Coteaux de la Loire, around the town of Ancenis, grow Gamay and a little Cabernet for light red and rosé, sold as VDQS Coteaux d'Ancenis. There is also Malvoisie (Pinot Gris), an off-dry specialty of Ancenis, which can make an excellent apéritif. Blends of Cabernet, Gamay, and Pinot Noir are used in the up-and-coming VDQS wines known as Fiefs-Vendéens, from the Atlantic coast region La Vendée, just south of Muscadet.

The name Vin de Pays du Jardin de la France is increasingly used for wines such as Chardonnay and Gamay from a wide area, which covers thirteen *départements*. Other *vin de pays* may put the name of the region on the label, including Marches de Bretagne, Retz, or the *département* name, such as Vin de Pays de Loire-Atlantique.

Leading Muscadet Producers

Domaine du Bois-Joly ☆☆
Le Pallet
The Bouchard family produces invigorating *sur lie* wines, especially the *cuvée* "Harmonie".

Boullault & Fils ☆–☆☆
La Touche, Vallet. 40 hectares
A fine sloping vineyard, run with great care by the Boullault family. The wines sell under the labels "Domaine des Dorices" or "Château la Touche", depending on the market. There is no difference between them. The domaine distinguishes three *cuvées*, however. The first, "Cuvée Choisie", which represents the major part of the production, is made for drinking young. The "Hermine d'Or" selection, and in great vintages, the "Cuvée Grande Garde" (which is kept as long as two years on its lees), benefit from three years or more of cellaring. Boullault also makes a *méthode traditionnelle* sparkling wine from Gros Plant.

Château de Briacé ☆–☆☆
Le Landreau. 10 hectares
The château is a private wine college, at which the students of viticulture and oenology work the vines. The Muscadet de Sèvre-et-Maine, Gros Plant, and various *vins de pays* are invariably clean, correct, and nicely made.

Chéreau-Carré ☆☆
St Fiacre-sur-Maine. 120 hectares. www.chereau-carre.fr
The Chéreau family is one of Muscadet's largest proprietors as well as an important négociant house specializing in Loire wine. It markets four million bottles yearly, half from purchased wines, half from one of six estates belonging to various family members. The domaines include Château de Chasseloir, which serves as Chéreau-Carré's HQ. A twenty-five-hectare property on the banks of the River Maine, it includes a three-hectare parcel of century-old vines vinified separately as "Comte Leloup de Chasseloir".

Enjoying Loire Wines

The wide range of Loire wines covers almost any gastronomic eventuality. For apéritifs there are excellent sparkling wines, and even better *crémants* (*demi-sec* or young *moelleux* are also served by the locals as an apéritif) of Saumur and Vouvray, or the pungent, dry Chenin Blanc wines of Savennières. Old *moelleux* may be rich enough to match *foie gras*.

For seafood, there is the incomparable match of Muscadet; for charcuterie Gros Plant du Pays Nantais, a young Pouilly-Fumé, Chenin Blanc, a light cool red, or a dry to off-dry rosé; for richer fish dishes with sauces, either more and better Muscadet or a Sancerre or Pouilly-Fumé two or three years old.

For *entrées*, Chinon, Bourgueil, and Saumur-Champigny provide either Beaujolais-style young wines, freshly fruity, or the weight of riper vintages with five or six years' maturity. Mature Savennières or Vouvray *sec* or *demi-sec* can make an interesting alternative to white burgundy for certain richly sauced creamy dishes.

Sancerre is the inevitable local choice with strong cheeses; with milder, ones the sweet wines of the Coteaux du Layon can be excellent.

Light, young Coteaux du Layon, appley, sweet and very cold, can be a remarkable picnic wine. The nobly rotten sweet wines of Bonnezeaux and Quarts de Chaume are some of France's finest dessert wines. Like the great German sweet wines, they are complete in themselves – perhaps better alone than with any food.

Château du Coing, a fifty-hectare estate on the confluence of the Sèvre and the Maine. Chéreau barrel-ferments selected batches from both châteaux du Coing and de Chasseloir in new-oak barrels. Probably the most elegant wines in the very good range.

Domaine du Bois Bruley is a twenty-hectare vineyard in Basse Goulaine. This property supplies Chéreau's Gros Plant du Pays Nantais as well as Muscadet de Sèvre-et-Maine *sur lie*. Grand Fief de la Cormeraie is a five-hectare vineyard in the commune of Monnière. "Commandeur" is the name of the splendid old-vines bottling. Château de la Gravelle is a twelve-hectare vineyard in Gorges. Its two *cuvées* of Muscadet de Sèvre-et-Maine include an old-vines bottling labelled "Don Quichotte". Château de l'Oiselinière de la Ramée is a ten-hectare vineyard in Vertou. The old-vines *cuvée* here is called "L'Aigle d'Or".

Xavier Coirier ☆
Pissote. 20 hectares
A dedicated grower in the VDQS Fiefs-Vendéens. Fresh, fragrant whites, rosés, and reds for summer quaffing.

Donatien-Bahuaud & Cie ☆☆
Château de la Cassemichère, La Chapelle-Heulin
A large négociant-grower, Donatien-Bahuaud markets ten million bottles of Loire wine a year, of which 25% is Muscadet. The firm's most famous Muscadet is "Le Master de Donatien", which represents *cuvées* selected after blind tasting by food and wine professionals. The selected *cuvées* are bottled at the property of the individual growers and are presented in seriographed bottles.

Donatien-Bahuaud also produces Muscadet from its own vines at Château de la Cassemichère as well as eight other Muscadets, including the early drinking "Fringant". One of the first Nantais domaines to market Chardonnay, the firm offers two bottlings: Chardonnay and Chenin Blanc form the blend for Donatien's "Blanc de Mer", also a *vin de pays*.

Domaine de l'Ecu ☆☆☆
La Bretonnière, Le Landreau. 21 hectares
Guy Bossard's estate pioneered organic and then biodynamic cultivation in the Sèvre-et-Maine. Bossard produces a wide range of wines from his medium-sized domaine. A fairly recent venture has been the coaxing of distinct and distinctive *cuvées* from different soil types: "Gneiss", "Orthogneiss", and "Granit". The richly textured, mineral "Hermine d'Or" *cuvée* shows the ability of his wines to develop in bottle. Other wines include a very fine Gros Plant du Pays Nantais, and a nuanced *méthode traditionnelle* made chiefly from Gros Plant.

la Ferme des Ardilliers ☆
Mareuil-sur-Lay
A progressive grower-négociant in the VDQS Fiefs-Vendéens, whose best wines are supple, easy-drinking Cabernets from his own vineyards.

Domaine de la Foliette ☆☆
La Haye-Fouassière. 32 hectares
A large, traditional estate producing rich, appley Muscadet de Sèvre-et-Maine *sur lie*.

Marquis de Goulaine ☆–☆☆
Château de Goulaine, Basse-Goulaine. 50 hectares

The showplace of Muscadet; westernmost of the great Renaissance châteaux of the Loire. The Château de Goulaine is now an efficient example of the stately home trade. Estate-grown grapes plus bought-in wine supply a wide range of wines: Gros Plant and Chardonnay as well as three different Muscadets, all bottled *sur lie*. The "Cuvée du Millénaire", the domaine's best wine, is a Muscadet made from fifty-year-old vines from Goulaine's four-hectare Clos la Tâche, blended with wines from several growers.

Guilbaud Frères ☆–☆☆
Mouzillon, Vallet. www.guilbaud-muscadet.com
Négociant company founded in 1927 producing three million bottles of above-average Muscadets under various names, including their own wines from Domaine de la Moutonnière and Domaine de la Pingossière. Each property produces two bottlings, a generic Muscadet de Sèvre-et-Maine *sur lie* and a deluxe *cuvée*, partially aged in old oak barrels. The "Clos du Pont", from La Moutonnière, is Guilbaud's finest wine; "Château de la Pingossière" is also commendable. "Le Soleil Nantais", Guilbaud's top-of-the-range négociant wine, maintains a good standard.

Domaine Guindon ☆☆–☆☆☆
La Couleuverdière, St-Géréon. 28 hectares
Pierre Guindon offers three qualities of Muscadet des Coteaux de la Loire, as well as Gros Plant and Coteaux d'Ancenis (Gamay red and rosé) and unusual off-dry Malvoisie (Pinot Gris). A specialty here is a Muscadet given extensive skin-contact before fermentation.

Domaine de la Haute-Févrie ☆☆
La Févrie, Maisdon-sur-Sèvre. 21 hectares
Claude Branger produces elegant Muscadet de Sèvre-et-Maine *sur lie*. "L'Excellence" is the name of his bottling from vines at least fifty years old. "Clos Joubert" is aged in barriques.

Domaine des Herbauges ☆☆
Bouaye. 40 hectares. www.domaine-des-herbauges.com
Luc Choblet makes superior Muscadet Côtes de Grand Lieu from vineyards west of Nantes airport. "Clos de la Sénaigerie" and "Clos de la Fine" are two notable single-vineyard bottlings. Choblet also produces pleasant Gros Plant du Pays Nantais.

Domaine de la Louvetrie ☆☆–☆☆☆
Les Brandières, La Haye-Fouassière. 26 hectares
Joseph Landron is an exciting grower who bottles his wines by soil type. His lightest *cuvée*, "Amphibolite", is named after its soils and is made to be drunk within the year. The "Hermine d'Or" and "Fief du Breil" bottlings come from harder soils – silica-streaked orthogneiss – and benefit from a year or more of cellaring. The latter, the domaine's prestige bottling, issues from old vines on a slope well-exposed to the south. There is also a "Cuvée Bois", an acquired taste.

Domaines Pierre & Rémy Luneau ☆☆–☆☆☆
Domaine Pierre de la Grange, Le Landreau. 35 hectares
A skilled winemaker and dedicated grower, Pierre Luneau produces a range of Muscadet *sur lie*: a lean, elegant Muscadet des Coteaux de la Loire and numerous Muscadets de Sèvre-et-Maine *sur lie*, including two single-vineyard

bottlings: "Les Allées" (from old vines) and "Les Pierres Blanches". There are also a barrel-fermented "Manoir la Grange" and the new-oaked *cuvée* "Le 'L' d'Or".

Louis Métaireau ☆☆–☆☆☆
La Févrie, Maisdon-sur-Sèvre. 29 hectares
All Métaireau wines are classic, fresh Muscadets without exaggerated flavour. He insists on finesse. The two deluxe bottlings, "Cuvée LM" and "Number One", exemplify this style. Métaireau also co-owns the twenty-eight-hectare Domaine du Grand Mouton. Grapes from this property are picked slightly underripe; the wines are *très sauvage* for the first one or two years (when they go well with shellfish). At three or four years they mellow enough to partner sole. Métaireau bottles about 10% of Grand Mouton directly off its lees, without filtration.

A tireless innovator, he has recently expanded his line with two Vin de Pays de Loire-Atlantique, made from Melon, as well as two Muscadets de Sèvre-et-Maine *sur lie* – "Premier Jour" and "10.5". The first is made from grapes picked on the first day of harvest; the second is low in alcohol.

Château la Noë ☆–☆☆
Vallet. 70 hectares
A lordly domaine, unusual in Muscadet, with a stately neoclassical mansion. The family of the Comte de Malestroit de Bruc has owned it since 1740. The estate produces a full-bodied Muscadet from low yields. Some is bottled *sur lie*, some not, but both benefit from a year of bottle-ageing.

Henri Poiron & Fils ☆☆
Les Quatre Routes, Maisdon-sur-Sèvre. 36 hectares.
www.henri-poiron.com
A grower with two properties producing three bottlings of meaty Muscadet de Sèvre-et-Maine *sur lie*, "Domaine des Quatre Routes", "Domaine du Manoir", and "Château des Grandes Noëlles". Gros Plant du Pays Nantais, Cabernet and Gamay Vin de Pays du Jardin de la France, and a *méthode traditionnelle* complete the selection.

Château de la Ragotière ☆☆–☆☆☆
Vallet-la-Regrippière. 68 hectares. www.freres-coulliaud.com
This estate, traceable back to medieval times, was acquired by the Coulliaud brothers in 1979. They produce a range of Muscadets, of which the most rich is often the "Vieilles Vignes", and some varietal wines, such as the Chardonnay. The Muscadet "Collection Privée" is aged for over two years *sur lie*.

Marcel Sautejeau ☆–☆☆
Domaine de l'Hyvernière, Le Pallet, Vallet. 90 hectares.
www.marcel-sautejeau.fr
One of the larger Loire-Atlantique négociants, family-run. The Domaine de l'Hyvernière is owned by Marcel Sautejeau and the Château de la Botinière is owned by associate Jean Beauquin.

The Muscadet is mechanically harvested and bottled *sur lie* to be drunk within two years. The "Clos des Orfeuilles" comes from a plot within L'Hyvernière. "L'Exceptionnel" is the firm's deluxe négociant bottling. Total turnover of wine from the whole of the Loire valley is more than seventeen million bottles a year.

Sauvion & Fils ☆☆
Château du Cléray, Vallet. 30 hectares

A flourishing family firm of growers and négociants, based at the historic Château du Cléray. The domaine *sur lie* wine is light and attractive, though the firm's special bottlings often upstage it. "Allégorie du Cléray" is Muscadet fermented and aged in new-oak barrels. "Sauvion's Découvertes" ("Discoveries") are estate-bottled Muscadets from small domaines whose wines have been selected after a blind tasting by wine professionals. "Cardinal Richard" is the proprietary name Sauvion gives to a grower's wine that has been placed first after several juried tastings.

les Vignerons de la Noëlle ☆–☆☆
Ancenis. 570 hectares. www.vignerons-de-la-noelle.com

Founded in 1955, this cooperative has 150 growers with vineyards spanning the Nantais and the western rim of Anjou. The majority of production is Muscadet, both Sèvre-et-Maine and Coteaux de la Loire, including estate-bottlings in each appellation: "Domaine la Mallonière" and "Domaine des Hautes-Noëlles" in Sèvre-et-Maine, and "Château de la Varenne" in the Coteaux de la Loire. It also produces Gros Plant du Pays Nantais, Gamay-Coteaux d'Ancenis (red and rosé), Anjou Coteaux de la Loire, Anjou Rouge and -Villages, and Crémant de Loire.

Daniel & Gérard Vinet ☆☆
La Quilla, La Haye-Fouassière. 13 hectares

The Vinet brothers are ambitious young growers producing prime Muscadet de Sèvre-et-Maine *sur lie*. "Domaine de la Quilla" is their fine base Muscadet; "Clos de la Houssaie" comes from a small parcel, producing 5,000 bottles annually. The prestige *cuvée*, "Le", is an *assemblage* of the Vinets' best *cuvées*, selected after numerous tastings.

Anjou-Saumur

Muscadet is the most single-minded of all French vineyards. Anjou, its neighbour to the east, has a gamut of wines as complete as any region of France. Its biggest turnover used to be in rosé, before spring frosts caused damage. However, Anjou's sparkling wine industry at Saumur is second only to Champagne in size, its best reds are considerable Cabernets, and its finest wines of all, sweet and dry Chenin Blanc whites, rank among the great apéritif and dessert wines of France. The wonderful 1989 vintage sparked a welcome revival.

Rosé d'Anjou is a sweetish, light pink from which nobody expects very much – a blend of mainly Grolleau with Cabernet, Cot, Gamay, and the local Pineau d'Aunis. It has not recovered its former hold on the export market – though it seems to play well in French supermarkets. Cabernet d'Anjou, whose market is primarily national, is fighting back. It is also rosé (not red) but an appellation to treat with more respect. Cabernet Franc (here often called the Breton) is the best red-wine grape of the Loire; its rosé is dry and can be full of its raspberry-evoking flavour, too. The best examples come from Martigné-Briand, Tigné, and La Fosse-Tigné in what is known as Haut-Layon – part of the Coteaux du Layon – which is also the most important district for Chenin Blanc white wines with an inclination to sweetness.

With one exception, all the considerable vineyards of Anjou lie along the south bank of the Loire and astride its tributaries, the Layon, the Aubance, and the Thouet. The exception is Savennières, the local vineyard of the city of Angers, which interprets the Chenin Blanc in its own way: as a forceful and intense dry wine. Savennières contains two small *grands crus*: La Roche aux Moines and La Coulée de Serrant. The wines of these, or of any of the top-quality Savennières growers, are awkward and angular at first, with high acidity and biting concentration of flavour. They need age, sometimes up to fifteen years, to develop their honey-scented potential. Drunk younger, they need accompanying food. It does seem that many producers are now making Savennières in a more accessible style, a commercial imperative, perhaps, but one that risks a loss of *typicité*.

Savennières faces Rochefort-sur-Loire across the broad river, complicated with islands. Rochefort is the gateway to the long valley of the Layon, where the Chenin Blanc may be dry (and acid and pernicious), but where all the fine wines are at least crisply sweet like an apple, and the best deeply and creamily sweet with the succulence of Sauternes. The district of Coteaux de Layon contains two substantial Grands Crus, Quarts de Chaume and Bonnezeaux, where noble rot is a fairly frequent occurrence (less so than in Sauternes) and sheer concentration pushes the strength of the wine up to thirteen to fourteen degrees.

Some great Layons are also made when the grapes are picked *passerillés* (shrivelled), or normally over-ripe. There is a return to harvesting grapes by *tri* and those from the Layon and the Aubance which meet certain specifications may carry the designation Sélection de Grains Nobles on their labels. Some, but by no means all, of these sweet wines are aged in barrels. They are, in a sense, the vintage port of white wines: like vintage port, bottled young to undergo all their development with minimum-possible access to oxygen. The eventual bouquet is consequently as clean, flowery, and fresh-fruity as the grape itself, with the resonance and honeyed warmth of age. Great old Vouvray is so similar that it would be a brave man (or a native) who could claim to know them apart. Like German wines of fine vintages, they perform a balancing-act between sweetness and sustaining acidity. But few German wines of modern times can hold their balance for half as long.

Trends in the sweet wine industry are being matched by progress in the production of the other styles of wine made in Anjou. The dry whites (Anjou Blanc) and the reds (both Anjou Rouge and Anjou-Villages) are similarly displaying a real improvement in quality. Anjou-Villages is the appellation which the top four-dozen red-wine communes are entitled to use.

Saumur is the centre of eastern Anjou, with a set of appellations of its own for dry or medium-dry white wines of Chenin Blanc (which is increasingly being bottled pure, though it can still be blended with up to twenty per cent Chardonnay and/or Sauvignon), and for *mousseux* versions of the same. Saumur's sparkling wine industry is built upon Chenin Blanc, which has the acidity to produce successful *méthode traditionnelle* wines. The main producers, many of whom are also négociants dealing in a range of Loire wines, are listed on the following pages. Many grapes are permitted in *crémants*, including a number of black ones, but not Sauvignon Blanc. There are also appellations in Saumur for red and rosé wines of Cabernet Franc and Pineau d'Aunis.

The red wine vineyards are scattered to the south of the city. Saumur-Champigny has enjoyed a recent leap to fame and fashion, with its light, savoury, herby reds. The exceptional vintages of 1976 and 1989, when the best wines took on deeper tones of real richness, were great boosts to their popularity. In normal years, such concentration is hard to attain.

Leading Anjou-Saumur Producers

Domaine de Bablut ☆☆–☆☆☆
Brissac-Quincé. 80 hectares
Under the stewardship of Christophe Daviau, this long-established family estate is taking exciting new directions, particularly in the production of Coteaux de l'Aubance and in pursuing organic viticulture. The top bottlings are "Vin Noble" and "Grandpierre", from botrytized grapes partially fermented and aged in new-oak barrels. It is as delicious as it is nuanced. The domaine also produces the rest of the Anjou roster of wines, and makes those of nearby Château de Brissac as well.

Domaine des Baumard ☆☆☆
Rochefort-sur-Loire. 43 hectares
Jean Baumard is a senior figure of the Loire, descended from a family who can trace their roots back to 1634 at Rochefort. He is a former professor of viticulture at Angers. His son, Florent, has now taken over the domaine. His vineyards are dispersed, with significant holdings in Quarts de Chaume, Savennières (including part of the Clos du Papillon), and Coteaux du Layon (Clos de Ste-Catherine). Five hectares of Cabernet Franc and five of Cabernet Sauvignon produce Anjou Rouge "Logis de la Giraudière". Chardonnay is grown, along with Chenin, to make Crémant de Loire. The Baumards use no wood as they prefer a reductive style. The "Clos de Ste-Catherine" is hard to classify: neither sweet nor dry but very lively – recommended with summer fruit or as an apéritif. The best wine is certainly the noble and elegant Quarts de Chaume.

Château de Bellerive ☆☆–☆☆☆☆
Rochefort-sur-Loire. 22 hectares
A major estate of the Grand Cru Quarts de Chaume, owned since 1993 by Serge and Michel Malinge. Almost Yquem-like methods are adopted, which means accepting a tiny crop from old vines and picking only nobly rotten grapes in successive *tris* around the vineyard. Fermentation, which takes place in barrels, requires most of the winter. The great difference between this and Sauternes (apart from the grapes) is that bottling is done at the end of April "when the moon is waxing", and all maturation takes place in bottle rather than barrel. The wine can scarcely be appreciated for five, sometimes ten, years – and it lasts for fifty.

Château du Breuil ☆☆
Beaulieu-sur-Layon. 35 hectares
A reliable family estate producing the entire range of Anjou wines. The most interesting are the several *cuvées* of Coteaux du Layon-Beaulieu, the deluxe bottling of which is the *vieilles vignes*, matured in new oak barrels.

Domaine de Brizé ☆☆
Martigné-Briand. 40 hectares
A fine family winery, run by fifth-generation Delhumeaus. The spectrum of Anjou wines is made, among them sturdy Anjou-Villages called "Clos Médecin", textbook Layon, dazzling Anjou-Gamay, and award-winning Crémant de Loire.

Philippe Cady ☆☆–☆☆☆
St-Aubin-de-Luigné. 20 hectares
Luscious, honeyed Coteaux du Layon-St-Aubin and some Chaume. The richest *cuvées* are called "Volupté", and the most concentrated is usually the "Cuvée Eléonore".

les Caves de la Loire ☆–☆☆
Brissac-Quincé. 1,800 hectares
A union of three cooperative cellars, at Brissac, Beaulieu-sur-Layon, and Tigné. They produce around one million cases of the general Anjou appellations with modern equipment.

Cave des Vignerons de Saumur ☆
St-Cyr-en-Bourg. 1,400 hectares. www.vignerons-de-saumur.com
The *cave cooperative*, with 300 members, makes the gamut of Saumur sparkling wines, including Saumur Brut (under a variety of labels), Saumur Rosé Brut, Crémant de Loire "Cuvée de la Chevalerie" Brut and Rosé, and a Rouge Mousseux *demi-sec*. In all, this accounts for around 30% of the production of each appellation.

Château de Chaintres ☆☆
Dampierre-sur-Loire. 20 hectares. www.chaintres.com
Owned by Baron Gaël de Tigny, this is a charming old country house. It was once a priory, and a notable producer of Saumur-Champigny from walled vineyards. The wine is unoaked.

Clos de Coulaine ☆☆
Savennières
A respected producer of fresh, floral Savennières and silky Anjou Rouge and -Villages. Since 1992, the domaine has been run by Claude Papin, one of the top producers of Coteaux du Layon (*see* Château de Pierre-Bise).

Clos Rougéard ☆☆☆
Chacé. 8 hectares
The Foucault family, now in its eighth generation here, produce three *cuvées* of Saumur-Champigny. "Les Poyeux" is an outstanding vineyard, and the wine is aged in one-year-old barrels; "Le Bourg", in contrast, is aged in new oak. Profound, long-lived wines.

Domaine du Closel ☆☆
Savennières. 16 hectares. www.savennieres.closel.com
An estate producing classic white Savennières, concentrated wine fermented mostly in tank, then aged in wood (excepting some *cuvées*, such as "Clos du Papillon", which still ferment in barrel), and a little Cabernet for Anjou or Anjou-Villages. "Les Caillardières" is a Savennières made in an off-dry style, and in some years the "Cuvée d'Avant" is made from old vines in a somewhat oxidative style.

Château de la Coulée de Serrant ☆☆☆–☆☆☆☆
Château de la Roche-aux-Moines, Savennières. 15 hectares. www.coulee-de-serrant.com

A beautiful little estate in an outstanding situation, chosen by monks in the twelfth century. The main vineyard is the Clos de la Coulée de Serrant, run by Nicolas Joly, whose highly individual methods of growing vines and making wine are based around the theory of biodynamism. He uses no fertilizers or artificial pesticides and no modern technological equipment; the results are wines of unusual ageing qualities. Joly also owns three hectares of La Roche aux Moines called the Clos de la Bergerie, and some parcels of Cabernet for "Château de la Roche". Another *cuvée* from Savennières, "Becherelle", has recently been added to the Joly stable. Chenin Blanc here makes some of its most intense dry (or off-dry) wines of extraordinary savour and longevity. With a yield of only about 1,700 cases, the top wine is on allocation at a suitably high price. No one questions Nicolas Joly's zeal, but some questions have been raised about the oxidative character some vintages acquire with ageing; Joly, however, insists the wine needs to be decanted for twenty-four hours to achieve its full grandeur and complexity.

Philippe Delesvaux ☆☆–☆☆☆☆
St-Aubin-de-Luigné. 15 hectares
An ambitious grower who lived in Paris until he came here in 1983. He produces pleasant Anjou Blanc sec and tasty Anjou Rouge, but pulls out all the stops with his Layon, particularly the *cuvées* from the *lieux-dits* La Moque and Clos du Pavillon, and the luscious Sélection de Grains Nobles. These are among the most concentrated of all the sweet wines of France.

Château de Fesles ☆☆–☆☆☆☆
Thouarcé. 35 hectares. www.vgas.com
An historic property, reputed for its remarkable Bonnezeaux from fourteen hectares. Long owned by the Boivin family, which had, quite literally, created the appellation, it has passed through different hands in the 1990s, and is one of sixteen estates now owned by Bernard Germain in Bordeaux and Anjou. All the white wines, dry and sweet, are fermented in 400-litre barrels. Although the estate produces a range of Anjou wines, the Bonnezeaux is the most sought-after: sumptuous and peachy, and marked by botrytis, it remains fresh for decades thanks to its vibrant but ripe acidity.

Domaine des Forges ☆☆–☆☆☆
St-Aubin-de-Luigné. 37 hectares
Claude Branchereau makes the gamut of Anjou wines, but his heart is in his Coteaux du Layon, of which he makes several marvellous *cuvées*, including an old-vines bottling from the Chaume *lieu-dit* Les Onnis (also spelled "Aunis"). The richest wines are the numerous Sélections de Grains Nobles, but the simpler wines can be just as enjoyable with their freshness and bright, appley fruit.

Château de la Genaiserie ☆☆–☆☆☆
St-Aubin-de-Luigné. 42 hectares
In 1990, Yves Soulez purchased a rambling old château with prime Layon vineyards after selling his share of the family domaine in Savennières. Of his many *cuvées* of Layon, the richest, most concentrated, and finest come from low-yielding old vines in the *lieux-dits* Les Petits Houx, Les Simonelles, and La Roche.

Domaine Jean-Yves Lebreton ☆☆–☆☆☆
St-Jean des Mauvrets. 52 hectares

The Lebretons pioneered red winemaking in Anjou. Today Jean-Yves's Cabernets remain among the best, especially the Cabernet Sauvignon-dominated "Cuvée Croix de Mission".

Domaine des Moines ☆☆
Savennières. 8 hectares
This property is a major proprietor in the top Savennières *cru* of La Roche-aux-Moines. The wines are traditional and long-lived.

Rémy Pannier ☆–☆☆
St-Hilaire-St-Florent. www.remy-pannier.com
The largest négociant of Loire wines, marketing thirty million bottles annually. It also owns the sparkling wine houses of Ackerman-Laurance and De Neuville (*q.v.*).

Domaine des Petits Quarts ☆☆☆
Faye. 12 hectares
Jean-Pascal Godineau specializes in Bonnezeaux, producing five different *cuvées*, three of which are from single vineyards. In some vintages he is able to produce an astonishingly sweet and concentrated *cuvée* called "Quintessence".

Château de Pierre-Bise ☆☆☆
Beaulieu-sur-Layon. 53 hectares
One of the top producers of Coteaux du Layon, Claude Papin bottles Layon by soil type, offering as many as a dozen different *cuvées*, including Layon-Chaume and Quarts de Chaume. Papin also produces excellent Anjou Blanc appellation, Anjou-Villages, and Anjou-Gamay, as well as Savennières from Clos de Coulaine (*q.v.*).

Domaine des Roches Neuves ☆☆–☆☆☆
Varrains. 21 hectares. www.roches-neuves.com
Thierry Germain, a young Bordelais, purchased this property in 1991 and ever since has been turning out flavoursome Saumur-Champigny, the two most concentrated being the "Cuvée Vieilles Vignes Terres Chaudes" and the "Cuvée Marginale", the latter aged in new oak. There is also an impressive white called "L'Insolite", from very old Chenin Blanc vines.

Domaine de la Sansonnière ☆☆☆
Thouarcé. 8 hectares
Mark Angeli goes his own way. A firm believer in biodynamic viticulture, he makes only white wines: two bottlings of superlative rich, Anjou and, in suitable vintages, Bonnezeaux.

Château Soucherie ☆☆–☆☆☆
Beaulieu-sur-Layon. 35 hectares
The property of the Tijou family since 1952. Most of the estate is in Coteaux du Layon planted with Chenin Blanc, with Cabernet and Gamay for red and rosé. His best Layons are often the *vieilles vignes*, the Chaume, and "Beaulieu Cuvée de la Tour", from ninety-year-old vines. Of the sweet wines, only the Beaulieu is vinified in new oak. An Anjou Blanc sometimes has 20% Sauvignon added to Chenin Blanc for aroma. Tijou also owns two hectares in Savennières called Clos des Perrières.

Domaine Pierre Soulez ☆☆–☆☆☆
Château de Chamboureau, Savennières. 25 hectares
Substantial producer of Savennières, both dry and *moelleux*.

The best of them often come from his parcel within Roche-aux-Moines. The red and rosé are of lesser interest.

Château du Suronde ☆☆☆–☆☆☆☆
Rochefort-sur-Loire. 8 hectares
Acquired in 1995 by Francis Poirel, whose background as a maritime economist has not prevented him from becoming the most passionate of the producers of Quarts de Chaume. Yields are minute – between 8 and 16 hl/ha depending on the vintage – and for one of his *cuvées*, "Trie Victor et Joseph", the grapes are picked berry by berry at exceedingly high ripeness levels.

Château de Targé ☆☆
Parnay. 25 hectares. www.chateaudetarge.fr
A four-towered *manoir*, in the Pisani-Ferry family since 1655, producing acclaimed Saumur-Champigny, especially the "Cuvée Ferry".

Château la Varière ☆☆–☆☆☆
Brissac. 95 hectares
Jacques Beaujeau is well-known for his robust Anjou-Villages, but he also makes sumptuous Bonnezeaux and Quarts de Chaume in top vintages such as 1997.

Château de Villeneuve ☆☆☆
Souzay-Champigny. 28 hectares.
www.chateau-de-villeneuve.com
Excellent family domaine run by Jean-Pierre Chevallier. The most powerful of the *cuvées* of Saumur-Champigny is the barrel-aged-old-vines bottling from the *lieu-dit* Le Grand Clos. There are two *cuvées* of Saumur Blanc, including "Les Cormiers", which is fermented and aged in new-oak barrels.

Sparkling Saumur

The in-built acidity of Chenin Blanc is the cause and justification of the Saumur sparkling-wine industry, which is based in the chalk *caves* of St-Hilaire-St-Florent, just west of Saumur. It uses the classic method to produce cleanly fruity, usually very dry wines at half Champagne prices, less characterful and complex, but just as stimulating. However, an increasing number of producers are now making Crémant de Loire; and there is a corresponding number of deluxe *cuvées*. A few of these begin to approach Champagne prices and, at times, Champagne quality (relatively speaking).

Leading Producers of Sparkling Saumur

Ackerman-Laurance ☆–☆☆
Saumur
The original firm, founded in 1811 when Ackerman, a Belgian, introduced the *méthode traditionnelle* to the Loire. Still a leader with the new extra-quality Crémant de Loire. Owned by Rémy Pannier (*q.v.*).

Bouvet-Ladubay ☆☆–☆☆☆
St-Hilaire-St-Florent, Saumur. www.bouvet-ladubay.fr

The second-oldest (1851) of the sparkling wine houses, Bouvet-Ladubay became part of the Taittinger group in 1974. Excellent sparkling Saumurs include "Bouvet Brut", "Saphir" (a vintage *brut*), "Rubis" (an off-dry red based on Cabernet) and three deluxe *cuvées*, each partially or entirely fermented in barrel: "Trésor", "Trésor Rosé", and a *demi-sec* "Grand Vin de Dessert".

An interesting new departure is the serious and concentrated "Nonpareils" range, controversial because of its use of new oak. Overall, annual production exceeds three million bottles.

Gratien & Meyer ☆–☆☆
Saumur. 20 hectares. www.gratienmeyer.com
A twin company to the Champagne house of Alfred Gratien. Twenty hectares of vineyards (Chenin Blanc and Cabernet) can be found over the cellars. Products include Saumur Brut, Saumur Rosé Brut, Blanc de Noirs, Crémant de Loire Brut, "Argent Extra Dry", and "Cuvée Flamme" – the top-drawer Saumur Brut.

Langlois-Château ☆☆
St-Hilaire-St-Florent, Saumur. 60 hectares.
www.langlois-chateau.com
This old house was bought by Bollinger in 1973. Principally it is a producer of fine sparkling Crémant de Loire (blanc, rosé, and vintage) but also of still Loire wines from Muscadet to Sancerre. The best of these come from the firm's own vineyards, Château de Fontaine Audon in Sancerre, and Domaine Langlois-Château for Saumur red and white. "Château de Varrains" is a Saumur-Champigny aged in new-oak puncheons.

De Neuville ☆
St-Hilaire-St-Florent
A firm producing sparkling Saumur and Crémant de Loire. Now belongs to Rémy Pannier (*q.v.*).

Other Anjou-Saumur Producers

Veuve Amiot ☆
St-Hilaire-St-Florent. www.veuve-amiot.com
Founded 1884, now owned by Martini & Rossi, this is an important producer of sparkling Saumur, Anjou, and Crémant de Loire. Its top bottling is the toasty "Cuvée Elisabeth Amiot".

Patrick Baudouin ☆☆☆
Chaudefonds-sur-Layon. 8 hectares.
www.patrick-baudouin-layon.com
Produces Coteaux du Layon from very low yields. The top *cuvées* are "Marie Juby" and "Après Minuit". Both are very intense, very sweet, and very expensive.

Château d'Epiré ☆☆–☆☆☆
St-Georges-sur-Loire. 11 hectares. www.chateau-epire.com
Family ownership of this estate dates back to 1749, and today it is run by Luc Bizard. The aim is Savennières made for long ageing, and the estate also pioneered an off-dry style.

Domaine Filliatreau ☆☆
Chaintres. 50 hectares
Paul Filliatreau was the grower who put Saumur-Champigny on the map, but quality has been overtaken by other estates in recent years.

Domaine les Grandes Vignes ☆–☆☆
Thouarcé. 51 hectares
Large, reliable estate producing a sound range of dry Anjou wines in all styles.

Château de la Guimonière ☆☆–☆☆☆
Rochefort-sur-Loire. 23 hectares
Bernard Germain bought this property in 1996, along with Château de Fesles (*q.v.*). With fifteen hectares in Chaume, he produces creamy, plump, sweet wines from one of the top properties in the region.

Domaine de Haute-Perche ☆–☆☆
St-Melaine-sur-Aubance. 34 hectares
Christian Papin's estate has expanded in recent years. He makes the entire range of Anjou wines. The best tend to be his warm, supple Anjou-Villages, honeyed Coteaux de l'Aubance, and delicious Anjou-Gamay.

Château du Hureau ☆☆–☆☆☆
Dampierre-sur-Loire. 21 hectares. www.domaine-hureau.fr
Philippe Vatan produces three exemplary *cuvées* of Saumur-Champigny, finely balanced between fruit and oak.

Domaine de Montgilet ☆☆
Juigné-sur-Loire. 37 hectares
Vincent and Victor Lebreton are very good producers of Coteaux de l'Aubance. The best *cuvées* are "Le Tertereaux" and "Les Trois Schistes".

Domaine Musset-Rouillier ☆–☆☆
Le Pelican, La Pommeraye. 28 hectares
Gilles Musset, a serious grower, joined forces with Serge Rouillier, another good young producer, in 1994. They produce exemplary Anjou Coteaux de la Loire, as well as admirable Anjou Blanc *sec* and Anjou-Villages.

Domaine Ogereau ☆☆
St-Lambert-du-Lattay. 23 hectares
Medium-bodied Coteaux du Layon-St-Lambert, deliberately made without extreme concentration. Lush "Cuvée Prestige" and single-vineyard "Clos des Bonnes Blanches". The white and red Anjou are also of impressive quality.

Château de Passavant ☆
Passavant-sur-Layon. 35 hectares.
www.perso.wanadoo.fr/passavant
Traditional producer of Anjou white, red, and rosé. Organic since 1998.

Domaine de Petit Val ☆☆
Chavagnes. 19 hectares
Denis Goizil makes very rich Bonnezeaux that is sometimes marred by high alcohol.

Joel Pithon ☆☆–☆☆☆
St-Lambert-du-Lattay. 10 hectares. www.domaine-jopithon.com

Enthusiast for ultra-concentrated Coteaux du Layon and Quarts de Chaume, but also makes fine, dry white Anjou.

René Renou ☆–☆☆☆
Thouarcé. 10 hectares
René Renou has, for some years, been the head of INAO, charged with defending the *typicité* of France's wine regions. His estate specializes in Bonnezeaux wines. The basic *cuvées* are dull, but "Anne" and "Zenith" are silky and elegant.

Domaine Richou ☆–☆☆
Mozé-sur-Louet. 36 hectares
Good Coteaux de l'Aubance, especially the "Trois Demoiselles" and "Pavillon", both from old vines. And very good examples of Anjou Gamay and Anjou-Villages.

Château de la Roulerie ☆☆
St-Aubin. 21 hectares. www.vgas.com
Like Château de Fesles, owned since 1996 by Bernard Germain, and made in the same way as Fesles and La Guimonière (*qq.v.*). Good Chaume.

Domaine de St-Just ☆–☆☆
St-Just-sur-Clive. 35 hectares. www.st-just.net
Good modern-style, fruit-driven Saumur-Champigny and white Saumur.

Domaine du Sauveroy ☆☆
St-Lambert-du-Lattay. 27 hectares.
www.isasite.net/domainesauveroy
Pascal Cailleau is winemaker at this family estate, using modern winemaking techniques to produce the Anjou reds and often outstanding Coteaux du Layon-St-Lambert "Cuvée Nectar".

Château de Tigné ☆☆
Tigné. 50 hectares
A substantial organic estate owned by actor Gérard Depardieu. The top *cuvées* are called "Mozart" and "Cyrano".

Château de Varennes ☆☆
Savennières. 7 hectares. www.vgas.com
Owned by Bernard Germain since 1996. The Savennières is fermented in new 400-litre barrels. An accessible style for drinking fairly young.

Domaine des Varinelles ☆–☆☆
Varrains. 40 hectares
The Daheuillers are a long-established family of predominantly red winemakers in Saumur-Champigny. Their *vieilles vignes* selection spends more time in wood.

Touraine

It is hard to define Touraine more precisely than as the eastern half of the central Loire, with the city of Tours at its heart and a trio of goodly rivers – the Cher, the Indre, and the Vienne – joining the majestic mainstream from the south.

Almost on its border with Anjou it produces the best red wines of the Loire. Chinon and Bourgueil lie on the latitude of the Côte de Beaune and the longitude of St-Emilion – a situation that produces a kind of claret capable of stunning vitality and charm. The Cabernet Franc, with very little, if any, Cabernet Sauvignon, achieves a sort of pastel sketch of a great Médoc, smelling of raspberries, begging to be drunk cellar-cool in its first summer, light and sometimes astringent, yet surprisingly solid in its construction: ripe vintages age almost like Bordeaux, at least to seven or eight years.

Much depends on the soil. Sand and gravel near the river produce lighter, faster-maturing wine than clay over tuffeau limestone on the slopes (*coteaux*). These differences seem greater than those between Chinon and Bourgueil, certainly than any between Bourgueil and its immediate neighbour on the north bank, St-Nicolas-de-Bourgueil, although this has a separate appellation of its own.

Touraine's other famous wine is Vouvray, potentially the most luscious and longest lived of all the sweet Chenin Blanc whites, though, like German wines, depending more on the vintage than the site for the decisive degree of sugar that determines its character. The best vineyards are on the warm, chalky, tuffeau slopes near the river and in sheltered corners of side valleys. A warm, dry autumn (1989 and 1997 were optimal) can overripen the grapes here by sheer heat; a warm, misty one can bring on noble rot to shrivel them. In either case, great sweet Vouvray will be possible, with or without the peculiar smell and taste of *Botrytis cinerea*. Cool years make wines of indeterminate (though often very smooth and pleasant) semi-sweetness, or dry wines – all with the built-in acidity that always keeps Chenin Blanc lively (if not always very easy to drink). One solution to overacid wines here, as in Saumur, is to make them sparkle by the *méthode traditionnelle*. The other is the production of a style known as *sec tendre*, which in practice means midway between truly dry and *demi-sec*.

It is an odd coincidence that each of the great Loire wines comes with a pair across the river: Savennières with Coteaux du Layon, Bourgueil with Chinon, Sancerre with Pouilly, and Vouvray with Montlouis. Montlouis, squeezed between the Loire's south bank and the Cher's north bank, is not regarded, except by those who make it, as having quite the authority and "attack" of great Vouvray. Its sites are slightly less favoured, its wines softer and more tentative. They can sparkle just as briskly, though, and ripen almost as sweet.

Outside these four appellations, Touraine, with its simple but all-purpose AC Touraine, has only a modest reputation, although these wines continue to improve. I suggest that the future lies with the general (and self-explanatory) Sauvignon and Gamay de Touraine; some of the top *cuvées* of Sauvignon and Gamay can give, respectively, Sancerre and Beaujolais a run for their money. They are not as fine as either, but an awful lot cheaper. Increasingly, the wine authorities are encouraging (indeed, in the case of Touraine-Mesland mandating) blends of Gamay, Cabernet, and Cot.

Leading Touraine Producers

Domaine Philippe Alliet ✩✩✩
Cravant-les-Côteaux. 9 hectares
Low yields are the clue to the impressive record of this small

Chinon estate, where the vines are planted on deep gravel soils. These are complex wines, all given long macerations, then aged in barriques, and bottled without filtration; they show suave textures and an unusual depth of fruit.

Domaine Yannick Amirault ✩✩–✩✩✩
Bourgueil. 17 hectares
Amirault produces St-Nicolas-de-Bourgueil as well as three *cuvées* of Bourgueil. All the wines are reliable, but vary in weight and style. The most concentrated is usually the splendid old-vine Bourgueil "La Petite Cave". Almost all the wines repay keeping for three to five years.

Domaine des Aubuisières ✩✩–✩✩✩
Vouvray. 22 hectares. www.vouvrayfouquet.com
Bernard Fouquet produces sublime *secs*, *demi-secs*, and *moelleux* from three different vineyards, Le Marigny, Les Girardières, and Le Bouchet. In certain vintages there is an ultra-rich *moelleux* selection called "Cuvée Alexandre". His sparkling Vouvray *méthode traditionnelle* is full-bodied and flavoursome.

Audebert & Fils ✩–✩✩
Bourgueil. 39 hectares. www.audebert.fr
One of the biggest négociant-growers in Bourgueil, St-Nicolas-de-Bourgueil, Chinon, and Saumur-Champigny. "Domaine du Grand Clos" and "La Marquise" are special *cuvées* from specific vineyards – easy wines for drinking cool in their youthful prime, although the "Grand Clos" has some tannic structure and can age.

Bernard Baudry ✩✩–✩✩✩
Cravant-les-Côteaux. 30 hectares
Baudry and his son Mathieu release separate *cuvées* of Chinon according to the provenance of the wine. Thus "Les Granges" and "Haies Martels" are from young vines, while "Les Grézeaux" comes from old vines on clay-gravel soils. The top bottling is usually "Cuvée Croix Boissée", which is powerful and long-lived. Baudry also produces an attractive white Chinon.

Marc Brédif ✩–✩✩
Rochecorbon. 20 hectares
Négociant-grower with hospitable cellars in the rock *caves* below Rochecorbon. The firm belongs to the de Ladoucette concern of Pouilly. The wines are all Vouvrays, in both still and sparkling forms. Brédif invented Vouvray *pétillant* in the 1920s. Some Chinon is also produced.

Domaine Cathérine & Pierre Breton ✩✩
Restigné. 14 hectares
Founded in 1982, this estate has been a leader in Bourgueil from the outset. There are various *cuvées*, but all the wines are made from vines cropped at no more than 40 hl/ha. "Clos Sénéchal" is usually the most elegant, "Les Perrières" usually the most lush. Red wines only.

Caslot-Galbrun ✩✩
Benais. 20 hectares
One of the oldest-established families of growers in Bourgueil, who produce some of the juiciest, deepest coloured, most age-worthy wine. The walled Clos de la Gaucherie at Restigné is theirs.

Cave du Haut-Poitou ☆–☆☆
Neuville de Poitou. 900 hectares
The VDQS zone of Haut-Poitou is well south of the Loire on the road to Poitiers, where forty-seven communes on the chalky soil of a plateau used to supply distilling wine to Cognac. In 1948, a cooperative was founded and succeeded in raising standards to the point where, in 1970, the region was promoted to VDQS. In September 1995, Georges Duboeuf of Beaujolais purchased 40% of the business. He ended its days as a cooperative but covered its considerable debts and bought himself a useful source of varietal wines – Sauvignon Blanc, Chardonnay, Gamay, and Cabernet. Ninety per cent of the appellation's wine is produced by the *cave*.

Cave des Producteurs la Vallée Coquette ☆–☆☆
Vouvray. 350 hectares
Founded in 1953, this is one of Vouvray's two cooperative cellars, and vinifies about 15% of the appellation. It specializes in sound sparkling Vouvray, *pétillant* and *méthode traditionnelle*, but the *moelleux* can be remarkably good. Vouvray's other cooperative, Cave de Vaudenuits, has had similar success with the same type of product.

Domaine de Cézin ☆☆
Marçon. 10 hectares
The Fresnau family has vineyards in Jasnières and more substantial holdings in the Coteaux du Loir. The Jasnières and the Pineau d'Aunis Rouge are rustic and personalized and have immense charm.

Domaine Champalou ☆☆–☆☆☆
Vouvray. 20 hectares
Dider and Catherine Champalou, both oenologists, created this estate in 1985. Their wines, dry and sweet, are consistently good, and in top vintages they produce a "Trie de Vendange" from the ripest botrytis grapes. The result is creamy and intense, and probably indestructible.

Domaine de la Chevalerie ☆–☆☆
Restigné. 33 hectares. www.domaine-de-la-chevalerie.com
Pierre Caslot is the thirteenth generation of his family to farm Cabernet vines, from which he makes firm, deep-toned Bourgueil, aged up to eighteen months in wood. The "Cuvée des Busardières" is made from fifty-year-old vines and is intended to age for five or more years.

François Chidaine ☆☆–☆☆☆
Husseau, Montlouis. 15 hectares
One of Montlouis's top producers. His superb sweet wine, "Les Lys", is made from vines that are sixty to ninety years old, picked grape by grape. He also makes firm dry wines.

Clos Baudoin ☆☆
Vallée de Nouy, Vouvray. 14 hectares
Maker of some immortal Vouvray from three top vineyards, Clos Baudoin, Clos des Patys, and Clos de l'Avenir. The fine vintages have what the owner, Prince Poniatowski, calls "race" – breeding – that takes twenty-five or thirty years to reach its full flowering. The 1854 in the cellar is apparently excellent. Recent vintages, however, lacked flair, though a new winemaker, Nicolas Renard, seems set to improve quality. Poniatowski does not print the style of the wine on the label, which can be confusing for consumers.

Clos Naudin ☆☆☆–☆☆☆☆
Vouvray. 12 hectares
Philippe Foreau is a perfectionist: no herbicides, very low yields, no added yeasts, no chaptalization, and all the wines are fermented in 300-litre barrels, but not in new oak. The dry wines can be very good here, but it's the supremely elegant *moelleux* wines that are truly memorable, with their flavours of apricots, pears, and dried fruits. The word *réserve* on the label signifies that the grapes were nobly rotten.

Confrèrie des Vignerons de Oisly & Thesée ☆–☆☆
Oisly. 310 hectares
A young (1961) cooperative with fifty-eight members. It has successfully created a new style and image for the Cher Valley in eastern Touraine. Almost half the production is of Sauvignon. Their aim is to design a well-balanced, light red and white using a blend of grapes. The white is Sauvignon, Chenin Blanc, and Chardonnay; the red Cabernet Franc, Cot, and Gamay. The co-op's brand for their top *cuvée* of each is "Baronnie d'Aignan"; "Château de Vallagon" and "Domaine de la Châtoire" are estate-bottled wines; "Excellence" is a new *cuvée* of both Sauvignon and Gamay, each hand-harvested from old vines. But labels can vary from market to market.

Couly-Dutheil ☆☆–☆☆☆
Chinon. 85 hectares. www.coulydutheil-chinon.com
A grower of Chinon and Saumur-Champigny and a négociant for other Loire wines, founded in 1910 by B. Dutheil, developed by René Couly, and now run by René's sons and grandson. Their vineyards are divided between wines of plain and plateau, sold as "Les Gravières d'Amador Abbé de Turpenay" (the lightest) and "Domaine René Couly", and the (better) wines of the *coteaux*, the "Clos de l'Echo" and "Clos de l'Olive". "La Diligence" is a new bottling from a recently purchased south-facing vineyard – for mid-term drinking. Another top wine is a selection labelled "Baronnie Madeleine", though the two "Clos" wines are usually superior. Most *cuvées* can be drunk young, but the *coteaux* wines can age for years into a harmonious mellowness. Admirably, the domaine retains small stocks of older vintages for sale.

Robert Denis ☆–☆☆
La Chapelle-St-Blaise. 4 hectares
A dedicated grower whose vineyards produce full-bodied rosés and fine-boned dry and off-dry Chenin Blanc, all barrel-fermented, in AC Touraine-Azay-le-Rideau.

Pierre-Jacques Druet ☆☆☆
Benais. 22 hectares
One of Bourgueil's finest producers, Druet offers five *cuvées* of Bourgueil and two of Chinon, including the "Clos du Danzay". In Bourgueil he produces a meaty, barrel-fermented rosé and, in order of age-worthiness, "Les Cents Boissellées", "Beauvais", "Le Grand Mont" and the often magnificent "Vaumoreau".

Domaine Dutertre ☆–☆☆
Limeray. 36 hectares
A family property producing Cabernet, Malbec, and Gamay for red and rosé Touraine-Amboise. The Dutertres also make sparkling and still dry whites in their rock-cut cellar.

Domaine du Four à Chaux ☆☆
Thoré la Rochette. 25 hectares

Dominique Norguet makes the best wine in VDQS Coteaux du Vendômois, particularly *vin gris* of Pineau d'Aunis and red blends, either of Gamay and Pineau d'Aunis or of Pinot Noir and Pineau d'Aunis.

Château Gaillard ☆☆
Mesland. 33 hectares
Vincent Girault cultivates his vines according to the principles of biodynamics. His best wine is his Touraine-Mesland *vieilles vignes rouge*, a fleshy blend based on Gamay supported by Cot and Cabernet.

Château Gaudrelle ☆–☆☆☆
Vouvray. 14 hectares
Alexandre Monmousseau makes a wide range of Vouvrays: *sec tendre*, sparkling, and *moelleux*. "Moelleux Réserve Spéciale" is a less concentrated style than "Réserve Personnelle", which is made from grapes picked at Sauternes-style levels of sugar.

Domaine des Huards ☆☆
Cour-Cheverny. 24 hectares
The Gendrier family vineyards are in AC Cheverny and in AC Cour-Cheverny. In Cheverny they produce estimable Sauvignon-based dry whites and Gamay- and Cabernet-based reds and rosés; in the latter they make some of the best examples of a unique dry white from the local Romorantin grape.

Domaine Huet ☆☆☆–☆☆☆☆☆
Vouvray. 35 hectares
Gaston Huet was perhaps the most respected name in Vouvray. In 1997, a few years before his death, he was still pouring his 1937 for admirers. Huet came from a family of growers which for generations had been making wine of the highest quality from three vineyards: Le Haut-Lieu, Le Mont, and Le Clos du Bourg – sweet or dry, still or sparkling – according to the season. Son-in-law Noël Pinguet is the winemaker and has converted the domaine to biodynamic viticulture. In 2003 the property was bought by Tokaji-producer István Szepsy and the American financier Anthony Hwang.

Charles Joguet ☆–☆☆☆
Sazilly. 38 hectares. www.charlesjoguet.com
An artist-*vigneron*, painter, and sculptor as well as one of Chinon's best winemakers, although he retired from active participation in the domaine in 1997. Joguet's best vines, over eighty years old, are in the Clos de la Dioterie. Clos du Chêne Vert is another noted vineyard. It is worth paying the slight premium for the top *cuvées*, as the other bottlings can be slight.

Lamé-Delille-Boucard ☆☆
Domaine des Chesnaies, Ingrandes de Touraine. 35 hectares
A considerable property, divided almost equally between four Bourgueil communes: Ingrandes, St-Patrice, Restigné, and Benais. The range of wines is quite distinctive: the "Cuvée Lucien Lamé" is delicate but not fragile, the *vieilles vignes* bottling is more robust and concentrated.

Domaine des Liards ☆☆
Montlouis. 19 hectares
A third-generation property run by the Berger family, 80% is planted with Chenin Blanc for still, sparkling, and *pétillant*

Montlouis, the rest with Sauvignon for Touraine Blanc, and Cabernet Franc for Touraine Rouge.

Domaine Frédéric Mabileau ☆☆
St-Nicolas-de-Bourgueil. 15 hectares
Mabileau has been running this family domaine since 1991, and the wines have gained in quality. All the wines are aged in barriques, but only "Cuvée Eclipse" spends time in new oak. With age, the wines develop a seductive gaminess

Domaine Henry Marionnet ☆☆–☆☆☆
Soings en Sologne. 60 hectares
Henry Marionnet at Domaine de la Charmoise is a modern-minded grower who has shown the true potential of Gamay and Sauvignon Blanc in Touraine. He uses *macération carbonique* to get a Beaujolais effect in his Gamay, and strives for round and fruity Sauvignon. There are special *cuvées*, including "M de Marionnet", a Sauvignon made from late-harvested grapes of his old vines; "Première Vendange", hand-harvested Gamay with no added sulphur, sugar or yeast; and the grapefruity "Provignage", a very rare bottling from century-old Romorantin vines.

Domaine Jacky Marteau ☆☆
Pouillé. 24 hectares
A reliable producer of superb Gamay de Touraine, Marteau also makes fine Sauvignon de Touraine, Cabernet, and rosé of Pineau d'Aunis.

Dominique Moyer ☆☆
Husseau, Montlouis. 12 hectares
A respected old family of growers (since 1830) with many very old vines (30% are over seventy years old). The Moyers go to the length of successive pickings to crush nothing but ripe grapes, making *sec* and *demi-sec* as ripe and round as possible. A little sparkling wine now made.

Domaine des Ouches ☆☆–☆☆☆
Ingrandes-de-Touraine. 14 hectares
The Gambier family has been making excellent wines here for decades. The top bottling is usually the *vieilles vignes*, aged, like most of the other wines, in old barriques.

Jean-Maurice Raffault ☆☆
Savigny-en-Véron. 50 hectares
In the last twenty-five years, M. Raffault, whose family have been *vignerons* since 1693, has expanded his vineyards and now has parcels scattered over seven communes, all within Chinon. He makes the wines of different soils separately. "Les Galluches", a light Chinon, comes from sandy soils; his longest-lived Chinons from the *lieux-dits* Les Picasses and Isoré. He favours a robust tannic style, and the wines can require many years of bottle-ageing.

Olga Raffault ☆☆
Savigny-en-Véron. 20 hectares
One of several Raffaults, not necessarily related, in and around this village at the western end of the Chinon appellation. (Another, Raymond, owns Domaine du Raffault). The estate keeps the wine of different sites separate. Clients can choose from a range of fruity and fairly full-bodied wines, of which the longest-lived *cuvée* is "Les Picasses Vieilles Vignes". Raffault also makes a tiny amount of Chinon Blanc.

Domaine du Roncée ☆☆–☆☆☆
Panzoult. 30 hectares. www.roncee.com

This property, formerly named Donabella, has been through various changes in ownership since the early 1990s. Jean-Martin Dutour now makes rich wines from two vineyards: "Clos des Marronniers" and "Coteau des Chenanceaux".

Domaine de la Taille aux Loups ☆☆☆
Montlouis. 14 hectares

Jacky Blot founded this estate in 1988 and picks selectively at very low yields. He likes to use new oak on certain wines, such as dry "Cuvée Remus". Its sweet counterpart, "Cuvée Romulus", is a rich mouthful of apples and honey with a spicy finish. A small quantity of dry Vouvray is produced from the Clos des Venise. All the wines, whatever their style, can be enthusiastically recommended as among the most characterful of the region.

Domaine Taluau & Foltzenlogel ☆☆
Chevrette, St-Nicolas-de-Bourgueil. 22 hectares

Despite the cumbersome name change, Joel Taluau is still in charge at this reliable estate. Vineyards in St-Nicolas and a few within Bourgueil produce fragrant and charming light red wines. Taluau ferments everything in stainless steel; and he doesn't believe in wood-ageing. Freshness and charm take precedence over power and intensity.

Vigneau-Chevreau ☆☆–☆☆☆
Chancay. 12 hectares

A biodynamic estate. Half the production is of sparkling wine. The *demi-sec* is often more harmonious than the austere *sec*, and the *moelleux* is intense, stylish, and tangy.

Other Touraine Producers

Domaine Allias ☆–☆☆
Le Petit Mont, Vouvray. 12 hectares

Daniel and son Dominique farm hilltop vines over the rock-cut cellars. Classic dry, *demi-sec*, and *moelleux* Vouvrays.

Domaine de Bellivière ☆☆
Lhomme. 9 hectares. www.belliviere.com

Excellent source of Jasnières and Coteaux du Loire from low-yielding vines.

Bourillon Dorleans ☆–☆☆
Vouvray. 19 hectares

Frédéric Bourillon has experimented with malolactic fermentation to give his dry wines greater softness – perhaps not a direction to pursue. Good *moelleux* wines.

Château de Chenonceaux ☆–☆☆
Chenonceaux. 35 hectares

The estate belongs to what must be the most beautiful of Loire showplace châteaux, complete with a well-equipped little winery in a courtyard. A range of wines is made.

Clos de la Briderie ☆–☆☆
Monteaux. 10 hectares

François Girault makes some of the most attractive wines in Touraine-Mesland, including a barrel-fermented white.

Clos des Quarterons ☆–☆☆
St-Nicolas-de-Bourgueil. 20 hectares

Thierry Amirault's property is well-distributed on the lighter soils of St-Nicolas. Fruity wines, with strong wood influence.

Clos Roche Blanche ☆☆
Mareuil-sur-Cher. 25 hectares

It isn't easy to be a successful producer within the basic Touraine appellation, as low prices don't encourage high quality. This property is one of the exceptions, releasing stylish varietal wines, such as Sauvignon and Cot.

Max Cognard ☆–☆☆
St-Nicolas-de-Bourgueil. 10 hectares

Good wines, with the delicacy and balance expected from St-Nicolas-de-Bourgueil.

Deletang ☆
St-Martin-le-Beau. 22 hectares

Good Montlouis and *méthode traditionnelle* wines from Chenin Blanc.

Catherine Dhoye-Deruet ☆☆
Vouvray. 5 hectares

Mme. Dhoye-Deruet stamps her personality on her wines, which are made without added yeasts and without chaptalization. Firm *sec*, and a range of *moelleux*, including "La Fontainerie", which is aged in new oak.

Jean-Pierre Freslier ☆☆
Vouvray. 9 hectares

Jean-Pierre has taken over from his father, André Freslier, and makes serious, dry Vouvray, tasty *moelleux*, and excellent Vouvray *pétillant*.

Domaine des Geslets ☆☆
Bourgueil. 16 hectares

A fine source of elegant Cabernets from both Bourgueil and St-Nicolas-de-Bourgueil. The "Cuvée de Garde" is made from very old vines. Since the estate only began production in 1998, it is hard to say how well these wines will age.

Jean-Pierre Laisement ☆–☆☆
Vouvray. 13 hectares

All his wines are made in 600-litre casks, stored in his chilly cellars. Good *moelleux*, sometimes with an unusual touch of austerity.

Levasseur ☆☆
Montlouis. 13 hectares

Producer of creamy, supple *moelleux* with flavours of apple and quince.

Domaine de la Perrière ☆☆
Cravant-les-Côteaux. 44 hectares

Christophe Baudry presents a sound range of Chinons, mostly red but also white.

Domaine Pichot ☆☆–☆☆☆
Vouvray. 27 hectares

Christophe and Jean-Claude Pichot have secured a good reputation for their wines, which succeed in all styles, from *sec* to the ultra-concentrated called "Les Larmes de Bacchus".

François Pinon ☆–☆☆
Vallée de Cousse, Vernou-sur-Brenne. 13 hectares

Pinon is scrupulous in both vineyard and cellar, producing high-quality *sec, demi-sec, moelleux,* and *liquoreux* as well as characterful *pétillant.* His regular bottling, "Cuvée Tradition", is a *demi-sec.* The *moelleux* is quite stylish, with appley overtones, but lacks intensity.

Domaine des Raguenières ☆
Benais. 19 hectares

A Bourgueil property making a little rosé as well as clean, fairly tannic, marvellously scented red. They can, though, be rather rustic and often vegetal.

The Upper Loire

It might well surprise the *vignerons* of Sancerre and Pouilly, the uppermost of the mainstream Loire vineyards, to learn what a profound influence their produce has had on forming modern tastes in white wine. It is an area of mainly small and unsophisticated properties – with one or two well-organized exceptions. But it has an easily recognizable style of wine, pungent and cutting, with the smell and acidity of Sauvignon Blanc grown in a cool climate. Although Sauvignon is planted on a far larger scale in Bordeaux, its wine never smelt and tasted so powerfully characteristic there as it does on the Loire. The Bordeaux tradition is to blend it with the smoother and more neutral Sémillon. But since Bordeaux has seen the world paying white burgundy prices for the assertive (some say obvious) Loire style, it is paying it the sincerest form of flattery.

One might say that the world discovered the Sauvignon Blanc and its singular flavour through the little vineyard of Sancerre and the even smaller one of Pouilly-sur-Loire. What is the flavour? It starts with the powerful aroma, which needs no second sniff. "Gunflint", the smell of sparks when flint strikes metal, is one way to characterize it. In unripe vintages tasters talk of cat's pee, and I am reminded of wet wool. Successful Sancerres and Pouilly-Fumés have an attractive smell and taste of fresh blackcurrants, leaves and all, and a natural high acidity which makes them distinctly bracing. Sancerre normally has more body and "drive" (and acidity) than Pouilly-Fumé; consequently it can benefit from two or three years' ageing. Pouilly needs only a year or so. Although there is no formal vineyard classification in Sancerre, some sites are widely recognized as exceptional, and their names sometimes appear on labels. The best-known are Le Chêne Marchand and Monts Damnés.

For reasons of tradition, the Pouilly vineyards also contain a proportion of the neutral Chasselas grape, which cannot be sold as "Fumé", only as Pouilly-sur-Loire: a pale, adequate, rather pointless wine, which must be drunk very young. Sancerre, on the other hand, is almost as proud of its Pinot Noir red and rosé as its Sauvignon white. They never achieve the flavour and texture of great burgundy, although those being made by the best producers can match lighter red burgundies. More commonly, they have the faintly watery style of German Spätburgunder (the same grape). Nor do they age so satisfactorily – at best for five to ten years. But they are highly appreciated at source.

Leading Sancerre Producers

Bailly-Reverdy ☆☆
Bué. 20 hectares

A distinguished traditional grower with vineyards in no fewer than fifteen sites. The bottling from the famous Clos du Chêne Marchand is now called "Caillottes". White from other vineyards is called "Domaine de la Mercy Dieu"; there is also a bottling from Monts Damnés. He looks for (and finds) a balance of fruit and finesse, particularly in his whites. The red Sancerre, which is succulent and tastes of cherries, accounts for around one third of production

Domaine Joseph Balland-Chapuis ☆–☆☆☆
Bué. 34 hectares. www.balland-chapuis.com

A well-established estate, with vines mostly in Sancerre but also in VDQS Coteaux du Giennois and a small parcel in Pouilly. Many *cuvées* of Sancerre, including two excellent whites, "Chêne Marchand" (aged in about 50% new oak) and "Comte Thibault". The deluxe red, "Comte Thibault Vieilles Vignes", matures in new oak. "Cuvée Pierre" and "Cuvée Marguerite Marceau" (a Giennois) are late-harvest Sauvignons, sweet to varying degrees and fermented in new oak. Now part of the Guy Saget (*q.v.*) group.

Domaine Henri Bourgeois ☆☆–☆☆☆
Bué. 65 hectares. www.bourgeois-sancerre.com

One of the most important grower-négociants in Sancerre. In addition to its vineyards, the firm acts as a négociant in Sancerre, Pouilly, Reuilly, Menetou-Salon, and Quincy. Bourgeois offers numerous high-end *cuvées*, including "La Bourgeoise" (red and white), "Grande Réserve", "Etienne Henri", and "Les Monts Damnés". The firm also sells the Sancerres of Domaine Laporte, an estate it bought in 1987. Overall, these are delectable wines, varying from *cuvée* to *cuvée*, yet all unmistakably Sancerre.

Cave Coopérative des Vins de Sancerre ☆
Sancerre. 200 hectares. www.vins-sancerre.com

Founded in 1963 and producing nothing but Sancerre. The cooperative moved into new cellars in 2001. A serious producer of typical Sancerre under a variety of labels. The prestige bottling is "Le Duc de Tarente".

François Cotat ☆☆
Chavignol. 2 hectares

A very small, totally traditional, and most prestigious grower. The Cotats do everything themselves, use an old wooden press, ferment in casks, and never fine nor filter. The vineyards are shared with Pascal-Francis Cotat (*q.v.*).

Pascal-Francis Cotat ☆☆
Chavignol. 2 hectares

A tiny property on the slopes of Monts Damnés. The emphasis is firmly on quality, but the search for maximum ripeness does mean that in some years the wines retain some residual sugar.

Domaine Lucien Crochet ☆☆–☆☆☆
Bué. 31 hectares

A family holding, three-quarters of it Sauvignon, the rest Pinot Noir. Crochet also buys in grapes for his modern, efficient cellars. Classic methods produce excellent wine, particularly his "Clos du Chêne Marchand" from his five hectares there (although the Chêne Marchand designation is no longer used). Bottlings include "La Croix du Roy" (both red and white) and the "Cuvée Prestige LC" (likewise), an old-vines bottling often released several years after the vintage. The "Cuvée Prestige" is oak-aged.

Domaine Vincent Delaporte ☆–☆☆
Chavignol. 20 hectares
About one-fifth of the production of Delaporte and son Jean-Yves is of Pinot Noir. Most wines ferment in stainless-steel tanks, although "Cuvée Maxime" is a limited production oaked Sancerre. The reds age in oak.

André Dezat ☆☆–☆☆☆
Verdigny. 38 hectares
André Dezat is an old-school grower, who works in clogs and a beret and loves his red wines as they age – though I prefer them young. He has vines in Pouilly as well as Sancerre. His whites are extremely fine, even elegant. Today he is assisted by his sons, Simon and Louis.

Gitton Père & Fils ☆☆
Ménétréol. 36 hectares. www.gitton.fr
A family estate in Sancerre, Pouilly, and Coteaux du Giennois, almost entirely Sauvignon, developed since 1945 and now run by Pascal Gitton. The wines are made in many different batches according to different soils – at least fifteen different Sancerre *cuvées* with different labels – "Les Belles Dames", "Le Gelinot", "Les Romains", and so on – and two Pouilly-Fumés. The whites are fermented in barrels or tanks and aged eight months in *cuves*; the reds fermented in *cuves*, then aged two winters in barrels. Altogether an original house, with a rich, supple style of its own.

Pascal Jolivet ☆☆–☆☆☆
Sancerre. 20 hectares. www.pascal-jolivet.com
A dynamic young grower and négociant with vineyards divided between Sancerre and Pouilly (*q.v.*). Jolivet does buy grapes and wine, but puts out a number of domaine bottlings. In Sancerre these include "Le Chêne Marchand" and "La Grande Cuvée", an old-vines bottling made only in good years. No oak is used for the white wines.

Château de Maimbray ☆
Sury-en-Vaux. 14 hectares
The Roblins, a trustworthy family of growers, produce sturdy Sancerre (red, white, and rosé) from their domaine.

Alphonse Mellot ☆☆☆
Sancerre. 48 hectares
Growers, négociants, and propagandists for Sancerre with an important holding of fifty hectares in good sites, mostly in La Moussière. The Mellot family, now headed by Alphonse, date back to the sixteenth century. Yields are modest here, and the wines are impeccable across the range. His deluxe bottlings are "Cuvée Edmond", which is partly aged in new oak, and "Génération XIX", which appears in both a red and a toasty white version. Mellot aims to produce wines that are capable of ageing, but are nonetheless accessible young.

Paul Millerioux ☆–☆☆
Crézancy. 17 hectares

An old-style grower with modern cellars who turns out flavourful Sancerres (red, rosé, and white). The wines are straightforward and far from complex, but no worse for that.

Henry Natter ☆☆
Montigny. 20 hectares. www.henrynatter.fr
Founded in 1974, the estate soon acquired a fine reputation for its deft, fruity wines, especially the zesty whites. The best wine is made from old vines and called "Cuvée François de la Grange".

Vincent Pinard ☆☆–☆☆☆
Bué. 15 hectares
A small estate that produces a number of different *cuvées*, all from hand-picked fruit. There is a strong emphasis here on red wines, although the whites are rich and elegant.

Pierre Prieur & Fils ☆☆
Verdigny. 12 hectares
A prominent family of growers for generations with several good sites, including Les Monts-Damnés (which is chalky clay) and the stonier Pichon, where an unusually high proportion of the property is Pinot Noir.

The white is made to age two or three years; the rosé of Pinot Noir mysteriously seems to share its quality – even its Sauvignon flavour. The red is made like very light burgundy. The deluxe "Cuvée Maréchal Prieur" is partially fermented and aged in new oak for twelve months.

Jean Reverdy & Fils ☆☆
Verdigny. 12 hectares
A succession of Reverdys since 1646 have farmed here. They have installed modern equipment in the cellar and make fine, classic wines, particularly the "Clos de la Reine Blanche" white, which can mature for three or four years.

Pascal & Nicolas Reverdy ☆☆
Maimbray. 12 hectares
A small estate producing elegant citric Sancerres. The "Cuvée Vieilles Vignes" is from sixty-year-old vines and bottled unfiltered. The red is unusually rich for Sancerre and is bottled without filtration.

Jean-Max Roger ☆☆
Bué. 27 hectares
Jean-Max Roger is an important grower-négociant with vineyards in Sancerre and Menetou-Salon.

Of particular merit is his Sancerre *vieilles vignes*, from his own vines, and numerous *cuvées* from some of the best sites in the region.

Domaine Vacheron ☆☆☆
Sancerre. 37 hectares
A particularly welcoming family of growers whose wines can be tasted in summer in the centre of Sancerre at Le Grenier à Sel. Jean Vacheron, who died in 1988, is succeeded by his sons Jean-Louis and Denis. They offer white "Le Paradis", red "Belle Dame", and rosé "Les Romains".

Their equipment and ideas are modern, but the red ages a year in Burgundian casks and is bottled without fining or filtration. Yields are restrained, and the red Sancerre in particular is one of the most concentrated and complex of the region.

André Vatan ☆☆
Verdigny. 12 hectares
Flowery white Sancerre and delicate red and rosé from a long-established grower.

Leading Pouilly Producers

Caves de Pouilly-sur-Loire ☆
Pouilly-sur-Loire. 200 hectares
The cooperative vinifies around 20% of the output of the appellation. The wines are solid and respectable and the Pouilly-Fumé "Les Vieillottes" is a bit more than that. The cooperative also produces VDQS Coteaux du Giennois.

Jean-Claude Chatelain ☆–☆☆
St-Andelain. 19 hectares
A leading grower-négociant, releasing numerous bottlings, including "St-Laurent-l'Abbaye", "Domaine des Chailloux", and the late-harvested but dry "Cuvée Prestige Vieilles Vignes". Chatelain and son Vincent are also shareholders in a new vineyard in the La Charité-sur-Loire area south of Pouilly, where they make Chardonnay and Pinot Noir.

Didier Dagueneau ☆☆☆☆
St-Andelain. 12 hectares
The appellation's best winemaker by far, the impassioned Dagueneau produces four decisive *cuvées* of Pouilly-Fumé; "En Chailloux", "Buisson Ménard", "Pur Sang", and "Silex". The last two ferment and age in new-oak barrels. There is also a tiny production of a wine called "L'Astéroïde", made from ungrafted vines.

Astonished many years ago by the quality of venerable bottles of Pouilly in private cellars, he changed his vinification and style from an easy-drinking white for early consumption to a well-structured, oak-aged wine capable of evolving fruitfully over many years. The style remains controversial, but Dagueneau is its master, and no other producer can rival the elegance and power of his wines. They brilliantly combine richness and minerality.

Serge Dagueneau & Filles ☆☆
St-Andelain. 15 hectares
A vineyard with a high reputation for typically fruity and full-flavoured Pouilly-Fumé and Pouilly-sur-Loire. His old-vines *cuvée* is "Clos des Chaudoux".

Pascal Jolivet ☆☆
Sancerre. 20 hectares
Pascal Jolivet is based in Sancerre but also has vines in Pouilly from which he produces numerous bottlings, including "Les Griottes" and "La Grande Cuvée", made from old vines in good vintages.

Domaine Masson-Blondelet ☆☆–☆☆☆
Pouilly-sur-Loire. 19 hectares
The Masson and Blondelet families (united by marriage in 1974) grow mainly Sauvignon and a small amount of Chasselas. Their best parcels are vinified separately: "Les Criots" is from fairly young vines, "Les Bascoins" is from older vines and has excellent finesse. "Tradition Cullus" is their *cuvée prestige*, partly oak-aged.

Château du Nozet ☆☆
Pouilly-sur-Loire. 52 hectares
The major producer and promoter of the fine wines of Pouilly, both from company-owned vineyards and from purchased wine.

The Baron Patrick de Ladoucette is the head of the family firm, which has three labels: "Pouilly-Fumé de Ladoucette", "Sancerre Comte Lafond" (from bought-in grapes), and a prestige *cuvée* "Pouilly-Fumé Baron de L". The Baron recently purchased Maison Cordier's vineyards on La Poussie in Sancerre. The Pouilly-Fumé wines are inexplicably expensive, and always have been.

Michel Redde ☆–☆☆☆
La Moynerie, St-Andelain. 35 hectares. www.michel-redde.fr
One of the best-known producers of Pouilly-Fumé, now in its seventh generation under Thierry Redde. The feisty Michel Redde was convinced that machine-harvesting delivers better-quality fruit, and was also content to have his wines go through partial malolactic fermentation to give them more roundness. "Cuvée Majorum" is the top wine from old vines, but Redde is adamantly opposed to oak-ageing. Pouilly-sur-Loire is also produced.

Guy Saget ☆–☆☆☆
Pouilly-sur-Loire. 240 hectares. www.guy-saget.com
A fifth generation growers' family affair run by the brothers Saget, expanded since 1976 into a négociant business. They now sell four million bottles of Loire wines annually, from twenty-five different appellations. Their technique is long cool fermentation with minimum disturbance of the wine and no malolactic fermentation to reduce the high natural fruity acidity. *See also* Balland-Chapuis.

Château de Tracy ☆☆
Tracy-sur-Loire. 28 hectares
The family of the Comte d'Estutt d'Assay has owned the Château, on the Loire just downstream from Pouilly, since the sixteenth century. The style is fairly rounded, and the wines are best enjoyed young. After a dull patch, the wines from the late 1990s show more concentration and precision.

The Minor Regions

The success of Sancerre and Pouilly has encouraged what were dwindling outposts of vineyards in less-favoured situations to the west of the Loire to expand their plantings. The names of Menetou-Salon, Quincy, and Reuilly are now accepted as Sancerre substitutes at slightly lower prices (but longer odds against a fine ripe bottle). Three other regions of the upper Loire have now gained VDQS status: Coteaux du Giennois, the tiny Châteaumeillant (good for its rosé), and Vins de l'Orléanais.

Much higher up the river where it cuts through the Massif Central, several scattered vineyard areas relate less to the Loire than to southern Burgundy and the Rhône. The most famous is St-Pourçain-sur-Sioule, once a monastic vineyard. Its wine is almost all consumed today to mitigate the effects of treatment at the spa of Vichy – but it is hard to see how it could ever have had more than a local following. Price remains the main thing in favour of the remaining areas of the heights of the Loire, but the quality is improving. The Côte Roannaises (now AC), and the AC Côtes du Forez and the VDQS Côtes d'Auvergne grow the right grapes for quality – Gamay, Chardonnay, some Pinot Noir, and Syrah.

Reuilly

Claude Lafond ☆☆
Le Bois St-Denis, Reuilly. 25 hectares
An energetic young grower, Lafond makes some of the best wine in the appellation, including a dry white "Clos des Messieurs", a dry rosé "La Grande Pièce", and a light Pinot Noir called "Les Grandes Vignes".

Menetou-Salon

Domaine de Chatenoy ☆–☆☆
St-Martin-d'Auxigny. 28 hectares
The ancestors of Bernard Clément have owned this estate since 1560, and now produce red, white, and rosé. Despite their freshness, they can reach thirteen degrees of alcohol. He recommends them as apéritifs as well as table wines.

Domaine Henry Pellé ☆–☆☆☆
Morogues. 40 hectares
A family winery producing vigorous whites and pleasant, light reds. The top white *cuvée* is "Clos des Blanchais", made from old vines.

Morogues, which abuts the Sancerre zone, is the only commune that may attach its name to that of Menetou-Salon on the label. There is also a small production of Sancerre.

Quincy

Domaine Mardon ☆–☆☆
Quincy. 14 hectares
A good family winery producing brisk whites – among the best in the appellation.

Coteaux du Giennois

Alain Paulat ☆☆
Villemoison. 5 hectares
Alain Paulat is a passionate young grower who cultivates his vines organically. He produces toothsome light reds from Gamay and Pinot Noir.

Balland-Chapuis & Gitton (*q.v.*) ☆☆
Sancerre
Also make reliable Coteaux du Giennois.

Vin de l'Orléanais

Clos St-Fiacre ☆
Mareau-aux-Près. 18 hectares
Engaging light reds from Pinot Meunier and Pinot Noir as well as light Chardonnays and somewhat vegetal Cabernets.

Châteaumeillant

Maurice & Patrick Lanoix ☆
Châteaumeillant. 19 hectares
Father (Maurice) and son (Patrick) produce pleasant reds and rosés (predominantly Gamay) under two labels: "Domaine du Feuillat" (Maurice's wines), and "Cellier du Chêne Combeau" (Patrick's).

Côtes d'Auvergne

Cave St-Verny ☆
Veyre-Monton
Founded in 1950 as a cooperative, the *cave* was purchased in 1991 by Limagrain, Europe's largest seed specialist. It produces nearly half the wine in the appellation in ultra-modern cellars, turning out clean whites, rosés (those from Corent are particularly noteworthy) and light red wines based on Gamay. The deluxe bottling is called "Première Cuvée".

Côtes du Forez

les Vignerons Foreziens ☆
Trelins. 200 hectares
The cooperative produces 98% of AC Côtes du Forez and 60% of the Vin de Pays d'Urfe. The former is Gamay; the latter predominantly Chardonnay.

Côte Roannaisses

Alain Demon ☆–☆☆
Ambierle. 4 hectares
From vineyards on the steep slopes above the Loire, Demon produces silky, characterful Gamays. His "Réserve" is made from 50- to 100-year-old vines.

Paul Lapandéry & Fils ☆–☆☆
St-Haon-le-Vieux. 8 hectares
A family winery with vineyards pitched at a vertiginous 72° angle. Lapandéry's highly personalized, light reds are based on very low yields and very long barrel-age.

St-Pourçain

Union des Vignerons ☆
St-Pourçain-sur-Sioule. 300 hectares
The cooperative (founded 1952), with 160 members, dominates this once-famous central vineyard, formerly a monastic stronghold. The varieties grown are Sauvignon, Sacy, Aligoté, Chardonnay, and Tresallier for whites, and Pinot Noir and Gamay for reds.

The cooperative produces up to 65% of the appellation's wine. Special bottlings include its popular "Ficelle", an easy-drinking Gamay; "Réserve Spéciale" (white and red); red and white wines from two estates and "Domaine de Chinière" and "Domaine de la Croix d'Or". A number of independent growers are also making great efforts and some progress.

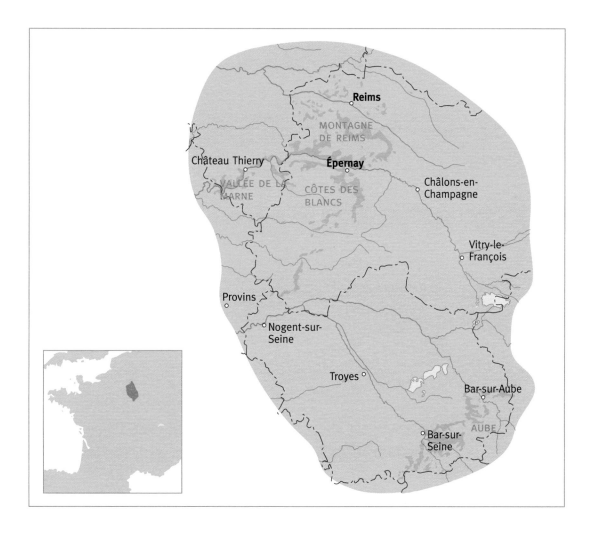

Champagne

Champagne is the wine grown in the northernmost vineyards of France: the local wines of Paris. The Champagne method (or traditional method, as Brussels insists that we now call it) is something that is done to the wine to make it sparkle – and can be done to any wine. Those who make wine sparkle in other regions would like us to believe that the method is all that matters. What really matters is the wine.

It was one of the best in France long before the method was invented. The difference between the best Champagne and the merely good is almost entirely a matter of the choice and treatment of grapes, their variety, their ripeness, their handling, and the soil that bears them. Outside France, the Champagne market is largely controlled by the *grandes marques*: the twenty or so great firms with the widest distribution.

These great merchants actually own only about ten per cent of the vineyards, and have to rely on 19,600 small farmers to provide them with grapes. Many growers in Champagne also sell their crop to cooperatives, though some – the *récoltants-manipulants* – make small amounts of Champagne of their own. All told, growers are responsible for 5,000 brands, though these are not necessarily vinified by

them. The best of these Champagne growers are described on pages 158–65.

Any merchant buying Champagne can think up a name (a "buyer's own brand") and print a label, so there is no limit to the number of brands. In itself this lends strength to the *grandes marques* with the best-known names, which are often bought simply as safe bets. But reputation and wealth also allow them to buy the best materials, employ the best staff, and stock their wine longest. (Time is vital to develop the flavours.) The great houses push to the limit the polishing and perfecting of an agricultural product.

The "method" began 200 years ago with the genius of a Benedictine monk, Dom Pérignon of Hautvillers, apparently the first man to "design" a wine by blending the qualities of different grapes from different varieties and vineyards to make a whole greater, more subtle, more satisfying than any of its parts. This blend, known as the *cuvée*, is traditionally the secret patent of each maker, though cellarmasters today will sometimes invite the wine trade and press to observe the blending process first-hand.

The best blends are astonishingly complex, with as many as thirty or forty ingredient wines of different origins and ages, selected by nose and palate alone. Houses with their own vineyards stress the character of the grapes they grow themselves; the heavier Pinot Noir of the Montagne de Reims or the lighter Chardonnay of the Côte des Blancs – each village is subtly different. Very few have enough to supply their own needs. Grape-prices are fixed by a percentage system (*see* page 164).

It was not Dom Pérignon but his contemporaries who discovered how to make their wine sparkling by a second fermentation in a tightly corked bottle – a process with dangers and complications that took another century to master completely. The principle of making Champagne is outlined diagrammatically on page 29. The sparkle is caused by the large amounts of CO_2 dissolved in the wine. The "mousse", or froth in the glass, is only part of it – you swallow the greater part. CO_2 is instantly absorbed by the stomach wall. Once in the bloodstream it accelerates the circulation, and with it the movement of alcohol to the brain. This is where Champagne gets its reputation as the wine of wit and the choice for celebrations. Other sparkling wines made by the same method can claim to have the same effect, but not the same taste.

Leading Champagne Producers

Besserat de Bellefon ☆☆–☆☆☆
Epernay. www.besseratdebellefon.com. Founded 1843. Owner: Marne et Champagne since 1992. Visits: appt. only. NV: Cuvée Blanc de Blancs, Brut, Cuvée des Moines Brut, Blanc de Blancs, and Rosé. Grande Tradition, Vintage, Grande Cuvée

A family business until 1959, the firm has had several corporate owners since then, the most recent being the giant Marne et Champagne. The Besserat house style is for very fine, light wines much appreciated in top French restaurants. The "Cuvée des Moines Blanc de Blancs" with its gentle sparkle and creamy flavour makes a good apéritif, while the "Cuvée des Moines Rosé" has great finesse. "Grande Cuvée" is a 50/50 blend of Chardonnay and Pinot Noir. France takes 80% of its total sales of 2.2 million bottles a year.

Billecart-Salmon ☆☆☆
Mareuil-sur-Aÿ. www.champagne-billecart.fr. Founded 1818. Owners: Roland-Billecart family. 6 hectares. Visits: appt. only. NV: Brut Réserve, Brut Rosé. Vintages: Cuvée Nicolas-François Billecart, Blanc de Blancs, Cuvée Elisabeth Salmon Rosé, Grande Cuvée

A small, highly respected Grand Marque, this family firm is currently producing exquisite Champagnes of the light and elegant kind. Always respectful of the traditional composition of its *cuvées*, Billecart nonetheless uses modern vinification techniques that involve a natural cold settling of the must and long, cool fermentations.

The result is wine of floral aromas and delicate flavours that belie its ability to live a long and distinguished life; a 1959 tasted in 1996 was still as fresh as a daisy. The "Brut Réserve" is quite exceptional; although dominated by the two Pinots, its 30% Chardonnay content gives an extra dimension of finesse and elegance. The subtle pale-salmon coloured rosé is Billecart's flagship wine in the United States. Outstanding vintage wines have a perfect balance of freshness and maturity, especially the late-disgorged "Grande Cuvée", the same wine as the vintage but given ten years, ageing on the yeasts.

Bollinger ☆☆☆–☆☆☆☆
Aÿ. www.champagne-bollinger.fr. Founded 1829. Owners: the Bizot family. Associated Companies: Langlois-Château (Loire), Chanson (Burgundy). 152 hectares. Visits: appt. only. NV: Special Cuvée Brut. Vintages: Grande Année Brut and Rosé, RD, Vieilles Vignes Françaises. Still wines: Aÿ, Côte aux Enfants

One of the "greats" of Champagne, a traditionalist house making muscular wine with body, length, depth, and every other dimension. Much of the harvest is barrel-fermented and wines are kept on their yeast as long as possible; in the case of RD "recently disgorged" about ten years, giving extra

Choosing Champagne

The knowledge essential for buying Champagne to your own taste is the style and standing of the house and the range of its wines. Other relevant points included in the entries on these pages are the ownership and date of foundation, whether you may visit the cellars, where most of the grapes come from, the annual sales and size of stock, and the principal markets of the house. To some extent you may deduce style and quality from the sources of grapes and their standing in the percentage table on page 164, in conjunction with the average age of the wine (the stocks divided by the annual sales).

Most houses offer wines in the following categories:

Non-vintage (NV) A *cuvée* maintained, as nearly as possible, to an exact standard year after year: usually fairly young. Standard gauge of "house style". Essentially apéritif wines.
Vintage Best-quality wine of a vintage whose intrinsic quality is considered too good to be hidden in a non-vintage *cuvée*. Normally aged longer on the yeast than non-vintage, more full-bodied and tasty, with the potential to improve for several more years. Their greater body makes them better at table.
Rosé A small quantity of still red wine from one of the Pinot Noir villages (often Aÿ or Bouzy) is blended with still white wine. This blend undergoes a second fermentation, which creates the bubbles. A very few producers, such as Krug, make rosé by a brief maceration of the grapes, but this is much harder to control than blending in red wine. In many cases, entrancingly fruity and fine, and one of the house's best *cuvées*.
Blanc de blancs A *cuvée* of Chardonnay grapes only, with great grace and less weight than traditional Champagne.
Blanc de noirs A *cuvée* of black grapes only, sometimes faintly pink or *gris*, and invariably rich and flavoury.
Cuvée de prestige (under many names) A super-Champagne on the hang-the-expense principle. Moët's Dom Pérignon was the first; now most houses have one. Fabulously good though most of them are, there is a strong argument for two bottles of non-vintage for the price of one *cuvée de prestige*. (See page 161.)
Crémant The old name for a half-pressure Champagne, preferred by some people who find a normal one too gassy – particularly with food. Since 1994, the houses have been forbidden to use the word on the front label.
Coteaux Champenois Still white or red wine of the Champagne vineyards, made in limited quantities when supplies of grapes allow. Naturally high in acidity, but can be exquisitely fine.
Brut, extra dry, etc. What little consistency there is about these indications of sweetness or otherwise is shown on page 163.

breadth of flavour. A tiny patch of ungrafted pre-phylloxera Pinot Noir in Aÿ and Bouzy gives "Vieilles Vignes Françaises": very rare and expensive, "combining the power of the New World with the elegance of the Old", in the words of Guy Bizot, great nephew of Madame Lily Bollinger. Sixty per cent of grapes come from Bollinger's own vineyards, average rating 97% on the *Echelle des Crus* (*q.v.*). Remainder bought from Côte des Blancs and Verteuil, Marne Valley. Production: 1.8 million bottles, and stock of seven million bottles.

Delamotte ☆☆–☆☆☆

Le Mesnil-sur-Oger. www.laurent-perrier.fr. Founded 1760. Owner: Laurent-Perrier. 5 hectares. Visits: appt. only. NV: Brut, Blanc de Blancs, Rosé. Vintage: Blanc de Blancs Vintage

The sixth oldest Champagne house. Since Laurent-Perrier's purchase of Salon (*q.v.*) in 1989, the two firms, housed in adjacent eighteenth century premises, have been managed jointly. The firm has some *grand cru* Chardonnay in Le Mesnil which, though producing only about 25% of the company's needs, certainly shapes the Chardonnay-led style of the Champagnes; fresh, aromatic, and long-lived.

The vintage-dated blanc de blancs is the most interesting: rich, peach-like, and especially successful in the great 1990 vintage.

Deutz ☆☆☆

Aÿ. Founded 1838. Owner: Louis Roederer. 110 hectares. Subsidiary and associated companies: Delas (Rhône), l'Aulée (Loire), Deutz (New Zealand). Visits: appt. only. NV: Brut Classic. Vintages: Brut, Blanc de Blancs, Rosé. Prestige: Cuvée William Deutz Brut and Rosé, Amour de Deutz

Like many great Champagne firms, this house was founded by German immigrants. Although the Lallier-Deutz family are still involved in the business, a majority stake was acquired by Roederer in 1993, since when quality has soared. The Roederer investment shows to good effect in the new "Brut Classic", a first-rate non-vintage *cuvée*, creamy, rich, yet decidedly dry in the Deutz tradition. The vintage-dated blanc de blancs "Amour de Deutz" made from *grand cru* grapes is exquisite, as is the "Cuvée William Deutz", a *prestige* blend of great vinous subtlety. *Echelle des Crus*: average of 97%.

Drappier ☆☆☆

Urville. www.champagne-drappier.com. Founded 1808. Owners: the Drappier family. 40 hectares. Visits: appt. only. NV: Brut Zero, Carte d'Or Brut, Carte Blanche, Dry Nature, Rosé Val des Demoiselles, Signature Blanc de Blancs. Vintage: Grande Sendrée Brut

Vignerons in the Aube since the time of Napoléon, this is a dynamic merchant-grower house producing hedonistic Champagne of great character. The heart of the business is the domaine planted mainly with Pinot Noir on the southern limestone slopes of Urville.

Meticulous winemaking in a pristine *cuverie* above cool, twelfth century Cistercian cellars results in some memorable bottles: the "Carte d'Or Brut" suffused with aromas and flavours of red fruits (the Drappier style); the impressive "Brut Zéro" – powerful, uncompromising, bone-dry, but in no way astringent or bitter; the *prestige* "Grande Sendrée" – mouthfilling, magnificent, and very Pinot, but with exactly the right amount of Chardonnay to add an extra touch of definition and refinement.

Duval-Leroy ☆–☆☆☆

Vertus. www.duval-leroy.com. Founded 1859. Owners: the Duval family. 150 hectares. Visits: appt. only. NV: Fleur de Champagne, Blanc de Noirs, Demi-Sec. Vintage: Fleur de Champagne, Femme de Champagne, Extra Brut, Blanc de Chardonnay, Cuvée des Roys, Cuvée Leroy Neiman

A quality-conscious family firm, which benefitted enormously from the acquisition of choice Chardonnay vineyards mainly on the Côte des Blancs. Until recently, much of the company's export business was in supplying "buyer's own brand" Champagnes to merchants in Britain, Belgium, and Germany. But in the late 1990s, the marketing strategy sought to establish the Duval-Leroy brand on world markets, and under the leadership of the current head of the company, Carol Duval, a formidably strong-willed widow, that ambition was largely achieved.

The style of the Champagne is subtle, fresh, aromatic, and well-illustrated by the Chardonnay-dominated "Fleur de Champagne". The superb blanc de blancs is a vintage wine, the classic 1990 a model of its kind.

Gosset ☆☆–☆☆☆

Aÿ. www.champagne-gosset.com. Founded 1584. Owner: Frapin Cognac. 100 hectares. Visits: appt. only. NV: Brut Excellence, Grande Réserve, Grand Rosé. Vintage: Grand Millésime. Prestige: Gosset Celebris. Still wine: Bouzy Rouge

Gosset has good claim to being the oldest wine house in the Marne, though Ruinart (*q.v.*) was the first to make sparkling Champagne on a serious scale. After 410 years of Gosset ownership, control of the firm passed to the quality-conscious Cointreau family of Frapin cognac in 1994. The new "Brut Excellence" is a brisk, racy wine dominated by Chardonnay (61%), and is ideal as an apéritif. The real stars of the range are the floral, rich, and complex "Grande Réserve", a classic blend of Pinot and Chardonnay from three great years, and the lustrous vintage-dated rosé: full, velvet-smooth, yet very elegant. Gosset Champagnes are built to last, the malolactic fermentation deliberately avoided to ensure a long life.

Alfred Gratien ☆☆–☆☆☆

Epernay. www.alfredgratien.com. Founded 1864. Owners: the Seydoux family of Gratien & Meyer (Saumur). No vineyards. Visits: appt. only. NV: Brut. Vintage: Brut Vintage. Prestige: Cuvée Paradis

Small traditionalist house, making 175,000 bottles per annum of excellent, very dry wines vinified in small barrels; the malolactic fermentation is avoided to ensure maximum vitality and long life. The vintage wines have an unusually high Chardonnay content, though the house style also favours a significant amount of Pinot Meunier in the blends in order to add notes of spices and luxuriant fruit. The *prestige* "Cuvée Paradis" ranks among the very greatest Champagnes, at once elegant and exotic; unlike many *prestige* bottlings, it is a non-vintage blend from the best vineyards.

Charles Heidsieck ☆☆☆

Reims. Founded 1851. Owner: Rémy-Cointreau. 70 hectares. (shared with Piper-Heidsieck). Visits: appt only. NV: Brut Réserve, Mis en Cave. Vintage: Brut and Rosé. Prestige: Blanc de Millénaire

The original Charles Heidsieck was the "Champagne Charlie" of the song, who made a fortune in the USA but almost lost it in the Civil War. Daniel Thibault was appointed winemaker in 1985, and within a few years the quality of the wines had improved greatly, especially the "Brut Réserve". Its outstanding character owes everything to natural vinification, technical treatments of the wine being kept to a minimum, and to the complexity of the blend, which is composed of 300 components with at least 40% reserve wines. Honeyed, fleshy, yet with a discreet vinosity, this is a Champagne *par excellence* to accompany fine cuisine. The *prestige* "Blanc des Millénaires" (great 1983 and 1989) is a magnificent blanc de blancs, a high-wire act of sharply defined, mature Chardonnay flavours and exotic fruitiness. An interesting initiative was the "*mis en cave*" ("bottled in cellar") programme, launched with the 1992 vintage. These are non-vintage wines, and the date refers to the year each bottling began its ageing process in the cellars. The extra bottle-age, and perhaps a superior blend, shows in round and toasty flavours.

Henriot ☆☆–☆☆☆

Reims. Founded 1808. Owner: the Henriot family since 1994. Associated company: Bouchard Père et Fils, William Fèvre. Visits: appt. only. NV: Brut Souverain, Blanc de Blancs, Brut and Rosé. Vintage: Cuvée des Enchanteleurs

Rémois merchants and wine-growers since the seventeenth century, the Henriots are as Champenois as the windmill of Verzenay. In 1994, Joseph Henriot took the firm back into family ownership. The price of independence from the LVMH group was the loss of the family's very fine, 100-hectare vineyards located mainly on the Côte des Blancs, though grapes are still sourced from these exceptional sites on a long-lease basis. Henriot Champagnes are very dry, pure-flavoured, and based exclusively on Pinot Noir and Chardonnay, the latter seemingly, if not actually, dominant. The blanc de blancs is a model of incisive but persistent Chardonnay flavours. The "Cuvée des Enchanteleurs" is a *prestige cuvée* that ages beautifully. In 1995, Joseph Henriot bought the Burgundy house of Bouchard Père et Fils (*q.v.*).

Jacquesson ☆☆☆

Dizy. Founded 1798. Owners: the Chiquet family. 33 hectares. Visits: appt. only. NV: Brut and Rosé Perfection. Vintage: Blanc de Blancs, Signature Brut and Rosé Vintage, Dégorgement Tardif

Johann Joseph Krug, founder of the *ne plus ultra* of Champagne houses, learned blending at Jacquesson, and this low-key firm is still one of the best exponents of classic Champagne-making. Subtly cask-aged reserve wines contribute significantly to the supple, rich, yet structured house style of the finished Champagnes. The Chiquet family's 95%-rated vineyards at Dizy, Aÿ, Hautvillers, and Avize account for 40% of their requirements. The "Perfection Brut" is a 70:30 mix of black grapes and Chardonnay, a wine of lovely Welsh-gold colour, the flavour soft and creamy yet long in the mouth. The outstanding vintage blanc de blancs is a pure Avize from the family vineyards. The 100%-wood-fermented "Signature" *prestige cuvées*, both white and rosé, are fascinating Champagnes of multi-layered complexity.

Krug ☆☆☆☆

Reims. www.krug.com. Founded 1843. Owner: Moët Hennessy-Louis Vuitton group (LVMH). 20 hectares. Visits: appt. only. NV: Grande Cuvée, Rosé. Vintage: Clos du Mesnil

The house of Krug sees itself as something apart from other Champagnes, and indeed its wines are quite unlike any other. All are fermented in small oak barrels and then aged on the cork for an uncommonly long time before sale. The "Grande Cuvée" has a high proportion of Chardonnay brilliantly assembled with Pinot Noir and Pinot Meunier into a masterly blend composed of seven up to ten vintages and twenty to twenty-five different growths. It has good claim to be among the finest of all Champagnes, very dry, elusively fruity, gentle yet authoritative at the same time. The Krug Rosé, first introduced in 1983, is another masterpiece of fruit and savour and is intended to accompany the finest culinary creations. The vintage is made in very small quantities and is not generally released until it is nine years old; these wines need long ageing, sometimes fifteen, twenty, even twenty-five years to reach their peak. This is especially true of the single-vineyard vintage "Clos du Mesnil", a pure Chardonnay Champagne, austere when young but with the potential to taste like a Corton Charlemagne with bubbles after a quarter of a century in bottle. The Krugs value the "Clos" because it reflects a remarkable terroir; they do not claim it is always superior to the vintage.

Lanson ☆–☆☆☆

Reims. www.lanson.fr. Founded 1760. Owner: Marne et Champagne. No vineyards. Visits: appt. only. NV: Black Label Brut, Demi-Sec, Rosé. Vintage: Brut and Rosé, Blanc de Blancs. Prestige: Noble Cuvée

Prospects looked bleak in 1991 when Lanson lost all 200 hectares of its magnificent vineyards as part of the terms of sale to the present owners. However, it does have access to 800 hectares belonging to Marne et Champagne. Initial misgivings now seem to have been ill-founded, for Lanson's long-serving *chef de caves*, the meticulous Jean-Paul Gandon, still makes the extremely popular "Black Label" as he has always done; the vivid, tingling style is shaped by a lot of Pinot Noir (50%) in the blend, and the avoidance of any malolactic fermentation, thus increasing the fruity character of the wine. The well-aged rosé is aromatic and fine-drawn: the *demi-sec* less cloying than many. Lanson vintage, dominated by Pinot Noir, is broad-shouldered, deep in flavour. Chardonnay (70%) is the motor of the "Noble Cuvée": floral, supremely elegant, but with a firm, durable structure, making it one of the most long-lived Champagnes.

Laurent-Perrier ☆☆–☆☆☆

Tours-sur-Marne. www.laurent-perrier.co.uk. Founded 1812. Owner: the Nonancourt family. 870 hectares. Associated companies: Salon, Delamotte. Visits: during working hours. NV: Brut, Ultra Brut, Rosé Brut, Demi-Sec. Vintage: Brut. Prestige: Grand Siècle NV and Vintage, Grand Siècle Alexandra Rosé

Laurent-Perrier non-vintage brut is now a consistent Champagne, fresh, racy, with a Chablis-like mineral character. Ultra brut is a dry, sugarless wine, but with no hint of the hair shirt as it is always made from grapes of a ripe year. The hugely successful rosé is made the hard way – by putting the Pinot Noir grape skins in contact with the juice to obtain the right colour, and then ageing the wine for four years. The real triumph of the house, though, is the "Cuvée Grand Siècle". Sumptuous, stylish, and long-maturing, it is a blend of three vintages, though it is occasionally sold with a vintage label. The vineyards, either owned or under long-term contract, are in the best sites of the Montagne de Reims, the Côte des Blancs, and the Marne Valley; the average rating is 96%.

Mercier ☆

Epernay. www.champagnemercier.fr. Founded 1858. Owner: LVMH group. 218 hectares. Visits: at regular hours. NV: Brut, Rosé, Demi-Sec. Vintage: Brut Millésimé

Mercier, like the rest of the Moët group, has the virtue of size, consistency of supply meaning reliability. The grapes come either from the firm's own vineyards, mainly in the Marne Valley, or under contracts with growers going back to 1945. The stress is on dry, brut Champagne in a soft, black grapes style. The rosé brut has a good balance of fruit and acidity; the excellent *demi-sec* is clean and incisive, thanks to the dominant Chardonnay (55%).

Eugène Mercier, the founder, was the pace-setter in bringing Champagne to ordinary French people during the late nineteenth century. For the Universal Exhibition held in Paris in 1889, he built a huge wine barrel; it took a team of twenty-four oxen three weeks to tow the cask to the capital. But his most enduring memorial is the labyrinth of cellars

beneath the crest of the hill on Epernay's Avenue de Champagne – sixteen kilometres (ten miles) long and connected by miniature electric train.

Moët & Chandon ☆☆–☆☆☆☆

Epernay. www.moet.com. Founded 1743. Owner: LVMH group. 630 hectares. Associated companies: Mercier, Ruinart, Domaine Chandon in California, Australia, Spain, Argentina, and Brazil. Visits: during office hours. NV: Brut Impérial, White Star Demi-Sec, Réserve Impériale, Brut Premier Cru, Rosé. Vintage: Brut Impérial and Rosé. Prestige: Dom Pérignon Blanc and Rosé

Moët's various *cuvées* maintain a style that is elegant, light, and easy to appreciate but also rounds out nicely with age. Very wide sources of supply ensure consistency of the huge quantities of Brut Impérial NV. The Brut Premier Cru, launched in 1996, is sourced from better-class grapes, the bottle carrying a back label explaining how the wine is made. The vintage is a true Champenois blend of the three principal grapes, and is always a good representative of the character of each vintage, yet with that supple, creamy style that runs through the whole Moët range.

The Rise of the Cuvée de Prestige

The success of Champagne has always been based on shrewd marketing, ensuring its reputation worldwide as the only suitable wine for any celebration. Individual Champagne houses go to great lengths to establish their own image. Veuve Clicquot sponsors fashionable events in the English season; Krug throws lavish and well-publicized parties instead.

When a Champagne house needs a shot in the arm, one way to supply it is to create a new product. Dom Pérignon was launched by Moët & Chandon for the first time in 1936, although the wine was from the 1921 vintage. Its success has been colossal, though fully justified by the quality of the wine.

Where Moët led, others soon followed. In the 1950s Taittinger created a luxury blanc de blancs, "Comtes de Champagne"; and Laurent-Perrier launched their "Grand Siècle". The 1960s saw the introduction of Perrier-Jouët's "Belle Epoque" in its unmistakable enamelled bottle, and Veuve Clicquot's "Grande Dame". Roederer's ultra-chic "Cristal" was originally created in the 1870s for the Russian court, and can plausibly claim to be the granddaddy of them all.

A *prestige cuvée*, by definition, is associated with luxury and rarity, so the price is high. With rare exceptions, such as Gratien's "Cuvée Paradis", the wines are from a single vintage, begging the

question of whether there is any significant difference between the vintage and the prestige *cuvées*. The answer is usually yes. Some houses will aim for an ultra-rich style. Charles Heidsieck's "Blancs de Millenaires" is in a powerfully toasty style, for example.

Other producers aim for the maximum finesse. This would be true of "Grande Dame" and even of "Dom Pérignon". Veuve Clicquot and Moët work hard to ensure there is a clear stylistic distinction between their excellent vintage Champagnes and their prestige *cuvées*. But even they would admit that in certain exceptional years, such as 1988 and 1990, the difference in quality between the two is fairly narrow, although the stylistic difference remains.

Krug would argue that its basic Champagne is the best possible "multi-vintage" blend and thus a prestige *cuvée* by price and definition. When Krug decided on a new product, they opted for a single-vineyard wine, "Clos du Mesnil". Very few other producers have opted for single-vineyard wines, although Philipponnat's "Clos des Goisses" is a noble exception, and Leclerc-Briant has persevered with this approach. This should not come as any surprise from the outset, the art of Champagne has been based on the art of blending.

Although some of these *cuvées* really are produced in very small quantities, being based on the most severe selection of grapes from the very finest of *grand cru* sites, others, notably "Dom Pérignon", are produced in surprising quantities. These Champagnes are not always as rare as their producers would like us to believe. For the last decade, exports of *prestige cuvées* have been at between five to six per cent of total Champagne exports, with the lion's share going to the USA.

There can be no disputing that many *cuvées de prestige* are exceptional Champagnes. In addition to those mentioned above, one could add "Cuvée Louise" from Pommery, "Grand Cordon" from Mumm, "Cuvée Sir Winston Churchill" from Pol Roger, and "Signature" from Jacquesson. Others, which it is kinder not to name, substitute heavyhandedness and vulgar packaging for real quality.

Exceptional winemaking by Richard Geoffroy, a former medical doctor, means that Dom Pérignon has been as fine as its reputation in such classic recent vintages as '82, '85, '88, and '90, distinctly luxurious yet also discreet and elegant. The Dom Pérignon Rosé – peach-coloured, subtle, *nuancé* – is outstanding. The Moët group owns parcels in ten out of seventeen *grand cru* vineyards. Grapes from these vineyards supply Ruinart (*q.v.*) as well as Moët.

Mumm ☆–☆☆

Reims. www.mumm.com. Founded 1827. Owner: Hicks, Muse, Tate & Furst, since 1999. 300 hectares. Visits: at regular hours. NV: Première Cuvée, Chardonnay Réserve Privée, Rosé Première Cuvée, Cordon Rouge, Cordon Vert (Demi-Sec), Mumm de Cramant. Vintage: Brut and Rosé, Blanc de Blancs. Prestige: René Lalou, Grand Cordon, Grand Cordon Rosé

It is hard to be categoric about the overall quality and style of Mumm Champagnes, as the range is very diverse. The wines made from a preponderance of Pinot Noir are mainly solid and straightforward. Cordon Rouge non-vintage remains bland, lacking a little character. The vintage rosé and lightly sparkling "Mumm de Cramant", made from Chardonnay grapes of a single year from the village of Cramant, are excellent. René Lalou is a very presentable top *cuvée* in a full-bodied, though sometimes austere, style.

The other *prestige* wine, "Grand Cordon", first introduced in the 1985 vintage from 50% Chardonnay, is the star: subtle and racy. Their vineyards have an average *échelle* (*see* box on page 164) of 94%, producing 20% of their needs. They are spread across the region, with the biggest concentrations in Mailly, Ambonnay, Bouzy, Vaudemanges, Avenay, Aÿ, Avize, and Cramant. Annual production is about nine million bottles. Since 1971, Mumm has been a leader of viticultural research in Champagne.

Bruno Paillard ☆☆–☆☆☆

Reims. www.champagnebrunopaillard.com. Founded 1981. Owners: the Paillard family. No vineyards. Visits: appt. only. Associated companies: Boizel, De Venoge. NV: Première Cuvée, Blanc de Blancs Réserve Privée, Rosé Première Cuvée. Vintage: Brut, Ne Plus Ultra

The youngest classic Champagne house, founded in 1981 by the perfectionist Paillard, a broker with deep roots in the industry. His wines are consistent models of elegance and refinement, very dry, almost austere, and built to last. The first-rate "Première Cuvée" is now partially fermented in wood, the "Réserve Privée" made by the old method for *crémant* (lightly sparkling Champagne). Paillard vintage wines are beautifully labelled, illustrated by prominent artists, and always mention the date of disgorging. The wines are as exceptional as the packaging. In 2000, Paillard launched a *prestige* wine called "Ne Plus Ultra", from barrel-fermented *grand cru* grapes, aged eight years before disgorgement. Sales are around 600,000 bottles a year.

Joseph Perrier ☆☆–☆☆☆

Châlons-en-Champagne. www.joseph-perrier.com. Founded 1825. Owner: Alain Thiénot and shareholders, since 1998. 21 hectares. Visits: appt. only. NV: Cuvée Royale, Blanc de Blancs, Cuvée Royale Rosé. Vintage: Cuvée Royale. Prestige: Cuvée Joséphine

The stylish, fruit-laden wines of this family owned Châlons

house go from strength to strength. The "Cuvée Royale" non-vintage is a benchmark of succulent, ripe Pinots (both Noir and Meunier) brilliantly blended with 35% Chardonnay. The Chardonnay-led *prestige* "Cuvée Joséphine" is usually a memorable bottle.

Their vineyards at Cumières, Damery, Hautvillers, and Verneuil supply one-third of the firm's requirements. Sales are around 650,000 bottles a year, with three years' stock for the NV. Vintage wines are not released until they are seven or eight years old.

Perrier-Jouët ☆☆–☆☆☆

Epernay. www.perrier-jouet.com. Founded 1811. Owner: Hicks, Muse, Tate & Furst, since 1999. 60 hectares. Visits: appt. only. NV: Brut. Vintage: Brut, Rosé. Prestige: NV Blason de France Blanc and Rosé, Belle Epoque Blanc and Rosé

Long respected for first-class, very fresh and crisp (but by no means light) non-vintage and luxury *cuvées* with plenty of flavour. "Blason de France", a blend of good vintages, is their rarest wine, complex and age-worthy. The much better-known "Belle Epoque", in its flower-painted bottle, is the flagship of the house: a *prestige cuvée* of consistently rich and harmonious style.

The choice vineyards include superb Chardonnay sites in Cramant and Avize, and Pinot sites in Aÿ. It is these that shape the hazelnut and creamy flavours of the excellent vintage wines. Grapes also come from thirty other *crus*. Sales average 3.3 million bottles from stocks of around ten million. In 1999, Perrier-Jouët, together with its sister house of Mumm, were purchased by an American investment company.

Piper-Heidsieck ☆–☆☆

Reims. www.piper-heidsieck.com. Founded 1785. Owner: Rémy-Cointreau. 70 hectares (shared with Charles-Heidsieck). Visits: open. NV: Brut. Vintage: Brut, Rosé. Prestige: Brut Sauvage, Champagne Rare

These well-regarded, very dry wines have changed a little in style since the firm was bought by Rémy-Cointreau in 1989. Although still very fresh, they now have an extra dimension of floweriness on the nose and fruitiness on the palate. The rosé is an exuberant expression of youthful Pinot Noir, yet it also ages well. "Brut Sauvage", a very dry style with practically no *dosage*, has now been phased out. The

Chardonnay-led "Champagne Rare" is exceptional, with long, citrus-like flavours and the potential to develop in bottle for up to fifteen years.

A medium-sized Grand Marque, sells about five million bottles a year, with eighteen million bottles in stock.

Pol Roger ☆☆☆
Epernay. www.polroger.co.uk. Founded 1849. Owners: Pol Roger family. 200 hectares. Visits: appt. only. NV: White Foil, Sec, Demi-Sec. Vintage: Brut, Brut Chardonnay. Prestige: Sir Winston Churchill, Réserve Spéciale PR

Smallish Grand Marque consistently regarded among the best half-dozen and a personal favourite of mine for over forty years. Outstandingly clean, floral, and crisp NV; stylish, long-lived vintage; one of the best rosés; and fragrant, exquisite Blanc de Chardonnay.

The Pinot-led "Sir Winston Churchill" (in homage to a family friend) is shamelessly sumptuous, exotically scented, and satin-textured. The "Réserve PR" is supremely elegant, being 50% Chardonnay; all the grapes come from 100% *échelle* vineyards. The cellars are said to be the coldest and deepest in the region.

The firm's vineyards are mainly in the Côte des Blancs. Production is about 1.8 million bottles, stock seven million bottles; 60% of sales are on export markets, the largest being Britain, followed by Germany and then Switzerland.

Pommery ☆–☆☆☆
Reims. www.pommery.fr. Founded 1836. Owner: Vranken, since 2002. Visits: at regular hours. NV: Brut Royal, Brut Rosé. Vintage: Brut, Rosé. Prestige: Louise Pommery, Flacons d'Exception

The LVMH group acquired this well-known Grand Marque in 1990, and re-established its tradition for very fine and notably dry Champagnes with the "Brut Royal", an elegant, pure-flavoured wine of low *dosage*. Delicacy and refinement are the hallmark of the vintage wines. "Louise Pommery" (since 1979) has been a revelation of Pommery quality: stylish, crisp, deeply winey, and well-structured.

Since 1996, mature vintage Champagnes in magnums, the "Flacons d'Exception", have been released in tiny quantities to connoisseurs. On receipt of the order, the wine is disgorged and delivered to the recipient's address within one month, for optimal freshness in the finished Champagne. (The 1979 is outstanding.)

In 2002, LVMH sold Pommery to Vranken, a house that is not known for its outstanding quality. Moreover, LVMH

Who Makes Champagne?

In 1970, there were 2,900 growers making their own Champagne. By 1997, that figure had risen, after fluctuations, to 5,100. The proportion of sales represented by grower-producers and cooperatives rose only slightly from twenty-five per cent in 1970 to twenty-eight per cent in 1997. Most of this growth was within France, at first by direct sales and mail order to private customers, more recently to high-quality, fashionable restaurants. The major houses continue to dominate the export trade, although their share is being increasingly challenged by cooperatives, and (to a lesser extent) by grower-producers, whose Champagnes may offer more value for money.

Dosage, Dryness, & Sweetness

When Champagne is disgorged, the loss of the frozen plug of sediment needs making good to fill the bottle. At this stage the sweetness of the finished wine is adjusted by topping up (*dosage*) with a *liqueur d'expédition* of wine mixed with sugar and sometimes brandy. A few firms make a totally dry wine, topped up with wine only, and known by names such as "Brut Natur" or "Brut Intégral". The great majority have some sugar added. The following are the usual amounts (g/l) of sugar in the *dosage* for each style (although they vary from house to house): Extra brut: 0–6g/l bone-dry. Brut: 3–15g/l very dry. *Extra sec*: 12–20g/l dry. *Sec*: 17–35g/l slightly sweet. *Demi-sec*: 33–50g/l distinctly sweet. *Doux*: over 50g/l very sweet.

---

retained the magnificently sited Pommery vineyards, with their average rating of over 99%. Pommery's cellars comprise fourteen kilometres (nine miles) of ancient Roman chalk-pits, some of which are decorated with bas-reliefs. Production: 6.6 million bottles, with stocks of twenty-eight million.

Louis Roederer ☆☆☆–☆☆☆☆
Reims. www.champagne-roederer.com. Founded 1776. Owner: Jean-Claude Rouzaud. 200 hectares. Associated companies: Roederer Estate, California. Ramos Pinto, Portugal. Château de Pez (Bordeaux). Visits: appt. only. NV: Brut Premier, Rich, Demi-Sec, Carte Blanche (sweet). Vintage: Brut, Blanc de Blancs. Prestige: Cristal Brut, Cristal Rosé

A very great family owned Champagne house whose peerless reputation rests on its marvellous vineyards (*échelle* 98%, and supplying 70% of its needs), and scarcely rivalled collection of reserve wines to maintain the highest standards for "Brut Premier". The house style is notably smooth and mature, epitomized by the excellent, full-bodied "Brut Premier" and the fabulous "Cristal", one of the most luscious Champagnes, racy but deeply flavoured. Recent vintages such as '85, '89, and '90 are among the greatest "Cristals" ever released.

The firm's 1980s venture in California sparkling wine at Roederer Estate (*q.v.*) has also been very successful. In the mid-1990s, the company diversified into other winemaking ventures, acquiring both port-producer Ramos Pinto and Château de Pez in St-Estèphe. Stock: a high twelve million bottles – over four years' supply. Up to 1917, half the sales were in Russia, where Czar Alexander III demanded crystal (clear) bottles.

Ruinart ☆☆☆
Reims. www.ruinart.com. Founded 1729 (the oldest recorded Champagne-making firm). Owner: LVMH group. 17 hectares. Visits: appt. only. NV: R de Ruinart Brut and Rosé. Vintage: R de Ruinart Brut Millésimé. Prestige: Dom Ruinart Blanc de Blancs, Dom Ruinart Rosé

Napoléon's Josephine enjoyed Ruinart – but, alas, refused, after her divorce, to honour the bills she ran up as empress. It is extremely stylish among the lighter Champagnes, both in non-vintage and vintage. The luxury "Dom Ruinart" is among the most notable blanc de blancs: uniquely fleshy and rounded owing to the Montagne de Reims Chardonnay grapes in the blend, and on a winning streak in recent vintages ('82, '85, '88, '89, '93). "Dom Ruinart Rosé" is equally outstanding.

The firm owns Chardonnay vines in the Montagne Grands Crus of Sillery and Puisieulx, the grapes reserved for the "Dom Ruinart" *cuvées*. Sales of 2.2 million bottles.

Salon ☆☆☆☆
Le Mesnil-sur-Oger. Founded 1920. Owner: Laurent-Perrier.
1 hectare
This unique house produces only vintage blanc de blancs Champagne from the village of Mesnil. Since 1920, vintages have been declared about three times a decade. Salon pioneered blanc de blancs wines and still leads in quality if not quantity, since production per vintage never exceeds 80,000 bottles. These are subtly rich and very dry wines, hand crafted and comparable in weight and complexity to *grand cru* burgundy. Not for those who like a fresh filly of a wine. Fifteen years is a good age for them. The 1990, Salon's

Champagne: A New Beginning

In the early 1990s, the Champagne industry was stricken by the worst economic crisis since the 1930s. The sharp fall in sales led to a collapse in prices and a swelling of stocks, compounded by bumper crops between 1989 and 1996. All types of Champagne producer – houses, co-ops, growers – were hit hard and huge losses were incurred.

By the end of the 1990s, the worst was over. Catastrophe was avoided by draconian measures, initiated by the Champagne authorities in 1992, to reduce yields in the vineyard and improve procedures for the pressing of the harvest – a critical stage in the making of Champagne. Only two pressings of the grapes (the *cuvée* and the *taille*) are now allowed. A third pressing has been effectively abolished, and rightly so, for with each successive press the quality of the juice diminishes. The wines are now generally aged for longer on the yeasts (three years for a non-vintage from a good house); the result is a leap in quality in the finished wines.

The Percentage System

Each harvest, the price a grower gets for his grapes is determined by a committee made up from the *Comité Interprofessionel du Vin de Champagne*, or CIVC, officials, growers, producers, and a government representative. Until a few years ago, the price was fixed by the CIVC alone, but this is no longer the case.

The CIVC is the official body that controls, promotes, and defends the industry. The vineyards of the region are rated on a percentage scale known as the *échelle des crus* (ladder of growths). Although this *échelle* is geographically based, it is essentially an index of price, graded on the reputed quality of grapes from particular wine villages. The seventeen *grands crus* rate 100% (*see* chart below); *premiers crus* 90–99%; *deuxièmes crus* 80–89%. Like most vineyard classifications, the *échelle's* chief weakness is that it makes no qualitative distinction between individual vineyard sites within the same *cru*. The best cellarmasters do not slavishly follow the rating of grapes when selecting them for use in their Champagne blends.

The leading vineyards, with their percentage ratings, are as follows:

Marne Valley

Avenay	93%	all grapes
Aÿ	100%	black grapes
Bisseuil	95%	black grapes
Champillon	93%	all grapes
Cumières	93%	all grapes
Dizy	95%	all grapes
Hautvillers	93%	all grapes
Mareuil-sur-Aÿ	99%	black grapes
Mutigny	93%	all grapes

Côte d'Ambonnay

Ambonnay	100%	all grapes
Bouzy	100%	all grapes
Louvois	100%	all grapes
Tauxières-Mutry	99%	all grapes
Tours-sur-Marne	100%	black grapes
Tours-sur-Marne	90%	white grapes

Côte d'Epernay

Chouilly	100%	white grapes
Chouilly	95%	black grapes
Grauves	95%	white grapes
Pierry	90%	all grapes

Côte des Blancs

Avize	100%	all grapes
Cramant	100%	all grapes
Cuis	95%	white grapes
Cuis	90%	black grapes
Grauves	90%	all grapes
Le Mesnil-sur-Oger	100%	all grapes
Oger	100%	all grapes
Oiry	100%	all grapes

Côte de Vertus

Bergères-les-Vertus	95%	all grapes
Vertus	95%	all grapes

Montagne de Reims

Beaumont-sur-Vesle	100%	all grapes
Chigny-Les-Roses	94%	all grapes
Ludes	94%	all grapes
Mailly	100%	all grapes
Montbré	94%	white grapes
Puisieulx	100%	all grapes
Rilly-la-Montagne	94%	all grapes
Sillery	100%	all grapes
Trépail	95%	white grapes
Verzenay	100%	all grapes
Verzy	100%	all grapes
Villers-Allerand	90%	all grapes
Villers-Marmery	95%	all grapes

thirty-third vintage release, only came onto the market in 2001. Salon's single hectare of vines only supplies about 15% of its needs, the rest of the grapes are bought in from growers owning *grand cru* Mesnil plots in the village, the same ones since the early twentieth century. Salon only releases around 30,000 bottles per year, yet stock is around 270,000 bottles (nine years' supply), which means it has one of the biggest sales/stock ratios in Champagne.

Taittinger ☆☆–☆☆☆
Reims. www.taittinger.com. Founded 1734 as Forest Forneaux, name changed to Taittinger in 1931. Owner: the Taittinger family. 270 hectares. Visits: appt. only. Associated company: Domaine Carneros. NV: Brut Réserve, Demi-Sec, Prestige Rosé. Vintage: Brut. Prestige: Comtes de Champagne, Comtes de Champagne Rosé

An important force in the Champagne world since 1945, and still family controlled. The style of the brut wines derives from the dominance of Chardonnay in the blend. Extra time in bottle greatly improved the NV in the late 1990s, although the *dosage* can be quite high. "Comtes de Champagne" is one of the most ageworthy, exquisitely luxurious *prestige cuvées*. "Taittinger Collection", a range packaged in designer-created bottles, is essentially the same wine as the vintage, released as a collector's item. Half the vineyards are planted with Chardonnay, and supply around half the house's needs. The main sources of grapes are Avize, Chouilly, Cramant, Mesnil, and Oger. Annual sales are around five million bottles; stock fifteen million bottles.

Alain Thiénot ☆☆–☆☆☆
Reims. www.alain-thienot.fr. Founded 1980. Owner: Alain Thiénot. 14 hectares. Visits: appt. only. Associated wine companies: Champagnes Joseph Perrier and Marie Stuart. Château Rahoul, Graves. Château Ricaud, Loupiac. Annual production: 600,000 bottles. NV: Brut. Vintage: Brut, Rosé. Prestige: Grande Cuvée

Formerly a broker from an old Champenois family, Alain Thiénot is a Champagne merchant to watch. The vineyards are in excellent sites, notably at Aÿ and Le Mesnil-sur-Oger. The house style aims for naturally very dry wines, characteristically and deftly blended from all three principal grape varieties. The NV is fresh and sprightly, yet with a good touch of maturity. The vintage rosé is fine-drawn but firmly structured; the exceptional "Grande Cuvée" allies beautiful, supple fruitiness with considerable complexity.

Veuve Clicquot-Ponsardin ☆☆☆
Reims. www.clicquot.com. Founded 1772. Owner: LVMH group. 286 hectares. Visits: by appointment. Associated wine companies: Cape Mentelle, Cloudy Bay. NV: Yellow Label, Demi-Sec, White Label Rich. Vintage: Gold Label, Rosé, Rich Réserve. Prestige: La Grande Dame, La Grande Dame Rosé

Large, prestigious, and influential house making excellent classic Champagnes in a firm, rich, full-flavoured style. The company's success was founded by "The Widow" Clicquot, who took over the business in 1805 at the age of twenty-seven, when her husband died. She invented the now universal *remuage* system for clarifying the wine, and produced the first rosé Champagne. Since 1928, there have been only four winemakers, the present *chef de caves* being Jacques Peters (since 1985). Notwithstanding its respect for tradition, winemaking is thoroughly modern, no wood has

been used since 1961. The *prestige* "La Grande Dame" is a masterpiece of balanced body and finesse, and since its first release in 1996, "La Grande Dame Rosé" has been lauded as one of the best pink Champagnes. The vineyards are very evenly spread across the classic districts, average *échelle* 97%. Production: eight million bottles; stock forty million bottles.

Other Champagne Producers

Includes grower-Champagne makers, the cooperatives, and merchant houses.

Agrapart ☆☆
Avize. www.champagne-agrapart.com
Blanc de blancs is the house specialty, a wine of raciness and elegance. Fine rosé too.

Ayala ☆–☆☆
Aÿ. www.chateau-ayala.fr
Once highly fashionable, a traditionalist Champagne house making sound medium-bodied wines, which are good value for money. The vintage blanc de blancs is the best wine.

Paul Bara ☆☆–☆☆☆
Bouzy
Leading *récoltant-manipulant* in Bouzy, making ample Pinot-led Champagnes. The "Grand Rosé" is exceptional.

Barancourt ☆☆
Bouzy. www.vranken.fr
Bought by Champagne Vranken (*q.v.*) in 1994, a small house specializing in a densely structured vintage blanc de noirs, and excellent still red Bouzy.

Edmond Barnaut ☆☆
Bouzy. www.champagne-barnaut.com
This grower uses an unusual *solera* method to produce his "Grande Réserve". Rich, winey blanc de noirs too.

Beaumont des Crayères ☆–☆☆
Mardeuil

The Mysteries of the Label

The Champagne industry uses a number of codes on the label to identify the source of the wine:

NM négociant-manipulant A producer who makes Champagne from purchased grapes.
RM récoltant-manipulant A producer who makes Champagne from his own grapes.
CM coopérative-manipulant Cooperative producer.
ND négociant-distributeur A company that sells, but does not produce Champagne.
SR société de récoltants A partnership, usually between family members.
MA marque d'achateur Champagne sold under the name of the seller, usually a supermarket as in a buyer's own brand (BOB).

Little co-op, just west of Epernay, makes good Champagne at reasonable prices. Fresh and fruity; Pinot Meunier dominated.

Boizel ☆☆
Epernay. www.champagne-boizel.fr
Family business founded in 1834, the majority of shares are now owned by Bruno Paillard (*q.v.*) and Chanoine Frères. Well-made, fruity wines; kind prices.

Alexandre Bonnet ☆☆
Les Riceys. www.champagnebonnet.com
Champagne grower and maker of the rare Rosé des Riceys. The family became merchants in 1932, and since 1998, this quality-conscious house has been owned by Bruno Paillard (*q.v.*). The grapes come from their own vineyards around Les Riceys and the Marne's top growths, especially the Côte des Blancs. The vintage "Cuvée Madrigal" can be a sumptuous wine.

Ferdinand Bonnet ☆
Reims
Now owned by Rémy-Cointreau and much expanded by the late 1990s, the firm has ten hectares of excellent Chardonnay on the Côte des Blancs. Stylish vintage blanc de blancs.

Bricout ☆–☆☆
Avize. www.chateau-bricout.com
Small, German-owned Champagne house, making light racy Champagnes. The Chardonnay-led *prestige cuvée* "Arthur Bricout" is by far the best wine.

Canard-Duchêne ☆–☆☆
Ludes. www.canard-duchene.fr
After a rough period during the early 1990s, when the wines did not live up to the firm's Grand Marque standing, things are now reforming here. Improved Pinot-based NV, lively and fresh; and rich *prestige* "Charles VII". Owned by LVMH.

de Castellane ☆
Epernay. www.castellane.com
An old-established house with a grand past, symbolized by its extravagant crenellated tower. Produces a sound, rather light NV and a more substantial vintage "Cuvée Commodore".

Rosé des Riceys

Within the borders of Champagne, lies one of France's most esoteric little appellations, specifically for a Pinot Noir rosé. Les Riceys is in the extreme south of Champagne. Most of its production is Champagne, but in good, ripe vintages the best Pinot Noir grapes, with a minimum natural alcohol of ten degrees, are selected. The floor of an open wooden vat is first covered with grapes trodden by foot. Then the vat is filled with whole unbroken bunches. Fermentation starts at the bottom and the fermenting juice is pumped over the whole grapes. At a skilfully judged moment, the juice is run off, the grapes pressed, and the results "assembled" to make a dark rosé of a unique sunset tint and, as its makers describe it, a flavour of gooseberries. The principal practitioner used to be Alexandre Bonnet (*q.v.*); his sons now continue this tradition. Between 1983 and 1996, the wine was made only five times. Also made by Defrance (*q.v.*).

Delbeck ☆☆
Reims. www.delbeck.com
A fine, small Champagne house that was bought by Bruno Paillard (*q.v.*) in 1994. *Grand cru* Champagnes are produced from different villages such as Aÿ and Bouzy. Fine vintage wines, too.

Jacques Defrance ☆–☆☆
Les Riceys
Another excellent producer of the rare and fine Rosé des Riceys. Full-bodied, Pinot-dominated Champagnes.

Daniel Dumont ☆–☆☆
Rilly-la-Montagne
Excellent Champagnes, especially the well-aged Pinot-dominated "Grande Réserve", and the fine *demi-sec*.

Egly-Ouriet ☆☆–☆☆☆
Ambonnay
From only eight hectares, this excellent little house produces rich, complex, Pinot-dominated Champagnes.

Nicolas Feuillatte ☆–☆☆☆
Chouilly. www.feuillatte.com
This brand is the creation of the eponymous M. Feuillate, a globetrotting promoter, and the Centre Vinicole de la Champagne (CVC), the largest cooperative in the region. Very modern winemaking and "correct" quality, with the occasional exceptional *cuvée*, such as the vintage "Palme d'Or". In 2001, it enterprisingly released bottlings from four different *grand cru* sites. Five million bottles were sold in 2001.

Georges Gardet ☆
Chigny-les-Roses. www.chateau-gardet.com
Rich, well-aged wines made mainly with Pinot Noir grapes from the Montagne de Reims. All the Champagnes are marked with the date of disgorging.

Gatinois ☆☆–☆☆☆
Aÿ
Grower, making concentrated, Pinot Noir-based Champagne from *grand cru* sites and still red Coteaux Champenois in good years. High quality.

René Geoffroy ☆☆
Cumières. www.chateau-geoffroy.com
Growers in the Marne Valley since the sixteenth century, with fine *premier cru* holdings. The best sort of traditional producer, using part-fermentation in wood and late-disgorging of vintage Champagnes. Also an excellent Cumières *rouge*.

Pierre Gimmonet ☆☆–☆☆☆
Cuis
Sizeable growers with enviably fine holdings on the Côte des Blancs, the Gimmonets are excellent winemakers, too: brilliant, bone-dry "Maxi-Brut" and the impressive "Cuvée Gastronome" – all finesse.

Emile Hamm ☆–☆☆
Aÿ
Formerly an Aÿ grower and a merchant house since 1930. Excellent, very dry Champagne.

Heidsieck Monopole ☆–☆☆
Epernay. www.vranken.fr
One of the oldest Champagne houses (founded 1777), this Grande Marque was sold by Mumm to the Vranken group in 1996. Quality of the "Brut Dry Monopole NV" slipped during the early 1990s; but the "Diamant Bleu" is still a real luxury *cuvée*: a powerful character to mature for many years.

Jacquart ☆–☆☆
Reims. www.jacquart-champagne.fr
This cooperative-turned-merchant is owned by Alliance Champagne, controls 850 hectares, and sells ten million bottles a year. The crisp, incisive "Brut Sélection" (mainly Chardonnay) is a bargain. The top range is called "Nominée".

Larmandier-Bernier ☆☆–☆☆☆
Vertus. www.larmandier.com
Excellent Chardonnay sites on the Côte des Blancs and Pierre Larmandier's own talent combine to create some of the most pure-flavoured blanc de blancs. Exceptional Cramant Grand Cru and ultra-dry, *non-dosé* Vertus Premier Cru.

Leclerc-Briant ☆☆
Epernay. www.leclercbriant.com
This firm owns thirty hectares in various communes, and has taken the innovative decision to produce "Les Authentiques": three single-vineyard Champagnes from *premier cru* sites. It is also converting to biodynamic viticulture.

R. & L. Legras ☆☆
Chouilly
Growers since the eighteenth century, and now a fashionable small house, with a niche market among France's Michelin-starred restaurants for its lovely *grand cru* blanc de blancs.

Mailly Grand Cru ☆☆
Mailly. www.chateau-mailly.com
Small and exclusive cooperative, each of its seventy member-growers own *grand cru* vines in Mailly on the Montagne de Reims. Full, muscular Champagnes (with at least 75% Pinot Noir) which need a minimum of four years on the cork to show their paces.

Serge Mathieu ☆☆–☆☆☆
Avirey-Ligney
Top-flight grower of the Aube, making Champagnes which are rich yet super-fine. Superb rosé and remarkably fresh and delicious Coteaux Champenois red.

Champagne & Food

There is no single classic dish for accompanying Champagne, but Champagne makers like to encourage the idea that their wine goes with almost any dish (even game and cheese). Vintage Champagne certainly has the fullness of flavour to go with most food – but many people find sparkling wine indigestible with food. Champagne is the apéritif wine par excellence, but can be marvellously refreshing after a rich meal. Meanwhile, there is the less fizzy *crémant* (meaning half-sparkling), and the non-sparkling Coteaux Champenois, white or red (notably Bouzy *rouge*).

Pierre Moncuit ☆☆–☆☆☆
Le Mesnil-sur-Oger
First-rate blanc de blancs from one of the best villages on the Côte des Blancs.

Philipponnat ☆☆–☆☆☆
Mareuil-sur-Aÿ. www.champagnephilipponnat.com
Small traditionalist house, now part of the Bruno Paillard group (*q.v.*), making well-constituted wines built to last. Especially fine and weighty single-vineyard "Clos des Goisses": a marvel of Pinot Noir concentration, made only in top vintages such as '85, '88, '89, and '90.

Alain Robert ☆–☆☆☆
Le Mesnil-sur-Oger. www.champagne-robert.fr
Outstanding Mesnil grower and perfectionist Champagne-maker. His "Mesnil Sélection", never less than twelve years old, is a great blanc de blancs. Many of his wines are only disgorged on receipt of orders.

Jacques Selosse ☆☆
Avize. www.champagne-selosse.com
Original grower, fermenting all his wines in wood. A rich, yet beautifully balanced range of top-class blanc de blancs includes a bone-dry *extra sec* and the "Cuvée d'Origine" vinified in new oak barrels. Opinions divide on whether these Champagnes are great or merely weird.

Tarlant ☆☆
Oeuilly. www.tarlant.com
Top-flight grower who ferments each individual vineyard's wine separately in wood to give best expression to their respective soils. The Krug-like "Cuvée Louis" is outstanding.

Union Champagne ☆☆
Avize
The leader in quality of all the Champagne cooperatives, its member growers owning magnificent Chardonnay plots on the Côte des Blancs. The principal brand is "De Saint-Gall". The *prestige* "Cuvée Orpale" is among the best blanc de blancs.

de Venoge ☆–☆☆
Epernay. www.champagnedevenoge.com
Now controlled by the Bruno Paillard group (*q.v.*), sizeable house making pleasant, soft, and supple Champagnes. Very good vintage blanc de blancs. Quality can be inconsistent.

Vilmart ☆☆
Rilly-la-Montagne. www.champagnevilmart.fr
Tiny firm making very high-quality wines fermented in wood and aged for a long time in bottle. Vilmart uses minimal herbicides and no fertilizers in its vineyards.

Vrancken ☆
Epernay. www.vranken.fr
"Demoiselle" is the leading brand of this Champagne group, which was created in 1976 by Paul-François Vranken, a Belgian marketing man. Light, Chardonnay-dominant wines of fair quality. "Veuve Monnier" and "Charles Lafitte" are other labels. The group gained control of Barancourt in 1994, Heidsieck Monopole in 1996, and Pommery in 2002 (*qq.v.*).

Alsace

After all the regions of France whose appellation systems seem to have been devised by medieval theologians, Alsace is a simple fairy tale. A single appellation, Alsace, takes care of the whole region. Alsace Grand Cru is for chosen sites.

Nor are there Germanic complications of degrees of ripeness to worry about. Alsace labelling is as simple as Californian: maker's name and grape variety are the nub. The difference is that in Alsace a host of strictly enforced laws means that there are no surprises. Varietal wines must be made purely from the variety identified on the label. The wines are correspondingly predictable and reliable. Their makers would like them to be considered more glamorous. In order to have their wines named among the "greats", they place increasing emphasis on late picking, on wines from *grand cru* and selected sites. What matters more to most drinkers is that Alsace guarantees a certain quality and a style more surely than almost any wine region. It makes brilliantly appetizing, clean-cut, and aromatic wine to go with food, and at a reasonable price.

The region is 113 kilometres long by two or three kilometres wide (seventy miles long by one or two miles wide). It forms the eastern flank of the Vosges Mountains in the *départements* of the Haut-Rhin and the Bas-Rhin where the foothills, between 180 and about 360 metres (600–1,200 feet), provide well-drained southeast and south-facing slopes under the protection of the peaks and forests of the mountains. The whole region is in their rain-shadow, which gives it some of France's lowest rainfall and most sustained sunshine.

On the principle that watersheds are natural boundaries, Alsace should be in Germany. It has been, but even since the Rhine became the frontier, it has been French. Its language and architecture remain Germanic. Its grape varieties are Germanic, too – but handled in the French manner they produce a different drink. What is the difference? The vineyards across the river in Germany can produce similar wines from similar varieties, but in general they have a different structure.

The Baden Rieslings are racy rather than rich, the Pinot Gris is often smothered in oak rather than allowed to express its glorious, musky spiciness without the distraction of wood. German Pinot Blanc is often aged in barrels, too. In contrast, many of the best Alsace wines are still fermented in oak. The barrels are antiques, thickly lined with tartrate crystals that prevent any flavours of wood or oxidation. Thus the aromatic (or otherwise) character of its grapes stands out cleanly and clearly.

Alsace wines are bottled as soon as possible in the spring (or latest in the autumn) after the vintage. Most are drunk young – which is a pity. Bottle ageing introduces the elements of complexity, which are otherwise lacking. A good Riesling or Gewurztraminer (no umlaut used in Alsace) or Pinot Gris is worth keeping at least four years in bottle and often up to ten. This is especially true of the sweeter wines that are being produced in ever larger quantities (*see page 169*). Sweet wines fetch higher prices, but they are no substitute for the combination of full and crisp flavours, which the region's best dry wines can deliver.

The centre of the finest area in Alsace lies in the Haut-Rhin, in the group of villages north and south of Colmar, with Riquewihr, an extravagantly half-timbered and flower-decked little town, as its natural wine capital: a sort of St-Emilion of the Vosges.

The climate is warmest and driest in the south, but scarcely different enough to justify the popular inference that Haut-Rhin is parallel to, let us say, Haut-Médoc. There is no suggestion of lower quality in the name Bas-Rhin; it is simply lower down the River Rhine. Even farther down, going directly north, are the German Palatinate vineyards. These produce the richest and some of the greatest of all the German Rieslings.

More important are the individual vineyard sites with the best soils and microclimates. Thirty or forty Vosges hillsides have individual reputations, which in Burgundy would long ago have been enshrined in law, but in Alsace only became so in 1983.

After hovering on the brink of listing certain vineyards as *grands crus* for many years, by the mid-1970s many growers felt that the time had come to make a proper classification of the great slopes of Alsace. A list of ninety-four *lieux-dits*, or possible sites, was drawn up, and from these, the first twenty-five received full *grand cru* status in 1983, followed by a further twenty-three in 1985, and finally two more in 1988. This total of fifty will probably not be exceeded for sometime. The *grands crus* represent a rather generous twelve per cent of the total vineyard area of Alsace.

A few of the *grand cru* names are well-established on labels. Schoenenbourg at Riquewihr is particularly noted for its Riesling; Kaysersberg's Schlossberg, Guebwiller's Kitterlé, Turckheim's Eichberg and Brand, and Thann's Rangen are other examples. Ownership of these vineyards is noted in the following list of producers.

Grand cru wines must come from specifically delimited slopes and may only be single ("noble") variety wines of Riesling, Gewurztraminer, Pinot Gris, Muscat, and (since 2001) Sylvaner. They have a lower permitted yield and a higher minimum alcoholic strength than other Alsace wines. Since 2001, proprietors within any *grand cru* have the right to set their own tougher rules and regulations than the basic AC requirements. Growers say that the *grand cru* legislation gives them the chance to demonstrate the terroir character of their best wines, but not all the great houses agree with this, and some (Trimbach, Beyer, Hugel) choose not to use *grand cru* names on their labels.

Another great success story in Alsace has been the remarkable growth in popularity of Crémant d'Alsace, produced since the turn of the century, but that is only recently seeing some success. *Crémant* is a *méthode traditionnelle* sparkling wine that may come from any Alsace grape – although in practice Muscat and Gewurztraminer are found to be too aromatic. Pinot Blanc is the most used, and some Chardonnay may also be added (although not permitted for the still wines).

Crémant rosé is 100 per cent Pinot Noir. The last ten years have also seen red wines re-emerging. They mean more, perversely, to Alsace growers and consumers than perhaps they do to outsiders who have the world's reds to choose from. Pinot Noir is the grape of choice.

In the past, it has been a struggle to find colour and substance in it here, but careful selection of Pinot Noir clones combined with careful colour and flavour extraction are making fuller, more characterful reds. On occasion, indeed, something akin to fine Burgundy.

Growers & Cooperatives

The vineyards of Alsace are even more fragmented in ownership than those of the rest of France. With 6,100 growers sharing the total of 14,400 hectares, the average individual holding is just over two hectares. (Although in truth, eighty-five per cent of the vineyard area is accounted for by just 2,000 of the growers.)

The chances of history established a score or more leading families with larger estates – still rarely as much as forty hectares. With what seems like improbable regularity, they trace their roots back to the seventeenth century, when the Thirty Years War tore the province apart. In the restructuring of the industry after the two World Wars last century, these families have grouped smaller growers around them in a peculiar pattern consisting of their own domaine plus a winemaking and merchanting business. They contract to buy the small growers' grapes and make their wine – very often using their own domaine wines as their top-quality range.

The small grower's alternative to a contract with a grower-négociant (or just a négociant) is to join the local cooperative. Alsace established the first group in France, at

Vendange Tardive

Late picking, Vendange Tardive, is the means by which Alsace growers are scaling the heights of prestige, which Burgundy and Bordeaux have so far monopolized. A hot summer and autumn (1989, 1990, 1994, and 1998 are the latest famous examples) provide such high sugar readings in the grapes that fermentation can stop with considerable natural sweetness still remaining. The wines reach an alcohol level usually greater than that of a German Auslese. The resulting combination of strength, sweetness, and concentrated, fruity flavour is still peculiar to Alsace. The Hugels of Riquewihr were instrumental in creating what has become the Vendange Tardive legislation. Very ripe grapes with a high sugar concentration, usually sweetened by noble rot, produce wines of enormous power, which are classified as Sélection de Grains Nobles (SGN).

In 2001, the rules were tightened, and the minimum potential alcohol for each grape variety was increased. For Vendange Tardive, Muscat and Riesling must be picked at a potential alcohol of at least 14% (up from 13.1%), Pinot Gris and Gewurztraminer at 15.3% (up from 14.4%). For SGN, Muscat and Riesling must be picked at a minimum of 16.4%, Pinot Gris and Gewurztraminer at 18.2% plus.

Such changes were long overdue. With crop-thinning and the phenomenon of global warming, it was not difficult for growers to attain high must weights. In short, far too much Vendange Tardive and even SGN was being produced. The best growers always exceeded the legal requirements and focused on quality; but some merchant houses and cooperatives simply obeyed the letter of the law and produced wines that fell far short of the standards originally set by the Hugels and others.

So the wines are likely to become richer and sweeter , and there will be a greater contrast between a *grand cru* Pinot Gris and a Pinot Gris Vendange Tardive of the future. It will be a pity if growers carry their passion for late harvesting to the point where their dry wines become second best.

the turn of the century, and it now has one of the strongest wine cooperative movements in the world. Their standards can be extremely high, and they often provide the best bargains in the region.

Leading Alsace Producers

Lucien Albrecht ☆☆
Orschwihr. 30 hectares. www.lucien-albrecht.fr
Jean Albrecht is the most important proprietor in *grand cru* Pfingstberg, from which he produces impressive Riesling, Pinot Gris, and Gewurztraminer. The more basic wines are fine and fruity, and always good value.

Jean Becker ☆–☆☆
Zellenberg. 18 hectares
The Beckers have been growers and merchants at Riquewihr since 1618. One quarter of their vineyards are *grand cru* (Froehn at Zellenberg and Sonnenglanz at Beblenheim), with other vineyards in Riquewihr, Ribeauvillé, and Hunnawihr.

Riesling is the major variety, and there is also some unusual Vendange Tardive and SGN Muscat. The Beckers seem to have a knack for excellent Gewurztraminer.

Léon Beyer ☆☆–☆☆☆
Eguisheim. 21 hectares
A family firm founded in 1867, although the Beyers have been making wine in Alsace since 1580. Their vines are all in Eguisheim. Beyer's best wines are full-bodied, powerful, and dry, clearly designed to go with food and often seen in top restaurants in France. Their finest wines are bottled under the "Cuvée des Comtes d'Eguisheim" label, and age extremely well.

Domaine Paul Blanck & Fils ☆☆☆
Kientzheim. 36 hectares. www.blanck.com
Top-quality estate founded in 1922. The holdings include part of the Kientzheim Grands Crus, Schlossberg and Furstentum – the Blancks have been registered Schlossberg owners since 1620 – and *grand cru* Mambourg.

The estate is close to organic, and all grapes are hand-picked. Fermentation is in stainless steel and temperature-controlled, with splendid results. Furstentum tends to give the richest wines, and many of the wines from here contain some residual sugar. Schlossberg, in contrast, has a more mineral character, and tastes (and usually is) drier. All Blanck wines are beautifully made at all levels, and the Pinot Noir from Furstentum is one of Alsace's best.

Bott-Geyl ☆☆
Beblenheim. 13 hectares
This essentially organic estate is run by Jean-Christophe Bott, and produces a good range of rich, ultra-ripe, spicy, though occasionally flabby wines from all the principal varieties. The *grand cru* sites here are Furstentum and Sonnenglanz, which deliver very exotic Pinot Gris.

Ernest Burn ☆☆–☆☆☆
Gueberschwihr. 10 hectares
Francis and Joseph Burn run this fine estate. Half the vineyards are in Clos St Imer with *grand cru* Goldert; it has

been in the family since 1934. The Pinot Gris can be remarkable: plenty of spice and honey, but never blowzy, and Muscat from the *clos* can be unusually elegant.

Domaine Marcel Deiss ☆☆–☆☆☆☆
Bergheim. 20 hectares
The Deiss family have been vignerons in Alsace since 1744, and founded the present domaine in 1949. Its best sites include 2.5 hectares of *grand cru* Altenberg de Bergheim and just under one hectare of *grand cru* Schoenenbourg.

Jean-Michel Deiss is determined that his wines should above all reflect their terroir, and the estate is run on biodynamic principles. Deiss insists that terroir is more important than mere varietal character, so his top wines are in fact blends. Low yields and late harvesting means, however, that many of his wines are distinctly sweet – too much so for some tasters.

Dirler ☆–☆☆☆
Guebwiller. 12 hectares
Together with Schlumberger (*q.v.*), one of the best estates (biodynamic since 1998) of southern Alsace, with holdings in *grand cru* Saering, Spiegel, Kitterlé, and Kessler. Jean Dirler makes varietal wines from all of them, so it is possible to compare their different characters. These are very serious wines, essentially dry and with plenty of fire and extract. With such a wide range of wines, there are misses as well as hits. The Muscat is a hit, the barrique-fermented white Pinot Noir a miss.

Dopff au Moulin ☆☆
Riquewihr. 76 hectares. www.dopff-au-moulin.fr
A family firm of seventeenth century origins, with the largest vineyard holdings of central Alsace, principally in the Schoenenbourg at Riquewihr for Riesling, and Eichberg at Turckheim for Gewurztraminer, with Pinot Blanc grown near Colmar specifically for Crémant d'Alsace, which Dopff pioneered in 1900.

Crémant is an increasing part of their business, which is known for delicate and individual wines. Wines from purchased grapes are bottled with a diamond-shaped label. The best still wines, without any doubt, are the *grands crus*, especially the Riesling from Schoenenbourg. Quality was mediocre until the late 1990s, when the arrival of a new winemaker rejuvenated the house.

Dopff & Irion ☆–☆☆
Riquewihr. 27 hectares. www.dopff-irion.com
One of the biggest grower/merchants of Alsace, buying regularly from 300 growers with 200 hectares between them. The Dopff and Irion families, whose forebears have made wine at Riquewihr for three centuries, combined in 1945; they also own the vineyards of Château Isenbourg at Rouffach.

The firm is best-known for its Riesling "Les Murailles" (from Schoenenbourg), Gewurztraminer "Les Sorcières", the very attractive Muscat "Les Amandiers", and Pinot Gris "Les Maquisards". Quality was middling for many years, but today the firm practises a greater selection, and lesser wines are sold under a different label.

Hugel & Fils ☆–☆☆☆
Riquewihr. 126 hectares. www.hugel.net

The best-known Alsace label in the Anglo-Saxon world. A combination of grower and grape négociant, in the family since 1639, with vineyards in Riquewihr producing their top wines, mostly from *grands crus* Schoenenbourg and Sporen. The Hugels, however, do not label any of their wines as *grands crus*. The house style is full, round, and supple, fermented dry but less apparently so than some. The Hugels pioneered late-harvested wines, which first won international acclaim in 1976.

The quality ladder for Riesling, Gewurztraminer, etc., goes Regular, Tradition, Jubilée, Vendange Tardive, and in certain years SGN. For blended wines made from purchased grapes, Hugel use registered names such as "Fleur d'Alsace" and "Gentil d'Alsace", which is a revival of the traditional "Edelzwicker" blend using quality grapes. The firm produces about 100,000 cases a year.

Josmeyer ☆☆–☆☆☆
Wintzenheim. 32 hectares. www.josmeyer.com

Grower and négociant since 1854, with vineyards at Wintzenheim and Turkheim (including *grand cru* Hengst and Brand). The full flavoured Gewurztraminers and vigorous Rieslings are particularly successful, but this house is most noted for its wide range of grapes, including Chasselas and Pinot Blanc, the latter unchaptalized to produce a light, refreshing wine. Since 2001, most of the estate has been cultivated biodynamically.

André Kientzler ☆☆–☆☆☆
Ribeauvillé. 11 hectares

Almost half the vineyards lie within the *grands crus* of Geisberg, Osterberg, and Kirchberg. Osterberg gives the driest, most pungent Rieslings; those from Geisberg are richer. Auxerrois and Chasselas from this domaine are among the best in Alsace, and the Pinot Gris is of high quality, too.

Marc Kreydenweiss ☆☆–☆☆☆
Andlau. 13 hectares

From holdings in the *grands crus* Wiebelsberg, Kastelberg, and Moenchberg, Kreydenweiss produces beautifully made, concentrated wines. The Rieslings from old vines in the steep Kastelberg site are made to last.

Fermentation is temperature-controlled, and the wines stay on their lees until shortly before bottling. Unusually, the domaine produces a late-picked Pinot Blanc, offered under the vineyard name "Kritt", linked with the old Alsatian name for Pinot Blanc: Klevner.

There is also a blend, "Clos du Val d'Eleons", from 70% Riesling and 30% Pinot Gris. In the 1980s, the wines were very austere, but since Kreydenweiss adopted biodynamic viticulture in 1989, they have gained in weight, in part because some of them go through malolactic fermentation.

Kuentz-Bas ☆–☆☆☆
Husseren-les-Châteaux. 17 hectares. www.kuentz-bas.fr

A family firm of growers and négociants, with vineyards in Husseren, Eguisheim, and Obermorschwihr. There are holdings in the *grands crus* Eichberg and Pfersigberg at Eguisheim. The house was founded in 1795 by Joseph Kuentz and became Kuentz-Bas in 1919.

These are firm, dry wines, well-balanced and elegant. The wines have excellent acidity, and the Vendange Tardive wines are superb. At Kuentz-Bas, the Vendange Tardive wines are labelled "Cuvée Caroline", the SGNs "Cuvée Jeremy". "Collection Rare" bottlings come from old vines and special parcels that are not *grand cru*.

Seppi Landmann ☆☆
Soultzmatt. 8 hectares. www.seppi-landmann.fr

The pride and joy of this small estate are the parcels in *grand cru* Zinnkoepflé, which has limestone soils and gives wines that age very well. Landmann is one of the rare specialists in the underrated Sylvaner, producing the variety in all conceivable styles, whether legally sanctioned or not.

Gustave Lorentz ☆☆
Bergheim. 30 hectares. www.vins-lorentz.com

Venerable family firm of growers and négociants. Their top vineyards are in *grands crus* Altenberg and Kanzlerberg at Bergheim – other grapes are bought in from nearby. "Cuvée Particulière" on the label denotes wines from their own vineyards.

Gewurztraminer and Riesling are the specialties. The house style is to produce wines with a fine and delicate nose that are quite round and rich on the palate, with relatively high acidity. The best thus have good ageing potential. Given that the firm produces almost two million bottles per year, quality is surprisingly high.

Albert Mann ☆–☆☆☆
Wettolsheim. 19 hectares

Maurice and Jacky Barthelmé run this fine property, with *grand cru* vineyards in Furstentum, Schlossberg, and Altenberg. They excel with lush, ultra-ripe Vendange Tardive and SGN from Gewurztraminer and Pinot Gris, and sometimes from Riesling.

Meyer-Fonné ☆☆
Katzenthal. 10 hectares

Riesling and Gewurztraminer are usually the best wines that are produced at this steadily improving estate. The most basic bottlings are excellent value, but the *grands crus* have far more personality.

Muré ☆☆–☆☆☆
Rouffach. 21 hectares. www.mure.com

A family of growers now in its eleventh generation. The heart of this organic domaine is the monastic Clos St-Landelin, a fifteen-hectare parcel within *grand cru* Vorbourg, which the Murés bought in 1935. The *clos* has warm, stony, and limey soil and notably low rainfall, and yields are kept very low. Its wines are full in character and round in style, intended as *vins de garde*.

The Pinot Noir and Muscat are some of the deepest and fullest in Alsace; the Riesling and Gewurztraminer are extremely rich, even a touch broad. Like Jean-Michel Deiss (*see* Domaine Marcel Deiss), René Muré believes terroir matters more than grape variety, so since 1998 the domaine has developed a blended wine from the *clos*. Wines made from purchased grapes are bottled under the "Côte de Rouffach" label.

Domaine Ostertag ☆☆
Epfig. 12 hectares

Alsace Grapes

Area of grapes occupied is expressed as a percentage of the total Alsatian vineyard.

Auxerrois This is a member of the Pinot family, but its precise identity is unknown. Wines from Auxerrois are richer and broader than its cousin Pinot Blanc. The area planted with Auxerrois in Alsace is not specified in official statistics.

Chasselas (1.0%) (In Germany Gutedel, in Switzerland Fendant.) Formerly one of the commonest grapes, rarely if ever named on a label, but used for its mildness in everyday blends, including the so-called "noble" Edelzwicker.

Clevner or **Klevner** A local name for the Pinot Blanc (*q.v.*).

Gewurztraminer (17.6%) Much the most easily recognized of all one-wine grapes, whose special spicy aroma and bite epitomize Alsace wine. Most Alsace Gewurztraminer is made essentially dry but intensely fruity, even to the point of slight fierceness when young. With age, remarkable scents of rose petals and citrus fruit often suggesting grapefruit and lychees, intensify. Gewurztraminer of a fine vintage, whether made dry or in the sweet, Vendange Tardive style, is worth maturing almost as long as Riesling. The fault of a poor Gewurztraminer is softness and lack of definition, or alternatively a heady heaviness without elegance. In a range of Alsace wines, Gewurztraminer should be served last, after Rieslings and Pinots.

Pinot Blanc (21.1%) An increasingly popular grape, giving the lightest of the "noble" wines; simply fresh and appetizing without great complexity. Now seen as Alsace's answer to Chardonnay. This is the base wine for most Crémant d'Alsace.

Pinot Gris, formerly Tokay d'Alsace (10%) After Riesling and Gewurztraminer, the third potentially great wine grape of the region. First-class Pinot Gris has a dense, stiff, intriguing smell and taste – the very opposite of the fresh and fruity Pinot Blanc.

It is almost frustrating to taste, as though it were concealing a secret flavour you will never quite identify. Pinots Gris mature magnificently into broad, rich, deep-bosomed wines whose only fault is that they are not refreshing. The name "Tokay" has been reclaimed by Hungary for its noble wine.

Pinot Noir (8.7%) A grape that is made into both red and rosé in Alsace, but it is sometimes necessary to read the label to know which is which. The must is often heated to extract colour, but the result in the past has been rarely more than a light wine, without the classic Pinot flavour found in, for example, Bouzy Rouge from Champagne. Fuller-bodied examples are emerging, including some extracted wines aged in barriques.

Riesling (23.3%) The finest wine grape of Alsace, as it is of Germany, but here interpreted in a totally different way. Alsace Rieslings are fully ripened and usually fully fermented, their sugar all turned to alcohol, which gives them a firmer structure than German wines. Dryness and the intensity of their fruit flavour make them seem rather harsh to some people. In fact, they range from light refreshment in certain years to some of the most aromatic, authoritative, and longest-lasting of all white wines. In recent years there has been a regrettable tendency to leave residual sugar in Riesling, but top producers such as Trimbach and Beyer are resisting the trend fiercely.

Muscat (2.3%) Until recently, Alsace was the only wine region to make Muscat grapes into dry wine. The aroma is still hothouse sweet, but the flavour is crisp and very clean, sometimes with a hint of nut kernels. It is light enough to make an excellent apéritif.

Sylvaner (14.2%) Steadily being pushed out by Pinot Noir and Pinot Blanc, but at its best (at Mittelbergheim, for example) a classy, slightly "*pétillant*", faintly vegetal but flavoursome wine, which ages well.

Biodynamic estate with a two-hectare holding in the Muenchberg Grand Cru vineyard (Riesling and Pinot Gris). The peculiarity of the estate is that some of its Pinot Blanc and Gris are aged in barriques (some of them new), in defiance of usual Alsatian practice. The results, not surprisingly, have proved controversial, but André Ostertag courageously sticks to his guns. Other specialties are Sylvaner *vieilles vignes* and Riesling from Muenchberg.

Rolly Gassmann ☆
Rorschwihr. 33 hectares
Founded in 1676, this estate is mainly in Rorschwihr and partly in Bergheim and Rodern. Gassmann specializes in Muscat and Auxerrois, the latter growing particularly well in the *lieu-dit* Moenchreben. Balanced wines, rounded with residual sugar, sometimes excessively so.

Domaines Schlumberger ☆–☆☆☆
Guebwiller. 140 hectares
The biggest domaine in Alsace, family owned, with vineyards at Guebwiller and Rouffach at the southern end of the region. Half of the estate is of *grand cru* vineyards: Kitterlé, Saering, and Kessler. Guebwiller's warm climate, sandy soil, and sheltered sites, allied with old-style methods, relatively small crops and ageing in wood, make Schlumberger wines some of the richest and roundest of Alsace, with sweet and earthy flavours of their own.

The best are from the Kitterlé vineyard and repay several years' bottle-ageing. The Vendange Tardive and SGN bottlings are named "Anne", "Christine", and "Clarice" after various family members, and are among the most refined examples of these styles in Alsace.

Schoffit ☆☆–☆☆☆
Colmar. 16 hectares
Bernard Schoffit's most important site is the Clos St Théobald, within *grand cru* Rangen at Thann. The wines are rich and silky, and because of the high ripeness levels of the most favoured sites, they sometimes contain residual sugar. Outstanding Riesling from Rangen, and spicy, concentrated Pinot Gris, with exceptional length.

Bruno Sorg ☆☆–☆☆☆
Eguisheim. 10 hectares
François Sorg is an exemplary grower, striving to achieve a balance between optimal ripeness and sensible alcohol levels. The basic wines, such as Sylvaner and Muscat, are great but, predictably, the most noble wines are the Rieslings and Pinot Gris from *grands crus* Florimont and Pfersigberg.

Pierre Sparr ☆–☆☆
Sigolsheim. 32 hectares
A family firm of growers and merchants, dating back to the

seventeenth century. Their own vines are in six communes between Turckheim and Bennwihr, including *grands crus* Schlossberg and Altenberg, *grand cru* Brand at Turckheim, and *grand cru* Mambourg at Sigolsheim. These are the company's top wines.

The basic range is called "Carte d'Or"; the next step up is "Réserve". The house style is to leave some residual sugar and produce rounded, supple wines. Specialties are the Kaefferkopff blend (75% Gewurztraminer and 25% Pinot Gris), Klevner de Heiligenstein, and the *crémants*.

Marc Tempé ☆–☆☆
Zellenberg. 8 hectares

The first vintage here was 1995, and the estate became biodynamic the following year. All the wines are vinified in casks, and most of them stay on the lees without racking for up to two years. Tempé, a former technician with INAO, has become a fashionable source, but the wines can be erratic.

F. E. Trimbach ☆☆☆–☆☆☆☆
Ribeauvillé. 25 hectares. www.maison-trimbach.fr

A historic (1626) family domaine and négociant house, with the highest reputation for particularly fine and racy dry wines. Their special pride is the Hunawihr Riesling "Clos Ste-Hune", indisputably the finest Riesling produced in Alsace. Sadly, they produce no more than 7,000 bottles.

A fascinating tasting of old vintages showed it at its best after about seven years. Each variety is made in the recently modernized cellar at three quality levels: standard (vintage), *réserve*, and *réserve personnelle*, the latter always coming from their own vineyards. The glorious Riesling "Cuvée Frédéric Emile" is sourced from *grands crus* Osterberg and Eichberg, though Trimbach doesn't use the term *grand cru* on the label. Gewurztraminer "Cuvée des Seigneurs de Ribeaupierre" is at the same quality level.

Domaine Weinbach ☆☆☆–☆☆☆☆
Kaysersberg. 23 hectares. www.domaineweinbach.com

A distinguished domaine of former monastic land, the Clos des Capucins was founded in 1898. Now run by the widow and daughters of the late Théo Faller, who is buried among his vines. Laurence Faller is in charge of the winemaking, Catherine the marketing.

Alsace Appellations

One of the "noble" grape names, or the term "Edelzwicker", meaning a blend of grapes, is usually the most prominent word on Alsace labels – although with the trend towards quality, "Edelzwicker" now appears less in favour of the noble names.

Appellation Alsace (including Crémant d'Alsace)

Wine from any permitted grape variety, with a maximum crop of eighty hectolitres per hectare.

Appellation Alsace Grand Cru

Wine from one of the "noble" grape varieties (Riesling, Gewurztraminer, Pinot Gris, or Muscat), growing in a designated *grand cru* site, with a maximum crop of fifty-five hectolitres per hectare (but with a PLC allowing a maximum of sixty-six!) and a minimum natural potential alcohol degree of 10 for Riesling and Muscat, 12 for Gewurztraminer and Pinot Gris (Tokay).

The family policy is to harvest as late as possible and use full maturity to give the wines maximum character, structure, length on the palate, and the potential to age. Ten years is not too much for the Rieslings. "Réserve Particulière" is the standard label for Riesling and Gewurztraminer, with various *cuvées* named after family members to single out special pickings or styles.

Riesling from *grand cru* Schlossberg is often seen as the epitome of elegance. Not content with Vendange Tardive and SGN in suitable vintages, the domaine, since 1989, has also produced a super-SGN called "Quintessence", which is quite literally picked berry by berry.

Alsace Willm ☆–☆☆
Barr. 15 hectares. www.alsace-willm.com

A very traditional firm, best-known for its seven hectares of Gewurztraminer, Clos Gaensbroennel, and its Riesling in the Kirchberg. The Gewurztraminer is well ripened and fermented completely dry, making it a firm and impressive *vin de garde*. Its delicate Riesling and very clean, fresh "Gentil" (Sylvaner and Gewurztraminer from Gaensbroennel) are both very attractive.

Domaine Zind-Humbrecht ☆☆☆☆
Turckheim. 40 hectares

The domaines of the Humbrechts of Gueberschwihr (since 1620) and the Zinds of Wintzenheim united in 1959, and are now run by Léonard and Olivier Humbrecht (one of the very few Masters of Wine). Léonard made wonderful Rieslings in his own right, but son Olivier has effectively been in charge since the early 1990s.

He is a fanatic for the individuality of each vineyard. He makes highly individual wines from four *grand cru* vineyards: Brand at Turckheim (opulent, sometimes exotic Riesling), Goldert at Gueberschwihr (full-bodied Gewurztraminer), Hengst at Wintzenheim (more full-bodied *vin de garde*), and Rangen at Thann, where his four-hectare Clos St-Urbain gives magnificent Rieslings.

Thirty wines are made in order to capture the very best aspects of terroir, all from specific *lieux-dits* such as Clos Windsbuhl and Clos Jebsal. Humbrecht insists on optimal ripeness and natural fermentation in large casks. Consequently some of the wines have residual sugar, but often there is so much power and extract that the sweetness is not detectable.

Alsace Cooperatives

Cleebourg ☆☆
Cleebourg. www.cave-cleebourg.com. Founded in 1946. 180 members with 180 hectares. 133,000 cases

This cooperative specializes in Pinots, especially Auxerrois. There are two *crémants*, one 100% Auxerrois and one 100% Pinot Gris.

Eguisheim ☆
Eguisheim. www.wolfberger.com. Founded 1902. 470 members with 670 hectares, including 51 Grand Cru. 1,250,000 cases

Specialties are varietals called "Armorie", sold in brown bottles embossed with a tiara as a reminder that Pope St-Léon

IX was born in Eguisheim. All sold with the brand name "Wolfberger". By far the biggest Alsace producer.

Hunawihr ☆–☆☆

Hunawihr. www.cave-hunawihr.com. Founded 1954. 130 members with 200 hectares, including 10 hectares Grand Cru. 175,000 cases

Specialties: Riesling and Gewurztraminer from *lieu-dit* Muehlforst, of which they are particularly proud. Also *crémant* called "Calixte".

Kientzheim-Kaysersberg ☆–☆☆

Kientzheim. www.vinsalsace-kaysersberg.com. Founded 1955. Generally reliable cellar for 150 members with 180 hectares, including 20 hectares Grand Cru. 140,000 cases

Specialties include *crémant*, Riesling Kaefferkopf, Gewurztraminer Altenberg, and Riesling Schlossberg.

Pfaffenheim ☆☆

Pfaffenheim. www.pfaffenheim.com. Founded 1957. 200 members with 235 hectares. 180,000 cases

Specialties include Pinot Noir, Pinot Gris "Cuvée Rabelais", Chasselas "Cuvée Lafayette", and a Gewurztraminer from the *grand cru* Goldert. Dry wines with reasonable concentration.

Ribeauvillé ☆–☆☆

Ribeauvillé. www.cave-ribeauville.com. Founded 1895. 40 members with a total of 262 hectares. 240,000 cases

The oldest growers' cooperative in France, making thirteen different *grands crus*. Specialties are "Le Clos du Zahnacker", (blending Riesling, Gewurztraminer, and Pinot Gris in equal proportions), and Rieslings from Altenberg and Osterberg.

Turckheim ☆☆

Turckheim. www.cave-turckheim.com. Founded 1955. 300 members with 310 hectares, including 18 Grand Cru. 280,000 cases

Specialties are Gewurztraminer "Baron de Turckheim", "Val St-Grégoire" (50:50 Pinot Blanc and Auxerrois), Pinot Noir "Cuvée à l'Ancienne" (*en barrique*), and "Crémant Meyerling". The cooperative resists the temptation to vinify in large lots, and there are numerous varietal wines from specified *lieux-dits* and *grands crus*, of which the finest is Brand.

Westhalten ☆–☆☆

Westhalten. Founded 1955. 180 members with 200 hectares. 250,000 cases

Specialties are the *crémants* "Producteur" (50:50 Pinot Blanc and Auxerrois), "Maréchal Lefèvre" (30% Auxerrois, 20% Pinot Gris, 50% Pinot Blanc), and "Madame Sans Gêne" (100% Pinot Blanc). Pinot Gris here tends to be a better bet than Riesling. Other label: "Heim".

Wolfberger

See Eguisheim

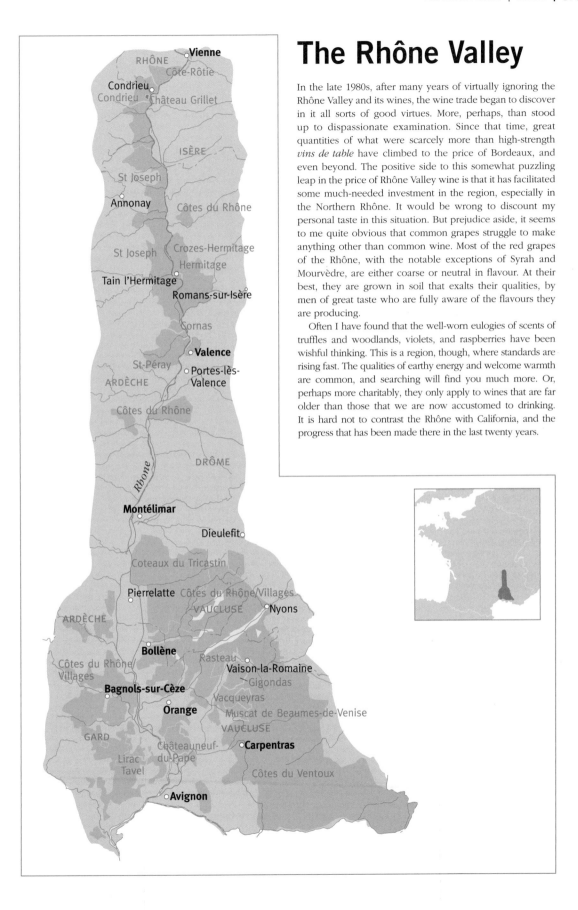

The Rhône Valley

In the late 1980s, after many years of virtually ignoring the Rhône Valley and its wines, the wine trade began to discover in it all sorts of good virtues. More, perhaps, than stood up to dispassionate examination. Since that time, great quantities of what were scarcely more than high-strength *vins de table* have climbed to the price of Bordeaux, and even beyond. The positive side to this somewhat puzzling leap in the price of Rhône Valley wine is that it has facilitated some much-needed investment in the region, especially in the Northern Rhône. It would be wrong to discount my personal taste in this situation. But prejudice aside, it seems to me quite obvious that common grapes struggle to make anything other than common wine. Most of the red grapes of the Rhône, with the notable exceptions of Syrah and Mourvèdre, are either coarse or neutral in flavour. At their best, they are grown in soil that exalts their qualities, by men of great taste who are fully aware of the flavours they are producing.

Often I have found that the well-worn eulogies of scents of truffles and woodlands, violets, and raspberries have been wishful thinking. This is a region, though, where standards are rising fast. The qualities of earthy energy and welcome warmth are common, and searching will find you much more. Or, perhaps more charitably, they only apply to wines that are far older than those that we are now accustomed to drinking. It is hard not to contrast the Rhône with California, and the progress that has been made there in the last twenty years.

Northern Rhône

The characteristic of the Northern Rhône is dogged single-mindedness: one red grape, the noble Syrah, a darkly tannic variety with concentrated, fruity flavour, grown on rocky slopes that need terracing to hold the soil.

Côte-Rôtie used to be a mere 100 hectares of terraced hill above the village of Ampuis. Somewhat controversially, the appellation has been enlarged to include, potentially, up to one hundred hectares of plateau land behind the *côte* proper. Côte-Rôtie means "roasted hill"; two sections of the hill, one with paler (more chalky) soil, and the other considerably darker, are known respectively as the "Côte Blonde" and the "Côte Brune". Their wines are normally blended by growers who have only a few hectares in total. There is rather more wine labelled "Côte" than can theoretically be produced – some growers appear to be using the terms *blonde* and *brune* as indicators of lighter or heavier styles, as there is no legal constraint on its use. The Syrah here was in the past grown and mixed with up to twenty per cent (but usually less and sometimes none) of Viognier. Partly from this aromatic component, but probably more from the singular soils or coolest microclimate of the hill, it draws a delicacy that makes Côte-Rôtie the finest, if not the most powerful. Between ten and twenty years of age, it moves closer to great Bordeaux than any other French wine, with an open, soft, fruity, perhaps raspberry bouquet that recalls the Médoc, yet with a warmer texture. Recent developments include perhaps more stress on new-oak flavours than the wine will stand.

Condrieu, where the once rare Viognier makes white wine, is only five kilometres (three miles) downstream from Ampuis, on the same south-facing right bank. Cloning has much improved this temperamental grape, which is now far more reliable. It is therefore enjoying a renaissance in the Rhône (and riding to fame in the South of France, California, and elsewhere).

St-Joseph covers a fifty-kilometre (thirty-mile), 300-hectare stretch of the same riverbank and its immediate hinterland, with some very good sites but no consistency. Legislation in 1992 has changed the territory covered by the appellation, to force a move off the plateau and valley floor back onto the slopes – although growers have until 2022 to make the move! A good example is clean, dark, and sufficiently fruity Syrah, without the grip or depth of Hermitage: wine to drink at four or five years.

The same in general is true of Crozes-Hermitage, the appellation for the east bank around Tain-l'Hermitage, without the advantage of the great upstanding mass of granite to help grill its grapes. It is the biggest AC of the Northern Rhône, and the least expensive, so its wines are often the consumer's introduction to Rhône wines. Efforts have been made to improve the basic quality level of Crozes. Growers such as Jaboulet and Graillot have shown what can be achieved here.

Few famous vineyards are as consistent as Hermitage. Its whole 130-hectare surface faces full south, at an angle that maximizes the warmth of the sun. Four-fifths are planted with Syrah, the rest with two white grapes, Roussanne and Marsanne, which produce a wine as splendid in its way as the red. A century ago, white Hermitage (then all Roussanne) was reckoned the best white wine in France, keeping "much longer than the red, even to the extent of a century". It is surprising to find white wine of apparently low acidity keeping well at all. Yet at ten years (a good age for it today) it has a haunting combination of breadth and depth with some delicate, intriguing, lemony zest.

St-Joseph and Crozes-Hermitage, incidentally, also make white wines of the same grapes, which can be excellent, though they do not share the longevity of white Hermitage

Red Hermitage has the frankest, most forthright, unfumbling attack of any of the Rhône wines. Young, it is massively purple-black, frequently uncomplicated by smells of new oak (although Jaboulet's "La Chapelle" now has a whiff about it), powerfully fruity, almost sweet, beneath a cloak of tannin, and it takes years to lose its opacity. Many people enjoy it in this state – or so it seems, because mature bottles are rare.

Cornas concludes the red-wine appellations of the Northern Rhône, with a sort of country cousin to Hermitage – another dark Syrah wine of macho vigour which only becomes a drink for fastidious palates after years in bottle. The delimited area is large – around 500 hectares – although only ninety-three hectares are currently planted, almost all on the steep slopes behind the village.

South of Cornas the appellations St-Péray is a surprising one for a *méthode traditionnelle* sparkling wine made from Marsanne and Roussanne grapes, which, providing you forget the finesse of Champagne or the *crémants* of northern France, has much to be said for it. It is a heavy-duty sparkler of almost sticky texture, even when it is dry. With age, it develops a very pleasant, almost nutty flavour. There is also a still St-Péray.

Leading Northern Rhône Producers

Thierry Allemand ☆☆–☆☆☆
Cornas. 3.5 hectares
Allemand served his apprenticeship with Robert Michel (*q.v.*) before setting up his own estate. The best wine is "Cuvée Reynards", made from vines over thirty years old. Small production, high quality.

Gilles Barge ☆☆
Ampuis. 7 hectares
Forward-looking grower of fine Côte-Rôtie and a little Condrieu. Good, sometimes excellent wines, needing ten years or so. Quality has been steadily improving, and the wines are gaining in finesse.

Bernard Burgaud ☆☆☆
Ampuis. 4 hectares
The forthright Burgaud believes in big, well-structured wines, scorning the inclusion of Viognier and the fad for multiple *cuvées*. He uses 20% new oak each year, and the wines are neither fined nor filtered. Impeccable quality.

Caves de Tain-l'Hermitage ☆–☆☆☆
Tain-l'Hermitage. 1,120 hectares
A high-quality co-op, offering excellent Crozes-Hermitage, Hermitage, St-Joseph, and Cornas. In 2001, a new director ordered immense investments in the winery to improve

quality further. Some of the top *cuvées*, such as Crozes "Hauts de Fief" and Hermitage "Gombert de Loche" are among the best within their appellations.

Emile Champet ☆–☆☆
Ampuis. 2 hectares
An old-fashioned estate producing rather old-fashioned, tannic Côte-Rôties that often retain a rustic edge.

Chapoutier ☆☆☆–☆☆☆☆
Tain l'Hermitage. 300 hectares (85 ha in Northern Rhône).
www.chapoutier.com
Founded in 1808, this is one of the most distinguished names of the Rhône, both as growers and négociants. They are the largest proprietor of Hermitage, with thirty-five hectares, and have significant holdings of Côte-Rôtie, Crozes-Hermitages, St-Joseph, and Châteauneuf-du-Pape.

When Michel Chapoutier took over the family firm in the late 1980s, he audaciously reversed the habits of decades. Old chestnut casks were replaced by barriques; yields were cut so severely that production was more than halved. Much of the domaine was converted to biodynamic viticulture. New luxury *cuvées* were introduced in each appellation, while maintaining the brands for which Chapoutier was best-known, such as Crozes "Meyssoniers" and the white Hermitage "Chante Alouette".

While all these changes were taking place at home, at the same time, Chapoutier bought and developed properties in Provence, Roussillon, and Australia. Some of the developments at Chapoutier have been controversial, but it is impossible to question the dedication to quality, the scrupulous attention to terroir, and the brilliant marketing of the house, which had been resting on its laurels for far too long.

Gérard Chave ☆☆☆☆
Mauves. 15 hectares
In 1981, Gérard Chave celebrated 500 years of direct succession in Hermitage. His red and white are among the best and longest-lived wines in France. His vineyards are divided among seven different terroirs within Hermitage, so each vintage requires careful blending to achieve the best results.

In the late 1980s, a special *cuvée* was introduced, "Cuvée Cathelin", but the "standard" Hermitage is so fine that it is rarely worth paying the considerable premium for "Cathelin". Son, Jean-Louis, is now taking over from his father, and has also created a small négociant business called J.L. Selections.

Auguste Clape ☆☆–☆☆☆
Cornas. 4 hectares
In addition to his Cornas vineyards, Clape owns parcels of St-Péray. His Cornas is dark-purple, almost black, and intensely tannic. Techniques are very traditional: ageing in old casks, no fining, and no filtration. The wines are very long-lived. There is also a bargain Côtes du Rhône, a pure Syrah from vines just outside the appellation, and the pure Marsanne St-Péray.

Clusel-Roch ☆☆–☆☆☆
Verenay, Ampuis. 4 hectares
There are two *cuvées* of Côte-Rôtie from this excellent property, the finer being "Les Grandes Places". There is no exaggeration here: no excessive alcohol, no over-indulgence in new oak. The wines are tight, balanced, and elegant.

Domaine du Colombier ☆☆
Mercurol. 15 hectares
Laurent Viale makes delicious wines from old parcels of vines in Crozes-Hermitage. The top *cuvée* is "Gaby", which is aged in older, 500-litre barrels. These are quite tannic, gamey wines that gain in complexity with age, and the white is peachy and exotic. There is also a small quantity of Hermitage.

Jean-Luc Colombo ☆☆–☆☆☆
Cornas
A consulting oenologist for many big names and guru of the producers' association, Rhône Vignobles, Jean-Luc Colombo makes big, plummy Cornas, built for long ageing ("Les Ruchets" is the top *cuvée*) from his own domaine. Under his négociant label, he produces a range of exciting wines from all the northern Rhône appellations including Hermitage, as well as Côtes du Rhône, and wines from a domaine near Marseille called "Côte Bleue". All his wines share certain characteristics: full ripeness, complete destemming, and a generous proportion of new oak.

Domaine Combier ☆☆–☆☆☆
Pont de l'Isère. 15 hectares
Laurent Combier doubles as a fruit farmer. Fruitiness is also a hallmark of his Crozes-Hermitage, red and white. The top *cuvée* is "Clos des Grives", which shows wonderfully pure, Syrah fruit and is one of the most hedonistic of all Crozes-Hermitage wines. The white is mostly Roussanne and is unusually spicy.

Courbis ☆☆–☆☆☆
Châteaubourg. 28 hectares
Serious property, using both tanks and barriques to age its St-Joseph, depending on the source and quality. The top bottling is "Les Royes". Also produces good Cornas, mostly from very old vines.

Pierre Coursodon ☆–☆☆
Mauve. 12 hectares
Family property of very old vines on the better slopes of St-Joseph. Both reds and whites demand to be aged. The arrival of the young Jérôme Coursodon in 1998 has given the estate a shot in the arm.

Yves Cuilleron ☆☆–☆☆☆
Chavanay. 25 hectares. www.cuilleron.com
Since Yves took over the domaine from his father in 1986, he has made spectacular improvements. Better vineyard practice, selective picking, and careful winemaking have resulted in superb Condrieus – particularly his unusual "Récolte Tardive". He also makes three *cuvées* of St-Joseph, of which the most intense is "Les Serines" from sixty-year-old vines, and a small quantity of Côte-Rôtie.

Delas Frères ☆–☆☆☆
St-Jean-de-Muzols. 14 hectares
Long-established growers and négociants, now owned by Deutz Champagne (and thus Louis Roederer). They have ten hectares in Hermitage (red and white), and buy from growers

in most appellations. The change in ownership revitalized the company, and new ideas, together with new investments, have increased quality dramatically since the late 1990s. The red wines in particular have gained in rich fruitiness, without losing their capacity to age and evolve.

Pierre Dumazet ☆☆
Serrières. 2 hectares

A tiny trickle of Condrieu to very smart restaurants and private clients. The late-harvested version is "La Myriade".

Ferraton Père & Fils ☆☆–☆☆☆
Tain l'Hermitage. 10 hectares

Four hectares of Hermitage, plus vines in Crozes, making solid, traditional wines. The red Hermitage spends at least two years in wood.

Pierre Gaillard ☆☆–☆☆☆
Malleval. 16 hectares

Gaillard is based in St-Joseph, but also owns parcels in Côte-Rôtie and Condrieu. He makes excellent, fairly oaky wines from all these appellations. By selling off wines he feels are not up to standard, in bulk, Gaillard maintains a consistently high level of quality.

Gerin ☆☆☆
Verenay, Ampuis. 9 hectares

Jean-Michel Gerin founded his domaine in 1990, and has gone from strength to strength. There are three *cuvées* of Côte-Rôtie, with "Les Grandes Places" and "La Landonne" aged entirely in new oak. These are modern, sleek, stylish wines in the Guigal mode, and have a devoted following. His Condrieu can also be excellent.

Alain Graillot ☆☆–☆☆☆
La Roche de Glun. 20 hectares

The domaine lies mostly in Crozes-Hermitage, with a few hectares in St-Joseph. Yields are deliberately low and the grapes picked when fully ripe to produce a very stylish white Crozes, which repays time in bottle. There is also an equally impressive red, "La Guiraude".

Château Grillet ☆☆
Verin. 3 hectares

The smallest property in France with its own *appellation contrôlée*, owned by the Neyret-Gachet family since 1830. The vineyard consists of perilous terraces forming a suntrap 150 metres (570 feet) above the bank of the Rhône. 22,000 Viognier vines yield on average 600–800 cases a year of highly aromatic wine, which is aged for eighteen months in oak. Opinions are divided about whether any sort of ageing improves Viognier wine. For some time, Château Grillet's reputation has wobbled, although prices have remained very high.

Bernard Gripa ☆–☆☆
Mauves. 10 hectares

A traditionalist producer of St-Joseph, fermented with stems and aged a year in wood. The resulting wines are dense and well-structured. His whites are 90% Marsanne.

E. & M. Guigal ☆☆☆☆
Ampuis. 43 hectares

The Guigal family are the leading producers of Côte-Rôtie, which they grow themselves on twenty hectares, and also buy in as grapes from many other small growers. They age the wine in new-oak barrels for three years, avoiding both fining and filtration if possible. The object is extremely long-lived wine.

The regular bottling is "Côtes Brune et Blonde"; in addition there are four *crus*: "La Mouline", "La Landonne", "La Turque", and (from 1995) "Château d'Ampuis". Whether Guigal's oak-scented style is true to the nature and traditions of Côte-Rôtie is a question on which I feel differently from the majority. It certainly attracts extravagant praise, a worldwide demand, and dizzying prices.

In 1985, the Guigals bought the firm of Vidal-Fleury (*q.v.*), and since then have absorbed De Vallouit and Jean-Louis Grippat, bringing the firm much sought-after St-Joseph and Hermitage sites. Guigal also produces sumptuous Condrieu and robust Hermitage, as well as good Gigondas and some of the very best Côtes du Rhône.

Paul Jaboulet Aîné ☆☆–☆☆☆☆
Tain l'Hermitage. 100 hectares. www.jaboulet.com

Growers and négociants since 1834, Jaboulet is actively run by members of the founding family. The house is a pace-setter for the whole Rhône, both as grower and merchant. Their domaine is focused in Hermitage and Crozes-Hermitage, and they produce a number of *cuvées* from each.

The red Hermitage "La Chapelle" in great vintages ('61, '78, '83, '85, '90, '99) is one of France's greatest wines, maturing over twenty-five years or more.

The white Hermitage "Le Chevalier de Sterimberg" is also memorable. Crozes-Hermitage "Domaine de Thalabert" is as fine as any wine from that appellation; likewise, the white Crozes "Mule Blanche".

Other excellent wines are St-Joseph "Le Grand Pompée", Côte-Rôtie "Les Jumelles", Cornas "St Pierre", Châteauneuf-du-Pape "Les Cèdres", and a very full and fruity Côtes du Rhône "Parallèle 45". In the late 1990s, Jaboulet bought the Domaine Roure in Crozes, thus acquiring some of that appellation's best sites.

Joseph Jamet ☆☆☆
Ampuis. 7 hectares

This domaine, of brothers Jean-Paul and Jean-Luc, comprises twenty-five separate plots in Côte-Rôtie. Their wine exhibits fine fruit and good structure, even in difficult years.

Robert Jasmin ☆☆
Ampuis. 5 hectares

A famous name, though a small property, with vines averaging thirty years old. Since the death of Robert Jasmin in 1999, the estate has been run by son Patrick. It retains a very traditional style of vinification, with 5% Viognier added to the black Syrah, and ageing in older barrels for twelve to eighteen months. The wines are not especially structured, and are best enjoyed around five years after bottling.

Robert Michel ☆☆
Cornas. 5 hectares

An old-fashioned family holding, partly on the hills giving the typically tough red, partly from the foot of the slope for lighter wines. Neither is filtered. The former is at least a ten-year-old wine. "La Geynale" is the top wine, from old vines on terraces facing due south.

Ogier ☆☆☆
Ampuis. 6 hectares

This family property in Côte-Rôtie is run with great energy by young Stéphane Ogier. The regular bottling is a splendid wine, infused with black fruits and liquorice. The top, new-oaked *cuvée*, "Belle Hélène", is far more massive; whether it is better is another question.

Domaine Pochon ☆☆
Château de Curson, Chanos-Curson. 15 hectares

There are two ranges of Crozes-Hermitage at this very dependable estate. The regular bottling is under the "Pochon" label, the best selections under the "Château de Curson" label. The latter is very much the more interesting wine, with an appealing juicy richness. Delicious whites, with more personality than most white Crozes.

Gilles Robin ☆☆☆
Mercurol. 10 hectares

A rising star in Crozes-Hermitage, with his first vintage being 1996. Robin wants to make wines in the same way his grandfather did: ploughing the vines, minimal treatments, and long fermentations. The results are sumptuous, fruity wines, with a characteristic Syrah gaminess.

René Rostaing ☆☆☆
Ampuis. 8 hectares

A splendid estate with some of the best vineyards in Côte-Rôtie (La Viallière, La Landonne). René Rostaing makes elegant, deeply coloured wines, as did his father-in-law (Albert Dervieux-Thaize) and uncle (Marius Gentaz-Dervieux) who left him their prime vineyards on their retirement in 1990 and 1993. First-rate Condrieu, too.

Domaine Marc Sorrel ☆–☆☆
Tain l'Hermitage. 4 hectares

Marc Sorrel's white Hermitage "Les Rocoules", and top red Hermitage *cuvée* "Le Gréal" are often some of the best of the commune. The Crozes-Hermitage is more modest.

Georges Vernay ☆☆–☆☆☆
Condrieu. 16 hectares. www.georges-vernay.fr

The leading figure in Condrieu, with vineyards mostly planted on reclaimed abandoned terraces. His wine is bottled in its first spring (or even winter) for freshness – and because demand outstrips supply. A small amount, from the oldest vines, spends longer in wood and becomes "Coteau de Vernon" and "Chaillées de l'Enfer", both distinctly superior wines. He also has two hectares of Côte-Rôtie and small vineyards in St-Joseph and Côtes du Rhône. There are two wines from Côte-Rôtie: the regular bottling and "Cuvée Maison Rouge", which is more oaky and peppery. Since 1997, the property has been run by his daughter, Christine.

J. Vidal-Fleury ☆–☆☆
Ampuis

The oldest (established 1781) and biggest domaine of Côte-Rôtie terraces, bought in 1985 by the Guigal family (*q.v.*) but run independently. The top Côte-Rôtie is "La Chatillonne"; the other wines are sound, but lack excitement.

François Villard ☆☆–☆☆☆
St-Michel-sur-Rhône. 6 hectares

This former chef has been making waves with his opulent wines from Condrieu, red and white St-Joseph, and Côte-Rôtie. He has followed the trend to produce late-harvested Condrieu, and his impressive version is called "Quintessence". He is also a partner in Vins de Vienne (*q.v.*).

Vins de Vienne ☆☆–☆☆☆
Seyssuel. 25 hectares

A joint venture among three St-Joseph growers; François Villard, Yves Cuilleron, and Pierre Gaillard (*qq.v.*). Essentially a négociant business, but they have also planted vineyards near Vienne with Syrah and Viognier. The wines, first made in 1999, come from all the major Rhône appellations, and are oaky and expensive.

Alain Voge ☆–☆☆
Cornas. 7 hectares

The Voge family, which is in its fourth generation here, makes Cornas by traditional methods, and sparkling St-Péray by the classic method.

Other Northern Rhône Producers

Albert Belle ☆☆
Larnage. 17.5 hectares

A sound producer of Crozes-Hermitage who also makes a very small quantity of red Hermitage.

Bonnefond ☆☆
Ampuis. 7 hectares

This family only started bottling its Côte-Rôtie and Condrieu in the 1990s, and has acquired a fine reputation for them.

J. F. Chaboud ☆
St-Péray. 13 hectares

Almost all the production here is classic-method St-Péray.

Bernard Chave ☆☆
Mercurol. 15 hectares

Bernard and son Yann produce lush, plummy red Crozes-Hermitage, and a white from ultra-ripe grapes. Very good, modern-style wines.

Caves des Clairmonts ☆
Crozes-Hermitage. www.cave-clairmont.com

Small, quality-conscious cooperative founded in 1972.

Collonge ☆
Mercurol. 38 hectares

A reliable producer of Crozes-Hermitage and St-Joseph, red and white.

Domaine des Entrefaux ☆–☆☆
Chanos-Curson. 24 hectares

Family disputes have muddied the waters at this Crozes-Hermitage estate. The best wine is the red "Les Machonnières" with its blackberry fruit.

Garon ☆☆
Ampuis. 2.5 hectares
Until 1995, the Garons sold their Côte-Rôtie grapes to Guigal, but now produce small quantities of bright, spicy, plummy wine.

Marcel Juge ☆–☆☆
Cornas. 1.5 hectares
A small grower of hearty, red Cornas. Methods are traditional, the wine "structured and fruity" – but not as fruity as his neighbour Clape's "Cuvée SC" is the top wine.

Jean Lionnet ☆☆
Cornas. 11 hectares
Good, rounded, fleshy Cornas wines – especially the oaky "Cuvée de Rochepertuis".

Niero-Pinchon ☆☆
Condrieu. 5 hectares
A small estate, from which Robert Niero coaxes two bottlings of Condrieu, and one of Côte-Rôtie.

André Perret ☆–☆☆
Chavanay. 10 hectares
Reliable producer of St-Joseph and Condrieu.

Domaine des Remizières ☆–☆☆
Mercurol. 27 hectares
A well-established domaine belonging to the Desmeure family. Numerous *cuvées* of slightly rustic Crozes-Hermitage and St-Joseph.

Southern Rhône

The catch-all appellation for the huge spread of Southern Rhône vineyards is Côtes du Rhône. It is not a very exigent title – the equivalent of AC Bordeaux Rouge. Big crops of up to fifty-two hectolitres per hectare (plus PLC) are eligible, so long as they reach at least ten degrees of alcohol.

The area covers a total 41,000 hectares of vineyards in more than one hundred communes north of Avignon, describing a rough circle among the low hills surrounding the widening Rhône. It leaves out only the alluvial bottom land around the river itself. In an average year, it makes almost twice as much wine as the appellation Beaujolais – indeed, not far short of the whole of Burgundy. Ninety-seven per cent of it is red or rosé.

In such an ocean of wine there are several estates that set standards of their own, and good négocians choose and blend well. The thing to bear in mind is that Côtes du Rhône is for drinking young, while it is reasonably fruity.

There used to be a tradition in the area of making a very light café wine known as *vin d'une nuit* – vatted for one night only. It has now been superseded by the adoption of Beaujolais tactics to make a Rhône *primeur*, with some of the qualities of new Beaujolais – but not with the exciting smell of the new Gamay grape. Regular red Côtes du Rhône is unpredictable, but compared with basic Bordeaux as a daily drink, it is warmer and more winey, less fresh and stimulating.

Côtes du Rhône-Villages is the inner circle. Over forty years ago, growers in two communes east of the valley, Gigondas and Cairanne, and two to the west, Chusclan and Laudun, raised their sights to making stronger, more concentrated *vin de garde*, modelling their wines on the *crus* of the Southern Rhône (Grenache base plus Syrah, Mourvèdre, and Cinsault). Limiting their crop to forty-two hecrolitres per hectare (plus PLC, as always) and ripening their grapes to give 12.5 degrees alcohol they made better wine, and got better prices.

A number of their neighbours followed suit. In 1967, the appellation Côtes du Rhône-Villages was decreed for a group of what has now risen to fifteen communes totalling 4,787 hectares. (The list of the group of qualifying communes is given on page 182.) The village name is permitted on the label for this group, but a total of sixty-four villages, covering 3,240 hectares, are still entitled to use "Côtes du Rhône-Villages" where the wine is not exclusively from the named village. Gigondas, Vacqueyras, and Rasteau have AC status, and this seems likely to happen to others in the group as they establish their identity and build their markets.

Certainly, Vacqueyras deserved its promotion to AC. As an example of the style of the area it might be compared with Gigondas. Tasted together, the Gigondas is fuller and rounder, with more "stuffing"; the Vacqueyras is more "nervous": harsh at first but developing a very pleasant, dusty, slightly spicy, bouquet. The wines from the best producers in both Vacqueyras and Gigondas are emphatically *vins de garde*; at five or six years they still need decanting – or keeping another three years.

There is a general and positive trend apparent in the Southern Rhône, which places greater importance on the use of better varieties in the blend (Syrah and Mourvèdre in particular) – with correspondingly less reliance on the workhorse Grenache, although this variety can give excellent results if yields are very low. Of the communes which are not -Villages, Uchaux, and Châteauneuf-de-Gadagne are areas of apparent promise. On about the same quality level as Côtes du Rhône comes the appellation Coteaux du Tricastin, inaugurated in 1974, for vineyards higher up the east bank of the river.

There is a small production of fortified wine in the Côtes du Rhône, of which by far the best known is the delicious Muscat from Beaumes-de-Venise, which manages to retain remarkable freshness and delicacy, despite its high alcohol. The wine, especially examples from the cooperative and from négociants such as Jaboulet, was extremely popular in the 1980s, but the fad has mysteriously faded away, even though the wine remains as delectable as ever. There is also some excellent *vin doux naturel* in Rasteau, mostly from Grenache.

Leading Southern Rhône Producers

Domaine des Anges ☆–☆☆
Mormoiron. 18 hectares
Irishman Gay McGuinness, owns this estate, which produces a fruity Côtes du Ventoux from Grenache and a Syrah especially for drinking young. The white is made mostly

from Marsanne and Roussanne, and there are also *vins de pays* bottlings of fairly simple Chardonnay and Cabernet.

Domaine Brusset ☆☆
Cairanne. 86 hectares. www.domainebrusset.com
Daniel Brusset's "Cuvée des Templiers" is a traditional Cairanne and one of the village's best. This estate also has a fine reputation for its Gigondas, especially "Les Hauts de Montmirail", which is aged in partly new barriques.

Cave de Cairanne ☆☆
Cairanne, 1,250 hectares. www.cave-cairanne.fr
Founded in 1929, this cooperative has 260 members, who own 80% of the Cairanne appellation. They offer a wide range of wines, the best of which are "Cuvée Antique" from eighty-year-old vines, and the smoky, concentrated "Réserve des Voconces".

Domaine du Cayron ☆☆☆
Gigondas. 15 hectares
Michel Faraud makes one of the finest Gigondas, from forty-five-year-old vines scattered all over the appellation. The winemaking is completely traditional: no de-stemming, no added yeasts, ageing in large casks, and bottling without fining or filtration.

Didier Charavin ☆–☆☆
Rasteau. 50 hectares
A family property going back to the years of the French Revolution, making classic, sweet Rasteau entirely from Grenache, and an old-style red from Grenache, Syrah, and Carignan, aged for one year in oak barrels. The top wine is usually the vigorous "Cuvée Parpaïouns".

Clos des Cazaux ☆☆–☆☆☆
Vacqueyras. 40 hectares
Enthusiastically run by the Archimbaud-Vache family, this estate produces a range of excellent Vacqueyras. "St Roch" is a traditional style, tasting of black cherries; "Cuvée des Templiers" is almost pure Syrah – less typical but delicious. The Gigondas, overwhelmingly Grenache from old vines, is released under the label "Tour Sarrazine", and is consistently fine and complex.

Domaine du Devoy ☆–☆☆
St-Laurent-des-Arbes. 40 hectares
Owned by the Lombardo brothers. An excellent Lirac property, producing full-coloured, distinguished, even elegant reds, with no wood-ageing. Also a little rosé.

Domaine Durban ☆☆
Beaumes-de-Venise. 57 hectares
The Leydiers are excellent producers of both Muscat de Beaumes-de-Venise and red Côtes du Rhône-Villages.

Domaine les Goubert ☆–☆☆☆
Gigondas. 23 hectares
Jean-Pierre Cartier's vineyards are spread over various appellations. His Beaumes-de-Venise is always good value, but his best wine is his Gigondas.

This wine comes in two versions; the first traditional, the other, "Cuvée Florence", barrique-aged. And it was one of the first wines oaked in Gigondas, a style that remains controversial, although it has proved very successful on the American market.

Domaine du Grand Montmirail ☆–☆☆
Gigondas. 35 hectares
Gigondas estate owned by Yves Cheron. The previously low production from old Grenache vines has been adapted with more Syrah, while Mourvèdre and Cinsault are now also used to make more assertive wines.

Château du Grand Moulas ☆–☆☆
Mornas. 29 hectares
From his vineyards in the Côtes du Rhône, Marc Ryckwaert makes three reds (the top label is the Syrah-dominated "Cuvée de l'Ecu") and a white, all very fine examples of the appellation. No wood.

Domaine Maby ☆–☆☆
Tavel. 55 hectares
A large and well-established family property in Tavel and Lirac. The Liracs, both white and red, are especially good. The red "La Fermade" has about 45% Mourvèdre, which gives the wine its backbone.

Gabriel Meffre ☆☆
Gigondas. No vineyards. www.gabriel-meffre.fr
In 1936, Meffre founded a domaine that grew to become the largest in France, with 800 hectares of vineyards. After his death, the property went through numerous changes, but since 1997 has been owned by former general manager Bertrand Bonnet with a selection of other investors.

The vineyards (Domaines des Bosquets, Raspail, and la Daysse in Gigondas) remained with the Meffre family, so the company now buys in grapes. It produces around 12% of all Gigondas. "Longue Toque" is a supple blend for early drinking, whereas "Laurus" is oak-aged and intended for top restaurants.

Domaine de la Mordorée ☆☆–☆☆☆
Lirac. 55 hectares
A forward-looking, organic estate, producing gently aromatic white, as well as robust Lirac. Its best-known wine, however, is probably the Châteauneuf "Cuvée Reine des Bois". By 1999, this had become the leading estate in Lirac.

Domaine de l'Oratoire St-Martin ☆☆–☆☆☆
Cairanne. 24 hectares
Frédéric and François Alary run one of the very best estates in this increasingly prized appellation. Their best wines are the unoaked "Cuvée Prestige" from old vines, and the oaky "Cuvée Haut-Coustias", red and white. These are modern wines with sleek tannins and great purity of fruit.

Domaine Les Pallières ☆☆
Gigondas. 25 ha. www.vignoblesbrunier.fr
The Roux family made wine in the manner of Châteauneuf-du-Pape in Gigondas for 500 years. With no heirs, it was sold in 1998 to the Bruniers of Vieux Télégraphe (*q.v.*). Their investments suggest that future vintages will be less rustic, but perhaps less individual, than those of the Roux's.

Domaine du Pesquier ☆☆–☆☆☆
Gigondas. 16 hectares

Côtes du Rhône-Villages

The fifteen communes entitled to this appellation are: Drôme: Rochegude, Rousset-lès-Vignes, St-Maurice-sur-Eygues, St-Pantaléon-lès-Vignes, Valréas, Visan, Vinsobres. Vaucluse: Cairanne, Roaix, Sablet, Séguret, Beaumes-de-Venise. Gard: Chusclan, Laudun, St-Gervais.

Traditional winemaking in tanks and large casks, and no filtration, giving sumptuous, gamey Gigondas with a silky texture.

Domaine de Piaugier ☆☆
Sablet. 30 hectares
Jean-Marc Autran makes serious Sablet and Gigondas from single vineyards. Some of them are quite unusual, such as "Cuvée Tenébi", which has at least 50% of the rare Counoise variety in the blend.

Domaine Rabasse-Charavin ☆☆
Cairanne. 68 hectares
A top producer of Cairanne, Corinne Couturier makes several wines, including a straight Syrah, and the "Cuvée d'Estevenas" from very old Grenache vines.

Domaine Raspail-Ay ☆☆☆
Gigondas. 18 hectares
One of the best domaines in Gigondas. Dominique Ay produces a very well-structured and fruity wine from his estate, where the average age of the vines is thirty years.

Cave de Rasteau ☆–☆☆
Rasteau. 750 hectares
A well-run cooperative producing sweet *vins doux naturel* (red and white), Côtes du Rhône-Villages, and, of course, more Rasteau by far than anyone else.

Domaine Richaud ☆☆☆
Cairanne. 40 hectares
Marcel Richaud may well be the best producer in Cairanne. The basic red is lively and fresh, and one of his best wines is the "Cuvée L'Ebrascades", from hundred-year-old Mourvèdre, Syrah, and Grenache vines.

The other red is "Les Estrambords", which he selects as the best wine of the vintage, usually a pure Grenache or pure Mourvèdre.

Château de St-Cosme ☆☆☆
Gigondas. 15 hectares
Louis Barruol is fortunate in owning vineyards with an average age of sixty years. The standard Gigondas is ripe and supple, and in top years Barruol makes "Cuvée Valbelle", aged in 50% new oak, magnificent in the 1998 vintage. There is also a small but high-quality négociant business.

Château St-Estève ☆–☆☆
Uchaux. 60 hectares. www.chateau-st-esteve-d-uchaux.com
The Français-Monier family have owned this estate since 1809. Uchaux lies on a sandy ridge north of Orange, which gives ripe, warm wines with body and character.

The property produces three red wines, and no fewer than three Viogniers, including the rare "Cuvée Thérèse".

Domaine St-Gayan ☆☆–☆☆☆
Gigondas. 38 hectares
Jean-Pierre Meffre has 400 years of Gigondas *vigneron* forebears. He produces much-appreciated, tannic Gigondas up to 14.5 degrees alcohol, reeking of crushed fruit, from ancient vines. Also big-scale Côtes du Rhône-Villages in Sablet and Rasteau. In addition, there is an oaked Gigondas called "Fontmaria". Meffre himself is not that keen on it, but it is made in response to strong demand from the American market for this style.

Château St-Roch ☆☆
Roquemaure. 65 hectares. www.chateau-saint-roch.com
This substantial Lirac property of Antoine Verda changed hands in 1998, when it was acquired by Château de la Gardine (*q.v.*) of Châteauneuf-du-Pape. The style is likely to change, given La Gardine's fondness for barriques, never previously glimpsed at St-Roch.

Domaine Sainte-Anne ☆–☆☆
St-Gervais. 33 hectares
The Steinmaier family makes concentrated Côtes du Rhône and -Villages, red and white; and good Viognier.

Domaine Le Sang des Cailloux ☆☆
Sarrians
Bought by Serge Férigoule in 1990, this is a source of good Vacqueyras, especially the rich "Cuvée Lopy" from eighty-year-old Grenache vines.

Domaine de Santa Duc ☆☆☆
Gigondas. 21 hectares
Yves Gras makes superlative Gigondas from dispersed vineyards, cultivated in an essentially organic way. The top bottling is the "Cuvée Hautes Garrigues", a blend of Grenache and Mourvèdre. Gras uses a good deal of new oak, but he dislikes the cult of overtly oaky wines, and insists that barriques are a tool to give greater complexity and texture.

Château La Soumade ☆☆–☆☆☆
Rasteau. 26 hectares
André Romero is the most dynamic of the Rasteau producers. He makes wines for long ageing, and both "Cuvée Fleur" and the rare "Cuvée Confiance" are from very old Grenache vines. The "Rasteau Doux" is a vintage wine, from 90% Grenache. All Romero's wines have high alcohol, and are not for the faint-hearted.

Tardieu-Laurent ☆☆☆
Lourmarin. No vineyards. www.tardieu-laurent.com
This négociant business is a joint venture between Dominique Laurent (*q.v.*) of Nuits-St-Georges, and Michel Tardieu. They buy wine from growers with very old vines, then age the wines in their own cellars. Rich, dense wines, from the northern Rhône as well as all the southern appellations, too extracted and formidable for some tastes but undeniably impressive. Expensive.

Château du Trignon ☆☆
Sablet. 53 hectares
An old (1898) family estate with modern ideas, making excellent wine. Charles Roux uses *macération carbonique* to make rich and savoury Gigondas, more fruity and less

tannic in youth than the old style, maturing up to, say, eight years. His vineyards are divided among Gigondas, Sablet, and Rasteau.

Château de Trinquevedel ☆☆
Tavel. 31 hectares

François Demoulin is one of the leading growers of Tavel, with interesting ideas on adapting his methods to the state of the crop, using partly old techniques and partly new (chilling and *macération carbonique*). He believes a little bottle-age improves his Tavel.

Château Valcombe ☆☆
St-Pierre-de-Vassols. 17 hectares

A high-quality estate in the Côtes du Ventoux. Sumptuous, new-oaked white "La Sereine" is from Grenache Blanc and Roussanne; its red counterpart is dominated by Syrah, and the new oak is remarkably well integrated.

Vieille Ferme ☆☆
Orange. www.lavieilleferme.com

The well-known négociant brand of the Perrin family, famous for its Châteauneuf-du-Pape "Château de Beaucastel". The excellent red is made as a *vin de garde* from the Côtes du Ventoux, and the delicate, fresh white from high vineyards on the Montagne de Lubéron. Both are exceptional value. Recently the range has expanded to include more serious wines from Gigondas, Vacqueyras, and other appellations.

Other Southern Rhône Producers

Daniel & Denis Alary ☆☆
Cairanne. 25 hectares

There are excellent red wines made here, especially "Cuvée Font d'Estévenas".

Clairette de Die

Clairette de Die is like a sorbet between the substantial main dishes of the Northern and Southern Rhône. The energy of the local cooperative has revived a fading appellation. Clairette de Die is at its best when made sparkling, but one or two traditional growers make a satisfying, nutty still wine. Sparkling Clairette must have 75% Muscat, whereas Crémant de Die must be pure Clairette.

Cave Coopérative de Clairette de Die
Three-quarters of the appellation is handled by the 500-plus members of this co-op, producing 273,000 cases of brut, Tradition, and still wines from 800 hectares.

The brut is a dry, sparkling wine with an aroma of lilac and lavender, it's claimed. Tradition is a sweet fizz of Muscat de Frontignan. The method involves fermentation in bottle (but, unlike Champagne, of the original grape-sugar), then filtering and decanting to another bottle under pressure. Other wines are Gamay red and Aligoté/Chardonnay white, for which they have their own AC Châtillon-en-Diois (fifty hectares).

Pierre Amadieu ☆
Gigondas. 130 hectares. www.pierre-amadieu.com

The largest estate in the region, producing wines from a range of appellations. The Gigondas, the hallmark wine, is rather tannic and leathery.

Château d'Aquéria ☆–☆☆
Tavel. 65 hectares. www.aqueria.com

A seventeenth century property with vineyards in Lirac, as well as Tavel. Robust and traditional wines.

Domaine de Cabasse ☆☆
Séguret. 20 hectares. www.domaine-de-cabasse.fr

This Swiss-owned property produces modern, sleek Gigondas and Côtes du Rhône Séguret. Fine rosé, too.

Caves de Vigneron de Chusclan ☆–☆☆
Chusclan

This is rosé country, and this co-operative produces excellent examples, as well as Côtes du Rhône based on old-vine Grenache.

Domaine de la Citadelle ☆–☆☆
Ménerbes. 40 hectares

One of the few serious properties in the Côtes du Lubéron. The best wine is the barrique-aged "Cuvée Le Gouverneur", a Syrah/Grenache blend.

Domaine de Deurre ☆
Vinsobres. 56 hectares

These Côtes du Rhône wines have a marked acidic structure. All are unoaked except for "Cuvée Jean-Marie Valayer", which can show bitterness from the barriques.

Domaine La Fourmone ☆–☆☆
Vacqueyras. 37 hectares. www.domaine-la-fourmone.com

Owned by the Combe family, this is a reliable producer of Vacqueyras and Gigondas (under the "Oustau Fouquet" label) for medium-term drinking.

Domaine du Gour de Chaulé ☆☆
Gigondas. 10 hectares

Owner Mme. Aline Bonfils makes powerful yet elegant wines for medium-term drinking.

Domaine Gourt de Mautens ☆☆–☆☆☆
Rasteau. 14 hectares

Jérôme Bressy is a rising star in Rasteau, where he makes unusually concentrated red and white wines, sold at considerably high prices.

Domaine de la Grapillon d'Or ☆☆
Gigondas. 23 hectares

Burly Gigondas with power rather than finesse, and peppery, plummy Vacqueyras.

Domaine Les Hautes Cances ☆☆
Cairanne. 16 hectares. www.hautescances.chez.tiscali.fr

Organic estate that made its first wine in 1995. Old vines and low yields ensure high average quality.

Domaine de la Monardière ☆☆
Vacqueyras

Christian Vache took over this estate in 1987, overhauled it, and began producing good wines with ample weight and fruit.

Domaine Pelaquié ☆
Laudun. 70 hectares. www.domaine-pelaquie.com
A large property, producing good but uninspired wines from this Côtes du Rhône village.

Château des Tours ☆
Sarrians. 39 hectares
This estate belongs to Emmanuel Reynard, proprietor of Château Rayas in Châteauneuf (*q.v.*). Here, too, Grenache reigns, giving supple Côtes du Rhône and Vacqueyras.

Tavel & Lirac

A similar area to Châteauneuf-du-Pape a few miles west, on the other side of the Rhône, has traditionally been famous for its rosé, made with the same grapes.

Tavel has a unique reputation for full-bodied dry rosé, made not by fermenting the wine briefly on its (red) grape skins, as most other rosés are made, but by a period of up to two days of maceration before fermentation starts. (The yeasts have to be inhibited by SO_2, or in modern cellars by cooling.) The wine is then pressed and fermented like white wine. I have never been attracted by this powerful, dry, rather orange-pink wine, any more than by similar rosés from Provence. It is regarded, though, as one of the classics. Like Racine, it should be re-read from time to time.

Lirac, the northern neighbour to Tavel, has been specializing more recently in red wines, which at their best can be very pleasantly fruity and lively, and in other cases, strong and dull.

Ventoux & Lubéron

Where the Rhône Valley merges with Provence to the east, the appellation Côtes du Ventoux has forged ahead in volume, now far out-producing the united Côtes du Rhône-Villages. Among some very reasonable reds, one of the outstanding wines is La Vieille Ferme (*q.v.*) of Jean-Pierre Perrin, brother of the owner of Château de Beaucastel (*q.v.*). The Côtes du Lubéron, the hills along the north of the Durance Valley (famous throughout France for its asparagus), also make a substantial contribution to this great source of red wine. Lubéron has been promoted to AC, and its reds and whites may appeal more for their crisp, well-defined flavours than some of the more pedestrian efforts of the Rhône. There is also some very adequate sparkling white Lubéron.

North of the Lubéron near Manosque, the VDQS Coteaux de Pierrevert is a further extension of these Rhône-style vineyards, making light wine.

Châteauneuf-du-Pape

Châteauneuf-du-Pape is much the biggest and most important specific southern Rhône appellation. If its 3,080 hectares of vines produced as plentifully as those of its neighbours, there would be almost as much Châteauneuf-du-Pape as Côtes du Rhône-Villages. But small crops are mandatory: the yield of Châteauneuf-du-Pape is set at thirty-five hectolitres per hectare; for Côtes du Rhône-Villages it can be up to forty-two hectolitres per hectare. Concentration is the very essence of this wine. Its vines grow in what looks like a shingle beach of big, smooth, oval stones that often cover the whole surface of the vineyard. Each vine is an individual low bush.

Where all other French appellations specify one or two, at most four, grape varieties of similar character, the tradition in Châteauneuf-du-Pape is to grow up to thirteen with widely different characteristics. It is not clear whether this is primarily an insurance policy, or simply accumulated tradition. Some growers assert that each of them, even the coarse or simply neutral ones, adds to the complexity of the wine.

New plantations, however, are tending to cut down the number to four or five. The base, always in the majority and sometimes as much as eighty to 100 per cent, is Grenache. Cinsault, Syrah, and Mourvèdre are also important. Varieties that could be described as optional are (red) Counoise, Muscardin, Vaccarèse, and Terret Noir and (white) Picardan, Clairette, Picpoul, Roussanne, and Bourboulenc. The white varieties were once used in the red wine, as well as made into white Châteauneuf-du-Pape on their own; these days there is a new demand for the white version.

Grenache and Cinsault are described as providing strength, warmth, and softness; Mourvèdre, Syrah, Muscardin, and Vaccarèse as adding structure, colour, "cut", and refreshment to the flavour, as well as the ability to live for long enough to develop a bouquet. Although the legal minimum is 12.5 degrees of alcohol, 13.5 degrees is considered the lowest acceptable by the best growers, and 14.5 degrees or more is not unusual.

And the result? We have all had great, dull, headachey wines called Châteauneuf-du-Pape. There is no distinct varietal handle by which to grasp either the aroma or the flavour. Commercial examples are usually made to be very warm and "giving", and slightly fruity.

The best estates, however, make magnificent *vins de garde* that start to open up after five years, and develop after ten or more. When a bouquet starts to develop, it is still elusive. It is rather part of a glowing, roast-chestnut warmth about the whole wine. Eventually, in the best examples, latent finesse and the essential sweetness of a great wine will emerge. The best I have ever drunk was a 1937, still in perfect condition in 1997. Recent vintages set to age splendidly include 1990 and 1998.

White Châteauneuf-du-Pape, formerly a long-lived wine – rich and elusive, is today more often made for drinking within three years at most. But from certain estates, the white can age for ten or more years. How this is possible is somewhat mysterious, given the low acidity of the wine.

Leading Châteauneuf-du-Pape Producers

Château de Beaucastel ☆☆☆–☆☆☆☆
Courthézon. 100 hectares. www.beaucastel.com

Brothers Jean-Pierre and François, the fourth generation of the Perrin family, make one of the best wines of the region on this big property, dating back to the seventeenth century. Their Châteauneuf vineyard is supplemented by Côtes du Rhône located just across the appellation boundary.

All thirteen authorized grapes, with relatively high proportions of Syrah and Mourvèdre, a 25 hl/ha crop, fifteen-day fermentation in square stone vats, and two years' ageing in oak give the wine depth and durability.

Organic methods are used in the vineyards, and the wine is bottled unfiltered, leading to some glorious bottles, but also occasionally to farmyard smells.

A small amount of delicious white Châteauneuf is made of 85% Roussanne and 15% Grenache Blanc. Even better is the magnificent "Cuvée Roussanne Vieilles Vignes". Their Côtes du Rhône (a notable bargain for this quality) is called "Cru de Coudoulet de Beaucastel". Also look out for their Côtes du Ventoux "La Vieille Ferme".

Domaine de Beaurenard ☆☆
Châteauneuf-du-Pape. 30 hectares. www.beaurenard.fr

Paul Coulon represents the seventh generation on this family property. He also owns over forty hectares of Côtes du Rhône at Rasteau. Both are planted with the same mixture of 70% Grenache and 10% each of Syrah, Cinsault, and Mourvèdre. He stresses careful, bunch-by-bunch selection in the vineyard and *cuvaison à l'ancienne* – long, carefully controlled vatting – in the cellar.

For a while, the estate favoured carbonic maceration, but has changed its mind. The top *cuvée* is called "Beaurenard": rich and massive but sometimes ungainly.

Domaine Bois de Boursan ☆☆☆
Châteauneuf-du-Pape. 15 hectares

Jean-Paul Versino has been enjoying great success with this property, founded by his Piedmontese father in 1955. In top years he produces "Cuvée des Félix", which is aged in older barriques to give a ripe, intense wine, with fruity rather than meaty or leathery flavours.

Henri Bonneau ☆☆☆
Châteauneuf-du-Pape. 6 hectares

From labyrinthine cellars in the village, Bonneau, a resolute traditionalist, produces "Cuvée Marie Beurier" and the "Réserve des Célestins", a solid, spicy, even massive red. The overall style is powerful and concentrated, sometimes funky.

Domaine Bosquet des Papes ☆☆–☆☆☆
Châteauneuf-du-Pape. 30 hectares

Maurice Boiron and son Nicolas produce traditional wine from very old vines. Since 1990, they have also made "Cuvée Chante Le Merle" from ninety-year-old vines, a splendid wine with overtones of coffee and leather.

Domaine Chante-Cigale ☆☆–☆☆☆
Châteauneuf-du-Pape. 40 hectares

The name means "the song of the cicada" – if song is the appropriate word. Noël Sabon, together with his son-in-law, Christian Favier, is the third generation to own this traditional property. The vineyards are 80% Grenache, 10% Syrah, and 5% each of Mourvèdre and Cinsault – no white grapes and no white wine. Old-style vinification and up to two years in cask make serious *vin de garde*.

Clos Mont Olivet ☆☆☆
Châteauneuf-du-Pape. 25 hectares

The three sons of Joseph Sabon are the fourth generation to make utterly traditional wine they describe as "well-structured, highly aromatic, and long in the mouth". The top *cuvée* is called "Papet", from old vines with very small yields. The wines are tannic and need plenty of ageing. Another eight hectares at Bollène (Vaucluse) produce Côtes du Rhône.

Clos des Papes ☆☆☆
Châteauneuf-du-Pape. 32 hectares

A property in direct descent from father to son for more than 300 years. The vineyards are planted with 70% Grenache, 20% Mourvèdre, plus Syrah, Muscardin, and Vaccarèse. Vincent Avril makes wines that balance power and structure against finesse. Not only the reds, but whites, too, are capable of long life in bottle.

Domaine Font de Michelle ☆☆
Châteauneuf-du-Pape. 30 hectares. www.font-de-michelle.com

Both red and white Châteauneuf-du-Pape are made at this domaine owned by the brothers Gonnet. The red is elegant rather than powerful: the white fresh and attractive. The top *cuvée* is named "Etienne Gonnet" after their father.

Château Fortia ☆
Châteauneuf-du-Pape. 30 hectares. www.chateau-fortia.com

The family estate of the instigator of the system of *appellations contrôlées*, Baron Le Roy, who in 1923 first defined the best vineyard land of the region in terms of the wild plants, thyme, and lavender – growing together – an early ecologist. Despite the domaine's reputation, quality has been disappointing for many years, with a persistent lack of concentration. Eight per cent of the production is white Châteauneuf-du-Pape.

Château de la Gardine ☆☆–☆☆☆
Châteauneuf-du-Pape. 54 hectares.
www.chateau-de-la-gardine.com

Half the vineyards are in Châteauneuf-du-Pape, the remainder in the Côtes du Rhône at Rasteau and Roaix. The Brunels aim for a reasonably "supple and elegant" wine rather than a pugilist. The top wine, the "Cuvée des Générations", is aged partly in new oak. The Brunels have been using barriques since 1980, so they know how to moderate overt oak influence. However, the white "Générations" is far too oaky, and the regular *cuvée*, which is delicious, is surely preferable.

Domaine Grand Veneur ☆☆–☆☆☆
Châteauneuf-du-Pape. 40 hectares.
www.domaine-grand-veneur.com

A large estate, with most of its vineyards in the Côtes du Rhône. In recent years, the Jaume family have made tremendous efforts here, especially with the rich, oaky

"Cuvée les Origines", with its flavours of chocolate and black fruits. There is also a soft, plump, all-Roussanne white called "La Fontaine".

Domaine de la Janasse ☆☆☆
Courthézon. 50 hectares

Christophe Sabon produces Côtes du Rhône and Châteauneuf-du-Pape from his domaine, planted mostly with old vines (some eighty to 100 years old in Châteauneuf). Low yields and a long *cuvaison* ensure very powerful wines, now among the best of the appellation. Top labels are "Cuvée Chaupin" (usually 100% Grenache) and *vieilles vignes* (95% Grenache). Also exceptional white wine, and, since 1996, a *cuvée prestige* aged in predominantly new oak, and containing 70% Roussanne.

Domaine de Mont-Redon ☆☆
Châteauneuf-du-Pape. 120 hectares.
www.chateaumontredon.fr

The biggest single vineyard in Châteauneuf, with a long history ("Mourredon", part of the episcopal estate, had vines in 1334), bought in 1921 by Henri Plantin and now run by his grandsons, Jean Abeille and Didier Fabre. Its immensely stony ground used to produce a benchmark Châteauneuf for endless ageing. Today it is a good middle-weight. Mont-Redon is the largest producer of white Châteauneuf, which is enjoyable young for its nutty freshness. The estate also includes twenty hectares of Côtes du Rhône at Roquemaure.

Domaine de Nalys ☆
Châteauneuf-du-Pape. 50 hectares

Nalys makes one of the fresher examples of Châteauneuf, at one time using carbonic maceration, and ageing the wine only up to a year in wood before bottling. The red remains mediocre, but the estate also makes notably good white wine for fairly early drinking.

Château de la Nerthe ☆☆☆
Châteauneuf-du-Pape. 90 hectares.
www.chateau-la-nerthe.com

One of the great names of Châteauneuf, quoted in the nineteenth century as being a separate and slightly better wine than Châteauneuf itself. Under director Alain Dugas, vintages of the 1990s have been innovative: fruitier and atypically new-oak-aged. The top *cuvées*, called "Cadettes" (red) and "Beauvenir" (white), have been outstanding. La Nerthe successfully attains complete ripeness without excessive alcohol.

Domaine du Pegau ☆☆
Châteauneuf-du-Pape. 12 hectares. www.pegau.com

Paul Féraud set up the domaine in 1987, and early acclaim seems to have gone to his head. There is, in addition to a good, leathery, basic wine, a plethora of special *cuvées*, mostly barrique-aged, and sold at extremely high prices. Yet, in my opinion, the wines can skirt perilously close to oxidation and mustiness.

Père Anselme ☆
Châteauneuf-du-Pape. No vineyards

The name recalls a wise old ancestor of the founder of this firm of négociants and winemakers, and the estate produces

most of the Rhône appellations. The "Jean-Pierre Brotte" label is used for wines sold to restaurants. Other ventures include a wine museum.

Château Rayas ☆☆☆
Châteauneuf-du-Pape. 13 hectares

A small but outstanding property, which is often cited as the best of Châteauneuf. Emmanuel Reynaud's estate is on slightly atypical clay soils and is overwhelmingly planted with ancient Grenache, the balance Cinsault and Syrah. He ages the red for two or three years in wood, depending on the vintage.

Although there have been rich and profound vintages of Rayas over many decades, quality can fluctuate wildly, although since Emmanuel Reynaud took over from his secretive uncle Jacques in 1997, the hand at the helm has been steadier. Reynaud uses "Pignan" as a second label. "Château Fonsalette" (a top Côtes du Rhône) is also made at Rayas. Fonsalette "Cuvée Syrah" is heroic for its appellation.

Domaine de la Vieille Julienne ☆☆–☆☆☆
Les Grès, Orange. 30 hectares. www.vieillejulienne.com

Jean-Paul Daumen owns ten hectares within Châteauneuf from which he produces three wines. The top *cuvées,* "Cuvée Réserve" and "Cuvée Vieilles Vignes", are not made every year. Although they are reds of magnificent concentration and dense fruit, they can, unfortunately, be marred by very high alcohol.

Vieux Donjon ☆☆–☆☆☆
Châteauneuf-du-Pape. 13 hectares

A classic estate, producing a ripe, slightly smoky white, and a single powerful red from 80% Grenache. The reds are firm and tannic, but always seem to have a core of ripe fruit. If the wines seem somewhat formidable when tasted young, they age beautifully, delivering sweet brambly fruit.

Domaine du Vieux Télégraphe ☆☆☆
Bédarrides. 70 hectares. www.vignoblesbrunier.fr

A long-established estate that takes its name from the old signal tower that still stands on the hill. It is worked by the third and fourth generations of the Brunier family who make 10,000 cases of a rather conservative, dark, peppery, and intense Châteauneuf.

The vines are 65% Grenache, 15% Syrah, and 15% Mourvèdre. The stony soil, low yields, and long fermentation of the whole bunches account for the deep concentration of the wine. They are also owners of another property here, Château de la Roquette.

Other Châteauneuf-du-Pape Producers

Domaine les Cailloux ☆☆
Châteauneuf-du-Pape. 22 hectares

This is a modern domaine, owned by André Brunel, which produces an accessible style of Châteauneuf-du-Pape. A new, silkier style of wine came with a change in vinification techniques (de-stemming and longer *cuvaisons*) in the late '80s.

Les Cèdres ☆☆
See **Paul Jaboulet Aîné**
The excellent brand name Châteauneuf of Paul Jaboulet Aîné.

Domaine Chante-Perdrix ☆☆
Châteauneuf-du-Pape. 18 hectares. www.chante-perdrix.com
A property south of Châteauneuf, not far from the Rhône River itself. Medium-bodied wine, showing finesse rather than power.

Les Clefs d'Or ☆–☆☆
Châteauneuf-du-Pape. 25 hectares
This is a traditional property – its vinification has not changed over the years. Excellent in good years, but inconsistent in weaker ones.

Domaine du Grand Tinel ☆
Châteauneuf-du-Pape. 53 hectares
This domaine is a traditionalist estate and is the property of Elie Jeune, the former mayor of the commune.

Domaine de Marcoux ☆–☆☆
Châteauneuf-du-Pape. 21 hectares
This, the first biodynamic estate in the region, has won a loyal following, but the wines have never been consistently convincing.

Domaine Roger Sabon ☆–☆☆☆
Châteauneuf-du-Pape. 15 hectares
Four different Châteauneufs are made, and inevitably the most basic, "Les Olivets", lacks weight. The top wine is the scarce "Les Secrets de Sabon" from 100-year-old vines.

Pierre Usseglio ☆☆
Châteauneuf-du-Pape. 22 hectares
Thierry Usseglio has won praise for his top wines, "Mon Aeuil" and "Deux Frères", but they can suffer from very high alcohol and burly tannins.

Domaine de Villeneuve ☆☆–☆☆☆
Courthézon. 9 hectares
A rising star since Philippe du Roy de Blicquy took over the domaine in 1993. Very old vines; plus biodynamic viticulture is practised.

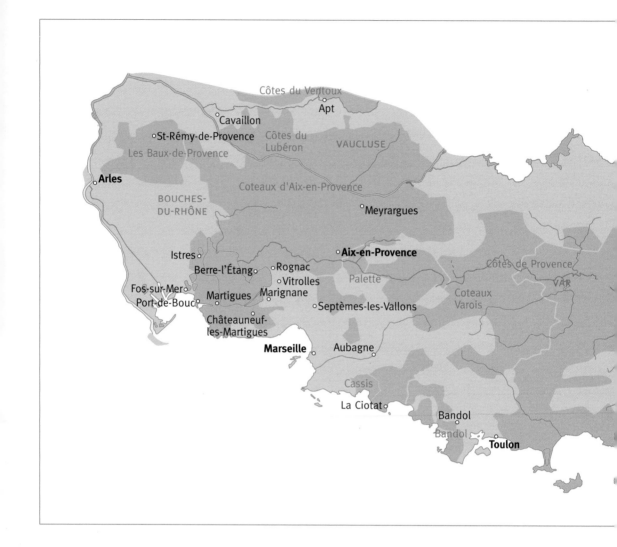

Provence

Not so long ago, it was just as well to approach Provence in an indolent frame of mind with serious judgement suspended. Most of its wine was passable at best, sunglass rosé with too much alcohol and too little taste. There were a few reds of character, and careful winemakers even made white wine that was almost refreshing, but the quality rarely justified the price. Wines as good could be found in the Rhône, and in the hills of the Midi, for less money.

Provence depended for too long on its captive audience of holidaymakers. In the past, I tried, but always failed, to enjoy traditional strong, dry rosé made from the non-aromatic grapes of the region, the same Carignan, Cinsault, and Grenache as the Rhône, with a small proportion of Syrah and Mourvèdre to give flavour.

Times have changed. There are now some deliciously light rosés, a much greater number of serious reds, and more well-made whites. There are sometimes aromas of herbs and pines: the heady, sun-baked smell of the land. Better grapes have been planted (there is growing emphasis on Syrah and

Mourvèdre, and Tibouren for rosés) and modern controls implemented. Côtes de Provence was promoted from a VDQS to an AC in 1977. For a few estates, it was recognition of their real quality. For the majority, it was more in anticipation and encouragement of the future progress, now apparent in the increased success of smaller estates. Individual growers have capitalized on the California-like climate and the wider availability of classic grape varieties.

In Provence, the estate or growers' name is all. Appellations are now a much more reliable guide to quality, too; Coteaux d'Aix-en-Provence and especially Les Baux-de-Provence have become serious contenders in the quality stakes. Areas of Côtes de Provence, such as Mont Ste-Victoire, now also have a number of good producers, especially of red wines.

Côtes de Provence was an alarmingly wide area for a single appellation, including the coast from St-Tropez to beyond Toulon to the west, and a great stretch of country inland, north of the Massif des Maures, back to Draguignan and the first foothills of the Alps. Before all this became an AC, however, there were already four little local appellations where the wine was considered consistently above-average.

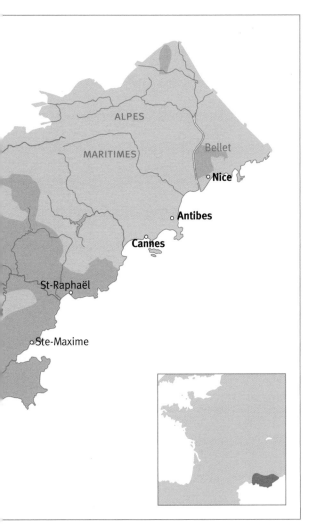

The biggest and unquestionably the best – indeed, a wine that must be included among France's most splendid reds – comes from Bandol, a sixteen-kilometre (ten-mile) stretch of coast and its hinterland just west of Toulon, with 1,420 hectares of vineyards. Good Bandol red has a quality that has traditionally been rare in Provence: tannic firmness that makes it a three-year wine at the very least, lasting without problems, but maturing in splendour up to ten years or more. The law requires Bandol vines to be at least eight years old for the wine to qualify for appellation status, and the wine must be aged at least eighteen months in cask. The reason is a high proportion (the legal minimum is fifty per cent, but many of the best estates will now use one hundred per cent) of Mourvèdre, which appreciates the heat of rocky terraces. Local lore has it that Bandol from nearer the sea, hence sometimes misty, is finer than that from further inland. There is also fine Bandol rosé, especially from Mourvèdre, and less consistent white. Farther west along the coast, almost in the outskirts of Marseille, the fishing port of Cassis, with 177 hectares of vines, is known for its (relatively) lively and aromatic white, for which the *bouillabaisse* restaurants of Marseille see fit to charge *grand vin* prices.

The wines of the district of Aix-en-Provence, north of Marseille, come under the AC Coteaux d'Aix-en-Provence (3,900 hectares). The microscopic forty-hectare enclave of Palette, an appellation area just east of Aix, is dominated by Château Simone (*q.v.*). Since the 1994 vintage, neighbouring Les Baux has achieved appellation status for its reds and rosés: Les Baux-de-Provence (for the present, the whites remain under the more general Coteaux d'Aix appellation). Many of the top-quality producers in Les Baux are using some Cabernet Sauvignon, and most adopt organic methods to grow their vines.

Behind Nice in the hills at the extreme other end of Provence, the forty-hectare appellation of Bellet is justified by wine that is considerably better than the generally dismal prevailing standard of its neighbours; the whites are better than the reds. The Côte d'Azur seems to disprove the theory that a sophisticated clientele spurs winemakers to make fine wine.

Some twenty estates in Provence use the title *cru classé*. This dates back to the 1950s and an attempt to raise local quality standards. It was originally used by producers who were the first to bottle their wines at the estate. The term should not be taken too seriously.

Leading Provence Producers

Bandol

Domaines Bunan ☆☆–☆☆☆
La Cadière d'Azur. www.bunan.com
The brothers Bunan, Paul and Pierre and Paul's son, Laurent, own steep vineyards at La Cadière (Moulin des Costes) and at nearby Le Castellet (Mas de la Rouvière). Some excellent and increasingly important, long-lived red (70% Mourvèdre, 30% Grenache – no Cinsault) is made, and in exceptional years, a special pure-Mourvèdre *cuvée* is produced under the "Château de la Rouvière" label. Varietal *vin de pays* (Mourvèdre and Cabernet Sauvignon) are also very good. The Bunans also rent the twenty-five hectare Domaine de Belouve.

Domaine de Pibarnon ☆☆☆
La Cadière d'Azur. 51 hectares
In 1977, Comte Henri de St-Victor gave up his day job in Paris and bought this run-down estate, and within ten years had developed it into one of Bandol's top properties. The red is almost pure Mourvèdre, and the rosé, which is from 50% Mourvèdre, can be surprisingly long-lived. When young, Pibarnon smells of violets and blueberries; with age, like other Bandols, it takes on overtones of tobacco and truffles.

Domaine Pradeaux ☆☆–☆☆☆
St-Cyr. 26 hectares
A highly traditional Bandol property, making robust wines that, with age, can resemble good Bordeaux. The vines are close to fifty years old, and low yields give the wines power and richness. Gamey with age.

Domaine Tempier ☆☆☆–☆☆☆☆
Le Plan du Castellet. 29 hectares

Lucien Peyraud is widely regarded as the "father of the Bandol appellation", for his part in rescuing it from decline. His sons and grandson, assisted by winemaker Daniel Ravier, make the finest wines of Bandol, hence of Provence: superbly flavoury and long-lived red and rosé. Many of the vines are up to seventy years old; the average age is thirty-five years. The red (two-thirds of production) has at least 70% Mourvèdre, the rest Grenache, Cinsault, and a little Carignan from very old vines. The outstanding "Cuvée Cabassaou" is 100% Mourvèdre, and the two single-vineyard wines, "La Tourtine" and "Le Migoua", are of comparable quality.

Domaine de la Tour du Bon ☆☆

Le Brûlat-du-Castellet. 12 hectares

Agnès Henri-Hocquard runs this fine domaine, with its plump rosé and a rich red from 70% Mourvèdre. The "Cuvée St Ferréol" is made from pure Mourvèdre, and partly aged in new oak.

Château Vannières ☆☆–☆☆☆

La Cadière d'Azur. 33 hectares. www.chateauvannieres.com

A leading Bandol producer, on an estate dating back to 1532. The stylish, medium-bodied red is made of 90% Mourvèdre and given long ageing in large casks.

Domaine de la Vivonne ☆☆–☆☆☆

Le Castellet. 15 hectares. www.vivonne.com

One of the leading lights in the Bandol appellation, Walter Gilpin makes robust wines in a traditional way, though sometimes a few new barriques supplement the casks. The wines are very deep in colour, and rich in black-cherry succulence.

Les Baux-de-Provence

Mas de la Dame ☆☆

Maussanne. 60 hectares. www.masdeladame.com

Mmes. Poniatowski and Misoffe produce one of the best wines in Les Baux from their organic estate. Since the late 1990s, consultant oenologist Jean-Luc Colombo has overhauled wine production, releasing as a top *cuvée* the "Coin Caché" from Grenache and Syrah: in its youth a tough and oaky red. It joins the other concentrated red, the "Cuvée de la Stèle".

Château Romanin ☆☆

St-Rémy. 51 hectares. www.romanin.com

A joint venture between financier Jean-Pierre Reynaud and Jean-Andre Charial, the owner of two top restaurants in Les Baux. The estate has been biodynamic from the outset. Some vintages have been rather herbaceous. One of the specialties here is the traditional *vin cuit*, made from heated must.

Domaine des Terres Blanches ☆☆

St-Rémy. 40 hectares

A substantial, organic estate in Les Baux, owned by Noël Michelin since 1968. Special *cuvées* are "Cuvée Aurélia" with Cabernet Sauvignon, made in exceptional vintages only ('90 and '95); and "Cuvée Berengere", mostly from Mourvèdre.

Domaine de Trévallon ☆☆☆–☆☆☆☆

St-Etienne-du-Grés. 20 hectares. www.trevallon.com

The rich, intense half-Cabernet Sauvignon, half-Syrah blend is the best wine in the district of Les Baux, but is not entitled to the appellation, as the INAO allows only 20% Cabernet Sauvignon. Consequently, since 1994, Eloi Durrbach produces his superlative wine as a red Vin de Pays des Bouches-du-Rhône, and he also makes a tiny amount of sumptuous white from 60% Marsanne and 40% Roussanne. In this case, the law is undeniably an ass.

Other Provence Appellations

Domaine les Bastides ☆☆–☆☆☆

Le Puy-Ste-Réparade. 28 hectares

(Coteaux d'Aix.) Jean Salen and daughter Carole produce a splendid "Cuvée Valéria" from Cabernet Sauvignon and Grenache, a complex wine made without recourse to small oak barrels. The rosé is unusually full-bodied.

Domaine des Béates ☆☆–☆☆☆

Lambesc. 27 hectares. www.domaine-des-beates.com

(Coteaux d'Aix.) Owned since 1996 by the Chapoutier family from the Rhône. The estate wine is a dark, rich, vigorous blend of Cabernet, Syrah, and Grenache, and the top (and wildly expensive) "Cuvée Terra d'Or" is a blend of Cabernet and Syrah, aged in barriques and intended for long ageing.

Château Calissanne ☆–☆☆☆

Lançon-Provence. 100 hectares

This large estate was bought in 2001 by industrialist Philippe Kessler. Under the previous owners, there were two excellent bottlings: the "Cuvée Prestige" and the new-oaked "Clos Victoire". The red "Victoire" was a fine blend of Cabernet Sauvignon and Syrah, and the rosé was a vivid, pure Syrah that tasted of strawberries.

Commanderie de Peyrassol ☆–☆☆

Flassans-sur-Issole

The Commanderie was founded by the Templars in 1204, and acquired by the Rigord family in 1790. The basic wine is the "Cuvée Eperon d'Or", while the "Cuvée Marie Estelle" is from older vines. Both reds have substantial percentages of Cabernet Sauvignon and Syrah, and new oak is used for ageing. They can be rather tough when young.

Château la Coste ☆☆

Le Puy-Ste-Réparade. 148 hectares. www.chateaulacoste.com

One of the largest estates in Provence. The Bordonado family owns this property and two associated estates: Domaine de la Grande Séouve and Domaine de la Boulangère. Winemaking techniques are modern for rosés and whites, but traditional for reds. For such large-scale production, the quality of the wines is high – especially for the reds. There are numerous bottlings, mostly defined by differing blends of grape varieties.

Domaine de la Courtade ☆☆–☆☆☆

Ile de Porquerolles. 35 hectares. www.la-courtade.com

An outpost of experimentation on an island west of Toulon, begun in 1983. The concentrated reds are almost pure Mourvèdre; the barrique-aged whites are from Rolle. Quality is very high, as are prices. The second label is "L'Alycastre".

Château de Crémat ☆☆
Nice. 12 hectares. www.chateau-cremat.com
This is a leading property in the tiny appellation Bellet in the hills above Nice, well-known to *habitués* of the Cote d'Azur. Since 1995, it has been owned by Jean-Pierre Pisoni, who has invested heavily in renovating the neglected vineyards.

Domaine du Deffends ☆☆–☆☆☆
Saint-Maximin. 14 hectares
One of the best estates in the sometimes overlooked Coteaux Varois. A *vin de pays* white is made from Rolle and Viognier, but red wine dominates production. The top *cuvée* is "Clos de la Truffière", which is a blend of Cabernet and Syrah, as much red fruit as truffle in its aromas.

Domaine des Féraud ☆–☆☆
Vidauban. 40 hectares
Owned by the Laudon-Rival family for three generations. Paul Rival, the former owner of Château Guiraud, Sauternes, ran this Côtes de Provence property for twenty-five years until 1955, then handed over to his nephew, Bernard Laudon. Médoc-inspired Cabernet Sauvignon, Syrah, and Grenache red; whites from Sémillon; also rosé from Tibouren.

Château de Fonscolombe ☆
Le Puy-Ste-Réparade. 150 hectares
The Marquis de Sapporta has two Coteaux d'Aix properties north of Aix – this noble Renaissance château (eighty-two hectares) and the Domaine de la Crémade (forty-four hectares). Both have been in his family since 1810. The Sapporta family has been notable for upgrading local wine quality, especially in whites. Modern techniques for whites and rosés, and traditional oak vinification for reds. The "Cuvée Spéciale" red has 15–20% Cabernet. Overall, the wines lack concentration, but are highly drinkable.

Domaine Gavoty ☆☆–☆☆☆
Le Luc. 25 hectares. www.gavoty.com
Bernard Gavoty was the music critic for *Le Figaro* in the 1970s. Today, this property, a producer of excellent Côtes de Provence, is run by Roselyne Gavoty. Bernard's pen-name was Clarendon, and the top *cuvée*, the often sumptuous "Cuvée Clarendon", is a fitting tribute. The red is mostly Syrah, the rosé mostly Grenache.

Les Maîtres Vignerons de la Presqu'île de St-Tropez ☆☆
Gassin. 690 hectares
This unusual enterprise unites nine domaines, each of which vinifies its own wines, which are then bottled and marketed by the *vignerons*. "Château de Pampelonne" is the top label, and "Château St-Martin-la-Touche" is also a single-vineyard wine. Good-value reds and rosés are bottled under "Cuvée du Chasseur", "Carte Noire", and other labels.

Château Minuty ☆–☆☆
Gassin. 100 hectares
Jean-Etienne Matton runs this sizeable property near St-Tropez, which has a serious reputation for its oak-aged red, "Cuvée Prestige Antica".

Domaines Ott ☆☆–☆☆☆
Le Castellet. 156 hectares. www.domaines-ott.com
Founded in 1896 by a native of Alsace, the family now owns three properties producing good, if high-priced, Provence wines by traditional, organic methods: limited yield, no sulphur, oak-ageing. Ott rosés in particular are superb. Estates owned are Clos Mireille (Côtes de Provence; white wines only), Château Romassan (Bandol), and Château de Selle (Côtes de Provence).

Château Réal Martin ☆☆–☆☆☆
Le Val. 30 hectares
Always dependable property for red and white Côtes de Provence. Much improved since the late 1990s, with weightier and better structured reds, especially the "Cuvée Optimum".

Château Revelette ☆☆
Jouques. 25 hectares
Owner Peter Fischer trained at UC Davis in California before acquiring this property in 1985. It lies high in the Coteaux d'Aix at 400 metres (1,300 feet), so the wines can have a certain austerity when young. The elevation also means that his Chardonnay has freshness as well as oakiness, and his red "Grand Vin", from Cabernet Sauvignon and Syrah, has intense berry fruit.

Domaine Richeaume ☆☆
Puyloubier. 22 hectares
German proprietor Henning Hoesch makes a red from Cabernet Sauvignon and Syrah, which is aged for two years in wood, and maintains that even his rosé and white are wines for keeping. Hoesch also produces unblended Syrah and a *rosé de saignée* from Grenache.

Domaine de St-André de Figuière ☆☆
La Londe-les-Maures. 16 hectares. www.figuiere-provence.com
Alain Combard's estate lies between St-Tropez and Toulon, producing good red and rosé. There are various levels of quality, the best being the *vieilles vignes*, closely followed by the red "Reserve", which is a focused barrique-aged Mourvèdre. Good rosé, too.

Château Ste-Roseline ☆☆–☆☆☆
Les Arcs-sur-Argens. 60 hectares. www.sainte-roseline.com
Property developer Bernard Teillaud bought and renovated this ancient monastic estate in 1994, replanting many of the vineyards. The Mourvèdre-dominated red "Cuvée Prieure" is the best wine made at this Côtes de Provence estate, closely followed by the rosé, which uses a good deal of Tibouren.

Château Simone ☆☆
Palette, Meyreuil. 17 hectares
One of two properties in the tiny AC Palette, and owned by the sixth generation of the Rougier family. The estate provides local restaurants with a very satisfactory specialty: slightly but agreeably rustic wines that really taste of the herbs and pines of the countryside. On average, the vines are sixty years old. The red ages well; the Clairette-dominated white could be considered an acquired taste, but often gains in grandeur after a few years in bottle. The rosé is lovely.

Châteaux Elie Sumeire ☆
Marseille. 140 hectares. www.chateaux-elie-sumeire.fr
The Sumeire family owns three estates (Château Coussin Ste-Victoire, Château de Maupague, and Château l'Afrique), in different parts of the Côtes de Provence appellation, making

it one of the appellation's largest landowners with 145 hectares. Whites and rosés are sold young, but they make a practice of ageing reds for a period of between six months and two years.

Domaine de Triennes ☆–☆☆
Nans-les-Pins. 40 hectares. www.triennes.com
This estate in Coteaux Varois has distinguished Burgundian co-owners: the de Villaines of Romanée-Conti and the Seysses of Domaine Dujac. Viognier and Syrah are the top wines here, together with the "Réserve" Cabernet and Syrah.

Château Vignelaure ☆
Rians. 60 hectares
The first estate to show the world that inland Provence could produce very good wines of more than local interest. Georges Brunet arrived in the 1960s and planted Cabernet with the local vines. He had already restored Château La Lagune in the Médoc. Although seen as making the best wine in the Coteaux d'Aix, Brunet sold the property in the mid-1980s, and thereafter quality declined as a succession of new owners arrived.

In 1998, the Irish O'Brien family became sole owners, having previously benefitted from the advice of co-owner and itinerant winemaker, Hugh Ryman. Strict selection has restored quality, and the O'Brien strategy is to use as much Cabernet Sauvignon as will ripen at this high altitude.

Other Provence Producers

Domaine du Bagnol ☆–☆☆
Cassis
Michelle Génovési's small estate produces good whites and an excellent rosé.

Château Bas ☆☆
Vernègues
A new team took over the running of this Coteaux d'Aix property in the late 1990s, with the aim of improving quality. The top bottling is the "Cuvée du Temple": a heavy white from mostly Rolle, and an extracted red from Syrah.

Domaine de la Bastide Neuve ☆–☆☆
Le Cannet des Maures
Hugo Wiestner makes his wines either in the traditional way with his "Cuvée d'Antan" – Syrah and Mourvèdre aged in oak – or uses *macération carbonique* for his "Cuvée Beaux Sarments" of Cinsault and Cabernet Sauvignon.

Château de Beaulieu ☆
Rognes
A huge, 240-hectare estate in the Coteaux d'Aix region. Reds contain 20% of wine aged in barriques, while the "Cuvée Exceptionelle" is entirely barrique-aged. The rosé is dull.

Château du Beaupré ☆
St-Cannat
Since the mid-1990s, the Double family have been improving the quality of their wines, using more barriques for the best, which are released under the "Collection label". However, the wines, though reliable, can lack concentration.

Château de Bellet ☆☆
Nice
Ghislain de Charnacé's ten-hectare property is one of only two sizeable ones in the tiny AC Bellet. The other is Château de Crémat (*q.v.*). The best wines are bottled under the "Cuvée Baron G" label.

Château La Bernarde ☆☆
Le Luc. 33 hectares
Well-located vineyards on stony, limestone soils. The best wines are bottled in top vintages as "Clos Bernarde". No oak is used here, and the wines are overpriced for the quality.

Château de Berne ☆
Lorgues. www.chateauberne.com
Despite the initial resemblance to Hollywood among the Provençal pine trees, this British-owned estate is producing some good-quality, modern-style Côtes de Provence. Two styles of red – a standard *cuvée* and a "Cuvée Spéciale" – are made.

Clos Ste-Magdelaine ☆☆
Cassis
A reliable white-wine property overlooking the Mediterranean, probably the best in Cassis, with ripe, lively, floral wines.

Vignobles Crocé-Spinelli ☆
Les Arcs
Monsieur Crocé-Spinelli owns three estates in Côtes de Provence: Château des Clarettes near Les Arcs, Domaine du St-Esprit, and Domaine de Fontselves near Draguignan. The wine from St-Esprit has a high percentage of Syrah, while the Clarettes relies more on Mourvèdre.

Domaine de Curebasse ☆–☆☆
Fréjus
A reliable producer of Côtes de Provence; half the production is rosé. The best red is a blend of Syrah and Cabernet; the white is Rolle. The excellent rosé has a high proportion of Tibouren.

Domaine Ferme Blanche ☆
Cassis
A leading property in this fashionable village, producing relatively floral white and rather hard red.

Domaine Le Galantin ☆☆
Le Plan du Castellet
The Pascal family are conscientious producers of slightly rustic but long-lived Bandol. By 2000, a new generation was in place, so the style may change.

Château du Galoupet ☆
La Londe-les-Maures. www.galoupet.com
This British-owned property aims to combine traditional grape varieties of the Côtes de Provence region with current winemaking techniques. The estate has been modernized since its current owners bought it in 1993. The château dates back to Louis XIV, and the older part of the cellar is Roman.

Château la Gordonne ☆
Pierrefeu du Var. www.listel.fr

A 188-hectare estate owned by Domaines Listel, producing red, white, and rosé Côtes de Provence from shale soil on the Maures foothills.

Domaine Hauvette ☆☆
St-Rémy. 12 hectares
A gradually expanding Les Baux organic estate, making fine reds from Grenache, Syrah, and Cabernet.

Domaine Lafran-Veyrolles ☆☆
La Cadière d'Azur. 10 hectares
Reliable red and rosé from Bandol, and an often exceptional "Cuvée Longe Garde".

Mas de Gourgonnier ☆☆
Mouriès. 42 hectares
A long-established, organic estate in the heart of the Les Baux Mountains. Rather rustic but enjoyable wines.

Mas Ste-Berthe ☆–☆☆
Les Baux-de-Provence. 38 hectares
A large and unapologetically commercial estate, producing reliably drinkable and inexpensive wines: red, rosé, and white.

Domaine Rabiega ☆☆
Flayosc
A small, Swedish-owned estate producing impressive, ripe oaky wines: "Clos d'Ière No 1" (mostly Syrah), and "No 2", (a blend of Grenache, Carignan, and Cabernet Sauvignon).

Domaine de Rimauresq ☆–☆☆
Pignans. www.rimauresq.net
This is a thirty-five-hectare property that has been under Scottish ownership since 1988. The property has some fifty-year-old vines, which are used to make the special "Cuvée 'R'". The wines are predominantly rosé and white Côtes de Provence.

Château de St-Martin ☆
Taradeau
A handsome old house with deep cellars, in the same family since the seventeenth century. The proprietor, Comtesse de Gasquet, makes reliable Côtes de Provence *cru classé* from forty hectares of vineyards.

Château Ste-Anne ☆☆
Ste-Anne d'Evenos
This estate has belonged to the Dutheil de la Rochère family for centuries. As well as Bandol, the estate produces Côtes de Provence rosé. The vineyards are terraced and planted on sandy subsoils that give a lighter, more elegant style. Since 1989, a "Vin de Collection" from pure Mourvèdre has been introduced.

Château du Seuil ☆☆
Puyricard
A large property quite high in the Coteaux d'Aix and prone to spring frost. The best wines are the "Grand Seuil" range. Quality has improved dramatically in the late 1990s.

Château la Suffrene ☆☆
La Cadière-d'Azur
Until the mid-1990s, this Bandol property sold its grapes to the cooperative, but now makes its own wine. The regular bottling of the red can be drunk young, the "Cuvée des Lauves", mostly Mourvèdre, benefits from ageing.

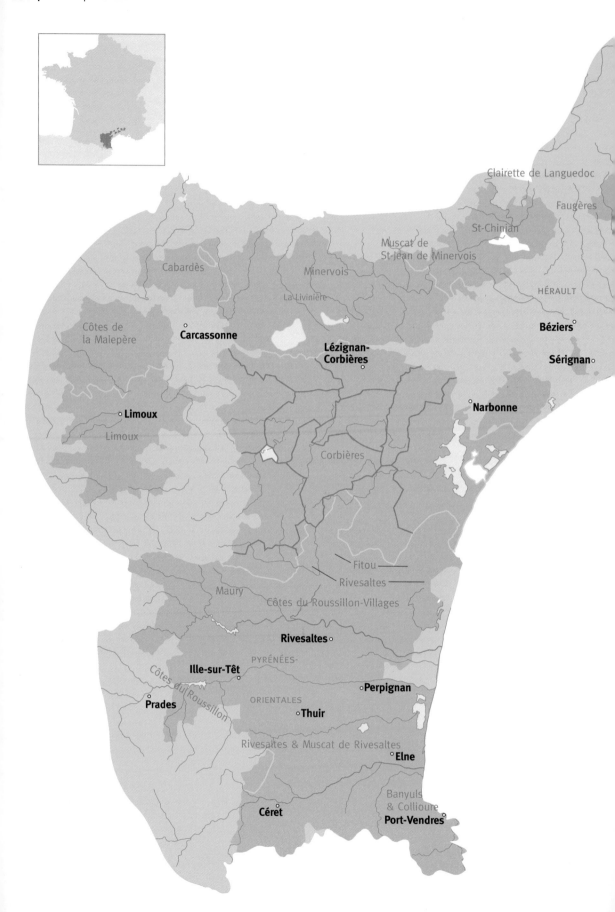

Clairette de Languedoc

Faugères

St-Chinian

Muscat de
St-Jean de Minervois

HÉRAULT

Cabardès

Minervois

La Livinière

Béziers

Côtes de
la Malepère

Carcassonne

**Lézignan-
Corbières**

Sérignan

Narbonne

Limoux

Limoux

Corbières

Fitou

Rivesaltes

Maury

Côtes du Roussillon-Villages

Rivesaltes

PYRÉNÉES-

Ille-sur-Têt

Côtes du Roussillon

Perpignan

ORIENTALES

Prades

Thuir

Rivesaltes & Muscat de Rivesaltes

Elne

Banyuls
& Collioure

Céret

Port-Vendres

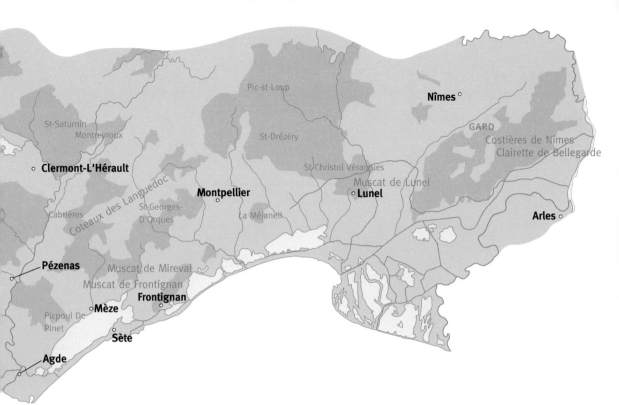

The Midi

The arc of country from the Spanish border to the mouth of the Rhône may well be France's oldest vineyard. It is certainly its biggest. Now it is where the experimentation is. Times have changed. Uncountable quantities of unwanted wine were once pumped from its plains, to the despair of politicians all over Europe.

Until fifteen years ago, there was not a great deal more to say. Traditions of better wine-growing persisted in the hills, but at such economic disadvantage that there seemed little future for them. Such traditions are being grafted onto new techniques to produce – at last – some memorable Midi wines. Interest and investment from Australia has made the locals sit up and take notice. The region is now coming to life again: the Languedoc hills, Corbières and Minervois, and also Roussillon.

There was no demand and no premium for extra effort until the 1960s, when educated winemakers and merchants began to realize that it was only the grapes that were wrong; the soils and climates of hundreds of hill villages have enormous potential. The penny dropped at the same time as California rose from its slumber. In the Midi, low morale, bureaucracy, peasant conservatism, and typically complicated land ownership have all been brakes on progress. Otherwise, there would long before have been famous Cabernets from the Corbières. But California has done it, so why not the South of France? The French way is to move cautiously along established lines: to improve wines, not to change them.

Upgrading started with the winemaking process, and then spread to the marketing of its produce. The introduction of *macération carbonique* was the vital first step. It extracted from dull grapes, such as Carignan, juicy flavours that nobody knew were there. The process is now a long way down the road, and a handsome list has emerged of properties and cooperatives with good wine to offer, from the "aromatic" grapes that the public want. It is now the estates rather than the cooperatives that lead the way in quality. Sadly, many cooperatives have become forces of reaction, failing to rein in their members' desires to keep on churning out large volumes of dull, dilute wines for which there is no longer any market. Other co-ops, however, have seen the future, and are tailoring their production and packaging to a generation of wine-drinkers seeking good, fruity wines at fair prices.

The Midi of quality wine divides into four distinct regions. Following the right-hand curve of the coast north from the Spanish border, they are Roussillon in the Pyrenean foothills, most famous for sweet apéritif and dessert wines; Corbières, red wine country; Minervois in the southernmost foothills of the Cévennes, also best-known for red wine; and the scattered Coteaux du Languedoc, producing red, white, and rosé in quality ranging from dire *vin ordinaire* to magnificent.

Precisely what constitutes a quality area and which are the "right" grapes for it are studied here with as much Gallic precision as on the slopes of Beaune. It is not long since VDQS was the senior rank in these parts. Now many areas have been promoted to AC (and others are about to matriculate) as their true potential becomes evident.

This is also the country of the *vin de pays*. Pages 227–230 give details of the innumerable "country-wine" districts. But to sell your wine as a *vin de pays* is also an interesting alternative to growers who find the panoply of appellation too oppressive. There is a danger of the situation arising, which Italy already knows, where the bright pioneer believes (and rightly) that his wine is more important than its label. Some of the best wines of the Midi are sold as *vin de pays* because Cabernet or Merlot is not cricket under the existing rules.

Roussillon

The wines of the baking Roussillon enjoy the prestige of an ancient and unique product, its *vin doux naturel*, practically unknown outside France, but so proud of its origins that it sees port (the equivalent) as an imposter.

Wines from the smaller properties in Roussillon are fast improving. They are now developing a "boutique" style: carefully using new wood for fermentation and maturation, and able to aim for quality, because they can sell their best wines to a waiting market. There is a trickle-down effect of these estates to the co-ops, smaller properties being a model to work towards, particularly for prestige wines.

The sheltered seaside hills around Perpignan, and inland up the valleys of the Agly and the Tet, make some formidable red wines: the biggest and most highly coloured of the many based on the Carignan around the coast. The best examples, stiffened with superior "aromatic" grapes, have some of the structure of, for example, Châteauneuf-du-Pape, though with more roundness and a softer texture.

Many are best drunk young when their fruit flavour is at its peak, but more and more growers are deliberately ageing in oak and sometimes in bottle, too, to add complexity to sheer beef. Better grapes are making headway, especially Syrah and Mourvèdre. The best red wines are entitled to the Côtes du Roussillon (4,750 hectares) or the Côtes du Roussillon-Villages (2,260 hectares divided among thirty-two communes) ACs. At the same time, growers such as Gérard Gauby (*q.v.*) are showing what can be done with white grapes, even in this very hot region.

One small, red-wine area at the seaside resort of Collioure (360 hectares) on the Spanish border, has had its own appellation since 1949 for a singular, concentrated wine in which Carignan plays little part: a blend principally of Mourvèdre and Grenache Noir, with intense flavours unlike anything else north of the Spanish border. Alas, it is a declining AC, as local development eats into the rocky vineyard area. Top producers include the Banyuls co-op, Château de Jau, and Domaine du Mas Blanc (*qqv.*).

The *vins doux naturels* apparently owe their origin to the revered figure of Arnaldo da Villanova, the thirteenth-century sage and doctor of Montpellier, who introduced the still from Moorish Spain. It was he who first added *eau de vie* to naturally very strong wine to stop the fermentation and maintain a high degree of natural sugar – hence the term *doux naturels*.

But whereas in port, the *eau de vie* represents a quarter of the volume and more than half the alcoholic strength, in *vins doux naturels* it is limited to ten per cent of the volume, while the natural strength of the wine has, by law, to reach no less than fifteen degrees. It is not for a foreigner, with the privilege of an education in port, to hold forth on the qualities of *vins doux naturels*. Aged, they acquire an oxidized flavour known by the Spanish term *rancio*. Traditional producers age them in thirty-litre, pear-shaped glass jars known as *bonbonnes* (again, from the Spanish: *bombonas*).

Vin doux naturel is made in many different styles and varying degrees of sweetness and age. Some esteemed examples can be aged for as long as twenty years or more in large casks. As well as Grenache blends sold simply as Rivesaltes (9,190 hectares), Banyuls (1,360 hectares), or Maury (1,670 hectares), or as the single-varietal Muscat de Rivesaltes (4,330 hectares), there is a growing fashion for "vintage" styles, closely modelled on vintage port. These are often called *rimage*.

Leading Roussillon Producers

Cave des Vignerons de Baixas ☆–☆☆
Baixas. 2,100 hectares. www.dom-brial.com
Founded in 1923, this is an important cooperative, producing a comprehensive range of wines from all permitted styles, still and fortified. "Dom Brial" is their brand name, "Château Les Pins" their top label. By far the largest producer of Muscat de Rivesaltes.

Château de Caladroy ☆
Bélesta. 120 hectares
A large estate, with a beautiful twelfth-century castle. It produced humdrum wines until the late 1990s, when quality took a turn for the better and some oak-ageing was introduced.

Domaine de Canterrane ☆–☆☆
Trouillas. 227 hectares. www.canterrane.com
An important estate in Roussillon, unusual in retaining and offering for sale substantial stocks of older vintages of Côtes du Roussillon. Thus, in 2002, the 1976 was still available. Good Rivesaltes, too.

Château de Casenove ☆☆
Trouillas. 50 hectares
Owned by former press photographer Etienne Montès, who has worked closely with oenologist Jean-Luc Colombo to improve quality. The white Côtes du Roussillon is good, if not especially aromatic, and benefits from bottle-age. The top red is usually "Cuvée Jaubert": a pure Syrah, partly barrique-aged.

Domaine Cazes ☆☆☆
Rivesaltes. 160 hectares. www.cazes-rivesaltes.com
The Cazes brothers, leading producers for decades, have continued to modernize their winery and replant their substantial vineyards with Grenache, Syrah, Mourvèdre, and Malvoisie. Their Rivesaltes and Muscat de Rivesaltes are utterly reliable, and the old-cask-aged bottlings such as "Cuvée Aimé Cazes" are well worth their cost. In recent years the Cazes have made great progress with their red Côtes du Roussillon, Côtes du Roussillon-Villages, and supple wines such as "Canon de Maréchal" made by carbonic maceration. In 1993, they launched "Credo", a Cabernet Sauvignon and Merlot *vin de pays*, designed, successfully, to show how well the Bordeaux grapes work in the region.

Domaine des Chênes ☆☆–☆☆☆
Vingrau. 30 hectares
Alain Razungles is an oenology professor at Montpellier, so you would expect him to make good wine at the family domaine. And indeed he does, with some rich *cuvées* of Côtes du Roussillon-Villages and some excellent whites based on Grenache Blanc.

Domaine du Clos des Fées ☆☆–☆☆☆
Vingrau. 9 hectares. www.closdesfees.com

This ambitious little estate focuses on intense and very oaky red Côtes du Roussillon-Villages, using modern techniques such as lees-stirring and micro-oxygenation. The owner, Hervé Bizeuil, was once a *sommelier*, and clearly has his eye on selling to top restaurants. Fine quality and high prices.

Coume del Mas
Banyuls-sur-Mer

A joint venture founded in 2002 by GICB (*q.v.*) and Dr. Alain Raynaud of Bordeaux. The idea is to produce a Banyuls aged in new oak called "Quintessence", and a Collioure called "Quadratur".

L'Etoile ☆–☆☆☆
Banyuls-sur-Mer. 152 hectares. www.banyuls-etoile.com

This cooperative was founded in 1921, and produces an enormous range of Banyuls and red and rosé Collioure. Most of the wines are cask-aged, and older examples are aromatic and subtle, with echoes of orange, coffee, and caramel. Vintage styles are also made, but not every year.

Domaine Força-Réal ☆☆
Millas. 40 hectares. www.forca-real.com

In a spectacular mountainside setting, Jean-Paul Henríques produces red and white Côtes du Roussillon and Rivesaltes from a vineyard which he has restored and replanted since 1989. The second wine of the estate is the easy-drinking "Mas de la Garrigue", while the top wine is the wood-aged Les Hauts de Força-Réal. His pride is a caramel-and-coffee-flavoured Rivesaltes "Hors d'Age".

Domaine Gardiès ☆☆
Vingrau. 45 hectares

Since the early 1990s, Jean Gardiès has produced some delicious Côtes du Roussillon-Villages, especially the Syrah-dominated "Tautavel". The estate takes pride in its "Cuvée La Torre", given tannic backbone by its high proportion of Mourvèdre.

Domaine Gauby ☆☆☆
Calce. 42 hectares

Gérard Gauby makes a fascinating collection of wines, including red and white Côtes du Roussillon in various blends, and *vin de pays*, some of them partially aged in new barriques. The white Vin de Pays des Côtes Catalanes (a blend of Carignan Blanc, Grenache Blanc, and Maccabéo) sells for more than the Côtes du Roussillon.

Vines that are fifty-years-old produce *vieilles vignes*. "Muntada" is Roussillon's most remarkable Syrah, infused with flavours of red fruits. Production is limited to around 7,000 cases, as Gauby's selection policy dispatches 60% of the crop to the local cooperative.

G.I.C.B. (Groupement Interproducteurs du Cru Banyuls) ☆–☆☆☆
Banyuls-sur-Mer. 1,200 hectares

This is a large-scale operation, three cooperatives, which also act as a négociant. Consequently, it dominates the Collioure and Banyuls areas, producing well over two-thirds of all their AC wines. There has been considerable investment in equipment, and the general quality is good. The major brand name used is "Cellier des Templiers". There are well over a dozen different styles of Banyuls on offer, mostly traditional but also Rimage, and Collioure, usually from 70% Grenache Noir, plus Mourvèdre, and Carignan.

Château de Jau ☆☆
Cases de Péné. 134 hectares

The Dauré family owns a trio of excellent properties in the region. At Jau, they make some of the best Côtes du Roussillon, plus outstanding Muscat, and good whites of Malvoisie and Maccabéo. The Côtes du Roussillon-Villages is a blend dominated by Syrah and Mourvèdre. Their other estates are the eighty-hectare Clos des Paulilles, which produces Collioure and Banyuls, and Mas Cristine, which focuses on Rivesaltes.

Domaine Lhéritier ☆☆
Rivesaltes. 35 hectares

Henri Lhéritier produces wines from two distinct terroirs. "Crest" is a Grenache grown and aged in barriques. "Romani" is unoaked and more overtly fruity. The range is completed with various Muscats and Rivesaltes, some bottled under the "Domaine de Moulin" label.

Mas Amiel ☆☆☆
Maury. 155 hectares

The appellation's best producer, offering traditional, cask-aged Maury, as well as the modern vintage style. Under Charles Dupuy, quality improved steadily throughout the 1990s, with better grape selection and vinification techniques. After Dupuy's death in 1999, Mas Amiel was bought by Olivier Decelle.

Domaine du Mas Blanc ☆☆–☆☆☆
Banyuls-sur-Mer. 21 hectares

Dr. André Parcé was for many years the leading producer of Banyuls and Collioure (and in his role as a member of the INAO inner circles, notorious for his opposition to the promotion of Château Mouton-Rothschild to *premier cru* status). The property is now run by his son, Jean-Michel. Its range of wines is still traditional, and includes rare styles such as Banyuls Blanc, Banyuls Dry, and a *solera*-aged wine. In the 1980s, Dr. Parcé re-terraced his Collioure vineyards at immense cost, and the estate produces a number of different *cuvées* of this powerful red wine.

Domaine du Mas Crémat ☆☆–☆☆☆
Espira de l'Agly. 30 hectares. www.mascremat.com

Owned by the Burgundian Jeannin-Mongeard family since 1990, this estate produces white and red Côtes du Roussillon from dark schist and limestone soils. The barrique-fermented Grenache Blanc is remarkable.

Domaine du Mas Rous ☆☆
Montesquieu-des-Albères. 40 hectares. www.mas-rous.com

José Pujol makes a complete range of Roussillon wines, including a spicy, oak-aged Côtes du Roussillon tasting of red fruits.

Vignerons de Maury ☆–☆☆
Maury. 1,700 hectares. www.vigneronsdemaury.com

Founded 1910, this substantial cooperative produces 85% of the Maury output. It first introduced the vintage style of Maury in 1982. The top *cuvée*, the vintage "Chabert", is predominantly Grenache. A large volume of Côtes du Roussillon and *vins de pays* is also made.

Vignerons de Pézilla ☆–☆☆
Pézilla-La-Rivière. 750 hectares
One of the most go-ahead cooperatives in the region, producing a fascinating selection of *vins de pays* (including Chardonnay and Viognier) as well as Côtes du Roussillon wines from separate domaines (Château de Blanes is vinified in 50% new oak), and a range of Rivesaltes.

Domaine Piétri-Géraud ☆☆
Collioure. 13 hectares
A small, mother-and-daughter estate producing unfiltered Collioure from Grenache and Syrah, as well as cask-aged Banyuls and Muscat de Rivesaltes.

Domaine Piquemal ☆☆
Espira de l'Agly. 50 hectares. www.domaine-piquemal.com
In a series of cellars in the centre of Espira de l'Agly, Pierre Piquemal makes a wide range of wines, including a Merlot-dominated red, rosé, and a Muscat Sec. Recent vintages of Côtes du Roussillon have been vinified in wood and emphasize soft tannins and ripe fruit. Also Rivesaltes.

Domaine La Pleiade ☆☆
Perpignan. 12 hectares
A small property, owned by the former director of the Maury cooperative. As well as Maury from pure Grenache Noir, there is a little Côtes du Roussillon-Villages.

Domaine de la Rectorie ☆☆–☆☆☆
Banyuls. 30 hectares. www.la-rectorie.com
Marc and Thierry Parcé run this excellent estate, which produces some of the finest Collioure and a range of Banyuls. There are also some *vin de pays* using varieties and blends not authorized for AC wines. Two unusual wines are the "Vendange Tardive", from super-ripe grapes without the addition of spirit; and "Vin de Pierre", a dry, *rancio* style.

Les Vignerons du Rivesaltais ☆
Rivesaltes. 1,600 hectares
A very large cooperative producing more Côtes du Roussillon and Rivesaltes than any other. Top *cuvée* of Côtes du Roussillon is "Arnaud de Villeneuve", which is aged in wood. Also increasingly producing *vins de cépage* – Vins de Pays d'Oc made from single grape varieties such as Malvoisie, Cabernet Sauvignon, Sauvignon Blanc, and Chardonnay.

Domaine Sarda-Malet ☆☆–☆☆☆
Perpignan. 48 hectares
This estate, run by the dynamic Suzy Malet, specializes in AC Côtes du Roussillon and Rivesaltes *vin doux naturel*. There are two Côtes du Roussillon whites, made from a blend of Grenache, Roussanne, Marsanne, Malvoisie, and Maccabéo grapes – one is tank-fermented and the other ("Etiquette Verte") is vinified in wood.

The range of red Côtes du Roussillon wines includes a wood-aged "Etiquette Noire", which requires ageing in bottle for four or five years. The top wine is a Syrah/Mourvèdre blend, called "Terroir Mailloles", that is aged in new oak. The *vins doux naturels* include red Rivesaltes and Muscat de Rivesaltes.

Domaine des Schistes ☆☆
Estagel. 16 hectares
Jacques Sire left the local cooperative in 1989. Since going solo, he has made some truly remarkable red wines from his schist soils. The best wine is "Les Terrasses" from 60% Syrah, plus Carignan, and Grenache, which is aged in 30% new oak.

Les Maîtres Vignerons de Tautavel ☆
Tautavel
Founded 1927, this cooperative makes, among other wines, fine Côtes du Roussillon-Villages red, including an oak-aged version, and rich Rivesaltes.

Cellier des Templiers
See GICB

Domaine Tour Vieille ☆☆–☆☆☆
Collioure. 13 hectares
Christine Campadieu and Vincent Cantié have together developed one of the best estates in the region. There are usually two *cuvées* of Collioure: one a Grenache/Syrah blend, the other from Grenache and Mourvèdre. A specialty is "Cap de Creus", a dry, *rancio* style which Mme. Campadieu says is one of the traditional wines of the region: dry and very strong.

Domaine Vaquer ☆☆
Tresserre. 32 hectares
The unusual specialty here is a white Maccabéo that can age for fifteen years without difficulty. The top red wines are "L'Exception", a blend of four varieties, and a lively, pure Carignan. All the wines are *vin de pays*.

Domaine Vial Magnères ☆☆
Banyuls-sur-Mer. 10 hectares
This small estate is run by a former food chemist, Bernard Sapéras. It produces good Collioure as well as various styles of Banyuls. His best wine is usually "Al Tragou", a *rancio* wine from Grenache Noir, made by a partial *solera* method.

Les Vignerons Catalans ☆
Perpignan. 10,600 hectares.
www.vigneronscatalans.com
An enormous producers' association that works both with Roussillon cooperatives and with private domaines in order to release three million cases a year. The wines, many of which are made by carbonic maceration (the association was a pioneer in this method) are released under a profusion of labels.

Corbières

Justice has been slow in coming to Corbières, until overdue promotion in 1985, the biggest VDQS area in France, now *appellation contrôlée*. It is a huge region, stretching from Narbonne inland almost to Carcassonne, and the same distance south to the borders of Roussillon. It rises and rolls in parched hills of pale limestone, suddenly embroidered in bold patterns with the green stitches of vines. The neutral Carignan grape has long been dominant, but must not now exceed sixty per cent of the blend. Syrah, Mourvèdre, and Grenache are blended with it.

A good site, combined with restraint in cropping and careful winemaking, make solid enough wines, but all too often they lack flavour and flair. Improvements are taking the form of winemaking with *macération carbonique* to coax at least an illusion of fruitiness from the grapes, and – more radically – replanting with varieties with more personality than Carignan. There is also greater use of wood (for fermenting and maturing) to add an extra taste component to the wines. A small but significant growth of white wine in the region is notable, some of it barrel-fermented and oak-aged. However, red wine still accounts for ninety-three per cent of production.

There are some big properties as well as the thousands of growers who contribute to the cooperatives, which vinify seventy per cent of the crop. Two areas in the southeast corner of Corbières, largely co-op country, have long enjoyed the appellation Fitou for their reds on the grounds that they are more age-worthy than the rest. There are 2,600 hectares entitled to the Fitou AC, though the wines can be labelled Corbières should the producers so wish. There has also been a more recent division of the Corbières appellation into eleven different zones to highlight the varying terroir; the climate ranges from maritime to arid.

The following listing describes the currently best-performing properties, district by district, together with entries for some of the promising ones: names to look out for in the future.

Total production of Corbières averages 5.5 million cases.

Leading Corbières Producers

Château Aiguilloux ☆☆
Thézan-des-Corbières. 38 hectares
François Lemarié runs this estate, producing structured, tannic red and fresh, fruity rosé.

Château la Baronne ☆–☆☆
Fontcouverte. 60 hectares
As well as Corbières made by carbonic maceration, the Lignières family has, since 1999, made a *prestige cuvée* from high vineyards on the Montagne d'Alaric. Called "Les Vals", it is dominated by Mourvèdre and given prolonged ageing in 30% new oak.

Château de Cabriac ☆
Douzens. 115 hectares
Corbières red and white are made here. Most of these wines are designed for relatively early drinking. In top years, a "Cuvée Spéciale" is made from Syrah and Mourvèdre.

Château de Caraguilhes ☆–☆☆
St-Laurent-de-la-Cabrerisse. 125 hectares
A large organic estate bought in 1998 by the Burgundy négociant house, Louis Max. As well as a standard Corbières, the property produces two special *cuvées*: "Prestige" and "Solus". The "Prestige" spends nine months in barriques; "Solus" is a special selection, half of it Carignan. Flavours of black-cherries war with the heavy oakiness, a problem

that also mars the whites. Prices of the top wines are at Burgundian levels.

Château Cascadais ☆☆
St-Laurent-de-la-Cabrerisse. 34 hectares
This property is owned by Philippe Courrian of Château Tour Haut-Caussan (*q.v.*) in the Médoc. The red is given some cautious ageing in new oak.

Cave Coopérative de Castelmaure ☆–☆☆
Embres-et-Castelmaure. 300 hectares
A well-run co-op, using modern techniques such as micro-oxygenation to moderate the rusticity of the Carignan. The best wines include the "Cuvée Pompadour", aged in barrique but without new oak, and the "Grande Cuvée" from Syrah and Grenache.

Château la Domècque ☆
Lézignan. 52 hectares
This property was established in 1985, when the Roger family left the local cooperative. In 1992, they set up a négociant business called "Frédéric Roger". "Grand Millésime" is often the top wine, with around 50% Syrah in the blend. The wines, white as well as red, are uncomplicated.

Château Etang des Colombes ☆☆
Lézignan. 77 hectares
The average age of the vines here is ninety years. Christophe Gualco produces a variety of wines, of which the best are the barrique-aged "Cuvée Bois des Dames" and the old-vine "Cuvée Centenaire" with its rich, cranberry fruit.

Domaine de Fontsainte ☆☆–☆☆☆
Boutenac. 45 hectares
Yves Laboucarié is one of the region's most dedicated and scrupulous winemakers, benefiting from excellent and varied vineyards. He makes an unusually fresh and spicy *vin gris*, and two red wines. The "Domaine" wine has limited oak-ageing, the "Réserve La Demoiselle" is made from very old vines and aged in older barriques for ten months. These are serious wines, capable of ageing with interest for a decade or more.

Château Gléon-Montanié ☆☆–☆☆☆
Villesèque-des-Corbières. 50 hectares.
www.gleon-montanie.com
The Montanié family's wines are marked by their vigour and liveliness. The top "Cuvée Gascon Bonnes" is more extracted, with rich fruit and dense tannins. But it is hard to beat the regular Corbières for vivid, peppery character.

Château du Grand Caumont ☆☆
Lézignan. 105 hectares
The Rigal family's old estate near the River Orbieu has been energetically modernized. The "Cuvée Tradition" is made by carbonic maceration, the "Cuvée Spéciale" is based on a selection of old Carignan vines.

Domaine du Grand Crès ☆☆–☆☆☆
Ferrals. 15 hectares
Hervé Leferrer is no fan of carbonic maceration and all his red grapes are de-stemmed. The "Cuvée Classique" is aged in older barrels. The ripe, fleshy "Cuvée Majeure" is

made from low-yielding Syrah and Grenache, and aged in 25% new oak which confers some discreet, deft, oak character. The estate also makes one of Corbières' better whites, an unwooded *vin de pays* from Viognier and Roussanne.

Château Grand Moulin ✩✩–✩✩✩
Lézignan. 60 hectares

Jean-Noel Bousquet started bottling his own wines from 1988. All the reds are de-stemmed. The two top reds are the "Fûts de Chêne Vieilles Vignes"; and "Terres Rouges", which has a higher proportion of Syrah in the blend. Both are aged in up to 50% new oak. The result are supple, but peppery and smoky reds, with a great deal of character and concentration. The oaked white is heavy.

Château Haut-Gléon ✩✩–✩✩✩
Villesèque-des-Corbières. 29 hectares. www.hautgleon.com

Owner Léon-Claude Duhamel is keen on oak-ageing for his best wines. The result is a rather clumsy white from Bourboulenc and Roussanne, but the Syrah-dominated "Cuvée Eric Liot" is very fine: slightly gamey on the nose, but with sleek red fruits on the palate. The buildings of the estate include a twelfth-century chapel, but the winery itself is thoroughly modern.

Château Hélène ✩✩
Barbaira. 42 hectares

Marie-Hélène Gau was a reliable producer of Corbières for many years. Her wines were named after Greek heroes and heroines: "Cuvée Penelope" had a good dose of Syrah; "Cuvée Ulysse" was a more traditional blend, aged in older barriques; and "Cuvée Hélène de Troie" was mostly Syrah, aged in new oak. There was also a white "Hélène de Troie" from Grenache Blanc and Roussanne. In 2001, Madame Gau sold the estate to Robert Baudoin.

Château de Lastours ✩✩–✩✩✩
Portel-des-Corbières. 170 hectares

This remarkable estate is based around a château that is a centre for the mentally handicapped, most of whom are employed on the estate. The vines are planted in a kind of sheltered bowl surrounded by rugged hills, that provide director Jean-Marie Lignières with tracks for four-wheel-drive races. But the wines are serious. The "Cuvée Simone Descamps" and "Arnaud de Berre" are complex reds with ageing potential. In top vintages they produce a very powerful, barrique-aged red, called simply "Château de Lastours".

Château Mansenoble ✩✩✩
Moux. 20 hectares. www.mansenoble.com

Guido Jansegers abandoned his budding career in Belgium in 1992 in order to pursue his love of wine. Mansenoble is now one of the region's top estates, which Jansegers attributes to his fanatical selective harvesting, ensuring that only fully ripe grapes are picked. No carbonic maceration is used. The "Réserve" has around 50% Syrah, and is given a long maceration before going into older barrels for ageing. "Cuvée Marie-Annick" has more Mourvèdre in the blend.

Château Meunier St-Louis ✩✩
Boutenac. 113 hectares

The basic *cuvées* here are good but not exceptional. The best wines are "A Capella": the white an oaky, creamy blend of Grenache Blanc and Vermentino; the red, mostly Carignan and Syrah, aged in 20% new oak to give a rounded, ripe, spicy wine of some elegance.

Domaine de Montjoie ✩
St-André-de-la-Cabrerisse. 37 hectares

Replanting has improved the vineyards, which deliver a stylish, full-flavoured red and a light rosé.

Cave Coopérative Mont Tauch ✩✩
Tuchan. 1,000 hectares. www.cru-fitou.com

This very successful cooperative has recently swallowed up some of its neighbouring co-ops such as Paziols. By 2000, it accounted for 60% of all Fitou production. Quality is ensured by ruthless selection once the grapes arrive at the winery. There are many wines from single domaines, such as the excellent "Château de Ségures", and impressive *prestige cuvées* such as "L'Exception", aged twenty-one months in oak.

Château de Nouvelles ✩
Tuchan. 77 hectares

The estate produces both Corbières and Fitou, the latter made with considerably less carbonic maceration. The wine is sturdy and old-fashioned, but reliable.

Château les Ollieux ✩✩
Montséret. 53 hectares

Only red wine is made at Mme. Surbézy-Cartier's estate. In 1988, she introduced a barrique-aged wine, although it is not a special selection. Much effort was made in the 1990s to improve both the vineyards and the winery.

Château les Palais ✩✩
St-Laurent-de-la-Cabrerisse. 100 hectares

This estate made a name for itself when it pioneered the use of carbonic maceration for Corbières back in the 1960s. It continues to make soft, fresh, fruity wines, which have made it one of the most familiar Corbières names.

Château de Pech Latt ✩✩–✩✩✩
Lagrasse. 124 hectares

A fine, former monastic property, with a wide range of red, rosé, and white wines. The basic white is pure Marsanne and lacks excitement. Among the reds, the best is "Cuvée Alix" from fifty-year-old vines, with its soft, black-fruits richness.

Domaine des Pensées Sauvages ✩
Albas. 11 hectares

This estate, owned by the Bradfords, an English family, concentrates mostly on one wine: a red Corbières aged in barriques and larger wood. They have recently planted more Syrah in the vineyard, and also Viognier, to make a white wine.

Château Prieuré Borde-Rouge ✩✩
Lagrasse. 23 hectares. www.borderouge.com

Alain and Natasha Devillers-Quénehen came from Paris in the early 1990s to develop this estate, which has very old Carignan and Grenache vines. Best wines are labelled "Signature"; the white is over-oaked, but the red is solid.

Domaine du Révérend/Domaine du Trillol ☆–☆☆
Cucugnan. 80 hectares. www.sichel.fr
Owned by the Bordeaux négociant Sichel, the property is divided between two estates. Domaine du Révérend, the larger, is in the pretty hill-village of Cucugnan, while Domaine du Trillol is in more remote country at Rouffiac. The wines are made in the Bordeaux manner, with considerable wood ageing. Both estates make white and red Corbières, while Domaine du Révérend also makes small amounts of rosé. The wine is sound, but rarely as good as it ought to be.

Roque Sestiére ☆☆
Ornaisons. 27 hectares
Jean Bérail and his daughter Isabel are atypical in that they focus mostly on well-crafted white wines from local varieties such as Grenache Blanc and Bourboulenc.

Château St-Auriol ☆☆–☆☆☆
Lagrasse. 97 hectares. www.saint-auriol.com
Red Corbières is the principal wine from this highly regarded estate run by Claude Vialade and her husband, Jean-Paul Salvagnac. They are great proponents of the different terroirs of Corbières, believing the region of Lagrasse gives a particularly mild climate for grape-growing. Their wines certainly are generous, the reds aged for six months, the white for three months in new oak. In the late 1990s, a new *cuvée* was introduced: "La Folie de St-Auriol", aged in mostly new oak, but balanced by refreshing acidity.

Château de Vaugelas ☆
Camplong. 110 hectares
Substantial estate with low yields. It changed hands in the mid-1990s and was bought by Gérard Daspet of St-Emilion.

Domaine de Villemajou ☆–☆☆
Boutenac. 70 hectares
One of many properties owned by the enterprising Gérard Bertrand. To be enjoyed young: the rosé is light but fresh; the reds, made mostly by carbonic maceration, supple and fruity.

Cave Pilote de Villeneuve ☆
Durban Corbières. 450 hectares
Founded in 1948, this Fitou co-op makes mostly carbonic maceration wines. Generic bottlings, plus domaine wines such as "Château de Montmal" and "Domaine de Courtal".

Château la Voulte-Gasparets ☆☆☆
Boutenac. 45 hectares
Ideal soil, together with careful use of carbonic maceration and wood-ageing, results in rich supple wines. The "Cuvée Romain Pauc" is the best wine, made mostly from very old Carignan, and given a mere touch of new-oak ageing. Quality from Patrick Reverdy's admired estate has been highly consistent for many years.

Crémant de Limoux

The most unexpected and original of all the wines of the Midi is the high-quality sparkling wine of Limoux, tucked away behind Corbières on the upper reaches of the River Aude above Carcassonne. There is substantial evidence that this lonely area of hilly farms produced France's first sparkling wine, about 200 years before Champagne. The wine used to be called Blanquette de Limoux – Blanquette coming not from the colour of the wine but from the white down that covers the underside of the leaves of the Mauzac (alias Blanquette) grape.

Mauzac is the white grape "with a slight smell of cider" that is the base for the rustic bubbly of Gaillac. (Gaillac was a Roman wine town; its antiquity may be immense.) Whatever its origins, the traditional Limoux formula was Mauzac for sprightliness plus Clairette for mildness, originally just *pétillant*, but now made by the *méthode traditionnelle* to full pressure and extremely high standards of delicate blending. Clairette has more or less dropped out of the blend, having made way for Chenin Blanc and, more importantly, for Chardonnay. The Burgundian grape contributes its full flavour to the best *cuvées*; if Blanquette has a fault, it is a slightly pinched, lemony leanness, which can benefit by plumping out.

There are a number of different styles within Limoux. Crémant de Limoux is a sparkling version, which must have ninety per cent Chenin and Chardonnay. Blanquette must have at least ninty per cent Mauzac, with up to ten per cent each of Chardonnay; the rare Blanquette *méthode ancestrale* is pure Mauzac.

Finally, still wines are permitted under the Limoux AC appellation, which was created in 1993; in 2003, Limoux Rouge was also given AC rank. Unlike the wines of Champagne and Burgundy, those from Limoux are best drunk within a year or two of production.

Seventy per cent of the entire production of the 3,200 hectares under vines is in the hands of the vast and ultra-modern cooperative, the Caves du Sieur d'Arques. Founded in 1946, the co-op now has some 460 members. Recently it has added to its repertoire a selection of the best red wine from its members' vineyards, which include a surprising proportion of Cabernet and Merlot. The brand for the still wines is the "Toques et Clochers" label, and varietal *vins de pays* are sold as "Le Sept Soeurs".

There are also a number of good individual producers, such as the Domaine de Martinolles near St-Hilaire, Domaine Collin, Domaine des Terres Blanches, Domaine de la Noureille, and Domaine de l'Aigle.

Minervois

The River Aude parts the last wrinkles of the Pyrenees from the first of the Massif Central, and Corbières from the Minervois. The Minervois is a sixty-five kilometre (forty-mile) stretch of its north bank, encompassing both the gravelly flats along the river and the very different hills behind, topped by a plateau at 180 metres (600 feet). Rivers have cut deep ravines in its soft brown rock, in one place leaving a mid-river island for the tiny town of Minerve. The plateau is dry, treeless *garrigue* where the vine struggles, and even the Carignan makes wine with nerves and sinews. Modern winemaking in the high Minervois has produced some deliciously vital, well-engineered wines with a structure not of old oak beams, as the word *charpente* seems to imply, but more like an air-frame: delicately robust. Some white wines are made here from southern French varieties, but they represent only around three per cent of production. The commercial centre of the region is below, on the plain. A group of ten cooperatives, produces large quantities of wine.

More recently, smaller estates have overtaken the cooperatives in importance. AC status was granted to Minervois in 1985, and a slow upgrading of the permitted grapes is taking place. More recently, in 1998, Minervois La Livinière was granted its own AC. The defined area covers 2,600 hectares, but at present only 165 are planted; the wine must be aged for at least fifteen months before release.

Total area: 18,000 hectares (of which 4,500 are in production) with around 180 private producers and twenty-four cooperatives. Also produced within the Minervois is the deliciously sweet Muscat de St-Jean-de-Minervois *vin doux naturel*.

Leading Minervois Producers

Domaine des Aires Hautes ☆☆
Siran. 27 hectares
The vineyard was substantially replanted in the 1970s, but only began bottling its wines in 1991. Syrah is the dominant variety in the two top *cuvées*: "Sélection" and the plummy "Clos de l'Escandil", which is aged in 30% new oak for up to twenty months.

Domaine de Barroubio ☆☆
St-Jean-de-Minervois. 25 hectares
The estate produces a simple Minervois, but is better-known for its splendid Muscats, especially the very rich, raisiny "Cuvée Nicolas".

Château Borie du Maurel ☆☆–☆☆☆
Felines-Minervois. 26 hectares
The vineyards here are planted in a kind of amphitheatre. Owner Michel Escande believes in keeping yields below 30 hl/ha. The grapes are picked at optimal ripeness, so the whites can be both alcoholic and a touch sweet.

The regular Minervois is soft and simple; the "Cuvée la Féline" a sleek wine from 70% Syrah. "Cuvée Sylla" is pure Syrah in a rather austere style that sells for a high price.

Clos des Centeilles ☆☆–☆☆☆
Siran. 15 hectares
Patricia Boyer-Domergue is passionately committed to this atypical property, which fashions what she regards as highly traditional wines, even though some of them fall outside AC regulations.

"Carignanissime" is a pure old-vine Carignan; "Cuvée Capitelle" a rare plummy Cinsault from low-yielding vines. Clos Centeilles itself is a walled vineyard with old Carignan, Syrah, Grenache, and Mourvèdre; its wine is aged two years in older barrels.

Sometimes she produces a Pinot Noir, and a botrytis wine from Grenache Gris called "Erme de Centeilles".

Château Coupe Roses ☆☆
La Caunette. 32 hectares

Françoise Le Calvez is both owner and winemaker of this property implanted on the sunny hillside of La Caunette.

Her "Cuvée Prestige" is a warm, sumptuous, pure Grenache; her "Cuvée Orience" a leaner, more elegant wine, mostly from Syrah. The white is made from Grenache Blanc and Roussanne.

Château du Donjon ☆–☆☆
Bagnoles. 50 hectares. www.chateau-du-donjon.com
An old family property, now run by Jean Panis. The best wine is the cherryish "Cuvée Prestige", which is barrique-aged. A Merlot *vin de pays* is bottled under the "Domaine La Gardinière" label.

Château de Fabas ☆☆
Laure-Minervois. 50 hectares
Roland Augustin bought this well-regarded property in 1996. It enjoys quite a high percentage of Syrah and Mourvèdre. Syrah dominates both the "Cuvée Tradition" and the "Réserve", though only the latter is barrique-aged. The Syrah gives the wine its spice. The top wine, "Cuvée Alexandre", has 60% Mourvèdre, giving the wine good structure and longevity.

Château de Gourgazaud ☆–☆☆
La Livinière. 90 hectares
Highly influential property that pioneered carbonic maceration in the region. Carignan has more or less disappeared from the vineyards, and been replaced by Syrah and Mourvèdre. "Cuvée Mathilde" has 80% Syrah; the "Réserve" is the same wine but aged in new oak. There is also a wide range of *vin de pays* from Cabernet, Chardonnay, Viognier, and other varieties.

Château la Grave ☆
Badens. 96 hectares
A large property belonging to the Orosquette family, producing supple Syrah-marked blends and aromatic whites.

Domaine Lignon ☆
Aigues-Vives. 26 hectares
The leading wine is a rounded Syrah called "Les Vignes d'Antan" made by carbonic maceration.

Cave Coopérative de La Livinière ☆☆
La Livinière
This excellent co-op benefits from the new appellation, and its leading wine is "Grand Terroir", essentially a blend of Syrah and Grenache. It has a supple texture and flavours of stewed red fruits.

Château Maris ☆☆
La Livinière. 60 hectares. www.comtecathare.com
This very important property is part of the Comte Cathare group. The best wine is the *vieilles vignes*, a remarkable, pure Carignan from very low-yielding vines, made by carbonic maceration and then bottled without filtration.

Cave Coopérative de Peyriac ☆–☆☆
Peyriac. 620 hectares
Founded in 1930, this dynamic cooperative has 200 members and is also known as Cellier Tour St-Martin. Only about half the wine produced is sold as AC, the remainder

being varietal *vin de pays*. One of the leading labels is "Château de Peyriac", the white from Marsanne, the red from Syrah and Mourvèdre and barrique-aged. "Domaine des Ginestières", in contrast, is mostly Grenache.

Domaine Piccinini ☆☆
La Livinière. 30 hectares

Maurice Piccinini is one of the movers and shakers that is responsible for the creation of the new La Livinière AC. His estate, Domaine Piccinini, is now run by his son, Jean-Christophe. The regular Minervois is reliable and fruity, but the best wine is the Syrah-dominated "Cuvée Line et Laetitia".

Domaine de Ste-Eulalie ☆–☆☆
La Livinière. 13 hectares

Bought and run by an oenologist couple since 1996, the "Cuvée Cantilène" is a plump supple wine bearing the new La Livinière appellation.

Domaine la Tour Boisée ☆☆
Laure-Minervois. 60 hectares. www.domainelatourboisee.com

Jean-Louis Poudou divides production between AC wines and single-varietal *vin de pays* directed mostly at the export market. The most vigorous of the white wines is the "Cuvée Marie-Claude" from old vines of local varieties. Its red counterpart is a Carignan and Syrah in a round, slightly jammy style.

Château de Villerambert-Julien ☆☆–☆☆☆
Caunes-Minervois. 75 hectares

The Julien family has been working this estate since 1852, and is a passionate promoter of AC wines. The use of carbonic maceration was phased out some years ago, and most of the wines are aged in barriques, though the Juliens are very sparing in their use of new oak. The basic range, which is good value, is called "Opéra"; the red is warm and supple, the rosé unusually lively and fresh. The top *cuvée* was formerly called "Trianon" and now bears the name of the château, and the blend varies from year to year.

Château de Villerambert-Moureau ☆–☆☆
Caunes-Minervois. 120 hectares

The three Moureau brothers produce good quantities of enjoyable, quaffable wines, mostly from Syrah.

Château de Violet ☆–☆☆
Peyriac. 40 hectares. www.chateau-de-violet.com

It is a pleasure to discover such an old-fashioned property (with hotel and small museum attached). The *vieilles vignes* bottling has 50% Mourvèdre, aged in older barriques. The unusual "Cuvée de Violet" is pure old-vine Carignan.

as growers begin to realize that Europe no longer has any use for a bottomless wine lake. But certain of its hillsides have AC status and a comparable potential for quality as Corbières and Roussillon.

A dozen areas, which are rather confusingly scattered across the map, produce worthwhile wines. In the 1980s, one domaine showed what could be done in terms of extraordinary quality: the highly individual Mas de Daumas Gassac at Aniane. Now, many other properties are rivalling Daumas Gassac for renown, quality, and price.

The region is vast, with around 8,500 hectares claiming the appellation. Confusingly, it has been divided into numerous terroirs with the right to append their names to the Coteaux AC on the label. They are: Cabrières, La Méjanelle, Montpeyroux, Picpoul de Pinet, Quatourze, St-Christol, St-Drézéry, St-Georges-d'Orques, St-Saturnin and Vérargues. Some of these are now agitating for independent AC status comparable to that enjoyed by Faugères, St-Chinian, and Clairette du Languedoc. In addition, the regulations recognize "climatic regions", such as the Terrasses du Larzac, Sommières, Pézenas, La Clape, Terrasses de Béziers, Pic-St-Loup, and Grès de Montpellier.

The main concentration of vineyards is to the north of Béziers, in the first foothills of the Cévennes where the River Hérault leaves its torrents to become placid and poplar-lined. Cabrières, Faugères, St-Saturnin are such foothill vineyards. The best-known of them are Faugères and St-Chinian, in the hills to the west towards Minervois. Their reds can be full-bodied, distinctly savoury wines. St-Chinian, partly on chalky clay and partly on dark-purple schist full of manganese, is worth careful study.

The variety of soils in these hills gives character to their wine. The Berlou Valley, on the schist soils, is outstanding for riper, rounder reds than the rest of the region. The most individual, and an area with plenty of exciting potential, is La Clape, the isolated limestone massif like a beached island at the mouth of the River Aude, between Narbonne and the sea. The soil and climatic conditions on La Clape have shown that they can produce highly distinctive white wines. Cool sea breezes give the hills a microclimate of their own. Several domaines have planted Chardonnay. St-Saturnin also makes stylish wines, often with a significant proportion of Syrah.

Many growers in the Coteaux now make use of the *vin de pays* regulations to make such non-conforming wine as Merlots and Chardonnays, which can be excellent: look for "domaine" names on labels otherwise identical to those of reputable châteaux. By law "château" must not appear on a *vin de pays* label. Early hopes that such varietal wines would offer a serious challenge to similar wines from the New world have yet to be realized.

Coteaux du Languedoc

The stress in this name is on the *coteaux*. The plains of the Languedoc between Narbonne and Montpellier are the notorious source of calamitous quantities of low-strength blending wine. The area is, however, shrinking

Leading Coteaux du Languedoc Producers
(including *vin de pays*)

Domaine Clavel ☆☆–☆☆☆
Assas. 44 hectares. www.vins-clavel.fr

Jean Clavel was a prime mover in establishing the Coteaux AC, and his son Pierre continues his father's dedication to quality. Their regular bottling is the juicy "Les Garrigues" from Syrah and Grenache, but Clavel has won most acclaim for its "Copa Santa", a Syrah/Mourvèdre blend, aged in oak for fifteen months and unfiltered. Robust and ripe, the wine has smoky aromas and remarkable length of flavour.

Domaine La Grange des Pères ☆☆☆
Aniane. 7 hectares
Laurent Vallié worked at some of the top estates of southern France before planting his own vineyards, which came on stream in 1992. Yields are minute, so ripeness levels are high. The wines, sold as *vin de pays*, are aged in wood for at least two years, share the power of their neighbour at Daumas Gassac, and exceed their prices. The red is from Cabernet, Syrah, and Mourvèdre; the white mostly from Roussanne.

Domaine La Grange de Quatre Sous ☆☆
Assignan. 8 hectares
A wide range of wines from a small property. By releasing them as *vin de pays*, Swiss owner Hildegard Horat can juggle with varieties such as Chardonnay, Cabernet Sauvignon, and Cabernet Franc.

Mas de Daumas Gassac ☆☆☆
Aniane. 25 hectares. www.daumas-gassac.com
The only begetter of this inspired estate, Aimé Guibert, can justly be said to have brought pride to the Languedoc for the first time. After he bought the undulating property on volcanic terrain, consultants from Bordeaux raved about the quality of the soil. They were right. Guibert's Cabernet Sauvignon is a massive, long-lived wine, with the structure of Bordeaux and the wild quality of the Languedoc *garrigue*. The white is a blend of Chardonnay and Viognier; a fatly aromatic wine. Guibert has also worked closely with local cooperatives to produce large-volume wines of good quality at fair prices.

Mas Jullien ☆–☆☆☆
Jonquières. 16 hectares
Olivier Jullien runs this innovative, biodynamic estate in the Terrasses du Larzac. He combines experimentation with a respect for tradition, using local varieties despite the commercial difficulties in selling them. The range of wines is wide. "Depierres" is mostly Syrah grown on schist soils; "Vignes Oubliées" is an unusual white blend of Terret, Carignan Blanc, and Grenache Blanc. Quality is inconsistent, but this remains an admirable property.

Domaine Peyre Rose ☆☆☆
St-Pargoire. 20 hectares
In a remote spot high on the *garrigue*, Marlène Soria makes just two wines, both of them mostly from Syrah but from different vineyards: "Clos Léone" and "Clos des Cistes". Yields are extremely low, at around 20 hl/ha, and the wines are aged in tanks and large casks, a welcome change from the prevailing trend for new oak with everything. Both wines are opulent, powerful, and long-lived, the "Clos des Cistes" denser and more tannic, the "Léone" with more immediately appealing berry fruit.

Prieuré de St-Jean-de-Bébian ☆☆–☆☆☆
Pézenas. 28 hectares. www.bebian.com
The former owner, Alain Roux, brought cuttings here from the finest estates of the Rhône, and as the vines matured, he began to fashion his own long-lived and powerful wines. In 1994, the property was bought by wine writer Chantel Lecouty and her husband, Jean-Claude Le Brun. Together, they modified the vinification and introduced barrique-ageing. Although the wine is perhaps more elegant, it unfortunately may have lost some of its wild individuality. Very expensive.

Domaine de la Prose ☆☆–☆☆☆
Pignan. 15 hectares
Alexandre de Mortillet bought this propery in 1990, and built modern cellars in 2000. The red is pure Syrah given prolonged ageing in new barriques; the white, from Vermentino and Grenache Blanc, is barrel-fermented and emerges as rather leaden. But the red "Grande Cuvée" and its less oaky counterpart, "Cuvée d'Embruns", are very successful.

Château Puech-Haut ☆☆–☆☆☆
St-Drézery. 100 hectares
Since 1995, this estate has been making really excellent wines. The red "Prestige" is mostly Grenache and, to be honest, rather earthy, but the top offering, the new-oaked "Tête de Cuvée", which is 60% Syrah, is extremely intense. Very good white wine, too, mostly from Roussanne and Marsanne.

Skalli ☆–☆☆☆
Sète. 7,000 hectares
Robert Skalli is the revolutionary producer of stylish Vins de Pays d'Oc from Cabernet, Merlot, Viognier, and Chardonnay. "Fortant de France" is his standard brand, based in the vast old wine warehouses of the port of Sète. He has quite recently expanded his activities by marketing wines from various parts of southern France, such as Minervois and Corbières, and is also the owner of Chateau St-Supéry (*q.v.*) in Napa Valley.

Coteaux du Languedoc Districts

Cabardès

This area was promoted to AC in 1999: 850 hectares, cultivated by sixteen private estates and the members of four cooperatives. The wines are ingeniously divided stylistically into Vent d'Est (Mediterranean varieties such as Syrah and Grenache) and Vent d'Ouest (Atlantic varieties such as Cabernet and Merlot). The AC rules require the use of forty per cent of each.

Château de Pennautier ☆☆
Pennautier. 300 hectares. www.vignobles-lorgeril.com
Almost half the Lorgeril family's extensive domaine is AC. The best wines, both barrique-aged, are "Grande Cuvée" and "L'Esprit de la Bastide"; the latter contains a good deal of Syrah. Because of the considerable volumes produced here, different labels may be encountered in different markets.

Domaine de Cabrol ✩✩
Aragon. 21 hectares

From south-facing vineyards, the Carayol family produce the two classic styles of the region: Vent de l'Est and the more succulent Vent d'Ouest: both concentrated, spicy, and tannic.

Cabrières

In the Clermont l'Hérault region of the Cévennes foothills, close to Faugères. Best-known for the light rosé, made without pressing, but the schist soils are also suitable for producing Syrah-spiced reds.

Cave Coopérative Les Coteaux de Cabrières ✩
Clermont-l'Hérault

By far the most important producer, this cooperative makes both Cabrières and Clairette du Languedoc. "Cuvée Cabanon" is a 90% Syrah red.

La Clape

A 1,000-hectare coastal area of limestone hills between Narbonne and the shore. Elevation and the constant wind gives good acidity and refreshing whites, but red wines are improving fast. AC rules are complex, but focus on typical southern French varieties. About thirty-eight growers and two cooperatives.

Abbaye des Monges ✩✩
Narbonne

This property changed hands in 1997. The "Abbaye" wines are unoaked, but the "Château des Monges" red is barrel-aged. Rather jammy reds but substantial, peachy whites.

Château de Capitoul ✩✩–✩✩✩
Narbonne. 66 hectares

Charles Mock runs one of the largest properties in the region. In the 1990s, he restructured the vineyards and modernized the winery. The standard range is called "Lavandines", and "Les Rocailles" is a selection of wines from older vines. Both lines are very well-made, especially the creamy, apricotty whites. The Viognier *vin de pays* is one of southern France's best, and in some years there is a rather oxidative late-harvest version.

Domaine de l'Hospitalet ✩–✩✩
Narbonne. 52 hectares

Not so much a wine estate as a tourist complex, with restaurants and museums. Founded by the Ribourel family, it was sold in 2002 to the Corbières-based négociant, Gérard Bertrand. Changes in ownership and direction have robbed the wines of consistency, but the vineyards are well-located, and the best whites have been models for the region.

Château de la Négly ✩✩–✩✩✩
Fleury d'Aude. 50 hectares

Until 1992 the wines were sold to a cooperative. After substantial replanting, Jean Paux-Rosset began bottling his wines in 1997. He has launched various bottlings, of which the best appears to be "La Falaise" from Syrah and Grenache. He has attracted much publicity by producing

some single-vineyard wines in minute quantities, at prices to which most Burgundy *grands crus* merely aspire.

Château Pech-Celeyran ✩✩
Salles d'Aude. 95 hectares.www.pech-celeyran.com

Large property, owned for generations by the St-Exupéry family, divided between La Clape and *vin de pays* sites. Known for Viognier, Chardonnay, and barrique-aged reds.

Domaine de Pech-Redon ✩–✩✩✩
Narbonne. 42 hectares

Restored old estate in a lovely situation high on the hills at La Clape, near the sea. Christophe Bousquet runs it with energy. As well as good AC wines, there are atypical offerings such as an unoaked Alicante, and a Mourvèdre and Cabernet Sauvignon (rather dry).

The best wine is often "La Centaurée", mostly Syrah and first made in 1998.

Château Ricardelle ✩✩–✩✩✩
Narbonne. 43 hectares

Bruno Pellgrini has made major efforts to improve quality here, and believes he finally succeeded in 2000. Two fine reds: "Closalbières" and the very oaky "Blason". The former seems more vigorous and better-balanced.

Château de Rouquette-sur-Mer ✩✩
Narbonne. 50 hectares

A remarkable site, once a hunting reserve, situated on the rocky slopes of La Clape near the sea. Modern winemaking results in fresh, well-crafted red, white, and rosé; perhaps the best of the area.

Coteaux de Vérargues

Near Lunel, between Montpellier and Nîmes. *See* Muscat de Lunel, page 208. Used to be famous for light café wines, but now produces soft, gamey blends of Syrah and Mourvèdre.

Useful reds from the Lunel-Viel co-op, which has planted Merlot, and from estates including Château de la Devèze.

Faugères

Westernmost of the Cévennes foothill districts. Some very competent producers of red and rosé. An AC since 1982, covering 1,865 hectares. Rules insist on at least 20% Syrah or Mourvèdre, and a maximum of 40% Carignan.

Domaine Jean-Michel Alquier ✩✩✩
Faugères. 27 hectares

Jean-Michel Alquier runs this impeccable property, which his father founded in the 1950s. Two *cuvées*, "Maison Jaune" and the Syrah-dominated "Les Bastides", are carefully aged in up to 50% new oak. There is nothing exaggerated about these wines, which are among the most elegant of the Languedoc. Impressive white and rosé, too.

Château des Estanilles ✩✩✩
Lenthéric. 35 hectares

Michel Louison is something of a maverick, producing wines to suit his fancy and not too bothered about the niceties of AC regulations. Although his regular Faugères bottlings are very good, he is rightly renowned for his pure Syrah, and for a remarkable barrique-fermented rosé from Mourvèdre. His daughter, Sophie, is increasingly involved.

Château la Liquière ☆–☆☆☆
Cabrerolles. 70 hectares
The Vidal family has been producing high-quality wines for many years. Bernard Vidal is a fan of Carignan from old vines, but only when vinified by carbonic maceration. His basic range is "Les Amandiers", and his best wine is the concentrated and almost jammy "Cuvée Cistus".

Château Moulin de Ciffre ☆☆
Autignac. 40 hectares
The Lésineau family were proprietors in Pessac-Léognan before moving here in 1998. They are off to a good start, with a svelte, elegant Faugères with a touch of eucalyptus; and an even more stylish and concentrated special *cuvée* called "Eole".

Montpeyroux

Northern district for full-bodied chewy reds from the foothills of the Larzac Mountains, near the famous Gorges de l'Hérault.

Domaine de l'Aiguilière ☆☆☆
Montpeyroux. 25 hectares
The domaine produces two exceptionally rich and opulent reds: "Côte Dorée" and "Côte Rousse", the former more structured, the latter more seductive.

Domaine d'Aupilhac ☆☆☆
Montpeyroux. 15 hectares
Sylvain Fadat is one of the Languedoc's most respected winemakers. His standard Montpeyroux is a highly traditional wine with good tannic backbone, but Fadat delights in variety, also producing a dense blackberry-toned pure Carignan, a pure Cinsault from 100-year-old vines, and a *vin de pays* "Plos de Baumes" from Bordeaux varieties. Perhaps the best wine of all is "Le Clos", a richly oaky and plummy blend of Grenache, Mourvèdre, and Syrah.

Domaine Font-Caude ☆☆–☆☆☆
Lagamas. 18 hectares
Alan Chabanon sells one-third of his crop to the cooperative in order to maintain quality. The regular Montpeyroux is free of rusticity, and he also produces special *cuvées* made from pure Merlot and from Grenache. Unusually, the white is from Chenin Blanc. In 2002, the estate officially became biodynamic.

Pic-St-Loup

A 600 metre (1,800-foot) peak due north of Montpellier. The AC here requires Grenache, Syrah, and Mourvèdre to comprise ninety per cent of the blend.

There are 800 hectares that are cultivated by thirty-six private estates and three cooperatives. Only nine per cent of production is of white wine, which must be sold as Coteaux du Languedoc.

Mas Bruguière ☆☆
Valflaunès. 20 hectares
Planted near Domaine de l'Hortus (*q.v.*) in a narrow valley, the well-drained vineyards are refreshed and kept healthy by steady breezes. The tank-aged "L'Arbouse" is a spicy, full-bodied blend of Grenache and Syrah. "La Grenadière" is the oaked version: stylish, and developing gamey aromas with age.

Château de Cazeneuve ☆☆
Lauret. 22 hectares
Belgian André Leenhardt bought this property in 1988, and his first vintage was in 1992. For some years it has been one of the region's most dependable estates. The white, mostly Roussanne, is for drinking young, as is the rich, black-fruited "Les Calcaires": a blend of Syrah and Mourvèdre. The estate's *prestige cuvée*, "Roc des Mates", is mostly Syrah, aged in 40% new oak. "Les Calcaires" is less weighty, but sometimes better-balanced.

Domaine de l'Hortus ☆☆☆
Valflaunès. 34 hectares
It was Jean Orliac who put this region on the map. Since the 1980s he has made excellent wines, especially reds. Both the basic "Bergerie de l'Hortus" and the oaked "Grande Cuvée" are exemplary. The oak is perfectly judged and the wines always in balance. The white is an unoaked blend of Viognier, Sauvignon, and Chardonnay.

Château de Lascaux ☆☆
Vacquières. 35 hectares
Jean-Benoît Cavalier's vineyards lie close against the foothills of the Cévennes. The top wine, "Nobles Pierres", is a relatively light, cherry-scented wine (mostly Syrah), and its white counterpart, "Les Pierres d'Argent", has a tendency to be overwhelmed by oak; indeed the unoaked version, also from Roussanne, Marsanne, and Vermentino, is quite often preferable. Consistent wines overall, but they can lack concentration.

Mas de Mortiès ☆☆–☆☆☆
St-Jean-de-Cuculles. 21 hectares
A good chunky Pic-St-Loup, a more supple but very enjoyable red Coteaux du Languedoc, and, disarmingly, a *prestige cuvée* called "Jamais Content", with a sweet, oaky nose and well integrated tannins.

Château La Roque ☆☆
Fontanès. 42 hectares
A former Benedictine estate, it was bought by Jack Boutin in 1985. Sound, mostly unoaked wines, with a solid, leathery "Cuvée Tradition", and a more weighty "Cuvée Mourvèdre". Boutin's top wine, "Cupa Numismae", is Mourvèdre and Syrah, aged in 50% new barriques: menthol, cherries, and hefty tannins.

Château de Valflaunès ☆☆–☆☆☆
Valflaunès
Numerous *cuvées* juggle with Grenache and Syrah and, in the case of "Un Peu de Toi", with 75% Carignan. "Tem Tem" is pure Syrah. Despite the air of whimsy, these are serious wines, with an unusual intensity and elegance for the Languedoc.

Picpoul de Pinet

The vines of Pinet overlooking the Etang de Thau produce the Picpoul grapes for a pleasant, dry white with 12% alcohol and a touch of freshness. Whether by design or chance, these wines are the perfect accompaniment to the oysters farmed in the nearby lagoons.

There are 650 hectares, farmed by twenty-three private estates and five co-ops. A regrettable fad for oaked versions, stirred up by foreign visitors, has fortunately been slow to catch on.

Cave de l'Ormarine ☆–☆☆
Pinet
This co-op accounts for half the sales of the region. The basic *cuvée* is "Carte Noire", with its fresh, lemon-grass scent. The more selective "Duc de Morny" bottling, however, is better.

Château de Pinet ☆☆
Pinet. 45 hectares
Carefully made Picpoul white, including a rare, late-harvested version.

St-Chinian

In the Cévennes foothills, to the west. An important zone promoted to AC in 1982. There are 3,000 hectares, cultivated by ninety private estates and ten co-ops. Carignan is in decline, and reds are increasingly made from blends of Syrah or Mourvèdre. Quality has been improving steadily.

Château Borie La Vitarèle ☆–☆☆
St-Nazaire-de-Ladarez. 13 hectares
Jean-François Izarn grows his St-Chinian on schist soils; his Coteaux on limestone. "Les Schistes" is his top wine, a blend of Grenache and Syrah, and "Cuvée Les Crès" is unusual in that the vineyard is exceptionally stony. The wines are rich but earthy.

Domaine Canet Valette ☆☆–☆☆☆
Cessenon. 18 hectares
This is an organic estate run by the perfectionist Marc Valette. "Mille et Une Nuits" is a gamey blend of traditional varieties; "Maghani", a low-cropped blend of Grenache and Syrah; and "Les Galejades", a remarkable late-harvested red with flavours of cherry compote. All expensive and highly individual.

Château Cazal-Viel ☆☆–☆☆☆
Cessenon. 67 hectares. www.cazal-viel.com
An important estate, run by the Miquel family. Syrah dominates all the red wines. The principal *cuvées*, varying in oakiness and intensity, are "Cuvée des Fées" and "Larmes des Fées", both of exceptional quality. *Vin de pays* include a rich Viognier.

Mas Champart ☆☆☆
Bramefan. 16 hectares
Varied soil types define the *cuvées* here. All the wines are excellent, including the flowery white Coteaux du Languedoc, but the star turn is "Clos de la Simonette", only made in top years and containing 70% Mourvèdre – a meaty wine built for the long haul.

Other Coteaux du Languedoc Producers

Abbaye de Sylva Plana ☆☆
Laurens. www.vignoblesbouchard.com
Since 2000, excellent "Cuvée Songe d'Abbé" from old vines in Faugères.

Abbaye de Valmagne ☆–☆☆
Mèze
A spectacular Cistercian abbey, its nave full of vast casks, and a more modern Coteaux du Languedoc vineyard, producing rich, barrel-fermented Roussanne and reds.

Domaine des Aurelles ☆–☆☆
Nizas
A small Coteaux du Languedoc property, producing unoaked red wines from Carignan, Grenache, and Mourvèdre; and a barrique-fermented "Aurel" from Roussanne and Clairette.

La Baume ☆–☆☆
A major export-oriented négociant house, owned by Australian giant Constellation-Hardy. There are three tiers of quality: varietal, "Sélection", and "Domaine de la Baume".

Bessière ☆–☆☆
Mèze
Founded in 1902, a conscientious, family owned négociant house, working with some thirty different domaines across the Languedoc.

Château de Camplazens ☆☆
Armissan
Owned by Dutch merchant Hans Walraven since 1998. A complex property with vineyards in La Clape and the Coteaux du Languedoc. Initial releases were impressive and beautifully packaged.

Domaine Capion ☆☆
Gignac
Owned by Adrian Buhrer, who also owns Saxenburg in South Africa. "La Garenne" is a Bordeaux blend, "Le Juge" a Rhône-style blend, both aged in new oak.

Domaine la Chevalière ☆–☆☆
Béziers
A replanted property acquired by Chablis producer M. Laroche in 1997. Most of the wines are made from purchased grapes. The top blend, made only in exceptional years, is "La Croix Chevalière", while the most basic range of varietal wines has, since 2002, been marketed as "M. Laroche South of France".

Clos Bagatelle ☆☆
St-Chinian
Good St-Chinian wines, especially the svelte new-oaked "Cuvée Gloire de Mon Père".

Clos Marie ☆☆
Pic-St-Loup
An acclaimed estate, but both the 50% Syrah "Olivette" and the top "Cuvée Simon" can suffer from excessive new oak.

Domaine de Clovallon ☆☆
Bédarieux

Catherine Roque produces a large range of wines, including the rare Clairette du Languedoc.

Comte Cathare ☆☆–☆☆☆

A quality-oriented négociant house founded in 1994 by Robert Eden and partners. The company owns five properties in different appellations, and also produces *vin de pays* from Syrah and other varieties.

Château Coujan ☆–☆☆☆
Murviel

Florence Guy runs this large domaine in St-Chinian. The best St-Chinian wine is the "Cuvée Gabrielle de Spinola", with 50% Mourvèdre, but the estate is even better known for its wide range of varietal wines.

Domaine Félines ☆–☆☆
Mèze

A good producer of Picpoul, with vibrant, crisp wines.

Château de Figuières ☆–☆☆
Narbonne

A La Clape estate owned by the Dupressoir family since 1994, and young Stephanie Dupressoir makes the wines. Various cuvees, but most of the wines are soft and spicy and best drunk young.

Château de Flaugergues ☆–☆☆
Montpellier. www.flaugergues.com

The best property in the small gravelly region of Méjanelle, in the hands of the Comtes de Colbert for three centuries. Good blends from Grenache and Syrah.

Foncalieu ☆–☆☆
Arzens. www.foncalieuvignobles.com

A company founded in 1967 to market the production of eighteen cooperatives farming 9,000 hectares. Most of the wines are sold as *vin de pays*, and the firm has a wide range of brands and an annual production of two million cases.

Domaine Fontaine Marcousse ☆☆
Puisserguier

The domaine only started bottling its St-Chinian wines in 1999. "Cuvée Quercus" is the most concentrated wine, aged in 50% new oak, and Carignan fans should note the supple "Cuvée Capellou".

Château Haut-Fabrègues ☆–☆☆
Faugères

Large property. Good oaked and unoaked reds.

Domaine Henry ☆–☆☆
St-Georges-d'Orques

The top wine from this domaine is the "Cuvée St-Georges-d'Orques". It has surprising delicacy, with flavours of strawberries and cherries.

Maison Jeanjean ☆
St-Felix-de-Lodez

A huge, family owned négociant house with wines drawn from the whole of southern France.

Domaine des Jougla ☆☆
Prades-sur-Vernasobres

A family estate founded centuries ago in the Cévennes foothills. Sound St-Chinian, mostly from schist soils.

Cave Coopérative de Laurens ☆
Laurens

About one-third of all Faugères is produced by this reliable co-op, as well as numerous *vin de pays*.

Listel
See **Domaines Viticoles des Salins du Midi**

Château Maurel Fonsalade ☆☆
Causses et Veyran

An exceptionally beautiful estate in St-Chinian, producing sleek wines with no trace of rusticity.

Domaine de Météore ☆
Cabrerolles

Liquorice flavours are the hallmark of the Faugères from this small domaine. The unoaked version is marginally preferable to the oaked.

Domaine de la Mirande ☆–☆☆
Pinet

Zesty, citric Picpoul de Pinet.

Domaine de Nizas Caux

A large property bought in 1998 by John Goelet, the owner of Clos du Val (*q.v.*) in Napa. Bernard Portet of Clos du Val oversees the winemaking.

Château Notre Dame du Quatourze ☆
Narbonne

The leading property in the Quatourze near Narbonne. Full-bodied Carignan thrives on the quartz soils.

Les Coteaux du Rieu-Berlou ☆
Berlou

A leading cooperative in St-Chinian, best-known for its "Schisteil" brand. The wines are correct but lack personality.

Cave Les Vins de Roquebrun ☆☆
Roquebrun

Best of the St-Chinian cooperatives, with some impressive whites from Roussanne, and Mourvèdre-dominated reds.

Château St-Martin-de-la-Garrigue ☆☆
Montagnac

There are seventeen varieties planted on Jean-Claude Zabalia's estate, so the range of wines is considerable. Both "Cuvée St-Martin", from Syrah and Mourvèdre, and "Cuvée Bronzinelle" (a Rhône-style blend) are excellent.

Cave Coopérative de St-Saturnin ☆–☆☆
St-Saturnin

Vineyards in the *garrigue* of the Cévennes foothills with a gamey, cherryish *cuvée* called "Seigneur des Deux Vierges".

Domaines Viticoles des Salins du Midi ☆–☆☆
Sète

A huge company, better known as Listel, producing salt

as well as good-value wines from 1,700 hectares of vineyards. As well as the vineyards on the phylloxera-free sands of the Golfe du Lion, the company owns 250 hectares in the Var at Pierrefeu and Ollières where it produces Côtes de Provence, Vin de Pays des Maures and Coteaux Varois.

Domaine du Tabatau ☆☆
Assignan
Bruno Garcia, former vineyard manager at Mas de Daumas Gassac, and his brother set up their own St-Chinian estate in 1997. Very extracted reds

Domaine Terre Mégère ☆–☆☆
Cournonsec
An estate with a rising reputation west of Montpellier. Good white blend "La Galopine" from Viognier and Chardonnay, and reliable red *vin de pays*.

The Muscats of Languedoc

Three small zones along the central south coast, between the wine port of Sète and the marshes of the Camargue, have appellations (and an antique reputation) for sweet Muscat *vins doux naturels* – 1,350 hectares in all. Frontignan is the biggest and best-known. Its vineyards stretch along the coast through Mireval (the second appellation) towards Montpellier.

The sole permitted grape is the Muscat à Petits Grains; its wine powerfully aromatic, brown and sticky, but lacking (at least as it is made today) the freshness and finesse of Muscat de Beaumes-de-Venise. Since the early 1980s, an independent producer, Yves Pastourel at Château de la Peyrade, has worked to improve this situation and succeeded in producing a lighter and more refined wine. The third area is Lunel, halfway between Montpellier and Nîmes, just inland from the Carmargue.

The cooperatives of Frontignan and Lunel are the major producers, and the cooperative at Vérargues also makes Muscat. High-quality private estates are few and far between. Other than La Peyrade, there is the Mas de Bellevue at Lunel, and Domaine Lacoste, also at Lunel, which also produces an unusual late-harvested version from grapes that have raisined on the vine.

Clairette du Languedoc

A scarcely merited *appellation contrôlée* for a generally dull and dispiriting dry white from Clairette grapes grown in several communes along the Hérault. Much of it is fortified as a cheap apéritif and sold under such names as "Amber Dry".

But some producers are attempting to make the most of what Clairette can offer, and some sweet versions are also produced. The best producers include Domaine de Clovallon (*q.v.*) in the Coteaux du Languedoc and Château St-André at Pézenas. The most important producer, inevitably, is the co-op: the Caves Coopérative de La Clairette d'Adissan at Adissan.

Costières de Nîmes

This rapidly improving region has for some time been in the throes of an identity crisis, unable to decide whether it forms part of the Languedoc or Provence. Its location, just south of Nîmes on undulating slopes with a view onto the Mediterranean, suggests the latter, but it is generally recognized as belonging to the former. It's a hot, stony region, with some slight maritime influence. It is also large, declaring production from around 3,300 hectares, cultivated by some eighty private estates and seventeen cooperatives.

The traditional varieties here are the usual suspects of the Midi, but in recent years much more Syrah has been planted, and with happy results. Syrah here gives intense, pure wines of great charm. Charm and suppleness are the present hallmarks of the Costières. This is not a region that shapes wines of great depth or complexity, though some producers see no reason why such styles should not emerge in the future. There is one other AC tucked within the Costières: the rather obscure forty-hectare Clairette de Bellegarde. Some attractive whites are also being made from Viognier, Marsanne, and Roussanne, not necessarily as AC wines. About one-third of production is of rosé wines. Estates tend to be large and many vineyards are picked by machine. Thus costs are relatively low, and this is reflected in the reasonable prices charged for even the best wines.

Château Beaubois ☆☆
Franquevaux. 60 hectares
The Boyer-Moutret family took over this property in 1985 and produces a well-balanced "Cuvée Tradition" and, in certain vintages, an oaked "Cuvée Elegance". Initially over-oaked, "Elegance" is now more harmonious. Fragrant white from Roussanne and Grenache Blanc.

Château de Belle Coste ☆☆
Caissargues. 65 hectares
This serious property is just outside Nîmes. The regular red is made from Grenache and Syrah; the top "Cuvée St Marc" has Mourvèdre to give the blend more backbone. The white has always contained a good deal of Viognier, which was permitted here on an "experimental" basis in the late 1980s, and has been in the wine ever since.

Château de Campuget ☆☆
Manduel. 160 hectares. www.campuget.com
The Dalle family own two good properties: Campuget and Château L'Amarine a few miles away. The winery is modern and well-equipped. Standard *cuvées* can lack concentration. The "Prestige" bottling is better, and the "Cuvée Sommelière", a pure Syrah aged in new 500-litre barrels, is first-rate, with a lovely red-fruit character and fine length of flavour.

Château Grande Cassagne ☆☆–☆☆☆
St-Gilles. 32 hectares
Since 1994, the Dardé brothers have made deliciously fruity red, white, and rosé. Rapid commercial success allowed them to be more selective, and in recent years they have introduced some new *cuvées*. The white "Hippolyte" is mostly Roussanne, vinified in oak, and the red "Hippolyte" is a selection of their best Syrah. "Cuvée Civette", in contrast, is mainly Grenache.

Mas de Bressades ☆☆–☆☆☆
Manduel. 22 hectares

Production here is divided between the "Cuvée Tradition" and "Cuvée Excellence". The white "Excellence" is mostly Roussanne fermented in new oak, and has a spicy, citric character. The red is mostly Syrah with some Grenache and can, in certain vintages, be a tannic wine. Excellent rosé.

Mas Carlot ☆
Bellegarde. 72 hectares

Owned by a Paris restaurateur, Mas Carlot, which also bottles its oaked wines as "Château Paul Blanc", has a sound reputation, but the red wines have often been too gamey, and the whites, heavy. Nathalie Blanc is also a significant producer of Clairette de Bellegarde.

Mas de Tourelles ☆
Beaucaire. 85 hectares

Hervé Durand's property is less remarkable for its Costières wines than for its painstaking re-creation of a Roman winery, complete with Roman-style wines aromatized with honey and seawater.

Château Masneuf ☆–☆☆
Vauvert. 120 hectares

The ebullient Olivier Gibelin is one of the best-known characters of the region, having been president of its *syndicat* since 1997. He bustles with energy and new ideas. He makes a very wide range of wines under many labels, including "Domaine de Pierrefeu". Quality swings widely.

Château Mourgues du Grès ☆☆–☆☆☆
Beaucaire. 40 hectares

François Collard favours a very ripe style for his red Costières. Sometimes it verges towards the jammy end of the spectrum, but usually it has lovely purity of fruit, reflecting the high proportion of Syrah he favours. His best selections are bottled as "Terre d'Argence", and there is also an oaked *cuvée* "Les Capitelles" that offers a different interpretation of the same excellent fruit. The rosé is one of the region's finest, with delicate strawberry aromas. There is also a rosé "Capitelles", mostly from Mourvèdre.

Château de la Tuilerie ☆–☆☆
Route de St-Gilles, Nîmes. 70 hectares.
www.chateautuilerie.com

An immaculately maintained estate owned by Mme. Chantal Comte. The property includes large peach and apple plantations. Her best wine is usually the *vieilles vignes*, mostly from Syrah and with unusual density and spice.

Corsica : L'Ile de Beauté

The importance of France's dramatically mountainous island of Corsica used to be almost entirely as a producer of bulk material for table-wine blends. When France lost Algeria, its winegrowers flooded into the island to plant the plains of the east coast with the basic grapes of Algeria and the Midi: Carignan, Grenache, and Cinsault. In the period

1960–'73, the island's vineyards expanded from 8,000 to 31,000 hectares. A scandal erupted in 1974, with accusations of fraud and illegal practices, and this resulted in a period of retrenchment, with 3,800 hectares being pulled up again. From 1983 the vineyards were restructured: many small properties vanished, and there was a growth in relatively big properties farmed for quantity rather than quality – with an average yield over the island of seventy-six hectolitres per hectare . The appellation Vin de Corse was instituted in 1976 as an encouragement to limit crops. The specific interest of Corsican wine lies in *crus* of Vin de Corse and three more limited appellations (Patrimonio, Cap Corse, and Ajaccio) relating to the best vineyards, which retain traditional grape varieties. These include the red Nielluccio (Italy's Sangiovese) and Sciacarello, which may be unique to Corsica, and the white Vermentino. Just over half the island's production from the present 7,500 hectares is red wine, which is traditionally made as varietals, but Syrah and Mourvèdre have now been planted for blending with Sciacarello. Corsicans do not much care for white wines, and tend to drink the island's powerful, dry rosés with fish in the restaurants of Bastia and Ajaccio. Patrimonio, in La Conca d'Oro in the north of the island, is relatively long-established for rosé and red made primarily of Nielluccio and whites from Vermentino, with one degree higher minimum alcohol (12.5) than the rest of the island's wines. Ajaccio, the capital, has Sciacarello red and rosé and Vermentino white. Calvi and the region of Balagne in the northwest have a relatively high proportion of AC wine. Cap Corse specializes in dessert wines, including sweet Muscat.

Porto-Vecchio and Figari, and the flat southeast, have more vineyards, but using a good proportion of Nielluccio. Sartène, around Propriano in the southwest, is the area with the highest proportion of appellation wines (seventy-five per cent), of Corsican grapes – mainly Sciacarello – and of traditional-style, small growers working on good hill slopes. Plantings of Cabernet Sauvignon, Merlot, Chardonnay, and Chenin Blanc on the eastern plain south of Bastia are included in increasingly interesting Vin de Pays de l'Ile de Beauté. Production is dominated by two large co-ops: the UVAL and UVIB, and by large companies such as Skalli, which uses the "Coteaux de Diana" label.

In Ajaccio the leading domaines are Clos d'Alzeto, Clos Capitoro (lean, elegant, long-lived reds), Alain Courreges, Domaine de Peraldi (good Sciacarello), and Domaine de Pratavone (leathery, raspberry-toned reds; floral whites). In Calvi, the top properties are Domaine d'Alzipratu and Clos Culumbu (both producing peppery rosés), and Domaine Maestracci. In Figari the leading estates are Domaine de la Murta (rich rosé), Domaine Petra Bianca, and Domaine de Tanella (especially "Cuvée Alexandra").

Patrimonio has a number of quality-conscious estates: Antoine Arena (serious reds and late-harvest Vermentino), Clos de Bernardi, Domaine du Catarelli, Dom Gentile (sound across the board), Domaine Leccia (very well-made, modern wines), Clos Marfisi, Orenga du Gaffroy (largest estate in the region, with a good, oaked "Cuvée des Gouverneurs"; Domaine San Quilico, under the same ownership, and Domaine de Pastricciola). The only serious estate in Porto-Vecchio is Christian Imbert's Domaine de Torraccia, with its outstanding "Cuvée Oriu", mostly from Nielluccio. In Sartène, the leading property is Domaine Fiumicicoli, with attractive whites and oaky reds, and Domaine San Michele.

The South West

The southwest corner of France exists in calm self-sufficiency. Its rich food and notable wines seem, like its beauty and tranquillity, to be its private business. To the east lie the great vineyards of the Languedoc; to the north Bordeaux; Spain lies beyond the towering Pyrénées to the south. In their foothills and the river valleys of the Tarn, the Garonne, the Lot, the Gers, the Adour, and the Gave, a different race of wines is grown, bearing no relation to the Midi and remarkably distinct from Bordeaux. Historically, some of these wines, notably Cahors and Gaillac, were exported via Bordeaux and known as the wines of the *hauts-pays*: the high country. Some use the Bordeaux grapes. But all except those closest to the Gironde, such as Buzet, have real character of their own to offer. A variety of grapes with extraordinary local names, some of them Basque, gives a range of flavours found nowhere else. In the 1990s, the world began to discover them and encourage the expansion of what was a depleted vineyard. Now fashion is swinging towards the regional idiosyncrasies the South West has to offer.

Bergerac

The vineyards of Bergerac flank the river Dordogne, which joins the Garonne downstream from Bordeaux. The growers could thus escape the greedy clutches of the Bordeaux merchants who controlled the passage of wines from other *hauts-pays* such as Cahors and Gaillac. Bergerac had free access to overseas markets – above all – the prosperous Dutch. The region's attachment to the Protestant religion caused many Huguenots to flee to Holland after the suppression of the reformed religion in 1698, and this reinforced Bergerac exports to that country. The Dutch preferred sweet white wines, which thus became and remained the pride of the Bergerac region. Monbazillac is its most famous name. But in the twentieth century, this style of wine was hard to sell. So the Bergeraçois tried red. Demand has switched to and fro between red and white, with Bergerac tending to be a step behind. The varieties planted are the Bordeaux red grapes, which perform excellently here, with Merlot in the majority. With a current near-equilibrium between red and white grapes, Bergerac is at last well-placed for the campaign it is waging to become better-known. The presence of a prosperous ex-pat community and the fact that foie gras could be considered the local sport are both factors to encourage winemaking enterprise.

Bergerac is not one simple appellation but, like Bordeaux, an all-embracing one with subsections determined by slopes, soil, and microclimates. Red Bergerac unqualified is light (minimum ten degrees alcohol), unmistakably claret-like by nature: an indistinguishable substitute for many light Bordeaux reds at a markedly lower price. Côtes de Bergerac are bigger, and more so still are the twelve-degree wines from the chalky eastern part of the region with its own appellation, Pécharmant (390 hectares) which, like claret, improve with ageing. The vintage of 2000 made some wines to convince any sceptic.

The dry white is sold as Bergerac Sec. Some growers exercise the option of introducing the flavour of Sauvignon into wine that is still predominantly Sémillon and, to a lesser extent, Muscadelle. A new generation of winemakers is working with barrique-ageing for their richest wines, but there is a genuine taste for the semi-sweet here which can produce wines of great charm to the open-minded.

No fewer than five inner regions of Bergerac enjoy appellations for sweet and semi-sweet whites (which rely on Sémillon and hope for a degree of "noble rot"). Just south of the town of Bergerac, Monbazillac (1,770 hectares), with its operatic château (the property of the local cooperative), is capable of truly luscious and powerful wines after the style of Sauternes. The best now share the miraculous harmony of fruity acidity that makes a great Sauternes – and their lives are no shorter. I have lingered long over forty-year-old Monbazillac that had turned a fine tobacco colour.

Saussignac is a tiny but growing appellation (62 hectares) for semi-sweet *moelleux* wines where some producers are making wines as rich as those of Monbazillac. There is much discussion about whether it would be useful to press for a new appellation for high-quality, botrytis-affected wines. Certainly this is a new name to look for.

North of the Dordogne, Montravel (378 hectares) is a (usually superior) Bergerac Sec – the names are interchangeable. The distinctions between the appellations Côtes de Montravel (*moelleux*), and Haut-Montravel (fully sweet) complicate an already complex situation for the Montravel growers, whose red wines previously could not be called Montravel (they had to be called Bergerac). The reds were sold as Bergerac until 2001, when the growers finally won the right to their own Montravel Rouge AC.

Rosette, an almost lost appellation, is having a mini-renaissance. It is another medium-sweet white, produced in the hills just north and west of Bergerac town.

Finally, Côtes de Bergerac, when applied to white wines, denotes a *moelleux* style to which producers are not entitled or choose not to apply one of the inner appellations. Its sweetness levels range from four to fifty-four grams of residual sugar. Quality is rarely special.

Leading Bergerac Producers

Basic red and dry white Bergerac is produced by most growers throughout the regions, even when they are entitled to use the name of an inner appellation. The listings that follow are somewhat capricious, since most Bergerac producers produce Monbazillac or other sweet wines, and vice versa.

Bergerac

Château Bélingard ☆–☆☆
Pomport, 90 hectares. www.chateaubelingard.com
Laurent de Bosredon is an enthusiastic producer of red and white Bergerac of reliable, if unexceptional, quality, and some fine, rich Monbazillac called "Blanche de Bosredon". He favours a racy, elegant style of Monbazillac in preference to a wine that is too weighty and tarry.

Château de la Colline ☆☆
Thénac. 17 hectares

A new property established in 1994. The red is overwhelmingly Merlot, and appropriately succulent, and the Sémillon-dominated white is barrel-aged. Old Sémillon vines are the source of a very rich, nobly rotten wine called "Confit de la Colline".

Château Grinou ☆☆
Monestier. 35 hectares

Guy Cuisset is an all-rounder making good red Bergerac, especially the oak-aged "Reserve", as well as both dry white Bergerac and fine Saussignac.

Domaine de la Jaubertie
Colombier. 50 hectares

A splendid property in disarray for many years. Nick Ryman developed the estate in the 1970s, and his son Hugh, later the best-known of all the flying winemakers, cut his teeth by making balanced and elegant reds and delicious whites, including a rare pure Muscadelle. Family rifts leave the property's future uncertain.

Château Masburel ☆☆
Ste-Foy-la-Grande. 25 hectares. www.chateau-masburel.com

Neil and Olivia Donnan have opted for a rich, powerful style of Bergerac, both red and white.

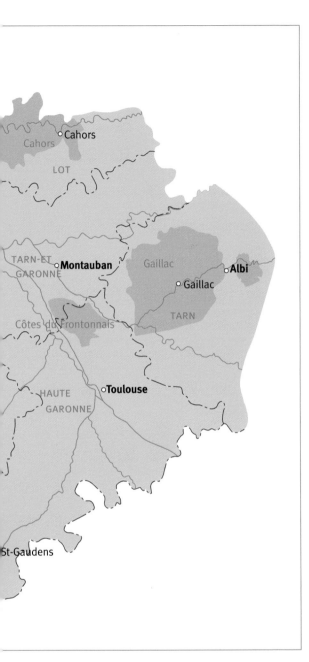

Château de Panisseau ☆
Thénac. 70 hectares
A well-known estate that was acquired by Groupe Suez in 1990. Sound wines, both white and red, with oaked and unoaked ranges.

Château Theulet ☆☆
Monbazillac. 50 hectares
An estate that goes back to the time of the special relationship with Holland. Owner Pierre Alard makes supple, highly drinkable red Bergerac, mostly from Merlot, and a zesty "Sec Prestige". The estate also makes good Monbazillac "Cuvée Prestige", aged in 50% new oak.

Château la Tour des Gendres ☆☆☆
Ribagnac. 44 hectares
Made from mostly biodynamic vineyards on diverse soils just south of Monbazillac, Luc de Conti makes stylish and distinctive wines. As well as a white Bergerac called "Moulin des Dames", "Cuvée des Conti" is mostly Sémillon, aged briefly in new oak. The wine has a distinct flavour of citrus fruits. A special *cuvée* called "Athologia" is made from late-picked Sauvignon, aged in oak. The red "Anthologia" is made by the severely artisanal method of fermenting in 500-litre barrels. The red wines, aged on their fine lees, are the most expensive in Bergerac: especially the "Moulin des Dames" from Cabernet and Merlot. Better value are the excellent, skilfully oaked wines labelled "Gloire de Mon Père".

Domaine les Verdots ☆☆–☆☆☆
Conne-de-Labarde. 21 hectares
David Fourtout produces a bewildering range of wines under a variety of labels. The best are offered under the simple but grand name of "Le Vin". The white is highly distinctive, including as it does a proportion of botrytized grapes. There is also a small quantity of Monbazillac made from leased vineyards, and what must be the only Bergerac *moelleux* aged partially in new oak.

Pécharmant

Château Beauportail ☆☆
Bergerac. 10 hectares
Fabrice Feytout's fairly small property close to the town produces a rich, discreetly oaky wine that should keep well.

Château Champarel ☆
Pécharmant. 8 hectares
Good, sturdy wine that needs a few years for its tannins and fruit to integrate.

Domaine du Haut-Pécharmant ☆☆
Bergerac. 45 hectares
The second-largest Pécharmant vineyard. Owner, Michel Roches, makes his long-lived wine in a traditional manner, with only the "Cuvée Prestige" being aged in oak. His most distinctive wine is "Cuvée Veuve Roches", made from 70% Cabernet Franc.

Domaine la Métairie ☆☆
Creyssensac-et-Pissot. 6 hectares
An oak-aged Pécharmant, and all the better for it. In recent years, the proportion of Merlot in the blend has been increasing. Owner Guy-Jean Kreusch also makes rich, dry, white Montravel.

Château Tiregand ☆☆
Creysse. 35 hectares
The biggest Pécharmant property, replanted after the 1956 frosts by the St-Exupéry family. Iron in the soil gives a structure in the wine which calls for ageing in bottle; only the best *cuvées* are lightly oaked. Wine from young vines is much lighter and sold as "Clos de la Montalbanie".

Monbazillac

Domaine de l'Ancienne Cure ☆☆
Colombier. 35 hectares

The owner and winemaker of this estate, Christian Roche, sells much of his production to wholesalers, therefore only the best wines are bottled by him. The regular Monbazillac bottling is fruity but lacks distinction. The better wine, made only in the good years, is "Cuvée Abbaye", from more carefully selected grapes and vinified in new barriques. He also makes an attractive dry "Abbaye Sec" from Sauvignon and Muscadelle, which is aged in older barrels, and the rich red, "L'Extase".

Château la Borderie ☆–☆☆☆
Sigoulès. 63 hectares

Armand Vidal has been a leading producer of Monbazillac and Bergerac for decades. His Monbazillac is of the highest quality, especially the "Cuvée Prestige" which is aged in barrels for eighteen months. The Vidals also own nearby Château Treuil de Nailhac, their older, smaller estate. "Treuil de Nailhac" has a distinct Muscat taste, due to the high proportion of Muscadelle grapes. By the early 2000s, the Vidals were contemplating retirement, and their son, Dominique, had decided to establish his own property at Château Fonmourgues (*q.v.*).

Château Caillavel ☆–☆☆
Pomport. 19 hectares

Since 1996, M. Lacoste, Caillavel's owner, has been fermenting his sweet wine in new oak, the wood imparting a certain creaminess. Cheaper and more commercial Monbazillac is sold under the name of another of his properties, " Château Haut-Theulet".

Cave Coopérative de Monbazillac ☆
Sigoulès. 800 hectares. www.chateau-monbazillac.com

About one half of the cooperative's production is of sweet wine. The best usually comes from the twenty-two hectares of the Château de Monbazillac, but other properties include Châteaux Septy, la Croix Poulvère, and la Brie. Quality slipped badly in the 1980s and '90s, but the arrival of a new director in 1999 was seen as part of a new strategy of improving standards. The wines used to be vinified only in tanks, but Château de Monbazillac is now barrel-fermented, which should give greater complexity.

Clos Fontindoule ☆☆
Monbazillac. 17 hectares

Gilles Cros is the archetypal, old-style *vigneron*, who, without the benefit of modern technology, has always made some of the most astonishing wines of the area. The only fertilizer is the manure from his own cows, and the grapes, in exceptional sites, have always been hand-picked, even before this became compulsory in Monbazillac in 1992. The wines are matured in huge old barrels and not bottled for at least six years, often longer. The style is thick, even tarry and rather orangey, and favours richness over elegance.

Château le Fagé ☆–☆☆
Pomport. 40 hectares

Although François Gérardin likes to think of himself as an all-rounder, it is his Monbazillac that attracts the plaudits, made from a high 90% Sémillon, with a fermentation at low temperature and long ageing in enamelled cement. In top vintages he also makes a "Grande Réserve", which is aged for over two years in barrels.

Château Fonmourgues ☆☆–☆☆☆
Monbazillac. 19 hectares

Dominique Vidal makes a richer, more opulent style of Monbazillac than his father at Château la Borderie (*q.v.*). He also makes red and dry white Bergerac of good quality.

Domaine Grande Maison ☆☆☆
Monbazillac. 20 hectares

Thierry Després took over this property in 1990 and promptly replanted much of the vineyards, which are cultivated organically. He uses individual techniques, such as chilling the botrytized bunches before fermentation. The oldest vines are destined for "Cuvée Diana", and his top oak-aged wine is bizarrely called "Les Monstres".

Château Haut-Bernasse ☆☆–☆☆☆
Monbazillac. 27 hectares

Jacques Blais is a cellist and self-taught winemaker. He takes his Monbazillac seriously and delays picking for as long as possible. Since the mid-1990s, all his wine has been barrel-fermented and aged for between eighteen and thirty-two months in oak.

Château Poulvère ☆–☆☆
Sigoulès. 86 hectares

A large estate producing a full range of Bergerac styles, including Pécharmant under the "Domaine les Grangettes" label. The Monbazillac is good but not exceptional.

Château Tirecul la Gravière ☆☆☆
Monbazillac. 9 hectares

This perfectionist estate is owned by oenologist Bruno Bilancini. The property is unusual in that half the vines are Muscadelle. Bilancini works as though this were a top Sauternes property: selective harvesting, high sugar levels, and a good deal of new oak for barrel-fermentation. The wines are marked by their richness and intensity. The almost syrupy top *cuvée* is called "Cuvée Madame". It is far more expensive than the regular Monbazillac, which is itself among the best of the region.

Saussignac

Clos d'Yvigne ☆☆–☆☆☆
Gageac-et-Rouillac. 20 hectares. www.cdywine.com

Half the production here is of red wine and a little good rosé, but it takes second place to the magnificent Saussignac. Owner Patricia Atkinson often waits into mid-November before harvesting to ensure the grapes are as botrytized and concentrated as possible. The wine is 90% Sémillon and aged in new oak. It is honeyed, tastes of dried apricots, and fetches a good price.

Château Court-les-Mûts ☆–☆☆
Razac. 68 hectares

Pierre-Jean Sadoux is an oenologist who did much to keep

the Saussignac flame burning after growers had abandoned its production. He also produces a full range of Bergerac, notably one of the best of the Bergerac reds from 50% Merlot and the two Cabernets.

Château la Maurigne ☆–☆☆
Razac-et-Saussignac. 6 hectares
Patrick and Chantal Gérardin bought this property in 1996 and have worked hard to make wines of high quality. The pineappley Saussignac is mostly Sémillon, and is aged in new barriques. They also make a dry Bergerac from very ripe grapes, and a slightly rustic red.

Château les Miaudoux ☆☆–☆☆☆
Saussignac. 18 hectares
Gérard Cuisset was one of the pioneers of the new-style, ultra-sweet Saussignac white wines, taking their cue from neighbouring Monbazillacs. Pressed direct into new wood, they are fermented and aged for about twenty months. The tiny yield from over-ripe grapes means, inevitably, that wine like this is not cheap.

Domaine Richard ☆☆–☆☆☆
Monestier. 18 hectares
The owner is Richard Doughty. Yes, an Englishman, also passionate about *liquoreux* Saussignac. Like Gérard Cuisset at les Miaudoux, he relies on his dry white Bergerac for a living, but his heart is in the sweet wine. The estate is farmed organically.

Montravel

Château Calabre & Château Puy-Servain ☆☆
Port Ste-Foy. 10 hectares
Owner Daniel Hecquet has been the leading grower pressing for higher quality and a shift to a sweeter richer style of *liquoreux*. The whites here are the thing. "Calabre" wines are made without wood, while "Puy-Servain" is oaked. The dry white is very dry, the oaked version (called "Marjolaine") having plenty of body and fat. The Haut-Montravel sweet wines reflect the current styles in Monbazillac and Saussignac, but as yet do not quite reach the level of the best from those two areas.

Domaine de Krével
Port Ste-Foy-et-Ponchapt
See **Domaine la Métairie (Pécharmant)**

Château Pique-Segue ☆☆
Port Ste-Foy. 76 hectares
A large estate, so some of the oaked wines appear under the "Château Dauzan-la-Vergne" label; these include a very oaky Merlot. The Haut-Montravel sweet wine is almost pure Sémillon, barrel-fermented and aged for around eight months. The wine is attractive and balanced, but not hugely concentrated.

Rosette

Very few estates still produce this aperitif wine. As a *moelleux* rather than a *liquoreux*, it competes with difficulty against the far richer wines from Monbazillac and Saussignac. Among the properties producing acceptable versions are Château Monplaisir and Domaine de Coutancie.

Cahors

Cahors is certainly the most celebrated red wine of the scattered regions of the South West. The ancient town on the River Lot with its famous fortified bridge is linked in the public mind with dramatic-sounding "black wine". This was because so much of the wine made in Bordeaux was thin and travelled badly, and the merchants needed something to give strength and body to their exports. Their position at the commanding mouth of the Garonne enabled them to call the tune at Cahors, whose growers they encouraged to produce a thick, dark brew by boiling some of their wine, even fortifying it. This was the famous "black wine", so celebrated, at least in myth, that Crimean winemakers produced a "Cahorski" in tribute.

Real Cahors wine has always been quite different, although the traditional methods of long fermentation and the universal use of the Malbec grape (called Auxerrois in Cahors) always produced a darker and more rustic wine than claret. Perhaps this explains why Cahors is still trying to live down the reputation it earned from its "black wine".

Cahors was destroyed by phylloxera in the 1880s, and nearly a second time by the great frost of 1956. It struggled back very slowly, with little to raise it above the second class of VDQS until the 1960s and '70s, when a business-like cooperative and a handful of old-time growers pulled the region together. It was promoted to appellation status in 1971 – not for a revival of its "black wine", but for well-balanced, vigorous, and agreeable reds. The Auxerrois may now be blended with the softer Merlot as well as Tannat (the grape of Madiran). No other varieties are allowed today.

Most of the 4,300 hectares are now on the alluvial valley land, which is very gravelly in places, although there are some expanding plantings on the *causses*, the limestone plateaux above the river. Despite the difference in the two terroirs, there is less distinction than might be imagined between the styles of *causse* and valley wines. Local growers suggest that the plateaux yield more elegant wines, and that the alluvial vineyards are more variable in quality. The real contrast is between the traditional methods of vinification and those adopted by the newcomers, the négociants turned *vignerons* and the financial entrepreneurs who have spent fortunes in creating modern wineries. All too often these provide textbook examples of the law of diminishing returns. Some have even tried to create a Beaujolais look-alike by *macération carbonique*, overlooking the fact that the Auxerrois grape, with its thick skin, is not suited to this technique. The result is invariably a clean enough, quaffable wine, but with no personality, let alone any resemblance to Cahors. For this reason, the best Cahors today are still mostly produced by the long-established growers and a few younger ones from the region who, like their counterparts in Madiran, understand the importance of keeping the *typicité* of their own wine. That *typicité* includes a certain robustness and vigour, power but not necessarily weight, and a hint of gaminess as the wine matures.

The structure of the Cahors industry is somewhat unusual in that a few families, such as the Vigouroux and the Rigals, tend to own or lease a number of estates, giving them a wider range of commercial options.

Leading Cahors Producers

Château de Caix ☆–☆☆
Luzech. 15 hectares. www.caix.com
Prince Henrik of Denmark is the owner of this property, which sold its grapes to the cooperative until 1993. The Cahors is distinctly fat and fruity, and is best drunk within five years. There is also a barrel-aged white wine from Sauvignon and Chardonnay.

Château la Caminade ☆–☆☆
Parnac. 35 hectares
The Resses family's estate is worth a visit for the architecture alone; a fine example of a Quercynois presbytery, turrets and all, now given over to high-class viticulture. In addition to its mainstream wine, the Château la Caminade produces an oaked premium wine called "Clos la Commendary" from pure Auxerrois, as well as a lighter and unwooded style called "Château Peyrouse".

Cave Coopérative les Côtes d'Olt ☆–☆☆
Parnac. 1,100 hectares
Over 300 growers participate in this forward-looking cooperative. The range of wines is large, and overall standards are sound. Unwooded wines include "Comte André der Monpezat" and "Château Vignals"; the oaked *cuvées* are "Impernal" and "Château les Bouysses". "Impernal" is pure Auxerrois, whereas "Les Bouysses" has 20% Merlot. Both are aged in 50% new oak. "Impernal" is the more discreet and structured of the two.

Château du Cèdre ☆☆☆
Vire-sur-Lot. 25 hectares
Pascal and Jean-Marc Verhaeghe have taken over from their father, but had the bad luck to see nearly all their 1995 crop destroyed by a freak summer hailstorm. They are certainly among the finest winemakers in the appellation. With more Auxerrois in their vineyards than most, the basic wine is finished with some Merlot, while in the "Cuvée Prestige" the Merlot is replaced by Tannat. Both wines are made using micro-oxygenation, and the "Prestige" is aged in about one-third new oak. There is also a new-oaked luxury *cuvée* called, simply, "Le Cèdre". Viognier was planted in 1988 and gives a rich, fat wine with a good deal of alcohol.

Château de Chambert ☆–☆☆
Floressas. 60 hectares. www.chateaudechambert.com
There were vineyards here in the eighteenth century, but the entire property was replanted in 1974. The soils are stony and impoverished, and viticultural practices are highly traditional. The wines are medium-bodied and elegant, though they lack some vigour and extract; and yet they age well.

Clos la Coutale ☆☆
Vire. 55 hectares. www.clos-la-coutale.com
The Bernèdes have been making wine here since before

the Revolution. Today, the wine is noted for its rich fruit underpinned by firm tannins, and is often successful in difficult years. Deeply coloured, the bouquet is often toasty, and there can be a hint of liquorice too.

Clos de Gamot & Château de Cayrou ☆☆–☆☆☆
Prayssac and Puy l'Evêque. 40 hectares
The colourful Jean Jouffreau, who died in 1996, was a hard act to follow at these two properties, but his son-in-law, Yves Hermann-Jouffreau is determined to maintain standards. The Clos de Gamot vineyard has been in the family since 1610 and is planted exclusively with Auxerrois. Château de Cayrou was bought in 1971 and is planted with a more modern mix of 73% Auxerrois, 20% Merlot, and 7% Tannat. The wines from both properties enjoy ultra-traditional production from a modern winery. The "Gamot", a chewy, concentrated wine, can last as long as great claret in a good year. "Cayrou" is a little lighter in style, and has considerable elegance.

Clos Triguedina ☆☆☆
Puy-l'Evêque. 60 hectares. www.clos-triguedina.com
Dating back to 1830, this large estate, owned by Jean-Luc Baldès, makes wines that need some ageing. In addition to the mainstream wine (from 70% Auxerrois), there is a special old-vine *cuvée* called "Prince Probus", which is generously oaked, and a lighter wine sold as "Domaine Labrande" for earlier drinking. In the mid-1990s, the winery re-created the black wine of Cahors, heating the must in tanks for thirty minutes, and ageing the wine is new oak. The result was tannic and jammy, and by no means preferable to the splendid "Probus".

Château Eugénie ☆–☆☆
Albas. 30 hectares
The Couture brothers claim to have been based here for 500 years. Whether this is true or not, they certainly understand their soils, so consequently each of the *cuvées* comes from and reflects a different terroir. Their premium wine ("Réserve de l'Aïeul") is almost exclusively from Auxerrois, and aged mostly in new oak. The other two wines, "Etiquette Noire" and "Cuvée des Tsars", are aged in older casks and barrels. The wines can lack fruit and show some rusticity, with tough tannins.

Château de Gaudou ☆–☆☆
Vire. 35 hectares. www.chateaudegaudou.com
Three *cuvées* are produced here from varied soils: the "Tradition", aged in large casks; the 85% Auxerrois barrique-aged "Prestige"; and the rather too oaky "Renaissance", exclusively from Auxerrois.

Château Gautoul ☆☆
Puy-l'Evêque. 30 hectares
The renowned Parisian chef, Alain Senderens, established this property, which was sold in 1998 to Eric Swenden. The wines are modern in style and can be enjoyed young.

Château Haut-Serre ☆–☆☆
Cieurac. 66 hectares. www.g-vigouroux.fr
These are the highest vineyards in Cahors, located on the plateau in a single stony parcel. A well-known property in the nineteenth century, says owner Georges Vigouroux, but it

was entirely replanted in 1972. Just one-third of the wine is aged in barriques to avoid overtly oaky flavours. There is also a special selection, "Géron Dadine", that often has a pronounced flavour of black-cherries.

Château les Ifs ☆☆
Pescadoires. 10 hectares
The Buri family's vineyards are located on rich, alluvial soil close to the river, but very good wine is made. Surprisingly full and generous, with the pronounced flavour of almonds and damsons so typical of the Auxerrois grape, these wines are good keepers.

Château Lagrézette ☆☆–☆☆☆
Caillac. 60 hectares. www.chateau-lagrezette.com
The estate that led the revival of the region in the 1980s. The owner, Alain-Dominique Perrin, is the head of Cartier and has spared no expense to make wine that is both concentrated and elegant.

The winemakers, overseen by consultant Michel Rolland, employ modern techniques, such as cold maceration and micro-oxygenation, to obtain the desired results. The flagship wines are "Le Pigeonnier", a pure Auxerrois from yields of 20 hl/ha and given prolonged ageing in oak, and "Dame Honneur". These are rich, sumptuous wines, perhaps not entirely typical of Cahors, and their price structure is ambitious.

Château Lamartine ☆☆–☆☆☆
Soturac. 30 hectares
A long-established property that uses very modern techniques to produce supple, oaky wines that give a great deal of pleasure, as well as the richer, more extracted "Cuvée Expression".

Château de Mercuès ☆☆–☆☆☆
Mercuès. 40 hectares
A luxury hotel as well as a wine estate, owned by the ubiquitous Vigouroux family. Supple, slightly chocolatey wines, plus a full-bodied special *cuvée* aged entirely in new oak.

Château Pech de Jammes ☆☆
Flaujac-Poujols. 9 hectares. www.g-vigouroux.fr
This American-owned vineyard is leased by the négociant Georges Vigouroux, whose presence in the region it is hard to ignore. Its position on the *causse* lends it power to age and considerable body; the bouquet often suggests red fruits, and even a hint of the truffles growing nearby.

Domaine Pineraie ☆☆
Puy-l'Evêque. 37 hectares
The Burc family have planted 85% Auxerrois, the rest being Merlot. The best wine, "Cuvée Authentique", is pure Auxerrois from the ground that rises up towards the *causse*. Sturdy yet stylish wines.

Prieuré de Cénac ☆☆–☆☆☆
Parnac. 35 hectares
Owned by the Rigal family since 1979, a property on varied soils, with about 80% Auxerrois and low yields. Rigal uses a good deal of new oak to produce one of the region's most structured wines.

Château St-Didier-Parnac ☆☆
Parnac. 70 hectares
Another property in the Rigal portfolio. Much of the wine is sold off, ensuring only the best is bottled. This is a good, fruity wine, not especially tannic or concentrated, but upfront, lush, and spicy.

Domaine des Savarines ☆☆
Trespoux. 4 hectares
Danielle Biesbrouck planted her vines in 1970 in the middle of nowhere up on the *causse*. The wine has good tannins and is attractively perfumed and soft in texture. The estate is now biodynamic.

Aveyron & The Upper Lot

One hundred and twelve kilometres (seventy miles) upstream from Cahors, the rolling limestone *causses* give way to the foothills of the Massif Central, and the landscape starts to close in on the River Lot. Wine has been made in this area for centuries, from grapes grown on almost perpendicular slopes, terraced and walled with back-breaking effort.

At Marcillac, the rich burghers of Rodez had their country homes where they employed resident winemakers to supply their needs; later, after the phylloxera epidemic, the wine was made to slake the thirst of the coalminers of Decazeville.

When the mines were closed down in the 1950s, the Marcillac growers formed themselves into a cooperative to raise standards of production and to find a new market for their wine. It is highly original, made entirely from the Fer Servadou grape, called locally Mansoi. It has a slight resemblance to Cabernet Franc: the same grassiness and flavour of soft, red fruits, redcurrants and blackcurrants, and sometimes blackberries. There is only red and rosé Marcillac. The 146 hectares have enjoyed *appellation contrôlée* status since 1990.

The local white wine comes from further up the river from nine hectares at Entraygues, where the Lot is joined by the Truyère, and at Estaing (a mere seven hectares). Here the Chenin Blanc grape is used to make a bone-dry, stylish, and surprisingly modern-tasting wine; at Estaing some Mauzac is also used. The production is very small, but locally important; the wines are seldom seen outside the area, but are on the lists of all the local restaurants.

Red wine, too, is made at both towns. Entraygues and Estaing both enjoy VDQS status, as do the wines grown in the upper valley of the Tarn in the vicinity of the town of Millau. Entraygues has no cooperative, and only seven or so producers, but Estaing and Millau both have small cooperatives in addition to a handful of private growers. Entraygues would be heading for extinction, were it not for the stubborn perseverance of a handful of growers such as François Avallon and Jean-Marc Viguier and the loyalty of some local restaurateurs. The same is true of Estaing, which is dominated – if that is the right word for such a tiny region – by Les Vignerons d'Olt.

At Millau, the only significant producers are the Cave des Vignerons des Gorges du Tarn and Domaine du Vieux Noyer.

Leading Aveyron Producers

Marcillac

Cave des Vignerons du Vallon ☆–☆☆
Valady
By far the largest producer, since the members farm 110 hectares. Most, but not all, of the wines are unoaked.

Domaine du Cros ☆–☆☆
Goutrens
Philippe Teulier has doggedly expanded his holdings to the present twenty-one hectares. Wines of substance, especially the "Cuvée Vieilles Vignes".

Jean-Luc Matha ☆–☆☆
Le Vieux Roche, Clairvaux
Two principal wines from fourteen hectares, one unoaked, the other the oak-aged "Cuvée Spéciale".

Gaillac

Gaillac is one of the most productive and economically important of the scattered vineyards of the South West. Historically, it has supplied not only Albi, the capital of its *département*, the Tarn, but places much further away – its reds having a name for amazing transportability and longevity. It was established as a vineyard during the first century after Christ, during the Roman occupation of the Midi, and long before vines were planted at Bordeaux.

Its unheard-of indigenous grape varieties, the bane of some modern producers but the pride and joy of others, encourage the idea of extreme antiquity. Its reds are the Duras (nothing to do with the wine area of that name) and the Braucol, the local name for Fer Servadou; its whites are Mauzac, Len de l'El (or Loin de l'Oeil), and Ondenc. Ondenc had almost completely disappeared until it was revived by Robert Plageoles, who replanted two hectares in 1983.

A century ago, just before phylloxera struck, the production of Gaillac was almost entirely of red wine. The little white that was made was either sweet or sparkling or both, or else of a style not unlike that of a light sherry. The reds were big and sturdy, mostly sold down the river to Bordeaux for blending. When the vineyard was replanted, the emphasis changed to white wine because of the competition in reds from the Midi.

The traditional white Gaillac grape, Mauzac, was exploited to produce sweet wines with an appley character. AC status was granted for the white wines in 1938. The red wines were only recognized in 1970, largely because the growers had failed to replant post-phylloxera with good-quality varieties and had stuck to the old, rather commonplace stocks.

The modern reconstruction of the industry, sparked off by big cooperatives, has opted for more standardized production. A tradition of bottling white wine before its first fermentation was over was dropped in favour of the Champagne method, despite the fact that the Gaillac process ante-dated the Champagne technique by several centuries. Sauvignon, Merlot, Gamay, and Syrah have been brought in, and where they are used, the wines are lighter and more neutral than they used to be.

In addition to the three cooperatives, there are today about one hundred private producers, which is ten times as many as there were in 1970. Some 3,100 hectares are under vine. Many producers are going back to the old Gaillac grapes in a search for *typicité* and distinctiveness. The modern range of Gaillac is thus bewildering; there are plain, dry white wines, or *perlé* – that is, dry with a slight prickle induced by keeping them on their lees; there are dry and *demi-sec* sparkling wines; and there are more or less sweet still wines.

There are oaked and unoaked reds and a *vin de l'année* after the style of, and often much better than, Beaujolais Nouveau. There are also rosé wines, of course. In terms of quality, there are marked variations, and the situation is complicated by the fact that some growers inevitably excel in some styles more than others.

Leading Gaillac Producers

Domaine de Balagès ☆–☆☆
Lagrave. 14 hectares
An atypical estate, in that only red wines are produced, notably the barrel-aged "Cuvée Rêveline".

Domaine de Causses Marine ☆☆–☆☆☆
Vieux. 13 hectares
Patrice Lescarret is known for his outstanding sweet wines. They are given proprietary names such as "Délires d'Automne" (an oxidative style) and "Grain de Folie", have varying degrees of intensity and are based on different grape blends. He also makes a wine under a *flor*-like layer of yeast which he calls "Mystère" and which resembles *vin jaune*.

Domaine de Gineste ☆–☆☆☆
Técou. 23 hectares
This estate earned its high reputation since its acquisition by Vincent Laillier in 1991. He is best-known for a wine called "La Coulée d'Or". Despite the muddle of the Gaillac AC rules, this wine doesn't qualify, as it is a late-harvest blend of Chardonnay and Mauzac. The dry red and white wines are not quite at the same level. Laillier has returned to his native Alsace, so the future direction of the estate is uncertain.

Domaine de Labarthe ☆☆
Castanet. 48 hectares
Jean-Paul Albert disappoints nowhere throughout his complete range of Gaillac. Especially to be recommended are his white *perlé* from Mauzac, his sweet white from Len de l'El called "Grains d'Or", his basic red wine, and his *rouge primeur* from Gamay. His top-of-the-range red, "Cuvée Guillaume", is quite markedly oaked.

Mas d'Aurel ☆☆
Donnazac. 13 hectares

Albert Ribot's vineyards are seemingly on top of the world just south of Cordes. His red wines are always reliable, especially his minty "Cuvée Alexandra", and he also has a fine reputation for his sweet "Cuvée Clara".

Mas Pignou ☆–☆☆
Laborie. 35 hectares

A property with a complete range of wine as well as the best view of Gaillac town and the valley of the Tarn. His dry white (50% Sauvignon, 50% Len de l'El) is allowed a second fermentation before being matured a further year in barrel; unlike most dry Gaillac, it ages well. The sweet wine is a stunner from Mauzac. The prestige red is "Cuvée Mélanie", but the basic red is excellent, too.

Château Montels ☆–☆☆
Souel-Cordes. 22 hectares

A sound range of red and white wines, of which one of the best is the "Cuvée Prestige" blend of Braucol and Cabernet Sauvignon.

Robert Plageoles ☆☆☆
Cahuzac-sur-Vere. 20 hectares

At his Domaine des Très Cantous, Robert Plageoles and son Bernard produce an astonishing range of varietal wines. Apart from the pure Sauvignon, all are from the traditional Gaillac varieties: a 100% Duras, a Gamay, dry and sweet whites exclusively from Mauzac, a dry sparkler made according to the old Gaillac method, sweet wines from 100% Ondenc, and another from Muscadelle.

The very sweet and honeyed "Vin d'Autan" and "Grain d'Autan" are made from late-harvested Ondenc, the latter from botrytized grapes. The range is rounded off with "Vin de Voile", very similar in character to a *vin jaune* from the Jura, though made from Mauzac. The entire region owes the Plageoles a great deal.

Domaine Rotier ☆☆
Petit-Nareye. 30 hectares

The Rotiers make a good range of wines in all the main styles found in Gaillac: red wine, barrel-aged white wines, and, of course, sweet wine. The best are labelled "Renaissance".

Cave Coopérative de Técou ☆
Técou. www.cavedetecou.fr

The best all-rounder of the three co-ops. The 220 members do not have the best terrain; most of the vineyards are on the south bank in the plain. But the quality of the winemaking is all the more remarkable for that. The top red is "Gaillac Passion": a blend of Braucol and Merlot aged in new oak.

Côtes du Frontonnais

The slopes around Fronton and Villaudric, twenty-four kilometres (fifteen miles) north of Toulouse and thirty-two kilometres (twenty miles) west of Gaillac, achieved AC status in 1975 for their ripely fruity red and rosé wines, which until then had been a secret kept by the people of Toulouse. The pink wines even today are billed as "Le Rosé de la Ville Rose". The local grape is Négrette, brought back from Cyprus at the time of the Crusades by the Knights Templar, who owned much of the land covered by today's vineyards at Fronton. For those who cannot resist the complications of ampelography, I should add that the Négrette turns up in the Charente (of all places) as Le Petit Noir. Its only appellation appearance is, however, in the Frontonnais.

Négrette, which by law must form at least fifty per cent of every Fronton vineyard, is, as its name implies, very dark-skinned and its juice is dark, too. The grapes are small and the skins are thin, which has encouraged at least one good grower to vinify by *macération carbonique*. The bouquet of Négrette is said to suggest violets, red fruits, and/or liquorice; the flavour often brings to mind cherries and almonds.

The problem with the Négrette grape, though, is that it is liable to grey rot, but given that the climate of Toulouse is hot and dry during the growing season, it flourishes well there. It is a very adaptable grape; on its own its low tannin and acidity can make a light quaffing style of wine of some considerable character; and blended with the two Cabernets, Gamay, and/or Syrah, it can also make a bigger wine, capable of four or five years' ageing.

Leading Frontonnais Producers

Château Baudare ☆
Campsas. 35 hectares

As well as Négrette, grapes such as Gamay and Syrah are also planted in Claude Vigouroux's vineyards. The result is a range of enjoyable medium-bodied wines to drink young, supplemented by *vins de pays*.

Château Bellevue-la-Forêt ☆–☆☆
Fronton. 115 hectares

Patrick Germain is one of the biggest private producers in the South West. He started from scratch in 1975, with advice from Emile Peynaud. His wines include a 100% light Négrette called "Ce Vin", originally styled by celebrated local restaurateur André Daguin, and a traditional red which is his biggest seller, as well as some oaked prestige wines such as "Cuvée Prestige" (mostly from Cabernet) and an unwooded "Cuvée d'Or". (Oak is controversial in Fronton, most growers believing that it does not suit the grape variety.) The rosé from this estate is popular and very good.

Château Cahuzac ☆
Fabas. 55 hectares

A long-established property owned by the Ferran family. Their most expensive wine, the "Fleuron de Guillaume", follows the fad for ageing in new oak and is not necessarily superior to their silky red, "L'Authentique".

Domaine de Callory ☆
Labastide-St-Pierre. 27 hectares
A traditional estate that eschews wood-ageing but makes a sound blend of Négrette, Syrah, and Cabernet Sauvignon.

Château Clamens ☆–☆☆
Caillol. 5 hectares
A small property that made its debut in 1998. The traditional wine has 50% Negrette, but the oaked *cuvée* is almost pure Cabernet Sauvignon.

Château la Colombière ☆
Villaudric. 20 hectares
Easy-drinking, red-fruited wines from Négrette made by carbonic maceration.

Château Joliet ☆–☆☆
Fronton. 20 hectares
Owners François and Marie-Claire Daubert specialize in an all-Négrette red, which is perhaps the best of its style in the region. There is no such thing as white Fronton, but Daubert makes a delicious, sweet *vin de pays* from the Mauzac grape.

Château Marguerite ☆
Campsas. 75 hectares
A very large property producing medium-bodied red wines and a surprisingly rich rosé.

Château Montauriol ☆–☆☆
Villematiuer. 35 hectares
A change in ownership in 1998 has led to improved quality in traditional-style wines made with at least 50% Négrette.

Château Plaisance ☆
Vacquiers. 24 hectares
Marc Pénavayre makes three styles of Fronton, in addition to a good rosé: a so-called *vin de printemps*, whose style speaks for itself; an excellent mainstream red; and an oaked "Cuvée Thibault de Plaisance", which has Syrah in the blend.

Château le Roc ☆☆
Fronton. 25 hectares
Frédéric Ribes makes wines that are more structured than most, and need some cellarage. Since 1995, he has selected the best Négrette and Syrah grapes for his "Cuvée Don Quichotte", which is both of high quality and fairly priced.

Château St-Louis ☆
Labastide-St-Pierre. 25 hectares
Good, rounded wines, and a fleshy, plump "Cuvée l'Esprit", which is aged in oak.

Lavilledieu-du-Temple

A small cooperative was built in this little town northwest of Montauban in 1949 by the growers of vines on the low-lying ground where the rivers Tarn and Garonne meet. They acquired VDQS status for their red and rosé wines in 1952, but the name was not much used until recent years, members preferring to use the names of various local *vins de pays*.

Today, the VDQS may be claimed for wines from 150 hectares of vineyards in thirteen communes; the wine must contain thirty per cent Négrette, and Gamay, Syrah, Cabernet Franc, and Tannat are also permitted. Such a cocktail does not add up to a particularly distinctive wine, but it is usually agreeable: rounded and fruity, soft, and easy to drink.

The Bordeaux Satellites

Côtes de Duras

The Côtes de Duras has the misfortune, like Bergerac, to lie just over the departmental boundary from Bordeaux – more particularly from Entre-Deux-Mers. Its wine is in every way comparable: half of it dry white, made increasingly from Sauvignon, though Sémillon and Muscadelle are widely grown, as well as small amounts of Ugni Blanc and Colombard. The red wines have as much as sixty per cent Cabernet Sauvignon, thirty per cent Merlot, and a little Cabernet Franc and Malbec.

Cooperatives are important here, but the best wines come from a handful among the fifty or so independent producers. There are about 2,000 hectares under vine, divided almost equally between red and white grapes.

Leading Côtes de Duras Producers

Domaine Amblard ☆
St-Sernin-de-Duras. 110 hectares
Fabrice Pauvert runs a huge property producing sound wines, all of which are aged in tanks. His dry white, based on Sauvignon, is sometimes found under the name of "Domaine la Croix-Haute".

Vignerons Landerrouat-Duras Berticot ☆
Duras. 1,000 hectares
Probably the best of the cooperatives, making fresh Sauvignons and a Merlot with the aid of carbonic maceration.

Château la Grave-Béchade ☆☆
Baleyssagues. 64 hectares
Daniel Amar's comfortable *gentilhommière* is the only winemaking property in the region aspiring to the status of a real château. Equipped with ultra-modern technology, it is making wines worthy of *bourgeois* château status in Bordeaux terms. A red wine estate, with both oaked and unoaked bottlings from Cabernet and Merlot.

Domaine Lafon ☆☆
Loubès-Bernac. 13 hectares
Well-exposed vineyards give very ripe wines, often released as varietal bottlings from Merlot and even Malbec. There is also a small production of *moelleux* wine.

Domaine de Laulan ☆☆
Duras. 30 hectares
Gilbert Geoffroy is a native of Chablis, and his white wines are outstanding. Made entirely from Sauvignon, they come both oaked and unoaked and are deliciously fruity, thus demonstrating how different this grape can be at a southern latitude.

Château la Moulière ☆–☆☆
Duras. 26 hectares
The brothers Blancheton cover the whole range of styles, taking particular pride in their *vin doux*. Although not botrytized, it is beautifully honeyed without being cloying.

Côtes du Marmandais

The 1,400-hectare Côtes du Marmandais lies right on the fringes of Bordeaux. Its light red (its major product) could for many years come under the heading of "claret", and its Sauvignon/Sémillon white is comparable to everyday Bordeaux Blanc. En route to AC status, granted in 1990, growers were required, with a view to ensuring *typicité* for Marmandais, to grow whatever they might choose from a list of grapes specific to the South West, including Malbec, Fer Servadou, and particularly a rare and local specialty called Abouriou.

In this way, Marmande wine has begun to acquire a character of its own, while retaining a fresh and fruity style. Two rival co-ops of roughly equal size make nearly all the wine, one to represent right-bank growers at Beaupuy, the other on the left bank at Cocumont.

Leading Marmandais Producers

Château de Beaulieu ☆☆
St-Sauveur-de-Meilhan. 29 hectares.
www.chateaudebeaulieu.com
The varieties planted here are Bordelais (with the addition of Syrah), and so, in general, is the style of the wine. Quality is consistently good, and there is a richer and very oaky "Cuvée l'Oratoire".

Les Vignerons de Beaupuy ☆
Beaupuy. www.cavedebeaupuy.com
The older (1948) of the two cooperatives works hard to meet the competition from its rival across the river. Right-bank wines are said to age more slowly than left-bank wines, so this co-op ages some of its wines in new wood. More Abouriou is grown on the right bank than on the left. About 40% of the production at Beaupuy is of Vins de Pays d'Agenais or *vins de table*, sometimes made from old grape varieties such as Bouchalès.

Cave de Cocumont ☆–☆☆
Cocumont. 1,000 hectares
With the benefit of AC status, this cooperative has invested in the latest state-of-the-art technology. The mainstream red wine, called "Tradition", is excellent in its class, better than the Bordeaux which the co-op makes for those of its members who have vines over the border. Those looking for an oakier version should seek out the "Cuvée Tap de Perbos". "Cuvée Beroy" gains structure from being made mostly from Cabernet Sauvignon.

Buzet

When Bordeaux was firmly limited to the *département* of the Gironde, one of the up-country sources of claret to be hardest-hit was the hills south of the Garonne to the north of the armagnac country, the Buzet. Happily, white wine for distillation was an alternative crop, but the gravel and chalky clay on good southeast slopes had long produced very satisfactory red wine. In the last thirty years, they have been reconstituted and are doing better than ever.

The cooperative at Damazan near Buzet dominates the 1,850-hectare area, making red wine to good Bordeaux standards. There are though, a handful of excellent private growers, continuing to contribute beneficial competition.

Leading Buzet Producers

Château Sauvagnères ☆
Ste-Colombe-en-Bruilhois. 20 hectares
Sound if unexciting red wines from the three principal Bordeaux varieties.

Les Vignerons Réunis de Buzet ☆☆
Damazan. 1,600 hectares. www.vignerons-buzet.fr
The overwhelming majority of Buzet comes from this model cooperative (with its own cooper), which has steadily expanded and improved the vineyards of the area since 1955, and can claim the credit for its promotion to appellation status in 1973. The red wines are aged in the homemade barrels, the new wood being given to the top range called "Baron d'Ardeuil", and then passed on to the second in line, "Carte d'Or", and finally to their least expensive range, called "Tradition". Small amounts of white and rosé wines complement the range. The co-op also makes wines for a number of individual properties, including Domaine Padère and Château de Gueyze (the best wine from this coop), and Châteaux du Bouchet, de Gache, Larché, de Piis, Bougigues, and Tauzia. There is tension between the co-op and some of the private growers. The former make no secret of their aim to establish a monopoly, which is a pity, because the latter are making wines with often more local character.

Côtes du Brulhois

This 200-hectare VDQS area adjoins Buzet to the east, but makes more rustic wines. Brulhois may, for example, contain Tannat, Malbec, and Fer Servadou in addition to the two Cabernets and Merlot. Some local growers have more rustic grapes still, but are not allowed to keep these and at the same time declare in a VDQS area, so many have given up altogether. Production is almost entirely in the hands of two cooperatives: the Vignerons du Brulhois at Dunes and the Cave de Donzac.

Madiran & Pacherenc

Madiran is the wine that came back from the dead. By 1948, the vineyard in the Vic-Bilh hills on the southern edge of the armagnac country, forty kilometres (twenty-five miles) north of Pau, had dwindled to fifty hectares. Today there are 1,300 and some would claim that Madiran is the best red of the South West, Cahors included. If it lacked the advantages of Cahors (fame and accessibility), it also avoided the identity crisis that still bothers the better-known wine. The name of "black wine" lingers, while the reality is merely a healthy red.

The peculiar quality of Madiran is to start life with a disconcerting bite, then to mellow quite rapidly into a wine with a most singular style and texture. The bouquet has the teasing qualities of a good Médoc or Graves. When I was looking for the right word for a nine-year-old 1973 from the main cooperative of the region, I was so struck by its silkiness on the tongue that I hesitated over the rather lame "liquid", then tried "limpid". Later I looked Madiran up in Paul de Cassagnac's *French Wines*, a little-known but extremely rewarding work of 1936. "An infinitely fluid savour" were the first words that struck my eye. So Madiran is consistent, despite its near demise; across fifty-five years it still caresses the palate in a seductively swallowable way.

This is the more odd in that de Cassagnac fulminates against "the inferior Tannat", a "common grape" being introduced to replace the Cabernet in the region for the sake of its bigger crop. All real Madiran, he says, is Cabernet. Yet today its producers tell us the secret of its character is the grape that sounds like tannin, and gives all the harshness its name implies; a smaller-berried cousin of the Malbec, Cot or (in Cahors) Auxerrois. A high proportion of Tannat, they say, is essential. So do the wine authorities, because a Madiran vineyard must by law consist of forty-sixty per cent Tannat, and some growers use Tannat alone. The best-known grower in the region, Alain Brumont, goes one stage further and believes that all other varieties should be banned from the appellation – and he should know.

The technique known as micro-oxygenation – the injection of controlled doses of oxygen into the wine during either fermentation or ageing – was developed here by Patrick Ducournau. It originated as a means of moderating the fierce tannins of Tannat. It seems to work well, and allows the wine to be broached and drunk at a younger age than before. (When applied to less robust varieties such as Merlot in St-Emilion, the technique is more controversial.)

The Vic-Bilh hills, a sort of piano rehearsal for the soaring Pyrénées, parallel to the south, give their name to the white wine called Pacherenc: a dialect equivalent of the French *piquets en rangs*, or "stakes in rows". Pacherenc sometimes lends itself as an alternative title to the Arrufiac grape, traditionally an important element in the wine. Gros and Petit Manseng and Petit Courbu are other grapes used. Traditionally, like Vouvray, it was as sweet a wine as the autumn permitted, but most growers today try to make

The Gers: Armagnac Country

Although a full range of wines is today made in the armagnac area, it is the dry white wines largely from the Colombard grape that have attracted much popularity. There are typical inexpensive examples produced at co-ops such as Condom and Nogaro, as well as the Plaimont trio, though none to merit particular attention. Most are sold as the Vin de Pays Côtes de Gascogne. Some independent growers are, however, producing wines of better class, of the sort that a buyer is likely to find in a good wine bar.

Growers include: The Grassa family: Château de Tariquet; Domaine de Rieux; Domaine de Planterieu; Domaine de la Jalousie; Domaine de Pagny; Domaine Mesté-Duran; Domaine de Lahitte; Domaine le Puts; Domaine de Bergerayre.

a dry and a sweet version by adopting different proportions of the grape varieties. Pacherenc was always a tiny local production, but nowadays most Madiran growers like to make some.

Leading Madiran & Pacherenc Producers

Château d'Aydie (Domaines Laplace) ☆–☆☆☆
Aydie. 65 hectares
The Laplace family is one of the few who never gave up on Madiran, and there are still some pre-phylloxera vines to prove it. Château d'Aydie is where the family now lives, and it gives its name to their prestige wine, from pure Tannat, aged in 50% new oak. A less-structured red is named after grandfather Frédéric Laplace and has 60% Tannat with equal quantities of the two Cabernets.

All these wines are completely faithful to the *typicité* of Tannat and thus of Madiran. "Fleury-Laplace" is the label given to wines from purchased grapes. Pierre Laplace thinks highly of the future for Pacherenc, and his own superb version of the sweeter style is made from grapes usually picked well into November and fermented in new oak.

Château Barréjat ☆☆☆
Maumusson. 16 hectares
Denis Capmartin has been the owner of this property since 1992, and he has enthusiastically taken up the technique of micro-oxygenation.

His top *cuvée* is "Vieux Ceps" from 80% Tannat. The general style is supple with a depth of blackberry fruit that is impressive and beguiling.

Domaine Berthoumieu ☆☆–☆☆☆
Viella. 24 hectares
There is something immediately attractive about Didier Barré's Madirans. They are much less stern and forbidding than some, and seem to come round more quickly than many, even though the *prestige* red "Charles de Batz" can be up to 90% Tannat and is aged in new oak. Barré selectively

harvests his white grapes no fewer than five times, and his sweet Pacherenc is made from the last three pickings.

Domaine Capmartin ☆☆
Maumusson. 10 hectares
Owned by Guy, the brother of Denis Capmartin (*see* Château Barrejat). The "Cuvée Tradition" is relatively accessible when young, but the oakier and more structured "Cuvée du Couvent" benefits from five years in bottle. It is a chunky, robust wine that attains harmony and texture with age.

Chapelle Lenclos
See **Domaine Mouréou**

Domaine du Crampilh ☆☆
Arions-sur-Idernes. 28 hectares
A well-known estate that has improved in quality throughout the 1990s. Alain Oulié employs micro-oxygenation to produce a range of flavoury wines, of which the most concentrated is the "Cuvée Baron" from 90% Tannat.

Domaine Labranche-Laffont ☆☆
Maumusson. 18 hectares
The Dupuy family, or at least its female members, are rapidly making a name for themselves in this male-dominated appellation. The "Cuvée Vieilles Vignes" comes from a small parcel of pre-phylloxera vines. These are rich, full-bodied wines, subtly softened by micro-oxygenation.

Château Laffitte-Teston ☆☆–☆☆☆
Maumusson. 40 hectares
Jean-Marc Laffitte's red Madirans are among the best the region has to offer, and include a 100% Tannat *vieilles vignes* bottling. Both his Pacherencs are consistently magnificent, too.

Château Montus and Domaine Bouscassé ☆☆–☆☆☆☆☆
Maumusson. 140 hectares. www.montus-madiran.com
Alain Brumont is the high priest of the Tannat grape. The premium wines from his two properties ("Montus Prestige" and "Bouscassé Vieilles Vignes") are both 100% Tannat, and are vinified for five weeks before being aged in new barriques. Not surprisingly they take several years to mature.

At gravelly-soiled Montus, the mainstream wine is 80% Tannat and 20% Cabernet Sauvignon, while at Bouscassé, where the soil is clay and limestone, 65% Tannat is complemented by 25% Cabernet Sauvignon and 10% Cabernet Franc. A third wine, "Domaine Meinjarre", is half Tannat, half Cabernet Franc and is priced at bargain level, and a fourth, Torus, described as *charnu, profond, puissant, chatoyant, fruit noir, cassis, mure*, (but not expensive) was introduced with the 2000 vintage.

There is a range of Pacherenc, too, in varying degrees of sweetness depending on the date of harvesting. Brumont is not above making good *vin de pays* and launched a range of varietal wines, many of them from obscure local varieties, in the mid-1990s.

At the other extreme he is always seeking to push the limits of his Madiran. "Montus la Tyre" is a Tannat grown in the region's highest vineyards, and in 1994 and 2000 he was moved to age some of his Tannat for 2,000 days in barriques. Despite the popularity of micro-oxyenation within Madiran, Brumont does not use the technique. Except

for "Meinjarre" and "Torus", these are wines that demand patience until their youthful aggression mellows.

Domaine Mouréou ☆☆
Maumusson-Laguian. 18 hectares
Patrick Ducournau is the think-tank of Madiran, much admired as one of the bright young hopes of the South West. Although a devotee of 100% Tannat wines – his premium wine "Chapelle Lenclos", for example – he is also keen to soften its tannins and round its edges. This he successfully does by applying the technique of micro-oxygenation that he pioneered.

His wines are very enjoyable, but perhaps lack the uncompromising *typicité* of those from Brumont and others. Delicious, sweet Pacherenc, too.

Domaine Pichard ☆–☆☆
Soublecause. 12 hectares. www.dom-pichard.com
A good source of rich, slightly old-fashioned Madiran from the southern slopes of the region. Aged in large casks, they have vigour and longevity as well as some rusticity.

la Cave de Crouseilles ☆–☆☆
Crouseilles. 520 hectares
A first-class co-op whose top bottling, "Château de Crouseilles" (a property which they own), can be among the best wines of the region. The mainstream Madirans and Pacherencs are good, too, and there is a large production of rosé and red Béarn, and *vin de pays*.

Côtes de Saint-Mont & Leading Producer

In 1974, André Dubosc created a cooperative of growers in the valley of the Adour, north of Madiran and south of armagnac. There are three branches at Plaisance, St-Aignan, and St-Mont. The co-op is thus called Plaimont. The object was to find an alternative market for the dry white wine locally produced for distillation into armagnac, because the demand for armagnac had started to decline. Dubosc had hit on a winner, because it was not long (1981) before he had created almost single-handedly his own VDQS under the name of Côtes de St-Mont, for wines of all three colours. He was also to attract members from the Côtes de Gascogne, whom he persuaded to improve standards with the Colombard grape. He attracted growers, too, from the northern part of the Madiran AC. Another cooperative, the Vignoble de Gascogne at Riscle, has followed the lead of Plaimont.

Producteurs Plaimont ☆☆
St-Mont. 2,500 hectares (of which 1,000 are St-Mont).
www.plaimont.com
Today the co-op produces Madiran and Pacherenc, both of excellent quality; St-Mont reds and whites, basically from the same grapes as Madiran and Pacherenc; and a full range of Vins de Pays Côtes de Gascogne which have become hugely popular: a sort of sub-Sauvignon style at a good price. In the 1990s, Dubosc developed new ranges of St-Mont wines, such as "Le Faite de St-Mont", from local varieties only, including some that were in danger of extinction, such as Pinenc.

Tursan & Leading Producer

The leading vineyard of the *département* of Landes. Almost the entire production comes from the cooperative at Geaune, Les Vignerons de Tursan, which has 250 members owning about 350 hectares out of a total area of 460 hectares of vines. The wines won VDQS status in 1958, although half of the production is still of Vin de Pays des Landes.

The reds are mostly Cabernet Franc with a little Tannat, while the whites are made principally from an obscure local variety called Baroque, with a little enlivening Sauvignon. There are Cabernet-based rosés, too.

The style is aimed at the holiday-makers of the Atlantic coast: light, fruity, and easy to drink, short *cuvaisons* at not too high a temperature for the reds, while the whites are given a cool fermentation. Their flagship red, from Domaine de Castèle, is made at the co-op.

Other Tursan Producers

Château de Bachen ☆☆
Duhort-Bachen. 20 hectares
The celebrated chef Michel Guérard has his elegant home here, and has built an architect-designed winery. Many of the wines are sold in his restaurants at Eugénie-lès-Bains. He specializes in white wine, of which the sweet version is still experimental. The vineyard is 50% Baroque, plus Gros Manseng, Petit Manseng, Sauvignon, and Sémillon.

There are two grades of dry white, "Château de Bachen" and "Baron de Bachen", the latter well-oaked. The wines are high-class, but hardly typical of the Tursan appellation. The reds are very simple.

Domaine de Perchade ☆
Payros-Cazautets. 15 hectares
Alain Dulucq produces a white that is 90–100% Baroque, a rosé mostly from Cabernet Franc, and a red from a mixture of Tannat and the two Cabernets.

Béarn & the Pyrénées

Béarn

Country-style wines have been made in the Béarn district for centuries. In recent times they rose to prominence largely on account of their rosé, which became fashionable throughout France in the middle of the twentieth century.

Today the red wines are overshadowed by Madiran and Irouléguy, and the whites by Jurançon, but good wines throughout the range are made at the cooperative at Bellocq near the pretty town of Salies-de-Béarn. The reds are from old local varieties, plus Tannat and the Cabernets. Growers in Madiran sell their rosé as Béarn AC, while those in Jurançon such as Clos Guirouilh sell Béarn red. Just one independent estate in Béarn proper makes very good

wine: the Domaine Lapeyre on the outskirts of Salies. It also uses the name Domaine Guilhémas. The Jurançon cooperative at Gan also makes Béarn.

Jurançon

All references to Jurançon start with the story of the infant King Henri IV, whose lips at birth were brushed with a clove of garlic and moistened with Jurançon wine – a custom said still to be followed in the Bourbon family, though without such spectacular results. The point is that Jurançon is strong, not just in alcohol but in character. Its highly aromatic grapes ripen on the Pyrenean foothills south of Pau in autumns warmed by the south winds from Spain. Its flavour is enhanced by small crops, in particular for the sweet wines. These should be made by harvesting very late, in November, when hot days and freezing nights have shrivelled the grapes (*passerillage*) and concentrated their juice.

The two principal grape varieties are the Gros and Petit Manseng, the latter not only smaller but with a much higher sugar content. Both give wines of high alcohol degree with a remarkably "stiff" and positive structure in the mouth, almost fierce when young but maturing to scents and flavours variously likened to such exotic fruits and spices as mangoes, guavas, and cinnamon.

The best sweet wines are made from pure Petit Manseng, whereas Gros Manseng is more commonly used for the dry wines. Some growers also use a little Petit Courbu in their dry wines to give them bite. Colette provided tasting notes I will not presume to rival: "I was a girl when I met this prince; aroused, imperious, treacherous as all great seducers are – Jurançon."

There are two appellations: Jurançon Sec and Jurançon, the latter applicable only to wines ranging from half-sweet to *liquoreux*. There is an important co-op at Gan, and nearly sixty private producers. Generally they make three styles of wine: *sec*, *moelleux*, and ultra-sweet, sometimes oaked. The great virtue of the sweet wine is that it retains high acidity, and thus freshness. It makes an excellent aperitif in the local restaurants. Many growers make repeated pickings, and consequently a succession of bottlings from grapes picked in October, November, and December at ever higher sweetness levels.

In the 1980s, production had declined and the wine had become little known. Fortunately, a few energetic growers boosted the region, and plantings doubled in about fifteen years to just over 1,000 hectares. Today the best wines are much admired and in great demand.

Leading Jurançon Producers

Domaine Bellegarde ☆–☆☆☆
Monein. 18 hectares
Pascal Labasse is the prototype new-wave Jurançon grower, remaining open-minded on the use of new wood. He produces a bone-dry *sec* which ages well, a *moelleux* called "Cuvée Thibault", and an ultra-sweet *cuvée*, "Sélection Petit Manseng", made entirely from that grape and modelled clearly on Henri Ramonteu's richest wines (*see* Domaine Cauhapé).

Domaine Bru-Baché ☆☆–☆☆☆
Monein. 8 hectares

Claude Loustalot took over from his uncle Georges Bru-Baché in 1994 and continues the same eccentric approach to sweet Jurançon, producing *cuvées* of increasing intensity. "Quintessence" is Petit Manseng aged in around 50% new oak, and exhibiting lovely flavours of apricot and quince. "L'Eminence", first made in 1991, is Petit Manseng picked in December and aged entirely in new oak.

Domaine Castéra ☆☆
Monein. 12 hectares

Christian Lihour scorns the oak, but makes very good wines in all three styles. The *sec* is entirely from Gros Manseng, and the *moelleux* almost so; the *liquoreux* is 100% Petit Manseng, and the best of it is bottled "Cuvée Privilège".

Domaine Cauhapé ☆☆–☆☆☆☆
Monein. 34 hectares

Henri Ramonteu is the best-known private grower of Jurançon, with the second-largest vineyard. He produces four *sec* wines, all from Gros Manseng, and one remarkable "Sec Noblesse du Petit Manseng", picked at high sugar levels and fermented and aged in some new oak. Equally unusually, his basic *moelleux* ("Ballet d'Octobre") is made exclusively from Gros Manseng.

Finally, there are two very small, ultra-sweet and very expensive productions called "Noblesse" and "Quintessence du Petit Manseng". "Quintessence" is made by snipping off raisined bunches and suspending them on wires from the vines, allowing them to attain even greater concentration. It is a wine of extraordinary intensity, with flavours of dried fruits and a discreet smokiness.

Cave des Producteurs de Jurançon ☆–☆☆
Gan. 550 hectares. www.cavedejurancon.com

Most of the production at this cooperative is of dry wine, of which there are three grades – the highest called "Peyre d'Or". There are three unoaked *moelleux* also, of which the top of the range, "Privilège d'Automne", is excellent. A fourth *moelleux* called "Croix de Prince" is aged in new wood.

Clos Guirouilh ☆☆
Lasseube. 7 hectares

Jean Guirouilh's *sec* contains 10% Petit Courbu but otherwise is all Gros Manseng. It has tremendous style and elegance, the taste of apples and pears giving way to citrus fruits with age. The *moelleux* is made of roughly equal parts of each of the Mansengs, the Petit being given some new oak. In good years he will make a *liquoreux* entirely from Petit Manseng.

Clos Lapeyre ☆☆–☆☆☆
La Chapelle-de-Rousse. 12 hectares

As well as the usual sec, Jean-Bernard Larrieu produces a special dry *cuvée* from old Gros Manseng called "Vitatge Vielh", kept one year in wood and needing some ageing. The finest of the sweet wines is the "Sélection", a superb 100% Petit Manseng with delightful flavours of mango and lemon.

Clos Uroulat ☆☆–☆☆☆
Monein. 7 hectares

Charles Hours has always been an enthusiast for the wines of the region, and is himself a producer of elegant and stylish, rather than fat and luscious wines. His superb *sec*, "Cuvée Marie", has both crispness and weight. Since 1990, he has used some new wood for his sweet wine from Petit Manseng.

Château Jolys ☆–☆☆
La Chapelle-de-Rousse. 36 hectares

Robert Latrille is the largest grower in Jurançon and helped revitalize the region in the 1980s. The vineyards of la Chapelle-de-Rousse are on much higher ground than those of Monein, usually in amphitheatre-like folds of the hills called *cirques*. Latrille has planted in vertical rows rather than on terraces. His wines are good middle-of-the-road Jurançon, the *sec* from Gros Manseng; the *moelleux*, 50% Gros and 50% Petit, and his *liquoreux* "Cuvée Jean" all from the Petit.

Cru Lamouroux ☆–☆☆
La Chapelle-de-Rousse. 6 hectares

Richard Ziemeck-Chigé now makes the wines at his former father-in-law's property, thoroughly traditionally and without regard to fashions such as new oak. He does not believe in Jurançon Sec, and makes wines only in varying degrees of sweetness as they always used to be hereabouts. The name of "Clos Mirabel", an adjoining property recently purchased, is used for the red Béarn AC using Cabernet Franc.

Other Jurançon Producers

Domaine Bordenave ☆☆
Monein

This old property began bottling its wines in 1993. The best wine is the oak-aged "Cuvée Savin" from pure Petit Manseng.

Domaine Gaillot ☆–☆☆
Monein

An old estate that has been bottling its wines from the 1970s. Assertive, dry Jurançon, and a fine, apricotty sweet "Sélection".

Domaine Larrédya ☆☆–☆☆☆
La Chapelle-de-Rousse

The *sec* is unoaked, but the three tiers of sweet wine all receive varying degrees of oak-ageing. The finest is "Cuvée Simon" (previously known as "François"), only made in top years and aged for two years in barriques: spicy and very concentrated with a citric tang.

Domaine de Souch ☆☆
Laroin

Biodynamic estate belonging to Yvonne Hégoborul. Many different bottlings make selection difficult, but most of the wines are flowery with good acidity and length.

Irouléguy

The Basque growers make wines to match the taste of their fellow-countrymen for rugby and bullfights; big, sturdy wines, trying to outdo Madiran, and a perfect match for the local cuisine. They are based, like Madiran, on the Tannat grape, plus the two Cabernets. The vines are grown on steep terraces, so all picking is done by hand.

Yields are small and the wines need time in bottle. The rosé is excellent, and there has been a small renaissance of the white wine, based on the Jurançon grape varieties. For many years the excellent cooperative had it all its own way, but there are now some good independent producers. With just over 200 hectares planted, this is an appellation to watch.

Leading Irouléguy Producers

Domaine Arretxea ☆–☆☆
Irouléguy. 6 hectares
A small, organic estate, with a powerful, oaked "Cuvée Haitza" from a large majority of Tannat. It needs to be aged for its spicy, berry aromas to emerge. The excellent white, from the Jurançon varieties, is called "Hegoxuri".

Domaine Brana ☆☆
St-Jean Pied-de-Port. 40 hectares
Jean and Martine's father, Etienne Brana, died tragically and suddenly just when the family, long-established négociants in the South West, had planted their vines in 1985. Scenically magnificent – the splendid winery is hewn out of the mountainside – with breathtaking views, the vines are planted in terraced rows on almost vertical slopes. Yields are tiny, and the wine expensive. There is only 30% Tannat, the rest of the red vineyard being divided more or less equally between the two Cabernets – the wines are very drinkable when young.

Domaine Etxegaraya ☆☆
St-Etienne-de-Baïgorry. 7 hectares
The Hillau family began bottling their wines, which are all unoaked, in 1994. The standard red is very good, even lush, and the remarkable "Cuvée Lehengoa" is made from 100-year-old vines.

Domaine Ilarria ☆☆
Irouléguy. 10 hectares
These wines are a benchmark for true Irouléguy. Two reds, made from 80 and 100% Tannat, are serious propositions. The latter is called "Cuvée Bixintzo" (the Basque name for St Vincent). *Cuvaisons* are long, and the wines aged in a mixture of new and old wood for eighteen months. It will soon be organic and some Petit Manseng have been planted.

Les Vignerons du Pays Basque ☆–☆☆
St-Etienne-de-Baïgorry. 130 hectares
Cooperative founded in 1952 to exploit the grant of VDQS status, raised to AC in 1970. There are 230 members, so many holdings are tiny.

Nearly half the production is of rosé, the basic version of which rejoices in the Basque name "Argi d'Ansa"; the better version, containing half each Tannat and Cabernet is called "Terrasses d'Arradoy".

The basic red is "Gorri d'Ansa", but there are special *cuvées*: "Domaine de Mignaberry" (old vines); "Domaine Iturritze" (quicker maturing); and "Domaine Mendisokoä". The small production of white wine is called "Xuri d'Ansa".

Vins de Pays

Throughout 1981 and 1982 a stream of decrees flowed from Paris, signed by the Minister of Agriculture, setting out the regulations for newly coined *vins de pays*. The object was to give pride to local production that had hitherto had no identity. Since that time, the junior rank of French country wines has undergone nothing short of a revolution.

Wines that were previously used entirely for blending, or dispatched label-less to the local bars, are now made to minimum standards and in regulated quantities. The names of over 140 *vins de pays* have come into active – sometimes hyperactive – use, with the south, the Midi, setting the pace. Outside interest, not least investment from New World wine countries, flying winemakers, and foreign supermarket wine-buyers, has raised standards and broken the mould of generations of cautious *vignerons*. The results are many of the best value for money wines of France.

This list of *vins de pays* is still changing long after the pioneers were promulgated. Some have been raised to VDQS and AC status. New *vins de pays* have appeared. From vintage to vintage, new ideas and new producers appear.

What follows is not a complete list, since many of the *vins de pays* are extremely obscure and very little wine is produced from them. The list gives some indication of the area delimited. Some are as local as three or four parishes; some are departmental (Vins de Pays de Loire Atlantique, for instance); some as sweeping as the whole of the Midi (Vins de Pays d'Oc) or the Loire Valley (Vins de Pays du Jardin de la France). The last regional *vins de pays*, of which there are four, were intended to give new life to traditional winemaking areas and be used as the vehicle for experimentation and new ideas – which they have done.

The second control is over the grape varieties to be grown. In some cases one or more classic grapes are prescribed as obligatory, while a number of others are tolerated up to a percentage. Some areas do not specify varieties at all. The most successful new *vins de pays* allow single-grape productions – eighty-five per cent of them from the Midi – and are generally seen as France's riposte to the varietals of the New World. The rules also specify yields, which tend to be far more generous than those for AC or VDQS wines.

Rhône & Provence

Most of the wine-growing areas of the Rhône and Provence are entitled to the wide-ranging appellations Côtes du Rhône or Provence. The *vins de pays* cover outlying, often interesting districts and one or two zones within the AC areas themselves. The wines, mostly red, are usually blends of the traditional grapes of the south, but increasingly the Bordeaux varieties are featuring.

Alpes-de-Haute-Provence
Provence. Mostly reds grown in the Durance Valley. Also some rosé.

Alpes-Maritimes
Provence. Restricted to the area around Nice. Rare.

l'Ardèche
Fourteen communes in the Ardèche and Chassezac valleys. Mainly reds from local and international varieties, and whites from southern French varieties plus Chardonnay.

d'Argens
Provence. From communes around Draguignan and les Arcs in the Argens Valley. Mostly red wines.

Bouches-du-Rhône
The wines come from three distinct but very large zones: the Aix-en-Provence area, the main Côtes de Provence vineyards in the east of the *département*, and the Camargue. Most of the wines are red, made from the southern grape varieties, with some Cabernet. Thanks to the disapproval of INAO, this is also the appellation proudly worn by one of the great wines of southern France: Domaine de Trévallon (*q.v.*).

Collines Rhodaniennes
Incudes the entire northern Rhône. Grapes, red and rosé: Syrah, Gamay, plus Pinot Noir, Merlot, and Cabernet Franc in some districts, plus secondary grapes up to 30%. White: traditional Rhône varieties plus Chardonnay in some districts.

Comtés Rhodaniens
One of the four regional *vin de pays* designations covering eight *départements* (the Ain, Ardèche, Drôme, Isère, Loire, Rhône, Savoie, and the Haute-Savoie).

Coteaux des Baronnies
Area around Rémuzat and Nyons, north of Mont Ventoux in the Alpine foothills, especially for red wines: Cinsault, Grenache, Gamay, Syrah, Pinot Noir, plus up to 30% others. White: Rhône varieties plus Aligoté and Chardonnay.

Coteaux du Verdon
Provence. From the northern Var, and mostly red and rosé from local varieties and/or Cabernet Sauvignon.

Drôme
The eastern part of the Rhône Valley, south of Valence and east of Montélimar. Over 80% is red, made from Carignan, Cinsault, and Syrah, supplemented by Gamay, Cabernet Sauvignon, and Merlot.

Maures
Provence. Red and rosé wines from the area around St-Tropez, mostly from local varieties but Cabernet Sauvignon and Merlot are also permitted.

Mont-Caume
Provence. Twelve communes around Bandol. One of the best such wines is the pure Cabernet Sauvignon from Bunan.

Principauté d'Orange
Around Bollène, Orange, Vaison-la-Romaine, and Valréas, east of the Rhône in the Côtes du Rhône Villages and Châteauneuf-du-Pape country. Many Grenache-dominated reds are produced.

Var
The most important *vin de pays* region in Provence, covering

the whole of the Var *département*. Much rosé and red made here from Grenache, Cinsault, Carignan, Syrah, and other varieties, including Cabernet Sauvignon.

Vaucluse
Includes the eastern part of the Côtes du Rhône and Côtes du Ventoux. Similar reds to Côtes du Rhône, although the blend includes Cabernet Sauvignon. The unmemorable white is from Ugni Blanc.

The Gard

The *département* of the Gard stretches from the Rhône at Avignon west into the hills of the Cévennes. The chief town is Nîmes. Most of the *département* is wine-growing country, and there is a *vin de pays* for the whole area: Vin de Pays du Gard. Other *vins de pays*, covering areas of varying size, are listed below. There are no specified grape varieties.

Mont Bouquet
Nineteen communes around Vézenobres, northwest of Nîmes.

Coteaux Cévennois
Twenty-four communes northeast of Alès in the Cévennes foothills.

Coteaux Flaviens
Nine communes southwest of Nîmes.

Coteaux du Pont-du-Gard
Nineteen communes around Remoulins, between Nîmes and Avignon. Most production comes from eight co-ops.

Sables-du-Golfe-du-Lion
Sand dunes and coastal strips in parts of twelve communes in the Camargue west of the mouth of the Rhône. Grapes, red and rosé: Cabernet Sauvignon, Cabernet Franc, Carignan, Cinsault, Grenache, Lladoner Pelut, Merlot, Syrah, and up to 30% others. White: Ugni Blanc, Clairette, Carignan, Muscats, Sauvignon, and up to 30% others.

Uzège
Twenty-six communes around Uzès, north of Nîmes.

Côtes du Vidourle
Fifteen communes around Sommières, west of Nîmes.

Hérault

This is France's biggest wine-producing *département*. Vin de Pays de l'Hérault covers the whole area. Twenty-seven local districts have their own sets of regulations. Some of the areas cover land in the St-Chinian and Minervois ACs, others include communes entitled to the Coteaux du Languedoc AC. The presence of one of the Midi's top estates – Mas de Daumas Gassac – proves that this is not only an area of inexpensive wines.

Ardailhou
Southernmost part of the *département* at the mouths of the Hérault and Orb. Co-ops at Portiragnes, Vias, Villeneuve-les-Béziers, Sérignan.

Cassan
Four communes around Roujan in the central Hérault.

Côtes du Brian
Thirteen communes in the eastern Minervois. Best-known producer is Clos des Centeilles for some more-daring wines.

Coteaux de Fontcaude
Six communes south of St-Chinian.

Coteaux du Libron
Six communes around Béziers.

Collines de la Moure
Twenty-seven communes around Frontagnan and Mireval. Widely used by private estates and co-ops alike.

Coteaux de Murviel
The eastern part of St-Chinian, with Château Coujan the best-known producer.

Côtes de Thau
Five communes around Florensac, near the coast at Agde.

Côtes de Thongue
Hérault. Red and white. Fourteen communes around Pézenas and Béziers. Quite commonly encountered.

Gorges de l'Hérault
Three communes in the upper Hérault Valley around Gignac.

Mont-Baudile
Around St-Jean de la Blaquière north of Clermont l'Hérault. Two-thirds production red, rest rosé and some white.

Aude

The entire *département* of the Aude, which stretches inland from Narbonne, is entitled to call the wines produced Vin de Pays de l'Aude.

Haute-Vallée de l'Aude
Fifty-five communes around Lomous. Grapes, red and rosé: Cabernet Sauvignon, Cabernet Franc, Cot, Merlot. White: Chenin, Chardonnay, Sémillon, Terret Blanc, Terret Gris.

Coteaux de la Cité de Carcassonne
Eleven communes around Carcassonne. A very wide range of grapes is permitted.

Cucugnan
Commune in the Corbières. Used mostly by the cooperative.

Coteaux de Miramont
Nine communes around Capendu east of Carcassonne.

Val d'Orbieu

This consists of twelve communes in the Orbieu Valley situated west of Narbonne. Grapes, red and rosé: Carignan, Cinsault, Grenache, Alicante-Bouschet, Picpoul, Terret Noir. White: Clairette, Macabeu, Bourboulenc, Carignan Blanc, Grenache Blanc.

Coteaux de Peyriac

Seventeen communes in the western Minervois.

Roussillon & Corbières

The Corbières hills, which the Pyrénées-Orientales *département* shares with the Aude to the north, have several interesting *vins de pays* that are listed here and under the Aude. Vins de Pays des Pyrénées-Orientales is the name used for the predominantly red wines produced in most areas of the *département*, except the southeast. The country to the south, consisting of plains and the foot-hills of the Pyrénées, uses the Catalan name for its two defined districts.

Catalan

Roussillon. Area stretching inland from Perpignan and Argelès.

Côtes Catalanes

Roussillon. North and west of Perpignan.

Côte Vermeille

Roussillon. The area around Banyuls and Collioure along the coast.

The South West

Nearly all of the South West is included in one or other of the many *vins de pays* now proliferating. Many of them overlap with or include the areas of AC and VDQS production described on pages 211–226. The best tend to be produced by growers for whom they are their first and only wines, rather than a bolt-on to wines of superior appellation.

l'Agenais

Covers the whole of Lot-et-Garonne from the armagnac to Cahors boundaries. It is mostly for red wines made by cooperatives.

Aveyron

Little seen except as one of the lines of the co-op at Aguessac, near Millau. The Millau VDQS is declassified if it contains too much Cabernet Sauvignon (!), and is sold as this *vin de pays*.

Bigorre

Hautes-Pyrénées. Certain communes around Madiran and Vic-de-Bigorre to the south. The Plaimont Producteurs and Brumont at Madiran (*q.v.*) also use Bigorre to describe some varietal wines.

Charentais

Charente and Charente-Maritime. Entire *départements*. Maximum yield 70 hl/ha. Grapes, red: Cabernet Franc, Cabernet Sauvignon, Merlot, Tannat (on the Ile de Ré only) plus up to 20% others. White: Chenin Blanc, Colombard, Folle Blanche, Muscadelle, Sauvignon, Sémillon, and Ugni Blanc. Usually lean and rustic.

Corrèze

One cooperative at Branceilles between Brive and the Dordogne and one private grower at Voutézac northwest of Brive (Domaine de la Mégénie) use this *vin de pays*.

Dordogne

A designation mostly applied by cooperatives to substandard or declassified red and white wines of growers from Bergerac.

Côtes de Gascogne

Almost the entire *département* of the Gers (armagnac country). Wide range of traditional and quality grape varieties.

Gers

Covers the whole *département*, overlapping Côtes de Gascogne. Many whites from Ugni Blanc and Colombard.

Côteaux de Glanes

Glanes is a village in the hills east of Bretenoux (Lot). A small cooperative is the sole producer. Attractive wine, much drunk in local restaurants, from Merlot, Gamay, and a crossing of Jurançon Noir and Portugais Bleu called Ségalin.

Coteaux & Terrasses de Montauban

For wines produced in the no-man's land between Côteaux de Quercy, Fronton, and Lavilledieu. Grape varieties include Gamay, Merlot, Syrah, Tannat, and the two Cabernets. Main producer: the cooperative at Lavilledieu.

Coteaux du Quercy

The area used to be called Bas-Quercy, the *causses* stretching south from Cahors. In the north, the Cahors grapes, Malbec, Merlot, and Tannat dominate, but further south Cabernet Franc, Gamay, and some Cabernet Sauvignon are also used.

Côtes du Tarn

Covers the Gaillac AC area and land to the south as far as the River Agout. Large and important production of dry white, rosé, and red wine.

The wines are sometimes declassified Gaillac, sometimes using grapes not permitted in AC, *e.g.* Jurançon Noir and Portugais Bleu. Mainstay of the cooperatives at Técou and Labastide-de-Lévis and featured by some independent Gaillac growers.

Thézac-Perricard

Southwest of Cahors, making red wines of similar but lighter style, as well as some rosé. The cooperative at Thézac is the only producer.

Comté Tolosan

Capable of designating most of the southwest, but in practice mostly used for the area of Toulouse, north to Montauban, and south towards Pamiers. Can be just about anything.

Pyrénées-Atlantiques

Covers the whole *département*, but mainly for wines grown in Béarn and Jurançon areas. Mostly red and rosé.

St-Sardos

The ambitious co-op in garlic-growing area west of Montauban aspires to VDQS. Reds and rosé from Syrah, Cabernet Franc, Gamay, and Tannat. Rosé is *saigné* from the same grapes, with a separate *cuvée* from black Muscat

Terroirs Landais

This covers the whole of the *département* of Landes. Used mostly for wines of the Gascon style (Colombard and Ugni Blanc for the whites, Tannat and Cabernets for the reds) produced over the border from the Gers; also smaller productions in the west of the *département*, especially *vin de table*, which is mostly from Cabernet Franc, grown near the Atlantic coast.

Loire

Coteaux Charitois

Area around la Charité-sur-Loire, south of Pouilly-sur-Loire. Mostly Sauvignon Blanc.

Coteaux du Cher & de l'Arnon

Ten communes around Quincy and Reuilly. Grapes, red and rosé: Gamay, Pinot Noir, plus 30% others. White: Chardonnay, Sauvignon, Pinot Gris, plus 30% others.

Jardin de la France

Most of the lower and mid-Loire basin. The vast zone covers thirteen *départements*. A successful appellation, often seen used for simple Chardonnays, for example, though Chenin and Sauvignon are also allowed.

Loire-Atlantique

From the Muscadet region. Reds and rosés are made from Gamay and Grolleau; whites from Muscadet, Gros Plant, and Chardonnay.

La Vienne

From Haut-Poitou. Reds and rosés from Gamay; whites from Chenin Blanc and Chardonnay.

Burgundy

l'Yonne

Usually Chardonnay from the northern stretches of Burgundy around Auxerre. This is the sole Burgundian *vin de pays* anyone is likely to encounter.

Midi & Corsica

Pays d'Oc

Covers the whole of Languedoc-Roussillon. This *vin de pays* is used for wines made from varieties not traditional to the region. This is thus Vin de Pays d'Oc made from Cabernet Sauvignon, Cabernet Franc, Merlot, Syrah, and Mourvèdre, with whites from Chardonnay, Sauvignon Blanc, Chenin Blanc, Viognier, and Vermentino.

Seventy per cent of production is of varietal wines. Many of the most interesting of the new wave of southern French wines are being made using this *vin de pays* name. Top producers include Skalli Fortant de France and la Baume.

L'Ile de Beauté

Corsica. Mostly red wines from a wide range of varieties, though Carignan and Cinsault may not exceed 25% and 50%, respectively, of the planted area. Some good wines are made.

Hamburg

Bremen

Elbe

Hanover

Berlin

Rhine

Leipzig

SAALE-UNSTRUT

Weser

Erfurt

SACHSEN

Bonn

Dresden

AHR   MITTELRHEIN

Koblenz

RHEINGAU

MOSEL-
SAAR-RUWER

Frankfurt

FRANKEN

RHEINHESSEN

Trier

Mannheim

Würzburg

NAHE

HESSISCHE-
BERGSTRASSE

Nürnberg

PFALZ

WÜRTTEMBERG

Main

Stuttgart

Baden Baden

Danube

BADEN

München

Freiburg

Bodensee

Germany

Until the 1970s, it was generally accepted that Germany made the world's finest white wines, with white burgundy as its only peer. No great dinner could begin without its Mosel or Rhein Spätlese. The Riesling was universally hailed as the queen of white grapes (while few people, believe it or not, had even heard of Chardonnay).

However it sometimes seems that, in the past decade or so, the international reputation or renown of every single wine-producing country has improved, with the exception of Germany. In the eyes of the outside world, German wine has been a more or less unmitigated disaster area.

The slide began with the German Wine Law of 1971, ironically coinciding with a truly magnificent vintage. The law came down firmly on the side of the little man, the cooperative member – whose vote, one can be forgiven for thinking, the politicians were eager to attract.

The new law allowed him to label his wine with grand names that bore almost no relation to its origin. It permitted the use of the word "quality" where it meant the opposite, while debasing such vital descriptive terms as Auslese to a mere matter of grams of sugar. It placed no restriction on yields, with the consequence that many, even most, wines soon came to taste like sugar water (with the stress on the water). Plummeting quality, in turn forced the price of German wine down to some of Europe's lowest levels. The country with the highest living standards and most expensive labour now makes some of western Europe's cheapest wine.

This sad recital is unfortunately a necessary prologue to understanding German wine today. The good news is that an ever-increasing number of proud producers is adopting an independent attitude, effectively bypassing legal minimum standards, which they regard as dismally permissive. Some are even redesignating their wine to make their own names more prominent (as brands) than the famous names of the sites they farm.

Many German vineyards are in northerly parts of Europe, and that makes vineyard location absolutely crucial. Think of the great loops of the River Mosel, where the sunshine on the vineyard varies with the shape, the steepness, and the exposure more than anywhere on earth. Free-draining slate or schist is vital for ripening Riesling here; the qualities of the best vineyards are known to everyone – and so is the impossibility of making fine wine on north-facing slopes or flat alluvial land.

Compare the Côte d'Or of Burgundy. Over centuries, it has been minutely divided into its grands crus, premiers crus, and villages sites. Its world fame rests on this classification; it simply works. The official German line is that such pinpointing of natural quality is "elitist" and undemocratic.

Even more fundamentally, red burgundy is pure Pinot Noir, white burgundy pure Chardonnay. But wine sold as "Bernkasteler" or "Piesporter" need not be Riesling at all. It can be made legally from such inferior bulk-producers as Müller-Thurgau and Kerner. If a region does not protect its own good name, nobody else will do it. Any French syndicat defines its role as the protection of its appellation; in Germany there is, alas, no appellation to protect. Hence the current débâcle.

On the other hand, what is true for the Mosel or the Rheingau, the regions where Riesling is the essential classic grape, is not necessarily true, or not true at all, for the Pfalz, or Baden in the south, or Franconia, where Silvaner comes into its own. Different soils and different traditions, not to mention longer growing seasons, offer other possibilities that thinking winegrowers must embrace.

In German thinking, and for understandable reasons, ripeness is everything. All German quality criteria (at least the government-regulated ones) are based on the accumulated sugar in the grapes at harvest time. There is no official ranking of vineyards as in France, no specific recipes for varieties of grapes as in Italy. German labels, at least those of quality wines, make unequivocal statements. Despite the difficulties of Gothic type, they can be the world's most consistent and informative – up to a carefully calculated point.

Since 1971, the wine laws have been subject to further revisions. But their strategy remains unaltered. They divide all German wine into three strata. The lowest, tafelwein, ("table wine") subject to relatively few controls, is correspondingly barred from claiming any specific vineyard origin. It is assumed to be a blend of wines that have required additional sugar. The only technical point to remember is the difference between Deutscher tafelwein, which must be German in origin, and tafelwein without the qualification, which may contain wine from other European countries (formerly Italy, now more often eastern Europe). A low-strength neutral base wine is easily cleaned up and given some superficial German characteristics by using very aromatic süssreserve ("sweet reserve": unfermented grape juice that may legally be added to finished wine). The use of heavily Gothic labels is obviously intended to encourage the innocent to believe that the wine is indeed German. A new category of tafelwein, called landwein, ("land" or "county" wine) with stricter rules, was introduced in 1982 as a sort of German vin de pays. But landwein is far from matching its French counterparts in popularity or enterprise.

More significant is the rebellious use of the tafelwein designation by proud growers who have despaired of official categories and consider their freedom to use their own judgement more important than official recognition.

The second category of German wine was christened Qualitätswein bestimmter Anbaugebiete: QbA for short. The term means "quality wine from a designated region". The use of the word "quality" in this context is really meaningless. Nonetheless, to a German, the difference between this and the top category of wine, Qualitätswein mit Prädikat, (QmP) is doubtless clear and simple. Unfortunately, the legislators did not take non-Germans into account, drinkers who are unaware that the two classes of Qualitätswein are far apart, distinguished by a basic difference. The first may be chaptalized during fermentation, as some added sugar will boost the alcohol level; the second is what used (before 1971) to be called, much more directly and succinctly, natur or naturrein; in other words the grapes had enough natural sugar to make wine. Mit Prädikat is hard to translate. "With special attributes" is the stilted official version. It certainly does not reflect the status of QmP wines as the top category in which, almost without exception, all the best wines of Germany are included. (The exceptions occur in vintages where the grapes did not ripen fully; in such cases, light chaptalization may improve a wine that might otherwise taste thin and undernourished.)

Qualitätswein mit Prädikat carry a designation of maturity of their grapes as part of their full names, in the following order; simply ripe grapes of the normal harvest are Kabinett; late-gathered (therefore riper) are Spätlese; selected very ripe grapes are Auslese. The precise sugar content (or "must weight") and therefore potential alcohol required for each category, in each region, is stipulated in the regulations.

At this point most wines begin to retain distinct natural sweetness. If an Auslese is fermented fully dry, it will be noticeably high in alcohol – often throwing it off-balance. Two levels of ripeness and selectivity beyond Auslese remain: Beerenauslese (BA), in which the individual berries are selected for extreme ripeness and concentration, and Trockenbeerenauslese (TBA), in which only berries dried and shrivelled by noble rot (occasionally by unseasonal heat) are selected. Sugar levels in such wines are commonly so high that fermentation is seriously hampered, and may take months to attain a modest degree of alcohol. TBAs (to use the current American abbreviation) are usually a stable conjunction of very modest alcohol level (usually around 5.5 per cent) and startlingly high sugar. They are less than half as strong in alcohol as Château d'Yquem, which is made in much the same way, and correspondingly twice as sweet (although great TBAs may be even more concentrated and intense than Yquem – but not necessarily better).

One further category of QmP wine deserves to be considered separately because of the way it is made. Eiswein is made by crushing grapes that have frozen solid on the vine. Crushing before they thaw means that the almost pure water, which constitutes the ice, is separated from the sugar, acids, and other constituents, which have a lower freezing point. The result, like a TBA, is intensely concentrated, but usually much less ripe and invariably more acidic. It can be extraordinary, its high acid giving it the potential for almost limitless ageing.

The name and ranking of a QmP wine is conventionally set forth on its label in the same order. First is the *gemeinde* (own or village) name; then the vineyard; then the grape; then the category of ripeness – Kabinett, Spätlese, and so on. In addition there may also be a stylistic guide: *trocken* or *halbtrocken*, which will be explained below.

A further complicating factor, and the major fault in the 1971 German law, prevents this formula from being crystal clear. It is the concept of the *grosslage*, or extended vineyard. Unfortunately, labels do not, and are not allowed to, distinguish between a single-vineyard site, known as an *einzellage*, and a group of such sites with very much less specificity: a *grosslage*. Grosslage groupings were made with the idea of simplifying the sales of wines from lesser-known *einzellagen*. Notoriety comes more easily to bigger units. But their names are in no way distinguishable from *einzellage* names and I have never met a person who claims to have memorized them. The consumer is therefore deprived of a vital piece of information. As a further confusing factor, in some areas, *einzellagen* are also groups of separate vineyards deemed to have a common personality. There is thus no truly clear-cut distinction between the categories.

At their worst, *grosslage* names are a con. Two well-known examples are Nierstein's Gutes Domtal and Piesport's Michelsberg. In both cases, these *grosslagen* need contain not a drop of wine from the village identified on the label; indeed, it is almost certain that a Gutes Domtal will contain nothing more than Müller-Thurgau grown on flat land better

suited for potato-growing. An exact French parallel would be that any Médoc could be sold as Margaux.

The often-quoted rule of thumb, based on the Kabinett-Spätlese-Auslese scale, is "the sweeter the wine, the higher the quality". While it is still true to say that quality is directly related to ripeness, the question of sweetness is now very much at the discretion of the winemaker (and the consumer). Sweetness in modern commercial German wines is adjusted to suit the market, by adding (or not adding) unfermented grape juice to fully fermented, fully dry wine just before bottling. Growers have also been encouraged by cooperatives and wholesalers to plant new crossings that attain very high sugar levels, the drawback being that they lack the acidity that is needed to balance sweetness, to prevent a wine from being cloying. The consequence is that crossings such as Albalonga and Optima can routinely produce grapes with Auslese sugar levels so routinely that the entire concept of Auslese is degraded.

But the sweetness in wine from Germany's top estates, especially in the Mosel, is wholly natural and intrinsic – a result of the fermentation stopping itself or being stopped. The grower looks for an harmonious balance between acidity, alcohol, and fruity sweetness in his wine.

The great change in German wine fashion over the past decade has been the demand for fully dry, unsweetened wines, to accompany food. To be so described as *trocken*, on the label, these must contain less than nine grams of sugar per litre. The taste for *trocken* wines has grown with, and in turn boosted, the use of what are typically French grapes, mainly of the Pinot family, to make true "table" or "food" wines of a kind Germany has traditionally lacked. It has fundamentally shifted the emphasis southward from the northernmost vineyards, where Riesling reigns, to such regions as the Pfalz and Baden, where the Pinots and similar grapes are fully at home. In tasting trocken wines of Riesling, it soon becomes clear how much a little natural sweetness adds to the charm, balance, and drinkability of most German wines; they have to have unusually good figures to survive such naked scrutiny. On the other hand, this is the area in which the most progress has recently been made by the most ambitious producers, especially in warmer Riesling regions such as the Pfalz. A halfway category, *halbtrocken*, with up to eighteen grams of sugar per litre, more often achieves the right balance of fullness and bite to make satisfactory mealtime wine.

German growers produce astonishing quantities. France, Italy, and other countries make low yields, which are a precondition for their appellations. In Germany, only sugar levels count. Average crops have grown from twenty-five hectolitres per hectare in 1900, to forty in 1939, and in the 1970s were averaging over 100. The year 1982 hit a record: a 173 hectolitres per hectare average, with a maximum close to 400. But this is the national average, including cooperatives, where anything goes.

A welcome move was made in 1989 by the government of the Rheinland-Pfalz (which controls two-thirds of German wine production) to tighten the law and prevent excessive production. It set maximum permitted yields according to region, grape variety, and quality classification. The Mosel-Saar-Ruwer was given an overall limit of 130 hectolitres per hectare for Müller-Thurgau; 120 hectolitres per hectare for Riesling. Other regions were given a sliding scale: in the Nahe, for example, growers can produce 120 hectolitres per hectare of table wine, 110 hectolitres per hectare of QbA wine, but only eighty-five hectolitres per hectare of *Prädikat* wine.

On the other hand many have doubted the serious intent of a law that permits over-production in one vintage to be held over to the next. It appears that the political will to frustrate over-production is far from resolute. Meanwhile, all serious growers attempting high-quality wines impose their own limits at a level well below the legal maximum. The average figure for Maximin Grünhaus and Robert Weil, for example, is fifty-five hectolitres per hectare; Dr. Loosen harvests at fifty hectolitres per hectare; and Egon Müller and Schlossgut Diel at forty-five hectolitres per hectare.

Another serious concern is that the current law, in setting simple minimum ripeness standards for Auslesen and the other top categories, simply invites growers to achieve that minimum and no more. The old rules allowed eager winemakers to differentiate between their standard and better-than-standard Auslesen, such terms as Feine or Feinste Auslese carrying considerable premiums. If the terms were open to abuse, they also rewarded the patient and ambitious perfectionist. Today he will still signal to his clients which are his best casks of wine, but often in an obscure semaphore of gold capsules, no less open to abuse because it is closed to the uninitiated.

The official answer to any doubts about the standards or authenticity of QbA and QmP German wines is that each wine is both analyzed and tasted officially before being issued with a unique *Amtliche Prüfungsnummer* (A.P.: "official inspection number") which appears on every label. The pass-mark for any wine at AP tastings is 1.5 out of 5, suggesting the examination is far from rigorous. All official tastings employ a points scheme, which is also used for the awarding of the gold, silver, and bronze medals at both national (DLG) and regional levels. But here again it is the self-imposed criteria of top growers which really set the standard. It is here that the *Verband Deutscher Prädikats-und Qualitätsweingüter* (VDP "Federation of German Prädikats and Qualitäts" wine estates) has firmly taken the lead in setting far stricter quality criteria than the government. Membership of the VDP is open to growers (there are about 200 at present) who sign up for self-discipline. Its standards are well policed and laggards lose their membership. The VDP imposes maxima of production and minima of must-weight far stricter than those decreed by government. The VDP has also supported a long overdue, though still unofficial, classification of the German vineyards (*see* box right). It is on the VDP and the pride of its members that the future of Germany's high-quality wine industry depends.

To be fair to the German wine authorities, they did launch a new initiative in 2001, creating two new categories of wine: Classic and Selection. The rules are complicated, but they are essentially as follows. Classic is a good-quality, single-variety QbA with no more than fifteen grams of residual sugar. Selection must be made from grapes cropped in a single vineyard, at no more than sixty hectolitres per hectare, with a potential alcohol of at least 12.2 per cent, and no more than twelve grams of residual sugar. The idea is to simplify the complicated German wine labels and to introduce concepts easily grasped by the consumer. The styles have been adopted by a few prestigious estates such as Selbach-Oster, Kruger-Rumpf, and Diel, but they are the exceptions. Whether these will be accepted in the crucial export markets is too early to say.

German Wine Regions

Germany's finest wines come from hillside vineyards facing the southern half of the compass. In this northern climate the

The New Classification

In the 1980s, progressive growers, especially in the Rheingau, sought to undo some of the damage inflicted by the 1971 wine law, by restoring the notion of a vineyard hierarchy. It was argued that no one could possibly memorize 3,000 individual sites. Better instead to highlight the best sites, and suppress the names of the lesser ones, by blending their production as a village or estate wine. The basis for vineyard classification throughout Germany would be the nineteenth century maps showing the tax band for each site: the better the vineyard, the higher the tax band. Not an infallible guide, but a sound starting point for classification.

The Rheingau proposals made sense, but encountered understandable opposition, especially from good growers not blessed with outstanding sites. Nonetheless, by the late 1990s, the Rheingau had evolved a system of vineyard classification that was legally approved. Unfortunately, the system of classification resulted in about one-third of the Rheingau being certified as First Growth, which is clearly far too high. The fatal error was to apply a complicated formula to vineyards based on the ripeness usually attained in those sites. This tended to benefit warmer and more precocious sites near the river, and penalize those further inland and higher up. To the dismay of some producers, some ordinary sites emerged as *erstes gewächs*, while others with a better track record were omitted.

Thus far, only a minute percentage of vineyards entitled to be labelled *erstes gewächs* are bottled as such. In practice, the estates are using the label as a kind of signal to identify their very top wines, produced according to the *erstes gewächs* rules and regulations. A few top growers, such as Franz Künstler in Hochheim, dismiss the whole system as meaningless and will have nothing to do with it. Others protest that there is no stylistic definition attached to *erstes gewächs* and that chaptalization is permitted for what is intended to be great wine.

In other regions – notably the Pfalz, Rheinhessen, and Nahe – different criteria were adopted in 2002 for a VDP initiative to classify dry wines from certain sites as First Growths (known as *grosses gewächs*). If all goes according to plan, it is probable that these are the criteria that will be adopted in almost all German wine regions in the years ahead. Some critics are surprised by the idea of classifying dry wines separately from sweet wines from the same vineyard and this may well change in the future. Criteria vary slightly from region to region, but those for *grosses gewächs* are as follows:

• Wines must be dry (up to eight grams of sugar). Nobly sweet wines such as BA or TBA are recognized as being of outstanding quality, but may not be labelled as *grosses gewächs*.
• Grape varieties must be traditional to the region.
• Maximum yield fifty hectolitres per hectare.
• Sugar content of grapes at harvest must be at least Spätlese level.
• Classified vineyards to be inspected regularly, and wines subjected to a tasting panel for approval.
• Special bottle and logo.

A second tier of vineyards is recognized as Klassifizierte Lagenweine. These are not First Growths, but are accepted as being high quality sites. The main difference from *grosses gewächs* is that yields may be sixty-five hectolitres per hectare.

All other wines must be sold as estate or village wines without any vineyard designation on the label.

Although this is a VDP initiative, it is intended that the system will be open to all producers who accept the quality criteria.

extra radiation on land tilted toward the sun is often essential for ripeness. Other factors also come into account: the climate-moderating presence of water; shelter from wind; and fast-draining and heat-retentive soil.

Germany in Round Figures

The total vineyard area of Germany is 105,000 hectares, farmed by some 75,000 growers. Of this number, however, only 5,415 growers bottle and sell more than ninety per cent of their wine themselves. The thirteen regions differ enormously in size. The following table shows the vineyard area in hectares per region, and in the line below the most important grape variety in that region, and the proportion of the area it occupies.

Region / Grape	Hectares
Mosel-Saar-Ruwer	11,239
Riesling (54%)	
Ahr	525
Pinot Noir (58%)	
Mittelrhein	547
Riesling (72%)	
Rheingau	3,219
Riesling (79%)	
Nahe	4,536
Riesling (25%)	
Rheinhessen	26,456
Müller-Thurgau (21%)	
Pfalz	23,460
Riesling (21%)	
Hessische Bergstrasse	456
Riesling (54%)	
Franken	6,030
Müller-Thurgau (40%)	
Württemberg	11,264
Trollinger (23%)	
Baden	15,880
Pinot Noir (32%)	
Saale-Unstrut	643
Müller-Thurgau (23%)	
Sachsen	445
Müller-Thurgau (23%)	

The following are the most widely planted grape varieties throughout Germany, followed by the percentage of plantings.

Variety	Percentage
Riesling	21%
Müller-Thurgau	19%
Pinot Noir	9%
Silvaner	6.4%
Kerner	6.2%
Portugieser	4.8%
Dornfelder	4.4%
Bacchus	3.1%
Scheurebe	2.8%
Pinot Gris	2.6%
Pinot Blanc	2.5%
Trollinger	2.5%
Pinot Meunier	2.3%
Faberrebe	1.4%
Other	12%

Fine German wines, in fact, come from almost every type of soil, from slate to limestone, clay to sand – given other optimal conditions. The effects of different soils on the character of wines from one grape, the Riesling, is a fascinating sub-plot of German oenology. But climate and microclimate, orientation, and angle of hill come first.

The thirteen principal wine regions fall into five broad divisions. The most important is the Rhine Valley, including its lesser tributaries, from the Pfalz (the Palatinate) in the south, past Rheinhessen, the Hessische Bergstrasse, the Rheingau and the Nahe, the Mittelrhein, and finally to the little tributary Ahr near Bonn in the north. Second comes the Mosel, flowing north with its tributaries the Saar and the Ruwer to meet the Rhine at Koblenz. Third comes the vast but scattered region of Baden in the south, from Heidelberg all the way to the Swiss border. Fourth comes Franken (or Franconia), the vineyards of the Main Valley in northern Bavaria. Fifth, and rarely spoken of outside Germany, comes the disjointed and diverse region of Württemberg.

On the export market, the Rhine and the Mosel are far and away the most important. The picture in Germany is rather different, with great loyalty (and high prices) for the wines of the last three. Foreigners tend to meet German wine either as a commercial blend ("Liebfraumilch") or as the produce of one of the many great historic estates of the Rhein or Mosel. (Liebfraumilch is a hazy category, required merely to have between eighteen and forty grams of residual sugar, and to be made from certain grape varieties from the most productive of Germany's wine regions.) Only rarely have the wines of the smaller local grower been offered abroad. Yet very often this small farmer-cum-innkeeper (for many of them sell their wine "open" by the glass in their own cheerful little *Weinstube*) epitomizes the style and vitality of his region. His wines are generally less fine than those of sophisticated noble estates. But they have character, often charm, and sometimes, brilliant dash and fire.

Glossary of German Wine Terms

For details of the main German white and red grape varieties, see pages 14–15.

Abfüllung Bottling (*see Erzeugerabfüllung*).

Amtliche Prüfung Certification of standard quality by chemical analysis and tasting. Compulsory since 1971 for all QbA and QmP wines (*qq.v.*). Each wine is given an AP number which must be displayed on the label.

Anbaugebiet The broadest category of wine region, of which (for "quality" wines) there are thirteen (*e.g.* Mosel-Saar-Ruwer, Baden).

Anreichern "Enriching"; adding sugar to the must to increase the alcohol, the equivalent of the French chaptalization. In Germany no sugar may be added to wines in the QmP categories (*q.v.*) but *tafelwein* and QbA wines are usually "enriched".

Auslese Literally "selected": the third category of QmP wines, made only in ripe vintages and usually naturally sweet. Auslesen often have a slight degree of "noble rot" which adds subtlety to their fruity sweetness. Good Auslesen deserve ageing in bottle for several years to allow their primary sweetness to mellow to more adult flavours.

Barriquewein Term for wines fermented and/or matured in small new-oak casks. Ageing in new oak is now standard practice for good red wines. White examples are more variable.

Beerenauslese Literally "selected berries": the category of QmP wine beyond Auslese in sweetness and price, and theoretically in quality. Only very overripe or "nobly rotten" grapes are used to make intensely sweet, often deep-coloured wines, which age admirably.

Bereich One of thirty-four districts or sub-regions (e.g. Bereich Bernkastel) within the thirteen Gebieten (q.v.). Bereich names are commonly used for middling to lower-quality wines (they are legal for QbA as well as QmP) blended from the less-distinguished vineyards of the district.

Bundesweinprämierung A national wine award presented by the DLG (q.v.) to wines selected from regional prizewinners. 3.5 points out of five wins a bronze medal, Four a silver medal, and 4.5 a "Grosser Preis". Winners normally display their achievements on a neck label on bottles of the winning wine.

Deutsche(r) "German"; distinguishes *tafelwein* grown in Germany from inferior mixtures of the wines of "various EU countries", often sold with pseudo-German labels.

Deutsches Weinsiegel A seal of quality awarded by the DLG (q.v.) for wines that achieve a set level of points higher than the standard required to obtain an

Amtliche Prüfungsnummer (q.v.). The standard seal is red, but there is a green seal for medium-dry wines, and a yellow for dry wines that meet DLG standards.

Diabetiker-Wein The driest category of German wines, with less than four grams of unfermented sugar per litre. It should be drunk by diabetics only after medical approval is given.

DLG *Deutsche Land-Wirtschafts-Gesellschaft* (the German Agricultural Society), the body that judges and presents the national wine awards. *See Bundesweinprämierung.*

Domäne "Domain" – in Germany, a term used mainly to describe the estates owned by Federal German States (e.g. in the Rheingau, Franken, Nahe).

Edelfäule "Noble rot". For a full explanation, *see* Château d'Yquem, page 66.

Einzellage An individual vineyard site. There are some 2,600 *einzellagen* in Germany. Officially, the minimum size for an *einzellage* is five hectares, although there are a number much smaller than this. Not all *einzellagen* are therefore in contiguous parcels, particularly in Baden and Württemberg. A *grosslage* (q.v.) is a unit of several *einzellagen* supposedly of the same quality and character. The *einzellage* or *grosslage* name follows the village (*gemeinde*) name on the label.

Eiswein Wine made by pressing grapes that have been left hanging on the vine into mid-winter (sometimes January), and are gathered and pressed in early morning, while frozen solid. Since it is the water content of the grape that freezes, the juice, separated from the ice, is concentrated sugar, acidity, and flavour. The result is extraordinarily sweet and piquant wines with almost limitless ageing capacity, less rich but more penetrating than BA or TBA, often fetching spectacular prices.

Erstes Gewächs *See grosses gewaches* below.

Erzeugerabfüllung "Estate-bottled"; the equivalent of the French *mis au domaine* or *mis au château*.

Fass A barrel. "*Holzfässen*" are oak barrels, the traditional containers in German cellars.

Flasche Bottle – the same word as the English "flask".

Flurbereinigung The term for the government-sponsored "consolidation" of vineyard holdings by remodelling the landscape, a process that has revolutionized the old system of terracing in most parts of Germany, making the land workable by tractors and rationalizing scattered holdings.

Füder The Mosel barrel, an oak oval holding 1,000 litres or about 111 cases.

Gebiet Region.

Gemeinde Village, parish, or commune. The village name always comes before the vineyard on German labels.

Grosses Gewächs "First Growth" vineyard, as established by the VDP classification.

Grosslage A "collective vineyard", consisting of a number of *einzellagen* (q.v.) of similar quality. Unfortunately, the wine law does not permit the label to distinguish between a *grosslage* and an *einzellage* name. *Grosslage* names are normally used for QbA wines, but also sometimes for such wines as TBA, when a single *einzellage* cannot produce enough grapes to fill even a small barrel.

Halbtrocken "Semi-dry" (*halb* = half) – wine with no more than eighteen grams of unfermented sugar per litre, therefore drier than most modern German wines, but sweeter than a trocken wine (q.v.).

Jahrgang Vintage (year).

Kabinett The first category of natural, unsugared, *Qualitätswein mit Prädikat*. Fine Kabinett wines have qualities of lightness and delicacy which make them ideal refreshment, not inferior in the right context to heavier (and more expensive) Spätlese or Auslese wines.

Kellerei Wine cellar; by inference a merchant's rather than a grower's establishment (which would be called a Weingut).

Landwein A category of *trocken* or *halbtrocken tafelwein* introduced in 1982. (*See* page 237.)

Liebfraumilch A much-abused name for a "wine of pleasant character" with between eighteen and forty grams of residual sugar, officially originating in the Pfalz, Rheinhessen, Rheingau, or the Nahe. It must be in the QbA category and should be mainly of Riesling, Silvaner, or Müller-Thurgau grapes. Since neither its character nor quality is remotely consistent, varying widely from shipper to shipper, its popularity can only be ascribed to its simple and memorable name.

Mostgewicht "Must weight". The density or specific gravity of the grape juice, ascertained with a hydrometer, is the way of measuring its sugar content. The unit of measurement is the "degree Oechsle" (*q.v.*).

Neuzüchtung New (grape) variety (*see* pages 14–15).

Oechsle The specific gravity, therefore sweetness, of German must is measured by the method invented by Ferdinand Oechsle (1774–1852). Each gram by which a litre of grape juice is heavier than a litre of water is one degree Oechsle. The number of degrees Oechsle divided by eight is the potential alcoholic content of the wine.

Offene Weine Wines served "open" in a large glass in a café or *Weinstube*.

Ortsteil A suburb or part of a larger community with a standing independent from its *gemeinde* or village. For example, Erbach in the Rheingau is an *ortsteil* of the town of Eltville. Certain famous estates (*e.g.* Schloss Vollrads) are allowed to omit the names of their villages from their labels.

Perlwein Slightly fizzy *tafelwein*, often artificially carbonated under pressure. A small measure of acidic carbon dioxide freshens up dull wines.

Prädikat *See* QmP.

Qualitätswein bestimmter Anbaugebiete (QbA) "quality wine of a designated region". The category of wine above *tafelwein* and *landwein* but below QmP. QbA wine has usually had its alcohol enhanced with added sugar. It must be from one of the thirteen *anbaugebiete* (unblended), from approved grapes, reach a certain level of ripeness before sugaring, and pass an analytical and tasting test to gain an AP number. In certain underripe vintages, a high proportion of German wine comes into this category, and can be very satisfactory, although never reaching the distinction of QmP wine.

Qualitätswein mit Prädikat (QmP) "Quality wine with special attributes" is the awkward official description of all the finest German wines, beginning with the Kabinett category and rising in sweetness, body and value to TBA. QmP wines must originate in a single *bereich* (*q.v.*) and are certified at each stage of their career from the vineyard on.

Rebe Grape (*rebsorte*: grape variety).

Restsüsse "Residual sugar": the sugar remaining unfermented in a wine at bottling, whether fermentation has stopped naturally or been stopped artificially. Some *trocken* German wines have less than one gram per litre.

In a TBA it may reach astonishing figures of more than 200 grams a litre, with very little of the sugar converted to alcohol.

Rosewein Pale pink wine from red grapes.

Rotling Pale red wine from mixed red and white grapes.

Rotwein Red wine.

Säure Acidity (measured in units per 1,000 of tartaric acid). The essential balancing agent to the sweetness in German (or any) wine. As a rule of thumb, a well-balanced wine has approximately one unit per 1,000 (ml) of acid for each ten degrees Oechsle (*q.v.*). Thus an eighty degree Oechsle wine needs an acidity of approximately 0.8.

Schaumwein Sparkling wine – a general term for low-priced fizz. Quality sparkling wines are called Sekt.

Schillerwein A pale red (Rotling) of QbA or QmP status, produced only in Württemberg.

Schloss Castle.

Schoppenweine Another term for *offene weine* – wine served "open" in a large glass.

Sekt Germany's quality sparkling wine, subject to similar controls as QbA wines.

Spätlese Literally "late-gathered". The QmP category above Kabinett and below Auslese, with wines of a higher alcoholic degree and greater body and "vinosity" than Kabinetts. Also often considerably sweeter but not necessarily so. A grower must notify the authorities of his intention to pick a Spätlese crop, and tasting panels establish a consensus of what constitutes proper Spätlese style in each vintage and region.

Spitzen "Top", a favourite German term, whether applied to a vineyard, a grower, or a vintage.

Stück The standard traditional oak cask of the Rhein, holding 1,200 litres or about 133 cases. There are also *doppelstücke* (double), *halbstücke* (half), and *viertel* (quarter) *stücke*.

Süssreserve Unfermented grape juice with all its natural sweetness, held in reserve for "back-blending" with dry, fully fermented wines to arrive at the winemaker's ideal of a balanced wine. This sweetening (which also lowers the alcoholic content) is often overdone, but a judicious hint of extra sweetness can enhance fruity flavours, and make an average wine more attractive.

Tafelwein "Table wine", the humblest category of German wine. (Without the prefix *Deutsche* it might not be German, however Gothic the label.) The origin, alcohol content, and grape varieties are all controlled, but *tafelwein* is never more than a light wine for quenching thirst.

Trocken "Dry" – the official category for wines with less than nine grams of unfermented sugar per litre. *Trocken* wines have become fashionable for drinking with food. Once frequently hollow and sour, they have improved greatly in recent years.

Trockenbeerenauslese "Selected dried grapes" (frequently shortened to TBA). Ironically, the precise opposite of the last entry. The "dry" here referring to the state of the overripe grapes when picked in a shrivelled state from "noble rot" and desiccation on the vine. Such is the concentration of sugar, acid, and flavours that Oechsle readings of TBA must (never in more than minute quantities) can reach more than 300 degrees. TBA wines are reluctant to ferment and rarely exceed seven degrees alcohol, the remaining intense sweetness acting as a natural preservative and slowing down maturation for many years.

Verband Deutscher Prädikats-und Qualitätsweingüter (VDP) An association of premium growers.

Weingut Wine estate. The term may only be used by growers who grow all their own grapes.

Weinprobe Wine tasting.

Weinstein The deposit of potassium tartrate crystals forming a glittering rock-like lining to old barrels.

Weissherbst A rosé wine of QbA or QmP status made from red grapes of a single variety, the specialty of Baden, Württemberg, and the Pfalz, but also the fate of some sweet reds of other regions which fail to achieve a full red colour. ("Noble rot" attacks the pigments and often makes red Auslesen excessively pale.)

Winzer Wine-grower.

Winzergenossenschaft, **Winzerverein** Cooperative.

Mosel-Saar-Ruwer

The Mosel twists and turns its way more than 193 kilometres (120 miles) from the German-French-Luxembourg border to its confluence with the Rhine at Koblenz. It cuts deep into the hill country of the Eifel and Hunsrück; a huge mass of slate, 400 million years of age, that weathers to give the stony grey soil. On the steep sides of its narrow valley, and those of its tributaries, the Saar and Ruwer, grow the brightest, briskest, most aromatic, and hauntingly subtle of all German Rieslings. This is essentially Riesling country, and no soil or situation brings out the thrilling and fascinating personality of the finest of all white grapes to better effect.

The complex topography and the cool, northerly climate result in huge microclimatic variations between vineyards that lie only a stone's throw from one another. The steep, south-facing slopes in sheltered positions give noble Rieslings that are expressive and elegant, while the flat vineyards on heavy soil produce mean, watery wines from high-yielding grape varieties such as Müller-Thurgau and Kerner. Unfortunately, the German wine law does nothing to differentiate between these two worlds; indeed, it confuses the two. Cheap generic wines are sold under plausible sounding *grosslage* names such as Piesporter Michelsberg and Ürziger Schwarzlay, although little or none of the wine in the bottle originates from the towns named. These wines are a world away from Rieslings which grew in the great Piesporter Goldtröpfchen and Ürziger Würzgarten sites.

The Mosel encounters its first few tentative vineyards in France, flows through Luxembourg, then enters Germany near Trier, once the effective capital of the Roman Empire. On either side of the city, it is joined by the rivers Saar and Ruwer. It is their side valleys, rather than the main stream, that have the first great Mosel vineyards. Upper Mosel (*Obermosel*) wines are at best light and refreshing. The ancient Elbling grape dominates here, giving appley, pleasantly tart, dry wines. Riesling also has difficulty ripening on the Saar and Ruwer. But when it does, on the best slopes, the results are unsurpassed anywhere on earth: quintessential Riesling, clean as steel, with the evocative qualities of remembered scents or distant music.

The Mosel Valley below Trier divides into two sub-regions, the Middle Mosel with its succession of famous vineyards strung along the river's course like pearls on a necklace. The wines are slightly fuller and more effusively aromatic than those of the Saar and Ruwer, but are equally long-living. The border between the Middle Mosel and the Terrassen Mosel ("Terraced Mosel" or *Untermosel*) has long been disputed, but Zell is the logical dividing line. Below this point, the vines tend to be planted on narrow terraces, rather than directly climbing the precipitous slopes as elsewhere in the region. Here grow the fullest, most supple Mosel Rieslings.

Outstanding Saar Vineyards

Ayler Kupp Some of the most charming and immediately appealing Saar wines. Most important owners: Bischöfliche Weingüter, Peter Lauer, Johann Peter Reinert.

Filzener Pulchen Sleek, steely wines with delicate apple and berry aromas. Most important owner: Piedmont.

Kanzemer Altenberg Very classic Saar Rieslings, subtlety and refinement married to racy acidity. Most important owners: von Kesselstatt, von Othegraven.

Obermmeler Hütte Monopoly site of the von Hövel estate. Elegant, long-living wines with pronounced floral aromas.

Ockfener Bockstein Sadly, substantially enlarged recently. Rieslings combining the forthright Mosel aromas with the steel of the Saar. Most important owners: Dr. Fischer, von Kesselstatt, Sankt Urbanshof, Dr. Wagner, Zilliken.

Saarburger Rausch Slow-developing, long-living wines with a pronounced citrus and mineral character. Most important owners: Dr. Wagner, Zilliken.

Scharzhofberg The greatest and most famous vineyard on the Saar, giving wines of the highest elegance and nobility in superior vintages. Their ageing potential is legendary, even Kabinett wines keeping for twenty-five years and more. This status was not ignored by the 1971 law, which made the twenty-eight-hectare vineyard an *ortsteil* of

Wiltingen; hence the village name does not appear on the label. Most important owners: Bischöfliche Weingüter (Hohe Domkirche), von Hövel, von Kesselstatt, Egon Müller-Scharzhof, van Volxem, Vereinigte Hospitien.

Serriger Schloss Saarstein Monopoly site of the Schloss Saarstein estate. Piercing acidity and a blackcurrant aroma make these very distinctive Saar wines.

Wiltinger Gottesfuß A small site yielding intense, succulent wines with a pineapple note that occures in good vintages. Most important owners: van Volxem, von Kesselstatt, Reverchon.

Wiltinger Braune Kupp Monopoly Riesling site of the Le Gallais estate, yielding substantial wines which often show a herbal character. Only QmP wines are sold as Braune Kupp; the *grosslage* name Scharzberg is for QbA wine, some of which is from Egon Müller's own estate. Kabinetts are light; higher qualities aromatic and spicy.

Outstanding Ruwer Vineyards

Eitelsbacher Karthäuserhofberg The monopoly site of the Tyrell family's formerly monastic Karthäuserhof

estate. Almost explosively aromatic wines that have a positively piquant interplay of fruit and acidity are produced here.

Kaseler Kehrnagel Sleeker than the Nies'chen wines, but otherwise with similar character. Most important owners: Bischöfliche Weingüter, Karlsmühle.

Kaseler Nies'chen Complex wines with a pronounced blackcurrant aroma and more body than most Ruwer Rieslings. Most important owners: Bischöfliche Weingüter, Karlsmühle, von Kesselstatt, von Beulwitz.

Maximin Grünhäuser Abtsberg This site forms the heart of the famous Grünhaus estate's vineyards. Like the Herrenberg, it is a monopoly of the von Schubert family. The wines are exceptionally elegant and refined, possessing decades of ageing potential.

Maximin Grünhäuser Herrenberg The red-slate soil of this famous site produces slightly leaner and more aromatic wines than those of its great neighbour, the Abtsberg. The names of the Grünhäuser sites recall the estate's monastic past; Herrenberg wines were made for the monks while those of Abtsberg, as the name suggests, were reserved for the abbot.

Egon Müller – A Great Saar Estate

German winemaking at its highest level can best be described as wine for wine's sake. In a fine vintage the producer is almost passive, like a painter before a sunset. Rather than try to mould the vintage to his preconceived ideal, he is dedicated to interpreting what nature provides. If one estate embodies this approach to wine it is that of Egon Müller-Scharzhof. Egon Müller IV's family has owned the Scharzhof manor at Wiltingen on the Saar, and eight hectares of the steep Scharzhofberg above it, since 1797. Their late-picked wines have frequently achieved world record prices at the annual auction of "The Grosser Ring", or Great Ring, of leading Mosel-Saar-Ruwer growers at Trier. Egon Müller's great-great-great-grandfather bought the estate, formerly church land like so much of Germany's best, after it was secularized under Napoleon. It is very much the old family house,

its hall lined with trophies of the chase, and its library with leather-bound books. A tasting of the new vintage with Egon Müller takes place in the half-light of the hall, standing at a round table of black marble with a ring of green bottles, and elegant tasting glasses. The Riesling that he grows on the grey slate of the Scharzhofberg is Riesling in its naked purity. Only Kabinett and better wines are sold under the estate and vineyard names, and each is fermented apart in its own cask. The samples at the tasting are of different casks. As the end of the harvest approaches, the differences between casks increase. The Kabinetts are often bottled as one wine, but Spätleses are usually kept in separate lots, and there may be five or six different Auslesen as each day's ripening intensifies the honeyed sweetness of the latest wines. It is very rare in the cool Saar to harvest grapes ripe enough for a BA; TBA are rarer still. But a "Gold Cap" Auslese (a gold capsule replaces the words Feinste Auslese) from Egon Müller has as much penetrating perfume, vitality, and "breeding" as any wine in Germany. Its measured sweetness is matched with such racy acidity that the young wine may almost make you wince. Yet time harmonizes the extremes into a perfectly pitched unity, a teasing, tingling lusciousness that only Riesling, only the Saar, only the Scharzhofberg can achieve. And when the Scharzhof does release a TBA, its quality and scarcity are such that only the richest collectors can afford it. A case of the 1994 TBA fetched the equivalent of $42,000 when auctioned in 2001.

Egon Müller jointly owns (with Gerard Villanova) a second Saar estate, the four-hectare Le Gallais, which makes up the entire Wiltinger Braune Kupp site. Its wines, vinified in the Scharzhof cellars, are richer but less fine than the Scharzhofbergers.

Outstanding Middle Mosel Vineyards

Bernkasteler Badstube (Alte Badstube am Doctorberg, Bratenhöfchen, Graben, Lay, Matheisbildchen) Small *grosslage* composed only of superior sites. Generally, sleek, racy wines that are the epitome of Mosel Riesling. In top vintages the Lay and Graben can give magnificent wines. Most important owners: Dr. Pauly-Bergweiler, Dr. Loosen, Dr. Thanisch, Heribert Kerpen, Joh. Jos. Prüm, S. A. Prüm, Selbach-Oster, Studert-Prüm, J. Wegeler (Deinhard), Dr. Weins-Prüm.

Bernkasteler Doctor Tiny, legendary 3.26-hectare site, which towers above the roofs of old Bernkastel. Intense, sleek wines which are capable of great finesse. Many experts claim to detect a smoky aroma. Most important owners: Dr. Thanisch, J. Wegeler (Deinhard).

Brauneberger Juffer Large site surrounding the great Juffer-Sonnenuhr, giving slightly less refined wines with similar body and minerally character. Most important owners: Fritz Haag, Willi Haag, Max Ferd. Richter.

Brauneberger Juffer-Sonnenuhr For centuries, the combination of minerally power and racy elegance made the wines from Brauneberg's top site the most sought-after Mosel Rieslings. Their reputation is once again on the rise. Most important owners: Fritz Haag, Willi Haag, Paulinshof, Max Ferd. Richter, Dr. Thanisch.

Drohner Hofberg Little-known site, the best part of which yields extremely juicy, appealing wines that show well from an early age. Most important owner: Bischöfliche Weingüter.

Erdener Prälat Nestling between massive red slate cliffs and the bank of the river, the tiny Prälat site enjoys the warmest microclimate in the entire Mosel-Saar-Ruwer. The result is rich wines with lavish almond, apricot, and exotic-fruit aromas, and great ageing potential. Most important owners: Bischöfliche Weingüter, Dr. Loosen, Mönchhof, Vereinigte Hospitien, Dr. Weins-Prüm.

Erdener Treppchen The Treppchen wines bear a family resemblance to those of the Prälat, but are more restrained and racy, many would say more classical. The eastern part of this site is the best. Most important owners: Bischöfliche Weingüter, Joh. Jos. Christoffel, Dr. Loosen, Merkelbach, Meulenhof, Mönchhof, Peter Nicolay.

Graacher Domprobst The deep slate soil of Graach's finest vineyard gives firm, intensely minerally Riesling, with a pronounced blackcurrant aroma. In hot years they are extremely long-living. Most important owners: Friedrich-Wilhelm-Gymnasium, Kees-Kieren, Heribert Kerpen, Max Ferd. Richter, Willi Schaefer, Selbach-Oster, Dr. Weins-Prüm.

Graacher Himmelreich Large site encompassing vineyards of variable quality. More charming and supple wines than those from the neighbouring Domprobst. Most important owners: Dr. Pauly-Bergweiler, Friedrich-Wilhelm Gymnasium, Kees-Kieren, Dr. Loosen, Markus Molitor, Joh. Jos. Prüm, S. A. Prüm, Willi Schaefer, Studert-Prüm, Dr. Weins-Prüm.

Josephshöfer 4.7-hectare monopoly site of the Kesselstatt estate yielding substantial Rieslings with a pronounced earthy note and excellent ageing potential.

Leiwener Laurentiuslay With the quality renaissance in Leiwen, this site's abilities to give Mosel Rieslings that are at once rich and refined has become more widely appreciated. Many old vines. Most important owners: Grans-Fassian, Carl Loewen, Rosch, Sankt Urbans-Hof.

Lieserer Niederberg-Helden This once famous site gives wines with a strong family resemblance to those from the nearby Brauneberg. Most important owner: Schloss Lieser.

Piesporter Domherr This small site within the famous Goldtröpfchen produces more delicate, but equally great Rieslings, which show their class both as young and mature wines. Most important owners: von Kesselstatt, Reinhold Haart, Kurt Hain.

Piesporter Goldtröpfchen The extremely deep slate soils of this site yield the most baroque of all Mosel Rieslings. When young, their explosive blackcurrant, citrus-fruit, and peach aromas may be too exotic for some, but with ageing they acquire great elegance. In hot years such as '89 and '83 many of the best Mosel wines come from here. Most important owners: von Kesselstatt, Reinhold Haart, Kurt Hain, Lehnert-Veit, Reuscher-Haart, Sankt Urbans-Hof, Weller-Lehnert.

Pündericher Marienburg The steep slopes below the Marienburg castle give the finest and richest Rieslings in this stretch of the Mosel Valley. Most important owner: Clemens Busch.

Thörnicher Ritsch Little-known site with excellent exposure, capable of yielding Rieslings with a Saar-like purity and steely intensity. Most important owner: Carl Loewen.

Trittenheimer Apotheke The best parts of this site are precipitously steep, with stony slate soil, giving wines with considerable elegance and subtlety. Most important owners: Ernst Clüsserath, Clüsserath-Weiler, Friedrich-Wilhelm Gymnasium, Grans-Fassian, Milz, Rosch.

Trittenheimer Leiterchen Tiny one-hectare monopoly site of the Milz estate in the heart of the Apotheke. The very rocky soil often gives wines with a herbal note.

Ürziger Würzgarten Its red sandstone soil results in astonishingly powerful, spicy Mosel Rieslings that need many years of ageing to reach their peak. Only the heart of this site is rated as first-class. Most important owners: Bischöfliche Weingüter, Joh. Jos. Christoffel, Dr. Loosen, Merkelbach, Mönchhof, Peter Nicolay, Dr. Weins-Prüm.

Wehlener Sonnenuhr The stony slate soil of this, the most famous of all Mosel vineyards, results in wines of almost supernatural grace and delicacy. Usually they are extremely charming from an early age, yet long-living. The highest-lying parts of this large site are the best. Most important owners: Dr. Pauly-Bergweiler, Heribert Kerpen, Dr. Loosen, Joh. Jos. Prüm, S. A. Prüm, Max Ferd. Richter, Selbach-Oster, Studert-Prüm, J. Wegeler (Deinhard), Dr. Weins-Prüm.

Zeltinger Sonnenuhr The best corners of this site are a match for the directly neighbouring and more famous Sonnenuhr vineyard of Wehlen. However, slightly richer soils result in more weighty, firmer wines. Most important owners: Markus Molitor, Joh. Jos. Prüm, Selbach-Oster.

Outstanding Terrassen Mosel Vineyards

Bremer Calmont This great amphitheatre of vines is the steepest vineyard in all of Europe. Its narrow terraces yield firmly structured Rieslings with pronounced minerally character. Most important owner: Reinhold Franzen.

Neefer Fraunenberg Much more floral, charming wines than Calmont. Most important owner: Reinhold Franzen.

Winninger Röttgen The aromatic, silky wines from this site, just downstream from the village of Winningen, have been famous for centuries. Most important owners: von Heddesdorf, Heymann-Löwenstein, Knebel.

Winninger Uhlen The great soaring wall of narrow terraced vineyards which forms the Uhlen is one of the most imposing vineyards on the entire Mosel – an impressive sight from the *autobahn* bridge where it crosses the river here. The firmly structured, minerally Rieslings produced from the Winninger Uhlen are arguably the finest of the Terrassen Mosel. Most important owners: von Heddesdorf, Heymann-Löwenstein, Knebel.

Leading Mosel-Saar-Ruwer Producers

Weingut Bastgen ☆☆
Kesten
Since Mona Bastgen and Armin Vogel took over this tiny four-hectare estate, it has begun to prove the true potential of sites such as the Kestener Paulinshofberg and Kueser Weisenstein. These are substantial wines, with plenty of fruit and character.

Weingut von Beulwitz ☆☆–☆☆☆
Mertesdorf
In 1982, Herbert Weis bought a hotel and a 5.5-hectare wine estate in the Ruwer, and continues to manage both. His best wines come from Kaseler Nies'chen, and are intensely fruity, though they can lack some zest.

Bischöfliche Weingüter ☆–☆☆
Trier. www.bwgtrier.de
This, the largest estate under a single management in the Mosel-Saar-Ruwer, was formed by the union in 1966 of three independent charitable properties: the *Priesterseminar* (Bishop's Seminary); the *Domkirche* (Trier Cathedral) estates; and the *Bischöfliches Konvikt* (Bishop's Hostel). In all, the property consists of 107 hectares, with excellent vineyards in Scharzhofberg, Kaseler Nies'chen, and

Trittenheimer Apotheke. The three charities maintain separate press houses; after pressing, all the juice is brought together in the venerable central cellar in Trier for fermentation and cask-ageing. Ninety-eight per cent of the whole estate is Riesling, mostly vinified in a *trocken* or *halbtrocken* style. After a period of unexciting performance during the 1980s, quality has improved steadily during the early 1990s. Older vintages, for which, inexplicably, there is only slight demand, are on sale at reasonable prices in the estate's sales outlet in Trier.

Weingut Joh. Jos. Christoffel ☆☆☆
Erben Ürzig
In 2001, Hans-Leo Christoffel, the owner of this tiny but highly regarded estate, decided to retire, and to lease his vineyards to his neighbour at Mönchhof (*q.v.*). They will continue to be released under the Christoffel label. These have long been the most polished, elegant Rieslings in this dramatic section of the Middle Mosel. Stars on the label (between one and five, the more indicating the better quality) are used to differentiate between the different bottlings of Würzgarten Auslese in fine vintages.

Weingut Clemens Busch ☆–☆☆☆
Pünderich
Clemens Busch is not only the Mosel's leading organic winemaker, but also makes the finest wines from the excellent Marienburg site. Highly individual, dry, lime-scented Rieslings are the specialty, although Busch is happy to make intense nobly sweet wines when climatic conditions oblige. Some of the dry wines can be too alcoholic, but there is no denying their mineral splendour.

Weingut Ernst Clüsserath ☆☆–☆☆☆
Trittenheim
A tiny three-hectare estate whose ever-improving wines have already won serious young owner/winemaker Ernst Clüsserath much acclaim. The yields here are very low, and the wines, whether dry or naturally sweet, are delicate and penetrating.

Weingut Clüsserath-Weiler ☆☆☆
Trittenheim. www.cluesserath-weiler.de
Half of Helmut Clüsserath's vineyards are in the Apotheke, and he is especially proud of a tiny parcel, planted with one-hundred-year-old vines, called Fährfels, which is bottled separately. All the wines are elegant, minerally, and medium-bodied, and a star system differentiates the different Auslese qualities.

Friedrich-Wilhelm Gymnasium ☆–☆☆
Trier. www.fwg-weingut-trier.com
The estate was founded by Jesuits in 1561 as an adjunct to their school, which still exists. The parents donated vineyards, many in excellent sites scattered from Ockfen to Graach. There is a range of non-Riesling wines packaged to appeal to younger drinkers, but it's the classic wines from good sites that are worth seeking out. Overall, standards are quite high, but there are few outstanding wines.

Weingut Fritz Haag ☆☆☆–☆☆☆☆
Brauneberg
This distinguished estate can trace its history back to 1605. It has long been one of the top addresses for perfectly made,

elegant, cask-matured Riesling wines, especially from Juffer-Sonnenuhr. Wilhelm Haag has rebuilt their once supreme reputation, although replantings in the early 1990s meant that the usual balance of the estate was disturbed, as there were too many young vines. At their best, the wines have a bracing minerality and power, without a trace of heaviness.

Weingut Willi Haag ☆☆
Brauneberg
Family problems caused a lapse in quality here, but this estate is back on form under Markus Haag, producing clean, attractive Rieslings from the best sites in Brauneberg.

Weingut Reinhold Haart ☆☆☆–☆☆☆☆
Piesport. www.haart.de
The quietly determined Theo Haart runs Piesport's leading estate, producing wines that combine the extravagant personality of these top-site vineyards with charm and delicacy. He also makes impressive wines from vines in the unclassified Wintricher Ohligsberg, which he purchased in 1990.

Weingut Grans-Fassian ☆☆☆–☆☆☆☆
Leiwen. www.grans-fassian.de
Gerhard Grans owns excellent parcels in Leiwener Laurentiuslay, Piesporter Goldtröpfchen, and Trittenheimer Apotheke, and he has done as much as anyone to show what the vines in Trittenheim and Leiwen are capable of. His Auslesen can be exquisitely elegant, and his Eiswein is always outstanding. The more basic qualities are excellent, too, showing an exemplary purity, both in dry and naturally sweet styles.

Weingut Kurt Hain ☆☆–☆☆☆
Piesport
Gernot Hain took over this well-established, five-hectare estate in 1988, and makes delicious wines, dry and naturally sweet, from the Goldtröpfchen.

Weingut Heymann-Löwenstein ☆☆☆–☆☆☆☆
Winningen. www.heymann-loewenstein.com
Reinhard Löwenstein's reputation as a rebel is well-deserved, not least because of the fanaticism with which he has pursued top quality, in an area where mediocrity is still largely the norm. He also scorns the use of such winemaking aids as cultivated yeasts, enzymes, and bentonite. His unusually full-bodied, dry Rieslings are among the best examples of this style in the region. As well as prized single-vineyard wines, there are appealing blends from slate soils called "Schiefferterrassen" and "Von Blauen Schieffer". He also produces some imposing late-harvest wines. The 1994 Riesling TBA from the Uhlen was the most expensive, and one of the greatest, wines ever made in the Terrassen Mosel.

Weingut von Hövel ☆☆
Konz-Oberemmel
The jovial Eherhard von Kunow makes some of the most immediately appealing Saar Rieslings. Rich and aromatic as young wines, they gain in elegance as they age. The Scharzhofberg wines are slightly more opulent than those from the estate's Hütte monopoly, from which many superb Auslese and higher *Prädikat* wines are made. At Kabinett and Spätlese level, the estates wines offer excellent value.

Weingut Immich-Batterieberg ☆☆–☆☆☆
Enkirch. www.batterieberg.de
Gert Basten bought this property, including a mansion that dates to the ninth century, in 1989. The monopoly Batterieberg was created by dynamiting the slate cliffs in 1844. Yields are low, so the grapes attain high ripeness levels conducive to dry wine production, which can be outstanding here.

Weingut Albert Kallfelz ☆☆
Zell-Merl. www.kallfelz.de
This estate, at the boundary between the Middle Mosel and the Terrassen Mosel, has expanded quite rapidly, and now consists of thirty-eight hectares. His best wines come from Merler Königslay-Terrassen, two-thirds of which are owned by the estate. Almost all the wines are *trocken* or *halbtrocken*.

Karlsmühle ☆☆☆
Mertesdorf. www.weingut-karlsmuehle.de
Peter Geiben has abandoned his former profession of hotelier to devote all his time to his vineyards in Kasel and his monopoly Lorenzhöfer vineyards. He makes Ruwer wines of tremendous personality, whether dry and pungent, or sweet and racy.

Karthäuserhof ☆☆☆
Trier-Eitelsbach
A beautiful old manor of the Carthusian monks in a side valley of the Ruwer, bought in 1811 by the ancestor of the present owner when Napoléon secularized church land. It stands at the foot of the steep Eitelsbacher Karthäuserhofberg vineyard, which is entirely owned by the estate. Since Christoph Tyrell took control of the estate in 1986, quality has improved in leaps and bounds. Today, the estate's dry and naturally sweet Rieslings are among the Mosel-Saar-Ruwer's finest. Intense blackcurrant and peach aromas and racy acidity are their hallmark. The bottle is unmistakable, with only a narrow label on the neck and none on the body.

Heribert Kerpen ☆☆–☆☆☆
Wehlen. www.weingut-kerpen.de
Martin Kerpen is fortunate enough to own three hectares of mostly ungrafted vines in Wehlener Sonnenuhr. He was a pioneer of dry wines in the Mosel, but his elegant floral Spätlese and Auslese wines with natural sweetness are consistently impressive.

Reichsgraf von Kesselstatt ☆☆–☆☆☆
Morscheid. www.kesselstatt.com
This was the greatest private estate of the Mosel-Saar-Ruwer when it was bought in 1978 by Günther Reh. Since 1983, the estate has been directed by his daughter, Annegret. The entire estate covers some of the greatest sites of the region: Scharzhofberg, Piesporter Goldtröpfchen, Kaseler Nies'chen, and the monopoly site Josephshöfer in Graach, and is planted with 100% Riesling. Between sixty and seventy per cent of the wines are *trocken* or *halbtrocken*, including the high-quality estate Riesling called "Palais Kesselstatt". Regardless of style, the wines are packed with fruit and have a vibrant, but never dominant, acidity.

Weingut Reinhard Knebel ☆☆☆
Winningen

A family split led to the creation of this excellent Terrassen Mosel estate in 1990. The Riesling *halbtrocken* wines are very good here, and the Auslesen from Uhlen are exceptional. Knebel also produces some fabulous TBAs from Röttgen, but in minute quantities.

Weingut Sybille Kuntz ☆☆
Lieser. www.sybillekuntz.de

Many of the Kuntz wines are dry, and the best of them is usually the cuvée called "Gold-Quadrat", made from ungrafted vines. When conditions permit, Kuntz also likes to produce ultra-sweet botrytis wines.

Weingut Schloss Lieser ☆☆☆
Lieser. www.weingut-schloss-lieser.de

Thomas Haag, son of Wilhelm Haag of Brauneberg, moved to the next village in 1992 to run the former Freiherr von Schorlemer estate. In 1997, he was able to buy the property, from which he produces concentrated, longlived wines. Not wines of tremendous power, but they have charm, raciness, and exceptional length of flavour.

Weingut Carl Loewen ☆–☆☆☆
Leiwen. www.weingut-loewen.de

Karl-Josef Loewen is something of a visionary by rescuing forgotten vineyard sites such as Thörnicher Ritsch. The *trocken* and *halbtrocken* wines are good, but by far the best wines are the Auslesen from Leiwener Laurentiuslay.

Weingut Dr. Loosen ☆☆☆☆
Bernkastel. www.drloosen.de

From old, ungrafted vines in great vineyards from Bernkastel to Erden, the dynamic Ernst Loosen produces some of the finest Rieslings made in the Mosel – and Germany – today. Their hallmarks are concentration, complex mineral, herb and spice flavours, and a distinctly drier balance than the norm for the region. The character of each site is extremely distinct. The crowning glory of the peaks in the estate's wide range are the majesterial Auslese wines from the Erdener Prälat. *See also* J. J. Wolf in the Pfalz.

Weingut Milz ☆–☆☆
Trittenheim

Founded in the seventeenth century, this estate is blessed not only with good parcels in the Apotheke, but with two monopoly sites in Trittenheim: Felsenkopf and Leiterchen. Quality varies from sound to excellent.

Weingut Molitor ☆☆☆
Wehlen. www.wein-markus-molitor.de

With thirty-five hectares, this is the largest estate on the Middle Mosel. Not all the sites are outstanding, but Markus Molitor has excellent parcels in Zeltinger Sonnenuhr. About half the production is of dry wines, but for many wine-lovers, it's the exquisite Auslesen from Wehlener Klosterberg that are the most appealing. Look out, too, for sensational, and very expensive, nobly sweet wines.

Mönchhof ☆☆–☆☆☆
Urzig

The old manor house of Mönchhof is a landmark at Urzig, and in its sixteenth century cellars repose classic Rieslings from Urzig and Erden. Very little dry wine is made. Sensible prices and high quality from the mid-1990s make this an excellent source for these wines. In 2001, the owner, Robert Eymael, leased the neighbouring Joh. Jos. Christoffel estate (*q.v.*).

Paulinshof ☆☆–☆☆☆
Kesten. www.paulinshof.de

This former monastic property has been owned by the Jüngling family since 1969. Klaus Jüngling has specialized in dry wines, picking as late as possible so as to have lower acidity levels. These dry and off-dry wines, especially from Brauneberger Juffer-Sonnenuhr and their monopoly site Brauneberger Kammer, are first-rate.

Weingut Dr. Pauly-Bergweiler & Weingut Peter Nicolay ☆☆–☆☆☆
Bernkastel-Kues. www.pauly-bergweiler.com

The marriage between Dr. Peter Pauly and Helga Pauly-Berres united some of the best vineyards in the Middle Mosel, including Bernkasteler Alte Badstube am Doctorberg, Graacher Domprobst and Graacher Himmelreich, Wehlener Sonnenuhr, Erdener Prälat, and Urziger Goldwingert (monopoly). Although many of the estate's wines are unashamedly *trocken* in style, Dr. Pauly also produces some fabulous sweet wines, such as sumptuous TBAs from Urziger Würzgarten and Eiswein from Bernkasteler Lay. The stars of the Nicolay range are usually the rich wines from the Urziger Goldwingert monopoly.

Weingut Piedmont ☆
Konz-Filzen

For many years, Claus Piedmont has made light, racy Saar Rieslings from the Filzener Pulchen, placing the main emphasis on dry wines.

Weingut J. J. Prüm ☆☆☆☆
Wehlen

The most famous estate of many belonging to the most famous family of growers of the Middle Mosel. The estate house, down by the river, looks across the water up to the great Sonnenuhr vineyard, of which it has one of the largest holdings. The huge sundials among the vines here and in Zeltingen were built by an earlier Prüm. The estate's signature is wine of glorious fruity ripeness, setting off the exquisite raciness of Riesling grown on slate, with deep notes of spice and honey. As very young wines, they often retain a yeasty aroma from fermentation, but this quickly dispenses. Their ageing potential is legendary: Spätlese and Auslese often needing ten years and more to reach their peak. Even the entry-level Prüm Riesling is a fine wine to age several years.

Weingut S. A. Prüm ☆☆
Wehlen. www.sapruem.com

Part of the great Prüm estate, which was originally divided among seven children in 1911. Since 1971, Raimund Prüm has made vigorous wines, especially from Wehlener Sonnenuhr. The Prüms as a whole are very conservative winemakers, but Raimund Prüm has had no qualms about using brightly designed labels to match the freshness of his wines. About seventy per cent of his wines are *trocken* or *halbtrocken*.

Weingut Johann Peter Reinert ☆
Kanzem

Johann Peter Reinert makes fruity wines of considerable charm from this four-hectare estate. The finest of these come from the Kanzemer Altenberg.

Weingut Max Ferd. Richter ☆☆–☆☆☆
Mülheim. www.maxferdrichter.com

This substantial estate, with holdings scattered through the Middle Mosel, is an extremely consistent producer of classic Mosel Rieslings, both in the dry and naturally sweet styles. Dirk Richter's finest wines are the powerful, minerally Rieslings from the top sites of Brauneberg, while Eiswein is made almost every year from his monopoly site, the Mülheimer Helenenkloster. Dr. Richter also runs a merchant business; the vinification is equally traditional and scrupulous, the only difference being that the grapes are purchased, mostly from growers with whom he has long-term contracts.

Weingut Josef Rosch ☆☆–☆☆☆
Leiwen

Werner Rosch is one of a number of growers behind the renaissance of the vineyards of Leiwein and Trittenheim. Although most of his wines are dry and somewhat austere, he also produces fine, naturally sweet wine, especially Auslesen of great elegance.

Weingut Sankt Urbans-Hof ☆☆☆
Leiwen. www.weingut-st-urbans-hof.de

Hermann Weis is a nurseryman who, with his son Nik, directs the third-largest privately owned wine estate in the Mosel-Saar-Ruwer. The dry Rieslings from Leiwener Laurentiuslay are very good, but outclassed by the mouth-watering naturally sweet wines from Piesporter Goldtröpfchen and Ockfener Bockstein.

Weingut Schloss Saarstein ☆☆
Serrig

The charming and dedicated Christian and Andrea Ebert run one of the most consistent wine estates on the Saar. Most of the wines come from their monopoly of Serriger Schloss Saarstein. Absolute purity of flavour and steely intensity are the qualities that typify both the dry wines and those with natural sweetness. The BA, TBA, and Eiswein are among the greatest in the entire Mosel-Saar-Ruwer, with enormous ageing potential.

Weingut Willi Schaefer ☆☆☆–☆☆☆☆
Graach

This miniature estate in the Middle Mosel, with a mere 2.7 hectares of vineyards, regularly produces the finest of Rieslings from the most excellent vineyards of Graach. This combination of extremely limited production and high demand means that the Auslese and higher *Prädikat* wines sell out almost instantaneously. It would be difficult to find Mosels with better ageing potential than these beautifully crafted, sleek, racy wines.

C. von Schubert, Maximin Grünhaus ☆☆☆☆
Grünhaus/Trier. www.vonschubert.ccm

This outstanding estate of the Ruwer is also one of Germany's finest. Acquired by the ancestors of Dr. Carl von Schubert in 1882, the vineyards consist of a unique undivided hill dominating the beautiful, formerly Benedictine-owned manor house, with its cellars dating back to Roman times.

The estate's three vineyards, Herrenberg, Abtsberg, and the less well-exposed Bruderberg, produce distinctly different wines. Since the early twentieth century, the estate's miraculously delicate wines have been sold under an extravagant *art nouveau* label. In spite of their lightness of body, even the "simplest" Grünhaus Rieslings age magnificently – the epitome of great German Riesling. The naturally sweet Auslesen of good vintages are sublime: infinitely subtle but surprisingly spicy and powerful, ageing twenty years or more. The estate is also one of the most reliable producers of dry Rieslings in the Mosel-Saar-Ruwer.

Weingut Selbach-Oster ☆☆☆
Zeltingen

Father Hans, and now his son, Johannes Selbach, make beautifully crafted Mosel Rieslings from eleven hectares. Below Auslese level the wines have a distinctly dry finish. The finest wines almost invariably come from their many parcels in Zeltinger Sonnenuhr, which gives wines that combine richness with great subtlety, and possess excellent ageing potential. The family also runs a high-quality merchant house under the name J. & H. Selbach.

Weingut Studert-Prüm ☆☆
Wehlen. www.weingut-studert-pruem.de

The Studert family, which has been growing vines since the sixteenth century, acquired the Wehlen vineyard holdings of the Benedictine St Maximin Abbey in Trier in 1805. Since the early 1990s, quality has taken a significant jump up here. The dry wines can be tart, but the naturally sweet Wehlener Sonnenuhr bottlings are delicious and make up the bulk of production.

Weingut Wwe Dr. H. Thanisch – Erben Müller-Burggraef ☆☆
Bernkastel

The Thanisch estate, which produced the legendary 1921 TBA from Bernkasteler Doctor, was divided between two branches of the family in the late 1980s. This is the larger of the two. Despite excellent vineyard holdings in Brauneberg and Wehlen as well as Bernkastel, quality was unexciting until the late 1990s, when it began to produce some excellent sweet wines. They have flamboyance rather than finesse.

Weingut Wwe Dr. H. Thanisch – Erben Thanisch ☆☆–☆☆☆
Bernkastel

This is the smaller of the Thanisch properties, and can be distinguished from the other by the VDP logo. Almost all the wines are naturally sweet, with some superb ranges from the Doctor vineyard. Their renown means they are very expensive, but the wines from other sites, such as Bernkasteler Badstube, are both very good and far less costly.

Vereinigte Hospitien ☆
Trier

This is one of the great charitable institutions of Trier, occupying Germany's oldest cellars, built as a Roman warehouse. The charity still runs a free hospital, largely financed by vineyards and other considerable estates. Although the Hospitien own excellent sites in Scharzhofberg and Goldtröpfchen and throughout the Saar, the wines are disappointing.

Van Volxem ☆☆☆
Wiltingen. www.vanvolxem.de

In 1993, the Van Volxem estate was bought by the Jordan family, who changed its name. But it was beset by problems, and in 2000 it was bought by Roman Niewodniczanski, heir to a brewery fortune. His mission has been to revive the tradition of great dry Rieslings from the Saar. These wines, from top sites such as Scharzhofberg and Wiltinger Gottesfüß, are not bone-dry, but taste dry thanks to their naturally high acidity. He also makes some resplendent sweet wines. The owner's personal wealth allows him to impose extremely low yields, which account for the wines' power and concentration.

Weingut Dr. Heinz Wagner ☆☆–☆☆☆
Saarburg

In the cavernous cellars below his imposing nineteenth century mansion close to Saarburg's railway station, Heinz Wagner produces unusually substantial Saar wines. The wines from the Bockstein are both subtle and seductive, while those from the Rausch are deep and long-living. One of the few reliable sources for dry wines, in a region where they are seldom harmonious.

Wegeler-Deinhard ☆
Bernkastel. www.wegeler.com

The Mosel estate of the once-famous Koblenz wine merchants started in 1900, with the sensational purchase of part of the Doctor vineyard. Today it owns seventeen hectares, mostly in outstanding sites. In 2001, Oliver Haag, brother of Thomas Haag of Schloss Lieser (*q.v.*), took over running the estate, so quality, already sound, is likely to improve further.

Weingut Dr. F. Weins-Prüm ☆☆☆
Wehlen

The shy Bert Selbach makes light but vivid Mosel Rieslings from a whole range of excellent vineyards. Almost all the wines are naturally sweet, and have a classic balance of fruit and acidity. Those from the Erdener Prälat and Wehlener Sonnenuhr usually have most character. They greatly repay ageing for five years or more.

Weingut Forstmeister Geltz Zilliken ☆☆☆
Saarburg

The family estate of the much-respected Ferdinand Geltz (1851–1925), Master Forester of the King of Prussia, is now run by his great-grandson, Hans-Joachim Zilliken. The wines are made very traditionally, in casks, and are designed for long age in bottle. The intensely minerally, racy wines from the Rausch are among the finest in the entire Saar. The Eiswein can be especially brilliant.

Ahr & Mittelrhein
Ahr

Perverse as it may seem, one of Germany's northernmost wine regions specializes in red wine. The Ahr Valley is an appealing landscape of steeply terraced vineyards, wooded hills and rocky terrain. The Ahr is a western tributary of the Mittelrhein and is not far south of Bonn. The valley's steep sides are clothed almost continuously in vines for sixteen kilometres (ten miles): 500 hectares, of which over two-thirds are Spätburgunder (Pinot Noir), Portugieser, and other red grapes. The remainder is planted with white grapes – Riesling and Müller-Thurgau are the most important. In its most sheltered corners, temperatures soar when the sun shines, and in a good summer Spätburgunder grapes ripen fully. The pale, thin, sweet-sour wines of the past came primarily from misconceived winemaking. Since the late 1980s, a handful of pioneers, working with proper maceration techniques and skilful barrel ageing, have proved that "real" red wines can also be made. Perfume and grace, rather than power and richness, are their strengths. The region's whites are usually dry, but are seldom capable of competing with those of the Mittelrhein or the Mosel-Saar-Ruwer.

Leading Ahr producers

Weingut J. J. Adeneuer ☆☆
Ahrweiler

The Adeneuers are relative newcomers to high-quality red wine production, but have learned fast. Most of the wines are aged in large casks, but the top *cuvées* are aged in up to one-third new barriques. Their top site is Walporzheimer Gärkammer; it is bottled separately. Their other outstanding bottling is their Spätburgunder "No. 1". These are wines to be enjoyed fairly young, at between three and five years.

Weingut Deutzerhof ☆☆☆
Mayschoss. www.weingut-deutzerhof.de

At no other Ahr estate has the quality improved so dramatically during the last decade as here. Half the production is deep-coloured Spätburgunder red wine, with a judicious touch of new oak. The top wines come from Altenahrer Eck, but there are also exceptional blends such as "Caspar C" and "Grand Duc". Some white wines, the late-harvest Rieslings especially, are also remarkable, but the reds are the wines to follow.

Staatliche Weinbaudomäne Kloster Marienthal ☆
Marienthal Ahr

The Ahr State Domaine's deliberately old-fashioned winemaking, with ageing mostly in older German barrels, produces typical examples of Ahr red wines. Yields are kept low, resulting in wines that display good character and depth. The ex-Augustinian convent that houses the estate is worth a visit for the architecture alone.

Weingut Meyer-Näkel ☆☆☆
Dernau. www.meyer-naekel.de

Ex-high-school teacher and self-taught winemaker, Werner Näkel was the dynamo of the red winemaking revolution of the 1980s. He makes the most elegant and sophisticated Spätburgunder red wines in the region, classifying these under an unusual personal system: "G" for light, early-maturing wines; "Blauschiefer" for the sophisticated wines from slate soils; and "S" for the most powerful, firmly-structured, slow-developing wines. He also makes excellent wines from the rare Frühburgunder variety. His subtle use of new oak is cautious and precisely judged. Werner Näkel's wines should lay to rest any remaining scepticism about the need to take the Ahr seriously.

Jean Stodden ☆☆–☆☆☆
Rech. www.stodden.de
Most of Gerhard Stodden's six-hectare estate is planted on steep terraces. The best wines, marked "JS" or, in top vintages, "JS☆☆☆", are aged in barriques, and tend to be very tannic. They are very expensive but enjoy a keen following in Germany.

Outstanding Mittelrhein Vineyards

Mention the Rhein and images immediately come to mind of the river coursing through the narrow gorge between Bingen and Koblenz, with its castles and vines clinging precariously to precipitous slopes. This, and the scattered vineyards between Koblenz and Bonn, make up the little-known Mittelrhein region. In wine terms, "Lower Rhein" might be a more appropriate name, since these are the last vineyards along the river's course.

Since 1950, the vineyard area has shrunk from 1,200 hectares to a mere 550. This is most regrettable because the most favoured vineyards here give Rieslings which are quite a match for those of the western Rheingau, and it has often been the best and steepest vineyards that have been abandoned. Fully seventy-two per cent of the region's vineyards are planted with the noble Riesling grape. The elegant, medium-bodied dry and naturally sweet Rieslings, made by the region's leading producers in recent years, have resulted in a renaissance of interest in Mittelrhein wines. So far, this has concentrated itself around Bacharach in the south, but competition is also beginning to hot up further north, around Boppard.

Bacharacher Hahn Arguably the best site in the southern Mittelrhein. Its stony, slate soil gives full-bodied Rieslings with rich, peachy fruit. The Hahn is virtually a monopoly site of the Toni Jost estate.

Bacharacher Posten Like Hahn, the Posten enjoys the warmth of the Rhein and can show richness and refinement. Most important owners: Fritz Bastian, Mades, Ratzenberger.

Bacharacher Wolfshöhle Archetypal Bacharach Rieslings: sleek, racy wines with a strong minerally character from the slate soil. Most important owners: Fritz Bastian, Toni Jost, Kauer, Mades, Ratzenberger.

Bopparder Hamm This giant amphitheatre of vines divides into five sites. Of them, the Feuerlay, Mandelstein, and Ohlenberg can all give magnificent Rieslings, but only a few local growers regularly realize this potential. Most important owners: Müller, August Perll, Walter Perll, Weingart.

Steeger St Jost This site yields steely Rieslings with the most intense bouquet of all Mittelrhein wines. Most important owners: Mades, Ratzenberger.

Leading Mittelrhein Producers

Bastian ☆☆–☆☆☆
Bacharach
A small estate specializing in firm steely Rieslings from top sites in the village. Very impressive *grosses gewächs* wines in 2001.

Weingut Toni Jost ☆☆
Bacharach
Peter Jost's richly fruity, dry and naturally sweet, Rieslings are real charmers. Their exuberance seems to match his own. Best are the concentrated late-harvest wines from the superb Hahn site. They can offer the finest Rheingau wines tough competition.

Weingut Dr. Randolf Kauer ☆
Bacharach
Dr. Kauer is a professor at the Geisenheim wine college. His organic three-hectare estate makes racy, Mosel-like Rieslings which need time to show their best. Few Kauer vines are in celebrated sites, yet the standard is very high, except in cool years when the grapes don't always ripen fully.

Weingut Lanius-Knab ☆☆–☆☆☆
Oberwesel
Until the quality renaissance at this estate during the early 1990s, Oberwesel's wines were completely overshadowed

---

Sekt

Germany has found a way of turning her awkward excess of under ripe wine, the inevitable result of her northerly situation, into pleasure and profit. They are turned into the national sparkling wine: Sekt. Sekt may be either fermented in bottle or in tank, may be made from any grapes from any region, and may even include imported wines.

All the better Sekts, however, fall within the German wine law as either *Deutscher* Sekt, (and thus the product of 100 per cent German-grown grapes), or *Deutscher* Sekt bA, entirely from German grapes from one of the eleven designated wine-growing regions.

Many of the best specify that they are entirely Riesling wines, and some specify their exact origins. There is, in fact, a huge range of qualities, from the banal to the extremely fine. The best examples have nothing in common with Champagne except bubbles: their flavour is essentially flowery and fruity, with the inimitable Riesling aroma in place of Champagne's greater depth of fruit and yeastiness. Leading specialists: Heymann-Löwenstein, Kesselstatt, Selbach-Oster, Dr. Wagner (Mosel); Ratzenberger (Mittelrhein); Diel (Nahe); Hans Barth, Georg Breuer, Johannishof, Schloss Reinhartshausen (Rheingau); Bergdolt, Koehler-Ruprecht, Rebholz, Wilhelmshof (Pfalz); Schloss Sommerhausen (Franken); Bernhard Huber, Schloss Neuweier (Baden).

by those of neighbouring Bacharach. Jörg Lanius's wines (dry and naturally sweet) are racy Mittelrhein Rieslings of crystalline purity.

Weingut Helmut Mades ☆
Bacharach

This tiny 3.5-hectare estate is among the most reliable producers in the Mittelrhein. Year in, year out, Helmut Mades' Rieslings from the top vineyards of Bacharach are full of fruit and well-balanced.

Weingut Matthias Müller ☆
Spay

Young Matthias Müller has already proved that he can make wines that reflect the true class of the Bopparder Hamm vineyards. The emphasis here is always on ripe fruit, freshness, and harmonious acidity.

August Perll ☆
Boppard

Thomas Perll makes surprisingly rich, deeply coloured wines that have fruit rather than freshness.

Weingut Ratzenberger ☆☆–☆☆☆
Bacharach

Jochen Ratzenberger maintains the high standards his father set. Yields here are low, thanks to selective harvesting. These are classic, racy Mittelrhein Rieslings, and remarkably long-lived. His Sekt, aged three years on the yeast, is excellent.

Rheingau

The Rheingau is the region that established Germany's reputation for world-class white wines in the early nineteenth century. A compact region, it lies on the right bank of the Rhein during the thirty-two kilometres (twenty miles) it flows from east to west from Wiesbaden to Bingen. Most of its vineyards lie on gentle slopes, with southerly exposure, that are well-protected from northerly air streams by the mass of the Taunus Mountains. Here, on soils ranging from slate to loess and marl, the Riesling vine can yield wines that are as aristocratic as the region's famous estates. It accounts for seventy-nine per cent of the vineyard area; next is Spätburgunder with twelve per cent.

This unique combination of natural and human factors makes the recent problems of the region hard to understand. Since the mid-1980s, a number of famous estates with glorious traditions have experienced difficulties, several changing hands and one closing its doors forever (Schloss Groenesteyn). Poor quality has been the main problem of the big estates, most of whom have been overtaken by a handful of ambitious young winemakers at the head of small, family-run estates. Thankfully, the combination of press criticism and competition from less famous neighbours has shaken most of the region's large estates out of their slumbers. Slowly but surely, the Rheingau is beginning to prove again that its white wines can be among the greatest anywhere in the world.

The Rheingau led the drive for vineyard classification, but regrettably made a botched job of it, with the result that one third of the vineyards are entitled to be produced, subject to various conditions, as *erstes gewächs*. In practice the proportion is far, far lower, as estates realize that the accolade of First Growth should only be bestowed on truly outstanding wines.

The region can be divided into several sub-areas. The first of these sub-areas is the island of vines at Hochheim on the River Main between Wiesbaden and Frankfurt, whose vineyards yield big, intense wines. The relatively fertile soils of the villages that lie close to the bank of the Rhine between Walluf and Winkel give the most typical Rheingau wines: elegant and subtle to the point of a slight austerity. Higher up, close to the Taunus Forest, the wines are more racy, with a pronounced minerally character from the soil. The wines from Johannisberg and Rüdesheim in the west share this general character, but are fuller-bodied. Assmannshausen is famous for its Spätburgunder red wine.

Outstanding Rheingau Vineyards

Assmannshauser Höllenberg The stony, slate soil of the fifty-five-hectare Höllenberg yields light, elegant, perfumed Spätburgunder reds. Most important owners: August Kesseler, Hotel Krone, Staatsweinger.

Eltville Sonnenberg Medium-bodied Rieslings with ample fruit and supple acidity that drink well from an early age, but also mature well. Most important owner: von Simmern.

Erbacher Hohenrain/Steinmorgen Racy Rieslings with firm acidity that need several years to unfold and reveal their class. Most important owners: Jakob Jung, von Knyphausen.

Erbacher Marcobrunn/Schlossberg/Siegelsberg The famous Marcobrunn gives the most powerful of all Rheingau Rieslings, its heavy marl soil giving them rich fruit, a firm structure, and long ageing potential. The neighbouring sites yield slightly lighter wines with a similar character. Most important owners: August Eser, Schloss Reinhartshausen (Schlossberg monopoly), Schloss Schönborn, von Simmern, Staatsweingüter.

Geisenheimer Fuchsberg/Kläuserweg With their heavy marl soils, these two sites give substantial Rieslings with assertive acidity, that need several years' ageing to reveal their full depths. Most important owner: H. H. Eser.

Geisenheimer Rothenberg A century ago, one of the Rheingau's most renowned vineyards. Its red-slate soil gives lavishly aromatic wines, often with exotic fruit aromas, with a beautiful fruit/acidity balance. Most important owners: Schloss Schönborn, J. Wegeler (Deinhard).

Hallgartener Schönhell The fullest and most harmonious of Hallgarten wines come from this site. Even so, the acidity can be pronounced in young wines. Most important owners: Fürst Löwenstein, Querbach.

Hattenheimer Nussbrunnen/Wisselbrunnen/Mannberg The famous Nussbrunnen yields full, aromatic wines whose ample fruit often masks their acidity, while the wines from the precocious Wisselbrunnen are sleeker and more elegant. Mannberg gives lighter, racy wines. Most important owners: August Eser, Schloss Reinhartshausen, Ress, Schloss Schönborn, von Simmern.

Hattenheimer Pfaffenberg Monopoly of Schloss Schönborn. Its light, sandy soil yields full, aromatic Rieslings with a particularly elegant acidity.

Hochheimer Domdechaney/Kirchenstück The two most famous vineyards of Hochheim yield dramatically contrasting wines. The Domdechaney's heavy marl gives powerful, earthy wines; while the lighter soil of the Kirchenstück yields elegant, refined wines. Most important owners: Künstler, Schloss Schönborn, Staatsweingüter, Domdechant Werner.

Hochheimer Hölle/Königin-Victoria-Berg Situated directly on the bank of the Main, these sites have an exceptional microclimate and deep marl-clay soils. This combination gives powerful, highly structured Rieslings. Most important owners: Hupfeld (Königin-Victoria-Berg monopoly), Künstler, Domdechant Werner.

Johannisberger Hölle/Klaus The Hölle's deep. stony soil gives firm, substantial wines with excellent ageing potential; those from the Klaus are more filigree and elegant. Most important owners: Prinz von Hessen, Johannishof, von Mumm.

Kiedricher Gräfenberg/Wasseros The stony phyllite slate soils of these steeply sloping sites give rich, aromatic wines with elegant acidity and enormous ageing potential. Most important owner: Weil.

Martinsthaler This site has similar soil and exposition to Rauenthal. Elegant, racy wines that drink well early.

Mittelheimer St Nikolaus The light soil and riverbank situation of this site results in ripe, juicy wines with plenty of charm. Most important owners: August Eser, Hupfeld.

Oestricher Doosberg/Lenchen The deep loess soils of Oestrich result in full-bodied, juicy wines with firm acidity; the Lenchen wines are slightly lighter and more elegant; the Doosberg wines are the more powerful, and often better than Lenchen in dry years. Most important owners: August Eser, Kühn, Querbach, Schloss Schönborn, Wegeler.

Rauenthaler Baiken/Gehrn/Nonnenberg/Rothenberg/Wulfen The Rieslings from the Rauenthaler *Berg* are among the most sought-after of all Rheingaus. The phyllite slate and excellent exposition high above the river result in extremely elegant, racy wines with pronounced "spice" and great ageing potential. The finest of all are those from the Baiken, the most vivacious those from the Rothenberg. Most important owners: Breuer (Nonnenberg monopoly), August Eser, von Simmern, Staatsweingüter.

Rüdesheimer Berg-Rottland/Roseneck/Schlossberg The steep vineyards of the Rüdesheimer Berg climb dramatically from the bank of the Rhine where its course

turns north again. Here the Riesling grape gives rich, supple wines, which nonetheless need long ageing to show their best. Most important owners: Breuer, Johannishof, Leitz, Dr. Nägler, Ress, Schloss Schönborn, Staatsweingüter.

Schloss Johannisberg Monopoly site of the eponymous estate. One of the greatest vineyard sites on the entire course of the Rhein. Its wines may not be the richest, but at their best they possess a sublime elegance.

Schloss Vollrads Set well back from the Rhein, this monopoly of the eponymous estate has underperformed for many years. With a new team in place since 1999, there are welcome signs of improvement.

Steinberg Planted in the twelfth century by the monks of Eberbach, this legendary walled vineyard in Hattenheim is comparable to the Clos Vougeot of Burgundy. At their best, its wines are racy, intense, and refined. It is a monopoly of the Staatsweingüter.

Wallufer Walkenberg This little-known site gives powerful, firm wines that need many years of ageing to show their best. Most important owner: J. B. Becker.

Winkeler Hasensprung/Jesuitengarten Directly next to the vineyards of Schloss Johannisberg, the Hasensprung gives similar but rather more succulent wines that develop more quickly. The Jesuitengarten wines from vines close to the riverbank are sleeker and more racy. Most important owners: Allendorf, August Eser, Johannishof, Wegeler.

Leading Rheingau producers

Weingut Fritz Allendorf ☆
Winkel. www.allendorf.de
A substantial estate with fifty-eight hectares in production, including a major holding in Winkeler Jesuitengarten. The wines are light and generally dry or medium-dry. They can be assertive and noticeably high in acidity.

Weingut Hans Barth ☆☆
Hattenheim. www.weingut-barth.de
This twelve-hectare estate is best-known for its Sekt, including the excellent "Ultra". The still, generally dry, Rieslings are more variable, but there are some excellent nobly sweet wines.

Weingut J. B. Becker ☆☆☆–☆☆☆
Walluf
The Becker estate was founded in 1893, and since 1971 has been run by the flamboyant but thoughtful Hans-Josef and his sister Maria. Their vineyards include substantial holdings in the excellent Wallufer Walkenberg, from where he makes powerful, dry wines. Indeed, the Auslese Trocken is often too powerful for its own good. He also produces good Spätburgunder, which was first planted in the Walkenberg in 1903. One peculiarity here is Becker's penchant for BA with high alcohol and relatively low residual sugar. This is an acquired taste.

Weingut Georg Breuer ☆☆–☆☆☆☆
Rüdesheim. www.georg-breuer.com
During the early 1990s, winemaker Hermann Schmoranz and director Bernhard Breuer made this one of the top Rheingau wine producers, and it remains at the top. A founding member of the Charta association of Rheingau estates, Bernhard Breuer was an outspoken promoter of a vineyard classification for the Rheingau. At his own estate an internal classification was introduced long ago; only the best dry and dessert wines from the very top sites (Berg Schlossberg and the monopoly site Rauenthaler Nonnenberg) are sold with a vineyard designation. Excellent wines are also sold under the names of "Rüdesheim" and "Rauenthal". The Sekt is serious and expensive, the Pinot Noir rather tough.

Weingut August Eser ☆
Oestrich. www.eser-wein.de
At this ten-hectare estate, owned by the family since 1759, Joachim Eser makes a full range, from dry to sweet. He maintains a generally high standard in all styles, but the estate needs a top vintage to really shine.

Weingut Joachim Flick ☆–☆☆
Flörsheim-Wicke
Reiner Flick makes some of the best wines from the eastern end of the Rheingau, although he owns few vines in top sites other than Hochheimer Hölle. The emphasis is on rounded accessible Rieslings. The reds from Spätburgunder and Dornfelder lack interest.

Weingut Prinz von Hessen ☆☆–☆☆☆
Geisenheim. www.prinz-von-hessen.com
The Count (Landgraf) of Hessen bought this large estate in 1958. After a period of underperformance during the late 1980s and early 1990s, the new director, Markus Sieben, has substantially improved the wine quality. The Auslese and higher *Prädikat* dessert wines have always been impressive.

Weingut Hupfeld ☆
Oestrich-Winkel
The Hupfeld family is best known as the owner of the well-known Königin Victoriaberg vineyard at Hochheim, where Queen Victoria stopped to watch the vintage in 1850. The original owners, the Pabstmann family, were not slow to commemorate the visit, getting the Queen's permission to rename the vineyard after her, erecting a Gothic monument and designing the most tinselly (now quite irresistible) label. It is not Hochheim's finest, but is full, soft, and flowery, and just what Queen Victoria might well have enjoyed. The family also owns vineyards in Oestrich-Winkel.

Schloss Johannisberg ☆☆
Johannisberg. www.eschloss-johannisberg.de
This marvellously situated property is surely the most famous estate of the Rhein, its name almost synonymous with the true Riesling vine. The first monastery was built on this hilltop commanding the Rhein in 1100; full flowering came in the eighteenth century under the Prince-Abbot of Fulda. Its vintage of 1775 was the first to be gathered overripe (the Abbot's messenger having arrived late with permission to pick); the term Spätlese and the appreciation of noble rot are said to have started with this incident, although such wines were already well-known in other parts of Europe.

The estate was secularized under Napoléon, and in 1816 it was presented by the Austrian Emperor to his Chancellor, Prince Metternich, for his diplomatic services. In 1942, the Johannisberg monastery-castle (but not its cellar) was destroyed in an air raid, and has since been totally rebuilt. The vineyard, in one block on the ideally sloping skirts of the castle hill, has been planted entirely with Riesling for 250 years. Technically it is an *ortsteil* – a local entity which needs no *einzellage* name.

At their best, the wines of Schloss Johannisberg are extraordinarily firm in structure, concentrated, and long-lived, with every quality of classic Riesling grown on an exceptional site. Wines from the 1860s and '70s, tasted recently, have proved still vigorous and bore traces of their original flavour. In 1992, this estate passed into the ownership of the huge Henkell & Söhnlein wine company, and the wines, except at the highest *Prädikat* levels, have lost much of their flair.

Weingut Johannishof ☆☆–☆☆☆
Johannisberg. www.weingut-johannishof.de
Hans Hermann Eser, now assisted by his engaging son, Johannes, comes from an old growers' family and has made a reputation for racy and full-flavoured wines, including the finest Johannisberg Rieslings. The deep cellars, nine metres (thirty feet) under the hill, are traditional: cold and damp with dark, oval casks for maturing wine of character. The recent addition of six hectares in Rüdesheim opens a new chapter in this fine estate's long history.

Weingut Jakob Jung ☆☆
Erbac. www.weingut-jakob-jung.de
Ludwig Jung's generally dry Rieslings offer rare value for money in an expensive region. Best are the elegant wines from the Erbacher Hohenrain.

Weingut Graf von Kanitz ☆☆–☆☆☆
Lorch. www.reinerwein.de
The noble von Kanitz family has only owned this property since 1926. The vineyards are planted on steep slopes at the northeastern extremity of the region. The wines are lively and assertive, with ample fruit, and age well.

Weingut August Kesseler ☆☆–☆☆☆
Assmannshausen. www.august-kesseler.de
A remarkable young estate, which is producing outstandingly successful, deep-coloured Assmannshausen Spätburgunder matured in barriques and sophisticated Rüdesheim Riesling with natural sweetness. Prices are high, but the wines have been taken up enthusiastically by top-quality restaurants and private customers.

Weingut Freiherr zu Knyphausen ☆☆
Erbach. www.knyphausen.de
This former monastic estate was bought in 1818 by the Freiherr's (Baron's) forebears. The property is run on traditional lines, making full-flavoured wines, seventy per cent dry or medium-dry. The quality here is consistent, but some wines lack the grip and concentration of the very finest from the Rheingau.

Weingut Robert König ☆☆
Assmannshausen

A rarity in the Rheingau: an estate that is almost entirely dedicated to red wine, from Spätburgunder and Frühburgunder. These are cask-matured wines that are traditional in style, but possess plenty of character.

Weingut Krone ☆☆–☆☆☆
Assmannshausen

This is the estate of probably the most famous hotel on the Rhein, the "Krone". Since the arrival of young winemaker Peter Perabo in 1995, the Spätburgunders have begun to challenge those of neighbour August Kesseler (*q.v.*). There are numerous *cuvées*, and a range of *Weissherbst* Auslesen too. The best place to sample these striking wines is at the hotel's restaurant, which carries 1,300 wines on its list.

Weingut Peter Jakob Kühn ☆☆☆–☆☆☆☆
Oestrich. www.weingutpjkuehn.de

Oestricher Lenchen and Doosberg may not be the Rheingau's most celebrated sites, but Peter Kühn makes marvellous wines, eighty per cent of them dry, from these vineyards. Kühn is a tireless experimenter, adopting and adapting techniques he observes on his travels. Full fruit and harmonious acidity are the qualities to be found right through the range. The late-harvested wines can be sensational here, as in 1998 and '99.

Weingut Franz Künstler ☆☆☆–☆☆☆☆
Hochheim. www.weingut-kuenstler.de

Gunter Künstler is one of the most talented young winemakers on the entire Rhein. His powerful, minerally, dry Rieslings catapulted him to fame during the late 1980s and continue to win blind tastings. However, his less well-known Auslese and higher *Prädikat* dessert wines also deserve the highest praise. In 1996, Künstler almost tripled his holdings by purchasing the renowned Aschrott estate in Hochheim, giving him access to more top sites. Künstler is unimpressed by the introduction of the *erstes gewächs* classification and proposes to ignore it.

Weingut Hans Lang ☆☆☆–☆☆☆
Hattenheim. www.lang-wein.com

This versatile grower produces light but elegant Rieslings, and a range of other wines: a pretty Silvaner, and barrel-fermented Grauer Burgunder and Weisser Burgunder. There's Spätburgunder, too, but it can be rather extracted. The Rieslings are the best wines, with plenty of character and acidity.

Freiherr Langwerth von Simmern ☆☆
Eltville

This aristocratic estate, which dates from 1464, is based at the beautiful Renaissance Langwerther Hof in the ancient centre of Eltville – one of the loveliest spots in the Rheingau. The richly heraldic (if scarcely legible) red label used to be one of the most reliable in Germany for classic Riesling, but standards slipped badly in the 1990s. At the end of the 1990s, a family member returned to take charge, and in 2001, a new winemaker, Dirk Roth, was appointed, and quality is once again on the rise.

Weingut Josef Leitz ☆☆☆
Rüdesheim. www.leitz-wein.de

When Johannes Leitz began making wine here in the mid-1980s, he followed the hi-tech model of the time. But he was unhappy with the results, and in the 1990s opted for low yields, natural yeasts, and ageing the wine on the fine lees after a slow fermentation. The improvement in quality was immediate. Leitz is now in the first rank of Rheingau growers, producing Rieslings of great individuality and elegance. Finest are the dry wines from Berg Rottland and the late-harvested, naturally sweet wines from Berg Schlossberg.

Weingut Dr. Nägler ☆
Rüdesheim. www.weingut-dr-naegler.de

For some time, quality here has been less than spectacular. However, Tilbert Nägler took over in 2001, so there are likely to be changes for the better. Prices are very reasonable.

Weingut Prinz ☆
Hallgarten

From a mere 1.6 hectares that belong to his wife, Fred Prinz,. who used to work alongside Bernhard Breuer, makes impressive dry and naturally sweet Rieslings from Hallgarten vineyards.

Weingut Querbach ☆
Winkel. www.querbach.com

In 1998, the Querbachs launched their own system of classification. "No. 2" for chaptalized Kabinett, "No 1" for Spätlese Trocken; there is also an *erstes gewächs* from Oestricher Doosberg. They have also bravely abandoned cork closures for their wines. Quality is good throughout the range.

Schloss Reinhartshausen ☆☆
Erbach. www.schloss-reinhartshausen.de

For more than a century, and until 1988, this large, eighty-two-hectare estate was owned by the Prussian royal family. Today it is owned by a consortium. Despite the size of the property, quality across the board is reliable. Best of all are the powerful, aristocratic wines from Erbacher Marcobrun and the racy wines from Hattenheimer Wisselbrunnen. Their drawback is their high price. Sekt is an important specialty here and is among the best in the Rheingau. Quality is set to improve further: after a period of instability, a new director, Andreas Blaurock, was appointed in 2000.

Balthasar Ress ☆☆
Hattenheim. www.ress-wine.com

Stefan Ress, now assisted by his son Christian, is a well-established merchant and grower, producing a wide range of wines from throughout the region. In 1978 he leased the four-hectare Schloss Reichartshausen, originally a Cistercian property but latterly rather neglected. This estate's wines are unashamedly modern in style, vinified in stainless steel and bottled early for maximum freshness. Quality is rather variable; most wines are best drunk young.

Domänenweingut Schloss Schönborn ☆☆–☆☆☆
Hattenheim. www.schoenborn.de

Since 1349, this vast, privately owned estate in the Rheingau, sixty-five hectares of mostly excellent sites, has been in the hands of a family of great political and cultural influence. Critics are divided over the recent performance of Schönborn wines. Some have described them as the

"Rubens of the Rheingau", while others have found them too heavy and clumsy. They come in vast variety, from the central Marcobrunn to Lorch at the extreme west of the region and Hochheim at the extreme east. Since the arrival of director Günter Thies in 1995, signs of improvement have been in evidence, but there is still a long way to go before Schönborn matches its performance of the decades prior to 1971.

Staatsweingüter Kloster Erbach ☆–☆☆☆

Eltville. www.staatsweingueterhessen.de

The State of Hessen's domain at Eltville is based on monastic vineyards ceded to the Duke of Nassau under Napoleon; then they passed to the Kingdom of Prussia, and eventually to the State of Hessen, whose capital is nearby Wiesbaden. For its ceremonial HQ, the domain has the magnificent and perfectly preserved Cistercian abbey of Kloster Eberbach (1135) in a wooded valley behind Hattenheim, and the most famous of its vineyards, the Steinberg, comparable to a walled Burgundian "clos". Kloster Eberbach is also the scene of prestigious annual wine auctions; and home to the German Wine Academy, which runs regular courses for amateurs and professionals. It was here that the word "cabinet" was first used (for the vintage of 1712) to designate reserve-quality wine – a meaning totally altered by modern laws.

The estates, 197 hectares in all, include properties in Assmannshausen and the Hessische Bergstrasse, which are discussed separately. Despite the weight of tradition, winemaking methods are extremely modern, and most wines are vinified in stainless steel. From the mid-1970s, this great estate's performance underwent a steady decline, despite owning some of the best sites in the region. The director since 2000, Dieter Greiner, understands precisely what needs to be done to restore the domain to its former excellence. Whether the politicians who are his masters will allow him to get on with the job remains to be seen.

Schloss Vollrads ☆☆–☆☆☆

Oestrich-Winkel. www.schlossvollrads.com

Few men did more to promote the Rheingau and its wines than Graf Erwein Matuschka-Greiffenclau, who presided over this magnificent old estate in the hills above Winkel, the latest in a long line of aristocrats who have inhabited Winkel since at least 1100. Their original Romanesque "Grey House" in Winkel, the oldest stone-built dwelling in Germany, is now a wine-restaurant. Their vineyards have been accepted as an *ortsteil*, a separate entity which uses no commune or *einzellage* name. Schloss Vollrads specialized in dry wines with minimal residual sugar, and Graf Matuschka also leased the Weingut Fürst Löwenstein (*q.v.*) in Hallgarten.

But the wines were rarely as good as they should have been, and practices such as machine-harvesting were tolerated at Vollrads. Despite his castle and fast cars, Graf Matuschka experienced growing financial difficulties throughout the 1990s, and this culminated in his suicide in 1997. The estate passed into the hands of his bankers, but after some anxious years, when it was feared that Vollrads might be split up, the Nassauische Sparkasse decided to keep the property intact and hired a new director, the experienced Dr. Rowald Hepp, to manage the property. Since 1999, there has been a distinct improvement in quality, which is set to continue.

Geheimrat J. Wegeler ☆☆

Oestrich-Winkel. www.wegeler.com

In the 1990s, this substantial fifty-five-hectare Rheingau estate, once linked to the Koblenz merchant house of Deinhard, was cruising on its former reputation. Then in 2000, Oliver Haag, the son of Wilhelm Haag of Brauneberg (*q.v.*) in the Mosel, was hired to take charge of the winemaking. There were already signs of improvement in 1999, and Haag will no doubt capitalize on them. The Wegeler vineyards are superb: Oestricher Lenchen, Winkeler Hasensprung, Geisenheimer Rothenberg, and the Rüdesheimer Berg. There is no reason why the it should not become as good as any in the Rheingau.

Weingut Robert Weil ☆☆☆–☆☆☆☆

Kiedrich. www.weingut-robert-weil.com

The historic Weil estate has been owned since 1988 by Japanese drinks giant Suntory, which made huge investments, including more than doubling the estate's vineyard area and building the most modern winemaking facility in the region. Important as these steps were, it is the work of director Wilhelm Weil that was decisive in pushing the estate back to the forefront of the region. Its late-harvested Riesling Auslese, BA, and TBA and Eiswein from the Kiedricher Gräfenberg are among the greatest wines of this style made in Germany. The grapes are harvested with repeated selections and must weights far exceed the legal minima, leading some to suggest that the Weil wines, while splendid, are exaggerated. The constant demand for the wines, despite their high prices, suggests the consumer is happy with the wines as they are. While the dry wines are of good quality, they do not begin to scale these heights.

Domdechant Werner'sches Weingut ☆☆–☆☆☆

Hochheim. www.domdechantwerner.com

The Werner family bought this superbly sited manor, overlooking the junction of the Rhine and Main, from the Duke of York in 1780. The buyer's son, Dr. Franz Werner, was the famous Dean (Domdechant) of Mainz who saved the cathedral from destruction by the French. The same family (now called Michel) still owns and runs the estate, making some of the most serious, full-flavoured Hochheimers from some of its best vineyards. Traditional barrel-ageing makes both dry and naturally sweet wines, which are both flavourful and long-lived.

Nahe

The River Nahe is a tributary of the Rhein, with which it has its confluence at Bingen. The best Riesling wines from its 4,600 hectares of vineyards have long been recognized as belonging to the finest Germany has to offer. Yet the region is one known to rather few people, either at home or abroad.

Since the Nahe's vineyards lie between those of the Mosel-Saar-Ruwer and the Rheingau, the conventional way of describing Nahe wines is as being transitional between Mosel and Rhein; some say specifically between Saar and Rheingau. This is true of the weight and balance, body and structure of the fine wines of the Middle Nahe; they do have the "nerve", the backbone, of the Saar, together with some of the meat of the weightiest and more densely flavoured Rheingau. The volcanic soil, however, adds something quite unique; to me the great Nahe wines often have a delicate hint of blackcurrant, with delicious and fascinating mineral undertones. In their delicacy yet completeness they make hypnotic sipping.

The greatest and most renowned vineyards of the Nahe lie in the rocky, winding strength of the valley upstream from Bad Kreuznach, particularly those of Niederhausen, Norheim, Traisen, and Schlossböckelheim. Their wines frequently achieve that miraculous balancing act between ripeness and freshness, of which only the Riesling grape is capable. Further upstream, where the valley is wider and more gently undulating, Monzingen has the best sites. Bad Kreuznach's wines come from heavier, more fertile soils, and are consequently more generous and juicy. In years with hot summers they can be bombastic; in less extreme years the epitome of charm and harmony. Downstream, towards the Nahe's confluence with the Rhein, the landscape once again becomes punctuated with south-facing cliffs and steep slopes in side valleys. Here, from Lower Nahe villages such as Münster-Sarmsheim and Dorsheim, the wines have similar minerally character to those of the Middle Nahe, but are fuller and more imposing.

Outstanding Nahe Vineyards

Altenbamberger Rotenberg This steep site with reddish rhyolite soil yields juicy, aromatic Rieslings with supple acidity. Most important owner: Gutsverwaltung Niederhausen-Schlossböckelheim.

Dorsheimer Burgberg/Goldloch/Pittermännchen
The reddish slate soil of the Goldloch and Burgberg gives full Rieslings with apricot fruit and a firm structure, while the grey slate of the Pittermännchen yields sleek, racy wines that possess an extraordinary resemblance to fine Mosel Rieslings. Most important owner: Diel.

Kreuznacher Brückes/Kahlenberg/Krotenpfühl
Bad Kreuznach's finest vineyards all enjoy sheltered positions on the outskirts of the town. The deep loam soils overlying reddish slate result in rich, fleshy wines. Most important owners: Anheuser, Anton Finkenauer, von Plettenberg.

Langenlonsheimer Rothenberg/Löhrer Berg The loam and reddish slate soils here yield medium-bodied Rieslings, full of ripe fruit, that drink well from an early age. Most important owners: Schweinhardt, Wilhelm Sitzius, Tesch.

Laubenheimer Karthäuser/St Remigiusberg Just north of Langenlonsheim, these vineyards have mostly loam soils, on which Riesling attains high ripeness levels, making it an excellent site for dry wines. Most important owner: Tesch

Monzinger Frühlingsplätzchen/Halenberg
These steep sloping sites have contrasting soils. The Frühlingsplätzchen is reddish slate, giving more immediately appealing, supple wines, while the blue slate of the Halenberg gives very elegant, racy Rieslings. Most important owners: Paul Anheuser, Emrich Schönleber.

Münsterer Dautenpflänzer/Kapellenberg/Pittersberg
The graceful sweep of these excellent vineyards can be viewed from the A61 *autobahn* as it crosses the Nahe. The slate over loess-loam subsoils on these sites gives intensely aromatic, racy Rieslings; those from the Dautenpflänzer have the most power, and the Pittersberg wines are the most elegant. Most important owners: Göttelmann, Kruger Rumpf.

Niederhäuser Hermannsberg/Oberhäuser Brücke These sites cover a single slope with southwesterly exposure and a stony porphyry-based soil. They are renowned for intense, minerally Rieslings. Most important owners Dönnhoff (Brücke monopoly), Gutsverwaltung Niederhausen-Schlossböckelheim (Hermmansberg monopoly).

Niederhäuser Hermannshöhle Since the Prussian classification of the Nahe vineyards (published in map form in 1901) this has been regarded as the greatest vineyard on the Nahe. Perfect exposure and an extremely stony soil composed of a complex mix of all the local soil types results in Riesling wines with the highest elegance and aromatic complexity. Most important owners: Dönnhoff, Jakob Schneider, Wilhelm Sitzius, Gutsverwaltung Niederhausen-Schlossböckelheim.

Niederhäuser Kertz/Klamm/Rosenheck Though these are not the greatest of Niederhausen's vineyards, they nonetheless give sophisticated, racy Rieslings with a strong minerally character from the porphyry soil. Most important owners: Crusius, Mathern, Jakob Schneider.

Norheimer Dellchen/Kafels/Kirschheck Extremely steep, terraced vineyards, with stony, porphyry soil, these are the least well known top sites of the Middle Nahe, yet they have the potential to challenge Niederhausen and Schlossböckelheim. Most important owners: Crusius, Dönnhoff, Lötzbeyer, Mathern, Jakob Schneider, Staatsweingut Bad Kreuznach.

Roxheimer Berg/Birkenberg/Höllenpfad/Hüttenberg/ Mühlenberg To the northwest of Bad Kreuznach, the best sites of Roxheim lie outside the Nahe Valley, but the combination of a southerly exposure and reddish slate soil gives ripe, aromatic wines of elegant acidity. Most important owners: Anheuser, Prinz zu Salm-Dalberg (Schloss Wallhausen).

Schlossböckelheimer Felsenberg/Kupfergrube The two great Schlossböckelheim sites stand side by side, but yield contrasting wines. The Felsenberg has been cultivated for centuries; its very stony, melaphry soil yields richly aromatic Rieslings with a silky acidity. The Kupfergrube was created out of a former copper mine in 1902, and yields sleeker, intensely racy wines which have remarkable ageing potential. Most important owners: Crusius, Dönnhoff, Gutsverwaltung Niederhausen-Schlossböckelheim.

Schlossböckelheimer In den Felsen/Königsfels The wines seldom match those of Schlossböckelheim's greatest sites, but they, too, give racy Rieslings with an extremely pronounced minerally character. Most important owners: Anheuser, Hehner-Kilz.

Traiser Bastei/Rotenfels The famous Bastei vineyard lies between the bank of the Nahe and the 180 metre (600-foot) high mass of the Rotenfels cliffs. Extremely stony porphyry soil yields powerful, pungently minerally wines. The neighbouring Rotenfels site gives similar, but less extreme wines. Most important owners: Crusius, Gutsverwaltung Niederhausen-Schlossböckelheim.

Wallhäuser Felseneck/Johannisberg/Pastorenberg
Commanding a sheltered position high up the Gräfenbach Valley these steep vineyards with their slate-rich soils give remarkably Mosel-like Rieslings. Most important owner: Schloss Wallhausen.

Wintzenheimer Rosenheck/Bretzenheimer Pastorei
These adjoining sites give similar, but slightly more elegant wines compared to the top vineyards of Bad Kreuznach. Most important owner: von Plettenberg.

Leading Nahe Producers

Weingut Paul Anheuser ☆
Bad Kreuznach. www.anheuser.de
This property can trace its origins back to 1627, and is the last surviving Anheuser estate in a town that not so long ago boasted three. In the 1880s, Rudolf Anheuser was the first to introduce Riesling to the Nahe. The estate is enormous, with sixty-eight hectares, and there are vineyards in many parts of the Middle Nahe. The wines mature in wood in deep, cool cellars. The aim is freshness and fruit. For some time the estate has failed to maintain the high standards set during the 1970s and 1980s.

Weingut Hans Crusius ☆☆–☆☆☆
Traisen. www.weingut-crusius.de
The Grand Seigneur of the Nahe wine industry, Hans Crusius, slowly handed over control of the thirteen-hectare family estate to his son, Dr. Peter Crusius, from the late 1980s. The Rieslings are very clean and quite beautifully crafted, and those from the Traisener Bastei and Rotenfels have force and personality.

Schlossgut Diel ☆☆☆
Burg Layen. www.schlossgut-diel.com
Winegrower, wine journalist, restaurant critic, and TV presenter, the multi-talented Armin Diel is one of the outstanding personalities on the German wine scene today. His substantial holdings in all three of Dorsheim's top vineyards make this the leading estate of the Lower Nahe. Dry and late-harvested Rieslings with natural sweetness form the bulk of the production, although the new-oak-aged Weisser Burgunder, Grauer Burgunder and "Victor" (a powerful blend of the two) also enjoy a high reputation, as does the Sekt. The difficult 2000 vintage was a great success here, and yielded some exquisite Auslesen.

Weingut Hermann Dönnhoff ☆☆☆☆
Oberhausen. www.doenhoff.com
Helmut Dönnhoff's Rieslings are the most perfect expressions of the great vineyards of the Middle Nahe. Behind his reserved manner lies a fanatical commitment to quality, and a remarkable natural talent for winemaking. Virtually every barrel from this cellar (and wood is an article of faith for Dönnhoff) is bottled separately, resulting in a confusingly wide range. However, such is the consistency and sheer quality that this hardly matters. The most powerful wines are those from the Oberhäuser Brücke, while those from the Hermannshöhle represent the ultimate in elegance and complexity. Dönnhoff's Eiswein is regularly among Germany's best.

Weingut Emrich-Schönleber ☆☆☆
Monzingen. www.emrich-schoenleber.com
Since the late 1980s, the Schönlebers' estate has been a rising star among Nahe producers. Their Rieslings, in both the dry and naturally sweet styles, are very pure and expressive, with vibrant fruit and racy acidity. The wines from the Halenberg are the more refined, those from the Frühlingsplätzchen more generous. Schönleber's Eiswein often rivals those from Dönnhoff for splendour and intensity.

Weingut Göttelmann ☆
Münster-Sarmsheim
Götz Blessing married into the Göttelmann family, and since 1984 has run the estate and makes the wines. The dry Riesling and Grauer Burgunder are often better than the naturally sweet wines, which can show some flabbiness. Quality is variable, but the best wines are very good indeed.

Weingut Hahnmühle ☆
Mannweiler-Cölln
Peter Linxweiler is best-known for sleek, steely, dry Rieslings from the rocky vineyards of the Alsenz Valley. The Chardonnay, from two sites in Oberndorf, is the specialty here.

Weingut Hehner-Kilz ☆
Waldböckelheim. www.hehner-kiltz.de
As well as running one of the best country inns in the Nahe, Georg and Helmut Hehner produce slightly erratic, but often good, dry, and naturally sweet Rieslings from the top sites of Schlossböckelheim.

Weingut Kruger-Rumpf ☆☆–☆☆☆
Münster-Sarmsheim. www.kruger-rumpf.com
This estate, with many of the best sites in Münster-Sarmsheim among its nineteen hectares, is deservedly admired for its firm, dry wines of great style from Riesling, Silvaner, Weisser Burgunder and Spätburgunder. In 2001, Stefan Rumpf crossed the border into Rheinhessen and purchased vines in the Binger Scharlachberg. All the wines can be tasted in the estate's excellent wine restaurant, which offers some of the best regional cooking in the Nahe.

Weingut Lötzbeyer ☆☆
Feilbingert
Adolf Lötzbeyer's impressive Riesling and Scheurebe dessert wines have attracted much praise, and a noticeable following in the United States. His Kabinett and Spätlese wines with natural sweetness can also impress, but the dry wines are rather rustic.

Weingut Mathern ☆☆–☆☆☆
Niederhausen. www.weingut-mathern.de
Helmut Mathern owns a fine selection of steep sites in

Niederhausen and Norheim, and in the 1990s has been making the most of them. The richly aromatic Rieslings, the majority of which are vinified with some natural sweetness, are of a consistently high standard. Indeed, the dry wines here can be somewhat tart. Mathern is not that interested in producing nobly sweet Rieslings, but his Auslesen in 1999 were superb.

Gutsverwaltung Niederhausen-Schlossböckelheim ☆☆–☆☆☆

Niederhausen. www.riesling-domaene.de
The former Nahe State Domain, once considered the finest in Germany, was founded in 1902 by Kaiser Wilhelm II. Its foundation pioneered viticulture on the steep slopes above the now-famous site of a former copper mine (the Kupfergrube) to grow Riesling. By 1920, its wines were acknowledged to be superlative and remained so into the 1980s. After a period of rather erratic performance in the early 1990s, a radical restructuring was undertaken and Kurt Gabelmann was appointed director; then, in 1998, the whole property was bought by the agricultural products manufacturer Erich Maurer. Gabelmann stayed on as cellarmaster. For a demonstration of the subtlety and finesse of great German wine, ranging from fine-drawn floweriness to sumptuous elegance, this estate's wines were as fine as any in the early 1980s, and Maurer is keen to restore the wines to that level. The Schlossböckelheimers are the most stylish and delicate; the Niederhäusers are fuller and more seductive; the Traisers big, ripe, and long-lived; and the wines from the Lower Nahe full-bodied and spicy. About 60% of the wines are dry.

Weingut Reichsgraf von Plettenberg

Bad Kreuznach
This domain has been in the Plettenberg family since the eighteenth century and produced outstanding wines in the 1970s. Despite owning well-placed vineyards around Bad Kreuznach, the estate has, alas, been on a downward slide in quality for many years.

Prinz zu Salm-Dalberg'sches Weingut Schloss Wallhausen ☆

Wallhausen. www.salm-salm.de
The organic estate belonging to Michael Prinz zu Salm-Salm, the national president of the wine estate association known as the VDP, lies in a little-known and unspoiled corner of the Nahe region. There are two brands, "Der Salm" and "Prinz Salm", offering easy-drinking varietal wines from mostly purchased fruit (and not necessarily organic). The most serious wines are single-vineyard bottlings from the estate. The dry Rieslings have an austere finesse, while the sweeter styles can sometimes lack concentration.

Weingut Bürgermeister Willi Schweinhardt ☆

Langenlonsheim. www.schweinhardt.de
This long established family of growers produces medium-sweet Rieslings and Scheurebes as well as full-bodied dry Weisser Burgunder and Grauer Burgunders. The grapey, light, and charming wines are best drunk quite young. This is a reliable and sensibly priced source of Riesling Eiswein.

Weingut Wilhelm Sitzius ☆–☆☆

Langenlonsheim. www.sitzius.de

Only half of the vineyards here are planted with Riesling. The basic wines lack excitement, but the top dry wines can be good, especially the ones from Niederhäuser Hermannshöhle. The Spätburgunder, aged in German oak, can be very appealing.

Weingut Tesch ☆☆–☆☆☆

Langenlonsheim. www.weingut-tesch.de
Founded in 1723, this used to be a highly regarded estate, and the new generation, in the form of Dr. Martin Tesch, is determined to restore its reputation. The best wines here are the dry Rieslings from Langenlonsheim and Laubenheim, sites that give good ripeness levels. The wines are generous, fruity, and quite broad-structured, but that also means they are approachable young. Tesch's best sweet wines come from Laubenheimer St Remigiusberg.

Rheinhessen

Anonymity behind the *nom de verre* of Liebfraumilch and other washed-out blends is the fate of most Rheinhessen wine. In volume terms, production is dominated by soft, gently flowery Müller-Thurgau; blunt, rustic Silvaner; and superficial, spicy wines from new varieties.

Only ten per cent of the 26,450-hectare vineyard is Riesling, concentrated in a few outstanding sites. The most important of these lie around Nackenheim, Nierstein, and Oppenheim, just south of Mainz; the rather unfortunately named "Rhein Front". The steep vineyards here give some of Germany's richest Rieslings, wines with the body and spice to take on the best of Alsace and Austria. In Bingen, at the region's northwestern extremity, vineyards with a similar quality potential – not always realized – yield more restrained and classical Rieslings.

Among the sea of vines covering the hill country that forms the bulk of Rheinhessen, are vineyards which can yield good dry Riesling, Weisser Burgunder, Grauer Burgunder, and traditional dry Silvaner. Efforts to give these wines more profile and to distinguish them from the mass-produced ones, such as the "Rheinhessen Selektion" programme, have been made, and the process has been accelerated by the introduction of the *grosses gewächs* vineyard classification. However, the success of a handful of dedicated producers on the Rhein Front and in the "Hinterland" is doing just as much to change the region's image.

There is a long way to go. Even growers anxious to improve their wines and move upmarket, find they are hampered by the low prices Rheinhessen wines usually fetch, which means that they cannot afford the necessary investment to improve their viticultural and winemaking standards. Fortunately, the success of growers such as Keller and Wittmann show what can be achieved – and that includes higher prices – so, with luck, steady improvement seems inevitable.

Outstanding Rheinhessen Vineyards

Binger Scharlachberg Elegant, refined Rieslings from the Taunus quarzite soil of this terraced, south-facing twenty-seven-hectare site. The historic heart of the vineyard was grubbed up in the 1980s and has not been replanted. Most important owner: Villa Sachsen.

Dalsheimer Bürgel A thirty-hectare site with some limestone soil, and planted with a good deal of Spätburgunder. Keller owns two hectares here.

Dalsheimer Hubacker Clay with some limestone. The best parcel gives Keller excellent Rieslings.

Nackenheimer Rothenberg The northern tip of the "Roter Hang", and a precipitously steep site with stony, reddish slate soil, and excellent exposure. It gives some of the most seductively aromatic and longest-living Rieslings on the entire Rhein. Virtually a monopoly of the Gunderloch estate.

Niersteiner Brudersberg Tiny monopoly site of Heyl zu Herrnsheim. Steep slopes, reddish, slate soil and perfect southerly exposition make for Rieslings with richness and elegance.

Niersteiner Heiligenbaum Only a small part of this site is highly regarded, due to the unremarkable loamy soil which dominates here.

Niersteiner Hipping Arguments rage about the merits of this site. However, all are agreed that the ripe pineapple aroma typical of its wines makes them extremely attractive from an early age. Most important owners: St Antony, Gunderloch, Heyl zu Herrnsheim, Schneider, Seebrich, and Strub.

Niersteiner Oelberg With the deepest soil of all Nierstein's top sites, the Oelberg gives powerful wines that need a long time to reveal their depths, but are also very long-lived. Most important owners: St Antony, Heinrich Braun, Guntrum, Heyl zu Herrnsheim, Rappenhof, Schneider, Seebrich, and Strub.

Niersteiner Orbel This steeply sloping, stony vineyard, west of Nierstein, yields wines that combine mineral intensity with racy acidity. Most important owners: St Antony, Braun, Schneider, and Strub.

Niersteiner Pettenthal Although enjoying identical exposition to the Nackenheimer Rothenberg, the Pettenthal's shallow soil results in quicker developing Rieslings with a very pronounced minerally character. Most important owners: St Antony, Braun, Heyl zu Herrnsheim, Rappenhof, Schneider, and Strub.

Oppenheimer Herrenberg/Kreuz/Sackträger The heavy marl soil of these sites gives completely different wines from Nierstein's top sites. Here, even the Riesling gives weighty, corpulent wines with a firm underlying acidity. They can be heavy and charmless if not vinified expertly. Most important owners: Guntrum, Carl Koch, Kühling-Gillot, and Rappenhof.

Westhofener Morstein Clay-loam above a limestone subsoil. Well-exposed, this gives fairly minerally wines. Most important owner: Wittmann.

Leading Rheinhessen Producers

Weingut Brüder Dr. Becker ☆☆
Ludwigshöhe. www.brueder-dr-becker.de
This organic estate, run by Lotte Pfeffer-Müller, rightly enjoys a good reputation for traditional style, cask-matured, dry Riesling and Silvaner, and vibrantly fruity, modern-style Scheurebe with natural sweetness. Some of the bottlings come from the calcareous loam of the Dienheimer Tafelstein site.

Weingut Gunderloch ☆☆☆☆
Nackenheim. www.gunderloch.de
Since the late-1980s, Fritz Hasselbach's concentrated, explosively aromatic Rieslings from the great Nackenheimer Rothenberg vineyard have shot him to international fame. His late-harvested Auslese and higher *Prädikat* wines are also exceptional.

The almost dry "Jean Baptiste" Riesling Kabinett is a model example of this classic German wine style. In the dry style, their "basic" Gunderloch Riesling also sets a high standard. Both are excellent food wines. With the acquisition of the Balbach estate in 1996, the company doubled in size. Simpler wines aimed at a more youthful market are packaged in brightly coloured labels under the "Balbach" name, while the "Gunderloch" label remains devoted to classic styles.

Weinkellerei Louis Guntrum ☆–☆☆
Nierstein. www.guntrum.com
This family business was started in 1824, and is now directed by the fifth generation. The estate wines can be ripe and lively with a wide range of flavours, each variety and site being bottled individually. In recent years, quality has been erratic, with many earthy wines.

Weingut Gutzler ☆–☆☆
Gundheim. www.gutzler.de
Gutzler's ten hectares are dispersed among various villages of southern Rheinhessen. The basic ranges here are unexciting, but there are some ambitious whites, such as a firm Riesling Spätlese Trocken from the Liebfrauenstift, and barrel-fermented Auxerrois. The reds are quite extracted and sometimes over-oaked.

Weingut Freiherr Heyl zu Herrnsheim ☆☆☆☆
Nierstein. www.heyl-zu-herrnsheim.de
Ex-astrophysicist Peter von Weymarn has been a pioneer of organic viticulture in Germany since the 1970s. He was also one of the first to focus on drier styles of Riesling. In 1994 he sold the estate to the Ahr family, who are maintaining the quality standard von Weymarn established, and have retained the large oak casks for ageing the wines. But the wine range has been simplified.

There are basic estate wines, a "Rotschiefer" (red slate) range for Silvaner, Weisser Burgunder, and Riesling; and the great single-vineyard wines from their monopoly site Brudersberg and from Pettenthal. These are wines of aristocratic reserve that frequently need several years' bottle age to show their best. A 1997 Spätlese launched the fifth edition of *The World Atlas of Wine* in Hamburg in 2002 in splendour. Although most of the wines are dry, there are also some rare and costly BAs and TBAs.

Weingut Keller ✩✩✩✩
Flörsheim-Dalsheim

This twelve-hectare estate has set new quality standards in the southern hill country of Rheinhessen. Their Rieslings and Rieslaners are remarkable wines, considering that Flörsheim-Dalsheim possesses no celebrated vineyards. But Klaus Keller and his son, Klaus-Peter, have identified the best parcels in vineyards such as Bürgel and Hubacker, with wonderful results. Yields are incredibly low, allowing the Kellers to make dry wines of full ripeness and intensity. Clarity, effusive fruit, and racy acidity are the hallmarks of the Keller wines, whether dry, with a touch of natural sweetness, or full-blown Rieslaner dessert wines.

Weingut Klaus Knobloch ✩✩
Ober-Flörsheim. www.weingut-klausknobloch.de

This thirty-hectare estate has been organically farmed since 1988. Knobloch produces an interesting range of red wines from varieties such as St Laurent and Lemberger, as well as Spätburgunder. Among the white wines, the best is often the rich Weisser Burgunder.

Bürgermeister Carl Koch Erben ✩
Oppenheim

Once a reliable source of wines from Oppenheim, this estate has not always shown consistency. But its sweet Rieslings, notably Auslesen, can be excellent.

Weingut Kühling-Gillot ✩–✩✩
Bodenheim. www.kuehling-gillot.com

Roland Gillot is best-known for his powerful, opulent dessert wines, which can be among Rheinhessen's best. His dry Rieslings are rather less remarkable, often tending to be too plump, as the vineyards in Bodenheim and Oppenheim have heavy soils.

Weingut Michel-Pfannebecker ✩✩
Flomborn. www.michel-pfannebecker.de

Since they started bottling their wines in the 1970s, the Pfannebecker brothers have restructured their eleven-hectare estate, eliminating many of the inferior grape crossings, and focusing on Riesling, Silvaner, and Spätburgunder. The Rieslings have elegance and length, but the Silvaners have more personality – in the case of the barrique-aged Silvaner, an unattractive personality. The Grauer Burgunder and Chardonnay can be zesty and complex.

Weingut Rappenhof ✩
Alsheim. www.weingut-rappenhof.de

With fifty-three hectares of vineyards, this very old family estate is one of the region's largest. Although Klaus Muth has invested great energy in experiments with Chardonnay, *nouveau*-style red wines and barrique-ageing, the quality is frequently unremarkable.

Weingut St Antony ✩✩✩
Nierstein. www.st-antony.com

Dr. Alex Michalsky has directed this twenty-three-hectare estate for its owners, the MAN truck- and bus-building company of Munich, for many years. It is endowed with a fine range of Roter Hang vineyards: steep and low-yielding. Well-established as a specialist in dry Rieslings, the estate has continuously pushed forward the limits of what is possible in this style. The result of this quest has been extremely powerful, concentrated wines that have won high praise on the one hand, and been criticized for being atypical German Rieslings on the other. They are certainly among the more austere dry Rieslings of the region, and need time in bottle to show their complexity. More recently, great efforts have been invested in the harvesting of naturally sweet Auslese and higher *Prädikat* wines. Unquestionably, this is now one of the region's finest estates.

Weingut Schales ✩–✩✩
Flörsheim-Dalsheim. www.schales.de

This long-established family property makes a wide range of wines from the limestone soil of Dalsheim, though none of the wines is vineyard-designated.

The powerful dry Grauer Burgunders and Weisser Burgunders can be impressive, though most of the wines, red as well as white, are made in a crowd-pleasing style, but are none the worse for that. The sumptuous, rather heavy, sweet wines are usually made from varieties such as Huxelrebe and Siegerrebe.

Weingut Georg Albrecht Schneider ✩✩–✩✩✩
Nierstein

By his own admission, no self-publicist or salesman, Albrecht Schneider makes some of the most elegant, finely crafted Rieslings from the top sites of Nierstein. Conscientious attention to detail in both the vineyard and cellar is the secret of the high standards set by this little-known estate.

Weingut J. & H. A. Strub ✩
Nierstein

This is an old family estate, which has a good name for producing gentle, mellow wines from some of Nierstein's top sites. They are enjoyable, but not especially memorable.

Weingut Villa Sachsen ✩–✩✩✩
Bingen. www.villa-sachsen.com

After a period of instability in the late 1980s and early '90s, this renowned estate was purchased by a consortium led by Michael Prinz zu Salm-Salm of Wallhausen in the Nahe. Production is divided between clean, simple, varietal wines, and fine Rieslings, especially *grosses gewächs*, from the Binger Scharlachberg. Most of the wines are dry, but there are some opulent, if somewhat broad, nobly sweet Rieslings from the Scharlachberg, too.

Pfalz

No wine-growing region in Germany enjoys a more generous climate than the Pfalz. Nowhere in Germany is it warmer and drier than the band of vineyards which runs for eighty kilometres (fifty miles) along the eastern flank of the Haardt Mountains, from the southern border of Rheinhessen to the French frontier, where the Haardt become the Vosges. The combination of climatic advantage and generally light, sandy soils results in many of Germany's best dry wines, and some remarkable dessert wines, too. In spite of the proximity to Alsace they have a completely different style to the wines from that area. Here the emphasis is firmly on fresh aromas and crisp acidity, rather than the savoury vinosity of Alsace – not that savoury vinosity is out of reach.

With almost 24,000 hectares of vineyards, the Pfalz is second only to Rheinhessen in size, though it often produces slightly more wine due to the intensive, highly mechanized viticulture practised in the flat vineyards down on the Rhine plain. Here it is possible to produce bulk wines more efficiently than anywhere else in Germany. However, it is with wines at the opposite end of the quality scale that the Pfalz has been attracting all the attention of late.

Traditionally, quality-wine production was associated with the Mittelhaardt area of the Pfalz, centred around the town of Bad Dürkheim. Here "the three Bs" – the great estates of Dr. von Bassermann-Jordan, Reichsrat von Buhl, and Dr. Bürklin-Wolf – and a clutch of smaller estates, established the region's reputation for noble Rieslings during the nineteenth and early twentieth centuries. At this time, the rest of the region, notably the southerly Südliche Weinstrasse, was seen as fit for producing nothing more than quaffing wines. The new generation has broken this mould, proving that the north and the south of the region can produce impressive white wines. Many of the best examples are from varieties that are relatively recent introductions: the Riesling crossings, Rieslaner and Scheurebe; the white Pinots (Weisser Burgunder and Grauer Burgunder); and the red Spätburgunder, St Laurent, and Dornfelder. Thankfully, the leading producers of the Mittelhaardt have responded to this challenge by redoubling their efforts, and quality competition is now intense.

The enterprise of the best young growers of the Südliche Weinstrasse made the owners of the great estates of the Mittelhaardt realize that their wines were not as good as they ought to have been. In the mid-1990s, this all began to change, as complacency gave way to energy, and a clear commitment to quality.

The VDP's vineyard classification was embraced fervently by almost all the top estates, and the *grosses gewächs* Rieslings and Pinot Noirs, and not just from the Mittelhaardt, are now among the greatest wines of Germany. Indeed, nowhere else in Germany can powerful, dry Rieslings be produced with such consistency.

The Pfalz may lack the dramatic scenery of the Mosel, Rheingau, or Mittelrhein, but its gently undulating, verdant country makes it one of the most charming of all Germany's winegrowing regions. The Pfälzer are renowned for their love of food and wine. This finds its fullest expression at Bad Dürkheim's famous *Wurstmarkt* ("sausage fair"), in September, where leading winemakers rub shoulders with local farmers while enjoying a *schoppen* (half-litre glass) of wine.

Outstanding Pfalz Vineyards

Birkweiler Kastanienbusch The only Pfalz site with stony, reddish soil which retains warmth and gives subtly aromatic Rieslings, with a silky acidity. Most important owners: Rebholz, Wehrheim.

Burrweiler Schäwer The Schäwer is the only vineyard in the region with a slate soil like that of the Mosel. This results in exceptionally refined, peachy Rieslings that are atypical for the region. Most important owner: Messmer.

Deidesheimer Grainhübel/Hohenmorgen/Kalkofen/Kieselberg/Langenmorgen/Leinhöhle/Maushöhle This cluster of small sites guarantees Deidesheim's excellent reputation as a producer of rich, succulent Rieslings. Traditionally, the Grainhübel is regarded as being the greatest of them. Like the Kalkofen, it has a limestone subsoil. The wines from these vineyards are slow to develop but long-lived. With its very light, sandy soil, the Leinhöhle is particularly sensitive to drought in hot years. Most important owners: Bassermann-Jordan, Josef Biffar, Reichsrat von Buhl, Bürklin-Wolf, Deinhard, Georg Siben, Werlé, W. G. Deidesheim.

Dürkheimer Michelsberg/Spielberg/Ungsteiner Herrenberg These three fine vineyards occupy the southern, western, and eastern side of a hill immediately to the north of Bad Dürkheim. The stony, limestone soil and excellent exposition result in intense, beautifully balanced Rieslings particularly well-suited to vinification in the dry style. Most important owners: Darting, Pfeffingen, Fitz-Ritter, Karl Schaefer.

Duttweiler Kalkberg Southeast of Neustadt, this light sand and loam site can give excellent Riesling and Pinot Noir. Most important owner: Bergdolt.

Forster Freundstück/Jesuitengarten/Kirchenstück/Pechstein/Ungeheuer The great vineyards of Forst occupy one of the most sheltered positions in the region. This, together with a light, quickly warmed topsoil and deep, water-retentive subsoil, results in remarkable Rieslings. Those from the Pechstein (so named because of the abundance of basalt in its top soil) are the raciest; those from the Ungeheuer are rich and fleshy; while the Jesuitengarten and Kirchenstück give wines with the greatest elegance. They have been recognized as the noblest sites of the Pfalz since at least the first half of the nineteenth century. Most important owners: Bassermann-Jordan, Reichsrat von Buhl, Bürklin-Wolf, Mosbacher, Eugen Müller, Karl Schefer, Deinhard, W. G. Forst, J. L. Wolf.

Gimmeldinger Mandelgarten Just north of Neustadt, this vineyard is of weathered sandstone, and is a *grosses gewächs* for Christmann (*q.v.*).

Haardter Bürgergarten/Herrenletten/Herzog The best sites of Haardt, close to Neustadt, have unusually deep and heavy soils for the Pfalz, which yield powerful wines with a firm, acidic structure and long ageing potential. At high levels of ripeness they can possess a ravishing apricot and pineapple bouquet. Most important owners: Müller-Catoir, Weegmüller.

Kallstadter Annaberg/Saumagen The limestone soil of the Saumagen and the southern exposition in the best part of this site make for extremely powerful, highly structured wines, which need years of ageing for the characteristic passion-fruit aroma to develop fully. The Saumagen lies in a kind of amphitheatre and is an extremely warm site. The Annaberg wines are less expansive, but in hot years they can possess a marvellous elegance, and their gunflint aroma is most distinctive. Most important owners: Henninger IV, Koehler-Ruprecht.

Königsbacher Idig Medium-bodied wines with a family resemblance to those of Ruppertsberg, but a slightly firmer structure. Most important owner: Christmann.

Mussbacher Eselshaut The very light, sandy soil here gives full-bodied wines with extravagant aromas, including exotic fruit notes. Most important owner: Müller-Catoir.

Ruppertsberger Gaisböhl/Nussbien/Reiterpfad The large area of good vineyards on the western side of Ruppertsberg generally yields Rieslings with pronounced floral aromas, which are charming from a very early age. Those from the Reiterpfad and Nussbien tend to be deeper and more complex. Most important owners: Bassermann-Jordan, Biffar, Reichsrat von Buhl, Bürklin-Wolf, Christmann, Deinhard, Werlé.

Siebeldinger im Sonnenschein The name says it all: a stony, sandy site bathed in sunshine. A top vineyard for Rebholz and Wilhelmshof.

Ungsteiner Weilberg This well-exposed site gives extremely typical, juicy, aromatic Pfalz Rieslings, which show well from their early youth, but will also age well. Most important owner: Pfeffingen.

Wachenheimer Belz/Goldbächel/Gerümpel/Rechbächel The top vineyards of Wachenheim yields Rieslings that combine the racy elegance of the Rheingau with the richness of the Pfalz. The Wachenheimer dry wines are every bit as impressive as the famous dessert wines. Most important owners: Biffar, Bürklin-Wolf (including the Rechbächel monopoly), J. L. Wolf.

Leading Pfalz Producers

Weingut Dr. von Bassermann-Jordan ☆☆☆–☆☆☆☆
Deidesheim. www.bassermann-jordan.de
Following the death of Dr. Ludwig von Basserman-Jordan in 1995, this famous and historic estate has passed to his daughter and widow. Since the early eighteenth century, when founder Andreas Jordan made the first vineyard-designated wines and the first Auslese in the region, this estate has been one of the most consistent producers of fine Pfalz Rieslings from superb vineyards in Deidesheim, Forst, and Ruppertsberg.

After an uneven period during the last years of Dr. von Basserman-Jordan's life, the appointment of talented winemaker Ulrich Mell, who made his name at Biffar (*q.v.*), has effected a dramatic return to top form. He put an end to practices such as centrifuging the must and machine-harvesting, and severely reduced the yields, which had been far too high. The stars of the range tend to be the dry Rieslings from the top vineyards, and the exceedingly concentrated nobly sweet wines.

Apart from the wine, the estate is worth a visit for the magnificent collection of Roman artefacts displayed in its cavernous cellars (by appointment only), among the wooden casks where the estate's wines continue to be made.

Weingut Friedrich Becker ☆–☆☆☆
Schweigen. www.weingut-friedrich-becker.de
Fritz Becker is best-known for the high standard of his red wines, principally from the Spätburgunder grape. There are three quality levels of Spätburgunder, the top one being immensely – indeed, excessively – expensive. The whites are more variable, but the dry Chardonnay, Weisser Burgunder, Grauer Burgunder, and Gewürztraminer often have the same combination of heady richness and ripe fruit as the red wines.

Weingut Bergdolt ☆☆–☆☆☆
Duttweiler. www.weingut-bergdolt.de
The loess-loam soils of Rainer Bergdolt's vineyards may set a limit to what he can achieve with the Riesling grape, but his dry Weisser Burgunders are among the finest wines made from this underrated grape in all of Germany. The dry Spätlesen are always beautifully balanced, but the Auslese Trocken can be wildly alcoholic. Few of the wines are barrique-aged, and those that are vinified in barrels are often dominated by the wood. In recent years, Rainer Bergdolt's Spätburgunders, all from Duttweiler Kalkberg, have made a big jump forward. They are made in a robust style, but have gained greatly in finesse since the late 1990s.

Weingut Josef Biffar ☆☆☆
Deidesheim. www.biffar.com
This twelve-hectare estate and the family's candied-fruits company are jointly directed by Gerhard Biffar and his daughter Lilli. With a string of concentrated, beautifully polished, dry, and naturally sweet Rieslings from the top vineyard sites of Deidesheim, Wachenheim, and Ruppertsberg, Biffar was catapulted into the first rank of Pfalz producers at the beginning of the 1990s, after Ulrich Mell was hired as cellarmaster. There were a number of changes of winemaker in the late 1990s and early 2000s, which slightly unsettled quality, but the estate seems back on course.

Weingut Reichsrat von Buhl ☆☆☆☆
Deidesheim. www.reichsrat-von-buhl.de
In the 1980s, this famous estate went through a bad patch; the grapes were harvested early to avoid risk, and yields were high. In the late 1980s, the owner, Freiherr von und zu Gutenberg, who had little interest in wine, leased the property to a group of Japanese investors. By the early 1990s, it was clear that von Buhl was still underperforming, given its portfolio of magnificent vineyards, and, in 1994, a new winemaker was taken on. Frank John had previously worked at Müller-Catoir (*q.v.*), and follows their non-interventionist style. He also severely reduced yields, and is highly selective at harvest. Riesling continues to dominate the vineyard plantings (eighty-eight per cent), but Grauer Burgunder, Spätburgunder, and Scheurebe have been introduced as specialties. A range of basic Rieslings in varied styles has been produced for export markets since 1992, but the best wines are the dry *grosses gewächs* from Forster Kirchenstuck and Pechstein. In suitable years, such as 1994, '96, and '98, John makes spectacular TBA and Eiswein here, and there are also delicious Rieslaner Auslesen among the sweet wines.

Weingut Dr. Bürklin-Wolf ☆☆☆☆
Wachenheim. www.buerklin-wolf.de
With eighty-six hectares of vineyards, this famous estate is one of the largest in Germany in private ownership. After taking over direction of Bürklin-Wolf in 1992, Christian von Guradze, who is married to proprietor Bettina Bürklin,

instituted a programme of radical changes which rapidly restored the estate to the first rank of Pfalz wine producers. Today, only the wines from outstanding sites are sold with vineyard designations, and subtle labelling (and price) differentiates those sites the von Guradzes consider *grand cru* from those they consider *premier cru*. Although Bürklin-Wolf once enjoyed the highest reputation for its Auslese, BA, TBA, and Eiswein dessert wines, the von Guradzes have rather lost interest in the style, preferring instead to focus their energies on their powerful, dry Rieslings.

Weingut Christmann ☆☆–☆☆☆☆
Gimmeldingen

In 1994, Steffen Christmann took over the family estate, and rapidly instituted a Burgundian-style hierarchy of wines. The vineyards are in the lower Mittlehaardt, and, as an ardent proponent of classification in the Pfalz, Christmann has selected his best sites – Ruppertberger Reiterpfad, Königsbacher Idig, and Oelberg – for his *grosses gewächs*. The Rieslings are mostly dry, though Christmann makes Auslesen and higher qualities when conditions permit. Christmann also produces rich, elegant Spätburgunder, but yields are so low as to be scarcely economically viable.

Weingut Kurt Darting ☆☆
Bad Dürkheim

In 1989, the Dartings left the local cooperative and established their own estate. Their wines are always fresh and vividly fruity, if rarely sophisticated. Best are the Rieslings from the Ungsteiner Herrenberg, but there are also excellent Scheurebes and sweet wines from Rieslaner and Muskateller. There is also a range of red wines, but these are of considerably less interest. The Darting wines are best enjoyed young, and have the bonus of being sensibly priced.

Weingut Dr. Deinhard ☆–☆☆
Deidesheim

A well-known estate founded in 1849 by the famous wine-producing Deinhard family of Koblenz. Although the property includes excellent vineyards in Deidesheim and Ruppertsberg, the wines are somewhat lacklustre. The Rieslings are bottled with a fair amount of natural carbon dioxide, giving them some zest when young, but they lack some weight and complexity.

Weingut K. Fitz-Ritter ☆☆
Bad Dürkheim. www.fitz-ritter.com

Konrad Fitz is the eighth generation of his family to run this estate, which, with its fine, classical eighteenth-century mansion (1785) set within a park, contains the largest maidenhair tree (*Ginkgo biloba*) in Germany. The Fitz family also started here (in 1837) one of the oldest Sekt businesses in Germany. Viticulture is close to organic. The modern-style wines are always fresh and fruity. Two-thirds of their vines are Riesling, but there are also some attractive red wines from Pinot Noir and Dornfelder.

Weingut Knipser ☆☆–☆☆☆
Laumersheim

The Knipser brothers have been among the leading figures in the Pfalz's red-wine revolution. Since the late 1980s, they have produced a string of impressively rich, tannic Spätburgunder, St Laurent, and Dornfelder red wines, from the little-known vineyards of Grosskarlbach and Laumersheim. Cabernet Sauvignon and Merlot were planted here in 1991, followed by Syrah in 1994. In general, the Spätburgunder is the best of the red range, and the Bordeaux and Rhône varieties can lack typicity. Their powerful, oak-aged white wines divide critical opinion, and barrique-aged Silvaner will always be a minority taste. However, the dry Rieslings are very good, though their dry Auslesen can be overly alcoholic. Their dessert wines can be magnificent.

Weingut Koehler-Ruprecht ☆☆☆–☆☆☆☆
Kallstadt

Koehler-Ruprecht specializes in two dramatically contrasting styles of wine. The dry Rieslings sold under the Koehler-Ruprecht label are perhaps the most traditionally vinified wines in the region, spending one or two years in wooden casks. Those from the Saumagen possess extraordinary power and ageing potential, and are among the greatest dry wines made in Germany.

The wines sold under the "Philippi" label are all vinified in 50–100% new-oak barriques in a deliberately international style. Among them, the Spätburgunder reds and Weisser Burgunder/Grauer Burgunder whites are frequently impressively concentrated and very well-made. The "Elysium" dessert wine, made from a range of grape varieties and aged for years in new barriques, is a dead ringer for a rather alcoholic Sauternes.

Weingut Lingenfelder ☆–☆☆
Grosskarlbach

This fifteen-hectare family estate produces rich, supple Riesling and Scheurebe in a fairly broad style that appeals to the export markets, which Rainer Lingenfelder has long cultivated. Some of his wines are innovative, such as "Ypsilon", a Silvaner aged in new Pfalz oak ovals. Lingenfelder was one of the pioneers of barrique-aged Spätburgunder in the Pfalz, but skilful vinification could not disguise the fact that the clonal material was not first-rate. The estate has had much deserved success with its juicy, cheerful Dornfelder.

Weingut Lucashof ☆☆
Forst

Klaus Lucas makes clean, crisp Riesling with plenty of character. The emphasis is on dry wines, the best coming from the first-class Pechstein and Ungeheuer sites of Forst.

Weingut Herbert Messmer ☆☆
Burrweiler

Founded in 1960, this twenty-six-hectare estate has long been one of the handful of dynamic properties that have changed the image of the Südliche Weinstrasse from that of being only a bulk wine producer. Gregor Messmer is a talented young winemaker with some remarkable vineyards at his disposal, including the first-class Burrweiler Schäwer, the only Pfalz vineyard with a slate soil like that of the Mosel. The elegant and tangy dry and late-harvested Rieslings from this site are frequently among the finest wines made from this grape in the entire region. The dry Weisser Burgunder and Grauer Burgunder are much more typical Pfalz wines, but equally well-crafted. Messmer's Spätburgunder, St Laurent, and Dornfelder reds are somewhat over-extracted. The best wines are labelled "Selection", which has nothing to do with the Wine Institute's category introduced in 2001.

Weingut Theo Minges ☆–☆☆
Flemlingen

Minges is typical of the Südliche Weinstrasse in producing a wide range of wines from many varieties. The white "Cuvée Libelle" (Weisser Burgunder/Grauer Burgunder/Chardonnay) is very attractive, more so than the more prestigious but woody barrique-aged versions of each separate variety. New oak is also somewhat too prominent on the reds from Spätburgunder and Dornfelder.

Weingut Georg Mosbacher ☆☆☆
Forst

This estate has long been a leading producer of Rieslings from the famous vineyards of Forst. Winemaker Richard Mosbacher is the very soul of modesty, but he sets the highest standards both for dry and dessert wines. Rich aromas, juicy fruit, and bright acidity are the hallmarks of the Mosbacher wines, and 1998 was a resounding success for the dry Rieslings. Mosbacher's daughter Sabine and her husband, Jürgen Düringer, both graduates of Geisenheim wine college, are now in the process of taking control. They have reduced yields even further, but the style of winemaking remains essentially the same.

Weingut Eugen Müller ☆☆–☆☆☆
Forst. www.weingut-eugen-mueller.de

Kurt Müller, now assisted by his son Stephan, owns, among his seventeen hectares of vineyards, the only old vines in Forst's top sites to survive the recent reorganization of the village's vineyards. The resulting wines are big, rich, and muscular. The regular Rieslings can be rather earthy.

Weingut Müller-Catoir ☆☆☆☆
Neustadt

Two complex personalities, owner Heinrich Catoir and winemaker Hans-Günther Schwarz have made this estate the undisputed leader in the Pfalz. (See Müller-Catoir: A Great Pfalz Estate, page 261.)

Weingut Münzberg ☆☆–☆☆☆
Godramstein. www.weingut-muenzberg.de

The Kessler family's estate, close to Landau, makes some of the Pfalz's best dry Weisser Burgunder, Chardonnay (the only white to be barrel-fermented), and Grauer Burgunder. The soils are rather heavy for Riesling, but this variety can be surprisingly fresh in the hands of the Kesslers. Their red wines have also improved dramatically in recent years. Barrique-ageing was introduced in 1989, and in the late 1990s the Spätburgunders gained in concentration.

Weingut Neckerauer ☆
Weissenheim. www.weingut-neckerauer.de

This isn't Riesling territory, as the soils here are sandy loam, and the Neckerauer estate fares better with Pinot varieties such as Grauer Burgunder. The red wines are distinctly patchy, and there can be some very rich sweet wines. But overall, the wines are inconsistent.

Weingut Karl Pfaffmann ☆☆–☆☆☆
Walsheim

Markus Pfaffmann graduated from Geisenheim in 1999, and came to join his father, Helmut, at this thirty-hectare estate.

This is a modern, commercial estate, with most vineyards machine-harvested and grapes vinified in stainless steel. The wines are very well-made, especially the crisp Rieslings and the delicate Gewürztraminer. About one-third of production is of red wine, notably Spätburgunder.

Weingut Pfeffingen ☆☆☆
Bad Dürkheim-Pfeffingen. www.pfeffingen.de

This highly regarded estate gained its reputation under Karl Fuhrmann from the 1950s to the 1970s. The property is now run by his daughter, Doris, one of Germany's leading women winemakers. Riesling dominates in the vineyards, notably the Ungsteiner Herrenberg, but Scheurebe is important, too, and produces juicily rich wines here. Pfeffingen Rieslings, whether dry or naturally sweet, have considerable finesse. Even wines from "off" vintages age long and gracefully.

Weingut Ökonomierat Rebholz ☆☆☆–☆☆☆☆
Sielbeldingen. www.oekonomierat-rebholz.de

The Rebholz family were the quality wine pioneers in the Südliche Weinstrasse, making the first BA and TBA wines in the area, when such rarities were considered the exclusive preserve of the Mittelhaardt. They are far better known, however, for their intense, dry wines. In the earlier 1990s, Hans-Jörg Rebholz's Rieslings could be very austere, but more recent vintages have been brilliant. Of the two *grosses gewächs*, the Kastanienbusch is laced with aromas of aniseed, while the Sonnenschein is more apricotty and opulent. Although Riesling dominates the estate's vineyards, Rebholz also has an excellent reputation for its Weisser Burgunder, Grauer Burgunder, Gewürztraminer, and Muskateller white wines, and Spätburgunder reds (the latter both with and without new oak ageing). All of these wines benefit from a year or two of bottle-ageing to shed their youthful assertiveness. The top wines are designated "R" on the label.

Weingut Karl Schaefer ☆
Bad Dürkheim. www.weingutschaefer.de

A family estate established in 1843, it is run on very traditional lines. Riesling dominates the vineyards, and the wines are fermented slowly in oak casks. After the death of the owner, Dr. Wolf Fleischmann, his daughter took over running the estate, and the wines seem to have lost some flair and concentration.

Weingut Georg Siben Erben ☆☆
Deidesheim

Wolfgang Siben was one of the first Pfalz growers to specialize in dry Rieslings. In 1997 he retired, handing over to his son, Andreas, the eleventh generation of Sibens making wine here. The wines are assertive and less opulent than many Pfalz Rieslings.

Weingut Thomas Siegrist ☆☆
Leinsweiler. www.weingut-siegrist.de

Thomas Siegrist was a pioneer of barrique-aged red wines in the Pfalz, producing his first vintage in 1985. Today, he is closely assisted by his son-in-law, Bruno Schimpf. They have created some red blends, such as "Johann Adam Hausch" (75% Spätburgunder/25% Dornfelder) and "Bergacker" (Spätburgunder/Dornfelder/Cabernet Sauvignon), but in general these are less successful than the complex Spätburgunders. These are ranked according to an in-house star system. The dry white wines were once rather severe, but

Müller-Catoir – A Great Pfalz Estate

The Pfalz's reputation as Germany's most dynamic winegrowing region would be unthinkable without the Müller-Catoir estate. It was founded in 1744 by the Huguenot Catoir family, but only in recent years has it written history. The estate is in Haardt, a suburb of Neustadt an der Weinstrasse. None of the Haardt vineyard sites attracted attention until the arrival, in 1962, of he shy owner of Müller-Catoir, Heinrich Catoir, and his ebullient winemaker, Hans-Günther Schwarz. Since then, they have perfected a dramatic new style of German wine from a palate of grape varieties, making the estate the undisputed number one in the Pfalz.

What is more remarkable about the achievement is that the estate does not own vineyards in the most prestigious villages such as Deidesheim and Forst. Instead they lie close to Neustadt, and have never been that highly regarded. Yet every Müller-Catoir wine, dry or sweet, exhibits a strong personality. The finest of them are unique expressions of the region's generous climate.

Riesling accounts for sixty per cent of the estate's twenty hectares of vineyards and gives some of the richest and most aromatic dry wines made from this noble grape, in the whole of Germany. It is, however, with rare grapes such as Rieslaner and unfashionable ones such as Scheurebe (both crossings of Silvaner and Riesling) that Catoir and Schwarz have made their names. In their hands, Rieslaner gives Auslese and higher-quality wines a scintillating freshness and unctuous richness, while their Scheurebes are lavish and exotic, yet silky and elegant. They each account for nearly ten per cent of the estate's vineyards.

In top vintages, Grauer Burgunder (3%) and Weisser Burgunder (8%) give dry wines as bombastic as the stone façade with which the baroque estate house was fitted at the turn of the century. Muskateller is a ravishingly perfumed dry wine, made only when nature smiles upon this fickle grape. With the 1993 vintage came their first successful Spätburgunder.

If the brilliance of the wines here is not primarily an expression of terroir, then one has to credit the skill of the winemaker. Yet Schwarz is no manipulator. Instead, when most German wineries were becoming ever more crowded with the latest technology and filters, Schwarz argued for minimal intervention. He had no truck with centrifuges, or de-acidification, or with cultivated yeasts, and if possible, fining was avoided, too. Schwarz was similarly exacting in the vineyard: eliminating fertilizers, ploughing the soil, and pruning severely to limit yields. But such practices are costly and time-consuming, so he was fortunate that Heinrich Catoir was willing to support this campaign for quality with his chequebook.

The Müller-Catoir wine style and commitment to quality have inspired an entire generation of young Pfalz wine-growers. Many of the region's leading young winemakers have worked at Müller-Catoir or are advised by Schwarz. Without him, the region's quality renaissance of the past three decades would have been unthinkable.

have gained charm lately, especially the Chardonnay and Weisser Burgunder.

Weingut Weegmüller ☆–☆☆
Neustadt. www.weegmueller-weine.de

The enthusiastic Stephanie Weegmüller is the winemaker here, producing a wide range of wines from many grape varieties and from vineyards scattered across three villages. That makes it hard to discern a consistent style, and some wines seem to lack verve. Haardter Herrenletten produces some very good dry Rieslings as well as Grauer Burgunder. The sweet wines from here are opulent, but a touch heavy.

Weingut Dr. Wehrheim ☆☆–☆☆☆
Birkweiler. www.weingut-wehrheim.de

Karl-Heinz Wehrheim makes some of the best dry Riesling, Weisser Burgunder, and Grauer Burgunder wines in the southern Pfalz. Rich and elegant, the best wines come from the steep slopes and stony, reddish soil of the Birkweiler Kastanienbusch, and from his other *grosses gewächs*, Birkweiler Mandelberg. The Weisser Burgunder is particularly successful here, and the reds are of interest, too. St Laurent was planted here as long ago as 1974, and there is

a Cabernet/Merlot blend called "Carolus", first made in the mid-1990s. It has yet to attain the elegance of the Kastanienbusch Spätburgunder.

Weingut Werlé Erben ☆☆☆
Forst

It is perhaps not surprising that a family which has lived in one of the most beautiful houses of the Pfalz for more than two centuries should be committed unswervingly to its winemaking tradition. Claus and Hardy Werlé make Riesling wines with an aristocratic reserve that makes some modern-style Pfalz wines seem almost uncouth. All of their wines need time to show their true depth and class. The most remarkable of them are those from the outstanding Jesuitengarten and Kirchenstück vineyards of Forst: Rieslings which live up to the legendary reputation of these sites.

Weingut Wilhelmshof ☆☆
Siebeldingen. www.wilhelmshof.de

The Roth family specializes in Sekt production, and makes some of the best sparkling wines in all of the Pfalz. There also worthwhile reds and some full-bodied Weisser Burgunders and Grauer Burgunders from the Im Sonnenschein vineyard.

Weingut J. L. Wolf ☆☆☆
Wachenheim. www.drloosen.de

In 1996, this poor, underperforming estate was taken over by a consortium headed by local businessman Christoph Hindenfeld and Ernst Loosen of the Dr. Loosen estate in Bernkastel, Mosel (*q.v.*). It did not take Loosen long to demonstrate that he is just as skilled at producing deliciously dry Rieslings as he is at making traditional, naturally sweet Mosel Rieslings. The wines, from top sites in Wachenheim, Forst, and Deidesheim, have purity and zest, and even the more basic Rieslings are excellent.

Pfalz Cooperatives

With so many excellent estates in all parts of the Pfalz, there is a diminishing role for the once-powerful cooperatives. At the top level they are still capable of producing good, well-made wine. The best of them are the Winzerverein Forst; Ruppertsberger Winzerverein "Hoheburg"; and Winzergenossenschaft Vier Jahreszeiten in Bad Dürkheim.

Hessische Bergstrasse

With its 450 hectares of vines clinging tenaciously to the terraced hills to the north of Heidelberg, the Hessische Bergstrasse is one of the most beautiful winegrowing regions in Germany. However, since most of its produce is drunk within the region, or sold to weekenders from the many large towns nearby, it is hardly known outside this area of Germany. This is a shame, because the best sites here are capable of giving elegant, sophisticated Rieslings which are of excellent quality.

The steep slopes of the Heppenheimer Steinkopf, the Bensheimer Kalkgasse, and the Streichling are the three top sites of Hessische Bergstrasse. The poor sandstone soil of the Steinkopf gives the most minerally and racy wines; the limestone of the Kalkgasse yielding more substantial, rounder wines; while the Streichling is famed for producing a delicate bouquet and subtlety. On the loess-loam soils of the lower-lying vineyards grow Weisser Burgunder and Grauer Burgunder, producing medium-bodied dry wines comparable with those of northern Baden – not surprisingly, since in effect this region is a continuation of Baden's northernmost vineyards. Müller-Thurgau is the workhorse grape, as in so many other regions of Germany.

Leading Hessische Bergstrasse Producers

Weingut der Stadt Bensheim ☆
Bensheim. www.bensheim.de

The town of Bensheim has a small estate of about thirteen hectares, mainly Riesling. Axel Seiberth has been the director here since 1987, and has stamped his style on the winery. The Rieslings are surprisingly soft, and this is due to the systematic malolactic fermentation to which the wine is subjected. This is unusual in Germany for Riesling. It results in supple wines for immediate drinking, but the wines emerge lacking in verve and typicity. The estate also makes some pleasant Spätburgunder aged in older barriques.

Staatsweingut Bergstrasse ☆–☆☆☆
Bensheim

Officially, this estate is part of the vast state domain of Hessen, based at Kloster Eberbach, but it has always enjoyed a high degree of autonomy. Heinrich Hillenbrand was the third generation of his family to direct the estate since its foundation in 1904, but he retired in 2001. His many achievements include the production of the first TBAs in the region's history in 1971, and its first Eiswein the following year. Today it is dry-style Riesling, Weisser Burgunder, and Grauer Burgunder that dominate the production, but the Eiswein can still be exceptional. Overall, this is the top estate in the region.

Weingut Simon-Bürkle ☆☆
Zwingenberg

This twelve-hectare estate was created by two ambitious young graduates of the Weinsberg wine school, at the beginning of the 1990s. Although the quality is still a little erratic, everything points to this producer becoming one of the quality leaders in the region, both for Riesling and the red St Laurent.

Franken

Eighty kilometres (fifty miles) east of the Rheingau, beyond the city of Frankfurt, the River Main, flowing to join the Rhein at Hochheim, scribbles a huge drunken "W" through the irregular limestone and red marl hills of Franken (Franconia), the northern extremity of Bavaria.

The centre of the region is the baroque city of Würzburg, which also contains the region's most famous vineyard, the Stein, within the city limits, on a slope down to the Main. The name *Stein* was once traditionally borrowed by foreigners to describe Franconian wine generically (as the English shortened Hochheim to "hock" for all Rhein wines). "*Steinwein*" comes in fat, dumpy flagons called *bocksbeutel*, thus distinguishing itself from almost all other German wines, which come in elegant bottles. This is probably the extent of popular knowledge. Franken wine enjoys local popularity, and its consistency and quality are such that drinkers are happy to pay good prices for the wines. This has prevented Franconian wines from becoming better known outside Germany.

The area, extending over 6,000 hectares, is exceptionally diffuse and hard to comprehend. Vineyards are found only on exceptional south-facing slopes. The most important sector is around Würzburg, and is known as the *Maindreieck* (Main triangle). Further east is the Steigerwald, which has heavier soils, and the westerly sector around Bürgstadt has a growing reputation for red wines. The Franconian climate is harsh, and serious frosts are common; the season is too short to achieve regular success with Riesling, though climatic changes in recent years have resulted in a growing number of excellent wines from this variety. Traditionally, however, Franken has made its best wine with Silvaner. Only here, and occasionally on the Rheinfront in Rheinhessen, does this variety make wine of arresting quality. Silvaner, grown in Franken, can produce full-bodied dry wines (and more rarely sweet ones) with a noble breadth and substance. They are sometimes compared with white burgundy, not for their flavour, but for their vinosity and ability to match rich food at the table.

Unfortunately, the Müller-Thurgau has now gained the upper hand, being planted in forty per cent of the vineyards. It can work well, when not overcropped, and makes easy-going, flavourful wines, although it rarely matches the remarkable low-key stylishness of Silvaner. Scheurebe can do better. Bacchus, still planted in twelve per cent of the vineyards, tends to be aggressively aromatic, but it enjoys a local following. Kerner is also too aromatic, although many people find it acceptable. In a ripe year, Rieslaner can produce excellent Auslesen, with the breadth of a Silvaner and the depth of a Riesling. And Rieslaner can also deliver exciting dry wines.

About half the wine is made by cooperatives. Würzburg itself, however, boasts three of the oldest, biggest, and best wine estates in Germany: the Bürgerspital, the Juliusspital, and the Staatlicher Hofkeller. But this mighty trio is being increasingly challenged by the growing ranks of small estates aiming for, and often achieving, the highest quality.

Outstanding Franken Vineyards

Bürgstadter Centgrafenberg The most western, first-class vineyard of Franken is also the warmest, lying on a sheltered south-facing slope in the small basin around the town of Miltenberg. The red-sandstone soil also combines to produce unusually aromatic and racy Franken wines. The Spätburgunder grape plays as important a role as Riesling.

Casteller Schlossberg This precipitously steep slope above the village of Castell is one of the top sites of the Steigerwald. The combination of excellent exposure and the heavy gypsum-marl soil, results in powerful, racy wines. Rieslaner, as well as Riesling and Silvaner, scale the heights here in more senses than one.

Escherndorfer Lump The "tramp" of Escherndorf is one of the most imposing vineyards in Franken; a great amphitheatre of vines in the crook of one of the Main's most dramatic bends. It is particularly renowned for rich, succulent, dry Silvaner.

Frickenhäuser Kapellenberg The finest vineyard of Frickenhäusen is also one of the least-known top sites of Franken. The south-facing slope lies directly adjacent to the bank of the Main. While the wines it produces may not be the most powerful in the area, they have ample fruit and lovely balance.

Homburger Kallmuth The towering wall of vines which forms the famous Kallmuth is one of very few top vineyard sites in Franken not to have been *Flurbereinigt* or reorganized by landscaping. Its wild flora, with a marked southern character, is famous. It was first documented in 1102. The reddish sandstone soil gives richly fruity wines with a powerful minerally character.

Iphöfer Julius-Echter-Berg/Kronsberg The vineyard named after the late-sixteenth-century Prince-Bishop, Julius Echter of Mespelbrunn, is indisputably one of Franken's greatest. Situated at the southwestern tip of the Steigerwald it enjoys optimum exposure, which, together with the gypsum-marl soil, gives wines of enormous power, with a strong, earthy character. The wines from the neighbouring Kronsberg are hardly less imposing.

RandersackererMarsberg/Pfülben/Sonnenstuhl/Teufelskeller The old town of Randersacker is blessed with more fine vineyards than any other in Franken. However much body and richness these wines have, they are less muscular than some other Franken wines. Beautiful balance and a subtle spicy-smoky character are their hallmarks. The differences between these vineyards, all of which have limestone soils, are primarily of exposure. First among equals is the fifteen-hectare Pfülben.

Rödelseer Küchenmeister The town of Rödelsee lies just to the north of Iphofen and its finest site. The Küchenmeister lies directly next to the top sites of its neighbour. The wines are similar in character, but a touch lighter.

Volkacher Ratsherr This imposing hillside vineyard lies only eight kilometres (five miles) north of the famous Escherndorfer Lump and enjoys a similarly favoured location, right next to the River Main. It gives rich, substantial wines with a good acid structure.

Würzburger Abtsleite/Innere Leiste Though less famous than the Würzburger Stein, both these sites enjoy excellent locations and are capable of yielding top-class Riesling and Silvaner wines. Indeed, the Innere Leiste, situated immediately below the Marienburg fortress, yields the town's most powerful wines. What the Abtsleite wines may lack in volume they more than make up for in racy elegance.

Würzburger Stein/Stein-Harfe The Stein and its sub-site the Stein-Harfe (solely owned by the Bürgerspital estate – *q.v.*) cover a slope that extends for more than eight kilometres (five miles), directly northwest of Würzburg. For a long time, the distinctive, smoky note of these wines was explained by the proximity of the main railway line, but since electrification it has been obvious that this character comes, in fact, from the limestone soil. No wines in Franken can excel the finest Rieslings and Silvaners from this site, in elegance or subtlety of fruit – the latter often distinctly citric, even slightly tropical.

Leading Franken Producers

Weingut Bickel-Stumpf
Frickenhausen. www.bickel-stumpf.de
Dry wines, even simple Kabinetts from Silvaner and Müller-

Thurgau, can be delicious here, often more so than the sweeter styles. On the other hand, the nobly sweet wines, such as the 1999 Scheurebe and Rieslaner TBAs, can be excellent. Reimund Stumpf has adopted the new "Classic" and "Selection" system, which will simplify his wine list.

Bürgerspital zum Heiligen Geist ☆–☆☆
Würzburg. www.buergerspital.de
A splendid charity, founded in 1319 for the old people of Würzburg by Johannes von Steren, it is now somewhat overshadowed by the even richer ecclesiastical foundation, the Juliusspital (*q.v.*). It owns 140 hectares, and has more Riesling planted than any other important Franken estate. It also enjoys the greatest share of Würzburg's famous Stein and other good south-facing slopes. The vineyards are 26% Riesling, 21% Silvaner, and 18% Müller-Thurgau; the rest include Kerner, Scheurebe, Spätburgunder, and several new varieties. The specialties of the house include Silvaner, of course, both dry and in a less successful, off-dry style called "Feinherb"; Riesling from the Stein, which doesn't quite live up to expectations; and broad, rich Weisser Burgunder. The wines can be sampled at the huge 500-seater *Weinstube* in the venerable hospital buildings. Quality has been mixed in recent years.

Fürstlich Castell'sches Domänenamt ☆☆–☆☆☆
Castell
Castell is a tiny principality, still complete with its own prince in a palace, and the vineyards and a chain of banks and other properties remain under family ownership. Until 1806, the Castells even had their own private army. The vineyards slope up to perfectly kept oak woods – the prince's other pride. In 1997, the present prince's son, Ferdinand, took over running the estate, and installed a new team prepared to make the changes required to improve quality further. Müller-Thurgau and Silvaner are the most important varieties, as well as Riesling and Rieslaner, the latter producing powerful, lush, and piquant sweet wines. The "Schloss Castell" range cites only variety and vintage on the label; these are attractive wines for early drinking. Far superior are the single-vineyard wines, and the best of these is invariably the Schlossberg. The sweet wines can be exceptional too: Silvaner Eiswein, and BA and TBA from Riesling and Rieslaner.

Weingut Michael Fröhlich ☆–☆☆
Escherndorf. www.weingut-michael-froehlich.de
Michael Fröhlich's fresh, clean wines are among the best in this part of the Main Valley, and the Rieslings are particularly commendable.

Weingut Fürst ☆☆☆–☆☆☆☆
Bürgstadt. www.weingut-rudolf-fuerst.de
Paul Fürst is one of the most talented winemakers in Germany. As well as producing impressive, if austere, dry Rieslings, he also makes some powerful Weisser Burgunder, aged in new oak. But he is best known, and deservedly so, for his majestic red wines: concentrated Spätburgunder and velvety rich Frühburgunder. The best of them are labelled "R", presumably for Reserve. There is also a blend of Spätburgunder and Domina called "Parzifal". This range constitutes the best red wines from Franken.

Juliusspital-Weingut ☆☆☆☆
Würzburg. www.juliusspital.de
This charitable foundation, on a scale even grander than Burgundy's Hospices de Beaune, was founded in 1576 by the Prince-Bishop Julius Echter von Mespelbrunn. With 160 hectares, it is now one of the largest wine estates in Germany, supporting a magnificent hospital and other charitable institutions for the people of Würzburg. Its low-vaulted cellar, 243 metres (800 feet) long, was built in 1699 and still houses casks full of wine. The vineyards are 40% Silvaner, 18% Müller-Thurgau, 18% Riesling. The remainder includes Gewürztraminer, Ruländer, Weisser Burgunder, Muskateller, Scheurebe, Spätburgunder (in Bürgstadt), and several new varieties. Today, the estate, directed by Horst Kolesch, is widely regarded as being the best of the great Würzburg estates. Silvaner appears in many guises, mostly single-vineyard bottlings, and gives vibrantly fruity, elegant wines; while the dry Rieslings demonstrate what this grape is capable of in this region. There is delicious, dry Rieslaner, and some rare BA and TBA from the Stein.

Weingut Fürst Löwenstein ☆☆–☆☆☆
Kreuzwertheim. www.loewenstein.de
After a period in the doldrums, this famous princely estate, which is under the same ownership as the estate in Hallgarten in the Rheingau (*q.v.*), has been enjoying a revival. The most exciting wines are the impressive, traditional-style Silvaners from the precipitous slopes of the exceptional Homburger Kallmuth site. Spätburgunder from the Bürgstadter Centgrafenberg can be spicy and stylish.

Weingut Gerhard Roth ☆–☆☆
Wiesenbronn. www.weingut-roth.de
Gerhard Roth's small estate in the Steigerwald is best-known for its tannic, oaky reds from Spätburgunder and Domina, but its fruity, substantial dry Rieslings deserve to be taken equally seriously.

Weingut Johann Ruck ☆☆☆
Iphofen. www.ruckwein.de
Since the late 1980s, Johann Ruck has been producing some splendid and meticulously made Franken wines. They marry beautifully the earthy and herbal qualities typical of the wines from Iphofen's famous vineyards, with great freshness and racy acidity. In addition to fine dry Riesling and Silvaner, Herr Ruck also makes the most concentrated dry Grauer Burgunder in the region, from old vines in Rödelsee. All his wines can be tasted at the historic estate house in the centre of Iphofen.

Weingut Horst Sauer ☆☆☆–☆☆☆☆☆
Escherndorf
This ten-hectare estate has risen swiftly to become one of the most consistent producers in Franken. The secret to Sauer's success is selective harvesting from the excellent Lump vineyard. The Silvaners are crisp and minerally, and the Rieslings too are racy and pungent. Sauer is extremely proficient at nobly sweet wines, and frequently succeeds in coaxing Silvaner Eiswein and Silvaner or Riesling TBAs from the Lump. Whether dry or ultra-sweet, these are wines of exemplary quality.

Weinbau Egon Schäffer ☆
Escherndorf. www.weingut-schaeffer.de

This miniature three-hectare estate once made seductively rich, dry Silvaners from the slopes of the famous "Lump" (or tramp) vineyard. But in recent years quality seems to have slipped.

Weingut Schmitt's Kinder ☆☆
Randersacker. www.schmitts-kinder.de
This estate was inherited by six sisters and one son in 1917, and rather than divide it up, they agreed to work together: hence the unusual name of this fourteen-hectare estate. Karl Martin Schmitt produces modern-style wines, and isn't afraid to use the latest technology to ensure clean musts. Yet the wines are usually aged in large casks, and quite a few wines are aged in barriques, though I can't say barrique-aged Müller-Thurgau is a particularly rewarding wine. But the Silvaners, even more so than the Rieslings, are brimming with fruit and aroma, very clean and pure in flavour. The Bacchus is rather too opulent, but the Rieslaners can be excellent.

Weingut Graf von Schönborn ☆
Volkach
The Schönborn family, who own a great estate in the Rheingau, also own this thirty-hectare property in Franken, which has been in the family since 1806. For some years the wines have been lacklustre, the dry wines a touch earthy, the sweeter styles rather bland.

Weingut Schloss Sommerhausen ☆–☆☆
Sommerhausen. www.weingut-schloss-sommerhausen.de
The Steinmanns were once hereditary stewards of this estate belonging to the castle at Sommerhausen, and in 1968 they became the owners of this twenty-hectare property. Dry Riesling, Silvaner, and Müller-Thurgau make up the bulk of the production, but Sommerhausen is best known for its wines from the Pinot family of white grapes (Weisser Burgunder, Grauer Burgunder, Auxerrois) and Chardonnay. It also produces a range of sparkling wines, of which the vintage Auxerrois bottling is often the most interesting.

Staatlicher Hofkeller ☆☆–☆☆☆
Würzburg. www.hofkeller.de
The superlative vineyards of the lordly Prince-Bishops of Würzburg, orginating in the twelfth century, and world-famous for its Tiepolo ceilings, are now (since 1816) the Bavarian State Domain. Although the prince's palace, the baroque Residenz, was largely destroyed during World War II, the great cellar beneath survived, and remains one of the most stirring sights in the world of wine. There have been changes in management in recent years, so quality has been somewhat uneven, which is regrettable, given the fine range of vineyards at the winery's disposal. Nonetheless, some of the dry Rieslings and the Rieslaners are object lessons in true Franconian style, balancing high acidity with powerful flavours. The Hofkeller is quite proud of its red wines, from Domina and Frühburgunder as well as Spätburgunder, but they can lack elegance. In 2001, the Hofkeller launched a blended white wine called "Franconia", stylishly packaged and aimed at the export market, since it is bottled in a burgundy bottle rather than the ungainly *bocksbeutel*.

Weingut Josef Störrlein ☆–☆☆☆
Randersacker. www.stoerrlein.de
This small estate has enjoyed a rapid rise since it was created out of nothing by Armin Störrlein in 1970. Störrlein knows precisely the style of wine he likes: entirely dry, yet not too acidic. This approach seems to work better with varieties such as Weisser Burgunder than Silvaner. The best range is labelled "SE". The top Spätburgunder is excessively oaky, but there is a softer, fruitier red blend (from Domina, Spätburgunder, and Pinot Meunier) called "Casparus".

Weingut Hans Wirsching ☆☆–☆☆☆
Iphofen. www.wirsching.de
A family firm since 1630, and now run by the fourteenth generation, this is the largest estate in Iphofen, with seventy hectares of vineyards. Silvaner is the principal variety here, and the best wines, invariably dry, carry the "S" designation. The Rieslings are zesty, and the top bottlings have a strong mineral tone. There are good wines from Scheurebe, Gewürztraminer, and Rieslaner, but not everyone will care for the Grauer Burgunder aged in one-third new Allier barriques. The reds are surprisingly lean in style.

Weingut Zehnthof ☆
Sulzfeld. www.weingut-zehnthof.de
The Luckert family acquired this twelve-hectare property in 1970, and today Wolfgang and Ulrich Luckert make sleek, supple dry wines from a wide range of white grapes (most importantly Silvaner, Müller-Thurgau, Riesling, and Weisser Burgunder) and superb dessert wines when conditions are right. The reds, from Domina and other varieties, can be too oaky and confected.

Württemberg

Three centuries ago, Württemberg was far and away Germany's largest wine-growing region. But wars and disease led to many sites being abandoned, and by 1963 there were only 7,000 hectares in production. Today that figure has risen to 11,250. Like those of Franken, its vineyards are very dispersed, but lie roughly between the cities of Heilbronn and Stuttgart. The region's identity derives from the fact that it is, other than the Ahr, the only one in Germany where red grapes dominate. Here they occupy sixty-two per cent of vineyards, and Württemberg accounts for fully forty per cent of Germany's red wine production.

Unfortunately, the red grape of choice here is the mediocre Trollinger. Visitors find it hard to discern the appeal of this pale, light red, but it has long been a vital part of the local Swabian diet, and is consumed in heroic quantities in the bars and restaurants of Stuttgart. However, there are other red grapes capable of producing more interesting wine. Schwarzriesling is the same as Pinot Meunier and, as one would expect, it doesn't often rise to great heights, but more serious wines are made from Lemberger, Spätburgunder, and Samtrot (a Pinot Meunier mutation).

Riesling is the most important white-wine grape, but gives completely different results compared to those of the Rhein or Mosel Valleys. The continental climate and gypsum-marl soils, which are so well-suited to the red grapes, yield white wines that are full, broad, and earthy. The challenge for winemakers is to give them at least a touch of elegance. The best of these come from steep, terraced vineyards in the Neckar Valley.

Sadly, at present, no wine-growing region in Germany has more unrealized potential than Württemberg. The ease with which wines of solid, everyday quality can be sold within the region seems to prevent more than a handful of winegrowers working for top quality – and recognition. But their ranks are growing, and the best estates are acquiring a solid reputation within Germany, although hardly any of the wines are exported.

The wine research institute at Weinsberg has busied itself creating new red-grape crossings that will give Württemberg wines more body and colour. At present they have been planted with caution, and are used almost entirely as components in a blend. The best red wine estates of Württemberg obtain good results by green-harvesting to ensure optimal maturity, and by getting to grips with the mysteries of barrique-ageing. In the early 1990s, many Württemberg reds were too tannic, too oaky, and too clumsy, but by 2000 many estates had corrected the over-enthusiasms of the past and were making well-balanced wines of character and even elegance.

The region is divided into three *bereiche*. Remstal-Stuttgart has some of the best sites, but the Württembergisches Unterland, which spreads across the Neckar Valley north of Stuttgart to the Bottwar Valley in the east, is by far the largest. And the smallest is the northern zone of Kocher-Jagst-Tauber, which, atypically, specializes in white wine.

Leading Württemberg Producers

Weingut Graf Adelmann ☆☆☆
Kleinbottwar. www.graf-adelmann.com
One of the best-known estates in Württemberg, its bottles are instantly recognizable by their pale-blue and red "lacy" labels, with the name "Brüssele" (after a former owner). The family castle, Burg Schaubeck is an enchanting but venerable stronghold, apparently with Roman origins, owned by the Adelmanns since 1914.

The estate, now run by Graf Michael Adelmann, is best known for its red wines, which, in the right vintage, can be among Germany's best. The most powerful of these are the Lembergers and the "Cuvée Vignette", a blend of Lemberger, Dornfelder, and Pinot grapes. Other *cuvées* include the Lemberger-dominated "Carpe Diem", aged two years in oak, and the softer "Herbst im Park". After some disappointing Rieslings during the early 1990s, considerable changes were made to the vinification of the white wines in favour of more fruit and freshness. Some Auslesen are marked by high alcohol and correspondingly less residual sugar, a style that is an acquired taste.

Adelmann has also created two white wine *cuvées*, of which the better is "Die Mauern von Schaubeck", made from Riesling and Silvaner. In the early 1990s, some of the wines were over-oaked, but these days the barrel-ageing is more skilfully monitored.

Weingut Gerhard Aldinger ☆☆–☆☆☆
Fellbach. www.weingut-aldinger.de
This twenty-hectare estate near Stuttgart is best known for its serious red wines, of which the blended "Cuvée C" is the

---

German Red Wines

Germany is best-known for its unrivalled Rieslings, and that's as it should be. But much of southern Germany enjoys a fairly warm climate, making it suitable not just for the production of dry white wines but of red wines, too. Pinot Noir, which thrives in this kind of climate, is obviously the most suitable and popular variety, but German winemakers yearn for wines with more richness and depth of colour. There are some wines made from the Bordeaux varieties, but there are few places where Cabernet Sauvignon will ripen regularly, and Merlot has never caught on.

The German solution to this has been to invent new varieties, especially at the wine institute at Weisenberg in Württemberg. New varieties such as Dornfelder and Domina have caught on, and a whole new wave of dark-coloured and dense crossings is coming on stream. The problem is that they contribute colour and tannin, but lack elegance. That is why most growers who have planted grapes such as Domina and Cabernet Cubin tend to use them for blending.

However, southern Germany has indigenous varieties that can give perfectly acceptable red wines on their own. Württemberg's Trollinger produces pallid wines with zero international appeal, but Lemberger, Schwarzriesling (Pinot Meunier), and Samtrot are all capable of giving lively, characterful red wines. If Californian red-wine producers have to struggle with "tannin management", their German counterparts must master "acidity management", but by picking at optimal ripeness it is perfectly possible, as the best winemakers have shown, to produce well-balanced red wines with depth of flavour and personality. It is more than a matter of simple climate, though, as the reds of the Ahr, near Bonn, can witness.

Organizations that have helped promote the best German reds are the Barrique Forum and, in Württemberg, the Hades group.

---

most impressive. This is a spicy, Bordeaux-style wine, aged for sixteen months in new barriques. Its white counterparts are "Cuvée S", a barrique-fermented Sauvignon Blanc from the Aldinger's monopoly site, Untertürkheimer Gips; and "Cuvée A", a bizarre blend of Riesling and Gewürztraminer, aged in new barriques. But it's the stylish reds that have made Aldinger's reputation.

Weingut Amalienhof ☆
Heilbronn. www.weingut-amalienhof.de
Since taking over the estate, with its monopoly Beilsteiner Steinberg site, in 1969, the Strecker family has built up a very successful property. The Rieslings are cleanly made, but better still are the traditionally vinified Lemberger and Samtrot red wines. In the late 1990s, the Streckers introduced a new Bordeaux-style *cuvée* called "Bariton".

Gräf von Bentzel-Sturmfeder ☆–☆☆
Ilsfeld-Schozach. www.sturmfeder.de
This is an estate with fourteenth century origins and eighteenth century cellars. Two-thirds of production here are of red wine, which is given prolonged cask-ageing. Lemberger and Samtrot are usually the most impressive wines. The Rieslings are rather broad and lack zest. The cellarmaster of thirty years, Hermann Blankenhorn, has recently retired, and a new team is in place, which may lead to improvements in quality. The wines last well, even when the acidity is relatively low, with barrel-ageing giving them stability.

Weingut Ernst Dautel ☆☆–☆☆☆
Bönnigheim. www.weingut-dautel.de

The Dautels have been grape farmers since the sixteenth century, but it was only in 1978 that Ernst Dautel withdrew from the local cooperative and began producing his own wines. Over the years he has established himself as one of the region's top winemakers. It is Dautel's red wines that have made the strongest impression. He has been using small oak barrels since 1986, employing oak from various countries. The simpler Spätburgunders lack interest, but at the top level, especially the reserve bottling labelled "S", the wine is truly sumptuous, with a firm, tannic finish. In 1995, Dautel introduced a blend called "Kreation" from Merlot, Cabernet Sauvignon, and Lemberger, the latter variety contributing a good acidic backbone to the wine. The pure Lemberger is fine, too. The Rieslings are surprisingly vigorous, and the Weisser Burgunder is preferable to the over-oaked Chardonnay.

Weingut Drautz-Able ☆☆
Heilbronn

Christel Able, and her brother Richard Drautz, run this eighteen-hectare estate, which produces an enormous range of wines. Although Riesling and Trollinger account for more than half the production, it is the powerful Lembergers aged in new oak, which have rightly attracted the most attention. There is also a complex blend called "Jodokus", formed from Cabernet Sauvignon and Lemberger, and aged two years in new oak. The white wines are good, but not spectacular. The barrique-aged Riesling is to be avoided.

Weingut Jürgen Ellwanger ☆☆
Winterbach. www.weingut-ellwanger.de

At this estate, east of Stuttgart, Jürgen Ellwanger cultivates twenty hectares, planted with a wide range of varieties. He is a fan of new oak, German as well as French, but wines such as "Nicodemus Candidus", a barrique-aged Kerner, are only for devotees of woodiness. The reds are more impressive, especially the fruity if tannic Zweigelt; the supple Dornfelder; an oaky Merlot; and the peppery, oak-aged Lemberger. The estate's Rieslings are rather less impressive.

Weingärtnergenossenschaft Grantschen ☆–☆☆
Grantschen. www.grantschen.de

This impressive cooperative has 200 members and offers a huge range of wines. The whites are disappointing, but two-thirds of the production is red wine. There's a fine, well-structured barrique-aged Lemberger, but the top wine is the "Grandor", Lemberger aged in new oak: a dense, peppery wine with excellent fruit.

Weingut Karl Haidle ☆☆–☆☆☆
Kernen-Stetten. www.weingut-karl-haidle.de

If Hans Haidle's estate is not better known in Württemberg, it is because he is a white-wine specialist in a region where red wines grab most of the limelight. His dry Rieslings and Weisser Burgunder are among the best in the region. The reds are by no means of lesser quality. They include a plummy Zweigelt, a herbal, barrique-aged Lemberger, and some elegant Spätburgunder.

Weingut Heinrich ☆–☆☆
Heilbronn. www.weingut-heinrich.de

Martin Heinrich focuses on Rieslings and an oaky red wine, which have attracted a good deal of attention. At the top of the range are the Lembergers and the powerful "Wollendieb" *cuvée*.

Schlossgut Hohenbeilstein ☆
Beilstein. www.schlossgut-hohenbeilstein.de

Hartmann Dippon took over the family estate in 1987, and promptly converted it to organic viticulture. Red wine remains the heart of the wide range, the best examples being made from the Spätburgunder grape. However, many of the reds, including Lemberger, seem to lack the fruit necessary to support the barrique-ageing.

Weingut Fürst zu Hohenlohe-Oehringen ☆–☆☆
Oehringen. www.verrenberg.de

A princely estate since the fourteenth century, with seventeenth century cellars, which even contains a cask dated 1702). The monopoly Verrenberg site is unusual in being a single sweep of vines, producing mostly dry whites. But the estate is best-known for its red wines, and barriques were first used here in 1983. There are three red-wine *cuvées*, of which the best-known is the somewhat jammy "Ex Flammis Orior".

Weingut Burg Hornberg ☆☆
Neckarzimmern. www.burg-hornberg.de

Baron Dajo von Gemmingen-Hornberg owns what may be the oldest wine estate in Württemberg, although it has only been in the hands of his family since the seventeenth century. Riesling is important here, occupying one-third of the vineyard, but there is also a good deal of Weisser Burgunder. The wines are made by traditional methods, and the best are full-bodied and impressive.

Weingut des Grafen Neipperg ☆☆–☆☆☆
Schwaigern

Documents prove the Neipperg family has been making wine here since 1248, shortly after the building of Burg Neipperg, the original castle. Two sites are monopoly vineyards: Schwaigener Ruthe, which is terraced; and Neipperger Schlossberg around the ruinous castle. There is a story that it was the Neippergs who introduced Lemberger to make red wine of colour and tannin. Graf von Neipperg does not believe it is true, but what is certain is that Lemberger came here from Austria, where it is known as Blaufränkisch, in the seventeenth century. It remains a specialty of the estate.

Their other specialty is spicy Traminer. The Rieslings, which have high acidity, are well thought of, and there is some delicious Gelber Muskateller. The best Lembergers are the single-vineyard bottlings from Ruthe and Schlossberg, and the oaked Samtrot is plump and attractive. Nobly sweet wines are rare, but occasionally Graf von Neipperg makes TBA from Gelber Muskateller. The Neippergs are also the owners of properties in St-Emilion, notably Château Canon-la-Gaffelière and La Mondotte, which are run by Stephan von Neipperg.

Weingut Albrecht Schwegler ☆☆–☆☆☆
Korb

It would be ridiculous to include an estate of such miniscule size (1.5 hectares) in a work like this, were it not for the fact that Albrecht Schwegler's rich, concentrated "Granat" is one of the finest red wines in Württemberg. It is mostly Merlot. Other *cuvées* are "Beryll" (Lemberger and Zweigelt), and "Saphir" (Merlot and Zweigelt). When, in 2000, conditions permitted a TBA to be made from grapes picked at 316 Oechsle, Schwegler appropriately bottled it under the name of "Monster".

Weingut Sonnenhof ☆☆
Vaihingen-Enz. www.weingutsonnenhof.de
This thirty-hectare estate's vineyards are mostly on steep slopes north of Stuttgart. Most of the wines are red, and the range includes an elegant oaked Lemberger.

Staatsweingut Weinsberg ☆
Weinsberg. www.lvwo.de
Founded in 1868 by Karl von Württemberg as the Royal Wine School, this estate is still attached to one of Germany's leading wine colleges. Riesling is the most important grape, with twenty per cent of the vineyard area, but Weinsberg is best-known for its red wines, which are made both in traditional and oak-aged styles. Many new crossings have been developed here, and some of them are bottled by the college as varietal wines. Among the more appealing of the traditional reds are the Clevner (Frühburgunder) and the Lemberger.

Weingut Wöhrwag ☆☆☆
Untertürkheim
With the entire Untertürkheimer Herzogenberg vineyard site at his disposal, Hans-Peter Wöhrwag has succeeded in making some of the finest Rieslings in Württemberg in recent years. They are atypical, in the sense that they are lean and racy rather than broad. They combine finesse and power. Wöhrwag tries to make Eiswein every year, and usually succeeds. There are two red *cuvées*, of which the better is "Philipp", a blend of Lemberger and Spätburgunder. Wöhrwag is one of the few winemakers in Germany to use must concentration – and admit to it.

Weingut des Hauses Württemberg Hofkammerkellerei ☆☆
Schloss Monrepos. Ludwigsburg. www.hofkammer.de
Founded in 1677, this forty-hectare estate is still in the hands of the dukes of Württemberg. They own some good sites: Riesling from Untertürkheimner Mönchberg tends to be rich and assertive, while the best Spätburgunder comes from the terraced Mundelsheimer Käsberg.

Baden

Like the Pfalz, Baden is gifted with a relatively balmy climate that makes it ideal territory for a whole range of wines, especially the Pinot varieties. By rights, it should be enjoying international renown – but it isn't. Its 16,000 hectares of vineyards, across the Rhein from Alsace, have undergone nothing other than a revolution in recent years: they have been almost entirely rationalized and remodelled by *flurbereinigung* and have doubled in size.

It is Germany's warmest (although not necessarily its sunniest) wine region, with correspondingly ripe, high-alcohol, and lower in acidity wines, in fact, the diametric opposite of Mosels in style and function. Baden produces good mealtime wines that have a warm vinosity that approaches the French style. It is the choice of grape varieties and the taste for a trace of sweetness that distinguishes them from Alsace wines. The difference is reinforced by a slightly less favourable climate than the suntrap of the Vosges foothills.

Eighty per cent of Baden's vineyards lie in a 130-kilometre (eighty mile) strip running from northeast to southwest, from Baden Baden to Basel, in the foothills of the Black Forest where it meets the Rhein Valley. Here the most important sub-regions, from north to south, are Ortenau (of which one quarter is planted with Riesling); Breisgau; the sun-drenched volcanic Kaiserstuhl; Tuniberg; and the Chasselas-dominated Markgräflerland.

The balance is of purely local importance. The vineyards lie southeast on the banks of the Bodensee (alias Lake Constance), north of Baden in the minor regions of the Kraichgau and Badischer Bergstrasse, respectively south and north of Heidelberg (but now united in one Bereich with both names), and far north on the border of Franken, a little region known logically enough as Bereich Badisches Frankenland. The main thrust of Baden viticulture is thus along the Rhein, from where it leaves the Bodensee to where it enters the Pfalz.

Baden is, even more than the southern Pfalz, the land of the cooperative, handling the production from 28,000 growers. 120 cooperatives process nearly seventy-five per cent of the crop, and half of all their output finds its way to the huge Badischer Winzerkeller central cellars in Breisach on the Rhein. This mega-cooperative bottles some 400–500 different types of wine. Baden has no powerful preference for one grape variety but the Müller-Thurgau has proved to be the workhorse, with twenty-six per cent of the vineyard area. Perhaps surprisingly, Spätburgunder for red and light rosé (*Weissherbst*) is now the most widely planted variety with thirty-two per cent. Then come Ruländer/Grauer Burgunder (Pinot Gris), Gutedel (Chasselas), Riesling, Silvaner, Weisser Burgunder, and Gewürztraminer. Baden's taste is clearly not for the highly aromatic new varieties, as the vast majority of its white wines are made from relatively "neutral" grapes. The best wine, however, is made from Riesling, Weisser Burgunder, and Grauer Burgunder.

Two factors account for the failure of Baden to punch its weight, especially on the international market. The first is the domination of cooperatives, most of which cater to a local market, and are reluctant to create products that might enjoy a wider appeal. Secondly, there is an over-proliferation of wine styles. It is not uncommon for a cooperative to offer ten or more different Spätburgunders – dry, lightly sweet, rosé, barrique-aged, and different quality levels of each style – which adds up to a marketing nightmare, whatever the quality of the wine. Those producers, such as Johner and Huber, who have trimmed down the range and committed themselves to high quality – justifiably charge high prices, which the domestic, but not the international, market is prepared to pay.

Outstanding Baden Vineyards

Achkarrer Schlossberg The steep slopes and stony, volcanic tuff soil of this site result in dry Weisser Burgunder and Grauer Burgunder wines that perfectly marry power with elegance.

Durbacher Plauelrain/Kapellenberg/Olberg/Schlossberg/ Schloss Grohl/Steinberg The south-facing vineyards in the Durbach Valley are some of the steepest in all Baden, and their granitic soil is ideal for Riesling, Scheurebe, and Gewürztraminer. The Plauelrain is the largest and best-known of these excellent sites.

Ihringer Winklerberg The steep, terraced Winklerberg at the southwestern tip of the Kaiserstuhl is the warmest vineyard in all of Germany. The volcanic tuff soil results in full-bodied, minerally, dry Grauer Burgunder and red Spätburgunder wines that belong to the finest Baden has to offer. The vineyard was expanded threefold in 1971 to its present 150 hectares, so quality can be inconsistent.

Neuweier Mauerberg/Schlossberg Close to Baden-Baden at the northern end of the Ortenau lie the terraced hillsides which form these fine south-facing sites. The Rieslings from here are intense and elegant, needing several years of ageing to show their best.

Oberrotweiler Eichberg/Henkenberg/Kirchberg The town of Oberrotweil, situated on the western flank of the Kaiserstuhl, boasts three first-class sites, all of which give impressively rich, firmly structured, dry Weisser Burgunder and Grauer Burgunder wines.

Ortenberger Schlossberg The narrow terraces of this small site, with poor granitic soil, yield perhaps the most intensely minerally Rieslings of the Ortenau. In the sole ownership of the Schloss Ortenberg estate.

Zell-Weierbacher Abtsberg The best of the vineyards to the east of the town of Offenburg, the Abtsberg yields some of the richest wines in the Ortenau. Riesling, Grauer Burgunder, and Gewürztraminer give the best results.

Leading Baden Producers

Weingut Abril ☆
Bischoffingen. www.abril.de
Hans Friedrich Abril's seven-hectare estate is a reliable source for full-bodied, dry Weisser Burgunder and Grauer Burgunder wines. Some interesting Spätburgunder, too.

Winzergenossenschaft Achkarren ☆
Achkarren
The 320 growers of this co-op produce a wide range from some of the best sites of the Kaiserstuhl. Grauer Burgunder can be rather good, if sometimes alarmingly high in alcohol.

Weingut Bercher ☆☆☆
Burkheim
Eckhardt Bercher and his brother, Rainer, run one of Baden's finest estates from an imposing seventeenth-century house in the beautifully preserved old town of Burkheim. Whether it is a simple Müller-Thurgau, sleek, dry Riesling Kabinett, or massive Weisser Burgunder Auslese Trocken, their white wines are of a uniformly high standard. Since the late 1980s they have also made superb oak-aged Spätburgunders that are among Germany's finest red wines. Although most of the estate's wines are drunk shortly after release, everything of Spätlese or higher quality will benefit from at least five years of ageing. This is an estate where it is really possible to speak of a successful marriage of tradition and innovation. The Berchers are masters of their trade, so these are wines that can be bought and enjoyed with complete confidence.

Weingut Bercher-Schmidt ☆☆–☆☆☆
Oberrotweil
Franz Schmidt has made a point of locating the original, and best, parcels in the much-enlarged vineyards of the Kaiserstuhl. Wines sourced from them are identified with a star system on his labels. The white wines are fresh and attractive, and see no oak. Schmidt has made great strides with the Spätburgunder and has planted French clones to increase quality further. The nobly sweet wines, such as the 2001 Muskateller TBA, can be splendid.

Weingut Blankenhorn ☆☆
Schliengen. www.gutedel.de
Since taking over the family estate in 1989, Rosemarie Blankenhorn has restructured it and switched to organic viticulture. The estate is best-known for its Gutedel, but there are also sound dry whites from Grauer Burgunder, Weisser Burgunder, and Müller-Thurgau. The whites are distinctly better than the reds.

Weingut Duijn ☆☆–☆☆☆
Bühl-Kappelwindeck. www.weingut-jacob.duijn.de
Dutchman Jacob Duijn, a former sommelier, specializes almost exclusively in high-priced Pinot Noir, aged mostly in new barriques, for up to twenty-one months.

Winzergenossenschaft Durbach ☆☆
Durbach. www.durbacher.de
One of the best cooperatives in Germany, WG Durbach specializes in dry Rieslings and Spätburgunder. The slopes of Durbach are ideal territory for Riesling, and most of them are cultivated by the cooperative's 320 members. Sauvignon Blanc, a rarity in Baden, is a specialty here, and can be very good.

Weingut Freiherr von und zu Franckenstein ☆
Offenburg
This estate's director/winemaker, Hubert Doll, produces juicy, elegant dry Rieslings, Grauer Burgunders and Gewürztraminers from fourteen hectares of vines on the granitic slopes of Zell-Weierbach and Berghaupten in the Ortenau.

Weingut Freiherr von Gleichenstein ☆☆
Oberrotweil. www.gleichenstein.de
This twenty-four hectare estate focuses on dry white wines, which are full-bodied and rich. Quality, always sound, is set to increase after the hiring, in 1999, of a new cellarmaster, Odin Bauer.

Weingut Dr. Heger ☆☆☆☆
Ihringen. www.heger-weine.de
Founded in 1935 by the country doctor Dr. Max Heger, this

estate has grown rapidly in extent and reputation. Thanks to the efforts of Dr. Heger's grandson, the dynamic Joachim Heger, it has become the best-known wine estate in Baden. This fame is primarily due to the powerful, dry Weisser Burgunder and Grauer Burgunder whites, the best of which see just a whiff of new oak. Other white varieties, such as Muskateller and Silvaner, even Riesling, can be extremely good here. During the 1990s, the estate's Spätburgunders, aged in new oak, also attracted a good deal of attention. They may not be the silkiest or most elegant Pinot Noirs in Germany, but for concentration they are hard to beat.

In 1997, Heger bought the sixteen-hectare Fischer estate in Bottingen, which in effect doubled the vineyards at his disposal. Top wines bear the "Dr. Heger" label; wines from lesser or leased vineyards are bottled as "Weinhaus Joachim Heger" and can also be of excellent quality.

Weingut Reichsgraf und Marquis zu Hoensbroech ☆–☆☆
Angelbachtal-Michelfeld

Ageing German Wines

Good-quality German wines have a much longer life span, and benefit much more from being kept in bottle than fashion suggests or most people suppose. This does not apply, of course, to the cheap blends and the major brands, which are specifically intended to be ready to drink within months of being bottled. With the enormous crops (and hence the high water content) of these wines, there is, indeed, no gain from keeping bottles more than a few months.

But almost all the superior-grade (QmP) Rieslings, delectable as they may taste in their flowery and fruity youth, have the potential to gain another dimension of flavour with maturity. When they are first offered for sale, they are at their most brisk and lively, with acidity and fruitiness often tending to cancel each other out in a generally tingling and exciting effect. Some fine wines (particularly Rieslings) at this stage have remarkably little aroma. Sometimes, after a year or two in bottle, the first rapture goes away without more mature flavours taking its place; the wine you bought with enthusiasm seems to be letting you down. Be patient. The subtle alchemy takes longer. It may be four or five years before the mingled savours of citrus and spice and oil emerge. The pale colour of a young Riesling will gradually evolve into a brilliant yellow-gold, and the aromas will become more honeyed and complex.

Each vintage has its own time span, but as a generalization, Kabinett wines from a first-rate grower need at least three years in bottle, and may improve for seven or eight; Spätlesen will improve for anything from four to ten years; and Auslesen and upwards will benefit from five or six years up to twenty or even more. The highly concentrated sweet wines – Eiswein, BA, and TBA – are more or less indestructible, but are usually at their peak at twenty-five years.

Riesling is the most age-worthy of German wines, but varieties such as Scheurebe and Rieslaner will also improve with bottle-age. Until the 1980s, red wines were almost always made for immediate consumption, but with the emergence of more concentrated wines in the 1980s, as well as a tendency to give red wines additional structure by ageing them in barriques, a good Spätburgunder from the Pfalz, Franken, or Baden can age for up to ten years.

Of Flemish origin, the Hoensbroechs have been in Germany since the seventeenth century, although this estate just south of Heidelberg is of much more recent origin. Their best wine is usually the powerful, dry Weisser Burgunder. The estate also has some red varieties, notably Lemberger and Schwarzriesling, more commonly encountered in Württemberg.

Weingut Bernhard Huber ☆☆☆
Malterdingen

Since leaving the local cooperative in 1987, Bernhard Huber has swiftly acquired an excellent reputation for his Spätburgunder. There are four *cuvées*, and the best of these – the "R" for reserve bottlings – are among Germany's finest red wines. His new-oaked "Malterer" is an idiosyncratic dry white (a blend of Pinot Blanc and the obscure local crossing Freisamer) with considerable character – more than the powerful but very oaky Chardonnay.

Weingut Karl H. Johner ☆☆☆
Bischoffingen. www.johner.de

In ten years, Karl Heinz Johner has not only built this estate up from scratch, but also made it one of Baden's most successful quality producers. No one has done more in Baden to simplify the range of wines on offer.

Almost all the wines are oak-aged dry varietals, and the best of them are reserve bottlings designated "SJ" (Selektion Johner). The finest wines are usually the Weisser Burgunder dry whites and Spätburgunder reds. Yields are kept very low, so the wines are concentrated and powerful, with sufficient structure to absorb the oak-ageing.

The oak exposure has, in any case, diminished: Johner used to age some of his wines entirely in new oak, but fifty per cent is more usual nowadays. Johner is unquestionably the most successful of the international-style producers of Baden.

Weingut Franz Keller/Schwarzer Adler ☆☆–☆☆☆
Oberbergen. www.franz-keller.de

For many years, Franz Keller has been a strong opponent of *süssreserve*; all his wines are allowed to ferment to dryness or come to a natural halt. Barrique-ageing has also been a feature for some years, with a number of wines being sold (at a very high price) as *tafelwein*.

The best place to sample the wines is at the family's "Schwarzer Adler" restaurant, one of the best in Baden, although it's easy to be tempted by its magnificent list of French wines. Today, Franz Keller's son, Fritz, runs the estate, has constructed expensive new subterranean cellars, and given the wines a fresher, more modern style. Production is considerably expanded by the purchase of grapes from neighbouring properties.

Winzergenossenschaft Königsschaffhausen ☆–☆☆☆
Königsschaffhausen. www.koenigsschaffhauser-wein.de

This Kaiserstuhl cooperative has an excellent reputation for its majestic sweet wines, and was the first Baden producer to market an Eiswein (in 1962). The Ruländer TBAs are especially fine. But no producer can survive on the basis of sweet wines alone, and Königsschaffhausen has also won acclaim for its dry wines from Weisser Burgunder, Grauer Burgunder, and Spätburgunder.

Unlike many cooperatives, this one soon mastered the use of barriques, and produces some balanced and long-lived oak-aged wines, white as well as red.

Weingut Andreas Laible ✩✩–✩✩✩✩
Durbach

No self-publicist, Andreas Laible's winemaking talents only came to the attention of a wider public during the 1990s. His elegant, intensely fruity, dry and naturally sweet Rieslings have almost Mosel-like character, being intense and racy. The top dry Riesling is labelled "Achat". Just as impressive are his powerful Scheurebe and Traminer Auslese, and higher *Prädikat* dessert wines, which are among Baden's finest wines.

Weingut Lämmlin-Schindler ✩✩
Mauchen. www.laemmlin-schindler.de

This organic estate, founded only in 1962, is today the leading quality-wine producer of the Markgräflerland. Its elegant Weisser Burgunder and Grauer Burgunder are among the most sophisticated dry white wines made in Baden, and even the simple Gutedel is extremely well-crafted. The Schindlers have been slow to get to grips with red-wine production, but there have been improvements in recent years.

Weingut Markgraf von Baden: Schloss Staufenberg ✩✩
Durbach

This homely old manor on a hill, with skirting vineyards, is a place of great charm, producing delicate and sometimes distinguished dry Rieslings. Both Riesling and Traminer were planted here in the eighteenth century, so this is an estate rich in tradition. The red wines lag behind the whites in quality.

Staatsweingut Meersburg ✩
Meersburg

Formerly the estate of the Prince-Bishops of Meersburg, this property became, in 1802, Germany's first state domain, its land largely in Meersburg, on the banks of the Bodensee (Lake Constance). The specialties are Müller-Thurgau of the gentler kind, and pinky-gold, *spritzig* Spätburgunder. Despite the Meersburg estate reputation as the most important estate on the Bodensee, quality is lacklustre.

Weingut Gebrüder Müller ✩
Breisach

Peter Bercher's ten-hectare estate boasts a sizeable holding in the great Ihringer Winklerberg vineyard in the Kaiserstuhl, and can claim to have made this site's reputation during the first half of the nineteenth century. Good as the dry white wines often are, it is the substantial Spätburgunder reds that rightly attract most of the attention.

Weingut Schloss Neuweier ✩✩✩
Neuweier. www.weingut-schloss-neuweier.de

Since purchasing the run-down Schloss Neuweier estate in 1992, Gisela Joos and her winemaker Alexander Spinner, have put this property back into the first rank of Baden's quality wine producers. The great majority of the production is dry Riesling of considerable sophistication and capable of long ageing. Those from the Mauerberg vineyard are distinctly minerally, those from the Schlossberg are a touch weightier.

Weingut Schloss Ortenberg ✩–✩✩
Ortenberg. www.weingut-schloss-ortenberg.de

The castle of Schloss Ortenberg belongs to the German youth hostel association, and its vineyards were purchased for them in 1950 by the regional council. A merger in 1997 with another estate brought the total area of its vineyards to forty-two hectares.

Ever since Winfried Köninger was appointed director in 1991, standards have improved considerably. A wide range of grapes is cultivated, with the best results coming from Riesling and Spätburgunder grapes.

Weingut Salwey ✩✩–✩✩✩
Oberrotweil. www.salwey.de

As well as producing some of the finest fruit brandies in the whole of Germany, Wolf-Dietrich Salwey also makes some of the finest white wines in the Kaiserstuhl. Unlike so many of his colleagues, he has resisted the temptation to experiment with ageing in new oak, and has remained true to the traditional vinification style. The result is rich but elegant dry Weisser Burgunder and Grauer Burgunder with excellent ageing potential.

His dry Spätburgunder *Weissherbst* wines from the Glottertal are among the finest of all German rosés. The estate's occasional dessert wines are also impressive. Only the red wines do not yet measure up to the highest standards.

Winzergenossenschaft Sasbach ✩
Sasbach. www.sasbacher.de

The smallest of the Kaiserstuhl cooperatives, this one specializes in Spätburgunder, which accounts for half of all its production. Sasbach has been a member of the German Barrique Forum since its inception in 1991. The wines retain good fruit, and are rarely overwhelmed by oak.

Weingut Hartmut Schlumberger ✩–✩✩
Laufen. www.schlumbergerwein.de

This old family manor, between Freiburg and Basel in the heart of the Markgräflerland, is mostly planted with Spätburgunder, Weisser Burgunder, and Gutedel. Hartmut Schlumberger has retained the old casks in his cellar, making this is a very traditional estate. It has received a further boost in quality since his son-in-law, Ulrich Bernhart, took over the winemaking.

Weingut Reinhold und Cornelia Schneider ✩✩–✩✩✩
Endingen. www.weingutschneider.com

Reinhold Schneider runs his eight-hectare estate along more or less organic lines. His soils are varied, though not exceptional, so rather than identify individual sites on the label, he has evolved a code to indicate the soil type: volcanic, loess, or loam.

Wines labelled "Trio" are a blend of all three. The wines are of a very high standard, exhibiting more freshness and zest than is usual in the Kaiserstuhl. The reds are rather less exciting.

Weingut Seeger ✩✩–✩✩✩
Leimen. www.seegerweingut.de

Located just south of Heidelberg, this eight-hectare estate has leapt vastly in quality over recent years. Thomas Seeger's Spätburgunders, aged in new oak, are well up there with Baden's best, although they can be very extracted and are decidedly expensive.

There is also a blend called "Cuvée Anna", from Spätburgunder, Lemberger, and Portugieser, which is aged twenty months – rather too long – in barriques. The estate's much improved Weisser Burgunder, Grauer Burgunder, and Riesling do, however, deserve to be taken seriously.

Weingut Rudolf Stigler ☆☆–☆☆☆
Ihringen

One of the best private estates in the Kaiserstuhl, known particularly for its Rieslings from the Winklerberg. These are wines with weight, minerality, and great length of flavour. Andreas Stigler's style is deliberately traditional, if not old-fashioned, emphasizing body and extract rather than the fruit itself.

Gräflich Wolff-Metternich'sches Weingut ☆☆
Durbach. www.weingut-metternich.de

Under director Ottman Schilli, this noble estate of thirty-six hectares made its way to the forefront of quality wine production in the Ortenau. After almost forty years at the helm, Schilli retired, and his place has been taken by Franz Schwörer.

Dry Riesling is important here, but the house specialty is Sauvignon Blanc, made from cuttings apparently brought here from Château d'Yquem in 1830. The wines benefit from bottle-age.

Saale-Unstrut

A short distance to the south of Halle and to the west of Leipzig lie the 640 hectares of vineyards which form the Saale-Unstrut region (until 1989 they lay within the former East Germany). The name "Saale-Unstrut" comes from the two idyllic river valleys which offer shelter to some of Germany's most easterly and northerly vineyards. The region itself is centred around the historic town of Naumburg, which is home to a splendid Gothic-Romanesque cathedral. It was in fact the church that brought serious viticulture to the region when the associated Cistercian monastery of Pforta was founded in 1137.

Even today, Saale-Unstrut still suffers from the hangover of the communist period. Almost half of the region's wines are made by the Freyburg cooperative and sadly, perhaps, the region is best-known in Germany for the Rottkäppchen Sekt Company of Freyburg – most of whose cheap, commercial sparkling wine is made from imported base wines.

A handful of independent growers, however, have managed to reclaim their vineyards, confiscated in the communist era, and have set about acquiring others. They are now managing to start demonstrating that the limestone soils of the best sites are in fact capable of producing subtly aromatic, mid-weight, dry Weisser Burgunder, Riesling, and Traminer, though Müller-Thurgau is the most widely planted grape.

Pinot Noir used to be a very common grape here a century ago, but it fell into disfavour in the 1960s because of difficulties with ripening and vinification; neither of these fitted into the industrial standardization of communist East Germany. Today, however, it is being revived, and Riesling, too, is on the increase.

Leading Saale-Unstrut Producers

Weingut Gussek ☆
Naumburg

André Gussek used to be the cellarmaster at Kloster Pforta (*q.v.*), but has been slowly establishing his own four-hectare estate. He is keen on red wines, which account for one-quarter of production, and the best of these is usually the Zweigelt. The Silvaner is sound and the Weisser Burgunders surprisingly rich in alcohol.

Landesweingut Kloster Pforta ☆
Bad Kösen

This property was established in 1899 by the Prussian state, and endowed with excellent terraced vineyards along the River Saale. It went through a period of instability in the 1990s, as directors came and went. By 2000, the situation was more stable. The estate has a higher proportion of Riesling than any other in the region, and both Riesling and Weisser Burgunder can have a firm, mineral quality. Overall, quality is disappointing considering the vineyards at the estate's disposal, but these are still early days.

Weingut Lützkendorf ☆☆–☆☆☆
Bad Kösen. www.weingut-luetzkendorf.de

After resigning as director of the Landesweingut Kloster Pforta following German reunification in 1989, Udo Lützkendorf founded his own wine estate. It is now run by his son, Uwe, who is already setting exemplary standards: his dry Weisser Burgunder, Riesling, and Silvaner are clearly the best wines made in the region. Full of fruit, crisp acidity, and enough vigour to improve with up to five years of bottle-ageing, they prove what the beautiful Saale-Unstrut region is capable of producing.

Sachsen

The 440 hectares of vineyards dotted along the Elbe Valley, around the historic cities of Dresden and Meissen, form the smallest wine-growing region in Germany. During the reign of Sachsen's mighty ruler, August the Strong, in the first half of the eighteenth century, the vineyard area was far greater than it is today, and records indicate that the wines from Sachsen's top vineyard sites were regarded as being among Germany's finest.

Since then, the phylloxera plague of the late nineteenth century, economic crises, war, and dictatorship came close to eradicating the region's great wine culture. As in Saale-Unstrut, the structure of the wine industry is dominated by only two producers: the cooperative of Meissen, which accounts for one-third of the region's production, and the Sächsisches Winzergenossenschaft, which makes up almost another third.

However, over the last five years, a dozen independent winegrowers have made increasingly sophisticated dry wines from a handful of grape varieties, which suggest that Sachsen may once again start producing wines of distinction. Traminer, Riesling, Weisser Burgunder, and

Grauer Burgunder have the most potential. The granite and ancient igneous rock soils result in wines that are more racy and minerally than those of Saale-Unstrut.

While it is too early to classify the region's vineyards, there are three obvious candidates: the Meissener Katzensprung, the Pillnitzer Königlicher Weinberg, and the Raebeuler Goldener Wagen.

Leading Sachsen Producers

Weingut Schloss Proschwitz ☆☆
Zadel uber Meissen. www.schloss-proschwitz.de
In 1991, Dr. Georg Prinz zur Lippe bought back his family's Meissen vineyards to recreate the ancient Proschwitz estate. Much work remains to be done in the vineyards, but some good wines have already been made, particularly dry Weisser Burgunder and Grauer Burgunder, which are clean, tight, and polished. The red wines remain rather thin.

Weingut Vincenz Richter ☆
Meissen. www.vincenz-richter.de
Thomas Herrlich supplements his eight-hectare estate with purchases from other vineyards. The wines, from Riesling, Weisser Burgunder, and Traminer, are mostly *trocken* and *halbtrocken*.

Weingut Schloss Wackerbarth ☆–☆☆
Radebeul. www.schloss-wackerbarth.de
The best sites belonging to this estate lie on terraced vineyards rising up behind the baroque mansion on the outskirts of Dresden. By 1989, the estate was in terrible shape, and much effort has been expended on renovating the vineyards and winery.

The turning point was 1999, when flabby, lacklustre wines were replaced by zestier bottlings. A large part of the output is of sparkling wine, most of it rather sweet and ungainly. Now owned by a local bank, Schloss Wackerbarth has the resources to improve quality further. Just to show what can be achieved, winemaker Jan Kux produced a Riesling TBA in 2000, apparently the first ever to be made in Sachsen.

Weingut Klaus Zimmerling ☆☆
Pillnitz
Sachsen's most intriguing wine estate came into existence in 1987, when Klaus Zimmerling, vintner, began clearing and replanting ancient vineyard terraces with the help of friends. Despite the climate, he has opted for organic viticulture, and yields are extremely low.

Today, he has a growing reputation for sophisticated, dry Rieslings, Traminers, and Grauer Burgunders. The labels are adorned with examples of his wife's sculpture, making this the most stylish packaging of any wine estate in the former East Germany.

Luxembourg

Luxembourg has some 1,350 hectares of vines along the upper Mosel, above Trier. There are about 1,000 small growers, but sixty-five per cent of the country's wine is made in cooperatives. The industry is highly organized and controlled. Since 1985, all wines are graded in one of five qualities: *non admis* (not passed), *marque nationale*, *vin classé*, *premier cru*, and *grand premier cru*. In 1991, a new appellation for Crémant du Luxembourg was created, supplementing the previous single appellation, Moselle Luxembourgeoise. These ultra-fresh sparkling wines can be bargains.

The grape varieties grown in Luxembourg are: Rivaner (Müller-Thurgau) about thirty-five per cent; Elbling about twelve per cent; Riesling and Auxerrois about ten per cent; with a little Gewürztraminer, Pinot Gris, Blanc, and Noir. Average yields are an astonishing 160 hectolitres per hectare, which makes its neighbour Germany look high-minded in comparison. Elbling produces very weak juice, but considerable quantities of light, often fizzy, and refreshing wines are made from a blend of Elbling and Rivaner. Rivaner is reliable; Auxerrois occasionally extremely charming – an original speciality with no real counterpart – especially from Wasserbillig; Riesling always lean but sometimes classic. Pinot Noir makes very pale but pleasant wines.

The Domaine et Tradition estates association, founded in 1988, promotes quality from noble varieties, largely by restricting yields to eighty-five hectolitres per hectare. Major producers are Caves Bernard-Massard at Grevenmacher (good "Cuvée de l'Ecusson" classic-method sparkling) and Les Domaines de Vinsmoselles at Stadtbredimus (the organization of cooperatives). Others are Cep d'Or at Hëttermillen (fine Crémant); Alice Hartmann at Wormeldange (elegant Riesling); Kohll-Reuland at Ehnen (good crémant); Aly Duhr at Ahn (nutty, oak-aged Pinot Blanc); Mathis Bastian, Caves Krier Frères, Caves Gales, and Caves St Rémy at Remich (also the H.Q. of the Government Viticultural Station); and Henri Ruppert (good Auxerrois) and Thill Frères at Schengen.

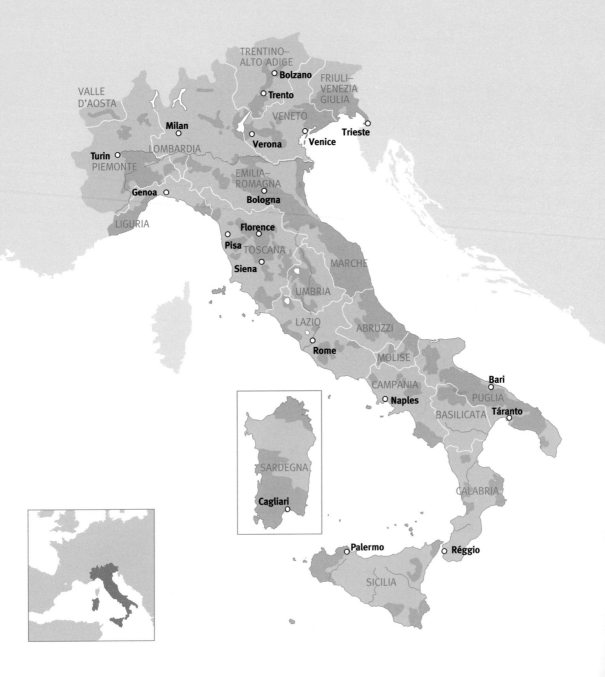

Italy

In the sheer quantity of wine she produces, Italy has for some years been running neck and neck with France, although as in most other wine-producing countries, both production and consumption are gradually declining. Nonetheless, every one of her twenty regions is in the wine business to a greater or lesser extent. Her geography, essentially a mountain range reaching south and east from the Alps towards the sub-tropics, offers as wide a range of vine-worthy sites and microclimates as nature has devised in any country. The palette is extraordinary, with some 1,000 grape varieties in cultivation, although only half of them are more than local curiosities.

It should be no surprise that some of the world's best wines come from Italy, and yet to most people it does. During the two-and-a-half centuries when France was building the formidable structure and reputation of her quality-wine industry and propagating her superlative vines, Italy was doing no such thing. Wine, like loyalty, remained very much a local, even a family, affair. Like bread, it was no less important for being taken for granted. But it was not measured even by national, let alone international, standards until well into this century. And when it was, Italy was inevitably judged as a source of low-priced wine, either for cheap-and-cheerful drinking or to be passed off as something else. To this day, an almost incredible quantity slinks anonymously out of the country in tankers to other parts of the EU. High-quality wine depends entirely on demand, and nobody demanded it in Italy.

The Italians have not helped themselves by rejoicing in ever-more-complicated wine labels. For non-Italians, even the most interested is often blocked by a lilting litany of tuneful polysyllables in which not just the name of the wine and its maker but that of his property – and often an additional fantasy name for good measure – all appear equally important.

Recent years have seen some dramatic changes in attitude and practice. The best winemakers are experimenting with untraditional ideas, grape varieties, and techniques. They are offering distinctive wines with designer labels (and bottles) at high-fashion prices not always justified by their quality. This producer-led revolution circumvents, or even ignores, the rules enshrined in the DOC system described below.

New developments at official level have proved equally important. New blood in the bureaucracy has seemingly meant an end to the scandal of deliberate wine surpluses: grapes grown to be distilled into unwanted industrial alcohol. Revisions of the law towards the French "pyramid" concept of regional appellations, with smaller, higher-quality zones within them, are very slowly beginning to work. Those DOCs that are virtually unused have now been revoked.

The wine-law of 1992 introduced a realization of the quality-pyramid philosophy. It peaks with wines which are subject to the strictest controls. DOCG (*Denominazione di Origine Controllata e Garantita*) and DOC (*Denominazione di Origine Controllata*) follow. There are over 325 of them, and they account for twenty per cent of Italian wine production. Half-way between the DOC wines and the next level, *vini da tavola* (table wines), is the new category of IGT wines (*Indicazione Geografica Tipica*); these are wines with grape-variety names, from a larger production area, and with more tolerant quality criteria than DOC wines. The IGT provides a clearer identity for much of what was the *vini da tavola* flood.

It also enables greater control of this production, as IGT wines, unlike *vini da tavola*, are subject to maximum crop limitations.

The method of access to the essentials in the following pages tries to make the problems of identifying and judging Italy's wines as simple as possible. This is how it works.

The country is divided into twenty regions. Each is treated separately, in two parts. First come the names and descriptions of the wines, then a wide selection of the better and bigger winemakers, with brief accounts of their standing, methods, size, and a list of the wines they offer. If you know the name of the wine or the maker but not the region, the only place to start is the index. If you know the region, go straight to the wine or the maker. Cross-referencing goes from maker to wine but not (to avoid a repetitive list) the other way round. The only list of producers, for example, of Chianti Classico is the list of winemakers in Tuscany, in which you will find that many Chianti makers also make other wines.

On the face of it, there is a radical division between officially controlled (DOC) wines and others. The DOC was instituted in 1963 as a necessary regulatory system for Italian quality wines – an approximate equivalent to the French AC.

A DOC is a very detailed legal stipulation as to the precise character, origin, grapes, crop levels, strength, methods, and ageing of a particular wine or group of wines, agreed between the consortium of its producers and an expert committee in Rome. The maximum crop is expressed in this book in hectolitres per hectare, to make it comparable with other countries, although the DOC regulations stipulate both the number of *quintals* (100 kilograms) of grapes that may be picked, and also what percentage of that weight may be processed into wine – the idea is to control the urge to press every last drop from the grapes.

Previous editions of this book have listed individual DOC regulations in considerable detail. In practice, however, most good producers obey those rules they believe contribute to the quality or typicity of a wine, while ignoring those (such as traditional excessive wood-ageing) that are, in their view, detrimental to quality. For example, until a few years ago, it was mandatory to include a proportion of white grapes in Chianti Classico. This absurd rule benefitted growers with a lot of Trebbiano in their vineyards. But it clearly could not improve the quality of a Sangiovese-based wine, so the best growers quietly ignored it. So, DOC listings below now focus on the most important features of each DOC rather than a list of detailed regulations.

In addition, an equal number of wines are listed that are not DOC and have no official delimitation. It is the great paradox of Italian wine today that a DOC freezes a type of wine in an historical moment. A DOC is essentially the definition of a tradition – at the very moment when wine technology has reached a pitch undreamed of before, when California (the outstanding example) is using its freedom to experiment to produce more exciting wine every year.

Not surprisingly, Italy's best winemakers are as eager to experiment with new ideas as anyone. They therefore either ignore DOC regulations or add to their traditional wares unconsecrated products representing their aspirations for the future. However good these have been – and they include almost all the great new wines of Italy – they have had to suffer the indignity of being officially classed as *vini da tavola*, the basic category for blended wine for everyday consumption. Some of these wines are now allowed to be labelled IGT, but can never be granted the accolade of DOC or DOCG.

The reader of this book, therefore, should make no absolute distinction between DOC and other wines, beyond that a DOC is "traditional" and subject to official regulation.

Another step in the regulation of certain DOCs has been instigated with an additional category: DOCG. The "G" stands for *Garantita*, inferring that the wines are guaranteed as Italy's best. They are, indeed, the best geographically controlled wines. The first four DOCGs were Barbaresco, Barolo, Brunello di Montalcino, and Vino Nobile di Montepulciano. Albana di Romagna was the next to be added to the list though anyone who tastes it may be forgiven for asking how seriously the "G" is to be taken). Candidates such as Carmignano and Torgiano go a long way to restoring faith. More recent DOCGs are Asti, Franciacorta (only the *spumante*), Gattinara, Taurasi, Vernaccia di San Gimignano, and Brachetto d'Acqui. Amarone di Valpolicella is likely to be one of the next.

It is hard to summarize the present state of Italian winemaking. Recent investments in modern equipment and new ideas have produced some wonderful results, but have also stripped old friends of their character. So far, the modern movement has succeeded in making both the most boring and the most brilliant wines. Those who feared Italy would be drowned in a tide of international varieties have been proven wrong. Although Italian producers are trying their hand at Cabernet Sauvignon, Merlot, Chardonnay, and Syrah (and why not?), they have also remained true to their traditional varieties. There is a balance to be found between tradition and technology (in grapes, cellaring, and every aspect of winemaking) and Italy is very busy looking for it.

Italy in Round Figures

1 The production by region of DOC wines in 1999 (in hectolitres)
2 Regional production as a percentage of national DOC total

	1	2
Piedmont	1,837,201	16.5
Valle d'Aosta	7,298	0.1
Lombardy	678,230	6.1
Trentino-Alto Adige	865,011	7.8
Veneto	1,965,086	17.4
Friuli	721,790	6.5
Liguria	27,075	0.2
Emilia-Romagna	1,001,423	9.0
Tuscany	1,368,584	12.3
Umbria	176,786	1.6
Marches	342,748	3.1
Latium	606,153	5.4
Abruzzi	687,089	6.2
Molise	40,580	0.4
Campania	134,564	1.2
Apulia	259,906	2.3
Basilicata	17,550	0.2
Calabria	53,708	0.5
Siciliy	166,834	1.5
Sardinia	194,342	1.7
Italy	**11,151,958**	**100.0**

Piedmont

Piedmont (in English and French, Piemonte in Italian), makes more wine than any other region of Italy. For uninhibited exploration of the varieties of grapes and what can be made from them, no part of Europe can compare. The vermouth of Turin witnesses that a good brew-up is part of local tradition. For ingredients, the hills of Piedmont offer such an assortment of indigenous grapes that the accepted international varieties have scarcely been planted at all. Each of the local grapes is a character with something to offer. Each is made into wine unblended, often in several styles, and also mixed with others in brews, which may be traditional or experimental, conventional or idiosyncratic. The former are frequently blessed with DOCs and DOCGs, the latter not – but this has no bearing on their respective qualities.

The emphasis is all on red wine. Only one Piedmont white has any history of other than local success before the last two decades, and that is Asti Spumante. The Cortese is a good white grape, now proving itself in Gavi, but the catechism of important Piedmont wines must start with a list of the red grapes that enjoy the harsh climate of this sub-Alpine area.

Nebbiolo comes first in quality. It takes its name from the fog (*nebbia*) that characterizes autumn here, not only closing Milan airport regularly but also creating quintessentially mellow, fruitful pictures of gold-leaved vines tilting up to the grey hilltop villages.

The 490-metre (1,592-foot) Langhe Hills south of Alba on the River Tanaro provide the slopes, shelter, soil, sunshine, and humidity that bring Nebbiolo to perfection in Barolo (southwest of Alba) and Barbaresco (to its east). The style of Barolo, a wine of the maximum concentration, tannin, and alcohol, has no very ancient history but it does have conviction, and its growers' palates are ready for as much power as their vines will give them. The inexperienced, the timid, and the claret-lovers should start with Nebbiolo in its milder, less explosive manifestations, such as Nebbiolo d'Alba or Roero.

Barbera comes first in quantity. But it, too, unlike the common grapes of the south of France, carries conviction. It can be clumsy, but good Barbera – which is to say, Barbera that has not been overcropped – is plummy and astringent in just the right measure.

Dolcetto is quite different. No other red grape succeeds in conveying such an impression of softness, while being sometimes startlingly dry. It sounds odd, but with rich food it makes a tantalizing meal opener; it is a marvellous complement to antipasti, especially the cold meats. Dolcetto is not normally for ageing.

In complete contrast, Freisa is inclined to be fizzy and sometimes even sweet, and again in contrast, Grignolino tends to the pale, mild but teasingly bitter style of wine, which is common in northwest Italy. Add the lively, light Bonarda and the Croatina and Vespolina and the range of possible cocktails is almost limitless.

The following list reflects the complexity of the region with more DOCs and DOCGs than any other – and lots of unofficial "table" wines besides. Piedmont now has three new DOC designations: Langhe, Monferrato, and Piemonte. These serve not only to give a legal home to huge quantities of not-yet-DOC wines, but also to legalize the blending of two or more varieties, by creating new appellations for such wines.

Nowhere in Italy, it's arguable, is the use of French oak as controversial as here. Traditionalists have always aged wines such as Barolo, Barbera, and Dolcetto in large casks, whereas modernists such as Elio Altare and Angelo Gaja began ageing their wines in barriques in the 1980s. There is little point coming down on one side or the other. There are great "traditional" Piedmontese wines, and great "modernist" ones. The quality of the fruit harvested is usually of far more importance than the container used to age the wine.

Would that there were space for more than a low bow towards the best fare of Italy: the truffles, the *fonduta*, the game, and all the simple but sensuous things that give these wines their proper context.

DOC & Other Wines

Barbaresco DOCG. Red wine. Province: Cuneo. Villages: Barbaresco, Neive, Treiso. Grape: Nebbiolo.

The immediate neighbour of Barolo, sharing most of its qualities of power and depth, youthful harshness, and eventual perfumed sweetness. Great Barbaresco has a style and polish it is hard to define; it is tempting, though inaccurate, to call it the Côte-Rôtie to the Hermitage of Barolo. Neither lives as long or develops so sumptuously as the best Rhône wines; but recent bottlings (particularly the wines from Gaja) have added new superlatives to Italy's wine vocabulary: the most luxurious, the most vigorous, silky, incisive, and memorable.

Barbera d'Alba DOC. Red wine. Province: Cuneo. Villages: many around Alba. Grape: Barbera.

Barbera wines are ubiquitous in Piedmont, but the best of them fall into one of three DOCs. Alba is considered the best area for full-bodied Barbera apt for ageing – though the style is entirely at the producer's discretion. It is also the case that the best sites in Alba are devoted to Nebbiolo, with Barbera being planted on sites that are less well-exposed.

Barbera d'Asti DOC. Red wine. Provinces: Asti and Alessandria. Villages: from Casale Monferrato to Acqui Terme. Grape: Barbera. Critics disagree on whether this or Alba gives the best Barbera. Over the past decade, Barbera, often planted on the best sites, since Asti is not primarily a Nebbiolo zone, yields outstanding results here.

Barbera del Monferrato DOC. Red wine. Provinces: Asti and Alessandria. Villages: a large number of the above provinces. Grapes: Barbera 85–90%, Freisa, Grignolino, and Dolcetto 10–15%.

The optional addition of other grapes allows this to be the least serious of the DOC Barberas, although some very good bottles exist.

Barolo DOCG. Red wine. Province: Cuneo. Villages: Barolo, Castiglione Falletto, Serralunga d'Alba, La Morra, Monforte d'Alba, Verduno, and parts of other communes. Grape: Nebbiolo.

If Barolo gives the palate a wrestling match, it makes its eventual yielding all the more satisfying. It takes practice to understand this powerful and astringent wine. For several years all flavour and most smell is masked and inaccessible. What is hidden is an extraordinary spectrum of scents (tar, truffles, violets, faded roses, incense, plums, raspberries have all been found).

Tasting notes on a 1974 Barolo in 1981 show just how slow the process can be: "Still a deep blackish plum colour, smelling harsh and indistinct. Strong and hard to taste, full of glow but ill-defined. More study reveals sweetness and fruit flavours, if not depth; sweetness, and a genial, roast-chestnut warmth grow with acquaintance (and air). Still no real development."

With such traditional Barolos, maturity comes on quite suddenly at about ten years and little is gained by keeping bottles beyond fifteen. The trend, though, is for more generous, though by no means easy, wines whose softer tannins make them more accessible sooner without shortening – indeed probably adding to – their long-term potential. In few areas anywhere has modern philosophy so successfully updated a natural classic.

The best vineyards are often signalled on the labels with the dialect words *sori* (meaning a steep sheltered slope) or *bricco* (a ridge). La Morra makes the earliest-developing wines, Monforte and Serralunga the slowest.

Barolo Chinato A domestic tradition among Barolo growers is to brew aperitifs and cordials with their wine. This, the best-known *amaro* (see page 279), is made bitter with an infusion of china bark. Another recipe includes green walnuts, tansy, garlic, cloves and cinnamon.

Boca DOC. Red wine. Province: Novara. Villages: Boca, part of Maggiora, Cavallirio, Prato Sesia, Grignasco. Grapes: Nebbiolo (Spanna) 45–70%, plus Vespolina and Bonarda Novarese (Uva Rara).

One of several dry reds from the hills north of Novara, where Nebbiolo is called Spanna. Blending with other grapes lightens this one. Tiny production.

Bonarda Piemontese Bonarda is a light red grape mostly grown in north Piedmont for blending. It can be fresh and pleasant on its own. Its own DOC is Piemonte Bonarda DOC.

Brachetto d'Acqui DOCG. Red wine. Provinces: Asti, Alessandria. Villages: Acqui Terme, Nizza Monferrato, and 24 others. Grape: Brachetto.

A light, sweet, fizzy red, with more than a touch of Muscat in the aroma. That made by Villa Banfi is a marvel: one of the best examples of Italian tradition updated for modern times. Like much Moscato d'Asti, Brachetto is very low in alcohol.

Bramaterra DOC. Red wine. Province: Vercelli. Villages: Massarano, Brusnengo, Cruino Roasio, Villa del Bosco, Sostegno, and Lozzolo. Grapes: Nebbiolo (Spanna) 50–70%, plus Croatina, Bonarda and/or Vespolina.

A big, solid, blended red from the Vercelli Hills, improving with age. Sold in Bordeaux-style bottles.

Bricco Manzoni A Nebbiolo/Barbera blend; the excellent invention of Rocche dei Manzoni at Monforte d'Alba and widely imitated.

Caramino A Spanna (Nebbiolo) blend from Dessilani in Fara DOC (*q.v.*). Well worth ageing for up to ten years.

Carema DOC. Red wine. Province: Torino. Village: Carema. A wine from the borders of Piedmont and Valle d'Aosta; a relatively lightweight Nebbiolo that can gain in finesse what it loses in power. The terrain is steep and terraced; the climate cool; and prices (especially in ski resorts) can be excessive.

Colli Tortonesi DOC. Red and white wine. Province: Alessandria. Villages: Tortona and twenty-nine others. Grapes: (red), Barbera 100%, or with up to 15% Freisa, Bonarda, and Dolcetto; (white) Cortese.

A good-quality Barbera blend with ageing potential, and a very light, dry Cortese white tending to sharpness and sometimes fizzy.

Cortese dell'Alto Monferrato DOC. White wine. Provinces: Asti and Alessandria. Villages: A large part of the above provinces. Grape: Cortese 85%.

An increasingly popular DOC for dry Cortese, still or sparkling, at a humbler level than that of Gavi (*q.v.*).

Dolcetto d'Acqui DOC. Red wine. Province: Alessandria. Villages: Acqui Terme and twenty-four others. Grape: Dolcetto.

A light, everyday red of good colour and certain character.

Dolcetto d'Alba DOC. Red wine. Province: Cuneo. Villages: Alba, Barolo, Barbaresco, La Morra, and thirty others. Grape: Dolcetto.

As with Barbera d'Alba, Dolcetto here is not planted on the best slopes, but the skill and renown of the producers may compensate and deliver a first-rate wine. The style varies from the traditional, soft, but dust-dry to something more fruity and refreshing. In most cases, youth is a virtue.

Dolcetto d'Asti DOC. Red wine. Province: Asti. Villages: Calamandrana, Canelli, Nizza Monferrato and twenty-one others. Grape: Dolcetto.

Less widely seen, but similar to Dolcetto d'Acqui.

Dolcetto delle Langhe Monregalesi DOC. Red wine. Province: Cuneo. Villages: Briaglia and many others. Grape: Dolcetto.

A rarely used DOC, established in 1974 for a lightweight Dolcetto, said to have more aroma than most.

Dolcetto di Diano d'Alba or **Diano d'Alba** DOC. Red wine. Province: Cuneo. Village: Diano d'Alba. Grape: Dolcetto.

An excellent Dolcetto, generally stronger and more focused than Dolcetto d'Alba.

Dolcetto di Dogliani DOC. Red wine. Province: Cuneo. Villages: Dogliani, Monchiero, and others. Grape: Dolcetto.

Possibly the original Dolcetto; often a good one with more "grip" (or less soft) than some. Some growers are aiming for a denser, richer style aged in barriques.

Dolcetto di Ovada DOC. Red wine. Province: Alessandria Villages: Ovada and twenty-one others. Grape: Dolcetto.

The best producers make very lively wine, with as fruity an aroma as every Dolcetto and capable of developing in bottle like good *cru* Beaujolais.

Erbaluce di Caluso, Caluso DOC. White wine. Provinces: Torino and Vercelli. Villages: Caluso and thirty-five others. Grapes: Erbaluce. Usually available vinified dry, but an excellent *passito* is also produced.

Fara DOC. Red wine. Province: Novara. Villages: Fara and Briona. Grapes: Nebbiolo (Spanna) 30–50%, plus Vespolina and Bonarda Novarese (Uva Rara).

Fara, Boca, and their neighbour Sizzano, similar reds of the same quality, were all early DOCs, but are still limited in production.

Favorita This dry white wine from the grape variety of the same name, grown in the Roero and Langhe Hills has recently made a comeback. Best drunk young.

Freisa d'Asti DOC. Red wine. Province: Asti. Area: the hills of Asti. Grape: Freisa.

A cheerful, fruity, sharpish red, sometimes sweet and often fizzy. It can be very appetizing, though the non-DOC Freisa d'Alba is often better-made, sometimes as a full-bodied red.

Freisa di Chieri DOC. Red wine. Province: Torino. Villages: Chieri and eleven others. Grape: Freisa.

Chieri, on the outskirts of Turin, specializes in the sweeter style of Freisa, often fizzy. Also capable of more serious reds.

Gabiano DOC. Red wine. Province: Alessandria. Villages: Gabiano and Montecestino. Grapes: Barbera 90–95%, plus Freisa and/or Grignolino. From the Gabiano village north of Asti. A very long-lived Barbera. Minute production.

Gattinara DOCG. Red wine. Province: Vercelli. Village: Gattinara. Grapes: Nebbiolo (Spanna), with up to 10% Bonarda.

The best-known Spanna (Nebbiolo) of the hills north of Novara, a quite separate enclave from Barolo and the Langhe, with a broader, juicier, less austere style of wine. Few, if any, Gattinaras reach top Barolo standards, but they are both impressive and easy to like.

Gavi or **Cortese di Gavi** DOC. White wine. Province: Alessandria. Villages: Gavi and three others. Grape: Cortese.

A recent international star, led to distinction by the La Scolca estate under the name Gavi di Gavi. It does not quite reach the standards of mingled acidity and richness that say "white burgundy"; too often its flavours are castrated by too-cold fermentation. But this area can grow this grape superbly well.

Ghemme DOC. Red wine. Province: Novara. Villages: Ghemme and part of Romagnano Sesia. Grapes: Nebbiolo (Spanna) 65–85%, plus Vespolina and Bonarda Novarese (Uva Rara).

A very similar wine to Gattinara, generally reckoned slightly inferior, though some (like me) may prefer the rather finer, less hearty style. The best bottles at five or six years incline towards a claret-like texture.

Grignolino d'Asti DOC. Red wine. Province: Asti. Villages: thirty-five communes in Asti. Grapes: Grignolino 100%, or with up to 10% Freisa. Good Grignolino is refreshing and lively, slightly bitter, and pale but not pallid.

Grignolino del Monferrato Casalese DOC. Red wine. Province: Alessandria. Villages: thirty-five communes (in the Monferrato Casalese). Grapes: Grignolino 100%, or with up to 10% Freisa. An additional Grignolino area to the north; gained DOC status a year after Grignolino d'Asti.

Lessona DOC. Red wine. Province: Vercelli. Village: Lessona. Grapes: Nebbiolo (Spanna) and up to 25% Vespolina and Bonarda. This remarkably fine, claret-weight Nebbiolo blend is scarce. Six years is a good age for it.

Langhe DOC. Red, white. Province: Cuneo. Grapes: almost all grapes grown in the province of Cuneo.

Recently introduced DOC as a catchment for declassified or not yet DOC-classed Langhe-wines: Langhe Bianco, L. Rosso, L. Nebbiolo, L. Freisa, L. Dolcetto, L. Arneis, L. Favorita, L. Chardonnay.

Loazzolo DOC. White. Province: Asti. Village: Loazzolo. Grape: Moscato.

A Moscato *passito*, with a history. Can be a sinful, sweet dream. Rediscovered in the 1980s by Giancarlo Scaglione and Giacomo Bologna, this is produced only in minute quantities. Forteto della Luja is the best.

Malvasia di Castelnuovo Don Bosco DOC. Red wine. Province: Asti. Villages: Castelnuovo Don Bosco and five others. Grapes: Malvasia di Schierano 100%, or with up to 15% Freisa.

A light, sweet, fragrant sparkling wine, either gently bubbly or fully sparkling.

Monferrato DOC. Red, white, and *rosato*. Provinces: Alessandria and Asti. Grapes: almost all grapes grown in this region.

DOC created in the mid-1990s to give greater respectability to many former table wines of the hills between the River Po and the Apennines: Monferrato Rosso, M. Bianco, M. Chiaretto, M. Dolcetto, M. Freisa, M. Casalese (a white from Cortese grapes).

Deciphering the Label

Abboccato Slightly sweet (*e.g.* Orvieto).
Amabile A little sweeter than *abboccato*.
Amaro Bitter.
Annata The year of the vintage.
Asciutto Totally dry.
Azienda (on a wine label) A wine estate.
Bianco White.
Botte Cask or barrel.
Bottiglia Bottle.
Cantina Wine cellar.
Cantina sociale or **cooperativa** A growers' cooperative cellar.
Casa vinicola a wine firm, usually making wine from purchased grapes. *See also* Tenementi.
Cascina Northern term for a farm or estate.
Chiaretto "Claret" – usually meaning very light red, but it can also refer to rosé.
Classico The "classic" heart of a DOC zone, by implication (and usually) the best part.
Consorzio A consortium of producers of a certain wine who join forces to control and promote it.
Dolce Fully sweet (technically, with between five per cent and ten per cent residual sugar).
Enoteca "Wine library" – Italy has many establishments with wide national or regional reference collections of wine. Also a wine shop.
Etichetta Label.
Fattoria Tuscan term for a farm or wine estate.
Fiasco (Plural *fiaschi*) flask; the traditional straw-cased Chianti bottle.
Frizzante Slightly fizzy, but with much less pressure than sparkling wine.
Gradazione alcoolica (grad. alc.) Alcoholic degree in percentage by volume.
Imbottigliato (or **messo in bottiglia**) **nel'origine** (or **del produttore all'origine**) Estate-bottled.
Liquoroso Strong, usually fortified, wine, whether sweet or not.
Marchio depositato Registered brand.
Metodo tradizionale or **classico** Now the mandatory term for sparkling wines made using the Champagne method.

Nero Black or very dark red.
Passito Wine made from grapes dried (either on mats in sheds or in direct sunlight) to concentrate them; strong and usually sweet.
Podere A farm or wine estate.
Produttore Producer.
Riserva, riserva speciale DOC wines that have been matured for a statutory number of years (the *speciale* is older). Except in the Chianti zone, the terms are gradually falling into disuse.
Rosato Rosé.
Rosso Red.
Secco Dry.
Semisecco Semi-dry (in reality, medium-sweet).
Spumante Sparkling.
Stravecchio Very old (a term regulated under DOC rules, not permitted elsewhere).
Superiore Superior in any one of a number of ways specifically designated by DOC rules; for example, high alcoholic degree.
Tenementi or **tenuta** Holding or estate.
Uva Grape.
Vecchio Old.
Vendemmia The vintage. It can also be used in place of *annata* on labels.
Vigna, vigneto Vineyard.
Vignaiolo or **viticoltore** Grape-grower.
Vin or **vino santo** Wine made from grapes dried indoors over winter and aged for many years in small casks. Usually sweet.
Vino da arrosto "Wine for a roast" implying a red of full body and maturity – "Sunday best".
Vino cotto Cooked (concentrated) wine.
Vino novello The wine of the current year, now used in the same sense as Beaujolais Nouveau.
Vino da pasto Everyday wine.
Vino da taglio Blending or "cutting" wine, of high degree and concentration.
Vino da tavola The regulation term for non-DOC wines, the equivalent of French *vin de table*.
Vite Vine.
Vitigno Grape variety.

Moscato d'Asti and **Asti** DOCG. White, usually sparkling (but can be still) wine. Provinces: Asti, Cuneo and Alessandria. Villages thoughout the communes.

Moscato d'Asti and Asti are basically the same, but regulations allow Moscato d'Asti to be slightly sweeter and lower in alcohol. Generally Moscato d'Asti is better than Asti, often made with great pains to be swooningly aromatic, sweet and slightly fizzy. It must be drunk as young as you can get it. Asti itself is one of Italy's inimitable classics: sweet, buxomly fruity but girlishly giggly with its scented froth. A major industry dominated by big names in the vermouth field, normally produced in tanks, hence the moderate price.

Nebbiolo or **Nebbiolo del Piemonte** An alternative title for any Nebbiolo wine. Not classified as DOC or DOCG. Ordinary to excellent wines.

Nebbiolo d'Alba DOC. Red wine. Province: Cuneo. Villages: Alba and sixteen others. Grape: Nebbiolo.

For those who can do without the stern majesty of Barolo, but love the flavours of its grape, this is the DOC to search out. Four years is usually enough to develop a delicious bouquet of fruit ranging from plums to raspberries and, with luck, truffles.

Piemonte DOC. Red, white, and *rosato* wines. Provinces: Alessandria, Asti, Cuneo. Grapes: Barbera, Bonarda, Grignolino,

Brachetto, Cortese, Chardonnay; Moscato: Pinot Bianco, Pinot Grigio, and Pinot Nero also for sparkling ("Piemonte DOC").

A new basket-DOC for the whole region of Piedmont. Includes Piemonte Barbera, P. Bonarda, P. Brachetto, P. Cortese, P. Grignolino, P. Chardonnay, P. Spumante, P. Moscato. Includes also new DOC for *spumante*, either *metodo tradizionale* or Charmat method.

Pinot Pinot Nero, Bianco, and Grigio are all grown in parts of Piedmont. Fontanafredda (*q.v.*) makes top sparkling Pinot Nero (Vigna Gattinera); there are also some interesting reds from the Langhe and Monferrato regions.

Roero DOC. Red wine. Province: Cuneo. Villages: nineteen in the province of Cuneo. Grapes: (red) Nebbiolo 95–98%.

A new category for red from Nebbiolo grown in the Roero hills north of Alba, but growers may still opt to produce Nebbiolo d'Alba or Roero. This zone makes attractive red wines, good young but sometimes capable of ageing beyond five to six years.

Roero Arneis DOC. White wine. Province: Cuneo. Villages: nineteen in the province of Cuneo. Grape: Arneis.

The Arneis grape grows in the Roero Hills. Soft, richly textured with a bitter-almond finish. Increasingly popular, especially the best-selling Blangé from Ceretto.

Ruchè de Castagnole Monferrato DOC. Red wine. Province: Asti. Villages: Castagnole Monferrato and six others. Grapes: Ruchè 90%.

A rare red grape, sometimes spelled "Rouchet", found only in the sub-Alps above Castagnole Monferrato where it makes a tannic wine that ages to something perfumed and fine.

Sizzano DOC. Red wine. Province: Novara. Village: Sizzano. Grapes: Nebbiolo (Spanna) 40–60%, plus Vespolina and Bonarda Novarese (Uva Rara).

Considered by many to be one of the best of the north Piedmont Spanna (Nebbiolo) blends, and is comparable with Boca and Fara. Has Potential to be a ten-year wine.

Spanna The alias of the Nebbiolo grape in the Novara and Vercelli Hills of north Piedmont, also used as a wine name for Gattinara-style wines.

Angelo Gaja

Angelo Gaja of Barbaresco has the highest profile of any grower in Piedmont today, aggressively taking his own line on techniques, grape varieties, style and price. The eighty-five hectares of Gaja vines produce almost 30,000 cases a year of Barbaresco and other Alba wines, including a Barolo, a Cabernet Sauvignon called Darmagi, two Chardonnays called Gaia & Rey, and a surprisingly long-lived Sauvignon Blanc. The wines that have always won the greatest acclaim are his single-vineyard Barbarescos such as Sorì San Lorenzo and the massively ripe and rich Sorì Tildin. So there was amazement when he announced in 2000 that he was declassifying them to Langhe Rosso. He explained that he wanted to bring attention back to his regular Barbaresco, but sceptics wondered whether the innovative Gaja was thinking of blending in some other varieties to his *crus*, a practice forbidden under Barbaresco DOC rules but allowed under Langhe rules.

Outside Piedmont, he has acquired the Brunello estate, Pieve di Santa Restituta in Tuscany, and created a new property on the Tuscan coast, Ca' Marcanda (*q.v.*), from which the first Bordeaux-style wines were released in 2002.

This most dynamic of Italian wine producers is still in his prime, untroubled by any controversy he stokes up, and as passionate as ever about his quest for the highest quality.

Leading Piedmont Producers

Alario ☆☆
Diano d'Alba, Cuneo
An enthusiastic grower of delicious Dolcetto, as well as fresh Barbera and concentrated Barolo "Riva".

Elio Altare ☆☆☆☆
La Morra, Cuneo
Despite the small size (nine hectares) of this vineyard, the wines have made international impact. In 1978, Altare shocked his family and neighbours by green-harvesting to reduce yields, and compounded the sin by ageing some of his wine in barriques. In short, he was the courageous

pioneer who helped create modern-style Barolo and Barbera of superb quality. His entire 1997 crop was wrecked by tainted corks and was withdrawn from the market.

Antichi Vigneti di Cantalupo ☆☆
Ghemme, Novara. www.cantalupovigneti.it
This thirty-hectare domaine is one of northern Piedmont's best producers, specializing in Ghemme.

Antoniolo ☆☆
Gattinara, Vercelli
A leading name in Gattinara, which has, if anything, improved in recent years.

Marchesi di Barolo ☆–☆☆
Barolo, Cuneo. www.marchesidicarolo.com
One of the larger Barolo houses, founded in 1861, and now producing 1.3 million bottles from all of the major Piedmontese varieties. The best wine is the Barolo Cannubi.

Batasiolo ☆–☆☆☆
La Morra, Cuneo. www.batasiolo.com
This very large winery is rapidly improving, using 105 hectares of excellent vineyards. Good Barolo and Dolcetto.

Bava ☆☆–☆☆☆
Cocconato d'Asti, Asti. www.bava.com
A large property, with a wide range of wines. Barbera d'Asti "Stradivario" is rich and complex, and the Chardonnay is zesty.

Bersano & Riccadonna ☆–☆☆☆
Nizza Monferrato, Asti. www.bersano.it
The second-largest producer in Piedmont, its 300,000 cases come from its own 170 hectares and from purchased grapes. Excellent Barbera, but others are humdrum. The wine museum created by the late Arturo Bersano is open five days a week.

A. Bertelli ☆☆☆
Costigliole d'Asti, Asti
From eight hectares, Bertelli produce a range of intense Barberas, and unusual, excellent wines from Rhône varieties.

Alfiero Boffa ☆☆☆
San Marzano Oliveto, Asti. www.alfieroboffa.com
Boffa is passionate about old Barbera vineyards, from which he makes a series of superb wines.

Braida-Giacomo Bologna ☆☆☆–☆☆☆☆
Rocchetta Tanaro, Asti. www.braida.it
More than just a talented winemaker, the late Giacomo Bologna was a prominent figure in Italian wine. He created a new style of modern, highly concentrated, long-lived Barberas, best exemplified by the estate's Bricco dell'Uccellone and Bricco della Bigotta. "Ai Suma" is a powerful, late-harvested Barbera made only when climatic conditions permit. Bologna died young, in 1990, but his standards are being maintained by his widow and children.

Cascina Castlet ☆☆–☆☆☆
Costigliole d'Asti, Asti
Maria Borio produces delicious Moscato and a range of Barbera d'Asti, including the late-harvested "Passum" from semi-dried grapes.

Caudrina ☆☆☆
Castiglione Tinella, Cuneo
The Dogliotti family is among the very best Moscato producers, with twenty-five hectares.

Ceretto ☆☆☆
Alba, Cuneo
The Ceretto brothers have expanded the family firm to include model estate wineries of Bricco Asili in Barbaresco, Bricco Rocche in Barolo, and the Blangé estate in Roero, where they make stylish Arneis. They are also part owners of I Vignaioli di Santo Stefano (for Asti and Moscato d'Asti) and the new Cornarea estate. Their Barolo and Barbaresco are first-rate examples of barrique-aged Nebbiolo.

Pio Cesare ☆☆–☆☆☆
Alba, Cuneo
A pillar of tradition in the Alba area, founded in 1881 by Pio Cesare, great-grandfather of Pio Boffa, who has given the winery a modern touch. Pio Cesare owns forty hectares in Barolo and Barbaresco, and also selects grapes from regular suppliers to make some excellent Piedmont wines.

Michele Chiarlo ☆☆–☆☆☆
Calamandrana, Asti. www.chiarlo.it
Sound, sometimes excellent, wines, especially from Barolo and Barbaresco from an expanding portfolio of vineyards.

Chionetti ☆☆☆
Dogliani, Cuneo
Outstanding producer of deep, rich, succulent Dolcetto di Dogliani.

Cigliuti ☆☆☆
Neive, Cuneo
New star in Barbaresco, also making excellent Barbera d'Alba. The Barbaresco is aged partly in casks, partly in barriques.

Francesco Cinzano ☆
Torino
Founded in the eighteenth century, Cinzano is best-known for its Asti and its sparkling wines: "Cinzano Brut" and "Principe di Piemonte Blanc de Blancs". Cinzano also controls the wine houses of Florio in Marsala and Col d'Orcia in Montalcino.

Clerico ☆☆☆☆
Monforte d'Alba, Cuneo
Domenico Clerico is a forward-looking producer who, since the early 1980s, has been releasing a range of superb Barolos, supple Dolcetto, and a barrique-aged blend called "Arte".

Aldo Conterno ☆☆☆–☆☆☆☆
Monforte d'Alba, Cuneo. www.aldoconterno.com
Conterno's skills as grower and winemaker, stem from five generations of forebears. His Dolcetto is soft; his Freisa brisk; his Barbera spicy; and his single-vineyard Barolos also bear the Conterno signature: notably harmonious, despite their massive chassis of tannin.

Giacomo Conterno ☆☆☆–☆☆☆☆
Monforte d'Alba, Cuneo

Brother of Aldo (see above), Giovanni Conterno, now assisted by his son, is particularly noted for his magnificent Barolo Monfortino, chosen from the best vintages and aged eight years in casks. All his wines are powerful and bold, among the finest expressions in the region of an ultra-traditional style.

Conterno-Fantino ☆☆☆
Monforte d'Alba, Cuneo

Very consistent producer of Barolo from Ginestra and Vigna del Gris, as well as a Nebbiolo/Barbera blend called "Monprà", and aged in new oak.

Giuseppe Contratto ☆☆–☆☆☆
Canelli, Asti. www.contratto.it

Founded in 1867, the firm is now owned by grappa-producer Bocchino. Excellent Asti and *metodo tradizionale* sparkling wines.

Coppo ☆☆–☆☆☆
Canelli, Asti

An established *spumante* house, now becoming as well-known for its splendid, vigorous Barberas and an intriguing barrique-aged Freisa.

Cordero di Montezemolo ☆☆☆
La Morra, Cuneo. www.corderodimontezemolo.com

Giovanni and Enrico Cordero, the sons of the founder, are building consistently on their father's reputation. With twenty-six hectares of their own vineyard, they produce, in particular, a fine Barolo, "Enrico VI", made for relatively young drinking, without losing depth and intensity.

Giovanni Corino ☆☆☆–☆☆☆☆
La Morra, Cuneo

Since 1995, all the wines from this seventeen-hectare estate have been barrique-aged. The single-vineyard Barolos are magnificent, tannic yet opulent. The Barbera "Pozzo" is built on the same massive scale and is certainly not for the faint-hearted.

Correggia ☆☆☆
Canale, Asti. www.matteocorreggia.com

A tragic accident deprived the Roero region of its most talented young winemaker, who had rapidly established a fine reputation for luscious Barbera and magnificent single-vineyard Roero, aged in barriques. His family is determined to maintain the standards he set.

Einaudi ☆☆–☆☆☆
Dogliani, Cuneo

Founded in 1897 by Luigi Einaudi, who later became president of Italy, the property remains in family hands. From thirty-three hectares, they produce first-rate Dolcetto di Dogliani, rich, dense Barolo Cannubi, and a fine blend of Piedmontese and Bordeaux varieties known as Langhe Rosso "Luigi Einaudi".

Luigi Ferrando ☆☆–☆☆☆
Ivrea, Torino. www.ferrandovini.it

Quality Carema, bottled with a special black label for fine vintages; and small amounts of unclassified sweet wines, such as his barrique-aged Solativa, from the Caluso zone.

Fontanafredda ☆–☆☆☆
Serralunga d'Alba, Cuneo. www.fontanafredda.it

The most impressive wine estate of Piedmont, founded in 1878 by Conte Emanuele Guerrieri, son of King Victor Emmanuel II, and based in a royal mansion in Serralunga. A major producer of Barolo and Asti, but quality was patchy until 1999, when a new winemaker, Danilo Drocco, arrived and swiftly turned things around. Fine wines across the range, from powerful, single-vineyard Barolo to juicy Dolcetto and characterful sparkling wines.

Angelo Gaja ☆☆☆☆
Barbaresco, Cuneo

See page 280.

Fratelli Gancia ☆
Canelli, Asti

A family firm that pioneered the traditional (Champagne) method in Italy. Also a producer of vermouth and spirits, Gancia remains a leader in sparkling wine with more than 1.5 million cases a year.

Bruno Giacosa ☆☆–☆☆☆☆
Neive, Cuneo. www.brunogiacosa.it

Bruno Giacosa is one of Piedmont's best winemakers, admired for powerful Alba reds (especially the Red Label Riservas made only in top vintages) that age with grace, and an excellent *tradizionale* made from Pinot Nero. His Barolo and Barbaresco are proof, if any were necessary, that great and complex Nebbiolo can be made without recourse to French oak. His best wines appear under the Falletto label.

Elio Grasso ☆☆☆
Monforte d'Alba, Cuneo

Quality rarely wavers at this estate. The single-vineyard Barolos are exceptional ("Chiniera" made in traditional style, "Runcot" aged in new barriques), and the Dolcetto and Barbera are rich and satisfying, too.

Marchesi di Gresy ☆☆
Barbaresco, Cuneo. www.marchesidigresy.com

Founded in the last century on the site of a Roman villa: Alberto di Gresy has been producing wine here since 1973. From thirty-five hectares of grapes planted in the prized Martinenga and Rabajà vineyards, di Gresy makes unusually elegant, medium-bodied Barbaresco, although the "Camp Gros" bottling has more body and weight than the "Martinenga" or "Gaiun".

Martinetti ☆☆☆
Torino

Franco Martinetti is an advertising executive and part-time winemaker, now assisted by his son, Guido. He owns no vineyards and buys in grapes from contracted vineyards. He is best-known for his three Barberas, including the magnificent "Sulbric", which contains some Cabernet. But his highly original full-bodied white wines, "Minaia" (a Cortese) and "Martin" (from the rare Timorasso grape), are both equally brilliant.

Bartolo Mascarello ☆☆
Barolo, Cuneo

A tiny Barolo maker that steadfastly relies on very traditional methods to carefully produce 2,000 cases of a single wine each year.

Giuseppe Mascarello ☆☆☆
Monchiero, Cuneo. www.mascarello1881.com

Mauro Mascarello's excellent and very traditional Barolo Monprivato comes from a seven-hectare family vineyard. Splendid Dolcetto, too.

Mauro Molino ☆☆☆–☆☆☆☆
La Morra, Cuneo

There are two single-vineyard Barolos here. "Conca", aged in 60% new oak, is more highly regarded than "Gancia", but both are excellent and extremely consistent. The concentrated and oaky Barbera "Gattera" is one of the best in the Alba region.

Nervi ☆☆
Gattinara, Vercelli

The best wine is the fine, single-vineyard bottling of Gattinara from Molsino.

Pecchenino ☆☆☆
Dogliani, Cuneo

Orlando Pecchenino is a single-minded producer, spearheading the revival of Dolcetto di Dogliani as a serious wine. His enthusiasm for barrique-ageing and micro-oxygenation is proving controversial, but the wines are of exceptional quality.

Pelissero ☆☆☆
Treiso, Cuneo. www.pelissero.com

One of the most gifted of the new generation of open-minded, modernist winemakers, Giorgio Pelissero produces rich Barbaresco "Vanotu" and sumptuous barrique-aged Barbera.

E. Pira ☆☆☆
Barolo, Cuneo

This tiny estate, run by Dr. Chiara Boschis, focuses on modern-style Barolo "Cannubi", powerful and fruity despite being aged entirely in new barriques.

Produttori del Barbaresco ☆☆–☆☆☆
Barbaresco, Cuneo. www.produttori-barbaresco.it

This exceptional cooperative, uniting fifty-six growers with ninety-six hectares of excellent vineyards, produces an array of single-vineyard Barbarescos, made with great care in a wholly traditional style.

Prunotto ☆☆☆
Alba, Cuneo. www.prunotto.it

Founded in 1904 as a cooperative, acquired by Alfredo Prunotto in 1920, the firm is now owned by Piero Antinori. Very careful, traditional winemaking produces benchmark Alba wines: gentle, plummy Nebbiolo, complex Barolo, and vibrant single-vineyard Barberas are first-class.

Renato Ratti ☆☆–☆☆☆
La Morra, Cuneo

The founder, the late Renato Ratti, was president of the consortium of Asti, and a respected author and local historian. His sons and nephew continue to make wines from thirty hectares of their own vineyards. After an uninspired patch, the wines are fast improving.

Vigna Regali ☆☆
Strevi, Alessandria

This is the Piedmontese branch of Villa Banfi, which also has immense estates in Montalcino. The Gavi "Principessa Gavia" is a particularly good example of a cold-fermentation modern white. Good Dolcetto d'Acqui and Brachetto, too, but sadly the delicious Moscato has been dropped.

Bruno Rocca ☆☆☆
Barbaresco, Cuneo

Imposing, modern style from *crus* "Rabajà" and "Coparossa", and a powerful if extracted Cabernet/Nebbiolo/Barbera blend called "Langhe Rabajolo". The succulent Dolcetto and Barbera are better-balanced.

Rocche dei Manzoni ☆☆☆
Monforte d'Alba, Cuneo

The innovative Valentino Migliorini makes splendid Barolos from forty hectares, plus his excellent Bricco Manzoni, a Nebbiolo/Barbera blend aged in barriques.

Luciano Sandrone ☆☆☆
Barolo, Cuneo. www.sandroneluciano.com

The owner, and his brother Luca, produce top-ranked Barolo and Barbera and admired Dolcetto from seventeen hectares of vines. Prices are high.

Scarpa ☆☆–☆☆☆
Nizza Monferrato, Asti

An outstanding Piedmont family firm, founded in 1854. Scarpa's wines are all models of their genre. As well as good Barolo, there is fine Brachetto and Barbera, a rare and remarkable rich red Rouchet and smooth Nebbiolo.

Paolo Scavino ☆☆☆–☆☆☆☆
Castiglione Falletto, Cuneo

His Barolo "Bric del Fiasc" is always outstanding, modern-style but not international. Enrico Scavino is also a master of Barbera and Dolcetto.

La Scolca ☆☆
Rovereto di Gavi, Alessandria. www.scolca.it

This fifty-hectare estate is run by Giorgio Soldati, the son of its founder, whose Gavi di Gavi made the world take the Cortese grape seriously. Also a good source of sparkling wines.

Sella ☆☆
Lessona, Vercelli

The Sella family is a leading producer of the rare wines from Bramaterra and Lessona.

Sottimano ☆☆☆
Neive, Cuneo

Andrea Sottimano produces four single-vineyard Barbarescos, each with a clearly discernible character from year to year, despite a high proportion of new oak. "Currà" and "Cottà" tend to stand out. Production is small but is set to expand.

La Spinetta-Rivetti ☆☆☆☆
Castagnole Lanze, Asti

The Rivetti family built their reputation on Barbera d'Asti and Moscato d'Asti, and over the past decade the dynamic Giorgio Rivetti has taken the wines to a new quality level. The wines are aged in mostly new barriques, but the intensely concentrated fruit is not overpowered by the wood. The Barberas are splendid, as are the dazzling, single-vineyard Barbarescos.

Vajra ☆☆☆
Barolo, Cuneo
The modest but perfectionist Aldo Vajra makes excellent Barolo, but his other wines are equally good: single-vineyard Dolcetto and Barbera d'Alba.

Mauro Veglio ☆☆☆
La Morra, Cuneo
Veglio produces four different Barolos from ten hectares. "Rocche" is built for the long term, while "Casteletto" is opulent despite very firm tannins. These wines need time to attain their majestic harmoniousness. Gorgeous Barbera d'Alba, too.

Vietti ☆☆–☆☆☆
Castiglione Falletto, Cuneo. www.vietti.com
Alfredo Currado presides over a substantial estate that once seemed mired in the past, but has moved forward, and is again producing fine Barolo and lively Barbera, as well as a range of other wines from the Alba region.

Vigna Rionda — Massolino ☆☆–☆☆☆
Serralunga d'Alba, Cuneo
A rising star, offering an impeccable range of well-structured, single-vineyard Barolos, and an intense Barbera d'Alba.

Roberto Voerzio ☆☆☆☆
La Morra, Cuneo
Many years ago, Roberto Voerzio split from the family winery (now run by Gianni Voerzio, his brother) to open his own operation, which is now one of the best Barolo estates. Yields are very low and the top wines are aged in barriques. Quality is dazzling, and prices are high.

Other Piedmont Producers

Anna Maria Abbona ☆☆–☆☆☆
Farigliano, Cuneo
An ambitious producer of Dolcetto di Dogliani, the best being "Maioli".

Gianfranco Alessandria ☆☆–☆☆☆
Monforte d'Alba, Cuneo
Modernist producer of sometimes over-tannic Barolo.

Ascheri ☆☆–☆☆☆
Brà, Cuneo
Founded in 1880 and still family owned, this estate makes very reliable Barolo and a Syrah called "Montalupa".

Azelia Castiglione Falletto ☆☆
Cuneo
Great Barolo "Bricco Fiasco".

Cascina La Barbatella ☆–☆☆
Nizza Monferrato, Asti
A good source for Barbera and Monferrato.

Terre del Barolo ☆–☆☆
Castiglione Falletto, Cuneo
A big cooperative with sound standards.

Bera ☆☆
Cuneo. www.bera.it
A rising star with Moscato d'Asti and Barbera.

Nicola Bergaglio ☆☆
Rovereto di Gavi, Alessandria
A widely admired maker of DOC Gavi.

Giacomo Borgogno & Figli ☆☆
Barolo, Cuneo. www.borgogno-wine.com
A traditional Barolo producer, making classic wines.

Gianfranco Bovio ☆☆–☆☆☆
La Morra, Cuneo
Bovio's excellent wines are best sampled at his famous restaurant in La Morra, Belvedere.

Brema Incisa ☆☆–☆☆☆
Scapaccino, Asti
Small quantities of outstanding Barbera.

Brezza II ☆☆
Barolo, Cuneo. www.brezza.it
Barolo "Sarmassa' is grandly old-fashioned and long-lived.

Bricco Maiolica ☆☆–☆☆☆
Diano d'Alba, Cuneo
Excellent range of wines: lush Dolcetto, fine Barbera, and oaky Nebbiolo.

Bricco Mondalino ☆☆
Vignale Monferrato, Alessandria
Renowned for excellent Barbera d'Asti and Grignolino.

Brovia ☆☆–☆☆☆
Castiglione Falletto, Cuneo. www.brovia.net
Highly consistent Barolo, with unusually elegant Dolcetto, too.

Burlotto ☆–☆☆
Verduno, Cuneo
Good Alba red wines right across the range.

Piero Busso ☆☆
Neive, Cuneo
Consistently good barrique-aged Barbaresco.

Ca' Bianca ☆–☆☆
Alice Bel Colle, Alessandria
Good Barbera d'Asti and Gavi from a winery that is part of the huge Gruppo Italiano Vini.

Ca' d'Carussin ☆–☆☆
San Marzano Oliveto, Asti
Bruna Ferro makes attractive, good-value Barbera d'Asti and a rare Barbera *passito*.

Ca' Romé ☆☆–☆☆☆
Barbaresco, Cuneo
Complex Barbaresco, especially "Maria di Brun".

Ca' Viola ☆☆–☆☆☆
Montelupo, Cuneo
The estate of respected oenologist Giuseppe Caviola, and a testing ground for his ideas. Excellent Dolcetto aand Barbera-dominated Langhe Rosso.

Giorgio Carnevale ☆☆
Rocchetta Tanaro, Asti
Sound Barbera, especially "Il Crottino".

Castellari Bergaglio ☆☆
Roverato di Gavi, Alessandria. www.castellaribergaglio.it
A leading Gavi producer.

Cavallotto ☆☆–☆☆☆
Castiglione Falletto, Cuneo. www.cavalotto.com
A highly traditional producer of long-lived Barolo.

La Chiara ☆–☆☆
Vallegge, Alessandria
Reliable Gavi producer.

Cogno ☆☆
Novello, Cuneo. www.elviocogno.com
Nine-hectare property. Sound Barolo and delicious Dolcetto.

Poderi Colla ☆☆
San Rocco Seno d'Elvio, Cuneo. www.podericolla.it
Traditional producer, offering both Barolo and Barbaresco of good quality, and a Dolcetto/Nebbiolo blend called "Bricco del Drago".

Giuseppe Cortese ☆☆
Barbaresco, Cuneo
Consistent Barbaresco from Rabajà.

Dessilani ☆–☆☆☆
Fara, Novara
The "Fara Caramino" and Gattinara are the most admirable wines from a large range.

Dezzani ☆☆
Cocconato, Asti
This estate is a large producer of sound Barbera and Dolcetto d'Ovada.

Fontanabianca ☆☆☆
Neive, Cuneo
Aldo Pola and Bruno Ferro have built a fine reputation on their barrique-aged, velvety Barbaresco "Sori Burdin".

Forteto della Luja ☆☆☆
Loazzolo, Asti
Acclaimed sweet Moscato *passito* from Giancarlo Scaglione under the Loazzolo DOC.

Gastaldi ☆–☆☆
Neive, Cuneo
Best-known for Dolcetto and his *rosso*, an unoaked Nebbiolo.

Gatti ☆☆
Santo Stefano Belbo, Cuneo
Delicious Moscato and Brachetto d'Asti.

Fratelli Giacosa ☆☆–☆☆☆
Neive, Cuneo
Very good, modern-style Barolo.

Gillardi ☆☆–☆☆☆
Farigliano, Cuneo. www.gillardi.it
Idiosyncratic producer, specializing in Dolcetto di Dogliani and a fine Syrah called "Harys".

Cantina del Glicine ☆☆
Neive, Cuneo
A minuscule wine house, producing consistently good-quality Barbaresco.

La Giustiniana ☆☆–☆☆☆
Rovereto di Gavi, Alessandria
Well-known producer of Gavi and Monferrato.

Silvio Grasso ☆☆–☆☆☆
La Morra, Cuneo
A fine, complex range of single-vineyard Barolos.

Domenico Ivaldi ☆☆
Strevi, Alessandria
Excellent Moscato *passito* "Casarito".

Luisin ☆☆☆
Barbaresco, Cuneo
Splendid traditional Barbaresco from one of the zone's top sites: Rabajà.

Malvirà ☆☆
Canale, Cuneo. www.malvira.com
A fine source of serious Roero and fresh Arneis.

Marcarini ☆☆
La Morra, Cuneo. www.marcarini.it
Hail destroyed most of the vineyards in 1986, so it has taken a while for production and quality to be restored. Elegant, medium-bodied Barolo.

Moccagatta ☆☆☆
Barbaresco, Cuneo
Excellent Barbaresco and superb barrique-aged Barbera.

Mossio ☆☆–☆☆☆
Rodello,Cuneo. www.mossio.com
Delicious Dolcetto from old vines. "Caramelli" is the top cru.

Fratelli Oddero ☆☆
La Morra, Cuneo
Respected family winery offering well-crafted, traditionally made, single-vineyard Barolos.

Orsolani ☆☆
San Giorgio Canavese, Torino. www.orsolani.it
Renowned for firm Erbaluce di Caluso and intense Caluso *passito* in tiny quantities.

I Paglieri ☆☆
Barbaresco, Cuneo
Steadily improving single-vineyard Barbaresco from Luca Roagna.

Armando Parusso ☆☆–☆☆☆
Monforte d'Alba, Cuneo. www.parusso.com
Tannic but accessible single-vineyard Barolos of fine quality.

I Vignaioli Elvio Pertinace ☆–☆☆☆
Treiso, Cuneo
A private cooperative producing good, if somewhat gamey, Barbaresco. "Nervo" is usually the best vineyard.

Punset ☆☆–☆☆☆
Neive, Cuneo
Small quantities of robust, sometimes austere, Barbaresco.

Fratelli Revello ☆☆–☆☆☆
La Morra, Cuneo
Impressive single-vineyard Barolos, aged in a high proportion of new oak, yet elegant too.

Albino Rocca ☆–☆☆☆
Barbaresco, Cuneo
Delicious Barbera "Gepin" here, but the single-vineyard Barbarescos are inconsistent: sometimes splendid, at others austere and bitter.

Rocche Costamagna ☆–☆☆
La Morra, Cuneo. www.rocchecostamagna.it
This is a traditional estate producing somewhat tough Barolos.

Gigi Rosso ☆–☆☆
Castiglione Falletto, Cuneo. www.gigirossso.com
A family firm, producing a full range of Alba wines. Reliable but rarely exceptional.

I Vignaioli di Santo Stefano ☆☆☆
Santo Stefano Belbo, Cuneo
Exceptional Moscato d'Asti from a small, private cooperative founded by Ceretto (*q.v.*).

Saracco ☆☆
Castiglione Tinella, Cuneo. www.paolosaracco.com
A specialist in white wines. Excellent Moscato, of course, but also good Chardonnay.

Scarzello ☆☆
Barolo, Barolo
A five-hectare estate producing Barolo that improves from year to year.

Scrimaglio ☆☆
Nizza Monferrato, Asti
Very consistent producer of Barbera d'Asti.

Mauro Sebaste ☆–☆☆
Alba, Cuneo
Robust Barolo that can sometimes lack fruit.

La Spinona ☆☆
Barbaresco, Cuneo

The Berutti family have for many years been making good, occasionally excellent, Barbaresco and Barolo.

Terre da Vino ☆
Moriondo, Torino
Owned by a group of cooperatives and estates in a joint-venture operation. Surprisingly good-quality Barolo for such a large company.

Travaglini ☆–☆☆☆
Gattinara, Vercelli
Forty hectares produce excellent Gattinara Riserva.

Vallana ☆–☆☆
Maggiora, Novara
Producer of long-lived Spanna and reliable Boca.

Castello di Verduno ☆☆
Verduno, Cuneo
Once the property of the Italian royal house, the estate is now owned by the Burlotto family, who produce sound traditional Barolo and Barbaresco, and the rare Pelaverga.

Gianni Voerzio ☆☆☆
La Morra, Cuneo
After the split with more illustrious brother Roberto (*q.v.*), Gianni took over the family winery. Excellent Barolo and Barbera.

Valle d'Aosta

The Valle d'Aosta is France's umbilical cord to Italy (and vice versa). It's narrow confines lead to the Mont Blanc Tunnel and St Bernard passes. Small vineyards perched in south-facing crannies along the valley manfully carry winemaking almost all the way from Piedmont to Savoie, with a corresponding meeting of their respective grapes.

Nebbiolo and Barbera from the south join Gamay and Petit Rouge (which tastes suspiciously like Mondeuse) from the north, with Swiss Petite Arvine, some Moscato and Malvoisie (Pinot Gris) and two indigenous grapes: Blanc de Valdigne and red Vien de Nus.

Quantities are very small; the skiers of Courmayeur and the townsfolk of Aosta prevent exports from the region. In 1986, Italy's most comprehensive region-wide DOC was established. Valle d'Aosta or Vallée d'Aoste takes in eighteen types of wine with their names in two languages. But even if classified, Aostan wines are interesting *sur place* but do not represent good value for money.

Leading Valle d'Aosta Producers

Anselmet ☆☆–☆☆☆
Villeneuve, Aosta
This is a tiny estate of 1.5 hectares, producing acclaimed oaked Chardonnay and Pinot Noir, and a late-harvest Pinot Gris.

Caves Coopérative de Donnas ☆
Donnas, Aosta. www.donnasvini.com
A small cooperative with tweny-five hectares, specializing in Nebbiolo-dominated reds.

Cave du Vin Blanc de Morgex et de la Salle ☆–☆☆
Morgex, Aosta
A cooperative with nineteen hectares specializing in Blanc de Morgex and Blanc de la Salle. At up to 1,040 metres (3,400 feet) their vineyards are some of the highest in Europe. The wine is light and can be sharp. A new addition is a late-harvest wine called "Chaudelune".

Cave des Onze Communes ☆
Aymavilles, Aosta
A cooperative with over 200 growers, but fewer than sixty hectares. Clean, fresh, varietal wines for early drinking.

Costantino Charrère ☆☆–☆☆☆
Aymavilles, Aosta
Charrère specializes in small quantities of wines made from obscure, low-yielding local varieties, often blended together. "La Sabla" is the fine, unoaked red made here from Petit Rouge, Fumin, and Barbera.

Coopérative de l'Enfer d'Arvier ☆
Arvier
A tiny cooperative, with 130 growers tending tiny plots. The only wine is a lightly oaked red dominated by Petit Rouge.

Les Crêtes ☆☆
Aymavilles, Aosta
A cooperative with a fine reputation for oaked Chardonnay, as well as unwooded wines from Petite Arvine, Syrah, and Pinot Noir.

La Crotta di Vegneron ☆☆
Chambave, Aosta. www.lacrottadivegneron.it
Cooperative offering sound Fumin, Muscat, and Pinot Gris, and lush *passito* wines from Moscato and Pinot Gris.

Di Barro ☆
Villeneuve, Aosta. www.mediavallee.it
Clean, fresh Chardonnay and Pinot Noir, and a Moscato *passito* unflatteringly called "Lo Flapì".

Grosjean ☆–☆☆
Quart, Aosta
The Grosjean family specializes in varietal wines from Gamay, Fumin, and Petite Arvine, and some Pinot Noir aged in barrique.

Institut Agricole Régional ☆☆–☆☆☆
Aosta. www.iaraosta.it
Experimental cellars of the regional agricultural school founded in 1969 and for many years directed by Joseph Vaudan, a priest. Some of the best wines of Aosta are produced here. There are two ranges, one for early drinking from varieties such as Müller-Thurgau, Petite Arvine, and Pinot Gris, the other more international in style and aged in barriques, including a Viognier ("L'Elite"); a Chardonnay; a Pinot Noir called "Sang des Salasses"; a Bordeaux blend called "Vin du Prévôt"; and a Syrah ("Trésor du Caveau").

La Kiuva ☆
Arnad, Aosta
A cooperative producing a mere 3,000 cases, with both oaked and unoaked Chardonnay.

Lo Triolet ☆–☆☆
Introd, Aosta
Marco Martin specializes in Pinot Gris and a Syrah-based red called "Coteau Barrage".

Albert Vevey ☆
Morgex, Aosta
Mario Vevey continues the family tradition, producing a fresh, aromatic Blanc de Morgex.

Ezio Voyat ☆☆–☆☆☆
Chambave, Aosta
These are classic Chambave wines, but Voyat sells them as *vini da tavola* under non-DOC names: "Rosso Le Muraglie" (mostly Petit Rouge); "La Gazzella" (Moscato); and "Passito Le Muraglie" (Moscato *passito*) – the latter superb.

Liguria

The crescent of the Ligurian coast, linking France and Tuscany, is scarcely regarded as a wine region and has never been an exporter. But in the centre of the crescent lies Italy's greatest port, and one of its most cosmopolitan cities, Genoa. Genoa demands, and gets, much better than ordinary whites for its fish and reds for its meat from the scattered vineyards of the hilly coast. Far more white than red is produced.

There are five DOC zones in Liguria: the Colline di Levanto in the hills behind La Spezia; white Cinqueterre in the seaside vineyards close to La Spezia; the red Rossese di Dolceacqua on the borders of France; the large Riviera Ligure di Ponente along the western Riviera; and the new white Colli di Luni in the lower Magra and Vora valleys behind La Spezia.

Liguria's wine list is a much longer one than its list of DOCs, but if the officially ranked wines are rarely exported, much less are the individualistic productions of its many small winemakers.

DOC & Other Wines

Cinqueterre DOC. White wine. Province: La Spezia. Villages: Riomaggiore, Vernazza, Monterosso, La Spezia. Aged one year for Sciacchetrà. Annual production: Cinqueterre 39,000 cases; Sciacchetrà 550 cases.

The largely legendary dry white (mostly Bosco, plus Albarola and Vermentino) of the beautiful Ligurian coast southeast of Genoa. It should be cleanly fruity. Sciacchetrà is the renowned specialty, made in tiny quantities from the same grapes, shrivelled in the sun to achieve concentration, sweetness, and a formidable sixteen degrees or more of alcohol. The vineyards are ledges on the rocky coast, sometimes only accessible by boat. If a pruner drops his secateurs there is a splash. How long will they survive?

Colli di Luni DOC. Red and white wines. Provinces: La Spezia, Massa e Carrara. Villages: eighteen communes in La Spezia and Massa e Carrara.

Wine has been made in this area since Roman times, but it only recently (1989) been elevated to DOC status. Good reds are made from Sangiovese-based blends, whites that can almost rival those of Riviera di Ponente predominantly from Vermentino and a dash of Trebbiano. Leading winemakers of the zone are investing heavily in new equipment and expertise, and look set to demand some respect in the future.

Riviera Ligure di Ponente DOC. Red and white wine. Province: Savona and Imperia. Villages: sixty-seven communes in Imperia, forty-six communes in Savona, plus two communes in Genoa. The red and white wines of this relatively new DOC west of Genoa are grown between Savona and Imperia. The main red varieties are Rossese and Ormeasco; the latter resembles Dolcetto. The whites, from Vermentino and Pigato, are best drunk young, the reds can improve with age.

Rossese di Dolceacqua or **Dolceacqua** DOC. Red wine. Province: Imperia. Villages: Dolceacqua, Ventimiglia and thirteen others.

The claret of the coast near the French frontier – a country wine from Rossese with a good balance of fruit and bite, best after two to five years, when it can develop a real bouquet to linger over.

Vermentino The commonest white grape of the coast, grown particularly to the west of Genoa. Standards vary, but it should be faintly aromatic and dry: much the best local fish wine. DOC in Riviera di Ponente, Colli di Luni, and in Cinqueterre blend.

Leading Liguria Producers

Walter de Batté ☆☆–☆☆☆
Riomaggiore, La Spezia
Probably the best producer both of Cinqueterre and Schiacchetrà.

Maria Donata Bianchi ☆
Diano Castello, Imperia
For those who like their Vermentino and Pigato fermented in French oak, this is the place to come. These *cuvées* are called "Eretico" and there are unoaked versions too.

Bisson ☆
Chiavari, Genoa
Piero Lugano's nine-hectare estate produces Vermentino and Ciliegiolo, and a red blend called 'Il Musaico'. A good source for Schiacchetrà del Cinqueterre.

Lunae Bosoni ☆☆
Ortonovo, La Spezia
A wide range of white and reds from Colli di Luni.

Riccardo Bruna ☆☆
Ranzo, Imperia
Some of the zone's finest Pigato but sadly only produced in small quantities.

Cane ☆☆
Dolceacqua, Imperia
Small production of admired Rossese, di Dolceacqua.

Colle dei Bardellini ☆☆
Sant'Agata, Imperia
Only five hectares, but zesty wines from Vermentino, Pigato, and Rossese.

La Colombiera ☆–☆☆
Castelnuovo Magra, La Spezia
A leading maker of fine Colli di Luni Vermentino; also a wine called "Terizzo" from Cabernet.

Cooperativa Agricola di Riomaggiore ☆–☆☆
Riomaggiore, La Spezia
Consistently good range of dry, white DOC Cinqueterre, with Sciacchetrà being the top wine.

Fèipu dei Massaretti ☆–☆☆
Albenga, Savona
Good Pigato and Rossese, and a blend (Rossese, Sangiovese, Brachetto) called Russu du Fèipu.

Foresti ☆☆
Camporosso, Imperia
Fifteen hectares of vines allow the Foresti family to make a range of impressive single-vineyard Rossese di Dolceacqua.

Forlini e Capellini ☆
Manarola, La Spezia
Family vineyard producing a good, full-bodied Cinqueterre.

Giuncheo ☆☆
Camporosso, Imperia
Excellent Vermentino and Rossese di Dolceacqua, in collaboration with oenologist Donato Lanati.

Enzo Guglielmi ☆
Soldano, Imperia
Guiglielmi's Rossese di Dolceacqua is consistently good.

Ottaviano Lambruschi ☆☆
Castelnuovo Magra, La Spezia
Very good DOC Colli di Luni Vermentino.

Lupi ☆☆
Pieve di Teco, Imperia
The Lupi family, ably advised by oenologist Donato Lanati, are among the region's top producers. Their Ormeasco, made from grapes grown in mountain vineyards, shows uncommon finesse and ages up to six years or more. Good Pigato and Vermentino, too.

Cascina delle Terre Rosse ☆☆–☆☆☆
Finale Ligure, Savona
Excellent Riviera Ligure di Ponente Pigato, and a red "Solitario" blend from Grenache, Barbera, and Rossese.

Vecchia Cantina ☆☆
Albenga, Savona
Specialists in rich Pigato and Vermentino from Riviera Ligure di Ponente.

Lombardy

Lombardy has always kept a low profile in the world of wine. It has no world-famous names. Oltrepò Pavese, its productive and profitable viticultural heart, is scarcely a name to conjure with. Valtellina, the last Alpine valley before Switzerland, commands more respect with its elegant Nebbiolo reds. The lakeside wines of Garda have some romantic appeal.

Local wine traditions are remarkably tenacious, but a region needs a flag-carrier which embodies its special qualities, and this Lombardy has only recently provided. An increasing number of DOCG Franciacorta *metodo tradizionale* sparkling wines are made, some of particularly high quality.

In contrast to Piedmont, with its proliferation of DOCs, Lombardy has a mere thirteen, but those of Oltrepò Pavese in particular, and Valtellina to a lesser degree, are umbrellas for a number of regulated brands or types of wine.

The grapes of Piedmont and the grapes of the northeast are all grown here, and frequently blended. It is inescapably a zone of transition, with rich possibilities but no clear identity to bank on. The producers are not greatly troubled by this, since they have a ready market in Milan and the other cities of the north, but there is, therefore, little incentive for them to jack up the quality of wines such as Oltrepò Pavese.

DOC & Other Wines

Barbacarlo An enclave of the Oltrepò Pavese (*q.v.*) near Broni, well-known for its unusual full-bodied, *frizzante* red from Lino Maga (*q.v.*), which can be dry or semi-sweet but always finishes faintly bitter.

Barbera One of the commonest red grapes of Lombardy, used both blended and alone. In Oltrepò Pavese it can be DOC.

Bonarda Another red grape with DOC rights in the Oltrepò Pavese. Dark, soft, and bitter on the finish.

Botticino DOC. Red wine. Province: Brescia. Villages: Botticino, Brescia, Rezzato. Grapes: Barbera, Schiava Gentile, Marzemino, Sangiovese 10–20%.

A fairly powerful and sweetish red; the local red-meat wine, best with three to four years of maturity.

Buttafuoco A forceful, concentrated red of blended Barbera, Uva Rara, and Croatina produced near Castana (under the umbrella DOC Oltrepò Pavese).

Capriano del Colle DOC. Red and white wine. Province: Brescia. Villages: Capriano del Colle and Poncarale. Grapes: (red) Sangiovese, Marzemino, Barbera, Merlot; (white) Trebbiano. A DOC for light local wines.

Cellatica DOC. Red wine. Province: Brescia. Villages west of Brescia. Grapes: Schiava Gentile, Barbera, Marzemino, and Incrocio Terzi No.l (Barbera/Cabernet Franc).

A respectable, mild red, best within two to four years, which has been enjoyed in the area since the sixteenth century.

Terre di Franciacorta DOC. Red and white wine. Province: Brescia: twenty-three communes south of Lake Iseo. Grapes: (red) for Franciacorta Rosso – Cabernet Franc, Barbera, Nebbiolo, Merlot, and others up to 15%; (white) for Franciacorta Bianco – Chardonnay and/or Pinot Bianco. Since 1995, this has been the DOC for the former "Franciacorta", as Franciacorta DOCG is now for sparkling wines only. Red Franciacorta is a very pleasant, light wine of some character.

Franciacorta DOCG. Awarded in 1995. Villages: as above. Grapes: Chardonnay and/or Pinot Bianco, and/or Pinot Nero, and/or Pinot Grigio.

Classic-method sparkling Franciacorta wine in white and *rosato* styles. From same province and villages as Terre di Franciacorta. This is Lombardy's best. Ca' del Bosco, Bellavista, Contadi Castaldi, Cavalleri, and Ricci Curbastro are among the top producers.

Garda and **Garda Classico** Recent DOCs for wines from the provinces of Brescia and Mantua made from local and international varieties of good quality. Too much of a catch-all to have any real identity. Shared with the Veneto.

Garda Colli Mantovani DOC. Red, white, and *rosato* wine. Province: Mantova. Grapes: (white) Garganega, Trebbiano Giallo and/or Trebbiano Toscano, and/or Pinot Bianco; (red and *rosato*) Rossanella (Molinara), Sangiovese, and Negrara. Lightweight local wines, though with a long history; Virgil mentioned them. The white resembles Soave.

Groppello A local red grape of southwest Garda.

Grumello A sub-region of Valtellina Superiore (*q.v.*).

Inferno A sub-region of Valtellina Superiore (*q.v.*).

Lambrusco Mantovano DOC. Red wine. Province: Mantova. Region: zones around the River Po and the border of Emilia-Romagna. Grapes: Lambrusco Viadanese and other sub-varieties; Ancellotta/Fortana (Uva d'Oro) up to 15%.

A DOC created in 1987 for a Lambrusco from the local Viadanese sub-variety; robust in the west, lighter towards the east of the zone. Wines are dry or more usually *frizzante*, and can hold their own with their counterparts from Emilia.

Lugana DOC. White wine. Provinces: Brescia and Verona. Region: the south end of Lake Garda between Desenzano and Peschiera. Grapes: Trebbiano di Lugano 100%, or with other light grapes up to 10%.

Formerly a glamorous rarity to be sought out in such lovely spots as Sirmione. Now a very pleasant, light, dry, white wine, scarcely distinguishable from a good Soave.

Merlot Increasingly grown as a "varietal" wine in Lombardy. Very satisfactory, though not included in a DOC. Part of blend in Franciacorta and Valcalepio.

Moscato di Scanzo Passito A great rarity from Bergamo: an excellent tawny dessert Muscat from a sub-zone of Valcalepio.

Müller-Thurgau This German grape is successfully grown in the Oltrepò Pavese, though not admitted in its DOC.

Narbusto Made from the Oltrepò red grapes, this is a long-lived *vino da tavola* (aged at least eight years).

Oltrepò Pavese DOC. Red and white wines. Province: Pavia. Area: Oltrepò Pavese. Grapes: (red) Barbera, Croatina, Uva Rara and/or Ughetta; (white) Pinot Grigio or Riesling Renano, others up to 15%.

The DOC for large volumes of reds and whites from the Oltrepò Pavese. Most of the more distinctive wines of the area are either specifically named (*e.g.* Barbacarlo, Buttafuoco) or have a specified grape variety dominant (eg Barbera, Pinot, Chardonnay, and Sauvignon).

Pinot Pinot Nero, Grigio, and Bianco are all widely grown in Lombardy. The Oltrepò Pavese is a major supplier of base wines of Pinot for *spumante* made in Piedmont and elsewhere.

Riesling The Oltrepò DOC includes both Italian and Rhine Rieslings without distinguishing them. Both grow well here.

Riviera del Garda Bresciano DOC. Red and *rosato* wine. Province: Brescia. Villages: thirty communes on western and southwestern shores of Lake Garda. Grapes: Groppello, Sangiovese, Barbera, and Marzemino.

The mirror image of Valpolicella and Bardolino from the other side of the lake. Commercial qualities at least are similar, although classic Valpolicella is much deeper in flavour. The village of Moniga del Garda makes a pale Chiaretto which is lively and good when very young. This has been partly replaced by the new Garda Bresciano DOC.

San Colombano al Lambro or **San Colombano** DOC. Red wine. Provinces: Milan and Pavia. Villages: San Colombano al Lambro, Graffignana, S Angelo Lodigiano. Grapes: Croatina, Barbera, Uva Rara; other reds up to 15%.

Hearty reds from the slopes around San Colombano. Best for drinking after two to four years.

Sangue di Giuda A fizzy, often sweet red called "Judas Blood" is the sort of wine that makes "serious" wine-lovers turn their eyes to heaven. It should be tried without prejudice. There are good ones.

Sassella A sub-region of Valtellina Superiore (*q.v.*).

Sfursat or **Sfurzat** or **Sforzato** Valtellina's equivalent of the Recioto of Valpolicella in the Veneto; a strong (14.5 degrees) red made of semi-dried grapes, in this case, Nebbiolo. Age certainly improves it as it turns tawny, but whether the final result pleases you is a personal matter.

San Martino della Battaglia DOC. White wine. Provinces: Brescia and Verona. Villages: Sirmione, Desanzano, Lonato, Pozzolengo, Peschiera. Grape: Tocai Friulano.

A distinctive character among Garda wines: dry, yellow, and tasty with something of the typical local bitterness in the finish. It is best drunk as young as possible. Also made as a fortified *liquoroso* wine.

Valcalepio DOC. Red and white wine. Province: Bergamo.

Villages: fifteen in the Calepio Valley. Grapes: (white) Pinot Bianco, Chardonnay, and Pinot Grigio; (red) Merlot and Cabernet Sauvignon.

A small production, principally red, of light wines with an ancient name but modern grape varieties. There is also a Moscato *passito* from Valcalepio.

Valgella A sub-region of Valtellina Superiore (*q.v.*).

Valtellina and **Valtellina Superiore** DOC. Red wine. Province: Sondrio. Sub-districts: Sassella, Grumello, Inferno and Valgella for superiore, Twelve communes for Valtellina. Grapes: Nebbiolo (called Chiavennasca) 70%, plus Pinot Nero, Merlot, Rossola, Brugnola or Pignola Valtellinese. *Superiore* is 95% Nebbiolo. Aged for not less than two years, of which one is in wood, and four years for *riserva*.

The most successful excursion of Nebbiolo outside its home region of Piedmont. Plain Valtellina can be expected to be a fairly "hard", light red. The named *superiores* develop considerable character as dry, claret-weight wines with hints of autumnal mellowness. Freshness and elegance should be the hallmarks of good Valtellina. It is hard to discern consistent differences between Sassella, Inferno, etc., but the first is generally considered the best. Switzerland (St-Moritz is just over the mountain) is a principal consumer. See also Sfursat.

Maurizio Zanella Cabernet Sauvignon and Franc with Merlot, blended wine grown in Franciacorta and named after its producer.

Leading Lombardy Producers

Bellavista ✫✫✫
Erbusco, Brescia. www.terramoretti.it
Vittorio Moretti's celebrated fifty-hectare estate has, for some time, been one of the very best producers of Franciacorta. These wines are stylish and very highly regarded, particularly the pure "Chardonnay Gran Cuvée Brut" and "Rosé". The still wines are also very good, especially the Pinot Noir. This estate is Ca' del Bosco's closest competitor and prices are high.

Guido Berlucchi ✫✫✫
Borgonato di Cortefranca, Brescia. www.berlucchi.it
Since 1962, this firm has grown to be one of Italy's largest producers of classic-method wines – over 400,000 cases. Berlucchi also owns Antica Cantine Fratta and produces *tradizionale* under that label.

Ca' del Bosco ✫✫✫–✫✫✫✫
Erbusco, Brescia. www.cadelbosco.com
Maurizio Zanella comes from a wealthy family, but he is no dilettante, and has thrown all his considerable energies into creating what is probably the outstanding estate of Lombardy.

If the "Pinero" Pinot Noir never quite justifies its high price, the Franciacorta sparkling wines are superb, as is the Chardonnay and the Cabernet/Merlot blend rather audaciously named "Maurizio Zanella". Often the best sparkling wine is the noble "Dosage Zéro".

Cavalleri ☆☆☆
Erbusco, Brescia. www.cavalleri.it
A fine source of Franciacorta, especially the "Collezione Brut", and the austere "Pas Dosé Brut". Also barrel-fermented Chardonnay "Seradina", and a French-style Cabernet/Merlot blend, "Tajardino".

Contadi Castaldi ☆☆☆
Adro, Brescia. www.contadicastaldi.it
Outstanding Franciacorta producer, also owned by Vittorio Moretti of Bellavista (*q.v.*). The top wine is the "Magno Brut"; other *cuvées* include the elegant "Satèn" and the austere "Brut Zero". Among the table wines there is a fine Cabernet Sauvignon called "Marconero".

Mazzolino ☆☆
Corvino San Quirico, Pavia. www.tenutamazzolino.co
A fine range of Oltrepò wines, with the emphasis on barrique-aged wines from Pinot Noir, Chardonnay, and Cabernet Sauvignon.

Monte Rossa ☆☆☆
Cazzago San Martino, Brescia. www.monterossa.com
The Rabotti family produces a range of excellent Franciacorta, especially the long-lived "Brut Cabochon".

Nino Negri ☆☆☆
Chiuro, Sondrio
Founded in 1897, but now part of the Gruppo Italiano Vini. The Valtellina region's largest cellars, benefiting from advanced technology and the direction of the experienced oenologist Casimiro Maule, it still remains a leading force. Excellent, subtle, sleek wines from all the regional *crus*, and wonderful Sfursat "5 Stelle". Production is approaching one million bottles.

Aldo Rainoldi ☆☆☆
Chiuro, Sondrio. www.rainoldi.com
Elegant and dependable wines from all of the major Valtellina *crus*. Rainoldi has mastered the use of barriques, especially in the remarkably stylish "Sfursat Fruttaio".

Conti Sertoli Salis ☆☆–☆☆☆
Tirano, Sondrio. www.sertolisalis.com
Ancient ruling house of the region, ambitiously revived with the '89 vintage. An excellent range of wines, using large casks and small barrels for ageing. Excellent Sforzato "Canua".

Triacca ☆☆☆
Villa di Tirano, Sondrio. www.triacca.com
Domenico Triacca has made enormous investments to select the best Nebbiolo clones, and to ensure they are skilfully vinified. "Prestigio" is a much acclaimed wine, but only for new-oak aficionados. Others may prefer the stylish *riserva*. Fine Sforzato, too.

Other Lombardy Producers

Agnes ☆☆
Rovescala, Pavia
Bonarda is the specialty of this respected Oltrepò Pavese

producer. "Millenium" is an interesting version made from late-harvested grapes.

Riccardo Albani ☆–☆☆
Casteggio, Pavia
Fresh, well-made Riesling Renano and Bonarda, and a fine red blend called "Vigna della Casona" from Barbera, Croatina, Uva Rara, and Pinot Noir.

Anteo ☆☆
Rocca de'Giorgi, Pavia
Major producer of *tradizionale* sparkling wines from Oltrepò Pavese, notably "Nature" from Chardonnay and Pinot Nero.

Balgera ☆☆
Sondrio
Good Valtellina.

Fratelli Berlucchi ☆
Borgonato di Cortefranca, Brescia. www.berlucchifranciacorta.it
Sound Franciacorta "Brut" and "Rosé".

Conti Bettoni ☆–☆☆
Cazzago, Cazzago San Martino, Brescia
Good Franciacorta, especially the top *cuvée*, which is called Tetellus.

Tenuta Il Bosco ☆–☆☆
Zenevredo, Pavia. www.ilbosco.com
Owned by Zonin, along with San Zeno at Stradella, and the base of a major *spumante* operation.

La Brugherata, ☆☆
Scanzorosciate, Bergamo
Leading producer of Valcalepio, white and red.

Ca' dei Frati ☆☆–☆☆☆
Lugana, Sirmione. www.cadeifrati.it
Top producer of Lugana and a lush *passito* wine made from Trebbiano and Chardonnay called "Tre Filer".

Cornaleto ☆☆
Adro, Brescia. www.cornaleto.it Luigi
Lancini produces very elegant Franciacorta as well as Terre di Franciacorta.

Costaripa ☆☆–☆☆☆
Moniga del Garda, Brescia
Mattia Vezzola, also the winemaker at Bellavista (*q.v.*), uses the new Garda Classico DOC here for a wide range of wines, some of them barrique-aged. "Pradamonte" is from Cabernet Sauvignon, "Maim" a pure Groppello.

Doria ☆☆
Montalto Pavese, Pavia.
Adriano Doria produces a range of wines from Oltrepò Pavese: barrique-aged Pinot Nero, the Barbera-dominated "Roncorosso", and Bonarda.

Faccoli Lorenzo ☆☆
Coccaglio, Brescia
A sound source of sparkling wines from Franciacorta.

Sandro Fay ✩✩
San Giacomo di Teglio, Sondrio
Good wines, including "Valgella Ca' Moreí", and barrique-aged "Valgella Carteria".

Ferghettina ✩✩–✩✩✩
Erbusco, Brescia
Although this house produces fine Franciacorta, it is also well known for its Merlot "Baladello" and Chardonnay.

Le Fracce ✩✩
Casteggio, Pavia. www.le-fracce.it
Very reliable, essentially varietal range from Oltrepò Pavese.

Frecciarossa ✩✩–✩✩✩
Casteggio, Pavia. www.frecciarossa.com
A 22-hectare estate founded in 1923 by the late Giorgio Odero, and now owned by his descendants.

Good Oltrepò Pavese, especially the traditional red blend "Villa Odero".

Lantieri de Paratico ✩
Capriolo, Brescia
Sound Franciacorta, both vintage and non-vintage.

After DOC?

A monumental effort of organization and definition produced, within twenty years from 1962, 300-odd DOCs covering over 1,000 styles of wine. It was precisely the discipline that Italy needed, both to concentrate her producers' minds on quality and to convince the rest of the world that she was in earnest, and that her labels were to be trusted.

The DOCs are accurate records of the regional practice of the time, when they were promulgated. Whatever a consensus of growers agreed as normal and satisfactory within the traditions of their area was, after consultation with Rome, engraved on the tablets.

What is not often clearly understood is that the practices being followed and approved were, in many, if not most cases, far from optimal. In the matter of grape varieties, the DOC enshrined what the farmers had planted in their vineyards, not what they should, or might, have planted to produce the best wine. It allowed for example, a proportion of white grapes in Chianti, which can almost make it a *rosato*.

The growers in most cases allowed themselves crops far larger than could be consistent with fine wine. They also set high minimum alcohol levels based on their old fear of unstable wine – whereas with modern techniques lower alcohol is both practicable and desirable.

Again, in their search for stability (and with their inherited taste for wines aged almost to exhaustion in oak) they set minimum ageing limits which run counter to the modern trends for clearly fruity and fragrant, or else bottle-aged and complex, wines.

Eventually, the slow-moving authorities acknowledged the seriousness of the problem, and introduced the new *Indicazione Geografica Tipica* (IGT) category, allowing much greater freedom to create wines that do not conform to the old rules. It also ends the anomaly by which some of the top wines of Italy were obliged to be labelled as lowly *vini da tavola*.

Lino Maga ✩
Broni, Pavia
This Oltrepò Pavese estate originated Barbacarlo (now a proprietary wine), one of Italy's most durable, bubbly reds.

Majolini ✩✩
Ome, Brescia. www.majolini.it
A rising star, with increasingly ambitious Franciacorta.

Villa Mazzucchelli ✩✩–✩✩✩
Ciliverghe, Brescia
Top *spumante* from blends of Chardonnay and Pinot Nero.

Monsupello ✩✩–✩✩✩
Torricello Verzate, Pavia. www.monsupello.it
Founded in 1893, this is a respected source of Oltrepò Pavese varietal wines, and of excellent sparkling wines from Pinot Nero.

Montelio ✩–✩✩
Codevilla, Pavia
Sound wines from Oltrepò Pavese, and surprisingly tasty Müller-Thurgau.

Mosnel ✩✩–✩✩✩
Camignone di Passirano, Brescia. www.ilmosnel.com
Excellent Franciacorta, and stylish, oak-aged Pinot Nero.

Nera ✩✩
Chiuro, Sondrio. www.neravini.com
A sound producer of Valtellina crus and Sforzato.

Pasini ✩✩
Raffa di Puegnago, Brescia. www.pasiniproduttori.it
Garda Classico "Montezalto" is a barrique-aged Cabernet Sauvignon, and the Groppello can also be recommended.

Pelizzatti ✩–✩✩
Perego, Sondrio, Sondrio
Old-fashioned producer of delicate Valtellina crus.

Cascina La Pertica ✩✩–✩✩✩
Polpenazze, Brescia
Ruggero Brunori's top wine is usually the Bordeaux-style red "Le Zalte", made with the advice of oenologist Franco Bernabei.

Barone Pizzini ✩✩–✩✩✩
Cortefranca, Brescia. www.baronepizzini.it
Respected producer of Franciacorta, especially the pure-Chardonnay "Satèn".

Ricci Curbastro ✩✩
Capriolo, Brescia. www.riccicurbastro.com
Rich, pure-Chardonnay Franciacorta "Satèn" and an oaky, still Pinot Nero.

Travaglino ✩✩
Calvignano, Pavia
A good source of Oltrepò Pavese from Riesling and Pinot Noir, and attractive sparkling wines, too.

Uberti Erbusco ✩✩✩
Brescia

Impressive, if expensive, *cuvées* of Chardonnay-dominated Franciacorta; "Francesco I Brut" and "Brut Magnificentia".

Bruno Verdi ☆☆–☆☆☆
Canneto Pavese, Pavia
Reliable source of Oltrepò Pavese from Bonarda, Pinot Grigio, and other varieties. You'll find "Sangue di Giuda Dolce" here, too.

Cantina Sociale ☆☆
La Versa, Santa Maria della Versa, Pavia. www.laversa.it
A respected cooperative in Oltrepò Pavese, its 750 members own 1300 hectares of vines and produce 8 million bottles annually. It sells a fraction of the production under its own label, most notably *spumante classico* and Pino Nero brut *tradizionale*. Delicious Moscato *passito,* too.

Virgili ☆
Montova
A leading producer of DOC Lambrusco Montavano.

Trentino-Alto Adige

The valley of the River Adige is Italy's corridor to the Germanic world and vice versa: a narrow, rock-walled but surprisingly flat-bottomed and untortuous trench among high peaks, which has carried all the traffic of millennia over the Brenner Pass, from the land of olives to the land of firs and back again.

So Germanic is its northern half, the Alto Adige, that its German-speaking inhabitants know it as the Südtirol and think of Italy as a foreign country. A large proportion of its wine production is exported for sale north of the border with the bottles labelled in German.

The Trentino has a more southern culture, but even Trento feels only halfway to Italy. The region's wines are correspondingly cosmopolitan, using most of the well-known international grape varieties.

The Alto Adige has made more and more successful interpretations of the white classics. The shelter and warmth of its best slopes, counterpoised by its altitude, give excellent balance of ripeness and acidity. Cooperatives are important in the region, and some of them pursue the same high standards as the very best private estates.

Farther south in Trentino, the trend is also toward whites. But happily, local taste still maintains the survival of the native reds. The Schiava, Lagrein, and Teroldego all seem to be mountain-bred versions of the grapes of Valpolicella. In slightly different ways they all share the smooth, inviting start and the lingering, bitter finish which you could call the *goût de terroir* of northeast Italy.

A quite different local specialty is Moscato Rosa, a sublimely perfumed pink Muscat, possibly of Sicilian origin, that miraculously combines intense aroma and delicacy with high levels of natural alcohol.

DOC & Other Wines

Alto Adige (Südtirol) DOC. Red, *rosato,* and white wine.

Province: Bolzano. Villages: Thirty-three communes with vineyards up to 700 metres (2,275 feet) high for red grapes and 1,000 metres (3,280 feet) for white. Grapes: 95% of any of the following: Moscato Giallo (Goldenmuskateller), Pinot Bianco (Weissburgunder), Pinot Grigio (Ruländer), Riesling Italico (Welschriesling), Müller-Thurgau, Riesling Renano (Rhein Riesling), Sylvaner, Sauvignon, Traminer Aromatico (Gewürztraminer), Cabernet, Lagrein *Rosato* (L. Kretzer), Lagrein Scuro (L. Dunkel), Malvasia (Malvasier), Merlot, Moscato Rosa (Rosenmuskateller), Pinot Nero (Blauburgunder), Schiava (Vernatsch), Chardonnay, plus 5% of any other; 85% Schiava and 15% of any other. Maximum permitted yields range from 98 hl/ha (for Schiava and Lagrein) down to 56 hl/ha (for Moscato Giallo).

The general DOC for a large zone, following the Adige and Isario valleys through the mountains, and including the Bolzano basin. Of the varieties allowed, the classic international grapes form the majority, several of them doing as well here as anywhere in Italy. Cabernet, Gewürztraminer, Pinot Bianco, and Rhein Riesling can all be outstanding. The local characters are the Lagrein, red or *rosato*, which makes a fruity, rich, smooth and flowing wine with a bitter twist, and the Schiava, which could be described as a jolly junior version of the same thing. The Traminer is also very much a local character, having its birthplace at Tramin (Termeno) just south of Bolzano. The same geographic area has several more restrictive DOCs (Santa Maddalena, or St Magdalener, for example) but they are not necessarily superior in quality.

Caldaro or **Lago di Caldaro** or **Kalterersee** DOC. Red wine. Provinces: Bolzano and Trento. Villages: nine communes in Bolzano and eight in Trento. Grapes: Schiava 85–100%, Pinot Nero and Lagrein 15%.

The German name *Kalterersee* is more common than the Italian for this light and often-sweetish red, originally grown around the lake southwest of Bolzano (now designated on labels as *classico*). The lake area has an exceptional microclimate for grape-growing. Like all Schiava, it is an acquired taste, with a bitter finish that helps to make it refreshing, though some of the bottles shipped to Germany are so revoltingly sweet and mawkish that putting them in the freezer is the only way of making them drinkable.

Castel San Michele A highly regarded Cabernet/Merlot blend produced by the regional agricultural college at San Michele, north of Trento. It needs five to six years or more bottle-age.

Casteller DOC. Red wine. Province: Trento. Villages: twenty-seven communes, slopes no higher than 600 metres (1,950 feet). Grapes: Schiava at least 30%, Lambrusco up to 60%, and Merlot, Lagrein, or Teroldego 20%.

The light, dry, everyday red of the southern half of the region from Trento to Lake Garda, but rarely seen outside.

Kolbenhofer. A superior Schiava red (and a Gewürztraminer) made at Tramin by Hofstätter.

Adige Meranese di Collina or **Südtiroler Meraner Hügel** DOC. Red wine. Province: Bolzano, Villages: around Merano, on both sides of the Adige River. Grape: Schiava. The local light red wine of Merano, for the young and hot to drink young and cool. Meraner Hügel is part of the Südtiroler DOC.

Nosiola DOC. Trentino native white grape. The wine is fruity, dry, and (surprise!) finishes with a bitter note; it has a distinctive hazelnut perfume (*nosiola* in Trentino-dialect means "hazelnut"). It is also the base of delicious *vin santo*.

San Leonardo One of the successful Cabernet/Merlot reds of the Trentino. *See* San Leonardo (Gonzaga).

Santa Maddalena or **St Magdalener** DOC. Red wine. Province: Bolzano. Villages: the hills to the north, above Bolzano (Classico is from Santa Maddalena itself). Grapes: Schiava, Lagrein, Pinot Nero up to 10%.

An obvious relation to Caldaro, but from better vineyards, more concentrated and stronger. Under Mussolini it was absurdly pronounced one of Italy's three greatest wines (Barolo and Barbaresco were the others). This and Lagrein Dunkel must be considered the first choice among the typical red wines of Bolzano.

Südtiroler Terlaner DOC. Was Terlano or Terlaner, but since 1993 part of the Alto Adige/Südtiroler-DOC. White wine. Province: Bolzano. Villages: Terlano, Meltina, Nalles, Andriano, Appiano, Caldaro (Terlano and Nalles are "Classico"). Grapes: 90% Chardonnay, Müller-Thurgau, Pinot Bianco, Riesling (Italico and Renano), Sauvignon, Sylvaner.

The best whites of the Alto Adige are grown in this part of the valley, particularly just west of Bolzano, where Terlano has excellent southwest slopes. Pinot Bianco, Riesling Renano, Sauvignon, and sometimes Sylvaner can all make wines of real body and balance, occasionally in the international class. Terlano without a grape name will include at least 50% of either Pinot Bianco or Chardonnay, and may include both; it is often a good buy.

Trento DOC. White and *rosato*. Province: Trento. Grapes: Chardonnay, and/or Pinot Bianco, and/or Pinot Nero, and/or Pinot Meunier. Classic-method sparkling and fifteen months' ageing on yeasts in bottle (thirty-six months for *riserva*) are obligatory. DOC for local traditional method sparkling wine. One of Trentino's most successful wines.

Teroldego Rotaliano DOC. Red wine. Province: Trento. Villages: Mezzocorona, Mezzolombardo, S. Michel all'Adige. Grape: Teroldego. Pergola-trained Teroldego vines, on the alluvial gravel deposited by the River Noce on the Campo Rotaliano, give the best of the typical smooth, well-fleshed reds of the region, with their characteristically bitter finish. The wines are attractive when young, but also have the potential to age well.

Trentino DOC. Red and white wine. Province: Trento. Villages: a long zone stretching from Mezzocorona north of Trento to 24 kilometres (15 miles) north of Verona. Grapes: Trentino DOC means twenty-five different wine types: Kretzer, Cabernet Franc, Cabernet Sauvignon, Chardonnay, Lagrein, Marzemino, Merlot, Moscato Giallo, Moscato Rosa, Rebo, Müller-Thurgau, Nosiola, Pinot Bianco, Pinot Grigio, Pinot Nero, Riesling Italico, Riesling Renano, Sauvignon, Traminer Aromatico, Rosso, Bianco, Vin Santo, Sorni Bianco, Sorni Rosso. Trentino

Rosso is a Cabernet/Merlot blend; Trentino Bianco is mostly Chardonnay and Pinot Bianco.

The southern counterpart of the DOC Alto Adige, with almost as great a range of wines, but with more emphasis on the reds. Cabernet is well established here with excellent results; Lagrein gives some of the best examples of the regional style. Merlot is common – best when blended with Cabernet. Pinot Bianco and Traminer are the best of the dry whites, while Moscato yields a potentially excellent dessert wine.

Trentino Sorni DOC. Red and white wine. Province: Trento. Villages: Lavis, Giovo, and S. Michele all'Adige, north of Trento. Grapes: (red) Schiava 70%, Teroldego 20–30%, and Lagrein up to 10%, (white) Nosiola 70%, and others 30%. DOC for reds and whites from around the village of Sorni. Both are light, dry wines for summer drinking.

Valdadige or **Etschtaler** DOC. Red and white wine. Provinces: Trento, Bolzano, and Verona. Villages: thirty-eight communes in Trento, thirty-three in Bolzano, and four in Verona. Grapes: (red) Schiava and/or Lambrusco 30% and the rest, Merlot, Pinot Nero, Lagrein, Teroldego and/or Negrara up to 70%; (white) Pinot Bianco, Pinot Grigio, Riesling Italico or Müller-Thurgau 20%; the rest, Bianchetta Trevigiana, Trebbiano Toscano, Nosiola, Vernaccia up to 80%. The catch-all DOC for most of the Adige Valley from Merano to Verona.

Südtiroler Eisacktaler DOC. (Was Valle Isarco or Eisacktaler; since 1993, part of Alto Adige/Südtiroler-DOC). White wine. Province: Bolzano. Villages: parts of twelve communes in the Isarco Valley northeast of Bolzano to Bressanone (Brixen). Grapes: Traminer Aromatico, Pinot Grigio, Veltliner, Sylvaner or Müller-Thurgau.

The white wines of this Alpine valley are all light and need drinking young, in contrast to the "stiffer" wines of Terlano, to the west.

Leading Trentino-Alto Adige Producers

Abbazia di Novacella (Stiftskellerei Neustift) ☆☆
Varna, Bolzano. www.kloster-neustift.it
A lovely twelfth century monastery producing Valle Isarco DOC. The top wines from Pinot Nero and other varieties are designated "Praepositus".

Ca' Vit (Cantina Viticoltori Trento) ☆–☆☆☆
Ravina, Trento. www.cavit.it
Founded in 1950, this consortium of thirteen cooperatives unites 5,600 growers owning 7,000 hectares; they produce about 75% of the wine of Trento province. Only a select part is issued under the Ca'Vit label.

In addition to varietal wines produced in large quantities from different sub-regions, there are small lots of exceptional wines, such as a *vin santo* from Nosiola, a Bordeaux blend, and a barrique-aged Chardonnay, the last two under the "Maso Toresella" label. This immense company achieves good quality at a reasonable price.

Cantina Produttori Colterenzio (Schreckbichl) ☆–☆☆☆
Cornaiano, Bolzano. www.colterenzio.com
An ambitious group of 310 growers with a range of Alto Adige, Terlano, St Magdalener and Kalterersee DOCs, with some single-vineyard bottlings. The Cornell label is used for selected wines, notably Chardonnay aged in barriques, and "Praedium" is the label designating a wine from an outstanding site.

Concilio ☆☆
Volano, Trento. www.concilio.it
Founded in 1972, a union of two older wineries, and now making very reliable varietal wines, with Merlot that is among the best in Trentino.

Donati ☆☆–☆☆☆
Mezzocorona, Trento
Marco Donati is an outstanding producer of Teroldego, especially the concentrated bottling called "Sangue del Drago".

Ferrari ☆☆–☆☆☆
Trento. www.cantineferrari.it
A firm founded in 1902 in the heart of Trento. For many years, the leading name in Italian classic-method sparkling wines, the winery is now run by the Lunelli family. The flagship wine is the consistently outstanding "Giulio Ferrari Riserva del Fondatore" *blanc de blancs.*

Foradori ☆☆–☆☆☆☆
Mezzolombardo, Trento. www.elisabettaforadori.com
Founded in 1930, this important estate, run by Elisabetta "Foradori" has long espoused the cause of Teroldego, and makes some of Trentino's best examples, notably the barrique-aged "Granato". Also excellent are the Bordeaux blend called "Karanbar" and a Syrah IGT called "Ailanpa".

Franz Haas ☆☆–☆☆☆
Montagna, Bolzano. www.franz-haas.it
A small property releasing elegant white wines, a fine Bordeaux blend called "Istante", and delicious Moscato Rosa.

J. Hofstätter ☆☆–☆☆☆
Termeno, Bolzano. www.hofstatter.com
Founded in 1907, this family business is now managed by Martin Foradori. For decades it has offered an excellent assortment of South Tyrolean wines, partly from forty-five hectares of estate vines. The Pinot Nero red from Barthenau is outstanding.

Istituto Agrario Provinciale San Michele all'Adige ☆☆
San Michele all'Adige, Trento. www.ismaa.it
The agricultural college built around Castel San Michele is a national leader in viticultural research. From its own vineyards, the college makes several wines both for experiment and commerce, including the excellent Castel San Michele (a Cabernet/Merlot blend) and many attractive white wines.

Alois Lageder ☆☆☆–☆☆☆☆
Magrè, Bolzano. www.lageder.com
This well-known family winery owns seventeen hectares, but manages and buys from 300 more to make some of the region's finest varietals. Most of them are different quality levels; the most dazzling wines are usually the "Löwengang" Chardonnay and the "Römigberg" Cabernet Sauvignon. A

separate range of IGT wines, "Casòn Hirschprunn", is produced from an estate Lageder bought in 1991.

Longariva ☆☆–☆☆☆
Rovereto, Trento. www.longariva.it
Admirable red wines here, from low-cropped Pinot Nero ("Zinzèle"), Merlot ("Tovi"), and other varieties. Stylish barrique-aged Chardonnay, too.

Pojer & Sandri ☆☆☆
Faedo, Trento. www.pojeresandri.it
Mario Pojer is the oenologist, Fiorentino Sandri the viticulturist. They produce some of Trentino's most brilliant white wines, including Chardonnay, Müller-Thurgau, Nosiola, and enjoyable Pinot Nero. The wines have a delicately floral scent and fruity crispness.

San Leonardo ☆☆☆
Avio, Trento. www.sanleonardo.it
Owner Marchese Carlo Gonzaga uses barriques to bring finesse to Bordeaux varieties, notably his Merlot and "San Leonardo", a blend that has become a Trentino classic.

Tiefenbrunner (Castel Turmhoff) ☆☆
Cortaccia, Bolzano. www.tiefenbrunner.com
Herbert Tiefenbrunner's long-established family winery produces some of the South Tirol's most exciting whites. The Feldmarschall (a Müller-Thurgau) comes from vineyards 990 metres/3,250 feet above sea level: the region's highest.

Vallarom ☆☆–☆☆☆
Avio, Trento. www.vallarom.com
The Scienza family produces good Marzemino and Chardonnay, and white and red blends called "Campi Sarni". Syrah shows promise.

Zeni ☆☆–☆☆☆
Grumo di San Michele all'Adige, Trento. www.zeni.it
Roberto Zeni has run this leading estate since 1975. He is a top winemaker; his Chardonnay and Pinot Bianco are perfumed, his Teroldego harmonious. Excellent Amarone too.

Other Trentino Producers

Arunda Vivaldi ☆☆–☆☆☆
Meltina, Bolzano
Josef Reiterer makes exemplary *tradizionale* sparkling wines from vineyards some 1,200 metres (3,900 feet) high.

Bolognani ☆☆
Lavis, Trento
A quality producer of white Nosiola, Müller-Thurgau, and Chardonnay.

A Cadalora ☆☆
Ala, Trento
A ten-hectare estate specializing in fresh, well-made white wines.

Barone de Cles ☆☆
Mezzolombardo, Trento

An historic estate, producing very good Teroldego Rotaliano and Lagrein.

Cantina Sociale Cornaiano (Girlan) ☆☆
Cornaiano, Bolzano. www.girlan.it
Sound varietal wines from a good cooperative, including some serious reds under the "Optimum" label.

Dorigati ☆☆
Mezzocorona, Trento
The Dorigati family is closely involved in running this winery, which produces excellent Teroldego.

Endrizzi ☆–☆☆
San Michele all'Adige, Trento. www.endrizzi.it
Good varietal wines, and interesting blends, red and white, called "Masetto".

Giuseppe Fanti ☆☆–☆☆☆
Pressano, Lavis
The top wines at this Trentino winery are usually the Chardonnay and the unusual white from Incrocio Manzoni (a Riesling x Pinot Blanc crossing), but Nosiola is good, too.

Gaierhof ☆☆
Rovere della Luna, Trento
Owner Luigi Togn produces fine white wines, notably Chardonnay, and good Teroldego Rotaliano. Some wines bear the label of his other estate at Maso Poli (*q.v.*).

Gojer-Glögglhof ☆☆
Bolzano
Good St Magdalener and barrique-aged red Lagrein Dunkel.

Haderburg ☆☆
Salorno, Bolzano
The Ochsenreiter family produces good sparkling wines, and the still Chardonnay and Pinot Nero are increasing in quality.

Cantina d'Isera ☆
Isera, Trento
A good cooperative, producing excellent Marzemino.

Kettmeir ☆–☆☆
Caldaro, Bolzano
A large long-established company, sold in the 1990s to the Santa Margherita winery of the Veneto. Good white wines.

Graf Kuenburg-Schloss Sallegg ☆–☆☆☆
Caldaro, Bolzano
First-class late-harvest Moscato Rosa and a fine range of red wines.

Letrari ☆☆
Rovereto, Trento. www.letrari.com
Founded in 1976 by Leonello Letrari. As well as sparkling wines, Letrari produce fine Moscato Rosa and a good Bordeaux blend called "Ballistarius".

Lunelli ☆☆–☆☆☆
Ravina, Trento

The still wine branch of Ferrari (*q.v.*). Good Chardonnay and Pinot Noir from single-vineyard sites, and a Bordeaux blend called "Maso Le Viane".

Karl Martini & Sohn ☆☆
Cornaiano, Bolzano
The "Sohn" is Gabriele Martini, who has raised quality to a high level. Very good Lagrein/Cabernet, and elegant Moscato Rosa.

Maso Cantanghel ☆☆
Civezzano, Trento
Produces a fine, barrel-fermented Chardonnay "Vigna Piccola", Pinot Nero, and Cabernet Sauvignon from their five-hectare vineyard.

Maso Furli ☆☆
Lavis, Trento
Delicious whites, especially the Traminer and Chardonnay.

Maso Poli ☆☆
San Michele all'Adige, Trento
Owned by Luigi Togn, this is an old estate producing good "Sorni Bianco" and Pinot Nero.

Cantina Mezzocorona ☆☆
Mezzocorona, Trento
An important quality-conscious cooperative producing good Teroldego and sparkling wines.

Klosterkellerei Muri-Gries ☆–☆☆
Bolzano
The ancient cellars of this Benedictine monastery (well worth a visit) produce a wide range of typical varietal wines under a number of Alto Adige DOCs. Lagrein is the specialty.

Niedrist ☆☆–☆☆☆
Cornaiano, Appiano
Elegant red and whites from Alto Adige, with successful Pinot Nero.

Pisoni ☆☆
Pergolese, Lasino. www.pisoniepisoni.it
Good white wines, notably "San Siro" (Chardonnay/Pinot Bianco) and *vin santo*.

Plattner-Waldgries. ☆–☆☆☆
Bolzano
A small family winery. Particularly successful are the Moscato Rosa and a *passito* wine called "Peperum".

Praeclarus ☆☆
San Paolo-Appiano, Bolzano
Noted *tradizionale* brut and extra brut.

Pravis ☆☆–☆☆☆
Lasino
A small, innovative estate producing a fine white blend, "Stravino di Stravino", and promising Syrah.

Castel Rametz ☆
Merano, Bolzano
Good Alto Adige Chardonnay and Riesling.

Cantina Rotaliana ☆–☆☆☆

Mezzolombardo, Trento. www.cantinarotaliana.it
Admirable Teroldego along with Lagrein and Trentino DOCs.

Hans Rottensteiner ☆

Bolzano
A sound range of DOCs including good St Magdalener.

Heinrich Rottensteiner ☆

Rencio, Bolzano
This is a dedicated grower making excellent St Magdalener and a spicy Cabernet/Merlot blend – unfortunately named "Putz".

Cantina Produttori San Michele Appiano (St-Michael) ☆☆☆

San Michele Appiano, Bolzano. www.stmichael.it
An outstanding cooperative, offering a very good range of Alto Adige DOCs. Top line is "Sanct Valentin" (includes Sauvignon, Chardonnay, Pinot Nero, Pinot Bianco).

Cantina Santa Magdalena ☆☆

Bolzano. www.kellereimagdalena.com
A sixty-five-member cooperative producing, among many other wines, excellent Lagrein.

Castel Schwanburg ☆☆

Nalles, Bolzano
Of Renaissance origin, this estate has developed a fine reputation for its Cabernet Sauvignon.

Armando Simoncelli ☆☆

Rovereto, Trento
A leading estate with a fine Marzemino and Lagrein, and fresh Pinot Bianco.

Enrico Spagnolli ☆–☆☆

Isera, Trento
A range of Trentino varietal wines, including a fine Marzemino and Müller-Thurgau.

De Tarczal ☆☆

Marano d'Isera, Trento. www.detarczal.com
An admirable range of Trentino DOCs, with an exemplary Marzemino and a Bordeaux blend called "Pragiara".

Cantina Terlano ☆☆–☆☆☆

Terlano, Bolzano. www.cantina-terlano.com
Elegant if pricey white wines, in ascending order of quality: "I Classici", "I Vigneti", and "Le Selezoni".

Cantina Produttori Termeno (Tramin) ☆–☆☆☆

Termeno, Bolzano. www.tramin-wine.it
Gewürztraminer is, of course, the specialty here, including a remarkable *passito* version.

Cantina Produttori Valle Isarco (Eisacktaler) ☆

Chiusa, Bolzano. www.cantinavalleisarco.it
A respected cooperative producing reliable "Isarco" white wines.

La Vis ☆–☆☆☆

Lavis, Trento. www.la-vis.com
An important cooperative, producing 10% of all Trentino DOC wine. The top ranges are "Ritratti" from outstanding terroirs, and "Ceolan" from Alto Adige grapes.

Elena Walch ☆☆☆

Termeno, Bolzano. www.elenawalch.com
Medium-sized producer with beautiful vineyards overlooking Lake Caldaro. Wines are from the Castel Ringberg and Kastelaz estates.

Hofkellerei W. Walch ☆–☆☆☆

Termeno, Bolzano
The Walch family buys in grapes locally to produce a sound range of varietal wines, the best of which appear under the "Janus" label.

Veneto

The hinterland of Venice is one-third mountain, two-thirds plain. Its northernmost boundary is with Austria, high in the Dolomites; in the south, it is the flat valley of the River Po. All the important wines of the Veneto are grown in the faltering Alpine foothills and occasional hilly outcrops, in a line eastwards from Lake Garda to Conegliano. Verona, near Lake Garda, is the wine capital, with a greater production of DOC wine from its vineyards of Soave, Valpolicella, and Bardolino than any other Italian region. So important are these three in the export market that Verona has a claim to being the international wine capital of the whole of Italy.

The nation's biggest wine fair, Vinitaly, takes place in Verona every April. To the east, Conegliano has another claim: to be the nation's centre of viticultural technology and research.

The Verona and Conegliano areas have strong traditions of using grape varieties peculiar to themselves: Garganega (the Soave grape), the Corvina of Valpolicella, and the Prosecco, which makes admirable sparkling wine at Conegliano, are unknown elsewhere. But less-established and self-confident areas, such as the Berici and Euganean hills and the Piave, prolific flatland vineyards on the borders of Friuli-Venezia Giulia to the east, try their luck with a range of international varieties: Pinots, Cabernets, and their kin. Merlot is the standby red of the region and is rapidly improving from acceptable to delicious.

For many years, a titanic struggle has been underway in the best-known regions such as Soave and Valpolicella. Here the cooperatives are all-powerful, and keep pushing the authorities to allow higher yields, as if they were not high enough. At the same time, a growing band of quality-conscious producers are trying to resist such proposals, and are also imposing on themselves ever more stringent restrictions to ensure the highest quality. Thus these DOCs include both wines of utter drabness and anonymity, and some of the finest wines of Italy.

DOC & Other Wines

Amarone *See* Valpolicella.

Arcole DOC. A new appellation, created in 2000, for vines grown in two areas southeast of Verona: flat, alluvial soils for blends; and higher land for varietal wines from Chardonnay, Sauvignon, Garganega, Merlot, Cabernet Franc, Cabernet Sauvignon, Raboso, and Corvina.

Bagnoli di Sopra DOC. Recent DOC covering fifteen communes in Padua. Mostly blended wines, plus Raboso.

Bardolino DOC. Red and *rosato*. Province: Verona. Villages: Bardolino and fifteen others. Grapes: Corvina Veronese 35–65%; Rondinella 10–40%; Molinara 10–20%; Negrara up to 10%; Rossignola, Barbera, Garganega, and Sangiovese up to 15%.

A pale red and even paler Chiaretto; a lighter version of Valpolicella with the same quality (in a good example) of liveliness. Bardolino is on glacial deposits which do not warm up as well as the limestone of Valpolicella. It is briskest and best in the year after the vintage. There is also a separate DOC for wines released shortly after the harvest: Bardolino Novello.

Bianco di Custoza DOC. White wine. Province: Verona. Grapes: Trebbiano Toscano 35–45%; Garganega 20–40%; Tocai Friulano 5–30%; Cortese, Riesling Italico, and Malvasia Toscano 20–30%.

The southern neighbour of Soave, this white is increasingly seen. Also a *spumante* (usually Charmat).

Breganze DOC. Red and white wine. Province: Vicenza. Villages: Breganze and Maróstica, and parts of thirteen other communes. Grapes: Breganze Bianco: Tocai, plus Pinot Bianco, Pinot Grigio, Riesling Italico, Sauvignon, and Vespaiolo, max. 15%. Breganze Rosso: Merlot, plus Marzemino, Groppello, Cabernet Franc, Cabernet Sauvignon, Pinot Nero, and Freisa, max. 15%. Breganze-Cabernet: Sauvignon or Franc. Breganze-Pinot Nero: Pinot Nero. Breganze-Pinot Bianco: Pinot Bianco and Pinot Grigio. Breganze-Pinot Grigio: Pinot Grigio. Breganze-Vespaiolo: Vespaiolo. Light and agreeable "varietal" wines from the birthplace of the great architect, Palladio. Pinot Bianco, Cabernet, and late-harvested Vespaiolo are the best (*see* Maculan under Producers).

Campo Fiorin An unusually serious interpretation of Valpolicella by Masi (*see* Producers). The wine is macerated with the skins of Recioto Amarone (*q.v.*) after pressing. The prototype for *ripasso* wines.

Colli Berici DOC. Red and white wine. Province: Vicenza. Villages: twenty-eight communes south of Vicenza. Grapes: seven varieties, with limited (10–15%) admixture of other local grapes. The range is Garganega, Tocai Bianco; Sauvignon, Pinot Bianco, Merlot, Tocai Rosso (sharp fruity young red), Cabernet.

These volcanic hills between Verona and Padua have clear potential for quality, best demonstrated by their Cabernet.

Colli di Conegliano DOC. From the slopes around Conegliano. Whites from Incrocio Manzoni, Riesling, and other varieties; reds from Cabernet Sauvignon, Merlot, and Marzemino.

Colli di Conegliano Refrontolo Passito DOC. A *passito* wine from Marzemino.

Colli di Conegliano Torchiato di Fregona DOC. White wines from Prosecco, Verdiso, and Boschera.

Colli Euganei DOC. Red, white, and sparkling wine. Province: Padua. Villages: seventeen communes south of Padua. Grapes: (red) Merlot 60–80%, Cabernet Franc, Cabernet Sauvignon, Barbera, and Raboso Veronese 20–40%; (white) Garganega 30–50%, Serprina 10–30% Tocai and/or Sauvignon 20–40%, Pinella, Pinot Bianco, and Riesling Italico max. 20%. Moscato Bianco can be still or sparkling.

Euganean wine, despite its long history, used to be rather dull, but is now being taken more seriously, as producers profit from the fine autumn climate and long growing season.

Gambellara DOC. White wine. Province: Vicenza. Villages: Gambellara, Montebello Vicentino, Montorso, and Zermeghedo. Grapes: Garganega 80–90%, Trebbiano di Soave up to 20%. Max. yield: 98 hl/ha (87 hl/ha for *classico*). Also made as a Recioto di Gambellara and as Vin Santo di Gambellara, aged for at least two years.

Soave's eastern neighbour, worth trying as an alternative. Its Recioto version is sweet (and sometimes fizzy). The *vin santo* is sweet and strong.

Lessini Durello DOC. White wine. Provinces: Verona and Vicenza. Area: seven communes in Verona and twenty-one in Vicenza. Grape: Durello min. 85%; Garganega, Trebbiano di Soave, Chardonnay, and Pinot Nero up to 15%. Steely, dry wines, both still and sparkling.

Lison-Pramaggiore DOC. Red and white wine. Provinces: Venice, Pordenone, Treviso. Area: eleven communes in Venice, two in Treviso, and five in Pordenone. Grapes: Chardonnay, Pinot (Bianco and Grigio), Riesling Italico; Sauvignon, Tocai Italico, Verduzzo, Cabernet (Franc and Sauvignon), Merlot, and Refosco del Peduncolo Rosso.

DOC comprising the former areas that produced Tocai di Lison Cabernet and Merlot di Pramaggiore. The wine list includes twelve types; the Pinot Bianco and Riesling Italico may also be *spumante*.

Merlot The major red grape of the eastern Veneto, included in the major DOC zones but often found as a *vino da tavola* which may be the sign of an individualistic product of quality. (*See* Villa dal Ferro-Lazzarini under Producers.) Its best wines are dark and nicely fruity, often ending with an astringent note. Others are light and grassy.

Montello e Colli Asolani DOC. Red and white wine. Province: Treviso. Villages: seventeen communes. Grapes: Prosecco for white, Cabernet or Merlot for red (up to 15% blending allowed).

DOC with a small supply of Cabernet, and more of Merlot and Prosecco, which is usually fizzy and often sweet. The hills around Asolo were a resort during the Renaissance, famous for Palladio's villas. The most famous wine estate of the area is Venegazzù (*q.v.*).

Piave or **Vini del Piave** DOC. Red and white wine. Provinces: Venice, Treviso. Villages: from Conegliano to the Adriatic sea. Fifty communes in Treviso, twelve in Venice. Grapes: Cabernet, Merlot, Pinot Bianco, Pinot Grigio, Pinot Nero, Raboso, Tocai, or Verduzzo.

A huge area, covering the path of the River Piave through flat country to the sea north of Venice (at Jesolo). Cabernet and Merlot both thrive well here, making rather dry wines that certainly benefit from ageing. The whites, however, need drinking young.

Pinot Bianco, Grigio, Nero All three Pinots are found in the Veneto; none achieves the quality found farther east in Friuli-Venezia Giulia. Some good Pinot *spumante* is made by Maculan, and Chardonnay *spumante* by Venegazzù (*q.v.*).

Pramaggiore *See* Lison-Pramaggiore.

Prosecco di Conegliano-Valdobbiadene DOC. White wine. Province: Treviso. Villages: Valdobbiadene, Conegliano, Vittorio Veneto plus twelve other communes. Grapes: Prosecco (85–100%), Verdiso, Pinot Bianco, Pinot Grigio, Chardonnay up to 15%, or Verdiso alone up to 10%. Min. alc.: 10.5 degrees *frizzante*, 11 degrees *spumante*. The native Prosecco grape gives a rather austere and charmless, yellowish, dry wine but responds well to being made fizzy, whether *frizzante* or *spumante*, particularly in its semi-sweet and sweet forms. Within Valdobbiadene is a restricted zone where the wines have a finer texture, greater length on the palate, and the right to the title Superiore di Cartizze.

Light-hearted consumers all over Italy tend to use the term "Prosecco" as a way of ordering any glass of fizz.

Raboso del Piave The local Raboso grape makes an astringent red wine, which is worth meeting, especially with four or five years' bottle-age. *See* Piave.

Recioto *See* Valpolicella.

Soave and **Recioto di Soave** DOC. White wine. Province: Verona. Villages: Soave and twelve others. Grapes: Garganega 70–90%, Chardonnay, Trebbiano di Soave, and Trebbiano Toscano up to 30%.

The most popular of all Italian white wines, from 5,500 hectares of vineyards. Its simple name seems to express its simple nature: smooth, light, and easy to drink. When it is well-made and, above all, fresh, it is hugely tempting. The zone is immediately east of Valpolicella, making Verona a singularly well-watered city. A central and hillier zone of Soave, with 1,300 ha planted, is entitled to the term *classico*. There are proposals under consideration to create a DOCG for wines from low-yielding vineyards, and an IGT for overcropped wines. Recioto di Soave is a concentrated, semi-sweet, and rich-textured version made of semi-dried grapes.

Tocai di Lison *See* Lison-Pramaggiore.

Valpolicella – Recioto/Amarone della Valpolicella DOC. Red wine. Province: Verona. Villages: nineteen communes in the hills north of Verona, the westernmost five of which are the *classico* zone. 5,600 ha. Grapes: Corvina Veronese 40–70%, Rondinella 20–40%, Molinara 5–25%, Rossignola, Negrara, Barbera, Sangiovese up to 15%. Recioto must have 14 degrees potential alcohol of which at least 12 degrees is actual.

Valpolicella, like Chianti, has too wide a range of qualities to be easily summed up. At its best, it is one of Italy's most tempting light reds, always reminding one of cherries,

combining the smooth and the lively and ending with the bitter-almond hallmark of almost all northeast Italian reds. In commerce it can be a poor, pale, listless sort of wine. *Classico* is better; the pick of the villa-dotted vineyards are in the hills skirted to the south and west by the River Adige, divided by the river from Bardolino.

At any Veronese gathering, the last bottle to be served is Recioto, either in its sweet form or its powerful, dry, velvety but sometimes, astringent version known as Amarone. Recioto is made by half-drying selected grapes to concentrate their sugars, then giving them a long fermentation in the new year. If the fermentation is allowed to go on to the bitter end the result is Amarone. Once marginal, Amarone is enjoying a spirited revival, and new styles have richness without astringency. Recioto is also made as a fizz.

Venegazzù della Casa The estate of Conte Loredan (*q.v.*) in the DOC Montello-Colli Asolani, but most famous for its non-DOC Cabernet/Merlot blend in the Bordeaux style, comparable perhaps to a powerful, rustic St-Emilion, and its *metodo tradizionale spumante*.

Leading Veneto Producers

Allegrini ☆☆☆–☆☆☆☆
Fumane di Valpolicella, Verona. www.allegrini.it
The late Giovanni Allegrini's three children, Walter, Marilisa, and Franco, now run the estate, which has choice plots in Valpolicella Classico. "Palazzo della Torre" is made from grapes harvested from pergola vineyards, by the *ripasso* method. "La Grola" is a barrel-aged Valpolicella without *ripasso*. "La Poja" comes from from a hilltop site planted solely with Corvina, and is one of Italy's most elegant red wines. Excellent Recioto and Amarone, too.

Anselmi ☆☆–☆☆☆☆
Monteforte d'Alpone, Verona
Roberto Anselmi was a pioneer of top-quality Soave, being one of the first to use barrique-ageing (for the single-vineyard "Capital Croce") and to create "I Capitelli", a Recioto di Soave as rich as a Sauternes. Since 1986, he has made a fine Cabernet Sauvignon called "Realdà".

Bertani ☆☆–☆☆☆
Arbizzano di Negrar, Verona. www.bertani.net
Founded in 1857, this respected family firm produces a wide range of vines from districts around Verona. From 200 hectares of family vines and even more belonging to suppliers, this venerable house makes model wines, notably Valpolicella, sparkling Recioto, the "Albion" Cabernet from its Villa Novare estate, and classic Amarone.

Bolla ☆–☆☆
Verona
Founded in Soave in 1883, the firm was bought by the American Brown-Forman company in 1999. Grapes acquired from more than 400 growers are processed in ultra-modern plants in the Verona area, to make nearly 2.5 million cases. Bolla, synonymous with Soave in the United States, is a leader in viticultural research through the Sergio Bolla Foundation. They also control the firm of

Valdo, which makes sparkling wines at Valdobbiadene. Bolla was one of the first companies to make single-vineyard wines, which are of much higher quality than their generic bottlings.

Corte Sant'Alda ☆☆☆
Mezzane di Sotto, Verona. www.santalda.it
This small fifteen-hectare estate has been run since 1978 by Marinella Camerani. She makes very good barrique-aged Valpolicella, sumptuous Amarone and good Recioto. Production is very limited, so prices are high.

Romano dal Forno ☆☆☆☆
Cellore di Illasi, Verona
Since 1983, Dal Forno has established himself as one of the most dedicated producers of Valpolicella and Amarone, modelling himself on the great Quintarelli (*q.v.*). Production is tiny, and most of the wines are aged in new French oak. They are high-priced and stylistically controversial, but magnificently concentrated.

Gini ☆☆☆
Monteforte d'Alpone, Verona
The Gini family produces a range of fresh, creamy Soaves, including Recioto, selectively harvested and aged either in tanks or in barriques. Pinot Nero shows considerable promise.

Guerrieri-Rizzardi ☆☆–☆☆☆
Bardolino, Verona
A family estate, dating back to the eighteenth century, with a small but interesting museum. From eighty hectares in Bardolino, Valpolicella, and Soave come splendid, gracious Verona wines. The Bardolino is admirably lively – one of the best of the pale breed.

Inama ☆☆–☆☆☆
San Bonifacio, Verona. www.inamaaziendaagricola.it
Giuseppe and Stefano Inama have rapidly joined the ranks of Soave's top producers, and are equally successful with varietal Sauvignon and Chardonnay. Curiously, their top wine, "Vigneto du Lot", is made from a high-yielding vineyard planted by Australian viticultural guru, Richard Smart.

Lamberti ☆☆
Lazise, Verona. www.giv.it
Part of the Gruppo Italiano Vini, Lamberti control 170 hectares of vineyards in Bardolino and Valpolicella, and purchase elsewhere. They produce reds and whites of good commercial quality. They were also pioneers of Bardolino Novello.

Maculan ☆☆☆☆
Breganze, Vicenza
Fausto Maculan must be the Veneto's most versatile winemaker. He has a sure hand with Cabernet Sauvignon (the "Fratta" bottling is outstanding), Merlot, and oaked Chardonnay "Ferrata", but also makes impeccable varietal wines from Pinot Grigio, Pinot Nero, and the local Vespaiolo grape. Vespaiolo is also the main variety used for his renowned barrique-aged "Torcolato" sweet wine, and the fully botrytized "Acini Nobili".

Masi ☆☆☆
Gargagnago, Verona. www.masi.it

The scholarly Sandro Boscaini presides over this splendid producer. For many years, "Campo Fiorin" has been a superb example of a *ripasso* Valpolicella, and the single-vineyard Reciotos and Amarones have always been outstanding. Boscaini has conducted research into local, and often near extinct, varieties and resurrected them in wines such as the Oseleta-dominated "Osar" and "Grandarella" from semi-dried Refosco and other grapes. Their deep red "Toar" is another *ripasso*-style interpretation of Valpolicella tradition. The firm also oversees the marketing of the excellent wines from the Serego Alighieri estate.

Pieropan ☆☆☆–☆☆☆☆
Soave, Verona. www.pieropan.it
Leonildo Pieropan is unwavering in his dedication to good viticulture and scrupulous winemaking. His top Soave, "La Rocca", is as good as Soave gets, and his "Calvarino" is not far behind. Exquisite Recioto di Soave, and other late-harvest wines complete the range.

Quintarelli ☆☆☆☆
Negrar, Verona
No one makes more profound, subtle Recioto and Amarone than the self-effacing Giuseppe Quintarelli. The quality begins in the vineyards with grapes rich enough to absorb the drying process, followed by prolonged fermentation, and years of ageing in large casks. The most individual of his hand-crafted wines is Amarone "Alzero" from Cabernet Franc, but even his least starry wine has a strong personality.

Le Ragose ☆☆–☆☆☆
Arbizzano, Verona. www.leragose.com
Maria Marta Galli, with her husband Arnaldo, makes impressive and highly consistent Valpolicella and Amarone from their fifteen hectares of vineyards.

Santa Margherita ☆
Fossalta di Portogruaro, Venezia
A very large company, producing wines from all over north and northeast Italy. Once a leading producer of Pinot Grigio, Santa Margherita has lost its edge. One of its more unusual wines is a fruity Malbec.

Cantina di Soave ☆
Soave, Verona. www.cantinasoave.it
This is unquestionably the biggest producer of Soave, with 1,200 members cultivating 3,500 hectares, 80% of whch are in the Soave zone. It also makes Valpolicella, Bardolino, and *spumante* wines. Some improvements in quality are noticeable in recent years, but the wines often lack personality.

Tedeschi ☆☆☆
Pedemonte, Verona. www.tedeschiwines.com
Renzo Tedeschi and his family are masters of all the styles that Valpolicella can produce. His top wines contain Corvinone as well as Corvina, setting them apart from most other expressions of Valpolicella. His ripasso Valpolicella, "Capitel San Rocco" and Corvina-based "Rosso della Fabriseria" are also delicious.

Venegazzù-Conte Loredan-Gasparini ☆☆
Volpago del Montello, Treviso. www.venegazzu.com
The eighty-hectare estate was founded in 1950 by Piero

Loredan, descendant of Venetian *doges*, and bought by Giancarlo Palla in 1974. The fine red wines include "Venegazzù della Casa" and "Capo di Stato", Bordeaux-style blends of great character and class, like a big, not exactly genteel, St-Emilion. After a prolonged bad patch, there are signs of revival.

Zonin ☆–☆☆☆
Gambellara, Vicenza. www.zonin.it
The Zonin family firm, founded in 1821, claims to be Italy's largest private winery with 1,800 hectares of vineyards, and a production of three million cases. The Veneto is the firm's base, but its eleven estates span northern Italy, the best-known: Castello d'Albola in Chianti Classico, and Ca' Bolani in the Friuli. One of the few producers of Recioto di Gambellara.

Other Veneto Producers

Adami ☆–☆☆
Colbertaldo di Vidor, Treviso. www.adamispumante.it
Reliable producers of Prosecco and Cartizze, both *frizzante* and *spumante*.

Bepin de Eto ☆–☆☆
San Pietro di Feletto, Treviso
A major producer of reliable reds and whites from Colli di Conegliano.

Desiderio Bisol ☆☆
Santo Stefano di Valdobbiadene, Treviso
A deservedly well-known producer of Cartizze and Prosecco di Valdobbiadene.

Boscaini ☆☆
Valgatara, Verona. www.boscaini.it
Since 1978, the Boscaini family have made highly typical wines from most of the major regions around Verona.

Brigaldara ☆☆–☆☆☆
San Pietri in Cariano, Verona
Stefano Cesari is a skilled specialist in Amarone and Recioto.

Brunelli ☆☆–☆☆☆
San Pietri in Cariano, Verona
Luigi Brunelli makes top Valpolicella, in all styles.

Tommaso Bussola ☆☆☆
Negrar, Verona
Specializes in top Recioto and Amarone di Valpolicella.

Ca' La Bionda ☆☆
Marano di Valpolicella, Verona
Less celebrated than some other Valpolicella estates, but a source of well-made wines in all styles.

Ca' Lustra ☆
Cinto Euganeo, Padua. www.calustra.it
A good address for varietal wines from the Colli Euganei.

Ca' del Monte ☆☆
Negrar, Verona
A sound source of Valpolicella and Amarone.

Ca' Rugate ☆☆–☆☆☆
Monteforte, Verona. www.carugate.it
Since 1986, the Tessaris have moved to the forefront as producers of classic Soave.

Canevel ☆
Valdobbiadene, Verona. www.canevel.it
A very reliable Prosecco.

La Cappuccina ☆☆–☆☆☆
Monteforte d'Alpone, Verona. www.lacappuccina.it
Good Soave, and unusual barrique-aged Cabernet Franc "Campo Buri".

Carpenè Malvolti ☆
Conegliano, Treviso
A family firm, founded in 1868 by Etile Carpenè and currently run by his descendants. The company is a leading name in Italian sparkling wine, but the quality of the produce is rarely special.

Case Bianche ☆
Pieve di Soligo, Treviso
Attractive Prosecco and white Colli di Conegliano.

Castellani ☆☆–☆☆☆
Marano di Valpolicella, Verona
Sergio Castellani produces good *ripasso* Valpolicella and a sumptuous Recioto.

Cantina del Castello ☆☆–☆☆☆
Soave, Verona. www.cantinacastello.it
Arthuro Stocchetti's Soaves are made with great care, especially the cask-aged "Acini Soavi".

Cavalchina ☆–☆☆
Sommacampagna, Verona
Good Bianco di Custoza and Merlot from Lake Garda.

Coffele ☆☆
Soave, Verona. www.coffele.it
Up-and-coming, medium-sized producer of dependable Soave.

Col Vetoraz ☆☆
Santo Stefano di Valdobbiadene, Treviso
Very reliable Prosecco and Cartizze.

Villa dal Ferro-Lazzarini ☆☆
San Germano dei Berici, Vicenza
The vineyards and cellars of this sixteenth century villa have been lovingly restored, and this is now a fine source of white and red wines from Colli Berici.

Foss Marai ☆
Valdobbiadene, Treviso. www.fossmarai.it
Dependable Prosecco and Cartizze.

Fraccaroli ☆
San Peschiera del Garda, Verona. www.fraccarolivini.it
Good Lugana.

Le Fraghe ☆☆–☆☆☆
Cavaion Veronese, Verona. www.fraghe.it

A small estate, producing enjoyable Bardolino and a powerful Cabernet (Sauvignon and Franc) called "Quaiare".

Nino Franco ☆☆
Valdobbiadene, Treviso
Founded in 1919, this firm, now run by Primo Franco, produces excellent Cartizze and Prosecco di Valdobbiadene (sparkling and still).

Lonardi ☆☆
Marano di Valpolicella, Verona. www.lonardivini.it
A tiny seven-hectare estate producing good, traditional Valpolicella and Amarone.

Masottina ☆☆
Castello Roganzuolo, Treviso. www.masottina.it
Good Prosecco and red and white blends from Colli di Conegliano.

Roberto Mazzi ☆☆
Sanperetto Negrar, Verona
The Amarone is usually the top wine at this small estate.

Merotto ☆☆–☆☆☆
Col San Martino, Treviso. www.merotto.it
Prosecco and Cartizze dominate production here, but there is also full-bodied Cabernet called "Rossodogato".

La Montecchia ☆☆
Selvazzano Dentro, Padua
Good wines from the Colli Euganei, and the rare Fior d'Arancio *passito*.

Montresor ☆☆–☆☆☆
Verona. www.montresorwines.com
A large and long-established firm offering a wide range of Veneto wines at a high overall standard.

Musella ☆☆
San Martino Buon Albergo, Verona. www.musella.it
As well as a good Amarone, Musella is perhaps best-known for the Corvina/Cabernet blend, "Monte del Drago".

Pasqua ☆☆
Verona. www.pasqua.it
Produces eighteen million bottles of Valpolicella and other wines, always reliable, rarely exceptional.

Piovene ☆☆
Porto Godi Villaga, Vicenza
A small producer of consistently flavoury red and white varietal wines from Colli Berici.

Umberto Portinari ☆☆–☆☆☆
Monteforte d'Alpone, Verona
Only four hectares, but outstanding Soave.

Prà ☆☆–☆☆☆
Monteforte d'Alpone, Verona
Excellent Soave, especially single-vineyard "Monte Grande".

Raimondi ☆☆–☆☆☆
Gargagnago, Verona

Small estate, recently founded, but already producing fine Valpolicella and Amarone.

Castello di Roncade ☆
Roncade, Treviso
An impressive fortress producing a worthy Cabernet/Merlot blend.

Ruggeri ☆☆
Valdobbiadene, Treviso. www.ruggeri.it
Excellent Prosecco and a rare sparkling Marzemino.

Le Salette ☆☆
Fumane, Verona
The Scamperle family has long been a reliable source of Valpolicella, Amarone, and Recioto.

Le Vigne di San Pietro ☆☆–☆☆☆
Sommacampagna, Verona
Owner Carlo Nerozzi produces charming Bardolino and Bianco di Custoza, and an oaky Cabernet Sauvignon: "Refolà".

Tenuta Sant' Antonio ☆☆–☆☆☆
Colognola ai Colli, Verona
A rising star in Valpolicella, with delicious Recioto, intense Cabernet Sauvignon, and a rare *passito* Chardonnay.

Santa Sofia ☆–☆☆
Pedemonte, Verona. www.santasofia.com
This estate offers a wide range of wines – Valpolicella, Soave, Bardolino – of reliable quality, and Amarone can be exceptional.

Santi ☆☆
Illasi, Verona. www.giv.it
Founded in 1843, the winery is now part of the Gruppo Italiano Vini complex. Unexpectedly good Soave and Lugana.

Sartori ☆–☆☆
Negrar, Verona. www.sartoriwinery.com
Despite a production of almost one million cases, the wines, most notably Amarone, can be impressive and firmly structured.

Serafini & Vidotto ☆☆–☆☆☆
Nervesa della Battaglia, Treviso
A top producer in the Piave zone, with delicious Bordeaux blends.

Speri ☆☆–☆☆☆
Pedemonte, Verona. www.speri.com
Steadily improving Valpolicella and Amarone producer.

Suavia ☆☆–☆☆☆
Soave, Verona. www.suavia.it
Giovanni Tessari makes small quantities of delicious Soave from various single vineyards.

Tommasi ☆☆
Pedemonte, Verona. www.tommasiwine.it
Recently much improved, Dario Tommasi's estate of forty-five hectares makes an Amarone of reliable quality.

Valdo ☆☆
Valdobbiadene, Treviso. www.valdo.com
Owned by Bolla (*q.v.*), this is a good producer of Prosecco.

Cantina Produttori di Valdobbiadene ☆–☆☆
Valdobbiadene, Treviso. www.valdoca.com
A large but reliable cooperative, producing some five million bottles of Cartizze and Prosecco.

Venturini ☆☆
San Floriano, Verona
Small, sometimes underrated producer of Valpolicella and Amarone.

Vignalta ☆☆
Torreglia, Padua
Lovely, Merlot-dominated red wines from Colli Euganei.

Viviani ☆☆☆
Negrar, Verona
Small-scale production – only 40,000 bottles are produced – so hard to find, but excellent Recioto and Amarone.

Zardetto ☆☆
Conegliano, Treviso
Founded in 1969, Zardetto has earned a good reputation for Cartizze and Prosecco.

Zenato ☆–☆☆☆
Peschiera del Garda, Verona
Located on the shores of Lake Garda, this well-known estate produces excellent Lugana and Valpolicella.

Friuli-Venezia Giulia

There is a tidiness about the DOC arrangements in Friuli-Venezia Giulia which is due to their recent emergence as an important part of Italian viticulture. There was little folklore to get in the way of a simple carve-up into geographical zones, whose wines are named for their grape varieties.

With six zones and some dozen varieties, the combinations still reach a head-spinning number. It helps to distinguish between them if you are clear that there is one very big DOC that embraces most of the region, two superior hill zones with Colli in their names, and three smaller and newer DOCs of less significance, in a row along the coastal plain.

The big zone is Grave del Friuli, DOC for the whole wine-growing hinterland from the Veneto border east to beyond Udine where the Alps reach down towards Trieste. The hills of Gorizia, right on the Slovenian border, are the oldest-established and best vineyards of the region. Today, this zone is generally known simply as "Collio". To the north is the separate DOC of the Colli Orientali del Friuli ("the eastern hills of Friuli") with similar growing conditions.

The coastal DOCs from west to east are Aquileia, Latisana, and Isonzo; the last, adjacent to the Gorizian hills, apparently having the greatest potential for quality. These coastal vineyards tend to stress red wine, whereas the reputation of the hills is mainly based on white – whether produced from such traditional grapes as Tocai Friulano, Malvasia, Picolit or Verduzzo, or more recent imports: the Pinot Bianco or Grigio, Sauvignon Blanc, and Rhine Riesling.

Together with Alto Adige, this is probably Italy's best white wine region, especially inland from the warmer coastlands. Barrique-ageing became fashionable, inevitably, in the late 1980s, but Friuli's white wines have such purity of flavour, at their best, that barrel ageing often seems superfluous. The region is also known for its delicate sweet wines, and has a growing reputation for reds based on Merlot and other varieties. Quality is remarkably high across the board in the hillier zones, and the wines fetch good prices.

DOC & Other Wines

Friuli Aquileia DOC. Red and white wine. Province: Udine. Villages: Aquileia and seventeen others. Grapes: Merlot, Cabernet, Refosco, Tocai Friulano, Pinot Bianco, Pinot Grigio, Riesling Renano, Sauvignon, Traminer Aromatico, Verduzzo.

Named after a Roman city, this DOC covers the varied production of the cooperative at Cervignano and other properties. The land is flat, the climate temperate, and efforts at quality production fairly recent. Light, fruity reds such as Cabernet and Merlot show the most promise.

Carso DOC. Red and white wine. Provinces: Trieste and Gorizia. Area: six communes in Gorizia and six in Trieste. Grapes: Terrano (85%), Pinot Nero, and Piccola Nera up to 15%; Malvasia Istriana (85%), other authorized light grapes up to 15%. A tiny hill region. Carso and Carso Terrano are virtually the same, both based on the Terrano (relative of Refosco) grape. Carso Malvasia is similar to other DOC Malvasia Istriana types.

Collio Goriziano or **Collio** DOC. White and red wine. Province: Gorizia. Villages: west of Gorizia. Grapes: Riesling Italico, Sauvignon, Tocai Friulano, Traminer Aromatico, Malvasia Istriana, Merlot, Pinot Bianco, Pinot Grigio, Pinot Nero, Cabernet Franc, Cabernet Sauvignon, Chardonnay, Müller-Thurgau, Picolit, Ribolla Giall, and Riesling Renano.

A DOC of such diversity of wines and styles that California comes to mind. Fruity, early developing reds of the Bordeaux varieties are less interesting than the white specialties, particularly the aromatic Tocai Friulano and Pinot Bianco and Grigio, which, at their best, balance Hungarian-style "stiffness" and strength with real delicacy. Clay and limestone soils predominate. Collio without a varietal name is a light, dry white of Ribolla and other local grapes. "Pinot Bianco" sometimes includes Chardonnay, and can develop burgundian richness with barrel-age.

Colli Orientali del Friuli DOC. White and red wine. Province: Udine. Villages: fourteen communes in the province. Grapes: Tocai Friulano, Verduzzo, Ribolla, Pinot Bianco, Pinot Grigio, Sauvignon, Riesling Renano, Picolit, Merlot, Cabernet, Pinot Nero, Refosco, Malvasia Istriana, Ramandolo (Classico); Rosato, and Schioppettino. 2,000 ha. The neighbouring DOC to Collio, with similar white wines, is perhaps slightly less prestigious except in its native Verduzzo (*q.v.*) and its rare dessert white, Picolit (*q.v.*). Merlot and Tocai are the major varieties in terms of plantings. The splendid rustic red Refosco and Cabernet are better than the Collio red wines.

Friuli-Annia DOC. Red, white, *rosato*. Eight villages of the province of Udine on southern coast. Grapes: Cabernet Franc, Cabernet Sauvignon, Refosco, Tocai, Pinot Bianco, Pinot Grigio, Verduzzo, Traminer, Sauvignon, Chardonnay, and Malvasia.

A DOC introduced in 1995. Not yet shining as brightly as Aquileia or Latisana, and will probably be best for early drinking whites and reds.

Friuli-Grave DOC. Red and white wine. Provinces: Udine, Pordenone. Area: Udine and Pordenone. Grapes: Merlot, Cabernet, Refosco, Tocai, Pinot Bianco, Pinot Grigio, Verduzzo, Riesling Renano, Pinot Nero, Sauvignon, Traminer Aromatico, and Chardonnay. 6,000 hectares.

This is the largest DOC of the region and Merlot accounts for half of its production. Grave Merlot is soft, dark and dry with a hint of grassiness – not as good as its Cabernet Sauvignon, which has more personality and life, nor as memorable as its fruity, bitter Refosco. Grave Pinot Bianco (sometimes Chardonnay) and Tocai can be as good as the Collio equivalents.

Isonzo DOC. White and red wine. Province: Gorizia. Area: twenty communes around Gradisca d'Isonzo. Grapes: Tocai, Sauvignon, Malvasia Istriana, Pinot Bianco, Pinot Grigio, Verduzzo Friulano, Traminer Aromatico, Riesling Renano, Merlot, Cabernet, Chardonnay, Franconia, Pinot Nero, Refosco dal Peduncolo Rosso, plus a Bianco, Rosso, and Pinot *spumante*. 1,000 hectares.

The DOC zone between the Collio and the Gulf of Trieste also specializes in Merlot, which can be better than that of Grave del Friuli, and Cabernet for drinking young. Its whites are light and pleasant, but they are rarely up to Collio standards.

Friuli Latisana DOC. Red and white wine. Province: Udine. Area: twelve communes in the province. Grapes: Merlot, Cabernet, Refosco, Tocai Friulano, Pinot Bianco, Pinot Grigio, Traminer Aromatico, Chardonnay, and Verduzzo Friulano. This DOC is dominated by Merlot, Cabernet Sauvignon, and Tocai, but Refosco is more robust and durable.

Picolit A native grape of the Colli Orientali del Friuli and its dessert wine, the Picolit is one of the almost-lost legends of the nineteenth century, along with the (really lost) Constantia of the Cape. It yields a powerful, smooth, even dense-textured wine, not necessarily very sweet, and finishing slightly bitter in the regional style.

Bottles of the wine I have tasted have clearly been too young to have developed the glorious bouquet and flavour that others have reported. It is rare, extremely expensive, and normally overpriced.

Schioppettino A native red grape of the Colli Orientali del Friuli, giving wine with some of the rasping fruitiness of a good Barbera from Piedmont.

Verduzzo A native white grape made either into a fresh, dry white "fish" wine or a sort of Recioto from partly dried grapes – *see* Ramandolo, Colli Orientali.

N.B. Verdiso is a different white grape, mainly grown in the Veneto.

Leading Friuli-Venezia Giulia Producers

Collavini ☆–☆☆
Corno di Rosazzo, Udine. www.collavini.it
Manlio Collavini is the third-generation winemaker at this well-known estate, which draws on most of the Friuli region for its grapes. Quality is reliable, but with the potential to do better. The best wines are bottled as "Collezione Privata".

Livio Felluga ☆☆☆
Brazzano di Cormòns, Gorizia. www.liviofelluga.it
This long-established family firm owns four different estates and a total of almost 150 ha. The barrel-aged white, "Terre Alte", blend is highly esteemed, and the Merlot Riserva and Picolit are usually magnificent, though very expensive.

Marco Felluga-Russiz Superiore ☆☆–☆☆☆
Gradisca d'Isonzo, Gorizia. www.marcofelluga.it
Marco Felluga, brother of Livio Felluga (*q.v.*), founded his wine house in 1956, the Russiz Superiore estate in 1967. In addition, he owns two other properties, of which the better known is the Castello di Buttrio.

The Marco Felluga label consists of the usual Collio varieties, mostly from grapes purchased from regular suppliers in Collio. Varietal wines, as well as blends such as "Molamatta", dominate the range. Russiz Superiore, a model of its kind, consists of sixty hectares of terraced vines.

Here, red wines such as Cabernet Franc and a Cabernet Sauvignon-dominated "Riserva degli Orzoni" take their place alongside the classic whites.

Walter Filiputti ☆☆☆
Rosazzo di Monzano, Udine
After decades working as a consultant to some of the best regional estates, the talented Filiputti set up his own winery in 1995. Unsurprisingly, the wines are excellent but expensive. "Ronco degli Agostiniani" is a Chardonnay-dominated white wine, aged in barriques, and "Ronco dei Domenicani" is its Cabernet-based red counterpart. There are rarities, too: a pure Pignolo, and a barrique-fermented Picolit.

Jermann ☆☆☆☆
Villanova di Farra, Gorizia
A family estate founded in 1880 and now expanded to seventy-six hectares, it has been run for many years by Silvio Jermann. Even as a very young man, Jermann showed an unerring touch with white wine vinification.

These are wines with ample fruit but perfect balance. Jermann ceased to use DOC labels many years ago, and all his wines are now IGT. As well as an impeccable range of varietal wines, there are delicious blends such as the Ribolla-dominated "Vinnae" and the justly celebrated "Vintage Tunina" (from Chardonnay, Sauvignon, Malvasia, Ribolla, Picolit) from twenty-three hectares of vines. Taste "Tunina" if you are a sceptic about Italian whites. Jermann has always enjoyed cryptic names for some of his wines. His expensive, barrel-aged Chardonnay was called "Where the Dreams Have No End..." and is now labelled "Were Dreams, now it is just wine!" Despite the larking about, Jermann's wines are serious but never ponderous.

Puiatti ☆☆–☆☆☆
Capriva del Friuli, Gorizia. www.puiatti.com

Giovanni Puiatti now runs the company founded by his respected father, Vittorio. Rather confusingly, he bottles wines under two labels: Collio wines appear under the "Puiatti" label; Isonzo wines under the "Giovanni Puiatti" label.

The Puiattis are passionate believers in unoaked white wines, and to prove their point, they release a range of bottle-aged, mature wines under the "Archétipi" label to prove that unwooded white wines can age very well – if made with the care which is characteristic of all the Puiatti ranges.

Rocca Bernarda ☆☆☆
Ipplis, Udine. www.roccabernarda.com

The Perusini family bequeathed their estate to the Knights of Malta. Standards have been maintained, and this remains an outstanding estate in Colli Orientali del Friuli. This is an utterly reliable source for white varietals made to an exacting standard, as well as for magnificent Picolit.

Schiopetto ☆☆☆☆
Capriva del Friuli, Gorizia. www.schiopetto.it

Founded in 1965 by Mario Schiopetto, on a thirty-hectare Collio property belonging to the *archbishopric* of Gorizia.

Schiopetto, now assisted by his son, Giorgio, is one of the most skilled and courageous winemakers of Italy. His whites, notably Pinot Bianco and Sauvignon, are among the most notable. With a few exceptions, they are unoaked, and have admirable purity of flavour.

Borgo del Tiglio ☆☆☆
Brazzano di Cormòns, Gorizia

Nicola Manferrari's small estate produces especially good Tocai and Malvasia, and fine Rosso della Centa (Merlot/Cabernet). The star, though, is the powerful Tocai/Riesling/Sauvignon blend called "Studio di Bianco".

Torre Rosazza ☆☆–☆☆☆
Oleis di Manzano, Udine

DOC: Colli Orientali del Friuli. This historic eighty-hectare estate was originally developed by the Generali insurance group, under the supervision of winemaker Walter Filiputti. Today Donato Lanati is the oenologist, as he is at the company's other estate at Borgo Magredo (*q.v.*). Red wines are successful here, notably "Ronco della Torre" (Cabernet/Merlot) and "L'Altromerlot".

Vie di Romans ☆☆☆
Mariano del Friuli, Gorizia

Gianfranco Gallo took over running this thirty-hectare Isonzo estate in 1978, and has turned it into one of Friuli's finest. (Originally named after himself, Gallo had to invent the current name after a certain Californian producer instituted legal proceedings for, one assumes, effrontery at sharing their name.)

The whites are very rich and usually attain rather alarming levels of alcohol. Chardonnay comes in unoaked and barrique-aged versions.

Le Vigne di Zamò ☆☆–☆☆☆☆
Manzano, Udine. www.levignedizamo.com

A new star in the Colli Orientali, helped to celebrity by consultant Franco Bernabei. Tocai is often the most dazzling wine, but Tullio Zamò also works wonders with Malvasia.

Villa Russiz ☆☆☆
Capriva del Friuli, Gorizia. www.villarussiz.it

Founded in 1869 by a French nobleman, Comte de la Tour, Villa Russiz has been run for some years by winemaker Gianni Menotti. An excellent range of Collio wines, with exceptionally elegant Sauvignon, Chardonnay, and Merlot.

Volpe Pasini ☆☆☆
Togliano di Torreano, Udine. www.volepasini.net

A thirty-four-hectare estate now owned by Emilio Rotolo. One of Italy's top oenologists, Riccardo Votarella, is the consultant winemaker here.

Tocai and Pinot Bianco are frequently the finest of these Colli Orientali wines, and the top range is labelled "Zuc di Volpe". "Le Roverelle" (Picolit, Sauvignon, Pinot Bianco, Chardonnay) and "Focus" Merlot are especially noteworthy.

Other Friuli Producers

Angoris ☆–☆☆
Cormòns, Gorizia

The Locatelli family produces good whites from their seventeenth century estate in Colli Orientali del Friuli.

Attems ☆
Lucinico, Gorizia

An estate dating back to medieval times, and now collaborating with a Tuscan counterpart, namely Frescobaldi. The wines at present are unexciting, but improvement is now likely.

Beltrame ☆☆
Bagnaria Arsa, Udine

A leading estate in Friuli-Aquileia, with attractive reds from Merlot and Tazzelenghe, as well as fruity whites.

Borgo San Daniele ☆☆☆
Cormòns, Gorizia

Rich whites, aged on the fine lees, and white and red blends called "Arbis".

Rosa Bosco ☆☆–☆☆☆
Manzano, Udine

Just two wines: Sauvignon Blanc and a delicious Merlot "Boscorosso".

Branko ☆☆–☆☆☆
Cormòns, Gorizia

Igor Erzetic makes only 2,000 cases, including fairly oaky whites, and a Merlot helpfully called "Red Branko".

Buzzinelli ☆–☆☆
Cormòns, Gorizia

Good Collio whites; those with partial or complete barrel-ageing are labelled "Ronc dal Luis".

Ca' Bolani ☆

Cervignano del Friuli, Udine. www.cabolani.it

One of a number of Friuli estates owned by Zonin (*q.v.*) of the Veneto, who also owns nearby Ca' Vescovo. The estates together have almost 600 hectares. Ca' Bolani mainly produces stylish Aquileia wines of fair quality.

Ca' Ronesca ☆☆

Dolegna del Collio, Gorizia. www.caronesca.it

Sergio Comunello produces a wide range of varietal wines, and fine Picolit.

La Castellada ☆☆☆–☆☆☆☆

Oslavia, Gorizia

Giorgio and Nicolò Bensa produce tiny quantities of fine Collio whites.

Borgo Conventi ☆☆–☆☆☆

Farra d'Isonzo, Gorizia. www.borgoconventi.it

The former walled convent, founded in 1876, is owned by Gianni Vescovo. This large property produces fresh white Collio wines, and an oaky Bordeaux blend called "Braida Nuova". In 2002, it was sold to the Tuscan house of Ruffino.

Dario Coos ☆☆

Ramandolo, Udine

Noted for elegant Ramandolo and Picolit.

Girolamo Dorigo ☆☆–☆☆☆

Buttrio, Udine

A leading estate, working closely with oenologist Roberto Cipresso. Concentrated white wines are the strength here, especially Chardonnay, Tocai, and Picolit. The top wines are bottled under the "Ronc di Juri" label.

Giovanni Dri ☆☆☆–☆☆☆☆

Ramandolo, Udine. www.drironcat.com

At his twenty-two-hectare Il Roncat estate, Dri has long made exquisite sweet wines: not only Picolit, but also the intense Ramandolo, with occasional special bottlings.

Le Due Terre ☆☆–☆☆☆

Prepotto, Udine

Unlike most Colli Orientali del Friuli estates, this focuses on blends, red and white, mostly from local varieties.

Fantinel ☆–☆☆

Pradamano, Udine

Fresh Collio whites. Gianfranco Fantinel also owns Santa Caterina where he also makes impressive Collio.

Conti Formentini ☆☆

San Floriano del Collio, Gorizia. www.giv.it

The sixteenth century castle and property have long belonged to the Formentini family, but since 1996, the winery is owned by Gruppo Italiano Vini and offers a reliable range of Collio varietal wines. The castle contains an *enoteca*, restaurant, and wine museum.

Villa Frattina ☆☆

Ghirano, Pordenone

A leading estate in Lison Pramaggiore, with steadily improving quality.

Viticoltori Friuliani-La Delizia

Casarsa della Delizia, Pordenone Cooperative. DOC: Aquileia, Grave del Friuli

Other: *spumante* wines. Annual production is more than a million cases from 1,500 hectares.

Friulvini ☆

Zoppola, Pordenone. www.friulvini.it

A joint venture among five cooperatives in Friuli-Grave. Soft, easygoing wines from over 600 hectares.

Isola Augusta ☆☆

Palazzolo della Stella, Udine. www.isolaugusta.com

Fruity Chardonnay, Cabernet, and other wines from Latisana.

Kante ☆☆☆

Aurisina, Trieste

A leading estate in Carso. Very high quality, but very low production and expensive.

Edi Keber ☆☆☆

Cormòns, Gorizia

Much of the production consists of blends, the red being mostly Merlot aged in older barriques. Often the splendid Tocai is better than the blend.

Lis-Neris ☆☆☆

San Lorenzo Isontino, Gorizia. www.lisneris.it

Alvaro Pecorari makes brilliant white wines from Pinot Grigio and Chardonnay, and a remarkable sweet wine, "Confini", based on Pinot Grigio.

Livon ☆–☆☆☆

Dolegnano, Udine. www.livon.it

A large winery, presenting its wines on a Burgundian hierarchy of *classica*, *cru*, and *gran cru*. The top white blend is the barrique-fermented "Braide Alte".

Borgo Magredo ☆–☆☆

Tauriano, Pordenone. www.borgomagredo.it

Owned by an insurance group, this estate is showing signs of improvement since oenologist Donato Lanati was hired.

Masut da Rive ☆☆–☆☆☆

Mariano del Friuli, Gorizia. www.masutdarive.com

New estate, in 1995, and already one of the best in Isonzo.

Miani ☆☆☆

Buttrio, Udine

A first-rate estate, run by Enzo Pontoni, but production is minute and prices astronomic.

Vigneti le Monde ☆☆

Prata, Pordenone. www.vignetilemonde.com

Owned by the Pistoni Salice family, the twenty-five-hectare estate produces attractive varietal wines from Grave del Friuli, and fairly tannic Cabernet Sauvignon and "Querceto" (Cabernet Sauvignon and Franc).

Moschioni ☆☆–☆☆☆

Cividale del Friuli, Udine

Just eleven hectares, but a fine range of wines, including rare barrique-aged Pignolo and Schioppettino.

Pierpaolo Pecorari ☆☆–☆☆☆

San Lorenzo Isontino, Gorizia. www.pierpaolopecorari.it

Top Isonzo wines from a low-yielding, twenty-hectare estate, and supple Merlot IGT.

Petrucco ☆☆

Buttrio, Udine. www.petrucco.com

Sound varietal wines from a well-located estate.

Pichéch ☆☆–☆☆☆

Cormòns, Gorizia

Full-bodied whites, notably the Collio Bianco from Ribolla, Tocai, and Malvasia.

Pighin ☆☆

Risano, Udine. www.pighin.it

Well-known family firm offering a range of wines from Collio and Grave. More than acceptable quality across the board.

Vigneti Pittaro ☆☆

Codroipo, Udine. www.vignettipittaro.com

Piero Pittaro is president of Italy's association of oenologists. His seventy-five-hectare estate produces supple reds from Grave del Friuli vineyards, as well as fresh varietal whites.

Plozner ☆☆

Spilimbergo, Pordenone. www.plozner.it

Sound varietal wines, from Grave del Friuli.

Idisoro Polencic ☆☆–☆☆☆

Cormòns, Gorizia. www.polencic.com

Impeccable and highly consistent Collio whites.

Primosic ☆☆

Madonnina di Oslavia, Gorizia. www.primosic.com

Excellent Bordeaux blend "Metamorfosis" sometimes outshines the reliable whites.

Alessandro Princic ☆☆☆

Pradis di Cormòns, Gorizia

This tiny Collio winery makes gorgeous Tocai.

Dario Raccaro ☆☆☆

Cormòns, Gorizia

Tiny production, so hard to find, but both the Tocai and Merlot are outstanding.

Radikon ☆

Oslavia, Gorizia

A once-admired Collio producer whose star has waned.

Rodaro ☆☆–☆☆☆

Spessa di Cividale, Udine

Classic whites from Colli Orientali, and an exotic blend called "Ronc" (Pinot Bianco, Sauvignon, Tocai).

Roncada ☆☆

Cormòns, Gorizia

Silvia Mattioni produces a dependable range of Collio varietal whites.

Il Roncat

See **Giovanni Dri**

Ronchi di Cialla ☆☆–☆☆☆

Prepotto, Udine. www.ronchidicialla.com

The Rapuzzi family pioneered the production of previously obscure local varieties such as Schioppettino, Refosco dal Peduncolo Rosso, and Verduzzo. It continues to produce exemplary versions.

Ronco del Gelso ☆☆–☆☆☆

Cormòns, Gorizia

Giorgio Badin makes top Isonzo wines: outstanding white varietals, and very good red wines from Cabernet Franc and Merlot.

Ronco del Gnemiz ☆☆☆

San Giovanni al Natisone, Udine

Low yields characterize Enzo Palazzolo's estate in Colli Orientali del Friuli. The flagship wine is named after the property, and is a blend of Cabernet and Merlot, bottle-aged for four years before release.

Ronco dei Tassi ☆☆☆

Cormòns, Grizia

Founded in 1989, this small estate has made great strides and produces utterly reliable Collio whites, especially the partly oaked blend "Fosarin", mostly Tocai and Pinot Bianco.

Roncus ☆☆–☆☆☆

Capriova del Friuli, Gorizia

Rich, full-bodied whites, but production is small.

Scubla ☆–☆☆☆

Premariacco, Udine. www.scubla.com

Roberto Scubla has built his reputation on the first-rate "Pomèdes" blend of Pinot Bianco, Tocai, and Riesling, matured in new oak.

Specogna ☆☆

Corno di Rosazzo, Udine

Leonardo Specogna is a reliable source of Colli Orientali del Friuli wines. Note the whites are usually better than the reds.

Castello di Spessa ☆☆–☆☆☆

Capriva del Friuli, Gorizia. www.castellospessa.com

This Collio estate is beginning to rival its illustrious neighbour Schiopetto (*q.v.*).

Subida di Monte ☆–☆☆

Cormòns, Gorizia

Good Chardonnay and Merlot, especially the "Selezione" range.

Valle ☆

Buttrio, Udine. www.valle.it

Cabernet and Merlot, as well as white varietals from Colli Orientali del Friuli.

Vazzoler ☆

Mossa, Gorizia

Good Pinot Grigio and Pinot Bianco from Collio.

Venica ☆☆–☆☆☆

Dolegna del Collio, Gorizia. www.venica.it

Vigorous Collio whites, and a substantial Bordeaux blend called "Ronco delle Cime".

La Viarte ✩✩✩
Prepotto, Udine. www.laviarte.it

As well as varietal wines from Colli Orientali del Friuli, the Ceschin family offer rarities such as a pure Tazzelenghe, and a blend of Picolit and Verduzzo. High quality across the range.

Tenuta Villanova ✩✩
Farra d'Isonzo, Gorizia

Ancient property; excellent Chardonnay and other wines.

Emilia-Romagna

It is to be expected that Italy's greediest culinary region, by all accounts, should put the emphasis on quantity rather than quality in its wine. Any ambition to produce better than simple thirst-quenchers is recent and limited to a select few. Bologna, the cooks' capital, is the hub of the region and the meeting place of its two component parts. Most of the land is the flat Po Valley, following the river to the Adriatic between Ravenna and Venice.

All the wine regions of interest lie in the foothills, however tentative, of the Apennines to the south, dividing the province from Tuscany. Fizzy red Lambrusco leads, not just in Emilia but in the whole of Italy, for volume production of a distinct type of wine. It is an ingenious and profitable way of achieving notoriety in deep valley soils where more conventional quality is unlikely.

Romagna produces nothing so exceptional. Its best-known wine is the white Albana, which has yet to distinguish itself. It is in the Colli Bolognesi and Piacentini, the hill areas nearest to Bologna and Piacenza, that progress is being made.

DOC & Other Wines

Albana di Romagna DOCG. White wine. Provinces: Ravenna, Forlì, and Bologna. Grape: Albana. May be made in *secco* (dry), *amabile* (off-dry), *dolce* (sweet), and *passito* styles. The standard white of Bologna and east to the coast. The Albana is a mild, not to say neutral, grape whose dry wine tend to flatness, finishing bitter to satisfy local taste. It gains more character when made *amabile* and/or *spumante*, or indeed *passito*.

Barbarossa di Bertinoro A vine not found elsewhere, cultivated on a small scale at Bertinoro, the centre of the Romagna vineyards, for a good, full-flavoured red with ageing potential. *See* Fattoria Paradiso.

Barbera The ubiquitous red grape is popular in the area of Piacenza and in the Colli Bolognesi and Colli d'Imola, where it is given DOC dignity.

Bianco di Scandiano DOC. White wine. Emilia. Villages: commune of Scandiano plus five others southwest of Reggio. Grapes: Sauvignon up to 85%, Malvasia di Candia and Trebbiano Romagnolo up to 15%. A white alternative to Lambrusco (*q.v.*) made semi-dry or distinctly sweet, sometimes fizzy and sometimes fully frothy.

Bosco Eliceo DOC. Red and white wine. Emilia. Provinces: Ferrara and Ravenna. Grapes: Trebbiano Romagnolo, Sauvignon/Malvasia di Candia, Fortana, Merlot, and Sauvignon. The Fortana is a rustic red from this DOC grown on reclaimed marshland.

Cagnina di Romagna DOC. Red wine. Villages: 16 communes in Forlì, five in Ravenna. Grapes: Cagnina, other varieties up to 15%. A sweet red wine classified as DOC in 1989. It is enjoyed locally as an accompaniment to roast chestnuts. Very small production.

Chardonnay Once an outlaw, Chardonnay is now permitted and being used in a range of DOCs in the region.

Colli Bolognesi DOC. Red and white wine. Emilia. Provinces: Bologna and Modena. Grapes: (white) Albana 60–80%, Trebbiano Romagnolo at least 20%, other whites up to 20%. For named varieties: Barbera, Merlot, Riesling Italico, Pinot Bianco, Cabernet Sauvignon, and Sauvignon Blanc 85%, with 15% neutral grapes allowed.

An umbrella DOC for the everyday wines of Bologna. More remarkable wines are being made in the same vineyards by growers experimenting with better grapes, including Sauvignon Blanc, Cabernet Sauvignon, and Chardonnay. Growing conditions are excellent.

Colli di Parma DOC. Red and white wine. Emilia. Province: Parma. Grapes: (red) Barbera 60–75%, with Bonarda or Croatina 25–40%, other dark varieties up to 15%; (Malvasia) Malvasia di Candia 85–100%, Moscato Bianco up to 15%; Sauvignon Blanc 100%.

In this DOC, the red resembles Oltrepò Pavese Rosso, the Malvasia may be either dry or *amabile*, usually *frizzante*; the Sauvignon Blanc usually still.

Colli Piacentini DOC. Red and white wine. Emilia. Province: Piacenza. Villages: twenty in Emilia. The region is known for a number of blended wines, such as the white Monterosso and Trebbiano Val Trebbia, and Gutturnio: a blend of Barbera and Bonarda.

Grapes: (white) Malvasia di Candia, Ortugo, Pinot Grigio, Sauvignon Blanc, Trebbiano Romagnolo; Barbera, Bonarda, Malvasia, Ortugo, and Pinot Nero. A high-volume zone, producing wines from innumerable varieties in every conceivable style.

Gutturnio dei Colli Piacentini *See* Colli Piacentini.

Lambrusco Lambrusco from Emilia was the smash hit of the Italian wine industry in the 1970s, selling like Coca-Cola (in more senses than one) in the United States.

It is simply a sweet, semi-sweet, or occasionally dry, fizzy red (or pink or occasionally white) wine such as any winemaker could produce who had the foresight to see the demand. The common qualities are scarcely drinkable by a discerning wine-lover, but this misses the point. The market is elsewhere. More discerning palates will choose one from a named region, of which the best is Sorbara.

Lambrusco accounts for approximately 5% of all Italian wine. Roughly a tenth of this is of DOC quality, and to be honest, only a fraction of this is really worth drinking. A select few producers show true genius with this wine.

Lambrusco Grasparossa di Castelvetro DOC. Red and *rosato*. Emilia. Province: Modena. Grapes: Lambrusco Grasparossa 85%, other Lambrusco and Uva d'Oro 15%.

Dark-coloured, tannic, rather strong, and always slightly sweet; comes from the hills southwest of Modena.

Lambrusco Reggiano DOC. Red and *rosato*. Emilia. Province: Reggio Emilia. Grapes: Lambrusco Marani, Salamino, Montericco, and Maestri either singly or together. 20% Ancellotta also allowed. Commonest, lightest, and usually fizziest Lambrusco.

Lambrusco Salamino di Santa Croce DOC. Red wine. Emilia. Province: Modena. Grapes: Lambrusco Salamino 90%, other Lambrusco and Uva d'Oro 10%.

Salamino di Santa Croce is a local sub-variety of the Lambrusco grape with a bunch said to resemble a little salami. Dark, soft, fruity, and at its best when dry.

Lambrusco di Sorbara DOC. Red and *rosato*. Emilia. Province: Modena. Grapes: Lambrusco di Sorbara 60% and Lambrusco Salamino max 40%.

A good Lambrusco di Sorbara is a delight: juicy, pink wine, racy, tingling and extraordinarily drinkable – a childish wine perhaps, but marvellously thirst-quenching with rich food. In-fact, the pink froth is a pleasure in itself.

Alas, off-putting chemical flavours are all too common, even in this premium Lambrusco; under no circumstances store bottles of any of them.

Merlot Widely grown in Emilia-Romagna mostly for blending. In the Colli Bolognesi it is DOC.

Montuni del Reno DOC. White wine. Emilia. Province: Bologna. Grapes: Montuni; other non-aromatic grapes up to 15%. The wine can be dry or semi-sweet and is usually *frizzante*.

Pagadebit di Romagna DOC. White wine. Provinces: Forlì and Ravenna. Grapes: Pagadebit; other whites up to 15%. The word means "debt payer" thanks to generous yields.

A white vine, rare in Tuscany, enjoying revival and modernization around Bertinoro in Romagna. Vinified as gently dry, or *amabile*. The commune of Bertinoro rates as a special sub-denomination.

Pinot Bianco Widely grown in Emilia-Romagna; DOC in Colli Bolognesi.

Pinot Grigio Increasingly being grown, Pinot Grigio is DOC in Colli Piacentini.

Pjcòl Ross An esoteric, dry, *metodo tradizionale* Lambrusco of high quality from only one grower: Moro of Sant' Ilario d'Enza.

Sangiovese di Romagna DOC. Red wine. Provinces: Ravenna, Bologna, Forlì. Grape: Sangiovese di Romagna. Romagna has its own strain of the red Sangiovese, distinct from the Tuscan one which is the basis of Chianti. It makes pleasant, light- to medium-weight red, often with a slightly bitter aftertaste. It is produced in enormous quantities and enjoyed young, often as the Sunday wine of the region.

Sauvignon Blanc An up-and-coming white grape in this part of Italy, possibly the best of the DOC Colli Bolognesi and the major partner in the DOC Bianco di Scandiano.

Trebbiano di Romagna DOC. White wine. Provinces: Bologna, Forlì, Ravenna. Grape: Trebbiano di Romagna. Taking over the area as the everyday white. Its style is clean-tasting and unobtrusive.

Trebbianino Val Trebbia *See* Colli Piacentini.

Leading Emilia-Romagna Producers

Castelluccio ☆☆☆
Modigliana, Forlì. www.ronchidicastelluccio.it
"Ronco dei Ciliegi" and "Ronco delle Ginestre" from Sangiovese, and "Ronco del Re" from Sauvignon Blanc, are fashioned into some of Romagna's finest bottlings under the experienced eye of wine consultant Vittorio Fiore.

Cavicchioli ☆☆
San Prospero, Modena. www.cavicchioli.it
Sandro Cavicchioli produces a million cases of very dependable Lambruscos from different DOCs. The top Sorbara is called "Vigna del Cristo" and takes its name from a seven-hectare vineyard.

Drei Donà: Tenuta la Palazza ☆☆☆
Massa di Vecchiazzano, Forlì
This is a small winery focusing on varietal wines of high quality, including a rich, barrique-aged Sangiovese; concentrated "Magnificat" Cabernet Sauvignon; and a Chardonnay IGT called "Il Tornese". Franco Bernabei is the consultant oenologist.

Giacobazzi ☆
Nonantola, Modena. www.giacobazzi.it
One of the largest producers, bottlers, and shippers of Lambrusco but now producing light, fizzy wines and a range of simple still wines such as Trebbiano and Sangiovese.

Fattoria Paradiso ☆☆☆
Bertinoro, Forlì. www.fattoriaparadiso.com
An estate that has been shaped into a viticultural paradise by Mario Pezzi and his family. From seventy-five hectares, Pezzi makes 40,000 cases of exemplary wine, including the unique red Barbarossa (of a vine only he grows), a Bordeaux blend called "Mito", Albana Passito, and white semi-sweet Pagadebit. There is also an *enoteca*, a museum and *tavernetta*, all open to the public.

Riunite ☆
Campegina, Reggio Emilia. www.riunite.it
Founded in 1950, Riunite is one of the world's largest winemaking operations, grouping twenty-six cooperatives, including seven outside the province of Reggio, with two bottling plants. Corrado Casoli presides over the complex, which includes 10,000 growers. Lambrusco is the principal product, but there are other local specialties such as Gutturnio and Sangiovese di Romagna.

San Patrignano Ospedaletto di Rimini ☆☆☆
Rimini. www.sanpatrignano.org
Quality has improved dramatically since Riccardo Cotarella was brought in as consultant winemaker in 1997. The highlights are the Sangiovese Superiore, and a dense, barrique-aged, Bordeaux-blend IGT called "Montepirolo".

La Stoppa ☆☆–☆☆☆
Ancarano di Rivergaro, Piacenza. www.lastoppa.it
A leader in Colli Piacentini owned by the Pantaleoni family. There is an attractive Cabernet Sauvignon, Barbera, and sweet Malvasia.

Terre Rosse (Vallania) ☆☆–☆☆☆
Zola Predosa, Bologna
Founded in 1965 by the late Enrico Vallania, a physician, whose genius and tenacity charted new directions in Italian viticulture. The Colli Bolognesi range includes excellent Sauvignon Blanc, Cabernet Sauvignon, Chardonnay, and Malvasia.

Tre Monti Imola ☆☆☆
Bologna. www.tremonti.it
An important estate, steadily improving with the help of consultant oenologist Donato Lanati. The white wines are often the best: Albana, of course, but also Chardonnay and Trebbiano.

La Tosa Vigolzone ☆☆–☆☆☆
Piacenza
An emerging estate making good Colli Piacentini wines from Cabernet Sauvignon, Sauvignon Blanc, and succulent Malvasia from partly dried grapes.

Fattoria Zerbina ☆☆☆
Faenza, Ravenna. www.zerbina.com
A family winery, run by Maria Cristina Geminiani, and now one of the top estates in Romagna. Their "Scacco Matto" is that rarity: an exceptional Albana. They also make "Marzieno" from Sangiovese with a little Cabernet Sauvignon, as well as a promising Sauvignon/Chardonnay blend called "Tergeno".

Other Emilia-Romagna Producers

Conte Otto Barattieri Vigolzone ☆☆
Piacenza
Good Colli Piacentini and a rare *vin santo* given extended barrel-ageing.

Francesco Bellei Bomporto ☆–☆☆
Modena
Highly regarded Lambrusco di Sorbara DOC and Pinot-Chardonnay *tradizionale*.

La Berta ☆☆–☆☆☆
Brisighella, Ravenna
Sangiovese is the mainstay of this estate, but you can also find a rare Alicante and an oaky Cabernet/Sangiovese blend called "Ca di Berta".

Bonfiglio ☆☆
Monteveglio, Bologna
Serious Pignoletto from the Colli Bolognesi.

Bonzara ☆☆
Monte San Pietro, Bologna
A small and steadily improving estate, offering a good range of Colli Bolognesi wines.

Le Calbane Meldola ☆☆
Forlì
Good Sangiovese Superiore and Calbanesco, a red *vino da tavola* from a mystery variety found in the vineyards of this small estate.

Cansetto dei Mandorli Predappio Alta ☆☆
Forlì
Good Romagna DOCs, including Sangiovese and Albana.

Casali ☆–☆☆
Scandiano, Reggio Emilia
One of the best Lambrusco Reggianos is made at this estate. Also bottle-fermented sparkling wines.

Celli Bertinoro ☆☆–☆☆☆
Forlì. www.celli-vini.com
This medium-sized winery takes Albana seriously and produces it in a range of styles. Other wines include rich Chardonnay and Sangiovese.

Cesari Castel San Pietro ☆☆–☆☆☆
Bologna. www.umbertocesari.it
Large producer. Specialities include Albana, Sangiovese, and Trebbiano di Romagna. The Sangiovese Riserva is delicious.

Cinti ☆☆
Pontecchio Marconi, Bologna. www.collibolognesi.com
Consistently reliable varietal wines from Colli Bolognesi.

Ferrucci Castelbolognese ☆☆–☆☆☆
Ravenna
Small estate makes very good, sweet Albana and Sangiovese Riservas, and a sweet Malvasia called "Stefano Ferrucci".

Cantina Sociale di Forlì ☆
Forlì
Good Sangiovese Superiore.

Luretta ☆☆–☆☆☆
Gazzola, Piacenza
A twenty-five hectare estate in the Colli Piacentini, producing very good Chardonnay and Cabernet Sauvignon.

Madonia ☆☆–☆☆☆
Bertinoro, Forlì
A small estate producing consistently good Albana and Sangiovese Superiore.

Moro Calerno di Sant'Ilario d'Enza ☆☆–☆☆☆
Reggio Emilia. www.rinaldinivini.it
Rinaldo Rinaldini produces Chardonnay and Cabernet, but is better known for his range of Lambrusco wines, including the rare house specialty: Pjcòl Ross.

Mossi Ziano ☆☆
Piacenza
Luigi Mossi produces a wide range from Colli Piacentini, specializing in Gutturnio. "Infernotto" is an unusual blend of Barbera, Pinot Nero, and Bonarda.

Pasolini Dall'Onda Montericco di Imola ☆☆
Bologna
Winemakers since the sixteenth century, the Pasolini Dall' Onda family owns properties in Romagna and Tuscany.

Poderi dal Nespoli ☆☆
Civitella di Romagna, Forlì. www.poderidalnespoli.com
A beautiful property, producing fine Albana Passito and an IGT from Sangiovese and Cabernet called "Borgo dei Guidi".

Il Poggiarello ☆☆–☆☆☆
Travo, Piacenza
Fine varietal wines from Colli Piacentini, still and sparkling. The top wine is "La Barbona" and is a blend of Barbera and Bonarda.

Cantine Romagnoli Villo di Vigolzone ☆
Piacenza
A complete range of Colli Piacentini DOCs, plus *spumante*.

Spalletti ☆☆–☆☆☆
Savignano sul Rubicone, Forlì
This winery is housed in the ancient Castello di Ribano. It produces a full range of Romagna specialties, from Pagadebit to Albana to Sangiovese. The "Rocca di Ribano Riserva" is often among the best Sangiovese di Romagna.

Tre Rè ☆
Faenza, Ravenna. www.trere.com
A reliable range of Romagna wines, from Albana to Sangiovese to *frizzante* Pagadebit.

Uccellina ☆☆
Russi, Ravenna
The property offers the usual range of Romagna wines, with two specialties: "Ruchetto" from Pinot Noir, and "Burson", named after the rare and tannic variety of that name.

Vallona ☆☆–☆☆☆
Castello di Serravalle, Bologna
A rising star in the Colli Bolognesi, producing a wide range of wines, with impressive Pignoletto and Cabernet Sauvignon.

Venturini Baldini Roncolo di Quattro Castella ☆☆
Reggia. www.venturinibaldini.it
Fine, full-bodied Lambrusco Reggiano, "Cuvée di Pinot" *tradizionale*; and Cabernet Sauvignon.

Zerioli ☆☆–☆☆☆
Ziano Piacentino, Piacenza. www.zeriolivini.com
The Zerioli family make a wide range of Colli Piacentini DOCs plus a good *vin santo* from Malvasia.

Tuscany

To find a national identity in such a federation of disparities as Italy is not as difficult as it sounds. The answer is Tuscany. For foreigners, at least, the old Tuscan countryside of villas and cypresses, woods and valleys where vine and olive mingle, is Italy in a nutshell.

And so is its wine. Nine out of ten people asked to name one Italian wine would say "Chianti". They would have many different ideas (if they had any at all) of what it tastes like – for if ever any wine came in all styles and qualities from the sublime to the gor-blimey it is Chianti – and this despite being the earliest of all regions, possibly in all Europe, to start trying to define and defend its wine. Certainly in modern times, the *consorzio* of its producers paved Italy's way to its DOC system.

Chianti started in the Middle Ages as a small region of constant wars and alarms between Florence and Siena. It is now the biggest and most complex DOCG in Italy. There is a real unity and identity, despite its varied soils, traditions, and microclimates, because they all grow the same basic red grape, or versions of it. The Sangiovese is what holds Chianti together, but that should not imply monotony. Individual inclinations show up strongly in the balance of the blend, the type of fermentation, the use or neglect of the "*governo*", the method and time of ageing.

Chianti has many departments and sub-regions, of which the most distinguished is Chianti Classico, the region between Florence and Siena. It also has several neighbours who claim superiority for their not-dissimilar wines, most notably Brunello di Montalcino and Vino Nobile di Montepulciano. Above all, it is the firing range for the army of ambitious producers who believe that a dose of Cabernet, some new-oak barrels, and a designer bottle and label add up to The Great New Italian wine. Their field marshal, Piero Antinori, has successfully demonstrated that it can.

White wine is a relative stranger here. There is no white Chianti. But several small traditional supply points are holding their own, and the most important is the popular Vernaccia di San Gimignano. Vermentino is proving popular along the Tuscan coast.

Indeed, the Tuscan coast, the Maremma, with its sub-regions (such as Bolgheri, Montescuadaio, and Scansano) has rapidly become the region's most fashionable area for wine production. Bordeaux varieties flourish here, and the path laid out by Sassicaia decades ago has been followed by numerous followers, such as Ornellaia, Guada al Tasso, and Tassinaia. No one could accuse the Tuscan wine industry of resting on its laurels.

DOC & Other Wines

Barco Reale DOC. *See* Carmignano.

Bianco dell'Empolese DOC. White wine. Province: Florence. Villages: communes of Empoli, and six neighbouring communes. Grapes: Trebbiano Toscano min. 80%, other whites up to 20%. Recent DOC, not well-known outside the hills of Empoli.

Bianco Pisano di San Torpè DOC. White wine. Provinces:

Livorno and Pisa. Villages: seventeen in Pisa and Collesalvetti. Grapes: Trebbiano Toscano 75%, other whites up to 25%.

DOC named after a (very) early martyr who was beheaded in AD 68 at Pisa. A pale, dry wine with some body and a touch of bitterness.

Bianco di Pitigliano

DOC. White wine. Province: Grosseto. Villages: Pitigliano, Sorano, part of Scansano and Manciano. Grapes: Trebbiano Toscano 50–80%, Greco (Grechetto), Sauvignon, Chardonnay, Pinot Bianco, and Riesling 30% together, but no more than 15% each.

Pitigliano is in the extreme south of Tuscany near Lake Bolsena, the home of Est! Est!! Est!!! (*see* Latium). Its soft, dry, slightly bitter white has no particular distinction.

Bianco della Valdinievole

DOC. White wine. Province: Pistoia. Villages: communes of Buggiano, Montecatani Terme, and Uzzano. Grapes: Trebbiano Toscano min. 70%, Malvasia del Chianti, Canaiolo Bianco, Vermentino max. 25%, other whites up to 5%.

A small production of plain dry, sometimes slightly fizzy, white from west of Florence. Production of *vin santo* is smaller still.

Bianco Vergine Valdichiana

DOC. White wine. Provinces: Arezzo and Siena. Villages: six communes in Arezzo and four in Siena. Grapes: Trebbiano Toscano 60–80%.

A satisfactory though pretty mild, mid-dry white from eastern Tuscany, often used as an apéritif in Chianti. A slightly bitter finish gives it some character.

Bolgheri

DOC. Red, white, and *rosato* wine. Province: Livorno. Grapes: Bolgheri Bianco – Trebbiano Toscano 10–70%, Vermentino 10–70%, Sauvignon 10–70%, others up to 30%; Bolgheri Rosso – Cabernet Sauvignon 10–80%, Merlot up to 70%, Sangiovese up to 70%, others up to 30%.

Small region on the coast south of Livorno. Until 1994, DOC only for white and *rosato*, now covers some of Italy's most sought-after and costly reds. Good, fresh Vermentino too. About 700 hectares.

Brunello di Montalcino

DOCG. Red wine. Province: Siena. Village: Montalcino. Grape: Brunello di Montalcino.

A big, dry red produced for many years by the Biondi-Santi family on "the Pétrus principle" – that nothing is too much trouble. But sold more in the spirit of Romanée-Conti: no price is too high. Made DOCG in 1980, the Brunello is a strain of Sangiovese which can be disciplined in this soil to give dark, deeply concentrated wines. The former requirement of prolonged barrel-ageing has been greatly modified, and most wines will now spend about two years in either large casks or in barriques, or a mixture of the two. Brunello still needs long bottle-age to coax a remarkable bouquet into its rich, brawny depths. Now it is made by about 150 growers, with inevitably varying standards. At its magisterial best, it is one of the great red wines of Europe.

Candia dei Colli Apuani

DOC. White wine. Province: Massa-Carrara. Villages: communes of Carrara, Massa, and Montignoso. Grapes: Vermentino Bianco 70–80%, Trebbiano and Malvasia Bianco (up to 20%). A DOC white wine rarely seen outside the marble-quarry coast.

Carmignano

DOCG. Red wine. Province: Florence. Villages: Carmignano, Poggio a Caiano (16 kilometres/10 miles) northwest of Florence). Grapes: Sangiovese 45–70%; Canaiolo Nero 10–20%; Cabernets Franc and Sauvignon 6–15%; Trebbiano Toscano, Canaiolo Bianco and Malvasia del Chianti up to 10%; other varieties up to 5%.

Best described as Chianti with a just-tastable dollop of Cabernet, justified to the authorities by the fact that the Bonacossi family introduced it from Bordeaux generations ago. Carmignano is consistently well made and justifiably self-confident. Posterity may well thank it for the inspiration to aim all quality Chianti in this direction.

A younger, easier-drinking version of Carmignano is Barco Reale (DOC) – made from the same grapes from a maximum crop of 70 hl/ha (only 56 is permitted for Carmignano). There are also a Carmignano Rosato DOC and a Carmignano Vin Santo DOC; the latter can be superb.

Chianti

DOCG. Red wine. Provinces: Siena, Florence, Arezzo, Pistoia, Pisa. Villages: 103 communes. Grapes: Sangiovese 75–100%, Canaiolo up to 10%, Trebbiano Toscano, Malvasia del Chianti up to 10%. Max. crop: 75 hl/ha.

There are two basic styles of Chianti: that made as fruity and fresh as possible for local drinking in its youth (still sometimes bottled in *fiaschi*, whether covered with straw or plastic), and drier, more tannic, and serious wine aged in barrels or tanks and intended for bottle-ageing; therefore bottled in Bordeaux bottles which can be stacked. The traditional grape mixture is the same for both – basically Sangiovese but with variable additions of dark Canaiolo.

White Trebbiano and Malvasia are added for quicker-drinking Chiantis, but serious producers worked hard to eliminate the rule that required a percentage of white grapes to be included. The *governo* is a local tradition of adding very sweet, dried, grape must (usually Colorino) to the wine after its fermentation to make it referment, boost its strength, smooth its astringency, and promote an agreeable fizz which can make young Chianti delicious. Few producers now use the *governo* for wine that is to be aged before bottling.

Fine old Chianti Riserva has marked affinities with claret, particularly in its light texture and a definite gentle astringency which makes it feel very much alive in your mouth. Its smell and flavour are its own – sometimes reminding me faintly of mulled wine with orange and spices, faintly of chestnuts, faintly of rubber. I have also found a minty "lift" in its flavour, like young burgundy. Its mature colour is a distinct, even glowing garnet.

The future of Chianti is under constructive debate. Many producers are systematically adding a little seasoning of Cabernet or Merlot, and ageing the best wines in new, rather than often reused, oak barrels. The region as a whole continues to benefit from viticultural research aimed at improving the selections of Sangiovese planted and seeing off the over-productive clones planted decades ago. The ultimate Chianti will be made when the ultimate strain of Sangiovese has been identified (as it has in Montalcino), propagated, and its use mastered. Chianti is betting its future on the qualities of its ancestral grape variety.

The seven sub-zones include:

Chianti Colli Aretini The country to the east in the province of Arezzo; a good source of fresh, young wines.

Chianti Colli Fiorentini The zone just north of Chianti Classico around Florence, especially east along the River

Arno. Several estates here are at least on a level with the best *classicos*.

Chianti Colline Pisane A detached area south of Pisa making lighter, generally less-substantial wine. A new DOC called Terre di Pisa is under consideration.

Chianti Colli Senesi A fragmented and inconsistent zone including the western flank of the *classico* area south from Poggibonsi, the southern fringes around Siena, and the separate areas of Montepulciano and Montalcino to the south. A wide range of styles and qualities.

Chianti Montalbano The district west of Florence that includes the separate DOC of Carmignano. Also good Chiantis, though lesser-known.

Chianti Montespertoli Created DOCG in 1997, apparently to benefit a single estate: Fattoria Sonnino.

Chianti Rufina A small area 24 kilometres (15 miles) east of Florence. Rufina is a village on the River Sieve, a tributary of the Arno. The hills behind, where the magically named Vallombrosa is hidden, contain some of the best Chianti vineyards (*see* Frescobaldi and Selvapiana).

Chianti Classico DOCG. Red wine. Provinces: Florence and Siena. Villages: Radda, Gaiole, Greve, San Casciano, Castelnuovo Berardenga. Grapes: Sangiovese 75–100%, up to 10% Canaiolo Nero, up to 6% Trebbiano and Malvasia, up to 15% other red grapes (such as Cabernet or Merlot). Max crop: 52.5 hl/ha. Since 1966 separated from "Chianti" and now an independent zone located between Florence and Siena. Most of its producers are members of the very active *Consorzio del Marchio Storico*, based near San Casciano, and seal their bottles with its badge: a black rooster.

Chianti Classico's progress during the last fifteen years has been some of the most impressive in all of Italy. In 1930,

when *vini tipici* were introduced, the original Chianti (which is today the *classico* region) was not able to satisfy the enormous demand for Chianti wine. So the neighbouring sub-zones that traditionally copied the Chianti style were officially granted the right to call their wines Chianti.

In 1963, when the DOCs were introduced, almost half of Tuscany was consequently incorporated in a huge Chianti-zone. The original style was therefore blurred and huge differences in character and quality between the sub-regions and producers were lost.

Since 1966, Chianti Classico, with independent status, has usually been the best and most expensive wine, but very good Chiantis also come from the redefined sub-zones Rufina and Colli Fiorentini.

Colline Lucchesi DOC. Red and white wine. Province: Lucca. Villages: Lucca, Capannori, and Porcari. Grapes: (red) Sangiovese 45–70%, plus Canaiolo, Ciliegiolo, and Merlot; (white) up to 70% Trebbiano.

A cousin of Chianti from nearer the coast, also made in both first-year and *riserva* styles. The white is as yet an unknown entity.

Elba DOC. White and red wine. Province: Island of Elba. Grapes: (white) Trebbiano Toscano (known as Procanico) 90%, other whites up to 10%; (red) Sangiovese at least 75%. The island off the south Tuscan coast, once a home for the exiled Napoléon, like a stepping stone to Corsica, has very adequate dry white wines to wash down its fish, along with increasingly structured Chianti-style red wines from some highly competent producers. The Elba specialty is the exquisite red *passito* wine from the Aleatico grape, and occasionally from the Ansonica variety.

Antinori – Charting Tuscany's Future

The Marchese Piero Antinori may well be to twenty-first century Chianti what the Barone Ricasoli was to the Chianti of the nineteenth and twentieth – the man who wrote the recipe. Antinori is persuasive with the eloquence of an aristocrat who does not have to raise his voice. He and his former winemaker, Giacomo Tachis, made this ancient Florentine house – based in the Palazzo Antinori, in the heart of the city – the modern pace-setter, not only for

exemplary Chianti but more prophetically for Tignanello, which is Sangiovese blended with Cabernet Sauvignon and aged, Bordeaux style, in new-oak barriques.

This set the trend for what became known as the Supertuscan. Since then, the Antinori family has moved on. It has expanded its vineyard holdings to almost 1,300 hectares in Tuscany (Santa Cristina, Peppoli, Badia a Passignano, and Chianti Classico at Bolgheri), Umbria (Castello della Sala), Piemonte (Prunotto), and Puglia. Extra grapes and extra wine are bought under contract. Renzo Cotarella supervizes wine production at this growing empire. The ultramodern winery is at San Casciano (near Santa Cristina) and the Palazzo Antinori in Florence has tasting facilities. The splendid Villa Antinori, portrayed on labels of the vintage Chianti Classico was destroyed in World War II. The Marchese also owns an estate at Montepulciano (Siena), La Braccesca, for DOC Nobile and Rosso di Montepulciano.

Nor is Antinori's vision confined to Italy. There have been substantial investments in Atlas Peak above Napa Valley, where the ambition to produce a great New World Sangiovese has yet to be realized; and a daring joint venture with Château Ste Michelle in Washington to produce a luxurious Bordeaux blend called "Col Solare". Despite the astonishing accomplishments of the house of Antinori, Piero Antinori and his children know full well that they cannot afford to rest on their laurels.

Galestro An ultra-modern white produced by a group of Chianti-makers using cold fermentation to instil zip and fruity freshness into Trebbiano (which often lacks these qualities). The name derives from a specific soil type. Galestro is the only Italian wine to have a ceiling on its alcoholic degree: 10.5.

Montecarlo DOC. White and red wine. Province: Lucca. Villages: hills of Montecarlo. Grapes: (white) Trebbiano Toscano 70%; Semillon, Pinot Gris, Pinot Bianco, Vermentino, Sauvignon, and Roussanne 30%; (red) Sangiovese 50–75%, Canaiolo Nero 5–15%; Ciliegiolo, Colorino, Malvasia Nera, Syrah 10–15%.

A good example of the improvements possible to Tuscan wines by allowing some more aromatic grapes to elaborate the essentially neutral Trebbiano. Montecarlo's smooth, unaggressive but interesting white can develop a very pleasant bouquet with two or three years in bottle.

Montecucco DOC. Province: Grosseto. Region southwest of Montalcino, producing wines more rustic than Brunello. Colle Massari is a leading estate.

Monteregio di Massa Marittima DOC. Province: Grosseto. Communes of Massa Marittima and Monterotondo Marittima. Grapes: (red) min. Sangiovese 89%; (white) Trebbiano 50%, Vermentino, Malvasia, and/or Ansonica 30%.

A Maremma appellation gradually assuming importance. Chateau Lafite and Chianti producer Castellare (*qq.v.*) are major investors here.

Montescudaio DOC. Red and white wine. Province: Pisa. Villages: Montescudaio and six other communes. Grapes: (red) Sangiovese 65–85%, plus Trebbiano Toscano and Malvasia, and other reds up to 10%. (white) Trebbiano Toscano 70–85%, Malvasia del Chianti and Vermentino 15–30%, other whites up to 10%.

Light white and rapidly improving red from near the coast west of Siena, although many top producers within the zone prefer to bottle their costly Cabernets and Merlots as IGTs. There is also distinguished and strong *vin santo*.

Morellino di Scansano DOC. Red wine. Province: Grossetto. Villages: Scansano and six other communes in the very south of Tuscany. Grapes: Sangiovese, plus up to 15% other red grapes.

DOC for a predominantly Sangiovese red increasingly admired. The wines at their best have body and richness but also remarkable finesse. A growing number of producers are already making extremely juicy wines and ageing them in barriques. Banfi, Frescobaldi, Fonterutoli, Rocca delle Macìe, Biondi-Santi, and Poliziano (*qq.v.*) are among the wine producers now planting in Scansano.

Moscadello di Montalcino DOC. White wine. Province: Siena. Village: Montalcino. Grapes: Moscato, plus max. 15% other white grapes. This sweet Moscato has been revived as a DOC due largely to Banfi. There is also a still sweeter *liquoroso* version, though rarely seen.

Parrina DOC. Red, white, and *rosato*. Province: Grosseto. Village: the commune of Orbetello. Grapes: (red and *rosato*) Sangiovese at least 80%; Canaiolo Nero, Montepulciano,

Colorino up to 20%; (white) Trebbiano 30–50%, plus Ansonica and/or Chardonnay up to 50%.

Lively wines, both red and white, from near the Argentario Peninsula in south Tuscany. Parrina Bianco caught young can be a good glass with seafood.

Pomino DOC. Red and white wine. Province: Firenze. Village: Pomino in the commune of Rufina. Grapes: (white) Pinot Bianco and/or Chardonnay (60–80%), Trebbiano max. 30%, other whites up to 15%; (red) Sangiovese 60–75%, Canaiolo and/or Cabernet Sauvignon and/or Cabernet Franc 15–25%, Merlot 10–20%.

The move for this DOC was led by the Frescobaldis. It applies to Pomino Bianco, which is based on Pinot Bianco and Chardonnay with Trebbiano. In 1716, the zone was cited by the Grand Duchy of Tuscany as one of the best wine areas.

Rosso di Montalcino DOC. Red wine. Province: Siena. Village: Montalcino. Grape: Brunello di Montalcino. Max. crop: 70 hl/ha.

A DOC made from Brunello grapes at Montalcino not deemed good enough to produce Brunello di Montalcino. Rosso varies greatly in quality. Some producers use the DOC as a kind of second wine; others take it seriously and set aside specific vineyards for its production. In fine vintages it can age well and offer very good value.

Rosso di Montepulciano DOC. Red wine. Province: Siena. Village: the commune of Montepulciano. Grapes: Sangiovese (Prugnolo Gentile) 60–80%, Canaiolo Nero 10–20%, other varieties up to 20% though no more than 10% white. Max. crop: 70 hl/ha. DOC that is enabling producers to make Vino Nobile better by declassifying some of it to *rosso*. Usually good value, especially in ripe years.

Sant' Antimo DOC. Red and white wine. Province: Siena. Village: Montalcino. Grapes: Chardonnay, Sauvignon, Pinot Grigio, Cabernet Sauvignon, Merlot, Pinot Nero.

A DOC created in 1996 that serves to create a specific appellation for the colourful quantity of innovative and experimental wines in the shadow of the big old Brunello di Montalcino estates.

Sassicaia DOCG. A remarkable wine that has proved the most influential of all in the shaping of Tuscan wine-growing. The late Marchesi Incisa della Rocchetta grew pure Cabernet Sauvignon on the coast at Bolgheri, south of Livorno – outside any recognized wine zone. What started as a whim became a sensation. He aged it in barriques like Bordeaux. His cousin, Antinori of Florence, used to bottle and sell it, but his son, Niccolò, moved the bottling to Bolgheri. A bottle should be surreptitiously slipped into top-level Cabernet tastings. (The 1975 has beaten all Bordeaux of this vintage.) Classified since 1994 as DOC Bolgheri, it now has its own DOCG.

Tignanello The firm of Antinori pioneered modern thinking about Chianti with this exceptional wine (and its Chiantis), Bordeaux-style winemaking, and ageing using barriques. Tignanello, a Sangiovese/Cabernet blend, is the obvious link between the highly individual Sassicaia and the traditional Chianti. It started the Tuscan revolution during the 1980s.

Val d'Arbia DOC. White wine. Province: Siena. Villages: ten along the Arbia River between Radda in Chianti and Buonconvento. Grapes: Trebbiano Toscano 70–90%, plus Malvasia del Chianti and Chardonnay. This is a DOC for a crisp, light, typically Tuscan white made in Chianti Classico country.

Val di Cornia DOC. Red, white, and *rosato*. Provinces: Livorno and Pisa. Villages: Campiglia Marittima, San Vincenzo, Piombino, and Suvereto in southwestern Tuscany. Grapes: (for red and *rosato*) Sangiovese 70–100%; Canaiolo Nero, Ciliegiolo, Cabernet Sauvignon, and/or Merlot at max. 30% but not more than 15% each; (white) Trebbiano Toscano 60–70%, Vermentino 15–30%, other white varieties up to 20%.

As in Bolgheri, Sangiovese gives only average results, and many estates are achieving remarkable results with Cabernet and Merlot grapes.

Vernaccia di San Gimignano DOCG. White wine. Province: Siena. Villages: the communes of San Gimignano. Grape: Vernaccia di San Gimignano.

Old-style Vernaccia was made as powerful as possible, fermented on its (golden) skins and aged in barrels for gently oxidized flavours to emerge. This was the wine Michelangelo loved. It can still be found like this, or in a modernized, pale version that can be good but can lack personality. There is also a San Gimignano DOC for red and other styles.

Vin Santo Wine of grapes dried in the loft until Christmas or later (to shrivel and sweeten them) is found all over Italy, but most of all at every farm in Tuscany. Although it can be red or white, white is far more common. Under several DOCs it is defined and regulated, but farmers make it regardless. The wine is fermented in very small barrels called *caratelli*, which are then sealed and placed in a loft to do their own thing for up to seven years. Inevitably, after such long ageing, some of it turns into vinegar, some into Madeira-like nectar. Traditionally, *vin santo* is sweet, but there are some dry versions, too. It should be at least three years old.

Vino Nobile di Montepulciano DOCG. Red wine. Province: Siena. Village: the commune of Montepulciano. Grapes: Sangiovese (Prugnolo Gentile) 60–80%, Canaiolo 10–20%. Other varieties up to 20%. Montepulciano would like to rival Brunello di Montalcino, also in the south of the Chianti country. It is highly debatable whether it has anything as exceptional as Brunello to offer. This is essentially Chianti, but professional winemakers have come to the fore and the DOCG is justified by an increasing number of excellent examples.

Leading Tuscany Producers

Castello d'Albola ☆☆–☆☆☆
Radda, Siena. www.albola.it
Zonin's base in Chianti Classico, a venerable castle with 150 hectares. The estate also produces "Le Elere", a pure Sangiovese from a single vineyard, and an oaky blend of Sangiovese and Cabernet called "Accaiolo".

Altesino ☆☆–☆☆☆
Montalcino, Siena

This highly respected small producer has wavered in direction, sometimes favouring Supertuscan styles over their excellent Brunello, then doing the opposite. "Palazzo Altesi" is barrique-aged Sangiovese, to produce an almost burgundy-like suppleness and fruitiness. The top Brunello is the single-vineyard "Montosoli", often of exceptional quality; and sometimes a delicious "Moscadello Ambro", a *passito* wine, is produced.

Castello di Ama ☆☆–☆☆☆
Lecchi in Chianti, Siena. www.castellodiama.com
Winemaker Dr. Marco Pallanti brought this eighty-hectare estate into the front rank of Chianti Classico by focusing on first-rate (and very expensive) single-vineyard wines such as his "Bellavista Riserva". The estate has, for many years, worked hard with international varieties such as Chardonnay, Merlot ("L'Apparita"), and Pinot Noir ("Il Chiuso"), but with mixed success.

Marchesi Antinori ☆☆–☆☆☆☆
Firenze. www.antinori.it
The present owner, Marchese Piero Antinori, is the latest in a line that began in 1385, and his daughters are poised to continue when he eventually retires. From his extensive power base in Tuscany, Antinori has expanded his holdings in regions as diverse as Umbria, Piemonte, and Puglia. *See* page 313.

Argiano ☆☆☆
Montalcino, Siena
This ancient estate has been through many changes of ownership; it now belongs to a member of the Cinzano family. Under winemaker Sebastiano Rosa, who left in 2002 to produce his own wine "Guidalberto", (*q.v.*), quality improved greatly. The Brunello is exceptionally rich, as is the magnificent "Solengo", a blend of Cabernet, Merlot, and Syrah, aged mostly in new barriques. All Brunello is vinified in the same way, then less satisfactory lots are declassified as *rosso*.

Avignonesi ☆☆–☆☆☆☆
Montepulciano, Siena. www.avignonesi.it
The sixteenth century Palazzo Avignonesi, over its thirteenth century cellars in the heart of Montepulciano, houses the family's barrel-aged Vino Nobile. The firm, which owns 218 hectares of vineyards, is owned and run by the three Falvo brothers. Their main focus is Vino Nobile, and their Merlot/Cabernet "Desiderio" and Chardonnay "Il Marzocco" can be rich and oaky. A second estate near Cortona makes exceptional dry Bianco Vergine Valdichiana, plus the Chardonnay and Sauvignon Blanc. Few would dispute that Tuscany's finest *vin santo* is made by Avignonesi, both the "regular" bottling and the rare and extremely costly "Occhio del Pernice". At the recently acquired Sovana estate near Pitigliano, they are also making a fine sweet Aleatico.

Badia a Coltibuono ☆☆☆
Gaiole, Siena. www.coltibuono.com.
The monks of this magical eleventh century abbey in the woods might have been the original growers of Chianti. The buildings, cellars, and gardens (with an excellent restaurant) are perfectly preserved by the Stucchi-Prinetti family,

owners since 1846. The hills are too high here for vines; the seventy hectares of vineyards are at Monti, to the south. There are few more consistently first-class Chiantis, as *riservas* back to 1958 prove. The top wine is usually "Sangioveto", an uncompromising barrique-aged pure Sangiovese that needs years to shed its youthful assertiveness.

Villa Banfi ☆–☆☆☆
Montalcino, Siena. www.castellobanfi

Founded in 1977 by major American wine importers with a yearning for their ancestral land, Banfi planted 650 hectares of vineyards and now produces a wide range of wines. The top Brunello di Montalcino is "Poggio all'Oro", and there are serious varietal wines from Pinot Noir ("Belnero"), Cabernet Sauvignon ("Tavernelle"), Syrah ("Colvecchio"), and two rich blends: "Excelsus" (a Bordeaux blend), and the new-oaked "Summus" from Sangiovese, Cabernet, and Syrah. There is also a large production of white wines, but these are mostly unremarkable. The firm found its feet under director Ezio Rivella, though today the wines are made by Rudy Buratti. There is also a sister winery in Piedmont.

Fattoria dei Barbi ☆☆
Montalcino, Siena. www.fattoriadeibarbi.it

Owned for two centuries by the Colombini Cinelli family, the Barbi estate has a long reputation. As well as reliable Brunello di Montalcino, they produce wines for earlier consumption, such as "Brusco dei Barbi", a Sangiovese made by the *governo* method. The estate is also developing vineyards in Scansano.

Biondi Santi – Il Greppo ☆☆☆
Montalcino, Siena. www.biondisanti.it

Founded in 1840 by Clemente Santi, whose grandson, Ferruccio Biondi Santi, is credited with creating Brunello di Montalcino. Early vintages, still alive in the bottle, are among Italy's most treasured wines. However, in the 1980s, quality slipped, and in the 1990s fungal problems affected the vineyards. Family feuding didn't help matters. By the early 2000s, the estate was back on course, though the astonishing improvement in quality throughout the region means that Biondi Santi is no longer as pre-eminent as it used to be. The family has acquired vineyards along the Tuscan coast, from which it is producing attractive and relatively inexpensive wines such as "Sassoalloro", a barrique-aged Sangiovese.

Boscarelli ☆☆–☆☆☆
Montepulciano, Siena. www.poderiboscarelli.com

Owned since 1962 by Paola de Ferrari Corradi. The thirteen-hectare estate is among the best in Montepulciano, producing Vino Nobile with depth, tone, and muscle. Fine Supertuscan "Boscarelli" is made with the aid of winemaker Maurizio Castelli.

La Brancaia ☆☆☆
Radda, Siena. www.brancaia.it

Owned by the Widmer family, this twenty-hectare estate produces delicious Chianti from pure Sangiovese, and the "Brancaia" Supertuscan IGT from Sangiovese, Merlot, and Cabernet. The wines are rich, concentrated, and sleek.

Castello di Brolio Barone Ricasoli ☆☆–☆☆☆
Firenze. www.ricasoli.it

The 227-hectare estate has been in the Ricasoli family since 1141. The great, grim, brick-built stronghold is the site where the great, grim Bettino Ricasoli, second prime minister of Italy in the 1850s, "invented" Chianti – or at least the blend of grapes and method of production. In 1971, the family granted control of the estate to Seagram, but this proved unsuccessful in the long-term. Eventually Francesco Ricasoli stepped in to revive the historic estate and restore its tattered reputation, largely by throwing out thousands of bottles he deemed of insufficient quality. He has had considerable success, especially with his top Chianti Classico named after the Castello and a Supertuscan IGT called "Casalferro".

Ca' Marcanda
Bolgheri, Livorno

Angelo Gaja, with a foothold in Tuscany at his Montalcino property, extended his holdings by purchasing and planting sixty-five hectares in the heart of Bolgheri with Bordeaux red varieties and Syrah. The first release was a wine called "Magari": half-Merlot, the rest Cabernet Sauvignon and Cabernet Franc. "Ca' Marcanda" itself will be similar, but with more Cabernet Sauvignon.

Tenuta Caparzo ☆☆–☆☆☆
Montalcino, Siena. www.caparzo.com

Under manager Nuccio Turone, Caparzo rose to become one of Montalcino's most consistent wineries. Fine Brunello, of course, especially the single-vineyard "La Casa", but also delicious "Le Grance" Chardonnay, and a Brunello/Cabernet blend called "Ca' del Pazzo". However, in 1999 the property was sold to Elisabetta Gnudi. She has also acquired the Borgo Scopeto estate in Castelnuovo Berardenga, which produces mostly Chianti Classico.

Tenuta di Capezzana ☆☆☆
Carmignano, Firenze. www.capezzana.it

Founded in the fifteenth century, and owned and run by Ugo Contini Bonacossi and his family. The ex-Medici villa of the Bonacossis, with its 110 hectares of vines, may be the first place Cabernet Sauvignon was grown in Tuscany. The excellence of their Carmignano assured the establishment of what seemed an alien DOC in the heart of Chianti (the finest is selected and sold as Villa Capezzana and Villa di Trefiano; named after the two estates where it is made).

Other innovations include the *rosato* "Vin Ruspo" and red "Barco Reale", and a fruity Cabernet/Merlot blend called "Ghiaie della Furba". A still Chardonnay has been introduced, but their immaculate *vin santo* is of greater interest. Their finest wine remains the firmly structured and long-lived Carmignano.

Casanova di Neri ☆☆☆–☆☆☆☆
Montalcino, Siena. www.casanovadineri.com

Giacomo Neri is a rising star in Montalcino. From thirty-five hectares, he makes regular Brunello, and two excellent single-vineyard wines: "Cerretalto" and the sensational "Tenuta Nuova". Neri doesn't apply a formula to his wines, adapting the wood-ageing to the quality and character of each vintage. There is also a pure but overpriced Cabernet called "Pietradonice".

Castelgiocondo ☆☆☆
Montalcino, Siena. www.frescobaldi.it

This 150-hectare estate is owned by the Frescobaldi family. Production, which began with the 1975 vintage, includes Brunello and Rosso di Montalcino, as well as various other wines such as the robust Merlot "Lamaïone".

Castellare ☆☆☆
Castellina in Chianti, Siena. www.castellare.it
This twenty-one-hectare estate, which belongs to Paolo Panerai, produces excellent Chianti and a range of other wines, including a pure Cabernet ("Coniale"), a pure Merlot ("Poggio ai Merli"), and a barrique-aged Supertuscan called "I Sodi di San Niccolò". Consultant winemaker Maurizio Castelli has masterminded the evolution of Castellare for twenty years.

Cecchi & Villa Cerna ☆☆
Castellina in Chianti, Siena. www.cecchi.net
Both owned by the merchant house of Luigi Cecchi. The main focus is on Chianti Classico and excellent Riserva, as well as a range of wines from other regions, including Scansano and San Gimignano.

Agricoltori del Chianti Geografico ☆☆
Gaiole Chianti, Siena. www.chiantigeografico.it
A cooperative founded in 1961. About two million bottles are produced from 570 hectares under a variety of labels. Other DOC wines include Vernaccia di San Gimignano and "Bianco Val d'Arbia"; IGTs include a pure Merlot called "Pulleraia".

The Rise of the Consultants

Almost every important estate in Tuscany now comes fully equipped with a consultant oenologist, who keeps a watchful eye on every aspect of an estate's viticultural and winemaking practices. Until the late 1960s, the Tuscan wine industry was dominated by large companies, but with the wine-production boom of succeeding decades, many growers decided to become winemakers, too. At the time, although these owners may have known a great deal about grape-farming, they probably knew very little about winemaking. Other estates that were already producing wine often had hopelessly outdated equipment.

They needed advice. There were profoundly knowledgeable winemakers in the industry, but they tended to be attached to a single company: Giacomo Tachis at Antinori, and Ezio Rivella at Banfi. So a new breed of consultants arose. As the wineries they advised gained in renown, so did the consultants. Oenologists such as Maurizio Castelli, Franco Bernabei, and Vittorio Fiore could add lustre to a wine estate, and their services, however costly, were keenly sought after. More recently, a younger generation is gradually taking their place: Riccardo Cotarela, Carlo Ferrini, Stefano Chioccioli, and Luca d'Attoma.

It is tempting to make fun of them, as they dash around Tuscany in their fast cars, mobile phones constantly beeping, but they have made an invaluable contribution to the success of Tuscan wines. They know about winemaking, can remedy faults, upgrade equipment – and they also know the competition and the market. Any fears that their multiplicity of clients could produce standardized wines are clearly, and most · fortunately, unfounded.

Col d'Orcia ☆–☆☆☆
Montalcino, Siena
A 130-hectare estate bought by Cinzano in 1973. Quality is high at the top of the range: the powerful Brunello, the pure Cabernet called "Olmaia", and Moscadello, though larger-volume wines such as "Rosso" are less impressive.

Costanti ☆☆☆
Montalcino, Siena
Owned by Andrea Costanti, with production overseen by consultant winemaker Vittorio Fiore. For many years, this has been an impeccable source of long-lived Brunello and Rosso di Montalcino. In the 1990s, Costanti introduced a single-vineyard wine called "Vermiglio", containing some Merlot and Cabernet as well as Sangiovese.

Fattoria di Cusona ☆☆–☆☆☆
San Gimignano, Siena. www.guicciardinistrozzi.it
Owned by Girolamo Strozzi and Roberto Guicciardini, this seventy-hectare estate dates back to the sixteenth century. It is an outstanding producer of Vernaccia di San Gimignano, under the direction of consultant winemaker Vittorio Fiore. Also Chianti dei Colli Senesi and the IGT Sangiovese, "Sòdole".

Fattoria di Felsina ☆☆☆☆
Castelnuovo Berardenga, Siena
Under manager Giuseppe Mazzocolin and winemaker Franco Bernabei, this estate is firmly in the top ranks of Chianti producers, especially with its *riserva* "Vigneto Rancia". The pure Sangiovese "Fontalloro" is first-rate, as is the barrel-fermented "Chardonnay I Sistri", and the *vin santo*.

Castello di Fonterutoli ☆☆☆–☆☆☆☆
Castellina in Chianti, Siena. www.fonterutoli.it
Owned by the Mazzei family since 1435, the estate is enjoying a revival. Filippo and Francesco Mazzei, with oenologist Carlo Ferrini, have abandoned their Supertuscan range in order to focus on modern-style Chianti Classico. Quality is outstanding. The Mazzeis have also developed a property in Scansano called Belguardo, to produce a delicious, uncomplicated Sangiovese Morellino.

Fontodi ☆☆☆–☆☆☆☆
Panzano, Firenze. www.fontodi.com
The Manetti family have been tile-makers since the eighteenth century, and have owned this estate since 1969. Giovanni Manetti, assisted by oenologist Franco Bernabei, has driven Fontodi to the top ranks. The Chianti Classico is consistently good, especially the "Vigna del Sorbo". The barrique-aged "Flaccianello" (pure Sangiovese) confirms this estate's position. Syrah and Pinot Noir show promise, but are not yet at the same level as the traditional wines.

Marchesi de' Frescobaldi ☆☆☆–☆☆☆☆
Firenze. www.frescobaldi.it
The Frescobaldis rival the Antinoris as the leading aristocratic wine family of Tuscany, tracing their ancestry back to 1300, and producing wines of outstanding quality, reliability, value, and originality. All Frescobaldi wines come from their eight estates east of Florence in Rufina, totalling 550 hectares. "Castello di Nipozzano" is their most famous red (a superior selection is called "Montesodi"). Other estates are Pomino and Poggio a Remole. "Pomino Bianco" is an excellent white

seasoned with Chardonnay; "Pomino Benefizio" is almost pure Chardonnay. Frescobaldi also manages Castelgiocondo (*q.v.*) at Montalcino, and participates in a joint venture with Robert Mondavi to produce a wine called "Luce".

Grattamacco ☆☆–☆☆☆
Castagneto Carducci, Livorno. www.grattamacco.com

Owner Pier Mario Meletti Cavallari built up a fine reputation for this ten-hectare estate in the hills behind Bolgheri. Its first success was with the Vermentino-dominated "Grattamacco Bianco", aged in barriques. "Grattamacco Rosso", made from Cabernet, Sangiovese, and Merlot, is sumptuous but very expensive. In 2002, Cavallari leased the property to a Swiss industrialist for twelve years.

Isole e Olena ☆☆☆–☆☆☆☆☆
Barberino Val d'Elsa, Firenze

On this justly admired, fifty-hectare estate-owner/winemaker Paolo de Marchi makes delicious Chianti Classico, the long-lived Sangiovese called "Cepparello", and excellent *vin santo*. Under the "Collezione" label, de Marchi produces some non-traditional wines such as Chardonnay, Cabernet Sauvignon, and a promising Syrah.

Le Macchiole ☆☆☆–☆☆☆☆
Bolgheri, Livorno. www.lemacchiole.it

Remarkable twenty-five hectare estate, run until his early death in 2002 by Eugenio Campolmi. "Paleo Rosso" was his best-known wine, originally a Cabernet-dominated blend, later a pure Cabernet Franc. Campolmi also created two scarce cult wines: "Messorio" (Merlot) and "Scrio" (Syrah). The wines are marvellous and astonishingly expensive.

Mastroianni ☆☆☆
Montalcino, Siena

Splendid quality from Gabriele Mastroianni's nineteen-hectare estate. As well as rich Brunello and Rosso di Montalcino, there'a a delicious sweet wine ("Botrys") from Moscato and Malvasia, and a fresh Sangiovese/Cabernet IGT called "San Pio". Mastroianni is full of ideas and enthusiasm, so this estate is likely to improve even further.

Melini ☆☆
Gaggiano di Poggibonsi, Siena. www.giv.it

An ancient 160-hectare property that now belongs to the Gruppo Italiano Vini complex. In the 1860s, Laborel Melini devised the strengthened Chianti flask which enabled shipping the wine, and consolidated the international following for Chianti. Best known for Chianti Classico Riservas, Vernaccia di San Gimignano, and other wines, notably the pure Merlot "Bonorli".

Monsanto ☆☆–☆☆☆
Barberino Val d'Elsa, Firenze. www.castellodimonsanto.it

Fabrizio Bianchi's improving seventy-hectare estate produces distinguished Chianti, notably the "Il Poggio" *riserva*. The IGT wines are impressive, too: the Sangiovese/Cabernet "Tinscvil", and a pure Cabernet called "Nemo".

Montevertine ☆☆☆
Radda, Siena

Founded by Sergio Manetti in 1967, and now run by his son, Martino, with consultant Giulio Gambelli. A fastidiously

tended little vineyard producing Chianti-like "Sodaccio" and "Le Pergole Torte", an oak-aged, all-Sangiovese IGT of unusual quality, and also a rather bizarre, oaky white wine from Trebbiano and Malvasia.

Ornellaia ☆☆☆☆
Bolgheri, Livorno

Forward-looking estate developed by Lodovico Antinori, with cellars designed by California's André Tchelistcheff, and advisers including Michel Rolland. "Poggio alle Gazze", a remarkably good Sauvignon Blanc, first issued in 1988, has now been phased out. The red "Ornellaia" is a blend of Cabernet Sauvignon, Merlot, and Cabernet Franc; an astonishingly voluptuous wine with wonderful depth of flavour. "Masseto" is pure Merlot, and usually more massive and powerful than "Ornellaia". Both are among Italy's greatest (and most expensive) red wines. In 2002, Mondavi took a controlling interest in the estate.

Il Poggione ☆☆
Montalcino, Siena. www.tenutailpoggione.it

Owners Clemente and Roberto Franceschi leave this well-known estate in the experienced hands of winemaker Fabrizio Bindocci. His Brunello di Montalcino is undeniably firm and structured, but the wine can lack the intensity and opulence of others. For those who prefer a more austere, traditional style of Brunello, Il Poggione is a good source.

Poliziano ☆☆☆
Montepulciano, Siena. www.carlettipoliziano.com

Owned by Federico Carletti who, with the help of Carlo Ferrini, makes juicy Chianti and Vino Nobile that is as fine as any in the region. Other impressive wines include "Elegia", a pure Sangiovese, and Cabernet-based "Le Stanze". He is also producing a delicious wine called "Lhosa" from vineyards in Scansano.

Fattoria Le Pupille ☆☆–☆☆☆
Magliano in Toscana, Grosseto. www.elisabettageppetti.com

The leading estate in Morellino di Scansano, producing a remarkable single-vineyard bottling from Poggio Valente. "Saffredi" is a Bordeaux blend with, unusually, a dash of Alicante. Two specialties are Vin Santo, and a sweet wine from Sauvignon and Traminer called "Solalto".

Fattoria Querciabella ☆☆☆
Greve, Firenze. www.querciabella.com

The Castiglioni family's estate does produce very good Chianti, but the main focus is on the succulent Supertuscan called "Camartina", and an oaked Chardonnay/Pinot Bianco blend called "Batar". Quality is impeccable, but prices are very high.

Castello dei Rampolla ☆☆☆
Panzano, Firenze

A beautiful property, owned for three centuries by the Di Napoli family. Very good Chianti Classico, but Rampolla's most celebrated wines are the Cabernet-dominated "Sammarco", which has a longer track record of excellence than most, and "Vigna di Alceo" – again Cabernet, but with a dash of Petit Verdot rather than Sangiovese.

Rocca delle Macìe ☆–☆☆☆
Castellina in Chianti, Siena. www.roccadellemacie.com

Founded in the 1970s, the Zingerelli's 220-hectare estate is one of the largest in the Chianti Classico. Their top wines are the *riserva* "Chianti Fizzano" and the "Ser Gioveto", a new-oaky pure Sangiovese. Because of the large scale of this operation, the wines are often underestimated, but at the top level they are excellent.

Ruffino ☆☆–☆☆☆
Pontassieve, Firenze. www.ruffino.com
The Folinaris have owned this property since 1877, but in 2000 there was a family split, and Ambrogio Folinari founded an offshoot company. Nonetheless, Ruffino retains its enormous holdings in Tuscany as well as the reputation established over many decades for its "Riserva Ducale". A Pinot Nero, "Nero del Tondo", is also impressive, as is the Sangiovese/Colorino blend called "Romitorio di Santedame". Ruffino also own the Greppone Mazzi estate at Montalcino.

San Felice ☆☆☆
San Gusmè, Siena. www.agricolasanfelice.it
Owned by a large insurance company, San Felice is not just a wine estate, but a beautifully restored tourist complex with a classy hotel and expensive restaurant. Winemaker Leonardo Bellacini has steadily improved the quality of its wines since he was hired in 1984. "Poggio Rosso", from a single vineyard, is one of Chianti Classico's finest *riservas*, and "Vigorello" is a tannic, assertive Supertuscan blend of Sangiovese and Cabernet Sauvignon.

San Giusto a Rentennano ☆☆☆
Monti, Siena
Owner Francesco Martini and his brother make a very traditional Chianti, but are better-known for the costly "Percarlo" (strong, pure, barrique-aged Sangioveto); a sumptuous Merlot called "La Ricolma"; and magnificent *vin santo* that is aged in cask for six years.

Tenuta San Guido-Sassicaia ☆☆☆☆
Bolgheri, Livorno. www.sassicaia.com
The late Marchese Mario Incisa della Rocchetta planted Cabernet Sauvignon on his 2,500-hectare seaside estate near Bolgheri, Tenuta San Guido, in 1944. Initially produced just for family use, Sassicaia emerged in the late 1960s as Italy's finest Cabernet. Consultant Giacomo Tachis insisted on ageing the wine in good oak rather than chestnut casks, and quality improved dramatically. Since Mario Incisa's death in 1983, his son Niccolò has taken personal control of the property. *See also* Guidalberto.

Selvapiana ☆☆☆
Pontassieve, Firenze
Founded in 1827 by the Giuntini family of Florentine bankers, it is still owned by descendant Francesco Giuntini, now assisted by Federico Masseti. Advised by oenologist Franco Bernabei, they produce highly traditional and long-lived Chianti Rufina. There are two beautifully structured, single-vineyard Chiantis, "Bucerchiale" and "Fornace", and glorious *vin santo*.

Castello del Terriccio ☆☆–☆☆☆☆
Castellina Maritima, Pisa. www.terriccio.it
The handsomely named Gian Anibale Rossi di Medelana Serafini Ferri owns a large estate south of Livorno. He only

began producing wine in the early 1990s, with consultant oenologists Carlo Ferrini (red wine) and Hans Terzer (white) giving their advice.

Terriccio produces two Chardonnays, the unoaked "Rondinaia" and the oaked "Saluccio". The star wine is the Cabernet-dominated "Lupicaia", aged eighteen months in new barriques. Sangiovese joins the Bordeaux variety in "Tassinaia", often overshadowed by "Lupicaia", but also of high quality. The Terriccio team is now working on new wines from Rhône varieties.

Val di Suga ☆☆☆
Montalcino, Siena
Owned by the Angelini family, who also own Tenuta Trerose in Montepulciano and San Leonino in Chianti Classico. Their Montalcino estate is divided between the north and south of the region, giving them a range of vineyards and grapes to work with.

There are two single-vineyard bottlings, both of exemplary quality: "Vigna del Lago" and "Spuntali".

Vecchie Terre di Montefili ☆☆☆
Greve, Firenze
Roccaldo Acuti established this small estate in 1980. As well as fine Chianti Classico, it produces an interesting white called "Vigna Regis", made from Chardonnay, Sauvignon Blanc, and Traminer. With its Cabernet/Sangiovese "Bruno di Rocca", this estate is a rising star in Chianti.

Castello Vicchiomaggio ☆☆–☆☆☆
Greve, Firenze. www.vicchiomaggio.it
This spectacular property has been owned by the Matta family since 1966, and is now run by John Matta. With its restaurant and accommodation in the castle, it's a popular tourist destination, but the wines have become increasingly impressive. Of the Chianti Classico wines, the most elegant is usually "La Prima", barrique-aged for nineteen months. There are two IGTs: "Ripa delle Mandorle", a Sangiovese/Cabernet blend designed to be drunk fairly young; and "Ripa delle More", a similar blend with longer barrique-ageing and more richness and power. In general, the wines are made in a plump, accessible style.

Villa Vignamaggio ☆☆☆
Greve, Firenze. www.vignamaggio.com
The beautiful fifteenth century villa where Mona Lisa probably lived, home of Michelangelo's biographer and one of the most prestigious Chiantis. Under guidance from oenologist Franco Bernabei, the owner, Roman lawyer Gianni Nunziante, has made substantial improvements in the vineyards and wines.

The Chianti Classico, especially the Riserva, is rich and complex, and there are also IGTs such as "Gherardino", a blend of Sangiovese and Cabernet Franc, and "Obsession", which sounds like a perfume but is in fact a new-oaked blend of Merlot, Syrah, and Cabernet Sauvignon.

Castello di Volpaia ☆☆☆
Radda in Chianti, Siena. www.volpaia.it
The medieval castle and its hamlet were high on the list of fifteenth century *crus*, and the village is now both a wine estate and a high-class tourist complex run by Giovanella Stianti Mascheroni. The vineyards are among the highest in

Chianti Classico, so it takes special care to ensure the grapes ripen fully. The Chianti is always a refined wine that needs a few years to reach its peak, and there are two impressive IGTs: "Balifico", a blend of Sangiovese and Cabernet Sauvignon, and "Coltassala", which is almost pure Sangiovese. In 2002, the leading oenologist Riccardo Cotarela became the consultant here, so the wines may well improve even further.

Other Tuscany Producers

Aia Vecchia ☆☆
Bibbona, Livorno
A rapidly expanding estate owned by Filippo Pellegrini. The sole wine at present is the richly oaky IGT "Lagone", from Merlot, Cabernet, and Sangiovese. Other wines will be released from 2005 onwards.

Aiola ☆☆–☆☆☆
Vagliagli, Siena
Thirty-four hectare property owned by the Malagodi family. Barrique-aged Chianti Classico, and an elegant Cabernet/Sangiovese blend called "Logaiolo".

Fattoria Ambra ☆☆
Carmignano, Firenze
The Rigoli family produce attractive, traditional Carmignano from their eighteen-hectare property.

Ambrosini ☆☆–☆☆☆
Suvereto, Livorno
A small estate producing a vigorous, oaky, Sangiovese/Merlot/Syrah blend called "Subertum", and an unusual Montepulciano IGT called "Riflesso Antico".

Jacopo Banti ☆☆
Campiglia Marittima, Livorno. www.jacopobanti.it
An eighteen-hectare estate in the Maremma hills. A wide range of wines, of which the best is "Peccato", a Cabernet/Merlot blend. Also produces a charming Ciliegolo.

Fattoria di Basciano ☆☆–☆☆☆
Rufina, Firenze
A rising star in the Chianti Rufina zone, with fine *riservas* an a Sangiovese/Cabernet blend called "I Pini".

Bindella ☆☆
Montepulciano, Siena. www.bindella.it
Swiss importer Rudolf Bindella makes fine Vino Nobile and a Cabernet Sauvignon called "Vallocaia".

Fattoria di Bossi-Marchese Gondi ☆☆–☆☆☆
Pontassieve, Firenze
The Gondis have owned this fine seventeen-hectare estate since 1592, and it is now run by Bernardo Gondi and his sister Donatella. Three different Chianti Rufinas are produced, and a splendid *vin santo*.

Fattoria del Buonamico ☆☆
Montecarlo, Lucca
The Grassi family produce Montecarlo Bianco and Rosso, and a Supertuscan blend called "Cercatoja".

Caccia al Piano ☆☆
Bolgheri, Livorno. www.cacciaalpiano.com
A new property founded and planted by Professor Marianno Franzini in 1997. Its two wines are the Merlot-dominated "Levia Gravia" and the Cabernet-dominated "Ruit Hora". Both wines are very concentrated but show signs of overripeness.

Castelli del Castelgreve ☆–☆☆
Mercatale Val di Pesa, Firenze
This cooperative is the largest Chianti Classico producer, with 185 members. The co-op produces a range of Chiantis, Morellino di Scansano, and Vernaccia di San Gimignano.

Castell' in Villa ☆☆
Castelnuovo Berardenga, Siena
Founded in 1968 by Riccardo and Coralia Pignatelli della Leonessa (the winemaker), the estate offers a consistent range of well-made Chianti Classico.

Castello di Cacchiano ☆☆–☆☆☆
Monti, Siena
A twelfth century estate near Gaiole, owned by Elisabetta Ricasoli Firidolfi, although half the estate is rented out to another family member. A reliable producer of good Chianti and excellent *vin santo*.

Villa Cafaggio ☆☆☆
Panzano, Firenze. www.girelli.it
Owned by the large firm of Casa Girelli. Fine Chianti Classico Riserva; pure Sangiovese called "San Martino" and a pure Cabernet called "Cortaccio", both of high quality.

Villa Calcinaia ☆
Greve, Firenze. www.villacalcinaia.it
Owned by the Caponi family since 1523, the estate produces reliable Chianti Classico.

Le Calvane ☆☆
Montespertoli, Firenze
A reliable source of Chianti Colli Fiorentini and Chardonnay.

Camigliano ☆☆
Montalcino, Siena. www.camigliano.it
The Ghezzi family produce dependable Brunello and Rosso di Montalcino from their eighty hectares of vineyards.

Campogiovanni ☆☆☆
See San Felice

Capaccia ☆☆
Radda, Siena. www.poderecapaccia.com
As well as good Chianti, this estate makes "Querciagrande", a pure Sangiovese aged in barriques.

Capannelle ☆☆–☆☆☆
Gaiole, Siena
A fourteen-hectare "boutique" winery, making admired but pricey IGT wines such as "Solare" from Sangiovese and Malvasia Nera.

Caprili ☆☆–☆☆☆
Montalcino, Siena. www.caprili.it
Excellent Brunello and Rosso di Montalcino.

Carpineto ☆–☆☆
Greve, Firenze. www.carpineto.com
This estate makes good Chianti and Vino Nobile, and white varietal wines.

Le Casalte ☆☆
Montepulciano, Siena
Owner Paola Silvestri produces dependable Vino Nobile.

Castellina Nittardi ☆☆–☆☆☆
Castellina in Chianti, Siena
Peter Femfert, aided by oenologist Carlo Ferrini, produces ultra-reliable Chianti Classico.

Cennatoio ☆☆–☆☆☆
Panzano, Firenze. www.cennatoio.it
Organic estate producing Chianti Classico and a range of varietal wines.

Cerbaiona ☆☆☆
Montalcino, Siena
The laid-back Molinaris, surrounded by their fifteen cats and three hectares of vines, produce tiny quantities of glorious Brunello, and a complex blend called "Cerbaiona".

Fattoria del Cerro ☆☆–☆☆☆
Montepulciano, Siena. www.saiagricola.it
Owner SAI Agricola, an insurance company, produce first-rate Vino Nobile and a Merlot called "Poggio Golo". *See also* La Poderina.

Chiappini ☆☆
Bolgheri, Livorno
Giovanni Chiappini is a farmer whose land happened to be in the heart of Bolgheri. He started making wine here in 2000: the unoaked, fruity "Felciaino" and the rich, Cabernet/Merlot blend "Guado de' Gemoli".

Chigi Saracini ☆
Castelnuovo Berardenga, Siena
An historic, eighty-hectare estate, now the property of a bank. Good *vin santo*.

Ciacci Piccolomini d'Aragona ☆☆☆
Montalcino, Siena. www.ciaccipiccolomini.com
Old estate emerging with fine Brunello di Montalcino and unusually rich *rosso*.

Villa Cilnia ☆☆
Montoncello, Arezzo
Twenty-hectare estate producing Chianti Colli Aretini and a wide range of other wines, including Chardonnays and a Sangiovese/Cabernet blend called "Vocato".

Colognole ☆–☆☆
Rufina, Firenze. www.colognole.it
Owned by the Contessa Spalletti, this twenty-seven-hectare property produces medium-bodied Chianti Rufina.

Dei ☆☆
Montepulciano, Siena
Caterina Dei is a leading producer of Vino Nobile from a fourty-four hectare estate.

Dievole ☆☆–☆☆☆
Vagliagli, Siena. www.dievole.com
The vineyards of this 100-hectare estate line a valley north of Siena. Their Chianti Classico is called "Vendemmia". Unusual late-harvest Sangiovese, "Novecento" and serious *governo* Chianti, "Rinascimento". Imaginative tours for visitors.

Fanti ☆☆–☆☆☆
Castelnuovo Abate, Siena
Steadily improving quality at this serious Montalcino estate.

Tenuta Farneta ☆☆–☆☆☆
Sinalunga, Siena
The estate has built its reputation on a fine, pure Sangiovese called "Bongoverno".

Fassati ☆☆
Montepulciano, Siena. www.fazibattaglia.it
Owned since 1969 by Fazi-Battaglia (*see* Marches). An important producer of Chianti and Vino Nobile di Montepulciano. Also owner of Greto delle Fate in Scansano.

Le Filigare ☆☆
San Donato in Poggio, Firenze
Elegant Chianti Classico and a stylish Sangiovese/Cabernet blend called "Podere Le Rocce".

Fuligni ☆☆☆
Montalcino, Siena
A small estate (under four hectares) with a big reputation. Roberto Guerrini ensures that quality at his family's property is impeccable, for both *rosso* and Brunello.

Castello di Gabbiano
Mercatale Val di Pesa, Firenze
Chianti Classico estate acquired by Beringer Blass in 2000.

Tenuta di Ghizzano ☆☆–☆☆☆
Ghizzano di Peccioli. www.tenutadighizzano.com
A small, fourteen-hectare property in the hands of the Veneroso Pesciolini family since the fourteenth century. Sumptuous IGT reds: "Nambrot", which is mostly Merlot, and "Veneroso", a Sangiovese/Cabernet/Merlot blend.

Il Greppone Mazzi
See **Ruffino**

Fattoria di Grignano ☆☆
Pontassieve, Firenze. www.fattoriadigrignano.com
This forty-hectare estate is a good source of Chianti Rufina.

Gualdo del Re ☆☆–☆☆☆
Suvereto, Livorno. www.gualdodelre.it
The Rossi family began bottling in 1982, but rarely reached the quality level of their illustrious neighbours. In 2000, they hired oenologist Barbara Tamburini to improve quality, and she seems to be succeeding. Pleasant white wines, but better reds, such as the fleshy "Gualdo del Re" Sangiovese, the previously Supertuscan and since 2000 pure Cabernet "Federico Prima", and the pure-Merlot "Rennero".

Guidalberto
Bolgheri, Livorno

A joint venture between Sassicaia and Marchese Nicolo's stepson, who owns vines adjoining Sassicaia. First vintage was in 2000 of a blend of Merlot, Cabernet, and Sangiovese.

Lilliano ☆–☆☆
Castellina in Chianti, Siena. www.lilliano.com
Owned by the Ruspoli family. Sound Chianti Classico from forty-five hectares.

Lisini ☆☆–☆☆☆
Montalcino, Siena. www.lisini.com
Consultant winemaker Franco Bernabei oversees the production of rich, reliable Brunello and delicious Rosso.

Mantellassi ☆
Magliano in Toscana, Grosseto. www.fatt-mantellassi.it
A producer of somewhat rustic Morellino di Scansano.

Fattoria di Manzano ☆☆☆
Manzano di Cortona, Arezzo.
Owned by the D'Alessandro family, this twenty-five-hectare property produces an oaky Chardonnay and outstanding Syrah called "Vigna del Bosco".

La Massa ☆☆☆
Panzano, Firenze
A twenty-seven-hectare estate bought in 1992 by a Neapolitan businessman. The top wine is "Giorgio Primo", a Chianti Classico aged in new barriques.

Massanera ☆–☆☆
Chiesanuova, Firenze
Aromatic Sangiovese wines, of which the best is "Prelato".

Castello di Meleto ☆☆
Gaiole, Siena. www.castellomeleto.it
A large, 180-hectare estate, now owned by Viticola Toscana. A new team, installed in 1996, has made great strides. All the Chiantis are pure Sangiovese, and the finest is "Fiore", which contains 10% Merlot.

Mola ☆☆
Porto Azzurro, Elba
An excellent Elba estate, producing an oaky Sangiovese-dominated red and a rich Aleatico.

Fattoria Montellori ☆☆
Fucecchio, Firenze
This is a large, fifty-five hectare estate that produces a wide range of wines: among them, a Sangiovese/Cabernet blend ("Castelrapiti"), a Cabernet/Merlot blend ("Salamartino"), and a pure Sauvignon. Ambition sometimes exceeds the results.

Montenidoli ☆☆
San Gimignano, Siena. www.montenidoli.com
Owner Elisabetta Fagiuoli produces highly drinkable Vernaccia di San Gimignano, and other wines in a wide range of styles.

Montepoloso ☆☆–☆☆☆
Suvereto, Livorno
Rapidly improving Swiss-owned Val di Cornia DOC property.

"Gabro" is mostly Cabernet, "Nardo" an opulent Sangiovese/Cabernet blend.

Moris ☆☆–☆☆☆
Massa Marittima, Grosseto. www.morisfarms.it
Increasingly well-known for its red wines, especially Morellino di Scansano.

Silvio Nardi ☆☆–☆☆☆
Montalcino, Siena. www.tenutenardi.com
Steady improvement at this seventy-five-hectare property, making traditional Brunello.

Siro Pacenti ☆☆☆
Montalcino, Siena
Powerful *rosso* and Brunello di Montalcino, but can show a heavy hand with the new barriques.

La Parrina ☆–☆☆
Albinia di Orbetello, Grosseto. www.parrina.it
Modest wines from the coast near Orbetello. The *riserva* is more serious, mostly Sangiovese, and aged eighteen months in new barriques.

Petra
Suvereto, Livorno. www.terramoretti.it
Owned by the Moretti family, who also own Bellavista (*q.v.*) in Franciacorta, Petra has its base at an astonishing new winery in San Lorenzo that resembles a tilted satellite dish. Ambition, money, and cask samples suggest that Petra will be worth keeping an eye on.

Fattoria di Petrolo ☆☆☆
Mercatale Valdarno, Arezzo. www.petrolo.it
Impressive wines from the Sanjust family: pure Sangiovese ("Torrione"), and pure Merlot ("Galatrona"), both excellent.

Fattoria di Petroio ☆☆
Quercegrossa, Siena
Owned by Pamela and Gian Luigi Lenzi, this thirteen-hectare property produces stylish Chianti Classico.

Agostina Pieri ☆☆☆
Montalcino, Siena
A small, seven-hectare property, releasing impressive Brunello and unusually rich Rosso di Montalcino.

Pieve di Santa Restituta ☆☆☆
Montalcino, Siena
Acquired by Angelo Gaja in 1994, the estate produces two principal Brunellos: "Rennina" and a single-vineyard wine called "Sugarille". They are aged for two years in large casks as well as barriques, and are improving from year to year.

La Poderina ☆☆–☆☆☆
Castelnuovo dell'Abate, Siena. www.saiagricola.it
Owned by the SAI Agricola insurance company, this twenty-hectare estate is making ever more stylish Brunello di Montalcino and Moscadello. *See also* Fattoria del Cerro.

Poggio Antico ☆☆☆
Montalcino, Siena. www.poggioantico.com
The Milanese banking family of Gloder bought this property

in 1984 and soon began to produce Brunello to a very high standard. In addition, there is a more approachable style of Sangiovese called "Altero", which can also age well.

Poggio Gagliardo ☆☆
Montescudaio, Pisa. www.poggiogagliardo.com

A large estate with an excess of wines. The best are the elegant "Vignalontana" from Chardonnay, the concentrated Sangiovese blend called "Rovo", and the oaky Cabernet Sauvignon labelled "Debbio del Falco".

Poggio San Polo ☆☆–☆☆☆
Montalcino, Siena

Sonia Fertonani's husband runs Val di Suga (*q.v.*); this is her pet project. First releases of Brunello and Rosso di Montalcino were very good, and there is an impressive Sangiovese/Cabernet blend called "Mezzopane".

Poggio al Sole ☆☆–☆☆☆
Greve, Firenze

Bought in 1990, owner/winemaker Giovanni Davaz produces excellent Chianti Classico. The best and richest Chianti is called "Casasilia". Impressive Syrah, too.

I Poggiolo di Roberto Cosimi ☆☆☆
Montalcino, Siena www.ilpoggiolomontalcino.com

Rodolfo Cosimi's boutique winery produces first-rate Brunello, especially the oaky but concentrated "Beato".

Poggiopiano ☆☆–☆☆☆
San Casciano, Firenze

Stefano Bartoli aims high, insisting on very low yields that give his Chianti and his new-oaked "Rosso di Sera" exceptional concentration.

Castello di Poppiano ☆☆
Montespertoli, Firenze

A good source of Chianti Colli Fiorentini; also produces Chardonnay and Syrah.

Castello di Querceto ☆☆–☆☆☆
Lucolena, Firenze. www.castello-querceto.it

Winemaker Alessandro François produces a variety of wines, either pure Sangiovese or Sangiovese-dominated blends, as well as "Cignale", a Cabernet with 10% Merlot. The top Chianti Riserva is called "Il Picchio".

La Regola ☆☆–☆☆☆
Riparbella, Pisa. www.laregola.com

Owned by the Nuti family, this twenty-hectare estate produces excellent red wines as Montescudaio DOC. "La Regola" is half Sangiovese, half Cabernet and Merlot, aged in mostly new oak. The second wine "Vallino delle Conche" is almost as good and excellent value.

Riecine ☆☆
Gaiole, Siena

Founded in 1971 by an Englishman, John Dunkley, who died in 1999. Winemaker Sewan O'Callaghan has maintained quality, with very fine Chianti Classico Riserva.

Rocca di Castagnoli ☆☆
Castagnoli, Siena

A seventeen-hectare property rented from the Cacchiano estate by Marco Ricasoli. Chianti Classico, a Bordeaux blend called "Geremia", and a pure Cabernet IGT, "Buriano".

Castello Romitorio ☆☆–☆☆☆
Montalcino, Siena. www.castelloromitorio.it

Fine *rosso* and Brunello from Alessandro Chia's impressive medieval property.

Russo ☆☆
Suvereto, Livorno

A small family estate beginning to produce impressive reds: the Merlot-dominated "Sasso Bucato" and the pure Sangiovese "Barbicone".

Salicuti ☆☆☆–☆☆☆☆☆
Montalcino, Siena

Francesco Leanza's Brunello estate is tiny, but quality is sensational.

Poderi San Luigi ☆☆–☆☆☆
Campo dell'Olmo, Piombino

This is a tiny, four-hectare property, producing a lovely blended wine called "Fidenzio", made from Cabernet Sauvignon and Cabernet Franc.

San Michele ☆☆
San Vincenzo, Piombino

Small Maremma estate with a flourishing focus on Syrah and Viognier.

Sangiusto ☆☆–☆☆☆
Piombino

Pierluigi Bonti is a warm-hearted man, whose personality is reflected in his generous wines. "Sangiusto" is a delicious blend of Sangiovese and Montepulciano, and "Rossi degli Appiani" is a similar blend but more dense and oaky.

Santini ☆☆–☆☆☆
Bolgheri, Livorno

New estate, with impressive first releases in 2000. Enrico Santini makes a delicious, supple red for early drinking ("Poggio al Moro"), and a richer, oakier blend of Cabernet, Merlot, and Syrah called "Monte Pergoli". Arresting quality.

Michele Satta ☆☆–☆☆☆
Castagneto Carducci, Livorno

Unlike more fashionable Maremma producers, Satta remains true to local traditions, making delicious Vermentino and a pure Sangiovese called "Vigna al Cavaliere", as well as a Bordeaux blend called "Pastraia".

Sorbaiano ☆☆
Montecatini, Pisa

The Picciolini family own this remote Motescudaio DOC property. All the wines have good acidity: "Lucestraia", a blend of Chardonnay, Trebbiano, and Vermentino, and the lean Sangiovese IGT "Rosso delle Miniere".

Talenti ☆☆
Montalcino, Siena

Pierluigi Talenti (formerly winemaker at Il Poggione *q.v.*) has aquired his own thirteen-hectare property, which is now run by son Riccardo. He produces attractive Brunello and Rosso di Montalcino.

Terrabianca ☆☆
Radda, Siena. www.terrabianca.com
Roberto Guldener of Switzerland bought this ancient property in 1988. The top Chianti Classico is "Vigna della Croce", and the estate is also known for its "Campaccio" (Sangiovese/Cabernet) and "Cipresso" (pure Sangiovese).

Teruzzi & Puthod – Ponte a Rondolino ☆☆
San Gimignano, Siena
Founded in 1975 by Enrico Teruzzi and Carmen Puthod, this estate was among the first to take Vernaccia di San Gimignano seriously. Eighty-four hectares provide exemplary Vernaccia and also a wood-aged *riserva*, known as "Terra di Tufi".

Tua Rita ☆☆☆
Suvereto, Livorno
The modest Besti family seem astonished by the acclaim their wines routinely receive. But they are excellent grape farmers, nurturing beautiful fruit. "Giusti di Notri" is their Bordeaux blend, "Perlato del Bosco" a pure Sangiovese, and their top wine is the marvellous Merlot "Redigaffi".

Castello di Verrazzano ☆☆
Greve, Firenze. www.verrazzano.com
The vineyards surround the castle where the explorer Giovanni da Verrazzano was born in 1485. Today it is owned by Luigi Cappellini.

Two IGT white wines are produced, from Trebbiano, Chardonnay, and other grapes. The Chianti Classico is sound but not exceptional, but there is an excellent Sangiovese/Cabernet blend called "Bottiglia Particolare".

Vignole ☆☆
Panzano, Firenze
Fine, reasonably priced Chianti Classico.

Vistarenni ☆
Gaiole, Siena
An eighty-hectare estate producing fairly lean Chianti Classico, and "Codirosso", a barrique-aged blend of Sangiovese and Cabernet Sauvignon.

Viticcio ☆☆
Greve, Firenze
Sound Chianti Classico; IGT Sangiovese called "Prunaio"; and impressive, new-oaked Cabernet called "Monile".

Umbria

If Umbria figured on a discerning wine-buyer's shopping list in the past, it was purely for Orvieto, its golden, gently sweet, and occasionally memorable specialty. Then the limelight (such as it was) turned to Rubesco, the noble red of Torgiano near Perugia, one of the best wines and best bargains in Italy.

If Torgiano could make such good wine, so (surely) could other hills in this inland region. Indeed, Sagrantino has recently become a fashionable local variety – and with good reason. It produces rich, full-bodied, and long-lived reds, and the best examples fetch high prices.

DOC & Other Wines

Assisi DOC. Red, white, and *rosato*. Province: Perugia. Communes: parts of Assisi, Perugia, and Spello. Grapes: (white) Trebbiano and Grechetto; (red and *rosato*) Sangiovese and Merlot. A recent DOC, created in 1997, as yet untested.

Colli Altotiberini DOC. Red, white, and *rosato* wine. Province: Perugia. Villages: a wide sweep of country in northern Umbria, including Perugia and eight other communes. Grapes (red and *rosato*) Sangiovese 55–70%, Merlot 10–20%, Trebbiano and Malvasia 10%; (white) Trebbiano Toscano 75–90%, Malvasia up to 10%, others up to 15%.

DOC from the hills of the upper Tiber. Production in the area is increasing. All its wines, including its dry red with Merlot, are intended for drinking young. Limited production.

Colli Amerini DOC. Red, white, *rosato*, and *novello* wine. Province: Terni. Villages: Amelia, Narni, and eleven others along the Tiber and Nera valleys between Orvieto and Terni. Grapes: (red, *rosato*, and *novello*) Sangiovese 65–80%, Montepulciano, Ciliegiolo, Canaiolo, Barbera and/or Merlot 20–35% (but no more than 10% Merlot); (white) Trebbiano Toscano 70–85%, plus Grechetto, Verdello, Garganega and/or Malvasia Toscana 15–30% (but no more than 10% Malvasia); (Malvasia) Malvasia Toscana 85–100%.

Production began only in 1990, and the wines have yet to establish a clear identity.

Colli Martani DOC. Red and white wine. Province: Perugia. Villages: from Bettona as far south as Spoleto; Gualdo Cattaneo, Giano dell'Umbria and parts of twelve other communes. Grapes: (white) Trebbiano min. 85%, Grechetto, or Grechetto di Todi; (red) Sangiovese min. 85%.

This is a fairly recent DOC, and the wines so far are promising. Of the three varietals, Grechetto seems to offer the brightest prospects.

Colli Perugini DOC. Red, white, and *rosato* wine. Provinces: Perugia and Terni. Villages: six communes in Perugia province; San Vananzo in Terni province. Grapes: (red and *rosato*) Sangiovese 65–85%, Montepulciano, Ciliegiolo, Barbera, and/or Merlot 15–35% (but no more than 10% Merlot); (white) Trebbiano Toscano 65–85%, Grechetto, Verdicchio, Garganega and/or Malvasia del Chianti 15–35%

(but no more than 10% Malvasia). DOC wine from the area between Perugia and Todi.

Colli del Trasimeno
DOC. White and red wine. Province: Perugia. Villages: nine communes around Lake Trasimeno. Grapes: (white) Trebbiano Toscano 60–80%, plus Malvasia Bianca, Verdicchio Bianco, Verdello and Grechetto; (red) Sangiovese 60–80%, Gamay, Ciliegiolo, Trebbiano Toscano, Malvasia Bianca.

Average-quality red and white from this zone on the borders of Tuscany. Gamay and Ciliegiolo give spirit to the red, and Grechetto gives the white a slight edge of acidity essential for freshness.

Grechetto or Greco
A "Greek" white grape which plays an increasingly important role here and in DOC Colli Martani farther south. Unblended, its wine, here an IGT, is somewhat more fruity, firm, and interesting than Trebbiano.

Lago di Corbara
DOC. Red wine. Province: Terni. Communes: Baschi and Orvieto. Grapes: Cabernet Sauvignon max. 70%, Merlot, Pinot Nero, or Sangiovese; other varieties max. 30%.

A recent DOC was created in 1998 and is proving popular and successful.

Montefalco Sagrantino and Montefalco Rosso
DOC/DOCG. Red and white wine. Province: Perugia. Villages: the commune of Montefalco and parts of four others. Sagrantino di Montefalco DOCG: Grape: Sagrantino. Montefalco Rosso DOC: Grape: Sangiovese 60–70%, Sagrantino 10–15%, other red grapes max. 30%.

Montefalco Bianco DOC: Grechetto min 50%, Trebbiano Toscano 20–35%, other white grapes max. 15%.

DOC for a small area south of Assisi, where the local Sagrantino grape makes very dark red wine, tasting of blackberries. Quality varies from dry and tannic to rich and opulent. The true specialty is the sweet and strong *passito* version, a notable dessert wine aged for a year. Plain Montefalco red uses Sagrantino as seasoning in a less original but still smooth and agreeable wine. The white is unexceptional.

Orvieto
DOC. White wine. Provinces: Orvieto and Terni. Villages: Orvieto and surrounding area; and eleven communes in Terni. "Classico" is from Orvieto itself. Grapes: Trebbiano Toscano (Procanico) 40–60%, Verdello 15–25%, Grechetto, Drupeggio and other whites 20–30%, Malvasia Toscana up to 20%.

The simple and memorable name that used to mean golden, more or less sweet wine, now suffers from the same identity crisis as many Italian whites. The taste for highly charged, then gently oxidized wines has gone. Modern vinification answers the problem with pale, clean, but almost neutered ones. Traditional Orvieto was laboriously fermented dry, was then re-sweetened with a dried-grape *passito* to be *abboccato*. If you found a good one it was memorably deep and velvety, but probably none too stable – like Frascati, a poor traveller.

Modern Orvieto is nearly all pale, but it should still have a hint of honey to be true to type. Much is dry and frankly dull, but the best producers release wines of freshness and character. In 1997, a new Orvieto Superiore was launched, requiring lower yields and a smaller proportion of Trebbiano. There is also a small production of botrytized Orvieto, this is very often labelled *muffa nobile* (noble rot).

Rosso Orvietano
DOC. Red wine. Province: Terni. Communes: Allerona, Baschi, Fabro, Orvieto, and others. This is a new catch-all DOC for red wine produced around Orvieto.

Torgiano
DOC. Red, white, and *rosato* wine. Province: Perugia. Village: Torgiano. Grapes: (red) Sangiovese 50–70%, Canaiolo 15–30%, Trebbiano Toscano 10%, Ciliegiolo and/or Montepulciano 10%; (white) Trebbiano 50–70%, Grechetto 15–40%, others up to 15%.

Virtually a one-man DOC; local tradition reshaped in modern terms by Dr. Giorgio Lungarotti (*see* Producers). This was Umbria's first DOC, its reputation built on the Lungarotti brands of "Rubesco" and "Torre di Giano".

Bianco di Torgiano and Rosso di Torgiano both have DOC status; the Torgiano Rosso Riserva became DOCG in 1990: the wines almost have the same name, but production rules differ (in the Italian way of creating transparency). For Torgiano Rosso Riserva, grapes are the same as for Rosso di Torgiano, the maximum crop is 65 hl/ha, and the wine must be aged for three years, with an annual production of up to 8,800 cases. There is also a range of varietal Torgiano, from Chardonnay, Pinot Grigio, Riesling, Cabernet Sauvignon, and Pinot Noir.

Leading Umbria Producers

Adanti ☆☆–☆☆☆
Arquata di Bevagna, Perugia. www.cantgineadanti.com
DOC: Montefalco Rosso, Sagrantino. Other: Rosso d'Arquata, Bianco d'Arquata, Rosato d'Arquata, *vin santo*.

This twenty-four-hectare estate is best-known for its Montefalco reds (stunning *passito* wines), but it also produces good Grechetto and IGT Rosso d'Arquata.

Barberani-Vallesanta ☆☆–☆☆☆
Baschi, Terni. www.barberani.it
This is a substantial, fifty-hectare estate, producing a full range of excellent Orvieto wines, including a peaches-and-cream *muffa nobile* called "Calcaia". Bracing, mineral Grechetto IGT; and succulent, if oaky, bottlings of Lago di Corbara.

Luigi Bigi ☆☆
Ponte Giulio di Orvieto, Terni. www.giv.it
Founded in 1881, and now part of the Gruppo Italiano Vini complex. This large company produces fresh, cherry-tinged Sangiovese, but is best-known for its ripe, flowery, single-vineyard Orvieto, "Torricella".

Arnaldo Caprai ☆☆☆–☆☆☆☆
Montefalco, Perugia. www.arnaldocaprai.it
Drawn from ninety hectares, Montefalco DOCs include a consistently fine, dry Sagrantino; even the more basic Rosso di Montefalco is excellent.

The top wine here, priced accordingly, is the plummy, toasty Sagrantino called "25 Anni", which is aged for thirty months in barriques.

Lungarotti ☆☆–☆☆☆

Torgiano, Perugia. www.lungarotti.it

Giorgio Lungarotti was, until his death in 1999, the leading personality in Umbrian wine. The Torgiano DOC, which accounts for about half the production here, is an official recognition of the quality of the wines he made in this village. Today, the estate is run by his daughters, Chiara and Teresa. The property is large, with 250 hectares of vineyards, and so is the production. The range of wines is enormous. The star is always the "Rubesco Riserva Monticchio DOCG", which is aged for years in bottle before release. "Torre di Giano" is the white. Cabernet (in an excellent blend called "San Giorgio") and Chardonnay are reliable and satisfying. "Giubilante" is a recent blend: a crowd-pleasing but delicious merger of Sangiovese, Cabernet Sauvignon, Montepulciano, and other varieties. Quality overall remains high, but perhaps not as stellar as when Giorgio Lungarotti was in his prime. Perhaps too many wines are being produced. The estate includes a popular wine museum and a charming hotel, and another museum devoted to the olive and its oil.

Castello della Sala ☆☆–☆☆☆☆

Sala, Terni

Antinori's Umbrian castle, run independently by Renzo Cottarella, has 140 hectares of vines. The outstanding wines are the floral and sometimes exotic "Cervaro della Sala" (80% Chardonnay, 20% Grechetto) and the superb, botrytized sweet wine, "Muffato della Sala". The estate's basic white wines are, of course, Orvieto, and the reliable and lemony Chardonnay. A cleverly oaked and well-balanced Pinot Nero is also produced here.

Other Umbria Producers

Antonelli Montefalco ☆☆

Perugia. www.antonellisanmarco.it

This long-established estate produces a full range of Montefalco reds, and Grechetto.

La Carraia ☆☆–☆☆☆

Orvieto, Terni

Founded in 1989, this rising star produces both classic honeyed Orvieto, and a fine Bordeaux blend called "Fobiano".

Cantina dei Colli Amerini ☆☆

Ternio Fornule di Amelia, Terni

A good source of red wines: Sangiovese IGT and a complex but inexpensive blend called "Carbio". Plus Chardonnay and Grechetto.

Colpetrone ☆☆–☆☆☆

Gualdo Cattaneo, Perugia. www.saiagricola.it

Owned since 1995 by the insurance company Saiagricola, this forty-hectare estate specializes in Sagrantino and Rosso di Montefalco.

Decugnano dei Barbi ☆☆–☆☆☆

Orvieto, Terni. www.deccugnanodeibarbi.com

A good source for Orvieto and, occasionally, the botrytized version; and renowned for "IL", a Sangiovese/Montepulciano blend, aged in barriques.

Duca della Corgna ☆–☆☆

Città della Pieve, Perugia

A small cooperative producing a typical range of wines, red and white, from the Colli del Trasimeno DOC.

Lamborghini/La Fiorita ☆☆–☆☆☆

Panicale, Perugia

A thirty-two-hectare property, best-known for its complex Sangiovese/Merlot blend called "Campoleone".

Milziade Antano ☆☆–☆☆☆

Bevagna, Perugia

This estate produces outstanding Montefalco reds, especially the Sagrantino *passito*.

La Palazzola ☆☆–☆☆☆

Terni

A small estate producing IGT reds, sparkling wines from Chardonnay and Riesling, and characterful sweet wines.

Palazzone ☆☆–☆☆☆

Orvieto, Terni. www.palazzone.com

Giovanni Dubini acquired this twenty-five-hectare estate in 1969. Good Orvieto, a honeyed, sweet wine from Sauvignon and Grechetto, and a concentrated Cabernet IGT called "Armaleo".

Pieva del Vescovo ☆☆

Corciano, Perugia

Supple red blends from Colli del Trasimeno.

Rocca di Fabri ☆☆–☆☆☆

Montefalco, Perugia. www.roccadifabri.com

A very reliable producer of complex Montefalco reds, with rich damson and liquorice fruit and robust tannins.

Scacciadiavoli ☆☆

Montefalco, Perugia

A venerable twenty-hectare estate that only produces red Montefalco.

Sportoletti ☆☆–☆☆☆

Spello, Perugia. www.sportoletti.com

With advice from Riccardo Cotarella (*see* Falesco, Latium), this estate produces interesting IGT wines: a good Grechetto and "Villa Fidelia", a Bordeaux blend aged in new oak.

Vaglie ☆☆

Baschi, Terni

Produces good Orvieto, but now better-known for its sensibly priced IGT reds: "Momenti" (Sangiovese/Merlot) and "Masseo" (Sangiovese/Cabernet).

Cantina Cooperativa Vitivinicola ☆–☆☆

Orvieto, Terni. www.cardeto.com

The best wines from the largest producer of Orvieto Classico (around four million bottles) are bottled under the "Cardeto" label. Red wine production is growing.

The Marches

The central slice of the Adriatic coast, from the latitude of Florence to that of Orvieto, is probably even better-known for its dry white Verdicchio than for the beaches and fishing boats that give the wine such a perfect context. The historic cities of Urbino in the north, and Ascoli Piceno in the south of the region, draw a proportion of its visitors inland, but the eastern flanks of the Apennines hardly rival the cultural crowd-pulling quality of Tuscany.

So the red wines of the Marches, potentially (sometimes actually) of good Chianti quality, are less well-known than they should be. The Montepulciano grape gives them a quality missing in most of those in Romagna to the north.

DOC & Other Wines

Bianchello del Metauro DOC. White wine. Province: Pesaro-Urbino. Villages: Eighteen communes in the valley of the River Metauro. Grapes: Biancame (Bianchello) 95%, Malvasia 5%.

A pleasant, sharp, plain white from the north of the region, for drinking young with fish.

Colli Maceratesi DOC. White wine. Provinces: Macerata and Ancona. Villages: Loreto and all of Macerata. Grapes: Maceratino min. 80%, plus Trebbiano, Malvasia Toscana, Verdicchio, and/or Chardonnay.

A minor DOC for another local dry seafood wine. Macerata is halfway from Ancona south to Ascoli Piceno.

Colli Pesaresi DOC. Red and white wine. Province: Pesaro-Urbino. Villages: thirty communes and part of six others in and around Pesaro. Grapes: (red) Sangiovese min. 85%; (white) Trebbiano min. 85%.

A little-used DOC for a red of limited character. Sangiovese is frequently used for non-DOC reds.

Esino DOC. White, red, and *rosato*. Province: Macerata. Villages: seven communes. Grapes: (white) Verdicchio min. 50%; (red) Sangiovese and/or Montepulciano min. 60%. A recent DOC from 1995. The white can be dry or *frizzante*; the red can also be made in a *novella* style.

Falerio dei Colli Ascolani DOC. White wine. Provinces: Ascoli and Piceno. Villages: entire provinces. Grapes: Trebbiano Toscano 20–50%, Passerina 10–30%, Verdicchio, Pinot Bianco, and/or Pecorino 10–30%, Malvasia Toscana up to 7%. Another of the local dry whites associated with restaurants on the beach.

Lacrima di Morro d'Alba DOC. Red wine. Province: Ancona. Villages: six south of Senigallia. Grapes: Lacrima min. 85%, Montepulciano/Verdicchio max. 15%. A DOC from around the ancient town of Morro d'Alba. Very small production.

Montepulciano Important in the Marches as a constituent grape of the best red wines, also sometimes sold unblended.

Rosso Cònero DOC. Red wine. Province: Ancona. Villages: five communes in Ancona and part of two others. Grapes: Montepulciano min. 85%, Sangiovese max. 15%.

A full-strength, full-flavoured red from Monte Cònero, near the Adriatic just south of Ancona. This is one of the most flourishing DOCs of central and eastern Italy. Good Rosso Cònero has fruit to mellow and tannin to sustain it.

Rosso Piceno DOC. Red wine. Provinces: Ancona, Ascoli Piceno, Macerata. Villages: a large number in the above provinces. Grapes: Sangiovese min. 60%, Montepulciano max. 40%, Passerina/Trebbiano max. 15%.

The standard red of the southern half of the Marches, varying widely in quality from unremarkable to hand-made and worth ageing, both in barrel and bottle. At its best it has Chianti-like weight and balance.

Verdicchio dei Castelli di Jesi DOC. White wine. Provinces: Ancona and Macerata. Villages: Twenty-six around the town of Jesi. Grapes: Verdicchio min. 85%.

This is the great commercial success of the Marches. Straightforward, dry, well-balanced, and clean; one of the earliest Italian whites to taste both modern and international, thanks to the skill of its promoters, initially the firm of Fazi-Battaglia (*q.v.*).

Their marketing flair produced the distinctive, amphora-shaped bottle seen among the fishnets in practically every Italian restaurant abroad – although better-quality wines are sold in normal Bordeaux-style bottles. The Verdicchio is a tricky grape to grow but clearly has quality. The wine is short-lived, however, and bottles held too long in stock are often undrinkable.

A current trend to leave some residual sugar in the wine is not to be encouraged. There is also a *tradizionale* sparkling version.

Verdicchio di Matelica DOC. White wine. Provinces: Macerata and Ancona. Villages: Matelica and seven others. Grapes: Verdicchio min. 85%.

Verdicchio from higher ground farther inland, it is widely said to be superior, but is hardly ever seen abroad. Another (non-DOC) with a similar reputation is Verdicchio di Montanello.

Vernaccia di Serrapetrona DOC. Red wine. Province: Macerata. Villages: Serrapetrona and part of Belforte del Chienti and San Severino Marche. Grapes: Vernaccia min. 85% Nera; plus Sangiovese, Montelpulciano, and/or Ciliegiolo. A locally popular, sweet, sparkling red, which has been made since the fifteenth century.

Leading Marches Producers

Brunori ☆☆–☆☆☆
Jesi, Ancona
Giorgio Brunori cultivates just six hectares, producing an unusually floral and elegant Verdicchio dei Castelli di Jesi, and the rare Lacrima di Morro d'Alba.

Fratelli Bucci ☆☆–☆☆☆
Ostra Vetere, Ancona. www.villabucci.com
Concentrated, peachy Verdicchio dei Castelli di Jesi from a twenty-six-hectare estate. And a good Rosso Piceno called "Tenuta Pongelli".

Cocci Grifoni ☆☆–☆☆☆
San Savino di Ripatransone, Ascoli Piceno
Guido Cocci Grifoni is an admirable producer, whose Rosso Piceno is one of the best, and whose Falerio has few rivals.

Colonnara ☆☆–☆☆☆
Cupramontana, Ancona. www.colonnara.it
The Cupramontana cooperative now goes under the name Colonnara, and is making some excellent, fragrant Verdicchio, still and sparkling.

Fazi-Battaglia ☆☆☆
Castelplanio, Ancona. www.fazibattaglia.it
Founded in 1949, this company was the first to win international recognition for Verdicchio dei Castelli di Jesi. Despite a total production of over three million bottles, standards remain very high, not just for dry Verdicchio, but also for a ripe, tobacco-scented Rosso Cònero and a botrytized Verdicchio called "Arkezia".

Garofoli ☆☆–☆☆☆
Loreto, Ancona
Still in family hands after a century of production, Garofoli produces delightful, refreshing Verdicchio dei Castelli di Jesi to consistently high standards. The oak-aged "Serra Fioresa" is perhaps an acquired taste, but the "Podium" bottling is impeccable. Garofoli was also a pioneer of vintage-dated sparkling Verdicchio.

Enzo Mecella ☆☆–☆☆☆
Fabriano, Ancona
Mecella is one of the region's most skilled and inspired winemakers, using purchased fruit to make a wide range of appellations, and an unusual IGT from Ciliegiolo called "Braccano".

Monte Schiavo ☆☆
Maiolati Spontini, Ancona. www.monteschiavo.com
A cooperative backed by farm-machinery manufacturer, Pieralisi, which competes in quality with top private wineries. From growers with 105 hectares come good Verdicchio Classico, *spumante*, and *passito*, as well as Rosso Cònero.

Sartarelli ☆☆☆–☆☆☆☆
Poggio San Marcello, Ancona. www.sartarelli.it
Small family estate that makes nothing other than highly concentrated, minerally Verdicchios, including a botrytized Verdicchio called "Contrada Balciana". Alberto Mazzoni is the winemaker.

Umani Ronchi ☆☆☆
Osimo, Ancona. www.umanironchi.it
Founded in 1960 by Gino Ronchi and now owned by the Bernetti family. One of the best-distributed brands of the Marches, producing over 300,000 cases of good-quality estate-bottled Verdicchio and Rosso Cònero.

Other wines are made from grapes that are bought in. The winery also offers some convincing red IGTs – "Cùmaro" (Montepulciano) and "Pelago" (Cabernet Sauvignon/Montepulciano) – and a rare sweet Sauvignon called "Maximo". Even the simpler wines, such as Rosso Cònero "San Lorenzo", are very well-made.

Vallerosa Bonci ☆☆–☆☆☆
Cupramontana, Ancona
A full-bodied, almondy Verdicchio dei Castelli di Jesi. The wine is made in all possible styles: dry, *passito*, and sparkling.

Villa Pigna ☆☆–☆☆☆
Offida, Ascoli Piceno. www.villapigna.com
With 120,000 cases from some 170 hectares of vines, the Rozzi family's Villa Pigna quickly emerged as a model large-scale estate. The Rosso Piceno Superiore closely resembles a claret. The IGT wines are also equally good: "Rozzano" from Montepulciano, and "Cabernasco" from Cabernet.

Other Marches Producers

Belisario ☆☆
Matelica, Macerata
The label used by a good cooperative specializing in Verdicchio di Matelica.

Boccadigabbia ☆☆–☆☆☆
Civitanova Marche, Macerata. www.boccadigabbia.com
A small, quality-focused estate specializing in expensive red IGTs from Cabernet ("Akronte"), Merlot, Sangiovese, and Pinot Nero.

Le Caniette ☆☆–☆☆☆
Ripatransone, Ascoli Piceno. www.lecaniette.it
Rich, chocolatey Rosso Piceno and unusual *vin santo* from Passerina.

Casalfarneto ☆☆
Serra de' Conti, Ancona. www.casalfarneto.it
Verdicchio only at this small estate founded in 1995.

Coroncino ☆☆☆
Staffolo, Ancona
Minute production of outstanding and complex Verdicchio dei Castelli di Jesi.

De Angelis ☆☆–☆☆☆
Castel di Lama, Ascoli Piceno. www.tenutadeangelis.it
A cherry-scented Rosso Piceno, but the estate is best-known for its intensely fruity Montepulciano/Cabernet IGT blend "Anghelos".

Lanari ☆☆–☆☆☆
Varano, Ancona
A small property producing nothing but Rosso Cònero of exceptional quality.

Mancini ☆☆
Pesaro
An atypical property, focusing on Pinot Nero.

Marchetti ☆–☆☆
Ancona. www.marchettiwines.it
Sound Rosso Cònero and Verdicchio, but quantities are very small.

La Monacesca ☆☆–☆☆☆
Matelica, Macerata

Industrialist Casimiro Cifola revived this estate in the late 1960s, and produced delectable Verdicchio di Matelica from old vines.

Moncaro/Terre Cortesi ☆☆–☆☆☆
Montecarotto, Ancona. www.moncaro.com

Very good cooperative producing four million bottles from 1,700 hectares. Impressive Verdicchio dei Castelli di Jesi, dry and *passito*, and structured Rosso Cònero Riserva. Also produces varietal IGTs.

Moroder ☆☆–☆☆☆
Montacuto, Ancona

Alessandro Moroder produces rich Rosso Cònero "Dorico" and (sometimes) a sweet Moscato/Trebbiano IGT from his small estate.

Oasi degli Angeli ☆☆–☆☆☆
Cupora Marittima, Ascoli Piceno

Tiny estate, just one wine: a new-oaked Montepulciano IGT called "Kurni", steeped in coffee and plums.

Saladini Pilastri ☆☆
Spinetoli, Ascoli Piceno

A large organic estate with supple, plummy Rosso Piceno.

Santa Barbara ☆☆
Barbara, Ancona. www.vinisantabarbara.it

Unusually powerful Verdicchio and a sound Cabernet/Merlot blend called "Rosso delle Marche".

Le Terrazze ☆☆–☆☆☆
Numana, Ancona

Antonio Terni makes good Rosso Cònero, a striking pink *tradizionale* "Donna Giulia" from Montepulciano grapes, and a pricey, but acclaimed red blend, intriguingly named "Chaos".

Velenosi ☆☆–☆☆☆
Ascoli Piceno. www.velenosivini.com

A diverse range of wines from a very modern winery: powerful Rosso Piceno, intense Chardonnay, and a classic-method sparkling wine.

Fratelli Zaccagnini ☆☆–☆☆☆
Staffolo, Ancona

From a range of Verdicchio dei Castelli di Jesi, the finest is the peachy, single-vineyard "Salmagina".

Latium

Rome can be compared with Vienna, as a capital city with wine so much in its veins that such artificial obstructions as bottles and corks have traditionally been foreign to it. The winemakers' taverns of Rome are slightly farther out of town than the *Heurigen* of Vienna, but are even more tempting as a summer outing, maybe to the cool of the wooded Alban Hills, or perhaps to the Castelli Romani south of Rome.

Frascati, the hub of the hills and their wine, has the air of a holiday resort. The spectacular Villa Aldobrandini and its beautiful gardens in the heart of Frascati show that the taste is both patrician as well as popular.

Latium, both north and south of Rome, is pock-marked with volcanic craters which are now placid lakes. The rich, volcanic soil of the region is highly suited to the cultivation of vines.

The choice of grape varieties, which is presumably based on the Roman taste for soft, young wines, has determined that they should remain local. The low acidity of the Malvasia, the grape that gives character to Frascati, makes it prone to disastrous oxidation once removed from storage in its cold, damp cellar, necessitating the introduction of such processes as pasteurization and, more recently, cold treatments, which have restored the balance of modern wines.

DOC & Other Wines

Aleatico di Gradoli DOC. Red wine. Province: Viterbo. Villages: Gradoli, Grotte di Castro, San Lorenzo Nuovo, Latera (in the hills above Lake Bolsena). Grapes: Aleatico.

Very limited production of a local specialty: sweet red wine with a faintly Muscat aroma made at both normal strength and *liquoroso* (fortified to 17.5 degrees of alcohol).

Aprilia DOC. Red, white and *rosato* wine. Provinces: Latina and Roma. Villages: Aprilia, Cisterna, and Nettuno. Grapes: (red and *rosato*) Merlot or Sangiovese; (white) Trebbiano. A vineyard area established by refugees from Tunisia after World War II. Merlot is reckoned its best product at two or three years of age. Although one of the first DOCs, the wines scarcely merit the dignity; however, recent experiments in vineyards and cellars are aimed at notable improvements.

Atina DOC. Province: Frosinone. Villages: Atina and twelve others. Recent DOC for red wines, notably Cabernet.

Bianco Capena DOC. White wine. Province: Roma. Villages: Capena, Fiano Romano, Morlupo, Castelnuovo di Porto. Grapes: 70–90% Malvasia di Candia, del Lazio and Toscana, and Trebbiano Toscano, Romagnolo and Giallo, Bellone and Bombino max. 20%.

Similar white wine to that of the Castelli Romani (*e.g.* Frascati) but from just north of Rome instead of south.

Castelli Romani DOC. Provinces: Roma and Latina. Name for the verdant region, otherwise known as the Colli Albani, where Frascati and its peers are grown. Whites from Malvasia and Trebbiano; red and *rosato* from a wide range of varietals.

Cerveteri DOC. Red and white wine. Provinces: Roma and Viterbo. Villages: eight northwest of Rome. Grapes: (red) Sangiovese and Montepulciano min. 60%, Cesanese Comune 25%, others up to 30%; (white) Trebbiano (Toscano, Romagnolo and Giallo) min. 50%, Malvasia max. 35%, others up to 15%. Standard dry wines from the country near the coast northwest of Rome.

Cesanese del Piglio DOC. Red wine. Province: Frosinone and Piglio. Villages: Piglio and Serrone, Acuto, Anagni and Paliano. Grapes: Cesanese min. 90%; plus Sangiovese, Montepulciano, Barbera, Trebbiano Toscano or Bombino Bianco. Dry or sweet, still or sparkling red from a zone just to the left of the Autostrada del Sole, heading southeast 65 kilometres (40 miles) out of Rome, where Anagni sits on its hilltop.

Another two Cesanese DOCs exist, Cesanese di Olevano (very scarce) and Cesanese di Affile (in practice defunct, since none is made!). All three were made DOCs in an excess of bureaucratic enthusiasm in 1973.

Circeo DOC. White, red, and *rosato* wine. Province: Latina. Villages: Latina, Sabaudia, San Felice, Circeo, and Terracina. Grapes: (white) Malvasia Bianca, Trebbiano, and others; (red and *rosato*) Merlot min. 85%. There is also provision for DOC wines from predominantly Trebbiano or Sangiovese.

Created in 1996, this is an all-purpose DOC for wines in all conceivable styles.

Colle Picchioni Surprisingly good, dry red of blended Merlot, Cesanese, Sangiovese, and Montepulciano grapes, made in the traditionally white (*i.e.* Marino) country of the Castelli Romani.

The superior "Vigna del Vassallo" is a Cabernet/Merlot blend.

Colli Albani DOC. White wine. Province: Roma. Villages: Ariccia and Albano, and parts of four others. Grapes: Malvasia Bianca di Candia max. 60%; Trebbiano Toscano, Romagnolo di Soave, and Giallo 25–50%; Malvasia del Lazio 5–45%; others up to 10%.

The local white of the Pope's summer villa at Castelgandolfo (and that of the Emperor Domitian, too, on the same superb site, with views west to the sea and east down to Lake Albano). Dry or sweet, still or fizzy.

Colli Etruschi Viterbesi DOC. White and red wines. Province: Viterbo. Villages: thirty-eight. Grapes: (white) Malvasia, Trebbiano, and others; (red) Sangiovese, Montepulciano, and others.

There is also provision for Moscatello (min. 85% Moscato Bianco) and wines from predominantly Grechetto, Merlot, or Montepulciano. Large new zone, established in 1996. Likely to be diffuse in character.

Colli Lanuvini DOC. White wine. Province: Roma. Villages: Genzano and part of Lanuvio. Grapes: Malvasia Bianca di Candia and Puntinata max. 70%; Trebbiano Toscano, Verde, and Giallo min. 30%; others max. 10%.

A lesser-known but recommended dry or lightly sweet white of the Castelli Romani. Genzano is on Lake Nemi, to the south of Lake Albano.

Colli della Sabina DOC. White, red, and *rosato* wine. Provinces: Rieti and Rome. Villages: twenty-five. Grapes: (white) Trebbiano min. 40%; Malvasia min. 40% di Candia or del Lazio; others max. 20%; (red and *rosato*) Sangiovese 40–70%, Montepulciano 15–40%, others max. 30%.

Large inland DOC created in 1996. Wines can be dry, sweet, sparkling, or *novella*.

Cori DOC. White and red wine. Province: Latina. Villages: Cisterna and Cori. Grapes: (white) Malvasia di Candia max. 70%, Trebbiano Toscano max. 40%, Trebbiano Giallo, Bellone max. 30%; (red) Montepulciano 40–60%, Nero Buono di Cori 20–40%, Cesanese 10–30%.

Cori is south of the Castelli Romani, where the country flattens towards the Pontine marshes. The red is soft and pleasant, but unfortunately, along with the white, it is rarely seen.

Est! Est!! Est!!! di Montefiascone DOC. White wine. Province: Viterbo. Villages: Montefiascone, Bolsena, San Lorenzo Nuovo, Grotte di Castro, Gradoli, Capodimonte, and Marta. Grapes: Trebbiano Toscano 65%, Malvasia Bianca 20%, Trebbiano Giallo 15%.

Very large quantities of unpredictable wine take advantage of this the earliest example of what is now called a fantasy name. The emphatic "It is" was the first three-star rating in history, antedating the well-known Michelin guide by some 800 years. More recent inspectors have had less luck, but now modernization of techniques and taste is producing an acceptable, usually dry, white.

Falerno or **Falernum** The most famous wine of ancient Rome, from the borders of Latium and Campania to the south. Then sweet and concentrated, now a good, strong red of Aglianico and Barbera, and a pleasant, low-acid white. The red has a DOC in Campania.

Fiorano The best of Rome's own wines, from one producer, Prince Boncompagni Ludovisi, on the ancient Appian Way south of the city. The red is a blend of Cabernet and Merlot like Bordeaux, the whites Malvasia di Candia and Semillon. The wines are aged in wood and set a standard far above the local DOCs.

Frascati DOC. White wine. Province: Roma. Villages: Frascati, Montecompatri, Monteporzio Catone, Colonna, and Grottaferrata. Grapes: Malvasia Bianca di Candia and/or Trebbiano Toscano min. 70%; Malvasia del Lazio and Greco max. 30%.

In legend, and occasionally in fact, the most memorable Italian white wine, though possibly the one that originated the notion of wines that "do not travel", even the 30 kilometres (18 miles) to Rome. Malvasia on volcanic soil gives a splendid sensation of whole-grape ripeness, a golden glow to the wine, encouraged by fermenting it like red on its skins. The dry variety should be soft but highly charged with flavour, faintly nutty, and even faintly salty. Sweeter (*amabile*) and sweeter still (*cannellino*) versions can be honeyed, too, but I would not count on it.

These are tasting notes made in a cool, damp, Frascati cellar. Notes on the bottled wine vary from neutral and sterile with no character to flat and oxidized, (occasionally) an approximation to the real thing. The best way to learn the difference between old-style and new-style Italian whites is to go to a restaurant in Frascati and order a bottle of a good brand, and also a jug of the house wine. Sadly, the luscious qualities of the latter are the ones that do not travel.

The best producers, however, do manage a very satisfactory compromise. Roman restaurants appear totally cynical about the whole affair.

Genazzano DOC. Red and white wine. Provinces: Rome and Frosinone. Communes: Genzano, Olevano Romano, San Vito Romano, Cave, Paliano. Grapes: (white) Malvasia Bianca di Candia 50–70%, Bellone and Bombino 10–30%; others max. 40%; (red) Sangiovese 70–90%, Cesanese 10–30%.

This is an obscure DOC, established in 1992, that permits high yields.

Marino DOC. White wine. Province: Roma. Villages: Marino and part of Rome and Castelgandolfo. Grapes: Malvasia Bianca di Candia max. 60%, Trebbiano 25–55%. Malvasia del Lazio 5–45%, others max. 10%.

First cousin to Frascati. Many Romans who dine out at Marino prefer to drink it fresh and unbottled.

Merlot di Aprilia *See* Aprilia.

Montecompatri-Colonna DOC. White wine. Province: Roma. Villages: Colonna, part of Montecompatri, Zagarolo and Rocca Priora. Grapes: Malvasia max. 70%, Trebbiano min. 30%, Bellone and Bonvino max. 10%. Another alternative to Frascati in the Castelli Romani.

Sangiovese di Aprilia
A strong, dry *rosato*. *See* Aprilia.

Tarquinia DOC. White, red, and *rosato* wines. Provinces: Rome and Viterbo. Communes: fifteen in Rome, fifteen in Viterbo. Grapes: (white) Trebbiano min. 50%, Malvasia max. 35%, others max. 30%; (red) min. 60% Sangiovese and Montepulciano (with at least 25% of each), max. 25% Cesanese, others max. 30%. A large zone, established in 1996, but permitting high yields.

Torre Ercolana
The highly recherché specialty of one producer (*see* Cantina Colacicchi, next column) at Anagni.

A red of Cesanese with Cabernet and Merlot, powerful in personality and maturing to outstanding quality.

Trebbiano di Aprilia
Rather strong, dull wine, *see* Aprilia.

Velletri DOC. White and red wine. Provinces: Latina and Roma. Villages: Velletri, Lariano, and part of Cisterna di Latina. Grapes: (white) Malvasia max. 70%, Trebbiano min. 30%, Bellone and Bonvino max. 10%; (red) Sangiovese 30–45%, Montepulciano 30–40%, Cesanese min. 15%, Bombino Nero, Merlot, and Ciliegiolo max. 10%.

South of the Frascati zone of the Castelli Romani, Velletri has a DOC for both its pleasant white and its mild red.

Vignanello DOC. White and red wine. Province: Viterbo. Communes: seven. Grapes: (white) Trebbiano 60–70%, Malvasia 20–40%; (red) Sangiovese 40–60%, Ciliegiolo 40–50%. Also a Greco di Vignanello from minimum 85% Greco.

Typical whites of the region, but the red is unusual in containing a high proportion of Ciliegiolo.

Zagarolo DOC. White wine. Province: Roma. Villages: Zagarolo, Gallicano. Grapes: Malvasia and Trebbiano 70–90%, Bellone and Bonvino max. 10%.

The smallest, indeed tiny, DOC of the Frascati group, with similar white wine.

Leading Latium Producers

Castel de Paolis ☆☆–☆☆☆
Grottaferra, Rome. www.casteldepaolis.it
This small property was created in 1993, and Franco Bernabei, its consultant winemaker, has brought its Frascati up to the highest standards (and prices). The floral "Vigna Adriana" contains a proportion of Viognier. The Syrah/Merlot IGT called "Quattro Mori" is one of Latium's finest barrique-aged reds.

Colli di Catone ☆☆
Monteporzio Catone, Rome
Antonio Pulcini makes good Frascati Superiore under the "Colli di Catone", "Villa Catone", and "Villa Porzina" labels. His two special versions of Frascati are both made from pure Malvasia; one, the single-vineyard "Colle Gaio", is made only in good years from low-yielding vines.

Cantina Colacicchi ☆☆–☆☆☆
Anagni, Frosinone
A family winery, made famous by the late Luigi Colacicchi. Best-known for "Torre Ercolana", the splendid but very rare red of Cabernet, Merlot, and Cesanese: intense, long-lived, and long on the palate. Only about 700 cases are made.

Falesco ☆☆☆
Montefiascone, Viterbo
The personal property of renowned oenologist Riccardo Cotarella, producing good Est! Est!! Est!!! (including a late-harvest version), as well as new-oaked red IGTs from Merlot and Cabernet Sauvignon. The "Montiano" Merlot is remarkably complex, with undertones of cassis and cinnamon.

Fontana Candida ☆☆–☆☆☆
Monteporzio Catone, Rome. www.giv.it
Part of the Gruppa Italiano Vini complex, owning extensive vineyards, cellars and bottling plants in the Frascati zone. The production of more than 600,000 cases includes a choice parcel of "Vigneto Santa Teresa", one of the best of all Frascatis.

Paola di Mauro (Colle Picchioni) ☆☆–☆☆☆
Marino, Rome. www.dimauro-sanpietrino.com
This small estate is run by Paulo di Mauro and son Armando, with advice from Riccardo Cotarella. From ten hectares they produce a remarkable traditional Marino and one of Rome's rare fine reds: a Bordeaux blend called "Vigna del Vassallo".

Sergio Mottura ☆☆–☆☆☆
Civitella d'Agliano, Viterbo. www.motturasergio.it
In northern Latium, Mottura produces IGT Grechetto in contrasting styles: oaked and unoaked. The oaked version is called "Latour", which seems presumptuous, but is a simple thank-you to Louis Latour of Beaune who provides the barrels. When vintage conditions permit, which is not every year, Mottura also makes a fine botrytis wine called "Muffo".

Villa Simone ☆☆–☆☆☆

Monteporzio Catone, Rome. www.pieroconstantini.it

Piero Constantini selects from twenty-four hectares of vines to make an impressive, full-scale Frascati Superiore, including the single-vineyard "Vigneto Filonardi" and the rare "Cannellino".

Conte Zandotti ☆☆

Rome. www.cantinecontezandotti.it

Acquired by the family in 1734, this twenty-five-hectare estate is now run by Enrico Massimo Zandotti. The cellars are carved into the vaults of an ancient Roman water cistern beneath the San Paolo villa. As well as a superb, dry Frascati Superiore, there is a Malvasia IGT tasting of tropical fruit.

Other Latium Producers

Casale del Giglio ☆☆–☆☆☆

Le Ferriere, Latina

A large property focused on IGTs from Syrah, Cabernet Sauvignon, and Chardonnay, all aged in barriques.

Cantina Cerveteri ☆–☆☆

Cerveteri, Roma

This cooperative, with 1,500 hectares, is a major producer of white and red Cerveteri.

Cantina Sociale Cesanese del Piglio ☆

Piglio, Frosinone

Sound Cesanese del Piglio DOC.

Gotto d'Oro ☆–☆☆

Frattocchie di Marino, Rome

This is the label of the Marino cooperative, whose members have 1,550 hectares of vines. As well as Frascati, it produces lightly effervescent red Castelli Romani.

Massimi Berucci ☆

Piglio, Frosinone. www.vignetimassimiberucci.it

This producer is a good source for the rare red Cesanese di Piglio DOC.

Italo Mazziotti ☆☆

Bolsena, Viterbo. www.mazziottiwines.com

This is an old family winery best-known for Est! Est!! Est!!! di Montefiascone, and a supple red IGT blend called "Volgente".

L'Olivella ☆☆

Frascati, Rome. www.racemo.it

Although located in Frascati, this twelve-hectare estate is better-known for its red wines, such as "Racemo" IGT from Sangiovese and Cesanese, and a unique blend of Shiraz and Cesanese.

Principe Pallavicini ☆–☆☆

Colonna, Roma

A noble estate that has been in family hands since 1670. It produces a good Frascati Superiore from some seventy hectares.

Palombo ☆☆–☆☆☆

Atina, Frosinone

A family estate specializing in Atina DOC, and a full-bodied Sauvignon Blanc called "Somiglio".

Cantina Sant' Andrea ☆☆

Borgo Vodice, Latina

An organic estate specializing both in Circeo DOC and in fine sweet Moscato.

Trappolini ☆☆

Castiglione in Teverina, Viterbo

A twenty-hectare family estate producing Est! Est!! Est!!! and, more interestingly, a sweet, rose-scented red Aleatico called "Idea".

Abruzzi

The Apennines rise to their climax in the 2,700-metre (9,000-foot) Gran Sasso d'Italia, which towers over L'Aquila ("The Eagle"), the capital of the Abruzzi.

The mountains only subside close to the sea, where Pescara is the principal town. Although it is close in proximity to Rome, the Abruzzi is a rather backward region with very simple ideas about wine, but their attachment to the red Montepulciano as chief grape is an extremely strong one.

Here, and in the even more rural Molise to the south, this grape makes a wine of vigour and style, if not exactly refinement. Whites at present are not remarkable, but only because the Trebbiano is the standard grape.

DOC & Other Wines

Cerasuolo *see* Montepulciano d'Abruzzo.

Controguerra DOC. Red, white, and *rosato* wines. Province: Teramo. Villages: Controguerra and four others. Grapes: (red): Montepulciano min. 60%, Merlot and/or Cabernet min. 15%, others max. 25%; (white) Trebbiano min. 80%, Passerina min. 15%, others max. 25%.

A DOC established in 1996, also permitting a range of varietal wines, plus red and white *passito* wines.

Montepulciano d'Abruzzo DOC. Red and *rosato* wine. Provinces: Chieti, Aquilia, Pescara, Teramo. Villages: many communes in the four provinces. Grapes: Montepulciano min. 85% . The production zone for this excellent red stretches along most of the coastal foothills and back into the mountains along the valley of the River Pescara, but the most complex Montepulciano comes from the Teramo Hills in the north. Standards in this large area vary widely, but Montepulciano at its best is as satisfying, if not as subtle, as any Italian red: full of colour, life, and warmth. Cerasuolo is the name for its DOC *rosato* – a pretty wine with plenty of flavour.

A recently introduced DOC sub-zone, "Montepulciano d'Abruzzo Colline Teramane", embraces the hills in the very north of Abruzzi, and produces wines from vines harvested at slightly lower yields.

Trebbiano d'Abruzzo DOC. White wine. Province: throughout the Abruzzi region. Villages: suitable vineyards (not exceeding 500–600 metres/1,625–1,950 feet) in the whole region. Grapes: min. 85% Trebbiano d'Abruzzo, and or Trebbiano Toscano; others max. 15%. A standard, mild, dry white, except in the case of Valentini (*q.v.*).

Leading Abruzzi Producers

Marramiero ☆☆–☆☆☆
Rosciano, Pescara. www.marramiero.it
Although only established in 1994, this estate has risen swiftly into the top ranks with barrique-aged Montepulciano "Inferi", good Trebbiano, and an IGT from Chardonnay aged in new oak.

Masciarelli ☆☆☆
San Martino sulla Marrucina, Chieti. www.masciarelli.it
The Masciarellis produce fine Montepulciano, especially the full-throttled "Villa Gemma", and a golden Trebbiano called "Marina Cvetic". Expensive.

Cantina Tollo ☆☆
Tollo, Chieti. www.cantinatollo.it
This large cooperative, producing one million cases each year, offers outstanding value for its Montepulciano and Trebbiano d'Abruzzo.

Valentini ☆☆☆
Loreto Aprutino, Pescara
Valentini makes artisan wine of the highest order, including a singular aged Trebbiano and a sumptuous Montepulciano. It is, however, expensive.

Ciccio Zaccagnani ☆☆–☆☆☆
Bolognano, Pescara. www.cantinazaccagnani.it
An increasingly admired estate acclaimed for fine Montepulciano "Castello di Salle". The range has expanded to include Chardonnay, Riesling, Cabernet Franc, and other wines.

Other Abruzzi Producers

Bosco Nocciano ☆☆
Pesaro. www.nestorebosco.com
Renowned for Montepulciano and a delicate IGT blend of Cabernet and Montepulciano called "Linfa".

Cataldi Madonna ☆☆–☆☆☆
Ofena, L'Aquila
Burly, full-bodied Montepulciano, both red and *rosato*.

Barone Cornacchia ☆–☆☆
Torano Nuovo, Teramo
Sound Montepulciano and Trebbiano d'Abruzzo, and a Controguerra DOC Cabernet Sauvignon.

Faraone ☆☆
Giulianuova, Teramo

A small but ambitious property, producing good Montepulciano and Trebbiano, and a Moscatello with flavours of dried apricot.

Fiarnese Vini ☆☆
Ortona
Successful new company marketing very sound Montepulciano d'Abruzzo from a splendid restoration of the battlements of Ortona.

Filomusi Guelfi ☆☆
Tocca da Causaria, Pescara
A small estate, only founded in 1982, with Montepulciano of power and grace.

Dino Illuminati ☆☆–☆☆☆
Controguerra, Teramo. www.illuminativini.it
A large but highly regarded estate, producing both Montepulciano and Trebbiano d'Abruzzo, and white wine, dry and sweet, under the Controguerra DOC.

Elio Monti ☆☆
Controguerra, Teramo.
Elio took over from his father Antonio in 1990. Good Montepulciano, likely to improve further now that ubiquitous consultant Riccardo Cotarella has been hired.

Camillo Montori ☆☆
Controguerra, Teramo
Good Montepulciano and Trebbiano d'Abruzzo, and lively Controguerra wines, red and white.

Nicodemi ☆☆
Notaresco, Teramo
Concentrated and fine Montepulciano, with flavours of plum, tobacco, and Indian spices.

Orlandi Contucci ☆☆–☆☆☆
Roseto degli Abruzzi, Teramo. www.orlandicontucci.com
Although this property makes good, supple Montepulciano, there is an atypical emphasis on varietal wines from Chardonnay, Sauvignon, and Cabernet Sauvignon. Donato Lanati is the consultant here.

Pasetti ☆☆–☆☆☆
Francavilla al Mare, Chieti
Rich Montepulciano, both red and *rosato*, and a plump, oaky Chardonnay/Trebbiano blend called "Testarossa".

Campania

The region of Naples and the Sorrento Peninsula may have been cynical about tourists' tastes in the past, and left some of its visitors with a nasty taste in their mouths, but in many ways it is superbly adapted for wine-growing. Volcanic soils, the temperate influence of the sea, and the height of its mountains give a range of excellent sites.

Its own grapes have character and perform well. The red Aglianico (the name comes from "*Hellenico*") and white Greco both refer in their names to the Greeks who presumably imported or at least adopted them in pre-Roman times. Fiano and Falanghina are other high-quality white grapes specific to Campania. Quality wines are made at Ravello on the Sorrento peninsula, on the island of Ischia, and above all in the Irpinian Hills north of Avellino, east of Naples, where the Mastroberardino winery has done more than anyone for the reputation of the region.

The last decade has seen a number of wineries making the most of the superb grape varieties and the remarkable volcanic soils of Campania.

DOC & Other Wines

Aglianico del Taburno DOC. Red and *rosato*. Province: Benevento. Villages: Monte Taburno, Torrecuso, and twelve other communes. Grapes: Aglianico min. 85%.

Recent DOC in an area where conditions are particularly suited to Aglianico. The wines are still rarely seen. There is also a Taburno DOC for a range of varietals (Greco, Falanghina, Coda di Volpe, Piedirosso) and a variety of styles, including *spumante* and *novello*.

Asprino or Asprinio A welcome refresher; sharpish, fizzy citric white without pretensions: Naples' universal café wine.

Aversa DOC. White. Provinces: Caserta, Naples. Villages: Aversa and twenty-one other communes. Grapes: Asprinio min. 85%.

Campi Flegrei DOC. Red and white wines. Province: Naples. Villages: parts of Naples and six other communes. Grapes: (red) Piedirosso 50–70%, Aglianico 10–30%, others max. 30%; (white) Falanghina 50–70%, Biancolella and/or Coda di Volpe 10–30%, others max. 30%. This DOC, with unusual sandy and volcanic soils, also permits varietal wines from Piedirosso (dry and *passito*) and Falanghina.

Capri DOC. White and red wine. Province: Naples. Area: the island of Capri. Grapes: (white) Falanghina and Greco, plus Biancolella up to 20%; (red) Piedirosso min. 80%.

A small supply of adequate dry white and a minute supply of light red to drink young are lucky enough to have this romantic name.

Castel San Lorenzo DOC. Red, white, and *rosato* wines. Province: Salerno. Villages: Castel San Lorenzo and seven other communes. Grapes: (white) Trebbiano 50–60%, Malvasia Bianca 30–40%, others max. 20%; (red) Barbera 60–80% , Sangiovese 20–30%, others max. 20%. Mostly dull wines, but this DOC also permits varietal wines from Barbera and Moscato.

Cilento DOC. Red, white, and *rosato*. Province: Salerno. Villages: Agropoli and seven other communes. Grapes: (Aglianico) Aglianico 85% min.; (red) Aglianico 60–75%, Piedirosso/Primitivo 15–20%, Barbera 10–20%, other reds up to 10%; (*rosato*) Sangiovese 70–80%, Aglianico 10–15%, Primitivo/Piedirosso 10–15%, others max. 10%; (white) Fiano 60–65%, Trebbiano Toscano 20–30%, Greco Bianco/Malvasia Bianco 10–15%; other whites up to 10%.

Created in 1989, this DOC is located in some outstanding terroirs and shows great promise.

Costa d'Amalfi DOC. Red, white, and *rosato*. Province: Salerno. Villages: Amalfi and twelve other communes. Grapes (white) Falanghina min. 40%, Biancolella min. 20%; (red) Piedirosso min. 40%, Aglianico max. 60%, others max. 40%. A DOC created in 1995, and including, for additional complexity, three sub-zones.

Falerno del Massico DOC. Red and white wine. Province: Caserta. Villages: Mondragone, and four other communes. Grapes: (red) Aglianico 60–80%, Piedirosso 20–40%, Primitivo and/or Barbera max. 20%; (white) Falanghina.

These wines, from a new DOC, show promise. Revived in their original area, they bear little similarity to their forbears but are worth watching. The rules also permit a varietal Primitivo.

Fiano di Avellino DOC. White wine. Province: Avellino. Villages: Avellino and fourteen nearby communes. Grapes: Fiano min. 85%, Greco, Coda di Volpe Bianco, and Trebbiano Toscano up to 15%. One of the best white wines of the south, light-yellow and nutty in scent and flavour with liveliness and length. It is also known as "Apianum", a Latin reference to bees, which apparently appreciated either its flowers or grapes – or juice.

Galluccio DOC. Red, white, and *rosato* wines. Province: Caserta. Villages: Galluccio and four other communes. Grapes (white) Falanghina min. 70%; (red and *rosato*) min. 70% Aglianico.

Small DOC established in 1997; it ought to produce wines of unusual elegance for the area.

Greco di Tufo DOC. White wine. Province: Avellino. Villages: Tufo and seven other communes. Grapes: Greco di Tufo min. 85%, Coda di Volpe Bianco max. 15%.

White wine of positive character, a little neutral to smell, but mouth filling with a good "cut" in the flavour: highly satisfactory with flavoursome food. Some bouquet develops with two to three years in bottle. It can also be made *spumante* (rarely seen).

Guardia Sanframondi DOC. Red, white, and *rosato*. Province: Benevento. Villages: Guardia Sanframondi and three other communes. Grapes: (white) Malvasia di Candia 50–60%, Falanghina 20–30%, others max. 10%; (red and *rosato*) Sangiovese min. 80%.

This DOC also permits varietal wines from Falanghina (dry and *spumante*) and Aglianico.

Ischia DOC. Red and white wine. Province: the island of Ischia. Villages: throughout the island. Grapes: (red) Guarnaccia 50%, Piedirosso (alias Per'e Palummo) 40–50%, others max. 15%; (white) Forastera 45–70%, Biancolella 30–55%, others max. 15%.

The standard red and white of this green island in the Bay of Naples are made to drink young and fresh – though newly ambitious producers are trying other ideas. The white should be sharp enough to quench thirst. Forastera, Biancolella, and Per'e Palummo grapes now have their own DOCs.

Lacrimarosa d'Irpinia A very pale, coppery *rosato* of good quality, aromatic to smell, faintly underripe to taste, made of Aglianico by Mastroberardino (*q.v.*).

Per'e Palummo The alternative name of the Piedirosso grape, meaning "dove's foot", applied to one of Ischia's best reds, refreshingly tannic and a shade "grassy" to smell.

Penisola Sorrentina DOC. Red and white wines. Province: Naples. Villages: Naples and twelve other communes. Grapes: (white) Falanghina min. 40%, Biancolella and/or Greco min. 60%; (red; still and *frizzante*) Piedirosso min. 4%, Sciascinoso and/or Aglianico min. 60%. Small DOC covering the Sorrento Peninsula in the Bay of Naples.

Ravello Red, white, and *rosato*, each good of its kind, from the terraced vineyards leading up to the ravishing hilltop town of Ravello. Sea mists, I suspect, keep the wines fresh.

Sannio DOC. Red, white, and *rosato* wines. Province: Benevento. Villages: all communes in the province. Grapes: (white) Trebbiano min. 50%; (red and *rosato*) Sangiovese min. 50%. Large, catch-all DOC, also permitting numerous varietal wines and classic-method *spumante*.

Sant' Agata de' Goti DOC. Red, white, and *rosato* wines. Province: Benevento. Village: Sant'Agata de' Goti. Grapes: (white) Falanghina 40–60%, Greco 40–60%; (red and *rosato*) Aglianico 40–60%, Piedirosso 40–60%.

Obscure DOC, which also permits varietal wines from Falanghina, Greco, Aglianico, and Piedirosso. Mustilli is the most important producer (*q.v.*).

Solopaca DOC. Red and white wine. Province: Benevento. Villages: Solopaca and eleven neighbouring communes. Grapes: (red and *rosato*) Sangiovese 50–60%, Piedirosso max. 30%, Aglianico 20–40%; (white) Trebbiano Toscano 40–60%, Malvasia, Coda di Volpe, and/or Falanghina max. 20%; others max. 20%.

A little-known DOC zone north of Naples with decent red but rather dreary white. Falanghina and *spumante* wines are also permitted.

Taburno DOC. *See* Aglianico del Taburno.

Taurasi DOCG. Red wine. Province: Avellino. Villages: Taurasi and fifteen other communes in the Irpinia Hills east of Naples. Grapes: Aglianico min. 85%.

Among the best reds of southern Italy, at least as made by Mastroberardino (*q.v.*). Aglianico ripens late in these lofty vineyards to make a firm wine of splendidly satisfying structure, still dark in colour even when mature at five years. It has a slightly roasted richness without being at all port-like. First-class but impossible to pin down by comparisons.

Vesuvio (Lacryma Christi) DOC. White, red, and *rosato*. Province: Naples. Villages: Boscotrecase, Trecase and San Sebastiano al Vesuvio, plus part of twelve other communes in Naples. Grapes: (white) Coda di Volpe and Verdeca min. 80%; (red) Piedirosso min. 80%, Aglianico max. 20%.

This DOC applies to the basic white, *rosato*, and red, while Lacryma Christi del Vesuvio applies to four superior versions that are capable of ageing three to six years or more. The white may also be sparkling.

Leading Campania Producers

Antonio Caggiano ☆☆☆
Taurasi, Avellino. www.cantinecaggiano.it
Caggiano founded this twenty-hectare property in 1991, and has resolutely focused on the excellent grape varieties typical of Campania. The Taurasi is magnificent, finely structured, and infused with the flavour of red fruits. "Fiagrè" blends Fiano and Greco, as does the late-harvested, sweet "Mel".

De Conciliis ☆☆–☆☆☆
Prignano Cilento, Salerno
A new star in Campania. The wines are IGTs, but they are true to local traditions: powerful, barrique-aged Aglianicos called "Zero" and "Naima", suffused with cherry and plum flavours, as well as crisp Fiano.

Feudi di San Gregorio ☆☆☆–☆☆☆☆
Sorbo Serpico, Avellino. www.feudi.com
The great success story of Campania is the swift rise of this large property to the top ranks of south Italian producers. The whites are brilliant – "Campanaro" and the barrique-aged, late-harvested "Privilegio" (both Fiano) – and the reds unusually profound: Taurasi, of course, but also a surprisingly voluptuous Aglianico/Merlot called "Serpico", and a succulent new Merlot called "Pàtrimo". (The Ercolino brothers, who own the property, point out that Merlot is traditional to the region.)

Molise

Molise, a slice of central Italy stretching from the Apennines to the Adriatic, is a relative newcomer to Italy's wine map. Bottles with labels on are a novelty in a land of bulk production. The first Molise DOCs date from 1983. They are Biferno, for red and white wine from forty-two communes in Campobasso province; and Pentro, for red and white wines from sixteen communes in the hills around Isernia. Both specify Montepulciano for red. In Biferno it is the dominant variety; in Pentro it is used half-and-half with Sangiovese. Both whites are based on Trebbiano Toscano, not a formula for quality. Both allow the addition of Bombino. In Biferno, Malvasia Bianco may also be added.

One outstanding Molise winery, and one of the most modern in Italy is:

Di Majo Norante ☆☆☆
Campomarino, Campobasso
Owned by Alessio di Majo Norante, with Riccardo Cotarella as the consultant oenologist. The Montepulciano is as good as the best of Abruzzo, and the Greco is fresh and lively.

Other Molise producers include:

Cantine Borgo di Colloredo ☆☆–☆☆☆
Campomarino, Campobasso
A family winery dedicated to the local grape varieties, and producing good Aglianico, Montepulciano, and Falanghina.

L.TA-Viticoltori del Tappino ☆
Gambatesa, Campobasso
Biferno DOC with the "Serra Meccaglia" and "Rocco del Falco" brands, as well as "Vernaccia di Serra Meccaglia" white.

Mastroberardino ☆☆–☆☆☆
Atripalda, Avellino. www.mastro.it
Founded in 1878 as a continuation of a long-standing business; now run by Antonio Mastroberardino and son Carlo. From seventy hectares of family owned vines in Irpinia and 250 of others under contract, the winery makes 200,000 cases. Cellars were renovated and expanded after being destroyed in the earthquakes of 1980, and the subsequent installation of ultramodern equipment signalled a new approach to the style of their white Fiano and Greco, now made in temperature-controlled, stainless-steel tanks.

The Mastroberardino firm split in two in 1994: Antonio keeps the winery in Atripalda, his brother Walter looks after the vineyards. Walter's label is "Vignadoria" (*q.v.*), located in Montefusco. Recent vintages of the once legendary Taurasi have failed to impress, but the extensive range of white wines remains exciting.

Montevetrano ☆☆☆–☆☆☆☆
San Cipriano Picentino, Salerno. www.montevetrano.com
Photographer Silvia Imparato produces, with advice from Riccardo Cotarella, a single wine, named after the estate, but it has become a cult wine, with a price tag to match. A blend of Cabernet, Merlot, and a dash of Aglianico, it is not unlike a fine Bordeaux.

Villa Matilde ☆☆☆
Cellole, Caserta. www.villamatilde.com
Riccardo Cotarella advises this sixty-two-hectare estate and helps to produce outstanding Falerno del Massico DOC Falanghina and Aglianico, and rare *passito* Falanghina IGT called "Eleusi", with its aromas of dried fruits.

The finest red is the rich and concentrated Aglianico from Vigna Camarato.

Other Campania Producers

D'Ambra ☆
Forio d'Ischia, Napoli. www.dambravini.com
Founded in 1888 by Francesco d'Ambra, this producer of Ischia DOC is loyal to local white varieties such as Biancolella and Forestera.

D'Ambra Corrado
Ischia
A member of the family sells his own production at his *enoteca* by the harbour. This could be the future.

D'Antiche Terre ☆☆
Manocalzati, Avellino
Especially good Greco and Fiano from an estate established only in 1993.

Ferrara ☆–☆☆☆
Tufo, Avellina. www.benitoferrara.it
A tiny property producing nothing but elegant, almondy Greco.

Galardi ☆☆☆
San Carlo di Sessa Aurunca, Casera. www.terradilavoro.com
A one-wine property. "Terra di Lavoro", like Montevetrano

(*q.v.*), is made by Riccardo Cotarella, but is based on local varieties Aglianico and Piedirosso.

Gran Furor ☆☆–☆☆☆
Furore, Salerno. www.granfuror.it
An excellent range of wines from Costa d'Amalfi DOC, using only indigenous varieties.

La Guardiense ☆
Guardia Sanframondi, Benevento
Large cooperative producer of typical Campania wines, from growers with almost 1,500 hectares of vines.

De Lucia ☆☆
Guardia Sanframondi, Benevento
An excellent source of Falanghina from Sannio DOC.

Luigi Maffini ☆☆☆
Castellabate, Salerno
A new property, using local grapes but releasing them as IGT. Outstanding Fiano called "Kratos".

Di Meo ☆
Salza Irpinia, Avellino. www.dimeo.it
Sound Greco and Fiano.

Michele Moio ☆☆–☆☆☆
Mondragone, Caserta. www.moio.it
Substantial Primitivo is released under the Falerno del Massico DOC.

Molettieri ☆☆–☆☆☆
Montemarano, Avellino
A small estate, but an impeccable source of powerful Taurasi, and a more accessible style of Aglianico called "Cinque Querce".

Mustilli ☆☆
Sant' Agata de' Goti, Benevento
Good wines from typical Campania varieties: Aglianico, Falanghina, and Greco.

Pietratorcia ☆☆
Forio, Napoli
Very attractive whites from Ischia.

Cantina del Taburno ☆☆–☆☆☆
Foglianise, Benevento. www.cantinadeltaburno.it
A quality-conscious cooperative producing excellent Aglianico, Falanghina, and other wines. The top Aglianico bottlings here are as fine as any in Campania.

Terredora di Paolo ☆☆–☆☆☆
Montefusco, Avellino. www.terredora.com
The spin-off Mastroberardino estate consists of 150 hectares, and produces very good Taurasi, Fiano, and Falanghina.

Antica Masseria Venditti ☆☆
Castelvenere, Benevento. www.venditti.it
The quality of this organic estate's Solopaca and Sannio wines has improved in recent years and continues to do so.

Puglia

The heel and hamstrings of Italy are its most productive wine regions. Their historic role has been to supply strength and colour for more famous but frail wines in blending vats farther north. The reds are very red indeed; very strong, and often inclined to portiness. The whites, which account for only twenty per cent of production, are the faceless background to vermouth. This is the one region where the best wines until recently were the rosés – or at least some of them. Today, things are changing rapidly.

The Salento Peninsula, the heel from Taranto southeastwards, is the hottest region. A few producers here are learning to moderate the strength and density of their reds to make good-quality, winter-warming wines – though a bottle still goes a long way. Their grapes are the Primitivo (California's Zinfandel) and the Negroamaro: "bitter black". North of Taranto the hills have well-established DOCs for dry whites, originally intended as vermouth base-wines, but with modern techniques increasingly drinkable as "fish" wines in their own right. As elsewhere in Italy, the existence of a DOC is better evidence of tradition than of quality. There is more interest in the fact that even in this intemperate region successful spots have recently been found to plant superior northern grapes – even Chardonnay.

Much the best-known DOC is Castel del Monte, and this is largely due to the crisp *rosato* of Rivera – which for many years has been one of Italy's best. The list of producers shows that things are changing; Puglian reds are no longer ashamed of their origin. Many of Italy's top wine producers are convinced that Puglia is capable of making outstanding wines at moderate prices. Antinori, Pasqua, and even the Californian Kendall-Jackson have invested heavily in the region.

DOC & Other Wines

Aleatico di Puglia DOC. Red wine. Area: the whole of Puglia. Grapes: Aleatico min. 85%. A dessert wine, approaching ruby port in its fortified (*liquoroso*) version. Small supply, and of local interest only.

Alezio DOC. Red and *rosato* wine. Province: Lecce. Villages: Alezio, Sannicola, plus parts of Gallipoli and Tuglie. Grapes: Negroamaro min. 80%. A DOC for the red and *rosato* of the tip of Italy's heel, and every inch a southern red: dark and powerful. It is moot whether to try ageing it or to take it on the chin as it is. Like many Puglian *rosatos*, the paler wine has more immediate appeal.

Brindisi DOC. Red and *rosato* wine. Province: Brindisi. Villages: Brindisi and Mesagna, just inland. Grapes: Negroamaro min. 70%.

The local red of Brindisi can age for five to ten years or more. Also makes a pleasant *rosato*. There is one outstanding example of Brindisi DOC: the "Patrigilione" from Cosimo Taurino (*q.v.*).

Cacc'e Mmitte di Lucera DOC. Red wine. Province: Foggia. Villages: Lucera, Troia, and Biccari. Grapes: Uva di Troia 35–60%; Montepulciano, Sangiovese, and Malvasia Nera 25–35%; others 15–30%.

Scholars tell us that the dialect name refers to a local form of *governo*, in which fresh grapes are added to the fermenting must. The wines mostly lack interest.

Castel del Monte DOC. Red, *rosato*, and white wine. Province: Bari. Villages: Minervino Murge and parts of nine other communes. Grapes: (white) Pampanuto and/or Chardonnay and/or Bombino Bianco, others max. 35%; (red and *rosato*) Uva di Troia and/or Aglianico and/or Montepulciano; plus varietal wines from Chardonnay, Sauvignon, Pinot Bianco, Pinot Nero, Cabernet (Sauvignon or Franc), Aglianico. Castel del Monte, the octagonal fortress of the medieval Hohenstaufens, lies 48 kilometres (30 miles) west of Bari near Minervino Murge. The leading DOC of Puglia deserves its name for an outstanding red and famous *rosato*. The red has a fat, inviting smell and considerable depth and vitality, with a certain bite and long, pruney finish. Rivera's "Il Falcone" is the best example (*q.v.*). The pale *rosato* has long been popular all over Italy for balanced force and freshness.

Copertino DOC. Red wine. Province: Lecce. Villages: Copertino and five other communes. Grapes: Negroamaro min. 70%.

A warmly recommended red made in some quantity south of Lecce on Italy's heel. The *riserva* is smooth with plenty of flavour and a bitter touch.

Five Roses A powerful, dry *rosato* from Leone de Castris (*q.v.*), so named by American soldiers who gave it one more rose than a famous Bourbon whiskey.

Galatina DOC. Red, white, and *rosato* wines. Province: Lecce. Villages: Galatina and six other communes. Grapes: (white) Chardonnay min. 55%; (red) Negroamaro min. 65%. Also varietal wines from Chardonnay and Negroamaro.

Small, marginal DOC established in 1997.

Gioia del Colle DOC. Red, white, and *rosato* wine. Province: Bari. Villages: Gioia del Colle and fifteen neighbouring communes. Grapes: (white) Trebbiano 50–60%; (red and *rosato*) Primitivo min. 50%.

Gioia is halfway from Bari south to Taranto. The Primitivo gives a pretty brutal red in these hot hills. With age it becomes more politely overwhelming. DOC rules also permit varietal Primitivo and the possibly extinct sweet Aleatico.

Gravina DOC. White wine. Province: Bari. Village: Communes of Gravina and Poggiorsini, and parts of Altamura and Spinazzola. Grapes: Malvasia Bianca 40–65%.

Dry white from around Gravina, best when containing significant amounts of Greco. A *spumante* is also permitted.

Leverano DOC. Red, *rosato*, and white wine. Province: Lecce. Villages: commune of Leverano. Grapes: (red and *rosato*) Negroamaro min. 50%, Malvasia Nera and/or Montepulciano and/or Sangiovese max. 40%, others max. 30%; (white) Malvasia Bianca min. 50%, Bombino max. 40%, others max. 30%. One of the 1980 class of DOCs for Salento wines. The red and the *rosato* stand with Salento's finest.

Lizzano DOC. Red, white, and *rosato* wine. Province: Taranto. Villages: communes of Lizzano, Faggiano, and part of Taranto. Grapes: (red and *rosato*) Negroamaro 60–80%; (white) Trebbiano Toscano 40–60%, Chardonnay and/or Pinot Bianco min. 30%, Sauvignon and/or Bianco di Alessano max. 25%, Malvasia Bianca Lugna max. 10%. Malvasia Nera and Negroamaro can also be *superiore* at 13 degrees.

Salento DOC, rarely encountered.

Locorotondo DOC. White wine. Provinces: Bari and Brindisi. Villages: Locorotondo, Cisternino, and part of Fasano. Grapes: Verdeca 50–65%; Bianco di Alessano 35–50%.

Locorotondo is famous for its round stone dwellings. With Martina Franca, it lies east of Bari at the neck of the Salento peninsula. Serious efforts are made to keep its white wine fresh and brisk.

Martina or **Martina Franca** DOC. White wine. Provinces: Taranto, Bari, and Brindisi. Villages: Martina Franca and parts of four other communes. Grapes: Verdeca 50–65%, Bianco di Alessano 35–50%.

Grapes and wine amount to much the same thing as Locorotondo.

Matino DOC. *Rosato* and red wine. Province: Lecce. Villages: Matino and part of seven other communes in the Murge Salentino, at the tip of Italy's heel. Grapes: Negroamaro min. 70%, Sangiovese and Malvasia Nera max. 30%.

An early (1971) DOC but still obscure.

Moscato di Trani DOC. White wine. Province: Bari. Villages: Trani and eleven other communes. Grapes: Moscato Bianco min. 85%. Min. alc.: 13 degrees plus 2 degrees of sugar for *dolce naturale*; 16 degrees plus 2 degrees of sugar for *liquoroso*. Sweet, golden, dessert Muscats of good quality from the north coast, west of Bari. Other Puglian Muscats, particularly those of Salento, can also be very drinkable.

Nardò DOC. Red and *rosato* wine. Province: Lecce. Villages: Nardò and Porto Cesareo. Grapes: Negroamaro min. 80%. Recent DOC for red and *rosato* wines. The red is best after three to six years.

Orta Nova DOC. Red and *rosato* wine. Province: Foggia. Villages: Orta Nova and five other communes. Grapes: Sangiovese min. 60%, Uva di Troia and Montepulciano 30–40%. Tiny production.

Ostuni and **Ottavianello di Ostuni** DOC. White and red wine. Province: Brindisi. Villages: Ostuni, and six other communes, including Brindisi. Grapes: (white) Impigno 50–85%, Francavilla 15–50%. Plus red Ottavianello.

The unusual white grapes give a very pale, mild, and dry "fish" wine. Ottavianello is a cheerful cherry-red dry wine, pleasant to drink cool and said to be related to Cinsault.

Primitivo di Manduria DOC. Red wine. Provinces: Taranto and Brindisi. Villages: Manduria and eighteen other communes along the south Salento coast. Grape: Primitivo.

The Primitivo grape variety, now known to be the same as California's Zinfandel, makes black-strap reds here, some sweet and some even fortified (*liquoroso*), as though 14 degrees were not enough in the first place. You may age them or not, depending on whether you appreciate full-fruit flavour or just full flavour.

Rosato del Salento *Rosatos* are perhaps the best general produce of the Salento peninsula. It is not a DOC but this name is widely used.

Rosso di Barletta DOC. Red wine. Province: Bari and Foggia. Villages: Barletta and four other communes. Grapes: Uva di Troia, plus others max. 30%. "Invecchiato" if aged for two years.

Some drink this relatively light red young and cool: others age it moderately and treat it like claret.

Rosso Canosa DOC. Red wine. Province: Bari. Village: Canosa. Grapes: Uva di Troia min. 65%, others max. 35%.

Canosa, between Bari and Foggia, was the Roman Canusium (an alternative name for the wine). Its wine is in a similar style to Rosso di Barletta.

Rosso di Cerignola DOC. Red wine. Province: Bari. Villages: Cerignola and three other communes. Grapes: Uva di Troia min. 55%, Negroamaro 15–30%, others max. 15%. A big, dry, heady red with faint bitterness. But almost extinct.

Salice Salentino DOC. Red, white, and *rosato* wine. Provinces: Brindisi and Lecce. Villages: Salice Salentino and six other communes in the centre of the Salento Peninsula. Grapes: (red and rosado): Negroamaro min. 80%, Aleatico: Aleatico min. 85% (*dolce* 15 degrees, *liquoroso* 18.5 degrees); (white) Chardonnay min. 70%; Pinot Bianco: Pinot Bianco min. 85%.

Typically big-scale southern reds which have a porty undertone accompanied by a balancing measure of astringency. I have found this to be a rather clumsy wine, but I am prepared to believe I have been unlucky; other Salento reds are often nicely balanced with an attractively clean finish. The *rosatos* can be fresh and flowery and complex with time, and are among the most distinctive of Italian rosés.

San Severo DOC. White, red, and *rosato* wine. Province: Foggia. Villages: San Severo, Torremaggiore, San Paolo Civitate, and part of five other communes north of Foggia. Grapes: (white) Bombino Bianco 40–60%, Trebbiano Toscano 40–60%, Malvasia Bianca and Verdeca max. 20%; (red and *rosato*) Montepulciano di Abruzzo min. 70%, Sangiovese max. 30%.

Inoffensive wines of no special qualities but offering good value for money.

Squinzano DOC. Red and *rosato* wine. Provinces: Lecce and Brindisi. Villages: Squinzano and eight others. Grapes: Negroamaro min. 70%.

Salento wines of moderate quality. The *rosato* is much less tiring to drink than the red.

Leading Puglia producers

Accademia dei Racemi ☆☆–☆☆☆
Manduria, Taranto. www.accademiadeiracemi.it
Founded in 1999, this is a kind of private cooperative almost entirely focused on Primitivo of the highest quality.

The wines are produced under various labels, such as "Pervini" and "Sinfarosa". Perhaps the most interesting of these is "Felline", which releases excellent Primitivo di Manduria DOC, and a remarkable IGT blend called "Vigna del Feudo" from Primitivo and Malvasia Nera.

Carrisi ☆☆–☆☆☆
Cellino San Marco, Brindisi. www.albanocarrisi.com
A small estate under the guidance of Franco Bernabei, Carrisi is best-known for its "Don Carmelo" Negro Amaro, and has won high praise for its opulent blend of Negroamaro and Primitivo called "Platone".

Leone de Castris ☆☆–☆☆☆
Salice Salentino, Lecce. www.leonedecastris.net
The estate of the Leone de Castris family is an ancient one, but the winery is ultramodern, producing 300,000 cases annually. It vinifies some of Puglia's best wine: rich and heady but not gross reds from Salice Salentino and (among others) Italy's first bottled *rosato*, "Five Roses", which remains a model of the genre.

Although there are some straightforward varietal wines from Verdeca, Sauvignon, and Aleatico, the top wines are usually "Donna Lisa" (a pure Negroamaro) and "Illemos", a voluptuous blend of Primitivo, Montepulciano, and other varieties.

Rivera ☆☆–☆☆☆
Andria, Bari. www.rivera.it
Founded by the De Corato family, the sixty-hectare estate began bottling in the early 1950s. Rivera makes about 100,000 cases of Castel del Monte from family vineyards and grapes from regular suppliers.

The popularity of the lively *rosato* overshadows the quality of "Il Falcone Riserva", one of Puglia's best-constructed reds. The Asti firm of Gancia has bought a share of the winery, and encouraged the production of varietal wines from Chardonnay, Sauvignon, and Primitivo.

The Chardonnay "Preludio No. 1" has become one of Puglia's best-known wines on the export market.

Rosa del Golfo ☆☆
Alezio, Lecce. www.rosadelgolfo.com
The Calò family has been selling wine from its estate near Gallipoli since 1938. It is best-known for its "Rosa del Golfo", one of Italy's most limpid and lovely *rosatos*, and produces other wines from Verdeca and Negroamaro.

Cosimo Taurino ☆☆☆
Guagnano, Lecce
After Cosimo Taurino died in 1999, his son Francesco became chief winemaker. Together with oenologist Severino Garofano, he makes admirable Salice Salentino and Brindisi DOC. To note especially is the famous Christmas-puddingy "Patrigilione", which is made from ultra-ripe grapes. "Notarpanaro" blends Negroamaro and Malvasia Nera.

Agricole Vallone ☆☆–☆☆☆
Lecce
A 150-hectare estate owned by Vittoria and Maria Teresa Vallone. They produce fine Brindisi *rosato* and Salice Salentino DOCs, and a splendid, perfumed Negroamaro IGT called "Gratticcaia", which is fermented only after drying the grapes for a few weeks in direct sunlight.

Other Puglia Producers

Michele Calò & Figli ☆☆
Tuglie, Lecce. www.michelecalo.it
Red, white, and *rosato* wines from Alezio DOC called "Mjère".

Borgo Canale ☆
Fasano, Brindisi
Good Locorotondo DOC and Primitivo.

Francesco Candido ☆☆–☆☆☆
Sandonaci, Brindisi. www.candidowines.com
A large, 160-hectare property producing robust Salice Salentino, and an impressive Negroamaro/Montepulciano blend calld "Duca d'Aragona".

Càntele Lecce ☆☆
www.cantele.it
A large winery, producing traditional wines such as Salice Salentino, and well-regarded Chardonnays.

Cantina Sociale di Copertino ☆–☆☆
Copertino, Lecce
The best co-op of Salento, with a huge production including good Copertino DOC.

Cantina del Locorotondo ☆☆
Locorotondo, Bari. www.locorotondodoc.com
Founded in 1932, this medium-sized cooperative focuses not only on crisp DOC Locorotondo, but on IGTs from Fiano, Pinot Nero, and various blends of local varieties.

Marco Maci ☆☆–☆☆☆
Cellino San Marco, Brindisi
Maci offers a large range of wines, both from international varieties such as Sauvignon and Pinot Bianco, and also from local varieties, all presented as IGTs.

Miali ☆
Martina Franca, Taranto. www.cantine-miali.com
A good range of wines, from Basilicata as well as Puglia.

Rubino ☆☆–☆☆☆
Brindisi. www.tenuterubino.it
This is an expanding estate with a growing reputation for a wide range of wines, both traditional and in an international style.

Santa Lucia ☆–☆☆
Corato, Bari. www.vinisantalucia.com
Emerging small estate with a good range from Castel del Monte, including fruity *rosato*.

Giovanni Soloperto ☆☆
Manduria, Taranto. www.soloperto.it
This fifty-hectare estate has focused for some time on Primitivo. Good fruit and dizzyingly high alcohol.

Cooperativa Svevo ☆☆
Lucera, Foggia
This cooperative, drawing grapes from 250 hectares, is one of the few producers of DOC Cacc'e Mmitte di Lucera, plus various red IGT blends from local varieties.

Tormaresca ☆☆
San Pietro Vernotico, Brindisi. www.tormaresca.it
The outpost in Puglia of Marchesi Antinori. Chardonnay is the major wine at present, and the principal red is a blend of Aglianico and Cabernet.

Conti Zecca ☆☆–☆☆☆
Leverano, Lecce. www.contizecca.it
The Zecca family own over 300 hectares in DOC Leverano, from which they produce a very wide range of wines. Their flagship wine is "Nero", a barrique-aged blend of Negroamaro and Cabernet Sauvignon.

Calabria

The vast mountainous peninsula that forms the toe of Italy has no famous wines, unless Cirò, with its athletic reputation, can be so called. Only about ten per cent of the region's 25,000 hectares of vines produce wine that is bottled locally. The rest is shipped out for blending. The local red grape is the Gaglioppo, a variety of deep colour and potentially very high alcohol, but the spots where it is grown to best effect are (with the exception of Cirò) high enough in the Calabrian Hills to cool its fiery temper.

The local grape for white wines is the Greco, which is used in the extreme south at Gerace to make a very good dessert wine which has the ability to age well, and which goes for a high price. With little established winemaking except of the most primitive kind, Calabria, like Sicily, is modernizing in a hurry. Its DOCs, though little-known, represent wines that meet up-to-date criteria, but only account for a trifling four per cent of production.

DOC & Other Wines

Bivongi DOC. Red, white, and *rosato* wines. Provinces: Reggio Calabria and Catanzaro. Villages: Bivongi and eight other communes. Grapes: (white) Greco, Mantonico, and Ansonica; (red and *rosato*) Gaglioppo and/or Greco Nero 30–50%; Nocera and/or Calabrese 30–50%.
Coastal DOC south of Catanzaro.

Cirò DOC. Red, white, and *rosato* wine. Province: Crotone. Villages: Cirò, Cirò Marina, part of Melissa and Crucoli. Grapes: (red and *rosato*) Gaglioppo min. 95%; (white) Greco Bianco min. 90%.
Cirò is a full diet, but a soporific rather than a stimulating one. Earlier picking and new cellar techniques have reduced its tendency to oxidize, though only the *riserva* can be aged beyond three to four years. White Cirò, as modernized, is a decent standard dry white to drink young.

Donnici DOC. Red, white, and *rosato* wine. Province: Cosenza. Villages: ten around and including Cosenza. Grapes: (white) Mantonico min. 50%, Greco or Malvasia Bianca max. 30%; (red and *rosato*) Gaglioppo min. 50%.
This wine is a relatively light and fruity red to drink young and fairly cool, from the central-western coastal hills of Calabria.

Greco di Bianco DOC. White wine. Province: Reggio Calabria. Villages: Bianco and part of Casignana. Grapes: Greco min. 95%.
A smooth, juicy, and intriguingly orange-scented sweet dessert wine made of Greco grapes at Bianco, where a few small vineyards make it their specialty. Bianco is on the south coast of the extreme toe of Italy.
More vineyards are expanding production. Bianco also produces a drier, more lemony, barrel-aged dessert or apéritif white called (after its grapes) Mantonico.

Lamezia DOC. Red, white, and *rosato* wine. Provinces: Catanzaro and Vibo Valentia. Villages: Part of ten communes around Lamezia Terme. Grapes: (red and *rosato*) Nerello Mascalese and/or Nerello Cappuccio 30–50%, Gaglioppo (known locally as Magliocco) 25–35%, Greco Nero (locally called Marsigliana) 25–35%, others max. 20%; (white) Greco max. 50%, Trebbiano max. 40%, Malvasia min. 20%, others max. 30%; Greco: Greco min. 85%.
A straightforward, fairly pale, dry red from around the Gulf of St-Eufemia on the west coast. Drink it young and cool. Lametina is the name of the local non-DOC sweet or dry white.

Melissa DOC. Red and *rosato* wine. Province: Crotone. Villages: Melissa and thirteen other communes. Grapes: (red) Gaglioppo 40–60%, Nerello 40–60%, Malvasia Nera, and others.
The light, yellow, dry seafood wine of the heel of the toe of Italy, around the port of Crotone. The wines resemble Cirò but don't match it for quality. Most of it is drunk locally where it represents good value.

Pellaro Powerful but light red or pink wines of imported Alicante vines grown on the Pellaro Peninsula in the extreme south.

Pollino DOC. Red wine. Province: Cosenza. Villages: Castrovillari, St Basile, Sarancena, Cassano Ionio, Civita, and Frascineto. Grapes: Gaglioppo min. 60%, plus Malvasia Bianca, Mantonico Bianco, Guarnaccia Bianco.
Monte Pollino is a 2,130-metre (6,922-foot) peak that divides northern Calabria from Basilicata. Its slopes produce a pale but powerful red.

San Vito di Luzzi DOC. Red, white, and *rosato* wines. Province: Cosenza. Village: San Vito. Grapes: (white) Malvasia Bianca 40–60%, Greco 20–30%, others max. 40%; (red and *rosato*) Gaglioppo max. 60%, Nerello max. 40%, others max. 40%.
Small DOC just north of Cosenza.

Sant' Anna di Isola di Capo Rizzuto DOC. Red and white wine. Province: Crotone. Villages: Isola di Capo Rizzuto and parts of the communes of Crotone and Cutro. Grapes: (red) Gaglioppo 75–95%; (white) Greco Bianco 80–95%.
A pale red/*rosato* to drink young and cool, from the easternmost cape (not an island) of the Calabrian coast. Almost extinct.

Savuto DOC. Red and *rosato* wine. Provinces: Cosenza and Catanzaro. Villages: fourteen communes in Cosenza and six in Catanzaro. Grapes: Gaglioppo 35–40%, Greco Nero

30–40%, Nerello Cappuccio, Maglicco Canino, Sangiovese, and Malvasia Bianca and Pecorino max. 25%.

A recommended red of moderate strength and some fragrance. Worth choosing the *superiore*. Odoardi the main producer (*q.v.*).

Scavigna DOC. Red, white, and *rosato* wines. Province: Catanzaro. Villages: Nocera, Tirinese, and Falerna. Grapes: (white) Trebbiano max. 50%, Chardonnay max. 30%, Greco max. 20%, and others; (red and *rosato*) Gaglioppo max. 60%, Nerello Cappuccio max. 40%, others max. 40%.

Coastal DOC west of Catanzaro. Odoardi the main producer here, too.

Verbicaro DOC. Red, white, and *rosato*. Province: Cosenza. Villages: Verbicaro and four other communes. Grapes (white) Greco Bianco, Malvasia Bianca, Guarnaccia Bianca, and others; (red and *rosato*) Gaglioppo and/or Greco Nero 60–80%, plus Malvasia, Greco Bianco, and others.

Northerly DOC along the coast near Campania.

Leading Calabria Producers

Caparra & Siciliani ☆☆
Cirò Marina, Crotone
A two-family venture, founded in 1963, and with Severino Garofano as the consultant oenologist. From over 200 hectares, the winery produces a complete range of Cirò wines, white, *rosato*, and red. The whites are vinified in steel, the reds aged in traditional large casks.

Dattilo ☆☆
Marina di Strongoli, Crotone. www.dattilo.it
A swiftly improving twelve-hectare estate, offering a fresh Chardonnay and gutsy red blends.

Cantine Enotria ☆–☆☆
Cirò Marina, Crotone
A cooperative with seventy growers cultivating 130 hectares. A full range of Cirò wines is produced, the smoky red *riserva* being a distinct notch up in quality.

Vincenzo Ippolito ☆–☆☆
Cirò Marina, Crotone
Founded in 1845 and now run by Antonio and Salvatore Ippolito. They produce a wide range of wines, the best being the Cirò, especially the *riserva*, which is only released after many years in bottle.

Cantine Lento ☆☆–☆☆☆
Lamezia Terme, Catanzaro. www.cantinelento.it
Fresh white wines and supple reds from DOC Lamezia. The best wines are labelled "Contessa Emburga" (IGT) and include an unusual Sauvignon given a little barrique-ageing.

Librandi ☆☆☆
Cirò Marina, Crotone. www.librandi.it
Founded in 1950 by Antonio Cataldo Librandi, and the best-known property in Calabria. Under the supervision of oenologist Donato Lanati, Librandi makes traditional Cirò using modern techniques (the best being the plummy

"Riserva Duca San Felice"). IGT wines include the rather leathery "Gravello", made from Cabernet and Gaglioppo; a pineappley Chardonnay called "Critone"; and, occasionally, a *passito* from Mantonico called "Le Passule". They are not cheap.

Odoardi ☆☆
Nocera Terinese, Catanzaro. www.odoardi.net
This progressive winery, with seventy hectares of vines, specializes in two DOC wines: Savuto and Scavigna red, white, and *rosato*. Indeed, they are the only significant producers of Scavigna. The white Scavigna is an aromatic blend of Chardonnay, Pinot Bianco, and Riesling, with a luxurious hint of tropical fruit on the palate.

Fattoria San Francesco ☆☆☆
Cirò, Crotone. www.fattoriasanfrancesco.it
In recent years, the Siciliani family have made great strides and now produce some of the best wines from Cirò: red, white, and *rosato*. The spicy red "Ronco dei Quattroventi" has a complexity unusual for the DOC.

Vintripodi ☆☆–☆☆☆
Archi, Reggio Calabria. www.vintripodi.it
This small property was founded in 1892 and is totally committed to local grape varieties, notably Nerello and Alicante. The reds are peppery and well-structured.

Basilicata

This mountainous region of the central south, almost entirely landlocked and chronically poor, would not feature on the wine list at all were it not for its romantically named Aglianico del Vulture, a close relation of Taurasi and one of the best reds of southern Italy.

DOC & Other Wines

Aglianico dei Colli Lucani A worthwhile red, from the Puglia side of Basilicata. It is worth tasting any wine made from this grape.

Aglianico del Vulture DOC. Red wine. Province: Potenza. Villages: fifteen communes north of Potenza. Grape: Aglianico. Monte Vulture, an extinct volcano, lies right in the extreme north of Basilicata, not far from the Iripinian Mountains where Campania's splendid Taurasi is made. The same grapes grown at high altitudes on volcanic soil give a well-balanced red wine of firm structure, which is sometimes offered as a young, sweet sparkler, but more often as a matured red with real quality and character.

Leading Basilicata Producers

Fratelli d'Angelo ☆☆–☆☆☆
Rionero, Potenza
Founded in 1944 and run by Donato (oenologist) and Lucio

d'Angelo, this is the best-known estate in the region, with twenty hectares under vine.

Famous for their consistently good Aglianico del Vulture, they also make a barrique-aged Aglianico called "Cannetto", which is as good but has a touch more elegance and no obtrusive oak flavours.

Basilisco ☆☆☆
Rionero in Vulture, Potenza

A small property located high on the slopes of Monte Vulture, and since 1992 producing a single wine: darkly fruity Aglianico del Vulture. It is late-picked and packs a punch.

Basilium ☆☆
Acerenza, Potenza

A medium-sized cooperative with a good reputation for sturdy Aglianico del Vulture.

Consorzio Viticoltori Associati del Vulture ☆☆
Barile, Potenza

An enterprise, founded in 1977, that markets the best Aglianico and *spumante* (dry and sweet) from six local cooperatives.

Cantina del Notaio ☆☆–☆☆☆
Rionero, Potenza. www.cantinadelnotaio.com

A newcomer, having been established only in 1998, but the "La Firma" Aglianico has already been hailed as outstanding. It is barrique-aged, and for those who prefer a more traditional style, there is another bottling called "Il Repertorio".

Paternoster ☆☆–☆☆☆
Barile, Potenza

Named after the proprietors, this estate produces a few different bottlings of Aglianico del Vulture, as well as a Moscato called "Clivus". The old-vine "Don Anselmo" Aglianico usually leads the pack.

Le Querce ☆☆
Potenza

An estate only founded in 1997, but already producing solid Aglianico of very good quality.

Sicily

Of all the regions of Italy, the island of Sicily has changed most in the past few decades. Thirty years ago it was an almost medieval land. The marriage of dignity and squalor was visible everywhere.

Its unsurpassed Greek ruins lay apparently forgotten. Syracuse was still a small city commanding a bay of incredible beauty and purity where you could easily imagine the catastrophic defeat of the Athenian fleet 2,000 years before. Palermo was sleepy, violent, indigent but magnificent.

As far as wine was concerned, there was Marsala, a name everyone knew but which nobody drank, and a few small aristocratic estates – the best-known on the ideal volcanic slopes of Mount Etna, and around Syracuse, from which

Marsala

An Englishman, John Woodhouse, started the Marsala industry in 1773. Nelson stocked his fleet with it. In a sense it is Italy's sherry, though without sherry's brilliant finesse or limitless ageing capacity. Its manufacture usually involves concentrated and/or "muted" (stopped with alcohol) musts, known as *cotto* and *sifone* – but the best, *vergine*, is made with neither: simply by an ageing system similar to the *soleras* of sherry. *Fine,* the basic style, is normally sweet and rather nasty; *superiore* can be sweet or dry, with a strong caramel flavour; *rubino* is an innovation, drier than *fine; vergine* is dry, with more barrel-wood flavour. Finest, and rarest of all, is *vergine stravecchio* or *riserva,* which must be aged ten years or more in cask and it can also be vintage-dated. *Speciali* used to be a strange aberration – Marsala blended with eggs, or even coffee – but is now no longer permitted under DOC regulation. Other recent changes to the DOC are the descriptions *oro* (gold), *ambra* (amber), and *rubino* (ruby); the first two refer to the wines based on white grapes, while the latter refers to the darker varieties less often seen.

Unfortunately, Marsala has been much abused over the years and came to be regarded as little more than a cooking wine. Nor has the proliferation of barely comprensible rules under the DOC helped the reputation or popularity of the wine. It took the single-mindedness of Marco de Bartoli (*q.v.*) to produce a well-aged, unfortified style that showed much more complexity and delicacy than most souped-up, "traditional" Marsalas. For his pains, his wines were denied the DOC. Commercial Marsalas from the best firms can nonetheless be very good, especially in drier versions. With Marsala, as with most other great wines, you get what you pay for: cheap can often be nasty, expensive can be sublime.

there was a trickle of legendary sweet Moscato. But the general run of wine was almost undrinkable, the best of it having been exported northwards for blending.

An apparently well-directed regional-development programme (for which Europe has paid millions) has changed all this, and the wine industry has become the biggest in Italy, and one of the most modern. Enormous new vineyards supply automated cooperatives, which churn out "correct", clean, and properly balanced, modern wines. Three-quarters of Sicily's wine is white. Eighty per cent of the colossal total is made in the cooperatives.

DOCs are almost irrelevant here; less than five per cent qualifies. It is a table-wine industry, based not on local traditions but on choosing appropriate grapes, converting cornfields into mechanized vineyards, and making wine with cool efficiency. None of this could have been achieved without New World techniques – and huge government grants.

The wine industry has grown far faster than its market. Although fair quality, good reliability, and modest prices have made one or two brands (above all "Corvo") famous on the international stage, most Sicilian wine remains a bulk product.

Yet the quality and success of producers such as Planeta (*q.v.*) are demonstrating the true potential of the island, and other quality-conscious wineries are bringing standards to a previously undreamt-of level.

DOC & Other Wines

Alcamo or **Bianco d'Alcamo** DOC. White wine. Provinces: Palermo and Trapani. Villages: around the town of Alcamo. Grapes: Catarratto Bianco Comune or Lucido plus Damaschino, Grecanico, and Trebbiano Toscano max. 20%. Wines from international varieties such as Cabernet and Chardonnay have recently been admitted by the DOC.

A straightforward, fairly full-bodied, dry white. "Rapitalà" is a far superior brand with some nuttiness and some astringency. "Rincione Bianco" is another similar brand.

Cerasuolo di Vittoria DOC. Red wine. Provinces: Ragusa, Caltanissetta, and Catania. Villages: ten communes in southeastern Sicily. Grapes: Frappato min. 40%, Calabrese max. 60% , Grosso Nero and Nerello Mascalese max. 10%.

An unusual pale "cherry" red of high strength, which the critic Luigi Veronelli recommends keeping for as many as thirty years. Little is made, but its reputation is high.

Contea di Sclafani DOC. Red, white, and *rosato* wines. Provinces: Palermo, Caltanissetta, and Agrigento.

A large district in the centre of the island, given DOC status in 1996, and presenting a wide range of mostly varietal wines, both local and international varieties.

Contessa Entellina DOC. White wine. Province Palermo. Commune: Contessa Entellina. Grapes: (white) based on Ansonica; (red and *rosato*) based on Calabrese and/or Syrah. DOC also permits varietal wines from Catarratto, Ansonica, Grecanico, Chardonnay, Sauvignon, Cabernet Sauvignon, Merlot, Pinot Nero.

New DOC for Palermo province. The main producer is Donnafugata (*q.v.*).

Corvo Perhaps the best-known of all Sicilian wines today, a highly successful brand from Duca di Salaparuta at Casteldaccia near Palermo (*q.v.*).

A green-labelled white is reasonably full-bodied but not over-strong and nicely in balance; a yellow-labelled one is very pale and delicate. The red is a brilliant piece of modern wine design: clean, warm, and satisfying without leaving any clear memory of scent or flavour.

There are also *spumante* and dry, fortified Stravecchio Corvo wines.

Eloro DOC. Red and *rosato* wine. Provinces: Ragusa and Siracusa. Villages: Noto and four other communes. Grapes: Nero d'Avola, Frappato, and Piganello min. 90% (alone or blended). Coastal region just south of Ragusa.

Etna DOC. White, red, and *rosato* wine. Province: Catania. Villages: Milo and twenty other communes on the lower eastern slopes of Mount Etna. Grapes: (white) min. 60% Carricante, Catarratto Bianco max. 40%, others max. 15%; (red and *rosato*) Nerello Mascalese min. 80%, Nerello Mantellato max 20%.

Until recently, this was the only quality table-wine area in Sicily. The volcanic soil of the still-fiery volcano and the cool of its altitude allow both reds and whites of vigour and some refinement.

The reds age well to a consistency not far from claret and the whites are brisk and tasty young. The leading estate is Villagrande (*q.v.*). A rare Bianco Superiore is made only in Milo and must contain 80% Carricante.

Faro DOC. Red wine. Province: Messina. Village: Messina. Grapes: Nerello Mascalese 45–60%, Nerello Cappuccio 15–30%, Nocera 5–10%, others max. 15%.

Limited production of a distinctly superior red, best aged three years or so. Undergoing a tentative revival.

Malvasia delle Lipari DOC. Dessert white wine. Province: Messina. Villages: islands of the Aeolian archipelago, especially Lipari. Grapes: Malvasia delle Lipari max. 95%, Corinto Nero 5–8%.

Well-known but scarcely exceptional wines (except in their lovely birthplace), made in both *passito* and *liquoroso* styles. There are many good dessert wines in Sicily; Moscato is much more interesting than Malvasia.

Marsala DOC. Apéritif/dessert wine. Provinces: Trapani, Palermo, and Agrigento. Villages: throughout the provinces but above all at Marsala. Grapes: (*oro* and *ambra*) Catarratto and/or Grillo, plus Inzolia max. 15%; (*rubino*) Perricone, Calabrese, Nerello Mascalese, plus whites max. 30%. Max. crop: 75 hl/ha for *oro* and *rosato*, 67.5 hl/ha for *rubino*. Min. alc.: 17 degrees by volume for fine; 18 degrees aged two years for *superiore* (sometimes called Garibaldi Dolce – or the appropriate initials); 18 degrees by volume aged five years for *vergine*. *See* box on page 342.

Menfi DOC. Red and white wine. Provinces: Agrigento, Trapani. Villages: Menfi, Sambuca, Sciacca, and Castelvetrano. Grapes: (white) any combination of Inzolia, Catarratto, Grecanico, Chardonnay min. 75%; (red) any combination of Nero d'Avola, Sangiovese, Merlot, Cabernet Sauvignon, Syrah min. 70% .

This DOC, confirmed in 1997, neighbours Sambuca in western Sicily. Many varietal wines are also permitted.

Moscato di Noto DOC. White dessert wine. Province: Siracusa. Villages: Noto, Rosolini, Pachino, and Avola. Grape: Moscato Bianco.

Little of this delicious Moscato is made, but the *liquoroso* is a very good example of this sumptuous genre. The Greeks introduced the Muscat grape here 2,500 years ago. It is also made in unfortified and *spumante* styles.

Moscato and **Passito di Pantelleria** DOC. White wine. Province: Trapani. Area: the island of Pantelleria. Grapes: Zibibbo. The island of Pantelleria is closer to Tunisia than Sicily. The Zibibbo grape is a variant of Moscato with a singular perfume, whether made as *spumante*, *naturale,* or best of all *passito* (which can also be fortified). This has become a cult wine; production has doubled over the past decade.

Moscato di Siracusa DOC. White wine. Province: Siracusa. Village: Siracusa. Grape: Moscato Bianco.

The celebrated old Moscato vineyard of Syracuse, once the greatest city of the Greek world, home of Plato, Theocritus, and Archimedes, is apparently extinct, like the matchless beauty of its bay before Sicily began to modernize.

The fact that it is no longer produced will not stop a bar selling you a glass of sticky aromatic wine at a high price as "Siracusa".

Regaleali The brand name of a good-quality range of wines, perhaps the island's best brand, from Conte Tasca d'Almerita (*q.v.*). The "Riserva Rosso del Conte" is as good as any Sicilian red; the white contains Sauvignon Blanc.

Sambuca di Sicilia DOC. Red, white, and *rosato* wines. Provinces: Agrigento and Palermo. Villages: Sambuca and seven other communes. Grapes: (white) Ansonica 50–75%, Catarratto and/or Chardonnay 25–50%, others max. 15%; (red and *rosato*) Nero d'Avola 50–75%, Nerello and/or Sangiovese and/or Cabernet Sauvignon 25–50%, others max. 15%.

A small DOC in western Sicily, also allowing varietal wines from Chardonnay and Cabernet Sauvignon.

Santa Margherita di Belice DOC. Red and white wines. Provinces: Agrigento, Palermo, and Trapani. Villages: Santa Margherita and eight others. Grapes: (white) Ansonica, Grecanico, Catarratto, and others; (red) Sangiovese and/or Cabernet Sauvignon 50–80%, Nero d'Avola 20–50%, others max. 15%.

A small region just north of Menfi in western Sicily. Some varietal wines are also permitted.

Leading Sicily Producers

Marco de Bartoli ☆☆☆
Marsala, Trapani

Marco de Bartoli selects grapes for a limited production of "Vecchio Samperi", his unfortified expression of Marsala Vergine, in its drier versions a heady compound of walnuts and iodine. But he so upset the authorities that his wines were denied the DOC, and more recently he had to rebut trumped-up charges against him that nearly drove him out of business.

He stubbornly and bravely persists in producing his excellent wines, of which the most sumptuous is the almost treacley "Bukkuram" *passito* from Pantelleria. His new dry Catarratto table wine is also outstanding.

Cottanera ☆☆–☆☆☆
Castiglione di Sicilia, Catania. www.cottanera.it

Although the Cambria family's property extends over forty-three hectares of vineyards, production is minute, and the wines, all IGTs, are expensive and hard to find. The wines range from the fashionable varieties, such as Syrah and Merlot, to the less usual, such as Nerello and Mondeuse. All are barrique-aged.

Donnafugata ☆☆–☆☆☆
Marsala, Trapani. www.donnafugata.it

Owned by Giacomo Rallo and family, this is a sophisticated, modern estate with 230 hectares in production. Using the Contessa Entellina DOC, they produce a wide range of blends, a fine Ansonica white called "Vigna di Gabri", and rich, apricotty Passito di Pantelleria. The wines are consistently well-made at all levels.

Feudo Principi di Butera ☆☆☆
Butera, Caltanissetta. www.feudobutera.it

This ambitious 180-hectare estate was established in 1997 by the Veneto firm of Zonin. Firmly turning its back on local traditions, it has produced standard international varietal wines – Chardonnay, Merlot, Cabernet – but to a high standard.

Firriato ☆☆–☆☆☆
Pacepo, Trapani. www.firriato.it

Despite a production of some four million bottles, this relatively new property, founded in 1985, maintains high quality standards.

The wines are all IGT, and most of them blend Sicilian and international varieties. "Altavilla", for example, is a barrique-aged blend of Grillo and Chardonnay, "Santagostino" a spicy, blackberry-toned blend of Nero d'Avola and Syrah. Yet the wines are remarkably harmonious.

Florio ☆☆–☆☆☆
Marsala, Trapani. www.cantineflorio.com

Founded in 1883 by Vincenzo Florio, and now owned by Illva Saronno, a group that also owns Duca di Salaparuta (*q.v.*). Florio was known in his day as "the king of the historic Marsala"; today the company has no vines but still makes Marsala. After a lacklustre spell, the wines have improved considerably in quality.

There are two vintage-dated *vergine* wines, "Baglio Florio" and the unfortunately named "Terre Arse". In addition, Florio has rightly won great acclaim for its lush, fortified Pantelleria called "Morso di Luce".

Carlo Hauner ☆☆☆
Salina, Messina

After the death of the famous owner, Carlo Hauner, who made Malvasia delle Lipari known worldwide, his descendants continue to run the property. With its rich tones of apricot and orange, the *passito* remains a remarkable wine.

Morgante ☆☆–☆☆☆
Grotte, Agrigento. www.morgante-vini.it

With the aid of oenologist Riccardo Cotarella, the Morgante family have, since 1992, been producing excellent wines from Nero d'Avola, of which the most concentrated is "Don Antonio", with its aromas of red fruits and coffee.

Salvatore Murana ☆☆☆
Pantelleria, Trapani

In 1984, Murana left the local cooperative to produce his own wines, and now offers an admirable range of Moscato di Pantelleria. All the wines are excellent, but the best, and most costly, is usually the intense "Martingana", a *passito* with fabulously complex spice and orange zest flavours.

Carlo Pellegrino ☆☆–☆☆☆
Marsala, Trapani

Founded in 1880, Pellegrino remains a major producer of good-quality Marsala. The 400-hectare property also supports a second range of wines under the "Duca di Castelmonte" label.

The line-up is enormous, ranging from international-style Chardonnay and Cabernet to sumptuous sweet wines from Pantelleria.

Planeta ☆☆–☆☆☆☆
Menfi, Agrigento. www.planeta.it

Although founded as recently as 1995, the Planeta family

winery has already made a huge impact, especially outside Italy. Under oenologist Carlo Corino, the winery has opted for rich, fruit-driven wines, essentially New World in style, but none the worse for that. As well as powerful, oaky Chardonnay, Merlot, and Cabernet Sauvignon, there are also wines from southern Italian grapes such as Nero d'Avola and the white Fiano.

Perhaps the barriques are sometimes applied with a heavy hand, but these are impressive wines of a consistently high quality.

Rallo ☆☆
Marsala, Trapani
Rallo is an important producer of Marsala, of which the best is the *vergine* "Solera Riserva". The firm also produces a substantial quantity of table wines, from Nero d'Avola, and such varieties as Chardonnay and Merlot.

Rapitalà ☆☆
Palermo
This estate is part of the GIV group and run by the French Comte Hugues de la Gatinais. An earthquake destroyed the winery in 1968, and it was rebuilt in 1971.

Its best-known wines are the almondy Alcamo DOC and the very reliable "Rapitalà Rosso", a wine of balance and finesse.

Duca di Salaparuta (Corvo) ☆☆–☆☆☆
Casteldaccia, Palermo. www.vinicorvo.it
The property may have been founded in 1824 by the Duca di Salaparuta, but today it is owned by the Illva Saronno group, and boasts an ultra-modern winery.

For many decades, "Corvo" has been the most famous brand of Sicilian wine. Production is about 830,000 cases, prevalently in Corvo Bianco and Rosso and the white "Colomba Platino", from grapes bought in the hills of central and western Sicily.

Of notable interest are the red "Duca Enrico", an aged, pure Nero d'Avola, one of the most successful new reds of all the south, and "Bianco di Valguarnera" from Inzolia and aged in small oak barrels.

Settesoli ☆☆
Menfi, Agrigento
This cooperative was founded in 1958, and is currently one of Europe's largest wineries. Its standards were established by renowned oenologist Carlo Corino.

The Syrah and Nero d'Avola are among the best of the red wines and both offer outstanding value. Inycon is the cooperative's best-known brand.

Tasca d'Almerita ☆☆☆
Palermo. www.tascadalmerita.it
A family estate founded in 1830, and today owned by Conte Lucio Tasca. Three hundred and sixty hectares of estate vineyards produce some of Sicily's finest dry wines, including the excellent "Rosso del Conte" (mostly Nero d'Avola) and "Nozze d'Oro" (a white blend mostly from Inzolia).

If one eye is trained on tradition, the other is fixed on innovation. Cabernet Sauvignon here is one of the best of southern Italy; Chardonnay is also particularly good. The winery's principal brand name is "Regaleali".

Other Sicily Producers

Abraxas ☆☆
Pantelleria, Trapani
Just one wine: a rich, honeyed Passito di Pantelleria.

D'Ancona ☆☆–☆☆☆
Pantelleria, Trapani
A highly dependable producer of Moscato and Passito di Pantelleria.

Benanti ☆☆–☆☆☆
Viagrande, Catania. www.vincolabenanti.it
A recent property, founded in 1992, and winning a high reputation for its IGT wines from international varieties and from Nero d'Avola and Nerello.

Calatrasi ☆☆–☆☆☆
San Cipirello, Palermo. www.calatrasi.it
A large property with numerous labels including "Terre di Ginestra" and the more basic "D'Istinto". The whites blend Catarratto and Chardonnay, while both Nero d'Avola and the Bordeaux varieties play their part in the reds.

Cantina Colosi ☆☆
Messina. www.cantinacolosi.com
As well as sturdy red wines from Nero d'Avola, Colosi produce sweet wines: good examples of Malvasia delle Lipari and Passito di Pantelleria.

COS ☆☆
Vittoria, Ragusa. www.cosvittoria.it
The name sounds like that of a cooperative, but is in fact composed of the founder's initials. Very good, traditional wines from Cerasuolo di Vittoria DOC, and a very ripe Nero d'Avola IGT called "Scyri".

Elorina ☆
Noto, Siracusa
A small cooperative producing sound Nero d'Avola and Moscato di Noto.

Grasso ☆☆
Milazzo, Messina
A good range of wines from local varieties in northern Sicily, and an apricotty Passito di Pantelleria.

Palari ☆☆–☆☆☆
Contrada Barna, Messina
A boutique winery, founded in 1990, which rapidly established a high reputation for its two red blends, both Nerello-based: "Palari", a Faro DOC, and the less complex "Rosso del Soprano", an IGT.

Abbazia Santa Anastasia ☆☆–☆☆☆
Castelbuono, Palermo. www.abbaziasantanastasia.it
A small but ambitious property producing both traditional wines from Nero d'Avola and acclaimed Cabernet called "Litra", and a Sauvignon/Chardonnay blend called "Gemelli".

Spadafora ☆☆–☆☆☆
Palermo. www.spadafora.com
Sound Alcamo DOC and fine-grained Cabernet Sauvignon

IGT called "Schietto". More fleshy and perhaps less refined is the Cabernet/Merlot/Nero d'Avola blend called "Don Pietro".

Terre di Ginestra
See Calatrasi

Cantina Sociale di Trapani ☆☆–☆☆☆
Contrada Ospedaletto, Trapani

This good cooperative's major brand is "Forti Terre di Sicilia", focused on varietal wines from Chardonnay, Nero d'Avola, and Cabernet Sauvignon. Rich, full-bodied wines.

Cantina Valle dell' Acate ☆☆
Acate, Ragusa

This property, founded in 1981, upholds the tradition of Cerasuolo di Vittoria DOC, and also makes sound varietal wine from Frappato and a Chardonnay/Inzolia blend.

Barone di Villagrande ☆–☆☆
Milo, Catania

This is a dignified old estate which made Etna wine respectable when little else in Sicily was. It is keeping up with the times.

Sardinia

Sardinia is a strange, timeless island adrift in the centre of things and yet remote, without Sicily's innate drama, without Corsica's majestic mountains or sour social history.

The modern world comes and camps on the coastline of Sardinia, the jet-set on the Costa Smeralda, the wine world on the opposite coast at Alghero, where one of Italy's most sophisticated and original wineries takes advantage of ideal natural conditions to break all the rules.

Sardinia's original wines are heroically strong, designed, it seems, by and for the supermen who built the *nuraghe* round fortress houses of colossal stones that dot the island. The most characteristic wine of the island is Cannonau, an indigenous red (but now known to be the same as Grenache) with a minimum alcoholic degree of 13.5 and often much more.

The traditional practice is to prevent all the sugar from converting to alcohol: to balance strength with sweetness in something faintly reminiscent of port. The sweet red is actually best: as *liquoroso*, fortified with brandy, when it goes all the way to a port-style dessert wine. The "Anghelu Ruju" of Sella & Mosca is the version of Cannonau most likely to appeal to untrained tastes. Two other grapes, Girò and Monica, make similar sweet and heady reds.

Nor are old-style Sardinian white wines any easier to cope with. Nasco, Malvasia, and Vernaccia are three white grapes that all achieve formidable alcohol degrees, often tempered, like the reds, with unfermented sugar left to sweeten them.

Sweet Malvasia is a serious specialty that can reach very high quality. Vernaccia, on the other hand, is best fermented dry and aged in the same way as sherry. (It even develops the same *flor* yeast that allows it to oxidize very gently to a nicely nutty maturity.) Old, dry Vernaccia needs no apology.

The modern movement in Sardinia consists largely of cooperatives. It was led by the Sella & Mosca winery at Alghero, and given greater credibility by the legendary Giacomo Tachis, Antinori's winemaker, who pointed out that Sardinian wine has been used to boost Tuscan for millennia.

DOC & Other Wines

Alghero DOC. White, red, *rosato*. Province: Sassari. Villages: Alghero and seven other communes. Grapes: Torbato, Sauvignon, Chardonnay, Cabernets Sauvignon and Franc, Sangiovese, Cagnulari, and Vermentino.

This is a fairly new and unproven DOC, but Sella & Mosca (*q.v.*) are almost certain to prove its worth given time.

Arborea DOC. Red, white, and *rosato* wine. Area: many communes in Oristano province. Grapes: (red and *rosato*) Sangiovese min. 85%; (white) Trebbiano Romagnolo or Toscano min. 85%.

Recent DOC with very limited production; the white also possibly *frizzante* or *amabile*.

Campidano di Terralba DOC. Red wine. Provinces: Cagliari and Oristano. Villages: Terralba and twenty-two communes nearby. Grapes: Bovale min. 80%.

A lightish dry red, pleasantly soft, best young and cool. Small production.

Cannonau di Sardegna DOC. Red and *rosato* wine. Province: whole of Sardegna. Grapes: min. 90% Cannonau. Min. alc.: 12.5 degrees for Cannonau di Sardegna (one year old: three years for *riserva*); 15 degrees for *superiore naturale*; 18 degrees for *liquoroso*.

The complicated set of DOC rules means that much Cannonau is sold as *vino da tavola* (without the DOC qualification "di Sardegna"), and is none the worse for a little less alcohol. It is the basic Sardinian red grape, traditionally both strong and sweet – in fact, anything but refreshing, however rich (which it is) in flavour. The most famous old-style Cannonau is that of Oliena, near Nuoro in the eastern centre of the island, which can be called Nepente di Oliena.

Carignano del Sulcis DOC. Red and *rosato* wine. Province: Cagliari. Villages: eighteen communes on the southwest coast. Grapes: Carignano min. 85%.

Both reasonable red and a quite smooth and fruity *rosato* are made from the French Carignan in this area of hilly islets and lagoons, known to the ancients as Sulcis. The red will take one to two years' ageing.

Girò di Cagliari DOC. Red wine. Provinces: Cagliari and Oristano. Villages: 72 communes. Grape: Girò.

Girò, like Cannonau, is a traditional red grape of formidable sugar content, most often seen as a sweet wine – impressive rather than attractive when it is made dry. Very limited production.

Malvasia di Bosa DOC. White wine. Provinces: Nuoro and Oristano. Villages: seven communes near the west coast south of Alghero. Grape: Malvasia di Sardegna. Min. alc.: 14.5 degrees plus 0.5 degrees of sugar for *secco*; 13 degrees plus

2 degrees of sugar for *dolce naturale*; 15 degrees plus 2.5 degrees of sugar for *liquoroso dolce naturale*; 16.5 degrees plus 1 degrees of sugar for *liquoroso secco*.

The most highly prized of several Sardinian amber whites that can best be compared with sherry – at least in function. They go through a shorter and simpler ageing process but acquire smoothness and some depth of flavour, ending in a characteristically Italian, bitter-almond note. Dry versions, served chilled, are good apéritifs.

Malvasia di Cagliari DOC. White wine. Provinces: Cagliari and Oristano. Villages: same 72 communes as for Girò di Cagliari. Grape: Malvasia di Sardegna.

Similar wines to the last but from less exclusively southern vineyards.

Mandrolisai DOC. Red and *rosato* wine. Provinces: Nuoro and Oristano. Villages: Sorgono and six other communes. Grapes: Bovale Sardo min. 35%, Cannonau 20–35%, Monica 20–35%, max. 10% others.

A new DOC for less-than-full-power Cannonau and *rosato* from modernized cooperatives.

Monica di Cagliari DOC. Provinces: Cagliari and Oristano. Villages: same 72 communes as for Girò di Cagliari. Grape: Monica.

This wine is made either dry or as a *liquoroso*.

Monica di Sardegna DOC. Red wine. Province: the whole island. Grapes: Monica min. 85%.

A standard dry red *vino da tavola* of acceptable quality, perhaps more enjoyable rather cool. Also *frizzante*.

Moscato di Cagliari DOC. White wine. Provinces: Cagliari and Oristano. Villages: same 72 communes as for Girò di Cagliari. Grape: Moscato Bianco.

The Muscat grape has a stronger tradition in Sicily than Sardinia. What is made here is reasonable local drinking. The fortified *liquoroso* is the most convincing.

Moscato di Sardegna DOC. White wine. Province: the whole island. Grapes: min. 90% Moscato Bianco.

A DOC for low-strength, sweet Muscat *spumante* – in fact the Asti of Sardinia. It can use the geographical term "Tempo Pausania" or "Tempio e Gallura" if the grapes are vinified at Gallura in the province of Sassari in the northwest.

Moscato di Sorso-Sennori DOC. White wine. Province: Sassari. Villages: Sorso and Sennori, north of Sassari. Grape: Moscato Bianco.

A near-extinct local Muscat DOC for a strong, sweet white, reputed better than that of Cagliari in the south. Also made as *liquoroso*.

Nasco di Cagliari DOC. White wine. Provinces: Cagliari and Oristano. Villages: same 72 communes as for Girò di Cagliari. Grape: Nasco. Min. alc.: 14.5 degrees (2.5 degrees of sugar) for *dolce naturale*; 14.5 degrees (0.5 degrees of sugar) for *secco*; 14 degrees for *liquoroso*; 17.5 degrees (2.5 degrees of sugar) plus 2 degrees of sugar for *liquoroso dolce naturale secco*. Another rustic, island white more appreciated sweet and strong by the locals, but in its modernized, lighter, and drier versions by visitors. Best producer is Argiolas (*q.v.*).

Nuragus di Cagliari DOC. White wine. Provinces: Nuoro and Cagliari. Villages: all communes in Cagliari, nine in Nuoro. Grapes: Nuragus min. 85%.

A light and essentially neutral, dry white wine, the standard resort of those who have been overwhelmed by Sardinia's more characteristic products.

Sardegna Semidano DOC. White wine. Area: entire island. Grape: Semidano min. 85%.

Semidano is believed to be an indigenous variety, and the best quality comes from the sub-zone of Mogoro. Can be dry, *spumante*, or *passito*.

Torbato di Alghero The fruit of modern technology and intelligent market planning applied to a number of Sardinian white grapes by Sella & Mosca (*q.v.*). Not exactly a thrilling wine, but an extremely well-designed dry white of just memorable personality, and just what is needed with the island's fish. In fact, it is a bargain anywhere.

Vermentino di Gallura DOCG. White wine. Provinces: Sassari and Nuoro. Villages: nineteen communes in the north of the island. Grape: Vermentino.

By tradition the sort of strong, dry white with low acidity that does the opposite of quenching your thirst – epitomized by the 14 degrees *superiore*. Recently promoted to DOCG.

Vermentino di Sardegna DOC. White wine. Area: the whole island. Grapes: Vermentino min. 85%.

The wine is dry white and may also be *amabile* or *spumante*. Standards are improving but remain behind Vermentino di Gallura.

Vernaccia di Oristano DOC. White wine. Province: Oristano. Villages: sixteen communes in centre-west. Grape: Vernaccia di Oristano.

On first acquaintance I found this the most appealing of all Sardinian wines: a sort of natural first cousin to Spain's Montilla, or an unfortified sherry. The grapes are slightly shrivelled before fermentation, the natural strength slows down oxidation while subtle, distinct flavours develop – such as the characteristic Italian bitterness lingering in the finish.

Leading Sardinia Producers

Argiolas ☆☆☆
Serdiana, Cagliari. www.cantine-argiolas.com
Good Cannonau and Vermentino, but really outstanding IGT "Turriga": a barrique-aged blend of Cannonau, Carignano, Bovale, and Malvasia. They also make a peachy Nasco di Cagliari called "Angialis".

Capichera ☆☆–☆☆☆
Arzachena, Sassario
A source of outstanding but very expensive Vermentino. Although entitled to the DOCG Vermentino di Gallura, the Ragnedda brothers, who own the property, spurned its use and bottle their wines as IGT.

In some years a late-harvested but still dry version is also produced. Carignano forms the basis of their less impressive red wines.

Attilio Contini ☆☆–☆☆☆
Cabras, Oristano. www.vinicontini.it

Founded in 1898. The specialty here is Vernaccia di Oristano, including "Antico Gregori", an unusual and nutty version aged for many years in a *solera* system.

There is also a cherryish "Nieddera" produced from this little-seen grape variety.

Cantina Sociale di Santadi ☆☆☆
Santadi, Cagliari. www.cantinasantadi.it

This cooperative produces wines every bit as good as those from the best private estates. Very good Carignano del Sulcis, of which the best is the *riserva* "Rocca Rubbia".

Also an outstanding IGT "Terre Brune" from Carignan grapes, and whites from Nasco and Vermentino. A new development is the late-harvested Nasco called "Latinia".

Sella e Mosca ☆☆–☆☆☆
Alghero, Sassari. www.sellaemosca.com

Founded in 1899 by the Piedmontese Emilio Sella and Edgardo Mosca, now owned by the INVEST group. The long-term winemaker is Mario Consorte. This very large property produces 500,000 cases of consistently well-made wines, focusing resolutely on local varieties.

The principal lines are Vermentino, Cannonau, chocolatey Cabernet Sauvignon ("Marchese di Villamarina") using the Alghero DOC, dry and *passito* Torbato, and the celebrated and port-like "Anghelu Ruju", made from partly dried grapes aged for many years in casks.

Other Sardinia Producers

Giovanni Cherchi ☆☆
Usini, Sassari

Producers of fresh, floral Vermentino di Sardegna, and a rare red Cagnulari.

Cantine di Dolianova ☆
Dolianova, Cagliari

A very large co-op producing reliable and inexpensive wines from Vermentino, Cannonau, Monica, and other varieties.

Cantina Sociale di Dorgali ☆–☆☆
Dorgali, Nuoro. www.csdorgali.com

A small cooperative specializing in Cannonau di Sardegna, the variety that also dominates its IGT blends "Noriolo" and "Fùili".

Giuseppe Gabbas ☆☆
Nuoro

Small producer with thirteen hectares making good Cannonau di Sardegna "Lillovè", and very good IGT "Dule", a blend of mainly Cannonau, Cabernet, Dolcetto, and Sangiovese, aged in new barriques.

Cantina Sociale Gallura ☆☆
Tempio Pausania, Sassari. www.cantinagallura.it

A good source for Vermentino di Gallura and Moscato di Sardegna. An unusual specialty here is Nebbiolo.

Meloni ☆☆
Serlargius, Cagliari. www.meloni-vini.com

This firm produces a wide variety of grapes from 250 hectares of vineyards: Vermentino, Cannonau, Nasco, and Malvasia. Sound quality.

Il Nuraghe/Cantina di Mogoro ☆–☆☆
Mogoro, Oristano

Mogoro is the heartland for the Semidano grape, and Il Nuraghe produces the best-known versions. Good Cannonau and Vermentino, too.

Cantina Sardus Pater ☆
Sant' Antioco, Cagliari. www.cantinesarduspater.com

The Sant' Antioco cooperative has had a makeover, and is now named after its best-known wine: a blend of Carignano and Cabernet Sauvignon. Attractive Vermentino, too.

Cantina del Vermentino ☆
Monti, Sassario. www.vermentinomonti.it

There is a large output from this 450-hectare cooperative, including DOC Vermentino di Gallura, red "Abbaìa", and *rosato* "Thaòra".

Chacolí de
Guetaria

Bilbao ○

Chacolí de
Vizcaya

ASTURIAS

GALICIA

PAÍS VASCO

Rías Baixas Ribeira Bierzo

Ribeiro Sacra

Valdeorras

Monterrei

Navarra

La Rioja

Ampurdán
Costa Brava

Somontano

Costers
del Segre

Pla de Bages

Cigales

Ribera del
Duero

Campo de
Borja

Conca de Barberá

Alella

Toro

Cariñena

CATALUNYA

Barcelona ○

Rueda

Calatayud

Priorato

Penedès

CASTILLA Y LEON

ARAGÓN

Terra
Alta

Tarragona

Madrid ○

Mondéjar

Méntrida

Vinos de
Madrid

VALENCIA

CASTILLA-LA MANCHA

Utiel-
Requena

Ribera del
Guadiana

La Mancha

Valencia ○

Binissalem

Manchuela

Palma ○

Pla I
Llevant

EXTREMADURA

Valdepeñas

Almansa

Valencia

Mallorca

Yecla

Jumilla

Alicante

Murcia ○

Bullas

Conado
de
Huelva

Sevilla ○

Montilla-
Moriles

ANDALUCÍA

Jerez-Xérès-Sherry
Manzanilla-Sanlúcar
de Barrameda

Málaga **Málaga**

○ **Gibraltar**

Spain

Throughout the last decade and more, viticultural Spain has continued to reinvent itself and redefine what it is trying to do in the world outside. Old attitudes have been changing, new ideas have been accepted – sometimes, admittedly, grudgingly – but the end result is that Spain produces more better-quality wines, with more regional credibility, even than it did five years ago. And it has been doing so without depending excessively on international grape varieties.

Part of the reason for this has been the re-establishment of real regional feelings of identity. The Franco years put Spanish winemaking into something of a state-controlled strait-jacket, from which only the most well-established – notably Rioja and sherry – managed to manifest their individuality. Twenty years after the new constitution restored some level of self-government to the regions, Catalonia, the Basque Country, and Galicia once again display their nationalist aspirations, in the bottle as well as in the ballot-box, and other regions are rediscovering a heritage which had been allowed to wither under the conformity and lack of investment which characterized the Franco era.

The last edition of this book listed fifty-one areas of Spain as having the *Denominación de Origen* (DO). Today there are fifty-nine regions with that status (and others queuing for promotion), and each of them claims its own individuality and heritage, fuelled by a reinvigorated local pride and the pragmatic acceptance that the market is, after all, king, and producers who want to be in it have got to make the effort to win it. There are two regions that qualify for the top rank of *DO Calificada* (DOCa): Rioja and Priorato.

This is not to say that all the DO zones produce wines of export quality or, indeed, that attitudes everywhere are as enlightened as they have been at the cutting edge of the Spanish wine business. Yet the fact remains that even the most stick-in-the-mud growers and *bodegueros* have noticed that their more enterprising peers are making something better, more easily saleable and, (most important of all), for a higher price than they themselves are getting. The Instituto Nacional de *Denominación de Origen* (INDO) in Madrid has always had a programme of education and encouragement for regions that genuinely want to improve their wine... But all the lecturing and cajoling in the world, it seems, is worth less than a sight of your neighbour's balance sheet.

Spain is Europe's second-biggest country (after France) and, with over 1.1 million hectares under vine, Europe's biggest vineyard. However, the hotter climate brings the need for sparser planting patterns and lower yields, so that France and Italy still make far more wine. Spain's viticultural map is dominated by the two great rivers, the Ebro and the Duero, both of which find their source in the mountainous Cordillera Cantábrica, which divides the cool, wet northwest from the continental interior. The Ebro runs southeast into the Mediterranean in the province of Tarragona, while the Duero flows southwest, through Portugal (where it is known as the Douro) and into the Atlantic at Oporto. These two rivers, and the mountain range in which they find their origins, are responsible for most of the microclimates of northern Spain.

South of Madrid, the sun is king; wider plantations of hardier grape varieties are the norm, and water, when it comes, is gratefully received by the spongy subsoils of the most successful wine-producing districts. The principal rivers in south-central Spain are the Guadiana, which waters the great central plains of La Mancha (with part of its course actually underground) and flows west then south into the Gulf of Cádiz, having formed the boundary between Spain and Portugal for its final stretch; the Tajo (or Tagus), which flows from the plateaux of Madrid west through Toledo and Extremadura into Portugal (where it is known as the Tejo) and thence into the Atlantic at Lisbon; the Júcar, which flows south and east from the mountains of Guadalajara through the winelands of the Levante, into the Mediterranean in the province of Valencia; and the Guadalquivír, which runs southwest from the central Meseta to skirt the sherry country. These rivers are nearly all the irrigation seen by most of the vineyards in the south of the country.

Climatic conditions are diverse. Most regions have a Continental climate: cold winters and baking summers. But elevation and maritime influence moderate some regions. This climatic variation, and the range of indigenous grape varieties (many now being re-discovered after years of neglect) within each region, help explain how a single country can produce wines that range from racy Albariño and salt-licked manzanilla to mighty reds from Ribera del Duero and Priorato.

The late 1990s saw regions previously dismissed as mediocre emerging as potentially splendid, now that the best growers are no longer content to make dreary wines. Cigales, Priorato, and Toro are three names that spring to mind. The well-established regions, such as Rioja, are not resting on their laurels. They have listened to the complaints of their critics and the increasing indifference of the international market, and are taking measures to improve quality. Jerez has kept its nerve and continues to produce glorious fortified wines, from the raciest manzanilla to the most profound oloroso.

Spanish Wine Regions

For all the inevitable complications of the system of *Denominación de Origen*, painstakingly worked out by the Spanish authorities over many years (and of which they can be proud), there is still a natural geographical logic to the different styles of wine of Spain. The entire country, mainland and offshore islands, divides into eight major wine-producing regions, each of which shares a common heritage, gastronomic culture, and climate. It is these factors, of course, that determine the way wine has evolved over the years anywhere in the Old World of wine.

The Northwest

This is the slice of Spain in the top left-hand corner, above Portugal, and along the coast of the Bay of Biscay towards France. Its southern border is the Cordillera Cantábrica, which shelters the rest of Spain from the excesses of Atlantic weather. The climate is comparatively cool and wet, the landscape is lush and green, and the original culture is non-Spanish. Celtic influences dominate in Galicia; Asturias was and is a separate principality under the Spanish Crown (exactly as is Wales in the United Kingdom); and the Basque Country has one of the oldest pre-Christian cultures in Europe. Add to this the local gastronomic culture – fish, fish, and more fish – and it is not surprising that the wines produced here have evolved to be mainly light, fresh, crisp, dry, and predominantly white. The DOs are as follows.

Region	DO	Hectares
Galicia:	Monterrei	550
	Rías Baixas	2,292
	Ribeira Sacra	1,550
	Ribeiro	3,000
	Valdeorras	1,300
Basque Country (north):		
	Chacolí de Guetaria	123
	Chacolí de Vizcaya	80

The Upper Ebro

In the shelter of the Cordillera Cantábrica, the climate is more Continental, with only the very highest vineyards (Rioja Alavesa, Navarra Estella) gaining some benefit from the influences of the Bay of Biscay. Politically, the area is sandwiched between the Spanish heartland of Castile-León and the resolutely non-Spanish region of Catalonia.

In the fifteenth and sixteenth centuries, the royal house switched capitals throughout the region as Castilian, Catalan, and Aragonés monarchs married each other and merged their kingdoms, so there were always rich and powerful people with money available for good-quality wine. The main gastronomic influence here is meat – whether from herds and flocks or running wild in the forests – so it is no surprise that this is predominantly red wine country.

The final quality "burnish" was provided towards the end of the last century when phylloxera devastated the French vineyards, and a vast but discerning export market opened up for this, the region closest to the French border. The DOs are as follows:

Region	DO	Hectares
La Rioja:	Rioja DOCa	59,000
Navarra:	Navarra	14,800
Aragón:	Calatayud	7,300
	Campo de Borja	6,270
	Cariñena	17,135
	Somontano	2,914

The Duero Valley

With one exception, this area has most of the attributes of the Upper Ebro: a Continental climate – although higher and rather cooler here – abundant food on the hoof, in the fields and forests, and a population of rich, influential people from Valladolid and Zamora, where royal courts once sat, to Salamanca, site of Spain's oldest university. So we may expect quality red wines to have been supplied to princes, bishops, and professors. The difference in style between the Duero and the Upper Ebro is export influence. In the Upper Ebro they made wine to please the French market, as well as themselves; in the Duero they made wine to please themselves. The result, traditionally, was wines with more fruit and more alcohol, and it is still apparent today. While Rioja was still devoted to long ageing in American oak, the Duero was shipping in new French barriques. The DOs are as follows:

Region	DO	Hectares
Castile-León:	Bierzo	3,700
	Cigales	2,533
	Ribera del Duero	15,265
	Rueda	6,600
	Toro	3,575

Catalonia & the Balearics

The culture here has always been a fiercely independent one. Catalonia (along with the Balearic Islands and other territories) was a Mediterranean power in the Middle Ages and, in its thinking, traditionally looks to sea rather than inland towards Madrid.

The style of cooking here is strongly Mediterranean in character – indeed, very similar to the neighbouring French region of Roussillon. Gastronomy leans heavily in favour of fish, of course; consequently, the wines that evolved naturally in the region were largely simple whites and *rosados* to suit the cookery.

The independent spirit of the region, however, encouraged early experimentation with non-Spanish grape varieties, and this continues today, as Catalonia is as strong on new-wave varietal wines as on its traditional styles. Most cava – Spain's best sparkling wine – is also produced here. The DOs are as follows:

Region	DO	Hectares
Catalonia:	Alella	330
	Ampurdán-Costa Brava	2,475
	Conca de Barberà	6,000
	Costers del Segre	4,165
	Montsant	1,700
	Penedès	27,540
	Pla de Bages	500
	Priorato	1,400
	Tarragona	11,000
	Terra Alta	9,000
	Cava	32,000
Balearics:		
	Binissalem (Mallorca)	300
	Plà i Llevant (Mallorca)	210

The Levante

The export culture evident in Catalonia is even better developed in this region. The hot, Mediterranean-maritime climate is ideal for the production of everyday wine. Local consumption of fish dishes (the paella was invented here) has resulted in the evoluion of a plentiful supply of adequate uncomplicated whites and *rosados*, but the region's main claim to fame is its resolutely "out-to-sea" vision.

Once it had aquired modern technology, the Levante has become the powerhouse of Spanish exports of low-cost wines. Valencia is the country's biggest wine port, from which wines are exported in road-, rail-, and sea-tankers as well as in bottle and cask, all over the world. The DOs are as follows:

Region	DO	Hectares
Valencia:	Alicante	13,820
	Utiel-Requena	41,000
	Valencia	17,500
Murcia:	Bullas	2,300
	Jumilla	41,280
	Yecla	4,200

The Meseta

The winemaking culture here is based on survival. There was no market for the wines of Spain's great central plateau until Madrid was founded in 1561. There was no chance of shipping them to the Levantine coast because in the south, the (nominally teetotal) Moors ruled until 1492.

Although food was abundant, the methods of cooking it were plain, and the climate is so searingly hot in the summer and freezing in the winter that only the very hardiest of vines could survive. As a result of these factors, the wine was poor and rustic and made in the cheapest available material (earthenware jars) because there was only the local market to satisfy.

The main contact with the outside world was the royal road from Madrid to Granada. One of the stopping-off places for official retinues was the town of Valdepeñas, and this ready market for better-quality wines still shows today. This isolation and the resulting low land prices led to massive redevelopment in the 1970s and '80s, with the result that many of today's everyday wines will have a La Mancha DO.

Until recently, the relatively new Mondéjar DO was devoted to bulk wines, but now a handful of wineries are beginning to suggest the region's potential. The DOs are as follows:

Region	DO	Hectares
Madrid:	Vinos de Madrid	11,760
Castilla-La Mancha:		
	Almansa	7,600
	La Mancha	193,130
	Méntrida	13,000
	Mondéjar	3,000
	Ribera del Guadiana	3,390
	Valdepeñas	29,100

Andalucía

This is the crucible of winemaking for Spain and a good deal of Western Europe. The Greeks and other winemakers from the eastern Mediterranean settled here some 3,000 years ago, and the wines they made were in the Levantine or Greek tradition: products of a fiercely hot climate with ameliorating influences around the coast in order to meet the demands of burgeoning export markets throughout the Mediterranean – especially during the Roman Empire – and the western European coast.

The Greek taste was for powerful, sweet wines with plenty of alcohol. Even so many years later, it is possible to see the legacy of the Greeks in the fortified wines of Andalucía. By the time of Shakespeare, the wines of southern Spain,

known then as "sack" after the Spanish word *saca*, meaning "withdrawal" (*i.e.* from the butt), were famous. Today, the wines of this area find their being in one of the world's greatest wines – sherry. The DOs are as follows:

Region	DO	Hectares
Andalucía:		
	Condado de Huelva	5,880
	Jerez/Xérès/Sherry	10,500
	Málaga	1,030
	Montilla-Moriles	10,000

The Canary Islands

The Canary Islands are in some ways a snapshot of what Spanish wine used to be like 500 years ago, when they were rediscovered and claimed for the Spanish crown. Varieties are grown here which died out on the peninsula centuries ago; production is small, and the "Canary-Sack" of Shakespearean fame is still made. Most of the production, however, evolved for local consumption and has developed to supply the tourist trade.

Those seriously ambitious bodegas are hampered by the sheer cost of shipping their wines to the mainland, let alone the markets of northern Europe. The DOs are as follows:

Region	DO	Hectares
Canarias:	Abona (Tenerife)	1,050
	El Hierro	250
	Lanzarote	3,270
	La Palma	880
	El Monte	450
	Tacoronte-Acentejo	1,715
	Valle de Güímar	530
	Valle de la Orotava	430
	Ycoden-Daute-Isora	875

Northwest Spain

Galicia

Galicia and the north coastal vineyards of the Bay of Biscay enjoy a wetter, cooler climate than the rest of Spain, and the wines are commensurately lighter and fresher. White wines predominate, although reds and *rosados* are widely made. In the ongoing search for the definitive white wine of Spain, this area is one of the leading contenders.

Monterrei

This is a very small region of white wines from the Godello and Doña Blanca grapes. Quality is potentially good, but with only a handful of bodegas affiliated to the *consejo regulador* it is difficult to give an overview. However, Bodegas Ladairo is worth watching.

Rías Baixas

In the province of Pontevedra on the Atlantic coast between Santiago and the Portuguese border. The most excellent wines are whites made from the Albariño grape, but planting on steep slopes and in small parcels means they lack economy of scale and are expensive. Most whites are vinified in tanks, but some producers are seeking greater complexity by putting the wine through malolactic fermentation and, in some cases, maturation in small oak barrels.

Ribeira Sacra

A beautiful area at the confluence of two rivers, the Sil and the Miño. Much of the winemaking is on a small and simple scale, but some winemakers have invested in new technology. The wines need a little more work, but there is some excellent Albariño and Godello. Although most producers make red wine from a grape called the Mencía, very few do it well. One that does is Adegas Moure.

Ribeiro

An old-established area in the province of Orense, lying just east of Rías Baixas. The vineyards are concentrated in the valleys of the Miño, Avía, and Arnoya rivers. Ribeiro is famous for its light, fruity, white wines. New development has provided it with some stars – mainly made from the Albariño, but also from the more widely planted (and much lower-priced) Treixadura. Caiño is the most important red variety. Overall, good-value whites that can be considered the poor-man's Rías Baixas.

Valdeorras

Both crisp, fresh whites and light reds are made: the whites from the excellent Godello variety, and the reds from the potentially good but usually under-achieving Mencía grape.

Basque Country

Chacolí de Guetaria (*Getariako Txakolina*) and Chacolí de Vizcaya (*Bizkaiko Txakolina*) are the two indigenous wines of the Basque Country. Most is white, made from the local Ondarribi Zuri grape. At its best it is a very crisp, grapey, thirst-quenching wine, although the quantity is so small that exports are virtually non-existent.

Leading Northwest Spain Producers

Bodegas Chaves ☆
Barrantes, Pontevedra
A small, family run bodega offering typically sharp and fizzy Albariños under the brand name of "Castel de Fornos".

Fillaboa ☆☆–☆☆☆
El Condado. www.fillaboa.es
A pioneer of barrel-fermentation for Albariño, as well as of keeping the wine in prolonged contact with the lees. Very consistent quality. In 2000, the winery introduced a new prestige bottling called "Selección de Familia".

Galegas ☆☆–☆☆☆
Salvatierra de Miño, Pontevedra
This relatively new winery, founded in 1995, specializes in

different styles of Albariño, including the barrel-aged "Veigadares" and "Gran Veigadares". The floral, citric "Gran Veigadares", made from rigorously selected grapes, has been hailed as one of Spain's very finest white wines.

Godeval ☆☆
O Barco. www.godeval.com
A small property located in the medieval priory of Xagoaza, and producing outstanding Godello white.

Lagar de Fornelos ☆☆
O Rosal
A bodega near the Portuguese border, making crisp, appley-tasting wine (labelled "Lagar de Cervera") from seventy-two hectares of their own Albariño vines. In 1988, the bodega was bought by Bodegas La Rioja Alta (*q.v.*), which has invested large amounts of money.

Martín Códax ☆
Cambados. www.martincodax.com
Eighty-five growers cultivating 190 hectares of vines send their Albariño grapes to an up-to-date, stainless steel winery north of Vigo. Good, clean, and fragrant dry wines are bottled under the "Martín Códax" label.

Gerardo Méndez Lázaro ☆☆–☆☆☆
Meaño, Pontevedra
A boutique winery producing outstanding Albariño, persistent in flavour, from extremely old vines.

Cooperativa Jesús Nazareno ☆
O Barco, Ourense
A substantial cooperative farming 2,000 hectares and bottling very adequate still red and white (DO Valdeorras) with the name "O Barco" ("The Boat"). Its top wine is a pure Mencía, called "Menciño" and aged in barriques.

Palacio de Fefiñanes ☆☆–☆☆☆
Fefiñanes, Pontevedra
The aristocrat of Galician wine, issuing from the small, modern bodega in the palace of Fefiñanes, near Cambados, owned by the Marqués de Figueroa. It is 100% Albariño, aged for up to six years (for *reservas*) in oak. It bears no resemblance to *vinho verde*, except in its remarkable freshness.

Rebolledo ☆–☆☆
A Rúa, Ourense
A Valdeorras property producing a pure Mencía red, and a successful Cabernet/Merlot, with upfront fruit that suggests it is best enjoyed young.

Cooperativa del Ribeiro ☆
Ribadavia
The biggest cooperative in Galicia, with 800 members cultivating 670 hectares, and very modern facilities. Its best white is crisp, clean, and faintly fragrant, only slightly *pétillant*, like a Portuguese *vinho verde*. The red "Alén de Istoria" is spicy, sharp, and an acquired taste.

Emilio Rojo ☆–☆☆
Arnoia, Ourense
A tiny Ribeiro property, which has rescued the almost extinct Lado variety, which Rojo uses in the blend of his one wine.

Santiago Ruiz ☆☆–☆☆☆
O Rosal

Small producer of high-quality white wine, commanding a high price. Unusual blend of Albariño, Loureira, and Treixadura grapes makes an especially aromatic, floral, dry white.

Salnesur ☆–☆☆
Cambados, Pontevedra. www.salnesur.es

A cooperative with 360 members cultivating 165 hectares of mostly Albariño, which they sell under the name of "Condes de Albarei".

Terras Gaudas ☆–☆☆
O Rosal. www.terrasgaudas.com

Since 1990, this estate has been built up into a major player in Rías Baixas, producing a pure Albariño, and a more complex blend of this grape with Caiño and Loureira.

Valderroa ☆–☆☆
Vilamartín de Valdeorras. www.valderroa.com

An organic estate producing grassy red Mencía, and a pure Godello called "Valdesil".

The Upper Ebro

This is the region of Spain that produces most (though not all) of the fine red wines for which the country is famous. Understandably, it tends to be dominated by Rioja, but recent developments in Navarra and, particularly, the Somontano region of Aragón, have brought the whole region forcefully to the forefront of quality winemaking in Spain.

La Rioja

As a wine region, Rioja claims a longer history than Bordeaux. Some French historians believe that the Romans may even have found the ancestor of the Cabernet in this part of Spain. Certainly the Romans followed the River Ebro up from the Mediterranean, much as they followed the Rhône, as a corridor of the climate and conditions they were accustomed to into a colder and more hostile land. High in the headwaters of the Ebro, over 600 metres up (1,950 feet), round its little tributary Río Oja, they found ideal conditions for wine of good quality – and possibly even the necessary grapes.

The post-classical history of Rioja was similar to that of all the Roman wine regions. Rapid decline (accelerated in Spain by the Moorish invasion), the dominance of the Church, a slow renaissance in the sixteenth century, but no real changes until the eighteenth or early nineteenth centuries. Then it was the influence of Bordeaux that reached Rioja, the new idea of barrel-ageing the best wines: as opposed to keeping them in animal hides. It was first tried in 1787, but was overruled by Luddite reaction, and finally introduced by reforming aristocratic landowners – in much the same way and at the same time as Chianti was "invented" by the Barone Ricasoli.

The first commercial bodegas of the modern age of Rioja were founded in the 1860s, by the Marqués de Riscal and the Marqués de Murrieta, with the Bordeaux château system very much in mind. Both used (and still use) grapes from their immediate districts. They sold their wine in bottle, and spread the reputation of the region at a most opportune moment. Phylloxera was invading Bordeaux, and French capital and technology were looking for a new region to develop. Before the end of the century, a dozen much bigger new bodegas had been built, drawing on grapes from a much wider area; the three regions of Rioja all contributed to their blends.

The railhead at Haro formed the nucleus for this boom, and the bodegas round it remain both physically and spiritually the embodiment of late Victorian technology. The cluster of huge, rather raffish buildings almost recalls Epernay, the Champagne capital, which grew during the same lush decades.

Phylloxera reached Rioja in the early years of the twentieth century. The disruption, followed by World War I, then by the Spanish Civil War, prevented the bodegas from capitalizing on the foreign markets they had successfully opened, despite the fact that in 1926 Rioja became the first wine region of Spain to set up a *consejo regulador* to supervise its affairs. During this period, the region was making and maturing some superlative vintages (examples can still be found occasionally). Yet Rioja remained the staple of connoisseurs only in Spain and Latin America until the international wine boom of the 1970s.

That decade saw the founding of a new wave of bodegas, a flurry of takeovers, and a vast increase in planting and production. It also saw modifications in winemaking techniques, which have added new styles to the already wide range produced.

Rioja is in fact three regions, with a total vineyard area of more than 59,000 hectares, following the valley of the Ebro from the Conchas de Haro, the rocky gorge where it bursts through the Sierra Cantábrica, to its much wider valley at Alfaro, ninety-five kilometres (sixty miles) east and nearly 300 metres (975 feet) lower in altitude.

The highest region, La Rioja Alta, has the city of Logroño as its capital, although the much smaller Haro is its vinous heart. Cenicero, Fuenmayor, and Navarrete are the other towns with bodegas. There are 24,450 hectares of vineyards. The soils are a mixture of chalky clay, iron-rich clay, and alluvial silt. The climate is cool here, and the rainfall relatively high. The minimum required strength for Rioja Alta wine is only ten degrees.

Rioja Alta wines have the highest acidity, but also the finest flavour and structure, finesse, and "grip" that sometimes allows them to age almost indefinitely.

The Rioja Alavesa, north of the Ebro in the Basque province of Alava, has more southern slopes and a more consistently clay soil. Its 12,050 hectares are largely Tempranillo, which here gives particularly fragrant, smooth, almost lush light wine, tending to be pale and quick-maturing. The minimum strength is eleven to 11.5 degrees. A dozen bodegas are based in four villages: Labastida, Elciego, Laguardia, and Oyón.

The Rioja Baja ("Lower Rioja"), with 20,900 hectares, has much the warmest and driest climate. Its soil is silt and iron-rich clay, its principal grape the Garnacha Tinta, and its wine stronger, broader and less fine, with a required minimum strength of twelve to 12.5 degrees. There are only six bodegas for ageing in the region, but nearly all Rioja bodegas buy some of their wine here, and several have been planting the finer grapes in the highest parts of the region.

It is probably true to say that most red Riojas are blends of wines from all three regions, although the old-established bodegas draw most heavily on the areas in which they were founded, and a few in Rioja Alavesa make a particular point of the regional style of their wines.

Rioja DOCa

From the 1991 vintage, Rioja was elevated to a new "super-category" called *Denominación de Origen Calificada*, which translates as "Qualified Denomination of Origin". The word "qualified" in this context means "quality-fied" rather than its normal English interpretation of "with reservations", and is an attempt to offer an extra guarantee to the customer, exactly like the DOCG in Italy. And, exactly like the DOCG in Italy, its introduction was marked by anger, recriminations, argument, opprobrium, and dismissal by the pundits as nothing more than a PR exercise. Certainly, it could have been done better, it could have been thought through more carefully, it could have changed the way Rioja is marketed... But it didn't. The main consequence that we see in the outside world is that bulk sales have been stopped, and all Rioja is now bottled in the region. The result, at least in the short-term, seems to have been that there is a lot less poor-quality wine appearing under the Rioja label. For many of us, that's good enough for a start.

Long ageing in Bordeaux-type barrels is the hallmark of traditional Rioja. It gives the wines, whether red or white, an easily recognized fragrance and flavour related to vanilla. The best wines, with a concentrated flavour of ripe fruit, can support a surprising degree of this oaky overlay. Lesser wines become exhausted by it, losing their fruity sweetness and becoming dry and monotone. Spanish taste leans to emphasis on oak; international taste inclines to less oak-ageing for reds, and little or none for whites. Many bodegas have therefore modified their old practice of bottling the wine at what they consider full maturity. By replacing time in barrel with time in bottle, they reduce the impact of the oak in favour of the more subtle bouquet of bottle-age.

Red wines make up three-quarters of the total production of the region. The range offered by a typical Rioja bodega includes some or all of the following:

Vinos Blancos

White wines, normally very dry, and gratifyingly low in alcohol (ten to eleven degrees). Principally made of the Viura grape (alias Macabeo), with or without Malvasía and/or Garnacha Blanca. They have good acidity and resist oxidation well. Made in the old way they had little grape aroma, but often very satisfying structure and balance.

Better whites were formerly all aged in old oak barrels for between about three and anything up to twelve years – the best longest. Outstanding examples of these *reservas* remain pale lemon-yellow and keep an astonishing freshness, roundness, and vigour beneath a great canopy of oaky fragrance. They can be compared with the best old vintages of white Graves. Sadly, this highly individual, if admittedly very old-fashioned, style seems to be losing ground to the vogue for fresh, crisp, white wines.

Many bodegas now make all or some of their whites by long, slow fermentation followed by almost immediate bottling, the object being to capture primary grape aromas in all their freshness. The Viura makes delicious wine in this style, possibly benefiting from some bottle-age. Most bodegas also make a compromise, semi-modern white, cold-fermented, and briefly oak-aged.

Sweet white Riojas are rarely a success. Noble rot is very rare in the dry, upland atmosphere; overripe grapes are simply half-raisined. But exceptional vintages have produced beautiful, delicate, and aromatic sweet wines of apparently limitless lasting power.

Vinos Rosados

Rosé wines, made in the customary way, normally dry and pale and not oak-aged.

Vinos Tintos

Many bodegas now call all their red wines *tinto*. The former custom was to divide them into *clarete*, light-coloured red wine of fairly low strength (ten to 11.5%) bottled in Bordeaux bottles; and *tinto* (sometimes called *Borgoña*) sold in burgundy bottles. *Tinto* in this sense is much darker, more fruity, fuller in body, and higher in alcohol. Both are made of a mixture of Tempranillo, the dominant red grape, with the luscious and aromatic Graciano, and the alcoholic Garnacha Tinta (the Rhône Grenache), often with some Mazuelo (or Cariñena), a cousin of the Carignan of the Midi. Cabernet Sauvignon is accepted as an "experimental" variety, but is occasionally included. Some bodegas make their wine from pure Tempranillo, but most blend. A little white Viura is also sometimes used in *claretes*. Both types are equally made up to the level of *reservas* or *gran reservas*, but Rioja's ultimate glories tend to be of the *tinto* type, which resists barrel-ageing better without growing thin and (although less fragrant) can grow marvellously velvety in the bottle.

All wines can be sold either as *joven* ("young"), which means "without oak ageing", or *con crianza*. A *vino de crianza* from Rioja is bottled at either three or four years old ("3 *años*" or "4 *años*"), of which at least one year must be in *barricas*, or 225-litre barrels. The rest will usually be in bigger oak containers. Wines of modest, medium, and good quality are all handled like this. *Reservas* are specially selected wines at least three years old, of which one year was in *barricas*. Now, however, any of the statutory period can be substituted by twice as long in bottle. White *reservas* have a minimum of six months in oak.

Gran reservas are wines of at least five years old, with at least two years in *barricas*, or twice as long in bottle. These requirements for ageing are much less than they were only a few years ago. The reason given is a change in customers' tastes, although commercial necessity points in the same direction. Reputable bodegas will, of course, only select wines of fine quality to mature as *reservas*, and top quality as *gran reservas* – although this is only implied, not required, by the regulations.

The excellent 1994 and 1995 vintages brought a revival of interest in this famous but often underperforming region. While the grand bodegas continued on their majestic way, and some of them continued to produce large volumes of well-made but rather washed-out wines, smaller, more innovative growers moved towards a more international style, using French rather than American oak, and only small barrels. Greater care was taken with fruit quality, too, with wines made from low-yielding vineyards and riper grapes. Traditionalists may worry that these sumptuous, and often high-priced, new wines lack Rioja *typicité*, but at present there is sufficient variety of style within the region to please everybody.

Leading Rioja Producers

AGE Bodegas Unidas ☆☆
Fuenmayor
A large, modern bodega, but one with a long history. It was established in 1967 with the joining of bodegas Romeral and Las Veras, and is now owned by Allied-Domecq. Though they own vineyards, most grapes have to be bought in. Best of the reds are the traditional *reservas*, "Marqués del Romeral", "Fuentemayor", and "Siglo Saco", sold in a sacking wrapper. White wines are all in the new fruity style and bottled young,

Finca Allende ☆☆☆
Briones. www.finca-allende.com
A small property run by Miguel Angel de Gregorio, who is fanatical about vineyard quality. Both Viura and Malvasía are used for the barrique-aged white. The highly aromatic, red-fruit-scented "Calvario" comes from a single vineyard, and "Aurus" is a top blend, aged, perhaps excessively, for two years in barriques. Production is 20,000 cases, and prices are high.

Artadi/Cosecheros Alaveses ☆☆☆
Laguardia, Alava. www.artadi.com
Founded in 1985, this winery has grown rapidly. Although it produces around one million bottles per year, quality is exceptional. All the wines are pure Tempranillo, and the best of them are aged in new barriques. They are single-vineyard wines or blends from very old vines, and have the structure to absorb the oakiness. The wines are first-rate, but their toasty, chocolatey tones may seem atypical to many Rioja admirers. Demand is strong, and prices very high.

Berberana ☆–☆☆
Cenicero. www.arcobu.com/berberana
Back in private hands (Arco Bodegas Unidas) after a period with Rumasa and then nationalization. The huge bodega in Cenicero (with no fewer than 34,000 barrels) dates from 1970. Grapes are from their own 130-hectare vineyard in Rioja Alta, though some are still bought in. There are two export labels: "Carta de Oro", which has 20% Garnacha in the blend, and "Viña Alarde", made in styles from *crianza* to rich, velvety *gran reservas*. The new Viura white is aged for six months in new American oak.

Bilbainas ☆–☆☆☆
Haro. www.grupocodorniu.com
The bodega was founded in 1901, and is now owned by the cava company, Codorníu. Seventy per cent of their grapes are grown in the company's own 260 hectares of vineyards in Haro (Rioja Alta) and Elciego, Leza, and Laguardia in Alavesa. They sell over 200,000 cases of wine a year. Their aim is a wide choice of wines rather than a strong house style, but all the wines are conservative: rather austere by modern standards. "Viña Zaco" is a high-quality *clarete*, while "Viña Pomal" is its more full-bodied *tinto* complement. "Pomal" *reservas* are the

biggest and longest-lived wines, but Codorníu has introduced a new barrique-aged range called "La Vicalanda".

Marqués de Cáceres ☆–☆☆
Unión Viti-Vinicola, Cenicero
Founded in 1970 by Enrique Forner (owner, with his brother, of Château de Camensac in Bordeaux), planned with the help of Professor Emile Peynaud, and now one of the most modern of wineries. Grapes come from dozens of local growers, including the Cenicero cooperative. Red wines spend fifteen to eighteen months in wood and fifteen to eighteen months in bottle (though the *reserva* and *gran reserva* spend up to thirty-six months in barrel and may be kept for ten years in bottle). They emerge less oaky than traditional Rioja, but well-balanced and fruity. The white, marketed young and without barrel-ageing, was the first of the new-style whites and, with its fruit and freshness, is still one of the best. Like many other Rioja wineries, Marqués de Cáceres has introduced a flagship wine called "Gaudium": a rich, tannic blend of Garnacha, Graciano, and Tempranillo.

Campo Viejo ☆–☆☆
Logroño
One of the largest bodegas, owned by Allied-Domecq. About 50% of production is from wine bought from cooperatives and 25% is from grapes bought in for vinification; 25% comes from its own vineyard of 500 hectares. "Campo Viejo" is consistently good value among the less ethereal red Riojas. "Marqués de Villamagna" is the bodega's top *gran reserva*, and there is a rich, barrel-fermented white called "Alcorta".

Viñedos del Contino ☆☆–☆☆☆
Laguardia, Alava. www.cvne.com
Founded in 1974 by CVNE (*q.v.*), this sixty-two-hectare property produces 30,000 cases of often exceptional, estate-grown *reservas* and *gran reservas*. The single-vineyard "Viña del Olivo", aged two years in small barrels, has both a savoury quality and a silky texture.

CVNE (Compañía Vinícola del Norte de España) ☆–☆☆☆
Haro. www.cvne.com
One of the top half-dozen Rioja houses, founded in 1879 by the Real de Asúa brothers and still owned by this family. Their 540 hectares provide 65% of the grapes needed for red wine. Other vineyards are under contract. They make consistently good wines. Reds include the excellent, vigorous "Cune"; the elegant, velvety "Imperial" (a *reserva* from the Rioja Alta); and the notably full-bodied, spicy "Viña Real" from Alavesa (made at Elciego). For white wines, CVNE used to be best-known for its traditional, oak-flavoured Viura white called "Monopole", but today the wine is only lightly oaked, whereas the Viña Real white is barrel-fermented in new oak. In 1989, the company invested £12 million in what was probably at that time the most modern winery in the world.

Domecq ☆–☆☆
Elciego, Alava. www.domecq.es
Founded in the early 1970s by the sherry house of Pedro Domecq (*q.v.*) and Canadian drinks giant Seagram. When the two parted company in 1974, Domecq built a modern bodega and began planting new vineyards and buying old ones in Alavesa. They now have 300 hectares, but still buy in

most of their grapes. White and red "Marqués de Arienzo" and the low-priced "Viña Eguia" are their main brands. "Marqués de Arienzo" is also made as *reserva, gran reserva*, and *reserva especial*. Annual sales reach 450,000 cases.

Faustino ☆☆
Oyón, Alava. www.bodegasfaustino.es

Founded in 1860 and still family owned and run. All grapes come from around the Oyón area in Rioja Alavesa, 40% from their own 650 hectares. "Faustino V", the red *reserva*; "Faustino I", the *gran reserva*; and the aromatic, lemony white in the new style, are made largely from their own grapes from first-class vineyards. The reds are given extra age in bottle rather than spending over-long in oak. Good *rosado*, too. A recent addition to the range is "Faustino de Autor", a new-style *reserva* aged two years in French oak.

Lopez de Heredia ☆☆☆–☆☆☆☆
Haro

One of the great bastions of Rioja tradition. A family owned bodega founded by Don Raphael Lopez de Heredia y Landeta in 1877; today the winemaker is his fifth generation descendant Maria-José Lopez de Heredia. The premises, on a railway siding at Haro, are a marvel of art nouveau design; the underground tasting room Wagnerian in its lofty, cobwebbed splendour; the cellars damp and chilly. Approximately half the grapes come from their own vineyards in Rioja Alta and most of the rest from small local growers. All the wines are fermented and aged long in oak: the minimum is three years. Indeed, the company has its own cooperage. Wines include weighty *rosado*, "Tondonia" (fine red and white not less than 4 *años*), "Bosconia" (a bigger red, at best sumptuous) and "Gravonia" (an oaky white), and "Cubillo", a red, and at 3 *años* their youngest wine. A 1964 "Tondonia Blanco" was still brilliantly fresh in 2002.

Martínez Bujanda ☆☆–☆☆☆
Oyón, Alava. www.bujanda.com

A century-old, family owned bodega, re-founded in 1988 and already making exceptional, modern-style wines from its 400 hectares of vineyards. The top wines are bottled under the "Conde de Valdemar" label. Other wines in their portfolio are a pure Garnacha, a resounding single-vineyard Rioja from the eighty-hectare Finca Valpiedra, and a blend of Tempranillo and Cabernet Sauvignon.

Muga ☆☆–☆☆☆
Haro. www.bodegasmuga.com

A small family firm founded in 1932 by Don Isaac Muga. His son, Don Isaac Muga Caño, took over on his father's death in 1969, and two years later moved to a new bodega by the famous Haro railway station. Muga claim to be the only producer in Rioja to use American oak exclusively throughout fermentation and ageing. Their own seventy hectares under vine provide 40% of their needs; the rest they buy from farmers in the Rioja Alta. Muga wines are almost alarmingly pale and ethereal, but very fragrant. Much their best wine to my taste is the darker and richer "Gran Reserva Prado Enea", a wine with some of the velvet pungency of burgundy. They also make traditional white of high quality. The launch of a *prestige cuvée* called "Torre Muga" has done much to raise the profile of the winery: it's a rich, oaky, fruity wine built for long ageing. Annual sales are 100,000 cases.

Marqués de Murrieta ☆☆☆–☆☆☆☆
Logroño

With Marqués de Riscal, one of the two noble houses of Rioja, the first two bodegas to be founded, still with a special cachet, and remarkably unchanged by time. Don Luciano de Murrieta y García-Lemoine founded this, the second-oldest, in 1872. In 1983, control passed to Vicente Cebrian, Count of Creixell. Their own vineyards at Ygay near Logroño supply the majority of grapes, and the new owner increased plantings to make the bodega self-sufficient, with 300 hectares in all. Wines are made by wholly traditional methods and maintain a very high standard. The small range includes a fruity 4 *años*, "Etiqueta Blanca", and their rare and expensive "Castillo Ygay" – released with a decade or more of age. The Creixells have also created a micro-winery called Dalmau, dedicated to eponymous *barrique*-aged wines, slightly jammy, but with immense concentration.

Bodegas Olarra ☆☆
Logroño. www.bodegasolarra.es

The most stylish bodega in Rioja, formed of three wings to symbolize Rioja's three regions, would look better in the Napa Valley than on an industrial estate outside Logroño. It owns no vines, but has rapidly made a name for typical and stylish wines, red and white (the white very lightly oaked and ageing extremely well in bottle). "Cerro Añon" is the label of the fatter and darker *reservas*. "Reciente" is a new-wave white. "Añares Crianza" is their best-seller of recent years, and in exceptional years such as 1995 they produce a rich, supple blend (Tempranillo/Mazuelo/Graciano) called "Summa".

Palacios Remondo ☆☆☆
Alfaro. www.vinosherenciaremondo.com

Founded by Don José Palacios Remondo in 1947 and still in the family. After Don José's death, there was a reorganization of the company, and the brilliant winemaker Alvaro Palacios took over, insisting on changes that would improve quality. Purchased grapes, mostly from Rioja Baja, supplement the production of the estate's 100 hectares. Brands are "Herencia Remondo", "Placet" (a barrique-aged Viura white), and the elegant, concentrated "2 Viñedos Vino de Guarda".

Remelluri ☆☆–☆☆☆
Labastida, Alava

An unusual organic estate, with 105 hectares planted at a high elevation, which gives the wines good acidic structure. After fermentation the reds are racked into large casks, and after twelve months of ageing, the maturation process continues in barriques for two years. Yet the wines are not excessively oaky; instead, they have deep colour, voluptuous fruit, and supple tannins. Viognier and Chardonnay have been planted to produce an unorthodox barrel-fermented white.

La Rioja Alta ☆–☆☆☆
Haro. www.riojalta.com

One of the group of top-quality firms round the station at Haro. Founded in 1890 and with descendants of the founders still on the board. They own 300 hectares at various sites in Rioja, and also buy in grapes from local producers. The reds are more distinguished than the whites. "Viña Alberdi" is the pleasant *crianza* red; "Viña Arana" is a fine light red (and a rather dull white); and "Viña Ardanza" a sumptuous, full *reserva* worth laying down. The top wines are the "Reserva 904" and "Reserva 890", selected for depth of colour and flavour to withstand, respectively, five and eight years in American oak and emerge in perfect balance. They also own a Rías Baixas bodega in Galicia, Lagar de Fornelos (*q.v.*).

Riojanas ☆☆
Cenicero. www.bodegasriojanas.com
A substantial and conservative bodega in Rioja Alta, conceived in 1890 as a sort of château in Spain, by families who still own the company today. Some grapes are bought in, the rest come from their own 200-hectare holding in Cenicero. Traditional methods are used to produce the *reservas*, "Viña Albina", and "Monte Real", a most pungent and admirable red. "Puerta Vieja" and "Canchales" are other brands.

Marqués de Riscal ☆☆–☆☆☆
Elciego, Alava. www.marquesderiscal.com
The oldest existing Rioja bodega, founded in 1860 by Don Camilo Hurtado de Amezaga, Marqués de Riscal. The bodega was designed by a Bordeaux *vigneron*, and most of the wines continue to have a light, elegant, almost claret-like character – the epitome of the Rioja Alavesa. Forty per cent of the grapes come from their own 210-hectare vineyards, twenty hectares of which are planted with Cabernet Sauvignon. Cabernet has always played an important part in the blends intended for long ageing. A 1970 *reserva* had 60% and an astonishing 1938, still vigorous in 1982, had 80%. The wines are aged in barrel for up to four years, then in bottle for a minimum of three, even ten. A new wine, based on the bodega's unique old plantations of Cabernet, is called "Baron de Chirel" and was first made in 1986. To save the blushes of the *consejo regulador*, its grapes are listed as 54% Tempranillo and 46% "others". White Riscal wines are not Riojas, but come from Rueda.

Riscal was one of the first large bodegas to respond to the ever-louder criticisms of falling standards within Rioja. They began reducing yields and hand-selecting the grapes; hired Paul Pontallier from Château Margaux as a consultant; and commissioned a dazzling new winery from Canadian architect Frank Gehry to be built in 2004.

Roda ☆☆–☆☆☆
Haro. www.roda.es
A rare boutique winery, owned by the Rotllant family. The two principal wines are "Roda I" and "Roda II", both from fifty-year-old vines, though "Roda I" is pure Tempranillo, aged for a longer period in mostly new oak. Devotees of 100% new oak should note the "Cirsion", produced from even older vines, but only made in minute quantities.

Other Rioja Producers

Alavesas ☆
Laguardia
Owned by the group Alter. They own over 360 hectares and also buy in grapes from local growers. They make typically pale, light, fragrant Alavesa wines, including *reservas* under the name "Solar de Samaniego". Other names include "Solar de Iriarte" and "Solar de Berbete".

Barón de Ley ☆☆
Mendavia, Navarra. www.barondeley.com
A steadily improving estate, among the best in Rioja Baja, with 150 hectares of vineyards. As well as the reliable standard range, there is a powerful single-vineyard "Finca del Monasterio" aged in barriques.

Beronia ☆
Ollauri. www.beronia.com
Owned by González Byass (*q.v.*), a reliable producer of fresh *crianzas* and white Rioja.

Ramón Bilbao ☆☆
Haro. www.bodegasramonbilbao.es
Founded in 1924; a family owned company which buys in most of its wine and grapes from private vineyards. The reds are pure Tempranillo, the barrique-aged white pure Viura.

Bretón ☆☆
Logroño
A large winery, with 100 hectares of vineyards, producing good red wines under many labels: "Loriñón", "Dominio de Comte", and the barrique-aged "Alba de Bretón".

Campillo ☆☆
Laguardia, Alava
Part of the Faustino group, and producing excellent *reserva* and *gran reserva*. The "Reserva Especial" has about 25% Cabernet.

El Coto ☆–☆☆
Oyón, Alava. www.elcoto.com
Founded in 1970 and considerably expanded since, the firm owns 150 hectares of vineyards in Cenicero and Mendavia. Soft, fruity reds, "Coto de Imaz" and "El Coto", are made almost wholly from Tempranillo, while "El Coto" white is made in the new style, almost entirely from Viura.

Franco-Españolas ☆–☆☆
Logroño. www.francoespanolas.com
A large winery owned by Marcos Equizábel Ramirez. The vineyards have been sold; they buy in grapes and wine from Rioja Alta and Alavesa. Traditional, oak-aged white "Viña Soledad" has been joined by an off-dry, unoaked white "Diamante". Traditional reds include a dark and flavoury (if rather coarse) bargain, "Rioja Bordon", and "Excelso" *gran reserva*.

Marqués de Griñón ☆☆–☆☆☆
Ollauri
Rich, fruity, modern-style wines made under a complicated joint-venture with Lagunilla and Berberana (*qq.v.*).

Lagunilla ☆
Fuenmayor. www.lagunilla.com
Modern bodega but a century-old firm, owned by the Arco group that also owns Berberana (*q.v.*). Buys in wine to make fresh whites and reds to age, including a powerful *reserva*.

LAN ☆–☆☆☆
Fuenmayor. www.bodegaslan.com
A large and very modern bodega founded in 1974 by Basque investors. Tempranillo, Mazuelo, and Viura from their own

seventy hectares in El Cortijo (Rioja Alta) provide some of their requirements. Most of the rest is bought from small growers, principally in Rioja Alavesa.

A willingness to pay high prices for good grapes has improved quality. The labels are "Lan", "Viña Lanciano" (a *reserva*), and the high-priced "Culmen de Lan", aged in barriques but still retaining fruit and complexity.

Montecillo ☆☆
Fuenmayor

Part of the Osborne sherry group. Using the labels "Viña Monty" and "Viña Cumbrero", it produces enjoyable, fruity Riojas of little complexity but great consistency.

Palacio ☆☆
Laguardia, Alava

Founded by Don Angel Palacio in 1894, and acquired in 1998 by Hijos de Antonio Barceló, owners of Viña Major in Ribera del Duero (*q.v.*). Formerly famous for its splendid "Glorioso", which is showing signs of regaining its reputation. They have small vineyards in Laguardia where they grow Tempranillo and Viura, but most grapes are bought in for their "Glorioso" and stylishly oaky white and red "Cosme Palacio" range, which was developed with the advice of Michel Rolland from Bordeaux.

Federico Paternina ☆
Haro. www.paternina.com

One of the largest bodegas, now owned by Marcos Equizábal Ramirez. Paternina buys in all its grapes from cooperatives and growers. Wines include "Banda Azul" (a variable but popular young red), "Viña Vial" (full and fruity *reserva*), a *gran reserva*, and a *reserva especial* "Conde de los Andes".

Primicia ☆☆
Laguardia, Alava

Medium-sized winery with forty-five hectares. It made waves in the late 1990s with complex, bottle-aged *reservas* under various labels: "Diezmo", "Julián Madrid", and "Carravalseca". Primicia also offers a rare single-variety bottling from Mazuelo.

Vinícola Real ☆☆–☆☆☆
Albelda de Iruega

A new star, south of Logroño, especially for the suave "Monges Reserva". The property was only founded in 1991, and is a fine example of the small-scale, vineyard-focused, yet forward-looking family bodega.

Viña Salceda ☆
Elciego, Alava

A bodega with forty hectares of its own vineyard making red wine only, using modern methods to make good wine with a leaning to the soft, Alavesa style. Recent expansion has enabled production to be increased. "Viña Salceda" is the regular quality; "Conde de la Salceda" the *gran reserva*.

Union de Cosecheros de Labastida ☆–☆☆
Labastida, Alava

Founded 1965. This co-op's 175 members are all in Rioja Alavesa with 500 hectares of admirable vineyards, and their cooperative competes on equal terms with the best bodegas.

The powerful reds range from the everyday pure-Tempranillo "Solagüen" range to the "Manuel Quintano" *reserva*, which is aged for almost four years in American oak. The white "Montebuena" is unoaked, in the modern manner, and one of the best of its sort.

Viña Villabuena ☆☆
Villabuena, Alava. www.izadi.com

A relative newcomer, having been founded in 1987. The wines are sold under the "Viña Izadi" label. The more basic qualities are easy-drinking wines, and the new-oaked bottlings, "Expresión" and "Selección", have been much admired as elegant wines for long ageing.

Navarra

Eastwards is the province of Navarra, which actually abuts Rioja and can lay claim to some of the vineyards of the Rioja Baja. Its limits are Catalonia in the east, the River Ebro in the south, and the Pyrenees to the north. The province has almost 15,000 hectares of vines, and utilizes the same grapes as Rioja but with more emphasis on the heavy, alcoholic Garnacha, which occupies over half the vineyards.

The best sites lie just south of the provincial capital, Pamplona, where the cooling influence of the Pyrenees can already be felt. The 7,000 growers are being encouraged to re-plant with Tempranillo, and some are also experimenting with small amounts of Cabernet Sauvignon.

Sterling work by the region's experimental laboratories at EVENA (*Estación de Viticultura y Enología de Navarra*) in Olite has meant Navarra has become one of the leading research establishments in Spain, and experimental plantations of all major grape varieties are under evaluation all over the region. New thinking has included barrel-fermentation of white wines such as Chardonnay, Tempranillo/Cabernet mixes, and a willingness to challenge even the mighty Rioja for quality red wines.

Nonetheless, *rosado* wines still account for one-third of production. The number of cooperatives has more than halved in twenty years, as growers take the decision to set up their own wineries in ever-greater numbers.

Leading Navarra Producers

Borgia ☆☆
Los Arcos

A 50,000-case winery owned by Faustino (*q.v.*) of Rioja. The medium-bodied "Marqués de Valcarlos" is a blend of Cabernet and Tempranillo, aged in new American oak. The flagship wine is called "Fortius", a pure Cabernet that is fresh and not too extracted.

Castillo de Monjardín ☆☆–☆☆☆
Villamayor. www.monjardin.es

A 160-hectare estate founded in 1988. Chardonnay is a specialty, both in oaked and unoaked versions.

The fruity *rosado* is made from Merlot, and in addition to new-style reds blending Cabernet Sauvignon, Merlot, and Tempranillo, there is a pure Cabernet and "El Cerezo", an unusual Pinot Noir.

Julián Chivite ☆☆–☆☆☆
Cintruenigo. www.bodegaschivite.com

The largest private wine company in Navarra, founded in 1860 and now with 550 hectares. Its "Gran Fuedo" crianza and *reserva* are pleasant, full-bodied, and oaky wines. The white "Gran Fuedo" is an unoaked Chardonnay. In 1988, Chivite bought an estate near Estella called Señorío de Arinzano, and this is the source of their top range, "Colección 125", mostly aged in new barriques. The "Colección" white is Chardonnay, the reds essentially Tempranillo. The superb "Vendimia Tardía", although from Moscatel, could easily be mistaken for a botrytis Semillon.

Guelbenzu ☆–☆☆☆
Cascante. www.guelbenzu.com

A small family owned property, run by lawyer Ricardo Guelbenzu. He has taken the decision to leave the Navarra *consejo* so as to be free to blend in grapes from his vineyards in other regions. The "Evo" *gran reserva* is a succulent Cabernet/Tempranillo blend, aged in barriques. At the top of the range is the elegant but costly "Lautus", mostly Tempranillo.

Irache ☆☆
Ayegui. www.irache.com

A traditional estate making a wide range of medium-bodied, fresh red and *rosado* wines from its own fifty hectares of vineyards in Tierra Estella and also from some purchased grapes.

Viña Magaña ☆☆
Barillas. www.vinamagana.com

This family owned, 120-hectare property has gone further than any other in Navarra in uprooting Garnacha, replacing it with Cabernet Sauvignon, Merlot, Cabernet Franc, and Syrah. Magaña wines share more than a passing similarity with good Bordeaux.

Vinícola Navarra ☆
Campanas

Century-old company with French origins, and a major exporter, now owned by Allied-Domecq. No great refinement, but reliable and increasingly tasty in the better qualities. "Castillo de Tiebas" is the full-bodied *reserva*, with Rioja-like oaky notes.

Nekeas ☆–☆☆
Valdizarbe

A private cooperative founded by eight families in 1994 and controlling 230 hectares of vineyards. The white is a blend of Viura and Chardonnay; the red is Tempranillo backed with Merlot.

Bodegas Ochoa ☆☆–☆☆☆
Olite. www.bodegasochoa.com

A locally popular, privately owned bodega in Olite, once the capital of the Kings of Navarra. The reds (including pure Tempranillo and barrique-aged Cabernet and Merlot) and *rosado* are soundly made, and the white Viura and the Moscatel are excellent, too.

Javier Ochoa has played a major part in backing EVENA and thus has contributed a great deal to the resurgence of quality within the region.

Bodega del Señorio de Otazu ☆☆
Echauri

The most northerly estate in Navarra, founded in 1989 by Carlos Biurrun. The barrique-aged reds blend Cabernet and Merlot, with Tempranillo playing a minor role. The white is pure unoaked Chardonnay.

Palacio de la Vega ☆–☆☆
Condesa de la Vega. www.palaciodelavega.com

Founded in 1991 this producer is owned by Pernod-Ricard. The winery does not own any vineyards and produces inexpensive, fruity Tempranillo and Cabernet, made from purchased grapes.

Príncipe de Viana ☆☆
Murchante. www.principedeviana.com

Set up in 1983 with the support of the regional government, Príncipe de Viana has amassed 280 hectares of vineyards. The brand used to be known as "Cenalsa", but for some time the basic wines have been bottled under the "Agramont" label, which offers good value. The "Principe" wines include barrel-fermented Chardonnay and a fine Cabernet Sauvignon.

Señorío de Sarría ☆☆
Puente la Reina. www.senoriosarria.com

The acknowledged finest wine estate in Navarra, unique in the region (almost in Spain) for its château-style approach and almost Bordeaux-like results. In 1981, the ancient estate was taken over by a bank, which completely overhauled the vineyards and cellars. In 2001, a new team was brought in to improve quality further. Tempranillo and Cabernet Sauvignon dominate the 150 hectares of vineyards. Its best *reservas* are better than most Riojas; even the light *joven* wines are very well-balanced.

Aragón

South and east of Navarra, astride the Ebro, lies the province of Aragón, whose climate tends more towards the Mediterranean. Aragón's once best-known *denominación*, Cariñena, is a byword for high-strength, dark, red wine with a rustic bite, though worth oak-ageing for two years to achieve a pleasantly smooth texture. The grape here is again largely Garnacha Tinta, despite the fact that the region gave its name to the great grape of France's Midi, the Carignan.

Cariñena lies in the south of the province of Zaragoza, with 17,135 hectares of vineyard. A small DO, Campo de Borja (with fourteen wineries and 6,270 hectares), lies halfway between Cariñena and the Rioja Baja. Borja (the origin of the Borgias) makes an even more rustic and alcoholic red, more in demand for blending than drinking. Calatayud, south of Borja, makes similar wines. Most interesting, however, is probably the DO Somontano in the Pyrenees, created in 1985 and updated in 1993. Incoming winemakers discovered that the sleepy local cooperative was actually turning out some excellent wines, and that the soils and microclimates were perfect for serious viticulture. Today, the region grows white Macabeo, Garnacha Blanca, and Chardonnay alongside the local – and splendid – Alcañón; reds are Tempranillo, Garnacha, and Cabernet Sauvignon alongside the indigenous

Parreleta and Moristel (not the Monastrell in spite of many references to the contrary). The co-op has modernized, and new wineries are now experimenting with everything from Pinot Noir to Gewürztraminer. Early results are extremely promising.

Leading Aragón Producers

Viñedos del Alto Aragón ☆☆
Salas Bajas. www.enate.es
A Somontano winery founded in 1991 by the Nozaleda Arenas family, with 400 hectares of vineyards and utilizing the "Enate" brand name. The oaked Chardonnay is nicely lean and pungent; the reds are complex blends of Tempranillo with Cabernet and Merlot, with the *reserva especial* aged in new oak, as is a new wine called "Merlot-Merlot", which speaks for itself.

The wines are ambitious, but not quite as concentrated as the high prices would lead one to expect, this is probably because the vines are still young. Nonetheless, this sophisticated operation is leading the way in the modernization of the region and its wines.

Aragonesas ☆
Fuendejalón. www.bodegasaragonesas.com
A large, traditional producer, drawing on 3,500 hectares belonging to two local cooperatives. The winery offers a good-value range of Campo de Borja wines that come under the "Coto de Hayas" label. Garnacha and Tempranillo dominate here.

Blecua ☆☆
Barbastro
A boutique winery, allied to Viñas del Vero (*q.v.*) and producing, since 2000, a single wine: a deep-coloured, black-fruited blend of Cabernet, Garnacha, and other varieties.

Bodegas Borsao ☆–☆☆
Borja. www.bodegasborsao.com
A Campo de Borja cooperative, offering red wines from 1,000 hectares of Cabernet Sauvignon, Garnacha, and Tempranillo. All good value.

Enate
See **Viñedos del Alto Aragón**

Grandes Vinos y Viñedos ☆
Cariñena. www.grandesvinos.com
A very large new enterprise, founded in 1997 and with access to over 5,500 hectares of vineyards. The winery produces close to one million cases from DO Cariñena.

Pirineos ☆–☆☆
Barbastro. www.bodega-pirineos.com
This 1,000-hectare property is a major player in Somontano, a former cooperative that groups together the vineyards of 200 growers. Pirineos, though very well-equipped, is still a custodian of tradition, using grapes such as Moristel and Parraleta, as well as Cabernet, Merlot, and Tempranillo. Various labels are used: "Montesierra", "Alquézar", and "Señorío de Lazán".

Cooperativa San José ☆
Aguaron
A 500-member co-op founded in 1955 and technically up to date. Very sound wines aged in oak casks. Both ranges, "Monasterio de las Viñas" and "Valdemadera", offer typical Cariñena reds, and whites from Macabeo.

Cooperativa San Valero ☆
Cariñena. www.bodegasanvalero.com
A large co-op with 700 members farming 4,000 hectares. San Valero enjoys a wide market in Spain for its "Don Mendo" and "Monte Ducay" wines. The sound reds are made mostly from Cabernet and Tempranillo.

Viñas del Vero ☆–☆☆
Barbastro. www.vinasdelvero.es
The new name of the Compañía Vitivinícola Aragonese. An ultra-modern, gravity-fed winery was built in 1993, producing a wide range of cleanly made Somontano wines from varieties as diverse as Gewürztraminer, Pinot Noir, Merlot, Chardonnay, and Viura. Some of the wines have high acidity and benefit from some ageing in bottle.

Duero Valley

Castile-León

Surprisingly, it is the very heart of the high plain of Old Castile, with some of the worst of Spain's savagely extreme climate, that is now producing wines of a quality that seriously challenges Rioja. Big, hot-country wines that they are, the red table wines of the Portuguese upper Douro and the Spanish Ribera del Duero seem to be kindred in their fine engineering. They have the structure, the cleanness, and "cut" of a massive Bordeaux – something not found (as far as I know) elsewhere in Spain.

Some of Spain's greatest reds, including her most expensive by far, grow along the Duero banks, the Ribera del Duero, just east of Valladolid towards Peñafiel. This was the "discovery" of the 1980s, and it has expanded steadily through the 1990s. There are 15,265 hectares in the Ribera del Duero *denominación*. The dominant variety is Tempranillo, known here as Tinto Fino. Vega Sicilia, aged ten years in cask, is the crown jewel, but even the *reservas* of the cooperative at Peñafiel echo the underlying quality of the region.

Rapid expansion means that many wines are inevitably based on young vines that cannot always support a prolonged regime of barrel-ageing, and thus not all the wines are worth the generally high prices demanded for them. Often the richly fruity crianzas offer more pleasure than tannic, over-extracted *gran reservas*.

It is strange to find an up-and-coming white wine DO only thirty-two kilometres (twenty miles) south of Valladolid, in the country that breeds such massive reds. Rueda made its name with a sort of sherry: a strong *flor*-growing, yellow wine of Palomino, grown on chalky clay not unlike the *albariza* of Jerez. Modern white wine technology has revolutionized Rueda. First the Marqués de Riscal from Rioja, then other investors, have seen enough potential here to call in the best advice from France and invent a new Rueda: a full-bodied, crisp, dry white of the kind Spain chronically needs. Here Verdejo is the traditional grape, and the wine must contain at least forty per cent. It is often blended with Sauvignon Blanc, which flourishes here.

Every other wine in Old Castile is red. Toro is Rueda's nearest neighbour: a massive wine from the dusty Duero Valley, between Valladolid and Zamora. Once regarded as a source of wine for blending, it is now home to modern wineries that are pushing Toro into the elite of Spanish DOs. Cebreros, from over the mountains to the south between Avila and Madrid, makes powerful *claretes*. Cigales, just north of Valladolid, is another region once known for rough *clarete*, but steadily improving in quality, with forty wineries in operation.

León itself is the commercial centre for the province. Its vineyards lie to the west, in Bierzo, over the mountains on the borders of cool Galicia. Vilafranca del Bierzo is the centre of a region of 3,700 hectares. Bierzo wines are correspondingly the lightest of León, with good acidity and not excessively strong.

Leading Castile-León Producers

Abadía Retuerta ☆☆–☆☆☆
Sardón de Duero
An ambitious project, established just outside the Ribera del Duero zone in 1996. The million-bottle production includes a wide range of wines from Tempranillo and Cabernet Sauvignon, offering good value within their price bands. Since 1996, St-Emilion winemaker Pascal Delbeck has been advising the winery.

Alión ☆☆☆
Peñafiel
This thirty-eight hectare property is a spin-off of Vega Sicilia (*q.v.*), producing modern-style wines entirely different in style from the mother estate. The production team is the same, headed by Vega Sicilia winemaker Javier Ausás. The wine is pure Tempranillo, but aged in new barriques.

Quality is very high: oaky, to be sure, but with fine tannins and exceptional length of flavour.

Ismael Arroyo ☆☆–☆☆☆
Sotillo. www.valsotillo.com
The Arroyo family began bottling in 1979. These Ribera del Duero wines are pure Tempranillo and mostly aged in American oak.

The simpler wines are released under the "Mesoneros" label; the top wines as "Val Sotillo". The *crianza* is delicious; the *gran reserva* overpriced for the quality.

Belondrade y Lurton ☆☆
Camino del Puerto
This firm was founded in 1994, and is the Rueda brainchild of Didier Belondrade and Brigitte Lurton, from the famous Bordeaux family.

Their principal wine is a barrrel-fermented Verdejo, rich in body and decidedly toasty.

Viños Blancos de Castilla ☆☆
Rueda. www.vinosblancosdecastilla.es
This 170-hectare property is the production centre for Marqués de Riscal white wines, since the company has never produced a white Rioja. The Verdejo sees some oak, but the Sauvignon Blanc is unwooded.

Bodegas de Crianza de Castilla la Vieja ☆☆–☆☆☆
Rueda. www.bodegasdecastilla.com
Owned by Ricardo Sanz, who comes from a prominent local family, this winery produces barrel-fermented Rueda from pure Verdejo, as well as racy, unoaked Sauvignon Blanc. There is also an occasional late-harvest Sauvignon. Rather confusingly, this estate uses the "Palacio de Bornos" label for its wines.

Condado de Haza ☆☆–☆☆☆
Roa de Duero
Alejandro Fernández of Pesquera (*q.v.*) founded this 250-hectare property in 1993. The wines, from Tempranillo only, are aged for fifteen months in American oak, and are exuberantly fruity and peppery examples of the less extracted style from Ribera del Duero.

Fariña ☆☆
Casaseca de las Chanas. www.bodegasfarina.com
It was Manuel Fariña who first put Toro on the map in the 1980s, with his rich, no-holds-barred Tempranillo reds called "Gran Colegiata", which are still among the most dependable and age-worthy wines of the region.

Alejandro Fernández ☆☆–☆☆☆
Pesquera de Duero
Fernández shot to stardom in the 1980s with "Pesquera", a red wine made from Tinto Fino grapes and aged for two years in new American oak. American critics are particular admirers of his dense, chewy style and powerful, tannic structure. He soon expanded his vineyards (to 200 hectares) and also production, and established Condado de Haza (*q.v.*) in 1993. The wines are not entirely consistent, but can be magnificent at the top level. His reserve of reserves is called "Janus".

Fuentespina ☆☆
Fuentespina, Burgos. www.avelinovegas.com
The Ribera del Duero outpost of the Avelino Vegas group, with vineyards of almost 400 hectares, and offering a sound range made solely from Tinto Fino. "Vega de Castilla" is a subsidiary label.

Mauro ☆☆☆
Tudela de Duero. www.bodegasmauro.com
Just outside the Ribera del Duero DO, this much admired estate is owned by Mariano García, formerly of Vega Sicilia. Yields are low, at between 25 and 40 hl/ha. The range includes a *crianza*, "Vendimia Seleccionada", and the prestige bottling "Terreus".

Viña Mayor ☆☆
Quintanilla de Onésimo. www.habarcelo.es
Owned by Hijos de Antonio Barceló, this is a 130-hectare estate producing substantial quantities of very reliable Ribera del Duero.

Hacienda Monasterio ✩✩✩
Pesquera de Duero

Founded in 1992, this is a quality-oriented estate, where Peter Sisseck of Pingus (*q.v.*) acts as consultant winemaker. The wines are aged in varying proportions of new barriques, with older barrels bought from Château Margaux. All the wines contain, in addition to the basic Tinto Fino, a small proportion of Cabernet, Merlot, and Malbec. After some years when the wines were inconsistent, quality is now impeccable.

Bodegas Emilio Moro ✩✩✩
Pesquera de Duero. www.emiliomoro.com

Since 1989, Moro has been producing traditional Ribera del Duero from pure Tinto Fino. In 2001, work on his new winery was completed, which should have the effect of raising standards even higher. The wines are splendid at all levels. In 1998, he introduced a flagship wine called "Malleolus", aged, unlike his other wines, entirely in French oak.

Pago de Carraovejas ✩✩–✩✩✩
Peñafiel

A successful estate owned by a consortium of Madrid restaurateurs. The seventy hectares of vineyards, planted in 1990, are well-drained and rarely affected by the spring frosts that can damage the vines of Ribera del Duero. The better qualities are aged only in French oak, and all the wines contain some Cabernet Sauvignon. Quality was uneven at first, but is now far more consistent.

Descendientes de J. Palacios ✩✩–✩✩✩
Villafranca del Bierzo

The famous winemaker Alvaro Palacios and his cousin are putting the Bierzo region on the map, producing plummy wines from very old Mencía vines, notably the high-priced *cuvée* "Corullon".

Viña Pedrosa/Pérez Pascuas Hermanos ✩✩–✩✩✩
Pedrosa de Duero. www.vinapedrosa.com

Founded in 1980, this 100-hectare estate is owned by the Pérez Pascuas brothers. The wines are classic Ribera del Duero, being aged in older American oak, for fourteen to twenty-eight months. Their *gran reserva* is made from forty-year old vines and the "Gran Selección" from a single vineyard containing even older vines. These are excellent wines, rich in black fruits, and only occasionally stepping over the boundary into portiness. They do not come cheap though.

Bodegas Peñalba-López/Torremilanos ✩✩–✩✩✩
Aranda de Duero. www.torremilanos.com

A small family firm, founded in 1903, with 200 hectares of vineyard planted with Tinto Fino, and a dash of Cabernet and Merlot. It makes fruity and well-balanced wines under the "Torremilanos" label: relatively light in style and among the best from this up-and-coming region.

A big expansion programme, including a new winery and thousands of new *barricas*, is testament to the family's confidence. The *reserva* "Torre Albéniz" contains a high proportion of Cabernet and Merlot. Peñalba-López is fond of new oak, so the wines can sometimes be tough and over-woody.

Estancia Piedra ✩✩–✩✩✩
Toro. www.estanciapiedra.com

A new star in Toro, belonging to an American, Grant Stein, and consisting of fifty-four hectares. The wines are dense and tannic, but by no means unapproachable, so vivid are the black fruit flavours.

Dominio de Pingus ✩✩✩
Peñafiel

Danish-born Peter Sisseck came to Ribera del Duero in 1990 and managed Hacienda Monasterio (*q.v.*), as he still does. He also founded what was the first *garagiste* winery in the region. He bought four hectares of very old and low-yielding Tempranillo vines, and aged the wine in new barriques for up to two years. Rave reviews from Robert Parker sent prices soaring, rather to his own amazement. The second wine, which is marginally more affordable and also of high quality, is "Flor de Pingus".

Protos ✩✩
Peñafiel. www.bodegasprotos.com

A long-established cooperative (founded in 1927) with 230 members, producing red wines worthy of a more famous region, well above normal co-op standards. "Ribera Duero" is their blackberryish red without oak-ageing. The "Cosecha" is slightly oak-aged. The *reserva* can be sensational, deep in colour and in its oak and mulberry fragrance, at ten years comparable to an excellent Rioja: long, soft, and delicious. In top years they produce a *gran reserva* especial.

Rodero ✩✩–✩✩✩
Pedrosa de Duero. www.bodegasrodero.com

Since 1991, Carmelo Rodero's eighty-hectare estate has been a rising star in Ribera del Duero. These are perfumed wines that always retain an intrinsic cherryish fruitiness; they are tannic, too, but never out of balance.

Telmo Rodriguez ✩✩–✩✩✩
Burgos

This brilliant and peripatetic winemaker also produces small quantities of outstanding Ribera del Duero from pure Tinto Fino. "Valderiz" is the main label, while the denser, spicier, and more concentrated "Matallana" is aged in French oak only. He is also producing excellent wines in Toro under a variety of labels, including "Gago" (*crianza*) and the complex and highly concentrated "Pago La Jara", aged in new barriques for seventeen months.

Señorío de Nava ✩–✩✩
Nava de Roa. www.senoriodenava.es

The former cooperative at Roa was taken over by VILE of León in 1986 and modernized, and the vineyards were adapted for mechanical harvesting. Cabernet and Merlot were planted alongside the traditional Tinto Fino. These are dense, chunky wines, short on finesse, but rich and chocolatey.

Valduero ✩✩–✩✩✩
Gumiel del Mercado, Burgos. www.valduero.com

A well-established property of 150 hectares, all Tinto Fino, producing delicious wines that are never overwhelmed by the new, mostly American oak used to age the *reserva* and *gran reserva*.

Vega Sicilia ☆☆☆☆
Valbuena de Duero

The most prestigious wine estate in Spain: a legend for the quality (and the price) of its wines. It was founded in 1864 on limestone hills 730 metres (2,373 feet) above sea level on the south bank of the Duero. The founder imported Bordeaux grapes (Cabernet Sauvignon, Merlot, and Malbec) to add to the local Tinto Fino, Garnacha, and Albillo. There are almost twenty hectares in production. The yield is very low and the winemaking completely traditional. Only the unpressed *vin de goutte* is used, fermented for fifteen days and matured in barrels of various sizes and ages for up to six years for the great *reserva* "Unica" (Vega Sicilia itself), and three or five for its younger brother "Valbuena". The result is a wine combining immense power and unmistakable "breeding".

The raciness of the flavour is astonishing, and the perfume intoxicating. Vega Sicilia is one of Europe's noble eccentrics, but if proof were needed of the potential of the Ribera del Duero for fine reds of a more conventional kind, "Valbuena" would be evidence enough.

The estate also produces an unusual wine called "Reserve Especial", which is a blend of old "Unica" vintages and some younger wines; it is a non-vintage wine and only 1,000 cases are produced. In 1998, long-time winemaker Mariano García left to take care of his Mauro property (*q.v.*), so Vega Sicilia has been going through some changes – none, as yet, revolutionary.

Other Castile-León Producers

Aalto
Roa de Duero. www.aalto.es

Two powerful figures within the region teamed up in 1999 to produce Ribera del Duero from old-vine vineyards. They are Mariano Garcia, the former winemaker at Vega Sicilia, and Javier Zaccagnini, the former head of the Consejo.

Palacio de Arganza ☆
Villafranca del Bierzo

Since 1805, the bodega that occupies the fifteenth century palace of the Dukes of Arganza has been the most important in Bierzo, but only joined the DO in 1992. It ages its potent *reservas* in oak casks.

Luna Beberide ☆–☆☆
Cacabelos

Good, mostly varietal wines from Bierzo, from Chardonnay, Gewürztraminer, Cabernet Sauvignon, and other grapes.

Bodegas Frutos Villar ☆–☆☆
Cigales

An important company, with vineyards in Ribera del Duero and in Toro (producing a wine labelled "Muruve"), and 110 hectares in Cigales, where their brand is "Calderona". Straightforward modern wines from Tinto Fino.

Matarromera ☆☆
Valbuena de Duero. www.gourmetel.com

Belonging to a group headed by Carlos Moro, this eighty-hectare property has been producing robust wines, rich in Tempranillo fruit, and very consistent from year to year.

Teofilo Reyes ☆☆
Peñafiel

Reyes was the winemaker for Pesquera and set up his own business in 1994, buying in almost all the grapes he required. The wines are surprisingly sumptuous: rich and lush on the nose, and packed with blackberry fruit on the palate.

Traslanzas ☆☆
Mucientes

A boutique winery demonstrating, since 1998, the remarkable potential of Cigales DO.

Vega di Toro ☆☆☆
Toro

The Eguren family in Toro own twenty hectares of old vines, from which they produce a small quantity of gorgeous, if very oaky wine, called "Numanthia".

Finca Villacreces ☆☆
Quintanilla de Onésimo

The spare-time project of Peter Sisseck of Pingus (*q.v.*): a fifty-hectare estate next door to Vega Sicilia producing a single wine packed with red fruit flavours, but with sufficient stuffing to ensure good ageing potential.

Catalonia & the Balearics

Your modern Catalan is proud of the autonomy of his privileged province. He basks in a temperate, mild-winter climate without the extremes of most of Spain. Catalonia lies on the same latitude as Tuscany, sheltered from the north by the Pyrenees, facing southeast into the Mediterranean. It can be considered as a southward extension of the best wine area of France's Côtes du Roussillon. Both have the capacity to produce ponderous and potent reds – and also to surprise with the quality of their white grapes.

Catalan wines astonish with their diversity. From Priorato, an inland enclave, come red wines of legendary colour and strength, now rightly regarded as some of the greatest wines of Spain. In contrast, over a century ago, the Raventós family of Penedès realized the potential of their native white grapes, naturally high in acid, for the Champagne treatment. Today Penedès produces ninety per cent of Spain's sparkling wine.

The latest development, but the most significant of all, has been the successful trial of the classic French and German grapes in the higher parts of Penedès. The Torres family, long-established winemakers of the region, have led the way with a judicious mixture of these exotics and the best of the well-tried Catalan varieties.

Among the native whites, Parellada and Xarel-lo are crisply acidic with low alcoholic degrees, Malvasía is broadly fruity, with low acidity, and Macabeo (the Viura of Rioja) is admirably balanced and apt for maturing.

Catalonia shares the best red grapes in Spain, above all the Tempranillo (here called Ull de Llebre), the Garnacha Tinta, and the deep and tannic Monastrell. The Cariñena (alias Carignan) is no more distinguished here than elsewhere.

Eleven zones in Catalonia now have *Denominación de Origen* status and, of the Balearic islands, Mallorca now boasts two DOs. *See* below.

Catalonia

Alella

Coastal valley just north of Barcelona, now reduced to 330 hectares of vines by urban sprawl – which is a pity, since Alella has some wonderful soils for viticulture. Most of its many small growers take their grapes to the cooperative. It used to be best known for a mildly fruity semi-sweet Xarel-lo, but little is produced today. Instead there is some good dry Chardonnay. The red is passable, but there are some experiments with Cabernet Sauvignon and Pinot Noir.

Ampurdán–Costa Brava

The northernmost DO centred around Perelada in the province of Gerona and situated behind the cliffs and beaches of the Costa Brava and bordering Roussillon. The 2,475 hectares produce mainly Cariñena rosé and international varieties such as Riesling and Syrah, as well as Tempranillo and Garnacha.

Conca de Barberá

This DO covers 6,000 sheltered hectares inland from the DO Tarragona, adjoining that and Costers del Segre in the northwest. Much of the grape production here is for the cava industry, although new ideas are becoming well-established and there are large plantations of Chardonnay – indeed, this is where Miguel Torres grows the grapes for his flagship barrel-fermented "Milmanda" (which is then, confusingly enough, labelled Penedès). But Macabeo

and Parellada are still the dominant varieties. Nonetheless, this is a region with promise.

Costers del Segre

This DO was ratified in 1988, really due to the influence of a single winery: Raimat. The vineyards are in the rugged, fertile western region of Lleida (Lérida), and the region is made up of the four geographically disparate sub-zones of Raimat, Artesa, Valls de Riu Corb, and Les Garrigues. Grape varieties are mainly traditional, but Cabernet Sauvignon, Merlot, and Chardonnay are also found. Most of the vineyards are cooperative-owned and devoted to producing the white wine traditional to the area, though modern methods and technological innovations are being introduced. Wines are of varying quality, with Raimat far in the lead.

Montsant

A recent DO, only dating from 2001, and adjoining Priorato. It used to be known as the Falset sub-zone of Tarragona. Some sectors resemble Priorato, others are less steep. The main varieties cultivated are Cariñena, Garnacha, and Syrah.

Penedès

The biggest DO of Catalonia ranges from the coast at Sitges back into 600-metre (2,000-foot) limestone hills. Its centres are Vilafranca de Penedès, best known for its table-wine bodegas (among them Torres), and Sant Sadurní d'Anoia, thirty-two kilometres (twenty miles) west of Barcelona, the capital of Spanish sparkling wine and headquarters of the vast firms of Codorníu and Freixenet.

The table wines of Penedès have been revolutionized in the last twenty years, and now rival Rioja. The reds are generally darker in colour and fruitier than Riojas, but add a concentration that Rioja normally lacks. Exceptional wines, especially those with a proportion of Cabernet, reach the best

The Torres Family

Such has been the contribution of this Catalan family to Spanish wine that their name has become as well-known in some quarters as Spain's most famous wine-producing regions. The reasons for this are two-fold.

First, in the 1950s, with the world recovering from war, the late Miguel Torres Carbó, and his wife Doña Margarita, travelled the world selling Torres wines and promoting the Torres name in countries as disparate as Belgium and Bali.

Second, their son, Miguel A. Torres studied chemistry at the University of Barcelona and went on to learn modern winemaking technology in Montpellier, before taking over the role of winemaker in 1962.

This combination of worldwide market share and new-wave winemaking skill contributed to the famous occasion in 1979 on which Torres "Mas la Plana" (then known as "Gran Coronas" Black Label) beat all-comers (including Château Latour) in a tasting of wines made principally from Cabernet Sauvignon.

Today, Miguel Torres oversees an empire which includes his sister Marimar's vineyards in California's Sonoma Valley, and his own large property in Curicó, Chile, but his heart remains in his native Penedès, where he maintains a vineyard of more than a hundred Catalan vine varieties as well as the classic Cabernet, Merlot, Sauvignon, and Chardonnay, which have made the family's name in international markets.

The Torres family is fully aware that is not enough to produce good wine; it is just as important to build up a loyal clientele of appreciative wine drinkers. To that end, Miguel Torres offers winery tours, and has founded cultural centres and other ventures that inform the present generation and educate the one to follow.

Miguel Torres has retained his essential modesty, and relishes harvest time, when he can taste the new wines and offer his thoughts on blending. Although there are other winemakers now producing costly bottles at the same level as Torres's best, no one can rival the consistent quality of his wines, from the cheapest to the most costly. That is no mean achievement.

international standards. Modern methods have brought the white wines, which still represent eighty per cent of production, under total control. There is now a benchmark dry, fruity Catalan white, which is certainly highly satisfactory if not exactly exciting. Unlike the best Rioja whites it does not (at least to my taste) take kindly to ageing in oak. Possibly less concentrated fruit, partly the result of bigger crops, is to blame.

Pla de Bages

A region some 100 kilometres (sixty-two miles) northwest of Barcelona around Manresa. Most of the production ends up as cava, and few wineries operate here. As well as indigenous varieties, some Cabernet and Merlot are grown here.

Priorato

The long viticultural course of the River Ebro, starting near Haro in the Rioja Alta, might be said to end without shame in the western hills of Tarragona with this memorable wine. Priorato lies within the much greater *denominación* of Tarragona, applying to some 1,400 hectares of steep, volcanic, hillside vines around the little tributary of the Ebro, the Montsant. Its fame was derived from the almost blackness of its red wine, traditionally a splendidly full-bodied brew of Garnacha and Cariñena that reached sixteen degrees alcohol or more, with the colour of crushed blackberries and something of their flavour.

Its wine, and reputation, began to change after a handful of innovative winemakers set to work in the tiny hilltop village of Gratallops. Each acquired seven hectares, and rebuilt the terraces of their vineyards. The group collaborated but sold their wines under their own labels. Soon, half a dozen like-minded boutique wineries were making stunning wines from low-yielding Garnacha, Cabernet Sauvignon, Merlot, and even Syrah, grown in soil over the schistose bedrock. Their names were Clos Mogador, Clos de l'Obac, Clos Dofi, Clos Martinet, and the best of all, Clos l'Ermita, which has a complexity that is astonishing. In 1992, the group broke up, but most of the winemakers are still active in the region.

Tarragona

The table wines from this DO are normally of blending quality without the extra distinction of Priorato. Its finest products are fortified dessert wines from Garnacha and Moscatel, but the great bulk of Tarragona's exports are of a more humble nature.

Terra Alta

A DO continuing south from that of Tarragona beyond the Ebro. Mora and Gandesa are the chief centres for the 9,000 hectares of vines in the hills that rise to the mountainous province of Teruel. Many of the grapes are used for cava, but the true potential of this region, with its fine soils and excellent drainage, is slowly being appreciated and exploited.

Cava

While technically a DO, this is not actually a geographical region. Cava is the official term for traditional method sparkling wine, and is produced predominantly in Penedès, though there are a few producers elsewhere in Spain.

It may have been the characteristic leanness of Catalan white wine that inspired the creation of cava. The Xarel-lo, Parellada, and Viura (locally called Macabeo) produce high-

acid musts of only slight flavour – ideal base material: the flavour of Champagne yeast comes through distinctly with its richness and softness. Wines that were stored in wooden vats (some still are) also picked up a very faint tarry taste, which added character. Chardonnay is increasingly used both in blends and in premium "varietal" cavas.

The cavas of Penedès today range from the extremely deft and delicate, to the fat and clumsy. The best can certainly be counted among the world's finest sparkling wines. It is only in the inevitable comparison with Champagne that they lose. Where Champagne finally triumphs is in the vigour of the flavours that it assembles so harmoniously.

The Balearics

Binissalem & Plà i Llevant

The Balearic Islands have a long vinous history, although Mallorca is the only one in the group that retains any vineyards at all. Binissalem, Spain's first offshore DO, was promoted in 1991, largely the result of the Ferrer (*q.v.*) bodega's campaign for recognition of the quality of its wines. In 1999, a new DO was created, Plà i Llevant, on the eastern side of the island. Son Bordils, founded in 1998, is another to watch. Majorcan wines are either primitive or modern.

Leading Catalan & Balearic Producers

Masía Bach ☆–☆☆
Sant Esteve Sesrovires. www.codorniu.es

Masía means farm. Bach was the name of two bachelor brothers who, in 1920, used a fortune made by clothing soldiers to build a Florentine folly in Penedès, with garages for forty cars and a winery, which grew in reputation and size until its cellars held 8,500 oak casks. It was bought by Codorníu (*q.v.*) in 1975, but continues to make the house specialty: an oaked sweet white called "Extrísimo Bach". High-quality varietal wines from Tempranillo and French grapes have also been added to the range. The red *reserva* "Extrísima" can be outstanding.

René Barbier ☆–☆☆
Sant Sadurní d'Anoia, Barcelona. www.renebarbier.com

An old-established bodega, now owned by Freixenet (*q.v.*), and producing a large range of varietal wines from Catalan and international varieties. The top "Selección" Cabernet and Chardonnay can be impressive.

Celler de Capçanes ☆☆
Capçanes

A Montsant cooperative with eighty members cultivating 300 hectares, and reorganized into a progressive private winery making the most of its members' old vines and excellent vineyards. Much of the crop is now sold off, leaving only the best to be aged and bottled here. Many of the wines are blends, but "Mas Torto" is a pure Garnacha of great power. The fortified "Pansal del Calas" hearkens back to local traditions, and tastes bright and raisiny.

Castell del Remei ☆☆–☆☆☆

Lleida (Lérida). www.castelldelremei.com

A long-established firm in Costers del Segre. Its eighty hectares of vineyards include Cabernet Sauvignon and Sémillon, and its wines have a good reputation. The white and red wines, bottled under the "Gotim Bru" and "Oda" labels are very well-made, though with a sweetish dimension that derives from the American oak.

Clos Mogador ☆☆☆

Gratallops

René Barbier (son of the René Barbier, who ran the bodega now belonging to Freixenet (*q.v.*) was a prime mover along with Alvaro Palacios in regenerating Priorato. His wine remains one of the very best, a blend of Cabernet, Cariñena, Garnacha, and Syrah drenched in red fruit flavours and very long on the palate. It bears some resemblance to a top Châteauneuf-du-Pape.

Costers del Siurana ☆☆–☆☆☆

Gratallops. www.costersdelsiurana.com

Carles Pastrana first made the renowned "Clos de l'Obac" in 1989, and it remains an impressive example of new-style Priorato, blending Cabernet and Merlot with traditional varieties. Vintages in the late 1990s were a tad inconsistent. Pastrana continues the local tradition for fortified wines by producing "Dolç de l'Obac", a warming blend of Garnacha, Cabernet, and Syrah.

José L. Ferrer ☆

Binissalem, Mallorca

The best-known bodega of the Balearic islands, now owned by the firm Franco Roja. The seventy hectares of vineyards are situated in the centre of the island. The local Manto Negro grape makes lively reds, and *reservas* can be extremely good. There is also a dry blanc de blancs sparkling wine.

Jean León ☆☆☆

Torrelavid, Barcelona. www.jeanleon.com

In 1964, Jean León started to plant what is now sixty hectares of Cabernet and Chardonnay in Penedès. The wines were first-rate and excellent value. In 1993, the company was bought by Torres, which runs the estate separately to maintain its identity. The Cabernet spends two years in casks, then three years in bottle, before release. Under Torres, Merlot has been added to the range. Quality has, if anything, improved further since the Torres acquisition.

Alvaro Palacios ☆☆☆–☆☆☆☆

Gratallops

Palacios is the prime mover behind the Priorato renaissance, and the creator of its costliest wine, "L'Ermita", an intense blend of mostly Garnacha with Cabernet, aged for twenty months in new barriques. Fortunately, Palacios also makes wines that are more affordable: the concentrated and persistent "Finca Dofí"; and the less structured but very enjoyable "Les Terrasses", which is essentially Garnacha and Cariñena. Low yields and rigorous grape selection are what lies behind the wines' splendour.

Parxet ☆☆

Tiana. www.parxet.es

The leading producer in Alella, with 200 hectares of vineyards.

White wines only, released under the "Marqués de Alella" label. The most vivacious wine is made entirely from the Pansà grape. The house also makes reliable cava, also from indigenous varieties.

Raïmat ☆–☆☆☆

Segrià, Lleida (Lérida)

The Raventós family of Codorníu has replanted the vineyards of the Castle of Raïmat, in the arid hill-region of Lérida, on a grand (2,200-hectare) scale, and re-opened a magnificent bodega built early in the twentieth century and subsequently abandoned. The property is run in an industrial yet sophisticated manner, with the grapes being picked at night by machine. Cabernet Sauvignon, Merlot, and Chardonnay are blended with native grapes, but also made as varietal wines. The results have been ultra-reliable if slightly lacking in personality, but that is being rectified as special bottlings of Chardonnay and Cabernet are coming onto the market.

Cellers de Scala Dei ☆☆

Scala Dei

Scala Dei was a great Carthusian monastery, now in ruins. The bodega, now owned by Codorníu, is in an old stone building nearby, making high-quality, oak-aged Priorato: deep, dark, and strong, but balanced with rich, soft-fruit flavours. The labels include "Cartoixa Scala Dei", a *gran reserva* made of pure Garnacha, and the less overwhelming "Negre", which is given shorter ageing in cask.

Torres ☆☆–☆☆☆☆

Vilafranca del Penedès. www.torres.es

An old family company (founded 1870), which has changed the wine map of Spain over the last thirty years, and put Catalonia on a par with Rioja as a producer of top-quality wines. The family has 2,000 hectares of vineyards, planted with Chardonnay, Gewürztraminer, Riesling, Sauvignon Blanc, Cabernet Sauvignon, Merlot, and Pinot Noir, as well as the traditional Penedès varieties, which Torres has been vigorous in preserving and propagating.

"Viña Sol" is a fresh Parellada white; "Gran Viña Sol" a blend with Chardonnay; "Fransola" mostly Sauvignon Blanc; "Milmanda" a single-vineyard Chardonnay, barrel-fermented. Of the reds, "Tres Torres" is a full-bodied blend of Garnacha and Cariñena, "Gran Sangre de Toro" an older *reserva* of the same, "Coronas" mostly Tempranillo, while "Gran Coronas Reserva" is Tempranillo with some Cabernet Sauvignon. "Mas Borras" is Pinot Noir, "Atrium" a Merlot. "Mas la Plana", the top wine, is a mighty and long-lived Cabernet Sauvignon, formerly known as "Black Label".

Miguel Torres is now absorbed in his mission to revive endangered Catalan varieties. The fruit of his research and hard work is the outstanding "Grans Muralles" from Conca de Barberá. The first vintages of this, rich, earthy and herby with dense soft tannins, promise real distinction with age. Total sales are around 2.5 million cases per year. (*See* page 365.)

Jané Ventura ☆☆–☆☆☆

El Vendrell. www.janeventura.com

A small but definitely quality-oriented estate, still loyal to Spanish varieties, white and red, although there is also a Cabernet on offer. The single-vineyard wines tend to be oak-aged and have an elegant, tannic structure. Good cava, too.

Other Catalan & Balearic Producers

Albet i Noya ☆☆
Vilafranca. www.albetinoya.com
Two brothers run this organic estate, best-known for its cava and juicy, fresh Tempranillo, but also producing good Cabernet and "Núria", a barrique-aged Merlot.

Alella Vinícola Cooperativa ☆
Alella
The long-established (1906) cooperative of the dwindling Alella region. The white *semisecco* is pleasant enough; the dry rather dull.

Cavas del Ampurdán ☆
Perelada
The sister company of Castillo de Perelada (*q.v.*), making pleasant still red, white, and rosé from bought-in grapes. Sparkling wines are bulk-produced by the *cuve close* method. This company was the defendant in a famous London court case, which took place in 1960, when the Champagne authorities succeeded in preventing it from using the term "Spanish Champagne".

Joan d'Anguera ☆☆
Darmós
An old Tarragona property dating from 1825 and owned by the Anguera brothers. Its calling card is the high percentage of Syrah in the wines. The new-oaked "El Bugader", with 70% Syrah, is the finest of them.

Anima Negra
Felanitx, Mallorca
A boutique winery producing a wine called "An" from the local red variety Callet.

Can Rafols del Caus ☆☆
Avinyonet del Penedès
A small property that has opted for mostly French varieties, and makes them well. The best are rich Merlot, and an unusually toasty Chenin Blanc called "La Calma".

Finca Carbonell ☆
Conca de Barberá
A former cooperative, privatized in 1988, and producing fruit-driven wines under Australian winemaker Richard Osborne.

Cims de Porrera ☆☆–☆☆☆
Porrera
The Porrera cooperative's "Classic" is a powerful and structured Priorato wine in a similar league to the acknowledged stars of the region.

Clos Martinet ☆☆–☆☆☆
Falset
Another new-style Priorato, from José Luis Pérez, who was one of the Gratallops pioneers. His best wines are usually labelled "Martinet Especial".

Cooperativa Agricola de Gandesa ☆
Gandesa, Tarragona
Old-established (1919) cooperative with 400 members now in the DO Terra Alta. The simpler, fruitier wines are best.

Masies d'Avinyò ☆
Avinyò, Pla de Bages. www.roqueta.com
Attractive, medium-bodied wines from Chardonnay and the Bordeaux varieties, all under the name of "Abadal".

De Muller ☆☆
Tarragona
The great name in the classic tradition of sweet Tarragona wines. A family firm founded in 1851, still in its old bodega by the harbour. The pride of the house are its altar wines, supplied to (among others) the Vatican, and its velvety, *solera*-aged Moscatel, Pajarete, and other dessert wines.

Naverán ☆☆–☆☆☆
Torrelavit. www.naveran.com
Medium-sized property, very much focused on red wines from Bordeaux varieties, plus Syrah. Cava is also produced.

Pedro Rovira ☆
Móra la Nova
An old family firm producing *solera*-aged dessert Tarragona, as well as everyday wines.

Puig Roca ☆☆
El Vendrell
A small estate that created a stir with its barrel-fermented Chardonnay and other varietal wines under the "Augustus" label. Fine quality.

Rotllan Torra ☆☆
Torroja del Priorat. www.rotllantorra.com
With twenty-four hectares of vineyards, Jordi Rotllan makes various *cuvées* of Priorato, of which the most exciting are the barrique-aged "Amadis" and "Tirant".

Jaume Serra ☆
Vilanova i la Geltrú
A low-key, but reliable producer of fresh Penedès whites and *rosado*, and some cava.

Celler Vall-Llach ☆☆
Porrera
A newcomer in Priorato, producing remarkably powerful wine given that the dominant variety is the less than thrilling Cariñena. Black-cherries and spice crowd the palate.

Leading Cava Producers

Conde de Caralt ☆–☆☆
Sant Sadurní d'Anoia. www.condedecaralt.es
A famous old sparkling-wine bodega, now part of the Freixenet group (*q.v.*). The name now appears on a range of still wines, including delicate red *reservas*.

Castillo de Perelada ☆☆
Perelada. www.perelada.com
A celebrated cava concern in a picturesque castle dating back to the fourteenth century, now housing a fine library,

collections of glass and ceramics, a wine museum – and a casino. Half the grapes come from the firm's vineyards. The best wine, "Gran Claustro", is one of Catalonia's most satisfying cavas; and a fine red, blending Bordeaux and Catalan varieties and aged in new barriques, appears under the same name. A sister company, Cavas del Ampurdán, produces the cheap and cheerful *cuve close* sparkling "Perelada".

Codorníu ☆–☆☆☆
Sant Sadurní d'Anoia. www.codorniu.es
The first Spanish firm to use the classic method, and now the second biggest sparkling wine house in the world, with 3,000 hectares under their ownership. The Raventós family has made wine in Penedès since the sixteenth century. In 1872, Don José returned from Champagne to imitate its methods. The establishment is now monumental, its vast *fin-de-siècle* buildings and thirty kilometres (eighteen miles) of cellars lie in a green park with splendid cedars. They include a considerable wine museum and attract enormous numbers of visitors. Codorníu is also the owner of other estates in Spain (Raimat, Masía Bach), Mexico, Argentina, and California. The wines range from simple and fruity ("Anna de Codorníu") to highly refined. The "Non Plus Ultra" and "Gran Codorníu" occupy the middle range, and the top bottling is "Jaume Codorníu", with 50% Chardonnay giving it greater elegance.

Freixenet ☆☆
Sant Sadurní d'Anoia. www.freixenet.es
The biggest Spanish cava house, and now the biggest sparkling wine producer in the world, overtaking the giant Codorníu. The top Freixenet wines are special vintage releases. "Brut Barroco" and "Brut Nature" are the best standard lines; "Cordón Negro" is the best seller. "Carta Nevada" is a cheaper brand, and a Brut Rosé is also made. Freixenet also owns "Castellblanch", a reliable brand.

Gramona ☆–☆☆☆
Sant Sadurní d'Anoia. www.gramona.com
Founded in 1921, this is a family owned cava house that has recently started producing a range of unusual table wines, such as barrique-aged Sauvignon Blanc, a Pinot Noir rosé, and an Icewine. Its vintage cavas are of exceptional quality: the "Celler Batlle" and "III Lustros", both traditional Xarel-lo and Macabeo cuvées and given long ageing on the yeasts.

Juvé y Camps ☆☆
Sant Sadurní d'Anoia
Sizeable family firm making superior and expensive cava from grapes grown in its own 300 hectares of vineyard, and from grapes bought in from carefully selected growers. Top cuvées are the vintage cava and "Gran Juvé y Camps". The grandly named "Reserva de la Familia" is a fruity cava, made in substantial quantities. Some still wines are also produced.

Segura Viudas ☆–☆☆
Sant Sadurní d'Anoia. www.seguraviudas.com
The three cava companies owned by Freixenet (*q.v.*) all shelter in the same cellars. Segura Viudas is the *prestige marque*, made in a modern winery surrounded by a 200-hectare vineyard that supplies part of its needs. Its best wine is the "Reserva Heredad", made solely from Catalan varieties and offered in a vulgar bottle with its own built-in coaster.

Other Cava Producers

Cavas Hill ☆
Moja. www.cavashill.com
The English Hill family arrived in Penedès in 1660. In 1884, Don José Hill Ros established this commercial bodega, which produces both cava and still wines. Labels include the very dry "Brut de Brut". The top red is the *gran reserva*.

Cavas Antonio Mascaró ☆
Vilafranca del Penedès. www.mascaro.es
An old family bodega with forty hectares, respected for its cava wines and fine brandy, and also making simple varietal wines such as Sauvignon Blanc.

Marqués de Monistrol ☆
Sant Sadurní d'Anoia. www.marquesdemonistrol.com
This is a long-established and reliable cava house, now owned by the Arco group (which owns Berberana in Rioja). It also produces good Penedès still wines from French grape varieties.

The Levante & Meseta

By far the greatest concentration of vineyards in Spain lies south and southeast of Madrid, in a great block that reaches the Mediterranean at Valencia in the north and Alicante in the south. This central band, with scattered outposts farther west towards Portugal in Extremadura, contained no great names, no lordly estates, no pockets of perfectionism. Its wines combined various degrees of strength with various degrees of dullness – but in the main, a generous helping of body. The last ten years have seen changes. Spain's membership of the EU has exposed the traditional cooperative producers of the region to the realities of competition. Modern market forces have prompted producers to invest in modern technology. Central Spain, like California's Central Valley, has a climate of extremes, but predictable extremes. This allows oenologists to "design" wines by regulating picking dates and controlling fermentation.

While large-scale cooperatives still make much of the wine, estates and smaller bodegas are emerging. The Marqués de Griñón's Cabernet Sauvignon from Toledo has made a mark, as have wines from Vinícola de Castilla in La Mancha (*qq.v.*). Experimental plantings are introducing French grapes; unsuspected flavours being coaxed by skilled winemakers from local varieties. Central Spain has a long road ahead of it, but it is no longer an unrelieved ocean of mediocrity.

The Tierra de Barros sub-zone, in the province of Badajoz, though producing some of the best wine from Extremadura, was never confirmed as a DO, although many sub-zones were regrouped in 1997 as the DO Ribera del Guadiana. The 40,000-odd hectares in Tierra de Barros are largely planted with a common white grape, the Cayetana, giving dry, low-acid, but high-strength wines – the curse of Spain, in fact. Its rarer red wines, however, have some merit.

Toledo province, southwest of Madrid, contains the DO of Méntrida, a 13,000-hectare spread of Garnacha vines supplying strong red wine. Until the 1980s, the minimum alcohol for its red wines had to be fourteen degrees, and some offenders reached eighteen. Today the wines are more balanced, but there is still some way to go.

By far the biggest wine region in the whole of Spain, demarcated or not, is La Mancha, the dreary plain of Don Quixote. It has around 193,310 hectares under vine, almost all of them planted with a white variety called Airén. The best that could be said of most Airén wine was that it had no flavour beyond that of its thirteen to fourteen degrees of alcohol, but some producers have been coaxing agreeable flavours from it by careful winemaking.

The one superior enclave of La Mancha is DO Valdepeñas, 160 kilometres (100 miles) south of Madrid, where the tradition is to blend Airén (almost eighty per cent of the vineyards being planted with this variety) with a small measure of dark red, made of Tempranillo (here called Cencibel) and Garnacha. So dark is the red that a mere ten per cent of it makes the wine, known as *aloque*: a *clarete* in colour, though it remains a soft and rather spineless wine, low in acid and tannin. The old method was fermentation in the tall clay *tinajas*, obviously descended from Roman or earlier vessels. Modern methods have shown clearly how much better the wine can be. Such producers as Los Llanos and Felix Solin now cool-ferment and oak-age their wines, with results worthy of the better parts of northern Spain.

The sorry tale continues with the DOP (provisional DO) of Manchuela, east of La Mancha, and making both white and red wine on its 8,000 hectares.

The smaller DO of Almansa around Albacete concludes the toll of the Castilian plain. Its 7,600 hectares are planted with dark grapes, mostly Monastrell.

The term "Levante" embraces six DOs of only very moderate interest at present, but some considerable potential as modern methods creep in. To the north, on the coast, is Valencia (and what was formerly called Cheste), liberal producers of alcoholic white wine and, to a lesser degree, red, although a handful of estates are demonstrating the true potential of the region for flavoury reds from good varieties.

Inland from Valencia lies Utiel-Requena, a hill region of black grapes (the principal one, the Bobal, as black as night) used expressly for colouring wine. The local technique is to ferment each batch of wine with a double ration of skins to extract the maximum colour and tannin: a brew called *vino de doble pasta*. Its by-product, the lightly crushed juice with barely any "skin contact" or colour, surplus to the double brew, makes the second specialty of the region: a racy, pale rosé more to the modern taste.

The DO Alicante covers both coastal vineyards, producing sweet Moscatel, and hill vineyards for red wines, *vino de doble pasta* and rosés. A little local white wine is (relatively) highly prized. Behind Alicante in the province of Murcia there are three *denominaciónes*: Bullas (mostly *rosado* wines), Yecla, and Jumilla, whose respective cooperatives are struggling to teach their inky material modern manners. So far, Jumilla seems to be marginally the more advanced of the three, with some wines showing surprising potential to age in bottle.

The striking achievements of the Marqués de Griñón in Castilla-La Mancha have stumped the DO authorities, who solved the problem by granting him his own appellation (*see* Dominio de Valdepuesa) in 2002.

Leading Levante & Meseta Producers

Ayuso ☆
Villarrobleda, Albacete. www.bodegasayuso.es
A family concern based in Manchuela. These La Mancha wines, released under the "Estola" label, used to be thin and faded, but have been gaining in body and fruit.

Miguel Carrión ☆
Alpera, Almansa
An improving producer of DO Almansa, situated to the east of La Mancha.

Casa de la Viña ☆
Alhambra, Ciudad Real
A major producer of agreeable, medium-bodied Valdepeñas. The property is part of the Bodegas y Bebidas group, and thus owned by Allied-Domecq.

Castaño ☆☆
Yecla. www.bodegascastano.com
A leading 350-hectare domaine in Yecla, well-equipped and producing a wide range of wines, mostly pure Monastrell, but also blends with Merlot and Cabernet. Most of the wines are unoaked; some are given a dose of American oak. They all offer excellent value. The top wines are bottled under the "Pozuelo" label.

Vinícola de Castilla ☆☆
Manzanares, Ciudad Real. www.vinicoladecastilla.com
This is a large, hi-tech, million-case winery that used to belong to Rumasa. The simple young wines are more enjoyable on the whole than the *gran reservas*, which can lack fruit. Pleasant Cabernet Sauvignon under the "Señorío de Guadineja" label.

Centro-Españolas ☆
Tomelloso. www.allozo.com
A modern and well-equipped La Mancha winery, working almost exclusively with the local varieties and bottling its wines under the "Allozo" label.

Dehesa del Carrizal ☆
Retuerta del Bullaque, Ciudad Real.
www.dehesadelcarrizal.com
A small property dedicated to a single variety, Cabernet Sauvignon, made in an elegant if oaky style.

Jesús Díaz e Hijos ☆
Colmenar de Oreja
One of the best-known estates in the DO Vinos de Madrid, with an emphasis on young wines for early drinking.

Gandía ☆–☆☆
Chiva, Valencia. www.gandiawines.com
This vast business produces four million cases, most of which is exported. Many of the better wines come from the Hoya de Cadenas property, which Gandía bought in the early 1990s. Cabernet Sauvignon plays a major part in the best wines, such as those released under the "Ceremonia" label.

Gutiérrez de la Vega ☆☆
Parcent, Alicante

A small family property, founded in 1978, showing the excellent quality that can be achieved using indigenous grapes such as Monastrell and Moscatel.

Bodegas Huertas ☆
Jumilla. www.bodegashuertas.es

Clean, well-made reds and *rosado* from Monastrell grapes, proving that Jumilla is not necessarily a bruiser of a wine.

InViOSA (Industrias Vinícolas del Oeste) ☆
Almendralejo, Badajoz

Best bodega of the DO Ribera del Guadiana, making red and white "Lar de Barros", though not from the typical grapes of the area. International varieties have been planted here since the early 1990s.

Cooperativa Jesús del Perdón ☆
Manzanares, Ciudad Real. www.yuntero.com

A large cooperative known particularly for its dry white, but the red has improved considerably in recent years. The brand name is "Yuntero", plus "Mundo de Yuntero" for organically grown Airén and Tempranillo.

Los Llanos ☆☆–☆☆☆
Valdepeñas, Ciudad Real. www.losllanos.com

The first house in Valdepeñas to bottle its own wines. The oak-aged *reservas* and *gran reservas* set new standards for the region. "Señorío de Los Llanos" *gran reserva* is a fine, aromatic, and silky wine by any standards, and the "Pata Negra" *gran reserva*, made only in top years, is even finer.

Finca Luzón ☆☆
Jumilla. www.fincaluzon.com

Modern-style wines from a new venture in Jumilla, which has grown rapidly to a production of one million bottles per year. All the reds are a blend of Monastrell, Tempranillo, and Cabernet Sauvignon.

Manuel Manzaneque ☆☆
El Bonillo, Albacete

A small property in the Meseta with some of the highest vineyards in Spain. The reds blend Cabernet and Tempranillo in varying proportions, and the best white is a full-bodied, oak-aged Chardonnay.

Luis Megía ☆
Valdepeñas

A very modern, mass-production facility, making sound and highly commercial wines under numerous labels.

Enríque Mendoza ☆☆–☆☆☆
Alfás del Pí. www.bodegasmendoza.com

A medium-sized Alicante estate, thoroughly international in its approach to reds, producing full-bodied Cabernet, Merlot, Shiraz, and French-style blends. Plus Moscatel, of course.

Cooperativa Nuestra Señora del Rosario ☆
Bullas

This very large cooperative is well-equipped and makes consistently fruity white (Macabeo), also *rosado* and red, both from Monastrell.

Piqueras ☆
Almansa

A large producer, and just about the only one in Almansa with aspirations to quality. A new winery was built in 2002. The reds are easily the best wines.

Salvador Poveda ☆☆–☆☆☆
Monóvar, Alicante. www.salvadorpoveda.com

An outstanding Alicante bodega, known especially for its rich dessert *fondillón*, a fortified Monastrell given long cask-ageing. "Viña Vermeta" is the label for the estate's finest Monastrell.

Cooperativa La Purísima ☆
Yecla. www.calpyecla.com

The major producer of Yecla wine. The huge bodega, working with the crop from 4,500 hectares, makes efforts to produce wines of moderate strength, but the result tends to mingle overripe and underripe flavours in rather thin wine. There is also an organic Monastrell.

Agapito Rico ☆–☆☆
Jumilla

This 100-hectare property has moved away from the traditional brawny style of Jumilla to produce fruity, straightforward red wines, mostly unoaked, from varieties such as Merlot and Syrah.

Cooperativa San Isidro ☆
Jumilla

The region's largest cooperative, processing the production of 20,000 hectares, much of which is sold in bulk. But wines bottled under the "Sabatcha" label can be of good quality.

Señorío del Condestable ☆
Jumilla

A member of the Bodegas y Bebidas group, now owned by Allied-Domecq. Best-known for its red "Señorío de Robles", a well-made, everyday wine from Monastrell, light in colour and flavour but with a fresh, almost cherry-like smell and pleasant texture. Some of the wines are sourced from other Spanish wine regions.

Félix Solís ☆☆
Valdepeñas. www.felixsolis.es

This family owned winery owns 1,000 hectares of vineyards, but also buys in grapes and must. It is a large-scale maker of reds and *rosados* with a reputation for oak-aged reds, especially "Viña Albali Reserva".

Dominio de Valdepusa ☆☆☆
Malpica de Tajo, Toledo. www.marquesdegrinon.com

The Marqués de Griñón founded this property in 1989, planting Bordeaux varieties and Syrah. The wines have been of exceptional quality and made in an avowedly French style, though they have their own personality, with more power than most Bordeaux or Rhône wines. Today the property is part of the Arco group (*see* Berberana), but the *marqués* remains fully involved.

El Vínculo ☆☆
Campo de Criptana

Alejandro Fernández of Pesquera (*q.v.*) has boldly ventured into La Mancha, creating this new property in 1999. The wine is very much in the Pesquera style: rich, tannic, and given long ageing in American oak.

Cooperativa Virgen de la Viñas ☆
Tomelloso, Ciudad Real

One of the bigger co-ops, known by its brand name "Tomillar" and for its Cencibel *reserva*.

Andalucía

The great fame and success of sherry were achieved to some degree at the expense of the other regions of Andalucía. From their long-established trading base, the sherry makers were able to buy the best from their neighbours to add to their own stock. Sherry may be the best *vino generoso* of Andalucía, but it is not the only one. Montilla can compete with very similar wines, and Málaga with alternatives at the sweeter end of the range.

Málaga

Málaga, on the Costa del Sol, is strictly an *entrepôt* rather than a vineyard centre. The grapes that make its sweet (occasionally dry) brown wines are grown either in the hills forty kilometres (twenty-five miles) to the east or the same distance to the north. East are the coastal vineyards of Axarquía, where the grape is the Moscatel. North around Mollina (in fact towards Montilla) it is the Pedro Ximénez (or PX). The rules require that all the grapes are brought to Málaga to mature in its bodegas. Various methods are used to sweeten and concentrate the wines, from sunning the grapes, to boiling down the must to *arrope*, as in Jerez. The styles of the finished wine range from a dry white of Pedro Ximénez, not unlike a Montilla amontillado, to the common dark and sticky *dulce color*, thickly laced with *arrope* (reduced grape juice used to make sweetening). The finest quality, comparable in its origins to the Essencia of Tokaj, is the *lágrima*, the "tears" of uncrushed grapes. The difference is that noble rot concentrates Tokay, in Málaga it is the sun. Other Málagas are Pajarete, a dark, semi-sweet apéritif style; the paler *semidulce*; and the richly aromatic Moscatel. The finer wines are made in a *solera* system like sherry, with younger wine refreshing older. A great rarity, a century-old vintage Málaga from the Duke of Wellington's estate, bottled in 1875, was a superlative, delicate, aromatic, and still-sweet dessert wine in 1995.

But Málaga is in decline. The large commercial wineries live on, but the the specialists such as Scholtz Hermanos, with their magnificent old *solera*s, have been forced by declining fashion and sales to shut their doors for good.

Montilla-Moriles

Montilla's wines are close enough to sherry to be easily confused with (or passed off as) its rivals. The soil is the same *albariza*, but the climate is harsher and hotter, and the Pedro Ximénez, grown here in preference to the Palomino, yields smaller crops, producing wines of a higher alcoholic degree and slightly lower acidity. The wines are fermented in tall clay *tinajas*, like giant amphoras, and rapidly develop the same *flor* yeast as sherry. They fall into the same classifications: fino, oloroso, or palo cortado – the finos from the first light pressing. With age, fino becomes amontillado, "in the style of Montilla". Unfortunately, however, the sherry shippers have laid legal claim in Britain (the biggest export market for Montilla) to the classic terms. Instead of a Montilla fino, amontillado, or oloroso, a true and fair description, the label must use "dry", "medium" or "cream".

Montilla has much to recommend it as an alternative to sherry. Its finos in particular have a distinctive dry softness of style, with less "attack" but no less freshness. A cool bottle of Montilla disappears with gratifying speed.

Last of the Andalusian *denominaciónes*, and most deeply in the shadow of Jerez, is the coastal region of Huelva, near the Portuguese border. Condado de Huelva (known in Chaucer's time as "Lepe") has exported its strong white wines for 1,000 years. The commercial power of Jerez has effectively kept it in obscurity. Until the 1960s, its wine was blended and shipped as sherry. Now that it has to compete with its old paymaster, times are not easy, and the region is increasingly making light white wines.

Leading Andalucía Producers

Alvear ☆☆–☆☆☆☆
Montilla. www.alvear.es

An independent firm, founded by the Alvear family in 1729. Today it is still owned and managed by family members. They have 130 hectares under vine in Montilla-Moriles, much of it in the superior Sierra district, and 17,000 butts of maturing wine in their bodegas. Fermentation in *tinajas* and ageing through the *solera* system are carried out according to the traditions of Montilla, producing wines of high quality. "Fino CB" is their biggest seller. "CB" is a slightly fuller fino, and other names and styles include "Carlos VII" amontillado, "Asunción" oloroso, and the *dulce* "Pedro Ximénez 1830".

Cobos ☆
Montilla

Wines of variable quality, but the "Pompeyo" fino and "Tres Pasa PX" are reliable.

Gracia Hermanos ☆–☆☆
Montilla

A bodega with high standards, owned by Pérez Barquero (*q.v.*). The fino, "María del Valle", is typically light and refreshing, and "Montearruit" a concentrated amontillado.

Larios ☆–☆☆
Málaga

Better known for its gin in Spain, but a Málaga bodega with an excellent sweet Moscatel and an oloroso called "Benefique". Owned by Pernod-Ricard.

López Hermanos ☆–☆☆
Málaga

This is now the leading Málaga bodega, since the sad demise in 1996 of Scholtz. The company has made a real effort to re-interest the foreign wine trade in Málaga wines, as well as rekindling interest at home. "Trajinero" is probably the best

Sherry Glossary

Almacenista a wholesaler or stockholder of wines for ageing, but also used for the individual old unblended wines he sells, which are occasionally offered as collectors' items.

Amontillado literally "a wine in the style of Montilla". Not at all so in fact, but a well-aged fino that has developed a nutty flavour with maturity in oak. The term is also loosely used for any medium sherry.

Añada the wine of one year, kept as such in a butt until (or instead of) becoming part of a *solera*.

Arroba the working measure in a sherry bodega. The standard 500-litre butt holds thirty *arrobas*.

Arrope a *vino de color*: wine reduced by boiling it to one-fifth of its original volume. The result is an intensely sweet and treacly black brew, used only for colouring and sweetening blends. *Sancocho* is similar.

Bristol the historic centre of the sherry trade in Britain, a name much used on labels to imply quality, but not a reference to any particular style of wine.

Brown sherry sweet sherry blended from olorosos and *rayas* to be sweeter and darker than a "cream".

Cream sherry a blend of sweetened olorosos, with or without *vino de color*. Harvey's Bristol Cream was the original. Croft's successfully introduced the idea of a pale (uncoloured) "cream" in the 1970s.

Dulce apagado intensely sweet wine made by stopping the fermentation of must by adding brandy. Used only for sweetening "medium" sherries.

Dulce de almíbar a mixture of young wine and invert sugar used for sweetening pale sherries without darkening them.

Dulce pasa dark sweetening wine made by leaving ordinary sherry grapes in the sun to concentrate the sugar, then stopping their fermenting must with brandy. Used for sweetening good-quality "cream".

East India now a fanciful name for a sweet, usually brown, sherry. It derives from the former custom of sending sherry (like Madeira) to the Indies and back as ship's ballast to speed its maturity.

Entre fino the classification of a young wine which shows fino character but not the required quality for the finest *soleras*.

Fino the lightest, most delicate, and literally finest of sherries. It naturally develops a growth of *flor* yeast, which protects its pale colour and intensifies its fresh aroma.

Fino amontillado a fino on the way to maturing as an amontillado.

Fino viejo, viejíssimo occasionally an old fino declines to enter middle age as an amontillado and simply intensifies its aristocratic finesse, growing formidably powerful, dusty, dry, and austere, while remaining straw-pale.

Jerez quinado a cordial or apéritif made by mixing quinine with sherry.

Macharnudo the most famous of the *pagos*, vineyard districts, northwest of Jerez; sometimes mentioned on labels.

Manzanilla the specialty of Sanlúcar de Barrameda. Sherries matured in its bodegas by the sea take on a singular sharp and even salty tang that makes them the most appetizing of all. Removed to bodegas elsewhere they revert to normal wines. Most manzanilla is drunk as pale and unsweetened fino. With age it becomes pasada, darker and slightly nutty with an almost buttery richness. Eventually it becomes a deeply nutty Manzanilla amontillado; one of the most vivid and intense of all sherries.

Moscatel sweetening wine made of sun-dried Moscatel grapes, for giving added sugar and fruity flavour to certain sweet blends.

Oloroso in its natural state, full-bodied dry sherry without the delicacy, fragrance, or piquancy of fino, but with extra richness and depth. It does not develop *flor* to the same extent, but picks up colour and oak flavours in the butt. Old, unblended olorosos are astonishingly dark, pungent, and so concentrated that they almost seem to burn your mouth. In practice nearly all oloroso is used as the base for sweet sherries, particularly "creams".

Palma a classification for a particularly delicate and fragrant fino. "Tres Palmas" is the brand name of a very fine one.

Palo cortado an aberrant sherry which shows the good characters of both amontillado and oloroso at the same time. Palo cortado is a highly prized rarity, nearly always kept apart and bottled as an unblended *solera* wine with only a little sweetening.

Pata de galina an oloroso which, in its natural state, shows signs of sweetness, derived from glycerine. Occasionally bottled as such, when it is incomparable.

Paxarete an alternative name for *vino de color*.

Pedro Ximénez (PX) The grape which, after sun-drying, produces the sweetest of all sherries. Often used for blending, but some shippers bottle pure PX, which resembles liquid treacle.

Raya the classification for an oloroso-type wine of secondary quality; the make-weight in most middle-range blends.

Vino de color colouring wine, *e.g. arrope*.

Vino de pasto "table wine": light, medium-dry sherry of uncertain quality, now rarely seen.

---

dry Málaga; "Cartojal" is a "pale-cream" *pálido*; and the flagship is the straight Málaga "Virgen", aged two years in cask without topping up.

Bodegas Pérez Barquero ☆
Montilla

A well-equipped winery producing a reliable range of different styles under the brand name "Gran Barquero".

Viños Telmo Rodríguez ☆☆
Burgos

The ubiquitous Spanish winemaker has sought out steep vineyards within Málaga to produce what he calls "mountain wine", a style popular centuries ago in Britain. It is an unctuous Moscatel, given greater suppleness with long barrel-ageing.

Toro Albala ☆☆–☆☆☆
Aguilar de la Frontera

Remarkable wines from Montilla, of which easily the best are the ancient *soleras* producing amontillado and very sweet PX styles of great concentration and swagger.

Cooperativa Vinícola del Condado ☆
Bollullos del Condado

The main cooperative of Huelva, with 4,500 hectares of vines. Responsible for large quantities of brandy, some table wines, and some good, *solera*-aged, sherry-style *generosos*.

Sherry

Sherry, like many Mediterranean wines, was first appreciated in and shipped to the countries of northern Europe for its strength, its sweetness, and its durability – all qualities that made it a radically different commodity from medieval claret. By Shakespeare's day, while spirits were still unknown, "sack" (as it was then called) was hugely popular as the strongest drink available. The warming effect of a "cup of sack", at perhaps seventeen degrees alcohol, was the addiction not just of Sir John Falstaff, but of every tavern-goer. Sack came from Málaga, the Canary Islands, and even from Greece and Cyprus. But the prince of sacks was "sherris", named after the Andalucían town of Jerez de la Frontera.

Jerez has had an international trading community since the Middle Ages. Until the rise of Rioja it was unique in Spain for its huge bodegas full of stock worth millions. The refinement of its wine from a coarse product, shipped without ageing, to the modern elaborate range of styles began in the eighteenth century. Like Champagne, (which it resembles in more ways than one) it flowered with the wealth and technology of the nineteenth century.

What its makers have done is to push the natural adaptability of a strong but not otherwise extraordinary, indeed rather flat and neutral, white wine to the limit. They have exploited its potential for barrel-ageing in contact with oxygen – the potentially disastrous oxidation – to produce flavours as different in their way as a lemon and a date. And they have perfected the art of blending from the wide spectrum in their paintbox to produce every conceivable nuance in between – and to produce it unchanging year after year.

The making of sherry today, folklore apart, differs little from the making of any white wine. A fairly light wine is rapidly pressed and fermented. Eventually it reaches a natural strength of between twelve and sixteen degrees. At this point it is fortified with spirit to adjust the strength to fifteen or eighteen degrees, depending on its quality and characteristics. This is where sherry's unique ageing process begins.

It is the wayward nature of sherry that different barrels (500-litre "butts") of wine, even from the same vineyard, can develop in different ways. The essential distinction is between those that develop a vigorous growth of floating yeast, called *flor*, and those that do not. All the young wines are kept in the "nursery" in butts filled four-fifths full. The finest and most delicate wines, only slightly fortified to maintain their finesse, rapidly develop a creamy scum on the surface, which thickens in spring to a layer several inches deep. This singular yeast has the property of protecting the wine from oxidation, and at the same time reacting with it to impart subtle hints of maturity. These finest wines, or finos, are ready to drink sooner than heavier sherries. They remain pale because oxygen is excluded. They can be perfect at about five years old. But their precise age is irrelevant because, like all sherries, they are blended for continuity in a *solera* (*see* box below).

Young wines of a heavier, clumsier, and more pungent style grow less *flor*, or none at all. A stronger dose of fortifying spirit discourages any *flor* that may appear. This second broad category of sherry is known, if it shows potential quality, as oloroso. These wines are barrel-aged without benefit of *flor*, in full contact with the air. Their maturation is therefore an oxidative process, darkening their colour and intensifying their flavour.

A third, eccentric, class of sherry is also found in this early classifying of the crop – one that combines the breadth and depth of a first-class oloroso with the fragrance, finesse, and "edge" of a fino. This rarity is known as a palo cortado.

These three are the raw materials of the bodega – naturally different from birth. It is the bodega's business to rear them so as to accentuate these differences, and to use them in combinations to produce a far wider range of styles. A fino which is matured beyond the life span of its *flor* usually begins to deepen in colour and broaden in flavour, shading from straw to amber to (at great age) a rich, blackish-brown. Every bodega has one or more *solera* of old finos, which have been allowed to move through the scale from a fresh fino, to a richer, more concentrated fino-amontillado, to an intensely nutty and powerful old amontillado.

Commercially, however, such true and unblended amontillados are very rare. In general usage the term has been more or less bastardized to mean any "medium" sherry, between dry fino and creamy old oloroso in style, but rarely with the quality of either. All sherries in their natural state, maturing in their *soleras*, are bone-dry. Unlike port, sherry is never fortified until fermentation is over – all sugar used up. Straight, unblended sherry is therefore an ascetic, austere taste: a rarity in commerce. The only exception is *dulce*: concentrated wine used for sweetening blends.

As the sherry ages in the bodega, evaporation increases both the alcohol content and the proportion of flavouring elements. Very old sherries still in wood often become

The Solera System

A *solera* is the bodega's way of achieving complete continuity in its essential stock-in-trade: a range of wines of distinctive character. It is a "fractional blending" system, in which wine is drawn for use from the oldest of a series of butts, which is then topped up from the next oldest, and so on, down to young wine in the youngest *criadera* in the series, which in turn is supplied with young sherry as close in character to its elders as possible. The effect of withdrawing and replacing a portion (normally about a third) of a butt at a time is that each addition rapidly takes on the character of the older wine to which it is added. An incalculable fraction of the oldest wine in the *solera* always remains in the final butt (or rather, butts, for the operation is on a big scale, and each stage may involve fifty butts). At the same time, so long as the *solera* is operating, the average age of the wine at every stage (except the new input) is getting gradually greater; thus the individuality of the *solera* is more pronounced. Certain famous *soleras* in Jerez, those that produce "Tío Pepe", for instance, or "San Patricio", were started over a century ago. Here the word "produce", however, is misleading. It is more accurate to say "give character to", for *solera* wine is rarely bottled "straight".

literally undrinkable in their own right – but priceless in the depth of flavour they can add to a blend. Classic sherry-blending is very much the art of the shipper, but anyone can try it for himself by acquiring, say, a bottle of a very old dry sherry such as Domecq's "Río Viejo" or González Byass "Duque", and simply adding one small glassful of it to a carafe of an ordinary "medium" sherry. The immediate extra dimension of flavour in the everyday wine is a revelation.

The former custom was for every wine merchant to have his own range of blends made in Jerez to his own specification. The more rational modern trend is for the shippers in Jerez to promote their own brands. The best of these will be the produce of a single, prized *solera*, usually slightly sweetened with *arrope*, a special treacly sweetening wine. A touch of near-black but almost tasteless *vino de color* may be needed to adjust the colour. Possibly a little younger wine in the same style will be added to give it freshness.

A common commercial blend, on the other hand, will consist largely of low-value, minimally aged *rayas* or *entre* finos (the term for second-grade wine in the fino style). A small proportion of wine from a good *solera* will be added to improve the flavour, then a good deal of sweetening wine to mask the faults of the base material. It is, unfortunately, wines made to this sort of specification that have given sherry the image of a dowdy drink of no style.

The sad result is that the truly great wines of Jerez, wines that can stand comparison in their class with great white burgundy or Champagne, are absurdly undervalued. In recent years, many of the major shippers have released new wines in order to stimulate fresh interest in sherry as a whole. Thus vintage-dated or age-dated sherries, and minute bottlings from the most ancient *soleras*, have been introduced onto the market, and in 2000 aged-dated sherries became an officially recognized category for the first time. For connoisseurs they are a true delight, but have had little impact on the overall sales and consumption of sherry, which continues to suffer from its stuffy image.

The Sherry Region

Jerez lies sixteen kilometres (ten miles) inland from the Bay of Cádiz in southwest Spain. Its vineyards surround it on all sides, but all the best of them are on outcrops of chalky soil in a series of dune-like waves to the north and west, between the rivers Guadalete and Guadalquivír. The Guadalquivír, famous as the river of Seville, from which Columbus set out to discover America, Magellan to circumnavigate, and Pizarro to conquer Peru, forms the northern boundary of the sherry region. Its port, Sanlúcar de Barrameda, Jerez, and Puerto are the three sherry towns. The land between them is the zone known as Jerez Superior, the heart of the best sherry country.

There are three soil types in the sherry region, but only the intensely white *albariza*, a clay consisting of up to eighty per cent pure chalk, makes the best wine. It has high water-retaining properties that resist summer drought and the desiccating wind, the Levante, that blows from Africa. It also reflects sunlight up into the low-trained bush vines so that the grapes bask in a slow oven as they ripen.

Barro, a brown, chalky clay, is more fertile but produces heavier, coarser wine. *Arena*, or sand, is little used now for vineyards at all.

Each distinct, low, vineyard hill has a name: Carrascal, Macharnudo, Añina, and Balbaina are the most famous of the *pagos*, as they are called, surrounding Jerez in an arc of *albariza* to the north and west. A separate outbreak of excellent soil gives rise to the *pagos* south and east of Sanlúcar, twenty-two kilometres (fourteen miles) from Jerez, of which the best-known name is Miraflores.

The regulations of the *consejo regulador*, the governing body of Jerez, stipulate that every bodega buys a certain proportion of its wine from the Superior vineyards – a rule scarcely necessary today, since eighty-five per cent of the region is Superior; the outlying low-quality vineyards have fallen out of use. Indeed, since the export market went into decline in 1979, there has been a massive reconversion in the sherry industry, with cash incentives to grub up excess vineyard land, and a spate of takeovers and mergers in the business. Sherry had boomed – give or take the odd war – from the Middle Ages until 1979, and planting reflected everyone's expectation that it would continue to do so. By 1997, the job was completed, and the vineyards today occupy 10,500 hectares.

Leading Sherry Producers

Antonio Barbadillo ☆☆☆
Sanlúcar de Barrameda. www.barbadillo.com
The biggest bodega in Sanlúcar, with a big stake in the manzanilla business and some wonderful old wines. It was founded in 1821 by Don Benigno Barbadillo. Five generations later, the company is still family-owned, although Harvey's has a shareholding. Offices (in the former bishops' palace) and the original bodegas are in the town centre.

In the surrounding *albariza* areas of Cádiz, Balbaina, San Julian, Carrascal, and Gibaldin, it owns 500 hectares of vines, producing a wide range of manzanillas and other sherries: "Solear", "Eva", "Pastora", "Tío Río", "Pedro Rodríguez", "Príncipe", "Ducado de Sanlúcar", and "Villareal". Barbadillo was a pioneer of dry white Palomino ("Castillo de San Diego") that has enjoyed phenomenal success on the domestic market. In the late 1990s, it launched "Manzanilla En Rama", drawn directly from cask and bottled with only the lightest filtration, and "Reliquias", a range of extremely old, rare, and costly sherries from ancient *soleras*.

Agustin Blázquez ☆–☆☆
Carretera de la Cartuja
A relatively small, high-quality bodega founded in 1795: part of the Domecq group (*q.v.*) since 1973 and operated independently. Its best-known products are a well-aged fino, "Carta Blanca", "Carta Roja" oloroso, a palo cortado called "Capuchino", and a noble old amontillado, "Carta Oro".

Bobadilla ☆
Jerez de la Frontera
A large company, founded in 1872. The original bodega was part of a monastery in Jerez, though the current premises are now modern. In 1990 it was bought by Osborne (*q.v.*), and today is better known for its brandies than its sherries.

John William Burdon ☆☆
Puerto de Santa María
Formerly an English-owned bodega, and one of the largest bodegas of the mid- to late nineteenth century. It is now

owned by Luis Caballero (*q.v.*). Wines are "Burdon Fino", a Puerto-style fino, "Don Luís Amontillado" and "Heavenly Cream". Wines have improved in recent years.

Luis Caballero ☆
Puerto de Santa María
Founded in the 1830s with a stock of wine from the dukes of Medina, this has been in the Caballero family since 1932, and is now run by Don Luis Caballero. All wines are supplied from own vineyards; major brands include "Troubadour" and a range called "Benito". Fino is the specialty, as Don Luis has his own formula, made by adding some very young wine to the wine drawn from *solera*. Don Luis is also the owner of Burdon and Lustau (*qq.v.*).

Croft ☆☆
Jerez de la Frontera
The port shipper (founded 1768) gave its name to the sherry division of International Distillers and Vintners in 1970. In 2001, the company was acquired by González Byass (*q.v.*). Rancho Croft on the edge of town is a huge complex of traditional-style buildings housing the most modern plant and 70,000 butts. Croft has planted 350 hectares of *albariza* land in Los Tercios and Cuartillos. Market research led the company to launch the first pale cream sherry, "Croft Original". "Croft Particular" is a pale amontillado, classic medium-dry, and "Delicado" a true fino. They also make a fine palo cortado.

Delgado Zuleta ☆☆–☆☆☆
Sanlúcar de Barrameda
Family firm founded in 1744 and still independent. The best-known wine is "La Goya", a manzanilla pasada. Other wines include the "Zuleta" amontillado and a fino called "Don Tomás".

Diez-Merito ☆
Jerez de la Frontera
An amalgamation of bodegas specializing in supplying "buyers' own brands". It was founded in France in 1884 as Diez Hermanos and is now controlled by Marcos Eguizábal Ramirez. The name was changed in 1979 when Diez took over the old house of Merito. It has 175 hectares, a huge new bodega in Jerez and one at Puerto de Santa María. Brands include "Fino Imperial" (a very old amontillado), a splendid oloroso "Victoria Regina", and the "Diez Hermanos" range. Diez-Merito has taken over Don Zoilo and Celstino Diez de Morales, and now markets the very fine "Don Zoilo" fino, amontillado, and cream.

Pedro Domecq ☆☆–☆☆☆
Jerez de la Frontera. www.domecq.es
The oldest, largest, and one of the most respected shipping houses, founded in 1730 by Irish and French families and including in its history (as English agent) John Ruskin's father. Today it is part of the Diageo empire. It owns 1,600 hectares of vines. The late head of the firm, Don José Ignacio Domecq, was recognized worldwide both literally and figuratively as "the nose" of sherry. The finest wines are the gentle "Fino La Ina"; "Sibarita", an old palo cortado; "Rio Viejo", a dark, rich but dry oloroso, and the luscious "Double Century". Tiny quantities of very old wines are released each year, under labels such as "Amontillado 51-1A" (average age: fifty years) and "Venerable PX".

Duff-Gordon
See Osborne

Garvey ☆–☆☆☆
Jerez de la Frontera. www.grupogarvey.com
One of the great bodegas, founded in 1780 by Irishman William Garvey, who built what for many years remained the grandest bodega in Spain: 170 metres (558 feet) long. It is owned by the Ruiz-Mateos family. A new winery and bodegas have been built on the outskirts of Jerez. Garvey has 500 hectares under vine in various *albariza* areas that produce consistently good wines. "San Patricio" (named after the patron saint of Ireland), a full-flavoured fino, is its best-known sherry. Others include "Tío Guillermo" amontillado, "Ochavico" dry oloroso, and "La Lidia" manzanilla. The wines overall are sound but lack concentration.

González Byass ☆☆–☆☆☆☆
Jerez de la Frontera. www.gonzalezbyass.es
One of the greatest sherry houses, founded in 1835 by Don Antonio González y Rodriguez, whose London agent, Robert Blake Byass, became a partner in 1863. The company is still directed almost entirely by the González family. They control 1,200 hectares of vineyards and have stocks of 132,000 butts. Their best-known sherry is the world's biggest-selling fino, "Tío Pepe", which is of outstanding quality. "La Concha" amontillado, "San Domingo" pale cream, and "Nectar" cream are exported throughout the world. There is a range of glorious old sherries, including "Amontillado del Duque" and "Apóstoles" dry oloroso. This was the first shipper to release vintage-dated sherries, beginning with 1963. They also make one of the greatest of all dessert sherries, "Matúsalem", and an astonishing PX called "Noë". Other interests include Bodegas Beronia in Rioja.

John Harvey ☆–☆☆☆
Jerez de la Frontera. www.domecq.es
The famous Bristol shipper was founded in 1796. In 1822 the first John Harvey joined the firm. It is now part of Allied-Domecq, and today Harvey works closely with its Jerez partner, Pedro Domecq (*q.v.*). The firm became famous as blenders of "Bristol" sweet sherries, above all "Bristol Cream", now the world's biggest-selling brand, and a huge export business. Only since 1970 has Harvey acquired extensive vineyards. "Bristol Cream", once the ultimate luxury sherry, is now merely good. Other brands are "Bristol Milk" (not sold in the UK), "Club Amontillado", "Bristol Dry" (in fact medium) and "Luncheon Dry", a dry fino.

Hidalgo ☆☆☆
Sanlúcar de Barrameda. www.vincola-hidalgo.es
Small bodega, founded in 1792 and is still owned and run by the Hidalgo family. They have 200 hectares of albariza vineyards in Balbaina and Miraflores. The principal brands include: the yeasty vibrant "La Gitana" manzanilla, "Jerez Cortado" (a *palo cortado*), "Napoleon" dry amontillado, and the outstanding manzanilla pasada "Pastrana".

Los Infantes de Orleans-Borbón ☆☆
Sanlúcar de Barrameda
The Danish royal family owns vineyards in southwest France; the Spanish royal family, in conjunction with Barbadillo, have their own bodega in Andalucía.

Good wines, especially the manzanilla "Torre Breva", amontillado "El Botánico", and "Carla PX".

Bodegas Internacionales ☆
Jerez

A public company founded in 1974 by Rumasa, but now under ownership of the Medina family. It is claimed to have the largest bodegas in the world, covering 530,000 square feet and containing stocks of 68,000 butts. Williams & Humbert is also part of the same group.

Emilio Lustau ☆☆–☆☆☆☆
Jerez de la Frontera. www.emilio-lustau.com

Founded in 1896, and since 1990 owned by Luis Caballero (*q.v.*), the company owns over 200 hectares and makes good-quality sherries under the "Solera Reserve" label. They include the rare amontillado "Escuadrilla" and the dry oloroso "Don Nuno". All wines from Caballero's own bodega are now released under the "Lustau" label. But the glory of the house is the range of rare almacenista sherries from small private stockholders. These stocks were built up by local professional families who sold the wines in bulk to the shippers. As shippers developed their own vineyards, the role of almacenistas diminished, so it was a bright idea on the part of Lustau in 1981 to bottle and market a selection of these excellent, hand-crafted wines. They come in all styles, from the most delicate manzanillas to a range of "Landed Age Rare Sherries" of which the "Rare Dry" oloroso and the amoroso are particularly fine.

Marqués de Real Tesoro ☆☆
Jerez

A somnolent company reinvigorated with new investment in the 1990s. The new owners have acquired the brand name "Tío Mateo" from Harveys. Clearly a bodega to watch.

Osborne ☆☆–☆☆☆
Puerto de Santa Maria. www.osborne.es

A large and expanding family owned bodega which was founded in 1772 by Thomas Osborne Mann from Devon. The family today is totally Spanish and the title of Conde de Osborne was created by Pope Pius IX. In 1872, Osborne took over Duff-Gordon (*q.v.*), and still uses that name in certain markets.

Osborne has extensive vineyards and stocks. Among its sherry brands are "Quinta" fino, "Coquinero" fino amontillado, and "10RF" oloroso. The finest sherries are limited *solera* bottlings under the "Rare" label. The Osbornes own food and wine businesses throughout Spain, and are major brandy producers, too.

Rainera Pérez Marín ☆☆–☆☆☆
Sanlúcar de Barrameda

A small company, with first-class manzanilla, especially "La Guita", the name by which the bodega is often known. Others include "Hermosilla" manzanilla and "Bandera" fino.

Sanchez Romate ☆☆
Jerez de la Frontera. www.romate.com

A respected small bodega, founded in 1781 and still an independent company owning eighty hectares of vineyards. Brands include "Marizmeño" fino; "NPU" (Non Plus Ultra) amontillado; and "Cardenal Cisneros PX".

Sandeman ☆☆
Jerez de la Frontera. www.sandeman.com

One of the great port and sherry shippers, founded in London in 1790 by George Sandeman, a Scot from Perth. It now belongs to Sogrape, but a descendant, David Sandeman, is chairman. After shipping sherries for many years, Sandeman founded its own bodega, and owns 650 hectares of vineyards on *albariza* soil.

The traditional methods used produce some fine sherries, and the company maintains old *soleras* for its top wines, such as the superb palo cortado "Royal Ambrosante", and the ultra-rich "Royal Corregidor" and "Imperial Corregidor" dessert sherries.

Terry ☆
Puerto de Santa María. www.domecq.es

A once famous name, now belonging to Harvey and thus Allied-Domecq. Terry still produces a small quantity of sherry, but is better-known for its brandy.

Valdespino ☆☆☆–☆☆☆☆
Jerez de la Frontera

Many sherry fanciers have long regarded this ultra-traditional house as the finest sherry producer of them all. The wines were uncompromising, especially the rich, dry palo cortado ("El Cardinal") and amontillado ("Tío Diego") styles.

"Coliseo" was the aficionado's amontillado: mouth-puckeringly dry, but explosive and intense in flavour. However, in 1999, the company was sold to the Estevez Group. No changes have been made to the production team or style, and one can only hope it stays that way.

Williams & Humbert ☆☆
Jerez de la Frontera. www.williams-humbert.com

Founded in 1877 by Alexander Williams and his brother-in-law, Arthur Humbert. Today the company is part of the Medina group, which also owns Bodegas Internacionales (*q.v.*). Vineyards on *albariza* soils in Carrascal, Balbaina, and Los Tercios produce good wines.

The best-known is "Dry Sack", which is a light oloroso in style and, despite its name, not dry. "Pando" is a fresh fino-amontillado; other brands are "Canasta Cream", "Walnut Brown", "A Winter's Tale", and the impressive palo cortado, "Dos Cortados". In the early 2000s, the company began to release rare and expensive vintage-dated wines.

Wisdom & Warter ☆☆
Jerez de la Frontera. www.wisdomwarter.es

Wisdom and Warter, although apparently a short-cut recipe for bargain sherry, are the names of the two Englishmen who founded the company in 1854.

It has long been a subsidiary of González Byass, but is run independently. The main brands are "Olivar" fino, "Royal Palace" amontillado, and the "Tizon" palo cortado.

The Canary Islands

Wine production varies from a cottage industry turning out tiny quantities of excellent wine made from museum varieties, which long ago died out on the peninsula, to quite large-scale wineries with real ambitions in the export department. However, even the largest winery in the largest DO (Bodegas Insulares in Tacoronte-Acentejo) admits that the lack of economy of scale on the islands, the eternal thirst of the tourist trade, and the sheer cost of shipping wine to mainland Europe are stacking the odds against them at the moment. However, the same used to be said of Australia and New Zealand, and there have been big developments there.

There are seven main islands, and DO wine is produced on four of them, with country wines on some of the others. Three of the DOs are island-wide.

Abona (Tenerife)
DO zone in the southwestern quarter of the island, planted in Listán Blanco and Listán Negro, and Bastardo Negro. Light wines in all three colours of no export significance.

El Hierro
The first vines on this island were planted by an Englishman, John Hill, in 1526. Today there are three sub-zones with vines planted on steep slopes up to 610 metres (2,000 feet) in altitude. As well as the staples Listán, Negramoll, Pedro Ximénez and Verdello, they also grow the rare Bujariego, Bremajuelo, Gual, Baboso, and Mulata. Some wines of exemplary quality, especially sweet wines and *rancios*, but the quantity is too small to be significant.

El Monte (Gran Canaria)
The DO covers the entire island, with production concentrated in the northeast sector. Listán Negro is the most important variety, though a wide range of others is also grown. Gran Canaria is best-known for its "mountain red" wine from Listán.

Lanzarote
Beguiling black volcanic soils are the hallmark of this island, with vines planted in hollows scooped out of the ground to protect them from the prevailing winds. Most of the cultivation is of Malvasía and the sweet, semi-fortified style is a descendant of the original "Canary-Sack" which was famed in Shakespeare's day. There are dry wines made from the same grape, as well as a growing production of dry white from Listán Blanco and Diego, and a tiny amount of red and *rosado*.

La Palma
The "Isla Bonita" is as famous for its banana plantations as for its wine, but there are three sub-zones, making anything from rustic, artisanal wines in the north to some respectable examples in the south. Grapes are Malvasía, Listán, Bujariego, Gual, Verdello, Bastardo, Sabro, and Negramoll, and wines come in all three colours. A handful are aged in French oak.

Tacoronte-Acentejo (Tenerife)
The Canary Islands' first and largest DO covers the northwest of Tenerife and, of all of them, has the best chance of achieving export markets. There are thirty bodegas in the area making good reds from Listán Negro and a few pleasant whites mainly from Listán Blanco and Malvasía. Production has been steadily increasing since the DO was granted.

Valle de Güímar (Tenerife)
This is almost a continuation of the vineyards of Abona, running up the southeastern coast of the island, with mainly Listán Blanco for mostly white wines of good, everyday quality. There is some small amount of *rosado* made from Listán Negro, and sweet Moscatel.

Valle de la Orotava (Tenerife)
On the northwest coast between Tacoronte in the north and Ycod in the south, in a valley running down from the volcano to the sea. Pleasant, light white and red wines are made here in roughly similar quantities, with a small amount of *rosado*. Grape varieties: Listán Blanco and Negro.

Ycoden-Daute-Isora (Tenerife)
This DO covers the extreme western part of the island and takes its name from the town of Icod de los Vinos, site of the famous 1,000-year-old "dragon tree". Mainly Listán Blanco and Negro. About two-thirds of production is white of good, clean, crisp style. There is also some light red and *rosado*.

Leading Canary Islands Producers

El Grifo ☆☆
San Bartolomé
The oldest bodega on the island – founded in 1775, and re-established in 1980. Wines are mainly white – including an excellent sweet Malvasía.

Vinícola del Hierro ☆
Frontera
A well-equipped winery producing fruity whites from Vijariego and red from Listán Negro.

Bodegas Insulares Tenerife ☆☆
Tacoronte
A bodega with all the latest kit and plenty of built-in room for expansion. The best wines are "Viña Norte Tinto Maceración", made from Listán Negro and Negramoll by carbonic maceration, and "Viña Norte Tinto Madera" made from the same grapes but aged for four months in oak. A quality leader in the islands.

Cueva del Rey ☆☆
Icod de los Vinos
Fascinating boutique winery run by Fernando González, an English teacher with a passion for white wines. He has a tiny bodega fitted with fibreglass tanks, and regales visitors with excellent tapas and a look round his museum. His wines, both white and red, are currently among the best of the DO.

Monje ☆☆
El Sauzal
A small but admired bodega in Tacoronte-Acentejo. The wines range from "Hollera Monje", made by carbonic maceration, to the oak-aged "Monje d'Autor".

Portugal

P ortugal, conservative as she is, was the first country in modern times to invent a new style of wine for export, and to get it so spectacularly right that it became one of the biggest-selling brands on earth. The wine, of course, is Mateus Rosé. With its competitors, it accounts for a large part of Portugal's wine exports.

It is the measure of Portuguese conservatism that neither the Mateus style, nor for that matter port, has ever caught on in a big way in their home country. With the rapid development of an urban middle class and a supermarket society outside Lisbon and Oporto, the Portuguese people are gradually being weaned onto more international styles of wine, although they are still largely made from indigenous grapes – the nature and variety of which are justifiably Portugal's pride and strength on the international wine front (*see* pages 15–16).

Yet this is no little backwater. The country produces six to seven million hectolitres per annum, which places it at eighth or ninth in the league of wine-producing nations, although less wine is now consumed in the home market. Portugal's position of third in the league of consumption per head has been dropping steadily, but average per capita consumption remains a thirst-quenching fifty litres.

Conservative they may be, but the Portuguese were the first to establish the equivalent of a national system of *appellation contrôlée*: the first delimited area being the Douro in 1756. Then came a wave of demarcations, starting in 1908 with Vinho Verde. Portugal had legally defined boundary, grapes, techniques, and standards, for all of what were then her better wines.

For many years, unfortunately, these have sat heavily on progress, leading to a distorted picture of where the best wines were really being grown. Happily, much of the confusion over regional boundaries has recently been resolved with the introduction of new legislation, more or less coinciding with Portugal's entry to the European Union.

The country now has a four-tier appellation system, which parallels that of France. The best wines qualify for DOC (*Denominação de Origem Controlada*) status, of which there are currently twenty-four. Next are the nine IPRs (*Indicações de Proveniência Regulamentada*), which are regions on a five-year probation for DOC status. In 1992, eight broader *vinhos regionais* were introduced. The fourth distinction is *vinhos de mesa* (table wines), which covers the rest.

During the long period while the regional system was out of date, many of Portugal's better wine companies took to using brand names that gave no indication of their origin. Regulations now insist, however, that all wines must have their region of origin indicated on the label, unless they are bottled as *vinho de mesa*, without a vintage date.

Another Portuguese peculiarity was the ascendancy of merchant companies over primary producers. This situation has now been reversed; encouraged by the availability of EU grants, and individual estates are very much the rising stars. The last twenty years have seen the rise of single quintas (estates): individual properties growing their own grapes and making their own wine. These are now making significant inroads, especially in Vinho Verde country, Bairrada, Dão, and the Alentejo.

Although there used to be relatively few big wine estates outside the Douro, (the port country in the north of Portugal), ever larger domaines are being created, especially in southern regions such as Palmela, the Alentejo, and Ribatejo. Esporão is one property with over 485 hectares of vineyards. Nonetheless, Portugal is still a land of smallholdings, with 180,000 growers tending small family vineyards. About half of them take their grapes to the country's cooperative cellars, of which there are over 100. Most of the rest who have wine to spare after supplying their families and friends, sell it to merchants. Most of the bigger and better merchants buy and bottle wine from each of the major areas; there is little regionality at this level, either.

Traditionally, the Portuguese practice was to divide all wines into two categories: *verde* or *maduro*, and these names are still used on the wine lists of many restaurants. Vinho Verde is unaged wine, and the use of the term is now legally limited to the northern province, the Minho; sparkling rosés would, however, logically fit into this category. *Maduro* means mature. It implies long ageing in barrel (or, frequently, in cement vat) and bottle. But the *verde/maduro* division is becoming blurred as more young wines, red and white, are now reaching the market.

The very real virtue of Portuguese wine made in the time-honoured way is its structure; it is engineered to last for decades, evolving from gum-withering astringency to a most satisfying texture, when firmness is rounded out to velvety smoothness without losing the feel of the iron fist within. Its vice is lack of flavour, and often only the shyest fragrance for such a potent wine. Such wines remain popular on the domestic market, but most go-ahead quintas and merchants are opting for a more international style: drinkable young, but also capable of bottle-age.

A peculiar piece of terminology is used for selected, long-aged wines. The word *garrafeira* has much of the meaning of *reserva*, but with the added implication that it is the merchant's "private" best wine, aged for some years in barrel and subsequently in bottle, to be ready for immediate drinking when sold. Alcohol levels for these wines should be at least 0.5 per cent above the legal minimum.

Portuguese Wine Regions & Styles

The wines of Portugal (excluding port) are described below, progressing geographically, as nearly as possible, from north to south.

The headings are the names of the officially recognized regions or DOCs. For port, *see* pages 386–91.

Vinho Verde

This is the largest wine region, accounting for about twenty per cent of the country's harvest, and which covers most of the northern province of the Minho from Oporto to the Spanish border. Its name is synonymous with the wines it produces: probably Portugal's most original and successful contribution to the world's wine cellar. What is "green" about Vinho Verde is not its colour (fifty-five per cent is red and the white is like lemon-stained water). It is its salad-days freshness, which seems to spring straight from the verdant pergolas where it grows in promiscuous polyculture with maize and vegetables.

Traditionally, the vines hang in garlands from tree to tree, or are trained on *pergolas* of granite post and chestnut lintel. Growing the grapes so high above the ground has several advantages. It slows their ripening and produces the desired sugar/acid balance; it counteracts the tendency to fungal diseases in a cool and rainy climate; it also allows for other cultivation below and between. However, modern vineyards are being trained on lower systems, making the operation easier to mechanize as well as producing wines with better acid balance.

The traditional method of making Vinho Verde is to encourage an active malolactic fermentation. The cool climate, the grapes cultivated (*see* page 16), and their elevated training result in very high levels of malic acid. The natural bacterial conversion of malic to lactic acid takes the rasp out of the acidity, and adds the tingle of its by-product, CO_2. In some country inns the jug wine from barrels is not unlike very dry, fizzy, and rather cloudy cider.

Nowadays, however, only a few jug wines are made in the traditional way, and almost no Vinho Verde undergoes malolactic fermentation in bottle, as this creates a sediment. The vast majority of commercial wineries finish the wine to complete bacterial stability, and then bottle it with an injection of CO_2 to arrive at approximately the same result. The last method also gives the winemaker the option of sweetening his wine (with unfermented must) without the danger of its refermenting.

The total dryness and distinct sharpness of "real" Vinho Verde is not to everyone's taste, so many bottlings that are exported are considerably sweet. In the red version, fermented stalks and all, it contrives with high tannin to make an alarmingly astringent drink, which foreigners rarely brave a second time.

The merchants' brands of Vinho Verde do not normally specify which part of the wide region they come from. Of the nine sub-regions, Amarante and Peñafiel, just inland from Oporto, produce the most white wine. Braga, the centre of the Minho, has good-quality, fresh red and white.

Lima, along the river of the same name north of Braga, specializes in slightly more full-bodied reds. Melgaço and Monção, along the River Minho on the Spanish border in the north, are most famous for their single-variety white: Alvarinho, much the most expensive (and most alcoholic) wine of the region, but only by courtesy, if at all, a Vinho Verde. Alvarinho is smooth and still, sometimes aged in wood and softly fragrant of apricots or freesias, rather than brisk and tinglingly fruity. It is mostly bottled young but, unlike ordinary Vinho Verde, it can be aged for two to three years in bottle.

Some of the best Vinhos Verdes are now being made by single-vineyard properties: members of a self-styled group of grower producers called APEVV (*Associação dos Produtores-Engarrafadores de Vinho Verde*).

Dão

The region of Dão, centred on the old cathedral city of Viseu, eighty kilometres (fifty miles) south of the Douro, is much the biggest and the most established and prosperous producer of *vinhos maduros* under a seal of origin. It is pine-forested country along the valleys of three rivers: the Alva, the Mondego, and the Dão, cut through hills of granite boulders and sandy soil. The vast majority of its 20,000 hectares of vineyard is planted with black grapes (several of which it has in common with the Douro).

The profile of a red Dão remains, despite the care and skill of several of the merchants who mature it, a rather dry, hard wine, strangely lacking in bouquet or lingering sweetness. With its cool nights, it is not always easy for the grapes to reach full maturation, so tannins can be quite tough.

Nonetheless, many observers are convinced that the Dão will one day produce wines of true greatness, and better site selection and grape selection is already yeilding impressive results.

The main reason for the Dão's poor image is that, until 1990, the ten local cooperatives had a near monopoly on production until the EU put a stop to that. There was, for many years, only one estate-grown Dão on the market – Conde de Santar. It no longer enjoys supremacy, though, as a number of single quintas now make very good wine. Now that the cooperatives have lost their monopoly, a number of producers have been encouraged by the release of this stranglehold and are starting to buy in grapes and make their own wines.

Sogrape is probably in the strongest position, having invested about four million pounds in a new winery at Quinta dos Carvalhais. Its wines have steadily improved. In the past, Dão was a blended wine, but today one of its components, Touriga Nacional, is increasingly being bottled as a varietal wine. Very impressive it can be, too.

Bairrada

Although it remained undemarcated until 1979, some seventy years after the Dão region, Bairrada is a real rival in the quality of its wines. The name applies to an area, between Dão and the Atlantic, north of Coimbra, and south of Oporto, with the towns of Mealhada and Anadia as its main centres. Its low, heavy-soiled, lime-rich hills have a greater vineyard area than Dão, and the same preponderance of red grapes (ninety per cent) over white. But its climate is more temperate, its grape varieties different, and its *adegas* more individual.

Two local grapes not found elsewhere have outstanding qualities. The red Baga is a late-ripening variety, high in tannin and acid, which give real authority and "cut" to a blend. As the dominant variety it needs fifteen to twenty years' ageing, but can eventually achieve the fragrance of fine claret. The aromatic local white grape is the Bical, which seems to have an exceptional balance of acidity and extract, aromatic of apricots, brisk and long-flavoured. Another grape, the more neutral Maria Gomes, forms the basis of Bairrada's sparkling-wine industry, which now has some very palatable products.

Garrafeira wines from almost any Portuguese merchant may contain or be based on Bairrada wines. The following firms are in the area and make good examples: Luis Pato (whose wines are from his own estate); Casa de Saima; São João; and Sogrape, which sources much of the base wine for Mateus from Bairrada.

The Douro

The mythology of the Douro reports that it was its terrible table wine that forced merchants to lace it with brandy and create port. It may have been so, but since 1991 the region has made great strides and today produces admirable table wines, among them Duas Quintas (from Ramos Pinto), Redoma (from Niepoort), Domingos Alves e Sousa (Quinta de Gaivosa and Quinta do Vale da Raposa), Quinta do Crasto and Quinta do Vale Meão.

The Douro also provides a number of well-known merchants' *garrafeiras* (private reserve), and, in the shape of Barca Velha, an old-fashioned red wine of international stature to put besides Spain's Vega Sicilia, from 160 kilometres (100 miles) farther up the same river.

Two of the new *vinhos regionais*, Trás-os-Montes, north of the Douro, and Beira Alta to its south, have well-balanced, not over-strong red wines to offer. (Beiras is the name for a catch all *vinhos regional* that includes Dão and Bairrada, as well as Portugal's entire centre.) The Lafões region in the wetter west of the Beira Alta has only recently been regulated and produces a wine that is similar in style to Vinho Verde, called *verdasco*.

Estremadura

The biggest Lisbon area, immediately north of the city, is the Estremadura, which, among its 32,000 hectares, includes three of the four historic wine regions. Carcavelos is nearest to extinction, with just one remaining vineyard: Quinta dos Pesos, which was launched in 1990. The quality of the wine does repay a search. It is a light-amber, velvety, not oversweet, slightly fortified dessert or apéritif wine like a soft, nutty, and buttery Verdelho or Bual Madeira.

More is heard of Bucelas, whose 160 hectares of vineyards lie sixteen kilometres (ten miles) due north of Lisbon. Despite its proximity to the capital, the region is enjoying a new lease of life. Until recently, there was only one producer, turning out a rather old-fashioned, oxidized style of white wine. Now there are four, the best being Quinta da Romeira, which produces Prova Regia, a distinctive, crisp, and fragrant, dry white from the aromatic Arinto grape.

Still more is heard of Colares, not because there is any quantity but because it is a true original. Its vineyards are an unplottable sprawl in the sand dunes of the Atlantic coast west of Lisbon, between Sintra and the sea. They grow the Ramisco: a tiny, bloomy, dark-blue bullet of a grape whose thick skin would tan an ox-hide. Grown in pure sand (the plants have to be planted at the bottom of deep pits, which are then progressively filled in) it makes wine of quite unreasonable inkiness and astringency. Grafting is unnecessary – phylloxera is baffled by sand. Production is dwindling.

The Estremadura is home to some giant cooperatives, such as Torres Vedras, Arruda, and São Mamede de Ventosa, as well as smaller, quality producers, including Quinta de Abrigada and Quinta de Pancas near Alenquer.

Indeed, Alenquer is the sub-region currently showing the most potential.

Terras do Sado

Across the Tagus, between the bridge and Setúbal on the far side of the Arrabida Peninsula, lies a region with nearly 20,000 hectares of vineyards, divided between good, plain, red wine and the sumptuously aromatic Muscat of Setúbal – a fortified wine with a minimum of 17% alcohol. It was apparently the creation of the firm of José Maria da Fonseca (*q.v.*) of Azeitão, who originally had a quasi-monopoly in the area (there are now other producers among whom J. P. Vinhos is leader).

Setúbal in this form is akin to a *vin doux naturel*, its fermentation stopped by the addition of spirit, in which the skins of more Muscat grapes, themselves highly aromatic, are steeped and macerated to give it the precise fragrance of a ripe dessert grape. The wine is barrel-aged and drunk without further ageing in bottle (though this does no harm), either at six years (when it is still amazingly fresh and grapey) or at twenty-five or more (when it has taken on more piquant notes of fragrance – I have noted geranium leaves – and developed the tobacco hue and satin texture of a fine, tawny port).

Ribatejo

The formerly undemarcated central coastal area, north of Lisbon, where Wellington held the famous battle lines of Torres Vedras, is now a *vinho regional* and has a series of IPRs. From here, eastwards to the far banks of the Tagus beyond Santarém, Ribatejo used to be bulk-wine country. For all that, it is a good source of wine, and has attracted the interest of a new generation of young winemakers. It is also one of the few regions in Portugal to grow commercial quantities of international grapes, including Cabernet Sauvignon, Merlot, and Chardonnay. Traditional ways are not dead, though: the Quinta do Casal Branco (*q.v.*) is one that continues to make good wines, especially its Falcoaria.

Alentejo

The vast area south of the Tagus was "discovered" in wine terms as recently as the beginning of the 1990s. Its brown hills are covered with the dark cork oaks that serve to furnish the world with its best-quality corks.

The Alentejo region as a whole has seen quite a dramatic improvement over the past decade in the quality of its wines, while certain sub-areas are now recognized for making the best wines, notably the DOCs Reguengos (home to Esporão and José da Sousa), Redondo, and Borba towards Elvas (of preserved-plums fame). Borba has a good cooperative and the Quinta do Carmo within its boundaries.

There are good IPRs, too: Evora (Cartuxa is the leader) and Granja-Amareleja which has an extraordinary cooperative. Herdade do Mouchão and Tapada do Chaves at Portalegre are making wines which can be outstanding.

Alentejo's potential has not been lost on the big merchants, either. Caves Aliança has invested at Borba and Sogrape in Vidigueira. These regions are virtually neighbours

of the Spanish Extremadura, and, as a result, their wines are correspondingly high in alcohol.

Algarve

The wines of the demarcated Algarve on the south coast are likewise high in alcohol, but that is the only characteristic this region shares with the Alentejo. Only a coarse, sherry-style white wine has any reputation at all – and that is an appalling one! In fact, the four DOCs of the Algarve risk being demoted, given the poor quality of their wines. In the early 2000s, the singer Cliff Richard sought to bestow much needed lustre on the Algarve by producing a wine called Vida Nova from his estate there.

Portuguese Rosé

The fabulous success of Mateus and subsequent Portuguese semi-sweet, semi-sparkling rosés was achieved by applying the idea (not the traditional technique) of Vinho Verde to red grapes from a region where the wine had no particular reputation: the hills north of the Douro round the town of Vila Real. It did not matter that this was not a demarcated region; rather the reverse. It meant that when the local grapes ran out, supplies could be found in other areas.

Today, rosés are made of grapes from almost anywhere in Portugal. The principal rosé winemaking areas are Bairrada and the Setúbal Peninsula south of Lisbon. It is a process, then, and not a regional identity that characterizes these wines. They are made with a very short period of skin contact after crushing to extract the required pink tinge, then fermented like white wine; the fermentation is stopped while about eighteen grams per litre of original grape sugar remain intact, then bottled with the addition of carbon dioxide under pressure.

Leading Portuguese Producers

Caves Aliança ☆–☆☆
Sangalhos. www.caves-alianca.pt
One of Portugal's principal still and sparkling wine producers. A public company controlled by the Neves family, based in the Bairrada, but offering Vinho Verde (the dry Casal Mendes), Dão, and Douro rosé as well as its admirable Bairrada red, "Aliança Tinto Velho", and very passable *méthode traditionnelle* sparkling wine. The company has invested substantially at Borba in the Alentejo, and its vineyard holdings are set to rise to 600 hectares. With the assistance of French oenologist Michel Rolland, Aliança has launched a sophisticated range of wines from individual properties, such as Quinta da Terrugem in the Alentejo.

Domingos Alves e Sousa ☆☆–☆☆☆
Santa Marta de Penagulão
Small producer with five properties in the Baixo Corgo sub-region of the Douro, which is now making some top red wines from local (port) grapes. The oak-aged "Quinta da Gaivosa" is rich and concentrated for keeping; "Quinta da

Vale de Raposa" produces a range of single-variety wines, as well as a new-oaked "Grande Escolha" in top vintages.

Quinta da Aveleda ☆
Penafiel. www.aveleda.pt

Each year this estate produces one million cases of the most famous brands of Vinho Verde: "Casal Garcia" and "Aveleda", both of which are medium-dry. "Quinta da Aveleda" is a more traditional, bone-dry wine, and "Grinalda" is a fragrant, crisp, dry wine from Loureiro and Trajadura, two of the best grapes in the region.

Adega Cooperativa de Borba ☆–☆☆
Borba

One of Portugal's most go-ahead cooperatives is to be found on the edge of the little Alentejo town of Borba. Balanced, fruity red wines and crisp white wines bottled as Borba, with a second wine known as "Convento da Vila".

Bright Brothers ☆☆
Estoril

Australian winemaker Peter Bright left J. P. Vinhos to found his own company. He has now joined the flying-winemaker set, making wines all over the world. He produces a broad range of Portuguese wines under the Bright Bros' label from the Douro, Beiras, Ribatejo, and Estremadura regions.

Casa Cadaval ☆☆
Muge

At this large Ribatejo property, winemaker Rui Reguinga produces a wide range of wines from Portuguese and international varieties. The spicy, concentrated Trincadeira is outstanding.

Quinta do Carmo ☆☆
Borba

This Alentejo estate, once the property of the Bastos family, is now owned by the Rothschilds of Château Lafite-Rothschild. The vineyards used to be dominated by Alicante Bouschet, which resulted in very long-lived wines, but the new owners have reduced the proportion to produce a wine that may be more elegant, yet lacks the solidity of vintages of yesteryear. Of the famous Alentejo growths, this shows the least typicity.

Fundação Eugenio de Almeida – Herdade de Cartuxa ☆–☆☆☆
Evora

This immense Alentejo property, managed as a charitable trust, has 200 hectares of vines close to the city of Evora. Fairly rigorous selection means the foundation's main label, Cartuxa, is a sweet, oaky red, but the best Trincadeira and Aragonez grapes are held back for "Pera Manca", which has quickly established itself as one of Portugal's leading wines, only released in outstanding years. Reds are rather more successful than the whites, although the white "Pera Manca" can also be magnificent. The remainder of the estate's production is bottled as *vinho regional*, or sold off to a local cooperative.

Quinta do Casal Branco ☆☆
Almeirim

A Ribatejo estate with 160 hectares, bottling its own wines since 1990. Best red and white wines are under the Falcoaria label. In 1996, it introduced a Cabernet Sauvignon called "Capucho".

Cortes de Cima ☆☆–☆☆☆
Vidigueira. www.cortesdecima.pt

The first vintage from this 95-hectare Alentejo estate was 1996, and it made its name by releasing an unauthorized Syrah called, appropriately, "Incognito". This remains its best-known wine, but the "Cortes Reserva", and the varietal Aragonez are equally rich and stylish.

Quinta do Côtto ☆☆–☆☆☆
Cidadelha

Based in a magnificent eighteenth century manor house, this estate was specializing in table wines from the Douro before it became fashionable to do so. Miguel Champalimaud, the owner, also produces port (*q.v.*), but it is less consistent than his red wine. The top *cuvée* is "Grande Escolha".

Quinta do Crasto ☆☆–☆☆☆
Sabrosa

Well-situated, family owned property in the Douro, making some inspiring, non-fortified Douro wines as well as port. David Baverstock, as winemaker, has managed to tame the hard tannins that mar so many Douro red wines, and his success is noticeable in a fruity young wine and also a full, fleshy *reserva*. Recent additions to the range include a Touriga Nacional and the tremendous new-oaked "Vinha Maria Teresa".

D. F. J. Vinhos ☆
Valada

This enterprising company is almost entirely focused on the export market. Although based in Ribatejo, it produces wines from all over Portugal, except for the Alentejo. D. F. J.'s main asset is its winemaker, José Neiva, a controversial figure who aims for rich, jammy, high-tech wines with a good dose of alcohol. The top range is called "Grand' Arte".

Herdade do Esporão ☆–☆☆☆
Reguengos de Monsaraz. www.esporao.com

The huge Esporão estate near Reguengos de Monsaraz in the Alentejo is owned by a company called Finagra. Planted in the 1970s, the vineyards extend over 650 hectares, and a further 350 are contracted to supply grapes. Esporão suffered a chequered start to life, but under the shrewd ownership and management of financier José Roquette, the investment is now paying dividends. Sales of red and white wines bottled under the company's three labels, "Alandra", "Monte Velho" and "Esporão", are buoyant both at home and abroad. The varietal bottlings, *reservas*, and "Private Selection" are their most exciting wines. Much of the credit for Esporão's success is due to Australian winemaker David Baverstock.

A. A. Ferreira ☆☆
Vila Nova de Gaia

Barca Velha, launched by port producer Ferreira in the 1950s, quickly established itself as Portugal's most prestigious red wine. Grapes, mainly Tinta Roriz, were grown at Quinta do Vale do Meão (*q.v.*) and trodden in big stone *lagares*, yielding about 4,000 cases a year. "Barca Velha" was only released in the best vintages ('91, '85, '83, '78, '66, and '65); lesser years are declassified to "Ferreirinha Reserva Especial". However, in 1999, the Quinta was sold, depriving Ferreira of its best grapes. In future, the Quinta da Leda will be the principal source. Owned by Sogrape (*q.v.*) since 1987.

José María da Fonseca ☆☆☆
Azeitão. www.azeitao.net

Founded in 1834, this is one of Portugal's leading wine companies, run by two brothers, Antonio and Domingos Soares Franco, descendants of the founder. Fonseca is famous for its superlative fortified Setúbal, but the quantity produced is minute compared to its range of red wines. "Periquita" is the best-known, made from a blend of local grapes of the same name (now known throughout Portugal as Castelão); "Quinta da Camarate" is a ripe blackcurranty blend of Castelão, Cabernet, and Touriga Nacional; and "Tinto Velho" from the José da Sousa *adega* in the Alentejo is a good, peppery blend of local grapes fermented in large clay amphorae. It also owns a winery in Dão, which bottles the "Terras Altas" brand. Other wines include *garrafeiras*, coded by letters (such as RA or TE) to indicate origin or grape blend, and a range of international varieties such as Sauvignon Blanc and Syrah under the "Colleccion Privada" label.

J. M. da Fonseca Internacional
Azeitão

This company was, for a while, owned by the American firm Heublein, but in 1996 it was sold back to the Soares Franco family, who are also its managers. The company is best known for the enormous sales of "Lancers Rosé", their semi-sweet, sparkling pink wine.

Quinta da Lagoalva de Cima ☆☆☆
Alpiarça

The grandfather of the Campilho brothers, who own this grand estate in the Ribatejo, was once ambassador to London. It was at Lagoalva that Portugal's first Syrah was produced, though most of the wines are made from local varieties such as Castelão, Touriga Nacional, and the white Arinto. Quality is high, and the wines have a welcome elegance.

Caves Messias ☆
Mealhada

A merchant house founded in 1926. Based in Bairrada, where it owns 160 hectares, including Quinta do Valdoeiro, which produces a fresh-tasting, appley, dry white from extensive Bairrada vineyards. Quinta do Cachão is a full, spicy Douro red. Also producer of the "Santola" brand of Vinho Verde, robust Bairrada *garrafeiras*, and a range of sparkling wines.

Herdade do Mouchão ☆☆☆–☆☆☆☆
Sousel

This small Alentejo estate, with 25 hectares of vines, turns out huge red wines relying heavily on low-yielding Alicante Bouschet grapes for colour and structure. When Mouchão is on form, it is the Alentejo at its very best: chunky, long-lived wines, with a long, spicy finish.

Niepoort ☆☆☆–☆☆☆☆
Porto

Of Dutch origin, this family owned port shipper has gone from strength to strength under Dirk Niepoort. "Redoma" is the name given both to their monumental Douro red, and to a powerful, oaky white from old vines. In 1999, Niepoort added "Batuta", an equally intense red from very low-yielding vines, and aged mostly in new oak. These are now among the most impressive dry wines of Portugal.

Palace Hotel do Buçaco ☆–☆☆
Mealhada

Within the cellars of this extravagant hotel matures one of Europe's most unusual wines. The hotel's vineyards are near Luso on the fringes of the Bairrada region, and grow its typical grapes. They are trodden (both black and white) in a stone *lagar* and their wine made exactly in the manner of the last century. Fermented in casks, the red wine is bottled at four to five years old; the white is aged for two to three years before bottling. Vintages available in the hotel go back to 1944 white and 1945 red, both still well preserved. The best vintages (*e.g.* white: '85, '84, '66, '65, '56; red: '82, '78, '70, '63, '60, '58, '53) have an exquisite hand-made quality, but some vintages are oxidized. The wines can only be purchased at the hotel bar or restaurant, both popular with the many visitors to this former royal hunting lodge.

Palacio de Brejoeira ☆☆–☆☆☆
Monção

The most prestigious producer of Alvarinho white wine from the Minho region.

Quinta de Pancas ☆☆–☆☆☆
Alenquer

Splendid sixteenth century quinta north of Lisbon. Some of Portugal's first Cabernet Sauvignon was planted and vinified here. The white wines include a delightful wine made from the Arinto grape (Quinta de Dom Carlos), and a soft, toasty Chardonnay. The top red wines, called "Special Selection", are high-priced varietal wines from Cabernet Sauvignon, Tinta Roriz, and Touriga Nacional.

Luis Pato ☆☆☆
Anadia

Luis Pato began making his own wines in 1980, and has subsequently established himself as one of the leading independent producers in Portugal. He farms 62 hectares in the heart of the Bairrada region, and relies heavily on the local Baga grape, continually monitoring its performance in a variety of different soils. This has resulted in two excellent single-vineyard wines: "Vinha Pan" and "Vinha Barrosa", the latter made from very old, low-yielding vines. All his top red wines are aged in French oak. Their high tannin and acidity makes them candidates for long ageing.

Pato has spent many years experimenting in the vineyard and the winery, with the result that there has been considerable variation in style from one vintage to the next. In 1994, he launched the remarkable "Quinta de Ribeirinho Pe Franco", a limited-production red made from incredibly low-yielding ungrafted Baga vines. Pato also makes attractive, dry white wines from the local Arinto, Cerceal, and Cercealinho varieties. There is also a single-variety white from Bical called "Vinha Formal". He also has a small amount of Cabernet Sauvignon and Touriga Nacional in his vineyards, which he usually blends with Baga grapes.

In 2001, Pato formally left the Bairrada DOC to free himself from bureaucratic restrictions.

J. P. Vinhos ☆–☆☆☆
Azeitao. www.jpvinhos.com

Australian winemaker Peter Bright is consultant winemaker for J. P. Vinhos (formerly known as João Pires and Filhos). New World influence is evident in the "Cova da Ursa", a barrel-fermented Chardonnay, the Cabernet-dominated "Quinta da Bacalhoa", and the pure Syrah known as "Sô". There are also robust wines from Portuguese varieties, including "Meia Pipa", a blend of Periquita and Cabernet, and "Tinto da Anfora", a warming, spicy red from the Alentejo. Ambitious sparkling wines are made at Quinta dos Loridos in Estremadura.

Quinta de Pellada ☆☆
Seia

Under the same ownership as Quinta de Sães, this Dão quinta specializes in rich, tannic, single-varietal wines from Touriga Nacional, Tinta Roriz, and Baga.

João Portugal Ramos ☆☆☆
Estremoz

This dynamic winemaker made his name as a consultant for many of the top estates in Portugal, as well as for cooperatives that are keen to improve the quality of their wines. In 1999, he built a modern winery in which to vinify his own expanding range of wines from his 100 hectares of vineyards in the Alentejo. His wines are marked by vibrant fruit, delicate oak, and impeccable balance. His most appealing wines are "Vila Santa", a blend from local varieties, and the sumptuous "Marques de Borba Reserva". There are also spicy varietal wines, including a splendid Syrah and Trincadeira.

Ramos Pinto ☆☆–☆☆☆
Vila Nova da Gaia

Under João Nicolai d'Almeida, port producer Ramos Pinto has launched its own Douro wines under the "Duas Quintas" label. Blended from two quintas, Bom Retiro and Ervamoira, the wines (especially the Reservas) are solid and appealing. A wine from a single estate, Quinta dos Bons Ares, combines the local grape, Touriga Nacional, and Cabernet in an 80:20 blend. In 1999, Ramos Pinto produced a very concentrated *reserva* from the oldest vines.

Real Companhia Vinícola do Norte de Portugal ☆
Vila Nova de Gaia

Royal Oporto, the old port monopoly company set up in the eighteenth century, is well-known for its wide range of wines that are produced in part from the four quintas under its ownership. The range includes a Vinho Verde called "Lagosta", as well as "Evel" and "Porca de Murça" brands from the Douro.

Quinta dos Roques ☆☆–☆☆☆
Abrunhosa do Mato

A forty-hectare family owned estate in the Dão region that has broken away from the local cooperative. Serious reds from Touriga Nacional and Jaen have seriously set the pace for the future of the Dão region. Also own Quinta das Maias.

Quinta de la Rosa ☆☆
Pinhão. www.quintadelarosa.com

The Bergqvist family broke links with port house Sandeman in 1988. The forty-hectare property now produces a good range of estate-bottled ports and Douro wines, the latter under the auspices of winemaker David Baverstock.

Quinta de Sães ☆☆–☆☆☆
Seia

Small property in the Dão region, owned by Alvaro Castro. Red and white wines from local grapes are refined and sophisticated. The top bottling is "Estagio Prolongado", which is aged in barriques for up to 18 months. Castro also owns another Dão property, Quinta de Pellada (*q.v.*).

Casa de Saima ☆☆–☆☆☆
Sangalhos

A twenty-hectare property in Bairrada, with winemaker Rui Moura Alves making outstanding red and white wines, mainly from the local Baga and Bical respectively. Their red *garrafeiras*, foot-trodden in *lagares*, age well.

Caves São João ☆☆
Anadia

Family owned producer with twenty hectares of vines in the heart of the Bairrada region. Two brothers, Alberto and Luis Costa, age, blend, and bottle some of the most impressive red wines from Bairrada and the neighbouring Dão region. Bottled respectively under the "Frei João" and "Porta dos Cavaleiros" labels, the *reservas*, sporting a cork label, have great depth and ageing potential. The company has recently launched a Cabernet-based wine called "Quinta do Poço do Lobo" from their own thirty-five hectare vineyard.

Soalheiro ☆☆☆
Melgaço

An outstanding producer of Vinho Verde from the Alvarinho grape. Limited production.

Sogrape ☆–☆☆☆
Porto

Portugal's biggest winemaker, and the producer of Mateus Rosé. Annual sales of over 2.5 million cases. The other wines are of impressive quality across the board. The Guedes family, which founded Sogrape in 1942, still controls the firm, and also owns Ferreira and Offley port (*see* pages 388–89). They have made a big investment in Dão, at Quinta dos Carvalhais, and at Herdade do Peso in the Alentejo. Other wines include "Grão Vasco", a good Dão made at the company's own winery near Viseu; the reliable "Vinha do Monte" from Alentejo; "Vila Regia", a ripe Douro red; and "Terra Franca", a soft, fruity Bairrada. The company also produces a deliciously oaky, dry white *reserva* wine from grapes grown north of the Douro River. New ventures include Touriga Nacional from Dão, and varietal wines from the Alentejo.

Quinta do Vale Meão ☆☆☆
Alto Douro

This historic estate was part of the Ferreira vineyards until its sale in 1999 to a former president of the company, Francisco Olazabal. The grapes for Ferreira's legendary "Barca Velha" were grown here, but now they are used for the Quinta's own red wine, a new-oaked superstar of the Douro.

Other Portuguese Producers

Alentejo: Ervideira (Evora), Herdade Grande (Vidigueira), Reguengos de Monsarraz cooperative (Reguengos).

Bucelas: Quinta da Romeira

Dão: Boas Quintas/Quinta Donte do Ouro (Mortagua)

Douro: Brunheda (Tua), Chryseia, Pintas (Pinhão), Poeira (Pinhão), Quinta do Fojo (Pinhão), Quinta do Portal (Sabrosa), Quinta de Roriz (São João de Pesqueira)

Estremadura: Casa Santos Lima (Alenquer)

Minho: Anselmo Mendes (Melgaço), Adega Cooperativa Regional de Monção, Paço de Teixeiró

Palmela: Hero do Castanheiro (Aguas de Moura)

Ribatejo: Quinta da Alorna (Almeirim), Falua (Almeirim)

Port

What the English have long known as port, and the Portuguese and other nations as porto, belongs with Champagne and sherry in the original trinity of great "processed" wines. Each is an elaboration on the natural produce of its region to enhance its latent quality. Being capital-intensive, requiring the holding of large stocks for long periods, their trade has become concentrated in the hands of shippers. Single-vineyard ports, and even single-vintage ports, are the exceptions in an industry, which lives day to day on long-established, unchanging blends.

Unlike Champagne and sherry, port was the child of political pressure. In the late seventeenth century, the British were obliged by their government to find alternatives to the French red wines they preferred. They turned to Portugal, an old and useful ally, for a convenient substitute for claret. Finding nothing to their liking in the existing vineyards (which is surprising; Lisbon had good wine, if Oporto did not) the enterprising traders pushed inland from Oporto up the valley of the Douro into the rugged hinterland. What they tasted there that made them persevere is hard to imagine. They could hardly have chosen a more difficult and inaccessible place, with a more extreme climate, to develop as a major new wine area. They started around Regua, about ninety-six kilometres (sixty miles – or three mule-days) upstream from Oporto where the river Corgo joins the main stream. Gradually, finding that the higher they went the better the wine became, they built terraces up the steep-sloped mountains surrounding the Douro and its tributaries: the Távora, the Torto, the Pinhão, and the Tua. They dotted the mountainsides with white-walled quintas, or farms, and demonstrated that once cultivated, the thin, arid soil of granite and schist became extraordinarily fertile. Today, not just the grapes, but the nuts, oranges, almonds, and even the vegetables of the Douro Valley are famous.

The first port was apparently a strong, dry, red wine, made even stronger with "a bucket or two" of brandy to stabilize it for shipping. It got a very cold reception from British claret-lovers, who complained bitterly. The shippers tried harder, and at some time in the eighteenth century hit on the idea of stopping the fermentation with brandy while the wine was still sweet and fruity. History is unclear on when this became the standard practice, since as late as the 1840s, the most influential British port shipper of all time, James Forrester (created a Portuguese baron for his services), was urging a return to unfortified (therefore dry) wines. Modern ideas provide surprising justification for Forrester's notions: today, the Douro is providing some of Portugal's best dry red table wine. Sweet or dry port was the most-drunk wine in Britain from the early eighteenth century to the early twentieth.

Today, port is one of the most strictly controlled of all wines. A series of statutory authorities regulate and oversee every stage of its making. All 40,000 hectares of vineyards are classified for quality on an eight-point scale by the register of each property (there are 33,000 growers), taking into account its situation, altitude, soil, inclination, grape varieties, standard of cultivation, fertility, and the age of its vines. It is then given an annual quota. Only forty per cent, on average, of the total Douro crop may be turned into port; the rest is just made into red wine. The maximum yield, allowed for vineyards classified as "A" on the eight-point scale, is 700 litres per 1,000 vines.

In the past, innumerable local varieties were planted together in the vineyards, and it took considerable research in the 1970s, mostly conducted by Ramos Pinto, to isolate the most important varieties: Touriga Nacional, Touriga Francesa, Tinta Roriz, Tinta Barroca, Tinta Cão, plus Tinta Amarela, and Sousão. Today they are planted separately, and later blended.

At harvest time, late September in the Douro, bureaucracy seems remote enough. The grinding labour of picking and carrying the crop from the steep terraces to the press-houses is carried on with amazingly cheerful, even tuneful, energy by gangs of villagers. On remote little farms, and with the best-quality grapes at some of the largest quintas, the crop is still trodden barefoot at night in open granite *lagares*, and then fermented in the *lagares* until it is ready to be "stopped" with brandy. In the case of most port shippers, however, much the greater proportion of the crop is machine-crushed and fermented in stainless steel, which allows better temperature control than the old closed concrete fermenting tanks of a kind introduced from Algeria, with a simple percolating system, operated by the natural build-up of carbon dioxide, to keep the juice constantly churning over the grape skins.

With either method, the moment comes when about half the grape sugar is fermented into alcohol. This is when the half-made wine is run off into barrels one-quarter full of brandy. Fermentation stops instantly.

The great majority of the port is moved, after its first racking off its gross lees, to the shippers' lodges to mature. These lodges are huddled together across the River Douro from Oporto, in Vila Nova de Gaia. In the past, the casks, known as pipes, were transported down-river on the beautiful Viking-style *rabelos*. But once the river was dammed for hydroelectric power, that was no longer feasible. It used to be obligatory for port to be shipped through Vila Nova da Gaia, but not any more. One important shipper, Noval, now moves its stock for maturation to air-conditioned warehouses upstream; while Sandeman and Cockburn keep substantial amounts of their port in the Douro.

Once in the shipper's lodge, port, like sherry, is classified by tasting and its destiny decided by its quality and potential for improvement. Most ports join a sort of perpetual blending system whose object is an unchanging product.

Simple, fruity, and rather light wines without great concentration are destined to become ruby port, aged for up to about two years in wood and bottled while their bright-red colour and full sweetness show no sign of maturity. This is the cheapest category.

Young wines with more aggressive characters and greater concentration – some outstandingly good, some of only moderate quality – are set aside to develop into tawnies, so-called from their faded colour after many years in wood. Tawnies include some of the greatest of all ports, kept for up to forty years in cask, then (usually) refreshed with a little younger wine of the highest quality. Tawnies also include some very ordinary mixtures with scarcely any of the character of barrel-age, made by blending young red and white ports (very popular in France as an apéritif). Their price varies accordingly. The best tawnies have an indication of age on the label; 20 years is old enough for most of them – the high premium for a 30- or 40-year-old wine is seldom worth it. Styles among top tawnies vary from the intensely luscious (*e.g.* Ferreira's Duque de Bragança) to refinement and dry finish (*e.g.* Taylor's 20-year-old). There is no legal requirement for all the wine in a 10-year-old, for example, to be at least that age; instead, the wine is required to match the tasting profile for that style, as determined by an expert tasting panel. Although the system is open to abuse, the top shippers maintain a high standard, as they wish to preserve their reputations.

The great majority of port falls into one or other of the above categories, which together are known as "wood ports"; their whole maturing process takes place in wood.

Vintage port, by contrast, is the product of one of the three or four vintages in a decade which come close to the shipper's idea of perfection – which have so much flavour and individuality that to make them anonymous, as part of a continuing blend, would be a waste of their potential. Whether or not a shipper "declares" a vintage is entirely his own decision. It is very rare that all do so in the same year. The Douro is too varied in its topography and conditions.

Vintage ports are blended in the particular style the shipper has developed over many years, using the best lots of wine from his regular suppliers – including, invariably, his own best vineyards. They are matured for a minimum of twenty-two and a maximum of thirty-one months in cask for their components to "marry", then bottled while they are still undrinkably tannic, aggressive, and concentrated in flavour. Almost all their maturing therefore happens in the airless, "reductive" conditions of a black-glass bottle with a long cork, designed to protect the wine for decades, while it slowly feeds on itself. Its tannins and pigments react to form a heavy, skin-like crust that sticks to the side of the bottle. Its colour slowly fades and its flavour evolves from violently sweet and harsh to gently sweet, perfumed and mellow. Yet, however mellow, vintage port is designed to have "grip": a vital ingredient in wine, which should never lose its final bite even in old age.

Between the clear-cut extremes of wood port and vintage port come a number of compromises intended to offer something closer to vintage port without the increasingly awkward need to cellar the wine for between ten and thirty years. Vintage character (or vintage reserve) is effectively top-quality ruby port whose ingredient wines were almost up to true vintage standards, but kept for four or five years in cask. These potent and tasty wines are "ready" when bottled, but will continue to develop, and may even form a slight "crust" in bottle if they are kept too long. The term "crusted" or "crusting" port is sometimes used for the same style (though not officially recognized in Portugal). Late-bottled vintage (or LBV) is similar, but is made of the wine of one "vintage" year, kept twice as long as vintage port in barrel: *i.e.* from 3.5 to six years. The label "LBV" carries both the date of the vintage and the bottling, and the wine is much lighter in colour and flavour than vintage port, but should have some of its firmness. It may or may not form a deposit in bottle according to its maturity on bottling, and the degree to which the shipper has chilled and filtered it for stability. Late-bottled vintage port, which forms a deposit, is usually labelled "traditional". LBVs from Warre and Smith Woodhouse are usually unfiltered.

A rare but sometimes succulent style of port is known as *colheita*. After decades in wood they acquire a fine intensity and elegance, but care must be taken to avoid oxidation. Except from masters of the style, such as Cálem, Burmester, and Niepoort, they are a risky purchase, as lesser examples can taste tired and astringent.

White port is made in the same way as red port, but of white grapes, usually fermented further towards dryness before being fortified with brandy. It is intended as an apéritif rather than a dessert wine, but never achieves the quality or finesse of, say, a fino sherry. Its underlying heaviness needs to be enlivened, and it can be far more enjoyable as a long drink with tonic water, ice, and a slice of lemon.

An increasingly popular compromise is to declare a single-quinta vintage port. Some properties, themselves single quintas, in contrast to shippers buying from a range of sources, are declaring this category almost every year. Quinta de la Rosa is probably the best-known example. But for some time, the major shippers have also declared single-quinta wines in lesser vintages, when no vintage wine under their own name is declared. Leading examples include Taylor's Quinta de Vargellas and Croft's Quinta da Roeda. They can do this because in lesser years, their top quintas may still produce outstanding wine that would, in top years, be a major contributor to the vintage wine. Single-quinta ports will mature sooner than classic vintages, but often have distinct and charming character. Being bottle-matured, these wines will of course form a crust, and will need decanting.

The number of single-quinta wines is growing from vintage to vintage. This means that the dominance of the market by the famous British shippers is diminishing, even if only slightly. Properties such as Quinta do Crasto, which once supplied the major shippers, are now nurturing and bottling their own vintage ports. Although there are some very fine examples, they can lack the consistency and reliability of the renowned names.

Leading Port Producers

A. A. Cálem & Filho ☆–☆☆
Porto. Vintages: 1935, '48, '55, '58, '60, '63, '66, '70, '75, '77, '80, '82, '83, '85, '91, '94, '97, and 2000
Founded in 1859 by a family already long-established in the port trade, Cálem was sold in 1989 to a group of local businessmen. The family retained the excellent Quinta da Foz at Pinhão, so the new owners will not be able to make use of the firm's best grapes. Cálem had a fine reputation for its *colheita* wines, but its vintage ports could lack consistency.

Churchill ☆☆–☆☆☆
Porto. Vintages: 1982, '85, '91, '94, '97, and 2000.
www.churchills-port.com
Founded in 1981 by John Graham and named after his wife, this is the first independent port shipper to be set up in the last fifty years. It has gone from strength to strength, making some splendidly concentrated wines from a number of well-situated quintas belonging to the Borges de Sousa family. Quinta da Agua Alta is bottled by Churchill as a single-quinta port. Churchill also make fine LBV, and an excellent dry white port which has been aged for around ten years in wood, and are one of the few shippers to have good stocks of delicious, mature, crusted port.

Cockburn ☆☆
Vila Nova de Gaia. Vintages: 1900, '04, '08, '12, '27, '35, '45, '47, '50, '55, '60, '63, '67, '70, '75, '77, '83, '85, '91, '94, '97, and 2000. www.cockburns-usa.com
Founded in 1815, Cockburn is one of the greatest names in port, owned by Allied-Domecq, but still run by descendants of its Scottish founders. Its properties are the Quintas do Tua (thirty hectares), da Santa Maria near Regua (eighteen hectares), do Val do Coelho and do Atayde near Tua where they are planting 250 hectares, and, since 1989, Quinta dos Canais in the Upper Douro. Cockburn's wines have a distinctive dry finish, or "grip", and the vintage ports can lack succulence. Martinez Gassiot (*q.v.*) is an associated company, sometimes rivalling the parent company in quality.

Quinta do Cotto ☆
Cidadelha
The Champalimaud family, who have owned their estate near Regua since the seventeenth century, are now the best-known of the new breed of grower-bottlers: their single-quinta vintage is made and matured in the Douro, and not moved down to Vila Nova de Gaia for bottling. Recent vintages have been less sweet than one would normally expect from a vintage style. They also make one of the Douro's best red table wines (*see* above).

Croft ☆☆–☆☆☆
Vila Nova de Gaia. Vintages: Croft – 1900, '04, '08, '12, '17, '20, '22, '24, '27, '35, '42, '45, '50, '55, '60, '63, '66, '70, '75, '77, '82, '85, '91, '94, and 2000. Quinta da Roêda – 1967, '70, '78, '80, '83, '87, '95. www.croft.com
Perhaps the oldest port firm, founded in 1678 and originally known as Phayre and Bradley, Croft was bought in 2001 by Taylor and the sherry house of González Byass. The jewel in its crown is the superb Quinta da Roêda with sixty-three hectares at Pinhão. Grapes from this quinta are responsible for the distinctive floweriness of their vintage wines, which are regularly among the finest of all vintage ports, early-maturing and well-balanced in style. Other wines from Croft include their sister brands Delaforce (*q.v.*) and Morgan. Croft is also well known as a sherry producer (*q.v.*).

Delaforce ☆☆
Vila Nova de Gaia. Vintages: 1908, '17, '20, '21, '22, '27, '35, '45, '47, '50, '55, '58, '60, '63, '66, '70, '75, '77, '82, '85, '94, and 2000. Quinta da Corte: '78, '80, '84, '87, '92 and '94, '95, '97
Founded in 1868, this firm is still run by the Delaforces, although in 2001 (like Croft, *q.v.*) it was bought by Taylor and

González Byass. The firm's finest wines, which have great freshness and elegance and are slightly drier than the Croft ports, come from the contracted Quinta da Corte vineyard in the Rio Torto valley. His Eminence's Choice is a superbly succulent 10-year-old tawny port.

Dow ☆☆☆☆
Vila Nova de Gaia. Vintages: 1904, '08, '12, '20, '24, '27, '34, ('42 & '44), '45, '47, '50, '55, '60, '63, '66, '70, '72, '75, '77, '80, '83, '85, '91, '94, '97, and 2000. www.dows-port.com
Since 1961, this venerable brand, shipped by Silva & Cosens, has been run by the ubiquitous Symington family. The firm's seventy-six-hectare Quinta do Bomfim at Pinhão, sometimes released as a single-quinta port, is one of the finest on the Douro. Supported by the Quinta Santa Madelena, nearby up the Rio Torto, and by Quinta da Senhora da Ribeira, Bomfim gives mightily tannic and concentrated vintage port, recognizable by its dry finish in maturity. Dow also sells a full range of ruby, tawny, and white ports.

A. A. Ferreira ☆☆–☆☆☆
Vila Nova de Gaia. Vintages: 1945, '47, '50, '58, '60, '63, '66, '70, '75, '77, '78, '80, '82, '83, '85, '91, '94, '95, '97, and 2000
An historic Portuguese house, Ferreira in the mid-nineteenth century was the richest in the Douro, ruled over by the famous Dona Antónia, who built the magnificent Quintas do Vesuvio and do Vale de Meão, colossal establishments in the remotest high Douro. The family members still own many vineyards, although the company was sold in 1987 to Sogrape (*q.v.*). Today, Ferreira sells more bottled port in Portugal than any other house. Its vintage wines are usually fairly light in style, and are outclassed by its superb tawny ports: "Superior", "Dona Antónia", and above all the superlative 20-year-old "Duque de Bragança". Ferreira was also a pioneer of table wines from the Douro, notably the legendary "Barca Velha".

Fonseca Guimaraens ☆☆☆☆
Vila Nova de Gaia. Vintages: 1904, '08, '12, '20, '22, '27, '34, '45, '48, '55, '60, '63, '66, '70, '75, '77, '80, '83, '85, '92, '94, '97, and 2000. www.fonseca.pt
Despite its name, Fonseca has been an English family business for over a century, and has been linked to Taylors since the 1940s. The firm started in the eighteenth century as Fonseca, and was bought by Manuel Pedro Guimaraens in 1822. Their vineyards of Quinta Cruizeiro (sixty-five hectares) and Quinta Santo António (forty hectares), both in the Val de Mendiz near Alijo, are splendidly sited. All their best wines are still made by treading. Fonseca Guimaraens is regularly one of the finest and richest vintage ports, and its "Bin No. 27" is an admirable premium ruby. They have an LBV and the single-quinta "Quinta do Panascal".

Gould Campbell
See **Smith Woodhouse**

W. & J. Graham ☆☆☆☆
Vila Nova de Gaia. Vintages: 1904, '08, '12, '17, '20, '24, '27, '35, '42, '45, '48, '55, '60, '63, '66, '70, '75, '77, '80, '83, '85, '91, '94, '97, and 2000. www.grahams-port.com
Graham, now part of the empire of the Symington family (with Warre, Dow, etc.), is renowned for some of the richest

and sweetest vintage ports. Graham's Quinta dos Malvedos on the Douro, near Tua, provides exceptionally ripe fruit for vintage port of great colour, body, and guts which mellows to a singularly sumptuous wine. Part of the crop is still trodden. "Malvedos" used to be the company's second wine, but now it is also issued as a single-quinta wine. Tawny and LBV follow the full-bodied, luscious style. Particularly good is the "Six Grapes" premium ruby port.

Kopke ☆
Vila Nova de Gaia. Vintages: 1934, '35, '42, '45, '52, '55, '58, '60, '63, '66, '70, '74, '75, '77, '78, '79, '80, '82, '83, '85, '87, '91, '92, '95, and 2000
In name at least, the oldest of all the port firms, Kopke was founded by a German in 1638. It now belongs to Barros Almeida (*q.v.*). Kopke has sixty hectares of vines and uses the names "Quinta de São Luiz" for vintages; "Old World" for tawny; "Bridge" for ruby.

Niepoort ☆☆☆
Porto. Vintages: 1927, '45, '55, '60, '63, '66, '70, '75, '77, '78, '80, '82, '83, '85, '87, '91, '92, '94, '97, and 2000
A small, Dutch, family owned company, founded in 1842, is currently being run by the fifth generation of Niepoorts. Sales amount to some 50,000 cases of robust, high-quality port a year, including a peculiar category, which is known as *garrafeira*. These are tawnies given further ageing in glass demijohns. Dirk Niepoort also makes a single-quinta wine from Quinta do Passadouro, a propery owned by his friend Dieter Bohrmann. Niepoort is a leading producer of high-quality, and expensive, table wines.

Quinta do Noval ☆☆☆☆
Vila Nova de Gaia. Vintages: 1904, '08, '12, '17, '20, '24, '27, '31, '34, ('41 & '42), '45, '50, '55, '58, '60, '63, '66, '67, '70, '78, '80, '82, '83, '85, '87, '91, '94, '95, '97, and 2000. www.quintadonoval.com
Perhaps the most famous, and one of the most beautiful quintas on the Douro, perched high above Pinhão. It belonged to the van Zeller family until 1993, when it was sold to AXA-Millésimes. A tragic fire in 1982 destroyed the historic records of the company and part of the stock. Old Noval vintages were some of the most magnificent of all ports. The '31 is legendary and the '27 was even better. A small plot of ungrafted vines still makes an astoundingly concentrated "Nacional" vintage port. The new owners have, if anything, improved quality even further, and in 1995 introduced robotic *lagares* that reproduce the process of foot-treading by mechanical means. Quinta do Silval is another property.

Offley ☆
Vila Nova de Gaia. Vintages: 1945, '50, '54, '60, '62, '63, '66, '67, '70, '72, '75, '77, '80, '82, '83, '85, '87, '94, '95, '97, and 2000
This firm was founded in 1737 by William Offley, and joined by James Forrester in 1803. His nephew, Baron Joseph James Forrester, was famous for mapping the Upper Douro, and saving the vineyards from a fungal disease in the 1850s. The company, formally known as Forrester & Co., was sold in 1929 and again in 1983 to Martini & Rossi – who have since sold to Sogrape. The vintage is rarely exceptional and the best wine is "Baron Forrester Tawny". Their style is generally considered to be early drinking, fat, and well-rounded.

Poças ☆
Vila Nova de Gaia. Vintages: 1960, '63, '70, '75, '85, '91, '94, '95, '97, and 2000
An independent family company founded in 1918, owning two Douro properties: the Quintas das Quartas and Santa Barbara, run on traditional lines. Their brands: "Poças Junior"; "Pousada", "Terras", "Almiro", and "Pintão" have substantial sales in Belgium and France. They are newcomers to vintage ports, having made their first declaration in 1960. These are sound, medium-bodied wines.

Quarles Harris ☆☆
Vila Nova de Gaia. Vintages 1908, '12, '20, '27, '34, '45, '47, '50, '55, '58, '60, '63, '66, '70, '75, '77, '80, '83 and '85, '91, '94, '97, and 2000
Together with Warre, Graham, Dow, etc. (*qq.v*), Quarles Harris is now part of the remarkable stable of the Symington family. There are no vineyards, but long-standing contracts with good growers along the Rio Torto maintain a style of very intense, full vintage port with a powerful bouquet. Harris (not Quarles) is the brand for tawnies, ruby, and white ports.

Ramos Pinto ☆☆–☆☆☆
Vila Nova de Gaia. Vintages: 1924, '27, '35, '45, '50, '52, '55, '60, '61, '70, '75, '80, '82, '83, '85, '91, '94, '95, and '97
Founded in 1880, and one of the most distinguished houses, now owned by Louis Roederer. Their properties include the famous Quinta Bom Retiro, with fifty hectares in the Rio Torto valley, the Quinta da Bons Ares, and Quinta da Ervamoira, the source of many of its fine tawnies. Tawnies are their specialties, but the company also produce two highly successful white ports as well as a reliable vintage. They also release excellent table wines. *See* also under wine producers.

Royal Oporto ☆
Vila Nova de Gaia. Vintages: 1908, '41, '43, '44, '45, '47, '54, '55, '58, '60, '62, '63, '67, '70, '77, '78, '79, '80, '85, '87, '95, and '97
"Royal Oporto" is the famous brand of the Real Companhia Vinícola do Norte de Portugal, which was founded in 1756 by the Marquis de Pombal to control the port trade. The company is now part-owned by the Casa do Douro (set up as the controlling body for the port trade), the result of a now infamous business deal. Its interests are now half in port and half in other wines. Quality was unremarkable for many years, but since the late 1990s there have been significant signs of improvement. *See also* under wine producers.

Sandeman ☆☆
Vila Nova de Gaia. Vintages: 1904, '08, '11, '12, '17, '20, '27, '34, '35, '42, '45, '47, '50, '55, '60, '63, '66, '67, '70, '75, '77, '80, '82, '85, '94, and 2000. www.sandeman.com
Founded in 1790, Sandeman are among the biggest shippers of both port and sherry. The firm – renowned for its logo of "the don" – was bought by Seagram in 1980, and then sold to Sogrape in 2001. But it is still chaired by George Sandeman, a direct descendant of the founder. The firm's vineyards are the Quintas de Confradeiro and Casal at Celeirós (forty-eight hectares on the Pinhão River). Quinta Laranjeira (214 hectares at Moncorvo) is a big new development in the highest Douro near Spain. Sandeman's vintage wines are fruity though not especially rich, and they seem intended for

medium-term drinking. Single-quinta port is produced from Quinta do Vao, near Pinhão. Their tawnies are attractively nutty, especially the 10-year-old "Royal". Companies associated with Sandemann are Robertson, Forrester, Diez Hermanos, and Rodriguez Pinho.

Smith Woodhouse ☆☆–☆☆☆
Vila Nova de Gaia. Vintages: 1904, '08, '12, '17, '20, '24, '27, '35, '45, '47, '50, '55, '60, '63, '66, '70, '75, '77, '80, '83, '85, '91, '94, '97, and 2000.
www.smithwoodhouse.com
Together with Graham, Warre, etc. (*qq.v.*), now part of the Symington family property. Smith Woodhouse also ships Gould Campbell vintage ports. Both come largely from the Rio Torto.

Gould Campbell vintages are big, dark, powerful, and very long-lasting wines; the Smith Woodhouse style is more fragrant and fruity and their tawnies notably so. Part of the crop is still trodden, and vintages reflect the quality of the year extremely accurately. Less expensive than the flagship labels of the Symington empire, they can be excellent value.

Taylor, Fladgate & Yeatman ☆☆☆–☆☆☆☆
Vila Nova de Gaia. Vintages: 1904, '06, '08, '12, '17, '20, '24, '27, '35, '38, '40, '42, '45, '48, '55, '60, '63, '66, '70, '75, '77, '80, '83, '85, '92, '94, '97, and 2000. www.taylor.pt
Founded in 1692, Taylor is one of the oldest and best shippers, still owned by descendants of the Yeatman family. The style of the tremendous vintage wines, of unrivalled ripeness, depth, and every other dimension, is largely derived from the famous Quinta de Vargellas (220 hectares), high on the Upper Douro above São João de Pesqueira.

In 1973, they bought the Quinta de Terra Feita (100 hectares) at Celeiros up the Pinhão Valley, and in 1998 bought two more properties near Pinhão. The vintage ports are still trodden by foot or by so-called robotic *lagares*; Taylor is experimenting with stainless-steel fermenters at its vinification centre for ruby ports near Regua. Both Vargellas and Terra Freita are sometimes released as single-quinta vintages. Fonseca (*q.v.*) is an associate company. Taylor's LBV is the biggest-selling one on the market. Its tawnies (particularly the 20-year-olds) are also exceptional.

Quinta do Vesuvio ☆☆☆
Vila Nova de Gaia. Vintages: 1990, '91, '92, '94, '95, '96, '97, '98, '99, and 2000. www.quinta-do-vesuvio.com
This magnificent Upper Douro estate used to be owned by A. A. Ferreira, but was acquired by the Symington family in 1989. Although technically a single-quinta port, it is made entirely in *lagares* and given the same care as all the other Symington vintage ports. Vesuvio aims to release a vintage every year, except when conditions are so dire, as in 1993, as to make this impossible.

Warre ☆☆☆☆
Vila Nova de Gaia. Vintages: 1904, '08, '12, '20, '22, '24, '27, '34, ('42), '45, '47, '50, '55, '58, '60, '63, '66, '70, '75, '77, '80, '83, '85, '91, '94, '97, and 2000.
www.warre.com
Dating from 1670, and the oldest English port firm, Warre is now one of the largest firms in the Symington group.

The vintage wines are based on the 40-hectare Quinta da Cavadinha near Pinhão, produced by modern methods. The single-quinta Quinta da Cavadinha is a recent introduction.

The style is extremely fruity with a fresh, almost herbal bouquet, and a firm "grip" at the finish. Recent vintages have been beautifully balanced and lingering. Warrior is a good vintage-character wine and Nimrod a fine tawny. "Warre's LBV" is particularly good.

Other Port Producers

Barros Almeida ☆
Vila Nova de Gaia. www.porto-barros.pt
This is a family owned substantial shipper of medium-quality ports, founded 1913. Also owns Kopke (*q.v.*) and Feuerheerd (*q.v.*).

Borges E. Irmão ☆
Vila Nova de Gaia. Vintages: 1945, '55, '58, '60, '63, '70, '79, '80, '82, '83, '85 and '94
Founded by the Borges brothers in 1884, this port house has banking connections and a substantial interest in table wines. Best wines are "Quinta do Junço", "Soalheira", and "Roncão". Quick-maturing vintages, but very average wines.

J. W. Burmester ☆☆–☆☆☆
Porto. Vintages: 1900, '10, '20, '22, '27, '29, '34, '35, '37, '40, '44, '48, '50, '55, '58, '60, '63, '70, '77, '80, '84, '85, '92, '95, '97, and 2000
A small, family owned Portuguese house, originally of English and German foundation in 1750. Grapes from their own vineyards and well-chosen wines from around Pinhão go to make their superb tawnies and sound vintages. The firm still lists *colheita* tawnies from 1900.

Feuerheerd ☆
Vila Nova de Gaia
Founded 1815. The formerly British-owned company now belongs to Barros Almeida (*q.v.*).

Martinez Gassiot ☆☆
Vila Nova de Gaia
An old firm founded in 1790 and bought by Harvey's in 1961. Now allied to Cockburn (*q.v.*). The best wines are fine tawnies, and there's an attractive single-quinta port from Quinta da Eira Velha.

Rebello Valente ☆
Vila Nova de Gaia. Vintages: 1945, '47, '55, '63, '66, '67, '70, '72, '75, '77, '80, '83 and '85
Now a subsidiary of Sandeman (*q.v.*), the firm of Robertson Bros. is the shipper of Rebello Valente vintage ports. The wines are of average quality.

Quinta de la Rosa ☆☆
Pinhão. www.quintadelarosa.com
This charming property near Pinhão produces a small quantity of elegant vintage port ideal for medium-term drinking. All the top ports are foot-trodden. Unlike most shippers, La Rosa aims to release a vintage wine every year, although 1993 proved impossible.

Rozès ☆

Vila Nova de Gaia. Vintages: 1987, '91, '94, '95, '97, '98, '99, and 2000. www.rozes.pt

A shipper, owned since 1987 by LVMH, selling mostly to France. Modest quality.

Wiese & Krohn ☆

Vila Nova de Gaia. Vintages: 1957, '58, '60, '61, '63, '65, '67, '70, '75, '78, '82, '84, '85, '91, and '95

Small, independent company without vineyards.

Madeira

The very existence of Madeira has been touch and go for a century and a half. No other famous wine region has suffered so much the combined onslaught of pests, diseases, disillusioned growers, and public neglect.

What has kept Madeira alive is the unique quality its old wines have of getting better and better over decades or even centuries. The remaining bottles of Madeira from before its troubles began are proof that the island can make the longest-lived wines in the world. At a century old, their flavours are concentrated into a pungency that would be overwhelming were it not so fresh. They leave the mouth so cleanly and gracefully as you swallow, that water could not be more reviving. Harmony between sweetness and acidity can go no further.

Madeira is the largest of a cluster of islands 643 kilometres (400 miles) west of the coast of Morocco. In the fifteenth century, the Portuguese, who landed on the island, set fire to the dense woodland that covered its slopes. The fire burned for years, the ashes from an entire forest enriching the already fertile volcanic soils.

Madeira flourished as a Portuguese colony. Prince Henry the Navigator ordered the sweet Malvasia grapes of Greece to be planted, as well as sugar cane from Sicily. Later, with the discovery of the West Indies, bananas became an important part of the island's harvest. The crops were, and still are, grown in a garden-like mixture on steep terraces that rise halfway up the 1,829 metre (6,000-foot) island-mountain. As in northern Portugal, the vines are trained on pergolas to allow other crops beneath. With its warm climate, Madeira was a natural producer of "sack", like Jerez and the Canaries. English legislation of 1665 settled its destiny by forbidding the export of European wines to British colonies except through British ports and in British ships. Madeira was presumably deemed to be in Africa, and so became the regular supplier for American vessels heading west. By the end of the seventeenth century, the American and West Indian British colonists used Madeira as their only wine.

Far from being spoilt by the long, hot voyage across the mid-Atlantic, the wine seemed to improve. Later, with growing British interests in the Far East, it was discovered to benefit even more from a voyage to India. So fine was their sea-matured Madeira that casks were shipped as ballast to India and back to give connoisseurs in Europe an even finer wine. It was during the eighteenth century that brandy was added, as it was to port, to sweeten and stabilize it.

In America, the appreciation of old Madeira became a cult – southern gentlemen would meet to dine simply on terrapin and canvas-back duck, before "discussing" several decanters of ancient wine, named sometimes for their grapes, or for the ship that carried them, or the families in whose cellars they had rested and become heirlooms. Thus a Bual might be followed by a Constitution, and that by a Francis, a Butler or a Burd. A popular pale blend, still sometimes seen, is known as Rainwater – because, apparently, of a similarity of taste. Almost the same reverence was paid to its qualities in England – and still is, by the few who have tasted such wines.

Quantities became far too great to transport through the tropics as a matter of course. In the 1790s, Napoléon's navy also put difficulties in the way of merchant seamen. A practical substitute was found in warming the wines in hot stores (Portuguese *estufas*) for several months, depending on quality. The least-good wine was heated the most, for the shortest period of time; the better for longer periods at more moderate temperatures. (The very finest wines received no artificial heat: rather, three to five years in cask in a sun-baked loft). The rules today stipulate 45°C (113°F) as the minimum temperature to which the wines must be heated.

Four principal grape varieties and three or four others were grown for different styles of wine. The original, the Malvasia or Malmsey, made the richest; the Bual a less rich, more elegant but equally fragrant wine; Verdelho a soft, much drier wine with a faintly bitter finish; the Sercial (thought to be a clone of Riesling) a fine, light wine with a distinct acid "cut". Tinta Negra Mole, reputedly an ancient forebear of Pinot Noir, was planted to make the red wine once known as "Tent". Bastardo, Terrantez, and Moscatel were also grown in smaller quantities.

Madeira was at the peak of its prosperity when a double disaster struck. In the 1850s came oidium, the powdery mildew. In 1873, phylloxera arrived; 2,400 hectares of vineyard were destroyed, and only 1,200 replaced with true Madeira vines. To save grafting, the remainder was replanted (if at all) with French-American hybrids, whose wine no longer has any claim to be called Madeira at all.

Since then, Madeira has lived on its reputation, kept alive by memories, by a meagre trickle of high-quality wines, and by the convenient French convention of sauce *madère*, which is easily enough satisfied with any wine that has been cooked. Half the wine from the island today is destined for sauce-making with no questions asked. Unfortunately, even the replanting of the original European vines, the four classics, was neglected in favour of the obliging Tinta Negra Mole.

Today, over eighty-five per cent of the crop (hybrids apart) is Tinta Negra Mole. It has to do service for the Malmsey, Bual, Verdelho, and Sercial (respectively 3.5, 1.8, 1.6 and 1.9 per cent of the crop) in all except the most expensive brands. Tinta, in fact, is picked either earlier or later, fortified during or after fermentation, "stoved" more or less, coloured and sweetened more or less, according to whether it is destined to be sold as Sercial, Verdelho, Bual or Malmsey.

Portugal's entry to the EU in 1986 has served notice on this practice. Its regulations require eighty-five per cent of a wine to be of the grape variety named. "Malmsey" can no longer be simply a style; it will have to be genuine Malvasia. The age of the wine can also appear on the label: 3, 5, 10, or 15 years. 3 and 5 are often disappointing, as they are not varietal wines but described with stylistic definitions on the label, such as "Finest Medium Rich" or "Finest Dry". It is invariably better to pay the small premium for 10 or 15 years.

Taking note of the EU regulations, the island's 4,000 growers are busy regrafting vines, 100,000 of them a year, to the classic varieties. It is their only hope. They cannot thrive on cheapness and low quality. They have no cash crop of "instant" wine; it all needs ageing. The *estufas* are expensive to run.

With the reputation of Madeira and its wines in steady decline, the authorities took the radical decision to ban all exports of bulk wines from 2002.

The maintaining of dated *solera* (as in Jerez) used to be standard practice, but is no longer permitted. Old *solera* bottlings still turn up at auction and can be outstanding value. The Madeira shippers still occasionally declare a vintage – always a rarer occurrence with Madeira than with port, and taking place not immediately after the vintage but some thirty years later.

Vintage Madeira is kept in cask for a minimum of twenty years, then may spend a further period in glass twenty-litre demijohns before bottling – when it is deemed ready to drink. In reality it is still only a young wine at this stage; it needs another twenty to fifty years in bottle to achieve sublimity.

In the early 2000s, the shippers introduced a new style of wine: the vintage-dated *colheita*. Blandy took the initiative with a 1994 Malmsey, and Henriques & Henriques and Justino Henriques soon followed suit with wines from 1995.

The late Noël Cossart, the fifth generation of the old firm of Madeira shippers Cossart Gordon, counselled, "Never to buy a cheap Sercial or Malmsey; these grapes are shy growers and must consequently be expensive; whereas Bual and Verdelho are prolific and develop faster and may be both cheaper and good."

Vintages

The most famous Madeira vintages up to 1900, bottles of which are still occasionally found, were 1789, 1795 (esp. Terrantez), 1806, 1808 (Malmsey), 1815 (esp. Bual), 1822, 1836, 1844, 1846 (esp. Terrantez and Verdelho), 1851, 1862, 1865, 1868, 1870 (Sercial), 1880 (esp. Malmsey).

Since 1900 over two dozen vintages have been shipped: 1900 (the last year Moscatel was made), 1902 (esp. Verdelho and Bual), 1905 (esp. Sercial), 1906 (esp. Malmsey), 1907 (esp. Verdelho and Bual), 1910, 1914 (Bual), 1915 (Bual, Sercial), 1916, 1920, 1926 (esp. Bual), 1934 (Verdelho), 1940, 1941 (esp. Bual), 1950, 1954 (esp. Bual), 1956, 1957, 1958, 1960 (Bual, Terrantez), 1965 (Bual), 1966 (Bual, Sercial), 1968 (Verdelho), 1969 (Terrantez), 1971, 1972 (Malmsey, Verdelho), 1973 (Verdelho), and 1974 (Terrantez).

Leading Madeira Shippers

Barbeito ☆☆
Funchal
This producer is 52% owned by a Japanese trading company. An impressive range of vintages is kept in stock, some of which were purchased after the founding of the company.

Henriques & Henriques ☆☆☆
Camara de Lobos
The biggest independent (still family run) and the only shipper to own vineyards (the largest on the island). The cellars are the most technically well-equipped on the island. Produces a wide range of well-structured, rich, toothsome wines including very fine old reserves and vintages.

Madeira Wine Company ☆☆☆
Funchal. www.Madeirawinecompany.com
In 1913, a number of shippers in the beleaguered trade formed the Madeira Wine Association to pool their resources and share facilities. Reconstituted in 1981 as the Madeira Wine Company, the group (owned since 1989 by port shippers Symington) controls twenty-six companies and accounts for about 60% of Madeira sales.

The main winery is in an old army barracks – blends corresponding to its 120 different labels are made up in the company's lotting rooms. One of its old lodges, next to the tourist office in Funchal, is open for visits and tasting.

Here you can buy vintage wines dating back to the nineteenth century. The wines are cellared together, but preserve their house styles.

The top labels include:

• Blandy's the main range is named after various British dukes and consists of 3-year wines from Tinta Negra Mole. The 5-year wines are varietals, as are the older blends. An innovation, launched in 2000, is a 1994 Harvest Malmsey, a kind of early vintage declaration. There are also glorious old vintages, mostly seen at auctions.

• Cossart Gordon established in 1745, and once the leading Madeira shipper. Wines slightly less rich than Blandy's.

• Leacock's and Miles (ex-Rutherford & Miles) other brands, midway in sweetness between Cossart Gordon and Blandy.

Other Madeira Producers

Artur Barros e Sousa
Tasting room in Funchal
A tiny producer.

H. M. Borges
Tasting room in Funchal

Justino Henriques
Canico

Pereira D'Oliveira
Funchal

Switzerland

So rare are Swiss wines outside their own country that it is easy to assume that they fall short of international standards and remain the special taste of a blinkered culture. The assumption is not wholly accurate. Many Swiss are critical and wine-conscious, most have money to spare – which is a good thing, for Swiss wines are expensive by almost any standards. Land prices and the cost of culture of their cliff-hanging vineyards are startlingly high. To justify inevitably high prices, there should, in principle, be every pressure on growers to concentrate on high quality. In practice, growers were, until very recently, cushioned against market forces by subsidies and protectionist measures. Red wine is imported in large quantities, as not enough is made to meet demand, but white wine production exceeds local demand, so stringently low import quotas were introduced to protect growers.

Now, however, the chill winds of competition are blowing through the vineyards, and white-wine import quotas have been relaxed. The imported wines significantly undercut the home-grown version. Producers are belatedly waking up to the fact that they must export to survive, and have made tentative attempts to sell their wines abroad, but their excessively high prices render the wines uncompetitive. The future for many looks bleak.

The emphasis was on red wines 150 years ago, the best of which came from Graubünden in the German-speaking east. The best whites came from the north shore of Lake Geneva between Lausanne and Montreux in the Vaud canton, where the steep south slopes ripened the local Chasselas to perfection. Further up the Rhône Valley, in the remote mountain area of the Valais, there was a largely part-time wine-growing tradition. Vineyards were irregularly planted with obscure grapes chosen for their dazzling sweetness and strength in the dry and sunny Alpine climate.

The modern industry began to take shape when the Chasselas spread up the Rhône Valley, when pressure for the sunny lake slopes of Lake Geneva as building land drove half the wines out of the Vaud, and when selected forms of the Pinot Noir and Gamay began to penetrate from France, via Geneva and then eastwards. Meanwhile, Müller-Thurgau, bred by the eponymous Swiss scientist a century ago at Geisenheim, began to invade the eastern cantons. (Nowadays in Switzerland his name is forgotten and the variety is referred to as Riesling-Sylvaner.) In 1945, the Italian-speaking Ticino (or Tessin) adopted the Merlot of Bordeaux as its main red grape variety.

Although in the last one hundred years the overall vineyard area has diminished considerably, selected areas such as German-speaking Switzerland, the Valais, Vaud, and Geneva have increased their hectarage. Plantings of red varieties are also increasing. Nevertheless, Switzerland remains a minnow in the grand scheme of wine, with only 15,000 hectares of vineyards accounting for just 0.2 per cent of global production.

The essential information given on the often rather taciturn, though frequently highly decorative, Swiss wine label is laid down by the federal government in the ODA

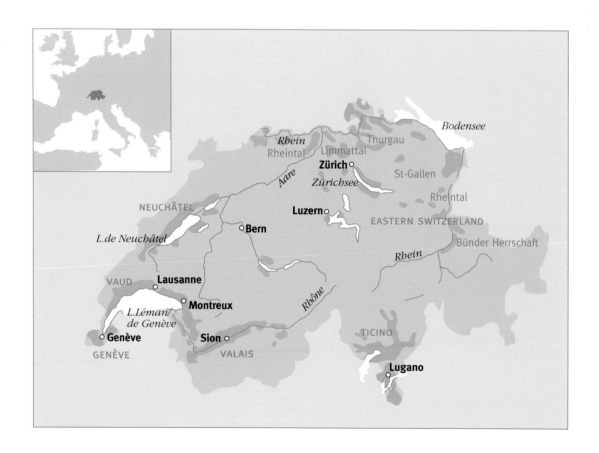

(the *Ordonnance sur les Denrées Alimentaires*). Generally speaking, for white wines, if there is no other indication of grape variety, assume Chasselas. Red wines will, in the main, be Pinot Noir and/or Gamay. Some German-Swiss labels use terms with no international validity – but then they not only never travel abroad, they seldom leave the confines of the canton in which they were grown. Italian-Swiss wine labels are simplicity itself as there are essentially only two types of wine: Merlot and the fast-disappearing Nostrano, made from a clutch of hybrid grapes.

The maker's name seems to be considered of little importance to the consumer and is often tucked away down at the bottom in small print. Pride of place may be given to a brand-name ("Les Murailles"), estate name (Château d'Allaman), or village name (St Saphorin). It is not always easy to tell which is which.

Although chaptalization is permitted, and quite commonly practised at the lower quality levels, all Swiss wines can be assumed to be dry unless a specific caution is included on the label: *mi-flétri* or *flétri* (literally "shrivelled") in the French-speaking cantons, Spätlese where German is the lingua franca. (Switzerland's multilingual community copes well with the need to have at least two different names for most things.) The Swiss also make wide use of screwcaps instead of corks for wines designed to be drunk young – which includes most Chasselas.

The French-Speaking Cantons

All the principal vineyards of the French-speaking cantons (Suisse Romande) lie along the south-facing right bank of the Rhône, from its emergence into the Valais (a suntrap sheltered on both sides by towering Alps), round the shores of Lake Geneva – simply a widening of the Rhône – to its departure through the gently rolling farmlands of Geneva canton into France. Also included in this group are the three lakes of Neuchâtel, Biel/Bienne, and Morat, each of which enjoys good, south-facing, lake-shore conditions. Three-quarters of all Swiss wine is grown in Suisse Romande, and most of it is white.

The Valais (Wallis)

The Valais (which begins, geographically, at the Grimselpass and ends at St Maurice on the right bank, and St Gingolph on the left) has Switzerland's driest and sunniest climate, frequently described as a cross between that of Spain and Provence. On its steeper vineyards, terraced on arid mountain slopes, irrigation by means of wooden channels known as *bisses* used to be common practice. Nowadays, irrigation is limited to periods of severe drought, and this only during the *période végétative*.

Wine-growing starts in earnest somewhere between Visp and Sierre, reaches a crescendo around Sion, the heart (and capital) of the Valais, and begins to wind gradually down after the Rhône has executed its sharp right turn at Martigny. At its upper extremes, the village of Visperterminen above Visp has what are reported to be Europe's highest vineyards at around 760 metres (2,500 feet) above sea level. In the upper Valais, the principal wine-growing villages are Salquenen/Salgesch, Sierre, and St Léonard; and in the lower Valais, Vétroz, Ardon, Leytron, Chamoson, Saillon, and Fully are the most important centres.

Action has finally been taken in the Valais in response to an awareness of the urgent need for some notion of *crus*. For too long, Fendant (*i.e.* Chasselas), which accounts for the largest quantity of wine produced in the Valais, was sold without mention of village or vineyard name. Since many were of poor quality (and the consumer had no way of differentiating), the result was that all Fendants, whether good, bad, or indifferent, tended to be tarred with the same bottom-of-the-market brush. Nowadays there will often be a village or vineyard name appended; the appellation Fendant may even be omitted. Sylvaner, known here as Johannisberg (sometimes Rhin, either Petit or Gros), makes aromatic, fuller-bodied yet dry wines; when late-harvested, they can be impressive indeed.

Lakes of Chasselas are one thing; the so-called "specialties" of the Valais, generally considered to be the great undiscovered potential of Swiss wines, are quite another. First comes the incomparable Petite Arvine, its name said to come from the Latin meaning "pale yellow". Distinguished by its fine nose and characteristic salty finish, it is usually vinified dry; some growers harvest a small proportion of the crop late to make a *mi-flétri* or *flétri*. Humagne ("vigorous vine" in Latin) is a nervy, stimulating wine once prescribed as a post-partum tonic to young mothers. It requires the best sites, performs rather irregularly, and ripens late – all of which had contributed to a gradual decline over the years, but that decline is happily now in reverse. Amigne, whose favoured sites are concentrated in and around Vétroz, is made in extremely limited quantities (since only twenty hectares remain) into a rich, velvety wine, almost always with some residual sugar but sufficient acidity and backbone to give it good keeping qualities.

Rarer still are a clutch of very old, quaintly named varieties, found mainly in the upper Valais around Visp. In centuries past they were harvested early to give quite sharp, thirst-quenching wines designed for vineyard quaffing after a hard day's work. Of these, the finest is Heida (or Païen), thought to be a relation either of Savagnin (the same grape as used in *vin jaune*), or of Traminer. Himbertscha, whose name sounds vaguely raspberry-related, apparently means "trellis-grown" in the upper Valais dialect, referring to the traditional method of training this particular grape, while Lafnetscha turns out to be the Blanchier of Savoie. Both give clean-tasting, rather acidic wines that need plenty of time to mature. Finally comes Gwäss (Gouais Blanc), another native of the Jura, sharply reminiscent of cider when young.

Of the non-indigenous but well-established varieties, the Marsanne grape thrives here under the name of Ermitage, giving (especially around Fully) a full-bodied wine with a striking nose and an elusively smoky flavour. Malvoisie (alias Pinot Gris) may be vinified dry (in which case it is often labelled Pinot Gris), or harvested late and made into a sweet wine – and often labelled Malvoisie. Muscat has been grown in the Valais since the sixteenth century, and is made here with all residual sugar fermented out, closer in style to a Muscat d'Alsace than to any other. Tiny quantities of Gewürztraminer, Riesling, Aligoté, Chardonnay, Chenin, and Pinot Blanc are also to be found.

Over half of Valais wine is red, and two-thirds of this is Pinot Noir, which acquits itself with some distinction, particularly around Sierre. The better growers are experimenting with Burgundy clones and varying proportions of new oak. Pinot Noir is also blended with Gamay and called Dôle, at its lower levels a good lunchtime wine quaffed throughout Switzerland in multiples of the decilitre to accompany uncomplicated meals. To qualify for the appellation, a Dôle must contain at least fifty-one per cent Pinot Noir and reach a certain minimum Oechsle level prescribed by the cantonal wine commission; if it misses the mark it is labelled Goron. Gamay is also vinified alone, especially from the villages around Martigny.

Of antique red grapes, there is Humagne Rouge (no relation of the white Humagne but reckoned by some to be Oriou, from the Valle d'Aosta). It makes robust, pleasantly tannic, and appetizing country wine. Cornalin (alias Landroter or Rouge du Pays) is an extremely rare variety whose irregular yield and uneven performance make it a tricky commercial proposition for most wine-growers. Its deep colour, good tannins, and superb fruit, however, make it an extremely interesting proposition for interested wine drinkers. Finally, in the upper Valais, Eyholzer Roter (the Mondeuse of Haute-Savoie) is to be found, which gives a tawny-reddish, rather rough country wine. Syrah, a fairly recent import, deserves special mention, particularly from around Chamoson; some Nebbiolo is also being grown.

Leading Valais Producers

Charles Bonvin ☆–☆☆☆
Sion. Owners: the Bonvin family. 22 hectares.
www.charles-bonvin.ch
Founded in 1858, Bonvin has some of its best vineyards at up to 2,275 feet (700 metres), on slate and chalk soils. There are three single-vineyard Chasselas wines on offer. Their barrel-fermented white wine is an attractive blend of Pinot Blanc, Chardonnay, and Petite Arvine. When climatic conditions are favourable, Bonvin produces a remarkable sweet wine from Silvaner and Amigne called "Cuvée d'Or", which is aged for two years in barriques.

Oskar Chanton ☆☆–☆☆☆
Visp. Owner: Josef-Marie Chanton. 6 hectares
Over twenty wines can be tasted in the venerable old Chanton cellar in Visp, including rarities from the upper Valais like Heida, Himbertscha, Lafnetscha, and Gwäss, rescued from oblivion by Josef-Marie Chanton. The Arvine is superb, as are the late-harvested Malvoisie and Gewürztraminer.

Gérald Clavien ☆–☆☆
Miège/Sierre. Owner: Gérald Clavien. 5 hectares
The wines of this young, dynamic grower (who was a chef before taking over his father's vineyards) feature on the lists of all the top restaurants in Switzerland. Sierre is the hub of red wine-growing in the Valais; Clavien's straight Pinot

Noir and "Tête de Cuvée" are notable, also the "Dôle Blanche" (a Rosé de Pinot Noir). Some full-bodied Humagne Blanc is also made.

Michel Clavien ☆–☆☆☆
Pont-de-la-Morge. Owner: Michel Clavien. 25 hectares
A prime mover in the *appellation d'origine* debate and a true marketing man right down to his fingertips, Michel Clavien has worked tirelessly to raise the image of Valais wines. The wines are elegant, the labels (especially of the "Fin Bec" line) extremely eye-catching. "Le Grand Sion" is a blend of Chasselas from a number of *lieux-dits* around Sion; "Dôle Fin Bec" contains 85% Pinot Noir and 15% Gamay; "Pinot Noir de la Follie" comes from the eponymous vineyard.

Germanier-Balavaud ☆–☆☆☆
Vétroz. Owners: the Germanier family. 180 hectares.
www.bonpere.com
Perhaps more famous locally for fragrant *eau-de-vie* from Williams pears, Bon Père Germanier is a producer of a wide range of wines of good concentration and length. In addition to Chasselas, it produces Malvoisie, Dôle, and Dôle Blanche, Pinot Noir, and a very attractive Amigne de Vétroz. Germanier also produce one of the richest Syrahs of the region by reducing yields to 40 hl/ha and ageing the wine in a good deal of new oak. In recent years they have made a great impression with "Mitis", a late-harvest Amigne fermented in new oak.

Adrian Mathier ☆☆
Salgesch. Owner: Adrian Mathier. 33 hectares.
www.nouveau-salquenen.ch
Interesting wines with personality, such as the "Cépages Nobles Topas" (from Pinot Gris, Marsanne, and Sylvaner) and a fine, late-harvest Amigne.

Simon Maye et Fils ☆☆–☆☆☆
St Pierre-de-Clages. Owners: the Maye family. 8 hectares
A small, top-quality grower making three highly prized Fendants ("Le Fauconnier", "Trémazière", and "La Mouette"), Johannisberg, Dôle, Pinot Noir, Humagne Rouge, plus some Chardonnay, Malvoisie, and dry and lightly sweet Petite Arvine. His richly spicy Syrah is widely regarded as one of the country's finest.

Domaine du Mont d'Or ☆–☆☆☆
Pont de la Morge. Owners: public company. 31 hectares.
www.montdor-wine.ch
The most famous property of Sion, established in 1847 on a steep, dry, sheltered hill by a soldier from the Vaud, one Sergeant-Major Masson, who installed the irrigation system by bisses which is still in operation. The domaine is best known for its Johannisbergs: "du Mont d'Or" when vinified dry, or "de la St Martin" (and more rarely "du 1er Décembre") when late-harvested. Also produced are a musky, weighty Malvoisie, a rather jammy Syrah, a magnificent honeyed Petite Arvine, and strong tannic and alcoholic Dôle.

Provins Valais ☆–☆☆☆
Fédération des Caves des Producteurs du Vins du Valais. Sion.
www.provins.ch
Highly regarded central cooperative of the Valais producing

some 30% of all Valais wines – and thus is one in only seven of all Swiss-bottled wines. Their "Capsule Dorée" range includes well-known brand names like "Pierrafeu Fendant", "Johannisberg Rhonegold", "Oeil-de-Perdrix Perdrizel" (a Rosé de Pinot Noir), and "Pinot Noir St Guérin".

To the usual vast Valaisan spectrum of grapes they add Pinot Blanc, Chardonnay, and Cabernet Sauvignon. Their "Chasselas St Léonard", made (exceptionally for Switzerland) without malolactic fermentation, is reserved for top restaurants. More recently they have made some truely outstanding sweet wines, such as the barrique-aged "Profil" from Marsanne and Pinot Gris, and the pure Marsanne "Grains de Malice".

Marc Raymond & Fils ☆–☆☆
Saillon. Owners: Marc and Gérard Raymond.
4 hectares
Tiny family business producing top Fendant, Johannisberg, Arvine (the pride of the house), Muscat, Malvoisie, and Dôle Blanche. Their reds are also notable, particularly Dôle and Pinot Noir. Marc Raymond is one of the few Valaisan growers to make Nebbiolo.

Eloi & Gérard Roduit ☆☆
Fully. Owners: Eloi and Gérard Roduit. 6 hectares
A small family business, run by an uncle and nephew, making the full range of Valais wines on some prime sites situated above the village of Fully. Of especial note are their Ermitage and Petite Arvine (vinified dry and *flétri*), Gamay, Pinot Noir (of which a proportion is oak-aged), and Syrah.

Bernard Rouvinez ☆☆
Sierre. Owners: Jean-Bernard and Dominique Rouvinez.
4 hectares
These brothers' estate lies next to a nunnery; they are the only men permitted to enter the nunnery grounds to tend the vines. On their own property, two-thirds of the grapes are red, predominantly Pinot Noir. They vinify excellent varietal Pinot Noir and Chasselas. However, their most notable creations are "Le Tourmentin", a Pinot Noir/Syrah/Cornalin/Humagne Rouge blend, and "Le Trémaille" (Chardonnay and Petite Arvine). These elegant, attractively presented wines indicate fresh thinking and a willingness to innovate – a hopeful sign in a sometimes overly tradition-bound region.

Varone ☆–☆☆
Sion. Owners: Jean-Pierre and Philippe Varone. 8 hectares.
www.varone.ch
A traditional producer, with, as yet, no plantings of fashionable varieties such as Cabernet or Syrah. Their best Chasselas comes from the Uvrier vineyard.

Maurice Zufferey ☆☆
Muraz/Sierre. Owner: Maurice Zufferey. 9 hectares.
www.maurice-zufferey-vins.ch
Sierre is red wine country and Zufferey's are particularly notable (though he also produces many other specialties). Three Pinot Noirs are made (one oak-aged), Dôle, a deeply coloured Humagne Rouge, and the tricky but infinitely rewarding Cornalin which Zufferey was among the first to revive in the Valais.

The Vaud

The canton of Vaud includes all the vineyards of the north shore of Lake Geneva and the Rhône, as high upstream as the border with the Valais at Bex: an eighty-kilometre (fifty-mile) arc of southern slopes.

It is divided into three main zones: Chablais, the right bank of the Rhône between Ollon and the lake; Lavaux, the central section between Montreux and Lausanne; and La Côte, from Lausanne round to Nyon at the border with Geneva. Further north, just short of Lake Neuchâtel, are the little enclaves of Côtes de l'Orbe and Bonvillars; half the villages in the Vully vineyard on Lake Morat also belong to Vaud. The canton has its own appellation systems, which control origin, grape varieties, and Oechsle levels.

The appellations of Chablais include the villages of Villeneuve, Yvorne, Aigle, Ollon, and Bex, all with good southwest slopes above the Rhône. Yvorne, with its minerally, gunflint character, real vigour, ripeness and length is generally considered to be the greatest of all Chablais wines. At its very best it is undoubtedly a match for (though subtly different from) the top wines from Lavaux.

Lavaux is certainly Switzerland's most scenic vineyard, piled high in toppling terraces above the lakeside villages. The view from among the vines is superb: the mountains of Savoie a great dark, jagged-topped bulk against the sun opposite, the lake surface below gleaming grey, wrinkled by white paddle-steamers gliding from village pier to village pier. Erosion is a serious problem: a brown stain in the lake after a night's heavy rain is bad news for a wine-grower.

Lavaux boasts the *crus* of Dézaley (for centuries considered to be the high point of Swiss white wine) and nearby Calamin, as well as six of Vaud's twenty-six appellations. Chasselas from the upper slopes takes on a liveliness and an almost aromatic quality which distinguishes it from the more austere dryness of the lower vineyards. Each village, however, has its committed supporters and the names of Epesses, St Saphorin, Rivaz, Cully, Villette, Lutry, Chardonne and others are writ correspondingly large on the label.

La Côte, situated between Lausanne and Nyon, has twelve appellations. The best-known of these are Féchy, Perroy, Mont-sur-Rolle, Tartegnin, Vinzel, and Luins. This is a more gentle, often southeasterly sloping vineyard whose wines rarely have the vigour or flavour of those of Lavaux or Chablais, but do make deliciously floral pre-prandial quaffing wines. For some unknown reason the term *grand cru* can be applied to any wine that comes from a *clos* or walled vineyard, regardless of its quality.

Chasselas dominates the Vaud vineyards, although a very small part is also made over to Pinot Gris, Pinot Blanc, and Riesling-Sylvaner. Pinot Noir and Gamay are also found in these vineyards, either vinified singly, or blended and designated Salvagnin (a so-called "label of quality" which has fallen somewhat into disrepute over the years). Overproduction in this area has been a serious problem here for some time, with average yields frequently surpassing 100 hectolitres per hectare, for red as well as white wines.

The wines – especially those made from Chasselas – enjoy an enthusiastic local following that can baffle those more used to the forthright flavours of Alsace or Australia.

Leading Vaud Producers

Henri Badoux ☆☆
Aigle. Owner: Henri Olivier Badoux. 50 hectares.
www.badoux.com
A substantial, second-generation, family owned business with vineyards in Yvorne, Aigle, Ollon, Villeneuve, St Saphorin, Féchy, Vinzel, and Mont-sur-Rolle. The two leading wines are the famous "Aigle les Murailles" (with the classic lizard label) and "Yvorne Petit Vignoble". Badoux's "Aigle Pourpre Monseigneur", a Pinot Noir from the Chablais district, benefits from some ageing.

Louis Bovard ☆☆
Lavaux. Owner: Louis Bovard. 16 hectares
A forward-looking estate, producing not only Chasselas from top sites in Epesses, St Saphorin, and Dézaley, but also good Sauvignon Blanc, Syrah, and Merlot.

Jean-Michel Conne ☆☆
Chexbres. Owner: Jean-Michel Conne. 10 hectares
By dint of wise buying of vineyards outside Lavaux, and by inheritance of the family vineyards, a considerable holding of good sites around Lake Geneva has been built up.
   Especially famous is their "Dézaley Plan Perdu", "St Saphorin Le Sémillant" (a *sur lie* bottling), and "Ollon L'Oisement". Several Pinot Noirs (of which the oak-aged is labelled "Cartige") are also produced.

Frères Dubois ☆☆
Cully. Owner: Jean-Daniel Dubois. 10 hectares. www.dubois.ch
The Dubois are believers in allowing Chasselas to go through malolactic fermentation. They offer a wide range of *crus*, including Epesses, St Saphorin, and Dézaley, all of which are capable of ageing for twenty years, after which they acquire a slight honeyed tone.

Hammel ☆–☆☆
Rolle. 24 hectares
This is a leading domaine and merchant house of La Côte, producing Chasselas from various Vaudois vineyards: Domaine Les Pierrailles and La Bigaire (La Côte), Domaine de Riencourt (Bougy), Clos du Chatelard (Villeneuve), and Clos de la George (Yvorne).

Alain Neyroud ☆–☆☆
Chardonne. Owner: Alain Neyroud. 7 hectares
A fifth generation business selling mainly to private clients in German-speaking Switzerland and to local restaurants. The Chasselas is labelled "La Petite Combe", the Gamay "La Perle Rouge", and the Pinot Noir "Au Coin des Serpents". Unusually for Vaud, about 50% of their production is red.

Obrist ☆–☆☆
Vevey. Owners: Schenk group (q.v.). 40 hectares. www.obrist.ch
One of the largest growers of Vaudois white, with a particular reputation for their Yvornes: "Clos du Rocher", "Clos des Rennauds", and "Pré Roc". Also famous is their "Cure d'Attalens" and Salvagnin "Domaine du Manoir".

Gérard Pinget ☆☆
Rivaz. Administrator: C. Pinget. 10 hectares
A traditional estate whose top wines include the steely "Dézaley Renard" (its label sports a fox), "St Saphorin", and "Soleil de Lavaux".

Schenk ☆–☆☆
Rolle. Owner: André Schenk. 37 hectares. www.schenk.ch
This, the largest Swiss wine firm, was founded and based at Rolle since 1893. Its principal estates are in Yvorne, Mont-sur-Rolle, Vinzel, and Féchy. Its subsidiary companies in Switzerland include Obrist (*q.v.*), Maurice Gay, and the Cave St Pierre in Vallais.

J. & P. Testuz ☆☆
Treytorrens-Cully. Owner: Jean-Pierre Testuz. 13 hectares. www.testuz.ch
The Testuz family (whose premises are actually in Dézaley) trace their wine-growing roots back to the sixteenth century. In 1865, they sold the first bottled wine in Switzerland. Their Dézaley, "L'Arbalète", is one of the finest of the area. Other Lavaux wines include the fine "St Saphorin Roche Ronde" and "Epesses". Chablais wines include "Aigle Les Cigales" and "Yvorne Haute-Combe".

Geneva

The canton is divided into three districts: the biggest – Mandement – to the north on the right bank of the Rhône, includes Dardagny, Russin, and above all, Satigny. South of the river (and of the city) is Arve-et-Rhône, centred around Lully-Bernex. The area which sets off around the other side of the lake is called Arve-et-Lac. Since the slopes are gentle and the vines well-spaced out, mechanical harvesting is a possibility, which gives the wines a useful price advantage.
   The area has increased its vineyards steadily and is now third in importance after the Valais and the Vaud. Chasselas (often, but not inevitably, known here as Perlan) accounts for about half the wine produced, a light, dry wine usually bottled with a slight prickle to make up for the character it frequently lacks. Some increasingly useful forms of Gamay have been introduced that suit both the conditions of the vineyard and the local taste, shaped by years of massive Beaujolais imports. Riesling-Sylvaner, Pinot Gris, Pinot Blanc, and Gewürztraminer are also to be found; impressive results are being achieved with Aligoté and Chardonnay.

Leading Geneva Producers

Pierre Dupraz ☆
Lully. Owner: Pierre Dupraz. 11 hectares
All Dupraz wines are labelled varietally (Chasselas, Aligoté, Chardonnay, Gamay, and Pinot Noir) with the domaine's name ("Domaine Les Curiades") appended. Some Chardonnay is oak-aged.

Charles Novelle & Fils ☆☆–☆☆☆
Satigny. Owner: Jean-Michel Novelle. 7 hectares
When Jean-Michel Novelle took over running the domaine in the 1980s, he replaced most of the Chasselas with seventeen other varieties, many of them international

rather than Swiss. Always experimenting, Novelle has made sweet wines from artificially dried Sauvignon and Petit Manseng grapes.

Claude Ramu ☆–☆☆
Dardagny. Owner: Claude Ramu

A range of mythologically named wines is produced in the district of Le Mandement, west of Geneva. Here the Pinot Gris, labelled "Domaine du Centaure", stands out. Other whites include the Chasselas (known in the Geneva vineyards as Perlan), an excellent Aligoté, Pinot Blanc, and Gewürztraminer. Reds are Gamay and Pinot Noir (some oak-aged), and a *crémant* labelled "Les Compagnons de Vénus" is also produced.

Bernard Rochaix ☆–☆☆
Peissy. Owner: Bernard Rochaix. 48 hectares.
www.lesperrieres.ch

Two-thirds of production is of white wines. As well as a fragrant Chasselas and lively Aligoté, Rochaix produces an attractive unoaked Chardonnay, often more enjoyable than his barrel-fermented version. The same is true of his Gamay, which also comes in two styles. Neither Pinot Noir nor Cabernet Sauvignon is really successful here.

Lakes Neuchâtel, Biel, & Morat

Vines grow all along the northern shores of all three lakes, sheltered by the Jura chain, which forms the backbone of the route from Geneva up to Basle. The best-known villages on Lake Neuchâtel are Cortaillod, Auvernier, Boudry, and St Blaise; on Lake Biel, the names of Schafis and Twann are famous; while on Lake Morat, the Fribourg villages of Praz, Nant, and Môtier enjoy a certain renown.

Chasselas reigns here once more, to give wines which are light, dry, and given to a natural prickle ("*l'étoile*") – a result of their being mainly bottled *sur lie*. There is no Gamay north of Geneva; Pinot Noir is the only permitted red variety. The limestone hills to the north and west of Lake Neuchâtel and the temperate climate seem to bring out some of the elusive finesse of the Pinot Noir grape.

Neuchâtel Pinots from reputable growers may be expected to have some distinction; in a good year they may be considered the best Pinots Switzerland can produce. The pale rosé, Oeil-de-Perdrix ("partridge's eye") – an appellation native to Neuchâtel, now widely used all over Switzerland – is an appealing Rosé de Pinot Noir.

Leading Neuchâtel Producers

Château d'Auvernier ☆☆
Auvernier. Owner: Thierry Grosjean. 30 hectares

One of the oldest-established houses, making nervy Neuchâtel blanc, Oeil-de-Perdrix, Pinot Noir d'Auvernier, Pinot Gris, and a small amount of Chardonnay. High-quality winemaking.

Samuel Châtenay ☆–☆☆
Boudry. 85 hectares

The are large quantities of white, rosé, and red wines made by this estate, the best of which include Chasselas and Pinot Noir from the seventeen-hectare Domaine de Château Vaumarcus.

Albert Porret ☆☆
Cortaillod. Owner: Pierre-André Porret

This is the family's fourth generation making Chasselas labelled "Domaine des Cèdres" (after the 200-year-old cedars outside the family house). Also Chardonnay, an Oeil-de-Perdrix, and a little Pinot Gris. "Pinot Noir Cortaillod" has a keen following.

The German-Speaking Cantons

Because the German-speaking cantons favour the same grape varieties and use broadly the same vinification techniques, they tend to be grouped together and called, for some obscure reason, eastern Switzerland. There are the usual concentrations around lakes (Constance, Zürich) and along rivers (Rhine, Aare, Limmat), with the odd microclimate thrown in (notably the four villages in Graubünden known as the Bündner Herrschaft).

Wine is grown in eight of the Swiss-German cantons: Graubunden, St Gallen, Thurgau, Schaffhausen, Zürich, Aargau, Baselland, and Bern. The most productive cantons today are Zürich (scattered between Wädenswil, home of the Federal School of Oenology and Viticulture, Winterthur, and the villages along the north shore of the lake); and Schaffhausen, where the Hallau vineyard is the largest in eastern Switzerland. Consumption of Swiss German-produced wines is almost exclusively local.

Up here north of the Alps, the colour balance changes and red begins to predominate in the shape of Pinot Noir (alias Blauburgunder, or Clevner on Lake Zürich). Riesling-Sylvaner is the main white variety, which performs well in the right (*i.e.* secateur-wielding) hands to give surprisingly aromatic, lively wines – frequently of more interest than run-of-the-mill Chasselas from further south.

Pinot Noir excels in the Bündner Herrschaft, whose warm autumn climate ripens it to real substance, with colour and a velvet touch. Elsewhere, the Swiss Germans exhibit a mystifying fondness for pale, slightly fizzy Blauburgunders, a penchant not inevitably shared by others.

Besides these two (plus a little Gewürztraminer, Pinot Blanc, and Pinot Gris) there are some specialties confined to the Swiss German cantons. Completer is an extremely rare, late-ripening, late-harvested specialty found in Graubünden, where it is long-matured and liquorous, and on the lakeshore of Zürich, where it is more austere. Its name is linked to the evening office of Compline, after which the monks were said to gratefully quaff a glass or two.

Räuschling is an old-established Zürich variety, which makes elegant, crisp white wines. Freisamer is a potentially promising cross between Sylvaner and Pinot Gris.

Leading Swiss German Producers

Schlossgut Bachtobel ☆☆–☆☆☆
Weinfelden. Owner: Hans-Ulrich Kesselring. 6 hectares
Schlossgut Bachtobel produces mostly Pinot Noir, plus Riesling-Sylvaner and tiny amounts of Pinot Gris, Chardonnay, and Riesling. There are three Pinot Noirs, each *cuvée* with a different number.

Donatsch ☆☆–☆☆☆
Malans. Owner: Thomas Donatsch. 5 hectares
The beautiful, old, wood-panelled restaurant Zum Ochsen in the patrician village of Malans has belonged to the family for over 150 years. This is the best place to sample Thomas Donatsch's superb Pinot Noirs and finely structured Chardonnays, although they are also found on the wine lists of most top Swiss restaurants. Both his Pinot Noir and Chardonnay are aged in barriques. Also produced are Riesling-Sylvaner, Pinot Blanc, Pinot Gris, and even some Cabernet Sauvignon.

Daniel Gantenbein ☆☆☆
Fläsch. Owner: Daniel Gantenbein. 4 hectares
Gantenbein's bread-and-butter wines are Riesling-Sylvaner, Chardonnay, and Pinot Gris, but he is best-known for his barrique-fermented Pinot Blanc and his outstanding and costly Pinot Noir, made from grapes that are left to dry after harvest.

Ruedi Honegger ☆
Stäf/Mutzmalen. Owner: Ruedi Honegger
Herr Honegger, at the wonderfully sited Itzikerhüsli, is one of the relatively small number of growers on Lake Zürich who bottles his own wine on the domaine. He makes fine Riesling-Sylvaner, Räuschling, Clevner (Pinot Noir), and rosé.

Andrea Lauber ☆☆
Malans. Owners: the Lauber family. 2 hectares
The lovely, onion-domed Gut Plandaditsch is a Malanser landmark. Especially notable is the Laubers' deep-ruby Pinot Noir, powerfully aromatic Pinot Blanc, late-harvested Freisamer, and Pinot Gris. The mouth-filling Chardonnay, produced in tiny quantities, spends up to seven months in new oak.

Anton Meier ☆–☆☆☆
Würenlingen. Owner: Anton Meier. 6 hectares
Anton Meier is a noted wine-grower, landlord of the Zum Sternen restaurant, and the owner of one of Switzerland's foremost vine nurseries. He produces a very fruity Riesling-Sylvaner, good Pinot Gris, a fine Gewürztraminer, some rosé (Pinot Noir), and a crisp *crémant*. His pride and joy, though, are the Pinot Noirs from Kloster Sion.

Nussbaumer ☆–☆☆
Aesch. Owner: Kurt Nussbaumer. 10 hectares
A small firm producing Riesling-Sylvaner, Chasselas, Pinot Gris, Gewürztraminer, Räuschling, and Pinot Noir in its Aesch and Arlesheim vineyards, just a stone's throw from the border with Alsace. A more recent addition is "Chrachmost", a classic-method sparkling Chasselas.

Hans Schlatter ☆
Hallau. Owner: Stefan Schlatter. 10 hectares.
www.weinbauschlatter.ch
Medium-sized grower and merchant of German Switzerland. The "Hallauer Blauburgunder Spätlese", "16-Fahre Wy", and "Tokayer" (Pinot Gris) are very popular locally.

Hermann Schwarzenbach ☆–☆☆
Meilen. Owner: Hermann Schwarzenbach. 6 hectares.
www.reblaube.ch
Small, old-established house with a range of wines, including Riesling-Sylvaner (some late-harvested as Beerenauslese), Freisamer, Sémillon, Räuschling, Chardonnay, Pinot Gris, and – the only grower still to make it on the lake – Completer. Pinot Noir is produced both straight and late-harvested, fermented in oak vats and recommended as a keeper.

The Italian-Speaking Cantons

The Ticino or Tessin divides into four main areas: north and south of Monte Céneri (Sopraceneri and Sottoceneri respectively), the shores of Lake Lugano (Luganese), and the districts of Mendrisiotto.

It is a delightfully uncomplicated area, producing mainly red wines, where Merlot holds sway over a bunch of miscellaneous black grapes (Bondola, Freisa, Barbera) blended into everyday table wine labelled Nostrano. The VITI "label of quality" is awarded by a commission of experts to Merlot wines of one year's bottle age which pass chemical analysis and taste tests. A few growers are successfully ageing some Merlots in new oak (often calling the result *riserva*). It gives them distinct character, no longer the typical, soft, one-dimensional Merlot del Ticino.

There is little white wine grown in Ticino: the soils are all wrong and the climate far too benevolent, though there is some Sémillon, Sauvignon, Pinot Gris, and a little Chardonnay to be found. The foxy *Vitis lambrusca* hybrid Americano is vinified less and less.

Leading Ticino Producers

Angelo Delea ☆–☆☆
Losone. Owners: Angelo and Leopoldo Delea. 20 hectares.
www.delea.ch
Restaurateur-turned-wine-grower, Angelo Delea produces some long-macerated, powerful Merlots in the Sopraceneri region. Each year he buys in 40% new barrels, into which goes his best Merlot (labelled *riserva*); the remainder is aged in used *pièces*.

Delea also produces a Chasselas, Pinot Blanc and – for old times' sake – an Americano: cherry-red and distinctly foxy.

Werner Stucky ☆☆–☆☆☆
Rivera. Owners: Werner and Lilo Stucky. 3 hectares
One of the young Swiss German pioneers of the region,

Werner Stucky produces tiny quantities of Merlot, straight and oak-aged, both of them sold out by year's end to private customers and a handful of top restaurants. His other specialty is "Conte di Luna", a blend of Merlot and Cabernet Sauvignon. These are tannic wines that gain in opulence from being bottle-aged.

Eredi Carlo Tamborini ☆–☆☆

Lamone. Owner: Claudio Tamborini. 35 hectares.
www.tamborini-vini.ch

An important Ticino house with steadily improving Merlot. "Vigna Vecchia" is its best, oak-aged from vines between thirty and sixty years old. "Collivo" is also good, and the "Vigneto ai Brughi" and "Castello di Morcote" excellent.

Fratelli Valsangiacomo ☆☆

Chiasso. Director: Cesare Valsangiacomo. 22 hectares

Cesare Valsangiacomo is the fifth generation of this distinguished old Ticino house, and produces some of the most respected bottles of the regions: "Roncobello", "Dioniso", "Rubro", "Riserva di Bacco", "L'Ariete", "Pedrinate del Piccolo Ronco" (all Merlots), "Cagliostro" (a Merlot rosé) and two Merlot bubblies. A swashbuckling brigand adorns the label of Valsangiacomo's fruity blend of Chasselas, Sémillon, and Sauvignon: "Il Mattirolo".

Vinattieri Ticinesi ☆–☆☆

Ligornetto. Owner: Luigi Zanini. 43 hectares. www.zanini.ch

Members of the Zanini family have invested heavily in vineyard and cellar. Bottles of their best Merlots bear vineyard names (sometimes complete with beautifully contoured sketch maps): "Ligornetto", "Tenuta ai Ronchi", "Roncaia"; all are oak-aged to some degree or other.

His other red wines include Syrah and Pinot Noir. With some good sites with chalky soils, Vinattieri even manages to produce creditable whites called "Verdor" and "Due Vittigni".

The Austrian Wine Law

CATEGORIES

Tafelwein Landwein Minimum 13° KMW (63 Oechsle). A *tafelwein* must come from a single wine area, maximum alcohol 11.5%, max. residual sugar 6g/l.

Qualitätswein From a single wine area, minimum 15° KMW (73° Oechsle), enriched up to maximum 19° KMW (94° Oechsle).

Kabinett Minimum 17° KMW (83.5° Oechlse), maximum 19° KMW (94° Oechsle), maximum 9g/l residual sugar, no chaptalization.

Prädikatswein *Qualitätswein* "of exceptional maturity or vintage": no chaptalization. The grades are:

  Spätlese late-picked grapes with minimum 19° KMW (94° Oechsle).

  Auslese Selected late-picked grapes with minimum 21° KMW (105° Oechsle).

  Eiswein Made from frozen grapes with minimum 25° KMW (127° Oechsle).

  Beerenauslese Selected late-picked overripe grapes with noble rot, minimum 25° KMW (127° Oechsle).

  Ausbruch Overripe, nobly rotten grapes which have dried naturally. Minimum 27° KMW (138° Oechsle).

  Trockenbeerenauslese Nobly-rotten, raisin-like grapes, minimum 30° KMW (150° Oechsle).

The Wachau has its own set of categories. The basic wine is Steinfeder, essentially an unchaptalized *Qualitätswein* with up to 10.7%. The next step up is Federspiel, essentially a dry Kabinett with a maximum alcohol of 11.9%. The ripest wines are called Smaragd, and are the equivalent of a Spätlese or indeed Auslese Trocken elsewhere in Austria.

Austria

Austria's wine history goes back at least two millennia – until shortly after the Roman conquered the Danubian provinces in sixteen BC. It is an interesting question why modern wine culture arrived here far later than elsewhere in Western Europe. Even during the 1920s and '30s only the very finest Austrian wines were sold in bottle. Still today, a significant proportion of Austrian wine is sold in wine inns run by growers (called *Heurigen* or *Buschenschenken*). The 1985 diethylene-glycol scandal put an end for some years to the industry's commercial success with off-dry and sweet white wines in the German mould (regulated by a German-style wine law introduced in 1972). Diethylene glycol was added to such wines by many large commercial bottlers. Whilst there is no evidence of anyone's health having been damaged by this illegal practice – in contrast to the Italian methanol scandal of the following year – enormous damage was done to the good name of Austrian wine.

The Austrian authorities responded by rushing through legislation to control the wine industry further. The 1985 law (amended the following year) is complemented by a system of controls and monitoring which make the nation's wine industry the most strictly controlled in the world.

The scandal also had entirely unexpected consequences. Instead of turning domestic consumers off their nation's wines, they switched from mass-produced wines to hand-crafted ones made by family-run estates. This coincided with a boom for dry white wines. The result was a renaissance for

regions such as the Wachau and Kamptal whose growers had previously made and sold good-quality dry white wines to loyal private customers in relative obscurity. In Styria, an entire new wine culture was born during the late 1980s as a number of producers switched from wines for everyday drinking in two-litre bottles (*doppler*) to quality varietals.

In the early 1990s, this was followed by a red-wine revolution during which dozens of younger Austrian producers, particularly in Burgenland, mastered the making of international-style red wines. Much of their inspiration came from across the Alps in Italy. Although France was the prime source of new grape varieties (Cabernet Sauvignon, Merlot, and to a lesser extent Syrah), these are usually blended with indigenous grapes to create sophisticated *cuvées*, an adopted word in the vocabulary of many young Austrian winemakers. Unlike the majority of fine Austrian wines, which are sold under vineyard (or *ried*) names, they tend to be sold under fantasy names such as "Comondor", "Bella Rex", or "Perwolff" in the mould of Italian wines such as "Sassicaia" or "Darmagi". Austria remains primarily a white-wine producer, and in this respect most wine-growers are true to their nation's winemaking traditions.

Austria's wine industry is founded on light- to full-bodied dry whites from the indigenous Grüner Veltliner grape. It accounts for a little over a third of Austria's 57, 105 hectares of vineyards, and gives wines with a distinctive aroma of white pepper. Lentils, and other vegetal notes, but at high levels of ripeness they are replaced by smokey and even exotic fruit aromas. The grape's flexibility – it will yield dry wines with anything from ten to fifteen degrees natural

alcohol, and impressive dessert wines – is its greatest strength. In international blind tastings, setting Grüner Veltliner against some of the world's great Chardonnays, the Austrian grape has performed very well.

Nonetheless, the white wines that have attracted most international praise have been the Rieslings. The noble white grape of Germany appears to have arrived in Austria towards the end of the nineteenth century, and there are still only 1,220 hectares planted with it in Austria. However, on the primary rock soils of the Wachau, the beautiful rocky gorge through which the River Danube flows between Melk and Krems, it yields great dry wines that can match the finest of Alsace and Germany. Such is the strength of domestic demand for the top Wachau Rieslings that importers from other countries must beg for every bottle from the top producers. Names such as Franz Hirtzberger, Emmerich Knoll, F. X. Pichler, and Franz Prager (qq.v.) are mentioned by Austrian wine-lovers in tones of awe. Similarly, fine, dry Rieslings come from parts of other regions in Lower Austria, most importantly Senftenberg and Stein in the Kremstal, and Langenlois-Zöbing in the Kamptal. A comparable discrepancy between supply and demand exists with the best Sauvignons and Morillons from Styria (a synonym for Chardonnay, which arrived in the region during the nineteenth century) where producers such as Polz and Tement (qq.v) are almost perpetually sold out.

Although it was almost exclusively dessert wines that were affected by the 1985 scandal, in this field, too, recent years have seen dramatic developments. The Neusiedler See-Hügelland region in the state of Burgenland has a recorded history of systematic dessert wine production, which goes back to 1617. For much of its history it was part of Hungary. This tradition is centred upon the town of Rust on the eastern bank of the shallow Neusiedlersee lake, the source of autumnal mists that promote the development of noble rot. However, during the 1990s, it has been the wines from Illmitz on the opposite bank of the lake that have attracted attention. The names of Illmitz winemakers Alois Kracher and Willi Opitz are now known around the world. Most of Austria's dessert wines are sold under the Trockenbeerenauslese and Beerenauslese names borrowed from the Germans during the 1960s. Today some are vinified in new oak casks like top Sauternes. Rust has its own tradition: a sweet wine midway in weight between a BA and TBA, and vinified to a higher alcoholic degree (and hence a lower level of residual sugar) than comparable wines from Illmitz. However, in recent years, top Rust growers have followed the stylistic norms set by Kracher for wines of great intensity and sweetness. Thus, in practice, a modern Ruster Ausbruch is hard to distinguish from an Illmitz TBA – but is none the worse for that.

Sadly, the worldwide fashion for Chardonnay has not left Austria untouched. Although a handful of winemakers produce powerful wines in the international style (most prominently Velich [q.v.] in the Neusiedlersee region), most results lag behind those achieved with traditional grapes such as Weissburgunder (Pinot Blanc), Grauburgunder (Pinot Gris), or aromatic grapes such as Muskateller and Traminer. The majority of Austria's fine dry white and dessert wines continue to be made from varieties such as these. Thankfully, the pendulum is beginning to swing back in the direction of tradition. Even the style-conscious yuppies of Vienna enjoy an evening in a *Heurige* drinking unpretentious local wine out of a glass mug (known as a *viertel* because it contains a quarter-litre!) while listening to *Schrammelmusik*: Viennese

folk music. The quality revolution of the late 1980s and 1990s has brought better and more diverse wines.

The wine regions of Austria are usually divided into four principal areas. Vienna (wth 680 hectares within the city limits), the Burgenland (14,560 hectares), Steiermark (*i.e.* Styria, with 3,300 hectares), and Lower Austria (30,000 hectares). The Burgenland is divided into four sub-regions: Neusiedlersee (8,325 hectares), which takes in all the vineyards north and east of the lake; Neusiedlersee-Hügelland (3,900 hectares) west of the lake, with Rust and Eisenstadt its principal towns; Mittelburgenland (1,875 hectares), and Südburgenland (450 hectares), red wine regions south of the lake and along the Hungarian border.

Styria is divided into three sub-regions, of which the most important is the Südsteiermark (1,740 hectares), plus the Süd-Oststeiermark (1,115 hectares) and the Weststeiermark (435 hectares). Styria is best-known as a white wine region, but Weststeiermark has a tradition of producing Schilcher, a markedly acidic rosé that has an ardent following within Austria itself.

Lower Austria is the most complicated region. Over half the production comes from the Weinviertel (15,890 hectares) to the north of Vienna, but with a few exceptions the wine is undistinguished. Far more important in terms of quality are the three sub-regions close to the Danube west of Vienna: the Wachau (1,390 hectares), Kremstal (2,175 hectares), and Kamptal (3.870 hectares), the source of Austria's finest white wines. Separating these regions from Vienna are the less significant Traisenthal (685 hectares) and Donauland (2,735 hectares). Immediately southeast of Vienna is Carnuntum (890 hectares), which can produce excellent red wines, while south of the capital is the Thermenregion, which includes the once famous heavy white wines from Gumpoldskirchen.

The estates below are divided into the four main regions, with sub-regions indicated within each producer entry.

Leading Lower Austria Producers

Leo Alzinger ☆☆☆
Unterloiben, Wachau. 8 hectares. www.alzinger.at
With both Riesling and Grüner Veltliner in top sites in Dürnstein and Unterloiben, the largely self-taught Alzinger makes sleek, elegant wines, with a fine acidic structure, lean but fruity, racy but never harsh. Invariably repay keeping.

Bründlmayer ☆☆☆
Langenlois, Kamptal. 60 hectares. www.bruendlmayer.at
The diffident, thoughtful Willi Bründlmayer runs one of the largest and most modern wine estates in Austria. Although he is best-known for his barrel-fermented Chardonnay and burgundy-inspired Pinot Noir, most of his production is traditional-style dry whites. Right across the impressive range the quality is excellent, the sublime Rieslings from old vines in the Heiligenstein site and magisterial Grüner Veltliner from the Lamm vineyard rank among Austria's greatest wines.

Winzergenossenschaft Dinstlgut Loiben ☆☆
Unterloiben, Wachau/Kremstal. 200 hectares. www.dinstlgut.at
Since Walter Kutscher took over the direction of this formerly

famous cooperative, quality has improved significantly. In 2002 he left, and was replaced by Rolf Clemens. The magnificent dessert wines Kutscher produced rightly attracted much praise, but the dry Rieslings and Grüner Veltliners have lagged behind, though they are well made.

Freie Weingärtner Wachau ☆☆–☆☆☆

Dürnstein, Wachau. 600 hectares. www.fww.at

Long one of Europe's finest winemaking cooperatives, quality took a leap forward with the appointment of Fritz Miesbauer and Willi Klinger as co-directors in 1995. Klinger left in 2000, but Rainer Wess continues his work.

Excellent Rieslings from the first-class Achleiten of Weissenkirchen and Singerriedel of Spitz, and Grüner Veltliners from the Kellerberg of Dümstein are the stars of the wide range produced. However, even the simpler wines, such as the "Terrrassen Thal Wachau" blend, are well-made and full of character.

The baroque Kellerschlössel entrance house to the extensive cellars dates from 1715, but the Freie Weingärtner's roots go back to at least the twelfth century.

Schloss Gobelsburg ☆☆

Gobelsburg, Kamptal. 35 hectares. www.gobelsburg.at

A monastic estate, this was leased by Willi Bründlmayer (*q.v.*) and Michael Moosbrugger in 1996, and they cultivate the vineyards organically. There is good Riesling from Heiligenstein and Gasiberg, and the Grüner Veltliners from Ried Lamm and Ried Grub can be massive wines, rich and alarmingly high in alcohol.

Franz Hirtzberger ☆☆☆–☆☆☆☆

Spitz, Wachau. 17 hectares

Franz Hirtzberger's natural optimism and talent for winning over opponents are mainly responsible for the success of the "Vinea Wachau" wine-growers association of which he is president. He is no less talented at making elegant, dry white wines. His Riesling from the great Singerriedel vineyard and his Grüner Veltliner from the first-class Honivogl site are among Austria's finest and most sought-after wines. The Hirtzberger's thirteenth-century estate house is one of the oldest and most beautiful in the Danube Valley.

Josef Högl ☆☆–☆☆☆

Spitz, Wachau. 5.5 hectares. www.weingut-hoegl.at

Modest, shy Josef Högl learnt quickly while he worked for the Prager and F. X. Pichler estates (*qq.v.*). Since going solo he has joined the first rank of Wachau producers with dry whites that combine power with clarity and polish.

Josef Jamek ☆☆–☆☆☆

Joching, Wachau. 25 hectares. www.jamek.cc

Josef Jamek pioneered dry, unchaptalized wines in the Wachau in the 1950s and remained one of the region's leading producers in the 1980s. His eponymous restaurant brought gastronomic culture to the region and became an institution. In 1996, his son-in-law, Hans Altmann, and daughter Jutta took over, and a new era began.

The best wines are the famous Rieslings from the first-class Klaus vineyard of Weissenkirchen and the dry Weissburgunder. Elegance, rather than power, has always been the Jamek hallmark. After a period when the wines lacked grip and minerality, quality had clearly recovered by the late 1990s.

Emmerich Knoll ☆☆☆☆

Unterloiben, Wachau. 13.5 hectares

Four generations of the Knoll family, all called Emmerich, are responsible for making this estate's unique wines. These are extremely long-lived wines that need years of bottle-ageing for their full, minerally character to emerge.

The dry Rieslings from the Schütt, Loibenberg, and Kellerberg sites are among Austria's finest white wines. In vintages when botrytis affects the vineyards, Knoll also produce sumptuous sweet wines.

Malat ☆☆

Palt, Kremstal. 35 hectares

Best-known for powerful, dry white wines, but Cabernet and Pinot Noir also show promise. He bottles his best Veltliner and Riesling under the confident label "Das Beste".

Mantlerhof ☆☆

Brunn im Felde, Kremstal. 14 hectares

Josef Mantleris best known for the rare white Roter Veltliner (Malvasia) grape, from which he makes rich, supple, dry wines. His Grüner Veltliners are also great and long-lived.

Markowitsch ☆☆☆

Göttlesbrunn, Carnuntum. 20 hectares. www.markowitsch.at

Gerhard Markowitsch is the most dynamic of the Carnuntum growers, equally adept with white and red wines. His Chardonnay is toasty and powerful, and his best red is the "Cuvée Rosenberg": an intense and deeply structured blend of Zweigelt, Merlot, and Cabernet Sauvignon. Markowitsch is also making progress with Pinot Noir.

Sepp Moser ☆☆

Rohrendorf, Kremstal. 50 hectares. www.sepp-moser.at

The roots of this estate go back to 1848, but in its present form it dates from the split-up of the erstwhile Lenz Moser company in 1986. With the help of son Nikolaus, Sepp Moser rapidly made it one of the nation's leading white-wine producers.

In 2000, Nikolaus Moser was given full responsibility for the winemaking. The barrel-fermented Chardonnay is among Austria's best, but it is the lush, complex, dry Riesling from the first-class Gebling site that is the real star. Increasingly good Burgenland reds, too.

Martin Nigl ☆☆☆

Senftenberg, Kremstal. 25 hectares. www.weingutnigl.at

In 1986, the Nigls left the local co-op, giving son Martin responsibility for their cellar. Since then, his sleek, minerally dry Rieslings and Grüner Veltliners have made the estate a leader in the Kremstal region. Top are the magnificent Rieslings from the first-class Kremsleiten and Piri sites.

Nikolaihof ☆☆–☆☆☆

Mautern, Wachau and Kremstal. 18 hectares

The recorded history of the Saahs family's organic estate goes back more than a millennium, and the magnificent buildings stand on Roman foundations.

Quality is somewhat mixed, but the best dry Rieslings are superb, both the Kremstal wines from the stony Steiner Hund site in Krems, and the Wachau wines from Mautern. These are wines that improve greatly with ageing. The excellent *Weinstube* is rightly as famous as the wine estate.

F. X. Pichler ☆☆☆☆
Oberloiben, Wachau. 10 hectares
Regarded as Austria's number one winemaker, Franz Xavier Pichler – frequently refered to simply as "F. X." – is a fanatical perfectionist. His great dry white wines are as concentrated as they are individual.

The most spectacular Rieslings and Grüner Veltliners come from the great Kellerberg vineyard of Dürnstein. Some of the richest wines are rather grandiosely labelled "M" (for "Monumental") or "U" (for "Unendlich"), referring to the prolonged finish. These wines can seem too massive for their own good, combining high alcohol and extract with some residual sugar. But their intrinsic quality and complexity are undeniable.

Rudi Pichler ☆☆–☆☆☆
Wösendorf, Wachau. 8 hectares
Rudi Pichler Jr. has been going from strength to strength as one of the Wachau's rising stars with lush, powerful, and aromatic dry Rieslings from Achleiten and Kirchweg, and minerally Grüner Veltliner from Hochrain.

Franz Prager ☆☆☆
Weissenkirchen, Wachau. 14 hectares. www.weingutprager.at
Since marrying Ilse Prager, Toni Bodenstein has consolidated the reputation of this excellent domaine, which has owned outstanding sites (Achleiten, Klaus, Steinriegl) for over three centuries. This he has done with a meticulous attention to detail. The dry Rieslings marry seductive, ripe fruit with minerally depth, and the Grüner Veltliners share their elegance.

Other Lower Austria Producers

Peter Dolle ☆☆
Strass, Kamptal. 28 hectares. www.dolle.at
A dynamic property and *Heurige*, producing a wide range of white wines, notably the Riesling from Gaisberg.

Ludwig Ehn ☆☆
Langenlois, Kamptal. 12 hectares. www.ehnwein.at
Ehn specializes in exotic, dry Riesling from the great Heiligenstein vineyard and rich "Ried Panzaun" from a mixed planting of ancient vines.

Forstreiter ☆☆
Krems, Kremstal. 14 hectares
Meinhard Forstreiter cultivates a range of varieties, but his best wines are the racy Grüner Veltliner, notably the "Alte Reben" and "Exlcusiv". Charming Gelber Muskateller, too.

Weinberghof Fritsch ☆☆
Oberstockstall, Donauland. 13 hectares. www.fritsch.cc
A leading producer of vibrant, dry Grüner Veltliner and a plummy red blend called "Foggathal", packed with blackberry fruit.

Walter Glatzer ☆☆
Göttlesbrunn, Carnuntum. 17 hectares
A leading property east of Vienna. He remains faithful to Austrian red varieties. His best Zweigelt is called "Dornenvogel", and there is a fine, Zweigelt-dominated blend called "Cuvée Gotinsprun", aged mostly in new barriques.

Schlossweingut Graf Hardegg ☆☆
Seefeld-Kadolz, Weinviertel. 43 hectares. www.grafhardegg.at
Proximity to the Czech border may explain the name of the top-selling wine, the Grüner Veltliner called "Veltlinsky". Also noteworthy are the Pinot Noir and the exotic Viognier. Occasionally, brilliant Riesling Eiswein is produced.

Hiedler ☆☆–☆☆☆
Langenlois, Kamptal. 17 hectares. www.hiedler.at
Hiedler's white wines are made for long age rather than instant gratification. His dry Riesling from the great Heiligenstein site, the powerful Veltliner "Maximum", and Chardonnay are among the region's finest.

Jurtschitsch ☆☆
Langenlois, Kamptal. 55 hectares. www.jurtschitsch.com
Reliable producer of super-clean, modern whites from around Langenlois. Good Sauvignon Blanc and Chardonnay, but the Rieslings and Grüner Veltliner are the stars.

Stift Klosterneuburg ☆☆
Klosterneuburg, Donauland. 100 hectares.
www.stift-klosterneuburg.at
Augustine monks of Klosterneuburg have made wine for nearly nine centuries, but the operation is now a commercial company owned by the monastery. Grapes from the vineyards, from Tattendorf south of Vienna to within the city limits of the capital itself, are supplemented by small producers in Burgenland and Niederösterreich. Top wines, from single vineyards, are bottled with the "Domäne" designation. A good reputation for white wines, such as Weissburgunder, and more recently for some formidable reds, such as the barrique-aged St-Laurent. The four-level cellars have three million bottles, including the Austrian State Wine Archive.

Loimer ☆☆☆
Langenlois, Kamptal. 21 hectares. www.loimer.at
Dynamic Fred Loimer produces a range of whites from traditional grapes. His finest wines are the barrel-fermented, old-vine Grüner Veltliner from the Spiegel site, and the Riesling from Steinmassl.

Lenz Moser ☆–☆☆
Rohrendorf, Kremstal. Owner: GHG. Estates: Klosterkeller Siegendorf, Siegendorf, Neusiedlersee-Hügelland, 24 hectares. Schlossweingut Malteser Ritterorden, Mailberg, Weinviertel, 50 hectares. www.lenzmoser.at
Dr. Lenz Moser (d. 1978) was a leading figure in the Austrian wine industry, remembered for the high-trellis vine-training system named after him. The company is now directed by his great-grandson, Lenz Moser V.

In the early 1990s, it grew to be the most important Austrian wine company. The basis of the huge range are the "Servus" of dry white and red Burgenland wines. The varietal "Lenz Moser Selection" wines is the next step up, and, like "Servus", these wines are made from grapes from contract growers. Indeed, the winery has access to some 2,500 hectares of vineyards. The estate-bottled wines form the pinnacle, of which the red *cuvée* "Kommende Mailberg" (Cabernet/Merlot) enjoys a particularly good reputation.

Ludwig Neumayer ☆☆–☆☆☆
Inzersdorf, Traisental. 8 hectares
The wines that put this region on the map include Neumayer's sophisticated dry Rieslings, Weissburgunders, and Grüner Veltliners from the Traisental. Top range is labelled "Der Wein vom Stein".

Pfaffl ☆☆–☆☆☆
Stetten, Weinviertel. 30 hectares. www.pfaffl.at
Roman Pfaffl's dry Grüner Veltliner, Sauvignon Blanc, non-oaked Chardonnay, and Riesling from just northeast of Vienna are arguably the Weinviertel's finest.

Pitnauer ☆☆
Göttlesbrunn, Carnuntum. 17 hectares. www.pitnauer.com
These wines come from vineyards close to the Slovak border. The powerful "Franz Josef" blend of Zweigelt and Cabernet is best, and there is an intriguing Syrah blend called "Pegasos".

Robert Schlumberger ☆
Bad Vöslau, Thermenregion. 10 hectares. www.schlumberger.at
Robert Schlumberger, son of a branch of the Alsace family, made Austria's first *méthode traditionnelle* Sekt in 1842. The Sekt side of the business is now based in Vienna, while the family firm has focused its attention on Bordeaux-style reds.

Schmelz ☆☆
Joching, Wachau. 8 hectares
Reliable and improving producer of juicy, substantial, dry Riesling and Grüner Veltliner.

Schmidl ☆☆–☆☆☆
Dürnstein, Wachau. 8.5 hectares
Franz Schmidl, who is also the local baker, has half his vineyards in the renowned Kellerberg, and makes underrated Riesling and Grüner Veltliner from this site.

Stadlmann ☆–☆☆
Traiskirchen, Thermenregion. 12 hectares.
www.stadlmann-wein.at
Some of the best wines of the Thermenregion from vineyards south of Gumpoldskirchen. Best are the dry Weissburgunder and Zierfandler (occasionally Zierfandler TBA).

Hofkellerei Stiftung Fürst Liechtenstein ☆–☆☆
Wilfersdorf, Weinviertel. 42 hectares. www.hofkellerei.at
This is a princely estate, producing sound wines from Grüner Veltliner and Zweigelt. Wines include the barrrique-aged Zweigelt "Profundo".

Weingut Salomon/Undhof ☆☆–☆☆☆
Stein, Kremstal. 20 hectares. www.undhof.at
Some of the best wines from the first-class vineyard of Krems' beautiful Gothic and Renaissance suburb, Stein. The soils of these are almost identical to those of the neighbouring Wachau. Most of his production is dry Riesling and Grüner Veltliner.

The estate has a fine reputation for delicate, late-harvest wines which are bottled under the "Reserve" label. The estate house dates back to 1792 and stands next to the Kloster Und wine center, which Erich Salomon founded.

Leading Burgenland Producers

Feiler-Artinger ☆☆☆
Rust, Neusiedlersee-Hügelland. 26 hectares.
www.feiler-artinger.at
Superlative Ruster Ausbruch; the finest is the intense "Essenz". In contrast are the flavoury red blends, both from Cabernet and Merlot, and "Cuvée Solitaire" from Austrian varieties.

Gesellmann ☆☆–☆☆☆
Deutschkreutz, Mittelburgenland. 25 hectares.
www.gesellmann.at
Albert Gesellmann has been taking an already admired estate to new levels, building on the reputation for red wines established by his father. Two powerful blends, "Opus Eximium" (Blaufränkisch, St-Laurent, and Blauburgunder) and "Bella Rex" (Cabernet and Merlot) are most impressive.

Martin Haider ☆–☆☆☆
Illmitz, Neusiedlersee. 12 hectares
Modest Martin Haider specializes in botrytis wines from a range of varieties. Those from Sauvignon Blanc and Weissburgunder can be exceptional. Dry wines are less successful.

Gernot Heinrich ☆☆☆
Gols, Neusiedlersee. 15 hectares
Gernot Heinrich is one of the rising stars among the new generation of Burgenland winemakers. His vineyards are split between white and red grapes, the latter giving fleshy, supple wines, particularly the single-vineyard "Gabarinza", which joins Austrian and French varieties in a blend rich in black-fruit flavours. His "Pannobile", a Zweigelt-dominated blend using a name shared by a number of growers who are members of the Pannobile association, is almost as good.

Juris (G. Stiegelmar) ☆☆☆
Gols, Neusiedlersee. www.juris.at
This sixteen-hectare estate is run by the untiring Stiegelmar family. Georg is the traditionalist, attached to the ancient Hungarian traditions of the Burgenland, but he has not stood in the way of his California-trained son, Axel. The best wines are the reds – St-Laurent, "Ina'mera" (Blaufränkisch with Cabernet and Merlot), and "St Georg" (St-Laurent and Pinot Noir).

The pure Cabernet is surprisingly plummy, and the Pinot Noir has more fruit than finesse. Unlike many Burgenland producers, the Stiegelmars do not pack their wines with more tannin than the wine's fruit structure can absorb, and they handle barrique-ageing with rare mastery. Delicious TBAs, too.

Kollwentz ☆☆
Grosshöflein, Neusiedlersee-Hügelland. 20 hectares.
www. kollwentz.at
Andi Kollwentz is one of Austria's most talented young winemakers, and has played an important role in the recent red-wine revolution. The dry whites are clean and crisp, but less exceptional than the reds. "Eichkogel" is an enjoyable blend of Blaufränkisch and Zweigelt; the "Cuvée Steinzeiler" has some Cabernet in the blend and is more concentrated.

Alois Kracher ☆☆☆☆
Illmitz, Neusiedlersee. 15 hectares
A perfectionist with a cosmopolitan perspective who remains

true to his roots in the sandy soil of Illmitz. In recent years his superbly crafted dessert wines have picked up almost every conceivable accolade. They combine honeyed richness with perfect balance. The "Zwischen den Seen" wines are traditionally made in tanks or old casks, the "Nouvelle Vague" wines in new oak, like Sauternes. "Grand Cuvée" is the designation Kracher gives to the best wine in any vintage.

Krutzler ☆☆☆
Deutsch-Schützen, Südburgenland. 10 hectares. www.krutzler.at

Reinhold and Erich Krutzler's silky reds are Südburgenland's finest and most elegant wines. Blaufränkisch is the dominant grape variety, and it attains unusual purity of blackberry and cherry fruit. Top of the range is the seductive "Perwolff", given more structure by the inclusion of some Cabernet.

Helmut Lang ☆☆☆
Illmitz, Neusiedlersee. 14 hectares

Lang is another master of sophisticated sweet wines from the Burgenland. Chardonnay, Sauvignon, and Welschriesling seem to give the best results, though Lang is greatly admired for his Scheurebe. Lang is keen on Pinot Noir, made in a dense, oaky style, remote from burgundy, but impressive on its own terms.

Hans & Anita Nittnaus ☆☆
Gols, Neusiedlersee. 22 hectares. www.weingut.nittnaus.at

The ever more sophisticated reds which Hans Nittnaus has made since the late '80s epitomize the red wine revolution occurring in Burgenland. Rich, powerful "Comondor", a Bordeaux blend, is serious competition for classified Bordeaux.

Josef Pöckl ☆☆☆
Mönchhof, Neusiedlersee. 20 hectares. www.poeckl.com

Pöckl is a Zweigelt enthusiast, which dominates his superb and consistent "Admiral" blend. "Rêve de Jeunesse" is quite different, blending Syrah with Zweigelt to give a rich, slightly confected wine. Pöckl is equally skilled with TBAs.

Engelbert Prieler ☆☆–☆☆☆
Schützen, Neusiedlersee-Hügelland. 20 hectares. www.prieler.at

The Prielers make some of the best wines of the Hügelland. The unoaked Pinot Blanc has more zest and individuality than the international-style, oaked Chardonnay. Blaufränkisch is delicious here, especially from Ried Goldberg. Prieler also makes tiny quantities of Cabernet Sauvignon with a slight herbaceous tone. Daughter Silvia is developing her own line of wines, notably a rich, rather tannic Pinot Noir.

Heidi Schröck ☆☆–☆☆☆
Rust, Neusiedlersee-Hügelland. 8 hectares. www.heidi-schroeck.com

An enthusiast for the local traditions of Rust, Schröck makes exemplary Ausbruch, and wines from ultra-sweet grapes are called "Elysium". She has helped to revive Furmint in Rust, although the dry wine is very austere and it works better as Ausbruch. Best red wine is the "Blaufränkisch Kulm".

Ernst Triebaumer ☆☆☆
Rust, Neusiedlersee-Hügelland. 15 hectares. www.triebaumer.at

Ernst Triebaumer has single-handedly demonstrated that the Blaufränkisch grape can produce great red wines if planted in the right place. This dark, rich, tannic wine is one of Austria's most sought-after reds. His Ruster Ausbruch dessert wines are also impressive, matching richness with harmony. And in complete contrast, his Chardonnay and Sauvignon Blanc are among Austria's best.

Umathum ☆☆☆
Frauenkirchen, Neusiedlersee. 25 hectares. www.umathum.at

It would be easy to mistake Josef Umathum's reds for French wines, although he works almost exclusively with traditional Austrian grapes. The most impressive is the red *cuvée* from the Hallebühl vineyard, a powerful, tannic blend of Zweigelt, Blaufränkisch, and Cabernet. The Zweigelt-Merlot *cuvée* from the Haideboden is equally rich, but more supple.

Velich ☆☆
Apetlon, Neusiedlersee. 9 hectares

This estate has the reputation of being one of Austria's leading white-wine producers. Impressive as the entire range is, the seductively rich, barrel-fermented "Tiglat" Chardonnay has to be singled out as outstanding, though to some palates it can seem excessively weighty. Excellent TBAs, too.

Other Burgenland Producers

Paul Achs ☆☆
Gols, Neusiedlersee. 20 hectares

Richly fruity, modern-style reds, particularly good Pinot Noir and red *cuvées*.

Braunstein ☆
Purbach, Neusiedlersee-Hügelland. 20 hectares. www.braunstein.at

Birgit Braunstein selects the best wines of any vintage to be oak-aged and labelled as "Oxhoft". The Chardonnay can be overblown, but both the St-Laurent and the "Cuvée Oxhoft" can be powerful, almost meaty wines.

Schlossweingut Esterházy ☆
Eisenstadt, Neusiedlersee-Hügelland. 45 hectares. www.esterhazy.at

The ancient princely family of Esterházy, patrons of Haydn and tamers of the Turks, have been making some of the best wine in the Burgenland since the seventeenth century. Vineyards spread around Rust, St Georgen, St Margaretten, Grosshöflein, and Eisenstadt.

Beneath the castle, 140 great casks line the cellars. At the same time, the zesty Chardonnay "Klassik" is a welcome reminder that this variety does not need to be heavily oaked to be enjoyable. Some of the best dessert wines of the Burgenland, such as their *strohwein* (straw wine), carry the "Esterházy" label.

Gsellmann & Gsellmann ☆☆
Gols, Neusiedlersee. 22 hectares. www.gsellmann.at

Two brothers join forces to produce a wide range of wines, from buttery Pannobile white blends to apricotty TBAs from Scheurebe. Their red wines are often too oaky, with assertive flavours of cherry compote and vanilla.

Schlosskellerei Halbturn ☆

Halbturn, Neusiedlersee. 48 hectares

A noble estate and a byword for mediocrity until 2002, when a new director arrived and began turning things around.

Hafner ☆☆

Mönchhof, Neusiedlersee. 22 hectares

Fine sweet wines, especially from Chardonnay, and a Zweigelt/Blaufränkisch blend called "Kashmir". Hafner is also Austria's leading producer of kosher wines.

Hans Igler ☆

Deutschkreuz, Mittelburgenland. www.weingut-igler.at

Hans Igler was a pioneer of serious, oak-aged reds. Since his death in 1994, his daughter and son-in-law continue to cultivate twenty hectares planted largely with red grapes. Best-known is the subtle, medium-bodied Blaufränkisch/Cabernet Sauvignon "Cuvée Volcano". In 1999, they launched "Ab Ericio", a Merlot-dominated blend, in an attempt to return the Igler estate to the esteem it enjoyed a decade ago.

Kerschbaum ☆☆

Horitschon, Mittelburgenland. www.kerschbaum.at

Paul Kerschbaum is a master of Blaufränkisch, and the exceptionally pure "Ried Hochäcker" is often preferable to the "Ried Dürrau", which can be overwhelmed by new oak. The splendid "Cuvée Impresario" blends Blaufränkisch with Zweigelt and Cabernet, and has exceptional elegance.

Josef Lentsch ☆☆

Podersdorf, Neusiedlersee. www.dankbarkeit.at

Tiny estate belonging to eponymous restaurant with first-class regional cooking. Excellent Pinot Noir and Pinot Gris, and fine dessert wines.

Münzenrieder ☆☆

Apetlon, Neusiedlersee

This eighteen-hectare estate, which only began bottling in 1991, has acquired a reputation for rich, full-bodied TBAs.

Gerhard Nekowitsch ☆☆

Illmitz, Neusiedlersee. www.nekowitsch.at

This four-hectare property has carved a niche for itself as a producer of *schilfwein*, made from bunches left to dry on reeds from the Neusiedler See. The peachy "Tradition" version is generally preferable to the somewhat cloying red-grape version called "The Red One".

Willi Opitz ☆–☆☆☆

Illmitz, Neusiedlersee. www.willi-opitz.at

Self-publicist Willi Opitz makes some remarkable dessert wines from ten hectares of vineyards, but dry wines lack flair.

Pittnauer ☆–☆☆☆

Gols, Neusiedlersee

As a member of the Pannobile group, Pittnauer makes a rich Zweigelt-led blend under this name. But his superb St-Laurent "Alte Reben", with its unusual peppery tone reminiscent of Syrah, is of comparable quality. The white wines are not on the same level.

Peter Schandl ☆☆

Rust, Neusiedlersee-Hügelland. www.schandlwein.com

Best-known for rich, traditional Ausbruch, including examples from the Furmint grape. But Schandl's white wines from Chardonnay and Pinot Blanc are very enjoyable.

Schwarz ☆

Andau, Neusiedlersee

Hans Schwarz works closely with Alois Kracher to produce two wines: a rich, jammy Zweigelt called "Rot", and the toasty, alcoholic white (Grüner Veltliner and Chardonnay). International-style wines at their least digestible.

Sommer ☆☆

Donnerskirchen, Neusiedlersee-Hügelland. www.weingut-sommer.at

A fine source of delicious white wines, especially the creamy Grüner Veltliner, "Premium Reserve".

Tinhof ☆–☆☆

Eisenstadt. Neusiedlersee-Hügelland

French-trained Erwin Tinhof makes a good range of dry wines, red and white, very oaky when young.

Wenzel ☆☆

Rust, Neusiedlersee-Hügelland

Robert Wenzel was an ultra-traditionalist, but his son Michael has freshened the style, and introduced modern, dry wines, including an Alsatian-style Pinot Gris aged in Austrian oak, and a dense, tannic Pinot Noir. An estate to watch.

Zantho ☆

Andau, Neusiedlersee. www.zantho.com

Unusual joint venture between Josef Umathum (*q.v.*) and the Andau co-op, to produce sizeable volumes of traditional Austrian reds, principally Zweigelt. The "Reserve" is delicious, but the venture will rise or fall on its Zweigelt "Classic".

Leading Wien (Vienna) Producers

Johann Kattus ☆

Major Vienna merchant dating from 1857, specializing in Sekt under the "Hochriegel" brand. The *méthode traditionnelle* "Alte Reserve", made from Riesling and Grüner Veltliner, is slightly fruity with a clean finish. Specialties include Gewürztraminer from Nussberg, in the Vienna suburbs.

Mayer am Pfarrplatz ☆☆

Heiligenstadt. 30 hectares. www.mayer.pfarrplatz.at

Franz Mayer is the largest grower in Vienna and runs a popular and authentic *Heurige*. His modern, well-run cellar produces a range of wines, of which the best are Riesling from the Nussberg and a zesty Grüner Veltliner.

Schlumberger ☆–☆☆

The best of the Viennese sparkling wine houses, offering a particularly fruity blanc de noirs underpinned by good acidity.

Wieninger ☆☆–☆☆☆

Stammersdorf. 21 hectares. www.wieninger.at

Vienna's leading estate makes everything from traditional, dry Riesling to barrel-fermented Chardonnay and deeply coloured Cabernet/Merlot from vines on outstanding sites such as the Nussberg and Bisamberg.

Other Vienna Producers

The proliferation of *Heurigen* in all the wine villages of Vienna means that a very wide range of wine is made. Most of it is consumed by thirsty customers and tourists, but the best *Heurigen* also bottle their wines. They can be of high quality and are usually sensibly priced. A selection of the best Vienna *Heurigen* estates should include: Hengl-Haselbrunner (Döbling), Reinprecht (Grinzing), Edlmoser (Mauer), Zahel (Mauer), Fuhrgassl-Huber (Neustift), Christ (Jedlersdorf), and Schilling (Strebersdorf).

Leading Styria Producers

Gross ☆☆
Ratsch, Südsteiermark. 20 hectares. www.gross.at
Alois Gross is one of the most consistent winemakers of the Steiermark, making elegant, aromatic wines from a wide range of grapes. Best are his Sauvignon, Gewürztraminer, and new-oak-aged Grauburgunder.

Erich & Walter Polz ☆☆☆
Spielfeld, Südsteiermark. 45 hectares. www.polz.co.at
The Polz brothers are leading figures in the wine revolution which began in Styria during the mid-1980s. They were pioneers in the move away from sweet wines and mass production in favour of quality dry wines. They produce two styles of wine: the lighter, very fresh "Steirische Klassik" wines; and the richer, slower-maturing, vineyard-designated wines. Best of the latter are the Weissburgunder, Morillon, and Sauvignon Blanc from the first-class Hochgrassnitzberg vineyard direct on the Austrian-Slovenian border. "Obegg" is an unusual oaked blend of Chardonnay and Sauvignon.

E. & M. Tement ☆☆☆
Berghausen, Südsteiermark. 35 hectares. www.tement.at
The interior of Manfred Tement's cellar may look rather like a Heath Robinson cartoon, but the dry white wines that come out of it are frequently some of Styria's finest. No other Austrian winemaker makes such judicious use

of new-oak casks for fermenting and maturing white wines. His Sauvignon Blanc and Morillon from the first-class Zieregg vineyard are masterpieces of this style: at once rich and refined. In contrast, the "Steirische Klassik" varietal wines are vividly fruity, very clean, and crisp.

Other Styria Producers

Burgweinbau Riegersburg ☆
Wildon, Süd-Oststeiermark
Once-great estate returning to form under Andreas Tscheppe. Good Sauvignon Blanc and non-oaked Morillon (Chardonnay) from four hectares within fortifications of medieval Riegersburg castle.

Sabathi ☆☆
Leutschach, Südsteiermark. www.sabathi.com
A rising star, with excellent steep sites such as the Pössnitzberg. Delicious Sauvignon and creamy Chardonnay with striking finesse.

Sattlerhof ☆☆–☆☆☆
Gamlitz, Südsteiermark. www.sattlerhof.at
Wilhelm Sattler was a leader of the dry-wine movement in Styria, and made some wonderfully rich whites at his twenty-hectare estate. Today it is run by his son Willi, who continues to produce long-lived Sauvignon, Chardonnay, and Grauburgunder.

Lackner-Tinnacher ☆☆
Gamlitz, Südsteiermark. www.tinnacher.at
This husband-and-wife-team make beautifully crafted traditional-style Steiermark whites from their sixteen hectares of vineyards. A particularly superb, dry Gelber Muskateller and rich Grauburgunder, but other wines are all good.

Eduard Tscheppe ☆☆
Pössnitz, Südsteiermark. www.tscheppe.com
A full range of clean white wines, including elegant Gewürztraminer and zesty Muskateller.

Winkler-Hamarden ☆☆
Kapfenstein, Süd-Oststeiermark. www.winkler-hamarden.at
A delightful property located (with a hotel and restaurant) in an old castle. The vineyards are on volcanic slopes, and although the majority of production is of traditionally made white wines, the estate is also well-known for its "Olivin", Styria's best Zweigelt.

Central & Eastern Europe

Hungary

The end of Communism in Eastern Europe had, and is still having, profound effects on wine industries that had been centrally directed for decades. Their markets had been almost exclusively the undemanding Soviet bloc. Existing sales channels disappeared almost literally overnight in 1989. For most of them, (Bulgaria being the exception) trading links with western markets had eroded. A fresh start was necessary.

Hungary, always the closest to the west, was the first to call in western aid and profit by flying-winemaker technology. But in any context, historical or cultural, Hungary is incontestably the regional leader. Indeed, in all of Europe, only France and Germany have older and more evolved traditions of quality winemaking than Hungary's most famous vineyards. Whether the Hungarians can recapture their former standing in the world of wine depends in part on

whether the world continues to prize the "international" grape varieties above all others, or whether, as in Italy, there is a real place for authentic ethnic traditions. The Hungarian words of appreciation for the country's traditional wines sum up their character and appeal. Hungarians call a good white wine "fiery" and "stiff" – masculine terms which promise a proper partner for the paprika in their cooking.

Such wines can still be found in the historical sites of Hungarian viticulture, the hill regions which dot the country from the southwest northwards, skirt the long Lake Balaton, then run up the Slovak border from near Budapest to Tokaj. Use of the traditional Hungarian grapes ensures that the wines remain very much individuals.

Despite the grubbing-up of old vines and massive plantings of international varieties in the 1960s and early '70s, Hungary remains rich in indigenous grapes of character that have the potential to contribute splendid wines to the world scene – grapes which often simply do not succeed elsewhere. The most notable of all is the vigorous Furmint, the dominant

The Classes of the "Great" Tokaji Wines

Tokaji Szamorodni This is Tokaji "as it comes" – *i.e.* the lesser "great" wines, sweet (*édes*) or dry (*száraz*) according to the quantity of aszú grapes used.

Tokaji Aszú Like Tokaji Szamorodni, *aszú* wines can only be made in years when there are sufficient high-quality *aszú* grapes – *i.e.* grapes infected with noble rot (*Botrytis cinerea*). Destalked, hand-picked *aszú* grapes are stored six to eight days, then kneaded to a pulp which is added to a base Tokaji wine, or to must, by the *puttony* (a hod of twenty to twenty-five kilos). The eventual sweetness depends on the number of *puttonyos* added to the 136–140-litre barrels (called *gönci*) of one-year-old base wine – usually 3, 4, and 5 *puttonyos;* 6 is exceptional. (The *putton* system describes a ration of paste to wine, as no one today uses these specific measures.) The sequence then is:

- maceration and stirring for twenty-four to forty-eight hours
- settling and racking the must
- fermentation period depending on number of *puttonyos*
- racking, fining, and filtering
- ageing in oak for not less than three years
- filtering prior to bottling
- if binned in Tokaji cellars, bottles are not laid on their sides but stood upright, and the corks changed every fifteen to twenty years.

Tokaji Aszú Eszencia Only individually hand-selected *aszú* grapes. Only produced in exceptional years from the best vineyards. Method as for Tokaji Aszú, but:

- quality cannot be measured by numbers of *puttonyos* as sugar content is higher than for 6 *puttonyos*
- fermentation takes several years (special yeast is used – Tokaji 22)
- minimum of ten years' ageing in oak.

Tokaji Eszencia Destalked hand-picked *aszú* grapes. While grapes are being stored (*see* Tokaji Aszú) the pressure of their own weight produces a minute amount of highly concentrated juice at the bottom of the tub (one *puttonyo* yields only 142 mm of this *eszencia*). The juice is then allowed to ferment extremely slowly for many years in oak casks. In practice, it scarcely ferments at all; the sugar content is too high.

grape of Tokaj, which not only rots nobly but in its dry form, yields strongly sappy and high-flavoured wine. The Hárslevelű or "linden leaf", is scarcely less notable: an excellent dry-climate late-ripener with abundant crops and good acid levels, as well as resistance to fungal diseases.

Szürkebarát, or "grey friar", is more familiar than it sounds, it is a form of Pinot Gris grown to splendid effect on the volcanic Mount Badacsonyi. The Kéknyelű ("blue-stalk") of the same vineyards north of Lake Balaton is a modest producer of concentrated and complex golden-green wines for the fish course. More widespread are three other white Hungarians: Ezerjó ("thousand blessings"), which is a good bulk-producer on the Great Plain, making fine wine only at Mór in the north; Leányka ("little girl") whose delicate, dry white is probably the best wine of Eger, again in the northern hills; and Mézesfehér ("white honey"), an archetypal description of the national view of a good glass of wine. The last is, regrettably, less grown now.

Most widespread of all is the Olaszrizling (same as the Austrian Welschriesling). The Great Plain makes most of its white from it, and on Mount Badacsonyi it rises to its maximum flavour and concentration.

The great Hungarian red grape is the Kadarka, which flourishes equally on the Great Plain producing a firm wine with a slight but convincing "cut", and at Eger and Szekszárd, producing a big, stiff, spicy red for ageing. Unfortunately, it is a late and unreliably ripening variety and its low yield has meant that the rather lighter Kékfrankos has been planted more and more as a substitute. The Austrian Zweigelt, on the other hand, is a newcomer with different virtues of softness, darkness, and a pleasantly sweet scent. There is also a long tradition of growing Pinot Noir in southern Hungary around Villány, and Merlot around Eger in the north.

Added to these are many grapes whose identification causes no problems: Szilváni, Cabernet (Sauvignon and Franc), Sauvignon Blanc, Pinot Blanc, Rajnairizling, Tramini, Muskat Ottonel or Muskotály.

Each of Hungary's notable wines is called by a simple combination of place and grape name. The place name has the suffix "-I". Thus Ezerjó from Mor is Mori Ezerjó.

Hungary has around 110,000 hectares of vines. Even under the former regime, even in Tokaj, the most important and famous area of all, many smallholders still owned land (a maximum of ten hectares) although their grapes had to be sold to the state farms for vinification. Today, although some vineyards remain in state ownership, the majority have now been wholly or partly privatized; substantial areas are owned by either major producers or cooperatives, but a very significant proportion is in the hands of small growers who, often with the assistance of foreign capital or partners, have invested in their own vinification and bottling facilities.

Currently there are twenty-two designated wine regions (although much very acceptable wine is produced outside them). Administration and appellation control is handled in each wine-producing "commune" by a local French-style *comité interprofessionel* (*hegyközség*), through regional *hegyközségek* to a national appellations board. Quality control is undertaken by an independent national institute in Budapest called OBI.

Even in 1990, it was already possible for a would-be buyer from abroad to form a joint-enterprise company with a group of smallholders (the first was formed in the village of Mád, in Tokaj). Their wines could then be bottled individually, without the intervention of the state cellars. There has been heavy foreign investment in major producers, particularly in the flagship region of Tokaj, where stakes have been taken by French insurance companies, the Spanish wine-producer Vega Sicilia, Japanese whisky firm Suntory, and others.

The Great Plain

The Danube divides Hungary almost down the middle. East of the river in southern Hungary lies the sandy Pannonian or Great Plain (Alföld): a vast expanse of steppe-like country which has a long tradition of wine-growing because vines help to bind the soil.

The Csongrád wine region embraces a total 5,800 hectares, producing wines almost entirely for the domestic market. The most common varieties grown here are Rajnairizling, Zöldveltelini (Grüner Veltliner), and Kékfrankos (the Austrian Blaufränkisch). The warm Hajós-Baja region, with more loess than sand, includes some 4,000 hectares, which give higher-quality wines, around half of which are exported. Principal grapes are Chardonnay, Cabernet Sauvignon, and Kadarka. Hajósi Cabernet has a particularly good name.

By far the largest region of the Great Plain is Kunság, which totals 30,000 hectares. Soil quality and water-table levels vary, the summers are dry, precipitation is low, and winters frosty. A quarter of Hungary's total wine production comes from this region. Seventy per cent of it is white, everyday wine, only some of which is bound for western Europe. Both still and sparkling wines, the latter mainly reflecting the domestic market's preference for sweeter wines, are made from indigenous and international grapes, including Kadarka, Kövidinka, Ezerjó, Olaszrizling, Kékoporto, Kékfrankos, Cabernets Sauvignon and Franc, Zweigelt, Zöldveltelini, and Ottonel Muskotály.

Northern Transdanubia

This great area includes much of the traditional wine-growing districts on the slopes of the old volcanic hills which run up from Lake Balaton to the Danube/Slovakian border, but it also embraces newer wine districts.

The 2,000-hectare Aszár-Neszmély region is dominated by a recently refurbished and re-equipped winery for white wine at Neszmély. Its entire production is exported. The moderate climate and good soils produce white wines that are fragrant, rich in acids, full-bodied, and keep well. Principal grape varieties of the region include Olaszrizling, Rizlingszilváni (alias Muller-Thürgau), Leányka, Sauvignon Blanc, Chardonnay, the Muscat-like Irsai Olivér, and Tramini.

Similar in size is the Badacsony region, a series of south-facing volcanic hills on the north shore of the eighty-kilometre (fifty-mile) long Lake Balaton. After Tokaji, this region is second-dearest to Hungarians and its basalt soils produce warming – sometimes fiery – full-flavoured and fruity white wines. The grapes are grown by cooperatives as well as by small individual producers and the wines sold largely on the domestic market.

There is a growing number of wine cellars opening their doors to the many tourists who visit the lake. Badacsony's best are reckoned to come from the Olaszrizling, Szürkebarát (Pinot Gris), and dryish Kéknyelű grapes, but Rizlingszilváni

and Ottonel Muskotály are also widely planted. The best producer is Huba Szeremley.

Farther east along the northern lake shore lies the Balatonfüred-Csopak region, some 2,800 hectares of red sand soils, less hilly than Badacsony, but likewise farmed by co-ops and smaller individual producers. A slightly warmer microclimate gives wines with more roundness, less "nerve". Overall, the style is softer than the Badacsony wines. Here the Olaszrizling makes notable wines, but Rizlingszilváni, Rajnairizling, Chardonnay, Sauvignon Blanc, Tramini, and Ottonel Muskotály are also widespread.

Almost behind the Badacsony region, on a second line of hills north of the lake, is the smaller (2,000 hectares) Balaton-Felvidék region. Here too, the vines are on south-facing volcanic slopes, but lack the benefit of the sun's rays being reflected from the lake's surface. Mainly small growers produce excellent Olaszrizling, Pinot Gris, and Rizlingszilváni, especially for the home market.

Thirty-two kilometres (twenty miles) west of Budapest is the small (1,620 hectares) Etyek-Buda region. A century ago the potential of its climate and loess and sand soils caught the eye of Champagne-trained József Törley for growing Chardonnay to produce sparkling wines. Törley's successor in the region today is Hungarovin (now owned by the huge German company Henkell & Söhnlein), joined by some small producers, growing Sauvignon Blanc, Zenit, Zefir, Pinot Blanc, and Zengő, among other varieties.

Smaller still is the Mór region, a 1,200-hectare stretch known principally for its robustly distinctive Móri Ezerjó wines, one of the country's best dry whites, although its quartz-rich soils over limestone also produce Sauvignon and a Rajnairizling which have acidity and "fire". Much of the production of Mór is exported.

Further north and closer to the Austrian border is the 1,000-hectare Pannonhalma-Sokoróalja region, lying at the foot of the Bakony hills south of Györ. A quarter of its area is owned by a cooperative, and virtually all of its production is consumed in the domestic market. The main grapes of the region are Olaszrizling, Rajnairizling, Chardonnay, Ottonel Muskotály, Rizlingszilváni, and Tramini.

Hungary's smallest region is Somló, just 400 hectares on the slopes of a single volcanic plug. Wine-growing is largely in the hands of small producers, some with as little as one hectare of vines, selling almost entirely to the domestic market. Characterful wines are made from Olaszrizling, Furmint, Tramini, Hárslevelű, and Chardonnay, and, most interesting of all, the sharp, bracing Juhfark. Béla Fekete and István Inhauser are among the best growers here.

The last of Northern Transdanubia's regions is Sopron, 1,800 hectares that run up to the border with Austria's Burgenland. A milder climate than most of Hungary and diverse soils are more favourable to red-wine production. Here Kékfrankos is the principal grape, although Zweigelt, Merlot, and Cabernet are also grown. There are whites too, made from Tramini, Leányka, Zöldveltelini, and some Chardonnay.

Southern Transdanubia

The area south of Lake Balaton and west of the Danube houses four of Hungary's best-known wine regions. The most recent is Dél-Balaton (meaning, "south" Balaton); 3,000 hectares of brown forest soils and sandy loess with a sub-Mediterranean climate, which means the springs are early, summers long and warm, and frosts rare, although rain (and frequently hail) is plentiful. Red and white wines are produced, from Olaszrizling, Chardonnay, Sauvignon Blanc, Kiráylánky, Kékfrankos, Merlot, and Cabernet Sauvignon. Most of the vineyard area is under the control of the Balatonboglár Winery (owner of the "Chapel Hill" export brand and itself owned by Henkell & Söhnlein), the rest is in the hands of small growers.

To the south, around the town of Pécs, is the Mecsekalja, a region of 1,315 hectares. It is the warmest of Hungary's wine regions and the wine produced here is almost all white, from local and imported varieties, including very respectable off-dry Olaszrizling, good Pinot Blanc, Furmint, Cirfandli (a specialty), Chardonnay, and Sauvignon.

One of Hungary's oldest and most renowned wine regions is Szekszárd in the south-central part of the country. It produces some of Hungary's best reds on gentle slopes of sandy loess, which follow the course of the Danube. It is the only region other than Eger permitted to produce Bikavér (Bull's Blood). It built its reputation for reds (likened to Bordeaux) on the Kadarka grape, but Szekszárd now depends mainly on the international varieties of Merlot and the two Cabernets, and the native Kékfrankos. White wines are made from Chardonnay and Olaszrizling. Foreign investors are beginning to show interest in the region. The best-known producers are Vesztergombi, Dúszi, Vida, and Takler.

Villány-Siklós is the combined name for two historic wine regions named after their principal towns. Red wines predominate in the Villány half where, on hills of stiff loess, the Kadarka has given way to the Kékoporto (probably the Blauer Portugieser) which takes full advantage of the mild winters and long, hot summers to produce some full-bodied wines which can take readily to oak. The two Cabernets, Merlot, Pinot Noir (producing some unmistakably Burgundian wines), Zweigelt, and the native Kékfrankos are also grown in the Villány half. There seems little doubt that this is Hungary's best region for serious, Bordeaux-style wines. In the Siklós part of the region, small producers concentrate predominantly on white grapes, notably Olaszrizling, Tramini, Chardonnay, and Hárslevelű. The best red-wine producers, and thus among the best in all Hungary, are Bock, Attila Gere, Tamás Gere, Vylyan, and Tiffan.

Northern Hungary

The lower slopes of the Bükk Hills and the sheltering Mátra Mountains north of the vineyards produce some of Hungary's best-known wines. Between Eger and the industrial city of Miskolc, the 2,700 hectares of the Bükkalja (-*alja* means "foothills") region benefit from a good microclimate and soils underlaid by tufa – perfect for vines. Cabernet Sauvignon, Leányka, Olaszrizling, Zweigelt, and Kékfrankos are the principal grapes. Most of the production is vinified by large wineries in Eger or Budapest.

To the south of the baroque city of Eger is the Eger wine region itself. Eger is famous for its Egri Bikavér (Bull's Blood) on which its reputation as a potent red-wine producer was built. Bikavér is in fact a style of wine, not a brand, made from a blend of Kékfrankos, Merlot, Cabernets Sauvignon and Franc, and Kékoporto. Kadarka is no longer the principal native grape in the blend. In fact, today there is a range of Bikavérs as individual producers determine the exact blending proportions and amount of ageing that suits their vineyards best. After a long spell in cellar, some extraordinarily powerful wines can emerge, although inevitably, perhaps, some export versions are all too variable.

In addition to Bikavér, Eger produces some fine, fresh, white wines, too, best of all from Leányka, a specialty of the region, but also using Chardonnay, Riesling, Olaszrizling, Tramini, and some Ottonel Muskotály. The underlying tufa may be the secret of Egri quality. The biggest producer, Egervin, now owns the impressive tufa-quarried cellars in the city, which are lined with vast red-hooped casks. The best producers in Eger, with an ever-expanding palette of grape varieties and blends, are G.I.A. (Tibor Gál), Thummerer, and Béla Vincze. The sommelier of the Tulipanka Restaurant is an up-to-date source of the latest releases.

Farther west, around the town of Gyöngyös, is the Mátraalja region, an almost exclusively white wine region of some 7,000 hectares. Today the region's biggest producers are two co-ops, Nagyréde and Danubiana. Nagyréde alone processes one-fifth of the entire crop. Under new German owners, Danubiana bought and re-equipped the huge Gyöngyös winery, and brought in Hungary's first "flying winemaker", Hugh Ryman. French and Australian investment has followed. Half of the region's total output is exported. Principal grape varieties include Olaszrizling, Pinots Gris and Blanc, Rizlingszilváni, Zöldveltelini, Leányka, Tramini, Hárslevelű (most famously from the town of Debrő), Chardonnay, Sauvignon Blanc, and the fragrant Ottonel Muskotály, which produces the region's dry Muscat specialty.

The final region is Tokajhegyalja, usually shortened to Tokaj, in the far northeast of Hungary, adjoining the Slovakian border. Tokaji Aszú is often thought to be the only wine of Tokaj (*see* page 410). There are in fact several table wines made from one or other of the four grape varieties permitted in the "great" Tokaji wines: Furmint, Hárslevelü, Sargamuskotály (Yellow Muscat or Muscat Lunel), and Oremus, a hybrid cross between Furmint and the Bouvier grapes which was only admitted to the Tokaji canon in 1994. A little Chardonnay also features.

Tokaji

Tokaji stands head and shoulders above the other wine regions of central and eastern Europe as the producer of their one undisputed wine of luxury and legend. Late-harvested, unctuously rich Tokaji (Tokay is the western spelling of the name) was the choice of Russian tsars, the kings of Poland, and emperors of Austria – even of Louis XIV of France.

It was almost certainly the first wine to be made purposely of botrytis-shrivelled grapes. The mid-seventeenth century is given as its known origin, at least a century before similar sweet wines were first made on the Rhein. Sweet Sauternes is also more recent in origin, though its start date is obscure.

By 1700, the wines of Tokaji were so important that their overlord, the prince of Transylvania (of the Rakoczi family) created the first recorded vineyard classification, grading the Tokaji vineyards into "*primae*", "*secundae*" and "*tertiae*" plots.

In some respects the Tokajhegyalya (Tokaj hills – the region's official name) compares with Burgundy's Côte d'Or. It occupies a similar area on the lower and mid-slopes, though of much higher hills. The best sites tend to be on the lower middle slopes, some on pure volcanic soil, some on warm light loess. Moreover the first-, second- and third-class growths correspond, up to a point, to the *grands* and *premiers crus* and – villages wines of Burgundy.

Like the Côte d'Or too, Tokaji has excellent cellars, but here they are narrow tunnels driven into the volcanic tufa, sometimes wandering for two miles or more, deeply lined with damp, black fungus and sheltering single or double rows of little 136-litre casks, or *gönci*, usually black with age. Vintage time is very late, delayed – ideally – until the hot sun, alternating with misty nights (the rivers Bodrog and Tisza skirt the hills), has induced a heavy infestation of botrytis. But unlike Sauternes, or any other wine, Tokaji Aszú is made in two stages: first a fully fermented "base" wine; then the collection of dry (*aszú*) grapes, shrivelled either by botrytis or simple raisining, which are macerated with the base wine or must and re-fermented to absorb their sweetness and highly concentrated aromas.

The amount of *aszú* added to each barrel is conventionally measured in *puttonyos* – a *putton* being a grape-carrying hod containing 20–25 kilograms. 3-, 4- and 5-*puttonyos* wines are the most usual; 6 is exceptional. Today the true measure is grams of sugar and "extract" after fermentation. A 6-putt wine, for example, must have at least 150 grams of residual sugar and forty-five grams per litre of extract.

Such wines, with their intense sweetness and concentrated, dried-fruit flavours, balanced by swingeing acidity, can be alarmingly penetrating when they are young, leaving the mouth with a whistle-clean sharpness despite their sugar content. With age they mellow to magical complexity and roundness, without losing their clean, fresh finish. Apparently, a century is not too great an age for them.

Eventually, even more important than the degree of sweetness, though, will be the singular quality of the vineyard. A handful of great sites have been celebrated for centuries, and will presumably be so again when their wines, unblended, are seen on the world market once more. Two sites in the commune of Tarcal have historically been regarded as the greatest of all: Szarvas (the property of the state) and Mezés Mály.

But Tokaji Aszús can no more be the only product of the region than can Ausleses in Germany. The regular drinking is dry, largely Furmint, table wine, which can be admirably lively and fiery. The less luxurious aperitif or dessert wine is Tokaji szamarodni – literally "as it comes"; which means the whole vineyard is harvested without any selection of *aszú* grapes. Szamarodni is edither *édes* (sweet) or *száraz* (dry) according to the proportion of *aszú* on the vines. At best it can be similar to sherry with its own distinctive "cut".

For those for whom the best is not good enough there remains a category richer even than a 6-putt wine: Tokaji Aszú Eszencia (or essencia). Such sweet intensity is overwhelming; years of maturity are needed to tame it.

The legendary Tokaji "Essence" goes even further. Its sugar content is so high (up to 800 grams per litre) that yeasts can make no impression on it; an interminable snail's pace fermentation was traditionally ended by the discreet addition of a little brandy. Essencia is the free-run juice of a pile of *aszú* bunches, pressed by their own weight alone to produce eggcup quantities. Since an eggcup of the elixir was reputedly enough to convert an imperial deathbed into something much more lively, Essencia has for centuries been the most highly prized of all wines – and virtually unobtainable.

The renaissance of the Tokaji region is now well under way, with over a dozen companies, including several major foreign investors, involved. There is much debate about the "authentic" style of Tokaji Aszú wines. During the Communist era, the wines were often pasteurized and sometimes lightly fortified: processes which (together with the inevitable attitudes of a command economy) tended to oxidize the wines prematurely. Modern practices, including regular topping-up of barrels, refermenting with must instead of base wine, and earlier bottling result in fresher wines with less of the marked Tokaj cellar character. The debate and the changes have been good for the region, and there will always be room for different interpretations of tradition. Great *aszús*, like great Sauternes, are wines to lay down for twenty years or more, so the jury will still be out for at least another decade.

Leading Tokaji Producers

János Arvay

The former winemaker at Disznókő (*q.v.*) has set up a joint venture in 2000 with a Hungarian now resident in the United States. They have bought fifty hectares, but no wine has yet been released.

Grof Degenfeld ☆☆
Tarcal. Owners: the Degenfeld family. 70 hectares.
www.grofdegenfeld.com
The noble Degenfeld family ended up in Romania in poverty in the 1950s, then migrated to Germany, where their fortunes revived. In their native Tokaji they bought and largely replanted vineyards, and bought back the family mansion. The style of the wines – only made from 1996 onwards – is relatively oxidative. As well as *aszú* wines, Degenfeld produce dry Furmint, and a grapefruity Muscat Lunel.

Disznókő ☆☆☆
Tokaji. Owner: AXA Millésimes. 100 hectares. www.disznoko.hu
One of the great old Tokaji estates, bought at privatization (1992) by the French insurance group AXA and directed initially by Jean-Michel Cazes of Bordeaux, and since 2001 by Christian Seely. AXA undertook a major investment in the splendid volcanic clay vineyards and a new winery. Under current winemaker Lászlo Mészáros, a full range of Szamorodni and *aszú* wines is produced in a zesty, modern style. The AXA team has been meticulous in its research into the vinification of Tokaji, and the results have been shared with other producers. Both French and Hungarian oak is used to age their wines, and if there are some who criticize the Disznókő wines as too similar to Sauternes, others hail them as among the region's very best.

Gundel ☆☆–☆☆☆
Mád. Owners: Ronald Lauder and George Lang
The most famous restaurant in Budapest, lovingly restored

in the 1990s, also produces its own wines here. High quality, especially for its *aszú* wines.

Hétszőlő ☆☆
Tokaji. Owners: Grands Millésimes de France, Suntory, and other investors. 47 hectares
A major foreign investment, with extensive vineyards replanted on the steep southern slope of the Tokaj mountain. Modern methods and commitment are making fine *aszú* wines and also Fordítas. Fordítas is made by pressing the *marc* again after the *aszú* mixture has been pressed, and then adding dry wine for a further fermentation.

The rather unsatisfactory outcome is a wine midway in style between Szamorodni and *aszú*. Wines from purchased fruit are bottled under the "Dessewffy" label.

Királyudvar ☆☆
Tarcal. Owner: Anthony Hwang. 96 hectares
After Chinese-American businessman Anthony Hwang tasted a wine made by István Szepsy (*q.v.*), he dashed to Tokaj to talk to him and persuaded him to oversee a new venture. Hwang has bought many top vineyards here, and restored a former seventeenth century winery in Tarcal.

Szepsy is in overall charge of wine production, with Zoltán Demeter running the winery on a daily basis. The usual range of typical Tokaj wines is supplemented by lightly sweet Furmint, and late-harvested Hárslevelü.

Châteaux Megyer and Pajzos ☆–☆☆
Sárospatak. Owner: Jean-Louis Laborde. 140 hectares
Major joint venture, initially between GAN (French insurance company) and a French-led consortium, but purchased in 1998 by Jean-Louis Laborde, owner of Château Clinet in Pomerol. The two properties are distinct, but used as a single source of grapes.

In general, Megyer is the lighter, more commercial wine, with Pajzos focusing on higher quality levels. Canadian-Hungarian Thomas Lászlo is the manager and winemaker. Quality has been variable, though some fine *aszú* wines have appeared under the Pajzos label. In addition there is a dry Furmint, Chardonnay (Megyer), and late-harvest single-varietal wines that are unoaked.

Oremus ☆☆☆
Tolcsva. Owner: Bodegas Vega Sicilia. 115 hectares.
www.tokajoremus.com
The name of the original 1630 Tokaj *Aszú* was bought at privatization by Vega Sicilia of Spain in 1993. Originally based in Sarospatak, they built a new winery in Tolcsva in 1999. *Aszús* were at first made in an oxidative style, but more recently the wines have become more intense and vigorous.

A good, dry Furmint, called "Mandolás", Fordítas, and late-harvest varietal wines supplement production. András Bacsó is the experienced manager and winemaker.

Royal Tokaji Wine Company
Mád. Owners: private investors. 106 hectares
Ambitious Anglo-Danish-Hungarian joint venture founded in 1990 (the first of the "Tokaji Renaissance") to specialize in *aszú* wines. Parcels in two second-class and four first-class sites in Mád and Tarcal produce single-vineyard Bojta, Betsek, Birsalmás, Nyulászó, Szt Tamás, and Mezés Mály.

"Blue Label" is a vintage-dated *aszú*; "Red Label" a slightly lighter blend. The aim is the maximum intensity of vineyard and cellar character, with lower alcohol than some *aszús* from other producers, and higher sweetness levels.

All *aszú* wines are at least 5 or 6 *puttonyos* in quality. (And hence are not rated because of Hugh Johnson's participation in the venture.)

István Szepsy ☆☆☆–☆☆☆☆
Mád. Owner: István Szepsy. 22 hectares
The Szepsys have been making Tokaji Aszú from Mád and Tarcal since the sixteenth century. There is a legend that his ancestor, Maté Szepsy, invented the *aszú* method, but the modest István Szepsy says that this is not so, although Maté did play a part in its creation.

In the 1980s, he came to realize that the mass-produced Tokajis from the state farm were a travesty of the real thing, and quietly continued producing authentic *aszú* from his family's vineyards. The first vintage to be released was 1993, and attracted much outside attention: so far production cannot meet the demand.

To keep up with it, Szepsy introduced "late-harvest" wines bottled without the customary barrel-ageing. Szepsy accounts for the quality by his vineyard practice: low-trained vines, hard pruning, green-harvesting, and rigorous selection of berries only at the peak of botrytis. Base wine added to the *aszú* grapes is must from the same vineyard. The wine is aged for as long as he deems necessary in Hungarian oak barrels. Production is limited to around 25,000 bottles.

Tokaj Kereskedöház/Tokaj Trading House Co. ☆–☆☆
Sátoraljaújhely. 80 hectares. www.crownestates.com
Former state-owned property with vineyard holdings much reduced from its heyday of 1,600 hectares, although the firm retains the first-class Szarvas vineyard and still purchases grapes from 2,600 growers. It makes dry and sweet wines (Furmint, Hárslevelü, Yellow Muscat, Szamorodni, *aszú* and "museum" wines aged for decades before release).

The company makes its top *aszú* wines in a style which has not changed greatly since the Communist years, but which its finest old *aszús* show to have been consistent for a century. In Britain, the wines are released under the not entirely accurate "Crown Estates" label, with dry wines bottled under the "Castle Island" brand.

Márta Wille-Baumkauff ☆☆
Abaújszántó. Owner: Márta Wille-Baumkauff. 7 hectares
In the 1970s, Mrs Wille-Baumkauff left Hungary to marry a German, and returned here in 1991 to develop her property in Mád. Quality has steadily improved.

Zemplén Ridge (Zemplén Hegyhát)
A new project of István Szepsy (*q.v.*) and Anthony Hwang, intended to supply lighter, less concentrated Tokaji that will appeal to a younger drinker. The wines will be aged in new 300-litre Hungarian barrels. First vintage 2002, and a new winery will be built by 2005.

Other producers to note include:
Bene, Bodnàr Bodrog-Varhegy (Chateau Dereszla), Demeter, Dobogó, Dusóczky, Evinor, Monyók, Tolcsva-Bor, and Uri Borok.

The Czech & Slovak Republics

Unlike Hungary, the quality of whose top wines was world-famous, these two republics have traditionally grown wine for their own use, rather than for export. Even with the advent of less repressive political regimes, they still do.

The former capital of both countries, Prague, may account for much of the consumption, but the wine-production capitals are Bratislava in Slovakia, and Brno in Moravia. Bratislava lies on the River Danube virtually on the Austro-Hungarian border; Brno is not far from the Czech border with Austria's Weinviertel.

Slovakia is the chief producer of the two republics, with some 36,500 hectares. About twenty per cent of this is planted with Rhine Riesling, Pinot Blanc, Gewürztraminer, Sauvignon Blanc, Pinot Gris, and Muscat Ottonel. Half is planted with lesser white varieties, of which Welschriesling, Grüner Veltliner, and Müller-Thurgau are much the most important. About a third is red, with Frankovka (Austrian Blaufränkisch, Hungarian Kékfrankos) and Svatovavrinecké (St-Laurent) the leading grapes. There are some 600 hectares of Cabernet Sauvignon and a few rare plantings of Pinot Noir on the hills between Bratislava and Pezinok. The big, old, state bottling companies of Raca (in the outskirts of Bratislava), Pezinok, some nineteen kilometres (twelve miles) to the northeast, and Nitra, another sixty-four kilometres (forty miles) farther on used to account for the vast majority of the entire state production.

Modra, just north of Pezinok has its own viticultural and oenology school as well as an independent bottling company. Nenince to the east along the Slovak-Hungarian border probably has a head start on quality production in the country. Kosice, far to the east is also surrounded by vineyard land. Names of breakaway cellars, which may yet come to the fore include Topolcany, Hurbanovo, Gbelce, Hlohovec, and Trnava, all of which have some fine vineyards to draw on. Although private cellars did develop throughout the 1990s, they have had limited impact outside the zones of production.

Slovakia's other special pride is in possessing a small corner of the Tokaji vineyard on the Hungarian border, growing 65% Furmint, 25% Hárslevelü, and 10% Muscat de Frontignan to produce her own Tokaji. Sadly, the wines are a pale shadow of the real thing, so it just as well that Slovakia owns no more than ten per cent of the region's vineyards.

Moravia's 11,000 hectares of vineyards lie between Brno and the Austrian border, and many of the grapes are similar to those of its neighbour. The industry is centred in the towns of Znojmo, Blatnice, Mikulov, and Velké Pavlovice, which produce both still and sparkling wines. Many growers have expanded their hitherto family production to offer bottled wines of fair quality for commercial distribution. White wines, such as Grüner Veltliners, Pinot Blanc and Gris, and Rieslings, are often lively and highly drinkable, the first choice in the *vinarnas*, the wine-bars of Prague, but the standard of red wines from St-Laurent, Zweigelt, and even Cabernet is gradually improving. Moravia's wines score in terms of both value and variety.

Bohemia, the western province with Prague at its heart, has a mere 1,000 hectares, including some Riesling of fair quality and some intriguing Pinot Noir-based reds. But full ripeness does not come easily here, and Moravian or Slovakian wine is the people's choice. The return, since 1989, of some noble families to their hereditary estates (and vineyards) is giving a boost to the home industry, but at present the quality sector remains small.

The Former Yugoslavia

Most of the countries that once made up Yugoslavia are in the wine business, some more traditionally and interestingly than others. Only land-locked and mountainous Bosnia-Herzegovina's production is negligible. Just two remain major exporters at present, both of them protected from the ravages of the 1990s: Slovenia, in the northwest, and Macedonia in the southeast. However, Croatia and Serbia traditionally had the majority of the former nation's vineyards, but the industry has yet to recover from the years of war.

Yugoslavia came tenth among the world's wine-producing countries and tenth among exporters: a respectable position for a country that had to build its wine industry almost from scratch after World War II. The industry roots are as old as Italy's, but long occupation by the Turks in the easterly regions of the country removed the sense of continuity.

The postwar reconstitution of the industry combined the Austro-Hungarian traditions of the north, the Italian influence down the coast, and some truly Balkan traditions in the east and south. In particular, Croatia's Dalmatian coast, and Madeconia likewise, have good indigenous grape varieties, whose origins can be traced back to ancient times, although these are threatened by the general trend in all these countries to move towards adopting the tried and trusted international varieties as part of the concerted effort to regain a slice of the export market.

The old wine industry was state-controlled, but always consisted almost half-and-half of small, independent growers and state-owned farms. The small growers (the law allowed them to own up to ten hectares of land) took their crops to the local, giant-sized cooperatives. These in turn supplied the larger regional organizations, which acted as négociants, blenders, and distributors. In the 1990s, many small, private producers are beginning to appear.

Slovenia

Slovenia, tucked into the Italian-Austrian-Hungarian north-west corner of the country, makes the best and most expensive wines of the countries that formerly made up Yugoslavia. The 24,200 hectares of vineyards are divided by a no-man's land strip, empty of vines, from the alpine border, past the capital, Ljubljana, down to the border with Croatia. There are three principal regions: Primorska (6,500 hectares), between Italy and Croatia along the coast; Podravje, just south of the borders with Austria and Hungary (10,200 hectares); and, east of Ljubljana, Posavje (7,500 hectares). The most attractive of the northerly Germano-Austrian style wines come from around Maribor, Ptuj, Ljutomer (or Lutomer), and Ormoz, between the valleys of the Mura (which forms in places the border with Austria and Hungary), the Sava, and the Drava tributaries to the Danube. The most exciting dry whites and reds produced in the Italian tradition come from the north of the Istrian Peninsula and up into the mountains alongside the Friuli border region.

These days, Slovenia is taking a lot of care in the grading of her wines. By the late 1990s seventy-five per cent of vineyards were privately owned, and quality is improving from year to year. This is also rapidly becoming a very pleasant, civilized country for the tourist to visit.

The combined influences of the Adriatic, the Alps, and the Hungarian plain make the climate moderate, while limestone subsoils favour white wine. The Adriatic influence gives more ripening potential for solid, dry wines and the better reds; the long, cool autumns of the alpine Maribor region and the only slightly warmer hillsides south of Hungary give lighter, more aromatic and grapey styles, the best of which are often sold under the Slovenian equivalent of the familiar Kabinett, Spätlese, Auslese, Beerenauslese, and TBA hierarchy.

The hills between Ljutomer and Ormoz, only eighty kilometres (fifty miles) from the west end of Lake Balaton, bear a vineyard almost as famous as Mount Badacsonyi, known by the name of Jerusalem from its crusader connections. The majority of the exports from this admirable region are unfortunately of Laski Rizling, although Pinots Blanc and Gris, Gewürztraminer, Sylvaner, and Rhine Riesling are also grown. It seems a pity to waste a first-rate vineyard on what is essentially a second-rate grape, however satisfactory its performance – and some of the late-picked wines here are more than satisfactory.

South of the Drava, the Haloze Hills produce a similar range of white wines. South again, the Sava Valley, continuing into Croatia and on to its capital, Zagreb, makes light red Cvicek of local grapes.

At the western end of Slovenia, on the Italian border, four small viticultural regions known collectively as Primorska have a mild Mediterranean climate. Their best-known wine is a vigorous, crisp, and tangy red called Kraski Teran. Teran is the Italian Refosco, and Kraski signifies that it is grown on the rugged limestone *karst* that stretches up the coast. Merlot, both Cabernets, and Barbera can be found, but tend to be used to produce relatively high-acid, Italian styles, which crave the company of oily foods. However, the weight and quality of the best of the dry whites, from Sauvignon Blanc, Pinot Blanc, and Pinot Gris to the earthy, slightly creamy, yellow Ribolla or Rebula, another Italian export, deserve real international acclaim.

At this end of the country, names such as Vipava, especially for fresh, delicate young whites; Brda, which has some extraordinary private vineyards; and Koper, south of Trieste, hold promise for the future. Tastings in 2002 showed a growing number of small estates clearly aiming for high quality in a wide range of styles, even if in many cases, quality was equated with a high degree of alcohol and long periods of ageing in mostly new oak barrels. Leading producers include Cotar in the Kras region, the cooperative at Goriska Brda, Movia (Primorska), Batic (Primorska), Princic, and Vinakoper in Koper (Primorska), Vinag (Podravje). Their ranks will continue to grow.

Serbia & Montenegro

The republic of Serbia was formerly the whole of the eastern landlocked third of Yugoslavia from Hungary to Macedonia. Now its northern section, north of the River Danube, comprises the region of Vojvodina. It has two more enclaves to the south: Montenegro on the southeastern coast and Kosovo, squeezed into a circle of mountains between Albania, Macedonia, and Serbia. It has, though, lost a significant southern slice adjacent to Albania, cut away to become Macedonia. The industry is dominated by the Navip company, which has access to 2,200 hectares and numerous wineries; it produces a complete range of wines as well as other drinks.

Including Vojvodina, Montenegro, and Kosovo, Serbia is still probably the major producer, with some 90,000 hectares of vines. It has been relatively conservative in its grape varieties, with the dark Prokupac as its chief red grape and Smederevka (Smederevo is near Belgrade) as its rarely exciting white, often made in an off-dry style. Its oldest and most famous vineyard is Zupa, 129 kilometres (eighty miles) south of the capital between Svetozarevo and Kruabzevac. Zupsko Crno ("Zupa red") is a blend of Prokupac with the lighter Plovdina. Prokupac is also widely used for rosé (*ruzica*). More and more Cabernet, Merlot, and Gamay is now being planted. Some individual vats of Sauvignon Blanc, Gewürztraminer, Cabernet Sauvignon, and Merlot, which rarely make it intact out of the country, suggest that, one day, this will be fine territory for all these varieties.

Vojvodina has a history of red winemaking (Carlowitz was once a famous example). Today a wide range of mainly white grapes makes nicely aromatic and balanced wines, the best of them in the Fruska Gora Hills by the Danube north of Belgrade. Gewürztraminer and Sauvignon Blanc can be particularly tasty, though I fear they are less widely planted than Laski Rizling. Further north and east, Subotica and Banat are the areas bordering on Hungary and Romania, both with sandy Great Plain soils and light wines; Subotica growing the Hungarian red Kadarka and white Ezerjó.

Kosovo had remarkable success for a relatively new exporting region. Its Pinot Noir-based pale red, made sweet for the German taste and labelled "Amselfelder", regularly left Belgrade in train-loads. Since war cut off supplies, this soft, empty style has been ruthlessly copied all over Eastern Europe for this single market. By 2002, Kosovo's wine industry was in crisis. Between 1998 and 2002, 2,200 hectares of vineyards were grubbed up, job losses mounted, and some wines were left unsold in tanks. Plans to privatize wineries may falter for lack of interest from investors.

The hearty, red, Vranac-based wines of Montenegro used to disappear to the Russian market. Since 1990, there have been some haphazard attempts to interest the West in them. They deserve to succeed, as the wines can be balanced, ripe, and quite intense, and appear to take well to wood-ageing.

This southerly end of the country, along the Bosnian coast, counts an unusually good unknown white variety among its potential surprises. I have found a touch of the apricot smell of the Zilavka grape, which makes me wonder whether its lightness is a clever piece of blending.

Croatia

With 52,000 hectares the old kingdom of Croatia musters the second-largest number of vineyards among the republics. It falls into two distinct and very different parts: Slavonia, the continental north between Slovenia and Serbia, between the Drava and the Sava rivers; and the coast, from the Istrian Peninsula in the north all the way south to Bosnia-Herzegovina, including the Dalmatian coast and its lovely islands.

Slavonia has half the grape hectarage, but its wines have neither the appeal of Slovenia's whites, close though they are, nor of some of the new wines of Vojvodina to the east. Wine shipped as Yugoslav Laski Rizling without further particulars often came from here. Grapes such as Traminer, Riesling, and Austria's Zweigelt are also grown here.

Croatia's best wines come from the regions of Istria and Dalmatia. Istria grows the same grapes as western Slovenia: Merlot, Cabernet, Pinot Noir, and Teran for reds – the Merlot is particularly good. The white wines include rich Muscats and Malvasias, and Pinot Blanc, the base of the local sparkling wine.

Dalmatia has Yugoslavia's richest array of original characters – mainly red. Plavac Mali (there seems to be no translation) is the principal grape, supported by Plavina, Vranac, Babic, Cabernet, Merlot, and "Modra Frankija" (Blaufränkisch). Plavac has its moments of glory. One is Postup, a concentrated, sweet red, aged for years in oak, produced on the Peljesac Peninsula north of Dubrovnik. A fifteen-year-old Postup is still bright-red, a strange sort of half-port with more than a hint of retsina, a big (14.2 degrees), well-balanced and structured wine that would appeal to those who like Recioto from Valpolicella. Dingac is very similar. Another is Faros from the island of Hvar, a degree lighter than Postup, and softly dry rather than sweet: a full-bodied, warmly satisfying wine without coarseness. The regular quality of coastal red is simply called Plavac. Some find Babic, when aged three or four years, a better wine. The dry rosé of the coast, made from several grapes, is called Opol.

White Dalmatian wines are in a minority, but in greater variety than red. The Marastina is the most widespread white variety and has its own appellation at Cara Smokvica. Grk is the oxidized, sherry-like specialty of the island of Korcula. Posip (which some equate with Furmint) makes heavy but not flat wine. Bogdanusa, especially on the islands of Hvar and Brac, can be surprisingly light, crisp, and aromatic. Vugava, grown on the remote island of Vis, is similar. Sometimes they are presented as separate varieties, sometimes in blends. It is hard to discover, in fact, whether some are different names for the same grape. But they certainly have old-style character to balance against the predictable correctness of Laski Rizling.

Dalmatia's dessert wines, whether of red or white grapes or both, are known as Prosek. The best Prosek tends to be a family matter, nursed in a little cask and given to guests in a thick tumbler with absolutely appropriate pride.

Macedonia

Thirty-thousand hectares of mostly red grapes, Vranac and Kratosija, which are mainly blended, set the scene. They are spiced up with more of the Cabernet and Merlot, which seemed to have been coming on so well just prior to the latest round of upheavals. Prokupac is the best-quality local red grape here, as in Serbia. Especially at the Povardarie winery, these reds are coming good, and beginning to reconquer the export market.

There seem to be one or two good whites in among the plethora of Smederevka, whose only salvation lies in the soda water so ubiquitously added to it. Some leafy but quite balanced and intense Chardonnay has appeared, and there are good reports of Zilavka.

Romania

The long-established quality and individuality of Romanian wine has suffered badly in the socialist era. The country speaks a Latin-based tongue and has both cultural and climatic affinities with France. Once the wines of Moldavia were drunk in Paris. Much of the white wine from the western part of the country, especially the hilly enclave of Transylvania, needed German terms on the labels to serve the needs of Romania's largest Western market. This has hardly helped the development or understanding of this still unnecessarily poor and secretive country. And yet Romania has well over 200,000 hectares of vines, which, since privatization, have been split into smallholdings; this in turn has made it difficult for ambitious investors to purchase substantial vineyards and cultivate them by modern means.

Since 1990, the most prosperous winemaking and bottling companies that led the export business have regrouped as shareholders of a private export marketing company with their major overseas agents. Companies such as the British importer Halewood International and the German Reh-Kendermann winery have invested and upgraded existing wineries. There are some French joint ventures as well, equally geared to the export market. Foreign winemakers have been taken on as consultants. The upshot has been the creation of bland, characterless brands. Quality is unlikely to improve further until the wineries can source better-quality grapes, or wait for their own new plantings to come on stream. Romanian wine exports are also bedeviled by the popular assumption that Romanian wine is extremely cheap. But some individual batches of wine have resulted, which show just what these beautifully sited vineyards can do.

Romania's wine-growing regions surround the central Carpathian Mountains. The main centres are Tarnave, at 488 metres (1,600 feet) on the Transylvanian plateau to the north; Cotnari to the northeast in Moldavia; Vrancea (including the once-famous Panciu, Odobest, Cotesti, and Nicoresti) to the east; Dealul Mare to the southeast; Murfatlar in the extreme southeast by the Black Sea; and in the south Stefanesti, Drăgăsani, and Segarcea. In the west, part of the sandy Banat plain to the west of Timisoara (where the 1989 freedom movement began) carries on the viticultural region and traditions of the Great Hungarian Plain. Around Minis, east of Arad, and Recas, east of Timisoara, some good red international grapes can be found, including Pinot Noir. The remainder of the vineyards are stocked with a mixture of international varieties (Merlot and Sauvignon Blanc predominate) and Romania's own white grapes, the Feteasca Alba, and Regala, Grasă, and Tămâñosă, and the red Băbeasca and Feteasca Neagră. Strangely, there is very little Chardonnay. Such as there is can be found mostly in Murfatlar, where it has superb but rarely realized potential.

Cotnari produces the most individual wine, although it has become quite rare. Despite its very northerly position near the Ukraine/Moldovan borders, long, fine, misty autumn conditions permit white grapes to overripen, shrivel, even develop noble rot in some years. Native grapes, Tămâîîosă Românească, Grasă (akin to Furmint and probably the better of the two), Fetească Alba, and Francusa are used to produce dessert wines aged in old oak casks.

Târnave produces a reasonable white blend called "Perla de Tîrnave" and "varietal" Fetească and "Riesling" (regrettably mostly Italian/Welsch/Laski rather than Rhein). Undoubtedly the best whites here are made from the rarer Pinot Gris and Gewürztraminer. Muscat Ottonel produces short-lived but highly scented styles, which may be sweetened.

Among a sea of very dull whites and some often good (but make sure it is the less-usual (brut) sparkling wine from Panciu, Vrancea's most notable wine is the pale, acidic, brisk red Băbească of Nicoresti.

The outstanding sixty-four kilometre (forty-mile) stretch of south-facing hill-slopes of the Dealul Mare overlooking the Bucharest plain specializes in Merlot, Cabernet Sauvignon, and the scarcer but potentially fine Pinot Noir. Urlat, Tohani, and Sahateni are among other names behind which lie some great potential. British investors have created the Prahova winery here, which dominates the export market.

Murfatlar, just inland from Constanza on the Black Sea, is traditionally a white- and dessert-wine area. Yields are low, fruit quality is intense but, all too often, good white grapes are left to overripen and produce a clumsy, sweetish, dessert-style wine from the likes of Chardonnay and Pinot Gris. There are, in fact, also excellent-quality red grapes in this area.

In the southern vineyards along the Danube tributaries such as the Olt, flowing down from the Carpathians to the river, Stefanesti and Drăgășani are better-known for whites, including Sauvignon Blanc; and Segarcea and Sadova for reds including Cabernet Sauvignon. The vineyards of Samburesti are among the best-managed and produce all the classics other than Chardonnay.

In all, Romania is a beautiful country except, unfortunately, for the very flat, dusty plains around the capital. It has enormous quality potential throughout its agricultural sector; it has coal, oil, and natural gas. It has a steel industry and, indeed, many of its state wineries show the benefits of this, as stainless steel is much more common here than elsewhere in Eastern Europe. Much of its infrastructure, especially in communications, remains dramatically underperforming long after the overthrow of the Ceausescus. Its agricultural output has decreased sharply through the disincentive of collective farming and rural depopulation. It would be tragic to lose any more of what could be some of Europe's greatest cool-climate vineyards for lack of a sense of direction.

Bulgaria

Of all the countries in Central and Eastern Europe, Bulgaria was the most adept at reprogramming its wine industry to earn Western currency. Since the late 1970s, Bulgarian wine has not been an occasional exotic excursion, but standard fare in several Western markets, since up to eighty-five per cent of production was exported. The industry succeeded by offering, with the help of generous government subsidies, excellent value for money in familiar flavours – above all in rich Merlot and well-hyped Cabernet Sauvignon, which satisfied palates that had been brought up on red Bordeaux. Post-Communist privatization put an end to that, and frequent changes of government (and policy direction), and the collapse of the country's banking system, led to a decline in the wine industry.

Wine is a major preoccupation of the whole country. Over 110,000 hectares is vineyard, marginally more planted in red varieties than white. Of the red vineyard, the majority, perhaps surprisingly, is Cabernet or Merlot, which together account for 40,000 hectares. The rest is Pamid and such other traditional varieties as Gamza (the Hungarian Kadarka), Melnik, and Mavrud, and a little Pinot Noir and Gamay.

The white vineyard caters much more for everyday local drinking and distillation – almost half is the lightly peachy Russian grape, Rkatziteli, backed up by Ugni Blanc, Rizling (here confusingly often referred to as Riesling), Red Misket, Dimiat (or Smederevka), and Muscat Ottonel, and growing plantings of Chardonnay, Rhein Riesling, Sauvignon Blanc, and Aligoté alongside small areas of Tamianka and Gewürztraminer. Of late, progress in the control of the vinification process has conclusively demonstrated that the better white varieties are as much at home here as their red counterparts. Chardonnay is beginning to show its natural superiority, with and without, the use of new-oak casks.

There are five main wine regions. The three major ones are grouped around the mountain range of the Stara Planina which forms the central backbone of the country from Serbia to the Black Sea. The fourth is perched in the high central valleys. Fifth is a small region tucked away around Melnik, on the southwest border. Conditions are cooler in the northern region, but both north and south can produce good, ripe, raw material.

Since 1978 there have been additions to the first twenty sub-regions officially recognized as appellations (Controliran Regions) for one or more grapes, and the number will continue to increase as quality and consistency improve. The Controliran Region wines have to comply with regulations issued by the Government, which cover grape varieties, cultivation techniques, and vinification technology. Levels of alcohol, acidity, and sugar are checked and the wines are approved by the National Tasting Committee. In 1985, a new classification was introduced, the Reserve category, for wines with ageing potential which have been matured in oak.

A long-term consequence of privatization has been a breakdown of the tidy system of grape delivery, which existed when vineyards were tied to a specific winery. There is now something of a free-for-all on the grape market each autumn. A great number of vineyards are in danger of falling out of production altogether. Many wineries, where they could afford it, have had to subsidize growers throughout the year in order to try to ensure that they would have a right to buy the resultant crop.

Slowly, in this far from favourable climate, some wineries, including Lovico Suhindol, Pavlikeni, Sliven, and Iambol, have managed to go private. Some of them have been acquired by the burgeoning Boyar Estates, which has also invested approximately 14.5 million euros in its new Blueridge winery.

The challenge for these new companies, and for foreign backers, is that the wine world equates Bulgarian wine with very low prices which diminish the profits that are needed for further investment.

Eastern Region

This cool region, between the mountains and the Black Sea, has thirty per cent of Bulgaria's vineyards and specializes in white wines, sparkling wines, and brandy. It includes many noted sub-regions, notably Varna, Shumen, Targovishte, and Razgad. The main grapes are Riesling, Rkatziteli, Aligoté, Chardonnay, Misket, Muscat Ottonel, Ugni Blanc, Dimiat, and Fetiaska.

The Varna district on the Black Sea was recognized in 1986 as a Controliran Region for Chardonnay. The Shumen district, which is experimenting with fermenting Chardonnay in small oak barrels, has three Controliran Regions producing Chardonnay, Gewürztraminer, and Sauvignon Blanc. Preslav, Khan Krum, and Targovischte Chardonnays are probably showing the most real quality potential to date.

Northern Region

The northern region has the River Danube as its northern boundary. It is known for its quality red wines – the main varieties being Gamza (the Kadarka of Hungary), Cabernet Sauvignon, and Merlot. The former state winery of Russe (now merged with Boyar) on the Danube's banks controls a lot of potentially good red grapes from all over the region. The wineries of Lovico Suhindol and Pavlikeni (which is now one private vineyard-owning cooperative) and Pleven in particular produce a lot of reliable Cabernet Sauvignons as well as good Merlots and silkily oak-aged Gamza.

Sparkling wine is another specialty of the region, benefiting from its relatively high acid levels. The area has several Controliran Region wines – the best being the Gamza, Cabernet Sauvignon, and Merlot of Suhindol, and

an Aligoté from Lyaskovets (which, like Targovischte, should probably be better-known now for its Chardonnay).

Southern Region

The southern region grows Cabernet and some Pinot Noir and Merlot, but also makes some well-known traditional wines such as Mavrud, Bulgaria's pride: a substantial, dark, Rhône-like wine needing four years' ageing. The winery at Assenovgrad, near Plovdiv, has a reputation for Mavrud. Another traditional grape variety, Pamid, makes a rather pallid everyday wine. Whichever way you look at it, however, the region's greatest potential lies more in the richly ripe Merlots of Stambolovo, Liubimetz, and in the Sakar Mountain region.

Southwest Region

A very small and distinct region on the Yugoslav border across the Rhodope Mountains in the southwest of the country. The Melnishki Controliran Region was designated in 1979 for the production of Melnik wine from Harsovo.

Bulgarians have the greatest respect for Melnik; its red wine, they say, is so concentrated that you can carry it in a handkerchief. It needs five years' ageing and will last for fifteen. However, finding a sample of this mythical stuff presents certain difficulties.

Sub-Balkan Region

This is the narrow strip south of the Balkan range, which includes the famous Sungurlare Valley where the Red Misket is grown, and the Valley of Roses (the source of attar of roses) which specializes in Muscats – "Hemus" is the brand name to look for. A fair proportion of Rkatziteli is also grown in this region where it can produce cool, delicate, white-peach aromas.

The Russian Empire

The former Soviet Union was the world's third-largest wine producer. It now has just under one million hectares of vines. In late Communist times, it was also a considerable net importer, and continues to consume much of its own produce. This is despite two enormous hiccups in its progress. First came Gorbachev's reforms, which caused nearly half the vineyard to be uprooted in 1985–'86 in the drive to reduce alcoholism. (Sales of vodka rose in response.) Second came the post-Communist break-up of the Soviet Union, with former republics such as Moldova and Ukraine becoming independent.

Although a number of people and companies have tried to collaborate with wine producers in these countries, the Western world has seen few, if any, Soviet wines and is still in ignorance of their historical traditions and undoubted potential, mainly because there is no infrastructure to support economical, regular quality production and transport. It is gradually shaping up, but is more likely to favour the home market first, because the locals see no reason to change their traditional styles to match the Western palate.

The vineyards can be found in a band stretching through the countries bordering first the Black Sea and then the Caspian. They are: Moldova (162,000 hectares), Ukraine (162,000 hectares), Belarus (105,000 hectares), Georgia (60,000 hectares), and on eastward into what might be thought of as more traditionally Muslim terrain, namely Azerbaidjan, Kazakhastan, Tadjikistan, Uzbekistan, Kyrgistan, and Turkmenistan, which together have a total of over 270,000 hectares. Armenia, too, has wine production, though it is perhaps better known for its excellent brandies.

The sweet wines – given particularly long ageing in large casks – deserve to be better known and can rival a fine *vin doux naturel* from southern France.

A glimpse of past glories appeared in London in 1990 at an auction by Sotheby's of dessert wines from the private estates of the tsar's and other great families in the Crimea. The Muscat wines of the imperial Massandra estate were outstanding among a variety of very well-made old "ports", "sherries", "Madeiras" and even "Cahorski".

The Russian republic (including the Crimea) is very much the greatest producer of wines of all qualities, with sparkling wine as its great specialty. Russia's sweet tooth is well-known, but the technical competence displayed, especially in drier *cuvées*, is beyond denial.

Moldova

President Breznev would come to Moldova to while away a weekend among not only the long-lived local Cabernet Sauvignons, but also some of the finest Bordeaux captured from the Germans during the last war. (Today, sadly, the condition of the old enamel-lined vats simply forces great quantities of the wine to deteriorate through metal contamination.) One look at the dark-soiled, rolling vineyards over fine limestone subsoils, and one taste of the immature wines, and enough to show that this could be a first-class producer, as could its more easterly neighbours. The climate, moderated by the nearby Black Sea, provides close to ideal growing conditions in the 105,000 hectares of vineyards. Bottles of the fragrant Cabernet blend, "Negru de Purkar", leave no one in doubt of Moldova's potential. Native grape varieties are similar to those of Romania, and there are substantial plantings of Aligoté, Rkatziteli, Sauvignon Blanc, Chardonnay, Merlot, Cabernet Sauvignon, and Pinot Noir. White wine represents approximately seventy per cent of production.

The first successful Western-style wines came out via the Hincesti winery (owned by the Vino Vitis company), briefly helped by the Australian giant Penfolds. The red Negru de Purkar was outstanding. In 2002 there was advance news of a range of new wines made with western help. Visitors will find sparkling wines made from Aligoté, *flor* "sherries", and other dessert wines, which can be truly remarkable.

Georgia

Though tiny in relation to Russia, Georgia has a far more ancient and original wine culture, with at least 500 indigenous vine varieties. Its most famous wine region is Kakhetià, east of Tbilisi, where the climate is at its most continental. The princely estate of Tsinandali was developed in the nineteenth century to make the finest Kakhetian wines, famous for fragrance and bite – and preferred by the poet Pushkin to burgundy.

Today, "Tsinandali" is the brand name of an adequate dry white; "Gurdzhani" and "Mukuzani" are others. Of these indigenous grapes, Saperavi, which accounts for seventy per cent of all red plantings, is worth watching, for, it gives a Syrah-like ripeness with a solid, peppery intensity. Visitors to Russia find Saperavi of several qualities on restaurant wine lists. It can be excellent.

To the west, towards the Black Sea coast, Imeretia has a more humid, less extreme climate and a winemaking tradition of its own, with scores of ancient indigenous grape varieties and a preponderance of white wines. However, the area under vine throughout the country has dropped precipitously from 112,000 hectares in 1990 to the present-day 60,000 hectares.

Ancient traditions remain well-preserved. Throughout Georgia private farmers can still be found using methods of pre-classical antiquity. The *kvevri*, a clay fermenting jar buried in the ground, is still found in many properties. Its strongly tannic produce is not for fine palates.

Georgia is also the home of a flourishing sparkling wine industry. Most of the wine is sweet, which is the preferred national taste. The locals drink it in awe-inspiring quantities and its legend has spread to attract a number of major players from the West, including both Champagne and cava companies, to invest in joint ventures. Despite the eagerness of many foreign investors to create joint ventures in Georgia, some have foundered, as companies found themselves bogged down in red tape, corruption, and poor infrastructure. One of the more successful has been Georgian Wines and Spirits, with backing from Pernod-Ricard.

Greece

The ancient Greeks were responsible for colonizing the Mediterranean and the Black Sea with the vine, exporting their wines in exchange for Egyptian grain, Spanish silver, and Caucasian timber. In the Middle Ages, the Peloponnese and Crete were valued sources of Malmsey sack for northern Europe. Her wine industry, though, was almost shut down by the occupying Turks for so long that not much remained when Greece was liberated in the nineteenth century – except a handful of interesting grape varieties.

The largely alkaline (in places, volcanic) soils and multifarious microclimates of Greece make her a natural country of the vine. With 163,000 hectares of grapes (not all for wine) she is a major producer. With entry into the EU imminent, there was a move towards varieties and systems of control that would lead to fine wine, and since then there has been very rapid progress. Since Greece's accession, progress in quality winemaking has been fast enough to astonish onlookers.

Under the earlier primitive conditions, with hot fermentations, the best qualities that could be produced were all sweet wines. The Greek taste remained faithful to what appears to be an ancient tradition of adding pine resin during fermentation to make retsina.

It goes too well with Greek cooking to be ignored, but today demand for this wine is falling, except among tourists, as the national palate turns increasingly to the fine Greek wines. A handful of producers attempt to make a high-quality retsina, in order to show that such a wine can exist.

At present, Greek wine can usefully be divided into national brands (usually blends); retsina, and other traditional and country wines for uncritical first-year drinking; and wines from defined areas now controlled by an appellation system in accordance with EU law. There are twenty-eight such areas. In addition, the past few years have seen the development of a number of small, but high-quality wine estates experimenting with grape varieties, also often outside the delimited areas, whose wines can only be sold as *vin de table* or *vin de pays*.

The Peloponnese has more than half of Greece's vineyards and produces more than a third of her wine.

Patras, at the mouth of the Gulf of Corinth is the main wine centre, with four appellations: Muscat, Muscat of Rio, Mavrodaphne, and plain Patras. Mavrodaphne can be the most notable of these: a sweet dark red wine of up to 16 degrees alcohol, something in the style of Recioto of Valpolicella, much improved by long maturing. (The excellent bottling from Spiliopoulos called "Nyx" has a strong resemblance to old tawny port.) Plain Patras white is for drinking young. Two other appellation of the Peloponnese are interesting: the region of Nemea for strong red with real ageing potential made of the Agiorgitiko (St George) grape, and Mantinia for a delicate, spicy white.

The 18,000 hectares of vines in the north of Greece, from Thrace in the east through Macedonia to Epirus, appear to have most potential for quality. Its most important appellation are: Naoussa (west of Thessaloniki) for potent though balanced and nicely tannic red; Amynteio, at 610 metres (2,000 feet) in the mountains of Macedonia, producing lighter red; and Zitsa (near Joannina in Epirus) for a light mountain white from the Debina grape. The most important recent development was the planting of the Sithonian Peninsula, the middle one of the three fingers of Halkidiki, with Cabernet and other grapes, by the firm of Carras (*q.v.*).

The island of Crete is second to the Peloponnese in hectarage, but only third in production (Attica has far more productive vineyards). Crete has four local appellation, all for dark and more or less heavy and sweet reds: Daphnes, Arhanes, Sitia, and Peza – Peza being the seat of the island's biggest producer, its cooperative. The grapes are all indigenous: Kotsifali, Mandelaria, and Liatiko.

Attica (including mainland Boetia and the island of Euboea) is Greece's most productive wine area, overwhelmingly for retsina, but there are now an increasing number of high-quality estates – Hatzimichelalis, Evharis, Semeli, and Strofilia among them. Savatiano is the principal grape from which retsina is made, but other important varieties grown in the Attica region include Assyrtiko, Cabernet Sauvignon, and Syrah.

Next in importance for hectarage and quality comes Cephalonia, which, with the other Ionian (western) islands musters 10,000 hectares. Cephalonia is known for its dry white Robola, its red Mavrodaphne, and its Muscat. Zakinthos to the south makes a white Verdea.

The central mainland region of Thessaly also has 10,000 hectares of vineyards, but only one important appellation: Rapsani, a middle-weight red from Mount Olympus, plus those of Messenikola and Anhialos.

The wines of the Aegean islands, the Dodecanese and the Cyclades, have more renown, notably the pale-gold Muscat of Samos, the luscious *vin santo* (see Boutari), and fresh, vigorous, dry white of the volcanic Santorini, from Europe's most punishing vineyards, the Muscat of Lemnos, and the sweet Malvasia and Muscat of Rhodes. (Rhodes's best wines are white "Villare" and red "Cava Emery".)

Malvasia is grown on many islands and is often their best product. Other island wines with esoteric reputations are the very dark-red Páros and the Santa Mavra of Levkas, whose grape, the Vertzani, is unknown elsewhere. Greek wine is advancing so fast that visitors should take every opportunity to try the latest bottlings.

Leading Greek Producers

Achaia-Clauss ☆
Patras

Once one of the the biggest and most famous Greek wine houses, producing up to two million cases per year, but it is now experiencing fierce competition from other expanding producers. "Demestica" is the best-known wine.

Otherwise they produce a large variety of dry and sweet wines from vineyards in the Peloponnese and Crete, and Mavrodaphne.

Antonopoulos ☆☆–☆☆☆
Patras

Established by Constantine Antonopoulos, who died in a car crash in 1994, this up-and-coming estate is now run by his cousins. Elegant white wines from Chardonnay and local varieties such as Moschofilero. The winery also excels at oaked Cabernet Sauvignon.

Biblia Hora ☆☆
Kavala, Macedonia

This is early days for a new venture between two of Greece's top winemakers: Vassilis Tasktsarlis and Evanghelos Gerovassilou (formerly of Carras *q.v.*).

Planting only began in 1999. Initial releases include a white blend of Sauvignon and Assyrtiko, a Cabernet/Merlot blend, and a Syrah rosé.

J. Boutari & Son ☆–☆☆☆
Naoussa, Thessaloniki

Long-established producer who has grown rapidly in recent years, covering several appellations with new wineries at each locality.

The main winery is in Naoussa specializing in Naoussa wines and obtaining good results from Xinomavro. The range is enormous, and in addition to the well-known top "Grande Reserve" red, there are excellent wines from Santorini, including a gorgeous *vin santo*, and varietal wines from indigenous varieties.

Cambas ☆☆
Kantza, near Athens

Another long-established producer with wineries in Kantza and Mantinia. It produces a wide range of table and sparkling wines, as well as ouzo and brandy.

Since 1992, Cambas has been owned by Boutari, but it is run independently. The flowery Mantinia is excellent, but the "Nemea Réserve" may be a touch too tannic for some modern tastes.

Domaine Carras ☆☆
Sithonia, Halkidiki

Developed primarily in the 1960s, this major estate was created by John Carras with advice from Professor Emile Peynaud of Bordeaux. The well-known "Château Carras" is a blend of the Cabernets Sauvignon and Franc with Merlot and Limnio, matured in French oak. There are several other labels under the appellation Côtes de Meliton.

In the 1990s, this huge 450-hectare estate and tourist complex ran into financial difficulties, and was sold in 1999. Its future is uncertain and quality has declined since the family relinquished control.

Gaia ☆☆–☆☆☆
Nemea. www.gaia-wines.gr
Founded in 1994, this estate has acquired a high reputation for its "Thalassitis", a Santorini white from very old vines, although the oak-ageing is very pronounced. The Agiorgitiko rosé, is wonderfully fruity, and there is a superb Nemea called "Gaia Estate", which needs time to shed its youthful tannins.

Gentilini ☆☆
Minies, Cephalonia. www.gentilini.gr
A small family estate, owned by Nicholas Cosmetatos, producing fine wines from the indigenous Robola, and a crisp Sauvignon Blanc. A cask-aged Sauvignon/Chardonnay ("Gentilini Fumé") is also produced.

Gerovassiliou ☆☆☆
Epanomi, Macedonia. www.gerovassiliou.gr
The former oenologist at Carras has his own thirty-three-hectare estate making outstanding whites from Malagousia, Viognier, and Chardonnay. The reds are steadily improving, with various blends employing Syrah, as well as a pure Syrah.

Hatzimichalis ☆☆
Atlantes, Athens-Lamia
An eighty-hectare private estate owned by Dimitri Hatzimichalis, which produces a range of wines from indigenous and international varieties. Using purchased grapes as well as his own vineyards, Hatzimichalis now produces around one million bottles. Overall, the reds are better than the whites.

Kokotos ☆☆
Stamata, Attica
This small estate northeast of Athens has its vineyards at a height of 450 metres above the plains of Attica. It uses the "Semeli" brand for most of its wines. Decent Savatiano and Roditis whites, and fine, tobacco-scented reds from Agiorgitiko and Cabernet Sauvignon.

Kourtakis ☆–☆☆
Athens. www.kourtakis.net
A family merchant house using the brand names of "Kouros" and "Calligas", and producing three million cases. There are very successful red and white Vins de Crète and Mavrodaphne of Patras made here. They also produce large quantities of the international best-selling retsina from the Savatiano grape of Attica. Given the volumes produced, quality is sound.

Kyr-Yanni ☆☆–☆☆☆
Naoussa
After Yannis Boutari left his family winery, he brought his skills to this fifty-hectare estate, working with grapes such as Xynomavro and Merlot. The blackberry-scented Syrah is a touch austere, but the Xynomavro is a fine tannic leathery wine with more than a passing resemblance to Nebbiolo.

Château Lazaridis ☆–☆☆
Drama, north Greece. www.chateau-lazaridi.gr
The fifty-hectare estate of one of two brothers producing fine wines in Drama. They use international varieties such as Sauvignon Blanc and Cabernet Sauvignon, but have also brought home varieties from southern Italy, which originated in Greece.

Domaine Kostas Lazaridis ☆☆–☆☆☆
Drama, north Greece
Main label is "Amethystos", red, white, and rosé. The red has a savoury, herbal character that is very individual. Also a high-class Tsiporou and increasingly confident use of barriques, particularly with Sauvignon and Cabernet.

Mercouri ☆–☆☆☆
Near Olympia, west Peloponnese
An old, private, family estate with an interesting wine museum. The main production is outstanding reds made from Mavrodaphne and from the Refosco grape, taken from Friuli in 1870. Good white Roditis, too.

Oenoforos ☆☆
Selinous, near Corinth
A small, recently developed estate with a gravity-fed winery, producing fresh, long-lived whites (especially "Asprolithi") from very high vineyards overlooking the Gulf of Corinth.

Samos Cooperative ☆☆–☆☆☆
Samos
With two wineries, this union of about 300 growers produces remarkable Muscat wines which are either naturally sweet or fortified, and exported widely. Top of the range, the "Samos Nectar", made from sun-dried grapes, is rich and golden, maturing continuously and darkening in bottle.

Skouras ☆☆☆
Argos. www.skouras.gr
Owned by George Skouras, a highly imaginative and talented French-trained winemaker producing magnificent Agiorgitiko and Nemea, but also experimenting successfully with Cabernet, Chardonnay, and Viognier.

His top red is usually "Megas Oenos" which is a blend of Agiorgitiko with Cabernet: a cherryish wine with a distinct oak influence.

Strofilia ☆☆
Anavissos, Attica
Exciting red, white, and rosé from an estate near to Cape Sounion. The three proprietors, all engineers, also run an excellent wine bar, "Strofilia", near the centre of Athens. In recent years, production has expanded greatly, and Strofilia is no longer a boutique winery. But quality remains high.

Tsantalis ☆☆
Aghios Pavlos, Halkidiki
Second-generation Macedonian merchant house, which made its name with Olympic ouzo. Various appellation areas supply a wide range of wines, such as the fine Rapsani and Agiorgitiko from Nemea.

To improve its supply of grapes, Tsantalis has recently planted 200 hectares of vineyards. Acceptable versions of international varieties (Chardonnay, Merlot, Syrah) are also being made.

Vaeni Naoussa Cooperative ☆–☆☆
Naoussa
Large cooperative in western Macedonia vinifying 70% of Naoussa production; mainly strong, above-average red wines from the Xynomavro grape. Once rather coarse, the wines have in recent years become softer and more mellow.

Cyprus

Wine culture in Cyprus, most easterly of the Mediterranean islands, has had seismic changes in fortune over the centuries. Cypriot wines were famed throughout classical, Byzantine, and early medieval times. In a bizarre international tasting known as the "Battle of Wines" at the French court, Cyprus was the outright winner. Then came three centuries of Islamic rule, and production went into dramatic decline. British government from 1878 brought stability – and a market. In more recent times it focused on the lower end of the market, selling vast quantities to the Soviet bloc and selling grape concentrate to the British. These markets are in steep decline, so Cyprus's wine industry has had to smarten up.

Modern Cyprus has no great range of wines to offer, but what she does she does well, producing low-cost "sherries", both dry and sweet, modelled on the Spanish (the term "Cyprus sherry" can no longer appear on the labels of wines for sale in the EU); smooth, dry, red and white table wines; and her own extremely luscious liqueur-wine, Commandaria, the modern successor to the classical wine "Nama", made of grapes dried on the vine, which was so highly prized over two and a half thousand years ago. Commandaria is to Cyprus what Constantia is to South Africa, or Tokaji is to Hungary.

Cyprus has, until very recently, been intensely conservative about grape varieties. Having never been afflicted with phylloxera, and intending to stay untainted, she spurned new-fangled introductions and planted only three grapes: Mavro the black, Xynisteri the white (which accounts for the vast majority of planting), and Muscat of Alexandria. Today there is a small but increasing volume of varietal wine made from international grapes, and wines from specific regions of the island. In 1990, after some thirty years of strictly controlled trials with non-native grapes, a few were made available for commercial cultivation. Among them Grenache, Carignan, Syrah, Merlot, and a minute amount of Cabernet Sauvignon now produce varietal wines; Malvasia Grossa and Palomino (of Jerez) are usually used in blends with the indigenous white varieties. The quest for better wine has renewed interest in the island's less-planted native varieties, the black Maratheftico and the less interesting Opthalmo: the former is difficult to cultivate but can produce outstanding wines. The traditional varieties can also produce good wines; Mavro particularly from high-altitude sites, provided its yield is restricted. Xynisteri has to be harvested most carefully, as the grapes are prone to oxidization.

All the island's vineyards lie on the south, mainly limestone, slopes of the Troodos Mountains, between 240 and nearly 1,500 metres (800–5,000 feet), the best located above 990 metres (3,250 feet), some on soils of igneous origin. Since 1990, total grape hectarage has decreased from a peak of over 50,000 hectares to 20,000 as the industry comes to terms with overproduction and a declining export market for its fortified and basic table wines. Most Cyprus wine is still made by a handful of very large wineries in the coastal towns of Limassol and Paphos (convenient for export) but, as part of the quality drive, the Cypriot government has supported the building of small, modern wineries within the vineyard areas themselves. The wines from these locations are just becoming commercially available.

The island's most distinctive wine, Commandaria, was given full legal protection of origin and production in 1993. Its delimited region comprises fourteen of the higher-altitude-wine-producing villages on the Troodos slopes. The most famous are Kalokhorio, Zoopiyi, and Yerasa. The best Commandaria is made from pure Xynisteri – a light-brown wine of considerable finesse, which can be drunk young.

Other commercially more important wines blend Xynisteri with Mavro to make a dark-tawny wine which can be superb after five or more years in barrel. The grapes are simply sun-dried for at least a week in the vineyard, then pressed and fermented. Long before all the grape sugars are turned into alcohol, fermentation stops naturally, giving a wine of at least ten degrees alcohol. Once fermentation is complete, the wine is fortified – usually to fifteen degrees, although the legal limit is twenty degrees. Maturation takes place in oak casks in Limassol and Paphos for a minimum of two years. Alas, prices – and hence quality – remain low.

Four concerns dominate the Cyprus trade. KEO produces the smooth red "Othello" and Commandaria "St John", as well as one of the best dry Cyprus "sherries", "Keo Fino", and light table wines using the "Laona" label. Its slightly fizzy "Bellapais" is a refreshing white. ETKO makes the "Emva" range of fortified wines, as well as a good white from Xynisteri called "Nefeli" and possibly the island's finest red, "INO": a single-estate Cabernet, produced in tiny quantities. Loel has a sound red "Hermes", Commandaria "Alasia", and a dry white made from the Palomino grape. Some of the best Cyprus brandies are also distilled by Loel. The cooperative SODAP, which has 10,000 members, has as its flagship wine the red "Afames". It also makes dry white under the "Arsinoe" brand and Commandaria "St Barnabas".

These are essentially products of the past, and the major wine companies know they must change their approach if they are to survive and prosper in international markets. KEO has hired a winemaker from New Zealand, who has rapidly been modernizing the production and trying to realize the full, remarkable potential of the best vineyards. At the same time, the company is working more closely with its contracted growers, for without good grapes there can be no good wines. As a cooperative, SODAP is moving more slowly into the modern era, and the other two companies will be introducing new ranges that will, they hope, have broader appeal.

Small, quality-conscious producers such as Vouni Panayia are beginning to provide strong competition to the big four, but only, as yet, on the domestic market.

Turkey

If Noah's vineyard on the slopes of Mount Ararat was really the first, Turkey can claim to be the original home of wine. Hittite art of 4000 BC is possibly better evidence that Anatolia (central Turkey) used wine in highly cultivated ways. In relation to such a time span, the long night of Islam has been scarcely more of an interruption than Prohibition was in the United States. Since the 1920s, Turkey has again been making good wines: much better than her lack of a reputation leads us to expect. One of the most surprising bottles of fine wine I have ever drunk was a 1929 Turkish red – at a friend's house in Bordeaux. I took it for a Bordeaux of that famous vintage.

Turkey has 600,000 hectares of vineyards, but only three per cent is made into wine – the rest being table grapes. Kemal Atatürk founded the twentieth-century wine industry in his drive to modernize the country, although it is held back by lack of a domestic market: ninety-nine per cent of the population is Muslim. The state monopoly, Tekel, is by far the biggest producer, with six wineries handling wines from all regions and dominating exports, particularly with popular bulk wines to Scandinavia. There are also twenty-five private wineries, two at least with very high standards. Wine production has been gradually increasing over the past decade, and in 2002 it stood at forty-eight million litres.

The main wine regions are Trakya, the Thrace–Marmara region on the European side of the Bosphorus, the Aegean coast around Izmir, central Anatolia around Ankara, and eastern Anatolia. The majority of the grapes are local varieties (of which there are over a thousand) whose names are unknown in the West, except in Trakya, where Cinsaut, Gamay, and Sémillon (supported by Clairette) make the best-known red and white. The Doluca company only began importing cuttings of Chardonnay and Cabernet Sauvignon in the early 1990s. A Gamay red called "Hosbag" (from Tekel) is not remarkable, but "Trakya Kirmisi", made of the Turkish Papazharasi and Adakarasi varieties, is a good, vigorous wine. *Kirmisi* is Turkish for red and *Beyaz* for white; *Sarap* for wine. "Trakya Beyaz" (a dry Sémillon) is a popular export.

Of the private firms, Doluca and Kavaklidere are the leaders. Doluca, at Mürefte on the Sea of Marmara, founded in 1926, has well-made reds: "Villa Doluca" of Gamay, Papazkarasi, and Cabernet. In my experience this is the best Turkish red. Doluca also makes Sémillon, Sauvignon Blanc, and Riesling. Kavaklidere, the largest independent firm, is based in Ankara but sources grapes from as far apart as Thrace and eastern Anatolia. It concentrates on Anatolia's indigenous grapes, producing "Yakut" and "Dikmen", red blends of Bogazkere, Kalecik Karese, and Oküzgözü (though Yakut may contain some Cabernet), and both sweet and dry whites from Narince, Emire, Sultanine (with a very fresh Primeur), and Cankaya.

Eastern Anatolia is also the home of the best-known of Turkish reds, the heavy and powerful "Buzbag", made of Bogazkere near Elazig. This is the produce of Tekel, the state enterprise, and remains Turkey's most original and striking wine. Turasan winery is based in Cappadocia, and mainly produces blends, dry and sweet.

The Aegean region counts Cabernet and Merlot (known, I believe, as "Bordo") among its reds, along with Carignan and Calkarasi. Most of the white is made of Sultanye, the seedless table grape with no real winemaking potential. Some Sémillon and Muscat is grown – the Muscat probably the best.

The Levant

Lebanon

What wine might be in the Levant, were it not for the followers of the Prophet, is a tantalizing topic. In 1840, Cyrus Redding had heard tell (he certainly had not been there), that "Syria makes red and white wine of the quality of Bordeaux". But there is current evidence that the eastern Mediterranean can make great wine. Noah's ancient land of Canaan, now the Beka'a Valley, emerged in the 1970s as a producer that compares with Bordeaux, just as Redding had reported.

In the early nineteenth century its reputation was for dry, white *vin d'or*. In 1857 Jesuits founded a vast underground winery at Ksara, northeast of Beirut, with over a mile of barrel-filled natural tunnels. It is still the largest (and oldest) Lebanese winery, producing a very good, fresh white. But the estate that fluttered the dovecots of the wine trade is Chateau Musar, at Ghazir, twenty-six kilometres (sixteen miles) north of Beirut. It was founded in the 1930s by Gaston Hochar, with vineyards in the Beka'a Valley. In 1959, his son Serge, after training in Bordeaux, became winemaker. Bottles started appearing in London. In 1982, he showed a range of vintages going back to the 1940s, which proved beyond doubt that the region can make extraordinarily fine and long-lived reds based on Cabernet Sauvignon with some Cinsaut and Carignan, aged in barriques – not at all unlike big Bordeaux of ripe vintages. Whites include an oaked version from the indigenous Obaideh grape, similar to Chardonnay, which is surprisingly capable of ageing a decade and more. During the civil war of the 1980s, Hochar, stoically carrying on making fine wine with Syrian tanks in his vineyards, became a figure of legend in the wine world. Some recent vintages, however, suggest that commercial success is stretching the supply.

The other well-established Beka'a Valley producer is the 300-hectare Kefraya, which makes a Cinsaut/Carignan blend called "Rouge de K" ("Chateau Kefraya" is reserved for the best years only) as well as rosé and white wines. The *cuvée de prestige* is the "Comte de M" blend from Cabernet, Syrah, and Mourvèdre, aged in new oak. Quality has improved since 2000.

The end of the civil war in Lebanon persuaded some brave entrepreneurs to create new wine estates. One of the most ambitious is Massaya, founded in 1998 by architect Sami Ghosn and benefiting from the advice of Hubert de Boüard, the owner of Château l'Angélus in St-Emilion, and Daniel Brunier of Châteauneuf-du-Pape. Initial releases of the reserve wines were impressive.

Domaine Wardy, launched in 2000, is making its mark with Sauvignon Blanc and Chardonnay, and will expand its range of varietals. The ancient Ksara winery has hired a French winemaker from Margaux to expand its range to twelve wines, including a Bordeaux-style blend. And Kefraya has a new neighbour in the form of Cave Kouroum de Kefraya.

The total area under vine in Lebanon is 1,100 hectares, so it remains small in terms of its production. However, the country now has a future as a wine producer, which was hardly the case ten years ago.

Israel

Winemaking in Israel dates back to ancient times, although the modern industry was established at the end of the nineteenth century with a gift to the state from Baron Edmond de Rothschild: the founding of wineries at Rishon le Zion, south of Tel Aviv, and Zichron Ya'acov, south of Haifa. These two wineries, which remain the largest in Israel, controlling sixty per cent of the business, sell their wines under the "Carmel" brand.

Israel now has 3,000 hectares of vineyards. The first to be planted were concentrated in the hot coastal regions of Samson and Shomron (which is still the largest wine-growing region) with predominantly Carignan, Grenache, and Sémillon grapes to make sweet sacramental wine. Interest was primarily kosher.

In the mid-1970s, the principal of the University of California at Davis, Cornelius Ough, identified the cool-climate Golan Heights as an ideal location for wine grapes. The improvement in quality was considerable. There are now vineyards up to 1,100 metres (3,600 feet), on a range of volcanic-basaltic soils in the Golan Heights and the Upper Galilee, producing the grapes for Israel's best wines.

The introduction of classic varieties, first Cabernet Sauvignon, then Merlot and Chardonnay in the 1980s heralded the beginning of a quality-wine industry and a move to producing dry table and sparkling wines that could compete internationally. By 2000, eighty per cent of all Israeli wines were dry. The Golan Heights Winery, in the small town of Katzrin high up in the Golan, leads the way, making oak-aged Chardonnay and Cabernet ("Yarden" is the premier label), classic-method sparkling wines, and complex Merlot. Barkan, Israel's third-biggest winery, makes Sauvignon Blanc and Cabernet Sauvignon of acceptable quality. Its production is now around 4.5 million bottles annually, and it has also set up a joint venture with a kibbutz to create another Golan winery, called Galil Mountain, with the emphasis on international varieties.

Among the newcomers are Dalton near the Lebanese border, which is establishing a reputation for barrique-aged Cabernet, Merlot, and Chardonnay; Tishbi, which is the renamed and revamped Baron winery; Recanati in Emek Hefer, and Cfar Tabor in Lower Galilee; and Domaine du Castel. This last winery is the most ambitious of all, ageing its red wines for two years in new French oak. The drawback is price, but its second wine, "Petit Castel", is almost as good and less overtly oaky.

North Africa

Nearly half a century ago, North Africa's wine-producing countries, Tunisia, Algeria, and Morocco, accounted for no less than two-thirds of the entire international wine trade. Algeria was by far the biggest producer of the three, with most of the vast quantity being exported to Europe (mainly to France) as blending wine. Independence from France resulted in an immediate decline, for there was practically no domestic market; political instability, and religious fervour inhibited investment in badly needed renovation of vineyards and wineries, and the trend has been either to pull up or neglect the vineyards. The drive, however, is towards improving wine quality from the best sites for export.

Tunisia

The institution of an *Office du Vin* in 1970 marked the start of Tunisia's coordinated plan to make wines for export. Her vineyard area devoted to wine production has been reduced from 50,000 hectares in its heyday to some 15,000 hectares, all in the vicinity of Tunis (and ancient Carthage) on the north coast. Muscats are the most characteristic wines here, as they are of the Sicilian islands lying not far off-shore. Reds, rosés, and whites are made of French Midi-type grapes, in many cases using modern methods. As in Algeria, the pale rosés are often the most attractive wines and constitute about two-thirds of production. Tunisia has adopted the French AOC system, and appellations include: Mornag (the largest), Grand Cru Mornag, Coteaux d'Ultique (near the sea north of

Tunis), Tébourba, Sidi Salem, and Kelibia. The biggest producer is the *Union des Caves Coopératives Viticoles* (UCCV at Djebel Djelloud), which makes sixty-five per cent of Tunisian wine. The Union makes an unusual dry white Muscat, "Muscat de Kelibia", from vineyards at the tip of Cap Bon to the northeast. It is highly aromatic, not over-strong, but nonetheless difficult to enjoy with a meal. The UCCV's best-quality red is "Magon", from Tébourba in the valley of the Oued (River) Medjerdah, west of Tunis. The Cinsaut and Mourvèdre in this wine give it both roundness and greater personality than the standard "Coteaux de Carthage". Other union wines include "Château Mornag" (red and rosé) from the Mornag hills east of Tunis; a pale, dry "Gris de Tunisie", a blend of Grenache and Cinsaut, from Tébourba; and a dry, Muscat-scented rosé called "Sidi Rais".

The most notable wines of the state-owned *Office des Terres Domaniales* are the earthy reds from Domaine Thibar, from the hills 137 kilometres (eighty-five miles) west of Tunis up the Medjerdah Valley, and "Sidi Selem" from Kanguet, near Mornag. Other noteworthy producers include the Société Lamblot for its red "Domaine Karim" from the Coteaux d'Ultique; Domaine Magon, now benefiting from German investment; Château Feriani, which makes one of Tunisia's tastiest red wines from the same area; Héritiers René Lavau for its "Koudiat", another strong red from Tébourba; and the *Société des Vins Tardi at Aïn Ghellal*, north of Tébourba, for its "Royal Tardi", which contains a touch of Pinot Noir. Better than these are the strong, sweet, dessert Muscats, which come under the appellation Vin Muscat de Tunisie.

The German firm of Langguth has produced and exported wine here since the 1960s, and more recently the Sicilian Calatrasi company has invested in large vineyards south of Tunis. Under the Selian label, Calatrasi produce gutsy, fruit-forward Carignan and Syrah. Such ventures should give the Tunisian wine industry a much-needed boost.

Algeria

The biggest and most intensely planted of France's former North African colonies has seen a reduction in her wine-grape vineyard from 365,000 hectares, its total of the 1960s, when Algeria was the world's sixth-largest wine producer, to around 35,000 today – and her productivity has gone down by an even greater proportion to a mere one per cent of pre-1962 levels. Wineries have closed their doors by the thousands, often under violent threats, their number shrinking from 3,000 over forty years to fifty. Many of the older vineyards on the fertile plains, which could never have produced good wine, have been converted to cereals, and viticulture has retreated to the hill vineyards, which produced superior wine in French days. A dozen *crus* were indeed given VDQS status before independence.

Of these, seven were recognized by the ONCV (*Office Nationale de Commercialization des Produits Viticoles*) as quality zones. They are all located in the hills about eighty kilometres (fifty miles) inland in the two western provinces of Oran and Alger. Of the two, Oran has always been the bulk producer, with three-quarters of Algeria's vines. The ONCV, which is responsible for the bulk of Algerian wine production, has standard labels that reveal nothing about the origin of the wine except its region – and in the case of its prestige brand, "Cuvée du Président", not even that. "Le Président" is a matured, faintly claret-like wine which, when last tasted, I did not find as good as the best regional offerings.

The western quality zone, the Coteaux de Tlemcen, lies close to the Moroccan border, covering north-facing sandstone hills at 760 metres (2,500 feet). Red, rosé, and white wines are well-made: strong, very dry but soft in the style the Algerians have mastered. The rosés and whites in particular have improved enormously with cool fermentation.

The Monts du Tessalah at Sidi-bel-Abbès to the northeast seem rather less distinguished; certainly less so than the Coteaux de Mascara, whose red wines in colonial days were frequently passed off as burgundy. Mascara reds are powerful and dark with real body, richness of texture, and, wood-aged as they are sold today, a considerable aroma of oak and spice. A certain crudeness marks the finish. This I have not found in the Mascara white; dry though it is, it would be creditable in the South of France: pleasantly fruity, not aromatic but smooth and individual – perhaps as good as any white wine made in North Africa.

At Dahra the hills approach the sea. The former French VDQS *crus* of Robert, Rabelais, and Rénault (now known as Tanghrite, Aïn Merane, and Mazouna) make smooth, dark, and full-bodied reds and a remarkable rosé with a fresh almost cherry-like smell, light and refreshing to drink – a skilful piece of winemaking.

Further east and further inland, in the province of Al-Jazair (Algiers), the capital, the Coteaux du Zaccar makes slightly lighter, less fruity wines. Again, the rosé, though less fruity than the Dahra, is well-made. South of Zaccar and higher, at 1,220 metres (4,000 feet), the Médéa hills are cooler, and finer varieties are grown along with the standard Cinsaut, Carignan, and Grenache. Cabernet and Pinot Noir go into Médéa blends, which have less flesh and more finesse than Dahra or Mascara. Easternmost of the quality zones is Aïn Bessem-Bouira, making relatively light reds and what some consider Algeria's best rosés.

Morocco

The vineyards of Morocco devoted to wine production now cover only 8,000 hectares: a sharp decline since independence in 1956, when there were 50,000 planted. It has the tightest organization and the highest standards of the three North African wine countries. The few wines that are "AOG" (*Appellation d'Origine Garantie*) have similar controls to French appellation wines, strictly applied. They are produced by a central organization, SODEVI, and the important cooperative, Les Celliers de Meknès. Quality here has improved in recent years, with some appealing Cabernet/Syrah and Cabernet/Merlot blends.

Four regions of Morocco produce fair wines, but by far the best and biggest is the Meknès/Fès area at 460–610 metres (1,500–2,000 feet) in the northern foothills of the middle Atlas Mountains, where the regions of Saiss, Beni Sadden, Zerkhoune, Beni M'Tir, and Guerrouane are designated. The last two have achieved remarkable reds of Cinsaut, Carignan, and Grenache, respectively sold abroad as "Tarik" and "Chantebled" (and in Morocco as "Les Trois Domaines"). "Tarik" is the bigger and more supple of the two, but both are smooth, long, and impressive. The 2,400-hectare Guerrouane also specializes in an AOG *vin gris*: a very pale, dry rosé of Cinsaut and Carignan, which substitutes for the white wines Morocco lacked until recently. Now a tolerable Sauvignon Blanc presages better things.

A little wine, but none of consequence, is made in the Berkane/Oujda area to the east near the Algerian border. The other principal areas are around Rabat, on the coastal plain, in the regions of Gharb, Chellah, Zemmour, and Zaër. The brand names "Dar Bel Amri", "Roumi", and "Sidi Larbi", formerly used for pleasant, soft reds from these zones, have been abandoned in favour of the regional and varietal names.

Further south down the coast, the Casablanca region has three wine zones: Zenata, Sahel, and Doukkala. The first produces a solid red marketed as "Ourika". South of Casablanca the firm of Sincomar makes the standard drinking of every thirsty visitor: the "Gris de Boulaouane". Boulaouane is the archetypal North African refresher: very pale, slightly orange, dry, faintly fruity, extremely clean, and altogether suited to steamy Casablanca nights.

Other labels that may be encountered are Castel Fréres' Atlas Vineyards, Domaine Ain Amhajir, the French-owned Domaines Delorme, and Domaine de Sahari, the last owned by Bordeaux négociant Williams Pitters.

Asia

The wine grape has been grown in the East for centuries. Chinese gardeners in the second century knew how to make wine, so did the Arabs, until they renounced alcohol in the eighth century – at least in theory. Afghan vineyards supplied the Indian Moghul court in the sixteenth century. But wine never became part of daily life in these countries, unlike the West. The reason, perhaps, is the nature of their cuisine. Strongly seasoned dishes are best washed down by a simple, refreshing liquid – even if each course is regaled by the local spirit. For all that, there are the beginnings of a modern industry in several Asian nations. Wines from Japan, India, and China reach Western markets but Thailand, South Korea, Vietnam, and Indonesia now have nascent industries, principally for local consumption. Even Nepal has two hectares of *vinifera* – the world's highest vineyard – while the tiny Himalayan kingdom of Bhutan has ventured into winemaking under the patronage of its royal family.

China

Vines were growing in China 200 years before they reached France. Wine, often sweet and fortified, has been consumed at Chinese banquets for centuries and is also used for medicinal purposes, infused with plants, herbs and, more unusually, animal organs, rodents, and reptiles.

Viticulture spread over the centuries throughout central and northwest China. The Autonomous Region of Xinjiang, in the far northwest, accounts for almost a quarter of the 140,000 hectares of vines in China, and for a third of the 1.5 million tonnes of grapes currently produced, but nearly all of the fruit is eaten fresh or as raisins. The major wine-producing regions are in the northeast – in Shandong, Hebei, and Jiangsu provinces, and around Beijing and Tianjin.

The modern industry is largely the product of foreign intervention. Under its "Four Modernizations" programme, beginning in the late 1970s, the Chinese government actively courted foreign interest in the modernization of its wine industry. The first to participate was Rémy Martin. In 1980, Rémy teamed up with a provincial farm bureau to establish a large-scale modern winery in Tianjin. Its "Dynasty" label quickly rivalled the longer-established "Great Wall", now also with a foreign joint-venture partner. It has subsequently become the market leader among the Western-style domestic wines, with sales of thirteen million bottles annually.

In the mid-1980s, two further foreign joint ventures established large-scale plantings of premium European varieties. The Huadong (East China) winery at Qingdao' on the northeast seaboard in Shandong Province was set up by Hong Kong-based investors. Allied-Domecq is now the foreign partner, and the wines can be of surprisingly good quality. About 200,000 cases are produced. Dragon Seal Wines is a joint venture between Pernod-Ricard and the Beijing Friendship Winery, and produces creditable Chardonnay and Cabernet Sauvignon. Both "Huadong" and "Dragon Seal" are now leading brands. The Marco Polo Winery in Hangzhou (the origin of willow-pattern porcelain) is a joint venture between Italian interests and a local rice-winemaker, producing the "Summer Palace" range of wines. And in a significant move upmarket, Rémy launched a premium sparkling wine, "Imperial Court", in 1992. It is made from the classic Champagne varieties grown at Rémy's Shen Ma Winery near Shanghai.

China's wine-grape production is currently some 300,000 tonnes, and output is growing. Five large, long-established wineries account for just under a quarter of the total. The Changu Yu Winery at Yantai in Shandong is the largest, bottling its wines under the "Marco Polo" label. The others – Beijing Yeguangbei, Lianyungang (Jiangsu), Great Wall, and Tong Hua (Jilin) – make about the same volume combined. Their production is a mix of traditional style and, more recently, western-style wines. Some now import bulk wine for blending or for bottling locally. In all, there are at least 200 smaller wineries, possibly many more, but only a handful are known outside China, mostly those with foreign interests.

Native grape varieties are used to make most of China's wine. Best-known is the Dragon's Eye, the grape used to make "Great Wall". Beichun, a hybrid of the *Vitis amurensis* species native to north China, is suited to the harsh climate of its border region. Other varieties are being tried, especially Rkatziteli, Muscat Hamburg (the backbone of the Dynasty operation), and Italian Riesling. Most impressive of all are the wines being made from the more recently introduced classic varieties: Chardonnay, Riesling, Pinots Noir and Meunier, Cabernet Sauvignon, and Gamay. Legally, wine in China need contain only seventy per cent fermented grape juice, but it is virtually certain that such questionable "wines" will be reserved for the domestic market.

More recent ventures include Lou Lan, a 400,000-case winery in the Gobi Desert run by Frenchman Gregory Michel and backed by investors from Hong Kong. Imported cuttings were planted in 1998: Cabernet, Merlot, Syrah, Chenin, Riesling, and other varieties. The top range of varietal wines is being released under the "Turpan Basin" label. In 2002, the Maotai Changli winery released wines from Cabernet Franc and other varieties. The Austrian Swarovski family, owners of Norton in Argentina, have invested in Shang-Li, where 300 hectares are being planted, mostly with Merlot and Cabernet.

India

India's first modern winemaking concern, the Andhra Winery and Distillery, was established in 1966 at Malkajgiri, Hyderabad, in the state of Andhra Pradesh. It is still the country's largest. The problem with most Indian wines is that they are made from table grapes, although in the 1990s the planting of international varieties became more common. It is estimated that there are about 13,000 hectares in production.

The first wine to cause a stir was the launch in 1985 by Chateau Indage, which started off as a joint venture with Piper-Heidsieck, of "Omar Khayyám", a sparkling wine based on Chardonnay, made near Poona in the Maharashtra Hills, southeast of Bombay. A sweeter "Marquise de Pompadour" followed for the domestic market, and there is a vintage *méthode traditionelle* called "Celèbre". The estate's dry red is made from the local Arkawati grape, the white from Ugni and Chardonnay. With almost 250 hectares of vineyards, Indage has a lot of grapes to use, and has launched two blends dominated by Cabernet: "Soma" and "Anarkali". The "Chantilli" range from Indage is aged in French oak. The wines from the forty-hectare Grover Vineyards at the base of the Nandi Hills near Bangalore are widely available in India. In 1995, Michel Rolland acted as a consultant. The white is mostly Clairette, and in the early 2000s Grover launched a medium-bodied Cabernet. Vineyards (Sauvignon, Chenin Blanc, and a blush Zinfandel) were planted in the late 1990s on fifteen hectares at the Sula Estate near Nasik, 193 kilometres (120 miles) northeast of Bombay, by American-educated Rajiv Samant.

Indonesia

The solitary enterprise in Indonesia, Hatten Wines, is located on Bali. It relies on black Isabella (*Vitis labrusca*) grapes grown in vineyards a few kilometres from the city of Singaraja in the north, where the slopes provide some respite from the tropical heat and humidity. So far, small batches of a medium-dry rosé have been produced, but Hatten's French winemaker is now experimenting with a sparkling wine.

Japan

The Daizenji Temple at Katsunuma, in the central Honshu prefecture of Yamanashi west of Tokyo, is the spiritual home of Japan's wine industry. Legend has it that the first vines were planted here in the eighth century by a holy man, although early interest in the grape was probably more for the medicinal value of the fruit. Winemaking came later, in the nineteenth century, although Yamanashi remained at the center, and is home to the most of the modern thirty-odd serious winemaking enterprises. Other wine-grape-producing regions are Nagano, an adjacent prefecture to the west; Yamagata, further to the north on Honshu island; and Hokkaido, the large island at Japan's northern extremity.

Growers must contend with unsuitable growing conditions – monsoonal weather patterns (central and southern regions); a long, severe winter (the north); drainage problems and acid soils – and high costs. The main focus of Japanese viticulture is on the growing of grapes for the table, rather than on providing top-grade raw materials for winemaking. This is reflected in the varieties and in viticultural practices.

Vitis labrusca varieties and hybrids, introduced over the course of the nineteenth century from North America, account for almost eighty per cent of Japan's total of some 25,000 hectares under vine. Kôshû, the local white and the *Vitis vinifera* descendant of the original vines planted at Katsunuma in the eighth century, provides the backbone of the industry's winemaking identity, if not the bulk of the wine produced. It is a heavy-bearing vine, producing big, round, pink-tinged berries, with which winemakers habitually do battle to extract colour, flavour, and body.

European varieties have been trialled since the 1960s. Seibel, a variety that looked promising in the experiments, was successfully crossed with the native vine to create a new variety called Kiyomi. It produces a conventional, though strongly acidic, wine with a resemblance to Pinot Noir. In more recent experimentation, Kiyomi has been crossed back to the native vine to produce a new commercial hybrid, Kiyomai, which will not need to be buried in soil for protection during the severe winter, as is the case with other varieties, Kiyomi included. The northern European varieties such as Müller-Thurgau and Zweigelt may well prove to be suited to the harsh winter conditions in Hokkaido.

The surprise is that there are some premium local wines (Semillon, Chardonnay, Cabernet, Merlot, and Kôshû) now being made in an attempt to keep pace with imports. Five huge, diversified beverage conglomerates, which together account for three-quarters of total output, dominate the industry. The brewer Suntory produces the most interesting (and costly) of all: Château Lion, a red Bordeaux-blend, and a very good Sémillon dessert wine. It vies for top position with soft-drinks giant Sanraku, which sells particularly good Chardonnay, Merlot, and Cabernet under the "Mercian" label. both Suntory and Sanraku produce over three million cases per year, dominating the domestic market. Manns Wine is emphasizing the local varieties Kôshû, Dragon's Eye, and local-Euro crosses which are adapted to Japan's rainy climate, as well as Chardonnay and a French-oaked Cabernet. Another brewer, Sapporo ("Polaire" label) and Kyowa Hakko Kogyo ("Ste Neige" label) are other big players. Smaller, family-owned wineries are likewise concentrated in Yamanashi, among them Marufuji ("Rubiat" label), Shirayuri ("L'Orient"), Maruki, and the quality-conscious Château Lumière. Such quality wines are, and are likely to remain, the exceptions; most wine labelled as "Japanese" is blended with imports from South America and Eastern Europe.

South Korea

With about 4,000 hectares of vineyards, South Korea has a wine industry of sorts. *Majuang* is the generic name for all local wine, mostly made from low-quality, imported bulk wine with some locally grown Seibel and Muscat Hamburg grapes added for "authenticity".

Thailand

The growing market for wine in Thailand has spawned some local winemaking ventures. Château de Loei is a 120-hectare vineyard and winery at Phurua, in the cooler Loei River district in northern Thailand. Château de Loei settled on Chenin Blanc as the base for its first commercial wine, released in 1995. Small quantities of red wine, made mainly from Shiraz, were available from the second vintage in 1996. Production has been less than 4,000 cases per vintage, but substantial expansion is planned. Prohibitive taxes and duties on imported wine provide a big incentive to meeting the challenge of growing wine grapes in this part of the tropics. The Siam Winery produces red and white wine under the "Chatemp" label, the red being from the grassy Pok Dum Rouge, the white from Malaga Blanc. A new estate, Domaine Saint-Lo, has planted Cabernet Sauvignon at 300 metres (1,000 feet), and harvests its grapes in February.

United States

U ntil the late 1960s, it was true to say that wine-growing was an exotic activity that had only succeeded in gaining footholds on the fringes of North America. The distribution of all American wine was regulated (as it still is) by the Bureau of Alcohol, Tobacco, and Firearms as though it were an ignitable, if not explosive, substance. Wine-drinking was an infrequent, low-profile, even faintly suspect activity. Prohibition had almost snuffed out the promise of healthy Americans, free of neuroses, freely accepting the happy legacy of Mediterranean culture.

During the past forty years, both the production and consumption of wine have vastly increased. In the world league of wine producers, the USA is now fourth, with California contributing ninety-five per cent to its total, and regularly makes approximately a quarter as much wine as France or Italy, the two giants of the wine world. Imports have soared. The per capita consumption has quadrupled from a mere 2.5 bottles to steady at eleven a year.

The figure is still modest, and the neurosis has not entirely departed, but wine has finally permeated America's soul as an essential part of the good life. Almost every state has aspiring winegrowers; a dozen have a wine industry. But it is the emphasis put on wine in restaurants and hotels, in publications and publicity, which proves that a great change has taken place. America in fact, has at last developed its own wine culture, with its own references, a budding appellation system, rating systems, and indigenous ideas about the use of wine with food. What is more, it is successfully exporting aspects of this new thinking to the rest of the world.

California

It now seems so natural to include California in the shortlist of the world's top winelands that it bears repetition that this status is relatively new. The 1970s was the decade when California decisively took up her position in the world of wine. She had had what proved to be a false start, though a very promising one, a century earlier. An adolescent America was not ready for what she (and wine in general) had to offer. The generation of winemakers that followed the repeal of Prohibition did indispensable groundwork for an industry that appeared to be remarkably friendless. Hardly anyone was prepared for the impact when, in the late 1960s, Americans started to change their habits, to look outwards for new ideas, to start thinking about their environment, their diet, and their health, and to discover that they had a well of the world's most satisfactory beverage in their own backyard.

From the early 1970s on, growth has been so rapid and change so breathless that one of the observers and critics closest to the scene in California, Bob Thompson, has compared an attempt to follow it to "taking a census in a rabbit warren". The figures hardly express the changes. In 1970, there were 220 wineries; in 1982, 591; in 2000, at least 850. (These figures refer only to bricks-and-mortar wineries. In addition, there are shared facilities, and winemakers that lease space. So the number of producers far exceeds those with physical wineries.) By 2000, wine-grape vineyards amounted to around 194,000 hectares (31,000 not yet in production), up from 68,800 in 1970. But beneath these figures, impressive as they are, everything was in ferment: grapes, men, priorities, areas, tanks, and philosophy. They still are.

Predictably, the other-drink businesses – brewers, distillers and soft-drink manufacturers – have moved in to control what they can of the mass-market production, although Gallo, the company that produces far more wine than any other in America, is still run personally by the families of the brothers who started it.

At the other extreme, in what rapidly and rather unkindly became known as boutique wineries, fashion has rocketed about from one winery to another, as drinkers even newer to wine than the winemakers tried to make up their minds what they liked, at the same time as discovering who made it – or if he made it again the following year. The cult of the winemaker is nowhere more developed than in California. A handful of them, and many are women, carry such kudos that any winery hiring them can charge enormous sums for their wines. This is not to cast doubts on the skills of those winemakers, but merely to remark that the prestige of the consultant winemaker counts for more in determining the commercial success of a winery, than such elusive factors as vineyards and terroir.

There are enduring landmarks, but they are few and far between. Essentially, this is an industry with no structure and very few rules.

There are four approaches to finding what you want in California, and you need them all. There is no escaping the dominance of the brand or winery name. The grape variety is the only firm information available about what is in the bottle. The area of production is a good clue to the style of the wine, but not, in many cases, its quality. And the vintage date at least tells you how old it is – and often considerably more. Access to the essentials in this chapter is therefore organized into three alphabetical directories: of wineries and brands, of grapes (and wine types) and of areas.

How good are the wines, and where do they fit into an international comparison?

In the last twenty-odd years, the top class of handmade wines have proved that they can outshine in blind tastings the very European wines they emulate. The reason they do this with almost monotonous predictability is inherent in their nature. It is the fully ripe grape that makes California wines comparable with the great vintages and the best vineyards of Europe.

There are also, however, the rate of ripening and the question of soil to consider. Both of these have more bearing on the long-term quality of wine than California is at present inclined to allow. The concomitant disadvantage of the super-ripe grape is the relentless force of flavour that it gives.

Heartiness suits Americans – at least today's Americans. It suits many wine-drinkers everywhere. The mood may waver, but only briefly. Not long ago, the terms of highest praise were "impressive fruit", "heaps of varietal character", "distinct notes of French oak". There followed a time when "delicacy", "balance", "harmony", and "elegance" became the bywords for quality. That moment turned out to be ephemeral. Within a very few years, "heaps" and "impressive" returned to fashion with greater vigour than before.

The American wine press has a disproportionately large role to play in deciding the fluctuating fortunes of any

Varietals & Varieties

The useful word "varietal" was coined in California as shorthand for a wine that is either made entirely from, or derives its character from, one named grape variety. Up to 1983, the law required that the named variety be a mere fifty-one per cent of the total. From 1983, the requirement is seventy-five per cent. Most high-quality varietals have long been closer to 100 per cent.

On a semantic note, varietal is an epithet that describes a wine. It is not a noun meaning a specific sort of grape. That noun is variety. The Chardonnay grape is a variety; its wine is a varietal wine.

winery. Only in Bordeaux is the wine writer's verdict so eagerly awaited. With hundreds of wineries producing expensive Cabernets from Napa and Sonoma, the poor consumer needs help in making a choice. They can be forgiven for concluding that the wine with the highest score in the wine press is "the best" or "the hottest". The press tends to reward richness and power over finesse. The splendid wines from Mondavi have sometimes won relatively low scores because they are less rich (but often more elegant) than those of their rivals.

The proprietors of a great many California wineries are keen on their wines making a splash in society. Indeed, it is a rare thing to come across an owner whose aspirations lean in the direction of a solid *cru bourgeois*, but an everyday occurrence to find one who wants nothing less than first growth status. Being, in the main, first-generation men and women in wine, these entrepreneurs and their winemakers must respond to the latest sales reports, rather than the voices of their fathers, or the voices of their often new vineyards. If society wants size, size it shall have, and California wine of late has become more top-heavy, and more alcoholic, than ever, with unabashed wines priced to appeal to princes.

Yet, there is a growing band of producers, often small-scale, that have worked a vintage or two in Gevrey-Chambertin or St-Julien, and who are trying to fashion wines with elegance as well as the hallmark lushness of California grapes. But it's not easy. California grape growers may talk of "cool-climate" regions, but California's climate is more Mediterranean than Bordelais or Burgundian.

Personal taste is the final arbiter – as I was reminded when I rashly asked a gathering in New York if they would really like all red Bordeaux to have the character of the great champion of modern vintages, 1961. "Of course," they said. What a fool I must be, not to want the most concentrated, the most overwhelmingly full-flavoured (but the least refreshing) of all wines with every meal. Perhaps they had a point. After all, the 1961 clarets are shy little things in the face of California's most outsized efforts.

The Climate

Since Prohibition ended or, more precisely, since the University of California at Davis became eminent in research, California has looked more to sun than soil for guidance as to where to plant which varieties.

Between 1940 and 1960, scientists at the university developed a system of five climate regions that governed planting in California for several decades, but is now substantially out of use. It was based on cumulative heat during an April 1 to October 31 growing season. The measure is "degree days" (a day's average temperature minus fifty).

The regions approximate roughly to: Burgundy (Region I, up to 2,500 degree days); Bordeaux (Region II, 2,500–3,000 degree days); the Rhône (Region III, 3,000–3,500 degree days); Sherry (Region IV, 3,500–4,000 degree days); and North Africa/Middle East (Region V, over 4,000 degree days).

The system worked well enough to steer growers to Monterey and the Santa Maria Valley in Santa Barbara in the 1970s, but mounting experience with climate regions has shown as many shortcomings as virtues. Chardonnay prospers in several locales where heat says it should not, and Cabernet refuses to ripen at sites where heat says it should.

The Soils

While, in California, the notion of climate regions rules, soil was thought to play a role only in so far as it drained well or poorly. Though a smattering of growers have begun to suspect a great role for it, soil has yet to be treasured in anything like the way it is in Europe.

Progress, to give the devil his due, will be slow. In the coastal counties where fine points matter most, soils are erratic, because California's geologically young Coastal Ranges are endlessly changing. Two examples may suffice.

At the grandest scale, the San Andreas fault marks two separate pieces of the North American tectonic plate. Soils on opposite sides of California's most famous manufacturer of earthquakes can be completely unrelated within a distance of mere inches – most strikingly so in the Santa Cruz Mountains.

On a far smaller level, what is now called the Russian River drained through the Napa Valley into San Francisco Bay, until geological activity caused Mount St Helena to rise, blocking its course, at which point it turned westwards to flow into the Pacific Ocean, leaving the Alexander and Napa Valleys to evolve in different ways.

It must also be remembered that the growers of St-Emilion, of Meursault, of Chianti, have had centuries to work out, essentially by trial and error, which grape varieties are best adapted to which soils. In those corners of California that have been growing grapes for a century or more, it is also possible to point to the best terroirs. But to say that Rutherford is the source of magnificent Cabernet is not the same as to explain why that should be the case.

Terroir, in California as elsewhere, is an infinitely subtle hodgepodge of factors, bundling together climate, soil, subsoil, drainage, wind strength, luminosity, clonal material, and many others. What is remarkable is how much California has achieved with so little understanding of its vineyards. When, in decades to come, that understanding has evolved, and been absorbed into the production of wine, the results could be even more spectacular.

American Viticultural Areas (AVAs)

As climate was losing ground and soil was failing to gain it, American grapegrowers, led by Californians, persuaded the US federal government to establish a rudimentary system of appellations of origin, beginning in the early 1970s. The regulations do nothing more than draw boundaries around more or less homogeneous areas. They imply no degree of quality. They impose no limitations on varieties, nor planting practices, nor yields. Indeed, they permit a wine to carry the area name when up to fifteen per cent of it comes from grapes grown elsewhere.

In spite of all that, the eighty-six California AVAs are proving useful, at least up to a point. They are forcing growers to look at which varieties grow better than others, and to plant them. Carneros and Chardonnay are one case in point, the Russian River Valley and Pinot Noir another. As a result, the viticultural areas are the most useful framework for any *tour d'horizon* of contemporary California.

NB: names with a black dot preceeding them indicate an important AVA. The principal sub-AVAs are then indented below the heading.

North Coast AVA This encompasses most of Lake County, Mendocino, Napa, Sonoma, and Marin, the major wine-growing counties north of San Francisco Bay.

• Napa County/Napa Valley AVA The most concentrated and prestigious region with 14,800 hectares and nearly 300 wineries. The cooler southern tip (Carneros) of a forty-kilometer- (twenty-five mile-) long valley, opens out onto San Francisco Bay. The warmer northern end (Calistoga) is sheltered by landmark Mount St Helena. The towns between, south to north, are Napa, Yountville, Oakville, Rutherford, and St Helena. Diverse soils and climates make it versatile, but history, old and new, favours Cabernet Sauvignon above all other varieties. Recent figures in hectares include: Cabernet Sauvignon (6,350), Merlot (3,000), Pinot Noir (1,150), Sangiovese (225), Syrah (315), Zinfandel (710), Chardonnay (3,320), and Sauvignon Blanc (830).

> **Atlas Peak AVA** Upland Valley AVA east of Stags Leap, recently developed with Sangiovese foremost in mind.

> **Carneros AVA** At the southern end of the valley, and shared with Sonoma County. Designed for Pinot Noir but Chardonnay is the gem, and Merlot and Syrah are coming up. Sparkling wine is a particular strength.

> **Yountville AVA** Valley floor of southern Napa Valley. Rather cool for Cabernet but excellent for Chardonnay.

> **Howell Mountain AVA** In the hills east of St Helena; historic home of Zinfandel, now more planted with Cabernet and Chardonnay.

> **Mount Veeder AVA** In hills west of Napa and Yountville; mostly Cabernet.

> **Rutherford AVA** The heart of the valley, where Cabernet has grown longest, and some would say, best.

> **Oakville AVA** Adjoins Rutherford on the south and extends Cabernet zone, but grows every grape variety from Chardonnay to Zinfandel surprisingly well. No white better than Sauvignon Blanc.

> **St Helena AVA** Adjoins Rutherford on the north; planted mainly with Cabernet Sauvignon.

Spring Mountain AVA The hills west of St Helena grow Cabernet and Chardonnay, and should grow more Riesling.

Diamond Mountain AVA In the hills west of Calistoga. Exceptional for robust Cabernet.

Stags Leap District AVA In the southeast quarter of the valley floor, devoted almost entirely to Cabernet Sauvignon, more supple here than elsewhere in Napa.

Chiles Valley AVA East of Howell Mountain, best for Cabernet and Zinfandel.

Wild Horse Valley AVA East of Carneros, a relatively cool upland valley. Only about fifty hectares planted.

Other AVAs are pending, notably Calistoga and Pope Valley (due north of Chiles, extending to the Lake County line, splendid for Sauvignon Blanc).

• **Sonoma County** Napa's nearest rival both physically and in terms of prestige. Sonoma sits between the Pacific and Napa. It is much larger in area than Napa, and more diverse, geologically and topographically.

There is no blanket AVA covering its 14,600 hectares of vines and 200-plus wineries. Nor is it synonymous with one grape variety. The major players in hectares are: Cabernet Sauvignon (4,600); Merlot (2,960); Pinot Noir (3,960); Syrah (616); Zinfandel (1,970); Chardonnay (6,260); Sauvignon Blanc (800).

Alexander Valley AVA Reaches north from Healdsburg to Mendocino County line; a warm valley, at its best with Cabernet Sauvignon and Zinfandel.

Carneros AVA Sonoma has more than half of the surface area in this, which is shared with Napa, but less than half of the vineyards. *See* Napa.

Dry Creek Valley AVA Ever warmer as it runs northwest from Healdsburg, superbly suited to Zinfandel, and showing promise with both red and white Rhône varieties.

Rockpile AVA Approved in 2002, 65 hectares in coastal hills of northwest Sonoma.

Knights Valley AVA Due north of Calistoga in Napa; mostly Cabernet, most of which goes to wineries outside this sparsely populated region.

Russian River Valley AVA Fog-cooled, broad expanse ranging from Healdsburg, south to Santa Rosa, southwest to Forestville and Sebastopol; shows best with Pinot Noir and Chardonnay for both still and sparkling, yet does well with Zinfandel, too. Sonoma – Green Valley (Chardonnay, sparkling wine) is the cooler sub-AVA of Russian River Valley; Chalk Hill (Chardonnay, Sauvignon) the warmer one. The valley remains best-known for its rich, spicy, and elegant Pinot Noirs, produced with consistent success for over twenty years

Grapes & Generic Wine Names

Alicante Bouschet A red, jug-wine standby, giving density and colour, but a few wineries produce single-varietal versions. 620 hectares.

Barbera High-acid variety planted mostly in hotter San Joaquin Valley for blending. Shows considerable promise in Sierra Foothills. 4,220 hectares.

Burgundy A fading term for any red wine, with the vague implication that it should be dark and full-bodied (unlike real burgundy). California burgundy is usually slightly sweet.

Cabernet Franc Plantings on the rise, especially in North Coast and Santa Barbara; mostly for blending with Cabernet Sauvignon and Merlot, but increasingly for varietals. 1,415 hectares.

Cabernet Sauvignon Makes California's best red: fruity, fragrant, tannic, full-bodied. Needs maturing in oak, and at least four years in bottle. The best comes from the central Napa Valley, parts of Sonoma, and the Santa Cruz Mountains. 29,945 hectares.

Carignane Some old vines survive in field blends in Sonoma and Mendocino, and lesser-quality vineyards in the San Joaquin Valley. Gradually declining. 2,700 hectares.

Carnelian A red crossing introduced in 1973, it added colour but not flavour to blends, and is now in decline.

Chablis Despite justified French protests that this is a part of France, it remains the uninformed American's term for (relatively) dry white wine from California, or anywhere else. Use almost entirely restricted to basic-quality wines.

Charbono Red grape of mysterious origins, giving inky, thick-textured wines. Sometimes made as a varietal.

Chardonnay California's most successful white grape, capable of great wines in the Burgundian tradition with maturation, and sometimes, fermentation in oak. Good judgement is needed not to produce over-intense, ponderous wines (especially in Napa). Parts of Sonoma and the Central Coast (Monterey) tend to have a lighter touch. At its pinnacle in Carneros, Anderson Valley; excels in Russian River Valley, cooler Napa Valley and (in a quirkier way) Edna Valley. Surprisingly good in Ukiah, even Lodi. Huge plantings – too many for use in commodity wines – have made it California's most-planted variety at 41,700 hectares. Problems of over-supply by 2002 meant that some vineyards were being grubbed up.

Chenin Blanc A surprisingly popular, usually rather dull white grape, appreciated for its high crop, good acidity levels, and clean, adaptable flavour. Pleasant when semi-sweet (although best dry); good in blends not needing age. Plantings peaked at 12,500 hectares in 1990; now dropped to 7,280 hectares.

Dolcetto This Piedmontese grape is being attempted by a dozen wineries, but so far they bear little resemblance to the toothsome original.

Flora An over-perfumed white grape that has virtually disappeared as a varietal.

French Colombard High-acid, white, blending variety mostly planted in hotter regions of San Joaquin Valley, where very high yields made it popular. Plantings have dwindled from a peak of 25,000 hectares down to 16,000.

Fumé Blanc *See* Sauvignon Blanc.

Gamay Beaujolais Not the Beaujolais grape, but a form of Pinot Noir. In the process of being phased out. 216 hectares.

Gewürztraminer After a hesitant start, a success in California, where its wine is oddly softer and less spicy than in Alsace.

Most successful in Anderson Valley, nearly as good in Russian River Valley, and parts of Salinas Valley. 620 hectares.

Gray Riesling Not a Riesling but a minor French grape, Chauché Gris, related to the Trousseau of the Jura. Heading for extinction.

Grenache A source of flavourful red or rosé in warmer Monterey areas. Most plantings in San Joaquin, often for port-style wines. Being taken more seriously as part of the Rhône variety revival. 4,430 hectares.

Grignolino Non-recommended red grape, presumably from Italy, used by one or two wineries in cool regions to make off-beat red or rosé.

Johannisberg Riesling (or White Riesling) Despite impressive results in both dry and late-harvest styles in Anderson Valley, Spring Mountain, and parts of Sonoma, Riesling has failed to find appreciation in US markets. 780 hectares.

Malbec Mostly used in California for blending in Meritage styles. Arrowood (*q.v.*) produces the best single-varietal version. Currently 390 hectares.

Malvasia Bianca The common Italian grape, recommended for dessert wines in hotter regions such as southern Monterey but capable of pleasant, soft, table wine in cooler areas. 400 hectares.

Marsanne From Mendocino to Santa Barbara, winemakers are trying their hand at Marsanne. No version has yet risen to great heights. Twenty-four hectares.

Meritage Term concocted, after a competition in 1988, to describe Bordeaux blends from California. By no means universally adopted on labels.

Merlot The Pomerol grape has become a runaway success as a varietal, especially when made bland and priced moderately. 20,770 hectares.

Mission The coarse old local grape of the Franciscan missionaries. Some 310 hectares are left in the hottest regions. A few Sierra Foothills wineries still bottle it, usually semi-sweet or fortified.

Mourvèdre/Mataro No examples of this grape from its Provençal heartland of Bandol can match the centenarian vineyards of Contra Costa County for longevity. The few producers with access to these vineyards make splendid wines.

Muscat or Moscato The best is Muscat de Frontignan or Moscato di Canelli, recommended for white table wines in cooler regions; for dessert wines in hotter areas. Its best production is a sweet, low-alcohol wine so unstable that it must be kept refrigerated. 480 hectares planted. Muscat of Alexandria is a hot-climate grape grown mainly for eating.

Napa Gamay To avoid confusion with Gamay Beaujolais (*q.v.*), this variety, which may have some distant kinship with Gamay itself, has been renamed Valdiguié. 270 hectares.

Nebbiolo Piedmont's noble grape, now up to seventy-five hectares in California. Fog is the very thing it likes best. Few convincing results as yet.

Petit Verdot Not widely planted but much-prized as a component in Bordeaux blends. 330 hectares.

Petite Sirah California's name for a low-grade French grape, Durif, and other equally obscure varieties. Can be intriguing, especially from Sonoma, Napa, and Mendocino, but mostly useful for giving colour and tannin to Rhône-style blends. 1,670 hectares.

Pinot Blanc Similar to a low-key Chardonnay, whether actually Melon (most of the total) or true Pinot Blanc. 355 hectares.

Pinot Gris Some families of Italian descent attempt a version styled like Pinot Grigio, but so far, Oregon has proved far more successful with this grape than California. 1145 hectares.

Pinot Noir Burgundy's red grape is widely regarded as the last great hurdle for California's winemakers – early results were over-strong, heavy, and dull. Recent years have seen increasing success, especially in Russian River Valley, Santa Maria Valley, Carneros, Arroyo Grande, and Santa Lucia Highlands. Much of the annual crop goes to make classic-method sparkling wines. 9,330 hectares.

Port A "generic" name taken from the Old World for sweet dessert wine, which rarely resembles the Portuguese original – although it may well have qualities of its own. Most are made from Zinfandel or Petite Sirah, a handful from the Douro varieties used for genuine port.

Roussanne There were blushes all around when it turned out that some delicious Roussannes from the later 1990s were, in fact, made from mislabelled Viognier vines. Authentic Roussanne grows in San Luis Obispo, with excellent results.

Ruby Cabernet Bred by H. P. Olmo at Davis to give balanced, Cabernet-like wines from warmest climates, it has proved very successful in San Joaquin Valley. Best performances in Monterey, Lodi, Madera. 3,330 hectares.

Sangiovese A new hope in the late 1980s, Tuscany's great red thus far has shown greatest promise in Amador, performing almost as well in Mendocino (Ukiah-Hopland), Sonoma (Alexander Valley), and Napa (Atlas Peak). 1,190 hectares.

Sauvignon Blanc Californians reject, or can't deliver, the New Zealand/Sancerre style, and prefer to oak-age Sauvignon Blanc to produce a Graves-style wine. Mondavi invented the term Fumé Blanc for oaked Sauvignon. Often fresher versions are best, vinified without aspirations to producing a poor-man's Chardonnay. 5,700 hectares.

Sémillon Bordeaux's sweet-wine and Australia's dry-wine grape, little exploited as yet in California, where it is generally too productive. 550 hectares.

Sherry California "sherry" has never achieved the standard of imitation of the Spanish original found in, for example, South Africa. Usually heated to mimic the oxidative character of genuine sherry.

Syrah In 1986, there were only fifty hectares planted across the state; today there are almost 6,000. Syrah flourishes just about everywhere: in Napa, the Sierra Foothills, Paso Robles, and Santa Barbara. Delivers rich, peppery wines of a quality that's improving from year to year.

Thompson Seedless A neutral white table, dessert, and distilling wine grape. Never mentioned on the label, but often present in many jug whites and *charmat* sparklers. Grown mostly for raisins; about one-third of its crop is crushed for wine such as "sherry".

Viognier Rhône Rangers couldn't resist trying their hand at this tricky grape. A handful succeed, but many California Viogniers are either too oaky or too alcoholic. 720 hectares.

Zinfandel California's own red grape, of Croatian origin, and identical to the Italian Primitivo. Immensely successful and popular for all levels of wine, from cheap blends to fresh, light versions, and to galumphing, sticky blackstrap. The best have excellent balance, a lively raspberry flavour and ample backbone. "White" (blush) Zinfandel is a commercial smash hit. 20,120 hectares.

Sonoma Valley AVA Stretches from Santa Rosa south through Kenwood and Glen Ellen to Sonoma town, where it opens to San Francisco Bay, without declaring a particular variety as premier. Cabernet-dominated Sonoma Mountain is a sub-AVA to Sonoma Valley; also, Sonoma Valley overlaps Sonoma's portion of Carneros.

Northern Sonoma AVA Covers all of the Russian River drainage. Sonoma Coast AVA is another catch-all, but includes some vineyards high in the coastal range that are proving excellent for Chardonnay and Pinot Noir.

● **Mendocino County/Mendocino AVA** Directly north of Sonoma County, Mendocino – and the Mendocino AVA – are splendidly schizophrenic. The region from Redwood Valley south through Ukiah and Hopland is warmer and drier than any part of Sonoma, but over a markedly shorter season.

The coastward Anderson Valley is as cool and rainy as California grape-growing areas can be. The county has about forty wineries and 5,670 hectares under vine. Principal varieties are: Cabernet Sauvignon (980 hectares); Zinfandel (770); Chardonnay (1,900); Sauvignon Blanc (295). Despite being rather thinly planted, Gewürztraminer (78) and Riesling (17) are important in Anderson Valley.

Anderson Valley AVA Anchored on Boonville on the cool west side of the county, the valley has made some of California's most extraordinary dry Gewürztraminer, long-lived Chardonnay, and Champagne-like sparkling wines, since its revival in the late 1960s.

McDowell Valley AVA A tiny, essentially one-winery area in the southeast corner of the county, which does well with Rhône varieties, red and white.

Potter Valley AVA A sparsely settled, upland valley northeast of Ukiah, which sends most of its grapes elsewhere. Chardonnay currently appears to lead.

Redwood Valley AVA Warm, inland area north of Ukiah, best for Cabernet and Petite Sirah.

Mendocino Ridge AVA Recently approved AVA between Anderson Valley and the Pacific, limited to vineyards high in the coastal mountains.

Minor Mendocino AVAs are Cole Valley and Yorkville Highlands.

● **Lake County AVA** North of Napa, east of Mendocino, Lake County is the smallest, warmest, and driest grape-growing region on the North Coast. Primary plantings in its 2,800 hectares of vineyard are: Cabernet Sauvignon (1,155), Chardonnay (280), and, most brilliant to date, Sauvignon Blanc (555).

Clear Lake AVA The majority of plantings (1,250 hectares) surround the lake that gives the county its name. From Lakeport to Middletown is where Sauvignon Blanc excels.

Guenoc Valley AVA A townless one-winery fiefdom bordering on Napa, where Cabernet is the prize, Chardonnay the surprise.

Benmore Valley AVA A small, high-elevation Chardonnay zone.

● **Central Coast** Where the North Coast is a compact though woozy 2:1 rectangle, the Central Coast is a scaled-down imitation of Chile, a 560 kilometre- (350 mile-) long snake-thin strip, running from southern San Francisco Bay all the way to Santa Barbara County. The principal wine-growing counties it includes are, north to south, Monterey, San Luis Obispo, and Santa Barbara, with Alameda and San Benito counties playing supporting roles.

● **Santa Barbara County** Significant viticulture has only been established here since the early 1970s, yet in this short career, Santa Barbara has begun to emerge as a distinctive region in its own right. It still has fewer than fifty wineries, and some 8,000 hectares of vines, with Chardonnay (3,680) and Pinot Noir (1,060) primary among them. The county is also showing great promise for Syrah (370) and Merlot (410).

Santa Maria Valley AVA Sea-fog-cooled, true east to west valley, running inland from the town of Santa Maria. Memorable, above all, for Pinot Noir.

Santa Ynez Valley AVA Pinot Noir excels in a fog-cooled stretch from Lompoc to Buellton; Cabernet, Sauvignon Blanc, and (unaccountably) Riesling, prevail in a sunnier and much warmer zone inland of Buellton, around Solvang and Los Olivos County.

Santa Rita Hills AVA Approved in 2001, this cool area lies at the western end of Santa Ynez Valley.

● **San Luis Obispo County** The county has a long history, mostly with Zinfandel, a durable presence in hills west of Paso Robles. Diversity arrived with the wine boom of the 1970s in the form of both more varieties and more growing regions, especially down on the cool plain stretching south from San Luis Obispo town. The county has sixty-four wineries, and more than 9,700 hectares of vines. Cabernet Sauvignon (2,890 hectares), Syrah (725), and Zinfandel (895) dominate red plantings. Chardonnay is the main white (1,725). Other than the AVAs listed below, there is a minor hill region called York Mountain.

Arroyo Grande AVA Based in the eponymous town at the southernmost corner of the county, Arroyo Grande was planted for sparkling wine, but still Pinot Noir and Chardonnay are now dominant.

Edna Valley AVA Lies between the towns of San Luis Obispo and Arroyo Grande; planted almost entirely with Chardonnay.

Paso Robles AVA Mountain-sheltered, relentlessly sunny, high inland valley; the hills west of Paso Robles town continue to produce heady Zinfandel; the rolling plain east of that town is newly famous for soft Cabernet. Muscat Blanc is an undiscovered treasure, Rhône varieties a hope for the future.

● **Monterey County/Monterey AVA** Monterey blossomed in the late 1960s as an easy answer to urban pressures on old vineyards in Alameda and Santa Clara counties, and then exploded in plantings in the early 1970s to a peak of 15,000 hectares. Most of the vines are in the Salinas Valley from Gonzales down through Soledad and Greenfield to King City. For lack of local wineries, most of the grapes go elsewhere as the basis of "Coastal" commodity wines. Leading grape varieties are Chardonnay and Cabernet Sauvignon. Also Merlot, Pinot Noir, Sauvignon Blanc.

Arroyo Seco AVA The floor of the Salinas Valley between Soledad and Greenfield grows whites well, especially lightsome Chardonnay.

Carmel Valley AVA Monterey's only ocean-facing district, with sheltered vineyards that grow some dark, intriguing Cabernet on high ground, where sea fog seldom reaches.

Chalone AVA High in the Gavilan Mountains above the east side of the Salinas Valley at Soledad is a virtual monopoly of Chalone Vineyards (*q.v.*).

Santa Lucia Highlands AVA The west hills of the Salinas Valley, from Gonzales down to Greenfield, recently planted, yet already producing some exquisite Pinot Noir.

Two other minor AVAs are Hames Valley and San Lucas.

● **Alameda County** Urban expansion has made the historic Livermore Valley virtually the last redoubt of grapes in the county. Livermore is the main wine town, Pleasanton its satellite. Leading varieties among a total 600 hectares: Chardonnay (242), Cabernet Sauvignon (140), Merlot (55), Sauvignon Blanc (28). San Francisco Bay AVA is a catch-all for Alameda County and the area south of San Francisco.

Livermore Valley AVA East of San Francisco Bay, anchored on the town of Livermore, Sauvignon Blanc, and Sémillon make inimitable wines in an historic district, but do not reign because Chardonnay rules the market.

● **Santa Clara/Santa Cruz Counties** In the nineteenth century, when Almaden and Paul Masson were powers, Santa Clara rivalled Napa, but those palmy times long since have given way to silicon in chips. Very little remains, but what does falls mostly within the well-regarded Santa Cruz Mountains AVA.

Santa Cruz Mountains AVA Encompasses parts of, from north to south, San Mateo, Santa Clara, and Santa Cruz counties. Acreage here is tiny and, owing to vine diseases, dwindling to around 330 hectares, tended by forty producers.

There are quite a few minor AVAs: Santa Clara Valley; San Ysidro, to the east of Gilroy; and Ben Lomond. Hecker Pass, west of Gilroy, never has attained AVA status, and likely will not, as housing supplants the few vineyards.

● **San Benito County** In its heyday, Almaden planted vines on several thousands of acres in San Benito, and successfully lobbied for some new AVAs to encompass them before abandoning them and the region. Most of the AVAs (and some of the vineyards) have fallen into disuse. Currently, only one AVA flourishes: Mount Harlan. The others are Cienega Valley, Lime Kiln Valley, Pacheco Pass, and Paicines.

Mount Harlan AVA High in the Gavilan Mountains and the fiefdom of Calera Winery (*q.v.*), Mount Harlan almost backs onto the similar fiefdom of Chalone (*q.v.*).

● **South Coast AVA** Covers the subtropical to desertous counties south of the Techachapi Mountains, most notably Riverside, where Temecula's 565 hectares dominate the region. Scattered small plantings are in Los Angeles, Orange, and San Diego counties, larger ones in San Bernardino (where historic Cucamonga is fading towards extinction as a growing area, due to urban pressure from Los Angeles).

San Pasqual AVA A one-vineyard AVA east of San Diego, too often beset with Pierce's Disease to have declared itself.

Temecula AVA In the southwest corner of Riverside County, along San Diego County's north boundary. Pioneered in the late 1960s, versatile in a modest way, with

André Tchelistcheff & the Consultants

Long before his death, aged ninety-two, in 1994, the California wine world had silently and unanimously bestowed the title of its "dean" on André Tchelistcheff. Born in Russia and trained in France, his career spanned the whole history of the industry, from Prohibition to the current decade; for thirty-six years (1937–73) at Beaulieu and thereafter, as consultant to many of the best wineries all over California and beyond. He threw out, or revamped, outdated winery equipment, introduced cold fermentation for white wines and malolactic for reds, and in the early 1940s introduced the idea of ageing red wine in small oak barrels. His "Reserve Cabernet" from top Rutherford vineyards, named after Georges de Latour, has served as a model for California winemakers ever since. Among the many winemakers who were at least partly trained by him, are the late Joe Heitz, Mike Grgich of Grgich Hills, Warren Winiarski of Stag's Leap, Richard Peterson of Folie à Deux, and Judy Matulich-Weitz.

Today, there is a new band of consultant oenologists whose usually well-publicized contribution confers instant cachet on any wine they help to produce. They tend to be experts in viticulture as well as winemaking, and are often no slouches when it comes to marketing either. At present, some of the names to conjure with are: Helen Turley, Heidi Peterson Barrett, Philippe Melka, Tom Eddy, and Marco diGiulio.

several of its twenty producers beginning to look beyond Chardonnay and Sauvignon to Rhône and/or Italian red varieties for a new lift. Pierce's Disease has destroyed many vineyards since the late 1990s.

• **The Interior** The huge San Joaquin Valley – modestly supplemented by the minnow Sacramento Valley – is California's Midi. Huge volume is generally the watchword in, from north to south, San Joaquin, Stanislaus, Madera, Fresno, and Kern counties. A few particular areas give definition; quickly sketched, they are:

Lodi AVA A low-lying, rich-soiled, reliably sunny part of San Joaquin County, at the mouth of the San Joaquin Valley. Long famous for Zinfandel, and more recently, a source of large volumes of reliable Chardonnay, Cabernet Sauvignon, and Merlot for, in particular, blending into commodity wines.

Clarksburg AVA In many ways a westward extension of Lodi into the Sacramento River delta. It grows a Chenin Blanc of more character than most in California, but plantings have turned towards Chardonnay in answer to a booming market.

Dunnigan Hills AVA Success by the pioneer R. H. Phillips winery is drawing other growers into a nascent region, just in the lee of the Coastal Ranges, near the Sacramento County town of Woodside. Chardonnay is important by hectarage, Sauvignon Blanc by result.

• **Sierra Foothills AVA** The AVA covers nearly all of the vineyards in four counties: Amador, Calaveras, El Dorado, and Yuba. Amador, at the centre, has unbroken history going back to the Gold Rush. Area under vine is modest (2,020 hectares) with Zinfandel dominant. Small wineries rule.

El Dorado AVA Covers all of the vineyards in the eponymous county. One centre is in the hills north and east of Placerville. Rhône and Italian varieties have replaced Bordeaux in the hearts of many growers. Most of the other plantings in the region circling around Somerset, are virtual extensions of Amador's Shenandoah Valley.

Shenandoah Valley-California AVA The historic heart of Gold Country wine-growing stretches eastward from Plymouth to Fiddletown. It has made its fame with heady Zinfandels. Here too, Syrah and Sangiovese are quickly becoming the new challengers.

Fiddletown AVA Anchored on the village of Fiddletown, is an eastward, more elevated extension of the Shenandoah Valley.

Leading Napa Valley Producers

It is a dull (and unusual) week in California when another new winery does not announce itself. All it takes is a hectare or two of vines, some leased facilities at a neighbour's winery, a label, a salesman, and a good review in the American wine press.

Specifically, each entry below states (if the information was available) the location of the winery, its ownership, vineyards owned (if any), website, and a brief description and assessment.

Inevitably, there are omissions, but the following entries include all the major players, the top-quality producers, and a selection of smaller, but quirky or interesting estates or labels.

Acacia Winery ☆☆–☆☆☆
Napa. Owner: see Chalone. 20 hectares. www.acaciawinery.com
Acacia Pinot Noir has exciting qualities of freshness, the berry smell and soft texture of burgundy – clear indication, since reinforced, that the Carneros district is right for the variety. In 1999, Acacia revived vineyard-designated Pinots, a practice abandoned some years earlier in favour of blends. An immediate leap in quality was evident. Fine as Acacia's Pinots are, its Chardonnays should not be overlooked.

S. Anderson Vineyard
Yountville. Owners: the Signorello family. 18 hectares. www.4bubbly.com
Carole and the late Dr Stanley Anderson founded their vineyard and winery in the 1970s, intending to make nothing but estate Chardonnay and classic-method sparkling wines.

With the slump in sparkling wine sales, production diminished, although quality remained high. In 2002, Carole Anderson sold the property to the Signorellos (*q.v.*).

Araujo ☆☆☆☆
Calistoga. Owner: Bart Araujo. 16 hectares. www.araujoestatewines.com
In the early 1990s, Bart Araujo bought one of the Napa's most famous vineyards, Eisele, and began producing the wine under his own label. The Cabernet remains a Napa classic, and there is splendid Syrah, too.

Artesa ☆☆
Napa. Owner: Codorníu S.A.. 70 hectares. www.artesawinery.com
The second major sparkling wine producer, established in Carneros by a Spanish cava house, Codorníu Napa is bold in architecture (glasshouse modern) but cautious in style. In the late 1990s, it changed its name from Codorníu, at the same time that it decreased sparkling wine production in favour of still wines from Chardonnay, Pinot Noir, and Merlot.

Atlas Peak Vineyards ☆
Napa. Majority owner: Piero Antinori. 200 hectares. www.atlaspeak.com
The first serious effort to make Napa Valley into Sangiovese as well as Cabernet country was spearheaded by Piero Antinori and his co-investors. Antinori selected the Sangiovese strain from Montalcino, yet it has taken many years for high-quality wines to emerge, and then only in the case of the reserves. "Consenso" is a Sangiovese/Cabernet blend, and there is also a Merlot.

Beaulieu Vineyards ☆–☆☆☆
Rutherford. Owner: Diageo. 485 hectares. www.bvwines.com
Founded by a French family, the de Latours, B.V. (as it

is familiarly known) set the pace in the Napa Valley throughout the 1940s, 1950s, and 1960s under a winemaker of genius, the late Russian-born André Tchelistcheff. At Beaulieu, he pioneered small-barrel ageing and malolactic fermentation for reds, cold fermentations for whites, and was one of the first to discover the virtues of the Carneros region for cool-climate varieties.

After the founding family sold to Heublein in 1969, and Tchelistcheff retired in 1973, Beaulieu went into a long period of drift. But by the late 1990s, there were signs of revival. There are many different ranges of wines. At the top are the reserves (including Carneros Chardonnay, the "Tapestry" Bordeaux blend, and Tchelistcheff's legacy, the Georges de Latour Private Reserve Cabernet Sauvignon). Also of interest is the "Signet Collection" of limited-production wines, often from Rhône or Italian varieties. In the middle is an extensive grouping of Napa Valley varietals, led by a vibrant Sauvignon Blanc. At the low end of the price scale is the "Coastal" line.

Beringer Vineyards ☆☆–☆☆☆
St Helena. Owner: Mildara-Blass. 1,000 hectares.
www.beringerblass.com
One of the great old stone-built wineries of Napa, with coolie-cut tunnels into the hills as its original cellars. Under the Beringers it declined, was bought in 1969 by Nestlé, which fixed it on an upward course. The late winemaker, Myron Nightingale, set a quiet, even reserved style after 1969. His specialty was a sweet Sauvignon made from grapes artificially botrytized. His successor, Ed Sbragia, who took over in 1984, favours bold wines. It was Sbragia who introduced the excellent barrique-aged "Private Reserves" from Cabernet, Chardonnay, and Merlot. The next range down is the "Appellation Collection" from North Coast grapes, while the more basic "Founder's Reserve" consists of varietal wines with the California appellation. Quality is remarkably consistent at all levels.

Biale ☆☆☆
Napa. Owners: the Biale family and partners. 3 hectares
This small winery bottles up to nine Zinfandels, one from its own Aldo's Vineyard (planted 1937), the others from outstanding old vineyards in Napa and Sonoma. Highly consistent.

Bouchaine ☆
Napa. Owner: Gerret Copeland and co-investors. 42 hectares.
www.bouchaine.com
Copeland was one of several Delaware businessmen who founded Bouchaine in an 1895 winery building in 1981. There has been some lack of direction, but today Bouchaine produces mostly Carneros Chardonnay, as well as Pinot Noir.

Bryant Family Vineyard ☆☆☆
Calistoga. Owner: Don Bryant. 4 hectares
One of Napa's cult Cabernets, immensely sweet and rich, selling for astonishingly high prices.

Buehler Vineyards ☆
St Helena. Owner: John Buehler. 26 hectares.
www.buehlervineyards.com
Since 1978, Buehler has been producing a wide range of wines; the "California Series" is made from purchased grapes.

Burgess Cellars ☆☆–☆☆☆
St Helena. Owner: Tom Burgess. 48 hectares.
www.burgesscellars.com
This often underrated winery has for many years been producing robust Cabernet Sauvignon and vibrant Zinfandel. "Bell Canyon Cellars" is a second label.

Cain Cellars ☆☆☆
St Helena. Owners: the Meadlock family. 34 hectares.
www.cainfive.com
"Cain Five" is an ambitious and solidly structured Bordeaux-style blend using estate and neighbouring Spring Mountain grapes. "Cain Cuvée" is its declassified, good-value sibling. The exotic Sauvignon is from Monterey plantings of the Musqué strain.

Cakebread Cellars ☆☆☆
Oakville. Owners: the Cakebread family. 33 hectares.
www.cakebread.com
The Cakebreads gained a good reputation for their weighty, dry Sauvignon Blanc. But the Cabernets are of much greater interest, especially those made from selected parcels: "Rutherford Reserve", "Three Sisters", and "Benchland Select". Fine quality, but expensive.

Cardinale ☆☆☆
Oakville. Owner: Jess Jackson. 85 hectares.
www.cardinale.com
A Jackson label, drawing on mountain vineyards in Napa and Sonoma. Very rich, and expensive, Cabernet/Merlot blends.

Carneros Creek Winery ☆
Napa. Owners: Francis Mahoney and Bill Hambrecht.
70 hectares. www.carneros-creek.com
A Carneros winery at the southern end of the Napa Valley that caused a sensation with its first Pinot Noir. The 1977 was the best I had tasted in California, with the combined velvet and carpentry of very good burgundy. Mahoney has worked closely with the University of California to isolate the best clones of Pinot Noir. Today the wines excite only at the top level. There are three tiers: the light "Fleur de Carneros"; the "Blue Label"; and the excellent "Signature Reserve".

Caymus Vineyards ☆☆–☆☆☆
Rutherford. Owner and winemaker: Chuck Wagner. 26 hectares. www.caymus.com
Caymus used to produce a wide range of wines, but by 2000, Wagner was focusing almost exclusively on Cabernet, especially the sleek and highly acclaimed "Special Selection". The Sauvignon Blanc is being phased out, and the successful white blend, "Conundrum", will be produced at a different facility. *See* also Mer Soleil (*q.v.*).

Chappellet ☆☆☆
St Helena. Owner: Donn Chappellet. 48 hectares.
www.chappellet.com
Donn Chappellet was the second man, behind Robert Mondavi, to build a new winery in the Napa. He has long been renowned for his deep-flavoured, austere, built-to-last Cabernet Sauvignon, from the uppermost slopes of his amphitheatrical vineyards.

In recent years, there have been two Cabernets. One, subtitled "Pritchard Hill", is approachable early. The other, "Donn Chappellet Signature", upholds the original premise and fulfils the original promise. Cabernet Franc is excellent and Chardonnay long-maturing. Chappellet is also one of the few reliable sources for dry, firm, long-flavoured Chenin Blanc as well as an extraordinary *moelleux*. A remarkable range includes Chardonnay, which ages admirably; big, easy, and charming Cabernet Franc; and an intense Chenin Blanc *moelleux*.

Chateau Montelena ☆☆–☆☆☆☆

Calistoga. Owner: Jim Barrett. 40 hectares. www.montelena.com
Old stone winery, north of Calistoga, at the foot of Mount St Helena, which has a thirty-year record of some of the best California Chardonnays and Cabernets from the estate vineyard. The Napa wines and their drinkers tend to be richer.

Two distinguished winemakers have set the style here: Mike Grgich up to 1974, followed by Jerry Luper up to 1981. Since 1981, Bo Barrett has maintained the highest quality. The Chardonnay, lean with very little new oak, is atypical of most from Napa, and much fresher. The "Calistoga Cuvée", from purchased grapes, is a much cheaper alternative to the costly Cabernet.

Chateau Potelle ☆–☆☆

**Mt Veeder. Owners: the Fourmeaux family. 120 hectares.
www.chateaupotelle.com**
Jean-Noël and Marketta Fourmeaux du Sartel came to California as agents of the French government, to measure California's wine industry. They liked what they saw enough to join up, beginning as négociants, and eventually buying vineyards and a winery high on Mount Veeder. They also buy in fruit from Paso Robles. Quality is inconsistent, but the best wines usually appear under the cryptic "VGS" label.

Chateau Woltner

Howell Mountain. Owner: Ladera Vineyards. 22 hectares
Françoise Woltner and Francis Dewavarin-Woltner sold their share of Haut-Brion in Bordeaux, and bought an old, long-idle Napa winery property called Nouveau Médoc in order to make… you guessed it, Chardonnay. They divided their high-elevation property into four vineyards, usually bottled separately. Their standards were rigorous, and the prices punishing. In 2000, they accepted that Howell Mountain was not really Chardonnay territory, and sold up.

Chimney Rock ☆☆–☆☆☆

**Stags Leap District, Napa. Owners: Stella Wilson and Terlato
Wine Group. 53 hectares. www.chimneyrock.com**
Winemaker Doug Fletcher's silky Cabernet epitomizes its region of origin. The winery's decision to source Chardonnay grapes from Carneros recognizes how fully attuned to Cabernet the Stags Leap District is. The founder, hotelier Sheldon Wilson, died in 2001.

Clos du Val ☆☆–☆☆☆

Napa. Owner: John Goelet. 120 hectares. www.closduval.com
Winemaker Bernard Portet was brought up at Château Lafite, where his father was manager. As in Bordeaux, he blends Merlot with Cabernet. His wines are reckoned supple by Napa standards, but they are still deep-coloured, juicy, and long on the palate. They can age beautifully. His Zinfandel is as strapping as they come, but Pinot Noir and Chardonnay tend to be less assured. Taltarni in Victoria, Australia, has the same owner.

Clos Pegase ☆☆

Napa. Owner: Jan Shrem. 140 hectares. www.clospegase.com
A major architectural competition was won by the American architect Michael Graves. The resulting winery is Napa's most striking post-modernist building to date, and it is also home to Shrem's imposing modern art collection. It produces steadily improving Chardonnay, Merlot, and Cabernet.

Colgin ☆☆☆

Oakville. Owners: the Colgin family. 3 hectares
Renowned for an extremely expensive, new-oaked Cabernet Sauvignon.

Corison ☆☆☆

St Helena. Owner: Cathy Corison. 4 hectares. www.corison.com
As winemaker at Chappellet from 1980 to 1989, Corison helped to solidify Chappellet Vineyard's reputation before launching out on her own. She makes nothing but Cabernet Sauvignon, in a rich but elegant style.

Cosentino ☆

**Yountville. Owner: Mitch Cosentino. 26 hectares.
www.cosentinowinery.com**
Cosentino buys in grapes from all over the North Coast and offers the countless visitors to his tasting room a wide range of wines. Many are excellent, but they are not always consistent.

Robert Craig Wine Cellars ☆☆☆

Napa. Owner: Robert Craig. 8 hectares. www.robertcraigwine.com
Craig specializes in rich, Cabernet-dominated blends from the mountains around Napa Valley.

Cuvaison ☆☆–☆☆☆

**Calistoga. Owners: the Schmidheiny family. 182 hectares.
www.cuvaison.com**
The winery took on its present form in 1979, when the Swiss Schmidheiny family bought the business. They bought a large vineyard property in Carneros and installed John Thacher as winemaker; both proved to be shrewd moves. Chardonnay remains the star turn, especially the reserve bottlings, but Cuvaison also produces very good Merlot and Pinot Noir.

Dalla Valle ☆☆☆–☆☆☆☆

Napa. Owner: Naoko Dalla Valle. 10 hectares
Massive wines from hillside vineyards have acquired cult status. The Cabernet and the Bordeaux blend called "Maya" are particularly sought-after and terribly expensive, and there's a good Sangiovese, too.

Darioush ☆☆–☆☆☆

**Napa. Owner: Darioush Khaledi. 16 hectares.
www.darioushwinery.com**
An ambitious new property, founded by Iranian-born supermarket tycoon Darioush Khaledi. Initial releases of Chardonnay, Cabernet, Viognier, and Shiraz are highly promising. The reserve wines are bottled under the "Signature" label.

Diamond Creek Vineyards ☆☆☆

**Calistoga. Owner: Al Brounstein. 9 hectares.
www.diamondcreekvineyards.com**
The Cabernet from these four small vineyards – Volcanic

Hill, Red Rock Terrace, Gravelly Meadow, and Lake – reflects four different soils and situations, a subject little enough studied in California. They are all big, tough, wildly expensive wines, designed for long ageing, and repaying it. Cabernet Franc, Malbec, and Merlot are added to the predominant Cabernet Sauvignon.

Domaine Carneros ☆☆

Carneros, Napa. Co-owners: Taittinger and Kobrand. 80 hectares. www.domaine.com

The winery, a pastiche of Taittinger's French château, makes a startling intrusion into the Carneros landscape; the wines, however, are a more graceful hybrid of Taittinger style and Carneros grapes. Still wines, especially Pinot Noir, are growing in volume at the expense of sparkling wines.

Domaine Chandon ☆☆

Yountville. Owner: LVMH. 445 hectares. www.domainechandon.com

The spearhead of France's invasion of California, a characteristically stylish and successful outpost of Moët in Champagne. A wine factory and an entertainment at the same time, with a first-class fashionable restaurant. All of the wines are excellent: the "Reserve Cuvée" is a show-stopper; "Etoile" is an intriguing blend of older vintages. Out of context in Europe, the sheer fruitiness of the Napa grapes makes the wines taste rather sweet, even though they are substantially drier than most *brut* Champagnes.

Dominus ☆☆☆

Yountville. Owner: Christian Moueix. 50 hectares. www.dominusestate.com

The maker of Pétrus found his ideal Napa vineyard (ex-Inglenook) in the early 1980s. Applying Bordeaux techniques made his wines massive but unfriendly at first. Since 1991, Dominus has relaxed enough to rank just below Napa's very best Cabernets, and fine-tuning continues.

Duckhorn Vineyards ☆☆☆

St Helena. Owner: Dan Duckhorn. 34 hectares. www.duckhornvineyards.com

Duckhorn is best-known for his splendid Merlots, which he was producing long before the variety became so fashionable. The Cabernet and Sauvignon Blanc are excellent, too. In recent years, Duckhorn has been expanding, not in Napa, but in cooler Mendocino, where it will be producing Pinot Noir from the Goldeneye Estate.

Dunn Vineyards ☆☆☆–☆☆☆☆

Howell Mountain. Owner: Randall Dunn. 10 hectares

Since 1979, this ex-Caymus winemaker has been making small lots of dark, stern Cabernet, both from his own Howell Mountain vineyards, and from purchased fruit.

Etude

Napa. Owner: Beringer Blass. No vineyards

Consulting winemaker Soter started making wines under the "Etude" label, almost as much to showcase his technical ability to potential clients as for commercial reasons. Soter's strength lies in Pinot Noir from Carneros, using varied clonal material. The company was bought in 2001 by Beringer Blass.

Evensen Vineyards ☆

Oakville. Owner: Richard Evensen. 2 hectares

Specializes in a sometimes admirable Gewürztraminer, as well as Chardonnay.

Far Niente ☆☆☆

Oakville. Owner: Gil Nickel. 95 hectares. www.farniente.com

A famous pre-Prohibition name, reborn in its original stone building, with its old vineyard replanted and now bearing fruit. Dirk Hampson has been here as winemaker since 1983, turning out extravagant, toasty Chardonnays; sumptuous, oaky Cabernets; and "Dolce", a sweet wine, modelled, ambitiously, on Yquem.

Robert Mondavi

Only the brothers Gallo have rivalled Robert Mondavi as a force in California winemaking, and they cannot match Mondavi when it comes to innovation.

When he left his family's Charles Krug winery to start his own company in 1966, he created the first new Napa winery of modern times. It was often forgotten what courage this took, and Mondavi came close to financial disaster, until a lawsuit decided in his favour, and this allowed him to put his fledgling winery on a more secure footing. Mondavi immediately established himself as a relentless experimenter on all fronts, and resolute champion of the Napa Valley as the New World's greatest wine region.

The mock-Franciscan mission winery buildings at Oakville still house endless experiments. Of the daunting quantities of Napa wine for sale under the Robert Mondavi name, the Cabernet Sauvignons (and now the Pinot Noirs too) trumpet his successes loudest, none more so than his gentle-but-gigantic reserves. Fumé Blanc (his globally accepted coinage for oaked Sauvignon Blanc) is a Californian style single-handedly created by Mondavi.

And yet these, and other wines under his name, are but the tip of the Mondavi iceberg. As an octogenarian, Robert presses on in ever-multiplying directions. Except for a brief pause in his seventy-sixth year (1989) to replace his worn-out, God-given knees with new, artificial ones, he maintains to this day a pace that would fell a marathon-runner.

In 1979 he brought the prestige of a Bordeaux first growth to Napa, when Baron Philippe de Rothschild became his partner in "Opus One". In 1995, in a reverse gesture, he joined his own name with that of the Frescobaldis in Tuscany. In between, he turned Mondavi-Woodbridge into a formidable player in the low-priced field; acquired more than 400 hectares of vineyard and the Byron Winery in Santa Barbara County; turned his company from private to a publicly owned corporation; became a partner in a Chilean winery; and acquired the Arrowood winery (*q.v.*) in Sonoma. Who could know what else he might have accomplished were he not on the road so much of every year, promoting wine to the world, as the beverage of civilization?

Flora Springs ☆☆–☆☆☆

St Helena. Owners: the Komes and Garvey families. 242 hectares. www.florasprings.com

After some years courting delicacy, especially in the Sauvignons, Flora Springs has turned gutsy in every wine on the list, especially in the reserve Cabernets from Rutherford, and the Bordeaux blend called "Trilogy". The latest project is a Supertuscan-style wine called "Poggio del Papa".

Folie à Deux ☆

St Helena. Owners: Dr. Richard Peterson & partners. 3 hectares. www.folieadeux.com

The current owners took over in 1995, and hired Scott Harvey as winemaker. He was a fan of old-vine Zinfandels from the Sierra Foothills, and has added a few splendid single-vineyard examples to the range here. The other wines tend to be rather light and simple.

Forman ☆☆☆

St Helena. Owner/winemaker: Ric Forman. 32 hectares

The former Sterling winemaker uses grapes from his own hill vineyards, and others down at Rutherford, to make classic "French-style" Chardonnay and Cabernet.

Franciscan ☆☆–☆☆☆

Rutherford. Owner: Constellation. 210 hectares. www.franciscan.com

With magnificently located vineyards in Rutherford and Oakville, it's hardly surprising that the winery is often at its peak with reds, most especially Cabernet Sauvignon and a Bordeaux blend called "Magnificat". Franciscan also has a fine reputation for "Cuvée Sauvage Chardonnay", fermented with natural yeasts. Other properties in the Franciscan group are Mount Veeder (*q.v.*), and Estancia (730 hectares in Monterey and Paso Robles). It was the Huneeus family that built up Franciscan's reputation in the 1990s, and it will be interesting to see if the new corporate owners can maintain that quality.

Freemark Abbey ☆☆–☆☆☆

St Helena. Owner: Legacy Estates Group. 120 hectares. www.freemarkabbey.com

This famous winery was established in an abandoned nineteenth century stone winery, just north of St Helena, by a group of leading Napa grape-growers. One partner (Brad Webb) had made history by pioneering small barrels at Hanzell (*q.v.*) in the late 1950s. The partners soon built up an excellent reputation for Chardonnay, and for rich Cabernets, none more so than an outstandingly concentrated and balanced wine from a Rutherford grower called Bosché (and so labelled). In 1973, they pioneered sweet, botrytized Riesling, labelled "Edelwein". In 2001, the ageing partners sold the property.

Frog's Leap Wine Cellars ☆☆☆

Rutherford. Owner: John Williams. 55 hectares. www.frogsleap.com

Originally a partnership located on the site of the one-time frog farm that led to the name, it is now solely owned, and has moved to drier land at Rutherford. But the wines, especially the Cabernet and Zinfandel, remain everything they were when the winery was earning its reputation. John Williams remains untainted by Napa glitz, and his wines, from organically cultivated vineyards, are balanced and immensely pleasurable. Perhaps it helps that Williams has one of the best senses of humour in Napa. Evidence: a white blend called "Leapfrogmilch", now, alas, discontinued.

Green and Red Vineyard ☆☆–☆☆☆

St Helena. Owner: Jay Heminway. 11 hectares

Tiny Chiles Valley winery that specializes in intense Zinfandel and Chardonnay.

Grgich Hills Cellars ☆☆–☆☆☆

Rutherford. Owners: Austin Hills and Mike Grgich. 100 hectares. www.grgich.com

Croatian by birth, Grgich has been making wine in Napa Valley since the early 1960s, notably at Beaulieu and Chateau Montelena. His forte is Chardonnay, but the Cabernet and Zinfandel are consistently good.

Groth ☆☆

Oakville. Owner: Dennis Groth. 66 hectares. www.grothwines.com

Groth shot to fame when Robert Parker awarded its 1985 Cabernet reserve a perfect score. But the stellar quality has been hard to maintain, and subsequent vintages of Chardonnay and Cabernet have been very good, but far from spectacular.

Hagafen Cellars ☆

Napa. Owner: Ernie Weir. No vineyards. www.hagafen.com

The original and still one of the leading producers of kosher wines from classic *vinifera* varieties.

Harlan Estate ☆☆☆☆

Oakville. Owner: Bill Harlan. 12 hectares. www.harlanestates.com

Bill Harlan founded the Merryvale winery, and established his own organic property in 1987. The top wine is a new-oaked Cabernet of impeccable balance and cult following.

Hartwell Vineyards ☆☆☆–☆☆☆☆

Napa. Owner: Bob Hartwell. 8 hectares. www.hartwellvineyards.com

Hartwell's Stags Leap vineyards yield exceptional Merlot and Cabernet Sauvignon.

Heitz ☆–☆☆☆

St Helena. Owners: the Heitz family. 140 hectares. www.heitzcellar.com

Until his death in 2000, Joe Heitz was known worldwide for his Cabernet, more locally for his Chardonnay and specialties such as Grignolino. Yet they all reflected the man, a sometimes gruff original. Most of the grapes are bought from friends, one of whom, Martha May, has already passed into legend as the name on "Martha's Vineyard", Heitz's flagship Cabernet: a dense and gutsy wine of spicy, cedary and gumtree flavours. "Bella Oaks Vineyard" is often of similar stature. Bacterial infections in the winery led to many disappointing bottles from the 1990s, but the problems seem to have been sorted out, and recent vintages have been back on form.

Hess ☆☆–☆☆☆

Napa. Owner: Donald Hess. 285 hectares. www.hesscollection.com

Swiss businessman and art collector, Hess (the winery is in fact a museum) aims high with wines from 115 hectares on Mt Veeder.

The "Hess Select" line, anchored in his even larger Monterey vineyards, is more for everyday drinking.

Jade Mountain
Napa. Owner: Chalone group. 7 hectares.
www.chalonewinegroup.com
Founded by Douglas Danielak, Jade Mountain was an early specialist in southern French varieties, especially Syrah and Mourvèdre. But in 2000, the name was sold to Chalone.

Judd's Hill ☆☆–☆☆☆
St Helena. Owner: Art Finkelstein. 6 hectares.
www.juddshill.com
Finkelstein was one of the owners of the successful Whitehall Lane (*q.v.*), but sold up in 1988 and built up his own property in the eastern hills. Exceptional "Estate Cabernet".

Robert Keenan ☆
St Helena. Owner: Robert H. Keenan. 20 hectares.
www.keenanwinery.com
High, cool vineyards on Spring Mountain Road produce Chardonnay and Cabernet Sauvignon, which is blended with Napa Merlot and oak-aged.

Even the Merlot, for which Keenan is now celebrated, can be tannic and astringent. The Zinfandel introduced in 1999 is considerably more ingratiating.

Charles Krug ☆☆
St Helena. Owner: Peter Mondavi and family. 485 hectares.
www.charleskrug.com
C. Mondavi & Sons is the company name at the oldest of Napa's historic wineries, now run by Cesare Mondavi's son, Peter. The other son is Robert, who left in 1966 to start his own winery, with spectacular success.

Krug, often underrated, produces a sound range of varietals at, for Napa, low prices; the reserve bottlings are especially good value. Chardonnays from Carneros vineyards and a Pinot Noir add depth to the range.

There is also a range of inexpensive wines under the "CK Mondavi" label, made from purchased fruit.

Laird Family Estates ☆☆
Napa. Owners: the Laird family. 810 hectares.
www.lairdfamilyestate.com
The Lairds own vast vineyards throughout Napa, and until recently they sold the fruit to other wineries. From 1999 they started producing their own wines, and Cristina Benz is the respected winemaker.

Lewis Cellars ☆☆☆
Napa. Owner: Randy Lewis. No vineyards. www.lewiscellars.com
Lewis buys in Napa Cabernet and Merlot, and Chardonnay from Russian River. The latter can be rather heavy, but the red reserves are superb.

Livingston-Moffett ☆☆☆
St Helena. Owner: John Livingston. 4 hectares.
www.livingstonwines.com
Long-lived Cabernet from the estate vineyards, as well as bought-in Cabernet, called "Stanley's Selection".

Markham Vineyards ☆–☆☆
St Helena. Owner: Sanraku. 140 hectares.
www.markhamvineyards.com
One of the first Napa wineries to take Merlot seriously. Markham, although sold to a Japanese company in 1988, continues to turn out a range of well-made varietal wines, which is dependable if not especially exciting.

Louis M. Martini ☆–☆☆
St Helena. Owner: E. & J. Gallo. 240 hectares.
www.louismartini.com
Gallo bought this historical company in 2002. Three generations of Martinis have their name on the shortlist of California's great individual winemakers. Martini Cabernets of the 1960s rank alongside Beaulieu in quality, but in a different and leaner style: more reminiscent of claret. The "Special Selection" Cabernets are still the best wines, and the more standard wines are decidedly modest, although Barbera and Zinfandel are true to type. The business was bought by E. & J. Gallo in 2002.

Mason Cellars ☆☆
Oakville. Owner: Randy Mason. No vineyards.
www.masoncellars.com
One of Napa's very few Sauvignon Blanc specialists, though red wines have been added to the range recently.

Mayacamas ☆☆–☆☆☆☆
Napa. Owner and winemaker: Robert Travers. 20 hectares.
www.mayacamas.com
Mayacamas is the name of the mountains between Napa and Sonoma counties. The Travers' predecessors, the Taylors, planted Chardonnay and Cabernet during the 1940s, in a spectacular natural amphitheatre 610 metres (2,000 feet) up. The sun, the fogs, the winds, the cold, and the rocks of the hills conspire to concentrate grape flavour into something you can chew. Travers' Cabernets are awe-inspiring in colour and bite for the first five years at least. Those weaned on thick, fleshy, valley-floor Cabernets find the Mayacamas style unacceptably austere, but to other tasters they are an authentic reminder of the way Napa Cabernets used to taste. The Chardonnay is individual, too: lean and flinty.

Merryvale ☆☆☆
St Helena. Owners: Jack Slatter and partners. No vineyards.
www.merryvale.com
Two of California's best winemakers, Bob Levy and Steve Test, have kept Merryvale at a high standard since the late 1980s. The basic range is known as "Classic", but it's the meticulously crafted reserve and prestige wines, such as "Silhouette" Chardonnay and the Bordeaux blend, "Profile", that make you sit up and take notice.

Miner Family Vineyards ☆☆–☆☆☆
Oakville. Owners: the Miner family. 35 hectares.
www.minerwines.com
A glitzy new winery on the Silverado Trail is the showroom for this new property, underwritten by a computer software fortune. Opulent, oaky wines, the best being from Napa.

Robert Mondavi ☆☆–☆☆☆☆
Oakville. Owners: Robert Mondavi and family. 650 hectares in Napa. www.robertmondavi.com

Mondavi's energy and enquiring mind took less than ten years to produce the most important development in the Napa Valley since Prohibition. He fits the standard definition of a genius better than anyone I know. His aim is top quality on an industrial scale. Inspiration and perspiration have taken him there (*see* page 441).

The winery is (in the local jargon) state-of-the-art. The "art" includes not only advanced analysis and every shiny gadget, but a personal knowledge of every French barrel maker worth a hoop. In 2001, they built an even more splendid winery, equipped with wooden fermentation vats, in emulation of many a top Bordeaux château. Each vintage is like a frontier, with the Mondavi family cheering each other on to reach it, and something new always develops. Bob Mondavi still comes into the office daily, but the operation of the Mondavi empire, and the winemaking, is in the hands of his sons, Tim and Michael.

Their best wine is their Cabernet Sauvignon reserve; a gentle titan you can drink after dinner with relish, but would do well to keep for twenty years. Their regular Cabernet is a model of balance between berries and barrels, and there are excellent, if high-priced, regional Cabernet bottlings from Oakville and Stags Leap, the latter being more graceful. Each vintage their Pinot Noir reserve grows more velvety and satisfying. Among whites, they are best known for Fumé Blanc, a Sauvignon/Sémillon blend with the body and structure (and barrel-age) of first-class Chardonnay. Their Chardonnay (notably the reserve) can be a touch too opulent.

The Mondavi empire reaches near and far beyond its Spanish mission-influenced building at Oakville. Opus One (*q.v.*) is right across the street, Byron (*q.v.*) is farthest afield, in Santa Barbara County. Mondavi-Woodbridge is the good-value, cut-price label, based in Lodi, the town where Robert Mondavi grew up.

Monticello Vineyards ☆
Napa. Owner: Jay Corley. 50 hectares.
www.corleyfamilynapavalley.com
"Monticello" is the label for the basic production; "Corley" goes on reserve bottlings. The reds are rather lean.

Mont St John Cellars ☆
Napa. Owner: Louis Bartolucci. 65 hectares
Rather rustic wines from well-established family vineyards in Carneros.

Mount Veeder ☆☆☆
Mt Veeder, Napa. Owner: Constellation. 25 hectares.
www.franciscan.com
Rocky vineyard known for concentrated, earthy, tannic Cabernets. Chardonnay was discontinued in the mid-1990s.

Mumm ☆☆
Rutherford. Owner: Allied Domecq. 45 hectares.
www.mummcuveenapa.com
For many years part of the Seagram empire, Mumm's focus on sparkling wines of ebullient fruitiness has made them popular California originals in both Europe, and on their home turf. "Blanc de Noirs" is the archetype; luxury *cuvée* "DVX" reaches for the other end of the stylistic pole. But the ever reliable "Cuvée Napa" is the best-seller that has made the *domaine*'s reputation.

Newton ☆☆☆
St Helena. Owners: Peter and Su Hua Newton. 42 hectares
Rich, enjoyable Chardonnay from bought-in grapes. The winery's own exquisitely landscaped vineyards on Spring Mountain produce highly rated Cabernet and Merlot, all aged in fine French oak.

The Graves-style Sauvignon Blanc, one of California's best, was phased out, as the Newtons couldn't charge enough to justify the high production costs. Newton was founder of Sterling, below in the valley, in the 1960s.

Niebaum-Coppola ☆☆–☆☆☆
Rutherford. Owner: Francis Ford Coppola. 80 hectares.
www.niebaum-coppola.com
Movie man Coppola and his winery have become a major force in the Napa Valley. He bought the hidden half of the historic Inglenook property in 1979, the showcase half in 1995, and continues to buy.

With the winemaking tuned up, Cabernet-based Rubicon at last begins to impress, now that it is no longer incurably tannic. The less expensive ranges, usually made from purchased fruit, are hit-and-miss, so the "Estate" wines (Merlot, Viognier) are the ones to go for.

Opus One ☆☆☆☆
Oakville. Owners: Robert Mondavi, Philippine de Rothschild.
42 hectares. www.opusonewines.com
Founded in 1979 as a fifty-fifty deal between the late Philippe de Rothschild and Robert Mondavi. Cabernet-based red, originally a sort of Mondavi "reserve of reserves", now has its own architecturally wondrous home, at the centre of an estate vineyard planted at Bordeaux densities.

In theory, styled to be Franco-American, but ripe, rich Napa grapes rule.

Pahlmeyer ☆☆☆
Napa. Owner: Jayson Pahlmeyer. 45 hectares.
www.pahlmeyer.com
Pahlmeyer has hired a succession of well-known consultant winemakers to satisfy his taste for very rich, alcoholic wines that have a devoted following. Recently he has been acquiring more vineyards in Atlas Peak and the Sonoma Coast.

Robert Pecota ☆☆
Calistoga. Owner: Robert Pecota. 16 hectares.
www.robertpecotawinery.com
Good Cabernet Sauvignon and an oak-aged Sauvignon Blanc. A delicious Muscat, "Canelli", is a Pecota specialty.

Pepi ☆☆
Napa. Owner: Kendall-Jackson. www.pepi.com
Robert Pepi was a California pioneer of Italian varieties, and especially Sangiovese. It is now part of Kendall-Jackson's Artisans and Estates group, and looking far beyond the original Napa vineyard for grapes. But the Italian flavour persists in wines such as "Arneis" and a Cabernet/Sangiovese blend called "Due Baci".

Joseph Phelps ☆☆–☆☆☆☆
St Helena. Owner: Joseph Phelps. 140 hectares.
www.jpwines.com
An ex-builder with an unerring sense of style, Phelps built his

beautiful redwood barn in the choppy foothills east of St Helena. His achievement is like a scaled-down Robert Mondavi's; all his many wines are good, and several are among the best. My favourites are a distinctly Germanic late-harvest Riesling, beautiful with bottle-age; Syrah – real Rhône Syrah; Cabernets – far from obvious but inspiring confidence. The "Insignia" label is for a strongly tannic Cabernet/Merlot blend on Bordeaux lines. "Phelps Chardonnay" is also restrained at first, but secretly rich. Winemaker Craig Williams shows a very sure hand when it comes to Rhône-style wines, Viognier as well as Syrah.

Pine Ridge Winery ☆☆–☆☆☆
Napa. Owner: Leucadia. 92 hectares. www.pineridgewinery.com
Separately bottled Rutherford and Stags Leap Cabernets teach delicious lessons about internal divisions of climate and soil in Napa. The white wines can be rather heavy.

Plumpjack ☆☆☆
Napa. Owners: Gordon Getty and partners. 21 hectares.
www.plumpjack.com
Founded in 1996, Plumpjack has rapidly established a reputation for rich, oaky Cabernet, especially the reserve bottling. The estate caused a sensation by releasing some of the 1997 wine with a screwcap closure.

Pride Mountain ☆☆☆–☆☆☆☆
St Helena. Owners: the Pride family. 32 hectares.
www.pridewines.com
The vineyards are high on Spring Mountain, and the results are very intense wines from Chardonnay, Cabernet, Merlot, and Viognier. Syrah is waiting in the wings.

Quintessa ☆☆☆
Napa. Owner: Augustin Huneeus. 68 hectares.
www.quintessa.com
After the sale of Franciscan (q.v.), Huneeus retained the isolated hillside Quintessa vineyard as his personal property, opening a new winery in 2003. The only wine is a polished and expensive Bordeaux blend.

Raymond Vineyards ☆☆
St Helena. Owners: the Raymond family and Japanese brewers, Kirin. 220 hectares. www.raymondwine.com
The "Napa Valley Reserve" line is high-quality, typically oaky – and taken one step further by the "Raymond Generations" range. Long-time residents of Napa, the Raymonds are pioneer growers of Pinot Noir in American Canyon (at the extreme southern end of Napa), and venturing into Monterey for less expensive "Amberhill" and "Estate" ranges.

Ritchie Creek ☆
St Helena. Owner and winemaker: Richard Minor. 3 hectares.
www.ritchiecreek.com
These Spring Mountains vineyards deliver good Chardonnay and lean Cabernet Sauvignon.

Rombauer Vineyards ☆
St Helena. Owners: the Rombauer family.
www.rombauervineyards.com
The Rombauers own vineyards but sell the entire crop to other wineries, obliging them to buy in fruit for their own range of classic varietals.

Round Hill Cellars
St Helena. Owner: Marko Zaninovitch. 15 hectares.
www.roundhillwines.com
Developed by the Van Asperen family, Round Hill supplies a wider market with good-value versions of distinct variety-plus-region character, notably Napa Cabernet and Merlot under the "Round Hill" and "Rutherford Ranch" labels. Its future direction is uncertain under new ownership.

Rudd ☆☆☆
Oakville. Owner: Leslie Rudd. 18 hectares. www.ruddwines.com
The former Girard estate was bought by delicatessen-king Rudd in 1996. Celebrated winemaker David Ramey fashioned the initial releases of Carneros Chardonnay and Napa reds, and has since been replaced by Charles Thomas.

Rutherford Hill Winery ☆
St Helena. Owner: Terlato Wine Group. 80 hectares.
www.rutherfordhill.com
Founded in 1976 by the partners of Freemark Abbey (q.v.), the winery's initially high reputation slipped in the 1980s, and in 1996 it was bought by its present owners. Quality has yet to return to its original high level, but Terlato seems keen to try.

St Clement Vineyards ☆☆–☆☆☆
St Helena. Owner: Beringer-Blass. 8 hectares.
www.stclement.com
Winemaker David Schlottman continues his predecessor's strategy of producing excellent Chardonnay from Carneros, a sleek, elegant Merlot, and a Bordeaux blend.

St Supéry ☆☆
Rutherford. Owner: Robert Skalli. 260 hectares.
www.stsupery.com
Sensibly priced Cabernet and Sauvignon Blanc from Dollarhide Ranch show what Napa's easterly, upland Chiles Valley can do with Bordeaux varieties, red and white. There's an excellent visitors' centre, too.

Saintsbury ☆☆☆
Napa. Owners: Richard Ward and David Graves. 22 hectares.
www.saintsbury.com
Burgundian inspiration here – Chardonnay and Pinot Noir are the only wines. The Pinot is exceptional, notably the reserve and the "Brown Ranch" bottlings.

V. Sattui ☆
St Helena. Owner and winemaker: Daryl Sattui. 60 hectares.
www.vsattui.com
Good Cabernet, Zinfandel, and Riesling draw thousands of customers to this hospitable tasting room, to which a deli and a picnic ground are attached.

Schramsberg ☆☆–☆☆☆
Calistoga. Owner: The Davies Family. 26 hectares.
www.schramsberg.com
Robert Louis Stevenson drank "bottled poetry" at Schram's ornate white, verandahed house, built by founder Jacob Schram in the 1860s. So have I, many times, under the Davies regime. Refounded in 1966, Jack Davies produced sparkling wines only, of a very high standard, none more so than his luxury cuvée, "J. Schram" (1989), which instantly set new

standards for California - although the old *cuvée* 1984 vintage was lovely in 2003, proving that Napa already made great sparkling wine. In 1998, Jack Davies died and Duckhorn (*q.v.*) took a minority share.

Screaming Eagle ☆☆☆☆
Oakville. Owner: Jean Phillips. 1 hectare.
www.screamingeagle.com
Napa's most costly trophy Cabernet, a dense, sweet wine of soaring and tenacious flavours, made by Heidi Peterson Barrett. The wine is full-bodied, rich, and oaky but unlike some cult Napa Cabernets, it has a remarkable purity and finesse. The 1995 is the most seductive vintage, with 1994 and 1998 close behind.

Sequoia Grove ☆☆–☆☆☆
Napa. Owners: the Allen family. 45 hectares.
www.sequoiagrove.com
Cabernet Sauvignon is easily the best wine here, especially the reserve.

Shafer ☆☆☆–☆☆☆☆
Napa. Owner: John Shafer. 80 hectares.
www.shafervineyards.com
Since 1978, John Shafer has produced immaculate "Stags Leap" Cabernet and Merlot. The top wine is the new-oaked "Hillside Select Cabernet", and the Sangiovese and Syrah are also good. The Carneros Chardonnay can be overblown.

Signorello ☆☆☆
Napa. Owners: the Signorello family. 40 hectares.
www.signorellovineyards.com
The Signorellos are grape farmers turned wine producers, offering luxurious and heavily toasted whites and reds.

Silver Oak Cellars ☆☆
Oakville. Owner: Raymond Duncan. 136 hectares.
www.silveroak.com
Silver Oak only makes Cabernet Sauvignon, in separate Napa and Alexander Valley bottlings. They differ in structure (the Napa is more tannic) but not in style, as both are aged exclusively in American oak, creating wines that can be drunk with pleasure on release. Co-founder and winemaker Justin Meyer sold his share to his partner in 2000.

Silverado Vineyards ☆☆–☆☆☆
Napa. Owners: the Disney family. 121 hectares.
www.silveradovineyards.com
Silverado's estate-grown Chardonnay, Sauvignon Blanc, and Cabernet Sauvignon are all ripe, supple, and sophisticated, with a growing reputation. Jack Stuart has been the winemaker since 1981.

Smith-Madrone ☆–☆☆
St Helena. Owners: Stuart and Charles Smith. 13 hectares
Vineyards at 520 metres (1,700 feet) up on Spring Mountain yield remarkable wines in a simple cellar. Sweet or dry lemony Riesling is easy to love, young or old. The Cabernet is lean and long-lived.

Spottswoode ☆☆☆
St Helena. Owner: Mary Novak. 15 hectares.
www.spottswoode.com

One of the most elegant and balanced Cabernets in California comes from Spottswoode, right in the town of St Helena. Wonderfully consistent wine that ages well, but is drinkable young. Intriguingly pure Sauvignon Blanc, too.

Staglin ☆☆☆
Rutherford. Owners: the Staglin family. 20 hectares.
www.staglinfamily.com
Blessed with magnificent vineyards in Rutherford, the Staglins produce fine, structured Cabernet and very good Sangiovese.

Stag's Leap Wine Cellars ☆☆–☆☆☆☆
Napa. Owner: Warren Winiarski. 48 hectares. www.cask23.com
Winiarski is a professor of Greek turned winemaker, whose Cabernets have startled the French with their resemblance to great Bordeaux. My notes are full of "harmony, elegance, feminine, finesse". "Cask 23" is a riper reserve Cabernet, and the Fay Vineyard bottling can be almost as fine. Stag's Leap Merlot and Chardonnay get good reviews, too, although my favourite remains the Cabernet. "Hawk Crest", the second label, offers good value.

Stags' Leap Winery ☆☆
Napa. Owner: Beringer Blass. 69 hectares.
www.stagsleapwinery.com
Unusually among Napa wineries, this has acquired a high reputation for its Petite Sirah.

Sterling ☆☆
Calistoga. Owner: Diageo. 485 hectares.
www.sterlingvineyards.com
The long, white building, like a Greek monastery, hugs the top of a lump in the valley floor big enough to need cable cars to get up it. British money built it in the 1960s; Coca-Cola bought it in 1978; and Seagram took over in 1983. The Sterling specialty used to be an austere Cabernet with a daring level of volatile acidity, but recent vintages have been more conventional. The stress now is on single-vineyard wines, notably a Merlot from Three Palms Vineyard, Cabernet from Diamond Mountain, and a Chardonnay from Winery Lake. The strong, dry Sauvignon Blanc can come as a relief after some of the more tropical-fruit flavours of the valley.

Stonegate ☆
Calistoga. Owner: Bandiera winery. 87 hectares
Stonegate developed a reputation for Merlot in the 1980s, but in the late 1990s the wines, essentially a varietal range, became soft and flat.

Stony Hill ☆☆
St Helena. Owner: Peter McCrea. 16 hectares.
www.stonyhillvineyard.com
Fred McCrea was the first of the flood of men from busy offices who realized that the Napa Valley offered something better. He planted white grapes in the 1940s and made twenty-five vintages of his own understated style of wine. Neither the variety nor the maturation grab your attention; the point seems to be boundless vigour and depth without an obvious handle. Eleanor McCrea continued her husband's total integrity of purpose after his death.

When she died, son Peter took up the reins with no compromise. The style, given the paucity of new oak, remains unfashionable, but is valid on its own terms. A second label, "SHV", uses non-estate grapes.

Storybook Mountain Vineyards ☆☆–☆☆☆
Calistoga. Owner: Dr. Jerry Bernard Seps. 17 hectares.
www.storybookwines.com
Jerry Seps revels in Zinfandel and produces nothing else. There are at least three blends, and they all tend to be splendid.

Sutter Home Winery ☆–☆☆
St Helena. Owners: the Trinchero family. 2,430 hectares.
www.sutterhome.com
A family operation (named after another pre-Prohibition family) that once specialized in small lots of red Zinfandel; later in huge volumes of White Zinfandel, sustained by enormous vineyards in inland areas. The winery now offers the usual varietals, most bearing California as an appellation, all at modest prices. In 1995 a new label, "M.Trinchero" was introduced for small lots of exceptional Chardonnay and Cabernet.

Swanson Vineyards ☆☆☆
Rutherford. Owner: W. Clarke Swanson. 56 hectares.
www.swansonwine.com
Following the increasingly common Napa practice, Swanson-owned vineyards range from Oakville to Carneros, to give a range of grape varieties their proper homes. And yet the

---

Labels

Two pieces of information included on the label of many good Californian wines give a helpful indication of what to expect in the bottle.

Alcohol content is measured in degrees or percentage by volume (the two are the same). Traditional wines vary between about 11.5 and 14 degrees, enough to make a substantial difference to taste and effect, with some fashionable Zinfandels attaining a natural but absurd level of 16.5%. But the law allows the labeller a remarkable latitude of 1.5 degrees from the truth. As a practical tip, if you find a he-man Napa Chardonnay, for example, too powerful for you at 13.5 degrees, there is no law against adding a drop of water. Perrier refreshes clumsy wines beautifully.

Residual sugar is most commonly reported on labels of Riesling and Gewürztraminer. It is the unfermented sugar left (or kept) in the wine at bottling. Below 0.5% by weight, sugar is undetectable: the wine is fully dry. Above about 1.5% it would be described as "sweet", above 3% as "sweet" and above 6% as "very sweet". A "selected bunch late-harvest" (roughly equivalent to a German BA) might have 14% and a "selected berry late-harvest" (roughly equivalent to a German TBA) as much as 28%. Measurement in grams per 100 millilitres is the same as measurement in percentages.

The Not the Whole Truth factor If a grape variety is specified on the label, only 75% of the wine needs to be made from that variety. If a county name, such as Sonoma, is cited, only 75% of the grapes need come from that county. If a specific AVA, such as Howell Mountain, is cited on the label, only 85% of the wine need come from that region. If a single vineyard is identified on the label, 95% of the wine must come from that site.

---

style still leans as heavily on new oak barrels as terroir. Banker Swanson also owns Avery's of Bristol. Some of the finest wines are from Sangiovese and Syrah.

Philip Togni ☆☆☆
St Helena. Owner/winemaker: Philip Togni. 4 hectares
From high on Spring Mountain, veteran British-born Togni makes sumptuous, long-lived Cabernet, and tiny quantities of an exquisite sweet wine from Black Hamburg, "Ca' Togni".

Trefethen ☆☆
Napa. Owners: the Trefethen family. 260 hectares.
www.trefethenwines.com
The Trefethens bought the former "Eshcol" vineyards near Napa, in 1968. The vineyards are relatively cool and thus better-suited for elegant Chardonnay, Riesling, and Cabernet Franc than for the often mid-weight Cabernet Sauvignon. Late-released "Library" wines show great ageing potential. Blended "Eshcol" table wines are some of the best value in the state.

Tudal ☆
St Helena. Owner/winemaker: Arnold Tudal. 3 hectares.
www.tudalwinery.com
A small operation, making full-flavoured but uneven Cabernets designed for laying down.

Turley ☆☆
St Helena. Owner: Larry Turley. 6 hectares.
www.turleywinecellars.com
The former partner of John Williams of Frog's Leap (*q.v.*), Larry Turley went his own way in 1994, specializing in Zinfandel and Petite Sirah from ancient vineyards. The wines are ultra-ripe and very alcoholic, which has made them controversial and, in the eyes of some, hard to swallow.

Turnbull ☆☆–☆☆☆
Oakville. Owner: Patrick O'Dell. 75 hectares.
www.turnbullwines.com
After purchasing the winery from its founders in 1993, O'Dell expanded the vineyard holdings and showed a willingness to think new thoughts, but thus far, the Cabernet continues to out-mint, out-spice even "Martha's Vineyard". Among the more unusual and delicious offerings are Syrah, Sangiovese, and a Rhône blend called "Old Bull Red".

Viader ☆☆☆
St Helena. Owner: Delia Viader. 9 hectares. www.viader.com
Argentinian-born Delia Viader makes just one wine from her organic hillside vineyards: a seductive blend of Cabernet Franc and Cabernet Sauvignon.

Vine Cliff ☆☆☆
Napa. Owner: Charles Sweeney. 16 hectares.
www.vinecliff.com
A major winery in the 1880s, this was revived in 1984, when terraced organic vineyards were planted. First releases were in 1993, and established an opulent style of high quality.

Whitehall Lane Winery ☆☆
St Helena. Owner: Thomas Leonardini. 45 hectares.
www.whitehalllane.com
Merlot is the top wine here. Its wines win extravagant praise, but some vintages can be a touch jammy.

ZD Wines ☆

Napa. Owners: the Norman de Leuze family. 16 hectares.
www.zdwines.com

Pinot Noir and Chardonnay, aged in American oak, are the focus; the philosophy is to find the right grapes.

Sonoma County

Alderbrook Vineyards ☆–☆☆

Healdsburg. Owner: Terlato Wine Group. 26 hectares.
www.alderbrook.com

Frequent changes of owner and winemaker occasioned numerous changes in style. In general, Alderbrook offers crisp whites and medium-bodied reds.

Alder Fels ☆

Santa Rosa. Owner/winemaker: David Coleman. No vineyards.
www.adlerfelswinery.com

A hilltop winery, buying in Sonoma grapes to make deeply flavoured whites and promising Sangiovese.

Alexander Valley Vineyards ☆

Healdsburg. Owners: the Wetzel family. 60 hectares.
www.avvwine.com

The dry, Burgundian-style Chardonnay is the estate's best-known wine, but there is also plump Cabernet Sauvignon and charming Cabernet Franc, all produced from Alexander Valley fruit.

Arrowood ☆☆☆–☆☆☆☆

Kenwood. Owner: Mondavi. 12 hectares.
www.arrowoodvineyards.com

Long-time Château St Jean winemaker Richard Arrowood set up on his own in the late 1980s. He buys in grapes from outstanding Sonoma vineyards. As well as the standard varietals, there is superb Viognier (sometimes late-harvest) and Malbec. In 2000, Mondavi bought the label, but Arrowood remains at the helm.

Belvedere ☆

Healdsburg. Owner: William Hambrecht. 200 hectares.
www.belvederewinery.com

Hambrecht is a Californian financier who also owns large vineyards in Sonoma, which supply his winery. The leading wines at present are Merlot and Chardonnay.

Benziger ☆☆–☆☆☆

Glen Ellen. Owners: the Benziger family. 35 hectares.
www.benziger.com

The late Bruno Benziger (d. 1989) and five sons started out to build a small, Sonoma-based winery. Within a decade they found themselves selling well more than one million cases a year of commodity wines, under the names "Glen Ellen Proprietor's Reserve" and "M. G. Vallejo". Dismayed, they sold those labels to Heublein in 1993, and returned to their original idea, this time producing wines under the family name.

They enjoy producing small quantities of unusual grape varieties, as well as various blends, and some of these are available under a new label they have created, called "Imagery Series".

Buena Vista ☆

Sonoma. Owner: Allied-Domecq. 550 hectares.
www.buenavistawinery.com

Historically important as the winery of Agoston Haraszthy, "the father of California wine". Restarted in 1943 by Frank Bartholomew, then sold to German owner Racke in 1979, and sold again in 2001. Most grapes come from Carneros, and Chardonnay dominates. Prices are modest, but so is quality.

Davis Bynum ☆☆

Healdsburg. Owner: Davis Bynum. 10 hectares.
www.davisbynum.com

Former newspaperman Davis Bynum was one of the first to realize the potential of Russian River Valley as a Pinot Noir region. Greatly assisted over the years by winemaker Gary Farrell (*q.v.*), he has released some delicious Pinots from some of the region's outstanding vineyards. The present winemaker is David Georges.

Carmenet ☆☆

Sonoma. Owner: Beringer Blass. 40 hectares.
www.carmenetwinery.com

Carmenet used to make delicious Edna Valley Sauvignon, but now focuses on red wines from its own mountain vineyards. "Moon Mountain Reserve" is the best Bordeaux blend, "Dynamite Cabernet" is a boisterously named basic wine.

Chalk Hill ☆–☆☆

Healdsburg. Owner: Fred Furth. 120 hectares.
www.chalkhill.com

Despite being an estate winery, it has been a medium in search of a message, or vice versa, for most of its career, changing names from Donna Maria to Chalk Hill in 1982, and changing styles to suit a succession of winemakers. The vineyards seem most suited to Sauvignon Blanc and Chardonnay.

Chateau Souverain ☆☆–☆☆☆

Geyserville. Owner: Beringer-Blass. 132 hectares.
www.chateausouverain.com

Souverain grows its own red grapes in Alexander Valley, but it's too hot here for Chardonnay, which is bought in, usually from Russian River Valley. The whites can be quite plump, but the reds are opulent and extremely drinkable. All wines, even reserves, sensibly priced.

Chateau St Jean ☆☆–☆☆☆

Kenwood. Owner: Beringer-Blass. 100 hectares.
www.chateaustjean.com

A showplace winery specializing in white wines of the sort of subtropical ripeness more often associated with the Napa Valley. In the 1970s and early 1980s, Richard Arrowood (*q.v.*) dazzled the wine world with his numerous single-vineyard white wines, both Sauvignon and Chardonnay. "Robert Young" Chardonnays are the biggest and lushest of all. I often prefer the more easily drinkable, multi-vineyard regular bottling.

After Arrowood's departure in 1990, the range was trimmed down, and some excellent red wines joined the list, none finer than the blend called "Cinq Cépages". Arrowood was also a master of formidable, sweet, late-harvest Rieslings and Gewürztraminers, but they are infrequently produced today.

Cline ☆☆–☆☆☆

Sonoma. Owner: Cline family. 60 hectares. www.clinecellars.com
The Clines own fabulous old vineyards in Contra Costa County that produce intense Zinfandel and Mourvèdre. In southern Sonoma they have planted Rhône varieties. The best wines are full of character and fire.

Clos du Bois ☆–☆☆☆

Healdsburg. Owner: Allied-Domecq. 365 hectares. www.closdubois.com
Clos du Bois wines were well-established before there was a winery. The best are the proprietary wines, such as "Marlstone Alexander Valley" (Merlot-based blend), "Briarcrest Alexander Valley Cabernet Sauvignon", "Calcaire Alexander Valley Chardonnay", and "Flintwood Dry Creek Valley Chardonnay".

Dehlinger ☆☆☆

Sebastopol. Owner/winemaker: Tom Dehlinger. 18 hectares
Dehlinger is devoted to Pinot Noir, and produces a number of different bottlings from different parcels of his vineyards. A rich style, highly regarded. There are also small amounts of Chardonnay, Syrah, and other varieties.

DeLoach ☆☆–☆☆☆

Santa Rosa. Owners: the DeLoach family. 400 hectares. www.deloachvineyards.com
From tiny beginnings, Cecil DeLoach built a substantial business by making wines that taste first and foremost of grape variety and vineyard. He cleverly bought up old-vine vineyards that growers were abandoning because yields were too low. But he also buys in fruit from all over California for his basic range. The very best wines bear the mysterious designation "OFS". Very good Zinfandel and Pinot Noir. Financial difficulties in 2003 led to a sharp drop in production.

Dry Creek Vineyard ☆☆–☆☆☆

Healdsburg. Owner: David Stare. 80 hectares. www.drycreekvineyard.com
Maker of one of California's best dry Sauvignon Blancs (Fumé Blanc), with other whites in the same old-fashioned, balanced, vital, but not-too-emphatic, dry style. Reserve Chardonnays are barrel-fermented and aged *sur lie*; while the Chenin Blanc, which is totally unoaked, is equally delicious. Very good Zinfandel and Petite Sirah head the range of reds.

Duxoup Wine Works ☆

Healdsburg. Owner: Andrew Cutter. No vineyards
Marx-inspired name (Groucho), but vibrantly fruity red wines, including a Syrah that has pleased local tasters, and a wild Charbono. All grapes come from Dry Creek Valley vineyards.

Everett Ridge ☆☆

Healdsburg. Owners: the Air family. 45 hectares. www.everettridge.com
Known as Bellerose until 1996, this property is now cultivated biodynamically. Most of the vineyards are in Dry Creek, but there are parcels in Mendocino and Sonoma. Peppery Cabernet, zesty Sauvignon, and spicy old-vine Zinfandel.

Gary Farrell ☆☆☆

Healdsburg. Owner/winemaker: Gary Farrell. 20 hectares. www.garyfarrell.com
The adroit former winemaker for Davis Bynum makes more particular wines for his own label, many of them from named vineyards in the Russian River Valley. Burgundian-style Pinot Noir "Allen Vineyard" is the memory-maker.

Ferrari-Carano ☆☆☆

Healdsburg. Owners: Donald and Rhonda Carano. 265 hectares. www.ferrari-carano.com
The Dry Creek winery and gardens are dramatic; so is the winemaking style. Reserves exceed even Texas-sized expectations. Reds are improving every year, especially the Supertuscan-style "Siena" and the Bordeaux blend, "Trésor".

Gloria Ferrer ☆☆–☆☆☆

Sonoma. Owner: Freixenet. 182 hectares. www.gloriaferrer.com
Catalonia rather than Champagne is the parent of this sparkling wine house, named after the wife of the president of Freixenet. A capacious winery and substantial vineyards spell serious intent. Thus far, the vintage-dated "Royal Cuvée" exceeds the rest of the range for depth and riches; the "Carneros Cuvée" is even toastier after seven years on the yeasts. As nationwide sparkling wine sales have slumped, Gloria Ferrer has made up the slack with a range of fairly light table wines, too.

Fisher ☆☆

Santa Rosa. Owner: Fred Fisher. 30 hectares. www.fishervineyards.com
Rich, bold wines from both Napa and Sonoma. The top red is usually the high-priced "Wedding Vineyard Cabernet".

Flowers ☆☆☆

Cazadero. Owners: Walt and Joan Flowers. 26 hectares. www.flowerswinery.com
This is the leading winery based in the highlands along the Sonoma Coast. The microclimate is cool but luminosity is high, so the wines, Chardonnay and Pinot Noir, show purity and intensity.

Foppiano ☆

Healdsburg. Owner: Louis J. Foppiano. 80 hectares. www.foppiano.com
One of the oldest family owned wineries, recently refurbished and raising its already respectable standards. "Foppiano" is the standard label; "Fox Mountain" a reserve label for Chardonnay and Cabernet, mostly from family vineyards. "Riverside Vineyard" is a second label.

Fritz ☆–☆☆

Cloverdale. Owner: Donald Fritz. 36 hectares. www.fritzwinery.com
Much Chardonnay here, some of it rather blowzy. Quality is not always consistent, but the most impressive red is usually the "Rogers Reserve Zinfandel" from Dry Creek.

Gan Eden ☆

Sebastopol. Owner: Craig Winchell. No vineyards www.ganeden.com
Light kosher wines, using only bought-in Sonoma grapes, which win prizes and praise.

Geyser Peak Winery ☆☆
Geyserville. Owner: Fortune Brands. 485 hectares.
www.peakwinesinternational.com
An old winery-turned-vinegar-works became a winery once
again in 1972. The former owners briefly had Australia's
Penfolds as a partner. Out of that deal, they kept sure-handed
Aussie winemaker Daryl Groom. Fumé Blanc and Shiraz are
the stars in a wide range of forward fruity wines, and "Cuvée
Alexandre" shows Groom can fashion a rich Bordeaux blend,
too. A second label is "Canyon Road".

Gundlach-Bundschu ☆☆
Sonoma. Owner: Jim Bundschu. 150 hectares.
www.gunbun.com
A famous San Francisco wine business, destroyed by the 1906
earthquake. Grapes from the old vineyards were sold until
1973, when the winery reopened. The range is excellent,
especially Cabernet and Merlot, and a Gewürztraminer, crisp
and refreshing like an Alsace wine. Chardonnay and Riesling
are also admirable. Some grapes are from 130-year-old
estate vineyards.

Hanna ☆☆
Santa Rosa. Owner: Dr Elias Hanna. 200 hectares.
www.hannawinery.com
After a hesitant start, the winery began hitting a stride in
the 1990s, especially with its whites. The excellent
winemaker, Jeff Hinchcliffe, was hired in 2000, so quality
should improve further.

Hanzell ☆☆–☆☆☆
Sonoma. Owner: Alex de Brye. 14 hectares.
www.hanzell.com
Scene of revolutionary winemaking in the late 1950s,
when James D. Zellerbach set out to make burgundy-style
wines in small, French-oak barrels. The steep, south-facing
vineyard gives high alcohol, but the concentration and
balance of both the Chardonnay and the Pinot Noir (though
occasionally funky) still makes them among California's most
impressive, demanding long maturation. The winery
is (vaguely) a miniature Château du Clos de Vougeot.
Bob Sessions made the wines here from 1973 until his
retirement in 2001.

Hartford Court ☆☆☆
Forestville. Owner: Jackson Family Estates. 20 hectares.
www.hartfordcourt.com
Don Hartford, a son-in-law of Jess Jackson, has overseen the
production of increasingly remarkable wines, made in an
artésanal fashion: single-vineyard Pinot Noirs and old-vine
Zinfandel from a number of different sites.

Iron Horse ☆☆–☆☆☆
Sebastopol. Owners: the Sterling family. 100 hectares.
www.ironhorsevineyards.com
I took an instant liking to Iron Horse Cabernet, tannic to start,
ripely sweet to finish, like good claret. Since then, vibrant
Chardonnay, and even more lively sparkling "Iron Horse"
have stolen the limelight.

Jordan Vineyard and Winery ☆☆
Healdsburg. Owner: Thomas Jordan. 112 hectares.
www.jordanwinery.com
When built in 1972, this was the most extravagant tycoon's
château in California yet. Today it is a Bordeaux-style
mansion and winery, deliberately set on producing claret like
the Médoc, in a setting of dark oaks and golden grassland,
beautiful even by Sonoma standards.

Both Cabernet and Chardonnay are still stylish wines, but
can lack personality. An affiliated company, "J", produces
one of California's most stylish classic-method *bruts*. In 1996,
the firm acquired Piper-Sonoma's winery and vineyard as the
basis for a rapid expansion of J.

Kenwood ☆☆
Kenwood. Owner: Gary Heck. 142 hectares.
www.kenwoodvineyards.com
Wide range of varietals from Sonoma grapes, including "Jack
London Vineyard" and "Artist's Series" Cabernet Sauvignons.
Reds are increasingly stylish, and the unfussy Sauvignon
Blanc is very good.

Kistler ☆☆☆–☆☆☆☆
Sebastopol. Owners: Stephen Kistler and Mark Bixler.
50 hectares
Hilltop vineyards on the Napa/Sonoma watershed, and
grapes purchased from Sonoma's top sites, deliver
Chardonnay grapes for artisan-method wines. The reclusive
Kistler practises non-interventionist winemaking, and
routinely produces some of California's greatest
Chardonnays. Recent vintages show him just as adept at
magnificent Pinot Noir.

Korbel ☆
Guerneville. Owner: Gary Heck. 400 hectares owned or leased.
www.korbel.com
Until Domaine Chandon came on the scene, this was
the first choice in widely available California "Champagne",
though then innocent of any Chardonnay or Pinot Noir.

It is still a reliable bargain, especially the extremely
dry "Natural". The flagship wine is the barrel-fermented "Le
Premier Reserve".

Kunde ☆☆–☆☆☆
Kenwood. Owners: the Kunde family. 325 hectares.
www.kunde.com
Long-time growers in the Sonoma Valley, the Kundes turned
to winemaking in 1990. The wines are well crafted and
accessible. The range is enormous, and there is some
remarkable old-vine Zinfandel.

La Crema ☆☆–☆☆☆
Geyserville. Owner: Kendall-Jackson. 100 hectares.
www.lacrema.com
Largely using Russian River Valley grapes, La Crema has a
growing reputation for Burgundian-style Chardonnays and
Pinot Noir. The "Sonoma Coast Pinot Noir" is a dependable
example of the new, leaner style of Sonoma Pinot Noir.

Lambert Bridge ☆
Healdsburg. Owners: the Chambers family. 2 hectares.
www.lambertbridge.com
After much instability, the Chambers family have revived this
Dry Creek winery, which buys in most of its grapes. The
wines are sleek and attractive, notably the Bordeaux blend
called "Crane Creek Cuvée".

Landmark ☆☆
Kenwood. Owner: Damaris Ethridge. 8 hectares.
www.landmarkwine.com
Highly regarded in California, but often exaggerates the toasty-buttery school, particularly noticeable in the Damaris reserve bottling, least in the "Overlook" blend.

Laurel Glen ☆☆☆
Glen Ellen. Owner: Patrick Campbell. 10 hectares.
www.laurelglen.com
Campbell studied philosophy at Harvard, then farmed vineyards for a Zen monastery before setting up his own small Sonoma Mountain winery in 1981. Very solid Cabernet Sauvignon, built to last. The second label, "Counterpoint", can be good value.

Limerick Lane ☆☆
Healdsburg. Owner: Ted Markoczy. 14 hectares.
www.wines.com/limericklane
Best-known for splendid Zinfandel, but the Hungarian owner also produces California's only wine, which is modelled on Tokaji Aszú.

Matanzas Creek Winery
Santa Rosa. Owner: Jess Jackson. 125 hectares.
www.matanzascreek.com
Having won acclaim with early vintages of Chardonnay, the estate suffered from a swollen head. Luxury lots of Chardonnay and Merlot, called "Journey", were priced to shame the French, but never justified the cost. In 2000, Jess Jackson bought the estate, and in 2001 there was a change in the winemaking team.

Peter Michael ☆☆☆–☆☆☆☆
Calistoga. Owner: Sir Peter Michael. 52 hectares.
www.petermichaelwinery.com
British media tycoon Peter Michael has, at vast expense, developed superb vineyards high above Knights Valley. The results are spectacular: some of California's best Chardonnay, Sauvignon, and, increasingly, red wines, too. Very expensive.

Michel-Schlumberger ☆
Healdsburg. Owner: Jacques Schlumberger. 26 hectares
Formerly Domaine Michel, this property is best-known for its Cabernet.

Mill Creek ☆
Healdsburg. Owner: Bill Kreck. 30 hectares. www.mcvonline.com
Soft and agreeable rather than competition wines, but the Cabernet and Merlot can be good.

Murphy-Goode ☆☆
Geyserville. Owners: Murphy and Goode families. 142 hectares
This estate produces three versions of Sauvignon Blanc, in ascending order of richness. Their other wines are good, too, though not exactly intense.

Nalle ☆☆☆
Healdsburg. Owner/winemaker: Doug Nalle. No vineyards.
www.nallewinery.com
One of too few in California who pays more than lip-service to terroir, Nalle produces only a single old-vine Zinfandel, which makes it immediately obvious why Dry Creek Valley

should be planted to more of the variety. The wines, beautifully balanced, are the perfect riposte to those who think Zinfandel has to have sixteen per cent alcohol to be drinkable.

J. Pedroncelli Winery ☆–☆☆
Geyserville. Owners: the Pedroncelli family. 42 hectares.
www.pedroncelli.com
An old-reliable for local country jug wines, now making Dry Creek Zinfandel, Gewürztraminer, Chardonnay and Cabernet Sauvignon to a higher and stylish standard, and at very reasonable prices.

Preston ☆☆
Healdsburg. Owner: Lou Preston. 40 hectares.
www.prestonvineyards.com
Grower first, vintner second, Lou Preston appropriately dotes on estate Sauvignon and Zinfandel from Dry Creek Valley – and turns increasingly towards Rhône and Italian varieties. Alas, retirement beckons to Preston, and production is diminishing.

Quivira ☆☆–☆☆☆
Healdsburg. Owner: Henry Wendt. 30 hectares.
www.quivirawine.com
Exemplary Zinfandel from Dry Creek Valley, and a reliable Rhône blend called "Dry Creek Cuvée".

A. Rafanelli ☆☆☆
Healdsburg. Owner/winemaker: David Rafanelli. 20 hectares
A rustic Dry Creek winery, but there's nothing rustic about these delicious Zinfandels and Cabernets.

Ravenswood ☆☆–☆☆☆
Sonoma. Owner: Constellation. 5 hectares.
www.ravenswood-wine.com
Joel Peterson first expressed his passion for Zinfandel and other red wines in an anonymous shed. Buying small lots of grapes from ancient vineyards, before the practice became fashionable, he made some remarkable wines.

In the 1990s, the business expanded a hundred-fold, but the top wines remained as good as before. In 2001, Peterson sold the winery. The Ravenswood motto is: "No Wimpy Wines".

J. Rochioli ☆☆–☆☆☆
Healdsburg. Owners: the Rochioli family. 65 hectares
Sonoma Pinot Noir producers queue up to buy Rochioli's grapes. These days there are even fewer to go around, as Tom Rochioli is now making wine himself. Expensive and hard to find, except on top restaurant wine lists.

St Francis ☆☆–☆☆☆
Kenwood. Owner: Kobrand. 162 hectares. www.stfranciswine.com
Merlot is usually the best wine, but the earthy, single-vineyard Cabernets and Zinfandels can also be impressive.

Sausal Winery ☆
Healdsburg. Owners: the Demostene family. 52 hectares.
www.sausalwinery.com
One of the Sausal Zinfandel vineyards was planted in 1877, and is the source of the winery's "Century Zinfandel". Other bottlings are from vines almost, if not quite, as venerable.

Schug ☆☆
Sonoma. Owner: Walter Schug. 17 hectares.
www.schugwinery.com

German-born Walter Schug made his name as the winemaker for Phelps (*q.v.*). Since 1990, with his own winery, he focuses on understated yet indelible Chardonnay and Pinot Noir, mostly sourced here in Carneros. The style is elegant.

Sebastiani
Sonoma. Owners: the Sebastiani family. 165 hectares.
www.sebastiani.com

A name intimately connected with the historic little city of Sonoma. Sebastiani moved from being a bulk producer to high quality with smooth speed, but family feuds resulted in a sale of most of its best-known brands in 2000. The winery, diminished in scale, remains in a state of flux, though its top wines can still be very good.

Seghesio ☆☆–☆☆☆
Healdsburg. Owners: the Seghesio family. 142 hectares.
www.seghesio.com

A long-established concern that only began to bottle its own wines in 1983. Zinfandel has been the signature, and there are usually five different wines to choose from. Sangiovese bottlings from the family's venerable vineyard and from newer plantings are among California's best. The whole line offers notable value.

Simi ☆☆–☆☆☆
Healdsburg. Owner: Constellation. 145 hectares.
www.simiwinery.com

Repeated changes in ownership have not helped the historic Simi winery to maintain a consistent image or quality. At their best, Simi's Alexander Valley Cabernet and barrel-fermented Chardonnay reserve are first-rate. Its Sauvignon Blanc is also splendid, and for some reason a range of Carneros wines has recently been added.

Sonoma-Cutrer ☆☆
Windsor. Owner: Brown-Forman. 445 hectares.
www.sonomacutrer.com

For years, Brice Jones's winery reigned as California's all-Chardonnay specialist, offering a range from named vineyards: "Les Pierres", "Cutrer", and "Russian River Ranches". "Les Pierres" was usually the best. In 1994, Jones broke Chardonnay's hegemony, adding Pinot Noir. Quality remained steady, but other Sonoma Chardonnays eventually came to match or even surpass those from Sonoma-Cutrer.

Stonestreet ☆☆☆
Healdsburg. Owner: Jess Jackson. 600 hectares.
www.stonestreetwines.com

Stonestreet can draw on Jackson's huge vineyard holdings in Alexander Valley. Quality is excellent: very good Chardonnay, and even better, the Bordeaux blend called "Legacy", and "Christopher's Vineyard Cabernet".

Rodney Strong ☆
Healdsburg. Owner: Klein Foods. 365 hectares.
www.rodneystrong.com

Rodney Strong, a veteran Sonoma producer, is no longer linked with the winery that bears his name, though winemaker Rick Sayre maintained continuity. The wines lack excitement, with the exception of the "Alexander's Crown Cabernet".

Joseph Swan ☆☆
Forestville. Owner/winemaker: Rod Berglund. 5 hectares.
www.swanwinery.com

The late Joseph Swan pioneered Dry Creek Zinfandel, and his son-in-law follows in his footsteps, though the Pinot Noirs can be as varied as the Zinfandels, and quality is erratic.

What the Jargon Means

References to California wine in current literature, on labels and from winery tour guides are full of racy jargon. Some of the less self-explanatory terms are:

Botrytized (Pronounced with the accent on the first syllable.) Grapes or wine infected, naturally or artificially, with *Botrytis cinerea*, the "noble rot" of Sauternes: hence normally very sweet.

Brix The American measure of sugar content in grapes, also known as Balling, approximately equal to double the potential alcohol of the wine, if all the sugar is fermented. 19.3 Brix is equivalent to ten per cent alcohol by volume.

Cold stabilization A near-universal winery practice for preventing the formation of (harmless) tartaric acid crystals in the bottle. The offending tartaric acid is removed by storing wine near freezing point for about fifteen days.

Crush A California term for the vintage; also the quantity of grapes crushed, measured in tons per acre.

Field-grafting A method much used recently for converting established vines from one variety to another – usually red to white. The old vine top is cut off near the ground and a bud of the new variety grafted on.

Free-run juice The juice that flows from the crushed grapes "freely" before pressing. By implication, superior. Normally mixed with pressed juice.

Gas chromatograph An expensive gadget for analyzing a compound (*e.g.* wine) into its chemical constituents.

Gondola A massive hopper for carrying grapes from vineyard to crusher, behind a tractor or on a truck.

Jug wines Originally, wines collected from the winery in a jug for immediate use – therefore of ordinary quality. Now standard wines sold in large bottles.

Ovals Barrels of any size with oval, rather than round, ends, kept permanently in one place and not moved around the cellar – the German rather than the French tradition.

Polish (as in shoes) filtration A final filtration through a very fine-pored filter to "polish" the wine to gleaming brilliance.

Pomace The solid matter – skins, pips, and stems – left after pressing.

Skin contact Alas, not that, but a reference to leaving the white-wine juice mixed with the skins before separating them. Some white wines gain good flavours from a few hours "maceration" with their skins, if healthy, before fermentation. Now out of favour, because of "whole-cluster pressing" (*q.v.*).

Whole-cluster pressing The practice of pressing white grapes, stems and all, as soon as they arrive at the winery. The advantage is a greater freshness in the wine; the drawbacks are, qualitatively, a possible loss of complexity, and, economically, a need for more presses because the stems take up so much room.

Topolos at Russian River ☆
Forestville. Owners: the Topolos family. 10 hectares.
www.topolos.com
Old-fashioned wines from organic vineyards are the Topolos hallmark. The Zinfandel and Alicante here are burly and robust: not for the faint-hearted.

Marimar Torres ☆☆☆
Sebastopol. Owner: Marimar Torres. 32 hectares.
www.marimarestate.com
The emphatically individualistic Torres does all in her power to subdue California fruitiness in favour of finesse, in her Chardonnay as well as her Pinot Noir. Marimar is the sister of the renowned Miguel Torres.

Trentadue ☆☆
Geyserville. Owners: the Trentadue family. 100 hectares.
www.trentadue.com
The Trentadues sell grapes to Ridge and others, but also make their own powerful reds from Zinfandel and Petite Sirah.

Viansa ☆☆
Sonoma. Owner: Sam Sebastiani. 36 hectares. www.viansa.com
Sam Sebastiani left his family winery to set up on his own in 1986. He has created a wide range of Italian-style wines. The less ambitious wines, such as the clean Arneis and Pinot Grigio, often succeed better than the more ambitious blends.

Williams & Selyem ☆☆☆–☆☆☆☆
Healdsburg. Owner: John Dyson. No vineyards
Artésanal to an extreme but never rustic, Burt Williams and Ed Selyem made Russian River and Sonoma Coast Pinot Noir for all it is worth, having taken Domaine de la Romanée-Conti as their philosophical model. Selyem retired in 1998 with back problems, and the label was sold to viticulturist Dyson, but Williams remains, for the time being, as winemaker alongside Bob Cabral.

Leading Mendocino Producers

Claudia Springs ☆☆
Philo. Owner: Bob Klindt. 10 hectares. www.claudiasprings.com
A low-key operation, but the wines, especially the Viognier, are highly enjoyable.

Edmeades ☆☆–☆☆☆
Philo. Owner: Jackson Family Estates. 25 hectares. www.kj.com
The Mendocino cog in Kendall-Jackson's Family Estates wheel specializes in named-vineyard wines, especially Pinot Noir, Zinfandel, and Petite Sirah. The wines are big and intense.

Fetzer ☆☆–☆☆☆
Hopland. Owner: Brown-Forman. 800 hectares. www.fetzer.com
Fetzer, operating from Mendocino County but reaching far beyond it, was among the first wineries in California to make good to outright excellent wines on a large scale. It was also a pioneer in operating at several different price levels by labelling wines clearly. In its case, Reserve is at the top, "Barrel Select" in the middle (and the most striking in value), while proprietary names such as "Sundial Chardonnay" and "Eagle Peak Merlot" mark the lower tier. The late Bernard Fetzer founded the winery as a retirement hobby. After his death in 1981, eight of his staggeringly energetic children built the business to three million cases per year, before selling it to Brown-Forman in 1992. The Bonterra brand is California's leading range of organic wines.

Fife ☆☆–☆☆☆
Redwood Valley. Owner: Dennis Fife. 15 hectares.
www.fifevineyards.com
Dennis Fife has vineyards in Napa as well as Mendocino, and produces very rich, intense wines from Zinfandel, Syrah, Petite Sirah, and other varieties.

Greenwood Ridge ☆☆–☆☆☆
Philo. Owner: Allan Green. 6 hectares. www.greenwoodridge.com
Green's best wines come from vineyards high on the Mendocino Ridges, which supply his Riesling, Merlot, and Cabernet. These are supplemented by Chardonnay and Sauvignon from other Mendocino sites. The robust Zinfandel is bought from Sonoma.

Handley Cellars ☆☆
Philo. Owner/winemaker: Milla Handley. 20 hectares.
www.handleycellars.com
Ex-Château St Jean winemaker Handley has won praise for Chardonnay, Gewürztraminer, and classic-method sparklers.

Husch ☆
Philo. Owner: Hugo Oswald. 100 hectares.
www.huschvineyards.com
Vineyards in Anderson Valley and Ukiah provide grapes for a full range of wines, of which the best are the Pinot Noir, Gewürztraminer, and Chardonnay.

Lazy Creek ☆
Philo. Owner: Josh Chandler. 8 hectares
The Gewürztraminer from this tiny Anderson Valley property is highly rated.

Lolonis ☆–☆☆
Redwood Valley. Owners: the Lolonis family. 120 hectares.
www.lolonis.com
The Lolonis family supply many wineries with their organic grapes and started producing their own wines in the 1990s. Initially rustic, the wines are now improving.

McDowell Valley Vineyards ☆☆☆
Hopland. Owners: the Keehn family. 135 hectares.
www.mcdowellsyrah.com.
This estate remains true to a cause, making a statement about the tiny, once-forgotten McDowell Valley in south Mendocino as a source of wines from Rhône varieties, most especially Syrah from vines planted in 1948 and 1959. Plus splendid Viognier and invigorating Grenache rosé.

Monte Volpe ☆☆
Redwood Valley. Owner: Greg Graziano. 8 hectares.
www.domainesaintgregory.com
Old Mendocino hand Graziano is doing intelligent work with Italian varieties, especially Barbera. Another label, "Enotria", is dedicated specifically to Piedmontese varieties. French varieties are labelled as "Domaine Saint Gregory".

Navarro ☆☆☆
Philo. Owners: Edward T. Bennett and Deborah Cahn.
35 hectares. www.navarrowine.com
Ted Bennett takes advantage of a relatively foggy area to make uncommonly long-lived wines, notably Chardonnay, Riesling and Gewürztraminer, in an Alsatian style.

Pacific Echo ☆☆
Philo. Owner: Champagne Pommery. 40 hectares.
www.pacific-echo.com
John Scharffenberger made his name as a sparkling wine producer. He runs this property, which produces classic-method sparklers, and Lonetree, from where he produces full-bodied Zinfandel and other wines.

Parducci ☆
Ukiah. Owner: Domain Hill & Mayes. 100 hectares.
www.parducci.com
The oldest winery in Mendocino, it was bought in 1996 by its current owners. The promised relaunch foundered and by 2001 the property was on the market.

Roederer Estate ☆☆☆
Philo. Owner: Jean-Claude Rouzaud. 142 hectares.
www.roederer-estate.com
A large-scale venture owned by the Champagne house, with vineyards in the cool Anderson Valley. The first vintage onwards is impressive. The vintage cuvée is "L'Ermitage", but the standard *cuvée*, "Estate Brut", sometimes rivals it in quality.

Leading San Francisco Bay Producers

Ahlgren ☆☆
Boulder Creek. Owner: Dexter Ahlgren. 10 hectares.
www.ahlgrenvineyard.com
Ahlgren's outstanding Cabernet comes from Santa Cruz Mountains fruit, but his other wines are sourced from various parts of the Central Coast.

Bargetto ☆
Soquel. Owners: the Bargetto family. 8 hectares.
www.bargetto.com
The most serious wines (Chardonnay, Merlot, Cabernet) come from the Santa Cruz Mountains, and the Italian varieties, to which Barghetto is increasingly turning, from the Central Coast. Quality is variable.

Bonny Doon ☆–☆☆☆
Santa Cruz. Owner: Randall Grahm. 56 hectares.
www.bonnydoonvineyard.com
Randall Grahm, the most sharp-witted man in the California wine business, became the foremost of the "Rhône Rangers" while operating from a modest barn in the Santa Cruz Mountains. There he continues to pursue Rhône-like wines (a Mourvèdre called "Old Telegram"; a Grenache called "Clos de Gilroy"; a red Châteauneuf-style blend called "Le Cigare Volant"; and a delicious Marsanne/Roussanne named "Le Sophiste"), but Grahm will try anything that's not Cabernet or Chardonnay. His Nebbiolo may be California's best, and he crusades for Riesling. At the same time, he produces populist blends that bring good, characterful wines to the masses.

David Bruce ☆☆–☆☆☆
Los Gatos. Owner: David Bruce. 6 hectares.
www.davidbrucewinery.com
A bottle of Richebourg converted dermatologist David Bruce to wine, and he set up shop high in the Santa Cruz Mountains. There he made brilliant Pinot Noir and Chardonnay, but disease in the vineyards and TCA problems sadly damaged his reputation. Today, the range, supplemented by purchased fruit from top vineyards in the Central Coast, is more diverse. There are still occasional disappointments, but top bottlings of Pinot Noir and Petite Sirah show that Bruce hasn't lost his touch.

Clos La Chance ☆☆
Saratoga. Owner: Bill Murphy. 2 hectares. www.closlachance.com
An eclectic range that includes fresh Chardonnay from Napa and Santa Cruz Mountains, and graceful Cabernet Franc and Cabernet Sauvignon.

Concannon ☆
Livermore. Owners: the Wente family. 80 hectares.
www.concannonvineyard.com
Founded by Col. Joseph Concannon to make altar wine, in the same year as the other great Livermore Valley winery, Wente Vineyard, it has been owned since 1991 by members of the Wente family, but run separately. There is renewed focus on estate Petite Sirah, Sauvignon Blanc, and "Assemblage", the proprietary name for red and white Bordeaux blends. Grapes for Chardonnay and other varietals are largely bought-in from Central Coast sources.

Cronin ☆☆–☆☆☆
Woodside. Owner/winemaker: Duane Cronin. 1.5 hectares
From the basement of his suburban house, Cronin produces mostly Chardonnay, from the best grapes he can find. Fluctuating sources have led to problems of continuity, but quality is high.

Thomas Fogarty ☆☆–☆☆☆
Portola Valley. Owner: Dr. Thomas Fogarty. 8 hectares.
www.fogartywinery.com
Gewürztraminer from Ventana (Monterey) is often stunning, as are the Pinot Noir, Chardonnay, and Merlot from the Santa Cruz Mountains.

Kalin Cellars ☆☆
Novato. Owner: Terrance Leighton. No vineyards.
www.kalincellars.com
A scientist-winemaker based in, of all unlikely places, Marin County, produces oaky, vineyard-denoted Chardonnays and Pinot Noir, released for sale only when Leighton thinks they are ready to drink.

Kathryn Kennedy ☆☆☆
Saratoga. Owner: Kathryn Kennedy. 3 hectares.
www.kathrynkennedywinery.com
Kennedy, and her son Marty Mathis, do mainly one thing, and do it well: rich, oaky Cabernet. Plus Santa Cruz Mountains Syrah and a Merlot-dominated blend. Extravagant prices.

J. Lohr ☆☆
San Jose. Owner: Jerry Lohr. 800 hectares. www.jlohr.com
If only there were more California wineries such as this one, focusing on sensibly priced varietal wines that are well crafted and full of fruit. Most of the grapes come from Monterey and Paso Robles.

Mount Eden ☆☆☆
Saratoga. Owners: Jeff and Eleanor Patterson. 16 hectares. www.mounteden.com
This renowned property was founded by Martin Ray, a difficult character who lost control of the winery in the 1970s. The vines are old and still produce tiny quantities of prodigious Chardonnay, Pinot Noir, and Cabernet Sauvignon; but the bulk of production is an Edna Valley Chardonnay.

Ridge ☆☆☆☆
Cupertino. Owner: Otsuka Co. 210 hectares. www.ridgewine.com
One of California's accepted first growths, Ridge is isolated on a mountain-top, south of San Francisco, in an atmospheric old stone building that is cooled by a natural spring. The adjacent vineyard produces "Montebello Cabernet", but Cabernet and Petite Sirah are also bought at York Creek, Napa; and Zinfandel from Geyserville, Sonoma, and Paso Robles. All the wines have a reputation for darkness and intensity without too much beef, and usually benefit from long ageing. For "Montebello" twenty years is not old; the Médoc is the natural point of reference. Paul Draper has been the winemaker here for over thirty years, and, unlike many California winemakers, he adapts his vinification techniques to the nature of the fruit harvested. Again atypically, he favours American oak over French barriques. For consistency as well as quality, Ridge is hard to beat.

Roudon-Smith Vineyards ☆
Santa Cruz. Owners: Roudon and Smith families. 5 hectares. www.roudonsmith.com
A two-family affair, producing a stylish Chardonnay, balanced somewhere between firm and smooth, just like a good Meursault. The Cabernet matches it well in style; the Zinfandel is more burly. Retirement is not far off for the owners, so production is declining.

Santa Cruz Mountain Vineyard ☆☆
Santa Cruz. Owner/winemaker: Ken Burnap. 6 hectares
A locally respected specialist in powerful Pinot Noir and Cabernet, which sometimes suffer from too much alcohol.

Savannah-Chanelle ☆☆
Saratoga. Owner: Mike Ballard. 6 hectares. www.savannahchanelle.com
Since 1996, when the present owner bought the property, it has risen to become one of the top estates. Sleek, oaky wines, notably estate-grown Cabernet Franc and Zinfandel.

Wente ☆☆
Livermore. Owners: the Wente family. 1,215 hectares. www.wentevineyards.com
One of the great wine dynasties of America. The founder, Carl, started with Charles Krug in the Napa Valley, and moved to the stony Livermore Valley in 1883 because land was cheaper. His sons Herman (d. 1961), Ernest (d. 1981), and Ernest's son Karl (d. 1977) are greatly respected names. Karl was a bold innovator, the first in California to build steel fermenting tanks outdoors, and a pioneer of Monterey vineyards. The fourth generation bought 250 more potential vineyard hectares in Livermore and planted in 1982–3. White wines made the "Wente" name. In the early 1960s their Sauvignon Blanc was my favourite; bold, sappy, old-Bordeaux style. Since then, Riesling and Chardonnay have done brilliant turns as well, and reds have become firmly ensconced in a broad, sound range. The basic range is "Family Selection"; estate-grown wines bear the "Vineyard Selections" label; and there are also reserve bottlings. The sparkling wine is serious, and spends five years on the yeast.

Leading Sierra Foothills Producers

Amador Foothill Winery ☆
Plymouth. Owners: Ben Zeitman and Katie Quinn. 4 hectares. www.amadorfoothill.com
This small, Shenandoah Valley vineyard, and the neighbouring ones from which it buys grapes, produce rugged, tannic Zinfandel, and juicy Sangiovese. The whites are disappointing.

Boeger Winery ☆–☆☆
Placerville. Owner: Greg Boeger. 34 hectares. www.boegerwinery.com
From vineyards at up to 915 metres (3,000 feet), Boeger produces innumerable wines, so quality is variable. The most reliable, and they can be excellent, are the Zinfandel, Barbera, Viognier, and blended reds.

Ironstone ☆
Murphys. Owners: the Kautz family. 1,780 hectares. www.ironstonevineyards.com
The Kautzes own only 28 hectares in the Foothills, but thousands more in Lodi and the San Joaquin Valley. From these sites they produce a range of simple varietal wines that are clean, fresh, and inexpensive. The Cabernet Franc is a specialty. The winery is the most spectacular in the Foothills, and has much in common with a theme park, made all the more engrossing as the theme in question is gold.

Karly ☆
Plymouth. Owner: Buck Cobb. 8 hectares. www.karlywines.com
Big, jammy Zinfandels are the Karly benchmarks, but the Mourvèdre is powerful, too, and there is delicious Orange Muscat.

Lava Cap Winery ☆☆
Placerville. Owners: the David Jones family. 24 hectares. www.lavacap.com
One of the most consistently stylish of the Sierra Foothills producers. The top range is called "Stromberg" and comes from vineyards planted at 975 metres (3,200 feet).

Madroña ☆☆
Camino. Owner: Dick Bush. 14 hectares. www.madrona-wines.com
Bush started planting his vineyards at 915 metres (3,000 feet)

in 1973. In some years the grapes don't fully ripen, but when they do, he produces a fine range of wines, white and red.

Monteviña ☆
Plymouth. Owner: Sutter Home. 160 hectares.
www.montevina.com
In 1988, the Trinchero family of Sutter Home bought Monteviña and began planting many Italian varieties. Despite a complete commitment to such wines, quality has rarely risen above the respectable, though there have been a few excellent wines under the Terra d'Oro label.

Renaissance ☆☆
Renaissance. Owner: Fellowship of Friends. 150 hectares.
www.renaissancewinery.com
A remarkable site producing remarkable wines: earthy, tannic, long-lived Cabernet and Zinfandel, as well as supple Sauvignon and exceptional late-harvest wines.

Renwood ☆☆☆
Plymouth. Owner: Robert Smerling. 280 hectares
Since 1992, Smerling has set out to make Amador Zinfandel more famous by making it to a still more heroic scale than previously, and raising the prices in proportion. There are up to seven different old-vine bottlings; the wines are remarkably sophisticated for Amador, and so are the Barberas. Smerling's team is now trying to crack the toughest nut of them all: Nebbiolo.

Shenandoah Vineyards ☆☆
Plymouth. Owner: Leon Sobon. 20 hectares.
www.sobonwine.com
Under the same ownership as Sobon (*q.v.*), Shenandoah offers a wide range of wines, though only the special reserve wines rival Sobon in quality. Excellent fortified wines.

Sierra Vista ☆☆–☆☆☆
Placerville. Owner/winemaker: John MacReady. 17 hectares.
www.sierravistawinery.com
MacReady makes some of the best Syrah in the Foothills, especially from Red Rock Ridge. Fine Viognier too, and a Tavel-style rosé called "Belle Rose". The Cabernet and Zinfandel are on the burly side of the spectrum.

Stevenot ☆
Murphys. Owner: Barden Stevenot. 20 hectares.
www.stevenotwinery.com
Ambitious winery well-launched with Chenin Blanc and Zinfandel, followed up by Cabernet and Chardonnay.

Domaine de la Terre Rouge ☆☆☆
Fiddletown. Owner: William Easton. 28 hectares.
www.terrerougewines.com
This new star from the Foothills produces Rhône-style wines, especially Syrah, under this label, as well as Zinfandel and Barbera under the Easton name. Quality is exceptional, for whites as well as reds, except when oak overwhelms the fruit.

Villa Toscano ☆
Plymouth. Owner: Jerry Wright. 42 hectares.
www.villatoscano.com
Pastiche Tuscan architecture and gardens, but the wines

from this new estate are more refined: lush Syrah and spicy Zinfandel.

Leading Monterey Producers

Bernardus ☆☆–☆☆☆
Carmel Valley. Owner: Bernardus Pon. 20 hectares.
www.bernardus.com
This well-funded winery, owned by a Dutch wine distributor, has acquired a reputation for classy, well-made, varietal wines, from Santa Barbara as well as Monterey, and for a splendid Bordeaux blend called Marinus.

Chalone ☆☆☆
Soledad. Owner: Chalone Group (of which the Rothchilds of Lafite are members). 120 hectares. www.chalonevineyard.com
For fifty years a lonely outpost of viticulture on a limestone hilltop near the Pinnacles National Monument, where all water had to be brought up by truck. Then Dick Graff stunned California with surprisingly Burgundian Pinot Noir and Chardonnay.

Pinot Blanc also does well on this elevated site, and the old-vine Chenin Blanc is one of California's best. Quality slipped in the 1990s, and bacterial problems crept into many of the wines. A new winemaker, Dan Karlsen, sorted out the problem, and since 1999 Chalone has been back on splendid form. Karlsen has added glorious Viognier and Syrah to the range.

Durney Vineyard
See **Heller**

Heller Estate ☆☆
Carmel Valley. Owner: Gilbert Heller. 50 hectares.
www.hellerestate.com
Carmel's first vineyard, on steep slopes not far from the ocean. The Cabernet is ripe, deep, and impressive, the Merlot more accessible and opulent and the Chenin Blanc a disciple of Vouvray. In the mid-1990s, the estate, then known as Durney, was bought by the present owner, who changed the name to his.

Jekel Vineyards ☆☆
Greenfield. Owner: Brown-Forman. 135 hectares
The whites (especially Riesling and "Gravelstone Chardonnay") produced by Jekel are among the best on offer in the region, ripe but not heavy.

Joullian ☆☆
Carmel Valley. Owners: Sias and Joullian families. 16 hectares.
www.joullian.com
For many years, Ridge Watson has run this estate on behalf of its Oklahoman proprietors. Sleek, fresh Chardonnays and ripe, elegant Cabernet are the best wines.

Mer Soleil ☆
Soledad. Owner: Charles Wagner. 158 hectares
Wagner of Caymus (*q.v.*) began planting in the Santa Lucia highlands in 1988 and has developed this brand of exotic Chardonnay, considered magnificent by some, overblown by others.

Mirassou ☆
San Jose. Owner: E. & J. Gallo. 400 hectares.
www.mirassou.com
An enterprising company with panache. Being squeezed out of increasingly urban San José, most of their vines are now in the Salinas Valley, where they pioneered field-crushing. Demand, and problems for a time with the Salinas climate, mean that more grapes have been bought in. Their wines were more exciting fifteen years ago.

Monterey Vineyard ☆
Gonzales. Owner: Diageo. 500 hectares
Monterey was founded as a vast cooperative in 1973. This winery has gone through numerous changes. The list has come to focus on sound, if commercial, Cabernet, Chardonnay, and Merlot.

Monterra.
See Delicato

Morgan ☆☆
Salinas. Owner: Dan Lee. 26 hectares. www.morganwinery.com
Founded in 1992, Morgan produces sound Chardonnay and Pinot Noir, and some wines from purchased Sonoma fruit.

Paraiso Springs ☆☆–☆☆☆
Soledad. Owner: Rich Smith. 730 hectares. www.psvwine.com
Rich Smith sells grapes to other wineries, but takes his pick for his own label. These are charming rather than structured wines, perfect for summer drinking. Syrah and Pinot Noir have performed best so far.

Talbott ☆☆
Carmel Valley. Owners: the Talbott family. 225 hectares.
www.talbottvineyards.com
The Talbott fortune derives from neckties. They sell most of their grapes, and the Chardonnay from Sleepy Hollow Vineyard is much sought after. Their own Chardonnays are lush and oaky.

Ventana Vineyard ☆☆–☆☆☆
Soledad. Owner: Douglas Meador. 120 hectares.
www.meadorestates.com
Doug Meador is an iconoclastic viticulturist, who believes he can attain high yields without compromising quality. His Sauvignon and Gewürztraminer grapes are sold to wineries across the state. His own winery releases standard varietal wines, but the top bottlings are sold under the "Meador Estate" label. Very promising Syrah.

Leading San Luis Obispo County Producers

Adelaida ☆☆–☆☆☆
Paso Robles. Owners: the Van Steenwyck family. 30 hectares.
www.adelaida.com
This quirky winery, tucked into the hills, produces Pinot Noir from thirty-five-year-old vines, and a powerful, barrel-fermented Chenin Blanc. Riesling comes from Monterey fruit and can be delicious.

Alban ☆☆☆–☆☆☆☆
Arroyo Grande. Owner: John Alban. 26 hectares
John Alban had a conversion experience in Condrieu, and in 1990 started planting Rhône varieties here. These are some of the best Rhône-style wines in California, powerful but balanced.

Arciero ☆
Paso Robles. Owners: Arciero brothers. 255 hectares.
www.arcierowinery.com
A large operation on the plateau east of Paso Robles. The wines are sound but never exciting. Another label is "Eos".

Claiborne & Churchill ☆
San Luis Obispo. Owners: Clay Thompson and Fredericka Churchill. No vineyards. www.clairbornechurchill.com
Unusually, this winery, buying in all its requirements, specializes in Alsatian-style wines, as well as exotic Chardonnay from Edna Valley.

Eberle ☆☆–☆☆☆
Paso Robles. Owner: Gary Eberle. 16 hectares.
www.eberlewinery.com
An intense loyalist to Paso Robles, particularly dedicated to Cabernet Sauvignon and Syrah, Eberle was the first to plant Syrah in the region, but the vineyard later succumbed to phylloxera. Many of Paso Robles' top winemakers worked here, and learned their craft from Eberle.

Edna Valley Vineyard ☆☆
San Luis Obispo. Owners: Chalone Group and Niven family.
400 hectares. www.ednavalley.com
This is a joint venture between Chalone and the family that owns the immense Paragon Vineyards in Edna Valley. Mostly Chardonnay, powerful and barrel-aged, and smaller quantities of Pinot Noir, Viognier, and, when the climate permits, late-harvest Riesling.

Justin ☆☆☆
Paso Robles. Owner: Justin Baldwin. 30 hectares.
www.justinwine.com
Retired banker Justin Baldwin and his wife Deborah came to this remote mountain location in 1982, and founded what has become one of the top Central Coast estates. All the wines under the "Justin" label are first-rate: lively Sauvignon; balanced Chardonnay; superb Cabernet; and a Bordeaux blend called "Isosceles". "Epoch" is the second label.

Meridian ☆–☆☆☆
Paso Robles. Owner: Beringer Blass. 2,835 hectares.
www.meridianvineyards.com
In effect the southern outpost of Beringer, producing a wide range of extremely well-made and moderately priced wines. Nor are the often excellent reserve bottlings overpriced. Paso Robles fruit finds its way into vigorous Syrah and plummy Petite Sirah.

Peachy Canyon ☆☆☆
Paso Robles. Owner: Doug Beckett. 16 hectares.
www.peachycanyonwinery.com
Since 1988, the Becketts have produced a splendid set of Zinfandels from various vineyards.

Seven Peaks ☆☆

San Luis Obispo. Owner: Southcorp. 400 hectares.
www.7peaks.com
Australia comes to California. In a partnership with the Niven family of Paragon Vineyards, Southcorp developed this brand of soundly made varietal wines with an Australian twang. However, in 2003 Southcorp, disappointed with the venture, sold its holding.

Stephan Vineyards ☆☆

Paso Robles. Owners: Stephan Asseo and Frank Benedict. 14 hectares. www.aventurewines.com
An ambitious project, launched in 1997. The main label is "L'Aventure", and prices are very high. Syrah, Zinfandel, and Viognier lead the charge.

Tablas Creek ☆☆

Paso Robles. Owners: the Perrin family. 50 hectares.
www.tablascreek
The Perrin brothers, owners of Beaucastel in Châteauneuf-du-Pape, founded a vineyard here in order to bring in much needed authentic plant material. As well as supplying vines to other estates, they have also begun producing white and red Rhône blends. Their initial releases were disappointing, but these are still early days, so perhaps worth keeping an eye on.

Talley ☆☆☆

Arroyo Grande. Owner: Brian Talley. 56 hectares.
www.talleyvineyards.com
Cabernet, the Talleys discovered, doesn't ripen here, but Burgundian varieties certainly do. The upshot is a range of impeccable and elegant Chardonnays and Pinot Noirs. "Bishop's Peak" is the second label.

Wild Horse Winery ☆–☆☆☆

Templeton. Owner/winemaker: Ken Volk. 20 hectares.
www.wildhorsewinery.com

Another Pinot Noir specialist, producing impressive results from mainly San Luis Obispo and Santa Barbara grapes. Volk will try his hand at anything – if you're searching for Negrette or Trousseau from California, this is the place to look. Quality varies, but Wild Horse wines are never dull.

Leading Santa Barbara County Producers

Au Bon Climat ☆☆–☆☆☆☆

Santa Maria. Owner: Jim Clendenen. 36 hectares
Few have done better than irrepressible Jim Clendenen at capitalizing on the great discovery about Pinot Noir in California. The vines must be shrouded in sea-fog for the wine to attain delicacy or depth. While Clendenen's single-vineyard Pinots from the Santa Maria and Santa Ynez Valleys are often superb, the whimsically named "La Bauge au-Dessus" sometimes stirs the soul more deeply. He is a Burgundian at heart, and strives for balance and elegance. Perhaps for that reason he is more admired in Europe than in his native land.

Babcock ☆☆–☆☆☆

Lompoc. Owner: Bryan Babcock. 35 hectares.
www.babcockwinery.com
Babcock made its name with its consistent Sauvignon Blanc, but red wines have grown in renown, especially the "Black Label Syrah" and the Bordeaux blend called "Fathom".

Beckmen ☆☆

Los Olivos. Owner: Tom Beckmen. 70 hectares.
www.beckmenvineyards.com
Beckmen follows the growing Santa Barbara trend towards Rhône varieties, both selling grapes and producing a growing volume of his own wines.

The Gallo Family

Ernest and the late Julio Gallo have done more to determine the direction and rate of growth of wine-drinking in the USA than anybody else in history. By far the biggest wine producers in America, and probably the world, E. & J. Gallo is still privately owned and directed by Ernest Gallo and the second and third generations of his and his brother's families.

The sons of an Italian immigrant grape farmer, they were brought up in Modesto in the Central Valley. They started making wine in 1933, when Ernest was twenty-four, and Julio twenty-three. Julio made the wine and Ernest sold it.

They built their first winery in 1935, where the present vast plant now stands, and in 1940 started planting vineyards to experiment with better grapes. They realized the limitations of Central Valley grapes and bought from growers in Napa and Sonoma. They were prepared to outbid rivals. Today they are said to grow or buy one wine-grape in three in California.

In the 1950s, the Gallos started a craze for flavoured "pop" wines with the fortified "Thunderbird", to be followed by a series of such enormously advertised and vastly popular gimmicks as fizzy "Ripple" and "Boone's" Farm apple wine. In 1964 they launched "Hearty Burgundy" which, with Chablis Blanc, set a new standard for Californian jug wines.

The Gallos have been moving slowly but steadily upmarket, taking America with them. In 1974, they introduced their first varietal wines, and in the mid-1980s bought and developed thousands of hectares in Sonoma, which formed the basis of Gallo Sonoma. In the 1990s, they proved they were capable of producing first-rate varietal wines from a range of individual Sonoma vineyards. This helped alter the image of Gallo from purveyors of jug wines to serious wine producers. This campaign was spearheaded by third-generation Gallos such as Gina and Matthew, who took charge of the Sonoma operations.

Impressive though this achievement has been, Gallo remains a Californian phenomenon, a business that single-handedly produces as much wine as all of Australia.

Brander ☆
Los Olivos. Owner: Frederic Brander. 17 hectares.
www.brander.com
Fred Brander makes outstanding Sauvignon Blancs, as well as Chardonnay and Merlot.

Byron ☆☆☆
Santa Maria. Owner: Mondavi. 260 hectares.
www.byronwines.com
Pioneer Santa Barbara winemaker Ken Brown sold the winery he founded to Robert Mondavi in 1990, but is still at the helm. Classic Santa Barbara Chardonnay and Pinot Noir: fresh and stylish. Often the regular bottlings are preferable to the very oaky reserves. Ultra-reliable from year to year. The "IO" label is reserved for lush, Rhône-style blends.

Cambria ☆☆–☆☆☆
Santa Maria. Owner: Kendall-Jackson. 565 hectares.
www.cambriawines.com
Jess Jackson bought much of the vast Tepusquet Vineyard in 1987, and uses it as the principal source for this Santa Barbara label. The reserve Chardonnay can be heavy-handed, and the simple bottlings are sometimes preferable. Charming Pinot Noir and sound Syrah, too.

Curtis ☆☆
Los Olivos. Owner: Kate Firestone. 26 hectares.
www.curtiswinery.com
Firestone acquired this Santa Ynez Valley winery and vineyard in 1987. More recently it has specialized in Rhône varieties, and the "Heritage Cuvée" proves it's possible to make highly drinkable Southern Rhône-style blends at a sensible price.

Firestone Vineyard ☆☆
Los Olivos. Owner: Suntory. 216 hectares.
www.firestonewine.com
Firestone (of tyre fame) pioneered the climatically quirky part of the Santa Ynez Valley around Los Olivos. This area does better by Cabernet and Merlot than it does by Pinot Noir, yet at the same time it also yields handsome Riesling and spicy Gewürztraminer. Among the reds, many prefer the Merlot to the Cabernet (though not I). The sweeter Rieslings appeal more than the drier ones. All of the wines are modestly priced for the quality.

Foxen ☆–☆☆☆
Santa Maria. Owners: Richard Dore and Bill Wathen. 4 hectares
Since 1987, this small winery has improved from year to year. Titanic yet silky Pinots and richly flavoured Chardonnays from single-vineyard sites.

Jaffurs ☆☆
Santa Barbara. Owner: Craig Jaffurs. No vineyards.
www.jaffurswine.com
Jaffurs buys in fruit from top vineyards to craft his exceptional Syrahs and other wines. The style can be on the lush side, with its emphasis on sweet American oak.

Koehler ☆☆
Los Olivos. Owners: the Koehler family. 40 hectares.
www.koehlerwinery.com
Santa Ynez grape farmers for many years, the Koehlers recently began producing their own wines. They are delightfully fresh and vigorous, but a new winemaker, Doug Scott, may impose changes.

Richard Longoria ☆☆
Los Olivos. Owner: Richard Longoria. 3 hectares.
www.longoriawine.com
A veteran Santa Barbara winemaker, Longoria makes a wide range of wines under his own name, emphasizing fruit rather than oak.

Mosby ☆
Buellton. Owner: Bill Mosby. 30 hectares. www.mosbywines.com
Mosby concentrates on Italian varieties, mainly Sangiovese, but also a host of others.

Andrew Murray ☆☆☆
Los Olivos. Owner: James Murray. 20 hectares.
www.andrewmurrayvineyards.com
Murray planted Rhône varieties on beautiful hillside vineyards from 1990 onwards, and his son, Andrew, turns them into gorgeously opulent wines, white as well as red. The yields are low, so the final wines are concentrated and imposing.

Fess Parker ☆☆
Los Olivos. Owner: Fess Parker. 265 hectares.
www.fessparker.com
Elderly readers may recall Parker in his most famous screen role as "Davy Crockett". Today he, and his son Eli, produce wine. The basic range carries the California appellation, but there are also estate wines. The style is full-bodied and oaky, and clearly finds favour with the countless visitors who flock to the winery and its restaurant.

Qupé ☆☆☆
Santa Maria. Owner/winemaker: Bob Lindquist. 5 hectares
Lindquist was one of the first winemakers to specialize in Rhône varieties, and his Syrah and Marsanne/Roussanne remain among the finest in California.

Rancho Sisquoc ☆
Santa Maria. Owner: James Flood. 130 hectares.
www.ranchosisquoc.com
The vineyards occupy a mere corner of a 15,400-hectare ranch. Better for whites than for reds. Recent changes in winemaker have resulted in inconsistency.

Sanford ☆☆–☆☆☆
Buellton. Owner: Richard Sanford. 145 hectares
Sanford has earned a name for characterful Chardonnay and lush Pinot Noir. Originally involved with the famous Sanford & Benedict Vineyard, Richard Sanford has more recently acquired the La Rinconada Vineyard, which began producing excellent Pinot Noir in 1999.

Santa Barbara Winery ☆☆
Santa Barbara. Owner: Pierre Lafond. 38 hectares.
www.sbwinery.com
Founded by Lafond in 1962, during the pre-history of Santa Barbara grape farming. The Chardonnay and Pinot Noir are very reliable, and sometimes there are delicious late-harvest wines from Sauvignon Blanc and Riesling.

Lane Tanner ☆☆–☆☆☆
Santa Maria. Owner: Lane Tanner. No vineyards

A gifted interpreter of Santa Barbara Pinot Noir and Syrah, whether blended or from named vineyards.

Zaca Mesa ☆☆–☆☆☆
Los Olivos. Owner: John Cushman. 182 hectares. www.zacamesa.com

Along with Firestone (*q.v.*), one of the first to plant in the Santa Ynez Valley. Pioneer vineyards on the 457-metre/ 1,500-foot flat-topped "mesa" (former cow country) are phylloxera-free and ungrafted. Crisp Chardonnay and Riesling were the first two successes, but since the mid-1990s it has shifted its focus to Rhône varieties. Syrah is the flagship, Viognier at the mercy of vintage variation. Cuvée Z is a blend of estate-grown Rhône varieties.

Other California Producers

Arcadian ☆☆☆–☆☆☆☆
Santa Ynez. Owner: Joseph Davis. No vineyards. www.arcadianwinery.com

Joe Davis trained in Burgundy, and it shows in his wines, which are made from blocks of vines he leases and farms himself. Yields are very low, and the wines, both Chardonnay and Pinot Noir, are finely poised and concentrated.

Bogle ☆
Clarksburg. Owner: Warren V. Bogle. 500 hectares. www.boglewinery.com

A standard range of varietal wines, almost always under the California appellation which permits inter-regional blending. Excellent Petite Sirah.

Calera ☆–☆☆☆
Hollister. Owner: Josh Jensen. 20 hectares

For Josh Jensen, burgundy is the Holy Grail, and limestone vineyards the path to it. So he found one of the few limestone areas in California and planted it with Pinot Noir. Rather funky wines from individual sites, plus less costly regional blends. Terrific Viognier.

Callaway ☆
Temecula. Owner: Allied Domecq. 300 hectares. www.callawaycoastal.com

The most considerable pioneer of varietal table wine in Southern California. For most of the 1980s, it specialized in unoaked Chardonnay and Chenin Blanc. In the 1990s, Pierce's Disease attacked many vineyards, so the company began purchasing grapes from California to supply its needs.

Constellation

Formerly known as Canandaigua, this corporation not only releases mediocre wines under such once renowned names as Inglenook, Paul Masson, and Alamaden, but has also been snapping up prestigious properties such as Franciscan, Simi, much of Sebastiani, and Ravenswood (*qq.v.*).

Delicato ☆–☆☆
Manteca. Owners: the Delicato family. 3,650 hectares. www.delicato.com

The Delicatos own the colossal San Bernabe Vineyard in southern Monterey. It recently began producing its own wines: the simple but clean "Blue Label" range, and the excellent "Monterra" range, which delivers beautiful fruit at bargain prices.

Ficklin Vineyards ☆☆–☆☆☆
Madera. Owners: the Ficklin family. 14 hectares. www.ficklin.com

California's most respected specialist in port-style wine, made by a *solera* system. It is neither vintage nor tawny in character, but it does age indefinitely like vintage. It needs careful, often early, decanting. Recently, Ficklin has revived the issue of vintage-dated wines.

E. & J. Gallo ☆–☆☆☆
Modesto. Owners: the Gallo families. 2,450 hectares. www.gallo.com

The world's biggest winemaker, still run by one of its founding brothers, Ernest Gallo (the other, Julio, died in a road accident in 1994). Everything about Gallo is stupendous. It owns the world's two biggest wineries to supply their incredible tank farm, which has a capacity of 265 million gallons, including a one million gallon storage tank and a ten-hectare warehouse. The bottling line starts with a glass factory. Through the 1960s, its "Hearty Burgundy" and bizarre assortment of "Chablis" (Blanc, Pink, Golden, Ruby etc.) were patiently and thoroughly designed for their huge markets. So too were Gallo sparklings ("Andre", "Ballatore"); dessert types ("Livingston Cream"); and brandies ("E & J").

With the 1970s, Gallo foresaw the market for generic wines dwindling in favour of varietals, and began to move in the latter direction. In the process it created numerous new labels for varietal wines. "Anapauma", "Zabaco", and "Turning Leaf" are but a few of the more recent. However, the venture that commands the greatest attention is Gallo Sonoma. That programme is housed in its own buildings in Dry Creek Valley, producing medium-sized lots of single-vineyard varietals from the family's ever-expanding holdings in Sonoma County (1,000 hectares and counting). Some of them are of high quality, which is more than can be said for the standard Gallo varietals, let alone their jug-wine brands.

Guenoc ☆–☆☆
Middletown. Owners: the Magoon family. 150 hectares. www.guenoc.com

A huge property straddling the Lake-Napa county line, where Lillie Langtry first planted vines in the nineteenth century. Chardonnay and Petite Sirah can be good here, and the range also includes red and white Bordeaux blends.

Kendall-Jackson ☆☆–☆☆☆
Santa Rosa. Owners: the Jackson family. 5,100 hectares. www.kj.com

Since the early 1990s, Kendall-Jackson expanded from a medium-sized company based in Lake County to one of the biggest players in California, and thus the world. The company structure is very complex, with varying ownership of vineyards, subsidiary wineries, and estates purchased over the years. Kendall-Jackson prides itself on using only "coastal" fruit, broadly defined as anything other than grapes from the torrid San Joaquin Valley.

Its "Vintners' Reserve" range of fruit-driven varietals has proved a huge success. The K.J. vineyards are analyzed as "flavour domaines": in other words, blending components for the major brands.

The more fascinating part of the story occured more recently when. Jackson scooped up nearly a dozen existing small properties, and then invented a couple more, for his Artisans and Estates division, (known as Jackson Family Vineyards). These included Cambria, La Crema, Edmeades, Hartford Court, Pepi, Lokoya, Matanzas Creek, and Stonestreet (*qq.v.*). Recently created labels for small-production wines in specific styles (and at high prices) include "Cardinale" (*q.v.*), "Verité", "Atalon", and "Carmel Road".

Leeward ☆
Ventura. 2 hectares
This winery buys in Chardonnay grapes from various Central Coast vineyards. Availability of grapes from year to year determines the range. There is occasional Napa Cabernet and Pinot Noir from Santa Barbara.

Littorai ☆☆☆
St Helena. Owner: Ted Lemon. No vineyards
Ted Lemon was the first Californian to be hired to make wines at a famous Burgundy estate: Roulot in Meursault. He has applied his Burgundian skills to the grapes that he buys from various sites in Sonoma and Mendocino. The results are great: highly impressive, elegant, and almost ethereal.

Lucas ☆☆☆
Lodi. Owner/winemaker: David Lucas. 8 hectares.
www.lucaswinery.com
Lodi's top producer of Zinfandels, the best of which is made from eighty-year-old vines.

Moraga ☆☆☆
Los Angeles. Owner: Tom Jones. 6 hectares
Hidden away in the canyons of star-studded Bel Air is this small vineyard, with a microclimate exceptional enough to allow it to produce sumptuous and expensive Cabernet Sauvignon.

Patz & Hall ☆☆–☆☆☆
Rutherford. Owners: Donald Patz, James Hall, and Ann Moses.
No vineyards. www.patzhall.com
An acclaimed négociant winery, specializing in Pinot Noir and Chardonnay from top-quality North Coast vineyards. The wines are sumptuous: a lot of (indeed, too much) new oak and alcohol.

R. H. Phillips ☆
Esparto. Owner: Vincor. 650 hectares. www.rhphillips.com
This once-lonely pioneer grower in Dunnigan Hills, northwest of Sacramento, now has company there. Consistently agreeable reds and whites from Rhône varieties enticed the rivals. In 2000, the founding Giguiere family sold the property to Vincor of Canada.

Quady ☆☆
Madera. Owner/winemaker: Andrew Quady. 6 hectares.
www.quadywinery.com

Quady uses Zinfandel from Amador County, but has planted the classic Portuguese varieties for a range of dessert wines and "port".

The celebrated "Essensia" is from Orange Muscat; "Elysium" is a red version from Black Muscat. Thanks to brilliant packaging and marketing, Quady has persuaded wine drinkers across the world to buy and enjoy his wines.

Ramey ☆☆☆
Glen Ellen. Owner: David Ramey. No vineyards
David Ramey, former winemaker for Matanzas Creek and Dominus, has his own label, devoted to subtle Chardonnay and a Bordeaux blend.

Rosenblum ☆☆–☆☆☆
Alameda. Owner: Kent Rosenblum. 14 hectares.
www.rosenblumcellars.com
Rosenblum is passionate about Zinfandel, and sources small parcels of grapes from throughout the estate, releasing up to ten versions each year.

Siduri ☆☆☆
Santa Rosa. Owner: Adam Lee. No vineyards. www.siduri.com
Lee buys Pinot Noir grapes from Oregon as well as California, and, using minimal intervention as a winemaker, fashions intense wines that have won wide acclaim.

Sine Qua Non ☆☆–☆☆☆
Ventura. Owner: Manfred Krankl. No vineyards
An Austrian restaurateur runs this eccentric operation, producing small lots of exotic wines sold mostly to collectors on his mailing list. He has collaborated with fellow Austrian sweet wine supremo, Alois Kracher (*q.v.*), on a range of dessert wines.

Steele ☆☆
Kelseyville. Owner: Jed Steele. 26 hectares.
www.steelewines.com
Jed Steele worked for Kendall-Jackson until a spectacular falling out took place. He buys in most grapes for his own label, and retains a fondess for Lake County and Mendocino fruit. Fleshy wines accessible young, as a whole.

Testarossa ☆☆☆
Los Gatos. Owners: Rob and Diana Jensen. No vineyards.
www.testarossa.com
Using grapes from top vineyards in Monterey and Santa Barbara, the Jensens produce a range of oaky but elegant wines that invariably show their vineyard origins clearly. Mostly Chardonnay and Pinot Noir, but some Syrah is now coming on stream.

Sean Thackrey ☆☆☆
Bolinas. Owner/winemaker: Sean Thackrey. No vineyards
Art dealer and winemaker, Thackrey has made some extraordinary Syrah and Rhône-style blends over the past two decades.

Unfortunately, as soon as he makes a vineyard famous, it ups its prices or sells to a rich buyer, so consistency of supply is a problem. Occasionally funky wines; never dull.

The Pacific Northwest

If, in the early 1970s, America was waking up to superlative quality from Napa and Sonoma, by the end of the decade the *avant-garde* were heralding the Pacific Northwest as the up-and-coming wine region, with strong hints that the new area would produce something that was closer to the European model: wines less overbearing than the California champions. Much of this expected potential has now been fulfilled.

In the early 1960s, a young man from Salt Lake City Utah, enrolled in a viticulture programme at the University of California at Davis. That man was David Lett. He became enamoured of Pinot Noir, but felt that, in most cases, California wasn't getting it right. He began studying climatological data from Oregon's Willamette Valley, and became convinced that the valley was the best place outside Burgundy to grow Pinot Noir grapes. In 1965, he moved to Oregon and began planting a vineyard. His Eyrie Vineyards made its first wine in 1970.

About the same time, a group of professors from the University of Washington began a winemaking project as a hobby, in a garage in Seattle. By 1967, they had made several very tasty wines from grapes grown in the Yakima Valley of central Washington. When the late André Tchelistcheff, then winemaker at Beaulieu Vineyards in Napa Valley, tasted their wines, he encouraged the men to produce more. Thus, Associated Vintners (now Columbia Winery) was born.

As early as 1979, Oregon Pinot Noir gained international accolades, when David Lett's 1975 Pinot Noir was placed second in a competitive blind tasting in Paris, organized by Robert Drouhin of Beaune; Drouhin's own 1959 Chambolle-Musigny won first place. Drouhin was so impressed that he visited Oregon several times, eventually establishing a vineyard and winery near Lett's in 1988.

In less than thirty years, the Pacific Northwest wine industry has burgeoned. Vineyards have expanded enormously. In Washington, there are now over 200 wineries, farming 11,300 hectares. In Oregon, there are 180 wineries and over 4,000 hectares of vineyards, of which half are planted with Pinot Noir. The two industries are as distinct as the geography that separates them.

North of the California border, in western Oregon, the Coastal Range acts as a very effective rain-catcher and offers shelter to the Umpqua Valley to the south, then further north, to the Willamette Valley, where seventy per cent of Oregon's vineyards are located. Umpqua is drier and warmer than Willamette; Cabernet will usually ripen there, but not further north.

Oregon's annual rainfall is a reasonable seventy-five to one hundred centimetres (thirty to forty inches), and the latitude the same as that of Bordeaux. For the most part, this is a gentle maritime climate, best-suited to cool-climate grape varieties. Although the star, to date, has been Pinot Noir, recent years have seen increased plantings of Pinot Gris, Chardonnay, and Pinot Blanc. The quality of Gewürztraminer is generally high, and the area also produces some good sparkling wines.

Oregon's occasional problems derive from unwelcome rainfall in autumn, often just before or during harvest. This leads to considerable vintage variation.

In complete contrast to Oregon, the vineyards of Washington have been planted two ranges back from the Pacific Ocean, east of the much higher Cascade Mountains, in an area with a mere twenty centimetres (eight inches) of rain a year: the Columbia River Basin, and within it, the more grape-specific, Yakima Valley. The region's deep, sandy soil; long, summer daylight hours; and hot sunshine, have proved ideal for wine grapes.

The latitude – 160 kilometres (100 miles) further north than Willamette – and the continental extremes of temperature (very cold in winter and surprisingly chilly even on a summer night) have proved particularly suited to the Bordeaux varieties: Sémillon, Sauvignon Blanc, Cabernet Sauvignon, Cabernet Franc, and Merlot with Syrah and Sangiovese as promising newcomers. Chardonnay, Riesling, and Gewürztraminer also fare extremely well in eastern Washington. Grapes ripen well while keeping remarkably high acidity, with a consequent intensity of flavour.

Four regional designations are permitted on Oregon labels: Willamette Valley (AVA: nine counties from Portland 160 kilometres (100 miles) south to Eugene); Umpqua Valley (AVA: Douglas County, centred on Roseburg, another eighty kilometres/fifty miles south); Rogue Valley (Jackson and Josephine counties, centred on Grant's Pass, eighty kilometres/fifty miles south again); and Applegate (a sub-zone of Rogue Valley).

Washington's vineyards are concentrated in the Yakima Valley, but its established wineries are centred around Seattle in suburbs such as Woodinville, which is still the stronghold for many of Washington's largest and most prestigious wineries. The five AVAs are Puget Sound (mostly planted with hybrids); Columbia Valley; Yakima Valley; Walla Walla Valley; and Red Mountain. In the past, the grapes were often transported the 240 kilometres (150 miles) over the Cascades to Seattle, but several companies have now built wineries near the vineyards. Sub-regions are being identified and developed. Watch out for such names as Ahtanum Ridge, Cold Creek, Wahluke Slope, and Canoe Ridge.

In the 1980s, Washington, with a climate promoting high acidity, was thought better for white grapes than for red. Today that view has changed, and fifty-seven per cent of production is now of red wine. With red grapes attaining lower alcohol levels than most of those from California, Washington can produce wines with finesse as well as ripeness. Merlot used to be considered the primary red grape, but it is now being overtaken by both Cabernet Sauvignon and Syrah. Moreover, as vintages go by, it becomes ever more clear which sites are producing the best grapes, and why. This is leading to a proliferation of single-vineyard wines with distinct personalities of their own.

Neighbouring Idaho, whose vineyards are east of Oregon along the Snake River, has sixteen wineries and has made a name for itself with its Chardonnays.

Oregon

Leading Willamette Valley Producers

Adelsheim Vineyard ☆☆
Newberg. Owners: David and Virginia Adelsheim. 65 hectares.
www.adelsheimvineyard.com
The winery first crushed in 1978, using mainly Washington grapes. The focus is now on fine Pinot Noir from its own and neighbouring vineyards. Also produced are Chardonnay, Pinot Gris, and fresh Pinot Blanc.

Amity Vineyards ☆
Amity. Owner/winemaker: Myron Redford. 6 hectares.
www.amityvineyards.com
Amity, established in 1976, produces about 15,000 cases a year. Its best efforts, at present, are dry and late-harvest Riesling, and Pinot Blanc. The quality of the Pinot Noir varies.

Archery Summit ☆☆☆
Dayton. Owner/winemaker: Gary Andrus. 45 hectares.
www.archerysummit.com
California-based Gary Andrus is owner of Pine Ridge in Napa Valley, and started buying vineyards here in 1992. The focus is Pinot Noir, with numerous bottlings. Wines such as "Red Hills Estate" are aged in new oak and high-priced, but quality is undoubtedly excellent. "Vireton" is an attractive white blend, dominated by Pinot Gris.

Argyle ☆☆☆
Dundee. Owner: Petaluma. 200 hectares.
www.argylewinery.com
The winery was founded in 1987 by a partnership including Brian Croser and Bollinger, with a view to making *méthode traditionnelle* sparkling wines. It also produces very good Chardonnay, Pinot Noir (notably "Nuthouse" and "Spirithouse" bottlings), and a delicious, dry Riesling.

Beaux Frères ☆☆☆
Newberg. Owners: Michael Etzel and Robert M. Parker.
13 hectares. www.beauxfreres.com
Beaux Frères is currently the darling of the Oregon wine industry, devoted to small quantities of intense, oaky Pinot Noirs from its 6.5 hectare vineyard. Co-owner Parker is the famous wine critic, winemaker Etzel his brother-in-law. The first wine was made in 1992. Initial releases packed too much of a punch; more recent vintages have been more stylish.

Bethel Heights ☆–☆☆
Salem. Owners: the Casteel family. 20 hectares.
www.bethelheights.com
Since 1984, Bethel Heights has been one of Oregon's most consistent Pinot Noir producers, known for its excellent vineyard in the Eola Hills and a roster of fine wines, which also includes Chardonnay, Pinot Gris, and Pinot Blanc.
Winemaker Terry Casteel picks his grapes late to give his wines a bold profile. Some additional Pinot Noir grapes are purchased.

Brick House ☆☆
Newberg. Owner: Doug Tunnell. 11 hectares.
www.brickhousewines.com
Doug Tunnell exchanged the life of a foreign correspondent for that of a vigneron, and produces small quantities of powerful Pinot Noir from organic vineyards.

Broadley ☆☆–☆☆☆
Monroe. Owners: the Broadley family. 8 hectares
The Broadleys only release high-quality Pinot Noir wines in fairly small quantities.

Chehalem ☆☆
Newberg. Owner/winemaker: Harry Peterson-Nedry.
70 hectares. www.chehalemwines.com
From its first commercial crush in 1990, Chehalem has become known for deep, intense, estate-grown Pinot Noirs. The 1994 vintage saw a collaboration between the winery and Burgundian winemaker Patrice Rion, in whose honour the top wine, "Rion Reserve", is named. Chehalem also makes Pinot Gris, Chardonnay, and Riesling.

Cooper Mountain ☆
Beaverton. Owner: Dr Robert Gross. 40 hectares.
www.coopermountainwine.com
A large organic property now converted to biodynamism. This commitment to sensitive viticulture seems to be reflected in the wines since 1999.

Cristom ☆☆–☆☆☆
Salem. Owner: Paul Gerrie. 27 hectares.
www.cristomwines.com
The Gerries bought this winery in 1992, and hired one of California's brightest and best – Steve Doerner, formerly of Calera – as their winemaker.
Cristom annually produces 7,000 cases of delicious Pinot Noir, Pinot Gris, and Chardonnay.

Cuneo Cellars ☆–☆☆
Carlton. Owner/winemaker: Gino Cuneo. 24 hectares.
www.cuneocellars.com
Formerly Hidden Springs Winery, it produces Pinot Noir from estate grapes, as well as a Nebbiolo and a Bordeaux blend. Top wines are bottled under the "Cana's Feast" label.

Domaine Drouhin ☆☆☆
Dundee. Owner: Robert Drouhin. 35 hectares.
www.domainedrouhin.com
The unique outpost of Burgundy in the Northwest, founded by Robert Drouhin in 1987. Drouhin's daughter Veronique has produced consistently fine wines.
Her regular bottling is of a high standard, but two barrel selections, "Laurène" and "Louise" are even better. Not surprisingly, this is the most Burgundian of Oregon estates. Chardonnay was added to the range in 1997.

Elk Cove ☆☆
Gaston. Owners: the Pat Campbell family. 40 hectares.
www.elkcove.com
Elk Cove was one of the pioneers, founded in 1977. In addition to much-improved Pinot Noir, well-oaked Chardonnay, Riesling, and Pinot Gris, the winery produces an ultra-sweet dessert wine called "Ultima".

Eola Hills Wine Cellars ☆

Rickreall. Owners: Investor group headed by Tom Huggins. 42 hectares. www.eolahillswinery.com

Eola Hills, near Salem, makes good and reasonably priced varietals from grapes grown on its own and neighbouring Eola Hills vineyards.

Erath ☆☆–☆☆☆

Dundee. Owner: Dick Erath. 54 hectares. www.erath.com

With the hiring of winemaker Rob Stuart, the former Knudsen Erath winery gained a new lease of life. The long-lived, dry Riesling is as delicious as ever, and Chardonnay has hit its stride; now the new Dijon clones from Burgundy are bearing fruit. There are various bottlings of Pinot Noir, as well as small quantities of Pinot Gris, Pinot Blanc, and tiny bits of Arneis and Dolcetto.

Evesham Wood ☆☆

Salem. Owner/winemaker: Russell Raney. 4 hectares

Small estate winery established in 1986, now producing approximately 3,000 cases of wine, including a bold and intense Pinot Noir, Chardonnay, Pinot Gris, and an exceptionally fine, dry Gewürztraminer.

Eyrie Vineyards ☆☆–☆☆☆

Dundee. Owner/winemaker: David Lett. 20 hectares

Delicate, pretty Pinot Noirs, oaky Chardonnays, and deliciously fruity Pinot Gris are this Oregon pioneer's stock in trade. Since his first vintage in 1970, David Lett has been a maverick; he sticks to his style, even though the industry around him has changed. His wines have proven remarkably and deliciously age-worthy. Also produces Pinot Meunier and dry Muscat.

Flynn ☆

Rickreall. Owners: the Flynn family. 45 hectares. www.flynnvineyards.com

With first vineyards planted in 1982 and first wines made in 1984, Wayne Flynn built a large new winery in 1990, and since then has devoted most of its efforts to sparkling wines, with still Pinot Noir and Chardonnay too. The inexpensive Cellar Select range is partly made with the use of oak chips.

Hinman ☆☆

Eugene. Owner: Carolyn Chambers. 3 hectares. www.silvanridge.com

Hinman is one of the largest and most advanced wineries in the state, with Chardonnay, Pinot Noir, and Pinot Gris. The top range is bottled under the Silvan Ridge label, as under a previous owner, Hinman's reputation was poor. Chardonnays are toasty, the Pinot Gris plump and spicy, the Pinot Noirs, stylish.

King Estate ☆☆–☆☆☆

Eugene. Owners: the King family. 75 hectares. www.kingestate.com

This huge, new, well-financed operation, managed by Ed King, is Oregon's largest winery. It supplements its own vineyard production by buying grapes from fifty growers. The château-style winery focuses on Pinot Gris, Pinot Noir, and Chardonnay, and the reserve wines can be excellent. Pinot Gris is King's best wine to date. First vintage was in 1992. Second label: "Lorane Valley".

Lange ☆

Dundee. Owner/winemaker: Don Lange. 6 hectares. www.langewinery.com

Transplants from Santa Barbara (California), the Langes have established a lovely vineyard and winery in Yamhill County, and since 1987 have produced some excellent wines, although the quality is inconsistent. Top attention-getters are their reserve Pinot Gris and reserve Pinot Noir.

Lemelson ☆☆

Carlton. Owner: Eric Lemelson. 37 hectares. www.lemelsonvineyards.com

1999 was the first vintage of this winery, but the inaugural Pinot Noirs showed great promise.

Montinore ☆☆

Forest Grove. Owners: Leo and Jane Graham. 115 hectares. www.montinore.com

A magnificent estate, planted in the early 1980s with a dozen different vine varieties. Today, under French winemaker Jacques Tardy, production focuses on medium-bodied reds and whites and occasional late-harvest wines.

Oak Knoll ☆

Hillsboro. Owners: the Vuylsteke family. No vineyards. www.oakknollwinery.com

One of Oregon's most venerable wineries, Oak Knoll at first made fruit and berry wines (their aromatic raspberry wine is still produced). These have been outshone by varietal wines, all from purchased grapes. The Pinot Noir can be coarse, but the white wines, especially Pinot Gris, are often excellent.

Panther Creek ☆☆–☆☆☆

McMinnville. Owner: Ron Kaplan. No vineyards. www.panthercreekcellars.com

Ken Wright (*q.v.*) used to make the wines here, but now has his own label. The present winemaker is Michael Stevenson. Kaplan buys in grapes from top vineyards, some of which are also managed by his team. Excellent, deeply flavoured Pinot Noir continues, along with a small quantity of Pinot Gris.

Ponzi ☆☆

Beaverton. Owners: the Ponzi family. Winemaker: Luisa Ponzi. 30 hectares. www.ponziwines.com

Pioneer Oregon winery; passed on to the second generation. The three Ponzi children control operations, and Luisa makes the wine. Still highly regarded for its dry Riesling, unctuous Chardonnay and Pinot Gris, and hefty Pinot Noir, Ponzi also experiments with Arneis and Dolcetto.

Rex Hill ☆☆–☆☆☆

Newberg. Owners: Paul Hart and Jan Jacobsen. 102 hectares. www.rexhill.com

From several vineyard sites throughout Yamhill County, winemaker Lynn Penner-Ash produces 30,000 cases of wine a year. The "Kings Ridge" range are easy sippers. More intense are the vineyard-designated Pinots and Chardonnays. Best wines are the reserve Pinot Gris, Pinot Noir, and Chardonnay.

St Innocent ☆–☆☆

Salem. Owner: St-Innocent. No vineyards. www.stinnocentwine.com

This producer was established in 1988; popular for its full-bodied Pinot Noir, Chardonnay, and a delightful sparkling wine. Winemaker Mark Vlossak purchases grapes from various Eola Hills vineyards.

Domaine Serene ☆☆☆
Dayton. Owner: Ken Evenstad. 62 hectares.
www.domaineserene.com
Ken Wright (*q.v.*) was the winemaker here until he left to concentrate on his own label; Tony Rynders took his place in 1998. These have always been impressive Pinot Noirs, and a new winery, opened in 2001, may raise quality even further.

Shafer ☆
Forest Grove. Owner/winemaker: Harvey Schafer. 13 hectares.
www.shafervineyardcellars.com
A firm belief that quality stems primarily from the vineyard motivates Shafer, whose Chardonnay and Riesling are highly regarded. But quality varies.

Silvan Ridge
See **Hinman**

Sokol Blosser ☆☆
Dundee. Owners: Bill and Susan Sokol Blosser. 17 hectares.
www.sokolblosser.com
One of Oregon's larger and more mature wineries, Sokol Blosser flagged in the late 1980s with changes in winemaker and general confusion. Today it is back on its feet with Russ Rosner producing very good wines.

Soter ☆☆
Yamhill. Owner: Tony Soter. 9 hectares
Tony Soter is one of Napa's most respected consultant winemakers. His own label, Etude (*q.v.*) was sold recently.

Torii Mor ☆☆–☆☆☆
McMinnville. Owner: Don Olson. 4 hectares.
www.toriimorwinery.com
The first commercial wines were made in 1993 from Olson's Dundee Hills vineyard. Joe Dobbes has replaced Patricia Green. Torii Mor doesn't lack ambition: prices for single-vineyard bottlings of Pinot Noir climb to $100.

Tualatin ☆
Forest Grove. Owners: Willamette Valley Vineyards.
60 hectares. www.wvv.com
All Tualatin wines come from grapes grown at the estate vineyard, established in 1973. Riesling and Chardonnay have long been the best wines here, but under winemaker Joe Dobbes, Pinot Noir has been coming into its own recently.

Tyee Wine Cellars ☆☆
Corvallis. Owners: the Buchanan family and Barney Watson.
4 hectares. www.tyeewine.com
Tyee excels in Pinot Gris, Pinot Blanc and Gewürztraminer, and also produces Pinot Noir and Chardonnay.

WillaKenzie Estate ☆☆–☆☆☆
Yamhill. Owner: Bernard LaCroute. 48 hectares.
www.willakenzie.com
Since 1995, LaCroute has invested a fortune in this fine estate and modern winery. His young French winemaker, Laurent

Montalieu, has produced delicious Pinot Gris and Pinot Blanc and some very promising Pinot Noirs.

Willamette Valley Vineyards ☆–☆☆
Turner. Owner: WWV. 40 hectares. www.wvv.com
One of Oregon's biggest producers. Most of the wines are unremarkable, but the top end of the range is first-rate, with single-vineyard Pinot Noirs made by winemaker Joe Dobbes.

Ken Wright ☆☆☆–☆☆☆☆
Carlton. Owner/winemaker: Ken Wright. No vineyards.
www.kenwrightcellars.com
Wright produces as many as 12 separate bottlings of Pinot Noir each vintage from parcels of vines he manages, but does not own. These are wines of great finesse and concentration, securing his reputation as one of Oregon's most experienced and gifted winemakers.

Yamhill Valley Vineyards ☆
McMinnville. Owners: Denis Burger and partners. 36 hectares.
www.yamhill.com
Established in 1983, this property has a sound reputation for fresh, lively wines from the Pinot family.

Leading Rogue Valley Producers

Bridgeview ☆
Cave Junction. Owner: Robert Kerivan. 90 hectares.
www.bridgeviewwine.com
Laurent Montalieu of WillaKenzie Estate (*q.v.*) brought this large, southern Oregon winery to prominence in the early 1990s with Pinot Gris, Pinot Noir, Chardonnay, Riesling, and Gewürztraminer. Bridgeview has developed a following for its "Blue Moon" range, especially the good-value Riesling.

Foris ☆☆–☆☆☆
Cave Junction. Owner: Ted Gerber. 25 hectares.
www.foriswine.com
The Gerbers began producing wine commercially in 1987. Winemaker Sarah Powell has pushed Foris to the top of the league in Rogue Valley, with a fine range of varietal wines.

Valley View ☆
Jacksonville. Owners: the Wisnovsky family. 12 hectares.
www.valleyviewwinery.com
Valley View has recently made great strides with red and white Bordeaux varieties. The reserve "Anna Maria" range is only bottled in outstanding vintages. Pioneer Peter Britt planted 200 varieties in experimental vineyards here in the 1850s.

Leading Umpqua Valley Producers

Henry Estate ☆
Umpqua. Owner/winemaker: Scott Henry. 18 hectares.
www.henryestate.com

Scott Henry is best-known as the inventor of a trellising system that has been adopted throughout the world. His estate, on the fertile valley floor, specializes in easy-to-drink Chardonnay, Gewürztraminer, Pinot Gris, and Pinot Noir. The "Barrel Fermented" and "Select" wines have pronounced American oak flavours. Gewürztraminer is probably Henry's best wine, but he is proud of his off-dry Müller-Thurgau.

Washington

Leading Columbia Valley Producers

Barnard Griffin ☆☆–☆☆☆
Richland. Owners: Deborah Barnard and Rob Griffin.
No vineyards. www.barnardgriffin.com
Rob Griffin used to work at the Hogue Cellars (*q.v.*) but as he always had a hankering for his own small winery and more experimental wines, setting up on his own came as a great opportunity. His success with Cabernet Sauvignon, Merlot, Sauvignon Blanc (Fumé-style), and Chardonnay is legendary.

Columbia Crest ☆☆–☆☆☆
Paterson. Owner: Stimson Lane. 1,200 hectares.
www.columbia-crest.com
Cellars are rare in the northwest: ninety per cent of Columbia Crest, Washington's largest winery, is underground, Doug Gore takes quality seriously. His best wines are Merlot, Cabernet Sauvignon, Sauvignon Blanc, and Chardonnay. His deft touch with Washington fruit and the Stimson ane marketing machine have proved a winning combination.

Preston ☆
Pasco. Owners: the Preston family. 72 hectares.
www.prestonwines.com
Since 1976, Bill Preston has released a wide range of varietal wines from a quality-conscious operation. Dependable and good value.

Leading Yakima Valley Producers

Chinook ☆
Prosser. Owners: Kay Simon and Clay Mackey. 1 hectare
A small winery, producing well-regarded but occasionally herbaceous Merlot, Sauvignon Blanc, and Chardonnay. Kay Simon was former winemaker at Château Ste Michelle (*q.v.*).

Covey Run ☆
Zillah. Owner: Constellation. 320 hectares. www.coveyrun.com
An attractive winery, making popular wines from a range of varieties. Good value.

Hedges Cellars ☆☆☆
Benton City. Owners: Tom and Anne-Marie Hedges.
26 hectares. www.hedgescellars.com
Founded in 1990 by a potato farmer with vision, Hedges now occupies an imposing château-style winery close to its vineyards on Red Mountain. The Cabernet/Merlot blend is juicy and good value, but the top wines are the "Three Vineyards", and the powerfully structured "Red Mountain Reserve".

Hogue Cellars
Prosser. Owner: Vincor. 160 hectares. www.hogue-cellars.com
This winery, founded by a long-established farming family, struck a chord from its earliest vintages. In 1997, it unveiled a new structure: a good varietal range called "Barrel Select"; reserves; and "Genesis", a label reserved for small lots of Syrah, barrel-fermented Sémillon, Pinot Gris, and other wines.

At all levels, the Hogues stressed value for money, and the quality of the reds became truly impressive by the mid-1990s. In 2001, the family sold the business.

Kiona ☆☆
Benton City. Owners: the Williams family. 30 hectares
This laid-back winery, a pioneer of Red Mountain fruit, now specializes in deep, dark Cabernet Sauvignon and Merlot, and delicious late-harvest Riesling and Gewürztraminer. The unusual Lemberger is worth looking out for, and Syrah joined the roster in 1997.

Paul Thomas ☆
Sunnyside. Owner: Constellation. 55 hectares.
www.paulthomaswinery.com
Paul Thomas makes a full line of fairly inexpensive varietal wines. The whites often have too much residual sugar; the reds lack concentration.

Washington Hills Cellars ☆☆–☆☆☆
Sunnyside. Owner: Harry Alhadeff. 45 hectares.
www.washingtonhills.com
Brian Carter is one of Washington's most gifted winemakers. He began working with Alhadeff in 1990 and soon had followers. He also makes the ultra-premium Apex wines – Chardonnay, Cabernet, Sauvignon Blanc, and late-harvest – under the auspices of Washington Hills.

Leading Walla Walla Producers

Canoe Ridge ☆☆☆
Walla Walla. Owners: Chalone Group and partners. 65 hectares.
www.canoeridgevineyard.com
The vineyard was planted from 1989 onwards along the Columbia River, confusingly next to Château Ste Michelle's (*q.v.*) Canoe Ridge Estate, but the winery is fifty miles away in downtown Walla Walla. John Abbott made its first wines – tantalizing Merlot, Cabernet, and Chardonnay – in 1993. These remain the winery's focus.

Cayuse ☆☆–☆☆☆
Walla Walla. Owner/winemaker: Christophe Baron. 14 hectares.
www.cayusevineyards.com

A Frenchman who worked in Australia as a flying winemaker, Baron has been making a fine reputation for himself here since 1997. Syrah is exceptional, and Tempranillo is a wine to watch.

Dunham ☆☆–☆☆☆
Walla Walla. Owner: Eric Dunham. 1 hectare.
www.dunhamcellars.com
Dunham used to be a winemaker at L'Ecole 41 (*q.v.*), and began his own label in 1995, producing a range of powerful oaky wines.

L'Ecole 41 ☆☆–☆☆☆
Lowden. Owner: Marty Clubb. 10 hectares.
www.lecole.com
Using, for the most part, purchased grapes from Walla Walla, this winery, based on a former schoolhouse, goes all out for opulent, showy wines, such as Merlot, Cabernet, and a powerful, barrel-fermented Sémillon.

Glen Fiona ☆☆☆
Walla Walla. Owner: Berle 'Rusty' Figgins. No vineyards.
www.glenfiona.com
Figgins, brother of Gary Figgins of Leonetti (*q.v.*), specializes in intense Syrah, but avoids the fad for new oak by ageing the wines in older puncheons.

Leonetti ☆☆☆
Walla Walla. Owner/winemaker: Gary Figgins. 20 hectares.
www.leonetticellar.com
Figgins has a legendary reputation, based on the splendid, dark-red wines he made in the 1980s, some of which are still going strong. Selected grapes from many vineyards and ample new oak make for expensive but very worthwhile Merlot and Cabernet. The wines are sold through a (full) mailing list, so are all but unobtainable.

Pepper Bridge
Walla Walla. Owner: Norm McKibben. 110 hectares.
www.pepperbridge.com
Norm McKibben has developed some of Washington's top vineyards, and since 1999 he has donned another hat as a wine producer. Quality is expected to be high.

Waterbrook ☆☆
Walla Walla. Owner/winemaker: Eric Rindal. 5 hectares.
www.waterbrook.com
Stylistically distinct, with clean, varietal flavours tempered with American oak, Waterbrook wines stand apart. They represent, for the most part, good value and excellent quality. Cabernet Sauvignon, Merlot, Sauvignon Blanc, and Chardonnay are now supplemented by red blends from Red Mountain vineyards.

Woodward Canyon ☆☆☆
Lowden. Owner/winemaker: Rick Small. 11 hectares.
www.woodwardcanyon.com
The first wines were made here in 1981, making Rick Small something of a Walla Walla pioneer. Woodward Canyon is noted for its toasty Cabernet and Merlot, and its ripe, rich, woody, love-it-or-hate-it Chardonnay.

Once known for its powerful white wines, today the winery is best-known for its "Old Vines Cabernet".

Other Columbia Valley Producers

Arbor Crest ☆☆
Spokane. Owners: Jim and Christina van Loben Sels.
No vineyards. www.arborcrestwinery.com
Good winemaking and ample capital led to early success for a winery working almost entirely with grapes from contracted vineyards. In 1999, a new generation took over, leading to a swift improvement in quality.

Château Ste Michelle ☆☆–☆☆☆
Woodinville. Owner: Stimson Lane. 500 hectares.
www.ste-michelle.com
Much the biggest concern in the northwest (800,000 cases annually), and with its top wines among the best. The large showpiece winery at Woodinville, twenty-four kilometres (15 miles) northeast of Seattle, was outgrown in 1983, when 26-million-dollar River Ridge facility, three times as big, was built on the Columbia River near Paterson. The wines produced cover the full spectrum: Riesling, Chardonnay, Sauvignon Blanc, Gewürztraminer, Chenin Blanc, Sémillon, Merlot, Cabernet Sauvignon, and "Port" – all notably well-made, the whites being especially successful in the local market.

Special emphasis in recent vintages has been laid on the winery's vineyard-designated Chardonnays, Cabernet Sauvignons, and Merlots, which rank among the northwest's finest. In the late 1990s, the company undertook some interesting joint ventures: with Antinori to produce a high-priced red blend from Horse Heaven Vineyard called "Col Solare"; and with Ernst Loosen in Germany to produce a sensational Riesling, called "Eroica".

Ste Michelle, by virtue of its size, its technical professionalism, and its marketing ability, is a worthy flagship for the whole winemaking industry in the northwest.

Columbia Winery ☆☆☆
Woodinville. Owner: Constellation. 150 hectares.
www.columbiawinery.com
One of the pioneers of the northwest, founded in 1962 by a group of professors at the University of Washington, and still one of the best. Since 1976, it has been directed by David Lake, a British master of wine.

Now making a wide variety of excellent wines including Gewürztraminer, Cabernet Sauvignon, Syrah, Merlot, Sémillon, Chardonnay, and Riesling. Lake has established close contacts (and contracts) with some of the best grape-growers, particularly Otis Vineyards and Red Willow and Wyckoff in the Yakima Valley.

DeLille Cellars/Chaleur Estate ☆☆☆
Woodinville. Owners: the Lill family and partners. 8 hectares.
www.delillecellars.com
The first vintage here was in 1992, and the winery's reputation was swiftly made. Winemaker Chris Upchurch focused from the start on ultra-premium, Bordeaux-style red and white wine blends sourced from eastern Washington vineyards.

"Chaleur Estate" is a complex and heady blend, selected from the best barrels. The white is a Graves-style blend. "Doyenne" is pure Syrah, given full oak treatment.

DiStefano ☆☆
Woodinville. Owner/winemaker: Mark Newton. No vineyards.
www.distefanowinery.com
Originally established to produce sparkling wine, Newton switched the emphasis to rich reds from Cabernet Franc, Cabernet Sauvignon, Merlot, and, more recently, Syrah.

Latah Creek ☆
Spokane. Owner/winemaker: Mike Conway. No vineyards.
www.latahcreek.com
Established in 1982, Latah Creek produces medium-bodied Merlot, Cabernet Sauvignon, Lemberger, and Chardonnay, all at moderate prices.

Quilceda Creek ☆☆☆
Snohomish. Owner: Alex Golitzin. 11 hectares.
www.quilcedacreek.com
Winery established in 1979. Quilceda's winemaker Paul Golitzin makes very good, new-oaked Cabernet in the Médoc tradition. Quantities are small and prices high.

SilverLake ☆
Woodinville. Owners: Washington Wine and Beverage Co.
92 hectares. www.washingtonwine.com
Founded in 1989, SilverLake astutely hired former Château Ste Michelle (*q.v.*) head winemaker Cheryl Barber-Jones to make varietal and sparkling wines from Yakima

Snoqualmie Winery ☆
Snoqualmie. Owner: Stimson Lane. 97 hectares.
www.snoqualmie.com
Founded in 1983, the winery was declared bankrupt in 1990 and sold to its present owners the following year. Makes 50,000 cases yearly of consistent and reasonably priced varietal wines at sister winery Columbia Crest (*q.v.*) by Joy Anderson.

Andrew Will ☆☆☆
Vashon. Owner/winemaker: Chris Camarda. 18 hectares
This small winery focuses on small quantities of highly concentrated Cabernet Sauvignon, Merlot, and barrel-fermented Chenin Blanc. There are now some five vineyard-designated Merlots as well as a Bordeaux blend called "Sorella". Camarda is gradually planting his own vineyards.

Idaho

Leading Idaho Producers

Ste Chapelle ☆☆
Caldwell. Owners: Corus Brands. www.stechapelle.com
Founder Bill Broich, an excellent if restless winemaker, left in 1985, having established a fine track record with Riesling, Chardonnay, Gewürztraminer, and sparkling wines made from Riesling, Chardonnay, and Pinot Noir.

Ste Chapelle was established in 1970 – the oldest and by far the largest of Idaho's dozen wineries, controlling almost half of the state's 400 hectares of vineyards, and producing 150,000 cases. It also buys in Washington grapes. The style is for crisp, elegant, and slightly floral wines, dictated largely by the climate, which does not reliably ripen the grapes.

Indian Creek Winery ☆☆
Kuna. Owners: Bill Stowe and partners
One of the half-dozen wineries grouped in the Caldwell area, southwest of Boise, and one of the state's most interesting properties.

With some eight hectares of vineyards, Bill Stowe produces a better-than-average Pinot Noir, including a stylish, dry white Pinot Noir, with smaller quantities of Riesling and Chardonnay. The winery's first vintage was in 1987.

Other Idaho Producers

Camas Winery ☆
One of Northern Idaho's oldest premium wineries, offering fourteen different wines.

Cana Vineyards ☆–☆☆
Established in 1990 on the site of the former Lou Facelli winery. Mostly Cabernet and Merlot.

Carmela Vineyards ☆–☆☆
Some twenty hectares in the Hagerman viticultural area. Best-known for Cabernet Franc.

Cocolalla Winery ☆
The state's northernmost winery, making an annual 400 cases of brut sparkling.

Hell's Canyon Winery ☆–☆☆
Established in 1980, and makes an annual 3,000 cases of Chardonnay and Cabernet Sauvignon from fifteen hectares.

Parma Ridge ☆–☆☆
Parma. www.parmaridge.com
A new property, planted in 1998 and a winery completed in 2000. Focuses on the classic international varieties.

Petros Winery ☆
Established in 1983 by Lou Facelli.

Rose Creek Vineyards ☆
This is a family run winery, established in 1984. After vineyards were wiped out by frost, owner Jamie Martin has had to buy in Idaho-grown grapes. Known for Riesling and Chardonnay.

Sawtooth ☆
The former Pintler Cellar, with six hectares of Riesling, Semillon, Chardonnay, Pinot Noir, and Cabernet Sauvignon.

Vickers Vineyard ☆☆
Kirby Vickers in the Snake River Valley produces small quantities of good Chardonnay.

Weston Winery ☆
One of Idaho's oldest and highest wineries – at 840 metres (2,750 feet).

Other Regions of the USA

For centuries the true wine-vine, *Vitis vinifera*, could not be successfully grown in the climate of most of North America. The problems are extremes of cold in the north and centre, and of heat and humidity in the south. The cold simply kills the vines in winter. Humidity brings rampant mildew; the heat of southern summers, a general malfunction of the vine (instead of respiring at night and building up sugar, the plant continues to grow; the sugar is used in excessive foliage and the grapes, despite months of broiling heat, are scarcely ripe).

Two regions, the northeast (led by New York State) and the southeast (led by Virginia), have strong wine traditions of their own, and are now enjoying a great revival. Until very recently, their wine industry was based on native grapes, adapted to the local climate, but most wineries today concentrate on *vinifera*. In the south, the grape is the Muscadine, or Scuppernong, a plant very different from the classic wine-vine (its berries are like clusters of marbles with tough skins that slip off the flesh). The powerful flavour of its sweet wine was once immensely popular in America in a famous brand called "Virginia Dare". Scuppernong still flourishes, but bears no relation to the wines of the rest of the world.

But now, almost every state of the union outside these areas has hopeful winemakers – hopeful of seeing their industry, fledgling or a century old, as some of them are, establish itself as part of the American wine boom. Only Alaska, North Dakota, and Wyoming are still winery-free.

A number of long-established wineries have distinct local markets. In the past, these tended to be a disincentive to experimenting with new grapes. When it was assumed for so long that *Vitis vinifera* could not be grown, it was a brave winemaker who did more than dip a toe in the water with a hectare or two of experimental planting. With modern knowledge, more and more dippers are reporting success. There are certainly quite large areas where the microclimate appears to make *vinifera* a practicable proposition after all. There are also new hybrid vines, crosses between *vinifera* and American natives, which show the hardiness of the natives without their peculiar flavours. These French-American hybrids have improved greatly over the past few years, but their overall importance in the eastern market has been overshadowed by recent successes with *vinifera*.

The wine boom is being led from the metropolitan areas of America, which have latched on to the varietal names of California. Riesling, Chardonnay, Cabernet Sauvignon are now household words. The best hybrids (Seyval Blanc, Vidal Blanc, Chambourcin) still have a long way to go. At present, in fact, wine-growers in the eastern and central states are looking three ways at once: at the old American varieties of *Vitis labrusca*, the exciting but risky *viniferas*, and the hybrids between the two. In the east, hybrids and *labrusca* will probably always play a role, but the majority of wine-growers are now betting on *vinifera*.

New York State and Virginia have the biggest and best-established wine industries, but there is no reason to think that they have overwhelming natural advantages. What the other regions lack is a bold entrepreneur to interpret their growing range of wines to the critical metropolitan public.

New York State

The New York State wine industry, long established around the Finger Lakes, south of Lake Ontario, has up to now been considered a maverick backwater by most wine-lovers. Originally based on varieties and chance hybrids of the native vine, *Vitis labrusca*, its wines were characterized by the peculiar scent of *labrusca* known as "foxiness". Most also had high acidity, usually masked by considerable sweetness.

Non-foxy French-American hybrids replaced *labrusca* in all but the most conservative wineries for almost forty years. Although it is usually acceptable and occasionally very good, little of the wine is exciting by European or Californian standards. Some companies in New York, as elsewhere in the east, still see *labrusca* as reliable: well-adapted to the stresses of the eastern climate. They also believe that its wine's distinctive flavours might provide them with a unique niche. At present, about forty per cent of New York wine is "hybrid"; forty per cent *labrusca* (mainly for less expensive "jug" wines); while most premium wine companies use *vinifera*, with a smaller amount of hybrids. Twenty years ago, *vinifera* accounted for only two per cent of the total vineyard hectarage; today, the figure is twenty per cent.

Since the mid-1950s, a vocal minority, first led by Dr Konstantin Frank, was dedicated to proving that *vinifera* vines could successfully be grown in the Finger Lake areas. Their successes, at least with white wines, convinced many. Most of the original vineyards have now planted at least some *vinifera*, and promising new vineyards are growing *vinifera* almost exclusively.

America's wine boom started to affect New York in the mid-1970s. In the late '80s, there were shifts in the industry that would influence the direction of New York wine-growing. First Seagram and then Coca-Cola decided that the industry could be expanded. Seagram bought Gold Seal, and Coca-Cola bought Taylor's and Great Western, the largest and most important wineries in the region. All three wineries have since closed, and Seagram and Coca-Cola have decided to get out of the Finger Lakes wine business altogether. Today, a new generation of wine producers (many of them descendants of the original growers who supplied Taylor's) is concentrating on the types of *vinifera* that do well in cool climates, especially Riesling, Chardonnay, and Pinot Noir.

In 1976, the state law was changed to encourage "farm wineries", lowering the licence fee for firms producing fewer than 21,000 cases a year, and easing restrictions on their sales. The result was the rapid start-up of exactly the small, open-minded enterprises New York needed to improve its image. Three-dozen small wineries were born or reborn, mainly in the Finger Lakes but also in the Hudson River Valley above New York City – which has a long history of nearly being a wine region – and on Long Island, where the maritime climate is kinder than upstate. It also gives the wines an elegant acidic structure, so that they have a very different personality than those from, say, Napa Valley.

Of the state's four wine regions, it is Long Island that is booming, its wineries benefiting from three AVAs: the Hamptons, North Fork, and Long Island itself. From small beginnings in 1973, when the Hargraves planted vines on North Fork, twenty-eight wineries now dot the map. Of note are Pindar (one of the biggest), Palmer, Paumanok, Pellegrini, Peconic Bay, and Bedell Cellars. The Hargraves began with Cabernet, Pinot Noir, Sauvignon, and later, Chardonnay. This last, and Merlot, seem to be the consumers' preferred choice, but growers are also trying Riesling, Gewürztraminer, Chenin Blanc, and Cabernet Franc.

Today, there are at least 125 wineries in New York State, and 13,000 hectares of vineyards.

Leading New York State Producers

Benmarl Wine Company ☆
Marlboro. Owner: Mark Miller. 15 hectares. www.benmarl.com
An historic vineyard in the Hudson River Valley, where the hybrid Dutchess was raised in the nineteenth century, which has been restored by Mark Miller, who runs it as a cooperative of some 1,000 wine-lovers, the Société des Vignerons. They help finance, pick, and drink Seyval and Baco Noir, and, more recently, Merlot, Syrah, Cabernet Sauvignon, and Zinfandel.

Bully Hill Vineyards ☆
Hammondsport. Owner: Walter S. Taylor. 52 hectares. www.bullyhill.com
The only Taylor still making wine – on the original family property on Lake Keuka. Hybrid wines and "Champagne" dominate production. Splendid labels.

Castello di Borghese
Cutchogue. Owners: Marco and Anne Marie Borghese. 22 hectares. www.castellodiborghese.com
The pioneering Hargrave family found ideal conditions for *vinifera* vines on the North Fork of Long Island, 113 kilometres (seventy miles) east of New York City, with the ocean close by on three sides. Their Chardonnay, Sauvignon Blanc, and Pinot Noir competed convincingly with top-rank California or Oregon wines.

In 1999, they sold the property, and the new owners will be adding Italian varieties such as Sangiovese and Nebbiolo to the vineyards.

Dr Konstantin Frank's Vinifera Wine Cellars ☆☆
Hammondsport. Owner: Willy Frank. 45 hectares. www.drfrankwines.com
Founded by Dr Konstantin Frank in 1962, and now run by his son. Vinifera Wine Cellars has produced good, fine, and sometimes brilliant white wine, including Rkatziteli and selected late-harvest Riesling; and reds from Merlot and Pinot Noir are much improved. Sparkling wines are released under the "Château Frank" label.

Fox Run Vineyards ☆☆–☆☆☆
Penn Yan. Owners: Scott Osborne and Andy Hale. 28 hectares. www.foxrunvineyards.com
The owners, who bought Fox Run in 1990, are convinced that European *vinifera* grapes can yield wine excellent enough to put the Finger Lakes in the ranks of the world's top wine producers. Their most recent Riesling, Chardonnay, and Merlot do indeed show great promise. Pinot Noir, Cabernets Sauvignon and Franc are coming along, and the company is also trying the little-known Lemberger grape.

Glenora Wine Cellars ☆–☆☆
Dundee. Owners: Gene Pierce and partners. 6 hectares. www.glenora.com
One of the best-regarded smaller wineries of the Finger Lakes, specializing in sparkling wines. Both hybrids and *vinifera* are produced, the latter including Chardonnay, very good Riesling, plus Merlot and Cabernet Sauvignon.

Hargrave Vineyard
See Castello di Borghese

Knapp Vineyards ☆–☆☆
Romulus. Owner: Doug Knapp. 32 hectares. www.knappwine.com
Doug Knapp's daughter, Lori Knapp, makes a palette of *vinifera* wines from Chardonnay, Sangiovese, and the Bordeaux varieties.

Lamoreaux Landing Winery ☆☆
Lodi. Owner: Mark Wagner. 60 hectares. www.lamoureauxwine.com
One of the best of the youngest generation of New York State wineries. Hybrids are being phased out, and production now focuses on Chardonnay, Cabernet Franc, Pinot Noir, and Cabernet Sauvignon.

Millbrook Vineyards & Winery ☆☆
Millbrook. Owner: John Dyson. 20 hectares. www.millbrookwine.com
In addition to Chardonnay (half the plantings), Cabernet Sauvignon, and Pinot Noir, Dyson is experimenting with Merlot, Zinfandel, Viognier, and other varieties. Located in the Hudson Valley, he is one of today's trailblazing producers of European-style wines, with a keen interest in Italian grapes such as Tocai, Pinot Grigio, and Sangiovese.

Palmer ☆☆
Aquebogue. Owner: Robert Palmer. 48 hectares. www.palmervineyards.com
An estate founded in 1986 that pioneered what one could call the classic Long Island style: clean, vibrant fruit, especially Chardonnay, and a Loire-style Cabernet Franc.

Standing Stone Vineyards ☆
Valois. Owners: Martha and Tom Macinski. 15 hectares. www.standingstonewines.com
Dry, well-balanced Riesling, Gewürztraminer, and the hybrid Vidal are the particular strengths here, but the future of the Cabernet Franc and Merlot is also looking good. Icewines from Riesling and Vidal are the house specialties.

Wagner ☆–☆☆
Lodi. Owner: Bill Wagner. 100 hectares. www.wagnervineyards.com
An attractive Finger Lakes winery; 85% of production is dry varietal table wines from hybrids and vinifera. The Chardonnay, including the barrel-fermented style, is excellent, as are the Gewürztraminer and Merlot.

Widmer's Wine Cellars ☆
Naples. Owner: Constellation. 90 hectares.
www.widmerwine.com

Large winery, best-known for wood-aged "sherries", "Lake Niagara", sweetish *labrusca* wines, and "Widmer"-brand hybrids, mostly with generic names. Now making dry *vinifera* wines (Cabernet, Chardonnay, and Riesling) and kosher wines.

Hermann J. Wiemer Vineyard ☆–☆☆
Dundee. Owner: Hermann J. Wiemer. 70 hectares.
www.wiemer.com

The Bernkastel-born ex-winemaker of Bully Hill (*q.v.*) has had striking success with Riesling (with a sparkling version and late-harvest) and with Chardonnay fermented in new French oak barrels. He credits Seneca, the biggest of the Finger Lakes, for the favourable microclimate. He is trying Pinot Noir, but Gewürztraminer suffers from bud injury in the cold.

Other New York State Producers

Cascade Mountain Vineyards ☆
Amenia. Owners: the Wetmore family. www.cascademt.com

Owns five hectares of hybrids and buys in from other growers in New York State. Careful producer of crisp, dry whites as well as rosé and fresh, young reds. Also an aged reserve red.

Gristina ☆–☆☆
Cutchogue. 40 hectares. www.gristinawines.com

The estate was bought in 2000 by businessman Vince Galluccio, who hired Michel Rolland as a consultant. Galluccio is expanding production and planting a new collection of varieties: Malbec, Carmenère, Petit Verdot, and Viognier.

Johnson Estate ☆
Westfield. Owners: the Johnson family. 55 hectares.
www.johnsonwinery.com

Good-quality, estate-bottled wines, which include a dry white Delaware. The hybrid whites are among the best of their kind.

Lenz Winery ☆☆
Peconic, Long Island. Owner: Peter Carroll. 27 hectares.
www.lenzwine.com

Close to the Hargrave Vineyard (*q.v.*). Produces very good estate-bottled Merlot and Cabernet, aged only in French oak.

North Salem Vineyard ☆
North Salem. Owner/winemaker: Dr George W. Naumburg.
www.northsalemwine.com

Seven hectares, planted with Seyval Blanc, Maréchal Foch, Chancellor, and De Chaunac. A Hudson River winery, which aims to make fresh, light white and red wines for drinking young.

Woodbury Vineyards ☆–☆☆
Fredonia. Owners: the Woodbury family. 12 hectares.
www.woodburyvineyards.com

An old farming family who were the first (in 1970) to plant *vinifera* in Chautauqua County, on a gravel ridge overlooking Lake Erie.

New England

Winemaking in New England is still on a very small and experimental scale. During the early years of the wine industry in the northeast, it was believed that the regional character should be asserted by developing only the best of the hybrids. While opinion about the relative merits of hybrid and *vinifera* vines has mostly shifted towards *vinifera* in recent years, hybrids will probably always play at least a minor role in New England, because of the extreme difficulty that growers experience in the growing conditions.

Off the Massachusetts coast, the climate becomes sufficiently moderated by the ocean for Chardonnay, Merlot, and even Zinfandel to do well. The wines produced at Chicama, on the aptly named island Martha's Vineyard, testify to this.

The state of Rhode Island, which is deeply invaded by ocean inlets, has around half a dozen small vineyards; the biggest, Sakonnet, growing both hybrid and *vinifera* vines. Sakonnet's Chardonnay, Gewürztraminer, Cabernet Franc, and Vidal have not only a very loyal local following, but are also becoming known in other parts of the east, and even in California. Prudence Island Vineyards, situated on Prudence Island in Narangansett Bay, has seven hectares of *vinifera* vines, the best being Chardonnay and Gewürztraminer.

Connecticut's first winery, Haight Vineyards at Litchfield, west of Hartford, managed to grow *vinifera* (Chardonnay and Riesling), and the hybrid Seyval. Several other wineries have followed. The most promising are Chamard and Stonington Vineyards, both along the coast. Chamard, founded in 1980, grows only *vinifera* (Chardonnay, Cabernet Sauvignon, Pinot Noir, and Merlot) on its eight-hectare vineyard.

Chamard wines are considered among the best in New England. Stonington Vineyards produces both *vinifera* and hybrid wines, including Chardonnay, Pinot Noir, and Seyval.

The Mid-Atlantic

There is growing conviction that Virginia may become the most promising wine-growing state in the east. The other mid-Atlantic states of Maryland, southern Pennsylvania, and perhaps a belt stretching inland into West Virginia, Kentucky, and Tennessee may have as much potential.

It is a well-publicized fact that Thomas Jefferson had no luck, but modern vines, sprays, and know-how have started to change the situation.

And so has foreign investment which has taken a thoroughly optimistic view of the regions potential – Virginia in particular.

Maryland & Pennsylvania

In the 1940s, Philip Wagner made history at Boordy Vineyards, near Ryderwood in Maryland, by planting the first French-American hybrids in America. These vines had been bred by the French to bring phylloxera-resistance to France, but ironically it was to be America that appreciated their virtues of hardiness and vigour.

Boordy then added Chardonnay (classic method sparkling) and Cabernet Sauvignon to its list, which includes the hybrids Seyval Blanc, Vidal, and Chambourcin, and now makes 10,000 cases per year. Currently there are twelve wineries in the state, employing both hybrids and *vinifera*. Basignani Winery has Cabernet, Chardonnay, and Riesling along with Vidal and Seyval. Elk Run Vineyards boasts of its all-*vinifera* vineyard, and also makes sparkling and dessert wines.

The southeast corner of Pennsylvania, a state with over seventy wineries in production, apparently has much in common with Maryland. Soils and climates are very variable; there are certainly good vineyard sites among them. Mazza Vineyards, which abandoned *vinifera* trials at the other end of Pennsylvania on Lake Erie when eight hectares were wiped out, is happy with its south Pennsylvania Chardonnay and Riesling, and even happier with white hybrids. Twin Brook, east of Philadelphia, on the other hand, has done quite well with Pinot Grigio. Eric Miller of neighbouring Chaddsford Winery makes excellent Chardonnay and Chambourcin, and a Bordeaux-style blend called "Merican".

Tim and John Crouch of Allegro Vineyards had five hectares of Chardonnay, Pinot Gris, and Cabernet Sauvignon, and made a Bordeaux blend called "Cadenza", but after Tim's death in 2000, the property was sold. Richard Naylor, at York near the Maryland border, is happy with Riesling and Cabernet Sauvignon, but more at ease with Vidal, Seyval, De Chaunac, Chambourcin, and a host of other hybrids.

Everybody believes hybrids are well-suited to the region's natural conditions, but consumers' reactions are pulling wine-growers increasingly towards *vinifera*.

Virginia

Lying between the cold weather extreme of the northeast, and the intense heat and humidity of the south (where the deadly vine ailment Pierce's Disease thrives), Virginia is the rising star in the east. The state now has sixty-five wineries, a remarkable number considering that the first successful *vinifera* grape wines were made here just over twenty years ago. In 2002, there were some 890 hectares under vine. Contributing to this success is an unusually supportive legislation, plus the affluent and educated customers in Washington D.C., who bolster the local wine industry.

Some Virginians are still wary of *vinifera*. Pioneers such as Meredyth Vineyards at Middleburg (which closed its doors in 2001) initially planted only hybrids, but later added Riesling, Chardonnay, and Cabernet. They ripened, but anti-rot treatments proved essential.

Foreign investors were the first to show confidence. It made a great stir in 1976 when Zonin, a big wine company from the Veneto in Italy, bought 280 hectares at Barboursville and planted fifty hectares of *vinifera*, including Cabernets Sauvignon and Franc, Gewürztraminer, and Italian classics such as Pinot Grigio, Nebbiolo, and Barbera. Like Barboursville, the French-owned Prince Michel is having success with Chardonnay, Riesling, Merlot, Cabernet Franc, and Cabernet Sauvignon. Others who have shown that *vinifera* can do well in Virginia are Ingleside Plantation, Oasis, and Linden. Horton Vineyards, in Orange County, has Marsanne, Mourvèdre, and the tricky Viognier. Horton is certainly the first Virginia property to plant Tannat and Touriga Nacional.

At least eighty per cent of the Virginia vineyard is now *vinifera*. The ultimate deciding factors will be the health of the vines and the prices the public will pay.

The Midwest

Lake Michigan and Lake Erie provide the heat storage to make life bearable for vines in the Midwest states of Ohio and Michigan. These large, relatively shallow bodies of water moderate temperatures to allow numerous families of grapes to be grown, including some of the more hardy vinifera varieties, as well as hybrids such as Vidal, Seyval Blanc, and Chambourcin. The Lake Erie Islands (known locally as the "Wine Islands"), lying in the shallow western basin of Lake Erie, are especially significant. For a dozen years a few hundred hectares of wine grapes, including Chardonnay, the two Cabernets, Riesling, Pinot Noir, and Gewürztraminer have produced successfully on the lime-rich soils. Most of these grapes are used by Firelands Winery, located on the mainland in Sandusky, Ohio; and by Meier's Wine Cellars, south of Cincinnati and the state's oldest and largest winery. Lake Erie's central basin, just east of Cleveland, also provides important microclimates that are hospitable to wine grapes. Chalet Debonné Vineyards of Madison and Ferrante Winery of Geneva make wines from both *vinifera* and hybrid grapes. Further east, towards the Pennsylvania border, Markko Vineyards in Conneaut makes high-quality Chardonnay, a Mosel-style Riesling, and a Cabernet. Harpersfield Vineyard in the Grand River Valley has been enjoying much acclaim for its Alsatian-style whites, as well as Pinot Noir and Cabernet Franc.

Michigan's vineyards and wineries are close to Chicago at the lake's southeastern corner. Notable ones include Tabor Hill, Fenn Valley Vineyards, and, biggest by far, St Julian. These family-owned companies supplement their own production with grapes bought in from Washington and California to make good-quality *vinifera* and hybrid wines. Château Grand Traverse cultivates only *vinifera* grapes, and has a fine reputation for its stylistically varied Rieslings.

There are wineries in the other northern Midwest states – in Indiana, Illinois, Wisconsin, even Minnesota, where small vineyards and dedicated growers often face sub-zero temperatures and other adverse growing conditions. Much of the production of Indiana and southern Ohio is located in the Ohio River Valley AVA, which borders the river from West Virginia to its junction with the Mississippi.

Missouri and Arkansas would seem improbable places to plant vines, but both states have long-established vineyards. Missouri, indeed, enjoyed the distinction of having the first official appellation granted to a viticultural area in the United States, in 1980, when the Bureau of Alcohol, Tobacco and Firearms declared Augusta, just west of St Louis, a designated region. Its first vines were planted in hills above the Missouri

River in the 1830s. Both states have strong research programmes at state-funded universities. Stone Hill, in Hermann, Missouri, is well-known for its annual collection of gold and silver medals in national competitions. It is far too cold here for most *vinifera* vines, but wineries including Stone Hill and Mount Pleasant at Augusta grow excellent hybrids such as Seyval and Vidal for full-bodied wines, somewhat different from the fruitier ones produced along the Great Lakes or in New York's Finger Lakes district.

Arkansas, to the south, has one unexpected outcrop of *vinifera* growing in the peculiar microclimate of a mountain plateau called Altus, settled in the 1870s by Swiss, Austrian, and Bavarian immigrants who understood mountains. According to Al Wiederkehr, whose Swiss family founded its winery in 1880, thermal inversion currents produce a very tolerable climate in which Riesling, Chardonnay, Sauvignon Blanc, Muscat Ottonel, Cabernet, Pinot Noir, and Gamay feel pretty much at home. Most of his hectarage is planted with these grapes, although he is not burning his boats with hybrids.

The Southwest

Much of the Southwest is too humid and subject, like the Deep South, to Pierce's Disease, to make it a viable region for vines, although growing grapes and making wine began here before the business took hold in California. Southern New Mexico and west Texas have the oldest commercial wine-growing regions in America. Catholic priests founded a mission with vineyards in El Paso on the Rio Grande in Texas around 1600, producing sacramental wine from the Mission grape. Nevertheless, only over the past two decades has there been a serious move towards establishing a modern wine industry of some quality.

Of the Southwest wine-producing states, Texas is the clear leader, being the country's fifth-largest producer, with twenty-seven wineries and 1,255 hectares of vineyards. (New Mexico has twenty-two wineries, Colorado thirty-eight, Arizona nineteen, Oklahoma fourteen, Utah six, and Nevada two.) The Texas vineyards are widely spread out across the vast state, whose total area is larger than France. The wineries range in size from boutique to fairly large. Ste. Genevieve, near Fort Stockton, has links with the state university and Domaine Cordier, and the biggest vineyards of the region – 400 hectares of *vinifera*, relying on drip irrigation and careful cultivation to survive the desert conditions. It is by far the largest winery in Texas, with an annual production of 750,000 cases.

Other promising Texan wineries include Sister Creek in the Texas Hill Country, which makes Pinot Noir, Chardonnay, Cabernets Sauvignon and Franc, and Merlot; Grape Creek Vineyard, also in the Hill Country, produces medal-winning Chardonnay and commendable Cabernet; Fall Creek Vineyards, north of Austin; and Paul Bonarrigo's award-winning Messina Hof Wine Cellars. The cool, dry climate of the high plateau area around Lubbock was the site of some of the first successful vineyards in Texas. Attention was drawn to the area by the premium wines from the Llano Estacado ranch, where the McPherson family and their partners pioneered *vinifera* vines. Kim McPherson, whose father was

at Llano in the early days, has been winemaker since 1992 at the noteworthy Cap Rock.

Some small wineries still successfully grow hybrids in the more difficult areas, although almost everywhere the shift is to *vinifera*. In the "dry" county of Springtown, La Buena Vida winery, led by winemaker Steve Smith, for long held out against the *vinifera* vogue, but it, too, is now producing good Chardonnay and Cabernet.

New Mexico now has twenty-two wineries, including La Chiripada Winery, north of Santa Fe, where the Johnson family produce award-winning wines from hybrids and *vinifera*, as does Madison Winery, a small family-run winery east of Santa Fe. Gruet represents the French influence in New Mexico (the winery is on the outskirts of Albuquerque; the vineyards are in southern New Mexico), with top award-winning sparkling wines from Chardonnay and Pinot Noir. Very good Chardonnay is also made at La Viña, one of New Mexico's oldest wineries, in the south of the state.

Colorado's production capacity continues to rise. Of its 165 hectares, eighty-five per cent are of *Vitis vinifera* and predominantly Chardonnay, although Merlot, Cabernet, Pinot Noir, Riesling, and Sauvignon are doing well, and one producer, Grande River Vineyards, is trying Viognier. Plum Creek Winery is well-known for Chardonnay, and has now planted Sangiovese.

Arizona's Callaghan Vineyards has widened the range to include Syrah, Mourvèdre, Grenache, Malvasia, Petit Verdot, and Zinfandel, but the blend of Cabernet/Merlot/Zinfandel called "Buena Suerte" draws plaudits. Nevada's single winery, Pahrump Valley Vineyards near Las Vegas, produces Merlot and Chardonnay, as well as light-hearted wines aimed at the substantial tourist market.

Canada

Canada was discovered, in fine-wine terms, in the 1970s, when old fears and prejudices about which vines could survive here were tossed aside. The formidable know-how that had been accumulating in new wine districts around the world provided answers to problems that had seemed insuperable. A massive grubbing-up programme in 1988 in the two leading provinces, Ontario and British Columbia, encouraged growers to pull out their hybrids in favour of vinifera. Canada now has some 5,670 hectares planted with wine grapes.

Ontario

Ontario took its place at the high table of the world's cool-climate wine regions in the 1980s. In the south of the province, the Niagara Peninsula, lake-locked and escarpment-sheltered, is Canada's natural vineyard, lying on the same latitude as northern Oregon. It is one of the designated viticultural areas in the Vintner's Quality Alliance (VQA), which sets standards to which all the leading estates adhere. Bitterly cold winters here produce conditions ideal for making one of the world's great icewines. Once a rarity, icewine now accounts for five per cent of all Ontario wine production. As well as this luscious specialty, Niagara produces Chardonnay, Riesling, Pinot Noir, and some wines from hybrids. The 1990s are seeing Niagara fine-tune its style, identify its most privileged sites, and build a world-class reputation. There are currently ninety wineries in Ontario as a whole.

Leading Ontario Producers

Cave Spring Cellars ☆☆–☆☆☆
Jordan. Owner: Leonard Pennachetti. 20 hectares.
www.cavespringcellars.com
Vinifera varieties were planted here in 1978, and the winery opened its doors in 1986. Best-known for its white wines, and winemaker Angelo Pavan has released some exceptional Riesling and Chardonnay, as well as dessert and icewines.

Château des Charmes ☆☆
St. David's. Owner: Paul-Michel Bosc. 110 hectares.
www.chateaudescharmes.com
Paul-Michel Bosc is a fifth-generation wine-grower who emigrated to Canada in the 1960s, and became the first to plant a wholly *vinifera* vineyard. Award-winning VQA estate wines include icewine, late-harvest, an impressive range of white and red varietals, as well as *méthode traditionnelle* sparkling wines. True to his roots, Bosc has more recently planted unusual varieties such as Auxerrois and Savagnin.

Clos Jordan
Niagara Peninsula. Owners: Vincor and Boisset. 55 hectares
A dazzling new venture, or it will be when renowned architect Frank Gehry has completed the winery. The only wines to be produced here will be Pinot Noir and Chardonnay, reflecting Boisset's Burgundian base, and the first bottles will only come onto the market in 2006.

Creekside Estate ☆☆
Jordan Station. Owner: Peter Jensen. 40 hectares.
www.creeksideestate.com
A property in the Annapolis Valley that is also developing the Paragon Estate on Niagara Peninsula. Creekside has a fine reputation for Sauvignon Blanc, and also produces good Pinot Noir, Bordeaux-style blends, and Vidal icewine.

Henry of Pelham Family Estate ☆–☆☆☆
St Catharines. Owners: the Speck family. 70 hectares.
www.henryofpelham.com
This estate was planted on land owned by the descendants of Henry Smith, who was awarded Crown land after the American Revolutionary War for being an Empire loyalist. For some years, winemaker Ron Giesbrecht has produced impressive varietal wines from vineyards on the Niagara Bench. The Cabernet/Merlot is among the best, and there is a remarkably fine Baco Noir. The flagship dessert wine is Riesling icewine.

Hillebrand Estates ☆☆
Niagara-on-the-Lake. Owners: Andrés. 40 hectares.
www.hillebrand.com
Canada's leading producer of VQA wines was bought by Andrés in 1993, but is operated independently, with winemaker Jean-Laurent Groulx at the helm. The top wines are released as "Showcase" wines, and the "Trius" range, including a Bordeaux-style red blend, is also of fine quality.

Inniskillin ☆☆–☆☆☆
Niagara-on-the-Lake. Owners: Vincor. 52 hectares.
www.inniskillin.com
Founders Donald Ziraldo and Karl Kaiser spearheaded the birth of the modern wine industry in Ontario. Since its establishment, Inniskillin has concentrated on varietal wines from Niagara-grown grapes. The winery is now housed in a 1920s barn, possibly designed by Frank Lloyd Wright, on the Brae Burn Estate. All Inniskillin wines have earned strong national and international recognition, especially the Icewine and late-harvest Vidal. In 1999, Inniskillin released no fewer than five single-vineyard Chardonnays. They also produce select late-harvest Vidal. *See also* Inniskillin Okanagan (British Columbia).

Konzelmann ☆☆–☆☆☆
Niagara-on-the-Lake. Owner: Herbert Konzelmann.
34 hectares. www.konzelmannwines.com
The Konzelmanns descend from a German wine-producing family. Herbert sought out the best possible lakeside sites to benefit from their special microclimate. Best-known for skilfully made Rieslings, plump and exotic Chardonnay, and very rich Vidal Icewine.

Magnotta ☆☆
Vaughan. Owners: Gabe and Rossana Magnotta.
www.magnotta.com
Icewine specialists, producing it not only from Riesling and Vidal, but also from Cabernet Franc. Like Inniskillin, they also make a sparkling Icewine.

Malivoire ☆☆–☆☆☆

Beamsville. Owner: Martin Malivoire. 20 hectares.
www.malivoirewineco.com

Malivoire has hired respected winemaker Ann Sperling, who produces rich and high-priced "Moira Vineyard Chardonnay" and Gewürztraminer here, and an excellent Maréchal Foch.

Pillitteri Estates ☆☆

Niagara-on-the-Lake. Owners: the Pillitteri family. 21 hectares.
www.pillitteri.com

Some of the vineyards here are fifty years old. The Bordeaux red varieties do well here, but the specialty is Icewines from Riesling, Vidal, and Gewürztraminer.

Thirty Bench Wines ☆☆–☆☆☆

Beamsville. Owners/winemakers: Tom Muckle, Yorgos Papageorgiou, Franz Zeritsch. 23 hectares.
www.thirtybench.com

A boutique winery, making its reputation by slashing yields to very low levels and by harvesting as late as the climate will allow. The result is very concentrated wines, perhaps exaggeratedly so.

Vineland Estates ☆☆

Vineland. Owner: John Howard. 30 hectares.
www.vineland.com

Hermann Weis from the Mosel planted *vinifera* and hybrid vines on the slopes of the Niagara Escarpment in 1979. The first bottling was in 1984. Vineland claims to have the best location for growing Riesling, but produces a wide range of red and white wines, dry, semi-dry, and sweet. Weis sold out to local businessman John Howard in 1992.

British Columbia

There are two distinct wine-growing regions in "BC": the Okanagan and Similkameen valleys in the central-southern part of the province, and the coastal areas of the Fraser Valley and Vancouver Island. Almost all production comes from the 160-kilometre (100-mile) long Okanagan Valley, which has 1,550 hectares of *vinifera* benefiting from its immense lake. The whole of the Okanagan is arid; its south end predominantly planted with classic red wine grapes (Pinot Noir, Merlot, and Cabernet Sauvignon); and the less arid north favouring white grape varieties (Riesling, Chardonnay, Pinot Blanc, Pinot Gris, Gewürztraminer, and Semillon). The province currently has sixty wineries.

Leading British Columbia Producers

Burrowing Owl ☆☆–☆☆☆

Oliver. Owner: Jim Wyse. 46 hectares. www.bovwine.com

A gravity-fed winery was built here in the southern Okanagan in 1997, and the wines are made with advice from consultant winemaker Bill Dyer of Sterling (*q.v.*) in Napa Valley. Initial releases were of Chardonnay, Pinot Gris, Merlot, and Cabernet, but Syrah and Pinot Noir will be added. The Bordeaux reds are the outstanding wines at present.

Calona ☆☆

Kelowna. Owner: Cascadia Brands. www.calona.kelowna.com

The Okanagan's oldest winery, which was established here under a different name in 1932. Howard Soon has been making the wines since 1980. Good Pinot Blanc and Pinot Gris, and a rare Icewine from Pinot Noir.

Gray Monk Estate ☆–☆☆

Okanagan Centre. Owners: the Heiss family. 13 hectares.
www.graymonk.com

Gray Monk is a family run winery overlooking Okanagan Lake. Winemaker George Heiss Jr. concentrates on varietals only. Included in the range are a late-harvest Ehrenfelser, and a Gewürztraminer reserve.

Inniskillin Okanagan ☆☆

Oliver. Owners: Vincor International. 9 hectares.
www.inniskillin.com

The pioneers of Inniskillin Ontario (*q.v.*) continue the tradition in Okanagan, and have produced Canada's first Chenin Blanc Icewine. Vineyards are located in the south of the valley, just north of the US border, in an area known as the Golden Mile. Oak-aged reserves are bottled under the "Pearl Label"; single-vineyard wines under the "Silver Label".

Mission Hill ☆☆

Westbank. Owner: Anthony von Mandl. 300 hectares.
www.misssionhillwinery.com

A huge and extravagant winery in one of the loveliest settings in the province. John Simes was formerly winemaker at Montana Winery (*q.v.* New Zealand). His innovative techniques and increased use of barrel fermentation and oak-ageing resulted in the launch of Mission Hill's "Grand Reserve" wines. The top red is a blend called "Oculus", and Syrah was planted in 1997.

Quails' Gate ☆☆

Kelowna. Owners: Ben and Tony Stewart. 50 hectares

One of the oldest producing vineyard sites in the Okanagan. The Stewarts were the first to introduce Chasselas, planting on the favoured south slope of Okanagan Lake in 1961. Very good wines are being produced by winemaker Jeff Martin, through careful vineyard management and a combination of New- and Old-World winemaking techniques.

Sumac Ridge ☆☆

Summerland. Owners: Vincor. 40 hectares

Sumac Ridge Estate produced its first vintage in 1980, supplementing its own grapes with fruit from other vineyards in the Okanagan and Similkameen valleys. In addition to the *vinifera* varietals, Sumac Ridge also produces sparkling and "port"-style wines, and an Icewine from Pinot Blanc. This is the largest winery in the province.

Tinhorn Creek ☆

Oliver. Owners: the Shaunessy and Oldfield families.
65 hectares. www.tinhorn.com

American-trained winemaker, Sandra Oldfield, makes Californian-style, fruit-driven whites from Pinot Gris and Chardonnay, much of it aged in American oak.

Central & South America

M any of the countries of Central and South America were beset by economic problems in the early years of this century, and their trail-blazing progress throughout the 1990s may have stalled. Chile remains a fine source of good-value wines, but the tremendous potential of Argentina has yet to be realized, although a handful of wineries are producing first-rate wines. Countries such as Mexico, Brazil, Peru, and Uruguay have also made a limited impact on the crucial international markets. Nonetheless, South America remains a continent of enormous promise and may surprise us all as this decade progresses.

Chile

Chile came of age as a wine-producing country in the 1990s. New regions were planted, adding to the diversity of Chilean wines, and scores of well-trained winemakers, many with international experience, took their places at the helm of the many new wineries. There was never any doubt about the quality of Chilean fruit, but for a long time, an uncritical domestic market and a rather naive approach to modern winemaking prevented flavours getting from the vineyard into the bottle. Now, however, Chile is firmly on the international scene and learning fast.

Wine has been made in Chile since the missionaries introduced vines in the mid-sixteenth century, but the first real quality developments only began when the copper-rich landowners of the nineteenth century paraded their wealth with vineyards. French vine cuttings were shipped to Chile in 1851, just before phylloxera hit Europe, thus ensuring a store of un-plagued rootstock and a unique marketing edge for future generations. The big leap came in the 1980s, when – prompted by the efforts of winemakers such as Miguel Torres – there was widespread investment in modern winemaking equipment.

The quality wine-growing region, in which over 100,000 hectares are planted, is spread across three main zones: the Aconcagua and Casablanca valleys; the Central Valley; and the southern region. Aconcagua incorporates the main east-west valley to the north of Santiago, but enjoys less coastal influence than the relatively new region of Casablanca, the source of Chile's best white wines. The Central Valley, where most wineries are based, is divided (moving north to south) into the four valleys of Maipo, Rapel, Curicó, and Maule, each irrigated by rivers flowing off the Andes, although channel irrigation is often being replaced by more controllable drip irrigation. These are all immense regions, so generalizations are tricky, but Maipo and Rapel are generally warmer than the other two. As Chilean growers learn more about their terroirs, sub-regions are being delineated. Two of the most exciting are Colchagua, and Apalta within Rapel.

The Chilean climate is perfect – almost *too* perfect, in that vines rarely have to struggle. Although rainfall increases as you move south, there is little difference between average temperatures in Maipo and Maule. The biggest variances are west to east, according to position relative to the Andean and Coastal ranges; it is easier to find wine style differences within valleys. Regions south of Maule, such as Bío-Bío and Triaguén, are attracting interest, especially for Chardonnay, but heavy rainfall can mar the crop.

With the isolationism of the Pinochet years long gone, the flow of knowledge, ideas, and technology into this 4,000-kilometre- (2,500-mile-) long nation has facilitated the harnessing of its viticultural resources. The belief that wine of international standards is made simply with stainless steel and new oak has switched to a philosophy of "vineyard first, winery second", bringing issues such as canopy management, irrigation, and soil study to the top of the agenda. Viticulturists are planting well-exposed slopes in preference to valley-floor sites on over-rich soils and many growers are not content supplying the big *bodegas*, but are going it alone.

Among red varieties, Merlot now shares as much of the limelight as easy-drinking Cabernet Sauvignon, which has traditionally been the most successful Chilean signature in export markets. A very few producers have managed to tame Pinot Noir, and Malbec shows great potential. In whites, Chardonnay and Sauvignon Blanc are the dominant pair, especially from Casablanca. In the 1990s, it became apparent that much of what was thought to be Merlot was in fact Carmenère, which is now enjoying some celebrity as Chile's unique grape variety (*see* box on page 478). Among other varieties, Syrah and Viognier show promise.

Yet, seventy per cent of all wines on the domestic market are sold in the same packaging as milk cartons. Prices and quality are low, and the prices for bulk wines have been declining. So it has become all the more imperative for wineries to focus on exports shipped in large volumes. It is scarcely possible for a Chilean winery to survive with a production of less than 100,000 cases, which is the main difference between its wine industry and that of other New World countries. At the same time, the emergence of large new wineries has stiffened competition, and there are serious doubts about whether there is a sufficiently large market for the growing volumes being produced.

This may spell trouble for some wineries, but will be a boon to consumers, who will continue to find sound, often excellent, wines at very attractive prices.

Leading Chile Producers

Francisco de Aguirre ☆☆
Limari. Owner: Pisquera Elqui. 420 hectares.
www.vinafranciscodeaguirre.cl
A brave venture in a remote and semi-arid northern valley, the estate began planting vineyards in 1992. The wines are of mixed quality, and the heavy oakiness of the *reservas* does not always disguise an occasional lack of ripeness.

Almaviva ☆☆☆☆
Maipo. Owners: Concha y Toro and Baroness Philippine
de Rothschild. 40 hectares. www.bpdr.com

This fascinating joint venture produces a single wine, the Cabernet Sauvignon-dominated "Almaviva". It effortlessly demonstrates the potential of the best Maipo vineyards – these were planted twenty-five years ago – but it can be argued that the wine is more Bordelais than Chilean. Nonetheless, it has been of excellent quality since the first vintage in 1996.

Aresti ☆–☆☆
Curicó. Owner: Vicente Aresti. 360 hectares. www.arestichile.cl
The Arestis are well-known fruit farmers and have owned vineyards since 1952. These have recently been expanded to their present size, and consist of four different vineyards, all hand-picked; 1999 was the first vintage here. The basic wines are released under the "Montemar" label, and top wines under the "Family Collection" label. The style is fruit-driven, fairly oaky, and essentially soft and commercial. The "Family Collection Cabernet Sauvignon" shows the concentration and vigour that many other wines lack. But these are still early days.

Viña Bisquertt ☆–☆☆
Colchagua. Owners: the Bisquertt family. 800 hectares.
www.bisquertt.cl
Bulk wine producers for many years, Bisquertt re-equipped its winery in 1993, switching attention to premium, bottled wine under the "Casa La Joya" label. Up till now, the wines have been inconsistent, but Don Osvaldo's son, Felipe, is developing new vineyards at El Rulo, which promise higher quality. The Chardonnay is attractive, but the best wines are the Merlot *reserva* and the very rich, plummy "Carmenère Cuvée Premium". "Zeus I" is an elegant, new-oaked Cabernet/Carmenère blend, produced as a non-vintage wine, made by a kind of *solera* system.

Chateau Los Boldos ☆☆
Requinoa. Owners: the Massenez family. 285 hectares.
www.chateauboldos.com
Of nineteenth century origin, this estate was bought in 1990 by an Alsace family. Both whites and reds are good, though rich and somewhat fatiguing. Top wine is an opaque Cabernet/Merlot blend called "Chateau Los Boldos Grand Cru".

Caliterra ☆☆–☆☆☆☆
Colchagua. Owners: the Chadwick and Mondavi families.
300 hectares. www.caliterra.com
Since 1995, Mondavi has been an equal partner in this dynamic winery, which has recently been developing a Colchagua estate (and label) called "Arboleda". The Sauvignon Blanc and Chardonnay are reliable if not outstanding, but the reds from "Arboleda" are showing real distinction, both the spicy, plummy Carmenère and the opulent Syrah.

José Cânepa ☆☆–☆☆☆☆
Colchagua. Owners: the Canepa family. 550 hectares.
www.canepa.cl
The Canepa vineyards were split up in 1996 (*see* TerraMater) but the descendants of José Canepa still have substantial holdings which are boosted by vineyards leased on long-term contracts. The reserve wines can be excellent: sleek, juicy Syrah; velvety Malbec; vigorous, toasty Casablanca Chardonnay. The top wines are the elegant Maipo Cabernet called "Finisimo", and the sumptuous, ultra-ripe "Magnificum", which blends Cabernet, Merlot, Malbec, and Carmenère perfectly.

Carmenère

The obscure Bordeaux variety Carmenère, virtually wiped out by phylloxera in its native land, thrived in Chile, where the louse was unknown. Carmenère, a very vigorous variety, grows differently from Merlot, and doesn't taste much like Merlot, yet for decades it was believed that Carmenère was in fact Merlot. And it was sold as such. Only in 1993 did eagle-eyed ampelographers from Montpellier spot the difference. Some wineries pretended not to notice, but others, notably Carmen, proudly bottled Carmenère as a varietal wine.

Carmenère is very vigorous and ripens three weeks later than Merlot. Its yields need to be reduced to ensure that by the time it is harvested it is fully ripe. Unfortunately, unripe examples of Carmenère are quite common, and can be spotted from their characteristic aroma of green peppers. But when fully ripe, Carmenère can be a lush, cherry-toned wine, with overtones of coffee and chocolate. Low acidity makes it unsuitable for cellaring, but it's a delicious wine when drunk young and fresh.

Carmen, Viña ☆☆☆
Maipo. Owners: Claro group. 475 hectares. www.carmen.cl
The oldest winery brand in Chile, but now boasts a state-of-the art winery in the Maipo Valley. It may be next door to its sister (Santa Rita), but in terms of technology and winemaking philosophy, the two are distant cousins. Former winemaker Alvaro Espinoza was a prodigious talent, focused as much on the vineyards as the winery.

Espinoza was a pioneer of organic wine production, and one of the first to recognize the potential merits of Carmenère. Since 2002, his place has been taken by María del Pilár González. The organic "Nativa Chardonnay" is the best of the whites, and the barrel-aged red reserves are highly recommended. The top wine is the voluptuous and tannic "Gold Reserve Cabernet Sauvignon".

Viña Carpe Diem ☆☆–☆☆☆
Itata. Owner: Fundacuón Chile. 170 hectares. www.vinosdelsur.cl
A leading estate in Maule in Central Chile, and the wine regions further south, producing rich, oaky, *gran reserva* reds and Chardonnay. Carpe Diem produced Chile's first Syrah.

Viña Casablanca ☆☆–☆☆☆
Casablanca. Owner: Santa Carolina (*q.v.*). 280 hectares
The winery, which, since 1992, has put the cool-climate Casablanca Valley firmly on the map. Inaugural winemaker Ignacio Recabarren used the pungent Sauvignon Blanc and citric Chardonnay as his ticket to international acclaim. The "White Label" series uses fruit sourced from various regions, but the best wines bear the Santa Isabel Estate designation. The whites from Casablanca are the winners, and the Merlot can also be exceptional. The oaky Cabernet/Carmenère blend called "Neblus" is the "icon" wine, but can be rather grassy.

Concha y Toro ☆–☆☆☆
Santiago. Owners: the Larraín and Giulisasti families. 3,740 hectares. www.conchaytoro.com
Founded in 1883, this has long been Chile's biggest winery. The planting programme over the last five years has enabled access to varied sources of fruit from seventeen sites. Reds are be led by the "Casillero del Diablo" Cabernet Sauvignon and Merlot. Other releases include the "Trio" range from Casablanca fruit, and the innovative "Terrunyo" range of single-vineyard wines, both overseen by Ignacio Recabarren. The flagship wine is "Don Melchor" from lush, Maipo Cabernet fruit.

Cono Sur ☆☆–☆☆☆
Chimbarongo. Owner: Concha y Toro. 300 hectares. www.conosur.com
Who would have thought a Chilean winery could forge its reputation on Pinot Noir? Cono Sur delivers this varietal (from Casablanca and Bío-Bío grapes) in four different guises: unoaked, reserve, "20 Barrels", and "20 Barrels Limited Edition". A new range of wines has appeared under the "Vision" label, including a Riesling from Bío-Bío and what may well be Chile's best Viognier. An organic range will be produced from the 2003 vintage.

Cousiño Macul ☆☆
Santiago. Owners: the Cousiño family. 550 hectares. www.cousinomacul.cl
Precariously close to the suburbs and smog of Santiago, Cousiño Macul is one of Chile's oldest and most beautiful wine estates. The Macul vineyard is also one of the closest to the Andes, and is affected by large diurnal differences in temperature. But urban pressures have led to the gradual selling off of the vineyards, and new vineyards in Buin, south of the city, are being acquired. A new Cabernet blend, "Finis Terrae", reveals a more modern and spicy style of red, in contrast to the renowned, if old-fashioned "Antiguas Reservas", which has the ability to age many decades.

De Martino
See **Santa Ines**

Echeverría ☆☆–☆☆☆
Curicó. Owners: the Echeverría family. 80 hectares. www.echewine.com
Since diverting attention from bulk-wine production to a premium range of varietals, Echeverría has been one of the leading boutique wineries. Self-sufficiency in grapes from vineyards surrounding the winery ensures control over quality. Cabernet Sauvignon is outstanding, particularly the "Family Reserve". The Sauvignon Blanc is stylish, the Chardonnay "Family Reserve" distinctly buttery. The overall style is delicate, rather than opulent, offering wines designed to be drunk with food, as Echeverría has focused its marketing on restaurants worldwide.

Luís Felipé Edwards ☆–☆☆☆
Colchagua. Owner: Luís Felipé Edwards. 300 hectares. www.lfewines.com
Founded in 1976, this beautiful estate, another of the emerging stars of the Colchagua Valley, only began bottling its own wines in 1994. The estate varietals are uninspired, although the new Syrah shows promise, but the reserves are rich and ripe. The flagship wine is "Doña Bernarda", a Cabernet Sauvignon marked by new oak.

Viña Errázuriz ☆☆–☆☆☆
Aconcagua. Owner: Eduardo Chadwick. 540 hectares. www.errazuriz.cl

Out on its own, to the north of Santiago, Errázuriz is best-known for the powerful and distinctive "Don Maximiano" Cabernet Sauvignon. California winemaker Ed Flaherty is pursuing projects such as "Wild Ferment" wines using wild yeasts to express a local character. Vineyards in Casablanca and the Central Valley provide Chardonnay, Sauvignon Blanc, and Merlot grapes for the range. Most of the wines are soft and forward, but there are single vineyard wines with far more character. In 1999, Eduardo Chadwick created a high-priced wine bearing his name, drawing on fruit from a vineyard in Maipo, close to Almaviva. It is made in a richer, spicier, more opulently oaky style than Don Maximiano.

Viña Gracia ☆☆–☆☆☆
Cachapoal. Owner: Córpora Group. 1,000 hectares.
www.gracia.cl
Founded in 1993, this winery buys in fruit from regions as varied as Aconcagua in the north, to Bío-Bío in the south. The best wines emerge from the "Reserva Superior" range, with fleshy Merlot, medium-bodied stylish Cabernet, and very well balanced Chardonnay from Bío-Bío. The recently launched flagship wine is "Caminante" from Aconcagua: a dense smoky blend of Cabernet, Merlot, and Carmenère. The Córpora Group also owns Viña Porta, which produces excellent Merlot, as well as other wines.

Haras de Pirque ☆☆☆
Pirque. Owner: Eduardo Matte. 142 hectares.
www.harasdepirque.com
Eduardo Matte owns a successful stud farm, and decided to plant vineyards – appropriately in the shape of a horseshoe – on the slopes around his Maipo property. A dazzling new winery, also horseshoe-shaped and reminiscent of Opus One in Napa, was ready for the first vintage in 2000. The basic range, "Equus", is at a far higher quality level than most Chilean equivalents, and the very concentrated "Character" and "Elegance" ranges are already among the most serious wines in the country. A new winemaker, Philippe Dardenne, is determined to take the wines to the highest possible level.

Casa Lapostolle ☆☆–☆☆☆☆
Colchagua. Owners: Joint venture between the Rabat and Marnier-Lapostolle families. 300 hectares.
www.casalapostolle.cl
Under the direction of oenologist Michel Rolland from Pomerol and winemaker Michel Friou, this Rapel Valley winery received acclaim from its first vintage in 1994. As you would expect from Rolland, his signature wine is a Merlot ("Cuvée Alexandre"), which is macerated for thirty days and aged in new oak for sixteen months. It is now joined by a very elegant Cabernet, "Alexandre". Profiting from very old vines in Apalta, Lapostolle has more recently released a rich, tannic, and expensive blend called "Clos Apalta". In general, these wines have a Bordelais-style elegance that is rare in Chile.

Viña Misiones de Rengo ☆☆
Rengo. Owner: Compania Chilena da Fosforos
Under the same ownership as Viña Tarapacá (*q.v.*), this new winery has achieved rapid success with its well-crafted, sensibly priced wines, of which the best appear under the "Gran Cuvée" designation.

Montes ☆☆–☆☆☆☆
Curicó. Owners: Aurelio Montes and partners. 550 hectares.
www.monteswines.com
Aurelio Montes is one of Chile's most talented winemakers, now drawing much of his finest fruit from extensive vineyards in the Apalta region. For many years, his "Montes Alpha" Chardonnay and Cabernet Sauvignon (and more recently Syrah) have been outstanding. Montes has not rested on those laurels, and has launched a superb red blend called "Alpha M" and what is certainly Chile's richest and most powerful Syrah: the high-priced "Folly" from Apalta.

Mont Gras ☆–☆☆☆
Colchagua. Owners: the Gras family. 300 hectares.
www.montgras.cl
The standard varietals and *reservas* here are not that different from those from a dozen other large wineries in Chile, although the Casablanca Chardonnay and the Merlot Reserve do stand out. Mont Gras's pride and joy is the unique vineyard called Ninquén, 90 hectares planted across the undulating slopes of a hilltop plateau. This is the source of its top wine, a Cabernet Sauvignon infused with flavours of plums and liquorice.

Viña Morandé ☆☆–☆☆☆
Casablanca. Owner: Pablo Morandé. 360 hectares.
www.morande.cl
While at Concha y Toro (*q.v.*), Pablo Morandé was the first winemaker to realize the potential of the Casablanca Valley. Today, his own winery is in Rapel, although half his vineyards are in Casablanca. The wines, mostly white, made from Casablanca fruit, are characteristically pure and elegant, and there are some impressive *gran reservas*, mostly reds, from Maipo grapes. His top wines are the "House of Morandé Cabernet Sauvignon"; and the sumptuous "Golden Harvest Sauvignon Blanc", from botrytis-affected grapes.

La Palmeria ☆–☆☆
Cachapoal Valley, Rapel. Owners: the Ossa family.
700 hectares. www.larosa.cl
One of the oldest wineries in Chile, La Palmeria (known locally as La Rosa) has only recently switched from selling bulk wines to producing premium-bottled wine. Extensive vineyards in the Cachapoal Valley and a new winery, combine to produce a sound range of varietals. Some of the best red wines come from the 120 hectares planted at the Palmeria estate, a unique plantation of over 1,000 Chilean palms as well as vines. The best wines include a lightly oaked Chardonnay *gran reserva*; a rich Merlot *gran reserva*; and a fruity Merlot/Cabernet rosé.

Paul Bruno ☆☆
Maipo. Owners: Paul Pontallier and Bruno Prats. 22 hectares.
www.aquitania.cl
This starry pair from the Médoc came across an exciting site in 1990, and launched their joint venture. The red wines are aged in 300-litre French oak barrels. The wines are good but not as exciting as one might have hoped. The vineyards are close to Santiago, and the owners are searching for new sites less prone to urban sprawl. An associated label is "SoldeSol", focusing on Chardonnay from the cool, wet Traiguén region.

Viña Pérez Cruz
Maipo. Owners: the Pérez Cruz family. 140 hectares
Tucked against the foothills of the Andes, is one of South

America's most spectacular wineries, sinuously shaped like an upended boat. Hardly any wines have been bottled, but a 2001 Malbec shows concentration and mintiness. If the 2002 cask samples are representative of what will eventually be bottled, the Carmenère and Syrah should prove outstanding.

Portal del Alto ☆–☆☆

Alto Jahuel. Owner: Alejandro Hernández. 170 hectares. www.portaldelalto.cl

Professor Hernández is one of Chile's best-known oenologists and teachers. At his own estate in Maipo, he and winemaker Carolina Arnello produce a wide range of wines. Rather surprisingly, the wines lack coherence and concentration, although a 2001 Syrah from Colchagua does show promise.

San Pedro ☆–☆☆☆

Curicó. Owner: Compania Cervecerias Unidas. 2,500 hectares. www.sanpedro.cl

Since 1994, San Pedro has belonged to Chile's biggest brewer, leading to substantial investment in a state of the art winery. The surrounding 1,200 hectares of vineyards make up one of the largest single estates in the Central Valley. In the 1990s, renowned consultant Jacques Lurton made enormous improvements in the "Gato Negro" and "Castillo de Molina" ranges, and since 2000, the talented Irene Paiva has kept the high standards. Despite the industrial size of the winery, the flagship wine, "Cabo de Hornos", is made in an old-fashioned way that would not be out of place in a small Burgundian cellar.

Santa Carolina, Viña ☆–☆☆

Santiago. Owner: private holding group. 650 hectares. www.vscwines.com

This is one of the easiest wineries for the traveller to visit, as the handsome old buildings are close to Santiago, although the home vineyards are now replaced by housing. However, Santa Carolina has planted extensively throughout all the main valleys, gaining a wide spectrum of fruit sources. Chardonnay, Malbec, and Cabernet Sauvignon come from close to the Cordillera in Maipo. Excellent Merlot is grown in extensive vineyards near San Fernando, and Chardonnay has been planted in Casablanca.

Santa Helena ☆–☆☆

Colchagua. Owner: Compañía Cervecerias Unidas. 1,100 hectares. www.santahelena.cl

Under the same ownership as San Pedro (q.v.), this is the largest of all the Colchagua wineries. The top range is "Selección del Directorioæ, offering wines of a sound but unexceptional quality.

Santa Inés ☆☆–☆☆☆

Isla de Maipo. Owners: the De Martino family. 300 hectares. www.santainesvineyards.com

This traditional estate has been organically cultivated since 2002. The style is rich, oaky, and powerful: a far cry from some of the bland ranges offered by other Chilean wineries. The winery is inexplicably proud of its atypical "Enigma Pinot Noir", but the Carmenère and Cabernet can be outstanding. The top range is the "Reserva de la Familia". Some wines carry the "De Martino" label.

Santa Mónica ☆–☆☆

Rancagua. Owners: the Solminihac family. 10 hectares. www.santamonica.cl

Santa Mónica switched from bulk production to bottled wine in 1981, but serious investment only really happened in the 1990s. However, most of the wines are neutral and lack personality, though further investments in the winery in 2000 may lead to an improvement. The Cabernets under the "Tierra de Sol" label are attractive but lack finesse.

Santa Rita, Viña ☆–☆☆☆

Buin, Maipo. Owner: Claro Group. 2200 hectares. www.santarita.cl

Erratic quality saw this long-established giant slip from the top, but expansion of its Buin estate and an extensive winery upgrade are rapidly turning things around. The whites mostly still lack appeal, but there are persuasively fruity reds under the "Medalla Real" label, and some excellent wines in the "Floresta" range, but they are made in small quantities. The flagship wine is the sleek, voluptuous Cabernet called "Casa Real", but the new "Triple C" from Cabernet Sauvignon, Cabernet Franc, and Carmenère, is even more complex.

Seña ☆☆☆

Aconcagua. Owners: the Errázuriz and Mondavi families. 16 hectares

Since 1995, two leading Pacific coast families have joined forces to produce an elegant, eucalyptus-tinged Cabernet Sauvignon from a vineyard at the cooler end of the Aconcagua Valley. Ed Flaherty, the Errázuriz winemaker, oversees production, and results have been consistently impressive.

Viña Siegel ☆

Curicó. Owner: Alberto Siegel. 600 hectares. www.siegelvinos.com

Alberto Siegel has long been Chile's leading wine broker, but his own venture as a wine producer has been dogged by severe problems. Since 2001 he has leased out his own vineyards and winery, and then in 2002 he himself leased new vineyards and a winery. The 2001 range was uninspired, and the top "Gran Crucero" label shows excessive oakiness.

Casa Silva ☆☆☆

Colchagua. Owner: Mario Silva. 800 hectares. www.casasilva.cl

The Silva family has produced bulk wines from its varied vineyards since 1977, but in 1997 began producing its own wine with advice from consultant winemaker Mario Geisse. First results have been very impressive. This is the only property in Chile to bottle a Sauvignon Gris: a richer, juicier grape than Sauvignon Blanc. And the flowery "Quinta Generación" blend is among the most complex whites in South America.

The basic "Classic" range is good value, and the reserves are substantially richer. The top reds are the supple "Quinta Generación" (Cabernet/Carmenère) and the very refined Cabernet/Carmenère/Merlot blend called "Altura".

Viña Tarapacá ☆–☆☆

Isla de Maipo. Owner: Compania Chilena da Fosforos. 600 hectares. www.tarapaca.cl

In 1996, this ancient winery switched its activity from the western side of the Maipo Valley to the Isla del Maipo, renovating the winery and acquiring vineyards in Casablanca. The Maipo vineyards are very diverse in soil structure and microclimate, permitting winemaker Sergio Correa to produce a range of six wines called "Terroir". The top red, a Bordeaux blend, is called "Zavala". Overall, quality is sound but unremarkable.

Terramater ☆–☆☆
Maipo. Owner: Cánepa sisters. 460 hectares. www.terramater.cl
After the splitting up of the original Cánepa estate (*q.v.*) in 1996, three sisters retained the Maipo vineyards, and there are other sites in Curicó and Maule. They are proud of their Zinfandels, a curiosity in Chile, but it can hardly compete with the better Californian examples. The other wines are lush and supple, but lack personality.

Terranoble ☆☆–☆☆☆
Talca. Owners: Mario Geisse, Patricio de Solminihac, and other investors. 90 hectares. www.terranoble.cl
This small Maule winery was founded in 1994 and has impressed with its richly concentrated *gran reserva* Cabernet and Merlot.

Torreón de Paredes ☆☆–☆☆☆
Rengo. Owners: the Paredes family. 150 hectares.
www.torreon.cl
A family run estate, with vineyards in the Cachapoal Valley. The reds (Merlot and Cabernet Sauvignon) are more impressive than the range of whites, although there is a good oaked Sauvignon Blanc. Alvaro Paredes lavishes passionate care and attention on improving the viticulture, with increasingly impressive results.

With French winemaker Yves Pouzet at the helm since 1996, the style has remained subtle and elegant. The flagship wine is "Don Amado", named in honour of the founder.

Miguel Torres ☆☆☆
Curicó. Owners: the Torres family. 400 hectares.
www.migueltorres.cl
When Miguel Torres set up his winery two decades ago, he ushered in a new era for the Chilean wine industry. The introduction of modern winemaking equipment – including stainless-steel fermentation tanks – allowed the white wines to be cold-fermented, while imported oak barrels replaced old *rauli* casks.

His innovations shocked the Chileans into realizing the true potential of their vineyards. The range is considerable, and even the more modest wines are well-made. Among the top bottlings are the barrel-fermented "Maqueha" Chardonnay; the robust "Manso de Velasco" Cabernet from very old vines; and a Carignan-dominated blend called "Cordillera".

Undurraga ☆☆
Talagante. Owners: the Undurraga family. 1,000 hectares.
www.undurraga.cl
A highly traditional winery that is currently undergoing something of a renaissance. The vineyards are split between Maipo and Colchagua – growing Sauvignon Blanc, Chardonnay, Merlot, Cabernet Sauvignon, and Pinot Noir. The whites are disappointing, but the reserve reds are richly fruity, and oak is used with discretion. The top wines are the "Founder's Collection Cabernet" and the rather overripe "Altazor", an old-vine Cabernet aged in new oak.

Valdivieso ☆☆
Curicó. Owner: the Mitjan Group. 100 hectares.
www.vinavaldivieso.cl
The biggest Chilean sparkling wine producer has also made considerable strides with still wine in recent years. Grapes are bought from various valleys, and some of their best fruit comes from unirrigated vineyards close to the coastal mountains. The white wines are bland and the reds mostly lack vigour and personality, but the arrival in late 2001 of talented New Zealand winemaker Brett Jackson should push up quality a few notches. The premium blend, Caballo Loco, is made by a *solera* system and thus carries no vintage date.

Los Vascos ☆☆
Colchagua. Owners: Partnership between the Eyzaguirre/Echenique family and Domaines Barons de Rothschild (Lafite). 500 hectares
Los Vascos is a French-Chilean collaboration, which has attempted to squeeze Chilean fruit into a Bordeaux mould. All, even the flagship Cabernet Sauvignon reserve, have yet to reach the level that this sort of potential suggests. A new winemaking team was installed in 2001, and a premium wine called "Dix" was launched, signalling an effort to rise above the mediocrity that has previously marked the wines.

Ventisquero ☆–☆☆
Rancagua. Owner: Agrosuper group. 1,500 hectares.
www.agrosuper.com
With amazing rapidity, Chile's largest chicken producer has developed vineyards and a series of ranges of wines targeted at different markets, under diverse labels such as "Yali" and "Southern Wind". Aurelio Montes is a consultant to the enterprise. Initial releases from 2001 were sound and fruity, but only noteworthy at *gran reserva* level, where the Carmenère and Cabernet stand out.

Veramonte ☆–☆☆
Casablanca. Owner: Constellation Wine Group. 400 hectares.
www.veramonte.cl
Launched in 1996, at the warm end of the Casablanca Valley, Veramonte even grows Cabernet and Merlot, though it also buys red grapes from Maipo. The whites are fresh and citric, but reds are disappointing, except for the top wine, "Primus", which is spicy and lively.

Villard ☆☆
Casablanca. Owners: Thierry Villard and partners. 20 hectares.
www.villard.cl
A partnership between Frenchman Thierry Villard and two Chilean growers. The basic range is called "Espreción", and the better wines are the barrique-aged "Esencia" and the dense, tannic, Bordeaux blend called "Equis".

Viu Manent ☆☆–☆☆☆
Colchagua. Owners: the Viu family. 400 hectares.
www.viumanent.cl
The red wines at this visitor-friendly estate are all sound, but special mention must be made of the Malbecs. No other Chilean estate produces a range of four Malbecs. All are attractive and two are outstanding: the full-bodied, spicy "Special Selection", and the intense new-oaked "Viu One". The Viu family is developing new vineyards that are potentially superb, so this is an estate to watch.

Argentina

Argentina, with its Hispano-Italian traditions, is the only country outside Europe with a natural wine culture, the fifth-biggest producer and consumer of wine in the world. During its forty-odd years of travail, first under Perón and then under assorted military authorities, Argentina was virtually a closed country. But the domestic market for wine was so enthusiastic (an annual ninety-odd litres a head, more recently falling, as elsewhere, to about half that level) that no one bothered about export – except in bulk to supply Japan's imaginary wine industry.

In the 1990s, that began to change. The government policy of pegging the peso to the US dollar gave the country a new era of stability. Foreign investors began to buy large vineyards and construct wineries with an eye on the export market. By 2000, there were 1,200 wineries, most of them in the Mendoza region. Yet exports never managed to rise above seven per cent overall.

Then, in late 2001, the economy collapsed, and the peso was devalued. Whatever hardship this caused many poorer Argentinians, it should have assisted the export industries, but initially had little impact. Nonetheless, the new investors, whether local or foreign, have not lost heart, and remain convinced of both the quality and commercial potential of Argentinian wines.

Argentina's principal grape-growing regions are (from north to south) Salta, Mendoza (with several sub-regions), San Rafael, and Río Negro. The vineyards of Salta reach as high as 2,000 metres (6,500 feet) in the Andean foothills, where the Cafayate Valley produces some notably aromatic, not over-heavy wine.

Mendoza City lies only a short distance from Santiago de Chile, but with the highest point of the Andes, Mount Aconcagua, in between. Its surrounding vineyards vary from the very warm plain of Guaymallén to the east, through the central, long-established Luján de Cuyo region just south of the city where the principal *bodegas* are, up to a height of 1,200-1,500 metres (3,900–4,041 feet) in the Tupungato foothills to the southwest, where cool conditions are making their impact.

Still in the province of Mendoza, but far south over the desert, the vineyards of San Rafael are irrigated by the Atuel and Diamante rivers. Further south, on the thirty-nineth parallel and equivalent to Hawke's Bay in New Zealand, is the Río Negro, where wine has, until recently, taken second place to fruit production, but recent releases show great promise.

Rainfall is rare in all these regions. The arid air cuts mildew and insect problems to a minimum. Hail, on the other hand, is a frequent scourge. Flood irrigation from the comprehensive canal network has been the rule. Intelligently used, it produces perfect grapes (it also rules out phylloxera), although many growers are now installing drip systems for greater control. Some vineyards are still trained on a pergola system, which, when properly managed, can give good results.

Red wines are what Argentina does best – so far. Such primitive grapes as Criolla are giving way to new plantings of international varieties, and Argentina also has large tracts of Italian table-wine grapes, among them Bonarda, Barbera, Sangiovese, and some Nebbiolo. The grapes that will make Argentina's name are Cabernet, Syrah, Merlot, and, most of all, Malbec. Just why Malbec, relegated from Bordeaux in favour of the Cabernets during the nineteenth century, makes such satisfying, juicy-textured wines here, no one is sure. One explanation may be that Malbec was brought here in the 1850s before phylloxera in France, so the plant selection may well be superior to that now in France. In France, Malbec sometimes ripens with difficulty, but in Argentina, ripeness is not a problem, so Malbec rarely has harsh tannins, and, depending on its handling in the winery, can exhibit flavours ranging from blueberry to mocha, from damsons to chocolate. Among the whites, Argentina's unique contribution is the Torrontés, an extremely aromatic variety, related to Muscat, usually vinified dry but difficult to find a place for at table.

The best *bodegas*, though, are turning out Malbecs and Cabernet blends of exciting potential, and some good Chardonnays. They are led, at a good distance, by Nicolás Catena, but many other wineries are moving swiftly to bring their quality up to comparable levels. Others focus their efforts on well-made and attractively priced commercial wines for the competitive export market.

At its best, Argentinian wine can probably surpass all but the best of Chile for vibrancy and character. Nonetheless, there are still too many dreary, even faulty wines that make it out of the country, usually heavily disguised as new "brands" for markets determined to purchase at the lowest-possible price regardless of quality. *Caveat emptor.*

Leading Argentinian Wine Producers

Achaval Ferrer ☆☆☆
Luján de Cuyo, Mendoza. Owner: a consortium. 64 hectares. www.achaval-ferrer.com
Achaval Ferrer produces only estate-grown wines, from some of Mendoza's oldest vines. Roberto Cipresso (from Montalcino) makes the wines, and has won a strong following for his highly concentrated and expensive reds, especially his Malbecs from Finca Altamira.

La Agrícola ☆☆
Maipú, Mendoza. Owners: the Zuccardi family. 580 hectares. www.familiazuccardi.net
This estate, founded by Alberto Zuccardi, was established in the 1960s, and a new winery was constructed in 1998. Some of the property is now organically cultivated. La Agrícola is technically innovative, having experimented successfully with techniques such as micro-oxygenation and mechanical punching down. The range of wines is broad, as production feeds a variety of export markets ("Santa Julia" is best-known in Britain, "Santa Rosa" elsewhere), and the top wines are smartly packaged under the "Q" label. These are well-made, commercial wines, rarely disappointing, rarely thrilling. Tempranillo is a house specialty.

Alta Vista ☆☆☆
Luján de Cuyo, Mendoza. Owners: the Aulan family. 115 hectares. www.altavistawines.com
Excellent Malbecs at all levels from this French-owned property. "Alto" is one of the top wines of Argentina: 80% Malbec, 20% Cabernet Sauvignon, from sixty-year-old vines, and aged in new barriques. Expensive but superb.

Altos Las Hormigas ☆–☆☆☆

Mendoza. Owner: Antonio Morescalchi. 40 hectares.
www.altolashormigas.com

A relatively small producer, offering delicious Malbec, especially the blueberry-tinged reserva.

Anubis ☆☆–☆☆☆

Luján de Cuyo, Mendoza. Owner: Dominio del Plata Winery.
45 hectares

A good-quality range of wines created by one of Argentina's best winemakers, Susana Balbo, and by Italian oenologist Alberto Antonini. Good red varietals, in a lush, slightly jammy style. Under the Anubis umbrella, Balbo also has her own wine, as does her husband, Pedro Marchevsky, who uses the "BenMarco" label. Balbo's Cabernet-dominated wine is called "Brioso" and combines power and stylishness. "BenMarco" is an unusual and somewhat gamey blend of mostly Malbec, plus Bonarda, Syrah, Cabernet, and Tannat.

Balbi, Bodegas ☆–☆☆

San Rafael, Mendoza. Owner: Allied-Domecq. 100 hectares.
www.bodegasbalbi.com

Founded 1930. A good, solid range of standard varietals, soft in texture and drinkable on release.

Valentín Bianchi ☆☆

San Rafael, Mendoza. Owners: the Bianchi family. 345 hectares. www.vbianchi.com

An important producer employing a number of labels, including "Elsa", "Los Primos", and "Famiglia Bianchi". Their best wines are usually the "Famiglia Bianchi" Cabernet Sauvignon and Chardonnay, the latter made in a sweetish, international style.

Luigi Bosca ☆–☆☆

Luján de Cuyo. Owners: the Arizú family. 650 hectares.
www.luigibosca.com.ar

An outstanding grape-grower, with vineyards that are close to organic. The cheapest range is "La Linda", and there is better quality and value among the "Viña Paraíso" line, with attractive Viognier. Red wines of mixed quality.

Canale, Bodegas Humberto ☆–☆☆

Río Negro, Mendoza. Owners: the Barzi family. 170 hectares.
www.bodegahcanale.com

Founded in 1913, this is the leading Río Negro winery, with very fair Sémillon, organic Merlot, and Malbec. The top export labels are "Black River" and "Diego Murillo".

Catena Zapata ☆☆☆

Agrelo, Mendoza. Owner: Dr. Nicolás Catena. 425 hectares.
www.catenazapata.com

Founded in 1902, Catena became Argentina's largest bulk wine producer. Dr. Nicolás Catena, while an economics professor at Berkeley, got to know the best wines of California and immediately began improving his own wines. Catena has been a pioneer of viticultural research, identifying the best clones of Malbec, and experimenting with high-density plantings.

Catena began exporting in 1991 and has consolidated its position as the leading producer of high-quality Argentinian wines. There are three *bodegas*. At the striking, new Mayan-style winery in Agrelo, Catena produces the wines sold under the "Alamos" (excellent value Chardonnay), "Catena", and "Catena Alta" labels. At Bodegas Esmeralda, they produce their largest brand, "Argento". At La Rural they produce brands for the domestic and American market such as "Rutini" and "Trumpeter". The two flagship wines are "Nicolás Catena", a magnificent and sumptuous, oaky, Napa-style Cabernet, and "Caro", a joint venture with Château Lafite, first made in 2000 and more sleek and confected than the "Nicolás Catena". Future projects include a range of single-vineyard Malbecs.

Finca La Celia ☆☆

San Carlos, Mendoza. Owner: San Pedro (Chile). 600 hectares

A new winery for this growing brand opened in 2002. Rich, juicy reserve Malbec from Uco Valley.

Bodegas Chandon ☆–☆☆

Agrelo, Mendoza. Owner: LVMH. 500 hectares

Producers of Baron B. and M. Chandon sparkling wine under Moët & Chandon supervision; 1995 saw a quality leap with the first Chardonnay/Pinot Noir blend. The company also produces a huge range of still reds and whites for domestic sale, and an excellent international brand, "Terrazas" (*q.v.*).

Colomé ☆☆–☆☆☆

Salta. Owner: Donald Hess (California). 30 hectares

From very old vineyards high in the Calchaquies Valley in the Cafayate area, Hess's winemaker "Randle Johnson" has, since 2001, been making a rich, complex blend of Malbec, Cabernet, and Tannat.

Bodegas Escorihuela ☆–☆☆

Mendoza. Owners: a consortium. www.escorihuela.com

This is the last remaining winery within the city of Mendoza. The partners who own the business include Dr. Nicolás Catena. The range of wines includes relatively inexpensive brands such as "Candela", "Gascon", and "High Altitude".

Bodegas Esmeralda

See **Catena Zapata**

Etchart ☆☆

Cafayate, Salta, and Luján de Cuyo, Mendoza. Owner: Pernod Ricard. 400 hectares

This venerable property was founded in 1850. In more recent times, it pioneered drip irrigation in Argentina. The basic range is "Río de Plata", and the top wine the Cabernet/Malbec blend. "Arnaldo B. Etchart" is among the best examples of an old-fashioned but elegant style.

Fabre Montmayou ☆☆–☆☆☆

Vistalba, Mendoza. Owner: Hervé Joyaux. 85 hectares

With a winemaker, Arnaud Meillan, originally from Pomerol, the French influence is strong here. Excellent Malbec, and spicy, oaky "Grand Vin" from ninety-year-old vines. The company also has vineyards in Río Negro, where it produces some increasingly impressive wines from Merlot and Malbec/Syrah under the "Infinitus" label.

Finca Flichman ☆–☆☆

Mendoza. Owner: Sogrape (Portugal) (*q.v.*). 300 hectares.
www.flichman.com

Bought by Sogrape in 1997, this estate is now undergoing

expansion and will double in size. The Merlot and Syrah reserves are disappointingly light, and the top Cabernet Sauvignon/Syrah blend, "Dedicado", is also made in a discreet, lean style.

Lagarde ☆

Luján de Cuyo, Mendoza. Owners: the Pescarmona family. 220 hectares. www.lagarde.com.ar

Decent commercial Merlot and Malbec, and promising Viognier, a variety first planted by this century-old estate.

Bodegas Lopez ☆

Maipú, Mendoza. Owners: the Lopez family. 1,060 hectares. www.bodegaslopez.com

If you weary of the bright, fruity styles of most Argentinian wines on export markets, then try the "Casona Lopez" range from this very traditional winery. These red varietals are slightly oxidative in style, since they are aged for many years in large old casks. They are by no means poor wines, but they are an acquired taste.

Bodegas Lurton ☆

Godoy Cruz, Mendoza. Owners: Jacques and François Lurton. 140 hectares

The ubiquitous Lurton brothers have been making wine in Argentina since the late 1980s. Yet their varietal ranges lack concentration and focus, and even the top wine, the "Gran Lurton" Cabernet/Malbec, lacks excitement.

Navarro Correas ☆–☆☆

Maipú, Mendoza. Owner: Diageo. 300 hectares

The estate was founded in 1798, but only began bottling its wines in 1984. After its purchase by the global Diageo corporation, Jeff Stambor from Beaulieu Vineyards (q.v.) in Napa was dispatched here to improve quality, which he did until 2002. There is a clear quality hierarchy: in upward order of quality, "Los Arboles", "Collección Privada", "Gran Reserva", and the new "Ultra". Overall the style is commercial and medium-bodied, perfectly acceptable yet bland. "Ultra", a new-oaked Bordeaux blend, is overpriced.

Nieto y Senetiner ☆☆–☆☆☆

Luján de Cuyo, Mendoza. Owner: Perez Companc (energy company). 300 hectares. www.nietosenetiner.com

Good-quality wines at all price levels – even the cheap "Ola" Barbera has ample fruit. The top Malbec is called "Cadus" and another top wine, the Bordeaux blend "Don Nicanor", is ripe, stylish, and balanced. Acceptable mass-volume wines are sold domestically under the "Santa Isabel" label, and exported under the "Valle de Vistalba" label.

Norton ☆☆–☆☆☆

Luján de Cuyo, Mendoza. Owner: Gernot Langes-Swarovski. 1,265 hectares. www.norton.com.ar

A classic Mendoza *bodega* acquired in 1989 by Austrian owners. The basic varietal range is humdrum, but the oaky *reservas* are very reliable, especially the vibrant, plummy Malbec. The top red blend is "Privada": a supple wine for medium-term drinking, and a very oaky, Merlot-dominated blend, "Perdriel", will soon join its side.

Viña Patagonia

See **Trivento**

Peñaflor

Maipú, Mendoza. Owner: DLJ consortium. 2,000 hectares

The country's biggest wine company, with four modern *bodegas* and a huge range of wines. Best-known labels have been "Michel Torino" (q.v.), "Santa Ana", and "Trapiche" (q.v.).

Finca El Retiro ☆–☆☆

Rivadavia, Mendoza. Owner: Pacífico Tittarelli. 650 hectares

The export brand of the large Pacífico Tittarelli company. Alberto Antonini was the consultant oenologist, and brought quality to a consistently high level. His departure in 2001 may have led to a slight decline in quality. Some of the best varietal wines are the Tempranillo, Bonarda, and Malbec.

Bodega La Riojana ☆–☆☆

La Rioja, Salta. Cooperative. 4,200 hectares. www.lariojana.com.ar

An enormous cooperative with 600 members, but with the help of consultant oenologists it has acquired a good reputation for its wines, especially for aromatic Torrontés. Well over half the production is of white wines. Labels include "Santa Florentína", "Rio Santo", and "Far Flung".

Bodegas La Rural

See **Catena Zapata**

Salentein, Bodegas ☆☆–☆☆☆

Tupungato, Mendoza. 340 hectares. www.bodegasalentein.com

This ambitious modern winery and estate was founded in 1998 and is owned by Salentein Argentina. The company has assembled a first-rate team here, led by the former owner of Trapiche (q.v.), Carlos Pulenta. The basic commercial range is called "El Portillo" or "La Pampa" (according to market); then there is the "Salentein" label, and finally the reserve (or "Primus") range. The stars of the "Salentein" range are the Merlot and Malbec, with Cabernet Sauvignon in hot pursuit. Winemaker Laureano Gómez is passionate about Pinot Noir, and has planted vines at 1,500 metres (4,041 feet) to supplement Pinot grown in their warmer vineyards. First vintages show promise, but it remains to be seen whether Salentein can succeed where so many others have failed.

Santa Julia

See **La Agricola**

Septima, Bodegas ☆

Agrelo, Mendoza. Owners: Codorníu. 300 hectares. www.bodegaseptima.com.ar

Since the first vintage, 2000, winemaker Ruben Calvo has issued a series of clean, bright, uncomplicated varietals.

Tapiz ☆–☆☆

Uco Valley, Mendoza. Owner: Kendall-Jackson. 1,400 hectares

This is the Argentinian property of the immense Californian wine company, Kendall-Jackson (q.v.). A new winery was completed in 2000 to produce a range of sound varietal wines under winemaker José Antonio Bravo. Some wines have previously appeared under the "Mariposa" label.

Terrazas ☆☆–☆☆☆

Perdriel, Mendoza. Owner: LVMH. www.terrazasdelosandes.com

From vineyards at an altitude varying from 750–1,200 metres (2,460–3,936 feet), the Terrazas team, led by Roberto de la

Mota, produces wines of excellent quality. "Alto" is the basic range, but the *reserva* and top "Gran" lines, aged mostly in French oak, are worth the extra cost. The "Gran" Malbec is packed with concentrated, black-cherry fruit, while the "Gran" Cabernet Sauvignon is smokier and more complex.

Michel Torino ☆–☆☆
Cafayate, Salta. Owner: Peñaflor. 720 hectares.
www.micheltorino.com.ar
Torino has benefited from enormous investments made by a succession of recent owners, culminating in Peñaflor's (*q.v.*) acquisition in 1999. Although Cafayate has a good reputation for its Torrontés, Torino's red wines are now distinctly better than the whites. The uninspired basic range is called "Collección"; the top wines are bottled as "Don David" and include an unusually zesty, spicy Don David Malbec. This mainstay of the Peñaflor group produces almost two million cases.

Pascual Toso ☆☆
Guaymallén, Mendoza. Owner: Enrique Toso. 300 hectares.
www.toso.com.ar
A small family concern best-known for fine Cabernets, made from very old vines, and for a million-case production of sparkling wines, some of which are made by the classic method.

Trapiche ☆☆
Maipú, Mendoza. Owner: DLJ consortium. 900 hectares.
www.trapichewinery.com
Once a proud independent label, Trapiche has for many years been a brand of the Peñaflor group. At the top level, long-term winemaker Angel Mendoza produces some very good wines, such as the supple "Medalla" Cabernet, the broad, plummy "Broquel" Malbec, and the pricey "Iscay" Malbec/Merlot blend, originally developed by former consultant oenologist, Michel Rolland.

Trivento ☆☆
Maipú, Mendoza. Owner: Viña Patagonia, itself owned by
Concha y Toro (Chile) (*q.v.*). 460 hectares. www.trivento.com
Trivento is the most important export label of Concha y Toro's Argentinian winery. The wines are far from complex, but they are inexpensive and well-made, with a fresh sappy Chardonnay, and damsony reserve Malbec among the best of them.

Viniterra ☆–☆☆
Luján de Cuyo. Owners: Adriano Senetiner and Walter Bressia.
40 hectares. www.viniterra.com.ar
Founded in 1997, this is a relatively small property created by the former owners of Nieto y Senetiner (*q.v.*). Young vine production is bottled under the "Omnium" label; the remainder under the "Terra" and "Viniterra" labels. Quality at the lower levels has been patchy, but there is impressive "Viniterra" Malbec with strong tones of plums and coffee.

Domaine de Vistalba
See **Fabre Montmayou**

Valle de Vistalba
See **Nieto y Senetiner**

Weinert, Bodegas ☆–☆☆
Luján de Cuyo, Mendoza. Owner: Bernardo Weinert.
35 hectares. www.bodegaweinert.com
A medium-sized winery, producing extremely old-fashioned reds, aged for years, even decades, in old casks. They seem to inspire admiration and bafflement in equal degrees.

Yacochuya ☆☆☆
Cafayate, Salta. Owners: Michel Rolland and Arnaldo Etchart
Pomerol owner and consultant Michel Rolland, a long-time devotee of Argentinian wines, is particularly excited about this vineyard, set at 2,035 metres (6,633 feet), from which he produces a predominantly Malbec wine, aged in new barriques for twelve months. It is dense and extracted, with far more power and tannin than is usually encountered with Malbec. A wine for the long haul.

Mexico

Given the world-class produce of its northerly neighbour, it would be surprising if Mexico were not producing very creditable wines. The oldest American wine industry is being revived with investment from abroad, and technical advice from the University of California at Davis. At present, there are 50,000 hectares under vine.

Vineyards have been part of the northern Baja California landscape since the 1880s, when Bodegas de Santo Tomás first opened its doors. The Guadalupe Valley, north of Ensenada, and San Vicente to its south, now have extensive vineyards, with fashionable European varieties ousting both the indigenous Mission grape, and other widely grown but less favoured grapes such as Chenin Blanc and Grenache. Most of the wine is exported, since there is little domestic demand, the wine-loving *bourgeoisie* of the cities preferring prestigious imported bottles.

Wente Vineyards of California and the historic Santo Tomás bodega recently joined forces to produce a Cabernet Sauvignon, with equal amounts of wine from either side of the border used to make "Duetto", a Bordeaux blend aimed at export markets. Another pioneer of the modern wine industry is L A Cetto (with almost 3,000 hectares of vineyards), making successful wines with Chardonnay, Nebbiolo (Cetto was a native of Piemonte), Cabernet, and Petite Syrah. But it was the investment of Pedro Domecq from Spain that set Mexican wine on a new course. Domecq now has vast vineyards in the Guadalupe Valley. Its premium wine, "Château Domecq", is a Nebbiolo/Merlot blend, its white counterpart a Sauvignon Blanc. Freixenet is the other principal Spanish interest, with forty hectares of vineyards and a predictable focus on sparkling wines. Two new notable wineries in the valley are the ambitious Monte Xanic, founded in 1988, which has full-bodied Cabernet and Merlot, and rich, barrel-fermented Chardonnays; and Château Camou, which first produced wines in 1995, and is turning out prize-winning Fumé Blanc and Chardonnay. The smallest wineries in Mexico are the Swiss-owned Mogor Badan, with a tannic Bordeaux blend; and Cavas Valmar, a quality-driven family operation, established on the outskirts of Ensenada in 1985. Its Cabernet Sauvignon is especially good.

Down south near Mexico City, Domecq and Freixenet have joined the pioneer, Caves de San Juan, in the mountains of Querétaro. Undoubtedly, Mexico has great potential, even if the local taste lags far behind the aspirations of her modern vineyards and wineries.

Brazil

The immense domestic market of South America's largest country has led some of the biggest names in drinks – Cinzano, Domecq, Heublein, Martini & Rossi, Moët & Chandon, Suntory, and National Distillers – to invest in Brazil.

By far the biggest and most important of Brazil's wine-growing regions is in the Rio Grande do Sul, high in the undulating hills around the towns of Bento Gonçalves and Garibaldi. Two hundred and fifteen metres (698 feet) above sea level, this sub-tropical region was settled by north Italians in the nineteenth century. Each family planted a small plot of vineyard on the steep slopes of land granted by the Brazilian government. Smallholdings remain important, with at least 16,000 owners cultivating their vines.

About eighty per cent of the 60,000 hectares of vines are non-*vinifera* varieties (with better disease resistance) for wines for the domestic market. The best producers are now making acceptable wines from classic varieties, notably Chardonnay, Cabernet, and Merlot, and are experimenting with better clones and trellising systems. Other producers are content with excessively high yields, with predictably uninteresting results.

The generally hot and sunny climate suits the vine, although rainfall is often in the form of torrential downpours. Early picking to avoid the risk of disease under these conditions often results in wine that is light in body, and rather high in acidity.

The Brazilian wine industry is dominated by Vinicola Aurora, a huge cooperative in Bento Gonçalves, which draws on 1,300 growers with 1,350 hectares. Sparkling wine has proved surprisingly successful, with Salton, De Lantier (owned by Martini & Rossi), and Chandon do Brasil all producing quaffable bottles. However, Brazil as a whole has been slow to adopt international standards of production and labelling, and will need to change fast to avoid losing out to its more dynamic neighbours.

Peru

One would be forgiven for not knowing that a Peruvian wine industry existed at all, yet wine was being produced close to Cuzco as long ago as 1560. Geographically (only ten degrees from the equator) and socio-economically (political turmoil coupled with hyperinflation of the past), conditions in Peru would not seem conducive to the hedonistic world of grape-growing and winemaking. Most of the country's 11,000 hectares of grapes go for distillation into the ubiquitous Pisco, to make the Pisco Sour that heals away the heat and dust of the day (despite its proximity to the equator the wine region is arid). The parched lunar landscape results from being on the wrong side of the Andes, and vines need irrigation to thrive.

Two hundred and ninety kilometres (180 miles) south of Lima along the Pan American Highway, lies the town of Ica, at the heart of Peru's wine region. Of the half dozen wineries located here, only one so far produces wines of quality.

Viña Tacama is by far the biggest, best, and most important winery in Peru. Founded in the sixteenth century, it has been solely owned since 1889 by the Olaechea family whose French winemaker, Robert Niederman, has been at the helm for every harvest since 1961, producing good Chenin Blanc, Sauvignon, Malbec, and even sparkling wine. Professor Emile Peynaud has acted as consultant here.

Other quality-focused wineries include Tabernero and Santiago Queirolo.

Other regions, among them Chincha, Moquegua, and Tacha, are now also making progress.

Uruguay

Uruguay is often called the Belgium of South America: small, flat, and with a population of just three million, it is dominated by its giant neighbours, Brazil and Argentina, both physically and oenologically. Its wine industry is supported by a thirsty local population, almost as avid wine-drinkers as the neighbouring Argentinians.

Uruguay has been making wine since the 1700s, variously influenced by France, Spain, Germany, and Italy. Its Mediterranean-type climate suggests that it is eminently suited to producing quality-wine grapes. At present, French grapes predominate. In addition to premium Chardonnay, Sauvignon Blanc, Cabernet Sauvignon, and Merlot, the Tannat (the grape of southwest France) is being widely planted – indeed, in greater quantities than in any other country. At present, Merlot and Tannat show particular promise. The country is principally divided into five wine zones which are simply called the Southern, South Western, Central, North Western, and Northern zones. The one showing most potential for quality is also the oldest and largest: the Southern zone, south of the capital Montevideo.

Uruguay's biggest producer is Dante Irurtia, which concentrates primarily on the bulk domestic market. The second-largest, Castillo Viejo, currently produces mainly bag-in-box rosés (some 2.1 million litres a year), but it is turning its attention to bottling quality varietal wines by initiating a joint venture with a French company. Its better wines are bottled with the "Catamayor" label. Other premium wineries include Pisano, Juanico, Pizzorno, Stagnari, De Lucca, and Cerro Chapeu.

Uruguay has the potential to make quality wines for export. Its first steps in this direction show much more promise than one might have thought.

Australia

Australian wine swept into favour around the world in the mid-1980s, with a suddenness that surprised almost everyone. The world was unprepared for such intensely fruity Chardonnay and Cabernet, lavishly seasoned with oak, at prices far below those for such wines from France or California. But then the world had resolutely ignored the quality of Australian wine for generations.

Until the revelation of the last ten years, it used to come as a real surprise to visitors to discover how important wine is in the country's life; how knowledgeable and critical many Australians are; how many wineries, wine regions, and "styles" (the favourite Australian wine word) this country, with a relatively small population, can profitably support. Extraordinarily little of the buzz of Australian winemanship penetrated overseas, largely because her best wines are made in vast variety but in small quantities, and partly because lack of any kind of central direction made Australian labels a pathless jungle.

By the early 1980s, open-minded critics overseas were acknowledging that Australia's best wines are excellent: different in flavour from California's but not a jot inferior, and presenting a far wider range of "styles". In Australia, Shiraz (the Syrah of the Rhône), Semillon (no é), and Riesling have been excellently grown for decades. First-class Chardonnay and Cabernet joined them in the 1970s. And the 1990s have seen Australian winemakers make progress with Pinot Noir, and a surge of interest in Rhône-style wines based on Grenache, Shiraz, and Mourvèdre (Mataro in Australia).

The whirlwind of change and innovation is no less strong in Australia than in California, but the establishment through which it blows is far older. Until recently, an astonishing number of wineries still belonged to the families that founded them over a century ago. They still have powerful traditions. Although nearly all have now changed hands, and most of their turnover today is likely to be in bulk wines sold in "cask", or "bag-in-box", they continue to make small, high-quality lots from their best grapes. Medium-sized and boutique wineries have proliferated in direct competition with these established classics, adding to the alarming number of good wines there are to choose from.

Australia long ago lost any inhibitions (if she ever had any) about blending wines from different grapes and different regions – even as much as 1,600 kilometres (1,000 miles) apart. And within these regions, until the recent boom, Australia's four main wine-growing states had only half-a-dozen quality areas of any importance.

New South Wales had the (then almost moribund) Hunter Valley, to the north of Sydney; Victoria had Rutherglen and its neighbourhood in the northeast, Great Western in the west (and the lonely Tahbilk in the middle).

South Australia, throughout the twentieth century much the greatest producer, had the Barossa Valley, Southern Vales, and Clare grouped round Adelaide, and Coonawarra in the remote south. Western Australia had the Swan Valley at Perth. The Murray River, flowing between the three eastern states, irrigated large areas for low-quality wine, most of which was distilled.

Each of these areas had four grapes at most, which it grew well for fine wines. And each was dominated by, at most, four or five considerable producers. Now, new vineyards have sprung up in a score of districts which are either entirely new to the vine but promise cooler growing conditions, or which (like many parts of Victoria) flourished as vineyards a century ago. Southeast Australia, from Adelaide to Sydney, is starting to look on the map like one great wine area. Soon, it seems, the same will be true of the southwest.

This explosion of new wine-growing areas has been accompanied by two significant developments: a passionate interest in regionalism, and the first stages in the formulation of an appellation system for Australia (the two being intimately related, of course).

Australian winemakers are increasingly realizing the benefits of connecting particular varieties or styles with particular regions – both from a marketing and wine quality point of view. Botrytis Semillon from Griffith, Cabernet Sauvignon from Margaret River, Riesling from Clare, Semillon from the Hunter, Shiraz from the Barossa – all these combinations and more are reinforced constantly in the consumers' mind. And winemakers are now prepared to admit that there may be something to the concept of terroir after all.

A body called the Geographical Indications Committee has been set up to undertake the long, laborious, and often controversial process of defining Australia's disparate wine areas. Once that process is finished, the regional names that appear on Australian bottles will be set in stone, and should convey unambiguously to the consumer a clearer idea about what to expect once the cork is pulled.

Recent years have seen a consolidation of the Australian wine industry, as large companies such as Southcorp and BRL Hardy have steadily swallowed up many other wineries, both large and small. Many fear that this will lead to a growing standardization at the level of huge-volume brands, that may prove to be the case. But the evidence so far suggests that the large, corporate owners are trying to respect and maintain the individuality and personality of the wineries they have ingested. We must hope that continues.

Australia's Wine Regions

New South Wales

Canberra 500-hectare region of small, newish wineries clustered around the Australian Capital Territory (ACT), many of them in decidedly cool spots at relatively high altitude.

Hunter Valley Australia's oldest wine region. The Lower Hunter, around Pokolbin, some 160 kilometres (100 miles) north of Sydney, is a long-established producer of serious Shiraz and age-worthy Semillon. Cloud cover mitigates the extreme summer heat, but rain often dampens the vintage. Chardonnay and Cabernet have been fairly successful in the past twenty years. The Upper Hunter, developed since the 1960s, is mostly a white wine area, well suited to Chardonnay.

Mudgee Small, long-established area 160 kilometres (100 miles) west of the Hunter Valley and 365 metres (1,200 feet)

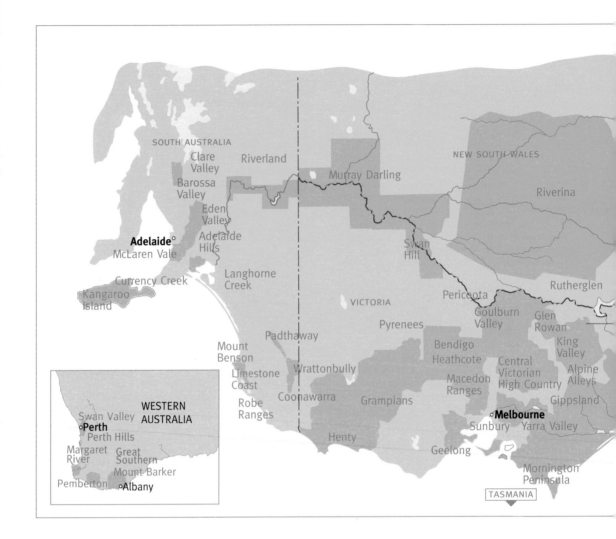

SOUTH AUSTRALIA
Clare Valley
Riverland
Murray Darling
NEW SOUTH WALES
Barossa Valley
Riverina
Eden Valley
Adelaide°
Adelaide Hills
McLaren Vale
Swan Hill
Langhorne Creek
Currency Creek
Rutherglen
Kangaroo Island
VICTORIA
Pericoota
Goulburn Valley
Glen Rowan
Pyrenees
Padthaway
Mount Benson
Bendigo
Heathcote
King Valley
Central Victorian High Country
Alpine Alleys
Limestone Coast
Wrattonbully
Macedon Ranges
Coonawarra
Robe Ranges
Grampians
Gippsland
°Melbourne
Sunbury Yarra Valley
Henty
Geelong
Mornington Peninsula
WESTERN AUSTRALIA
Swan Valley
•Perth
Perth Hills
Margaret River
Great Southern
Mount Barker
Pemberton °Albany
TASMANIA

higher, with a sunnier, later season. Wines from Mudgee are usually full-flavoured, with Chardonnay often the best wine.

Orange 2,750 kilometres (1,709 miles) west of Sydney, this region, which has volcanic soils, was planted in the 1980s at elevations above 365 metres (1,200 feet). Ripeness is problematic at the highest elevations. The region is best-known for Shiraz, Chardonnay, and Riesling. About 1,000 hectares.

Riverina Fertile, flat, fruit-growing land around Griffith, 480 kilometres (300 miles) west of Sydney. Known predominantly for unexciting bulk wines until the mid-'80s, when extraordinary botrytis-affected Semillon emerged as the area's specialty. More sophisticated methods of irrigation are upgrading the table wines, too.

Other Areas There are a handful of exciting new wine regions which have emerged across New South Wales in the last twenty years, including the warm Hastings Valley in the north, and the cool regions of Cowra and Hilltops in the centre of the state. Southwest of Canberra, Tumbarumba is proving to be a good region for Chardonnay and other grapes destined for sparkling wines.

Victoria

Central Victoria This is a diffuse region, spreading from around the old gold-mining towns of Bendigo and Ballarat, and encompassing the area of Heathcote.

All wineries are relatively new, and some excellent wines are produced, with the especially minty, intense, powerful Shiraz styles.

Geelong This cool area southwest of Melbourne was, in the last century, one of Victoria's most promising. It fell victim to phylloxera, but was re-established in the 1960s. Pinot Noir is very successful.

Goulburn Valley Important small, historic area 160 kilometres (100 miles) north of Melbourne. Marsanne is a regional specialty.

Grampians Region 225 kilometres (140 miles) west of Melbourne, with fairly new wineries jostling with some very old ones at places like Great Western. The Shiraz is rich and flavoursome.

Strathbogie Ranges About 1,000 hectares planted at elevations of around 365 metres (1,200 feet) on stony granite soils. Good for Riesling and Chardonnay, has potential for Pinot Noir.

Yarra Valley This region has been a vine-growing region since the nineteenth century; forty-eight kilometres (thirty miles) east of Melbourne, it is now re-established and realizing its full potential. Small wineries rub shoulders with some of the state's largest ones to produce exceptional, cool-climate wines – among Australia's best.

Other Areas Whether it is the scattered, disparate wineries of Gippsland, southeast of Melbourne, or the wineries strung along the Great Dividing Range that cuts a swathe through central Victoria and up into New South Wales, there are numerous other regions that add to the state's viticultural colour.

South Australia

Adelaide Hills Still one of Australia's most talked-about "cool-climate" regions, around the Mount Lofty Ranges southeast of Adelaide. Some remarkable Sauvignon Blanc, Pinot Noir, and Chardonnay are produced.

Adelaide Plains Formerly important vine-growing area, including recently restored Penfolds' Magill estate, now largely swallowed by the city suburbs.

Barossa Valley Oldest and most important region, 56 kilometres (35 miles) northeast of Adelaide, settled by Germans in the 1840s. Good all-round producer and home to many of Australia's largest wineries. Renowned for powerful Shiraz.

Clare Smaller area, sixty-four kilometres (forty miles) north of Barossa, with as long a history as the Barossa. 396-metre (1,300-foot) hills give it a cooler season in which Riesling does especially well, though Semillon, Shiraz, and Cabernet can also be fine.

Coonawarra Remote area 400 kilometres (250 miles) southeast of Adelaide, on an eccentric flat carpet of red earth over limestone with a high water table. Its latitude makes it relatively cool; its soil is absurdly fertile. The result is some of the best wines in Australia, though in some vintages, Cabernet Sauvignon struggles to ripen.

Eden Valley Cooler region to the south of the Barossa, home to a handful of high-quality wineries, and a useful source of premium grapes for others.

Langhorne Creek Tiny historic area, 75 kilometres (47 miles) southeast of Adelaide on rich, alluvial soil. Red wines are soft and wonderfully generous.

McLaren Vale Warm region immediately south of Adelaide. A combination of old, traditional wineries and younger, more modern wineries, most producing particularly good red wines.

Macedon Ranges Small, cool, hilly region north of Melbourne, with a growing handful of wineries. Sparkling wine very good indeed. Sunbury to the south, slightly warmer and possibly more suited to red wines.

Mornington Peninsula Cool, fashionable, maritime-influenced region south of Melbourne, with a surprisingly large number of small wineries.

Northeast Victoria Illustrious area, between Milawa and Rutherglen on the New South Wales border, famous for superb dessert wines, especially Muscat. Recent developments include large new vineyards in the King Valley, and smaller ones in the Ovens Valley, Beechworth, and the Victorian Alps.

Northwest Victoria Long-established, mainly irrigated area along the Murray River, stretching from the huge vineyards at Mildura and Robinvale, through Swan Hill and down to Echuca. Source of much of Australia's good-value bulk wine.

Pyrenees Hilly region around the town of Avoca, 193 kilometres (120 miles) northwest of Melbourne. A handful of wineries turn out solid, rather earthy wines.

Principal Grape Varieties

Chardonnay Far and away Australia's most popular white grape variety, planted almost everywhere, and produced in a variety of styles, from green-tinged, unwooded wines that are light and crisp, to deep-yellow, barrel-fermented wines that are rich and creamy. Destined to be hugely popular until the end of time.

Shiraz The quintessential Australian red grape, currently enjoying massive interest both at home and overseas. Styles rich, deep, chocolatey wines in warmer climates such as the Barossa Valley and McLaren Vale; through smooth, soft, and relatively delicate ones in the Hunter Valley; to dusty, peppery, elegant examples in cooler areas such as southern Victoria and Western Australia.

Cabernet Sauvignon Like Chardonnay, planted right across Australia, and relatively successful in most areas. At its best in fashionable regions such as Margaret River, Coonawarra, and the Yarra Valley, usually when it is blended with varying proportions of Merlot and Cabernet Franc to produce "Bordeaux blends" that bear little resemblance to Bordeaux.

Semillon At its best, in the Lower Hunter, Semillon is a total (and thoroughly undervalued) triumph: a light, dry white wine, Chablis-green when young and lively, ageing superbly for up to twenty years. Also promisingly grassy in Margaret River, but most examples in the Barossa or Clare are masked by heavy-handed oak maturation. Also widely used for cheaper sparkling wines, and often blended with Chardonnay.

Riesling Despite a growing confidence on the producers' behalf – leading to the dropping of the "Rhine" prefix – the much-touted revival of interest in Riesling among consumers has yet to take hold fully. This means some of Australia's best white wines – excitingly perfumed, crisply dry, and full of the ability to age superbly – are also some of the best value. Outstanding in Clare and Eden Valley.

Secondary Grape Varieties

Cabernet Franc Initially planted and mostly used to blend with Cabernet Sauvignon, but occasionally crops up as a brightly flavoured, purple varietal.

Chenin Blanc Mainly used as a blending grape, but also occasionally appears on its own as a fresh white wine.

Durif A Shiraz-like grape used occasionally in northeast Victoria for interesting dark wine.

Gewürztraminer Mostly used to produce cheap, sweet, grapey white wine, blended with Riesling, but some makers treat it seriously and with great success.

Grenache Overshadowed by Shiraz, but dry-farmed old vines in Barossa and McLaren Vale yield powerful, succulent Rhône-style reds.

Marsanne Once almost solely confined to the vineyards of Tahbilk, producing remarkably long-lived, aromatic whites, now another beneficiary of the interest in Rhône-style wines, and cropping up in all sorts of places.

Merlot On the verge of creeping onto the list of principal varieties, this red grape started life in Australia as a blender, but is increasingly beginning to prove itself on its own. Plantings have shot up since 1998.

Mourvèdre Yet another Rhône-style rediscovery, Mourvèdre (or Mataro, as it used to be known in its less trendy days) is often found in blends with Shiraz and Grenache.

Muscadelle Occasionally used in dry white blends, but most impressive in its dark, luscious dessert form (known as Tokay) in northeast Victoria.

Muscat Brown Muscat used in northeast Victoria for superbly luscious dessert wines; lesser variety, Muscat Gordo Blanco, or Lexia, used to make a fruity, sweet white in the irrigated areas.

Pinot Gris Some increased plantings in the cooler areas, but it has yet to take off and capture public enthusiasm.

Pinot Meunier Important variety for sparkling winemakers, but not exactly widely planted.

Pinot Noir After years of promise and occasional brilliance, Pinot Noir producers finally began to consistently crack it in the early 1990s, and continue to make rapid progress. A candidate for promotion to the principal grape variety list.

Sauvignon Blanc Nowhere near as successful as in New Zealand, but in certain places such as the Adelaide Hills, central Victoria, Margaret River, and Coonawarra, produces pungent, racy wines.

Trebbiano Also known as Ugni Blanc, and chiefly used as a blending variety in cheap, bulk white wine.

Verdelho Surprisingly good, gently aromatic white variety. Often overlooked but can be delicious.

Other Varieties Currently produced on a very small scale (either by one or just a handful of winemakers) but nevertheless providing exciting glimpses of the future include: Barbera, Dolcetto, Nebbiolo, Roussanne, Petit Verdot, Sangiovese, Viognier, and Zinfandel.

Riverland The Murray continues its way across the border from Victoria, and the region becomes known as the Riverland. The majority of Australia's bulk production comes from these huge vineyards and wineries, as do some good-value bottled wines.

Other Areas Coonawarra is not the only area suited to the vine in the vast tracts of land south of Adelaide. Neighbouring Wrattonbully has similar soils, and Padthaway has for a long time been an important source of good, cooler-climate grapes. Now joined by huge new vineyards in places such as Koppamurra, north of Coonawarra, and Mount Benson, over on the South Australian Limestone Coast.

Western Australia

Geographe New name for the long coastal plain between Perth and Margaret River, home to a handful of diverse wineries.

Great Southern This is a sprawling region of diverse topography and soil, and includes the regions of Mount Barker and Frankland River. There are a growing number of wineries that are attracted to the cool, slow-ripening conditions here.

Margaret River Western Australia's top-quality wine region, 322 kilometres (200 miles) south of Perth, on a promontory with markedly oceanic climate. It does well with a variety of wines, especially sensational Cabernet and Chardonnay.

Pemberton New, much-hyped region with great potential. The cool-climate has provided some exceptional Pinot Noir and Chardonnay, and fruit from the region is already sought after by wineries in the eastern states.

Swan Valley Old, hot, vine-growing area on the outskirts of Perth, traditionally known for jammy reds, dessert wines, and the famous Houghton "White Burgundy", but recently producing some surprisingly good wines.

Queensland

Minor wine-producing state. Most vines are grown in the Granite Belt region just across the border with New South Wales. Although Queensland well deserves its name as the "Sunshine State", the best wineries here are at high altitude and a little cooler.

Tasmania

Following the search for a cooler climate to its logical conclusion, a number of wineries have consequently sprung up in Tasmania, near Launceston in the north of the island and Hobart in the south. Sparkling wines from this region (as you would expect from the relatively chilly conditions) are extremely good, as are Pinot Noir Riesling and Chardonnay.

Northern Territory

The proud possessor of a single winery, Château Hornsby, at Alice Springs, obstinately irrigating in the fierce heat, and producing passable wines, too.

Leading New South Wales Producers

Vineyard holdings are somewhat misleading, since it is very common for estates to supplement their own estate-grown grapes with fruit bought in from neighbouring properties, or even from other regions entirely. Moreover, with a spate of recent mergers and acquisitions, vineyard holdings are often, sometimes rather confusingly, shared among various wineries within the group.

Canberra

Clonakilla ☆☆
Murrambateman. Owners: the Kirk family. 7 hectares.
www.clonakilla.com.au
One of the first, and one of the best, producers in the Canberra district. The Kirks' Riesling is good; experimental batches of Viognier are very exciting; but the most characterful wine is the gamey Shiraz.

Lark Hill ☆☆–☆☆☆
Bungendore. Owners: the Carpenter family. 10 hectares.
www.larkhillwine.com.au

The highest, and one of the best, wineries in the Canberra region. Winemaker Sue Carpenter's wines include Chardonnay, Shiraz, delicate Germanic Riesling, and often remarkable Pinot Noir.

Hunter Valley

Allandale ☆☆–☆☆☆
Pokolbin. Owner: Wally Attallah. 7 hectares.
www.allandalewinery.com.au
Since the late 1980s, Bill Sneddon has made good wines with grapes from a variety of sources: estate vineyards, other Hunter growers, Mudgee, and the cooler region of Hilltops.

Arrowfield ☆☆
Upper Hunter. Owners: Hokuriku. 60 hectares.
www.arrowfieldwines.com.au
The firm has now established a reputation for very good value. Best are a smoky, cedary Shiraz; big, California-style Chardonnay; and powerful "Show Reserve" wines. Yet Arrowfield lacks a stylistic signature.

Brokenwood ☆☆☆
Pokolbin. Owners: Iain Riggs and partners. 15 hectares.
www.brokenwood.com.au
Originally set up by a partnership of Sydney wine-lovers that included wine author James Halliday, Brokenwood is now guided by the phlegmatic Iain Riggs. Multi-regional blends are produced here, but it is the estate wines – in particular superb, limey "ILR Reserve" Semillon and (atypically sturdy for the region) "Graveyard Vineyard" Shiraz – that impress most. Their most popular wine by far is the ripe, gently oaky "Cricket Pitch" Sauvignon/Semillon.

Drayton's Family Wines ☆–☆☆
Pokolbin. Owners: the Drayton family. 55 hectares.
www.draytonswines.com.au
This old family company has been making wine since the 1850s. Traditional Hunter styles predominate, with the best Shiraz held back for five or more years to be released at its peak (and at a suitably inflated price). The basic range is called "Oakey Creek".

Evans Family Wines ☆☆–☆☆☆
Pokolbin. Owners: Len Evans and family. 8 hectares
Australia's "Mr. Wine", Len Evans, and son Toby, produce small, single-vineyard lots of well-received Semillon, Chardonnay, Pinot Noir, and Gamay from their small family vineyard. The wines are mostly exported.

Hope Estate ☆☆
Broke. Owner: Michael Hope. 90 hectares.
www.hopeestate.com.au
Standard Hunter varietals, plus Merlot. Fresh wines, not too extracted.

Hungerford Hill ☆☆
Pokolbin. Owner: James Kirby. No vineyards.
www.hungerfordhill.com.au
Part of Southcorp for many years, the winery was sold to a businessman in 2002 and given a new lease of life. Under

winemaker Phillip John's direction, Hungerford Hill offers smartly packaged wines produced only from fruit grown in newish wine areas in central and south New South Wales, such as Young, Cowra, and Tumbarumba.

Successes include Tumbarumba Sauvignon, Clare Riesling, and Hilltops Cabernet.

Kulkunbulla ☆☆
Pokolbin. Owner: Gavin Lennard and partners. 7 hectares.
www.kulkunbulla.com.au
The brainchild of Lennard, fleeing from corporate life, and based on his vineyard in Rothbury's former Brokenback estate. Fruit is also purchased. Production since 1997 has been limited, but the winery is set to expand. Classic "Glandore" Semillon, extremely buttery "Brokenback" Chardonnay, and a spicy, toasty Petit Verdot add novelty to the range.

Lake's Folly ☆☆☆
Pokolbin. Owner: Peter Fogarty. 12 hectares.
www.lakesfolly.com.au
First the hobby, then the passion of a distinguished surgeon from Sydney, Max Lake. He started the first new Hunter winery in forty years, ignoring tradition, to prove that Cabernet can be the same splendid thing under Hunter skies as elsewhere. Then he did the same with Chardonnay. In 2000, the property was sold, but son Stephen Lake remains as consultant, so the style is unlikely to change.

McGuigan Brothers ☆–☆☆☆
Pokolbin. Owner: A public company. 4,000 hectares
(managed and controlled). www.mcguiganwines.com.au
After selling Wyndham Estate (*q.v.*) to Orlando, the McGuigan brothers set up on their own winery in 1992, and started to build another empire. Neil left, but Brian is still there, larger than life and still the marketing supremo he always was. The vineyards are dispersed throughout NSW and South Australia, so the range of wines is enormous, with "Black Label" the basic line, followed by the "Bin" series, and then "Personal Reserve" at the top.

Meerea Park ☆☆
Windella. Owners: the Eather family. No vineyards.
www.meereapark.com.au
The Eathers were grape farmers who sold their vineyards to in order to finance their winery. Winemaker Rhys Eather buys grapes mainly from Hunter Valley. Among the white wines there is fresh, clean Verdelho and apricotty Viognier. Shiraz is the best red: "The Aunt's" from two old vineyards, and "Munro", from old vines, which is bottle-aged before release. These are unusually rich and damsony for Hunter Shiraz.

Petersons ☆☆
Mount View. Owners: the Peterson family. 20 hectares:
www.petersonswines.com.au
An accomplished small winery whose first releases were in 1981. The range includes an exceptional Shiraz, Chardonnay, a good Semillon, and Cabernet.

Reynolds ☆☆
Cudal. Owners: Cabonne Limited. 900 hectares.
www.reynoldswine.com.au

Despite the change in ownership, former Wyndham Estate winemaker Jon Reynolds is still making the wines here, mostly from Orange fruit. "Little Boomey" has been the inexpensive range, with more serious lines including "Moon Shadow" Chardonnay and the earthy, oaky "Jezebel" Cabernet Sauvignon.

Rosemount Estate ☆–☆☆☆
Denman. Owners: Southcorp Wines and the Oatley family.
1,500 hectares. www.rosemountestates.com
One of the country's most confident wineries, with some of Australia's most popular wines in export markets. From the winery in the Upper Hunter (where the famous Roxburgh Chardonnay vineyard is situated), winemaker Philip Shaw drew fruit from across the country to produce a staggering array of good wines. Shaw has been dispatched to oversee Southcorp winemaking, leaving Andrew Koerner as head winemaker at Rosemount. Recent successes include rich, oaky Chardonnays from the Roxburgh Vineyard and from Orange, and some delicious, heady Shiraz, especially the "Balmoral" (oddly labelled "Syrah"), from McLaren Vale. There is a new emphasis on regional wines such as the "Hill of Gold" range from Mudgee; Grenache/Syrah/Mourvèdre "GSM" from McLaren Vale; and, also from McLaren Vale, the "Traditional" blend of Bordeaux varieties. The crowd-pleasing wines are the "Diamond"-labelled varietals.

Rothbury Estate ☆–☆☆☆
Pokolbin. Owners: Beringer Blass. 300 hectares.
www.beringerblass.com
Long-lived Semillon, in the true old Hunter style, made the reputation of this impressive winery when it belonged to Len Evans and partners; Syrah backed it up. In 1995, it fell victim to an aggressive takeover, leaving much bitterness in its wake. Production is now concentrated on barrel-fermented and matured Chardonnay. Shiraz is the main red wine. Top wines, including spicy, high-flavoured Chardonnays, bear the "Reserve" label. Neil McGuigan is the winemaker and many of the wines, especially the Semillons, are of high quality.

Saddler's Creek ☆–☆☆
Pokolbin. Owner: John Johnstone. 12 hectares.
www.saddlerscreekwines.com.au
Horse-breeder Johnstone owns this property, with most wines made from purchased fruit from Langhorne Creek as well as the Hunter. The best-known brand is "Bluegrass" Shiraz and Cabernet Sauvignon, aged in American oak. The oaky sweetness makes the wines accessible young. They are commercial yet sophisticated, but the reds can be tiring.

Scarborough ☆☆
Pokolbin. Owners: the Scarborough family. 40 hectares.
www.scarboroughwine.com.au
Unusually for this area, the main focus here is Chardonnay. The lemony "Blue Label" is from early picked grapes, the "Yellow Label", a richer style, is aged in mostly new oak.

Tempus Two ☆☆
Pokolbin. Owners: McGuigan Family.
www.tempustwo.com.au
A subsidiary label for McGuigan (*q.v.*), and an imposing new winery that is due to come into production in 2003.

Outstanding early releases included a fine "Hollydene" Cabernet Sauvignon.

Tower ☆☆☆
Pokolbin. Owner: Len Evans and partners. No vineyards.
www.towerestatewines.com.au
Since 1999, Evans and winemaker Dan Dineen have selected small parcels of outstanding fruit from the Hunter, Clare, the Adelaide Hills, Tasmania, and other regions, the idea being to produce exceedingly good wine in maximum lots of 1,000 cases each. The stars of the 2001 range were the Adelaide Hills Sauvignon and Chardonnay, Hunter Shiraz, and Coonawarra Cabernet. Supple, perfumed wines of great elegance.

Tyrrell's ☆☆–☆☆☆☆
Pokolbin. Owners: the Tyrrell family. 470 hectares in Hunter and South Australia. www.tyrrells.com.au
Murray Tyrrell was one of the main architects of the Hunter revival of the 1970s, building on a traditional Semillon and Shiraz base, but startling Australia with his well-calculated "Vat 47 Chardonnay", the wine that really led the way for the variety in Australia. Despite success with long-lived "Vat 9 Pinot Noir", Tyrrell's strength now lies in Shiraz ("Vat 9"); individual vineyard wines such as "Stevens Semillon" and the reliable "Old Winery"; and rather plain "Long Flat" commercial ranges. Andrew Spinaze has been making the wines since the 1970s.

Wyndham Estate ☆–☆☆
Dalwood. Owners: Orlando Wyndham. 150 hectares.
www.wyndhamestate.com.au
This is one of Australia's oldest wineries and is now also one of the most popular. For a time, under the brash charge of Brian and Neil McGuigan, Wyndham's wines were seen everywhere. Now that the winery is part of the huge Orlando Wyndham group, quality is just as reliable, but some of the spark has, however, gone. The basic "Bin" series plays it safe, but the "Show Reserves" are considerably more exciting.

Mudgee

Botobolar ☆–☆☆
Mudgee. Owners: Kevin and Trina Karstrom. 22 hectares.
www.botobolar.com
The winery sticks to organic principles, and produces some of Mudgee's most engaging wines, especially Shiraz.

Huntington Estate ☆☆–☆☆☆
Mudgee. Owners: the Roberts family. 40 hectares
One of Mudgee's most serious quality wineries. Winemaker, Bob Roberts has been succeeded by daughter Susie, who continues to produce some lovely wines, especially refined but substantial Cabernet blends and Shiraz.

Miramar ☆
Mudgee. Owners: Ian MacRae and partner. 33 hectares.
www.miramarwines.com.au
One of the most competent wineries in Mudgee, bringing out powerful characteristics in each variety, especially Chardonnay, a Chardonnay/Semillon blend, Cabernet, and Shiraz. Also a clean rosé and "vintage port".

Orange

Bloodwood Estate ☆☆
Orange. Owner: Stephen Doyle. 8 heactares
www.bloodwood.com.au
Stephen and Rhonda Doyle were pioneers in the high region of Orange. Toasty Chardonnay, exotic Riesling, spicy Cabernet, and a ludicrously juicy Malbec rosé.

Brangayne ☆–☆☆
Orange. Owner: Don Hoskins. 25 hectares.
www.brangayne.com
The Hoskins family owns this small property, with vineyards high up in Orange. Rather heavy, toasty Chardonnay, but elegant medium-bodied Pinot Noir, made under contract by Simon Gilbert.

Highland Heritage ☆
Orange. Owners: D'Aquino Family. 15 hectares.
First releases were in 1997, and the greatest initial success was the rich, toasty Chardonnay.

Logan ☆–☆☆
Northbridge. Owners: Logan family. 14 hectares.
www.loganwines.com.au
Since 1997, this winery has specialized in wines from Orange, of which the Chardonnay is usually the best.

Riverina

De Bortoli Wines (Griffith) ☆–☆☆☆
Bilbul. Owners: the De Bortoli family. No vineyards.
www.debortoli.com.au
Mostly everyday wines under the "Sacred Hill" label, but best known for "Noble One", its remarkable botrytis Semillon.

McWilliams ☆☆–☆☆☆☆
Chullora. Owners: the McWilliam family. 140 hectares.
www.mcwilliams.com.au
A single-minded family business, with three centres of operation in New South Wales. The majority of production – bulk wines, and occasional beauties such as botrytis Semillon – is based at Hanwood in the Riverina, while flagship wines such as the extraordinary, long-lived "Elizabeth" and "Lovedale" Semillons are made at the legendary Mount Pleasant winery in the Hunter Valley. A new vineyard at Barwang in the Hilltops area is producing encouragingly flavoursome, cooler-climate style wines. The great achievement of winemakers Philip Ryan and Jim Brayne is to maintain the exemplary standards of the Hunter Semillons, and indeed, Shirazes from old-vine vineyards: wines that remain underappreciated but are Australian classics.

Other Areas

Cassegrain ☆–☆☆
Port Macquarie. Owner: Gerard Cassegrain. 154 hectares.
www.cassegrainwines.com.au
A fascinating development in the warm region of the Hastings Valley, in the north of the state. Part of the vineyard is being run on biodynamic principles. Wines can be very

impressive – especially a softly spicy, generous Merlot, and an unusual, vibrant, purple-coloured Chambourcin.

Trentham Estate ☆
Mildura. Owners: Anthony and Patrick Murphy. 50 hectares. www.trenthamestate.com.au
A minnow compared to the very big vineyards just across the river in Victoria, but a popular and reliable producer, nonetheless. Whites are clean and tasty, and reds – particularly good Merlot and Shiraz – are characterized by soft, approachable, sweet fruit.

Leading Victoria Producers

Central Victoria

Balgownie ☆☆
Maiden Gully. Owners: the Forrester family. 33 hectares. www.balgownieestate.com.au
Mildara bought this property in 1986, and in 2001 it was sold again. Its founder, Stuart Anderson, built one of the best names in Australia for Cabernet Sauvignon structured like Château Latour. Recent performance has been patchy, with occasional superb Cabernet Sauvignon, but new investment may bring more consistency.

Jasper Hill ☆☆☆–☆☆☆☆
Heathcote. Owner/winemaker: Ron Laughton. 18 hectares
Remarkable wines from an organically run vineyard in central Victoria. Riesling is as fragrant as you could wish for; reds ("Georgia's Paddock", a straight Shiraz; "Emily's Paddock" a Shiraz/Cabernet Franc blend) are massively structured but also gorgeously approachable. Demand far outstrips supply.

Yellowglen ☆☆
Smythesdale. Owners: Beringer Blass. 14 hectares. www.yellowglen.com.au
Established to make Australia's best sparkling wines, Yellowglen quickly became the provider of some of its best value – but not necessarily best quality – instead. But quality improved through the 1990s, and the results, especially in the biscuity, crisp "Cuvée Victoria", have been encouraging.

Geelong

Bannockburn Vineyards ☆☆–☆☆☆
Bannockburn. Owner: Stuart Hooper. 25 hectares
Winemaker Gary Farr has worked in Burgundy during the vintage for over a decade, and this experience shines through in the exceptional Chardonnay and tight, long-lived Pinot. Recently, a change in winemaking style, which was influenced by Alain Graillot at Crozes-Hermitage, has also resulted in a remarkably Rhône-like, dusty Shiraz. *See also* By Farr.

By Farr ☆☆☆
Bannockburn. Owner/winemaker: Gary Farr. 5 hectares
Gary Farr, winemaker for Bannockburn Vineyards (*q.v.*)

has, since 1999, had his own label for two wines; "Chardonnay by Farr" and "Pinot Noir by Farr". Both are first-rate, if very oaky.

Scotchman's Hill ☆☆–☆☆☆
Drysdale. Owners: the Brown Family. 50 hectares. www.scotchmanshill.com.au
This winery is the leading light on the Bellarine Peninsula, south of Geelong, and is a favourite in trendy Melbourne bistros. The intense fruit flavours of the Chardonnay and Pinot Noir, made by Robin Brockett, have ensured them a quick rise to the top.

Goulburn Valley

Mitchelton ☆☆
Mitchellstown, Nagambie. Owner: Petaluma. 120 hectares. www.mitchelton.com.au
An extraordinary edifice, looking like a 1970s monastery, on the banks of the lovely Goulburn River. A lookout tower, aviary, and restaurant were built to attract tourists. But the wines are another matter entirely. The Mitchelton label is used for estate wines: peachy Marsanne, aged in cask and distinctly aromatic for this grape; well-made Riesling; hefty Chardonnay; and excellent "Print" Shiraz. Other labels include "Blackwood Park" and "Preece".

Tahbilk ☆☆–☆☆☆☆
Tahbilk. Owners: the Purbrick family. 168 hectares
Victoria's most historic and attractive winery, and one of Australia's best. The old farm, with massive trees, stands by the Goulburn River in lovely country, its barns and cellars like a film set of early Australia. Dry, white Marsanne starts life light, but ages to subtle roundness; Riesling is crisp but full of flavour and also ages well. The Shiraz is consistently one of the best value in Australia, and "1860 Vine" Shiraz (from the remaining rows of original vineyard) remarkably Old World in style. The Cabernet Sauvignon is more earthy, but also long-lived.

Grampians

Best's Wines ☆☆–☆☆☆
Great Western. Owners: the Thomson family. 50 hectares. www.bestswines.com
A famous old name in Victoria, highly picturesque in its original buildings at Great Western. "Bin O" Shiraz is reliably good and surprisingly elegant; "Thomson Family" Shiraz (exclusively from 130-year-old vines) is a much more serious affair: dark, chewy, and glorious.

Mount Langi Ghiran ☆☆–☆☆☆
Buangor. Owner: Yering Station. 95 hectares. www.langi.com.au
Organic estate, and one of Australia's foremost exponents of rich, peppery, Rhône-like Shiraz, also producing fine Cabernet from Limestone Coast, Pinot Gris, and Riesling. Too early to guess the consequences of a change of ownership in 2002.

Seppelt Great Western ☆☆–☆☆☆☆
Great Western. Owner: Southcorp Wines. www.seppelt.com.au

The old cellars at Great Western are now also home to a vast new development that handles sparkling-wine production for Southcorp. Seppelt sparklings are still very much the focus here, from the great-value "Great Western" to the flagship "Salinger". A revamped range of Seppelt table wines, all from Victorian fruit, have brightened this winery's image. Single-vineyard wines (such as "Great Western" Shiraz, "Drumborg" Cabernet, and others from the company's South Australian vineyards) are released when mature, and are excellent. At another facility in the Barossa, Seppelt process a fabulous range of fortified wines from Rutherglen and South Australia; Muscats, "ports", and "sherries" are all first-rate.

Macedon Ranges

Bindi ☆☆☆
Gisborne. Owners: the Dhillon family. 5 hectares
Estate producing tiny quantities of greatly sought-after Chardonnay and Pinot Noir. Yields are kept low to maximize the fruit concentration, yet the wines, despite prolonged oak-ageing, are rarely heavy or excessively dense.

Cope-Williams ☆☆
Romsey. Owners: the Cope-Williams family. 20 hectares.
www.cope-williams.com.au
In a setting that feels remarkably like a country garden in Sussex, the Cope-Williams family (originally from the old country) produce delicate, cool-climate wines, the best of which is one of Australia's finest bubblies.

Craiglee ☆☆☆
Sunbury. Owners: the Carmody family. 10 hectares
The self-effacing manner of Pat Carmody hides a skilful grape-grower and winemaker. His Chardonnay is tight and gently toasty, but it is the supremely elegant, enticingly peppery Shiraz that really shines from this historic winery.

Hanging Rock ☆☆
Newham. Owners: the Ellis family. 12 hectares.
www.hangingrock.com.au
Reliable wines under the (cheap) "Rock" or "Victoria" labels, but exceptional quality to be found in wines made from estate fruit. "Jim Jim" Sauvignon Blanc can be almost searing in its grassy intensity; and "Heathcote" Shiraz is a powerfully oaky expression of the grape.

Virgin Hills ☆☆
Kyneton. Owner: Michael Hope. 12 hectares
The dream of Melbourne restaurateur Tom Lazar, this cool-climate vineyard has been through many changes of ownership, culminating in the present proprietor, who also owns a winery in Hunter Valley (*q.v.*). The sole wine is a blend of Cabernet, Shiraz, and Merlot.

Mornington Peninsula

Dromana Estate ☆–☆☆☆
Dromana. Owner/winemaker: Garry Crittenden. 30 hectares.
www.dromanaestate.com.au
Glorious Cabernet, Pinot Noir, and Chardonnay are made here. Other good wines, made from bought-in grapes, are

sold under the "Schinus" label, joined recently by a range of Italian varietals (Arneis, Dolcetto, Nebbiolo, etc.) from King Valley, under the Crittenden "I" label. With so many wines on offer, quality is variable, but Garry Crittenden's enthusiasm and courage are admirable.

Hickinbotham ☆–☆☆
Dromana. Owners: the Hickinbotham family. 6.5 hectares.
www.hickinbothamwinemakers.com.au
A family of innovative winemakers, closely associated with many of the most significant developments in Australian wine production, but ambitious plans have been scaled down, and the winery now focuses on Mornington Peninsula fruit, mostly purchased.

Paringa Estate ☆☆☆
Red Hill South. Owner/winemaker: Lindsay McCall. 4 hectares.
www.paringaestate.com.au
The reputation and success of this tiny winery is completely out of all proportion to its size. Perfectly sited, trellised vineyards produce exceptional fruit. Chardonnay is intense and lingering; Pinot is wild and spicy; Shiraz teeters on the edge of greenness, but pulls it off in dusty, peppery style.

Stonier ☆☆–☆☆☆
Merricks. Owner: Lion Nathan. 20 hectares.
www.stoniers.com.au
Now arguably the region's foremost winery, consistently successful. Tod Dexter produces complex, extremely well-made Chardonnay, and silky and raspberry-packed Pinot. Not surprisingly, the reserve range is substantially superior to the standard wines, which, nonetheless, are still good.

T'Gallant ☆☆–☆☆☆
Main Ridge. Owners/winemakers: Kevin McCarthy and Kathleen Quealy. 25 hectares
Talented couple pioneering unusual, quirkily packaged wines, such as hugely ripe and spicy Pinot Gris; yeasty, gently bronzed, white Pinot Noir; crisp, unwooded Chardonnay; and "Holystone": a good, dry rosé. Very successful with the trendy café set in Melbourne.

Northeast Victoria

All Saints ☆–☆☆☆
Wahgunyah. Owner/winemaker: Peter Brown. 65 hectares
Traditional old winery (established 1864), producing a full range of table, fortified, and sparkling wines. Bought in 1991 by Brown Brothers (*q.v.*) and lavishly renovated. In 1998, Peter Brown became sole owner. Fabulous "Museum" releases from ancient *soleras* of Muscat and Tokay.

Bailey's ☆☆–☆☆☆
Glenrowan. Owner: Beringer Blass. 60 hectares.
www.beringerblass.com.au
The famous makers of heroic Shiraz, a caricature Aussie wine with a black and red label rather like a danger signal. A thickly fruity wine, which ages twenty years to improbable subtlety. Even better (and amazing value, too) are the dessert Muscats and Tokays, profoundly fruity, intensely sweet and velvety.

Brown Brothers ☆☆

Milawa. Owners: the Brown family. 160 hectares. www.brownbrothers.com.au

This old Victorian family winery seems to be continually expanding and innovating. As well as a wide, reliable range of conventional wines, Brown Brothers also experiments with new varieties and styles (mostly sold cellar-door only), such as excellent, ultra-cool-climate Sauvignon Blanc and Italian varietals. An Epicurean Centre restaurant and tasting facility has proved successful.

Bullers ☆–☆☆☆

Rutherglen, Victoria, and also at Beverford. Owners: the Buller family. 32 hectares at Rutherglen, 33 hectares in Beverford. www.buller.com.au

Old family firm producing superb fortified Muscat and Tokay at Rutherglen, and some enormously flavoursome – and highly alcoholic – red wines at Beverford.

Campbells of Rutherglen ☆☆–☆☆☆

Rutherglen. Owners: the Campbell family. 56 hectares. www.campbellswines.com.au

Under Colin Campbell, this traditional Rutherglen winery has recently begun to smarten up its image and modernize its approach. Superlative Muscat and Tokay (especially "Merchant Prince" and "Isabella" labels) are still the backbone, but wonderfully spicy "Bobbie Burns" Shiraz and a stout, impressive Durif called "The Barkly Durif" are also very good.

Chambers Rosewood ☆–☆☆☆

Rutherglen. Owners: the Chambers family. 50 hectares

Bill Chambers is a veteran winemaker, eccentric but hugely respected for his old Liqueur Muscat and Tokay. The "Rare" range contains wines up to ninety years old. The dry wines are of astonishing mediocrity, however.

Morris Wines ☆☆☆

Rutherglen. Owner: Orlando Wyndham. 90 hectares

Dave Morris's Liqueur Muscat is Australia's secret weapon: an aromatic, silky treacle that draws gasps from sceptics. The old tin winery building is a treasure-house of ancient casks of Muscats and Tokays, so concentrated by evaporation that they need freshening with young wine before bottling.

Stanton & Killeen ☆☆–☆☆☆

Rutherglen. Owner/winemaker: Chris Killeen. 45 hectares. www.stantonandkilleen.com.au

A small, old, family winery that has been gradually expanding its range and volumes. Its "Moodemere" reds, Cabernet, Shiraz, and Durif are among the best in northeast Victoria. Muscats, Tokays, and "ports" are not luscious in the regional tradition, but light and elegant.

Northwest Victoria

Deakin Estate ☆

Red Cliffs. Owner: Freixenet. 300 hectares. www.deakinestate.com.au

The rather plain (but successful) "Sunnycliff" brand was relaunched in 1995 as "Deakin Estate", with spanking-new labels and a breezy marketing approach. The change worked wonders, and the wines are now some of the most popular – and best value for money – the country has on offer. The reserve range is called "Deakin Select".

Lindemans ☆–☆☆☆

Karadoc. Owner: Southcorp Wines. Vineyards in Hunter Valley, Sunraysia, Coonawarra, and Padthaway. www.lindemans.com

One of Australia's great wine companies, now part of its largest, Southcorp. Started in 1870 in the Hunter Valley, the wines produced under the Lindemans name now come in a range of guises, and from a variety of sources. The Hunter Valley winery has been run down, and most production is based here in Victoria. At the base of the pyramid is "Bin 65" Chardonnay, one of the world's most easily recognized white wines. Other wines include a solid range from Padthaway, and the Coonawarra reds "Limestone Ridge" (Shiraz/Cabernet), "St George" Cabernet, and the "Pyrus" blend.

Pyrenees

Blue Pyreenes ☆–☆☆

Avoca. Owners: Bill Anderson and John Ellis. 185 hectares. www.bluepyrenees.com.au

Originally established as Château Remy for brandy-making, this estate now offers a wide range of varietal wines and also reserves. Sparkling wines (especially "Midnight Cuvée", a blanc de blancs made from grapes that are picked by hand under spotlights at night) have improved considerably. In 2002, the estate was sold, but the new owners are likely to retain the policy of making rarely exciting but good-value wines.

Dalwhinnie ☆☆☆–☆☆☆☆

Moonambel. Owner/winemaker: David Jones. 18 hectares. www.dalwhinnie.com.au

Possibly the best producer in the region, with powerful Chardonnay (sensibly balanced by savoury, toasty oak); chunky, ripe, black Cabernet; and vibrant, resinous, lingering Shiraz. In 2000, an elegant Pinot Noir was added to this impressive range.

Redbank ☆☆–☆☆☆

Redbank. Owner/winemaker: Neill Robb. 15 hectares. www.redbankwines.com

Neill Robb's Redbank wines sometimes show the hard, unyielding quality that the Pyrenees region can bestow, but the top label, "Sally's Paddock", a Cabernet/Shiraz-based blend, is, in good years, one of the best red wines in the area: complex, spicy, and satisfying.

Taltarni ☆☆

Moonambel. Owner: John Goelet. 115 hectares, also 20 hectares at Clover Hill in Pipers Brook, Tasmania, for sparkling-wine production. www.taltarni.com.au

The brother winery to Clos du Val (*q.v.*) in the Napa Valley: extremely modern and well-equipped. Since 1976, Dominique Portet made brawny Cabernet Sauvignon and Shiraz in a powerful, tannic style, and the wines aged well. More Merlot and Cabernet Franc have been added to recent vintages, bringing extra subtlety. Whites are less sure-footed, but Sauvignon Blanc is good. With the departure of Portet in 2000 to set up his own winery (*q.v.*), the style appears to be becoming more supple and user-friendly.

Warrenmang Vineyard ☆☆
Moonambel. Owners: the Bazzani family. 10 hectares.
www.bazzani.com.au

The passionate venture of local Italian restaurateur, Luigi Bazzani, this attractive, inviting vineyard has produced some good, weighty, earthy Shiraz and chocolatey Cabernet over the years, as well as, more recently, lighter, more approachable, bistro-style wines under the "Bazzani" label.

Yarra Valley

Coldstream Hills ☆☆–☆☆☆
Coldstream. Owner: Southcorp Wines. 180 hectares.
www.coldstreamhills.com.au

Founded by the country's leading wine critic, James Halliday, the estate succumbed to a takeover in 1996 from Southcorp. Production has been greatly expanded and Sauvignon was introduced. Yet, Coldstream Hills still makes some of Australia's most stylish Pinot Noir and Chardonnay, as well as elegant Cabernet Sauvignon and Merlot. Andrew Fleming makes the wines, with James Halliday as consultant.

De Bortoli (Yarra Valley) ☆☆–☆☆☆
Dixons Creek. Owners: the De Bortoli family. 155 hectares.
www.debortoli.com.au

The Victorian arm of the successful New South Wales wine family. Wines made from fruit grown across Victoria appear under the good-value "Windy Peak" and "Gulf Station" labels. Wines from the Yarra Valley vineyards are better quality, especially the citrus-tangy Chardonnay, the fruity, dry Cabernet Rosé, and the dark, berry-fruited Cabernet.

Diamond Valley ☆☆☆
St Andrews. Owner/winemaker: David Lance. 4 hectares

David Lance makes outstanding Pinot Noir, as well as Chardonnay and Cabernet. Lance has rightly won acclaim for his powerful and complex "Close-Planted" Pinot Noir, with its earthy aromas and rich, plummy flavours. Wines from purchased fruit are released under the "Blue Label".

Domaine Chandon ☆☆☆
Coldstream. Owner: LVMH. 100 hectares. www.chandon.com

Exciting Yarra Valley investment, established with the foreign expertise of Moët and the local knowledge of Tony Jordan, one of Australia's foremost wine consultants. Wines are made from both estate and bought-in fruit, and aged two years on the yeast. The first commercial classic-method sparkler was released in 1989, and quickly rose to the top of Australia's competitive sparkling wine hierarchy. Smaller production of blanc de blancs, blanc de noirs, and a *cuvée prestige* (aged six years and vintage-dated) represent exceptional quality. Under the "Green Point" label, Chandon is making great progress with still Chardonnay and Pinot Noir.

Mount Mary ☆☆☆
Lilydale. Owners: Dr. John and Marli Middleton. 12 hectares

A near-fanatical doctor's pastime which has become very serious indeed. His "Quintet" Cabernet blend is like a classic Bordeaux: mid-weight, complex, and intensely fruity. The

Chardonnays are strong, rich, and golden; new-oak fermented and, like the Cabernets, easily ten-year wines. Exceptional Pinot Noir is also made, but not every year. Dr. Middleton is impervious to fashion or criticism, yet there is no shortage of demand for his very expensive wines.

Dominique Portet ☆–☆☆
Coldstream. Owner/winemaker: Dominique Portet.
1.5 hectares. www.dominiqueportet.com

After retiring from Taltarni (*q.v.*), Portet took time off before setting up shop in the Yarra Valley. The range is very limited at present, and initial releases were more forward and friendly than the Taltarni wines. An estate to watch.

St Huberts ☆☆
Coldstream. Owner: Beringer Blass. 35 hectares.
www.beringerblass.com.au

The modern re-incarnation of one of the Yarra's nineteenth-century showpieces. Since Beringer Blass (*q.v.*) acquired the property, quality has remained good, even though production has increased threefold.

Seville Estate ☆☆☆
Seville. Owners: Brokenwood. 5 hectares

Tiny vineyard and winery in the southern Yarra Valley. In 1997, it was bought by Brokenwood of Hunter Valley (*q.v.*), so Iain Riggs is now in charge of production. Particularly elegant wines, with juicy Cabernet, spicy Shiraz, and low-key, deeply flavoured Chardonnay.

Tarrawarra ☆☆☆
Yarra Glen. Owners: the Besen family. 75 hectares.
www.tarrawarra.com.au

Single-mindedly striving to produce the region's best Chardonnay and Pinot Noir from a very impressive, expensive winery, and occasionally coming close to achieving that aim. Winemaker Clare Halloran has been careful to avoid the excessive extraction that marred some previous vintages.

Yarra Burn ☆☆–☆☆☆
Yarra Junction. Owners: Constellation-Hardy. 10 hectares.
www.brlhardy.com.au

Good Yarra producer used by BRL Hardy as a production base for its steep, cool-climate Yarra vineyard, Hoddles Creek – a vineyard so steep that it has inspired a new range of wines rather amusingly called "Bastard Hill". The "Bastard Hill" Chardonnay is first-rate: toasty yet vigorous. Fine Pinot Noir and Shiraz, too.

Yarra Ridge ☆☆
Yarra Glen. Owner: Beringer Blass. 80 hectares.
www.beringerblass.com.au

After this estate, founded by lawyer Louis Bialkower, was bought by Mildara Blass (*q.v.*) in the mid-1990s, the wines went through a dip in quality, but the estate is now back on course. These are medium-bodied wines, well-made but for early drinking.

Yarra Yarra ☆☆–☆☆☆
Steels Creek. Owner/winemaker: Ian Maclean. 9 hectares.
www.yarayarravineyard.com.au

So good they named it twice? A small property, focusing on

Sauvignon/Semillon blends that age surprisingly well, and a Cabernet Franc and Cabernet Sauvignon blend called "Cabernets", aged in French oak. It is medium-bodied, elegant, understated. In 2000, a rounded, plummy Shiraz was made for the first time.

Yarra Yering ☆☆☆
Coldstream. Owner/winemaker: Dr. Bailey Carrodus. 34 hectares
Dr. Carrodus is an individualist who initiated the wine revival of the Yarra Valley, with an unirrigated vineyard producing small yields of high-quality fruit. He is not keen on varietal labelling; a Bordeaux-type blend is called "Dry Red No. 1", a Rhône-type, "Dry Red No. 2". Both wines are widely admired for harmonious composition. Pinot Noir he makes straight. Since the late 1990s he has added Viognier, Sangiovese, and a port-style wine to his range. All his wines are characterized by their vibrancy and aromatic pungency.

Yeringberg ☆☆–☆☆☆
Coldstream. Owner/winemaker: Guillaume de Pury. 2 hectares
The remnant of a wonderful old country estate near Melbourne, making some excellent wines, still in the hands of its Swiss founding family. Pinot Noir, Marsanne, Chardonnay, Cabernet, and Merlot are delicate and charming. The potential of the old estate shows, though production is tiny.

Yering Station ☆☆–☆☆☆
Yarra Glen. Owners: the Rathbone family and Champagne Devaux. 115 hectares. www.yering.com
This historic old winery, now completely modernized, was one of Victoria's first, and its renaissance in the mid-1990s was exciting, while wine quality was not always so. It has been expanded by the Rathbones, and its joint venture with Champagne Devaux has resulted in a sparkling wine called "Yarrabank". All the wines are well-made and balanced, but it's the reserves that stand out as exceptional.

Other Areas

Bass Phillip ☆☆☆
Leongatha South. Owner/winemaker: Phillip Jones. 15 hectares
This tiny Gippsland winery closely resembles a small domaine in Burgundy – in size, approach, passion, and much more than occasionally in the glass. Few other Australian wineries even come close to making Pinot Noir as well as Phillip Jones. The three grades of quality are always eagerly sought-after.

Delatite ☆–☆☆☆
Mansfield. Owners: the Ritchie family. 25 hectares. www.delatitewinery.com.au
Ros Ritchie produces very remarkable white wines and characteristically minty reds from these very cool vineyards. Riesling and Gewürztraminer are among the best. His other wines include Pinot Noir, Malbec, and Sauvignon Blanc.

Giaconda ☆☆☆–☆☆☆☆
Beechworth. Owner/ winemaker: Rick Kinzbrunner. 6 hectares. www.giaconda.com.au
Small, fashionable winery in northeast Victoria that produces good Pinot Noir and some of Australia's most reserved, complex Chardonnay, easily often mistaken in blind tasting for a finer white burgundy. Some of the other wines include a Chardonnay/Roussanne blend called "Nantua Les Deux", and a pure Roussanne called "Aeolia". Quantities are tiny and sold to mailing-list devotees and top restaurants.

Other Victoria Producers

Elgee Park ☆☆
Merricks North. www.elgeeparkwines.com.au
The oldest winery in the Mornington Peninsula, producing extremely good wines in frustratingly minute quantities. Viognier and Chardonnay in particular can be very impressive.

Kooyong ☆☆
Shoreham, Mornington Peninsula. www.kooyong.com
A Mornington Peninsula winery that made its first wines from thirty-four hectares in the year 2001. It has since attracted admiration for light, elegant Pinot Noir and Chardonnay.

Oakridge Estate ☆☆
Seville
Although this Yarra Valley winery produces good Shiraz, Merlot, and Chardonnay, it unfortunately experienced severe financial problems which led to a change of ownership in 2001, when it was acquired by Western Australian winery Evans & Tate (*q.v.*).

Turramurra ☆☆
Dromana
This Mornington Peninsula estate has been producing rich Pinot Noir and Sauvignon Blanc in limited quantities.

Wantirna Estate ☆
Wantirna South
A tiny estate located in the suburbs of Melbourne, where owner/winemaker Reg Egan produces an extremely good Pinot Noir, a most suave, gentlemanly Cabernet/Merlot blend, and tiny quantities of other very well-made wines.

Leading South Australia Producers

Adelaide Hills

Knappstein Lenswood Vineyards ☆☆☆
Lenswood. Owner/winemaker: Tim Knappstein. 25 hectares. www.knappsteinlenswood.com.au
Once Tim Knappstein had let go of his eponymous winery, he was free to concentrate on wines from his excellent cool-climate vineyards at Lenswood. Pinot Noir is deep, stone-fruity, and gamey; Chardonnay is as rich as they come; and impossibly intense Sauvignon Blanc is possibly Australia's best.

Nepenthe ☆☆–☆☆☆

Lenswood. Owners: the Tweddell family. 60 hectares.
www.nepenthe.com.au

Peter Lenske, a winemaker with considerable experience in Burgundy, has brought this estate to the top ranks since the mid-1990s. The crisp Riesling and sophisticated Chardonnay are the stars among the white wines, their red counterparts being the leafy Pinot Noir and a Cabernet/Merlot blend called "The Fugue". The style of the wines is tight and elegant, so they benefit from some bottle-ageing.

Petaluma ☆☆–☆☆☆☆

Piccadilly. Owner: Lion Nathan. 500 hectares, in the Adelaide Hills, Coonawarra, and Clare. www.petaluma.com.au

Despite the takeover of this wonderful property by the New Zealand brewer, Petaluma remains one of Australia's leading wineries. All the wines bear the stamp of its brilliant and dedicated winemaker, Brian Croser. He lends his name to the very good sparkling "Croser". The range consists of the gloriously limey Riesling from Clare, and the long-lived Chardonnay from the Piccadilly Valley, which continues to shine. "Coonawarra", a Cabernet blend, is clean, tight, and slow to develop. Recent additions are the Shiraz and the very complex (and expensive) single-vineyard "Tiers" Chardonnay. The second label, "Bridgewater Mill", provides more immediate, approachable wines, and Croser's "Sharefarmers Vineyard", just north of Coonawarra, produces a red and a white of impeccable quality.

Shaw & Smith ☆☆–☆☆☆

Balhannah. Owners: Martin Shaw and Michael Hill-Smith. 26 hectares

The fortuitous pairing of winemaker Martin Shaw with restaurateur, master of wine, and cousin, Michael Hill-Smith has resulted in one of the best wineries in the Adelaide Hills. Unwooded Chardonnay is one of the best in the country: all crisp, apple fruit. Reserve Chardonnay is at the other end of the spectrum, with powerful, creamy, oak treatment; and Sauvignon Blanc often rivals the best of Marlborough with its mouth-watering fruitiness. As for the red wines, Merlot is proving exceptional.

Geoff Weaver ☆☆☆

Lenswood. Owner/winemaker: Geoff Weaver. 11 hectares.
www.geoffweaver.com.au

Former Hardy's chief winemaker, Geoff Weaver, is now ensconced at his own Adelaide Hills winery, and is producing some wonderful, classy wines. Sauvignon can be pungently fruity; Chardonnay invariably brilliant; Riesling floral and limey; and Cabernet/Merlot uncommonly elegant. Without exception, these are wines of impeccable balance and clarity.

Adelaide Plains

Primo Estate ☆☆☆

Virginia. Owner/winemaker: Joe Grilli. 40 hectares.
www.primoestate.com.au

Joe Grilli is deceptively softly spoken but a true innovator: his wines simply shout their flavours and quality. Deliciously fruity Colombard, silky Shiraz, and "Sparkling Red", with its dry finish, share the limelight with serious, Amarone-style Cabernet.

Barossa Valley

Barossa Valley Estates ☆☆–☆☆☆

Marananga. Owners: Valley Growers Cooperative and Constellation-Hardy. Vineyards: 65 growers across the Barossa Valley. www.bve.com.au

This winery produces and exports wines under the "Barossa Valley Estates" labels and some more upmarket, extremely powerful wines under the "E & E" label. Typical Barossa Shiraz: jammy, sweet flavours, enhanced by American oak. The top wines are the "E & E Black Pepper" and "Ebenezer" Shirazes.

Basedow ☆☆

Tanunda. Owners: Hill International. No vineyards.
www.basedow.com.au

A sometimes excellent Barossa winery, buying in all its grapes, since the vineyards were sold off in 1982. In the late 1970s, its Shiraz reached real heights of richness and complexity. In the 1990s, Chardonnay and Semillon were the stars. A recent addition to the range is the "Johannes" Shiraz.

Beringer Blass

Barossa. www.beringerblass.com

A very complex history of mergers has led up to the creation of this giant Australian wine company. Mildara was a Coonawarra winery, best-known for its highly popular "Jamieson's Run" brand. A marriage with Wolf Blass led to the formation of a new company, Mildara Blass, which subsequently swallowed up the large Napa-based Beringer company. Under its new name of Beringer Blass, it continued to acquire wineries. Such well-known labels (brands) as "Quelltaler", "Saltram", "Annie's Lane", "Rothbury", "Yellowglen", "Baileys", "Coldstream Hills", "Yarra Ridge", "Krondorf", and of course, "Wolf Blass" itself, are now part of the empire. Each of the twelve brands has its own winemaker to preserve the individual style and identity of the wineries.

Bethany ☆☆

Tanunda. Owners: the Schrapel family. 37 hectares.
www.bethany.com.au

Traditional growers and winemakers with an understated style that manages to avoid clumsy portiness for the red wines. There is good Riesling from Eden Valley, and stylish Grenache that acquires cherry fruit and a whiff of tobacco as it ages.

Leo Buring ☆☆–☆☆☆

Nuriootpa. Owner: Southcorp Wines. 60 hectares.
www.australianwines.com/leoburing

Although the original Leo Buring winery in the Barossa Valley has now been transformed into Richmond Grove (*q.v.*), wines under the Leo Buring label continue to be produced at Penfolds, around the corner. Reds are impressive, Chardonnay also, but it is the Rieslings, among Australia's best, that continue to shine the brightest.

Elderton ☆☆

Nuriootpa. Owners: the Ashmead family. 30 hectares.
www.eldertonwines.com.au

Winemaker Neil Ashmead is a tireless self-publicist, but the quality of the wines usually matches the hype. Traditionally huge, chocolatey, alcoholic reds have amassed a clutch of awards at shows, among them the infamous Jimmy Watson trophy for a particularly liquorous Cabernet. "Command" Shiraz is made from vines planted between 1895 and 1905, and this American-oaked wine is as rich and jammy as one would expect.

Grant Burge ☆☆–☆☆☆

Tanunda. Owners: Grant and Helen Burge. 400 hectares.
www.grantburgewines.com.au

After his Krondorf winery was snapped up by Mildara in 1986, Burge set up on his own. His own vineyards are substantial, but he also buys in fruit. The Riesling and Chardonnay come from Eden Valley, but he is best-known for the excellent "Holy Trinity", first made in 1995, and a blend of Grenache, Shiraz, and Mourvèdre. Its sleek texture and vibrant fruit are oddly reminiscent of a medium-bodied Zinfandel. His blockbuster "Meshach" Shiraz, a "Grange" pretender, is also worth seeking out, as is the "Shadrach" Cabernet, a blend of fruit from Coonawarra and Barossa, aged in new oak.

Greenock Creek ☆☆☆

Seppeltsfield. Owners: Michael and Annabelle Waugh

Rave reviews for its Shiraz from the American press has given cult status to this winery. The vineyards are dry-farmed and low-yielding, so the wines have all the concentration and power one could wish for. Numerous *cuvées* of Shiraz and Cabernet are produced. Tasted side by side with other Greenock Creek Shirazes, the "7 Acre" seemed the most complete.

Henschke ☆☆☆–☆☆☆☆

Keyneton. Owners: the Henschke family. 110 hectares.
www.henschke.com.au

A fifth generation family firm, with two justly famous brands of Shiraz: "Hill of Grace" (deep wine from ancient vines) and "Mount Edelstone" (easier, more elegant red). Other wines include a crisp, dry, and delicate Riesling; and elegant blends such as "Keyneton Estate" from Shiraz, Cabernet, and Malbec; and "Johann's Garden" from Grenache, Mourvèdre, and Shiraz. The intense "Cyril Henschke" Cabernet comes not from Barossa but from Eden Valley. The top reds are easily capable of ageing and improving for fifteen years or more. The dream team of winemaker Stephen Henschke and viticulturist Prue Henschke hit their stride ten years ago and has not faltered.

Kaesler ☆☆

Nuriootpa. Owners: the Hueppauff family. 24 hectares.
www.kaesler.com.au

Medium-bodied wines, the best being designated "Old Vine". The most impressive wine is the "Old Bastard Shiraz" from vines planted in 1893. Winemaker Reid Bosward keeps the tannins nicely under control, and the red wines acquire a leathery warmth with age.

Peter Lehmann ☆☆–☆☆☆

Tanunda. Owner: A public company. 50 hectares.
www.peterlehmannwines.com.au

Peter Lehmann is one of the great showmen and pillars of Barossa, founding his winery when the market for grapes dried up in 1978. The wines that appear under his name are equally expressive, and bask in their sense of place. Rieslings, from both the Barossa and Eden valleys, can be wonderful, and Cabernet and Shiraz can be as rich and full as you'd wish. "Clancy's" is a good-value red blend, while flagship wines "The Mentor" (a Cabernet blend), "Stonewell"

Penfolds

Few wine companies anywhere else in the world could lay claim to being the undisputed number one in their particular country, but Penfolds undoubtedly occupies that enviable position in Australia.

Since 1844, when Christopher Rawson Penfold and his wife, Mary, established a vineyard at Magill, on the outskirts of Adelaide, the Penfold name has been synonymous with consistency and quality in wine. Initially, of course, and until the middle of the twentieth century, after Penfolds had moved to its current huge winery in the Barossa Valley, most of that wine was fortified.

But from the 1950s on, when winemaker Max Schubert began to release his "Grange Hermitage" onto an unsuspecting market, the Penfolds banner was held aloft by rich, oaky, quintessentially South Australian reds. More recently, the white wines in the portfolio have begun to show the same kind of consistent quality, but it is still the reds that most wine-lovers associate with the name.

The cornerstone of Penfolds' success is the extraordinary range of choice vineyards – often old and low-yielding – that the company has amassed over the years. These vineyard resources allow almost unlimited flexibility when it comes to blending (the soul of Penfolds – indeed Australian – winemaking), and ensure remarkable consistency of style year after year. This consistency is enhanced by the characteristic Penfolds' trademark: lavish, unrestrained use of new American oak.

Not surprisingly, Penfolds has been through a succession of owners over the years, moving from a family empire, through the hands of a couple of major brewers, and finally ending up as the flagship of Southcorp Wines, itself a part of the multi-billion dollar Southcorp Holdings. The Southcorp group, which also includes other great wine companies such as Seppelt, Lindemans, and Wynns, as well as such outstanding smaller wineries as Coldstream Hills, is Australia's largest wine producer (and one of the top ten biggest wine companies in the world), but it is the Penfolds name that is firmly at the top of the Southcorp hierarchy.

Shiraz, and "Seven Surveys" (a supple blend of Shiraz, Mourvèdre, and Grenache) are worthy newcomers to the pantheon of Barossa legends.

Charles Melton ☆☆
Tanunda. Owner/winemaker: Charlie Melton. 28 hectares.
www.charlesmeltonwines.com.au
One of the nicest men in the Barossa, Charlie Melton produces some of the region's best wines. Cabernet and Shiraz stuffed with ripe fruit; "Rosé of Virginia", an intriguing cross between a heavy rosé and a light red; and a deep-flavoured Shiraz/Grenache/Mataro blend called "Nine Popes", the catalyst for the revival in interest in Rhône styles.

Orlando ☆☆
Rowland Flat. Owners: Pernod Ricard. www.orlando.com.au
One of the biggest wine companies in Australia, and known worldwide for the phenomenally successful "Jacob's Creek", produced by winemaker Philip Laffer and his team. Beyond that brand, however, lurk some far better wines.

The "Gramp's" wines are packed with succulent fruit; "Carrington" sparkler is good, (slightly more pricey "Trilogy" is better); "Steingarten" Riesling, from an individual, rocky vineyard is beautifully steely and tight; and Coonawarra Cabernets such as "St Hugo" and "Jacaranda Ridge", while very oaky, can be very enjoyable. Morris of Rutherglen, Richmond Grove, and Wyndham Estate (*qq.v.*) in the Hunter, are also part of the empire.

Penfolds ☆☆–☆☆☆☆
Nuriootpa. Owner: Southcorp Wines. 8,000 hectares.
www.penfolds.com
While "Grange" may no longer be the only true first-growth of the Southern Hemisphere (arguably, Henschke's "Hill of Grace" has swelled the number to two), Penfolds remains Australia's most esteemed red-wine company (*see* opposite page). Classic Penfolds wines include "Kalimna" Shiraz, "Magill Estate", and "Bin 707" Cabernet Sauvignon. "Ports" are excellent, with "Grandfather" a legend, and white wines are slowly improving.

Its flagship white, the tight, citric "Yattarna" Chardonnay, has won praise, but few believe it justifies its high price. After decades as winemaker, John Duval stepped down in 2002, and his place has been taken by the equally competent Peter Gago.

Richmond Grove ☆☆–☆☆☆
Tanunda. Owner: Orlando Wyndham. 10 hectares.
www.richmondgrovewines.com
Richmond Grove now has its home in the heart of the Barossa, in the old Château Leonay winery established by Leo Buring at the end of the nineteenth century. Fittingly, John Vickery, the winemaker who made some remarkable, seemingly immortal Rieslings under the Leo Buring label during the 1960s, '70s, and '80s, is back at Château Leonay, after a brief spell in retirement. Not surprisingly, the new Richmond Grove Rieslings are good, but so, too, are other wines from this revamped winery.

Rockford ☆☆☆
Tanunda. Owner: Tanunda Vintners. No vineyards.
www.rockfordwines.com.au

Small Barossa winery with one of the region's true characters, the reticent Rocky O'Callaghan, at the helm. Styles are particularly regional and thoroughly traditional: big, brawny Grenache and "Basket Press" Shiraz are totally seductive, as is the exceedingly rare but worth searching for "Sparkling Black Shiraz", which has achieved an almost cult following.

St Hallett ☆☆–☆☆☆
Tanunda. Owner: Lion Nathan. 40 hectares.
www.sthallett.com.au
Across the board, the wide variety of styles made here by winemaker Stuart Blackwell are good, but the "Old Block" Shiraz (one of the first wines to exploit the marketing potential of the Barossa's ancient viticultural heritage) is consistently top of the tree.

Saltram ☆☆–☆☆☆
Nuriootpa. Owner: Beringer Blass. 18 hectares
For a while, in the '60s and '70s, when Peter Lehmann was winemaker, Saltram produced classic red wines such as "Mamre Brook" Cabernet, and "Metala" Shiraz/Cabernet. During the '80s, under the ownership of Seagrams, quality was reliable but sluggish. After the takeover by what is now Beringer Blass (*q.v.*), there were fears for Saltram's future, but winemaker Nigel Dolan has steered Saltram back to its former exalted position, especially for Shiraz.

Seppelt
Seppeltsfield. *See* Victoria listing

Tollana ☆☆
Nuriootpa. Owner: Southcorp Wines. 130 hectares.
www.australianwines.com.au/tollana
Although the winemaking for Tollana is based in the Barossa, most of the fruit is sourced from the Eden Valley and Adelaide Hills. Consequently, wines such as the Tollana Cabernet, Shiraz, Sauvignon Blanc, and Botrytis Riesling all tend towards bright, fruity elegance, and a refreshing lightness of touch.

Torbreck ☆☆☆
Tanunda. Owner: David Powell. 36 hectares. www.torbreck.com
Torbreck has, since 1995, specialized in small quantities of wines that feature various blends of Shiraz and Viognier, with the exception of "The Steading", which blends Grenache and Mourvèdre. "The Factor" is the most expensive *cuvée*, but "Run Rig", from 120-year-old Shiraz vines, is as good. These wines are plummy and tannic, as old-vine Shiraz should be, but they are never overblown, and the oak handling is masterly. In 2002, marital problems led to the estate going into receivership, but the banks have sufficient confidence in Powell and his team to maintain the status quo.

Veritas ☆☆–☆☆☆
Tanunda. Owner/winemaker: Rolf Binder. 28 hectares
Rolf Binder's Austrian and Hungarian origins are reflected in the names of his wines. In every other respect they are typical Barossa, hewing fine Grenache and Shiraz from vineyards he considers outstanding. A zest for experimentation means that most of the wines are available only in tiny quantities, which has helped some of them achieve cult status.

Wolf Blass ☆–☆☆☆

Nuriootpa. Owner: Beringer Blass. 140 hectares.
www.wolfblass.com.au

The ebullient Wolf Blass arrived in Australia thirty years ago, and immediately put his skills as a blender and marketer to good use, gradually building up one of Australia's most widely recognized wine empires. If anyone was a pioneer of what have become known as "fruit-driven wines", it was surely Wolf Blass. Although he is no longer involved in the day-to-day running of the company, Blass's presence still makes itself felt in every bottle of wine that bears his name (and there are twenty million of these produced each year). The popularity of Wolf Blass continues unabated, with some wines – impressive Rieslings and richly oaky reds – even confounding the meanest critics. Drink them for oaky fruit, not for finesse or terroir character.

Yalumba ☆☆☆

Angaston. Owners: the Hill-Smith family. Vineyards: plantings at Coonawarra, Koppamurra, and at Oxford Landing on the Murray River. Also three other estate vineyards: Heggies, Pewsey Vale, and Hill-Smith Estate, all in Eden Valley.
www.yalumba.com

The sixth generation of the Hill-Smith family is active in this distinctively upper-crust winery that has an air of the turf about it. Their finest wines in the past were "ports", but since the planting of higher and cooler land in the 1960s, dry whites have been very good and hugely popular.

Yalumba wines range from the bargain bubbly "Angas Brut", through reliable stalwarts such as "Galway Shiraz", elegant Coonawarra Cabernet "The Menzies" to "The Signature" from Cabernet and Shiraz, and the flagship Shiraz, "Octavius" (aged in ninety-litre American barrels called octaves). Wines from the Hill-Smiths' cooler vineyard estates are also very good. "Hill-Smith" Sauvignon Blanc is crisp and grassy; "Pewsey Vale" Riesling is a classic wine, honeyed and long-lived; "Heggies" Cabernet and Merlot are brambly and fine; and "Heggies" Viognier is the best Australian example of this grape yet made. The recent "Vinnovation" range allows the winemakers to enjoy themselves with unusual grape varieties (in Australia) such as Nebbiolo and Petit Verdot.

Clare

Tim Adams ☆☆

Clare. Owner/winemaker: Tim Adams. No vineyards.
www.timadamswines.com.au

All wines made by this talented winemaker display solid regional character. Riesling is crisp and limey; Semillon, lemony and balanced with good oak; "Aberfeldy" Shiraz, full of big, jammy, red-fruit flavours; and "The Fergus" (85% Grenache), suitably heroic.

Jim Barry ☆☆–☆☆☆

Clare. Owner: Jim Barry. 240 hectares. www.jmbarry.com

One of the largest wineries in Clare, where winemaker Mark Barry produces a wide range. Whites include Chardonnay, Sauvignon, and both dry and sweet Rieslings. Among the reds are a fine "McCrae Wood" Cabernet, and a remarkable single-vineyard Shiraz called "The Armagh"; thick with prune and cherry and spice.

Grosset ☆☆☆–☆☆☆☆

Auburn. Owner/winemaker: Jeffrey Grosset. 7 hectares.
www.grosset.com.au

One of Australia's best small wineries. Jeffrey Grosset is a fastidious but open-minded winemaker, producing quite delicious Riesling ("Watervale" for drinking young, "Polish Hill" for the long haul), and a Cabernet blend called "Gaia" from his and others' vineyards in the Clare Valley, as well as smaller quantities of intense Chardonnay and gamey Pinot from vineyards in the Adelaide Hills.

Knappstein Wines ☆☆–☆☆☆

Clare. Owner: Lion Nathan. 100 hectares.
www.knappsteinwines.com.au

This well-known Clare winery, originally known as Enterprise Wines, is now owned by Petaluma (*q.v.*), and winemaking is overseen by Andrew Hardy. Although Tim Knappstein is no longer involved (he's now wrapped up with his Lenswood Vineyards [*q.v.*]) the reputation he established is in good hands.

Riesling and Gewürztraminer are still fragrant and flowery, and Cabernet is as chunky and fruit-packed as it ever was. So is the mighty "Enterprise" Shiraz.

Leasingham ☆☆–☆☆☆

Clare. Owner: Constellation-Hardy. 260 hectares. Winemaker: Richard Rowe. www.leasingham-wines.com.au

New ownership meant a revamp for this famous old winery. Old labels such as the "Bin 56" Cabernet/Malbec and "Bin 7" Riesling have been reintroduced, and a premium range, "Classic Clare", added. Riesling is excellent, so is Shiraz – especially the resinous, thickly textured "Classic Clare".

Mitchell ☆☆–☆☆☆

Sevenhill. Owner/winemaker: Andrew Mitchell. 65 hectares

A very reliable Clare producer, known for memorable lime-scented "Watervale" Riesling, plus good Semillon, and vigorous "Peppertree" Shiraz and Cabernet. All are among Clare's best.

Mount Horrocks ☆☆–☆☆☆

Auburn. Owner/winemaker: Stephanie Toole. 3 hectares.
www.mounthorrocks.com

This vivacious winemaker, one of Clare's best international ambassadors, produces impeccable dry Riesling, and a fascinating sweet "Cordon Cut" Riesling, made by snipping the stems and leaving the cut bunches on the vine to desiccate. Red wines are increasingly fine, too, especially the plump, berry-stashed Cabernet/Merlot.

Sevenhill Cellars ☆☆

Sevenhill. Owner: the Manresa Society. 53 hectares.
www.sevenhillcellars.com.au

This old Jesuit church and winery is one of the most attractive places in Clare, and the wines produced by Brother John May are somewhat old-fashioned, but nonetheless among the region's best. Monumental in stature, with abundant fruit and spice, the reds, based on Shiraz, Cabernet, Malbec, and Grenache, are surprisingly drinkable when young, but also capable of ageing for long periods. Whites, including an unusual dry Verdelho and a fragrant Riesling, are also good.

Taylor ☆–☆☆☆
Auburn. Owners: the Taylor family. 560 hectares.
www.taylorwines.com.au
An extremely large vineyard, with an similarly large winery, located in a region where such facilities are rare. The Taylors produce substantial quantities of middle-of-the-road wines, although the Riesling can often be exceptional. Since 1999, the best wines have been bottled under the "St Andrews" label, with Cabernet and Shiraz clearly the most exciting wines. There is a sharp upward curve in quality with the "St Andrews" range. In some markets, the wines are sold as "Wakefield" (to avoid any conflict with a well-known port house).

Wendouree ☆☆☆–☆☆☆☆
Clare. Owner/winemaker: Tony Brady. 10 hectares
This small, old vineyard has produced some of Australia's most powerful, concentrated red wines for decades. Thankfully, it seems that nothing is set to change, as Tony Brady sees himself merely as the guardian of a great tradition, preferring to interfere as little as possible during the fruit's passage from vineyard to bottle. An ardent Australian following means these wines are almost impossible to find.

Coonawarra

Bowen Estate ☆☆–☆☆☆
Coonawarra. Owner/winemaker: Doug Bowen. 25 hectares
An ex-Lindemans winemaker, Doug Bowen offers a near-model Coonawarra Cabernet which can age well. The "Ampelon" Shiraz is an uncommonly opulent example from this area. Bowen built a handsome new winery in 1982, and expanded again in 1995.

Hollick ☆☆
Coonawarra. Owners: Ian and Wendy Hollick. 72 hectares.
www.hollick.com
Small Coonawarra producer making a successful range of varietals: Cabernet and Pinot Noir for the reds; Chardonnay, Sauvignon, and Riesling for the whites. Hollick's Cabernet has won the important Jimmy Watson Trophy. "Ravenswood" is their flagship Cabernet.

Katnook Estate ☆☆–☆☆☆
Coonawarra. Owner: Freixenet. 150 hectares.
www.katnookestate.com.au
Owned until 2001 by the large Wingara Wine Group, which was then bought by Spanish cava giant, Freixenet. Katnook Estate is one of Coonawarra's most unusual wineries, in that its best wines are often not red but white. Certainly, Cabernet and a varietal Merlot can be good, but the Katnook Chardonnay, delicious Riesling, and exceptional, long-lived Sauvignon Blanc are often the best. Second label "Riddoch" offers some great value for money. Katnook does, however, produce one outstanding red: the cedary "Odyssey" Cabernet.

Leconfield ☆☆–☆☆☆
Coonawarra. Owners: the Hamilton family. 32 hectares
In the hands of former winemaker Ralph Fowler, quality at Leconfield improved dramatically, and is continuing to be maintained by current winemaker Paul Gordon. A fine

"Old Vines" Riesling is still in production, but the reds from Cabernet and Merlot are the real strength: tight, elegant, and very stylish.

Majella ☆☆
Coonawarra. Owners: the Lynn family. 60 hectares.
www.majellawines.com.au
Much of the crop supplies other wineries, but estate-bottling is on the rise here. The star is the Shiraz/Cabernet blend called "Mallea": oaky but stylish.

Parker Estate ☆☆☆
Coonawarra. Owners: the Parker and Fairfax families.
20 hectares
Parker specializes in Bordeaux-style wines from Coonawarra. The finer is called "First Growth" (easily dismissed as arrogance until you try the superb wine inside the bottle), the second a cassis-flavoured pure Cabernet that comes close to matching "First Growth" in quality. Chris Cameron makes the wine, with seeming ease and confidence.

Penley Estate ☆☆–☆☆☆
Coonawarra. Owner/winemaker: Kym Tolley. 90 hectares.
www.penley.com.au
Born into a wine family so with wine in his blood, Kym Tolley did his apprenticeship at Penfolds (*q.v.*), before setting up on his own. He now produces some seriously good wines in Coonawarra, especially a dark, dense, multi-layered Cabernet.

Rouge Homme ☆☆
Coonawarra. Owner: Southcorp Wines. 90 hectares
Old Coonawarra winery, set up by the Redman family (hence the terrible pun of a name), then owned by Southcorp until sold in 2002. The Cabernet has been outstanding, but the winery's future seems uncertain.

Rymill ☆☆
Coonawarra. Owners: Peter and Judy Rymill. 165 hectares.
www.rymill.com.au
From excellent and extensive vineyards, winemaker John Innes manages to fashion very good wines for comparatively low prices. Showpiece winery building and elegant packaging complete the picture.

Wynns ☆☆–☆☆☆
Coonawarra. Owner: Southcorp Wines. 850 hectares.
www.wynns.com.au
The Wynns were an important Melbourne wine family making their greatest impact in South Australia. They took over the old Riddoch winery in Coonawarra, and promptly carved a name for the region with some spectacular Shiraz and Cabernet. Both remain reliably brilliant (with the former excellent value), and have been joined by Chardonnay, Riesling, and a Cabernet/Merlot/Shiraz blend. Two flagship wines, "John Riddoch" Cabernet and "Michael" Shiraz – hugely-structured, massively ripe, opulent wines – crown the range. Given the scale of production here (around 250,000 cases), quality remains gratifyingly high.

Zema Estate ☆☆–☆☆☆
Coonawarra. Owners: the Zema family. 60 hectares.
www.zema.com.au

The personable Zema family stoically continue to produce some of the region's richest, most powerful wines, while all around them, things are increasingly dominated by the larger companies.

Eden Valley

Mountadam ☆☆–☆☆☆

High Eden Ridge. Owner: Cape Mentelle (and thus Veuve Clicquot). 50 hectares. www.mountadam.com

Adam Wynn, whose family founded the Coonawarra-based firm now owned by Southcorp, trained in Bordeaux and established this high-altitude winery with the help of his father, David. The grapes grown here go into the Mountadam range of first-class varietals. A second label, called "David Wynn" includes Chardonnay, Cabernet, Shiraz, and Riesling. They are made from bought-in Eden Valley grapes, and see very little oak-ageing. The "Eden Ridge" range of organic wines is also successful. Adam Wynn remains at the helm, despite the sale of the property in 2000.

Langhorne Creek

Bleasdale Vineyard ☆☆

Langhorne Creek. Owner/winemaker: Michael Potts. 55 hectares

The fifth generation of the pioneering Potts family operates this working slice of Australian history (it still has the huge, old, red-gum beam press). In this arid area the vineyards are irrigated by flooding through sluices from the Bremer River. The wines are supple and consistently good value.

Bremerton ☆☆

Langhorne Creek. Owners: the Willson family. 120 hectares. www.bremerton.com.au

Founded in 1985 by Craig Willson, Bremerton's winemaking has now been placed in the capable hands of his daughter, Rebecca. The best wines, not surprisingly, are red: the delicate Bordeaux blend called "Tamblyn", and a jammy Shiraz called "Old Adam".

McLaren Vale

Andrew Garrett ☆☆

McLaren Vale. Owner: Beringer Blass. 200 hectares. www.andrewgarrett.com.au

This highly successful winery, now part of Beringer Blass (q.v.), is responsible for making a best-selling range of varietals. The reds include Cabernet/Merlot and good-value Shiraz. "Ingoldby" is another label that is also produced here.

Chapel Hill ☆☆–☆☆☆

McLaren Vale. Owner: the Schmidheiny family. 44 hectares. www.chapelhillwine.com.au

In 2000, this well-known property was sold to the Swiss owner of Cuvaison in Napa Valley (q.v.). Pam Dunsford stayed on as consultant winemaker to fashion some of McLaren Vale's best wines at this modern winery, even though they are often multi-regional blends. Riesling is good, Chardonnay (wooded and unwooded) is very good, but the reds, especially the soft, concentrated Shiraz wines, are exceptional.

Clarendon Hills ☆☆☆

Blewitt Springs. Owner/winemaker: Roman Bratasiuk. 1 hectare

Pharmacist Roman Bratasiuk sources fruit from old, dry-grown, low-yielding vineyards in McLaren Vale, and uses traditional techniques such as natural yeasts and minimal sulphur additions to produce huge, concentrated wines. Mighty Shiraz and Grenache, but Pinot Noir does not fit well into this stylistic approach.

Coriole ☆☆☆

McLaren Vale. Owners: the Lloyd family. 40 hectares

Wonderfully ripe Shiraz is the main focus here, but Semillon and Chenin Blanc can be refreshingly grassy. Pioneering work with Sangiovese (and olive oil) is most exciting. The top Shiraz is the sumptuous, minty "Lloyd Reserve", with all the power and concentration that anyone could desire from a McLaren Vale red.

D'Arenberg ☆☆–☆☆☆

McLaren Vale. Owners: the Osborn family. 60 hectares. www.darenberg.com.au

Once one of McLaren Vale's most traditional producers, making good, rustic wines, and most famous for Grenache/Shiraz called "d'Arry's Original Burgundy". With younger-generation winemaker Chester Osborn at the helm, the family company has become more innovative, with forays into the world of obscure varietals (sparkling Chambourcin, Mourvèdre) and huge big reds such as the "Dead Arm" Shiraz particularly impressive. Just as good is the gamey but vigorous "Laughing Magpie" Shiraz/Viognier, and in some vintages, Osborn produces an amazingly raisiny "Noble" Riesling.

Edwards & Chaffey ☆–☆☆

McLaren Vale. Owner: Southcorp Wines. 150 hectares. www.edwardsandchaffey.com.au

This is what is left of the former Seaview property. It is now a sparkling-wine production centre for both the Seaview and Edwards & Chaffey labels. Good wines, mostly based on Chardonnay.

Simon Hackett ☆–☆☆

McLaren Vale. Owner/winemaker: Simon Hackett. 40 hectares

Hackett makes a wide range of wines, such as "Old Vine" Grenache, "Foggo Road" Cabernet, and "Anthony's Reserve" Shiraz – all well-made, yet lacking some flair and concentration.

Hardy's ☆–☆☆☆

McLaren Vale. Owner: Constellation-Hardy. Winemakers: Peter Dawson, Tom Newton, Steve Parnell, Ed Carr. 1,200 hectares at Padthaway, Coonawarra, Koppamurra, Elgin Valley, Langhorne Creek, and Hoddler Creek (Yarra Valley). www.brlhardy.com.au

One of the great old Adelaide wine dynasties, now merged with the Berri Renmano group, and owner of some of Australia's most exciting wineries. The family's origins were in McLaren Vale, where rich and fruity reds are still made – including top-of-the-range labels such as "Eileen Hardy" Shiraz and "Thomas Hardy" Cabernet – but pioneering vineyard moves into Padthaway and other new South Australian regions have resulted in fruit for a wide range of other well-known wines, such as the "Nottage Hill" varietals and the "Stamp Series". Quality is increasingly encouraging. The BRL Hardy group has also absorbed many important wineries, such as Houghton, Leasingham, Yarra Burn, and Chateau Reynella (*qq.v.*). In 2003, it merged with the vast, American-based Constellation group.

Hillstowe ☆☆
Hahndorf. Owners: Lion Nathan. 30 hectares.
www.hillstowe.com.lau
Under the ownership of the Lawrie family, the fruit quality in Hillstowe wines was more often than not exemplary: clean, full of freshness and life. The new ownership leaves the future direction uncertain.

Geoff Merrill Wines ☆☆–☆☆☆
Woodcroft. Owner/winemaker: Geoff Merrill. 60 hectares.
geoffmerrillwines.com
Geoff Merrill is one of Australia's highest-profile winemaking characters. Serious, surprisingly understated, and elegant wines are released under his eponymous label, while much more approachable, fruity wines come out as "Mount Hurtle". Shiraz has become the house specialty, with powerful yet refined reserves. At the top of the range is the high-priced "Henley Shiraz".

Pirramimma ☆–☆☆
McLaren Vale. Owners: the Johnston family. 180 hectares
This long-established wine estate is still making bulk wine, but it is also using its own label for clean, blackberryish Cabernet, aromatic Riesling, and a vibrant, chocolatey Petit Verdot.

Reynella ☆☆
Reynella. Owner: Constellation-Hardy. 10 hectares.
www.brlhardy.com.au
The former Chateau Reynella, with an historic cellar and vineyard just south of Adelaide, was bought by Thomas Hardy in 1982. The name was truncated to signify wines made here by Steve Pannell, of which the best are under the "Basket Pressed" range.

Richard Hamilton ☆☆
Willunga. Owners: the Hamilton family. 68 hectares.
www.hamiltonwines.com
Producer of generous, rich wines from old vineyards in McLaren Vale and younger ones in Coonawarra. Whites include Chardonnay and Semillon, while the reds are based on Cabernet, Shiraz, and Grenache, with recent small and exciting releases of Merlot.

Seaview
See **Edwards & Chaffey**

Tatachilla ☆☆–☆☆☆
McLaren Vale. Owner: Lion Nathan. No vineyards.
www.tatachillawinery.com.au
Tatachilla buys in grapes from many parts of South Australia.

The winemaker here, the enthusiastic Michael Fragos, makes wines that seem to reflect his personality. These are wines that have swagger without coarseness. The reds, especially the peppery Grenache/Shiraz and the ultra-ripe "Clarendon" Merlot, are usually considerably better than the whites.

Wirra Wirra ☆☆–☆☆☆
McLaren Vale. Owners: Greg and Roger Trott. 40 hectares.
www.wirra.com.au
The resurrection (in 1969) of a fine old ironstone winery has resulted in the production of essentially more graceful wines than the macho style that more usually emanates from McLaren Vale. This estate was once best-known for its white wines, but Wirra Wirra has since attained a fine reputation for its reds. "Church Block" is a Cabernet/Merlot/Shiraz blend. "RSW" Shiraz is dark and resinous, and "The Angelus" blends Cabernet from Coonawarra and McLaren Vale to achieve remarkably harmonious results, with the former's berry fruit and the latter's chocolatey density.

Woodstock ☆–☆☆
McLaren Flat. Owner/winemaker: Scott Collett. 75 hectares.
www.woodstockwine.com.au
Woodstock began producing wines in 1982. It now makes a wide range of varietals, including Cabernet, Shiraz, and Chardonnay, as well as an excellent sweet botrytis white and tawny "port".

Other South Australia Producers

Angove's ☆
Renmark. www.angoves.com.au
A conservative old family company, with 500 hectares in the Riverland irrigated area, well-known for producing good-value lines.

Annvers ☆☆
Kangarilla. www.annvers.com.au
The first vintage at this Adelaide Hills winery was 1998, using estate grapes and fruit from other SA regions. Plump, rich Cabernet and Shiraz.

Burge Family Winemakers ☆☆
Lyndoch, Barossa
Rick Burge likes Rhône wines, and his best wines are the peppery "Old Vine" Grenache and Shiraz, both of which pack a punch.

Cape Jaffa ☆☆
Cape Jaffa. www.capejaffawines.com.au
This is the first winery built in Mount Benson actually to produce some wine. Initial releases, such as the Sauvignon/Semillon and Cabernet/Merlot, were stylish, but these are early days.

Crabtree of Watervale ☆☆–☆☆☆
Clare
A fine, if little-known, source of elegant Riesling and Shiraz.

Dowie ☆☆
Doole
Three partners combined to form this McLaren Vale winery. So far the Shiraz has been their best wine.

Dutschke ☆–☆☆
Lyndoch, Barossa
Strictly for fans of porty, oaky Barossa Shiraz.

Fox Creek ☆☆
Willunga, McLaren Vale. www.foxcreekwines.com
A relative newcomer, with first releases in 1995, Fox Creek has swiftly gained a good reputation for rich and bold reserve bottlings of Shiraz and Cabernet.

Glaetzer ☆☆
Tanunda. www.glaetzer.com
Ben Glaetzer has no vineyards of his own, but buys in fruit from good Barossa sites and makes some sturdy Shiraz.

Haan ☆☆
Nuriootpa. www.haanwines.com.au
Ambitious Barossa producer, with bright, jammy Merlot "Prestige" and a Bordeaux blend called "Wilhelmus" that has concentration and swagger.

Henry's Drive ☆☆
Padthaway
First vintage here was 1998, with American-oaked Shiraz the leading wine.

Hewitson ☆☆
Unley
Dean Hewitson was a winemaker at Petaluma before starting his own négociant business. Access to outstanding vineyards is reflected in the quality of the wide range of wines.

Stephen John ☆☆
Watervale
Good wines, mostly from Clare, with succulent Riesling and Merlot.

Lake Breeze ☆☆
McLaren Vale
Good-quality red wines from Greg Follett, especially the Cabernet Sauvignon.

Normans Wines
Clarendon
The company went into receivership in 2001, but has been bought by Xanadu (*q.v.*) in Western Australia.

Penny's Hill ☆
McLaren Vale. www.pennyshill.com.au
A sound range of varietal wines, with somewhat jammy fruit, and inclined to be slack in structure.

Pertaringa ☆–☆☆
McLaren Vale
A joint venture between Geoff Hardy and viticulturist Ian Leask. The Shiraz is a bit of a bruiser, but there is also Cabernet, Sauvignon, and Semillon on offer.

Skillogalee ☆☆–☆☆☆
Sevenhill
A fine Clare property benefiting from vineyards that were planted in 1970 to give concentrated Riesling and a rich Cabernet blend.

Turkey Flat ☆☆–☆☆☆
Tanunda. www.turkeyflat.com.au
Full-bodied, spicy reds, often from very old Barossa vines. Exemplary Shiraz and a fine Grenache/Mataro/Shiraz blend under the alarming name of "Butchers Block".

Leading Western Australia Producers

Great Southern

Alkoomi ☆☆–☆☆☆
Frankland. Owners: Mervyn and Judith Lange. 70 hectares. www.alkoomiwines.com.au
This estate is the pace-setter for the new Frankland area, best enjoyed as dense, full-flavoured Cabernet and clean, tannic Shiraz. Riesling is light and sometimes sweetish on the finish.

Frankland Estate ☆☆
Frankland. Owners/winemakers: Judi Cullam and Barrie Smith. 30 hectares. www.franklandestate.com.au
Frankland Estate has, for many years, backed the cause of Riesling in Western Australia, and its "Isolation Ridge" Riesling is one of the best: lemony with mineral undertones. "Olmo's Reward" (a Bordeaux blend) is initially tight and intriguingly austere.

Goundrey ☆–☆☆
Mount Barker. Owner: Vincor. 185 hectares. www.goundreywines.com.au
Goundrey is one of the Great Southern region's most dramatically ambitious wineries. Huge investment and rigorous winemaking have resulted in some good wines, especially the brooding "Reserve Shiraz". In 2002, the property was sold to Vincor of Canada, so its future direction is unknown.

Howard Park ☆☆–☆☆☆
Denmark. Owners: Jeff and Amy Burch. 230 hectares. www.howardparkwines.com.au
Howard Park draws on its own vineyards, and those of contracted growers, to make blends incorporating the best properties of various Western Australian regions. It produces fragrant, sometimes austere Riesling, intense Shiraz, and tight, long-lived Cabernet. Vintage variation is important here, and acidity levels can be very high in certain years. "Madfish" is the label used for simpler wines.

Plantagenet Wines ☆☆–☆☆☆
Mount Barker. Owners: Lionel Samson and Co., and Tony Smith. 40 hectares. www.plantagenetwines.com
The senior winery at Mount Barker, with Gavin Berry in

charge of winemaking since 1994. Chardonnay (either the excellent unwooded "Omrah" or spicy, wooded "Plantagenet") and perfumed Riesling are the white wine successes here, and Shiraz, with dusty, edgy flavours, is remarkably Rhône-like. The Cabernet Sauvignon is tight, even austere, in its youth, but blossoms with eight years in bottle.

Wignall ☆☆
Albany. Owners: the Wignall family. 16 hectares
This vineyard is stuck out on its own near the remote town of Albany, but has forged an impressive reputation with some of the state's best Pinot Noir. Shiraz shows promise.

Geographe

Capel Vale ☆☆–☆☆☆
Capel. Owners: Dr. Peter and Elizabeth Pratten. 200 hectares.
www.capelvale.com
Successful winery, sourcing fruit from a number of regions for its wines. Dr. Pratten, a former radiologist, says he wants to make Old World wines from New World fruit. Those under the second "CV" label can be good value; wines under the "Capel Vale" label – especially the single-vineyard range – can be very good indeed. These include the delicate "Frederick" Chardonnay, with its nuance of mandarin oranges; the burly, almost porty "Howecroft" Merlot; and the silky, red-fruits "Kinnaird" Shiraz.

Peel Estate ☆☆
Baldivis. Owners: Will Nairn and partners. 15 hectares.
www.peelwine.com.au
Strong California influence shows in this blossoming estate. Chenin Blanc aged in oak is modelled on the lovely Chappellet Napa wine. Zinfandel is clean and aromatic, while Shiraz with fifteen months in French and American oak seems to be a wine for long ageing.

Margaret River

Amberley Estate ☆☆
Yallingup. Owners: investment group. 32 hectares.
www.amberley-estate.com.au
This medium-sized company has established a good name for itself with clean, reliable, sometimes very good wines, including fruity, fresh, off-dry Chenin Blanc and medium-bodied, juicy Cabernet blends. In 2000, it launched "Charlotte Street", which employs fruit from all over the state.

Ashbrook Estate ☆☆☆
Willyabrup. Owners/winemakers: Brian and Tony Devitt.
12 hectares
Remote, family run winery in the middle of a red-gum forest. Excellent and much sought-after white wines are produced, including "Gold Label Rhine Riesling", rich Semillon, crisp Sauvignon Blanc, and rich, intense Chardonnay. The wines are sold mostly through a mailing list, so are hard to find.

Brookland Valley ☆☆–☆☆☆
Willyabrup. Owners: Malcolm Jones and Constellation-Hardy.
16 hectares. www.brooklandvalley.com.au

One of Margaret River's newer success stories, Jones manages to combine a popular approach to wine tourism at his Flutes restaurant, with some downright delicious wines. The unoaked Sauvignon/Semillon is particularly good, with intense grass and pea flavours. The Cabernet/Merlot and reserve Cabernet are often outstanding: spicy and beautifully structured. As well as the estate wines, there is a less expensive range called "Verse 1", first made in 1998.

Cape Mentelle ☆☆☆
Margaret River. Owner: Veuve Clicquot-Ponsardin.
150 hectares. www.capementelle.com.au
One of the great success stories of the Margaret River. David Hohnen, Cape Mentelle's founder and original winemaker, trained in California, and that shows in his drive and dedication. Not content with making one of Margaret River's best Cabernets, Cape Mentelle also pioneered the Semillon/Sauvignon blend in this area, and produce excellent Chardonnay, elegant, spicy Shiraz, and chunky, thoroughly idiosyncratic Zinfandel. Hohnen also established the remarkable Cloudy Bay in New Zealand and, more recently, bought the Mountadam (*q.v.*) property in South Australia. Long-term winemaker John Durham has maintained consistently high quality.

Clairault ☆☆
Willyabrup. Owner: Bill Martin. 230 hectares.
www.clairaultwines.com.au
Clairault's wines are less obviously fruity than some of its neighbours', and include excellent Cabernet Sauvignon and Semillon/Sauvignon, a style increasingly identified as particularly suited to this region.

Cullen ☆☆☆
Cowaramup. Owner: Diana Cullen. 30 hectares.
www.cullenwines.com.au
Cabernet/Merlot made the Cullens' reputation, especially the brilliant reserve, but this organic estate, one of Margaret River's first, is also producing quite excellent and incredibly flavoursome Chardonnay and oak-aged Sauvignon/Semillon, under the shrewd eye of winemaker Vanya Cullen. A recent addition to the range is the delicious, perky "Mangan": an unusual blend of Petit Verdot and Malbec.

Devil's Lair ☆☆☆
Margaret River. Owner: Southcorp Wines. 114 hectares.
www.southcorp.com.au
Phil Sexton set up the enormously successful Matilda Bay Brewing Company in Perth, and applied the same entrepreneurial skills to this winery before selling it in 1997. The dynamically packaged wines are quite excellent, with zesty, citric Chardonnay and generously flavoured, oaky Cabernet leading the way. Despite the acquisition by the vast Southcorp company, quality has remained very high. The second label, "Fifth Leg", offers good value.

Edwards Vineyard ☆☆–☆☆☆
Cowaramup. Owners: the Edwards family. 40 hectares.
www.edwardsvineyard.com.au
This is a fairly new estate that is offering the styles that are becoming Margaret River classics: a citric Semillon/Sauvignon blend, an elegant Shiraz, and a robust, black-fruits Cabernet Sauvignon.

Leeuwin Estate ☆☆–☆☆☆☆
Margaret River. Owners: the Horgan family.
130 hectares. www.leeuwinestate.com.au
Winemakers: Bob Cartwright, Philip Tubb

A substantial modern winery (built with advice from California's Robert Mondavi) in the green hills and woods of the Margaret River – although the ocean is only a jog away. The Chardonnays are sensational, with aromas, liveliness, richness, and grip to out-do anything else in Australia and most in California. Rieslings have varied from excitingly steely to melon-rich. Cabernets are rich but not overripe. After a period of some uncertainty, Leeuwin's star is again shining as bright as ever. The second label, "Prelude", is no shelter for mediocre wines, and can be of high quality.

Moss Wood ☆☆–☆☆☆
Margaret River. Owner/winemaker: Keith Mugford. 18 hectares.
www.mosswood.com.au

The winery that put the Margaret River among Australia's top-quality areas. Moss Wood Cabernet seems to define the style of the region: sweetly clean, faintly grassy, intensely deep, and compact – almost thick, in fact, but without the clumsiness that implies. Definitely for very long ageing. Good, citric Chardonnay and a rather weary Pinot Noir are also produced. The Cabernet, including the separately bottled "Glenmore" Cabernet, is head and shoulders above the other wines.

Pierro ☆☆–☆☆☆
Margaret River. Owner/winemaker: Dr. Michael Peterkin.
18 hectares

Pierro is a high-quality winery producing small quantities of well-received wine, including what has come to be recognized as one of Margaret River's best barrel-fermented Chardonnays. The Sauvignon/Semillon can be herbaceous. The best red wine is the cedary Cabernet/Merlot.

Suckfizzle ☆☆–☆☆☆
Augusta. Owners: John Britton and partners. No vineyards

A venture with a Rabelaisian name, founded in 1997, and run by two leading winemakers: Janice McDonald and Stuart Pym. The range is eclectic, and includes an elegant, oaky Semillon/Sauvignon, a pure, intense Margaret River Cabernet Sauvignon, an assertive and rather bizarre Sangiovese/Cabernet blend, and, of all things, a rose-petal-scented Pink Muscat.

Vasse Felix ☆☆–☆☆☆
Cowaramup. Owners: the Holmes à Court family. 170 hectares.
www.vassefelix.com.au

One of the Margaret River pioneers, and still up there with the best under the stewardship of Clive Otto, who has been making the wines since 1992. The basic and good-value range is called "Classic Dry" White and Red. The Chardonnay, especially the top "Heytesbury" bottling, can be a touch over-oaked. The Cabernet/Merlot is quite a substantial wine, but cannot match the pure Cabernets, with their voluptuous taste of blackberries and slight mintiness.

Voyager ☆☆☆–☆☆☆☆
Margaret River. Owner: Michael Wright. 100 hectares.
www.voyagerestate.com.au

Despite the size of this property, there is no second label here. Any wine that does not please the owner, or the winemaker Cliff Royle, is sold off. Royle makes outstanding Chardonnay that is toasty, but always backed by good acidity. The Shiraz is more Rhône than Barossa in style, and the Cabernet/Merlot is an opulent wine with cassis aromas and a long earthy finish. The top *cuvée* is a barrel-selection called "Tom Price", the white being a Graves-style blend rather than a Chardonnay. These are wines that try too hard to impress, and their sheer power can unbalance them.

Xanadu ☆☆
Margaret River. Owners: the Lagan family. 130 hectares.
www.xanaduwines.com.au

Vastly improved Margaret River winery, (whose name was, not surprisingly, inspired by Coleridge's poem), producing fine Semillon in the whites, and some of the region's finest, earthiest Cabernets. In 1999, the Lagans bought Normans (*q.v.*) in South Australia, and embarked on a programme of expansion. Their basic range is called "Secession", unashamedly fruit-driven in style. Greater complexity is delivered under the "Show Reserve" and "Lagan Estate" labels. Quality is variable, but may improve and stabilize in future.

Pemberton

Picardy ☆☆–☆☆☆
Pemberton. Owners: Bill and Sandra Pannell. 7 hectares.
www.picardy.com.au

The Pannells were the founders of Moss Wood (*q.v.*), and this is their retirement project, the goal being to produce intense, Burgundian-style Chardonnay and Pinot Noir, although their Shiraz can be splendid, too. First releases were in 1997. The finest wines are labelled "Tête de Cuvée", but are only made in minute quantities.

Salitage ☆☆
Pemberton. Owner: John Horgan. 20 hectares.
www.salitage.com.au

What Dennis Horgan has done for Margaret River with the Leeuwin Estate (*q.v.*), brother John hopes to do for the new, cool West Australian region of Pemberton. Winemaker Patrick Coutts produces complex, Burgundian Chardonnay, and some hedonistically rich Pinot Noir from this state-of-the-art winery.

Swan Valley

Paul Conti ☆☆
Woodvale. Owners: the Conti family. 17 hectares

A (stylistically) leading Swan Valley producer, with well-placed vineyards at Marginiup and Yanchep. Elegant Shiraz, and clean, balanced Chardonnay.

Evans & Tate ☆–☆☆
Jindong. Owners: public company. 190 hectares.
www.evansandtate.com.au

The largest estate in Western Australia, and on its way to becoming one of the largest in Australia, since its purchase of

Cranswick in 2002. The basic range is called "Gnangara", and the prestige label is "Redbrook". The wines as a whole are rather dull, though competently made, but the arrival of dynamic young winemaker Virginia Willcock may add more individuality to the wines. Barrel-aged but restrained Semillon is consistently excellent, as is the "Redbrook" Cabernet.

Houghton ☆☆–☆☆☆
Middle Swan. Owner: Constellation-Hardy. 500 hectares.
www.houghton-wines.com.au
The most famous name in Western Australia, the wines at this Swan Valley winery were, for fifty vintages, made by the legendary Jack Mann. Now, as part of the Constellation-Hardy group, and benefiting from newer vineyards in cooler parts of the state such as Margaret River and Pemberton, Houghton's lustre has revived. Winemaker Larry Cherubino, with much experience in Bordeaux, has worked wonders in recent years. "Moondah Brook" is a basic range from Great Southern vineyards; "Crofters" is a range from cool-climate vineyards. In 1999, Houghton introduced regional wines, such as the bright, elegant "Frankland River Shiraz", the lush, concentrated "Margaret River Cabernet", and a milk-chocolatey "Gladstones Shiraz". "Jack Mann", a blend of Cabernet and Malbec, remains the top wine: opaque and damsony.

Sandalford ☆☆
Caversham. Owners: Peter and Debra Prendiville.
182 hectares. www.sandalford.com
This old-established winery on the Swan River now relies almost entirely on fruit from its more southerly vineyards, and is producing some excellent wines. Chardonnay and Verdelho are the best of the whites, and a spicy, elegant Shiraz and tight, earthy Cabernet Sauvignon share the honours as the best of the reds. The cheaper range, called "Elements", provides good value. Sandalera is a splendid, long-aged dessert wine in the Iberian style. After a bad patch in the 1990s, winemaker Paul Boulden, appointed in 2001, has been making good progress in improving quality.

Westfield ☆☆
Baskerville. Owner/winemaker: John Kosovich. 24 hectares.
www.westfieldwines.com.au
A Swan Valley miniature, notable for exceptional Chardonnay, good Cabernet, and Verdelho, and some exciting wines under the "Bronze Wing" label from the vineyard at Pemberton. Kosovich, who made his fiftieth vintage in 2002, also releases fortified wines, such as "Liqueur Verdelho", but they can be coarse.

Other Western Australia Producers

Ferngrove Vineyards ☆
Frankland. www.ferngrove.com.au
Since 1997, Murray Burton has not only planted over 400 hectares of vineyards but has also built a winery and tourist complex. Initial releases were medium-bodied and lively.

Lenton ☆☆–☆☆☆
Brae
A small Margaret River winery, producing stunning Chardonnay and stylish Cabernet and Cabernet/Merlot.

Palandri ☆
Cowaramup. www.palandri.com.au
An ambitious new Margaret River venture, with 350 hectares planted. First releases have been competent but unexciting. But these are early days.

West Cape ☆☆
Howe, Denmark
A good range of varietal wines are made here from the Great Southern vineyards.

Leading Queensland Producer

Ballandean Estate ☆
Ballandean. Owners: Angelo and Mary Puglisi. 18 hectares
Angelo Puglisi is known as the godfather of winemaking in Queensland, and Ballandean Estate, while the first, is still one of the best in the Granite Belt area. The eclectic range includes Shiraz and Merlot, fortified wines, and an unusual sweet white from the rare (in Australia) Silvaner variety.

Leading Tasmania Producers

Domaine A ☆☆
Campania. Owner: Peter Althaus. 11 hectares.
www.domaine-a.com.au
Swiss engineer Peter Althaus is passionate about Bordeaux, and despite an unfavourable climate for Bordeaux varieties, makes an intense, oaky Cabernet by keeping yields extremely low. In complete contrast, he also produces a zesty, unoaked Sauvignon. The second label here is "Stoney Vineyard".

Freycinet ☆☆☆
Tasman Highway, East Coast. Owners: the Bull family.
9 hectares
One of Tasmania's top wineries, producing refreshing Riesling, as well as superb, complex, beetroot-and-spice Pinot Noir.

Heemskerk
See **Piper's Brook**

Stefano Lubiana ☆☆
Granton. Owner: Steve Lubiana. 6 hectares.
www.stefanolubiana.com
From relatively small vineyards, Lubiana makes a wide range of wines, from sparkling, traditional-method brut, to Pinot Noir, Riesling, and Pinot Grigio. All the wines are well-made, yet can lack personality.

Moorilla Estate ☆☆–☆☆☆
Berriedale. Owners: a private partnership. 26 hectares.
www.moorilla.com.au

One of the first bold souls to look for quality in Tasmania back in 1958, and in a cool corner at that. Frost, birds, and underripeness are persistent problems. Riesling does best to give Moselle-like flavours; Gewürztraminer can be as steely as Alsace; Pinot Noir as supple as those from the Côte d'Or. Cabernet Sauvignon and Syrah can be remarkably dense and fruity, given the climatic conditions.

Piper's Brook ☆☆–☆☆☆
Piper's Brook. Owner: Kreglinger. 220 hectares.
www.pipersbrook-vineyard.com.au
The bold enterprise of an eclectic mind in search of ideal conditions: cool but not too cool. Dr. Andrew Pirie stresses that vines work most efficiently where evaporation is not too high – "when the grass stays green".

His hilltop vineyards within sight of the island's north coast (and reach of sea winds) make superb dry Riesling and austere Chardonnay, very characteristic Pinot Noir, Cabernet with lively and intense flavours, and one of Australia's most complex sparkling wines. "Ninth Island" is the second label: wines with less intensity, but no less attractive. In 1998, Piper's Brook bought the well-known Heemskerk estate and the less well-known Rochecombe, but in 2001, was itself acquired by a Belgian company. Dr. Pirie has now departed.

Spring Vale ☆☆
Cranbrook, East Coast. Owners: Rodney and Lyn Lyne.
4 hectares
One of the wineries to confirm the east coast of Tasmania as a great place to grow Pinot Noir. The "Spring Vale Pinot" is round, earthy, and deliciously spicy.

Leading Northern Territory Producer

Château Hornsby ☆
Alice Springs. Owners: Denis and Miranda Hornsby. 3 hectares
Maverick, tourist-oriented winery, with heavily irrigated vines, in the searing heat of the outback. Reds are full and clean-flavoured.

New Zealand

While almost every Australian settler, it seems, planted vines for wine, the new New Zealanders did much less to exploit the temperate climate and fertile soils of their islands. No real wine industry, beyond isolated missions and private estates, existed until Dalmatian Kauri-gum workers and Lebanese immigrants started to provide for their own needs in the Auckland area early in the twentieth century. Their products were crude, from poor vines unsuited to the warm humidity of Auckland. Phylloxera forced them to plant hybrids. Most of the wine was fortified and probably deserved its unflattering title of "Dally plonk". And the small, strait-laced Anglo-Saxon community, frequently muttering about Prohibition, hardly provided an encouraging marketplace. Until 1961, it was illegal to drink wine in restaurants and there were other irksome restrictions on consumption.

Matters began to change quite briskly in the late 1960s, as New Zealanders developed both a tentative export market to Australia and Great Britain – and also a taste for wine themselves. In 1960, almost half of the total 390 hectares of vines was in the Auckland area, and most of the rest in Hawke's Bay on the central east coast of the North Island. The 1960s saw a trebling of the Auckland hectarage and the development of Waikato, sixty-five kilometres (forty miles) south; the Hawke's Bay vineyards doubled in size and an important new area sprung up at Poverty Bay near Gisborne, north of Hawke's Bay.

Results were encouraging, even if the first mass plantings were decidedly unambitious. The market's chief interest was in cheap fortified wines – made all the cheaper by the illegal addition of water. For table wines, Müller-Thurgau was widely considered to be as high a mark as New Zealand could profitably reach. Early planters mistakenly took German advice that their climate was closer to that of Germany than of France.

Experiments with Sauvignon Blanc and then with Chardonnay in the 1970s proved, however, that the climate of the main fruit-growing region, the east coast of North Island, was not so much German as central French. These east-coast areas flourished in the 1970s, quintupling their vineyards, while Auckland's actually shrank slightly. But the 1970s also saw the vine move to the South Island of New Zealand: by 1980, Marlborough had nearly 800 hectares, and trial planting had moved as far south as Canterbury and Central Otago.

New Zealand's true potential as a producer of fine wine burst upon the world in the mid-1980s: to be precise, in February 1985, when British wine critics, buyers, and journalists attended a tasting (now an annual event) held at New Zealand House in London. Those present are unlikely to forget the excitement of that morning, as it became apparent that a dozen different wineries had produced a number of white wines of a racy vitality and tingling fruitiness that are only met with on rare occasions elsewhere in the world.

The best Sauvignon Blancs were the most memorable, giving an extra dimension to this essentially second-league

variety. It was unanimous: New Zealand had jumped into the first division of the world's white wine producers.

Subsequent tastings confirmed the fact, adding Chardonnays of extremely sound quality, a few Rieslings, Chenin Blancs, and Gewürztraminers of fine quality by any standards, and some promising red wines. Any shortcomings in the early quality of the reds were more due to inexperience than to the quality of the grapes. Significant developments, especially with Pinot Noir, which benefits from the cool climate from Martinborough southwards, and advances in vinification techniques, have proved their worth. Cabernet Sauvignon/Merlot blends, especially from Hawke's Bay, have also improved, again with better vinification techniques, better viticulture, and site selection. In general, there has been a considerable widening of the range of grape varieties planted. Several wineries now produce Syrah, and Zinfandel is out of quarantine. There is Viognier and great interest in Pinot Gris, Sangiovese, and other varieties.

An enormous growth in vineyards has been witnessed. Existing wineries have planted new vineyards and there has been a large increase in the number of winemaking facilities. New viticultural areas are being considered, with isolated wineries appearing in unexpected places. Such expansion also brings danger as some outlying valleys in Marlborough and Hawke's Bay are proving awkwardly susceptible to frost.

By the late 1990s, the best winemakers had learned to temper the sometimes over-herbaceous or vegetal character of their wines, especially in the Cabernets and Merlots. It had also become apparent that the star turn, among red wines, was going to be Pinot Noir, especially from Martinborough and Central Otago. (By 2003, there were over 2,000 hectares planted). For the present, however, it is still with white wines that New Zealand conquers. If international taste should begin to tire of the powerfully flavoured Marlborough Sauvignons, there is no shortage of superb Rieslings.

New Zealand's natural gift is what the winemakers of Australia and California are striving for: the conditions that give slowly ripened, highly aromatic fruit. The wines are developing the strength, structure, and delicacy of those from (for example) the Loire, Alsace, possibly the Médoc, possibly Champagne – with a freshness and vigour that are New Zealand's own.

The potential for sparkling wines has been nurtured, using classic methods and nearly always with Pinot Noir and Chardonnay grapes. Restrictive EU legislation has forbidden the importation of New Zealand's sweet and botrytis wines, but visitors to the country can attest to the splendid quality of its best botrytis Rieslings and Semillons.

North Island Wine Regions

Auckland

464 hectares. Until the 1970s this was New Zealand's largest grape-growing region, but its almost subtropical climate, with considerable cloud cover and frequent autumn rain, was never suited to the vine. It is now eclipsed as a wine region

(both in terms of quantity and quality) by Gisborne, Hawke's Bay, and Marlborough to the south. Urban sprawl has turned vineyards into shopping malls, but many important wine companies are still based here. *See also*: Waiheke Island.

Wineries include: Babich, Collard Brothers, Coopers Creek, Delegat's, Kumeu River, Lincoln Vineyards, Matua Valley, Montana, Nobilo, Selak's, Soljans, Villa Maria, and West Brook.

Gisborne

1,800 hectares. This sunny and fertile area on the east coast of the North Island is well-suited to white grape varieties, notably Chardonnay, although it suffers from autumn rains which force the harvest forward, and from active phylloxera, which has resulted in almost total replanting. Wineries are few, as most grapes are sent for blending to the major producers in Auckland.

Wineries include: Matawhero, Millton, and Montana.

Hawke's Bay

3,600 hectares. One of the top-quality regions, situated on the east coast south of Gisborne, and in the rain shadow of the island's volcanic mountain centre. Its sunshine and its glorious mixture of soils – silt, shingle, and clay – provide enormous potential for red and white grapes and the number of wineries is growing. Together with Waiheke Island, this is one of the few spots where Bordeaux varieties usually ripen fully. Growers are now identifying the best sub-regions, such as Gimblett Gravels and the Ngatarawa Triangle.

Wineries include: Brookfields, Craggy Range, Kim Crawford, Esk Valley, Kemblefield, Matariki, Mission, Montana Church Road, Ngatarawa, C. J. Pask, Sacred Hill, Sileni, Te Mata, Trinity Hill, and Vidal.

Northland

This rainy, humid region in the extreme north of the island was the site of New Zealand's first vineyard in 1819, but it is ill-suited to grape-growing. A growing number of wineries are trying to prove its suitability, however, especially in the Matakana Valley. Now, there are also a couple of isolated wineries even further north; Longview at Whangarei, and Okahu Estate at Kaitaia.

Wineries include: The Antipodean, Ascension, Heron's Flight, and Ransom.

Waikato Bay of Plenty

136 hectares. A small, rainy region, spreading eastwards from Waikato, about seventy-two kilometres (forty-five miles) south of Auckland, to the Bay of Plenty. Most of the larger wineries, such as Morton Estate, source their grapes from Hawke's Bay, Gisborne, or elsewhere in New Zealand.

Wineries include: Firstland, Morton, and Rongopai.

Wairarapa

600 hectares. This is the region at the southern end of the North Island, just north of Wellington, with the small town of Martinborough at its centre. Wairarapa's combination of good soil, low rainfall, and autumn sunshine first prompted the

planting of vineyards in 1978. Four wineries had their first vintage in 1984 and three of them, Martinborough Vineyards, Dry River, and Ata Rangi, have since established a firm reputation for Pinot Noir from low-yielding vines.

Since 2000 there have been substantial plantings in Te Muna, a few miles from Martinborough. Sauvignon and Chardonnay are good, too, but the record with red Bordeaux varieties and Syrah is more patchy.

Wineries include: Alana, Ata Rangi, Dry River, Escarpment, Gladstone, Martinborough Vineyards, Palliser, and Te Kairanga.

Waiheke Island

A small island in the Hauraki Gulf with a far drier climate than Auckland (thirty per cent less rainfall) and better soil (lighter and freer-draining). Vines were first planted by the Goldwaters in 1978, then by Stephen White at Stonyridge. Others followed suit, mainly planting Bordeaux varieties.

Wineries include: Goldwater Estate, Mudbrick, and Stonyridge.

Canterbury

520 hectares. One of several newer wine regions in the South Island, around Christchurch on the mid-east coast. Its coldish climate and low rainfall lured an increasing number of small wineries into the area during the 1980s, and resulted in some impressive Riesling and Pinot Noir. The plains around Christchurch, however, tend to be very prone to frost, which causes problems. There is, though, considerable potential in Waipara, north of Christchurch, where the climate is distinctly warmer and the soil limestone-based, proving suitable for Pinot Noir and Chardonnay, and resulting in a growing number of wineries and vineyards.

Wineries include: Giesen, Kaituna Valley, St Helena, and Waipara Springs.

South Island Wine Regions

Central Otago

570 hectares. The southernmost vineyards in the world on the forty-fifth parallel, with dramatic scenery in the Gibbston Valley, close to Queenstown; other vineyards overlook the shores of Lake Wanaka and cower beneath schist outcrops around the town of Alexandra. Otago is currently the fastest-growing vineyard area in New Zealand, especially around Cromwell.

The climate in this region is more continental than the other regions, and vintages can vary quite considerably. This is proving an outstanding region for rich, savoury Pinot Noir, and good Chardonnays and Rieslings are made here, too.

Wineries include: Akarua, Black Ridge, Chard Farm, Felton Road, Gibbston Valley, Mount Difficulty, Mount Edward, Peregrine, Quartz Reef, Rippon, and Waitiri Creek.

Marlborough/Blenheim

6,400 hectares. Sunny, stony-soiled Marlborough, the region around the town of Blenheim at the northeastern tip of the South Island, has proved the making of New Zealand's wine industry. Since it was pioneered by Montana in 1973, it has produced some of the world's best Sauvignon Blanc, and is easily the country's largest grape-growing region.

Marlborough's excellent soil, low rainfall (irrigation is essential here, at least for young vines) and cool autumns, combined with its position in New Zealand's sunniest corner, make it ideal for growing well-flavoured fruit, especially for white wines: Sauvignon Blanc, Chardonnay, and Riesling have all proved successful, and there is some delicious Pinot Noir. Wind, and in some valleys, frost, are the only serious problems for Marlborough growers.

Wineries include: Cellier Le Brun, Cloudy Bay, Forrest, Framingham, Fromm, Highfield, Huia, Hunter's, Isabel, Jackson Estate, Montana, Mount Riley, Mud House, Nautilus, Saint Clair, Allan Scott, Seresin, Vavasour, Wairau River, and Wither Hills.

Nelson

425 hectares. Small, somewhat inaccessible region to the west of Marlborough, which shares some of that region's beneficial conditions, but suffers from autumn rainfall. The vineyards are mostly undulating, and most of the growing number of wineries are boutique, rather than large concerns. The quality of the wines is excellent.

Wineries include: Greenhough, Neudorf, Seifried Estate, and Te Mania.

Leading New Zealand Producers

Ata Rangi ☆☆☆
Martinborough. Owners: Clive and Alison Paton, and Oliver Masters. 20 hectares. www.atarangi.co.nz
Outstanding Pinot Noir from Martinborough, with a silky texture, complexity, and intensity. They produce Chardonnay from Hawke's Bay as well as Martinborough, and "Celebre", a Cabernet/Merlot/Syrah blend in varying proportions, depending on the vintage. A peppery Syrah, launched in 2001, shows promise.

Babich ☆☆–☆☆☆
Henderson, Auckland. Owners: the Babich family. 240 hectares. www.babichwines.co.nz
A large, old Auckland family winery, highly respected for consistent quality and value. The Babich reputation is largely based on Chardonnay, notably the Irongate Vineyard.

There is also an Irongate Cabernet/Merlot blend, and two wines in the flagship "Patriarch" range: Cabernet Sauvignon and Chardonnay. Less-usual varieties, such as Syrah and Pinotage, are bottled under the "Winemaker's Reserve" label.

Cellier Le Brun ☆☆–☆☆☆
Renwick, Marlborough. Owner: Tony Nightingale. 26 hectares. www.lebrun.co.nz

Daniel Le Brun's family were Champagne-makers in Epernay and brought *méthode traditionnelle* to the Marlborough region. There is a non-vintage brut, a vintage, blanc de blancs vintage, and a rosé – all from riper fruit than the French versions. The range of still wines, "Terrace Road", is varied and attractively priced.

Chard Farm ☆☆–☆☆☆
Gibbston, Queenstown. Owners: Rob and Greg Hay.
27 hectares. www.chardfarm.co.nz
Named after the Chard family who came out from the eponymous Somerset village. Riesling and Pinot Noir are the specialties here, the former limey and zesty, the latter very perfumed and supple.

Cloudy Bay ☆☆☆
Blenheim, Marlborough. Owner: Veuve Clicquot Ponsardin and David Hohnen. 150 hectares. www.cloudybay.co.nz
Founded in 1985 by the Australian David Hohnen, whose Western Australian winery Cape Mentelle had already received great acclaim, Cloudy Bay rapidly became the spearhead of New Zealand's assault on the international wine market in the late 1980s. Its pungent, nettle-sharp Sauvignon Blanc, made from vines grown in Marlborough's stony soil and near-ideal climate for white wines, has been one of the benchmarks for the finest expression of this grape's varietal character to be found anywhere, and sells out all around the world within weeks of its release – it includes some Semillon and a small amount of oak. Winemakers Kevin Judd and James Healy have gradually introduced a barrel-fermented Sauvignon ("Te Koko"), an excellent, oaky Chardonnay, Pinot Noir, and lush Gewürztraminer. Other successful extensions to the range include "Pelorus" classic-method sparkling wine, and first-rate "Late Harvest Riesling".

Coopers Creek ☆☆
Huapai, Auckland. Owners: Andrew and Cynthia Hendry.
40 hectares. www.cooperscreek.co.nz
Successful, small winery with high-quality varietals and popular blends. Well-known for Chardonnay, Coopers Creek also produces substantial red blends from Hawke's Bay.

Craggy Range ☆☆☆
Havelock North, Hawke's Bay. Owner: Terry Peabody.
165 hectares. www.craggyrange.co.nz
The shrewd investment of Brisbane businessman Peabody and the viticultural and winemaking skills of Steve Smith MW have fused to launch a lavish new winery, with extremely impressive releases right from the outset. Numerous bottlings of Sauvignon, Chardonnay, Riesling, and Merlot reflect different vineyard sites, in Te Menu near Martinborough as well as Hawke's Bay. Initial releases of Syrah and Cabernet Sauvignon in 2001 showed remarkable concentration and focus. Early days, but the "Prestige" range is likely to ascend rapidly into the top ranks of New Zealand wines.

Delegat's ☆☆–☆☆☆
Henderson, Auckland. Owners: Jim and Rosemari Delegat.
1,200 hectares. www.delegats.co.nz
Streamlining of production in the mid-1980s and good winemaking skills (from Brent Marris and now from Michael Ivicevich) led to a significant improvement. This is a family winery, and the only brother-and-sister team in New Zealand. The best wines are the reserves from Hawke's Bay, and the Marlborough wines, which are sold under the "Oyster Bay" label.

Dry River ☆☆☆–☆☆☆☆
Martinborough. Owner/winemaker: Neil McCallum.
18 hectares.
Small estate with finely crafted and magisterial wines. Complex Pinot Noir, made by blending different techniques and barrels, lush Pinot Gris, and lovely Riesling and Gewürztraminer. These are among the most sought-after wines in New Zealand, and this acute demand is reflected in the wines' very high prices.

Esk Valley ☆☆–☆☆☆☆
Napier, Hawke's Bay. Owner: Villa Maria (*q.v.*). shares vineyards with Villa Mariz. www.eskvalley.co.nz
Formerly a large family firm, Esk Valley produces some of the country's best reds under winemaker Gordon Russell. All the wines are made from Hawke's Bay fruit. It offers a wide range of wines, the basic range being "Black Label"; the superior bottlings being the "Reserves"; and the remarkable "The Terraces": a scarce red Bordeaux blend produced only in outstanding vintages.

Felton Road ☆☆☆
Bannockburn, Central Otago. Owner: Nigel Greening.
30 hectares. www.feltonroad.com
Although Felton Road bottlings are among the most sought-after wines in New Zealand, the first releases were as recent as 1997. Blair Walter has been the winemaker from the outset. He produces two Rieslings (one dry, the other less so); two Chardonnays (unoaked and barrique-fermented); and a range of superb Pinot Noirs made in a non-interventionist style. The most sought-after Pinots are the acclaimed "Block 3" and "Block 5" bottlings, but the regular wine is almost as good at a fraction of the price. The "Cornish Road" label is used for wines from that particular vineyard near Cromwell.

Fromm ☆☆–☆☆☆
Blenheim, Marlborough. Owner: Georg Fromm and family.
21 hectares. www.frommwineries.com
Unusually for a Marlborough winery, Fromm has specialized in Pinot Noir since 1992, and the "Clayvin Vineyard" bottling can be outstanding. The wines are supple and elegant and also age well. The Chardonnay reserve, however, shows heavy-handed oak influence, but the Riesling is plump and vigorous.

Gibbston Valley ☆☆☆
Gibbston, Queenstown. Owner: Mike Stone. 60 hectares.
www.gvwines.co.nz
Alan Brady, originally from Ulster, pioneered grape-growing in Central Otago in 1981, but sold this successful winery in 1997 to set up his own handcrafted operation at Mount Edwards (*q.v.*). Under winemaker Grant Taylor, Riesling can be delicious and Chardonnay impressive, but Pinot Noir is the best wine, especially the Burgundian-style reserve, which is aged in new oak.

Giesen ☆☆
Christchurch. Owners: Marcel, Alex, and Theo Giesen.
435 hectares. www.giesen.co.nz

The Giesen brothers came originally from the Palatinate, where their father had just one hectare of vines as a hobby – they now have the largest winery in Canterbury, although most of their vineyards are in Marlborough. They make stylish, dry Riesling, which develops with bottle-age, and in the right years, some lovely late-harvest wines.

They have a fine track record with Chardonnay, and are also working hard on their Pinot Noir. The first sparkling wine was released in 1995: a Pinot Noir and Chardonnay blend.

Goldwater Estate ☆☆

Waiheke Island. Owners: Kim and Jeanette Goldwater. 10 hectares. www.goldwaterwine.com

The Goldwaters planted the first vines on Waiheke back in 1978, on an island vineyard which benefits from a warm, dry microclimate. They concentrate on fragrant, delicate Bordeaux blends, and on Sauvignon and Chardonnay. The Sauvignon, and some of the Chardonnay, comes from Marlborough.

Grove Mill ☆–☆☆☆

Renwick, Marlborough. Owners: local investors. 85 hectares. www.grovemill.co.nz

From small beginnings, Grove Mill has grown to be a substantial operation, with a brand-new winery. The Pinot Noir can be dour, but both the Sauvignon and the reserve Riesling are exemplary. Cheaper, attractively priced ranges are bottled under the "Sanctuary" and "Frog Haven" labels.

Huia ☆☆–☆☆☆

Renwick, Marlborough. Owners: Claire and Mike Allan. 20 hectares. www.huia.net.nz

Founded in 1996, Huia is a quality-conscious estate, using an unusually high proportion of natural-yeast fermentation. All the wines are beautifully crafted and impeccably balanced. A very dependable source of Sauvignon Blanc and Pinot Noir.

Hunter's ☆☆–☆☆☆

Blenheim. Owner: Jane Hunter. 37 hectares. www.hunters.co.nz

After the death of pioneering Ernie Hunter in 1987, his widow Jane Hunter has maintained this family winery as one of the South Island's best. The varietal range includes good barrel-fermented Chardonnay and ripe and fruity Sauvignon Blanc, as well as Riesling and oaky Pinot Noir. The excellent "Miru Miru" sparkling wine is produced exclusively for export.

Isabel Estate ☆☆☆

Renwick, Marlborough. Owners: Michael and Robyn Tiller. 54 hectares. www.isabelestate.com

The Isabel vineyards are planted at an unusually high density – far higher than that commonly encountered in New Zealand. Michael Tiller, who also makes the wines, uses indigenous yeasts whenever possible. The resulting wines are zesty and concentrated, the stars being the Chardonnay, and the spicy, complex Pinot Noir.

Jackson Estate ☆☆–☆☆☆

Blenheim. Owners: John and Warwick Stichbury. 100 hectares. www.jacksonestate.co.nz

Jackson is best-known for its pungent Sauvignon Blanc, citric, spicy Chardonnay, and graceful Riesling, both in dry and botrytized styles. In the late 1990s, the Stichburys planted new clones of Pinot Noir, which are now producing refined and charming wines.

Kumeu River ☆☆☆

Kumeu, Auckland. Owners: the Brajkovich family. 25 hectares. www.kumeuriver.co.nz

Kumeu River specializes in serious Chardonnay, with the Maté Vineyard given the full Burgundian treatment. Winemaker Michael Brajkovich MW is also skilled with lesser varieties such as Pinot Gris and Pinot Blanc, and there are some stylish Bordeaux blends such as "Melba" from Merlot and Malbec. Michael is a fervent exponent of the Auckland area for grape-growing, despite controversy. "Brajkovich" is the second label.

Martinborough Vineyards ☆☆☆

Martinborough. Owners: Duncan and Derek Milne. 22 hectares. www.martinborough-vineyard.co.nz

One of Martinborough's founding wineries. Winemaker Larry McKenna spent time in Burgundy and produced elegant, Burgundian-style wines with intensity and delicacy. After his departure to set up his own winery, Escarpment (q.v.), his place was taken by Claire Mulholland. The winery's reputation for Pinot Noir means that its excellent Chardonnay, Riesling, and rich, barrel-fermented Pinot Gris are sometimes overlooked.

Matariki ☆☆☆

Hastings, Hawke's Bay. Owner: John O'Connor. 55 hectares. www.matarikiwines.co.nz

Matariki is located in the heart of the Gimblett Gravels region, where O'Connor has most of his vines. Until 1997, he produced bulk wines, and since then has overseen a rapidly improving range of rich and full-flavoured varietals. The zesty Chardonnay is sometimes preferable to the hefty, oaky reserve, but reserve bottlings of Merlot and Syrah are excellent, and a new Sangiovese shows promise. The house specialty is the Bordeaux blend, "Quintology": concentrated and vibrant. "Stony Bay" is the second label: delicious Chardonnay.

Matua Valley ☆–☆☆☆

Auckland. Owner: Beringer Blass. 148 ha. www.matua.co.nz

California-style winery just north of Auckland, founded in 1974 by Ross and Bill Spence. It was Ross who isolated and propagated the single clone of Sauvignon, which has been planted in New Zealand for the past twenty years. "Ararimu" is the top label for Chardonnay and Cabernet Sauvignon, and there are some excellent wines under the "Matheson" label from Hawke's Bay. Marlborough wines are sold under the "Shingle Peak" label. With the sale to Beringer Blass in 2001, the future direction remains uncertain, although the Spences remain as directors.

Millton ☆☆–☆☆☆

Gisborne. Owners: James and Annie Millton. 20 hectares. www.millton.co.nz

It takes a brave person indeed to establish a biodynamic estate in Gisborne, but James Millton has studied the approach thoroughly and has no doubts about its effectiveness. He produces an interesting range of styles, which includes a fresh Viognier, luscious, oaked Chenin, and fine, botrytized Riesling.

Mission ☆☆

Taradale, Hawke's Bay. Owner: the Catholic Society of Mary. 50 hectares. www.missionestate.co.nz

Founded in 1851, this is the oldest winery in Hawke's Bay, located in a beautiful spot at the foot of grassy hills. The reserve range is very reliable, and the top range appears under the "Jewelstone" label: Chardonnay, Cabernet/Merlot, a youthful Syrah, and Noble Riesling.

Montana Wines ☆–☆☆☆

Auckland. Owner: Allied Domecq. 2,900 hectares. www.montanawines.com

For many years New Zealand's biggest wine company, it has recently grown even larger by acquiring Cooks and Corbans. Today, Montana is responsible for almost sixty per cent of all New Zealand wine production. It played a major role in the 1970s, when it pioneered the new Marlborough region, where there is a showcase winery. There are other wineries at Auckland, Gisborne, and Hawke's Bay. The Marlborough wines include a very dry Sauvignon Blanc, slightly spicy Riesling, and an excellent Chardonnay. Montana's Church Road Estate in Hawke's Bay focuses on Chardonnay and red varieties, especially Bordeaux blends. Montana has for some years had a joint venture with Champagne Deutz to produce "Deutz Cuvée Marlborough", which is at a higher level than their well-known "Lindauer" sparkling wine. Wines appear under the guise of numerous brands, the best-known being "Brancott", "Church Road", "Longridge", and "Stoneleigh". Given the immense scale of the operation, quality can be surprisingly high.

Morton Estate ☆–☆☆☆

Katikati, Bay of Plenty. Owner: John Coney. 420 hectares. www.mortonestatewines.co.nz

This winery (its façade in an attractive Cape Dutch style) benefited in the 1990s from the talents of John Hancock, one of the country's best winemakers (now running Trinity Hill [*q.v.*]). Morton's reputation stands on Chardonnay, with the "Black Label" and (since 1998) "Conchiglie" bottlings the top of the range, followed by "Reserves" and the "White Label".

Mount Difficulty ☆☆–☆☆☆

Bannockburn, Central Otago. Owners: four vineyard owners. 40 hectares. www.mtdifficulty.co.nz

Since the first vintage in 1998, Matt Dicey has turned out some delicious wines from Chardonnay and Pinot Noir: both big wines with a lot of swagger and style.

Mudbrick ☆☆–☆☆☆

Waiheke Island. Owner: Nick Jones. 10 hectares. www.mudbrick.co.nz

Many of the grapes are bought from Marlborough, but the reds come mostly from estate vineyards on the island. The Syrah is intense and peppery, and the "Shepherds Point" Cabernet/Merlot is supple, oaky, and concentrated.

Neudorf ☆☆–☆☆☆

Upper Moutere, Nelson. Owners: Tim and Judy Finn. 23 hectares. www.neudorf.co.nz

One of Nelson's leading wineries, owned by a friendly husband-and-wife team. A 100-old clapboard building houses the winery. The new-oaked Chardonnay is often the best wine, showing considerable complexity. The Riesling and Sauvignon are good, too, and the Pinot Noir improving all the time.

Ngatarawa ☆–☆☆☆

Hastings, Hawke's Bay. Owners: Alwyn and Brian Corban. 23 hectares. www.ngatarawa.co.nz

The Corbans have been making wine in New Zealand for over a century, although the winery that bears their name now belongs to Montana. Ngatarawa is housed in an attractive winery building, around old racing stables. Top of the range is the "Alwyn Reserve": a high-priced wine made only in top vintages. Also of high quality is the "Glazebrook" label, which includes a Merlot/Cabernet blend, Chardonnay, and a botrytis Riesling. The "Stables" range is more accessible in style.

Nobilo ☆☆

Kumeu, Auckland. Owners: Constellation-Hardy. 670 hectares. www.nobilo.co.nz

The Nobilos originally came from Dalmatia, and worked hard on the red varieties that ripen well in the warm, damp Auckland climate. Since its takeover by Australian wine giant BRL Hardy, Nobilo has grown to become New Zealand's third-largest wine company. The range is very broad, and so is quality. Some of the best wines come from Nobilo's sister winery, Drylands, in Marlborough.

C. J. Pask ☆☆–☆☆☆

Hastings, Hawke's Bay. Owner: Chris Pask, John Benton, and Kate Radburnd (also winemaker). 90 hectares. www.cjpaskwinery.co.nz

Chris Pask, pilot-turned-viticulturist, was the first person to plant on what is now the highly rated Gimblett Road area – with silt over shingle in old river bed vineyards. He concentrates on Bordeaux varieties, plus Chardonnay, Merlot, and Syrah. The flagship wine is "Declaration", a concentrated, peppery blend of Cabernet Sauvignon and Malbec. The reserve wines are rich and powerful, and are aged in new oak.

Pegasus Bay ☆☆–☆☆☆

Amberley, Waipara. Owners: Ivan and Christine Donaldson. 30 hectares. www.pegasusbay.com

Winemakers Matt Donaldson and Lynette Hudson have worked wonders for this Waipara winery. Their white wines, even the Sauvignon Blanc, are unusually lush and creamy, and there are exceptional late-harvest wines both from Riesling and Chardonnay. Perhaps their best-known wine is the top Pinot Noir called "Prima Donna". Wines made from fruit not grown in Waipara are bottled under the "Main Divide" label.

Rippon ☆☆☆

Wanaka. Owner: Lois Mills. 15 hectares. www.rippon.co.nz

Rolfe Mills planted the first vines in the region (apart from the nineteenth century settlers) in 1976, choosing an exquisite site on the shores of Lake Wanaka. The best wines here are Pinot Noir and Riesling. Young Pinot vines are bottled under the "Jeunesse" label; the top Pinot Noir is delicate yet long-lived. The same is true of the powerfully dry Riesling. In 1999, Rippon produced an astonishing TBA-style Riesling called "La Nina" – sadly, a one-off. After the death of Rolfe Mills, his son Nick, who honed his winemaking skills at Burgundy's top estates, returned in 2002 to take control.

Sacred Hill ☆☆☆
Napier, Hawke's Bay. Owners: the Mason family. 145 hectares. www.sacredhill.com
From a range of vineyards in Hawke's Bay and Marlborough (having bought the former Cairnbrae estate there), winemaker Tony Bish makes a variety of impressive wines. The basic range is called "Whitecliff". These are sound and good value, but it's the "Special Selection" that attracts attention. These include the very stylish "Sauvage" Sauvignon (barrique-fermented with indigenous yeasts); the toasty, peachy "Rifleman's" Chardonnay; the powerful but harmonious Bordeaux blend called "Helmsman's"; and the smoky, opulent "Broken Stone" Merlot.

Saint Clair ☆☆–☆☆☆
Blenheim, Marlborough. Owner: Neal Ibbotson. 55 hectares. www.saintclair.co.nz
This ambitious winery produces three tiers of wine: basic Marlborough bottlings, single-vineyard wines, and reserves. The single-vineyard wines show clearly the differing character of the increasingly dispersed Marlborough vineyards. All the wines are well-made (since 1996 by Matt Thomson) and the best include the "Fairhall" Riesling, the "Wairau Reserve" Sauvignon, the "Omaka Reserve" Chardonnay and Pinot Noir.

Allan Scott ☆☆–☆☆☆
Blenheim, Marlborough. Owner: Allan Scott. 60 hectares. www.allanscott.com
Scott is an experienced viticulturist who set up his own winery in 1990. It has grown to become one of the largest privately owned estates in the region. The wines are consistently well-made and stylish: exemplary expressions of Marlborough fruit with its refreshing acidity.

Seifried Estate ☆☆
Appleby, Nelson. Owners: Hermann and Agnes Seifried. 150 hectares. www.seifried.co.nz
A fast-growing and ambitious enterprise; the Seifrieds have built a new winery, not to mention restaurant and conference centre. The Seifrieds' son, Chris, is now responsible for the winemaking. Basic wines are sold under the "Old Coach Road" label, while the best wines appear under the "Winemaker's Collection" label. Some good dry and late-harvest Riesling; also good Chardonnay and Pinot Noir. A new vineyard has been planted on exceptionally stony soil at Brightwater, which, it's hoped, will eventually deliver red wines of exceptional quality.

Seresin ☆☆☆
Blenheim, Marlborough. Owners: Michael Seresin and Brian Bicknell. 98 hectares. www.seresin.co.nz
Seresin is a film maker based in London, Bicknell a winemaker. Both share the same vision: an organic estate (moving towards biodynamism) and a reliance, whenever possible, on indigenous yeasts.

The white wines are delicious: racy Riesling and Sauvignon, elegant, dry Pinot Gris, and Chardonnay in unoaked and oaked styles. The sparkling wine, "Moana", spends three years on the yeasts. The Pinot Noir is rich but lacks finesse. The commitment to quality at Seresin is commendably rigorous.

Stonyridge ☆☆☆
Waiheke Island. Owner/winemaker: Stephen White. 5 hectares. www.stonyridge.co.nz
Stonyridge focuses on Bordeaux varieties, and its finest wine is the excellent and high-priced Cabernet blend called "Larose". The second label is "Airfield". Serious, perfectionist winemaking can be found here, with intense attention to detail and passionate commitment to quality.

Te Kairanga ☆☆–☆☆☆
Martinborough. Owner: numerous shareholders. 30 hectares. www.tkwine.co.nz
As well as the range of varietals and Reserves, the rapidly expanding Te Kairanga makes inexpensive wines under the "Castlepoint" label. Te Kairanga established its reputation under Australian winemaker Chris Buring, who has been replaced by Peter Caldwell. Quality here is impressive, especially for Pinot Noir and Syrah.

Te Mata ☆☆☆
Havelock North, Hawke's Bay. Owners: John Buck, Michael Morris, and partners. 156 hectares. www.temata.hb.co.nz
One of the oldest wineries in New Zealand, recently restored and renowned for its "Coleraine", one of the country's best Cabernet/Merlot blends. (The restorations have resulted in an attractive winery complex, with a barrel cellar that would not be out of place in the Médoc). Winemaker Peter Cowley aims to make long-lived wines with plenty of acid backbone. The whole range is reliable, but the best bottles tend to be the "Castle Hill" Sauvignon, "Coleraine" Cabernet/Merlot, the lighter but more accessible "Awatea" Cabernet/Merlot, and "Elston" Chardonnay. "Bullnose" Syrah is a more recent introduction. Since 1996, other wines have been emerging from Te Mata's expanding new estate, also in Hawke's Bay, called Woodthorpe Terraces.

Trinity Hill ☆☆–☆☆☆
Hastings, Hawke's Bay. Owners: John Hancock and partners. 60 hectares. www.trinityhillwines.com
John Hancock built his reputation as the winemaker for Morton Estate (*q.v.*) before setting up his own winery in 1996. Most of the best wines come from vineyards in the Gimblett Road area, and Hancock has a fondness for obscure (by New Zealand standards) varieties, such as Montepulciano and Tempranillo. "Trinity" is a decent blend of Merlot, Cabernet Franc, and Syrah, but the outstanding wines are usually the Syrah and the Cabernet/Merlot blend. The best wines sport a black label.

Vavasour ☆☆–☆☆☆
Awatere Valley, Marlborough. Owners: numerous shareholders, including Peter Vavasour. 30 hectares. www.vavasour.com
Vavasour is unusual in setting up shop in the Awatere Valley (south of Blenheim and running parallel to the Wairau Valley). Other Marlborough wineries have now planted vines there. The emphasis is on Sauvignon and Chardonnay – and successfully, too, and they have also turned their attention to Pinot Noir. The second label is "Dashwood". The hallmark here is elegance rather than power.

Vidal ☆☆–☆☆☆

Hastings, Hawke's Bay. Owner: Villa Maria (*q.v.*). 78 hectares. www.vidal.co.nz

One of the oldest wineries in Hawke's Bay, dating from 1905, Vidal is now part of the Villa Maria group, offering aromatic Gewürztraminer, restrained Chardonnay, promising Pinot Noir, and a Cabernet with sweet and lively flavours. It has established a serious reputation for its red wine, especially the reserves, and have recently developed an organic vineyard on the Gimblett Gravels with grapes destined for the reserve label. since 1994, Vidal has produced a series of sumptuous botrytis Semillons.

Villa Maria ☆☆☆

Auckland. Owner: George Fistonich. 1,150 hectares. www.villamaria.co.nz

Villa Maria is New Zealand's largest privately owned winery. In decreasing order of quality and volume, the ranges here are "Reserve", then "Cellar Selection", and then "Private Bin". Gisborne, Hawke's Bay (for good reds), and Marlborough are the main grape sources. Given the large volumes, quality is astonishingly high, especially at "Cellar Selection" and "Reserve" levels, and the wines are sensibly priced. Sauvignon Blanc, Riesling, Chardonnay, Pinot Noir, and botrytis Riesling are often outstanding. A new winery and visitors' centre is set to open near Auckland airport in 2004.

Wairau River ☆☆–☆☆☆

Blenheim. Owners: Chris and Phil Rose. 120 hectares. www.wairauriverwines.com

Phil Rose is a farmer-turned-grape-grower, initially for Montana. For many years John Belsham has been the winemaker, focusing on ultra-typical Marlborough Sauvignon and Chardonnay, and is adding Riesling, Pinot Noir, and Pinot Gris to the range. The reserve Sauvignon is barrel-fermented and one of the more successful examples.

Wither Hills ☆☆☆

Blenheim, Marlborough. Owner: Lion Nathan. 150 hectares. www.witherhills.co.nz

Brent Marris couldn't keep the smile off his face in 2002. And no wonder, since the brewery group Lion Nathan had just paid an enormous sum for the estate he and his father, John Marris, had developed in only eight years. Nobody begrudged the Marrises their good fortune, as they had built up one of New Zealand's top estates with skill and hard work, especially in the vineyard. The formula was simple: varietal wines (Sauvignon, Chardonnay, Pinot Noir) of exemplary purity and balance.

Other New Zealand Producers

Akarua ☆–☆☆

Bannockburn, Central Otago. Owner: Sir Clifford Skeggs. 50 hectares. www.akarua.com

A recently established estate that is concentrating on Pinot Noir and Chardonnay. The quality is sound and set to improve as the vines age.

Alana ☆☆

Martinborough. Owner: Ian Smart. 20 hectares. www.alana.co.nz

Smart's first vintage was 1997. The whites, both Sauvignon and Chardonnay, are fresh and mouthwatering, and the Pinot Noir, while light, has great charm.

Alpha Domus ☆☆

Hastings, Hawke's Bay. Owners: the Ham family. 30 hectares. www.alphadomus.co.nz

Serious if extracted reds from Hawke's Bay: Bordeaux blends under the "Aviator" and "Navigator" labels.

Black Ridge ☆☆

Alexandra, Central Otago. Owners: Sue Edwards and Verdun Burgess. 7 hectares

Burgess was a pioneer in an extremely tough region of schist cliffs and thin soils. He has focused on firm, dry, and age-worthy Rieslings, fresh Chardonnay, and somewhat earthy Pinot Noir.

Brookfields ☆☆

Taradale, Hawke's Bay. Owner: Peter Robertson. 24 hectares. www.brookfieldsvineyards.co.nz

The emphasis is on reds that will age in bottle: a pure Cabernet, a Cabernet/Merlot blend, and Syrah. The hefty, oaky "Marshall Bank" Chardonnay is fermented and aged in barriques.

Carrick ☆☆

Bannockburn, Central Otago. Owners: a partnership of local vineyard owners. 25 hectares. www.carrick.co.nz

Established in 2000, producing zesty, high-acidity whites, and gently oaky Pinot Noir.

Collard Brothers ☆☆

Henderson, Auckland. Owners: the Collard family. 20 hectares.

A well-established, small company, which is very much a family concern. Geoffrey concentrates on the vineyards and Lionel runs the business. Rothesay Chardonnay is one of their best wines, which disproves the theory that Auckland is no good for vines. Serious, meticulous attention is also paid to the Chenin Blanc from Hawke's Bay. The Riesling is stylish and elegant, and the Pinot Noir shows potential.

Kim Crawford ☆☆

Hastings, Hawke's Bay. Owner/winemaker: Kim Crawford. 56 hectares. www.kimcrawfordwines.co.nz

Crawford controls some vineyards in Marlborough, but most of his grapes are purchased from Gisborne and Hawke's Bay to make a wide range of négociant wines.

Escarpment

Martinborough. Owner: Larry McKenna. 24 hectares. www.escarpment.co.nz

Larry McKenna left Martinborough Vineyards (*q.v.*) in 2001 to set up his own winery, with vineyards in the Te Muna district. The first estate wines are from the 2002 vintage, and barrel samples show great promise.

Forrest ☆☆

Renwick, Marlborough. Owner: Dr. John Forrest. 60 hectares. www.forrest.co.nz

A deservedly respected source of typical Marlborough Riesling and Sauvignon, and, since 2000, of Pinot Noir too.

Framingham ☆–☆☆☆

Renwick, Marlborough. Owners: Rex Brooke-Taylor and partners. 30 hectares. www.framingham.co.nz
This winery has the oldest Riesling vines in Marlborough, and consequently it produces some of the finest expressions of this variety in New Zealand. The "Dry" is dry, the "Classic" off-dry; both exemplary. The other white wines and the Pinot Noir, can lack concentration, however. The Montepulciano – how did this grape end up in Marlborough? – is juicy and attractive.

Gladstone ☆☆

Carteton, Wairarapa. Owners: Christine and David Kernahan. 14 hectares. www.gladstone.co.nz
White wines are the focus here, especially racy Sauvignon and crisp Pinot Gris.

Greenhough ☆☆–☆☆☆

Hope, Nelson. Owners: Andrew Greenhough and Jennifer Wheeler. 9 hectares. www.greenhough.co.nz
A rising star from Nelson, with good Chardonnay, and often dramatic and spicy Pinot Noir.

Heron's Flight ☆☆

Matakana. Owners: David Hoskins and Mary Evans. 6 hectares. www.heronsflight.co.nz
David Hoskins has done much to counter the view that Northland is too wet for vines. He makes a Cabernet/Merlot blend and Chardonnay, but since 1996 has focused strongly on Italian varieties such as Sangiovese and Dolcetto.

Highfield ☆–☆☆

Blenheim, Marlborough. Owners: Tom Tenuwera and Shin Yokoi. 5 hectares. www.highfield.co.nz
Good, straightforward varietal wines, notably Chardonnay. The "Elstree Brut" is a rich, toasty, traditional-method sparkling wine, one of New Zealand's best. Almost all the grapes are purchased.

Kemblefield ☆☆

Hastings, Hawke's Bay. Owners: John Kemble and Kaar Field. 80 hectares. www.kemblefield.co.nz
John Kemble, once closely involved with Ravenswood in Sonoma Valley (*q.v.*), takes credit for introducing Zinfandel to New Zealand. The best wines are grandly known as "The Distinction" and there are also "Reserves" produced only in top vintages. The white wines are very good, but the red wines, with the occasional exception of the reserve Cabernet, lack depth.

Lake Chalice ☆☆

Renwick, Marlborough. Owner: Phil Binnie. 40 hectares. www.lakechalice.com
Fiery Sauvignon and delicate, unoaked Chardonnay. The best wines in outstanding years – usually Chardonnay, Merlot, and Cabernet Sauvignon – are bottled under the "Platinum" label.

Lawson's Dry Hills ☆☆–☆☆☆

Blenheim, Marlborough. Owners: Ross and Barbara Lawson. 44 hectares. www.lawsonsdryhills.co.nz

The Lawsons are grape-growers who began producing wine in 1992. Today they purchase about half their requirements. The white wines are best: lush Gewürztraminer, benchmark Sauvignon, and appley Chardonnay. The Pinot Noir shows great promise.

Lincoln Vineyards ☆–☆☆☆

Henderson, Auckland. Owner: Peter Fredatovich. No vineyards. www.lincolnwines.co.nz
With no vineyards of its own, Lincoln buys in fruit from Auckland, Marlborough, and Gisborne. The "Heritage Collection" ranges are aged in American oak, the "President's Selection" in French oak. Lincoln used to be known for its fortified wines, and its venerable "Archive" ports are splendid, but declining stocks make them an endangered species.

Matawhero ☆–☆☆

Gisborne. Owner/winemaker: Denis Irwin. 30 hectares.
A highly individual, small-scale family operation whose hand-made wines have won acclaim, notably the dry, aromatic Gewürztraminer, a discreet Chardonnay, and Bordeaux blends. Performance can be erratic.

Mills Reef ☆☆–☆☆☆

Tauranga, Bay of Plenty. Owners: the Preston family. 20 hectares. www.millsreef.co.nz
Excellent wines under the top "Elspeth" label, especially lush Syrah, fleshy Merlot and Malbec, and an impressive Cabernet/Merlot blend, suggesting plums and blackberries.

Mount Edward ☆☆–☆☆☆

Gibbston, Central Otago. Owner/winemaker: Alan Brady. No vineyards.
Alan Brady, the founder of Gibbston Valley (*q.v.*), sold the winery when it grew too large for his comfort, and in its place he set up this boutique winery, where he could control the entire process. Using minimal equipment and intervention, Brady produces sleek and concentrated Pinot Noir.

Mount Riley ☆☆

Blenheim, Marlborough. 120 hectares. www.mountriley.co.nz
First releases date from 1996, and the wines are consistently fresh and even elegant. The top wines are the "17 Valley" Chardonnay and Pinot Noir, both well-balanced and extremely enjoyable.

Mud House ☆☆

Renwick, Marlborough. Owner: John Joslin. 24 hectares. www.mudhouse.co.nz
A good range of wines, made by Matt Thomson: minerally Sauvignon, light Pinot Noir, and oaky Merlot. First releases of Pinot Noir from the Terravin Vineyard show more savoury character. "Le Grys" is the export label for Mud House.

Nautilus ☆☆

Renwick, Marlborough. Owner: Yalumba. 38 hectares. www.nautilusestate.com
This Marlborough property is expanding fast. Chardonnay is delicious, and Pinot Noir is steadily improving.

Olssens ☆☆

Bannockburn, Central Otago. Owner: John Olssen. 13 hectares. www.olssens.co.nz

Fresh, supple, well-balanced wines from Chardonnay and Pinot Noir.

Palliser ✩✩–✩✩✩
Martinborough. Owner: a public unlisted company. 60 hectares. www.palliser.co.nz

One of the leading Martinborough wineries, and a source of delicious Riesling and Sauvignon. More recently, Alsatian-style Pinot Gris has been added to the range, and the Pinot Noir has been improving steadily and impressively.

Peregrine ✩✩–✩✩✩
Queenstown, Central Otago. Owner/winemaker: Greg Hay. 50 hectares. www.peregrinewines.co.nz

A rising star in Central Otago, with weighty Pinot Gris, spicy, cherry-tinged Pinot Noir, and powerful, vibrant, dry Riesling.

Pleiades ✩✩
Blenheim, Marlborough. Owner/winemaker: Winston Oliver. 1.5 hectares

Winston Oliver does one thing only, and does it well: a Malbec/Merlot blend called "Maia": dense and plummy.

Quartz Reef ✩✩
Cromwell, Central Otago. Owner/winemaker: Rudi Bauer. 15 hectares. www.quartzreef.co.nz

Austrian winemaker Rudi Bauer has spent a decade or more in New Zealand, and is now installed at Quartz Reef, which opened its doors in 1998. As well as good Pinot Gris and Pinot Noir, Bauer produces delicious "Chauvet" sparkling wine in a joint venture with the Champagne house of that name.

St Nesbit
Papakura, Auckland. Owner/winemaker: Anthony Molloy. 5 hectares

The red wines, from Bordeaux varieties, attracted a strong following until diseased vines necessitated a complete replanting. The 2002 will be the first vintage from new vines.

Selak's
Kumeu, Auckland

Now owned by Nobilo (*q.v.*).

Sileni ✩✩–✩✩✩
Hastings, Hawke's Bay. Owners: Graeme Avery and partners. 100 hectares. www.sileni.co.nz

Together with Craggy Range (*q.v.*), this is the most stunning winery complex in Hawke's Bay. But vast expenditure and a succession of serious frosts in the vineyards have proved troublesome. The wines are cleanly made and balanced, and there is an unusual focus on Semillon, both dry and sweet.

Staete Landt ✩✩
Blenheim, Marlborough. Owners: Ruud Maasdam and Dorien Vermaas. 21 hectares. www.staetelandt.co.nz

This enthusiastic Dutch couple are aiming for perfection in their wines, conducting rigorous soil analysis and selection during harvest.

First releases were in 2000, so these are early days, but the wines, especially Sauvignon and Pinot Noir, show great promise.

Stonecroft Wines ✩✩
Hastings, Hawke's Bay. Owner: Alan Limmer. 16 hectares. www.stonecroft.co.nz

Alan Limmer pioneered Syrah in New Zealand. His first vintage, 1987, was released in 1990, and he has repeated its success in subsequent years. Limmer is very keen on trying different grape varieties, especially from the Rhône, and has also taken some Zinfandel from Kemblefield (*q.v.*). Gewürztraminer can be excellent, too.

Te Mania ✩–✩✩✩
Richmond, Nelson. Owner: Jon Harrey. 8 hectares. www.temaniawines.co.nz

This is a small winery with a wide range of wines. Riesling comes from Marlborough as well as Nelson, and both are enjoyable, the Nelson wine having a stronger sweet-and-sour character. Chardonnay is tangy and citric, and the Pinot Noir reserve is surprisingly rich and concentrated.

Valli ✩✩✩
Gibbston, Central Otago. Owner/winemaker: Grant Taylor. No vineyards

Grant Taylor, the winemaker at Gibbston Valley (*q.v.*), has his own label for purchased Pinot Noir from single vineyards. Handcrafted and delicious.

Waipara Springs ✩✩
Waipara, North Canterbury. Owners: the Grant family and partners. 26 hectares. www.waiparasprings.co.nz

Waipara Springs is one of the pioneers of the area, concentrating on Pinot Noir, Chardonnay, and Gewürztraminer.

Waitiri Creek ✩✩
Arrowtown, Central Otago. Owners: Paula Ramage and Alistair Ward. 8 hectares. www.waitiricreek.co.nz

A new property with promising first releases of Pinot Noir.

West Brook ✩
Waimauku, Auckland. Owner/winemaker: Anthony Ivicevich. 8 hectares. www.westbrook.co.nz

With Auckland's vineyards in irreversible decline, Ivicevich has to bring fruit in from Marlborough and Hawke's Bay. The result is a wide range of wines, to enjoy young.

South Africa

Despite a history of wine production dating back to the 1660s, South Africa entered the New World fine-wine league in the mid-1970s – a decade later than California and Australia. (The Cape's one historically famous wine was the dessert Muscat of Constantia, which in Napoléon's time fetched prices as high as any wine in the world, but by the twentieth century it had become a historical relic.) South Africa has been struggling to catch up with the rest of the so-called New World, partly for self-imposed reasons.

The government purposely limited both the supply of good grapevines and the land to grow them on. Nor could the welcome establishment of the Wine of Origin system in 1973 make much headway, given the isolation of South Africa during the apartheid era. International sanctions inhibited the importation of good quality vines and cuttings, and South African winemakers, however skilled, could not stay fully in touch with the viticultural and other developments in the rest of the wine world. But now that South Africa is no longer a pariah among nations, the full potential of its vineyards is slowly being realized.

There are those who argue that the natural conditions of the Cape for the vine are as good as any on earth, and a growing number of wines since 1998 are showing this to be

the case. The essential grape varieties are now at last being planted, and some spectacular wines are emerging from the lovely estates of Stellenbosch and Franschhoek, and from the remoter regions of Robertson and Swartland.

The natural advantages of the coastal region of the Cape are impressive. Ideal slopes can be found facing every point of the compass. There is an eight-month growth period; never any frost, never any hail, autumn rain is rare, and there are very few of the diseases that plague other vineyards. An important quality factor is the wide range of temperatures: cool nights between hot days, the Cape pattern, reduce night-time respiration from the vine leaves. The plant, unable to consume sugars accumulated during the day, stores more of them. None of these conditions is a guarantee of good wine, but taken together, with intelligent handling, they encourage optimism.

On the down side, while most coastal-region vineyards need soil pH adjustment, the major problems facing South Africa's growers in the past two decades have related to the quality of planting material. It was only in the mid-1980s that the authorities liberalized regulations governing the importation of vines. This followed the "Chardonnay scandal", in which it became clear that the draconian agricultural legislation left the *avant-garde* farming community with no alternative but to smuggle in premium varieties unavailable from the nurseries. Moreover, the vineyards established – particularly of Cabernet – were severely virus-infected, often inhibiting ripening and leading to harshly tannic wines. More recent plantings are all on virus-free material, but only in recent years have nurseries been able to cope with the demand from growers.

Many grape farmers were not wine drinkers. South Africa has long been a brandy, rather than a wine, culture. Non-white Prohibition ended in 1962; grocers could only sell wine from 1979. Government regulation encouraged the planting

of vines for eventual distillation, or for the production of cheap fortified wines. So when South Africa finally emerged from the nightmare of apartheid, its vineyards were dominated by grapes – notably Chenin Blanc and Colombard – not associated with fine wine production.

Given this background, it is astonishing how swiftly South Africa has progressed. There is growing domestic demand, and the swift replacement of poor-quality vineyards with plantings of good modern clones in carefully selected sites. That bastion of conservatism and protectionism, the KWV – an organization founded in 1918 to protect grape farmers from low wine prices, by fixing a minimum price and distilling the surplus – has had its powers curtailed throughout the 1990s. This has left the industry free to develop in ways more attuned to the requirements of an increasingly international market. Successful brands have been created to provide inexpensive wine of sound quality, and at the opposite end of the spectrum, new estates have sprouted like mushrooms. By 2002, a new cellar was opening its doors every eight days – even if many of them were the tiniest of boutique wineries. At the same time, "empowerment" projects are burgeoning, as landowners find ways not only to provide good working and living conditions for their (mostly black) farm workers, but also to involve them more actively in the business.

The old staple grape of South Africa was Steen, the local name for Chenin Blanc, which was used for everything from thirst-quenchers (it was saved by its relatively high acidity and could be very pleasant) to "sherry" – which was the country's biggest international success. If there was a red equivalent, it was Pinotage, an odd cross between Pinot Noir and Cinsault peculiar to the Cape, making a dark, scented wine not to everybody's taste. Now Sauvignon Blanc has proved a hit, with strong demand on domestic and export markets and Chardonnay (absent from the Cape until the 1970s) is steadily improving, while there are attempts to revive wines from Chenin and Semillon, which can be excellent if yields are kept low, from the few old vineyards that have not been grubbed up. Cabernet and Pinotage are now the mainstays of red wine production, but there is increasingly elegant Pinot Noir from Walker Bay, lush Merlot from Stellenbosch, and some splendid Shiraz from all the major wine regions. Dozens of young winemakers, still in their twenties, have worked vintages in regions as diverse as Priorat and Burgundy, and have brought their knowledge and experience back to South Africa. If the actual achievement is not quite as stellar as the South Africans themselves would have us believe, there is no doubt that the potential for great wines will soon be realized.

Regions of Origin

The Wine of Origin system was introduced in 1973, dividing wine-producing areas into four regions (Breede River Valley, Coast, Olifants River, and Little Karoo), fourteen districts, and fourty-three wards. The most important are listed below.

Breede River Valley An immense region that includes the important districts of Worcester, Robertson, and Swellendam.

Cape Point A very cool, one-winery designated area on the other side of the mountains from Constantia.

Coastal Region A catch-all appellation that may be given to wines made from grapes grown all of the following regions: the Stellenbosch, Durbanville, Swartland, Paarl, Constantia, and Tulbagh districts.

Constantia Once the world's most famous Muscat wine, from the Cape. The ward in which it was produced is now a highly regarded cool-climate area. There are only five estates, but all maintain high quality.

Durbanville A small, hilly district just north of Cape Town. Durbanville Hills is by far the most important producer based in this distinctly cool area.

Elgin A cool area, east of Cape Town, with shale and clay soils. Although long championed by Neil Ellis, Paul Cluver is the only winery here, although others are now being developed.

Elim A tiny region east of Walker Bay, but with a growing reputation for Sauvignon and other cool-climate wines.

Franschhoek A beautiful and narrow valley east of Stellenbosch, and named after the Huguenots who settled here. It is now the self-proclaimed gastronomic centre of South Africa, and home to many high-quality and ambitious estates.

Klein (Little) Karoo The easternmost Wine of Origin district. Very little rainfall and all irrigated vineyards. Best for dessert wine and brandy, though some good Chenin Blanc is also produced. A vast and elongated area.

Olifants River Northerly Wine of Origin district, with a hot, dry climate. Once known mostly for wine for distilling from irrigated vineyards, Olifants River is now producing a growing range of value-for-money wines, notably from the vast Vredendal cooperative. Includes the wards of Koekenaap, Lutzville Valley, Spruitdrift, and Vredendal.

Overberg Southern, coastal Wine of Origin district. Contains the Walker Bay and Elgin wards (*qq.v.*), with some of the Cape's coolest vineyards.

South Africa in Round Figures

South Africa is the world's seventh-largest wine producer, with three per cent of total world production. The vineyard area of 106,331 hectares, however, places the country in seventeenth position, with just 1.5 per cent of the world's vineyards. Fifty-nine per cent of the grapes are white.

Wine production stood at some 746 million litres in 2001, of which seventy-seven per cent was used for wine production, the remainder for brandy and grape juice concentrate. Fortified wines represent about seven per cent of the domestic market. There are sixty-seven cooperatives, and 340 estate wineries and private cellars.

Paarl A region of growing importance, eighty kilometres (fifty miles) northeast of Cape Town. It boasts some of the country's best vineyards, both red and white. Includes the wards of Franschhoek (*q.v.*) and Wellington, the latter of which tends to be warmer than the rest of Paarl.

Piketberg A small, western Wine of Origin district north of Tulbagh, towards the Olifants River. A warm, dry climate gives mainly dessert wine, but also an expanding range of table wines.

Robertson A Wine of Origin district inland and east of Cape Town. Irrigated vineyards with alluvial and calcareous soils along the Kogmanskloof and Breede rivers provide some high-quality white and much-improved red table wines, as well as fine fortified wines.

Stellenbosch The beautiful old Cape Dutch town and its demarcated region fifty kilometres (thirty miles) east of Cape Town, extending south to the ocean at False Bay. Most of South Africa's best estates, especially for red wine, are in the mountain foothills of the region. Includes the wards of Bottelary, Devon Valley, Jonkershoek Valley, Papegaaiberg, and Simonsberg.

Swartland A warm Wine of Origin district around Malmesbury, between Tulbagh and the west coast. Most of the growers here supply cooperatives, but the excellent conditions that exist for Mediterranean varietals are now encouraging new estates to establish themselves in their own right. The district includes just one cool coastal region, that of Darling.

Tulbagh A demarcated district sheltered in the hills north of Paarl, and best-known for white wines.

Walker Bay Southeast of Cape Town and close to the coastal town of Hermanus is this region that has already won a high reputation for Burgundian varietals.

Worcester Demarcated wine region around the Breede and Hex river valleys, bordering Robertson to the east. Rainfall is usually high enough for good table wine; southeast to Swellendam irrigation is necessary.

Its nineteen cooperatives produce around twenty-five per cent of all South Africa's wine.

Leading South African Producers

Allesverloren ☆☆
Swartland. Owners/winemakers: Danie and Fanie Malan. 180 hectares. www.allesveloren.co.za
Although this estate produces good Cabernet and Shiraz, it is best-known for its reliable and succulent ports.

Alto ☆☆–☆☆☆
Stellenbosch. Owners: Distell. 93 hectares
A superbly sited vineyard, running straight up a mountainside near the sea for a mile and a half (in which it

Cape Independent Winemaker's Guild
This loose grouping of thirty-odd ambitious winemakers was founded in 1983, and two years later launched its annual auction, at which members offered very small quantities of their finest wines (often no more than a single barrel) for sale. These special bottlings have often shown the full potential of Cape wines, setting new standards for quality and style. The equally well-known Nederburg auction is only open to the wine trade; the guild auctions are open to all.

rises nearly 300 metres (975 feet) yielding long-lived Cabernet and a red blend called "Alto Estate".

L'Avenir ☆☆–☆☆☆
Stellenbosch. Owner: Marc Wiehe. 56 hectares
This is an extremely unlikely joint venture, created in 1992, between urbane Mauritius sugar broker Marc Wiehe and enthusiastic winemaker Naudé. Chardonnay, velvety Pinotage, and cassis-infused Cabernet Sauvignon are exceptional here.

Backsberg ☆–☆☆
Paarl. Owner: Michael Back. 180 hectares. www.backsberg.co.za
Backsberg was established by the late Sydney Back, one of the Cape's pioneering estate wine producers, and has an enviable reputation for high-quality, value-for-money wines. The emphasis is on well-crafted wines that are enjoyable on release.

Beaumont ☆☆
Walker Bay. Owners: Raoul and Jayne Beaumont. 50 hectares. www.beaumont.co.za
Since 1993, a reliable source of flavoury Pinotage, Shiraz, and Chenin Blanc.

Graham Beck ☆☆–☆☆☆
Robertson. Owner: Graham Beck. 165 hectares. www.grahambeckwines.co.za
Beck's property is divided between two sites: the major part is in Robertson, and the remainder, which vinifies grapes from cooler coastal sites, is based at a separate winery in Franschhoek. Although Beck is well-known for its excellent sparkling wines, its table wines are becoming increasingly impressive, especially the single-vineyard "Ridge" Shiraz, "Old Road" Pinotage, and intense, tannic "Cornerstone" Cabernet Sauvignon.

Beyerskloof ☆☆–☆☆☆
Stellenbosch. Owners: Beyers Truter, Simon Halliday, and Krige family. 5 hectares. www.beyerskloof.com
Beyers Truter is the respected winemaker at Kanonkop (*q.v.*), but this is essentially his own label, specializing in tannic, structured Cabernet and lush Pinotage. In 2001, Truter introduced a new blend from Pinotage, Merlot, and Cabernet.

Boekenhoutskloof ☆☆☆
Franschhoek. Owners: Boekenhoutskloof Investments Ltd. 20 hectares
Since 1996, when this property was founded, Marc Kent has been its winemaker and was rewarded for his brilliance

by being offered a share of the business. He is a non-interventionist winemaker, using mostly natural yeasts and ageing the wines in barrel with minimal racking. His barrique-fermented Semillon resembles an opulent and waxy white Graves, and ages well. His Syrah is equally remarkable, and often more complex than the very concentrated Cabernet Sauvignon. These wines are only made in small quantities. Larger-volume bottlings- that are still of excellent quality are released under the "Porcupine Ridge" label.

Le Bonheur ☆☆

Stellenbosch. Owners: Distell. 50 hectares

Le Bonheur's vineyards, on the generally north-facing slopes of the Klapmutskop mountain, have been extensively replanted over the last twenty years. This estate produces a fine Cabernet; a Bordeaux blend "Prima"; and good, unwooded Sauvignon Blanc.

Boplaas ☆☆

Klein Karoo. Owner/winemaker: Carel Nel. 65 hectares. www.boplaas.co.za

One of the Cape's leading port-type wine producers, and a good source for Pinotage and fortified Muscadel.

Boschendal ☆–☆☆

Franschhoek. Owners: Anglo American Farms. 300 hectares. www.boschendal.com

One of the Cape's largest single estates, with coolish vineyards stretching along the Simonsberg. Many of their wines are blends, but they rarely rise to any great heights. However, despite the fact that Boschendal has been up for sale for some time, quality has been creeping up, especially for its "Grand Reserve" red.

Bouchard Finlayson ☆☆☆

Walker Bay. Owners: Peter Finlayson and partners. 16 hectares. www.bouchardfinlayson.co.za

Winemaker Peter Finlayson, formerly with Hamilton Russell Vineyards (q.v.), has been involved since 1990 in a joint venture with Paul Bouchard, formerly of Bouchard Aîné. Some grapes are bought in, but increasing volumes of their own plantings are gradually coming into production. These are extremely distinctive, cool-climate wines, and the rather citric "Kaaimansgat" Chardonnay, from vineyards at 700 metres (2,296 feet), together with the "Galpin Peak" Pinot Noir, can be said to be among the Cape's finest expressions of these varieties.

J. P. Bredell ☆–☆☆☆

Stellenbosch. Owner/winemaker: Anton Bredell. 95 hectares

Since 1991, some of the Cape's best ports have been produced here, and red wines are growing in quality.

Buitenverwachting ☆☆–☆☆☆

Constantia. Owners: Richard Mueller and Lars Maack. 95 hectares. www.buitenverwachting.com

Part of Van der Stel's original Constantia farm and a consistently good Cape producer. The wines are nurtured by winemaker Hermann Kirschbaum, who has been here since 1993. "Buiten Blanc" is its crowd-pleasing white blend, but more impressive wines include the rich Sauvignon Blanc, and the excellent Cabernet/Merlot blend called "Christine".

Cabrière ☆–☆☆

Franschhoek. Owner/winemaker: Achim von Arnim. 30 hectares. www.cabriere.co.za

The flamboyant Achim von Arnim has long been recognized as one of the Cape's leading producers of *méthode traditionnelle* sparkling wines under the "Pierre Jourdan" label. Although the sparkling wines can be very good, Cabrière's reputation for Pinot Noir is perhaps less easily understood.

Cape Point ☆☆

Noedhoek. Owner: Sybrand van der Spuy. 36 hectares. www.cape-point.com

A remarkable patchwork of vineyards, along the very cool coastline south of Cape Town. Initial releases of Sauvignon and Chardonnay from winemaker Emmanuel Bolliger were impressively minerally, though over-oaked. In 2002, Bolliger was succeeded by Anneke Burger, formerly of Boschendal (q.v.). Red varieties such as Merlot and Shiraz are about to come into production. The delicious late-harvest Semillon tastes of quince.

Clos Malverne ☆☆–☆☆☆

Stellenbosch. Owner: Seymour Pritchard. 25 hectares. www.closmalverne.co.za

Attractive Sauvignon and Pinotage, and a brambly red blend (Cabernet/Merlot/Pinotage) called "Auret".

Paul Cluver ☆☆

Elgin. Owner: Dr Paul Cluver. 84 hectares. www.cluver.com

At present, this is the only winery located in the Elgin region. Until 1997, the grapes were sold to Nederburg (q.v.). Winemaker Andries Burger is Cluver's son-in-law, and has worked at Château Margaux. The appley Chardonnay and silky Pinot Noir are impressive, but Cabernet Sauvignon can be austere.

Constantia Uitsig ☆☆

Constantia. Owner: David McCay. 31 hectares. www.constantiauitsig.co.za

Bought in 1988 as a run-down property, Constantia Uitsig has been entirely replanted. Some of the wines are made in both a wooded and unwooded style. Although the Merlot is very enjoyable, the strength here lies with white varietals such as Sauvignon, Semillon, and Chardonnay.

Cordoba ☆☆–☆☆☆

Stellenbosch. Owner: Jannie Jooste. 31 hectares. www.cordoba.co.za

A boutique winery specializing in a stylish, oaky Cabernet Franc/Merlot blend called "Crescendo".

Darling Cellars ☆☆

Darling, Swartland. Owner: consortium of shareholders. 1,500 hectares. www.darlingcellars.co.za

Winemaker Abé Beukes produces two ranges of wine from the company's extensive vineyards: the single-vineyard "DC" wines, and the top "Onyx" line. Cabernet and Shiraz are the stars of both ranges.

Delaire Vineyards ☆☆–☆☆☆

Stellenbosch. Owner: Masud Alikhani. 22 hectares. www.delairewinery.co.za

This ailing estate was acquired by London-based international businessman Masud Alikhani, and under its winemaker, Bruwer Raats, it has won a fine reputation for Chardonnay, new-oaked Merlot, and other rich reds.

Delheim ☆☆
Simonsberg, Stellenbosch. Owners: the Sperling family. 150 hectares. www.delheim.com

Delheim has long produced traditional, Cape-style reds, tannic and short on fruit, as well as off-dry white wines from Riesling and Gewürztraminer. Recent vintages have shown greater ripeness, especially the plummy "Vera Cruz" Shiraz.

De Toren ☆☆☆
Stellenbosch. Owner: Emil den Dulk. 20 hectares. www.de-toren.com

A new star, De Toren's sole wine is a dense, voluptuous Bordeaux blend called "Fusion V", first produced in 1999. This exceptional wine is made by the youthful Albie Koch, who, despite his tender years, has had extensive winemaking experience in California and France.

De Trafford ☆☆–☆☆☆
Stellenbosch. Owner/winemaker: David Trafford. 5 hectares. www.detrafford.co.za

Former architect David Trafford makes most of his wines from purchased fruit, employing natural-yeast fermentation. As well as rich, powerful Cabernet and Merlot, he produces luscious Chenin Blanc with complex aromas of cooked apples. His apricotty "straw wine" is also made from Chenin.

De Wetshof ☆☆–☆☆☆
Robertson. Owner/winemaker: Danie de Wet. 208 hectares. www.dewetshof.co.za

Danie de Wet was trained in Germany, and brought back boundless enthusiasm for white wines of styles not then found in South Africa. His experimental work with Riesling, Sauvignon Blanc, and Chardonnay, and with his noble-rot sweet wine, "Edeloes", shook old ideas about the Robertson area, and about South African whites in general. He is one of the leading producers of Chardonnay in the Robertson region, with several different *cuvées*, ranging from "Finesse" (lightly wooded) to Chardonnay "d'Honneur" and "Bateleur" (both barrel-fermented).

These Chardonnays are remarkable for their citric freshness and lack of heaviness. Twelve hectares of Pinot Noir are now beginning to produce some fragrant, raspberry-scented wines of undoubted potential.

Diemersfontein ☆–☆☆
Wellington. Owners: David and Susan Sonnenberg. 48 hectares. www.diemersfontein.co.za

The Sonnenbergs, who founded Woolworth's in South Africa, bought this farm in 1942, and in the 1990s converted it into a luxury hotel and wine estate. Most of the wine appears under the "Diemersfontein" label, but top selections bear the "Carpe Diem" label. The focus is on Pinotage, Merlot, and Shiraz, and the style is reminiscent of some Australian wines, with a surfeit of upfront, jammy, oaky fruit. But they seem set to enjoy considerable commercial success.

Distell
Stellenbosch. www.distell.co.za

A vast company, formed by the amalgamation of the Distillers and Stellenbosch Farmers groups. Principal estates are Alto, Le Bonheur, Uitkyk, Neethlingshof, and Stellenzicht, but other ventures include Nederburg, Zonnebloem, Fleur du Cap, Le Roux, and Durbanville Hills. All told, Distell, in 2002, controlled about 30% of all Cape wine production.

Dornier
Stellenbosch. Owner: Christoph Dornier. 60 hectares. www.dornierwines.co.za

Ian Naudé is the winemaker at this new property, which is focusing on rich, red wines. The initial releases, of Merlot and Cabernet in 2001, were ultra-ripe and lacked finesse, but these are early days.

Durbanville Hills ☆–☆☆☆
Durbanville. Owners: Distell. 770 hectares. www.durbanvillehills.co.za

An ambitious joint venture between majority shareholder Distell and a group of leading local growers. Large new cellars were built in time for the 1999 vintage, and veteran winemaker Martin Moore (formerly of Groot Konstantia [*q.v.*]) was hired to supervise production. There are three ranges: basic varietals; the mostly new oaked "Rhinofields" wines; and single-vineyard wines, aged in new French oak. The standard varietal wines are for early drinking, and the Sauvignon Blanc can be vegetal. The single-vineyard "Caapmans" Cabernet/Merlot, and "Luipardsberg" Merlot are rich and fleshy.

Eikendal ☆–☆☆
Stellenbosch. Owners: Substantia company. 65 hectares. www.eikendal.com

The wines at this Swiss-owned estate have long been sound, if not always exciting, but quality is set to improve under the new winemaker Liselle Gerber.

Neil Ellis ☆☆☆
Stellenbosch. Owners: Neil Ellis and Hans Pieter Schroeder. 105 hectares. www.neilellis.com

Since 1988, Neil Ellis has set himself up as a leading winemaker/négociant at the top end of the Cape wine market. He sources grapes from vastly different microclimates to produce a range of wines, each with striking individuality. The "Premium" wines are very reliable, and the "Vineyard Selection" range is often outstanding, if pricey. Several Sauvignon Blanc *cuvées*, some of them emphatically grassy, as well as some top Cabernets have confirmed his reputation.

Ernie Els ☆☆
Stellenbosch. Owner: Ernie Els. No vineyards. www.ernieelswines.com

Although this grotesquely expensive Bordeaux blend bears the famous golfer's name, the fruit comes mostly from Rust-en-Vrede (*q.v.*), where the wine is also made. The result: an international-style red, sleek and oaky.

Fairview ☆☆–☆☆☆
Paarl. Owner: Charles Back. 350 hectares. www.fairview.co.za

No one has his finger more firmly on the pulse of the international market for Cape wines than Charles Back, who has enjoyed great success with Shiraz above all. The "Goats Do Roam" range (his take on Côtes du Rhône) has combined a fun-loving image with good-quality wines. Back himself admits that he barely understands the structure of his own company, since it is constantly evolving. He is also the sole proprietor of the former joint venture, Spice Route (*q.v.*).

Flagstone ☆☆

Cape Town. Owner/winemaker: Bruce Jack. No vineyards. www.flagstonewines.com

Bruce Jack buys in fruit from forty vineyards to make a wide range of wines, including characterful, grassy Sauvignon Blanc from Elim, Pinotage, and a complex red blend called "Longitude".

Ken Forrester ☆☆–☆☆☆

Stellenbosch. Owner: Ken Forrester. 33 hectares. www.kenforresterwines.com

Former restaurateur Forrester is an ardent champion of unfashionable varietals, in his case Chenin Blanc and Grenache. The wines are made by Martin Meinert (*q.v.*), and the dry Chenins are among the Cape's finest, as is his botrytized version called "T": a glorious confection of apricot and cream. Also noteworthy are the delicate Sauvignon Blanc, and the fresh and spicy Grenache/Syrah blend.

Glen Carlou ☆☆–☆☆☆

Paarl. Owners: the Finlayson and Hess families. 65 hectares. www.glencarlou.co.za

Under winemaker David Finlayson, Glen Carlou has risen to the top ranks within Paarl. The stalwarts of the range include a rich Chardonnay Reserve, and the fine Bordeaux blend "Grande Classique".

Grangehurst ☆☆☆

Stellenbosch. Owner/winemaker: Jeremy Walker. No vineyards. www.grangehurst.co.za

The gifted Walker has long focused on two wines: an elegant Pinotage, and a fine Cabernet/Merlot blend. In the late 1990s, he added a new wine, "Nikela": a concentrated yet vigorous blend of Cabernet, Pinotage, and Merlot.

Groot Constantia ☆

Constantia. Owners: Groot Constantia Trust. 90 hectares. www.grootconstantia.co.za

The original farm, founded by the Cape's first governor, Simon van der Stel, in 1685, and the source of the legendary Constantia dessert wine of the eighteenth and nineteenth centuries. An extensive replanting programme and renovation of the cellar have contributed to an improvement in the wines, but direction by committee allows little initiative on the part of the winemakers. The best wine is usually the "Gouverneurs' Blend", aged in new oak.

Groote Post ☆☆

Darling. Owner: Nick Pentz. 100 hectares. www.grootepost.com

Relatively cool vineyards yield fine Sauvignon, Chardonnay, and Merlot.

Hamilton-Russell Vineyards ☆☆–☆☆☆

Walker Bay. Owner: Anthony Hamilton Russell. 65 hectares

The first of the new generation of cool-climate producers focused on Pinot Noir and Chardonnay. By 1998, mediocre clones had been replaced, and recent vintages have consolidated Hamilton Russell's position in the front rank of producers working with these varieties. These are arguably the most Burgundian of Cape Pinots, with great purity and length of flavour. Credit for their success is shared between the Hamilton-Russells and their foresight, and the skills of long-term winemaker Kevin Grant.

Hartenberg ☆–☆☆

Stellenbosch. Owner: Hartenberg Holdings. 85 hectares. www.hartenbergestate.com

A substantial investment programme has contributed to noteworthy improvement in the estate's formerly rustic wines. There is good Shiraz, Cabernet, and Merlot, but the white wines still lag behind.

Havana Hills ☆☆–☆☆☆

Tygerberg. Owners: Kobus du Plessis and Nico Vermeulen. 48 hectares

A new star in the Cape, especially for the "Du Plessis Reserve" range: red wines that show elegance and restrained use of oak.

Iona ☆☆

Grabouw. Owner: Andrew Gunn. 14 hectares. www.ionawines.com

A new venture near Elgin. The 2001 Sauvignon Blanc was the delicious and gently herbaceous first release, and a Merlot-dominated red will follow.

Jordan ☆☆–☆☆☆

Stellenbosch. Owners/winemakers: Gary and Kathy Jordan. 100 hectares. www.jordanwines.com

After successful careers, Kathy (an economist) and Gary (a geologist) Jordan returned to the family farm, and immediately established it as a quality avant-garde producer; healthy, virus-free vineyards and meticulous cellar practices have contributed to their success. Their top wine is the concentrated and chocolatey "Cobbler's Hill Reserve": a Cabernet-dominated blend aged in new oak, but quality is high throughout the range.

Kanonkop ☆☆☆

Stellenbosch. Owners: the Krige family. 100 hectares

Winemaker Beyers Truter is devoted to Pinotage, and regularly produces one of the Cape's richest and best. Equally remarkable is his long-lived Bordeaux blend, "Paul Sauer": rustic in the best sense, since it never lacks fruit despite its rude vigour. Long-established vineyards and traditional vinification techniques, such as fermentation in shallow troughs, ensure consistent quality.

Kanu ☆☆–☆☆☆

Stellenbosch. Owners: Hydro Holdings. 150 hectares. www.kanu.co.za

The first vintage here was 1998, made by Teddy Hall. The most important wine here, unusually, is the crisp Chenin, which retains lively acidity. Sauvignon and Chardonnay are equally good, and there is a supple, smoky Cabernet/Merlot blend called "Keystone".

Klein Constantia ☆☆–☆☆☆
Constantia. Owners: the Jooste family. 75 hectares.
www.kleinconstantia.com
An historic property, which was part of Van der Stel's original Constantia farm. The Joostes bought the estate in 1980 and renovated it, and in 1984 hired Ross Gower as winemaker. Cool vineyards, state-of-the-art viticulture, and a well-managed cellar ensure a high overall quality for all the estate wines. Sauvignon, Semillon, and Chardonnay are attractive and vigorous, but the red wines can sometimes be lean. Lowell Jooste and Ross Gower have revived the famous sweet wine of Constantia, which they sell as "Vin de Constance". It is made from unfortified late-picked Muscat à Petits Grains, replanted here in 1982, and has flavours of dried apricot and, sometimes, marmalade. Nobody knows how close it comes to its legendary forebear, but it is a very clean, intense wine which will undoubtedly mature for many years.

KWV International ☆–☆☆
Paarl. www.kwv-international.com
The national wine cooperative was established in 1918, with statutory powers to govern the wine industry. Initially it was founded to protect grape-growers in their price negotiations with wholesale merchants, but its role changed into that of policeman for the entire wine industry. Embroiled in politics and numerous conflicts of interest, it has had to be entirely restructured in the 1990s and early 2000s. As a wine producer, it has churned out large volumes of bland varietal wines under the "KWV" and "Roodeberg" labels, the Chenin Blanc always good value. Quality improved with the introduction of the new-oaked "Cathedral Cellars" range, led by the Bordeaux blend called "Triptych". In 1996, KWV launched "Perold", a dense Shiraz of good quality and outrageous price.

Laborie ☆–☆☆
Paarl. Owner: KWV International. 35 hectares.
www.kwv-international.com
A very attractive estate on the slopes of the Paarl Mountain, owned by the KWV, and used as a guesthouse. The wines, made by Gideon Theron, are easygoing and well-made, if not especially concentrated.

Land's End ☆☆
Elim. Owners: Private partnership. 35 hectares
A label created for wines made from grapes sourced from the handful of growers who planted in ultra-cool Elim in 1997. Initial releases showed great promise: exotic Sauvignon and zesty Semillon.

Landskroon ☆–☆☆
Paarl. Owners: the de Villiers family. 275 hectares.
www.landskroonwines.com
The eighth generation of a Huguenot family who have made wine at the Cape for three centuries. Long-established property, with a reputation for steadily improving red wines and excellent Cape "ports".

Lievland ☆☆
Stellenbosch. Owner: Paul Benadé. 65 hectares
Winemaker Abé Beukes transformed this estate into a leading producer of Shiraz, and a Cabernet/Merlot blend called "DVB". Beukes has moved to Darling Cellars (q.v.), and has been succeeded by Jean Pienaar.

Longridge ☆☆
Stellenbosch. Owner: Winecorp. www.winecorp.co.za
A négociant winery, producing consistently good red wines for fairly early drinking.

Meerlust ☆☆☆
Stellenbosch. Owner: Hannes Myburgh. 160 hectares.
www.meerlust.co.za
Hannes Myburgh occupies the same exquisite manor house that his ancestors called home in 1756. Since 1978, the winemaker has been the untamed north Italian Giorgio Dalla Cia, whose love for Bordeaux was matched by the then owner, Nico Myburgh, who had started planting Cabernet Sauvignon in the 1960s, followed by Merlot, Cabernet Franc, and Pinot Noir following in the 1970s.

Meerlust's top wine is the Bordeaux blend called "Rubicon", but the Merlot and idiosyncratic Pinot Noir are almost as fine. It took Dalla Cia eleven years to be satisfied with his Chardonnay, first released in 1995, and, unexpectedly, a dead ringer for Meursault. And his "grappa" is a dead ringer for the real thing. All the wines, Chardonnay included, benefit from five years of bottle-age. "Rubicon", in its youth, can have assertive tannins and dour pickle tones, but with patience, the wine becomes cedary and harmonious.

Meinert Wines ☆☆☆
Stellenbosch. Owner/winemaker: Martin Meinert. 13 hectares.
www.meinertwines.com
Martin Meinert established the reputation of Vergelegen (q.v.). Since the late 1990s, he has focused on his own label. His Cabernet and Merlot are rich and profound, and it's arguable whether his top red blend, "Synchronicity", is superior.

Middelvlei ☆☆
Stellenbosch. Owners: the Momberg family. 130 hectares.
www.middelvlei.co.za
An estate with a long-established reputation for Pinotage, and recently for Cabernet Sauvignon and Shiraz.

Mont du Toit ☆☆–☆☆☆
Wellington. Owners: Stephan du Toit, Bernd Philippi, and Bernhard Breuer. 28 hectares. www.montdutoit.co.za
Founded in 1997, this South African/German venture first made its mark with a powerful 1998 Syrah/Cabernet/Merlot blend.

Morgenhof ☆☆–☆☆☆
Stellenbosch. Owners: Alain and Anne Cointreau-Huchon.
60 hectares. www.morhgenhof.com
Since 1993, the Cointreau-Huchons have extensively renovated the homestead and vineyards, and built a massive subterranean barrel-maturation cellar. The wines are extremely reliable and good-value, especially the lush Bordeaux blend "Première Sélection".

Morgenster ☆☆
Somerset West. Owner: Giulio Bertrand. 40 hectares.
www.morgenster.co.za
Piedmontese industrialist, Bertrand, bought the run-down property in 1993 in order to develop olive groves. Inevitably vineyards followed, the aim being to produce a

St-Emilion-style wine with the help of Cheval Blanc winemaker Pierre Lurton. The first vintage was 2000: ripe, oaky, and stylish. The second wine is the lighter, cherry-tinged "Lourens River Valley".

La Motte ☆☆

Franschhoek. Owner: Hannelie Koegelenberg. 108 hectares. www.la-motte.com

La Motte traces its origins back to the Huguenots. Under its present owner, Hannelie Koegelenberg, daughter of Dr. Anton Rupert, the property has been fully restored, and is now one of the country's leading producers of Shiraz. Veteran winemaker Jacques Borman has also achieved great success with the Cabernet/Merlot blend, which sells under the "Millennium" label.

Mulderbosch ☆☆☆

Stellenbosch. Owner: Hydro Holdings. 27 hectares. www.mulderbosch.co.za

Mulderbosch has the reputation of being the Cape's answer to New Zealand's Cloudy Bay: several highly successful Sauvignon Blanc vintages together with some excellent Chardonnay have contributed to this image, though winemaker Mike Dobrovic is too eclectic a personality to fit easily into so simplistic a comparison. The Sauvignon is surely the most mouth-watering of all those the Cape can offer. The Chenin, as invigorating as a bite into a freshly picked apple, and a plummy Merlot/Cabernet blend sold under the "Faithful Hound" label, complete an impressive range.

Nederburg ☆–☆☆☆

Paarl. Owners: Distell. No vineyards. www.nederburg.co.za

Although most of the wines from this large estate are thoroughly commercial, Nederburg has become renowned for its annual auction, featuring both its own top wines and special bottlings from throughout the Cape. Nederburg has a well-deserved reputation for its rich, sweet wines made from botrytized Chenin Blanc, and sold under the proprietary name of "Edelkeur".

Neethlingshof ☆–☆☆

Stellenbosch. Owner: Distell. 210 hectares. www.neethlingshof.co.za

Hans-Joachim Schreiber, a retired German banker, bought Neethlingshof in 1985. He invested heavily in the property, and established its reputation for sound Chardonnay and Shiraz, and for outstanding botrytized Riesling. It is now part of the Distell group.

Nitida ☆☆

Durbanville. Owner/winemaker: Bernhard Veller. 12 hectares. www.nitida.co.za

The first vintage here was 1996, and Nitida soon established a well-deserved reputation for its Sauvignon Blanc. The flagship wine is the Merlot/Cabernet blend called "Calligraphy", which can be somewhat hard and austere in some vintages.

L'Ormarins ☆☆

Franschhoek. Owners: the Rupert family. 200 hectares. www.lormarins.co.za

A Franschhoek property, extensively replanted and restored.

Good Cabernet-based reds (notably the new-oaked "Optima"), fine Cabernet, and widely distributed Blanc Fumé.

Overgaauw ☆☆–☆☆☆

Stellenbosch. Owners: the van Velden family. 75 hectares

Long-established, family-owned property, producing one of the best Cape "ports" as well as the Cape's only Sylvaner. Merlot and Cabernet are increasingly impressive, as is the Bordeaux blend "Tria Corda", which a decade ago was fiercely astringent.

Plaisir de Merle ☆☆

Franschhoek. Owner: Distell. 380 hectares. www.plaisirdemerle.co.za

Once a supply farm for Nederburg (q.v.), Plaisir de Merle subsequently acquired a reputation as one of the Cape's "First Growth" properties, with advice from outside consultant, Paul Pontallier – director of Château Margaux. The Cabernet and Merlot are often excellent.

Rudera ☆☆–☆☆☆

Somerset West. Owner: Teddy Hall. 18 hectares. www.rudera.co.za

This is the private label of the winemaker at Kanu (q.v.), vinifying grapes sourced mostly from leased vineyards, and producing delicious Chenin Blanc in both dry and nobly sweet styles.

Rupert & Rothschild ☆☆–☆☆☆

Paarl. Owners: Benjamin de Rothschild and Rupert families. 50 hectares. www.fredericksburg.co.za

When two multi-millionaires teamed up to establish this new venture, it was done on a lavish scale. Yet first releases in 1997 were unsatisfactory. The range was revamped and quality soon improved. Despite the untimely death of co-founder Anthonij Rupert in 2001, the estate he helped to create goes from strength to strength, especially with the voluptuous "Baron Edmond" bottling.

Rust-en-Vrede ☆☆–☆☆☆

Stellenbosch. Owners: the Engelbrecht family. 50 hectares. www.rustenvrede.com

Until the late 1990s, this historic estate produced highly regarded, Cape-style reds that were tannic and often astringent in their youth. Since 1998, Jannie Engelbrecht's son, Jean, has been in charge, and he hired winemaker Louis Strydom to make wines in a fleshier, more accessible style. Eventually the estate will release just one wine under the prestigious Rust-en-Vrede label, the elegant "Estate" blend: a far cry from the more robust and earthy vintages of a decade ago. Other wines from the estate, it's planned, will be released under the "Guardian Peak" label.

Rustenberg ☆☆☆–☆☆☆☆

Stellenbosch. Owner: Simon Barlow. 100 hectares. www.rustenberg.com

Perhaps the most beautiful estate in the Cape: low, white, Dutch buildings shaded by enormous trees, and with extensive vineyards on south-facing slopes. Recent replanting, substantial cellar investment, and a change of winemaker (Adi Badenhorst) have all confirmed Rustenberg's place in the front rank of South Africa's producers. The flagship red is the superb "Peter Barlow"

Cabernet blend; the top white, the "Five Soldiers" Chardonnay. "Brampton" is the second label.

Sadie Family Vineyards ☆☆☆
Swartland. Owner: Eben Sadie and family. 6 hectares
The youthful Sadie was the much-lauded winemaker at Spice Route (*q.v.*), but in 2002 devoted himself full-time to his own venture. He only produces one wine, "Columella", which is made in small quantities from vineyards leased and controlled by Sadie. Sadie is passionate about the potential of old-vine Shiraz from the Swartland valleys, and "Columella" is predominantly Shiraz with a slight addition of Mourvèdre. Yields are exceptionally low and vinification both non-interventionist and meticulous. The lush, ripe, first vintage, 2000, proved to be one of the most profound wines South Africa has yet produced.

Saxenburg ☆☆–☆☆☆
Stellenbosch. Owner: Adrian Bührer. No vineyards.
www.saxenburg.co.za
Saxenburg is widely regarded for its red wines, particularly those sold under the "Private Collection" (reserve) label. The Shiraz and Cabernet have been particularly successful. Winemaker Nico van der Merwe is exceptionally skilled, but some of the wines are too expensive for the quality.

Simonsig ☆☆–☆☆☆
Stellenbosch. Owners: the Malan family. 200 hectares.
www.simonsig.co.za
After early emphasis on varietals, Frans Malan and his three sons had runaway successes with blended, wood-matured whites, and were the first in the Cape to make a true *méthode traditionnelle* sparkling wine. Simonsig's reputation for red wines is based firmly on Pinotage, but new wines have been added to the range: "Frans Malan Reserve" (Pinotage/Cabernet/Merlot) and the charming and cedary Bordeaux blend called "Tiara".

Spice Route ☆☆–☆☆☆
Malmesbury. Owner: Charles Back. 110 hectares
Founded in the late 1990s by a group of winemakers and wine writers, this successful brand is now wholly owned by Charles Back of Fairview (*q.v.*). Under winemaker Eben Sadie, Spice Route swiftly established a reputation for rich, full-flavoured, slightly gamey wines from Mediterranean varieties, with a preference for dry-farmed bush vines. In 2002, Charl [sic] du Plessis took over from Sadie, and he will expand the range with white wines from Darling, and a flagship red blend to be called "Caldera".

Springfield ☆☆☆
Robertson. Owner/winemaker: Abrie Bruwer. 140 hectares.
www.springfield-estate.com
Springfield sold its production to bulk-wine producers until 1995. Since then, Bruwer has gone from strength to strength, focusing on quality to such an extent that production has dropped by two-thirds. The winemaking is artisanal, with the exception of the racy Sauvignons. All other wines are made from uncrushed berries fermented with natural yeasts, and are bottled without filtration. His most remarkable wines are called "Cuvée Ancienne", the red being pure Cabernet, minty and peppery; the white, a rich Chardonnay. Just for fun, Bruwer has also made a brave facsimile of Hungarian Tokaji Aszú.

Stark-Condé ☆☆–☆☆☆
Stellenbosch. Owner/winemaker: José Condé. 40 hectares
A new star in Stellenbosch, Condé is an American who, since 1998, has been producing small quantities of sumptuous, concentrated, herbal Cabernet Sauvignon and Pinotage.

Steenberg ☆☆
Constantia. Owner: Adrian Gardiner. 64 hectares.
www.steenberg-vineyards.co.za
This is a relative newcomer to this historic region, although the original Steenberg farm was planted in 1682. In the 1990s, the estate was revived as a tourist-and-leisure complex, and a winery was added in 1996. It has enjoyed great success with its melony Semillon, as well as aromatic Sauvignon. In addition, there are some attractive reds, a Cabernet/Merlot blend called "Catharina", and a brave stab at Nebbiolo.

Stellenbosch Farmers' Winery
See Distell

Stellenbosch Vineyards ☆☆
Stellenbosch. Owners: private consortium. 1,000 hectares.
www.stellvine.co.za
A new company formed by the merger of four cooperatives, pooling substantial resources. "Kumani" is their best-known brand; "Versus" is a vehicle for high-volume wines; and their top range is called "Genesis".

Stellenzicht ☆☆
Stellenbosch. Owner: Distell. 123 hectares.
www.stellenzicht.co.za
Under winemaker Andre van Rensburg, Stellenzicht achieved international recognition, especially for its Shiraz. Since 1998, Guy Webber has been the winemaker, and the estate is now part of the Distell group, but the emphasis remains on Pinotage and Shiraz. The principal range of varietal wines is "Golden Triangle", but the "Stellenzicht Vineyards" wines (Syrah, an estate blend, and Semillon) can be exceptional.

Thelema ☆☆☆
Stellenbosch. Owners: the Webb and McLean families.
52 hectares
This beautiful estate lies high up in the hills. Although the soils are relatively fertile, the skills of winemaker Gyles Webb have won Thelema a worldwide reputation for its finely structured Cabernet Sauvignon, Cabernet Sauvignon/Merlot, Sauvignon Blanc, and Chardonnay.

The range is remarkable for its consistency from year to year, and the Merlot reserve, a wondrous confection of black fruits, oak, and chocolatey nuances, is one of the Cape's finest.

Tokara
Stellenbosch. Owner: G. T. Ferreira. 40 hectares
Overseen by Gyles Webb of Thelema (*q.v.*), this fledgling venture had a lavish new winery and restaurant to show by late 2002, but no wines. At present they are being released under the second label of "Zondernaam", until owner

Ferreira and winemaker Miles Mossop consider they deserve the "Tokara" label.

Uiterwyk ☆–☆☆☆
Stellenbosch. Owners: the de Waal family. 115 hectares.
www.uiterwyk.co.za
A beautiful estate (one of the less flamboyant), bottling a small quantity of its best wines in a traditional cellar. Consistently good red wines, including an "Estate" blend and Pinotage, especially the old-vine bottling called "Top of the Hill". By 2001, all the best wines were being released under the "De Waal Wines" label.

Van Loveren ☆
Robertson. Owners: the Retief family. 250 hectares
One of the more important producers in the Robertson area: easy-drinking wines, a good Chardonnay, and an extensive range of interesting varieties such as Fernão Pires.

Veenwouden ☆☆☆
Paarl. Owner: Deon van der Walt. 15 hectares
Veenwouden, owned by South Africa's most celebrated tenor, made a remarkable debut in 1993. Deon van der Walt and his winemaker brother Marcel planted their vineyard with a view to producing Pomerol-style wines.

Veenwouden's Merlot and Cabernet/Merlot "Classic" blend may not be easily mistaken for right-bank Bordeaux, but they are wonderful wines, nonetheless: rich and concentrated, but showing far more elegance than most Cape wines in this style.

Vergelegen ☆☆☆–☆☆☆☆
Somerset West. Owner: Anglo American Farms. 120 hectares.
www.vergelegen.co.za
Vergelegen is one of the Cape's oldest properties (dating back to around 1700). It has been extensively renovated since being purchased by the Boschendal (q.v.) owner (Anglo American Farms) in 1987, and a new hilltop winery was built.

Winemaker Martin Meinert put Vergelegen on the map, and since 1997, Andre van Rensburg has consolidated its reputation. Although best-known for Sauvignon and Chardonnay, the red wines – Cabernet, Merlot, and the superb "Estate" blend – are increasingly rich and complex.

The Cabernet combines plums, liquorice, and cloves; the Merlot is slightly sweeter and plumper; while the Estate blend is smokier and with even greater length.

Vergenoegd ☆☆
Stellenbosch. Owners: the Faure family. 100 hectares
This 300-year-old estate once supplied bulk grapes to wholesalers, such as the KWV. Today it bottles all its own wine, and since the late 1990s, quality has increased dramatically, with firm, tannic Cabernet and age-worthy Merlot, as well as good Cape-style port.

Villiera ☆☆
Stellenbosch. Owners: the Grier family. 300 hectares
This cooler-than-average estate is strongly focused on value-for-money, high-quality wines.

Villiera has been particularly successful with Merlot and Merlot/Cabernet blends, and a complete range of classic-method sparkling wines.

Vredendal
***See* WestCorp**

Vriesenhof/Talana Hill/Paradyskloof ☆☆–☆☆☆
Stellenbosch. Owners: Jan Boland Coetzee and partners.
35 hectares. www.paradys.co.za
On the Helderberg side of Stellenbosch, Vriesenhof's mountain slopes are cooled by the breeze coming off False Bay. The estate has a good reputation for Cabernet and Cabernet-based blends, sold either under the premium "Talana Hill" label, or as Vriesenhof.

The Bordeaux blend called "Kallista" can be rather tough, but there is fine Chardonnay and Pinotage, and a growing enthusiasm on winemaker Coetzee's part for Pinot Noir. In 2002, Boland regrouped his three labels under the name of "Domaines Paradyskloof".

Warwick Estate ☆☆–☆☆☆
Stellenbosch. Owners: the Ratcliffe family. 75 hectares.
www.warwickwine.co.za
Very much a family business, this leading property is run with both energy and charm by Norma Ratcliffe and her son Michael.

For some years, its top wine has been the successful Bordeaux blend "Trilogy", but recent additions to the range are "Three Cape Ladies": a blend of Cabernet, Merlot, and Pinotage, and a Chardonnay and Sauvignon. Warwick also has a good reputation for its blueberry-scented Cabernet Franc.

Waterford ☆☆–☆☆☆
Stellenbosch. Owner: Jeremy Ord. 50 hectares.
www.waterfordwines.com
After Ord bought this hillside farm in 1998, he constructed a charming Tuscan-style cloistered winery, and hired Kevin Arnold, formerly of Rust-en-Vrede (q.v.), to make the wines. Initial releases have shown great promise, especially the reds from Cabernet and Shiraz.

Welgemeend ☆☆–☆☆☆
Paarl. Owner: Louise Hofmeyr. 16 hectares
A tiny estate by South African standards, but an influential pioneer of red wines. Billy Hofmeyr demonstrated the merits of picking early, blending the two Cabernets with Merlot, Malbec, and Petit Verdot, and maturing for up to eighteen months in small, new-oak barrels. His daughter, Louise, now follows admirably in his footsteps.

The first Cape estate to produce traditional Bordeaux-style blends, Welgemeend now offers several different combinations. The standard estate wine is predominantly Cabernet, while "Douelle" contains mainly Merlot and Malbec. Current vintages of the "Amadé" have Rhône varieties and Pinotage in the blend.

WestCorp ☆
Olifants River. 4,600 hectares
The immense and successful Vredendal cooperative made great inroads into the British market with brands such as "Goiya Kgeisje".

In 2002 the company merged with Spruitdrift, also in Olifants River, to form a new company called WestCorp. The wines are highly commercial, but good examples of their kind.

Wildekrans ☆☆
Walker Bay. Owners: Bruce Elkin and Eric Green. 40 hectares
A good source for Chenin Blanc, Semillon, and Pinotage, all in a fresh, elegant style.

Zandvliet ☆–☆☆
Robertson. Owners: the Paul de Wet family. 155 hectares.
www.zandvliet.co.za
The Shiraz was a pioneering red from Robertson, and today the winery produces at least three bottlings. The "Astonvale" range focuses on value-for-money varietal wines.

Zevenwacht ☆–☆☆
Stellenbosch. Owner: Harold Johnson. 150 hectares.
www.zevenwacht.co.za
Zevenwacht's Kuils River vineyards are cooled by breezes off False Bay. They yield easy-drinking red wines with flavour rather than weight, as well as several successful whites, notably Chenin Blanc.

Zimbabwe

Zimbabwe lies on the same line of latitude as much of Bolivia and southern Brazil, and climate conditions are by no means perfectly conducive to growing quality grapes for making wine (heat and sunshine in abundance, but also frost during the growing season, and summer rains which affect the harvest). An industry of sorts began in 1965. The first wines were of poor quality and dubious grapes – Jacques, Issor, and Farrazza – which have since been replaced by the planting of noble varieties, imported from South Africa. The vineyards are mainly located some 1,200 metres (4,000 feet) above sea-level, north of Harare.

Since the early 1980s, tremendous progress has been made. The use of irrigation, cold fermentation, modern equipment, winemakers trained in Germany, Australia, and South Africa, together with the consultation of "flying winemakers" has brought about an upsurge in quality.

The political unrest and violence that marred Zimbabwe in the early years of the twenty-first century have inevitably complicated life for the handful of functioning estates, such as Worringham, where wines were first made in the 1960s. Mukuyu at Marondera, sixty kilometres (thirty-seven miles) from the capital, cultivates 100 hectares and produced 185,000 cases a year, including Merlot and Cabernet Sauvignon, until the troubles curtailed production. The wines are made by Australian-trained Sam Pfidzayi. African Distillers (Stapleford Wines) is based in Gweru, north of Harare, and produces some 555,000 cases (Sauvignon Blanc, Muscat, a Cabernet/Merlot blend, and a very exciting Pinotage) from 180 hectares of vineyards in Bulawayo, Gweru, and Odzi. It also buys in grapes from private growers. The "Private Cellar" label is top of the Stapleford range.

England & Wales

The fact that England and Wales are at the farthest northern limit of the zone where grapes will ripen has not discouraged some 350 landowners from planting vineyards, great and smalll. The revival of English winegrowing (it was probably introduced by the Romans, and was widespread in the Middle Ages) started slowly in the 1950s, and accelerated rapidly in the 1970s. The excellent summer of 1976 encouraged many to think that winegrowing could be more than a hobby. In spite of a succession of dismal harvests in the late '70s, with vintage rain a regular occurrence, the industry has consolidated its position, helped by global warming in the '90s. In total, almost 850 hectares are in production, across southern England and Wales, with concentrations in the traditional fruit-growing areas of Kent and Sussex, Essex and Suffolk, along the south coast through Hampshire as far as Cornwall, and north through Berkshire, Wiltshire, and Somerset as far as Hereford and Worcester. Total annual production is now averaging 18,000 hectolitres – some 2.4 million bottles – almost all of it white.

It is too early to say that any regional styles have emerged. English wine is a light, refreshing, often slightly tart summer drink. Its best qualities are floweriness, delicate fruitiness, and crisp, clean freshness. Its acidity should be noticeable and matched with fragrant, fruity flavours, whether dry or semi-sweet. Winemakers now produce bottle-fermented sparkling wines, which develop good lees character from two to three years' ageing, and still wines aged in oak. More complex flavours are evolving as the vines age and the winemakers grow more skilful. Good English wines clearly benefit from bottle-age; indeed, they need it, particularly in vintages of high acidity.

In this cool climate, with uncertain weather, early ripening and resistance to rot are two major factors governing the choice of grapes. But some growers, especially the larger ones, are moving away from grapes such as Müller-Thurgau and Schönburger, and from varietal wines, in favour of blends. New German varieties designed to ripen well in cool weather, and the (excellent) hybrid Seyval Blanc are still prominent, although classic French varieties are increasingly used. There are also some serious dessert wines being made, mainly from botrytis-infected Bacchus and Huxelrebe.

The industry's regulatory body, the United Kingdom Vineyards Association can grant a "Seal of Quality" to non-hybrid wines over fifteen per cent total potential alcohol, but it is little-used as it excludes Seyval Blanc. From 1996, the UK can produce regional wines – equivalent to the French *vins de pays* – made from *vinifera* and non-*vinifera* grapes, and may include table wines, although they need no longer be labelled as such.

Leading Producers

Breaky Bottom ☆–☆☆
East Sussex. Owner/winemaker: Peter Hall. 2 hectares. Visits. www.breakybottom.co.uk
Seyval Blanc and Müller-Thurgau are planted on chalk downland. Wines made in a non-interventionist style by Peter Hall have attracted a loyal following. Since 1994, a very good classic-method sparkling has been made from Seyval Blanc. These are lean wines that definitely benefit from bottle-age.

Chapel Down Winery ☆☆
Kent. Owners: Chapel Down Wines Ltd. www.chapeldownwines.co.uk
One of the largest wineries in the UK, handling grapes from all over the southeast (it has no vineyards of its own), and since 1995 the owner of Tenterden (*q.v.*). "Epoch" red is one of the best in England, and the sparkling wine is of excellent quality. Some of the wines have been selected by British Airways.

Chiddingstone ☆☆
Kent. Owners: the Quirk family. 15 hectares
Pinot Noir can be good, compares favourably with French styles, and has been served at royal banquets. Supplies several airlines.

Denbies ☆☆
Surrey. Owner: Adrian White. 106 hectares. Visits. www.denbiesvineyard.co.uk
The UK's largest vineyard, planted with twenty varieties, mainly Müller-Thurgau. The winery is perhaps the most modern in Britain. A comprehensive range of wines, with some award-winning ones, especially Bacchus and dessert wine. A blend of Dornfelder and Pinot Noir makes a plump, attractive red.

Halfpenny Green ☆
Staffordshire. Owner: Martin Vickers. 6 hectares. Visits
Produces a range of white and red wines in all styles. Single varieties include Huxelrebe and good Madeleine Angevine.

Hidden Spring ☆–☆☆
East Sussex. Owners: Graham and Sue Mosey. 3 hectares. Visits
Property with a range of varieties including Pinot Noir, Seyval Blanc, Ortega, Müller-Thurgau, and Faber. Striking labels and good wines, especially oak-aged and red.

Llanerch ☆
Vale of Glamorgan, Wales. Owners: Peter and Diana Andrews. 2 hectares. Visits. www.llanerch-vineyard.co.uk
The largest and most commercial vineyard in Wales, with vines (including Reichensteiner, Bacchus, Kernling, Huxelrebe, Seyval Blanc, and Triomphe) on south-facing slopes in the Ely Valley. The estate wines are released under the "Cariad" label, including various dry whites, one rosé, and a sparkling, which have netted a number of international awards.

Northbrook Springs ☆
Hampshire. Owner: Brian Cable. 5 hectares
This chalky downland location looks to be very promising. The wines, made with advice from consultant John Worontschak, are good and improving; with occasional excellent late-harvest wines, and a Fumé-style Reichensteiner and Bacchus blend.

Nyetimber ☆☆–☆☆☆
West Sussex. Owner: Andy Hill. 20 hectares. www.nyetimber-vineyard.co.uk
The estate that, since 1992, has proved that England can make sparkling wines from traditional Champenoise varieties. Stuart and Sandra Moss were the owners behind this success story. Nyetimber wines have won innumerable awards. In 2002, they sold the property but still manage it. Chardonnay and Pinots Noir and Meunier are planted, solely for sparkling-wine.

Penshurst ☆
Kent. Owner/winemaker: David Westphal. 5 hectares.
www.penshurst.co.uk
Well-established with modern winery. Good range of wines, especially Müller-Thurgau and Seyval Blanc. All wines are vegetarian (no fining) and are not released for at least two years.

Ridge View Estate ☆☆–☆☆☆
East Sussex. Owner/winemaker: Mike Roberts.
6.5 hectares. www.ridgeview.co.uk
Ridge View has followed the lead of Nyetimber by planting only Chardonnay and Pinots Noir and Meunier, and producing traditional-method sparkling wines. The first vintage was 1993 and quality since has been consistently high and rewarded with critical acclaim. This is the English wine closest to Champagne in flavour.

Sandhurst ☆
Kent. Owners: J & C Nicholas. 5.5 hectares. Visits
Well-run vineyard on a mixed farm. Good, oak-aged Bacchus and Pinot sparkling; red wine production is set to expand.

Tenterden ☆
Kent. Owner: Chapel Down. 7.5 hectares.
www.chapeldownwines.co.uk
Müller-Thurgau and Seyval Blanc vines planted in 1979 now produce a range of wines from very dry to sweet, a rosé, and sparkling. There is an award-winning, oak-aged Seyval. The property is now owned by Chapel Down (*q.v.*). It is also the base for New Wave Wines, a company that markets wines from Tenterden, Lamberhurst, and Chapel Down (*qq.v.*), including a new range of English varietals under the "Curious Grape" label.

Three Choirs ☆
Gloucestershire. Owner: limited company. 30 hectares.
www.threechoirs.com
The largest producer in the west of England, but the wines, especially the reds, can be inconsistent in quality. The range includes vintage sparkling, white (including oaked), rosé, red, and dessert wines, plus an unusual *nouveau* style.

Valley Vineyards ☆☆–☆☆☆
Berkshire. Owner: Jon Leighton. 8 hectares.
www.valleyvineyards.com
Serious estate, with winemaker John Worontschak producing good to very good wines. Especially recommended are the oak-aged white and red, and sparkling wines. Few other English wineries, if any, can match its tally of show medals. Other labels used are "Clocktower" and "Heritage".

Other Producers

Bearsted ☆
Kent. www.bearstedwines.co.uk
From a mere two hectares, the Gibson family produce eight wines, including a fresh rosé and sparkling wine.

Boze Down ☆–☆☆
Oxfordshire
Two hectares of mixed varieties, with an interesting selection of high-quality, oaked reds.

Bruisyard ☆
Suffolk
Four hectares of Müller-Thurgau, established in 1974. The Berwicks produce a full range of wines styles. They retired in 2002, and put the vineyard up for sale.

Cane End ☆
Berkshire. 5 hectares
Rosé and Bacchus dessert wine can be good.

Carr Taylor ☆
East Sussex. 8 hectares
Well-known sparkling-wine house merged in 2000 with Chapel Down (*q.v.*). Wines will now be made at Tenterden (*q.v.*).

Chilford Hall ☆
Cambridgeshire. www.childfordhall.co.uk
Long-established vineyard, with many German grapes, has enjoyed much success at annual shows.

Dunkery ☆
Somerset. Owner/winemaker: Derek Pritchard.
An estate within the Exmoor National Park. The specialties are Pinot Noir and sparkling wines.

Gifford's Hall ☆
Suffolk. 4 hectares. www.giffordshall.co.uk
Good wines. The "Medium Dry" regularly wins awards.

Lamberhurst ☆
Kent. 11 hectares
Founded in 1971 by Kenneth McAlpine, it acquired a solid reputation, and on his retirement the property was sold. Merged with Chapel Down (*q.v.*) in 2000.

New Hall ☆
Essex. 36 hectares. www.newhallwines.co.uk
A large vineyard, that also sells grapes to other wineries. Bacchus and sparkling wines are regular award-winners.

Sedlescombe ☆
East Sussex
Organic vineyard, making a wide range of wines from three hectares of mixed varieties.

Sharpham ☆–☆☆
Devon. Owner/winemaker: Mark Sharpham. 4 hectares.
www.sharpham.com
This winery produces red wines from Dornfelder, Pinot Noir, and others, and occasional prize-winning dessert wine.

Wickham ☆
Hampshire. Owners: Angela Baart and Gordon Channon.
www.wickhamvineyard.com
Under John Charnley, Wickham acquired a good reputation for sparkling rosé; a Pinot Noir/Triomphe blend; and for an oaked white, supplied to the House of Commons. In 2000, Wickham was sold to its present owners.

Wyken ☆
Bury St Edmunds, Suffolk
Small, two hectares planted in 1988, it makes a prize-winning Bacchus and a creditable red.

Enjoying Wine

Enjoying Wine

It is the inquisitive who enjoy wine most. The essence of the game is variety; you could taste a different wine every day of your life and yet not learn it all. Each wine evolves with time. There will always be new wines to taste, and new combinations of wine with food to try. There will also always be more to learn about yourself, your palate, and its reactions.

No single attitude or set of rules can apply to a commodity that can be either a simple foodstuff as basic as bread and cheese, or one of the most *recherché* of luxuries, or anywhere in between. There are enamel-mug wines and Baccarat-crystal wines, and there is no point in pretending that one is the other.

This chapter is concerned with choosing, buying, storing, serving, and appreciating wine that is above the *ordinaire* or jug level. Once a wine has a named origin (as opposed to being an anonymous blend) it reflects a particular soil, climate, culture, and tradition. For better or worse, the wine then has some character.

The mastery of wine consists in recognizing, bringing out, and making the most of that character. I cannot improve on the late André Simon's definition of a connoisseur: "One who knows good wine from bad, and appreciates the distinctive merits of different wines." Thank heaven all white wines are not Sauvignon Blancs, however fresh, flowery, and fragrant, or all reds great thumping Cabernets.

It is a crucial (but also a common) misunderstanding of the nature and variety of wine to say that a Barolo, for example, is better than a Rioja, or a Pauillac than a Napa Cabernet. The secret is to learn to understand and enjoy each of them for what they are.

There is only one essential I would press on you, if you are going to spend more than a bare minimum and buy wines above the jug level: and that is to make a conscious act of tasting. Become aware of the messages your nose and mouth are sending you – not just about wine, but about all food and drink. Seek out new tastes and think about them.

By far the greater part of all fine wine, and even – perhaps especially – of the best, is thrown away by being used as a mere drink. A great bottle of wine is certainly wasted if nobody talks about it, or at least tries to pinpoint in his or her own consciousness the wonderful will-o'-the-wisp of fragrance and flavour.

Buying Wine

To buy wine and get exactly what you expect is the exception rather than the rule. Wine is a moving target: a kaleidoscope of growers and vintages that never stands still. If this bothers you, there is a solution – stick to a brand. But you will be sacrificing the great fascination of wine, its infinite variety, not to mention the fun of the chase: the satisfaction of finding a winner (and the chagrin of backing a dud).

There are few cardinal rules in such an open field, where one day you may be buying from the corner store, the next by mail order, and the third direct from the producer. But it is certainly better to think carefully about what you want to buy before you buy it. Sometimes, of course, you will just want a decent bottle to accompany a dish you are preparing for guests that very day, but whenever possible, buy ahead of your needs.

Nobody can take in all the offerings of a well-stocked store at a glance. Do your wine-buying when you are in the mood and have time to browse, to compare prices, to make calculations, to use reference books. By far the best place to do this is at home, by comparing the price lists of alternative suppliers. Avoid traders who have no list and rely on you to fall for this week's "special".

Your wine needs time to rest. Although many modern white and light red wines are so stable that you could play skittles with them and do them no harm, all mature red wines need a settling period of at least several days after being moved. Your chances of serving a wine at its best are far greater if you can prepare it calmly at home.

Given time you can make an order that qualifies for a discount. Buying by the case, even the mixed case, is invariably cheaper than buying by the bottle.

In the past, wine-buyers had to rely on either their own knowledge and experience or those of their wine merchant. Today there are many more ways to acquire information. This edition of the *Wine Companion* includes, for the first time, the website addresses of all producers who have them. These sites vary in quality, but most give detailed information about the range and styles of wines produced, and provide email addresses so that, should you wish, you can obtain further information from that producer.

Moreover, there are many websites that specialize in providing information to consumers in the form of tasting notes, vintage notes, news about changes in the industry, and so forth. These sites may or may not be linked to sites selling wine. Some of the more rarefied and detailed wine websites are pay sites; many others are free.

An Investment in Pleasure

An investment in future pleasure is often one of the most profitable of all. Inflation aside, when you come to drink the wine, now better than when you bought it, the expenditure will be a thing of the past; the pleasure will seem a gift from the gods.

In fact, very little money is needed to convert you from a bottle-by-bottle buyer to the proud possessor of a "cellar". Calculate what you spend on wine in three months, or two months, or at a pinch only one month – and spend it all at once in a planned spree. Put the wine away. Then continue to buy the same quantity as before but use it to replenish your stock, instead of for instant drinking. All you have done is to borrow three, two, or one month's wine money and the interest on that is your only extra expenditure. Your reward is wine you have chosen carefully and kept well, ready when you want it, not when you can get to the shops.

Make an effort to be clear-headed about what you really need. Do not spend more than you can comfortably afford. Think twice before buying unknown wines as part of a package. Do not buy a quantity of wine you have never tasted and may not like. Consider whether home delivery is really practicable: will there be someone at home to answer the door? Can you easily lift the forty or fifty pounds (twenty or twenty-five kilos) that a case of wine weighs?

One of the wiliest ways of broadening your buying scope is to join with a small group of like-minded people to form a syndicate. A syndicate can save money by buying bigger lots of wine, thus bringing within reach extraordinary bottles at prices that would make you, on your own, feel guilty for months. Three or four friends who have never tasted Château Latour or Romanée-Conti will enjoy them more if they buy and open them together, sharing their opinions (and their guilt). While there may be laws that prevent an unlicensed citizen from selling wine, even to a friend, there is nothing to stop them sharing its cost.

The Wine Trade

The structure of the wine trade has changed radically in recent years from a fairly rigid pattern of brokers, shippers, agents, wholesalers, and retailers to an intricate but fluid mixture of ingredients, some old and some new. It is not surprising that such a pleasant vocation has more volunteers than the army. The great growth areas have been in "experts", writers and consultants, and in ingenious methods of selling with or without a shop.

In America the period has seen wine change from being a minority – even a faintly suspect minority – interest to a national pastime. The wine trade has recruited regiments of specialists at every level. Locally, the retailers are the most prominent, nationally, the marketing men. But what remains sovereign (and to the foreigner most bizarre) is the changing legislation from state to state. Scarcely two are alike. New York, California, Texas, Florida, and a few more states are relatively free to benefit from all the rich possibilities; the remainder are more or less inhibited by local legislation, especially laws that prohibit the dispatching of wine across certain state lines. This denies consumers the freedom to buy and ship wine directly while protecting the interests of local retailers. Even individual counties can stick their oar in and say what you may and may not drink. However, in recent years, the grip exercised by local retailers on interstate shipments has relaxed slightly, or been prised open by determined legislators, and unless neo-Prohibition rears its ugly head, it should, in the future, be easier rather than more difficult for wine-lovers to buy the bottles they want from the source of their choice.

In Britain, the wine-drinking consumer is relatively fortunate. Changes started in the 1960s with the ponderous tread of the brewers, fearful that a growing taste for wine would erode their sales of beer, buying scores of traditional local wine shops and replacing them with chains tied to national brand-marketing ideas. Unfortunately, many of these new shops were dismal, and the rising generation of vocational wine merchants – as opposed to accountants – wanted nothing to do with them. They found it easy to reinvent the old individualistic wine trade for the new generation of better-travelled and more knowledgeable (if less wealthy) wine-lovers. Today there is a specialist for almost every area of the wine-growing world, as well as well-stocked independent merchants in city and countryside alike.

Traditional wine merchants offer the old virtues of personal service, storage or delivery to your door, and credit (at a price). Personal service consists largely of word-of-mouth recommendations based on a regular customer's known tastes and resources. Some firms offer cellar plans, recommending wines for laying down, storing them, and advising when they are becoming ready to drink. Many merchants offer wines *en primeur* (or, as Americans know it,

as "futures"), that is, many months in advance of bottling and shipping. The supposed advantage is a more favourable price and the opportunity to secure wines from the most sought-after properties. For the purchaser, the disadvantage is having to part with your cash well in advance of delivery for a wine you yourself have had no opportunity to taste and assess. Such firms are skilful at offering the best wines of a new vintage early, while they are still in their makers' cellars and long before they are even bottled, at "opening" prices that usually rise once the wines come on the general market.

At the opposite extreme, making wine available and tempting to every shopper, are the supermarkets, offering at first a rather simple and limited range, sometimes under their own brand names, and now a remarkable collection including fine wines and esoteric discoveries. For European wine-drinkers, the supermarkets and national chains are now the primary source for their purchases. Some supermarkets and chains select with care to build a constantly evolving range of interest and value; the majority buy primarily on price, and quality can be dismal. A further source of wine is the wine club, often linked to national newspapers or periodicals; some of them, such as The Wine Society in Britain, offer a more extensive range of services, including storage.

In wine-producing regions it is common to buy direct from the producer. Just about every wine-drinking household in Tours or Stuttgart or Vienna will have its favourite producers, visited on a regular basis for a congenial hour in the cellars while the latest vintage is loaded into the car. In regions where the vine struggles to grow, or is not even planted, it is more practical to buy from merchants or via the internet.

Buying wine over the ether is practical and easy. Often the range of wines on offer is good and varied, and special offers and discounts are constantly being dangled before the consumer and can be good value. The drawbacks are those common to most forms of e-commerce: credit card security (or lack thereof) and lack of recourse when something goes wrong. Should a delivery arrive very late, or should the wines delivered not correspond to what you ordered, or should some of the bottles be smashed, you may well be able to obtain refunds or other redress, but the process can be laborious. On the other hand, many buyers find the advantages far outweigh the drawbacks.

The Marketing Man Cometh

Remember that, for many large wine companies, wine is not the supreme drink but a mere "product". Produced in enormous volumes, it needs to be marketed and sold as aggressively as possible. Supermarkets and national retailers usually lack qualified staff, and recommendations take the form of cards quoting favourable reviews from wine writers – which may or may not be reliable indications of quality and value. Many wines are discounted or offered as part of "special promotions"; nothing wrong with that, except that such offers form part of a trade war between the largest companies, battling each other for shelf space.

Packaging is an essential part of the armoury of marketing. Stylish labelling is always welcome, but is hardly the most important component of a bottle of wine. Be on your guard whenever you see "original" bottles, such as those coated with a simulacrum of dust, or those with laddish labels along the lines of "Sad Old Git" or "Miserable Bastard".

With so much energy going into subsidiary matters such as packaging, the wine inside the bottle is unlikely to be memorable.

Learn While You Drink

Mention has already been made of websites as good sources of information, as indeed is the welcome proliferation of books on every conceivable subject and wine region. There are other, more personal ways of expanding one's knowledge and purchasing skills. Wine clubs and some leading merchants often offer a great deal of information about the wines they sell, and some of them organize periodic tastings, which feed the urge to learn while you drink. Such tastings are often tutored by the best experts in the field, who will give participants the opportunity to question and talk to notable authorities on wine.

Many wine fairs are restricted to wine professionals. Some others, however, are specifically designed to appeal to the general public. They are often organized either by major retailers or by wine magazines. For a modest fee, they can give you access to an enormous number of fine wines which are usually poured by those who either make the wine or own the property, again giving those present the opportunity to quiz the experts directly. Such consumer wine fairs are increasingly common and popular events on both sides of the Atlantic. These events are often linked to "winemaker dinners" or master classes, at which some of the most prestigious figures in the wine world pour and discuss their wines. These can be expensive, but often give you a rare opportunity to taste rare older vintages in the company of the producer.

If the one-day wine fair merely whets the appetite, then you might consider a wine tour. These have become popular in England, and can be an extremely effective way to learn about wine. They tend to be package tours for small groups, led by experts in the region being visited. It is as close as the enthusiastic amateur will get to the life of the professional: walking the vineyards, tasting from barrel in the cellar, questioning the winemakers, and, twice a day, enjoying Rabelaisian meals with excellent wines.

Wine Auctions

In the past twenty years or so, auctions have come to epitomize both the scholarship and the showmanship of wine. At first, it was Michael Broadbent at Christie's; then a succession of auctioneers at Sotheby's and elsewhere, became wine's ringmasters and at the same time the repositories of esoteric vinous knowledge. Auctions are now regularly used in the USA, Germany, South Africa, and many countries besides Britain to sell and publicize at the same time. But the London auction houses have another role simply to turn over private cellars, surplus stocks, and awkward small amounts of wine that complicate a wine merchant's life. There is a steady flow of mature wine, young wine, and sometimes good but unfashionable wine at absurdly low prices. Anyone can buy, but the bargains are often in lots larger than an individual may want. It is common practice to form syndicates to buy and divide such lots.

But bear in mind that much wine is consigned to auction for a good reason: a restaurant or private collector may be offloading stock surplus to requirements. On the other hand,

a collector may also have found the wine disappointing and decided to get rid of it. Beware especially of the eleven-bottle case, often a sure sign that bottle number twelve has already been drunk – without pleasure. There is always an element of risk in buying wine at auction (the wine may be splendid, but it may also have been stored in abysmal conditions), but they can provide you with genuine bargains. Before bidding it is crucial to become familiar with current prices for top growths; tables are often found in leading wine magazines.

Speculating in Blue Chips

The auction houses established a flourishing market in old wines whose value had been unknown before. In their wake, a new class of, so to speak, second-hand wine merchants or brokers has sprung up, led by Farr Vintners in London. Their business can be compared with antiquarian booksellers: finding rare wines on behalf of collectors – for collectors there certainly are today, as there never were in the spacious days when a gentleman filled his cellars with First Growth claret as a matter of course.

Those who buy such blue-chip wines in quantity these days are more likely to be engaged in the less gentlemanly game of speculation. Wine is a commodity susceptible to buying cheap and selling dear – but happily, with no certainty of success.

The more expensive the wine, the greater the chance of its appreciation. But other factors come into it, too: the vintage and its reputation (which will shift, not always predictably, as time goes on); the general financial climate; the popularity of the château or grower in question; perhaps most of all the proven ability of the wine to age. It is the classed growths of Bordeaux and vintage port that are known or presumed to have the longest potential life span – therefore the biggest spread of opportunity for reselling at a profit. Modern burgundies and German wines, even Champagne, are considered relatively poor risks, with or without justification. The very best Italian, Australian, and Californian wines, and such rarities as Tokaji Eszencia, also have a certain following.

Who Do You Believe?

In the past, most wine writers were historians, connoisseurs, or dilettantes. Today there is a new breed: the wine critic, whose primary role is to assess individual wines for the benefit of the consumer. Robert Parker was the first to introduce the now widely adopted system of marking wines on a 100-point scale. There are obvious flaws to such a system, the principal one being that it gives the impression that a tasting note is a definitive assessment rather than a snapshot taken of a living product in a constant state of evolution and transformation. Such a system affects certainty where there can be no such thing.

Yet there can be no doubt that many, perhaps most, wine-drinkers find such scoring systems positive and useful, assisting them in their choices. Scores are usually accompanied by some kind of commentary on the flavour or style of the wine in question, which may be more useful than the score itself. Most wine-drinkers lack the opportunities to taste dozens, even hundreds, of wines each week, and are grateful to the tasting professionals who are willing to submit to the endurance test.

Scores are only as reliable as the critic making the score. If you find your own judgment concurring with one critic more than another – or with one newspaper columnist more than another – then you have grounds for trusting his or her judgment. The wine score may be a blunt and flawed instrument, but it serves a useful purpose. Just don't expect infallibility.

Choosing Wine

One of the many advantages of living in a winemaking country is the way it simplifies your choice. You drink the local wine, preferably made by friends. You tend to suit your diet to it; if the wine is delicate you will go easy on the seasoning; if it is strapping you will make meals of garlic and peppers. All bets are off in California, where your friends and neighbours may make anything from a relatively fragile Sauvignon Blanc to a galumphing Zinfandel or Chardonnay, but most wine regions arrived at a balanced food-and-wine regime years ago.

In a country or region with no such traditions things are more complicated. In Britain, or the eastern United States, where the shops offer every wine there is, it is hardest of all to know where to start. Our wonderful variety makes a wonderfully difficult choice.

The realistic starting point, of course, is the price. The poorer you are, the easier your choice will be. Together with the price goes the company and the occasion. If your companions are as interested in wine as you are, you will want to seize the opportunity of discussing a good bottle with them. If they are indifferent, no matter how much you love them, remember that the wine itself is an occasion; it does not have to be fascinating, too – unless to save you from death by boredom.

A Moment in the Limelight

In short, before you choose a wine, decide whether it is going to spend even a moment in the limelight – and who, beside yourself, will be drinking it. Test yourself with your reaction to the reported behaviour of Voltaire, who habitually gave his guests Beaujolais while he drank the finest burgundies himself.

Whether you give priority to the food or the wine is the next question. Ideally they should share the stage as harmonious equals – no more rivals than a hero and heroine. In a restaurant, the menu and the wine list should be offered to you at the same time.

In practice the proposition is probably either "What shall we drink with the lamb tonight?" or "What shall we eat with this bottle of Pomerol"? You need, in fact, a two-way frame of reference: a mental image of the flavours of both food and wine so that you can match them to bring out the best in both.

It is surprising how often I am asked, "You don't have to drink red wine with meat and white wine with fish, do you?", usually with a sort of indignation that implies that this simple piece of lore is a savage attack on liberty and the Constitution. Of course you don't have to. You may please yourself. But if you want to please yourself, you could do worse than follow such sensible guidelines, based on sound reasons and centuries of practice.

The reasons are both chemical and aesthetic. The appetizing, refreshing quality of white wine is provided by acids that enhance the flavour of fish, while the saltiness of fish in turn emphasizes the fruity grape flavours of the wine. By contrast, the "edge" of a red wine is not acidity but tannin, which can react disastrously with the salt, which makes it bitter, and the fishy oils, which leave a lasting metallic tang in your mouth.

Of course there are exceptions. Certain fish (and, best of all, lampreys) are cooked in red wine to make a dish that goes excellently with a full-flavoured red – not Beaujolais but St-Emilion. Pinot Noirs, low in tannin, are now becoming almost *de rigueur* with salmon or tuna, or indeed all except very oily fishes.

But on the aesthetic side, the association of white wine with pale fish, and for that matter pale meat, is no accident, either. Each foodstuff has its appropriate colour. The eye tells the brain what kind of flavour to expect. And the eye finds it natural to associate pale drink with pale food.

Some of the traditional associations have even simpler reasons. We drink dry white wine with goats cheese, for example, because the cheese's salty dryness makes us thirsty. Some associations are simply negative; we do not drink red wine with sweets because sugar, like salt, makes tannin taste bitter. Strong, savoury, protein-rich meat and game dishes are the natural partners of vigorous red wines; their tannin finds a match, and so does their colour. But light, grapey reds ask for a less strenuous marriage with poultry or veal or pale lamb.

What the French so evocatively call *la cuisine douce*, such rich things of gentle savour as foie gras, sweetbreads, quenelles, and cream cheeses, has a similar affinity for sweet, or at least fat and unctuous, white wines.

Clearly there are broad classes of wine that are more or less interchangeable. They can be matched with similar classes of dishes to achieve satisfactory harmonies, if not perfect ones. There are other dimensions of taste that have to be taken into account, too.

Intensity is one; a powerful flavour, however appropriate, will annihilate a bland or timid one. Unfortunately this is the effect many strong cheeses have, even on splendid, full-scale red wines. Style is another; there are hearty, rustic tastes and pronounced urbane ones: garlic, if you like, and truffles. The wine and the food should belong to the same culture. Peasant and aristocrat rarely show one another off to advantage: neither will bread and cheese and great claret.

The total context of the meal is important. Is it leisurely or hurried? Fine wine deserves time. Is the day hot or cold? Even air-conditioning fails to make big red wines a good idea in tropical heat.

There are a few dishes that destroy the flavour of wine entirely. The commonest is salad dressed with vinegar. Surprisingly, even some of France's best restaurants serve violently acetic salads. Vinegar is best avoided altogether; lemon juice makes a better salad dressing in any case. Salad dressings with vinegar include the red "cocktail sauce" of American restaurants, too.

Chocolate is another flavour that dominates and spoils the taste of most wines. In my view, most desserts are better served without wine; creamy, highly perfumed concoctions fight wine rather than complement it. So do syrupy, fruity ones. Citrus fruit is particularly guilty. The one wine that challenges this rule is the recently revived classical Hungarian Tokaji Aszú: the best examples are so richly penetrating that they handle desserts with aplomb. Where a very rich gâteau is on the menu, I sometimes drink a glass of Madeira or even brandy with it. On the other hand, raspberries and strawberries, and particularly wild strawberries, are a wonderful match for fine red wine. In Bordeaux they pour claret rather than cream over them.

There are times when no single wine will fit the bill. It happens in a restaurant where everyone is eating something different: one shellfish, another game, a third a dish with a creamy sauce. The cop-out answer is a neutral wine that will offend nobody. Liebfraumilch, "blush" wines and Portuguese rosés made fortunes by offering themselves as the safe bet. A more swashbuckling (albeit less digestible) choice would be Champagne. My suggestion is to start with a bottle of white wine that will match almost any hors d'oeuvre, and then (if it is a party of four or more) continue with both white and red. There is no good reason not to have both on the table at the same time.

The structure of a more formal meal with a succession of wines is the great opportunity of gastronomy. To achieve a graduated harmony of successive flavours, it is worth taking pains. The ground rules are simple: follow lighter and more delicate with heavier and more pungent – both in wine and food. The fresh and hungry palate is susceptible to the subtlest flavours. Feeding fatigues it. It needs more powerful stimuli as the meal proceeds.

Occasionally the best way to bring out the singularity of a wine is to serve it concurrently with another which is similar and yet distinct: say, either slightly younger or from a neighbouring property.

Wine Divided Into Ten Basic Styles

I have risked a rather arbitrary division of the infinite variety of wine into ten categories, and associated each category with a selection of dishes, as a guide to where to start to look, whether your starting point is the wine or the food.

No such generalization can be defended in every particular case, but it is true to say that certain criteria of flavour, age, and quality can be applied across the board. Some wines could appear equally in two different categories, but for the sake of clarity I have put them firmly where, in my judgement, they most often belong.

The Alcohol in Wine

The amount of alcohol in wine varies considerably. While alcohol provides much of the "body" in many wines, it needs to be balanced by the flavouring elements: sugar, acidity, tannin, and extract. These, combined with the alcohol, give richness of flavour. Alcohol alone makes a wine fierce and unpleasant. Typical alcoholic strengths, per cent by volume, are:

German Kabinett	8.0 – 9.0
French vin de table	9.0 – 12.0
German Beerenauslese	9.0 – 14.0
German Qualitätswein	10.0 – 12.0
German Auslese	10.0 – 10.5
Beaujolais	10.0 – 13.5
Bordeaux Cru Classé	10.5 – 13.0
Red Bordeaux	11.0 – 12.0
Chablis Premier Cru	11.0 – 13.0
Beaune	11.0 – 13.5
Alsace Riesling	11.5 – 13.5
California Chardonnay	11.5 – 14.5
Valpolicella	11.5 – 13.0
California Cabernet	12.0 – 15.0
Muscadet	12.0
Montrachet	12.0 – 13.5
Chianti	12.0 – 13.0
California Zinfandel	12.5 – 16.0
Chambertin	12.5 – 13.0
Rioja Reserva	12.5 – 13.0
Châteauneuf-du-Pape	12.5 – 14.5
Australian Shiraz	12.5 – 14.5
Barolo	13.0 – 14.0
Sauternes	13.0 – 15.0
Château d'Yquem	13.5 – 15.0
Fino sherry	15.0 – 16.0
Oloroso sherry	18.0 – 20.0
Vintage port	19.0 – 20.0

Dry white wines of neutral, simply "winey" flavour

Among the cheapest wines, generally useful but too plain to be exciting, or to be particularly pleasant as apéritifs without the addition of extra flavour (such as blackcurrant or grenadine syrup).

These wines are better with simple food, especially with strong-flavoured or highly seasoned dishes, e.g. hors d'oeuvres (antipasto), aïoli or fish stew, mussels, herrings and mackerel (which need a rather acid wine to cut their oil), salade niçoise, red mullet, grilled sardines, terrines and sausages, curry or Chinese food (both of these are better for a little sweetness in the wine, e.g. Australian Chardonnay or a Pinot Gris from Alsace). All should be served very well chilled (about 8˚C/46˚F).

Examples are: most branded "jug" whites; Entre-Deux-Mers, Gaillac, Muscadet (Gros Plant du Pays Nantais or Aligoté for more acidity); Swiss whites such as Fendant; most standard Italian whites (including Soave, Verdicchio, Orvieto Secco, Frascati, Pinot Bianco, and Pinot Grigio); most standard Spanish and Portuguese whites; central and east European "Welschrieslings" or Pinot Blancs (i.e. Hungarian, Yugoslav, Bulgarian, etc.); many Chenin Blancs; and South African Sauvignon Blanc.

Light, fresh, grapey white wine with fruity and sometimes flowery aromas

This is the category of wine that has grown most in recent years at the expense of the dry whites. Modern techniques, especially cold fermentation, capture whatever flavour the grape has (some have much more than others) and add as little as possible. The very aromatic, German-style grapes are nearly always in this or the sweet, white-wine category. All these wines make excellent apéritifs or refreshing between-meal or evening drinks, most of all in summer. Those with relatively high acidity are also good with many first courses, but are dominated by seriously savoury dishes and lack the substance to be satisfying throughout a meal. Suitable dishes to accompany them include: poached trout, crab salad, cold chicken. They need slightly less chilling than the previous category.

Wines include: German *Qualitätswein*, most Kabinetts and some Spätleses; light French Sauvignons from Bergerac and Touraine; Savoie whites (Crépy, Apremont); Portuguese Vinho Verde and Spanish Albariño; certain California Chenin Blancs; Australian Rieslings; some New Zealand Sauvignons and English Müller-Thurgaus and Seyval Blancs; and simpler Austrian Grüner Veltliners.

White wines with body and character, aromatic from certain grapes or with the bouquet of maturity
Fine French dry whites all come into this category. High flavour often makes them taste rich even when fully dry.

Without food, these wines can be too assertive; they are best matched with a savoury dish which is also rich in flavour and pale in colour, *e.g.* oysters, clams, lobsters and prawns, smoked fish, frogs' legs, snails, onion or leek tart, ballotines, prosciutto, salmon, turbot, and other rich fish in butter, hollandaise or other rich sauces, scallops, poultry, sweetbreads, hard Swiss cheeses. Wines should only be lightly chilled (10°–13°C/50°–55°F).

Examples are: all good mature Chardonnays (*e.g.* white burgundies after two or more years depending on their quality); their equivalents from California and Australia; Alsace Riesling, Gewürztraminer and Pinot Gris; Sancerre and Pouilly Fumé and Savennières from the Loire; fine white Graves; mature white Rhône wines (*e.g.* Hermitage Blanc) and young Condrieu; exceptional Italian whites (the best examples of Frascati, Soave Classico, Verdicchio, Cortese di Gavi, Pomino, or Chardonnay); best-quality mature Rioja, Rueda, and Penedès whites from Spain, manzanilla sherry or Montilla fino; Hungarian Szürkebarát (Pinot Gris); Austrian Rotgipfler and top Grüner Veltliner; Ruländer (Pinot Gris) from Baden; Australian Semillons and dry Barossa and Coonawarra Rieslings with three or four years in bottle.

Sweet white wines
Varying from delicately fruity and lightly sweet to overwhelmingly luscious, these wines are to be sipped slowly by themselves and are rarely improved by food.

Very rich and highly flavoured desserts, however delicious, tend to fight sweet wines. Chocolate and coffee ones are fatal. If you want anything at all, the best choice is a dessert such as French apple or raspberry tart, crème brûlée, plain sponge cake or such fruit as peaches or apples. Sweet white wines are usually drunk after meals, but in France often as apéritifs, too. They are normally served very well-chilled.

The finest natural sweet wines are produced by the action of "noble rot". These include Sauternes and Barsac and the best qualities of Ste-Croix-du-Mont and Monbazillac, which are the most potent, Vouvray and Anjou whites of certain years, late-gathered wines of Alsace and Austria, and the rare and expensive very late-harvested wines of Germany, Beerenauslesen, and Trockenbeerenauslesen (which have lately been imitated with real success in parts of the New World). German wines offer every gradation between the light flowery whites and the intensely sweet ones with the same delicately acid flavour. None of them is really a mealtime wine. Tokaji Aszú, on the other hand, the "botrytis" wine recently revived in Hungary (*see* pages 412–14), finds matches at both the start of a banquet (with foie gras) and with fruity and/or creamy desserts at the end. Sweet Muscats are found in most wine countries. They range from the feather-light, such as those from Asti in northern Italy, where the very low-strength base wine for *spumante* is delicious; to the richer fortified *vins doux naturels* made in the south of France at Beaumes-de-Venise. Heavier Muscats are made in Languedoc and Roussillon (Rivesaltes), southern Italy (especially Sicily), on the east coast of Spain, at Setúbal in Portugal, in Greece and Russia, and (best of all) in northeast Victoria, Australia.

Rosé wines
Rosés are usually workhorse, compromise wines of adequate quality, made by fermenting the juice of red grapes very briefly with the skins, then separating it and making it like white wine. The great exception is pink Champagne, which, although generally made in the same way as still rosé (before undergoing a second fermentation in the bottle), is very highly sought-after. Few things are more delicious.

Rosés divide broadly into two camps: the light, pale-purply-pink, usually faintly sweet Loire style, and the drier, more orange-pink, stronger, and more sunburnt Provençal variety. Portuguese carbonated fizzy rosés and Californian "blush" wines fit into the first category. Tavel from the Rhône and most rosés from Spain and Italy are stronger and drier. A third group that can be classed as rosé are *vins gris*, red-grape white wines merely shaded with colour, more grey than pink, and a fourth, *pelure d'oignon* ("onion skin"), which are very pale orange-brown. Both are usually made very dry; the gris more fruity and the onion skin more alcoholic.

Rosés are best in summer with salads and on picnics, and the Provençal style with oily and garlicky or even oriental dishes. They have possibilities with such hors d'oeuvres as artichokes, crudités, salami or taramasalata. Pink wines need to be served really cold: colder than most whites. If this is difficult to arrange on a picnic, choose a light red wine instead.

Grapey young reds with individuality, not intended to mature
Beaujolais is the archetype of a light red wine: made to be drunk young while it is still lively with fresh, grape flavour. Beaujolais-Villages is a better, stronger, and tastier selection. Simple young Bordeaux, burgundy and Rhône reds, Cabernet from Anjou, and Mondeuse from Savoie should have the same appeal. Similar wines are now made in the Midi (Corbières, Minervois, Roussillon, St-Chinian) by the Beaujolais technique of carbonic maceration and also of most of the popular red grape varieties: light wines to drink young.

Italy's Valpolicella and Bardolino, Barbera and Dolcetto, and even Chianti, can be freshly fruity if they are caught young enough. Fizzy red Lambrusco is a sort of caricature of the style. Spain provides few examples, although Valdepeñas has possibilities and no doubt will be made fresher in the future. Portugal's red Vinho Verde is an extreme example not to everyone's taste. The heat of the vineyards of California, Australia, South Africa, and South America have proved inimical to this style of wine. Light Zinfandels and Gamays from California sometimes achieve it.

In its liveliness and vigour this is perhaps the safest and best all-round class of red wine for mealtimes, appetizing with anything from pâté to fruit and often better than a more "serious" or older wine with strong cheese, in mouthfuls rather than sips. For the same reason it is the easiest red wine to drink without food. It is usually best served cool. Ideal dishes include: pâtés and terrines (including those made from vegetables), quiches, salads, hamburgers, liver, ham, grilled meats, many cheeses, and soft fruits such as raspberries, plums, peaches, or nectarines.

Plain everyday or "jug" reds These are unpretentious and anonymous blended wines with little body or flavour. French brands, and the country wines of Italy, Portugal, or Spain, as well as California's "jug" reds, come into this category. Often a slight sweetness remains in the wine to disguise its lack of body.

Most inexpensive imports from southern, central and eastern Europe, North Africa, Argentina, Chile, South Africa, and Australia are in the classes that follow.

Like the "neutral" cheap whites, these are essentially wines for mealtimes, a healthy and stimulating accompaniment to almost any homely food. They are always best served rather cool. As drinks on their own they are improved by being iced in summer (as Sangria, with orange juice added) and "mulled" on the stove with sugar and spices in winter.

Mature reds of light to medium strength and body This category includes most of the world's finest red wines, epitomized by claret (red Bordeaux) and most of the typical wines of Burgundy and the Rhône, although some of the greatest fall into the next class, depending on the ripeness of the vintage. These wines need more care in serving than any others since they often throw a deposit in maturing.

They are wines for meat and game dishes with the best ingredients and moderate seasoning. Lamb, beef, veal (also sweetbreads and tongue), chicken, duck, partridge, grouse, pheasant are all ideal, although very gamey birds may need wines from the next category. Only mild cheeses should be served with these relatively delicate wines. They need to be served at a temperature of between 15°C and 18°C (60° F and 65°F) to bring out their flavour.

Wines in this category (apart from French) include the best of Rioja and Penedès from Spain; Chianti Riservas, Tuscans such as Tignanello, Carmignano, and Venegazzú; traditional Portuguese reds from Dão, Alentejo, and Bairrada; top California, Oregon, and Washington Cabernets and Pinot Noirs with the exception of a few mentioned in the next category; Coonawarra, Western Australian, and some Hunter Valley reds; top South African estates; Argentinian Malbec; Chilean Cabernet; Chateau Musar from the Lebanon; and Bordeaux blends from New Zealand.

Exceptionally concentrated, full-flavoured, and powerful reds, usually but not always needing to mature In Europe this category depends more on the vintage than the producer. Wines that achieve this status fairly regularly include Pétrus in Pomerol, Chambertin and Corton in Burgundy, Hermitage and Châteauneuf-du-Pape (Côte-Rôtie is more often in the previous category), exceptional Roussillons (not for maturing); Barolo and Barbaresco, Brunello di Montalcino, Recioto and Recioto Amarone from Valpolicella; Spanish Vega Sicilia, Pesquera, and Priorato; Portuguese Barca Velha and other Douro reds; Dalmatian Posip and Postup. Occasional vintages produce many such wines: 1961 in Bordeaux, 1971 in Burgundy, and more recently 1990 for both.

California, Australia, and South Africa find it hard not to make such big reds. Most of their best wines are carefully restrained in ripeness, but in California a number of wines, especially Zinfandel, are made to be larger than life. Australia makes many such wines, especially in Victoria and Barossa and the Southern Vales in South Australia. Top Shiraz such as Penfold's "Grange" and Henschke's "Hill of Grace" are the supreme examples.

Well-hung game and strong-flavoured cheeses are the obvious candidates for these wines, although those in the appropriate price bracket are also excellent with barbecues and on picnics – when someone else is driving.

Fortified wines Wines whose natural strength is augmented with added alcohol, either during the fermentation to preserve the natural sweetness (as in port) or after they have fermented to dryness, as a preservative (as in sherry). Since the role of these wines is largely determined by their sweetness, which is at their makers' discretion, all that can usefully be said is that dry versions (whether of port, sherry, Madeira, or their regional equivalents) are intended as apéritifs, while sweet ones are used either before or after meals according to local taste and custom.

The French, for example, prefer sweet apéritifs, the Italians bitter ones, and the British, who divide everything along class lines, some sweet and some dry. In all cases, smaller glasses are needed because the alcoholic strength is higher than that of table wine.

They also have their uses with certain foods. Dry sherry is always drunk in Spain with tapas, which are infinitely various savoury snacks. It is one of the best wines for smoked eel and cuts the silky sweetness of fine Iberian ham. Old oloroso sherry, whether dry or with added sweetness, is very good with cake, nuts, and raisins. Port, both vintage and tawny, is often drunk with cheese. Madeira has a cake especially designed for it.

Other wines in this category include Spanish Málaga and Tarragona, Sicilian Marsala, Cypriot Commandaria, French *vins doux naturels* (*e.g.* Banyuls) and a host of wines, usually with borrowed names, in the New World.

Storing Wine

The greatest revolution in the history of wine was the discovery that if air could be excluded from wine, its life span was increased enormously. And, even better, that it could take on an undreamed-of range of flavours and a different, less grapey and infinitely more subtle and interesting smell.

The invention that made airtight storage possible was the cork, which came into use some time in the seventeenth century. It is possible that the ancient Greeks knew the secret, but all through the Middle Ages and up to the seventeenth century, the premium was on new wine, not old. The latest vintage often sold for twice as much as the remnants of the previous one, which stood a good chance of having become vinegar. The only exceptions were the class of high-strength and possibly sweet wines generally known as "sack", products of hot sunshine in the eastern Mediterranean, southern Spain, and later, the Canary Islands. Their constitution allowed them to age in barrels in contact with air and take on the nuttiness and warmth of flavour we associate with sherry.

Maturity Comparisons

Every bottle proceeds at its own pace towards maturity with almost incredible differences between the fastest and the slowest, between even similar types from the same regions, varieties, and seasons.

It is interesting to plot the life span of a range of wines in a graphic form. In these diagrams I have assumed a notional (and unmeasurable) "optimum" for each wine: the time when all its potential is realized. The better the wine, the longer this "plateau of perfection" is likely to be. The "drinkability" of each wine up to the optimum is the vertical dimension of each diagram. For clarity it assumes that all wines are equally perfect at some stage of their lives. The horizontal scale shows time measured from the vintage in years (or months, as indicated).

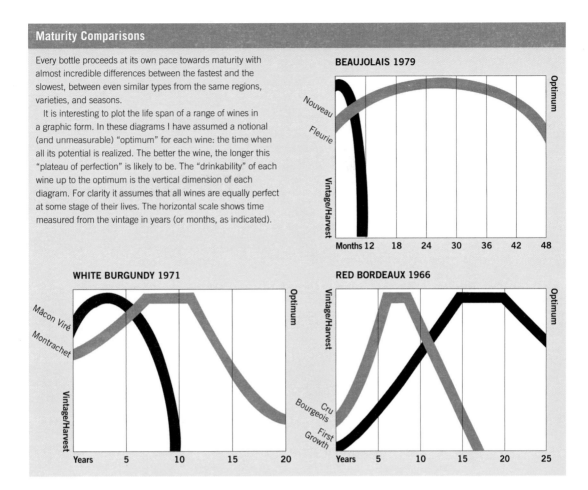

Ageing in bottles under cork is a totally different process. Instead of oxidizing, or taking in oxygen, the wine is in a state of "reduction" – in other words, what little oxygen it contains (absorbed in the cellars, while being "racked" from one cask to another, and in being bottled) is being used up (reduced) by the life processes within it. So long as it lives (and wine is a living substance with a remarkable life span), it is the battleground of bacteria, the playground of pigments, tannins, enzymes: a host of jostling wildlife preying on each other. No air gets through a good cork as long as it is kept wet, in contact with the wine, so that there is no risk of the vinegar process starting.

Whether the reduction process is beneficial, and for how long, is the determining factor in deciding when a bottled wine will be at its best.

Today, an increasing number of wines are being sealed with screwcaps. Most of them are intended for rapid consumption, but others, such as Australian Rieslings, can be kept for up to ten years. The wines, if properly stored, will age well, but retain more freshness than a corked version of a similar style.

Which Wines to Store

The great majority of wines are made with the intention of being ready to drink as soon as possible. This is true of all bulk wines, most white wines except very sweet and particularly full-bodied ones, nearly all rosés, and the whole class of red wines that can be compared with Beaujolais – whose character and charm lie in a direct flavour of the grape. Reduction spoils their simple fruitiness. The only table wines that benefit from storage are a minority of sweet or very concentrated, intensely flavoury whites and those reds specifically made, by long vatting with their skins and pips, to take up pigments and tannins as preservatives – which includes, of course, all the world's best.

Precisely how much of these elements combine with the juice and how well they act as preservatives is only partly in the hands of the winemaker. The overriding decisive factor is the vintage. And no two vintages are exactly alike. The analysis of the grapes at harvest time may be similar, but each crop has stood out in the fields through a hundred different days since the vine flowers opened. The number and size of the grapes, the formation of the bunches, the thickness of the skins, and the yeasts they gathered will always be subtly different. No two vintages develop in the same way or at precisely the same speed. But the better wines of each vintage will always last longer and mature further, to more delicious flavours, than the less good.

Thus laying down wines for maturing is always an exploratory business. Experts will give their opinion that the 1990 Bordeaux need from five to fifteen years to reach their best, depending on their quality. Such a margin will be safe enough, although it is scarcely a very helpful guide.

It is worth bearing in mind that later harvesting at higher ripeness levels – not just in Bordeaux but throughout the wine world – is giving richer, more supple wines with softer tannins. There is no reason to doubt that such wines will age as well as the best wines of the 1960s and '70s, but they are also accessible at a younger age. In the past, many red wines needed long ageing in bottle because they contained a measure of unripe tannins that made the wine unpalatable when young, while whites wines were dosed in sulphur dioxide that also made the wine disagreeable in its youth. The wines of today are far more approachable, and whether you like a fine burgundy or Bordeaux or Shiraz in its dazzling youth or in its mellow, subtle, old age is finally a matter of taste.

Wine Merchants & Brokers

In the past, only the grandest producers were capable of maturing and bottling their wine satisfactorily, marketing was an idea that was entirely unknown to them. The key to what the consumer wanted was held by the merchants, who blended wine to the customers' tastes. Today, buying wine direct from the maker has largely changed the shape of the wine trade.

It is the broker's job to know his region in the finest detail, to be a sort of family doctor to the small grower's wine, to advise him on its condition, choose samples with him, and take them to the right merchant. To the merchant, the broker is a valued talent-spotter who can gather and submit the right samples. The merchant's traditional function is to finance the wine while it is maturing, to make sure it suits the customers' tastes, then to bottle and ship it. In many cases he and his agents create both the wine and the market. His agents provide the link with the wholesalers, who are stockholders for retailers. The possible permutations of the system are endless. Its advantages are that each aspect of the chain from grower to table has its highly experienced expert, whether in knowing the right time to bottle or the turnover of a nightclub's refrigerator.

Is it Time to Try?

Happily, there are always plenty of other people opening bottles of every vintage and adding to a general pool of information about it, transmitted through wine books and magazines and catalogues. You will never have to look very far for an indication of whether it is time to try the wine you

Bottle Size, Shape, & Capacity

Each European wine region has a long-established traditional bottle-shape that helps to preserve an identity in the public mind. In most cases the New World wines based on the same grape varieties are also sold in the appropriately shaped bottles to help identify the style of their wineries.

Colour of glass is as important as shape. All Rhine wines are bottled in brown glass, all Mosels in green. White Bordeaux is in clear glass, red Bordeaux is in green.

For table wines whose origin is not important the "cubitainer" or "bag-in-box" is a plausible invention. The wine is in a plastic foil bag inside a cardboard box. As it is drawn off through a tap, the bag collapses, theoretically protecting the remaining wine from harmful contact with air. But in practice, no wine is well-served by such a device.

Red Bordeaux comes in several sizes. The bigger the bottle the longer the wine keeps, the slower it matures, and the better it will become.

Champagne is the only other wine with the same range of bottle sizes – but in this case, the various sizes available are for purely celebratory reasons.

are storing. You can even tell a certain amount about the maturity of red wine without opening the bottle, by holding its neck up to a strong light; the depth and quality of colour are quite readable through the glass.

The more difficult decision, assuming you intend to lay down some wine, is how much of which vintages to buy. It is probably a mistake to plump too heavily for one vintage – you never know whether the next one will be better. It is more sensible to buy regularly as good vintages turn up, which in Bordeaux in the 1980s was about two years out of three, but in the 1990s the success rate was lower: one year in three, in Burgundy one out of three, in the Rhône two out of three, and in California, for the sort of reds we are talking about, the same.

Since there is rarely enough space (and never enough money) it is worth making a calculation of how much dinner-party wine you are likely to use, which in turn depends on how many of your friends share your passion. Let us suppose that you give an average of one dinner party a month for eight people, and each time use four bottles of mature wine (in addition to such current items as young white wines and possibly Champagne). Your annual consumption will be about forty-eight bottles. Perhaps you use another bottle a week on family occasions (or alone). That makes about eight dozens a year.

The theoretically ideal stock is arrived at by multiplying the annual consumption by the number of years it stays in the cellar. Since this number varies from perhaps two, for fine white wines, to ten or more for the best reds, a finer calculation is needed. Let us say that two of the eight dozens are two-year wines, four are five-year wines, and two are ten-year wines. The total is 2x2 + 4x5 + 2x10 = 44 cases.

Besides table wines, two other kinds of wine are worth laying down: Champagne and vintage port. Champagne is a relatively short-term proposition. Vintage Champagne almost invariably gains a noticeable extra depth of flavour over two or three years. Lovers of old Champagne will want to keep it far longer, up to ten or even twenty years, until its colour deepens and its bubbles quieten. In Britain, it is worth keeping non-vintage Champagne for a year or two as well, but I have found that in America it is usually mature (sometimes overmature) by the time it reaches the customer.

Vintage port is an entirely different matter. The way the wine goes through almost its whole life cycle in the bottle is explained in the section on port. It needs cellaring longer than any other wine – except the almost unobtainable vintage Madeira. All good vintages need twenty years or more to reach their hour of glory.

The practical arrangements for storing wine are a challenge to most householders. The ideal underground cellar is even more remote than its ideal contents. But the storage conditions that make an underground cellar ideal are relatively easy to reproduce upstairs (at least in temperate climates) if the space is available. If money is no object and you have sufficient space, there are various temperature- and humidity-controlled storage systems that can be installed in your house and buried in your garden.

The conditions required are darkness, freedom from vibration, fairly high humidity, and a reasonably even temperature. Darkness is needed because ultraviolet light penetrates even green glass bottles and hastens ageing prematurely. Vibration is presumed to be bad (on what evidence I am not sure; it would have to be pretty violent to

keep any normal sediment in suspension). Humidity helps the corks to stay airtight, but much more important is that the wine remains in contact with the corks inside the bottle. It is essential to store all wine horizontally, even if you only expect to keep it for a month or two. Excess humidity is a serious nuisance; it rapidly rots cardboard boxes and soon makes labels unreadable. My own answer to the label problem is to give each one a squirt of scentless hair lacquer before storing it away.

Temperature & Time

Temperature is the most worrisome of these conditions. The ideal is anything between a steady 7°C and 18°C (45°F and 65°F). A 10°C (50°F) cellar is best of all, because the white wines in it are permanently at or near the perfect drinking temperature. It is highly probable that wines in a cold cellar mature more slowly and keep longer than wines in a relatively warm one.

Chemists point out that chemical reaction rates double with each 10°C (18°F) increase in temperature. If the maturing of wine were simply a chemical reaction this would mean that a wine stored in a cellar at 19°C (68°F) would mature twice as fast as one in a 10°C (50°F) cellar. But it is not so simple; wine is alive. Its ageing is not just chemical but a whole life process.

One should not exaggerate the effects of fluctuation, either. My own (underground) cellar moves gradually from a winter temperature of about 8°C (48°F) to a summer one of over 15°C (60°F) without the wine suffering in any detectable way. The most common difficulty arises in finding a steadily cool place in a house or apartment heated to 21°C (70°F) or more in winter, when the outside temperature can range from 15°C (60°F) plus to well below freezing. The answer must be in insulating a small room or large cupboard near an outside wall. In practice, fine wines are successfully stored in blocked-up fireplaces, in cupboards under the stairs, in the bottoms of wardrobes… ingenuity can always find somewhere satisfactory.

The same applies to racks and "bins". A bin is a large, open shelf (or space on the floor) where a quantity of one wine is laid, bottle on bottle. In the days when households bought very few wines, but bought them a barrel at a time, the bin was ideal. For collections of relatively small quantities of many different wines, racks are essential. They can either be divided into single-bottle apertures (either one or two bottles deep) or formed into a diamond pattern of apertures which are large enough to take several bottles – a half-dozen or a dozen depending on the quantities you usually buy. I find it convenient to have both single-bottle and dozen-bottle racks.

A much more complex problem, as a collection grows, is keeping track of the bottles. It is difficult not to waste space if you deplete your stock in blocks. Where space is limited you want to be able to use every slot as it becomes vacant. This is the advantage of the random storage system. But its efficaciousness depends entirely on dedicated book-keeping. If this is not your line you are likely to mislay bottles just when you want them.

Very fine wines – most classed as growth Bordeaux, for instance – are shipped in wooden packing cases that are perfect storage while the wine matures. If you do buy such wines by the complete case, there is no point in unpacking it until you have reason to think the wine will be nearing maturity.

If possible, make allowance in your storage arrangements for bigger-than-normal bottles. The "standard" 75-centilitre bottle has been accepted by generations as the most convenient regular size – though whether it was originally conceived as being a portion for one person or two is hard to say. But bigger bottles keep wine even better. Length of life, speed of maturity, and level of ultimate quality are all in direct proportion to bottle size. Half-bottles are occasionally convenient, particularly for such powerful and expensive sweet wines as great Sauternes or Beerenauslese, where a little goes a long way. Otherwise, bottles are better, and magnums better still. Double magnums begin to be difficult to handle (and how often can you assemble enough like-minded friends to do justice to one?). The counsel of perfection is to lay down six magnums to every twelve bottles of each wine on which you pin really high hopes.

It is not necessarily only expensive wines that are worth laying down. Many Australian reds, for example, will evolve from a muscle-bound youth into a most satisfying maturity. One of my greatest successes was a barrel of a three-year-old Chilean Cabernet, which I bottled in my amateurish way in my own cellar. It reached its delectable peak ten years later.

Experiment, therefore, with powerful, deep-coloured, and tannic reds from whatever source. Be much more circumspect with white wines. Most of those that have proved that cellaring improves them beyond a year or two are expensive already: the better white burgundies, the best Chardonnays, Sauternes of the best châteaux, and outstanding German Auslesen – which probably provide the best value for money today.

The neglected areas to add to these are fine Chenins from the Loire (both sweet and dry), top-quality Alsace wines, and what was once considered the longest-lived of all white wines, the rare white Hermitage of the Rhône.

Glasses

Each wine region has its own ideas about the perfect wine glass. Most are based on sound gastronomic principles that make them just as suitable for the wines of other regions, too. Perhaps the most graceful and universally appropriate is the shape used in Bordeaux. A few are flamboyantly folkloric – amusing to use in their context but as subtle as a dirndl at a dinner party. The traditional *römer* of the Rhine, for instance, has a thick trunk of a stem in brown glass ornamented with ridges and excrescences. It dates from the days when Rhine

A "tulip" glass has the rim turned in to concentrate the bouquet. This is the classic Bordeaux model.

A glass with an out-turned lip is conventional for top red burgundies. Some of these glasses are large enough to hold half a bottle comfortably.

Types of Glasses
You can argue that there is only one perfect wine glass, equally ideal for all table wines but there is also a case for enjoying the traditional, sometimes fanciful, shapes adopted by different regions to promote the identity of their products.

wine was preferred old and oxidized, the colour of the glass, and presumably when Rhinelanders wanted something pretty substantial to thump the table with. The Mosel, by contrast, serves its wine in a pretty, shallow-bowled glass with a diamond-cut pattern that seems designed to stress the wine's lightness and grace. Alsace glasses have very tall, green stems that reflect a faint green hue into the wine. Glasses like these are pleasant facets of a visit to the wine region, adding to the sense of place and occasion, but you do not need them at home.

The International Standards Organization (ISO) has pre-empted further discussion by producing specifications for the perfect wine-tasting glass. Its narrowing-at-the-top shape is designed as a funnel to maximize the smell of the wine for the taster's nose. For ordinary table use, this feature can be less pronounced. In all other respects it has the characteristics that any good glass should have: it is clear, unornamented, of rather thin glass, with a stem long enough for an easy grip and an adequate capacity. Capacity is important. A table-wine glass should never be filled more than half full. A size which is filled to only one-third by a normal portion (about 11 cl/4 fl.oz or an eighth of a bottle) is best of all. Anything larger is merely ostentatious – and more likely to get knocked over.

"Correct" glassware has become something of a fetish in some circles. The Austrian glassware designer Georg Riedel has devised countless models, each intended to complement a particular style of wine. Perhaps they do, but how many of us want a dozen or more styles of glass in our crowded cabinets? The styles illustrated below are more than sufficient to make the most of each type of wine.

Displaying the Bubbles

Sparkling wines are best served in a slightly smaller but relatively taller glass filled to about three-quarters of its capacity, giving the bubbles a good way to climb – one of the prettiest sights wine has to offer. They should never under any circumstances be served in the shallow *coupes*, now very rarely seen.

Dessert wines, being stronger, are served in smaller portions in smaller glasses, usually filled to between a half and two-thirds of their capacity. Their scents are more pungent than table wines; to plunge your nose into a wide bowl of port fumes would be almost overpowering.

When several wines are being served at the same meal it saves confusion if each has a slightly differing glass. In any case, guests should be told that the order of pouring is from

White wines are served in smaller glasses than reds. A matching set is useful for dinners when more than one wine is being served.

A slender tulip glass is a good shape for displaying the bubbles in Champagne or other sparkling wine.

A smaller version of the red burgundy glass for white wine served at table or as an apéritif. Good for aromatic whites such as Chardonnay and Riesling.

Port, sherry or Madeira are usually served in a glass with an in-turned rim which concentrates the bouquet.

left to right (*i.e.* the first wine is poured into the left-hand glass and so on in order). I imagine this tradition is for the practical reason that a right-handed drinker is less likely to knock over this first glass in reaching for his second. As a further precaution against confusion (if two or more similar wines are being poured) it is a simple matter to slip a little rubber band around the stem of one of the glasses.

Wine glasses should be as clean as you can possibly make them – which is, unfortunately, beyond the capacity of any dishwasher. Detergents leave a coating, which may or may not have a taste or smell, but is always detectable to the touch. It even affects the fizz of Champagne. There is only one way to achieve a perfectly clean, polished, brilliant glass. After washing with soap or detergent to remove grease, it should be thoroughly rinsed in clean hot water, then not drained but filled with hot water and only emptied immediately before it is dried. A clean linen or cotton cloth polishes a warm, wet glass perfectly (and very quickly) whereas it leaves smears and fluff on a cold one.

The best place to keep glasses is in a closed cupboard, standing right way up. On an open shelf they collect dust. Upside down on a shelf they pick up odours of wood or paint. An alternative to a closed cupboard is a rack where they hang upside down, but dust on the outside of a glass is no better than dust on the inside.

Serving Wine

The no-nonsense approach to serving wine takes up very little space or time. The cork is out before discussion starts. There are times, and wine, for this can-of-beans attack which it would be pretentious to deny. But here I put the case for taking trouble to make the most of every bottle. On the basis that anticipation is a part of every great pleasure, I argue that you should enjoy reading the label, be aroused by handling the bottle, relish removing the capsule, feel stirred by plunging in the corkscrew.

Sensuous enjoyment is the entire purpose of wine. The art of appreciating it is to maximize the pleasure of every manoeuvre, from choosing to swallowing. The art of serving wine is to make sure that it reaches the drinker with all its qualities at their peak.

No single factor is as important to success or failure as temperature. The characteristic scent and flavour of wine consists of infinitely subtle volatile compounds of different molecular weights, progressively heavier from "light" white wines to "heavy" reds. It is the temperature that controls their volatility: the point at which they vaporize and come to meet your sense of smell.

Each grape variety seems to behave differently in this respect. The Riesling scent is highly volatile; a Mosel sends out its flowery message even when it is too cold to drink with pleasure. Champagne's powerful fragrance of grapes and yeasts can hardly be suppressed by cold (although I have known people who seem to try). The Sauvignon Blanc is almost as redolent as the Riesling; the Chardonnay much less so – less so, in fact, than the Gamay; Beaujolais is highly volatile at low temperatures. The Pinot Noir vaporizes its ethereal sapidity even in a cool Burgundian cellar, whereas the Cabernets of Bordeaux hold back their aromas,

particularly when they are young. In a Bordeaux *chai* it tends to be the oak you smell more than the wine. California and other warm-climate Cabernets are often more forthcoming.

Are Aromas Everything?

It will be seen that these observations tally more or less with the generally accepted norms of serving temperatures shown on page 553. Not that aromas are everything. We expect white wines to be refreshingly cool; we expect red wines to awaken our palates with other qualities of vigour and completeness. It is fascinating to test how much your appreciation is affected by temperature. Taste, for instance, a good mature Meursault and a Volnay of the same quality (they are the white and red wines of neighbouring vineyards, made of grapes with much in common) at precisely the same fairly cool temperature and with your eyes shut. You will find they are almost interchangeable.

It is time to forget the misleading word "chamber" to describe the right temperature for red wines. Whatever the temperature of dining-rooms in the days when it was coined (and it must have varied from frigid to a fire-and-candle-heated fug), the chances of arriving at the right temperature by simply standing the bottle in the room where it is to be drunk are slight. An American dining-room at 21˚C (70˚F) plus is much too warm for wine. At that temperature the alcohol becomes unpleasantly heady. Mine, at 15˚C (60˚F), is good for burgundy but too cold for Bordeaux.

Everybody has, in his refrigerator, a cold place at a constant temperature that can be used for cooling white wine. Nobody I have met has a 16˚C (63˚F) oven. On the other hand, since an ice bucket is a perfectly acceptable (in fact, by far the most efficient) way of chilling wine, why not a warm-water bucket for red? Water at 21˚C (70˚F) will raise the temperature of a bottle from 15˚C–18˚C (55˚F–65˚F) in about eight minutes, which is the same time as it would take to lower the temperature of a bottle of white wine from 18˚C–13˚C (65˚F–55˚F) in a bucket of icy water. (Ice without water is much less efficient in cooling.) In a fridge, incidentally, where air rather than water is the cooling medium, the same lowering of temperature would take about one hour.

Bear in mind that the prevailing temperature affects the wine not only before it is poured out but while it is in your glass as well. Serve white wine on a hot day considerably colder than you want to drink it. Never leave a bottle or glass in the sun; improvise shade with a parasol, the menu, a book, under your chair… anywhere. At one sumptuous outdoor buffet in South Africa, the white wine was admirably cold but the red wine was left on the table in the sun. Not only was it ruined beyond recognition but I nearly burned my tongue on it. There are circumstances where the red wine needs an ice bucket, too.

Cooling Vessels

Failing the ideal arrangement of storing white wine permanently at the perfect drinking temperature – that of a cool cellar – the most efficient way to chill it rapidly is by immersing the entire bottle in ice-cold water. A refrigerator takes up to ten times as long as an ice-bath to achieve the same effect. Ice-cubes or crushed ice alone are inefficient. Ice must be mixed with cold water for rapid conduction of heat from the bottle. The perfect ice bucket is deep enough to immerse the whole bottle, neck and all: otherwise you have to put the bottle in upside down to start with to cool the neck. Insulated cooler sleeves, which are kept in the freezer and placed around the bottle when needed, are also effective. There is also a sort of open-ended Thermos flask that keeps an already chilled bottle cool by maintaining a wall of cold air around it.

Do You Decant?

Wine-lovers seem to find a consensus on most things to do with their subject, but decanting is a divisive issue. There is one school of thought, the traditional, that holds that wine needs to "breathe" for anything from a few minutes to a few hours, or even days, to reach its best. Its opponents, armed with scientific evidence, proclaim that it makes no difference or (a third view) that it is deleterious. Each is right about certain wines, and about its own taste. But they are mistaken to be dogmatic.

There are three reasons for decanting. The most important is to clean the wine of sediment. A secondary one is the attraction of the plump, glittering, glowing-red decanter on the table. The third is to allow the wine to breathe. Nobody argues with the first two. The debate revolves around when the operation should take place.

The eminent Professor Peynaud, whose contribution to gastronomy in general and Bordeaux in particular should make us listen carefully, writes (in *Le Goût du Vin*), "If it is necessary to decant [at all], one should always do it at the last possible moment, just before moving to the table or just before serving [the wine]; never in advance." The only justification Peynaud sees for aeration, or letting the wine breathe, is to rid it of certain superficial faults that sometimes arise. Otherwise, he says, decanting in advance does nothing but harm; it softens the wine and dulls the brilliance of its carefully acquired bouquet.

Scientifically minded Americans have come to much the same conclusions, although their consensus seems to be that decanting makes no difference that can in any way be reliably detected. My own experience is that almost all wines change perceptibly in a decanter, but whether that change is for the better or worse depends partly on the wine and partly on personal taste.

There are wine-lovers who prefer their wine softened and dulled; vintage port in particular is often decanted early to soothe its fiery temper; its full "attack" is too much for them. They equate mellowness with quality. Tradition in Spain

equates the taste of oak (as in Rioja) with quality. Who can say they are wrong about their own taste?

The English have always had strong ideas about how their wines should taste. One hundred years ago they added Rhône or Spanish wine to claret; it was altogether too faint for them without it. There are surely some people who preferred the burgundies of the days before the strict application of the appellation laws to the authentic, straight-from-the-grower burgundy we drink today. The Californians, too, have their own taste. They love direct, strong-flavoured wines that often seem as though the transition from fruit juice was never completed. Not surprisingly, ideas about decanting differ.

There are certain wines that seem to curl up when you open the bottle – like woodlice when you turn over a log. The deeply tannic Barolo of Piedmont shows nothing but its carapace for an hour or sometimes several. If you drink it during that time you will have nothing to remember but an assault on your tongue and cheeks. But in due course, hints of a bouquet start to emerge, growing stronger until eventually you are enveloped in raspberries and violets and truffles and autumn leaves.

The standard French restaurant practice is not to decant burgundy. If it is true that the Pinot Noir is more volatile than the Cabernet, the practice makes sense – the contact with the air when pouring from bottle to carafe wakes the Bordeaux up; the burgundy does not need it.

Those who believe in decanting would give several hours' airing to a young wine, one or two to a mature wine (these terms being relative to the expected maturing time), and treat an old wine as an invalid who should be kept out of draughts. Yet, strange to say it is an often repeated experience of those who have tasted very old and very great wines (Château Lafite 1803 was a case in point) that they can add layer upon layer of bouquet and flavour hour after hour – even, in some cases, tasting better than ever the following day. I regularly finish the bottles the evening after opening them. The only general rule I have found is that the better the wine, taking both origin and vintage into account, the more it benefits from prolonged contact with the air.

Sometimes a wine that is a distinct disappointment on opening changes its nature entirely. A bottle of Château Pontet-Canet 1961 (in 1982) had a poor, hard, loose-fitting cork and, on first tasting, a miserable, timid smell and very little flavour at all (although the colour was good). Twenty-four hours later it seemed to have recharged its batteries; it opened up into the full-blooded, high-flavoured wine I had expected. The moral must be to experiment and keep an open mind.

The pros and cons of decanting are much more long-winded than the process itself. The aim is simply to pour the wine, but not its sediment, into another receptacle (which can be a decanter, plain or fancy, or another bottle that has been well-rinsed).

If there is enough advance warning, take the bottle gently from its rack at least two days before you need it and stand it upright. Two days (or one at a pinch) should be long enough for the sediment to slide to the bottom. If you must decant from a bottle that has been horizontal until the last minute you need a basket or cradle to hold the bottle as near its original position as possible, but with the wine just below cork level (*see* page 550).

Cut the capsule right away. Remove the cork gently with a counter-pressure corkscrew. Then, holding the decanter in

The French Way with Burgundy

Serving burgundy, if you follow the French practice and do not decant it, presents more of a problem. Restaurants often serve it from a cradle: the worst possible system because each time the bottle is tipped to pour and then tipped back, the sediment is stirred into the remaining wine. The Burgundian answer to this is the splendid engine that tips the bottle continuously, as in the motion of decanting, but straight into the guests' glasses. Without such a machine I decant burgundies at the last minute – but only when they have sediment. Unless they are very old they are often clear to the last drop.

Decanting

There is much debate about whether and when to decant wine; whether "breathing" is a good thing or not. Modern "scientific" opinion tends to be against it. Certainly its effects are hard to predict, but if a rule of thumb is called for, I suggest the following:

Vigorous young ("young" in this context relates to the vintage – a great vintage is young at ten years, a poor one up to four or five) red Bordeaux, Cabernets, Rhône reds, Barolo and Barbaresco, heavy Zinfandels, Australian Shiraz, Portuguese reds, and other similar tannic wines: decant at least one hour before drinking, and experiment with periods of up to six hours.

"Young" red burgundy, Pinot Noirs and Spanish wines: decant just before serving.

Wine for decanting needs to be held in a position as near to horizontal as possible. The purpose of a wine basket is to hold a bottle in this position while it is being opened prior to decanting. It should never be used for pouring wine at table.

The corkscrew being used here is the Screwpull, which draws the cork up into itself with almost infallible ease. The worm is Teflon-coated, which means the cork can be drawn with a smooth, single, screwing action.

Pour the wine into the decanter in one continuous movement, holding the bottleneck over a light so that you can watch the sediment. As soon as it approaches the neck, stop pouring.

A special silver funnel has been devised which has a perforated strainer in the base and a spout curved sideways to prevent the wine from splashing down the neck of the decanter.

The Temperature for Serving Wine

Nothing makes or mars any wine so much as its temperature. The following chart serves to show the ideal temperatures for each category of wine. It is wrong, however, to be too dogmatic. Some people enjoy red wines several degrees warmer than the refreshing temperature I suggest for them here, and some like their white wines considerably colder than the moderate chill I advocate for the best appreciation of scent and flavour.

It is also worth remembering that on a hot day, "room temperature" may be considerably higher than that listed below, so red wines may need to be immersed briefly in an ice bucket.

DOMESTIC FRIDGE TEMP.	CELLAR TEMPERATURE ▼ THE IDEAL CELLAR	ROOM TEMP. ▶

SWEET WHITES	DRY WHITES	LIGHT REDS	FULL-SCALE REDS

Temperature scale: C° 4 · 5 · 6 · 7 · 8 · 9 · 10 · 11 · 12 · 13 · 14 · 15 · 16 · 17 · 18
F° 39 · 41 · 43 · 45 · 46 · 48 · 50 · 52 · 54 · 55 · 57 · 59 · 61 · 63 · 64

Wine	Approx. serving temperature (°C)
MUSCADET	6–7
CHABLIS	8–9
MACON	7–8
CHINON	10–11
BEST WHITE BURGUNDIES & GRAVES	12–13
RED BURGUNDY	15–16
BORDEAUX BLANC	7–9
BEAUJOLAIS CRU	11–12
SAUTERNES	5–7
BEAUJOLAIS NOUVEAU	8–10
GEWURZTRAMINER	5–7
COTES DU RHONE (RED)	12–13
TOP RED RHONE	15–16
SANCERRE/POUILLY	6–8
VINTAGE PORT	16–17
GROS PLANT	4–6
ALSACE/RIESLING	7–9
MIDI REDS CORBIERES, ETC.	12–13
MUSCATS	4–5
SYLVANER	6–7
ORDINARY RED BORDEAUX	14–15
ALIGOTE	5–6
FINO SHERRY	8–9
TAWNY PORT	10–11
CREAM SHERRY	12–13
TOKAJI	5–6
AMONTILLADO	11–12
MADEIRA	13–14
CAHORS	15–16
FINE RED BORDEAUX	16–17
NON VINTAGE CHAMPAGNE	6–8
MONTILLA	11–12
MADIRAN	15–16
VIN JAUNE	10–11
BANDOL	16–17
SPARKLING WINE SEKT, CAVA, ETC.	4–7
BEST CHAMPAGNE	8–10
EISWEIN	4–6
GOOD GERMAN & AUSTRIAN WINES	8–9
BEST DRY GERMAN WINES	10–11
BEST SWEET GERMAN WINES	12–13
LIEBFRAUMILCH	4–6
SWEET LOIRE CHENIN BLANCS	4–8
FRASCATI	6–8
VALPOLICELLA	10–11
ORVIETO	6–8
FIASCO CHIANTI	12–13
SOAVE	8–9
SICILIAN REDS	12–13
VERDICCHIO	7–9
HUNGARIAN WHITES	10–11
"BULLS" BLOOD	12–13
VINHO VERDE	4–7
BARBERA	12–13
FENDANT	7–9
VALDEPENAS	10–11
DOLE	10–11
LIGHT ZINFANDELS	12–13
RETSINA	4–6
LAMBRUSCO	7–9
YUGOSLAV RIESLING	7–9
SOUTH AFRICAN CHENIN BLANC	7–9
CALIFORNIA/AUSTRALIAN/OREGON PINOT NOIR	15–17
LIGHT MUSCATS	4–6
CHARDONNAY	7–9
TOP CALIFORNIA/AUSTRALIAN CHARDONNAYS	10–11
NZ SAUVIGNON	7–9
BEST CALIFORNIA CABERNETS & ZINFANDALS	16–17
JOHANNISBERG RIESLING	6–9
CALIFORNIA	10–11
BAROSSA RIESLING	7–9
SAUVIGNON BLANC	9–10
OLD HUNTER VALLEY WHITES	12–13
LIQUEUR MUSCATS	9–11
TOP AUSTRALIAN CABERNET/SHIRAZ	16–17
VIN ROSE	7–9

the left hand, pour in the wine in one smooth movement until you see the sediment advancing as a dark arrow towards the neck of the bottle. When the sediment reaches the shoulder, stop pouring.

It makes it easier to see where the sediment is if you hold the neck of the bottle over a candle-flame or a torch, or (I find best) a sheet of white paper or a napkin with a fairly strong light on it. Vintage port bottles are made of very dark glass (and moreover are usually dirty), which makes it harder to see the sediment. If the port has been lying in one place for years, its sediment is so thick and coherent that you can hardly go wrong. If it has been moved recently it can be troublesome, and may even need filtering.

Clean, damp muslin is the best material; I have found that coffee filter papers can give wine a detectable taste.

Opening Sparkling Wine

Five easy steps to openeing a bottle of sparkling wine:
1. Tear off the foil hiding the wire "muzzle" to uncover the "ring". Tilt the bottle and untwist the ring, being careful not to point the bottle at anyone.
2. Remove the muzzle. Tilt the bottle, holding the cork down firmly with your thumb. Ease the cork sideways and upwards with the other thumb.
3. When the cork feels loose, grasp it firmly and twist, keeping the bottle tilted, with a glass beside you to take the first foam.
4. Specially made pliers are sometimes used when a Champagne cork is very stiff, or when opening a number of bottles.
5. Butlers in the great Champagne houses pour Champagne by holding the bottle with a thumb in the indentation known as the "punt".

Opening Vintage Port

Bottles of vintage port older than about twenty years often present a special problem – the cork becomes soft and crumbly and disintegrates in the grip of a corkscrew. Spongy corks are almost impossible to remove. The answer is to cut the top off the bottle, which can be done in either of two ways.

Port tongs are specially made for the job. Heat them until red-hot over an open flame, than clamp the tongs around the upper neck of the bottle for a minute. Wipe quickly around the hot neck with a wet rag – it will crack cleanly all round and the top with the cork will come away easily.

An equally effective and more spectacular way of opening an old bottle of port is to grasp it firmly in one hand and take a heavy carving knife in the other. Run the back of the knife blade up the neck of the bottle to give a really sharp blow to the "collar". The neck will crack cleanly. Practise before making your début at a dinner party. Confidence is all.

Retaining the Sparkle

Sparkling wines should be spur-of-the-moment, celebratory drinks. When opening expensive bottles, it is a good idea to have a stopper that will keep the fizz intact if the celebration should be short-lived.

If a port cork crumbles into the bottle, it is possible to filter the wine through a clean, muslin-lined glass or plastic funnel, or to use one of the handsome old-fashioned silver funnels which has a built-in strainer.

Corks & Corkscrews

The first corks must have been like stoppers: driven only halfway home. There is no known illustration of a corkscrew until 100 years after corks came into use.

Although screwcaps, crown closures and synthetic corks now offer cheaper and simpler ways of keeping the wine in and the air out, cork remains the way fine wine is still sealed. What makes cork so ideal as a wine plug? Certainly its lightness, its cleanness, and the simple fact that it is available in vast quantities. It is almost impermeable. It is smooth, yet it stays put in the neck of the bottle. It is unaffected by temperature. It very rarely rots. It is extremely hard to burn. Most important of all it is uniquely elastic, returning, after compression, to almost exactly its original form. Corking machines are based on this simple principle: you can squeeze a cork enough to slip it easily into the neck of a bottle and it will immediately spring out to fill the neck without a cranny to spare.

As for its life span, it very slowly goes brittle and crumbly, over a period of between twenty and fifty years. Immaculately run cellars (some of the great Bordeaux châteaux, for example) re-cork their stocks of old vintages approximately every twenty-five years, and one or two send experts to recork the château's old wines in customers' cellars. But many corks stay sound for half a century.

The only thing that occasionally goes wrong with a cork is a musty smell that develops. Corks are carefully sterilized in manufacture, but sometimes one or two of the many cells that make up the cork (there are twenty to thirty in a square millimetre) are infected with fungus. When these cells are in contact with wine, the wine picks up the smell and becomes "corky" or "corked". The problem is fairly rare, but when it happens, it is instantly noticeable – and, naturally, disappointing. There is nothing to be done but to open another bottle. Sometimes the taint is slight and only detectable to someone who knows how the wine in question ought to taste at this stage in its development. In such cases we simply have to live with our disappointment, though we are likely to blame the wine rather than the real culprit, the cork, for our dismay.

Good-quality corks produce no other problems. Poor ones do. Many cheaper wines have very hard, small, low-grade corks in necks that are narrower than the norm. They make it extremely tough going for the corkscrew, which sometimes pushes the cork in instead of pulling it out. If you have wiped the top of the cork clean with a damp cloth before starting to open the bottle, no harm is done. Synthetic corks can also provide a challenge for many corkscrews; brute force may be the only solution, but may result in a broken corkscrew, lost in the cause of opening a mediocre wine. A gadget made of three parallel lengths of thick wire

Types of corkscrew

Quite simply, all that is required from a corkscrew is some sort of leverage against the rim of the bottle. A foil cutter (shown centre bottom) cleanly removes the top of the foil capsule before the corkscrew is inserted into the exposed cork. Out of a catalogue of thousands of devices, these corkscrews are some of the most popular and effective in current use.

with a wooden handle is made for fishing for lost corks. It is reasonably effective, but a simpler answer is to leave the cork in and pour the wine out, holding the cork down with a knife or a skewer until it floats clear of the neck.

The quality of the corkscrew is extremely important. Enormous ingenuity has been expended on the engineering of corkscrews. The simple screw-with-a-handle has long since been improved on by designs that use counter-pressure against the bottle. The straight pull is strictly for the young and fit; it can take the equivalent of lifting eighty pounds to get a cork out.

Various dodges are used to provide leverage, but the most important factor of all is the blade – the screw – that pierces and grips the cork. At all costs avoid narrow gimlets on the one hand and open spirals of bent wire on the other. The gimlet will merely pull out the centre of a well-installed cork; the bent wire will simply straighten if it meets with resistance. A good corkscrew blade is a spiral open enough to leave a distinct chimney up the middle, and made like a flattened blade with a sharp point and two cutting edges on its horizontal sides. The points of corkscrew design are illustrated above.

Types of Corkscrew

Endless ingenuity has been applied to the mechanical problem of grasping a cork in a bottle and pulling it out without exertion. A straight pull with the bottle between your knees is neither dignified nor necessary; all you need is some sort of leverage against the rim of the bottle. A foil cutter (shown centre bottom on page 553) cleanly removes the top of the foil capsule before the corkscrew is inserted into the exposed cork.

The Unfinished Bottle

A wine, once exposed to air, will gradually, or even swiftly, deteriorate. Nonetheless, leftover wine can be conserved for enjoyment the next day. Devices such as the Vacuvin, which employs a simple pump to extract the oxygen from the bottle, which is at the same time sealed with a rubber "cork", are imperfect but useful nonetheless. It is worth keeping a small supply of clean half-bottles into which small volumes of leftovers can be poured, thus reducing the amount of oxygen to be pumped out. Another device is a spray of nitrogen gas, which acts as a barrier between the remaining wine and the oxygen above it.

Opened bottles seem to keep better when refrigerated, and this applies to red wines as much as white. The ability of an opened bottle to survive depends not only on the storage conditions, however, but also on the style of the wine. Big, oaky Chardonnays seem more prone to swift oxidation than an intense, reductive Riesling. Saying this, though, there are no tested formulae.

Champagne bottles need to be re-sealed with a special stopper, which is available from most wine merchants. The bizarre method of placing an upended spoon in an opened Champagne bottle is unreliable.

Leftover wines are often best dedicated to the stew or the sauce, and even corked wines can be used for cooking without imparting their musty flavours to the dish.

Tasting Wine

There are wine tastings on every level of earnestness and levity, but to taste wine thoroughly, to be in a position to give a considered opinion, demands wholehearted concentration.

A wine-taster, properly speaking, is one who has gone through a professional apprenticeship and learned to do much more than simply enjoy what he tastes. He is trained to examine every wine methodically and analytically until it becomes second nature.

Although I am by no means a qualified professional taster, I often find myself, ridiculously, putting a glass of tap water through its paces as though I were judging it for condition and value. If I do not actually hold it up to the light, I certainly sniff it and hold it in my mouth for a moment while I see how it measures up to some notional yardstick of a good glass of water. Then naturally I spit it out.

Whether or not you have any desire to train your palate (it has its disadvantages, too; it makes you less tolerant of faulty or boring wines) it makes no sense to pay the premium for wines of character and then simply swallow them. It is one of the commonest misunderstandings about wine that if it is "better", it will automatically give more pleasure. To appreciate degrees of quality you need conscious, deliberate awareness. You need to know what sort of quality you are looking for. And you need a method to set about finding it.

Pierre Poupon, one of the most eloquent of Burgundians, has written: "When you taste, don't look at the bottle, nor the label, nor your surroundings, but look directly inwards to yourself, to observe sensations at their birth and develop impressions to remember." He even suggests shutting your eyes to concentrate on the messages of your nose and mouth.

Before dinner parties become like prayer meetings, let me say that there is a time and place for this sort of concentration. But if you apply it at appropriate moments it will provide you with points of reference for a more sociable approach.

What, to start with, are you tasting for? A very basic wine-tasting for beginners might consist of five wines to show the enormous variety that exists: a dry white and a sweet one; a light young red and a fine mature one, and a glass of sherry or port.

The point here is that the wines have nothing in common at all. Another very effective elementary tasting is to compare typical examples of the half-dozen grape varieties that have very marked and easily recognized characters.

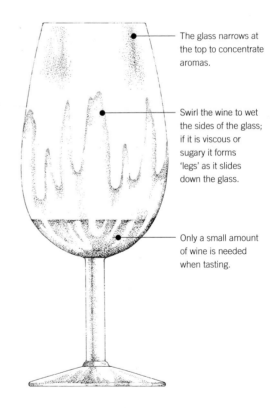

The glass narrows at the top to concentrate aromas.

Swirl the wine to wet the sides of the glass; if it is viscous or sugary it forms 'legs' as it slides down the glass.

Only a small amount of wine is needed when tasting.

An ideal tasting glass, to the specifications of the International Standards Organization, is about 6 in (152 mm) high and would hold 7 fl. oz (215 ml). For tasting purposes it is usually only filled to about one-fifth of capacity. The tall funnel shape is designed to capture the aroma, or bouquet, for the taster's nose. It needs a long enough stem to keep the hand away from the bowl. (Professional tasters often hold their glass by its foot.) The thinner the glass, within reason, the better. Wine is tasted more vividly from thin glass.

How to Taste Wine

The secret of getting the maximum pleasure out of wine is to remember that we smell tastes: it is our noses and the nerves high in the brain behind the nasal cavity that distinguish nuances of flavour – not our tongues, lips, or palates. The mouth detects what is sweet, sour, salt, bitter, burning, smooth, oily, astringent. But the colour and character of a flavour lie in its volatile compounds, which need the nose to apprehend them. Thus the procedure for tasting wine pivots around the moment of inhalation: the first sniff is crucial, since the sense of smell rapidly wearies.

First look carefully at the precise colour, clarity, and visual texture of the wine. Using a piece of white paper can help.

Swirl the wine to volatize its aroma while you concentrate. The glass should only be filled to about a fifth of its capacity.

Try to exclude all other thoughts and sniff. First impressions are crucial and should trigger recognition.

Take a generous sip, a third of a mouthful, and "chew" it so that reaches all parts of your mouth.

The final judgement comes when the volatile compounds rise into the upper nasal cavity.

At a professional tasting you must spit out all the wine: it is essential to keep a clear head.

Most tastings are intended to compare wines with an important common factor, either of origin, age, or grape variety. A tasting of Rieslings from a dozen different countries is an excellent way of learning to identify the common strand, the Riesling taste, and judge its relative success in widely different soils and climates. A variant of this, more closely focused, would be to take Rieslings of the same category of quality (Kabinett or Spätlese) from the principal wine regions of Germany.

Vertical & Horizontal Tastings

Tastings of the same wine from different vintages are known in the jargon as "vertical"; those of different wines (of the same type) in a single vintage are known as "horizontal".

Professional tastings concerned with buying are nearly always horizontal. The important thing here is that they should be comparing like with like. It is of no professional interest to compare Bordeaux with burgundy, or even Chablis with Meursault; if the Chablis is a good Meursault it is a bad (because atypical) Chablis.

A Médoc that tasted like a Napa Valley wine would be a poor Médoc – although it might be hard to convince a Napa grower that the converse was true. Most of us, of course, drink most of our wine with meals. We judge it, therefore, partly by how well it goes with the sort of food we like. Professional and competitive tasters always judge wine either by itself or in company with other wines, which gives them a different, and clearer, point of view. It is clearest of all when you are hungry and not tired; the end of the morning is the time most professionals prefer to attend a tasting.

The ideal conditions, in fact, are rather unattractively clinical: a clean, well-lit place without the suggestive power of atmosphere, without the pervasive smell of wine barrels, without the distraction of friendly chatter – and above all without the chunks of cheese, the grilled sausages, and homemade bread that have sold most of the world's second-rate wine since time immemorial.

Whether you should know what you are tasting, or taste "blind" and find out afterwards, is a topic for endless debate. The power of suggestion is strong. It is very difficult to be entirely honest with yourself if you have seen the label; your impressions are likely to reflect, consciously or otherwise, what you think you should find rather than simply what your senses tell you – like a child's picture of both sides of a house at once.

If I am given the choice, I like to taste everything blind first. It is the surest method of summoning up concentration, forcing you to ask yourself the right questions, to be analytical and clear-minded. I write a note of my opinion, then ask what the wine is or look at the label. If I have guessed it right, I am delighted; I know that my mental image of the wine (or memory, if I have tasted it before) was pretty close to reality. If (which is much more frequent) I guess wrong, or simply do not know, this is my chance to get to know the wine, to taste it again carefully and try to understand why that grape, in that vineyard, in that year, produced that result. This is the time to share impressions with other tasters.

It is always interesting to find out how much common ground there is among several people tasting the same wine. So little is measurable, and nothing is reproducible, about the senses of smell and taste. Language serves them only lamely, leaning on simile and metaphor for almost everything illuminating that can be said.

The convenient answer, normally used at competitive tastings, is the law of averages. Ask a group of tasters to quantify their enjoyment, and reduce their judgement to scores, and the wine with the highest average score must be the "best". The disadvantage of averaging is that it hides the points of disagreement, the high and low scores given to the same wine by different tasters who appreciate or dislike its individual style, or one of whom, indeed, is a better judge than another. At a well-conducted tasting the chairman will therefore consider an appeal against an averaged score and encourage a verbal consensus as well, especially where gold medals hang on the result.

This is as close to a final judgement on wine quality as fallible beings can get. But at best it represents the rating by one group of one bottle among the wines they tasted that day. It takes no account of other wines that were not tasted on the same occasion. All one can say about medal-winners is that they are good of their sort.

For competitive tastings, taster against taster, "blindness" is the whole point of the exercise. The individual (or team) with the widest experience and the best memory for tastes should win. For competitive tastings, wine against wine, it is the only fair method. But it can nonetheless produce misleading results. It tends to favour impact at the expense of less obvious but ultimately more important qualities. When California Cabernets are matched against red Bordeaux of similar age, the Californians almost always dominate. They are like tennis players who win by serving ace after ace.

The Grand Tour

The act of tasting has been anatomized by many specialists. To me there are five aspects of wine that convey information and help me gauge its quality: origin, age, the grape varieties involved, and how long it will keep (and whether it will improve). They constitute the grand tour of its pleasures, the uplift excepted. To take them in order they are its appearance, smell, the first impression the wine makes in your mouth, its total flavour as you hold it there, and the taste it leaves behind. I take each of these into account, note each separately (writing a note is not only an *aide-mémoire*; it forces you to make up your mind) and then draw a general conclusion. Tasting is a demanding discipline, quite distinct from the mere act of drinking. It sometimes has to be a quick and private little ceremony at a party where wine is not an accepted priority. Yet to contract the habit and apply a method of one kind or another is the only way to get full value out of your wine.

There is more to appearance than simply colour. Fine wine is brilliantly clear. Decanting should make sure that even old wine with sediment has the clarity of a jewel, capturing and reflecting light with an intensity that is a pleasure in itself.

Wine is more or less viscous, at one extreme forming heavy, slow-moving "legs" on the walls of the glass, at the other instantly finding its own level like water. The more dense it is, the more flavour-giving "extract" and/or sugar it contains – which, of course, is neither good nor bad in itself; it must be appropriate to the kind of wine. On the other hand a deposit of crystals in white wine does not imply poor quality; it is certainly not, under any circumstances, a fault.

"Colour [I quote Professor Peynaud] is like a wine's face. From it you can tell age, and something of character." That is, you can if you have certain other information about the wine, which the smell will soon provide.

The best way to see its colour clearly is to hold the glass against a white surface – a piece of paper will do – and to tip it slightly away from yourself so that you are looking through the rim of the liquid. Shallow silver tasting-cups are common in parts of France – particularly Burgundy – where wine is kept in dark cellars. It is easier to judge the colour of red wine in a shallow layer over the brightly reflecting silver than in a glass, where it is in a greater mass. The *tastevin* worn on a ribbon around the neck has become the ceremonial symbol of Burgundy.

White wines grow darker as they age; reds go through a slow fading process from purplish through red to a brickish reddy brown (which can be seen even through the green glass of the bottle by looking at the neck against a light). In young wines, the colour in the glass is almost uniform from edge to edge (making allowance, that is, for greater density where you are looking through more wine). In older wines the rim is usually decidedly paler. A browning rim is a sure sign of maturity in red wines.

Sheer redness is an indicator of quality rather than a virtue in its own right. The famous 1961 Bordeaux vintage can often be recognized from right across the room by its extraordinary glowing darkness – even in maturity a colour of pregnancy and promise. Red burgundy rarely has the same deep tints, and never precisely the same hue as Bordeaux. Rioja is generally rather pale, but this is because it has been aged for so long in cask, while Beaujolais is light-coloured in a different way; it has more the translucent purple of grape juice.

In general, hot-country wines of good grape varieties, the Cabernets, for example, from Australia, California, and South Africa, have more intensity of colour than their cool-country equivalents. Vintage port is deep purple-red, ruby port a much lighter, more watery colour, and tawny port, aged in wood for many years, can be anything from the brown-red of old claret to a clear, light amber when it is very old – the most extreme example of a red wine fading.

White wine has scarcely less variety than red. Chablis has a green light in its pale gold, which is uncommon in other white burgundies. Mosels also have a touch of green, with less of the gold, while Rhine wines tend to a straw colour, deepening almost to orange in old sweet examples. Sherry is coloured by oxidation: young finos only very slightly, old olorosos to a mahogany brown. When great sweet Sauternes ages, it goes through all the tints of gold to arrive at a deep, golden brown.

Hold Your Nose

You have only to hold your nose while you sip to realize that it is the organ that does most of the serious work of tasting. Unfortunately, our sense of smell is our least cooperative, least stable faculty. While taste, like hearing and sight, is constantly awake, the sense of smell rapidly wearies. This is apparent if you sniff more than half a dozen times in rapid succession at the same glass (or the same rose); its message becomes dimmed. Your nose needs a different stimulus.

For this reason, wine-tasters place a great deal of faith in their first impression. They swirl the wine once or twice to wet the sides of the glass and volatize as much of the smell as possible. Then they exclude all other thoughts and sniff. The nerves of smell have instant access to the memory (their immediate neighbour in the brain). The first sniff should trigger recognition: possibly the memory of the identical wine tasted before. If the smell is unfamiliar it will at least transmit this piece of negative information, and suggest where in the memory-bank partially similar smells are to be found.

The smell will also be the first warning sign if there is something wrong with the wine: perhaps a slight taint of vinegar, the burning sensation of too much sulphur, or a mouldy smell from an unsound cork or an unclean barrel. Most wines have a more or less agreeable but simple compound smell of grapes and fermentation, and in some cases barrel-wood: the smell we recognize as "winey". At its simplest, the better the wine, the more distinctive and characteristic this smell, and the more it attracts you to sniff again.

At this stage, certain grape varieties declare themselves. The eight "classics" all set a recognizable stamp on the smell of their wine. Age transmutes it from the primary smell tasters call the "aroma" to a more complex, less definable, and more rewarding smell. This scent of maturity is known, by analogy with the mixed scents of a posy of flowers, as the "bouquet".

The essence of a fine bouquet is that you can never put your finger on it. It seems to shift, perhaps from cedar to wax to honey to wildflowers to mushrooms. Mature Riesling, for example, can smell like lemons and petrol, Gewürztraminer like grapefruit, Chardonnay like butter – or rather, they can fleetingly remind you of these among many other things.

By the time the glass reaches your lips, then, you have already had answers, or at least clues, to most of the questions about the wine: its overall quality, its age, perhaps its grape (and by deduction, possibly its origin).

If all is well, the taste will confirm the smell like the orchestra repeating the theme introduced by a soloist, adding the body of sound, the tonal colours that were missing. Only at this stage can you judge the balance of sweetness and acidity, the strength of the alcohol, and whether it is counterpoised by the intensity of fruity flavours, and the quantity and quality of tannin.

Each wine has an appropriate combination of these elements; its quality is judged on whether they harmonize in a way that is both pleasant in itself and typical of its class. In fact, typical comes before pleasant. A young red wine may be disagreeably tannic and astringent; the taster's job is to judge it for the latent fruitiness that in time will combine with the tannins.

Different parts of your mouth pick up different facets of flavour. It is the tip of your tongue that recognizes sweetness, so sweetness is the first taste you become aware of. Acidity and saltiness are perceived by taste buds along the sides of your tongue and palate, bitterness by the soft back part of your tongue.

The tastes switch off in the same order: sugar after a mere two seconds or so; salt and acid after rather longer. Bitterness, which you notice last, lingers – a quality the Italians appreciate; many of their red wines (Valpolicella is an example) have a slightly bitter aftertaste.

Science can measure many (not all) of the chemical constituents that provide these sensations. It has identified more than 400 in wine up to now. But our perception of them is entirely personal. A few tasters, like a few musicians, may have "perfect pitch", but most people probably have slight blind spots. Someone who takes three spoonfuls of sugar in coffee must have a high threshold of perception for sweetness. If you need to smother your food with salt you will hardly pick up the subtle touches of saltiness in wine.

Sweet, sour, salt, and bitter in any case hardly start to express the variety of sensations that evolve in your mouth between sipping and swallowing. The moment of maximum flavour is when the wine reaches the soft palate and you start to swallow. Its vapour mounts directly to the olfactory nerves through the channels that link mouth and nose. At a serious tasting, where it is essential to spit the wine out to keep a clear head and stay the course, this moment can be maximized by holding a small quantity in the very back of the mouth and breathing in through slightly parted lips. The grimace and the gurgling are a small price to pay for the redoubled concentration of flavour achieved.

Red wines contain more or less tannin, the substance that turns hide to leather. Very tannic wine is so astringent (like walnut or broad-bean skins) that your mouth can begin to feel leathery and further tasting can be difficult. Tannin varies in taste and quality, too, from fully ripe, agreeable astringency, or the mouth-drying astringency of oak, to unripe, green harshness.

Acids vary from harsh to delicately stimulating – not just in their concentration, or their power (measured in units of pH), but in their flavours. Of the wine acids, malic is green-appley, citric is fresh and lemony, tartaric is harsh. Acetic is vinegary, lactic is mild, and succinic is a chemical cousin of glutamic acid. We owe much of the lip-smacking, appetizing taste of wine to tiny traces of succinic acid generated as a by-product of fermentation.

As for the alcohol itself, in low concentrations it merely has a faintly sweet taste, but at about eleven per cent by volume it begins to give the mouth the characteristic feeling of winey warmth known as "vinosity". (Lighter wines, such as many German ones at eight to nine per cent, lack this feeling.)

Add the ability of your tongue to differentiate between (more or less) fluid or viscous, to pronounce that one liquid feels like satin, and another like velvet, and the permutations begin to be impressive.

Finally, add the all-important element of persistence – how long the final flavour lasts. Really great wines have more to offer at the beginning, in the beauty of the bouquet, and at the end, in the way they haunt your breath for minutes after they have gone. Logical in all things, French scholars have even invented a measure of persistence; one second of flavour after swallowing is known as a *caudalie*. According to one theory, the hierarchy of the wines of Burgundy is in direct proportion to their *caudalie* -count.

Order of Tasting

In tasting wine, as in serving it at a dinner party, take care to organize a crescendo of flavour. Powerful, strong-flavoured wines followed by lighter ones, however good, make the latter appear as pygmies. The conventions are to follow younger with older, lighter with heavier, drier with sweeter, and to put red after white. Bordeaux professionals, however, will often taste red before white. It is worth trying both methods.

Tasting: Further Reading

In recent years, a number of excellent books tackle this subject in great detail. Michael Broadbent's *Winetasting* is both concise and authoritative; Michael Schuster's *Essential Winetasting* is probably the best of a large number of how-to books on this topic.

BORDEAUX CHATEAUX INDEX
(General Index follows)

INDEX

(Wines and wine properties that share the same names are indexed together. Bordeaux châteaux are indexed separately: see pages 561–4.)